W9-BQK-227

Encyclopedia of GLOBAL BRANDS

2nd Edition

Encyclopedia of GLOBAL BRANDS

VOLUME 1

2nd Edition

ST. JAMES PRESS
A part of Gale, Cengage Learning

Detroit • New York • San Francisco • New Haven, Conn • Waterville, Maine • London

GALE
CENGAGE Learning

Encyclopedia of Global Brands, 2nd Edition

Written and edited by Kepos Media, in collaboration with Thomas Riggs & Company

Project Editor: Peggy Geeseman

Editorial: Miranda Ferrara

Composition and Electronic Prepress: Evi Seoud

Manufacturing: Rita Wimberley

Product Manager: Michele LaMeau

Cover Photograph: London Bus in Motion, © StockPhoto.com/Maciej Noskowski.

For product information and technology assistance, contact us at
Gale Customer Support, 1-800-877-4253.
For permission to use material from this text or product,
submit all requests online at **www.cengage.com/permissions.**
Further permissions questions can be emailed to
permissionrequest@cengage.com.

LIBRARY OF CONGRESS CATALOGING-IN-PUBLICATION DATA

Encyclopedia of global brands. — 2nd edition.
volumes cm
Includes bibliographical references and index.
ISBN 978-1-55862-227-2 (set) — ISBN 978-1-55862-228-9 (vol. 1) —
ISBN 978-1-55862-229-6 (vol. 2)
1. Brand name products–Encyclopedias. 2. Corporations–Encyclopedias.
I. St. James Press.
HD69.B7E534 2013
338.703—dc23 2013012023

Gale
27500 Drake Rd.
Farmington Hills, MI 48331-3535

ISBN-13: 978-1-55862-227-2 (set) ISBN-10: 1-55862-277-6
ISBN-13: 978-1-55862-228-9 (vol. 1) ISBN-10: 1-55862-228-4 (vol. 1)
ISBN-13: 978-1-55862-229-6 (vol. 2) ISBN-10: 1-55862-229-2 (vol. 2)

This title is also available as an e-book.
ISBN 13: 978-1-55862-854-0 ISBN 10: 1-55862-854-1
Contact your Gale, a part of Cengage Learning, sales representative for ordering information.

Printed in Mexico
1 2 3 4 5 6 7 17 16 15 14 13

Contents

Preface

The *Encyclopedia of Global Brands, 2nd Edition,* is an update of St. James Press's *Encyclopedia of Consumer Brands* (*ECB*). This reinvigorated product is based on a survey of marketing textbooks (both domestic and international), current brand management services, business journal and trade publication brand rankings, and discussions held with business school professors.

The growing importance of the Internet and the global market inspired a more international focus for the *Encyclopedia of Global Brands.* The *Encyclopedia* also endeavors to present a more consistent definition of the term "brand," putting the entry's focus on the product's branding rather than on the product itself.

The *Encyclopedia of Global Brands, 2nd Edition,* is intended as a reference for students, businesspeople, librarians, historians, economists, investors, job seekers, researchers, and others who want to learn more about the world's most influential brands. It provides substantive information on the brand names and brand marks of products that have been international leaders in their respective categories.

The *Encyclopedia*'s two volumes highlight 269 of the most popular brands in the world. The brands covered represent products currently on the market, ranging from those whose branding history extends a century or more to newcomers who have quickly established their strength in the 21st-century global marketplace.

INCLUSION CRITERIA

Brands included in this volume were selected by the editors and advisory board members, who chose brands possessing a combination of elements including strong public awareness of the brand, high financial valuation, dominance in sales and market share in the product's category, and the brand's potential for future success and global expansion. Although the editors and advisory board selected brands from a wide range of categories and geographic locations, because of the increasingly vast number of global brands, some significant ones were inevitably left out.

ENTRY FORMAT

Each entry begins with the *At a Glance* section, which lists the brand name; a brief *Synopsis* that describes the brand; the name, address, and website URL of the brand's parent company; the *Sector* name, industry, and industry group of the product; the product's *Performance* in terms of global sales and market share; and the brand's *Principal Competitors*.

The body of each entry describes the *Brand Origins*, analyzes the *Brand Elements* (the images, words, and other physical qualities that make the brand distinctive), examines the *Brand Identity*, provides an overview of the *Brand Strategy*, evaluates the *Brand Equity*, assesses the level of public *Brand Awareness*, forecasts the *Brand Outlook*, and suggests articles for *Further Reading*.

SOURCES

Entries have been compiled from publicly accessible sources both in print and on the Internet, such as general and academic periodicals, books, and annual reports.

HELPFUL INDEXES

The *Encyclopedia of Global Brands* includes cumulative indexes to people and companies, brand sectors, and countries that make it easy to locate not only featured brand names but also other pertinent brand names, companies, and people mentioned in the articles, as well as to identify brands by the geographic locations of their parent companies.

SUGGESTIONS WELCOME

Comments on this title, and suggestions for how to make subsequent and similar titles better, are always welcome. Please write:

The Editors
Encyclopedia of Global Brands, 2nd Edition
Gale, Cengage Learning
27500 Drake Rd.
Farmington Hills, MI 48331-3535

Gale, Cengage Learning, and St. James Press do not endorse any of the companies or brands mentioned in this title. Companies and brands appearing in the *Encyclopedia of Global Brands, 2nd Edition,* were selected without reference to their wishes and have in no way endorsed their entries. All brand names mentioned in the *Encyclopedia* are trademarks or registered trademarks of their respective parent companies.

ACCENTURE

AT A GLANCE

Brand Synopsis: Management consulting and technology services firm Accenture wants corporate clients to know it delivers high performance.
Parent Company: Accenture plc
1 Grand Canal Square
Grand Canal Harbour
Dublin
Ireland
http://www.accenture.com
Sector: Information Technology
Industry Group: Software & Services
Performance: *Sales*—US$25.5 billion (2011).
Principal Competitors: BearingPoint Europe Holdings B.V.; HP Enterprise Services, LLC; International Business Machines Corporation (IBM)

BRAND ORIGINS

- Accenture began in 1953 as the consulting division of accounting firm Arthur Andersen & Co. installing the world's first data processing computer for the General Electric Company.
- In 1989 the company, known then as Andersen Consulting, introduced Business Integration, a service for aligning a client's employees, technology, and strategy for enhanced business performance.
- In 2001 Andersen Consulting severed ties with Arthur Andersen and underwent a crucial rebranding campaign that included changing its name to Accenture.
- The newly emerged brand Accenture booked US$5.6 billion in new contracts in 2001 and ended the year with earnings of US$11.4 billion, a 17 percent increase over the previous year.

Accenture was started in 1953 as the business and technology consulting division of Arthur Andersen & Co., an accounting firm. The firm was asked by the General Electric Company (GE) to conduct a feasibility study to determine the best course of action for automated payroll processing and manufacturing. Arthur Andersen researched possible solutions and recommended the installation of a Universal Automatic Computer (UNIVAC), the world's first data processing computer. With the help of employee Joe Glickauf, Arthur Andersen instituted an administrative services division, which became the world's first data-processing business. A long line of clients soon followed GE, and Arthur Andersen's consulting division established itself as a provider of systems integration, strategy, software development, and technology.

In 1989 partners at Andersen Consulting, as the division was then called, joined to formally establish the firm as its own separate unit under parent corporation Andersen Worldwide Société Coopérative. Andersen Consulting provided consulting and technology services dedicated to managing large-scale systems integration and enhancement of business performance. In the same year, Andersen Consulting introduced Business Integration, a system for aligning a client's employees and technology with its overall strategy, which enabled all aspects of the client's organization to work toward enhanced business performance.

The company grew steadily for a decade and by 2000 earned annual net revenues of more than US$9.5 billion. In 2001 Andersen Consulting, which had grown far beyond the bounds of a consultation practice, was at last allowed to sever ties with its founding company, Arthur Andersen. Following a series of legal battles to make the severance permanent, Andersen Consulting thrived, undergoing a massive rebranding campaign that included changing its name from Andersen Consulting to Accenture. In 2001 Accenture's partners elected to form a public company and registered the firm as a Bermuda corporation. The company booked US$5.6 billion in new contracts and ended 2001 with revenues of US$11.4 billion, a 17 percent increase. This growth rate doubled the industry standards. In 2009 the company changed its place of incorporation and moved its headquarters to Ireland. Because Accenture is a global organization that does not operate under a U.S. holding company structure, it performs primarily as a group of locally owned partnerships in more than 54 countries. The information services offered by Accenture have become a staple for many of the companies on *Fortune* magazine's Fortune 1,000.

BRAND ELEMENTS

- Accenture's name change in 2001 represents the accelerated growth of its services and capabilities. The company introduced a new advertising campaign and slogan, along with its logo and accompanying symbol.
- Accenture created an advertising campaign that featured case studies of client success, including that of Marriott International, whose website became one of the top retail sites in the world after Accenture implemented a new online platform for the company.
- In 2011 Accenture appointed TBWA/Chiat/Day to handle creative development and made use of business-to-business marketing, including airport ads in 35 countries.

Accenture, the name adopted by the company in 2001, represents the swift growth of the services and capabilities the brand offers. Accenture's rebranding campaign included the new slogan "High performance. Delivered." The campaign crossed every brand touch point, including print, online, and broadcast advertising, social media, mobility platforms, and employee communications across six continents. To promote the positive response from its clientele, Accenture ran a series of results-focused case studies highlighting client success. These case studies included ads featuring clients such as Olympus and Unilever. One case study detailed how Accenture helped hospitality company Marriott International create one of the top 10 retail sites in the world through implementation of a platform supporting nine websites in seven languages. This allowed customers to book reservations more easily and generated US$7 billion in annual sales for Marriot.

The rebranding campaign featured a bold color palette and engaging imagery, as well as the "Accenture symbol," a simple, right-pointing arrow that has been part of the brand's logo for more than a decade. Subsequent campaigns would make use of business-to-business marketing and high-impact installations, showcasing the brand's ability to create innovative and effective advertising. Accenture appointed TBWA/Chiat/Day as its agency of record for creative development in 2011, while the production agency Tag Worldwide translates and implements the brand's campaigns worldwide.

BRAND IDENTITY

- Accenture's aim is to accelerate their client business performance through long-term collaboration.
- Accenture has maintained long-standing relationships with more than 75 percent of the companies on *Fortune* magazine's Global 500, including 92 of the top 100.
- Accenture offers a combination of industry knowledge and foresight into technology trends to design solutions for clients.

Accenture is a global powerhouse with clients in more than 120 countries. As such the company has focused on building a brand identity that conveys competence, a deep level of experience, and high performance. Accenture is distinguished in the marketplace by the brand's extensive industry experience, evolving service offerings, a history of technology and innovation, and a commitment to the long-term development of the brand's employees. The Accenture brand is shaped by a desire to improve its clients' business performance and create long-term relationships through which clients achieve excellence. By enhancing the brand's consulting and outsourcing expertise with alliances, Accenture's clients benefit from the exceptional service provided through the brand's global network.

Accenture considers diversity to be essential to the brand's ability to deliver high performance to clients and counts an inclusive culture as a key element in its capacity to compete in the global marketplace. Accenture offers a combination of industry knowledge, technological capability and a foresight into new business and technology trends that allows the brand to develop specialized solutions for clients up-to-the-minute. This dedication to client satisfaction has contributed to Accenture maintaining long-standing relationships with more than 75 percent of the companies on Fortune Global 500, including 92 of the top 100.

BRAND STRATEGY

- Accenture's global growth strategy focuses on industry differentiation, leadership in technological services, and geographic expansion.
- The brand has increased investment in particular industries, including the health care industry, in which it connects fragmented health care ecosystems with new forms of health care delivery.
- Accenture established Accenture Property and Casualty Services after acquiring the software company Duck Creek Technologies.
- Accenture consolidated its mobility expertise and skills to create Accenture Mobility Services.

Accenture's fiscal success in 2011 was due in part to its concentration on global growth, a strategy that comprised three aims: industry differentiation, technology leadership, and geographic expansion. Accenture prioritized its investments with regard to specific industries, such as the health care industry. Clients responded favorably to the opportunities Accenture offered for connecting health care ecosystems with new forms of health care delivery. Accenture acquired the software company Duck Creek Technologies in 2011, which resulted in the enhancement of Accenture's insurance capabilities and led to the establishment of Accenture Property and Casualty Services.

Accenture has continued to expand its services across a range of technology and business initiatives, including mobility, digital marketing, and smart grid and cloud computing. The brand consolidated its mobility skills and expertise through the formation of Accenture Mobility Services and established innovation centers in the United States and Europe to advertise the brand's analytical assets. Its progress in smart grid technology brought Accenture more than 100 smart grid projects in more than 20 countries. Accenture's strategic aims are typically market-focused. The brand concentrates on adapting to accommodate a broad range of markets. Accenture also focuses on operating as a high-performance business, expanding use of its global network to improve delivery across its range of services and streamline its internal operations.

Accenture is notable in the marketplace for its expertise in business transformation outsourcing and its history of technological innovation, including research and developmental capabilities. The brand's dedication to client satisfaction has resulted in long-standing relationships with its clients. In fiscal year 2011, 99 of Accenture's top 100 clients had been clients for at least five years, and 92 had been clients for approximately 10 years. In 2012 Accenture extended its Skills to Succeed project, which equips individuals with the skills to start businesses, by granting US$3.65 million to international aid organization Plan and US$962,000 to Ashoka France to help those organizations in their initiatives to provide job readiness training and teach entrepreneurial skills.

BRAND EQUITY

- In 2011 Accenture achieved growth through industry differentiation, superior technology services, and geographic expansion.
- Accenture ranked 92nd on *Fortune* magazine's 2012 list of the best companies to work for.
- Accenture's annual revenue in 2011 was US$25.5 billion, with earnings per share of US$3.40 and an operating margin of 13.6 percent. Its balance sheet generated a free cash flow of US$3 billion.

In 2011 Accenture achieved profitable growth through industry differentiation, leadership in technology, and geographic expansion. In 2012 Accenture ranked 92nd on *Fortune* magazine's list of the best companies to work for. Additionally, Accenture ranked 11th in the technology sector of BrandZ's Top 100 Most Valuable Global Brands.

In 2011 Accenture posted its highest-ever annual revenue at US$25.5 billion, an increase of 15 percent. Its earnings per share grew to US$3.40, an increase of 28 percent. Accenture returned cash to shareholders through more than US$2.8 billion of share purchases and dividend payments and achieved an operating margin of 13.6 percent. Its balance sheet generated a free cash flow of US$3 billion.

BRAND AWARENESS

- Accenture has been recognized as a global business leader by Wall Street, the FTSE, and the Nikkei.
- In 2002 Accenture boosted its brand recognition to 34 percent through the "I'm your idea" brand campaign.
- Accenture was included in the Fortune 500 from 2005 to 2012.
- Accenture ranked 11th in the technology sector of BrandZ's Top 100 Most Valuable Global Brands.

Accenture has been recognized as a global business leader from Wall Street to the FTSE to the Nikkei. In 2002, shortly after Accenture had emerged from what remained of Anderson Consulting, the new brand launched the "I'm your idea" campaign, which resulted in Accenture's brand recall growing from 29 percent to 34 percent. This was followed in 2003 with a new campaign starring professional golf star Tiger Woods, which further lifted Accenture's brand recognition (the brand would latterly have to extricate itself from that particular association due to bad press on the part of Woods).

Accenture was included in *Fortune* magazine's Fortune 500 from 2005 to 2012. In 2012 Accenture ranked

139th on *Barron's* magazine's list of the 500 largest publicly traded companies in the United States and Canada, categorized among those companies that had most increased their sales and cash flow. The BrandZ Top 100 Most Valuable Global Brands, published by the *Financial Times*, ranked Accenture 45th (up from 49th place in 2011) and 11th in the technology sector. Accenture was consistently among the top-ranked firms in *Forbes* magazine's Global 2,000 from 2008 to 2012. From 2009 to 2012, the brand was recognized as a top corporation by the Women's Business Enterprise National Council.

BRAND OUTLOOK

- In 2004 Accenture undertook a US$10 billion contract with the U.S. government to build and install a security system that combines various technologies to identify all foreign nationals entering or exiting the United States.
- Under the leadership of William D. Green, from 2004 to 2008 Accenture's fiscal status increased by US$10 billion.
- Accenture achieved net revenues of US$25.5 billion for the fiscal year 2011.

In 2004 Accenture undertook a US$10 billion contract with the U.S. government to build and install a security system that combines fingerprint analysis, facial scans, and other technology to identify all foreigners entering or exiting the United States. This contract reflected Accenture's new brand name (reminding the public of its separation from Arthur Andersen, Inc.) and symbolized its broad range of services.

Between 2004 and 2008, under the leadership of William D. Green, Accenture's fiscal status increased from US$15 billion to US$25 billion. During this period, Accenture's services were divided into the following sectors: Communications and High Technology; Financial Services; Products (including Automotive, Consumer Goods, Retail, and Health and Life Sciences); Public Services; and Resources.

In fiscal year 2011 Accenture had net revenues of US$25.5 billion. As of 2012, the company employed more than 249,000 people, including 5,000 senior executives.

FURTHER READING

Accenture plc. "Accenture Unveils 'Connected Vehicle Integrated Solution' to Help Manufacturers Meet Customer Demand for In-Vehicle Services—From Wi-Fi Access to Mobile Payments and Safety Devices." Accessed September 27, 2012. http://newsroom.accenture.com/article_display.cfm?article_id=5373

———. "2011 Letter from Our Chief Executive Officer." Accessed September 14, 2012. http://www.accenture.com/us-en/company/annual-report/Pages/annual-report-2011-ceo-letter.aspx.

"Accenture Ltd. Sets Price on $1.8 Billion IPO." *Chicago Tribune*, June 11, 2001.

Banks, Howard. "House Divided." *Forbes*, November 3, 1997.

Covell, Jeffrey L. "Accenture Ltd." *International Directory of Company Histories*. Ed. Jay P. Pederson. Vol. 108. Detroit, MI: St. James Press, 2010.

"Crowd Computing—The Future?" *Computing News Middle East*, January 19, 2012. http://www.cnmeonline.com/insight/crowd-computing-the-future/.

Gordon, Joanne. "A Rose by Any Name." *Forbes*, March 4, 2002, 86.

Manor, Robert. "Accenture Grows into Life on Bermuda, Land of Few Taxes or Rules." *Chicago Tribune*, July 20, 2001.

Pearlstein, Steven. "How Accenture Seized Tomorrow." *Washington Post*, June 4, 2004.

ADIDAS

AT A GLANCE

Brand Synopsis: A leading global sports apparel and gear brand, adidas is considered innovative and is primarily associated with sports such as soccer, baseball, football, and track and field.
Parent Company: adidas AG
Adi-Dassler-Strasse 1
D-91074 Herzogenaurach
Germany
http://www.adidas-group.com/
Sector: Consumer Discretionary
Industry Group: Consumer Durables & Apparel
Performance: *Market share*—22 percent worldwide (2010); 11.7 percent in the United States (2011). *Sales*—US$17.3 billion (2011).
Principal Competitors: ASICS; Converse; K-Swiss; New Balance; Nike; Puma; Skechers; Under Armour

BRAND ORIGINS

- Adidas was founded in 1948 in Germany by Adolf Dressler, after a 20-year partnership with his brother ended.
- Adidas became the number-one sporting apparel company in the world in the early 1970s.
- Adidas slipped to number-two worldwide in 1980 behind Nike, the position it still holds in the early 21st century.

Adidas footwear had its origins in Germany in 1920 when brand founder Adolf Dassler made his first pair of sports shoes because of his personal interest in athletics. Throughout the 1920s and 1930s, he and his brother Rudolph produced running shoes, soccer shoes with nailed studs, track shoes with hand-forged spikes, and the first tennis shoes. By the end of 1937, the line of Dassler shoes included styles designed for eleven specific sports.

During this time period, the Dasslers gave free shoes to athletes and used the Olympic Games as a way to promote their shoes, something they would continue to do after adidas was founded. Adolf Dassler also took input from athletes, trainers, doctors, and materials specialists. He used his findings to continuously improve his shoes.

The Dasslers' partnership ended in 1948 after years of bitter fighting. The brothers then formed two separate companies. Adolf Dassler named his venture "Addas." Then he changed the name to "adidas," a combination of his nickname, Adi, and a shortened form of Dassler. The brand founder adopted a lower case "a" to further distinguish his brand. Rudolph created the Puma Company, which rivaled adidas for years.

The brotherly rivalry played out at the Olympic Games, where adidas and Puma fought to equip more athletes. Adidas dominated at the 1952 Summer Olympics in Helsinki, when it introduced track shoes with changeable spikes and its first accessory, sports bags. In 1954 the German soccer team won the world championship wearing adidas shoes. The team wore the first shoes with screw-in soccer studs. In 1956 adidas revolutionized the game of soccer with the introduction of nylon soles. In 1963 it moved into nonsports shoes with the first adidas-branded soccer balls, and its first training suit came out in 1967.

Until the late 1960s, adidas remained primarily a European brand. Adidas shoes were not launched in the United States until 1968, when the Summer Olympic Games were held in Mexico City. The brand soon caught on in the United States, and by 1972 adidas had a major portion of the U.S. market and had become the world's largest sports-shoe brand.

During the 1970s, adidas capitalized on the running craze with technological improvements such as interchangeable spikes and sharkskin soles for traction. It helped triple the brand's sales between 1976 and 1979 to over US$500 million. By the end of the 1970s, adidas led the industry in sales and expanded into more sports. At the height of its popularity, adidas had 100 different shoe styles and between 30 percent and 40 percent of the sports-shoe market.

Beginning in 1979, however, adidas lost significant market share in the United States and, later, the world because of the popularity of newer brands like Nike and Pony which had more aggressive advertising and innovation. Adidas controlled 25 percent of the American market in 1978, then 20 percent in 1979. By 1980 Nike had passed adidas in market share in the United States, though adidas remained the worldwide leader. Adidas tried to regain its market share in the 1980s but misstepped in marketing and ignored such major American sporting trends as aerobics, basketball, and cross-training.

In 1989 the family-owned adidas was reorganized as a public German corporation. By this time, it had 15 percent of the global athletic shoe market, compared to Nike's 17 percent, and was in a downward spiral. In 1990 the company and brand were acquired by Bernard Tapie Finance G.m.b.H. The new owners cut the product line, but adidas still struggled with competition from Nike and Reebok and made poor marketing decisions. By 1992 adidas had only 3 percent of the U.S. market and 40 percent of the German market.

In February 1993 adidas was purchased by Robert Louis-Dreyfus, and a plan was put in place to broaden its appeal to the youth market. Though adidas was on the verge of becoming a second-tier brand by the mid-1990s, it soon reemerged stronger, with a sharper focus and new campaigns to raise brand awareness. The brand formed high-profile alliances with athletes and sports teams like the New York Yankees beginning in 1997. In 1998 adidas, seeking to appeal to runners in the United States, launched the provocative, million-dollar campaign "Runners. Yeah, We're Different." The ads eventually were used globally, ran through 2000, and led to record-high brand awareness in markets like the United States.

But adidas still struggled in the U.S. market, dropping behind Nike, Reebok, and New Balance. In the first nine months of 2003, sales sagged 16 percent. Still challenging market leader Nike and fighting for market share, adidas bought the rights to sponsor the 2004, 2008, and 2012 Summer Olympic Games. It also gained other high profile sponsorships, including Major League Soccer and FIFA (including the World Cup). In 2004 adidas launched its largest-ever advertising campaign, "Impossible Is Nothing," a year-long global effort that linked past and present sports stars in ads. The US$50 million campaign led to an 11 percent increase in sales.

As the adidas brand gained strength, its parent company bought a major competitor, Reebok, in 2006. Further honing its approach, adidas began focusing on increasing brand-desirability to increase revenue, and it targeted older consumers in developed markets and younger consumers in emerging markets. The decisions paid off with strong global sales and double-digit growth in 2011. While adidas was again a strong brand, it remained number two to Nike both globally and in the United States.

BRAND ELEMENTS

- The three-stripes logo was introduced in the 1940s as part of a support device for sports shoes produced by the Dassler brothers.
- The three stripes have defined the adidas brand.
- As adidas moved into apparel, it created the trefoil logo, which incorporated the three stripes.

The adidas brand is tied to its well-known three-stripes logo. The trademarked three-stripe design found on adidas shoes, apparel, and gear was introduced in 1941 as part of the support structure for sports shoes produced when the Dassler brothers were still partners. The three-stripe device was not registered as a trademark until 1949, and soon it had a related slogan, "The Brand with the 3 Stripes."

After the Dassler brothers split up and Adolf launched adidas, he and his brother Rudolph, the founder of Puma, fought for the rights to equip more athletes. Adidas's trademark three-stripe device made its shoes stand out from other brands. Standing out became increasingly important as media attention, beginning in the 1950s, focused on sporting events.

In 1967 adidas moved into sportswear with its first training suit. Seeking to distinguish its branded sportswear as well, in 1971 the brand adopted the trefoil, a geometric image with a triple intersection and three stripes running through it. Its clothing was often decorated with three stripes extending down the arms or legs as well. The trefoil logo eventually became the company's corporate symbol and was used on adidas Originals apparel in the early 21st century.

Yet another version of the three-stripes logo was created in 1997 and called the "three bars." It was originally placed on adidas sporting equipment. Inspired by how the three stripes appear on footwear, the three bars form the shape of a mountain, symbolizing the challenge to be faced.

BRAND IDENTITY

- Adidas was one of the first sports apparel brands to use athletic endorsements to build the brand.
- Adidas is especially linked to soccer, baseball, and the NBA.
- In 2011 its "adidas is all in" campaign was launched.

Adidas was among the first sportswear manufacturers to use athletic promotions and endorsements to make the brand synonymous with serious, successful athletes. Regularly serving as an official sponsor of the Summer Olympic Games, adidas continued to use promotions at major sporting events as primary advertising vehicles throughout the 20th and 21st centuries. Adidas's expanded line of sports shoes and apparel spread to encompass a wide variety of sports.

Many of the leading soccer players and teams have worn adidas, beginning with the 1954 World Cup-winning German soccer team. In 1971 both Muhammad Ali and Joe Frazier wore adidas in their "Fight of the Century." By the mid-1980s tennis star Ivan Lendl was the star of a global marketing campaign for the brand. In 1997 adidas began a long-term sponsorship of the New York Yankees baseball team, launched with the advertising campaign "Yankee Fans." Adidas began sponsoring New Zealand's Rugby Union team in 1999.

Soccer, though, remained key for adidas, which signed a 10-year agreement to sponsor Major League Soccer in the United States beginning in 2004 and a seven-year sponsorship of FIFA, including World Cup events, beginning in 2005. In 2006 adidas signed a US$400 million, 11-year global merchandising deal as the official uniform and apparel provider for the NBA.

Adidas's advertising emphasized its heritage in sports. Its extremely successful "Impossible Is Nothing" campaign was launched in 2004. It included television commercials with Muhammad Ali running with David Beckham, the British soccer star, and other leading athletes of the 1990s and early 2000s. In 2011 its "adidas is all in" campaign included soccer stars, NBA players, and pop star Katy Perry. This effort underscored the broadening of the brand's audience and appeal and its new emphasis on digital strategies to market itself to athletes and nonathletes alike.

BRAND STRATEGY

- Adidas began with sports shoes and expanded into sporting equipment in 1963.
- In 1967 adidas moved into sportswear.
- In 2002 adidas reorganized its brand structure.

From its founding, adidas has focused on innovation in the sports apparel industry. Founder Adolf Dassler began with sports shoes in the 1930s and 1940s, improving his designs with input from athletes, trainers, and materials experts. By linking his shoes with the world's leading athletes, Dassler helped adidas become known as one of the leading sports apparel companies by the mid-20th century.

In 1963 adidas moved into sporting equipment when it introduced its own brand of soccer balls. By 1970 the World Cup had adopted adidas's as its official ball. In 1967 it moved into sportswear with its first training suit. It was then that the brand adopted the trefoil logo with three stripes running through it to distinguish its branded sportswear. All the while, adidas introduced shoes, apparel, and equipment for more and more sports, and it continued to innovate and refine its lines.

In 2002 adidas reorganized its brand structure to further develop its customer base and increase growth. Moving away from divisions of footwear and apparel, the brand organized into Sports Performance (for serious athletes but with appeal to be worn outside of sport), Sports Heritage (which included original adidas designs for lifestyle wear), and Sport Style (stylish, forward-looking sportswear). In 2007 Sports Style was merged into Sports Heritage.

To further promote the brand, adidas opened retail stores in markets worldwide, including concept stores, those dedicated to Sports Performance and Sports Heritage lines, and factory outlets. It also had an online retail presence. Because adidas especially targeted developing markets like China, it focused on opening stores that adapted to those markets. In 2011 adidas also sought to build new markets in countries like Russia.

BRAND EQUITY

- Adidas is the number-two sports apparel brand in the world, after Nike.
- Adidas had significant growth in 2011, though it did not overtake Nike.
- Adidas has high brand equity and is considered a leading green brand.

For decades, adidas has been the number-two sports apparel manufacturer after Nike, both globally and in the United States. Though the worldwide economic downturn affected the brand's fortunes, it had significant global growth in 2011 and 18.5 percent growth in the United

States in the first half of 2012. For the adidas Group, its biggest market in 2011 was Western Europe (35 percent), followed by North America (20 percent), Greater China (12 percent), Other Asian Markets (15 percent), Latin America (13 percent), and European Emerging Markets (5 percent).

Because of adidas's growth, its brand equity remained high and it was admired as a leading and environmentally friendly brand. Interbrand's list of *Best Global Brands 2012* ranked adidas at number 60. Its brand value was US$6.699 billion, an increase of 9 percent over 2011. Interbrand also ranked adidas at number 22 on its list of *Best Global Green Brands 2012*. Forbes ranked adidas at 53 on its 2012 list of *The World's Most Powerful Brands*, a ranking of brand performance that measures both consumer perception and brand value. Its brand value was US$6.8 billion. In 2012 Brand Finance's *Global 500 2012* said adidas had a brand value of US$7.150 billion and an enterprise value of US$11.457 billion, and it was ranked 135th, up from 139th in 2011. Brand Finance also ranked adidas 11th on its list of the *German Top 30* in 2012 with a brand value of EUR5.393 billion.

BRAND AWARENESS

- Adidas has worked to build its brand awareness since its inception.
- Though adidas is no longer the number-one sporting apparel brand in the world, many sports fans identify it as a leading brand because of its strong ties to leading athletes and events.
- Adidas has worked to broaden its appeal through ads featuring nonathletes like Katy Perry.

Adidas's founder focused on building brand awareness from the first by linking adidas with the world's leading athletes. Initially these were Olympic track and field athletes and soccer players, but later adidas linked to athletes in many sports, from basketball to baseball to tennis. Though it lost its status as the number-one sporting apparel brand in the world, many sports fans identify it as the leading sports brand. Over the years, effective advertising campaigns helped build brand awareness. From 1998 to 2000, the "Runners. Yeah, We're Different." campaign celebrated the quirky habits of committed runners, and it was effective in highlighting the adidas brand globally. In 2011 "adidas is all in" used pop star Katy Perry in an attempt to broaden its appeal and brand awareness. Based in Germany, adidas is a favorite brand among German consumers and is highly regarded in markets such as the United States, the United Kingdom, and India. Surveys and studies emphasize adidas's high brand awareness and popularity. For example, the Reputation Institute's *Global RepTrak 100* ranked adidas at number 11 in 2012. Also in 2012, adidas made the *Top 25 Global Corporate Reputation Index*, a list of the companies with the strongest corporate reputations that was put together by Burson-Martseller, Landor, PSB, and BAV.

BRAND OUTLOOK

- After adidas saw significant global growth in 2011, it focused its marketing on Russia, North America, China, and other less-developed market areas.
- In 2010 adidas released its five-year strategic plan, "Route 2015," which outlined how it would pursue increased market share and sales.
- Also in 2010 adidas released its "Environmental Strategy 2015," which explained how it would become a zero-emissions company by 2015.

Though adidas had a 6 percent decline in sales in 2009 because of the ongoing worldwide economic recession, there was still high demand for sporting goods and sporting apparel. The brand saw significant global growth in 2011 and in the United States in 2012, and adidas planned to increase its revenues through growth in Russia, North America, Greater China, Latin America, Japan, and the United Kingdom. Adidas also hoped that by targeting older consumers in developed markets in Europe and North America and younger consumers in developing economies, it would gain market share and increase revenues. The brand was helped by high-profile, long-term sponsorships, including its forthcoming sponsorship for the FIFA World Cup 2014.

Though it was unclear if adidas could surpass Nike and regain its position as the number-one sports apparel brand in the world, the company released a five-year strategic plan in 2010 called "Route 2015" that it hoped would help it achieve that goal. The plan outlines the ways in which the brand plans to outperform its major competitors and increase market growth. That same year, adidas unveiled "Environmental Strategy 2015," a five-year plan focused on changing the brand's environmental impact and help it become a zero-emissions company, with energy use cut by 20 percent. Adidas was already one of the most sustainable companies in the world, having been included in the Dow Jones Sustainability Index every year since 1999.

FURTHER READING

"Adidas." *Forbes*. Accessed January 24, 2013. http://www.forbes.com/companies/adidas/.

"Adidas." RankingTheBrands.com. Accessed January 24, 2013. http://www.rankingthebrands.com/Brand-detail.aspx?brandID=220.

Adidas Group. *Adidas: The Story of a Logo*. Accessed January 24, 2013. http://www.adidas-group.com/en/ourgroup/assets/History/pdfs/logohistory-e.pdf.

———. *Adidas Group History*. Accessed January 24, 2013. http://www.adidas-group.com/en/ourgroup/history/history.aspx.

———. *Annual Report 2011*. Accessed January 24, 2013. http://adidas-group.corporate-publications.com/2011/gb/.

"Best Global Brands 2012." Interbrand. Accessed January 24, 2013. http://www.interbrand.com/en/best-global-brands/2012/Best-Global-Brands-2012.aspx.

Brand Finance. "Adidas." *Brandirectory*. Accessed January 24, 2013. http://brandirectory.com/profile/adidas.

Dougal, April S. "Adidas." *Encyclopedia of Consumer Goods*. Ed. Janice Jorgensen. Vol. 2. Detroit, MI: St. James Press, 1994.

Hall, James. "London 2012 Olympics: Adidas Aims to Beat Nike to Second Place at Games." *Telegraph* (London), May 29, 2011.

Skidmore, Sarah. "Adidas Enters Barefoot Shoe Race." *Huffington Post*, August 23, 2011. Accessed January 24, 2013. http://www.huffingtonpost.com/2011/08/23/adidas-barefoot-shoe_n_934484.html.

ADOBE

AT A GLANCE

Brand Synopsis: As a leading digital media and digital marketing solutions developer, Adobe is "changing the world through digital experiences."
Parent Company: Adobe Systems Inc.
345 Park Avenue
San Jose, California 95110-2704
United States
http://www.adobe.com
Sector: Information Technology
Industry Group: Software & Services
Performance: *Market share*—43 percent of the creative software market (2009).
Principal Competitors: Infosys Technologies Ltd.; Hitachi Solutions Ltd.; SAP Americas Inc.; CA Inc.; Electronic Arts Inc.

BRAND ORIGINS

- Adobe was founded in 1982 by John Warnock and Charles Geschke, both former employees of Xerox Corporation's Research Center in Palo Alto, California.
- In 1987 Adobe introduced Adobe Illustrator, a design and illustration software program.
- In 1993 Adobe realized its goal of enabling incompatible computer systems to communicate via the introduction of its Adobe Acrobat software.
- Adobe solidified its position in the desktop publishing market in 1994 when it acquired Aldus, the maker of the industry-leading PageMaker desktop publishing software.
- In 2005 Adobe and Macromedia Inc. merged in a US$3.4 billion deal, one of the largest ever in the software industry.

Adobe was founded in 1982 by John Warnock and Charles Geschke, both former employees of Xerox Corporation's Research Center in Palo Alto, California. At Xerox, Warnock conducted interactive graphics research, while Geschke directed computer science and graphics research as the manager of the company's Imaging Sciences Laboratory. Believing in the profitability of an independent venture, they left Xerox to establish their own business, which they named Adobe, after a creek that ran by their homes in Los Altos, California.

Shortly after it was launched, Adobe introduced PostScript, a powerful computer language that essentially described to a printer or other output device the appearance of an electronic page, including the placement of characters, lines, or images. The introduction of PostScript proved integral to the desktop publishing revolution. With a personal computer (PC) and a laser printer equipped with PostScript, users could produce polished, professional-looking documents with high-quality graphics.

In 1987 the company introduced Adobe Illustrator, a design and illustration software program. Enabling users to create high-quality line drawings, Illustrator became popular among graphic designers, desktop publishers, and technical illustrators. The company also released the

Adobe Type Library, which contained a large selection of type fonts, many of which were original typefaces Adobe had created especially for the electronic medium. The Type Library eventually became the most widely used collection in the industry.

Adobe ended the 1980s by acquiring all rights to Photoshop, an image editing application. Photoshop, which was designed especially for artists and desktop publishers, was slated for market in conjunction with the Apple Macintosh. Designed to work with type, line art, and other images, Photoshop provided users with a complete toolbox for editing, creating, and manipulating images. Other unique Photoshop features included color correction, retouching, and color separation capabilities.

In 1993 Adobe realized its goal of enabling incompatible computer systems to communicate. Adobe Acrobat software was designed to turn computers into information distributors that would allow Macintosh users to view a document in its original form, with formatting and graphics intact, even if the document had been created on an IBM. Analysts hailed Acrobat as a tool that could facilitate electronic distribution of everything from interoffice memos to magazines.

Adobe solidified its position in the desktop publishing market in 1994 when it acquired Aldus, the maker of the industry-leading PageMaker desktop publishing software. Adobe released a number of products in 1999, including InDesign. InDesign was Adobe's first offering in the high-end professional publishing segment, which had been dominated by Quark products.

In 2005 Adobe and Macromedia Inc. merged in a US$3.4 billion deal, one of the largest ever in the software industry. The merger brought significant new capabilities to Adobe, and in January 2006 a new engagement platform was unveiled that married technology from Adobe Reader with Macromedia's Flash Player. This new technology proved invaluable in moving Adobe into the mobile device market.

BRAND ELEMENTS

- The Adobe brand is represented by a logo featuring a white, triangular "A" element that is superimposed on a square red background. The word "Adobe" appears in black type below the logo.
- In 2013 Adobe utilized the tagline, "Changing the world through digital experiences," which encompassed the company's dual focus on digital media and digital marketing solutions.
- Adobe provides its customers with opportunities to immerse themselves in the Adobe brand through unique experiences.

The Adobe brand is represented by a logo featuring a triangular element that represents the letter "A." This element typically is white, and is superimposed on a square red background. The word "Adobe" appears in black type below the logo. Other versions of the logo use the same elements but display the white square background and brand name in white, superimposed against a red background. In this latter version, the triangular "A" element appears in red. In addition to its main logo, Adobe has created specialized logos for some of its well-known products, including Adobe Acrobat and Flash.

In 2013 Adobe used the tagline, "Changing the world through digital experiences." This encompassed the company's dual focus on digital media and digital marketing solutions. Adobe's digital media offerings include applications for functions such as desktop publishing, digital publishing, web authoring, and photo editing. Within the digital marketing space, Adobe provides publishers, advertisers, and marketers with solutions for monitoring and optimizing campaigns and customer experiences.

Adobe provides its customers with opportunities to immerse themselves in the Adobe brand through unique experiences. One example is the Photoshop & You Experience, which took place in 2011. The event brought together Adobe Photoshop experts, camera manufacturers, industry leaders, and photographers in what the company described as "a celebration of the iconic Photoshop brand and all things related to digital imaging," according to a July 25, 2011, *Business Wire* release. Attendees had the opportunity to engage in how-to sessions and learn photography, printing, and photo editing techniques.

BRAND IDENTITY

- Among creative professionals, Adobe has long been the top choice for traditional publishing and imaging solutions.
- In 2010 the Adobe brand took a serious beating when Apple prevented the use of Flash technology on its popular iPod Touch, iPhone, and iPad devices, leading to Flash's eventual demise.
- The death of Flash prompted Adobe to alter the focus of its brand, along with the way it interacted with consumers.
- Adobe's more comprehensive brand position is communicated through the tagline, "Changing the world through digital experiences."

The strong popularity of applications like Photoshop, Acrobat, and InDesign has given the Adobe brand a choice position among creative professionals, including graphic designers and photographers. Passion for Adobe has resulted in the emergence of individuals who identify themselves with unofficial titles like "International Design Heroes" and "Adobe Evangelists." These proponents share their expertise and passion for the brand with others at Adobe sanctioned events and other venues.

Beyond the creative community, the vast majority of everyday consumers have experienced the Adobe brand through a handful of ubiquitous applications. A prime example is Flash, which was long the dominant personal computer multimedia software. In 2010 the Adobe brand took a serious beating when Apple prevented the use of Flash technology on its popular iPod Touch, iPhone, and iPad devices.

According to a July 21, 2010, *Daily Finance* article, the late Apple CEO Steve Jobs effectively sealed Flash's fate when he wrote: "Flash was created during the PC era for PCs and mice. The mobile era is about low-power devices, touch interfaces and open web standards, all areas where Flash falls short." Adobe's stock dropped nearly US$3 per share five days after Jobs' remarks, and during the first half of the year the value of the Adobe brand plummeted 43 percent, from US$7 billion to US$4 billion.

Other technology giants, including Google and Microsoft, jumped on the bandwagon with Apple, supporting other technologies, namely HTML5, as a better alternative to Flash. In November of 2011 Adobe threw in the towel, announcing it would stop offering Flash Player for mobile devices, resulting in a US$97 million restructuring charge and the elimination of 750 employees.

In its November 9, 2011, issue, *eWeek* described the public's reaction: "When Apple made it clear it was never bringing Flash to the iPad or iPhone, Adobe thought for sure the customers would complain and force Apple to change its stance. But now years later, it's clear that they didn't care that much one way or another. They just wanted their mobile devices to work reliably no matter what underlying technology they connected."

The death of Flash prompted Adobe to alter the focus of its brand, along with the way it interacted with consumers. The company began offering applications on a hosted basis through its Creative Cloud and developing software that could be used on tablet devices. Finally, Adobe expanded into the realm of digital marketing, offering tools publishers, advertisers, and marketers could use to optimize their campaigns. Collectively, these changes marked Adobe's evolution into a more comprehensive brand focused on "Changing the world through digital experiences."

BRAND STRATEGY

- A major aspect of Adobe's brand strategy is maintaining strong connections with the creative professionals who utilize the majority of its products.
- On the interactive front, Adobe personalizes its connection to consumers in different global markets through the establishment of local online communities.
- Adobe's brand strategy has evolved beyond digital media, in which it has enjoyed a long-time leadership position, to include digital marketing solutions.

A major aspect of Adobe's brand strategy is maintaining strong connections with the creative professionals who utilize the majority of its products. The creative community's passion for Adobe has resulted in the emergence of individuals who identify themselves as "International Design Heroes" and "Adobe Evangelists." These brand advocates share their expertise and passion for the brand with others through official venues such as Adobe Design for Impact, a virtual event where experts from international markets such as Paris and Barcelona engage with participants from across the globe to offer insight and exchange ideas.

Adobe MAX, a conference attended by more than 5,000 creative professionals throughout the world, is another example of Adobe's brand engagement strategy. The annual event provides Adobe users with a venue for experiencing the brand together. This is accomplished through collaborating, exploring software and project ideas, pushing boundaries, and achieving inspiration through more than 300 different labs and breakout sessions.

On the interactive front, Adobe personalizes its connection to consumers in different global markets through the establishment of local online communities. For example, in 2013 Adobe maintained dedicated Facebook pages for customers in markets such as Taiwan, Hong Kong, Korea, India, and Southeast Asia. Likewise, dedicated Adobe websites served specific global markets, providing a consistent message regarding the brand's offerings, but with a local focus. In China, Adobe's site is presented in the Chinese language, with pictures of Chinese creative and business professionals utilizing the company's products.

Adobe's brand strategy has evolved beyond digital media, in which it has enjoyed a long-time leadership position, to include digital marketing solutions. This includes tools that publishers, advertisers, and marketers use to optimize campaigns and customer experiences. It represents Adobe's evolution into a more comprehensive brand focused on "Changing the world through digital experiences."

BRAND EQUITY

- Adobe ranked 78th on Interbrand's listing of the 100 Best Global Brands.
- According to Interbrand, the Adobe brand was valued at US$4.56 billion in 2012, representing an increase of 9 percent from the previous year.
- *FORTUNE* magazine ranked Adobe as the second-leading computer software company on its World's Most Admired Companies list for 2012.

According to Interbrand, the Adobe brand was valued at US$4.56 billion in 2012, an increase of 9 percent from the previous year. Adobe ranked 78th on Interbrand's listing of the 100 Best Global Brands.

Adobe's brand equity also is evident by its placement in rankings compiled by leading business publications. For example, Adobe ranked as the second-leading computer software company on *FORTUNE* magazine's World's Most Admired Companies list for 2012. Adobe also was included on *FORTUNE*'s 100 Best Companies to Work For list that year. Additionally, Adobe secured the number-eight spot in the *Financial Times*' ranking of the 25 most valuable U.S. software and computer services companies in 2011.

BRAND AWARENESS

- By 2012 Adobe's digital media products were the solutions of choice by the majority of creative professionals and its digital marketing solutions were used by approximately 5,000 of the world's top brands.
- Photoshop Touch, Adobe's photo editing tool for tablet users, earned it Editors' Choice honors from *PC Magazine* and made iTunes' App Store Best of 2012 list.
- Adobe ranked 54th on *Forbes'* World's Most Innovative Companies list in 2012.

The Adobe brand has long benefited from strong levels of top-of-mind awareness. By 2012 the company's digital media products were the solutions of choice by the majority of creative professionals. Adobe Photoshop alone was used by 90 percent of creative professionals worldwide. The company's newer digital marketing solutions were used by approximately 5,000 of the world's top brands.

Awareness of the Adobe brand extends beyond desktop applications. For example, in 2012 Adobe Photoshop enthusiasts lauded the introduction of Photoshop Touch, a photo editing tool for tablet users. The product's robust array of tools for manipulating images earned it Editors' Choice honors from *PC Magazine* in 2012. In addition, the app's popularity among consumers resulted in its being named to the App Store Hall of Fame and making iTunes' App Store Best of 2012 list.

In 2012 Adobe ranked 54th on *Forbes'* World's Most Innovative Companies list. That year, analysts took note of Adobe's ability to move beyond the demise of its Flash technology and develop new offerings for the mobile device market. For example, IDG's InfoWorld Test Center recognized Adobe's PhoneGap development tool, which could be used to create mobile apps with HTML5, with the Technology of the Year Award.

BRAND OUTLOOK

- After the setback associated with the collapse of its Flash technology in 2011, Adobe has taken strides to ensure the continued relevancy of its brand, including the development of tablet-friendly versions of its software.
- Adobe's evolution into a brand that focuses on both digital marketing and digital media means that it has a more comprehensive range of solutions to offer its customers.
- Adobe's transition to a subscription-based model for its products positions the company to generate a higher volume of recurring revenue and reach customers who might not otherwise purchase Adobe products and experience the brand.
- Despite extremely high levels of adoption across many industries, Adobe estimated that the market for Acrobat still included tens of millions of potential customers in 2012.

After the setback associated with the collapse of its Flash technology in 2011, Adobe has taken strides to ensure the continued relevancy of its brand moving forward. This has been accomplished in several ways, including the development of tablet-friendly versions of Adobe software, such as Photoshop Touch, which earned Editors' Choice honors from *PC Magazine* and made iTunes' App Store Best of 2012 list. Another example is Adobe's PhoneGap development tool, which could be used to create mobile apps using technologies such as HTML5.

In addition, Adobe's evolution into a brand that offers digital marketing solutions means that it has a more comprehensive range of solutions to offer its customers. As the company explains in its 2011 annual report, Adobe's foray into digital marketing complements the digital media side of its business by "bringing together the art of creating content with the science of measuring and optimizing it, enabling our customers to achieve optimal business outcomes."

Adobe's transition to a subscription-based model, which it calls the Adobe Creative Cloud, positions the company to generate a higher volume of recurring revenue. From a financial standpoint, this offers the prospect of a more stable and predictable income stream. In addition, the software-as-a-service (SaaS) approach provides access to customers who might not otherwise purchase Adobe products and experience the brand.

Innovation is critical for the continued evolution of organizations and their brands, and Adobe is no exception. The company continues to make substantial developments in research and development initiatives, ultimately leading to the development of new digital marketing and digital media products. In 2011 Adobe devoted US$738.1 million to research and development initiatives compared to US$680.3 million in 2010 and US$565.1 million in 2009.

Although Adobe continues to introduce a wide range of new products and solutions, significant opportunities still exist for existing, less glamorous offerings. An excellent example is Adobe Acrobat, which traces its roots back to the early 1990s. Despite extremely high levels of adoption across many industries, Adobe estimated that the market for Acrobat still included tens of millions of potential customers in 2012. In particular, growth opportunities existed among both small and midsized businesses.

Electronic signatures present another opportunity for growth within Adobe's document services business. Through the acquisition of EchoSign, Adobe was able to offer digital signature technology to customers without the need for digital certificates, scanning software, or signature pads. Significant opportunities existed for this technology as it was integrated into Adobe's cloud-based offerings. The new solution provided millions of global users with the capability to sign contracts faster and eliminate the need for sending paper documents via express delivery services.

FURTHER READING

"Adobe Announces Integrated Video Publishing, Advertising and Analytics Platform." Benzinga.com, February 27, 2012.

"Adobe Highlights Digital Marketing and Revenue Link." *Marketing Week*, February 23, 2012.

"Adobe Systems Inc." *International Directory of Company Histories*. Ed. Derek Jacques and Paula Kepos. Vol. 106. Farmington Hills, MI: St. James Press, 2010.

"Adobe Takes Major Step to Bring Broadcast TV Online." *Newsbytes US*, November 16, 2012.

"Adobe Unveils Photoshop & You Experience in San Francisco." *Business Wire*, July 25, 2011.

Elliott, Stuart. "To Stand out, Campaign for Adobe Gets Blunt." *New York Times*, October 23, 2012.

"Information Technology: Adobe Makes Pledge to Be Loud and Proud Brand." *Marketing Week*, March 17, 2011.

Reisinger, Don. "Adobe Lost the Mobile Flash Battle with Apple 10 Reasons Why." *eWeek*, November 9, 2011.

"The 10 Biggest Brand Disasters of 2010: Adobe." *Daily Finance*, July 21, 2010.

AEON

AT A GLANCE

Brand Synopsis: Aeon and its subsidiary brands represent thousands of stores of various kinds—most notably supermarkets and convenience stores—in Asia and Australia and are identified with social and environmental consciousness.
Parent Company: Aeon Co., Ltd.
1-5-1 Nakase, Mihama-ku, Chiba-shi
Chiba 261-8515
Japan
http://www.aeon.info/en/
Sector: Consumer Staples
Industry Group: Food & Drug Retailing
Performance: *Sales*—JPY4.7 trillion (US$58.1 billion) (2012).
Principal Competitors: The Daiei, Inc.; Isetan Company Ltd.; The Seiyu, Ltd.

BRAND ORIGINS

- With thousands of stores in Asia and Australia, Aeon is a major retailer.
- In the 1970s, the retail chains owned by Takuya Okada, Kazuichi Futagi, and Jiro Inoue combined to form the Japan United Stores Company (JUSCO).
- Jusco stores are located in Hong Kong, China, Taiwan, Thailand, and Australia.
- Aeon's international partnerships include alliances with British, American, and French companies.

Aeon is a retailer through and through. It has more than 1,500 supermarkets, 600 general merchandise stores, 220 shopping centers, 4,100 convenience stores, 3,400 specialty stores, 2,800 drugstores, 100 discount stores, and other affiliated companies. Many of these stores are in Japan, although the company has 100 overseas supermarkets, general merchandise stores, and other types of stores. A general merchandise store (also known as a superstore or hypermarket) is a store that combines a supermarket and a department store under one roof.

In addition to its Jusco supermarkets and general merchandise stores, the company has other stores, subsidiaries, and affiliated companies. These include the Ministop convenience stores as well as its CFS Corporation, Welcia, and Aeon Wellness drugstores. These stores are in Japan and throughout the rest of Asia.

Aeon has long been a multipart corporation. Takuya Okada's Okadaya Co., Ltd., originally began as a kimono and clothing store in the 1700s and grew to become a department store chain after World War II. Okada observed that larger chains could cut costs by buying and selling items in large numbers and thereby enjoy administrative benefits. Meanwhile, Kazuichi Futagi and Jiro Inoue both had their own chains of stores in Japan. By the 1970s, Okada's, Futagi's, and Inoue's businesses combined to form the Japan United Stores Company, JUSCO (or Jusco). The company changed its name from Jusco to Aeon in 1989.

Although founded in Japan, the company has been an international presence for some time. Jusco's first overseas store opened in Malaysia in 1985. Jusco would later open stores in other areas, including Hong Kong, China, Taiwan, Thailand, and Australia. Other Aeon stores, such as Ministop drugstores, can be found in Japan, China, the Philippines, Vietnam, South Korea, and Indonesia.

Aeon has partnered with companies from other countries. In 1984 it began a partnership with the British women's clothing and home goods company Laura Ashley, and since 1990 it has operated the Japanese stores of another British company, the Body Shop, known for its lotions and soaps. Aeon's partnerships with American companies include its 1988–2010 involvement with the women's clothing company Talbots and its involvement with the Sports Authority, a sporting goods chain, and Claire's, a chain that sells fashion accessories.

Aeon's international business continues to grow. It acquired stores of the French company Carrefour in Japan in 2005 and in Malaysia in 2012. In addition to its stores, Aeon is affiliated with companies like the AIC Corporation, a retail consortium that imports goods for Aeon's stores. As an importer, AIC has offices all over Asia in addition to its head office in Chiba, Japan. Another of Aeon's international efforts is the Tasmania Feedlot, a beef-producing cattle operation on the island of Tasmania near Australia. These affiliations demonstrate that Aeon is a global company with global concerns.

BRAND ELEMENTS

- The Aeon name comes from a form of the Latin word for eternity.
- The Aeon logo includes a horizontal ring in the middle of the E of Aeon that links the letters A, E, and O.
- Aeon's Ministop logo includes a house and a tree, symbols of "warmth and comfort," according to the company.
- Other Aeon logos include a butterfly symbol used by the Aeon Wellness drugstores in Malaysia.
- The logo for Topvalu, Aeon's private brand, includes a rectangular shape with a semicircle projecting from the top.

The company took the Aeon name from a form of the Latin word for eternity. On its website, the company adds that the name also means "a future of limitless promise." The name's connection to the Latin language can be seen in the Aeon logo, which uses a ligature (the A and the E are attached to each other), resulting in "ÆON." The Aeon logo also has a horizontal ring shape for the middle bar of the E in Aeon. This ring also connects the A and O of the word as well.

The logo for the Jusco stores is reminiscent of Aeon's logo. This logo is in capital letters, like the Aeon logo. In addition, the S and the C in the middle of Jusco are intertwined, echoing the way the horizontal ring of the Aeon logo connects the letters A, E, and O. In addition, both logos often use the colors magenta and white. The similarities of these logos reinforce the brand's visual presence.

The brand symbol for Aeon's Ministop stores is evocative. According to a Ministop website, the logo symbolizes "'your refreshment station on a street corner.' It shows a house and a tree for its motif, with an arc encircling the MINISTOP inscription. The logo represents our desire to provide family-like warmth and comfort. It also expresses that MINISTOP is an indispensable existence for the local community, and provides a variety of products and services to create a future of limitless promise by transforming daily life." Other company symbols include a stylized butterfly that is used for Aeon Wellness, Aeon's chain of Malaysian drugstores.

Other Aeon brand elements include logos for its private brand, Topvalu. The Topvalu logo consists of the word TOPVALU in capital letters in a rectangle. A semicircular shape projects from the top central portion of this rectangle. Usually this semicircle features the capitalized words QUALITY AND TRUST above three stars. For Topvalu Select products, the semicircular shape features the word PREMIUM above a maple leaf and the word SELECT under the rectangle/semicircle shape. Topvalu Bestprice products feature the Topvalu rectangle, the semicircular QUALITY AND TRUST and stars portion, with BESTPRICE under the rectangle/semicircle shape.

BRAND IDENTITY

- Aeon embraces the three principles of peace, people, and community.
- Self-service counters and baby rooms are amenities Aeon provides for its customers.
- Aeon's charitable and community interests include donations for natural disaster relief and its 1 Percent Club.
- In 1991 Aeon created the Aeon Group Environment Foundation, which established an international environmental award, the MIDORI Prize for Biodiversity.
- Aeon has planted more than seven million trees throughout the world, promoted recycling, and opened the ecological shopping center Aeon LakeTown.

According to Aeon's website, the customer is at the center of the brand's identity. This is emphasized by a diagram showing the customer in a circle bounded by a triangle whose three corners represent the basic principles of the Aeon philosophy: peace, people, and community. Discussing its commitment to peace, the company notes that "AEON is a corporate group whose operations are dedicated to the pursuit of peace through prosperity." Discussing people, it adds that "AEON is a corporate group that respects human dignity and values personal relationships." Discussing community, it concludes that "AEON is a corporate group rooted in local community life and dedicated to making a continuing contribution to the community." Reflecting the parent company's customer-centered philosophy, Aeon's Jusco stores feature special amenities like self-service counters and baby rooms, which are rooms where mothers can feed babies, change their diapers, and let them rest.

The company embodies its commitment to peace, people, and community through involvement in charitable activities. It donates to natural disaster relief in Japan and other countries and in 1989 founded the 1 Percent Club, which uses 1 percent of the member companies' pretax profits to fund initiatives. These initiatives include a teenage ambassadorship program, projects involving education and culture, and environmental efforts. In this manner Aeon promotes its brand as more than just a retail operation.

Aeon has long been interested in environmental matters and has promoted them as part of its brand. Since 1990 it has been a partner of the Body Shop, a company committed to human, animal, and environmental issues. In 1991 Aeon created the Aeon Group Environment Foundation, which established an international environmental award, the MIDORI Prize for Biodiversity. Aeon has established an extensive tree planting campaign that has helped plant more than seven million trees in Japan and in other places, including Malaysia, China, Kenya, Vietnam, Laos, Cambodia, Indonesia, and the island of Miyakejima. In addition, the company has promoted recycling and has opened an ecological shopping center in Japan, Aeon LakeTown.

BRAND STRATEGY

- Topvalu and Jusco Selection are Aeon's private brands.
- Introduced in 1994, Aeon's Topvalu brand includes around 6,000 products and earned JPY530 billion (US$6.47 billion) in 2012.
- Since Topvalu is a private brand, Aeon does not have to spend as much money to produce or promote it.
- In 2010 Aeon began opening R.O.U stores, which cater to female shoppers in their 30s.
- After the 2011 earthquake and disaster, Aeon was able to reopen stores to serve its customer base without hiking prices.

Aeon uses private labels, like Topvalu and Jusco Selection, as a major part of its strategy to strengthen and expand the overall Aeon brand. Like Aeon's customer commitment, the company's strategy for its private brands has three parts. Not surprisingly, the first part of Jusco's private brand strategy involves listening to customers. According to a company website, the second part is Aeon's goal to use its private brands "to deliver incremental profitability, sales, and strengthening AEON's competitive advantage through differentiation." The third focus of its brand strategy is to use private brands to unify the company.

One private brand, Topvalu, is a vital part of Aeon's success. Introduced in 1994, this brand encompasses around 6,000 products and includes food and beverages, clothing, and pet products. Writing in the *Wall Street Journal*, Hiroyuki Kachi noted that since Topvalu is a private brand, Aeon does not have to spend as much money to produce or promote it. It delivers much in return, though. Kachi observed that the Topvalu brand earned JPY530 billion (US$6.47 billion) in 2012. Topvalu products appear in Aeon stores in Japan and China. Japan's Maruetsu supermarkets, which partner with Aeon, also carry the Topvalu brand.

In keeping with its strategy of listening to consumer needs, the company launched a new type of store in Japan in 2010. Called R.O.U, the store caters to female shoppers in their 30s and features health and beauty products, household goods, and stationery. Unlike other Aeon group stores, these stores do *not* include Aeon's private store brands.

Aeon's strategy of focusing on customers served it well after the devastating earthquake and tsunami that struck northeast Japan in March 2011. As reported in the *Wall Street Journal* on April 12, 2012, Aeon stores were able to reopen soon after the disaster with enough inventory to meet demand and without raising prices to take advantage of those in desperate need. This ability to return to normal helped maintain consumer confidence in the brand.

BRAND EQUITY

- Aeon is the largest mall developer in Japan and one of the country's largest retailers.
- In 2007 Aeon operated 518 of Japan's 2,700 shopping centers for a 19.2 percent share of that market.
- In 2012 Aeon held around 14 percent of the Japanese superstore market.
- Aeon's Ministop stores claimed about a 23 percent share of the convenience store market in the Philippines in 2012.
- Aeon's Topvalu brand is Japan's biggest private brand.

As a large company operating in different countries, Aeon participates in a number of markets. It is the largest mall developer in Japan and one of the country's largest retailers. In 2007 Aeon operated 518 of Japan's 2,700 shopping centers for a 19.2 percent share of that market. In addition, Aeon held approximately 14 percent share of the Japanese superstore market in 2012.

In other markets, Aeon's Ministop stores accounted for about a 23 percent share of the convenience store market in the Philippines in 2012. According to 2010 reports, Ministops accounted for 9 percent of South

Korea's convenience store market and a 3.8 percent share of Japan's convenience store market.

The company's dominant retail presence extends to its brands. With its thousands of products and billions of yen in sales, Aeon's Topvalu brand is Japan's biggest private brand.

BRAND AWARENESS

- In 2011 to raise brand awareness, Aeon gave the Aeon Mall name to its shopping malls with Aeon supermarkets as their anchor stores.
- Aeon Malls exist throughout Japan and China and often include stores affiliated with Aeon, like Laura Ashley.
- In a 2011 poll by Nikkei Business Publications, consumers named Aeon the third most environmentally responsible company in Japan.
- The International Council of Shopping Centers has given the Asia Shopping Centre Awards to Aeon for design and development.

In 2011 Aeon's shopping mall division sought to raise its brand awareness. It gave the Aeon Mall name to its shopping malls with Aeon supermarkets as their anchor stores. Aeon Malls exist throughout Japan and China. They often include stores affiliated with Aeon, such as Laura Ashley, and thus reinforce Aeon's ties to other companies.

Consumers have taken note of Aeon's extensive environmental efforts. In 2011 consumers named Aeon the third-most environmentally responsible company in Japan. This poll, conducted by Nikkei Business Publications, gave Aeon high marks for its efforts regarding global warming, energy conservation, recycling, waste reduction, biodiversity, and conservation of nature.

These environmental efforts have also earned awards for Aeon. Its shopping centers have won Asia Shopping Centre Awards for design and development, and for sustainable design, from the International Council of Shopping Centers, Inc. (ICSC). Other Aeon shopping centers have won other honors from the ICSC, including awards for shopping center renovations that lower carbon dioxide emissions and address the needs of elderly consumers. These awards reflect Aeon's commitments to its customers and the environment.

BRAND OUTLOOK

- In 2008 Aeon introduced new Topvalu items, Topvalu Barreal beer and the clothing line Topvalu Collection.
- In November 2011, Aeon expanded by acquiring Marunaka and Sanyo Marunaka, two Japanese supermarket companies.
- Aeon opened multiple Jusco stores and introduced the Topvalu brand in China in 2012.
- Founded in 2012, the Aeon ECO Project aimed to achieve environmental goals beyond the company's efforts to reduce carbon dioxide emissions.

Aeon continues to develop its various brands and to expand its business. In 2008 it introduced new items for its Topvalu line, Topvalu Barreal beer and the Topvalu Collection, a clothing line. In November 2011 it acquired more businesses by buying Marunaka and Sanyo Marunaka, two Japanese supermarket companies.

The company experienced a number of interesting international developments in 2012. In that year, it opened multiple Jusco stores in China and introduced the Topvalu brand into the country. Later in 2012, however, Chinese protests prompted the closure of several Aeon supermarkets in China and the vandalizing and looting of a few stores. Most of the stores reopened a few months later. These protests were related to a territory dispute between China and Japan over islands in the East China Sea. In other international news in 2012, Aeon bought Carrefour's Malaysian stores, expanding the company's already sizable presence in Malaysia.

In addition to its retail and geographical expansion, Aeon continues its environmental commitments. After meeting its goals in reducing its carbon dioxide emissions, it established the Aeon ECO Project in 2012 to set additional environmental goals.

FURTHER READING

Aeon Co., Ltd. "Aeon Review 2012." Accessed October 30, 2012. http://www.aeon.info/en/investors/library/annual.html.

"Aeon Co., Ltd." *International Directory of Company Histories*. Ed. Tina Grant and Miranda H. Ferrara. Vol. 68. Detroit, MI: St. James Press, 2005.

Aeon Mall. "Topics." Accessed November 1, 2012. http://www.aeonmall.com/en/csr/topics.html.

"Brand Symbol." Ministop. Accessed October 31, 2012. http://www.ministop.co.jp/english/about/brand.html.

Current Survey of Commerce by Ministry of Economy, Trade and Industry. "Major Group Companies' Market Share in Japan (Nonconsolidated)." 2010. Accessed October 30, 2012. http://webcache.googleusercontent.com/search?q=cache:WejXWxlmwCEJ:www.7andi.com/dbps_data/_template_/_user_/_SITE_/localhost/_res/en/ir/library/co/pdf/2010_07.pdf+aeon+japan+market+share&hl=en&gl=us.

Groover, Joel. "Japan's Top Mall Landlord Is Also a Big Tenant." *Shopping Centers Today*, July 2007. Accessed October 30, 2012. http://www.icsc.org/srch/sct/sct0707/retail_aeon.php.

Kachi, Hiroyuki. "Aeon Reports Record Profits." *Wall Street Journal*, April 12, 2012.

Nikkei Business Publications. "Eco Brand Survey 2011." Accessed November 1, 2012. http://www.nikkeibp.com/news/110906.html.

AIRBUS

AT A GLANCE

Brand Synopsis: One of only two major players in commercial aircraft production, Airbus strives to be known as the leader in technology and innovation.
Parent Company: European Aeronautic Defence and Space Company EADS N.V.
Mendelweg 30
2333 CS Leiden
The Netherlands
http://www.eads.com
Sector: Industrials
Industry Group: Capital Goods
Performance: *Market share*—56 percent by revenues (2011). *Sales*—EUR33.1 billion (US$42.97 billion) (2011).
Principal Competitors: Boeing Company; BAE Systems plc; Aviation Industry Corporation of China; Lockheed Martin Corporation; Northrop Grumman Corporation; Raytheon Company; General Dynamics Corporation

BRAND ORIGINS

- In 1970 Aérospatiale of France, Deutsche Airbus of Germany, VFW-Fokker of the Netherlands, and Hawker Siddeley of the United Kingdom combined to create Airbus Industrie.
- Airbus released its first aircraft, the A300, in 1972.
- In 1999 Airbus overtook its main rival, Boeing, for the first time as the top manufacturer of commercial airliners with more than 100 seats.
- In 2000 three of the four Airbus partners merged to form EADS.
- In 2006 the European Aeronautic Defence and Space Company (EADS) became the sole owner of Airbus Industrie.

Airbus began in 1970 as Airbus Industrie, a consortium created to compete with American aircraft manufacturers. The consortium was formed by Aérospatiale of France and Deutsche Airbus of Germany and, to a lesser degree, VFW-Fokker of the Netherlands and Hawker Siddeley of the United Kingdom. The following year, Construcciones Aeronáuticas SA (CASA) of Spain acquired a share in Airbus.

In 1972 Airbus leaped ahead of its American competitors by rolling out its first aircraft, the A300, ahead of schedule. The A300's efficiency made it popular with airlines, especially as the global fuel crisis mounted in the 1970s. Forty A300s had been ordered by the end of 1975. In 1978 American airlines Eastern Air Lines and Pan American World Airways (Pan Am) began placing orders for the A300. That same year, Airbus expanded its line of aircraft by launching a second model, the A310.

In 1977 British Aerospace, which in 1999 would become BAE Systems, acquired Hawker Siddeley. Two years later British Aerospace acquired a 20 percent share of Airbus, making it a principal shareholder of the aircraft manufacturer. Aérospatiale and Deutsche Airbus each reduced their share to 37.9 percent, while CASA rounded it out with a 4.2 percent share.

Within a decade of its formation, Airbus had surpassed Lockheed Corporation and McDonnell Douglas in worldwide jet production, although the company still lagged behind Boeing. In 1983 Airbus began work on the A320, which was considered a model of efficiency, with computerized controls for the rudders, wing flaps, and elevators. Airbus received 100 orders for the aircraft before its first flight. By that time the company had also begun manufacturing executive and private jets, as well as freight planes.

In 1986 Airbus reached a milestone by receiving its 500th order. The following year would also prove to be a landmark one for the airline manufacturer. Amid fanfare that included a ceremony with guests like the Prince of Wales and the French prime minister, the Airbus A320 made its maiden flight, eventually becoming the best-selling single-aisle aircraft in the world. That same year, Airbus introduced its A330 and A340 lines of aircraft to the medium, long-haul, and very long-range markets.

In 1992 United Airlines announced it had leased 50 planes from Airbus, a major score for the consortium considering that United Airlines had previously used planes exclusively from Airbus's rival, Boeing, up to that point. In 1999 Airbus finally surpassed Boeing to become the world's top manufacturer of commercial airliners with more than 100 seats. The following year, Airbus upped its market share to 55 percent, and it would grow to 60 percent by 2001.

Not long after the company's founding, it became clear that Airbus had developed far beyond a temporary collaboration intended to produce a single aircraft. This fact necessitated Airbus's eventual transition from being a consortium to operating as a traditional company. During the 1990s Daimler-Benz acquired Deutsche Airbus, becoming DaimlerChrysler Aerospace, and in 1999 British Aerospace merged with Marconi Electronic Systems to become BAE Systems. In 2000 three of the four Airbus partners (DaimlerChrysler Aerospace, CASA, and Aérospatiale's successor, Aérospatiale-Matra) merged to form the European Aeronautic Defence and Space Company EADS N.V. (commonly referred to as EADS), giving the newly formed company an 80 percent share of Airbus Industrie. In 2006 BAE Systems sold EADS its 20 percent stake in the company, leaving EADS the sole owner of Airbus.

Although share prices of airplane manufacturers plummeted after the terrorist attacks of September 11, 2001, Airbus continued to grow. In the first decade of the 21st century the company began developing its 555-passenger A380 model, became embroiled in an international trade disagreement between the United States and the European Union, and began new cost-saving efforts, including the auctioning off of its six European plants in 2007. In 2011 Airbus set new records in orders with its A320neo, a more fuel-efficient model of the A320. That same year the company had a year-end order backlog of nearly 4,500 aircraft.

BRAND ELEMENTS

- The term "airbus" was used in the airline industry in the 1960s to refer to a plane of a certain size and range.
- Airbus used the same logo from its founding until 2010, when slight changes were made to give the logo a sleeker, more modern feel.
- In 2011 Airbus announced new branding, colors, and names for its corporate jets.

When Airbus Industrie was founded in 1970 as a consortium between several European companies, the term "airbus" was used in the airline industry to refer to a plane of a certain size and range. The two main players in the consortium, Aérospatiale of France and Deutsche Airbus of Germany, began their negotiations in the late 1960s, discussing the need for an airbus that could carry at least 100 passengers over short or medium distances for a relatively low cost. As the name "Airbus" was deemed linguistically acceptable to the French, the company name was decided.

Airbus's original logo, used from the company's inception until 2010, featured a ball shape next to the word "AIRBUS," written in thick, all-capital letters slanting slightly to the right. Both the company name and the ball shape (meant to represent the partnership between Airbus's founding companies) appeared in a deep blue color. The logo was updated in 2010 but remained very similar to the original version. The new logo featured the same ball shape next to the company name, both in the same dark blue, but the two elements appeared cut by a laser rather than painted by a brush, while the company name was updated with a new typeface. These subtle changes gave the logo a sleeker and more contemporary feel.

The 2010 logo change did not accompany any major rebranding efforts by the company, but in 2011 Airbus announced new branding, colors, and names for its corporate jets. The jets were updated with metallic blue shading highlighted by flowing curves on most of the fuselage and tail. The company also created a new logo for its corporate jets, while "Airbus ACJ" replaced the "A" designation on all corporate jet model names (e.g., the A318 model became the Airbus ACJ318). These updates were an effort to reflect improvements in Airbus's aircraft and to represent the company's "culture of innovation and family commonality."

BRAND IDENTITY

- As of 2012, Airbus was one of two producers of airplanes with 100 or more seats for the global commercial airline industry.
- The lightweight and fuel-efficient A300, the first Airbus model, helped establish Airbus's reputation for advanced technology and creative thinking.
- In 2007 the A380, the world's largest passenger airliner, entered commercial service, challenging Boeing's monopoly of the large-aircraft market.
- Since the 1990s Airbus has been in tight competition with Boeing, and the two companies are considered a duopoly in their industry.

Along with Boeing, Airbus is one of two producers of airplanes with 100 or more seats for the global commercial airline industry. Its leading position and commitment to innovation are two of the most important elements of the Airbus brand identity.

Airbus's creation was largely an effort by its European founders to steal away a portion of the large market share held by American aircraft manufacturers in the 1960s. Airbus executives knew the company needed to go above and beyond, employing advanced technology and creative thinking to generate aircraft models in a different class than those available from competitors. The company's first aircraft, the Airbus A300, reflected those ideals, with the model's fuel efficiency and light weight propelling Airbus to popularity with airlines.

Airbus continued this tradition of inventive thinking and advanced technology in its later models, including the A320, which made its first flight in 1987 and went on to become the best-selling single-aisle aircraft in the world. The A320 was considered revolutionary at the time for its use of a computerized system that controlled the plane's rudders, wing flaps, and elevators. In 2007 the A380, a double-deck, wide-body, four-engine jet airliner, entered commercial service. Considered the world's largest passenger airliner at the time of its introduction, the A380 was so big that many airports had to alter their facilities in order to accommodate it.

That Airbus designed the A380 to challenge Boeing's dominance in the large-aircraft sector was appropriate, because the company's longstanding rivalry with Boeing forms a significant part of its identity. Since the 1990s the two companies have been locked in a fierce battle over market share and aircraft orders. In the 21st century Airbus has frequently managed to outsell Boeing, but as of 2012 Boeing's products in service outnumbered Airbus's in-service products three-to-one. However, Boeing's lead in that area could be due in part to the fact that it entered the airliner market almost 15 years earlier than Airbus.

BRAND STRATEGY

- Since its inception, Airbus has focused on leading the commercial airline industry in innovation and technology.
- Airbus's main focus is on commercial aircraft production, although it also manufactures executive jets, freight planes, and military aircraft.
- Latin America and India are considered important emerging markets for Airbus in the 21st century.
- In 2012 Airbus announced it expected a 60 percent market share for its new, more fuel-efficient A320neo.

Since its inception Airbus has focused on being a leader in innovation and technology, seeking to develop increasingly lightweight and fuel-efficient aircraft capable of rivaling anything on the market. Although the company also manufactures executive jets, freight planes, and aircraft for the military, Airbus's main focus is on commercial aircraft production. Parent company EADS, which also operates subsidiaries that supply helicopters and civil and military space systems, earns more than two-thirds of its revenues from commercial aircraft manufacturing. While EADS is headquartered in the Netherlands, Airbus is headquartered in Toulouse, France, where final assembly production is based. The company's remaining factories are located in Germany, Spain, and China, while Airbus subsidiaries exist in the United States, Japan, China, and India.

Since the 1990s the brand has been battling Boeing for dominance in the commercial aircraft market, particularly among prominent U.S. and European airlines. Throughout the company's history, the largest percentage of jetliners sold throughout the company's history has been bought by North American customers. In the 21st century India and Latin America have proven to be growing markets for the manufacturer. Latin America accounted for 8 percent of Airbus's deliveries in 2011, and that same year the company broke records when it received the largest order in Mexican history for 44 airplanes.

Predicting that airlines will consider fuel efficiency critical when replacing older models, Airbus continues to focus on making its planes more fuel efficient. In October 2012 Airbus said it expected a 60 percent market share for the new A320neo, a more fuel-efficient version of the popular single-aisle jet. In November, Airbus and Boeing attacked each other in dueling advertising campaigns, with Boeing first claiming its 737 MAX would be cheaper for airlines to operate than the A320neo. Airbus then countered with an ad picturing a Boeing 737 MAX with its front stretched out like the nose of Pinocchio.

BRAND EQUITY

- With a brand value of US$4.8 billion, Airbus was ranked 213th on Brand Finance's Global 500 2012 list.
- Airbus set new records in commercial aircraft deliveries and number of orders in 2011.
- In 2011 Airbus held a 54 percent market share by revenues and a 64 percent market share by industry orders.

In 2012 Airbus was ranked 213th on Brand Finance's Global 500 list, with a brand value of US$4.8 billion. This was a significant gain from 2009, when Airbus held the 372nd spot on the same list. Airbus's main competitor, Boeing (which also produces defense, space, and security systems), held the 97th spot in the Global 500 2012 rankings, with a brand value of US$9 billion.

According to the EADS 2011 annual review, Airbus set a new record of 534 commercial aircraft deliveries in 2011. The company also received a record number of orders that year, thanks largely to the launch of its fuel-efficient A320neo. Consolidated revenues for 2011 were EUR33.1 billion (US$42.97 billion), an increase of 10 percent from the previous year, reflecting higher commercial deliveries. Also in 2011 Airbus held a 54 percent market share by revenues and a 64 percent market share by industry orders, with the remaining percentages held by Boeing.

BRAND AWARENESS

- Airbus was ranked in 70th place on the 2012 Global RepTrak 100 brand popularity survey by the Reputation Institute.
- Among the most popular brands in the United Kingdom, the Centre for Brand Analysis ranked Airbus 37th in 2012.
- A trade dispute regarding government subsidies created widespread publicity for Airbus and Boeing in 2005 and 2012.

In its 2012 Global RepTrak 100 brand popularity survey, the Reputation Institute ranked Airbus in 70th place, up from 74th in 2011. Boeing was 56th, and Lockheed Martin was 97th. The worldwide survey of more than 150,000 ratings from about 47,000 consumers indicated how people perceive businesses and how this influences their buying habits. Only the world's largest and most reputable companies were included.

Another survey, the Business Superbrands Official Top 500 by the Centre for Brand Analysis, ranked Airbus in 37th place among the most popular brands in the United Kingdom, down from 21st in 2011 but up substantially from 87th in 2008. BAE Systems was 13th in 2012, Boeing was 18th, and Lockheed Martin was 79th. Survey participants included the Business Superbrands Council and thousands of business professionals on the YouGov panel.

In 2005 and again in 2012 the Airbus brand was involved in a legal dispute between the European Union (on behalf of Airbus) and the United States (on behalf of Boeing). Each claimed that its competitor had received an unfair advantage in the form of government subsidies and loans amounting to billions of dollars. The litigation was widely publicized, keeping the two brands in the news for long periods of time.

BRAND OUTLOOK

- Airbus expects a 60 percent market share for its fuel-efficient A320neo, scheduled to enter service in 2015.
- Airbus sees growth opportunities in building planes with better fuel efficiency and lower carbon emissions.
- The fuel-efficient A350 will enter into service in 2014 and compete with the Boeing 787 Dreamliner.
- Airbus expects future growth from sales in the Latin American and Indian markets.

In October 2012 Airbus said it expected a 60 percent market share for the new A320neo, a fuel-efficient version of its popular single-aisle jet, recording 1,469 orders as compared to 858 firm orders for Boeing's competing 737 MAX. The A320neo is scheduled to enter service in 2015.

As concerns grow regarding aircraft emissions, Airbus researchers have been testing alternative fuels and fuel cells in an effort to reduce the carbon emissions of aircraft. In 2010 Airbus began work on the A350, a commercial airplane made primarily of carbon-fiber-reinforced polymer that would offer better fuel efficiency. The A350 was also designed to be a competitor to Boeing's 787 Dreamliner, which entered commercial service in 2011. As of 2012, Airbus had received more than 500 orders for the A350, which is expected to enter service in 2014.

Although it sells its aircraft to airlines around the world, Airbus has seen recent growth in the markets of Latin America and India. Latin America accounted for 8 percent of the company's deliveries in 2011, while Airbus predicts that India, the fourth-largest market in terms of annual passenger traffic growth, will need more than 1,000 aircraft through 2030. In 2012 Airbus remained in a stable duopoly with Boeing, a trend company representatives said they expect to continue into the foreseeable future.

FURTHER READING

"Airbus Industrie." *Notable Corporate Chronologies*. Detroit, MI: Gale, 2010.

"Aircraft." *Encyclopedia of Global Industries*. Ed. Lynn M. Pearce. Detroit, MI: Gale, 2012.

Brand Finance. "Global 500 2012." *Brandirectory*. Accessed November 5, 2012. http://brandirectory.com/league_tables/table/global-500-2012.

European Aeronautic Defence and Space Company EADS N.V. "EADS Annual Review 2011." Accessed November 28, 2012. http://www.eads.com/eads/int/en/investor-relations/annual-report/2011.html.

"European Aeronautic Defence and Space Company EADS N.V." *International Directory of Company Histories*. Ed. Derek Jacques and Paula Kepos. Vol. 109. Detroit, MI: St. James Press, 2010.

"Largest Commercial Jet Makers in Europe, 2008, 2010, 2012." *Market Share Reporter*. Ed. Robert S. Lazich and Virgil L. Burton, III. Detroit, MI: Gale, 2010.

Pearson, David. "Airbus Keeps Top Spot over Boeing." *Wall Street Journal*, January 18, 2012.

Walker, Karen. "EADS in merger talks with BAE Systems." *Air Transport World*, September 12, 2012. Accessed November 5, 2012. http://atwonline.com/airline-finance-data/news/eads-merger-talks-bae-systems-0912.

"World's Most Valuable Aerospace and Defense Brands, 2011." *Business Rankings Annual*. Ed. Deborah J. Draper. Detroit, MI: Gale, 2013.

AIRTEL

AT A GLANCE

Brand Synopsis: Bharti Airtel, commonly known as Airtel, is a telecommunications service that aims to become a global provider inspired by a desire to "seize the day."
Parent Company: Bharti Airtel Limited
Bharti Crescent, 1 Nelson Mandela Road
Vasant Kunj, Phase II
New Delhi, 110 070
India
http://www.airtel.in
Sector: Telecommunications Services
Industry Group: Telecommunications Services
Performance: *Market share*—27.61 percent (2011). *Sales*—US$12.89 billion (2012).
Principal Competitors: Nu Tek India; Idea Cellular; Reliance Comm; Tata Comm; Tata Teleservice

BRAND ORIGINS

- Bharti Airtel began as part of the entrepreneurial endeavors of Sunil Bharti Mittal in the late 1970s.
- In 1986 Mittal created a joint venture with German company Siemens AG and incorporated as Bharti Telecom Limited.
- Bharti Cellular Limited, a subsidiary, won bids to provide cellular service in regions across India.
- In 2006 the publicly traded division Bharti Tele-Ventures changed its name to Bharti Airtel Limited.
- In 2009 Bharti Airtel began its global expansion by establishing service in Sri Lanka and Kenya.

Airtel began as part of the entrepreneurial endeavors of Sunil Bharti Mittal, whose early business ventures included trading bicycle parts and hosiery yarn and importing Suzuki generators and push-button telephones, from 1979 to 1983. The technology for push-button telephones had not yet reached India; thus, in 1986 Mittal created a joint venture with German manufacturer Siemens AG and incorporated as Bharti Telecom Limited (BTL). The business evolved quickly, branching into sales of other telecommunications products, and entered the mobile market in the 1990s. BTL was granted a mobile network license in Delhi in 1994, becoming the first cellular service in the region. As other companies dropped out of competition, Bharti Enterprises (as the parent company was now known) moved in to fill the niche and become the first Indian company to export products to the United States. Bharti Cellular Limited was established as a subsidiary of the company, with plans to offer cellular services under the brand name Airtel.

In the years that followed, Bharti Cellular Limited won bids to provide cellular service in Mumbai, Maharashta, Gujarat, Haryana, Uttar Pradesh, Madhya Pradesh, Kerala, Tamil Nadu, Karnataka, Andhra Pradesh, Himachal Pradesh, and Chennai. These services accounted for 87 percent of all mobile phone use in India. The brand also released three post-pay plans (Airtel Dream, Airtel Delight, and Airtel Paradise) and one prepay plan called Airtel Magic. After experiencing massive growth in their customer base following the extension of service to Punjab, the sector of Bharti Enterprises titled Bharti Tele-Ventures Limited filed for an initial public offering in 2002.

In 2004 the Airtel brand partnered with Research In Motion to introduce a Blackberry Wireless solution in India, giving Airtel business customers the opportunity to use secure, integrated wireless technology via their Blackberry devices. In the same year, Airtel announced it would be the first private sector mobile service to operate in the Jammu and Kashmir state. This expansion provided a high level of connectivity to the Himalayan mountain region and created approximately 200 jobs for residents of the area. In the following year, Airtel launched mobile services in the Andaman and Nicobar islands, as well as Assam, making the brand the first mobile carrier in the country to represent all of India's 23 telecommunications circles, or cellular zones.

In 2006 Bharti Tele-Ventures changed its name to Bharti Airtel Limited. The same year, Airtel entered into another joint venture, this time with the Walt Disney Company. The introduction of Disney Mobile Theatre was intended to expand Disney India's presence in the country. Airtel also took its first major step in marketing its products outside of India by convincing the British telecommunications giant Vodafone to buy a 10 percent stake in Airtel. Citigroup Global Markets Limited and UBS AG London were later issued 95,089 equity shares of the Airtel brand.

From 2007 to 2008 the number of Airtel users increased to 75 million. The beginning of 2009 saw the brand successfully expanding into Sri Lanka through its subsidiary Bharti Airtel Lanka Private Limited. To combat falling market shares, Airtel enacted significant changes to its business structure, assembling the company into nine segments run by separate CEOs. In mid-2009 Airtel made inroads into Africa by acquiring Zain Africa BV and investing US$150 million in Kenya's mobile market.

BRAND ELEMENTS

- Bharti Airtel's logo symbol is a graphic representation of a lowercase "a."
- Airtel maintains a connection to underprivileged children in India through the Bharti Foundation, the philanthropic arm of Bharti Enterprises.
- In 2011 Airtel used "Wave" as the name for the brand's new symbol.

Bharti Airtel's logo is a graphic representation of a lowercase "a". The red color of the symbol and text is intended to convey warmth and life and the dynamism of the energy connecting Airtel and its customers. The use of the lowercase letter represents "the need for humanity," recalling Airtel's dedication to social responsibility through its patronizing of the Bharti Foundation, the philanthropic arm of Bharti Enterprises, which seeks to help underprivileged children in India. By 2010 the brand was also an outspoken advocate for clean energy and was among the first companies globally to introduce initiatives to reduce its carbon footprint.

In 2011 Airtel decided to use "Wave" as the name for the brand's new symbol. The name was decided by a contest in which the brand's customers were invited to name the logo, another example of Airtel's effort to maintain a close connection with its customer base of 220 million people.

The Airtel brand comprises Mobile Services, Broadband & Telephone (B&T) services, and Enterprise services. All services are offered under the unified "Airtel" brand directly or through a subsidiary (of which Airtel owns 113).

BRAND IDENTITY

- Bharti Airtel is India's leading telecommunications service provider.
- The Airtel brand prides itself on energy, creativity, and determination to succeed.
- Airtel launched a new brand vision in 2010, one designed to propel the brand into a global arena.

The Airtel brand, India's leading telecommunications service provider, prides itself on its energy, creativity, and determination to succeed, abetted by team efforts to "seize the day." In 2010 Airtel unveiled a new worldwide vision of the brand: a unified Airtel that promised to deliver innovative services and a superior brand experience. The new face of Airtel is intended to be youthful, international, inclusive and dynamic, and representative of the journey of the first Indian brand to go global. With the new identity the company wishes to underline Airtel's emphasis on everything that is new, fresh, and original.

Of the brand's promise to customers, Airtel states, "Enriching lives means putting the customers at the heart of everything we do. ... Only then will we be thought of as exciting, innovative, on their side and a truly world class company."

BRAND STRATEGY

- Bharti Airtel began its expansion into Africa with a leadership meeting in Kampala, Uganda, in 2010.
- In 2010 Airtel made partnership deals with IBM, Ericsson, NSN, Huawei, Spanco, Avaya, and Tech Mahindra.
- In 2011 Airtel launched innovative prepaid and subscriber services in Nigeria, the Democratic Republic of the Congo, and Kenya.
- In 2011 Airtel launched Airtel App Central, the largest global operator-driven app store, in India and South Asia.

In 2003 Airtel engaged in a joint project with the Bank of Punjab, in which 131 of the bank's automatic tellers also served as recharge facilities for Airtel Magic subscribers. This enabled the bank's customers to manage their accounts using their phones.

In 2010 Airtel made a major step forward in the telecom industry when it established operations in Africa, thus changing the scale of the brand's operations and altering the size of the global telecom space. With this expansion, Bharti Airtel became a truly global brand. The first leadership meeting in Kampala, Uganda, projected the 2015 Vision for Airtel Africa, stating that, by 2015 Airtel would be the best-known brand on the continent. This projection was followed by the leadership team's making a 16-country trip across Africa. Airtel also made partnership deals with IBM, Ericsson, NSN, Huawei, Spanco, Avaya, and Tech Mahindra. Intending to appeal to the leading entertainment interests in its African market (that is, soccer and music fans), Airtel created the soccer-themed ad campaign "Kabutu," partnered with the English Premier League leader Manchester United, and launched "Airtel Rising Stars," a soccer program for under-17 boys and girls in 15 countries. Product innovation was also a key part of Airtel's strategy in Africa. Airtel launched 2Good, a prepaid service, in Nigeria; Loba Nayo, a plan offering special rates to subscribers, in the Democratic Republic of the Congo; and MNP (Mobile Number Portability) in Kenya in 2011.

In India and South Asia, Airtel expanded its product line with Airtel App Central, the world's largest operator-driven app store. Believing that data would be the growth inducer for the next decade, Airtel also brought 3G wireless service to 13 circles and broadband wireless access to 4 circles, the better to extend Internet access to its customers throughout India. These actions contributed to the overall growth of non-voice services and led to an increase in total mobile revenue of 15 percent.

In partnership with Novatium and Tally, in 2011 Airtel launched Net OC Plus, software for bookkeeping and stock management, thus shifting the company's focus from core carriage services to managed services. The shift brought an increased emphasis on new service portfolios like Strategic Network Outsourcing, Network Integration, and Hosted Services.

BRAND EQUITY

- In 2012 Airtel's brand value was US$5,221 million.
- Airtel was rated the strongest corporate brand in India in 2009.
- Airtel reported revenues of US$12.89 billion in 2012.

According to Brandirectory, in 2012 Airtel's brand value was US$5,221 million. The brand was ranked 27th in the Top500 Telecom Brands and 187th in the Global 500. In 2010 Airtel was ranked fifth in the India 50. Bharti Airtel was considered the strongest corporate brand in India in 2009 and won numerous awards for being India's top brand from 2010 to 2012, including Best Mobile Service Provider and Most Trusted Brand (both in 2012).

In 2012 Airtel reported revenues of US$12.89 billion. It claimed a market share of 27.61 percent in early 2011. The brand held cash and cash equivalents of INR9.68 billion (US$133.82 million) and a net profit of INR60.57 billion (US$837.35 million, a decline of 33 percent from the previous year). Airtel paid out total dividends of INR616 million (US$8.52 million).

BRAND AWARENESS

- Composer A. R. Rahman wrote an Airtel signature tune in 2002 that became the most downloaded ringtone in India that year.
- In 2009 Airtel was named "Top of the Mind," of the telecommunications brands in India.
- In 2012 Bharti Airtel was second to Vodafone with respect to amounts of overall advertising space.

In 2002 Airtel signed on music composer A. R. Rahman to compose an Airtel signature tune which would appear along with the brand slogan "Live every moment." The tune was later the most downloaded ringtone in India, greatly contributing to Airtel's brand recall.

In 2009 Bharti Airtel was given the distinction of being "Top of the Mind" of the telecommunications brands with a recall of 60 percent. In 2012 Bharti Airtel entered India's mobile advertising space and soon was second only to Vodafone in the amount of telecom advertisements recorded over 68 ad routes, as observed by the Indian Proof of Performance Data Services.

BRAND OUTLOOK

- In 2011 Airtel upgraded its DSL service to a minimum broadband speed of 512 kbps.
- Bharti Airtel expanded its international network coverage to include more than 50 countries in 2011.
- Airtel predicts that cloud computing services, with per-use payments, will be adopted by all enterprises.

Broadband penetration in India is currently around 1 percent; this figure, along with latent demand for high broadband speeds, indicates a strong potential for growth for Airtel. In 2011 Airtel upgraded its DSL service to a minimum broadband speed of 512 kbps and pioneered 50 Mbps broadband, the fastest wireline broadband in the country. The company also expanded its international network coverage to more than 50 countries and boosted the brand's presence in Sri Lanka.

India has become the global hub for cloud computing. Consumers are able to pay as they go for public cloud computing services, which they can access via mobile apps for phones or web browsers. Airtel predicts that such ease of use will encourage the technology's adoption by all enterprises.

FURTHER READING

Bharti Airtel. "2010–2011 Annual Report." Accessed November 1, 2012. http://www.airtel.in/AnnualResults/Bharti_Airtel_annual_report_full_2010-2011.pdf.

"Bharti Airtel Looks Good in Telecom Space: Anand Tandon." Moneycontrol.com, November 1, 2012. Accessed November 1, 2012. http://www.moneycontrol.com/news/stocks-views/bharti-airtel-looks-goodtelecom-space-anand-tandon_776423.html.

"Bharti Airtel Nets 57 percent Rise in Profit." *Times of India*, April 26, 2008.

"Bharti Airtel's Revenue Market Share up 1.1 Percent after Falling for 9 Quarters." *Economic Times*, August 27, 2012.

Caudill, Chrystal. "Bharti Airtel Limited." *International Directory of Company Histories*. Ed. Karen Hill. Vol. 128. Detroit, MI: St. James Press, 2012.

Chandler, Clay. "Wireless Wonder: India's Sunil Mittal." *Fortune*, January 17, 2007.

"Tata Motors, Bharti Airtel Lift Sensex by 56 Points." *Hindu*, November 1, 2012. Accessed November 1, 2012. http://www.thehindu.com/business/markets/tata-motors-bharti—lift-sensex-by-56-points/article4054513.ece.

ALLIANZ

AT A GLANCE

Brand Synopsis: The Allianz brand is strongly associated with insurance and also offers investment products in several different countries.
Parent Company: Allianz SE
Königinstrasse 28
80802 Munich
Germany
https://www.allianz.com/
Sector: Financials
Industry Group: Insurance; Diversified Financials
Performance: *Market share*—17.5 percent of the German life insurance market (for Allianz Leben) (2012). *Net income*—EUR2.804 billion (US$3.7 billion) (2011).
Principal Competitors: American International Group, Inc.; AXA; Talanx AG; Zurich Financial Services AG

BRAND ORIGINS

- Allianz was originally founded as Allianz Versicherungs-Aktien-Gesellschaft in 1890.
- By unifying its mergers and restructuring its company accordingly, Allianz has built a consistent brand.
- Since the 1970s Allianz has been a major international company and brand.
- The September 11, 2001, terrorist attacks against the United States and various economic problems in the early 2000s have challenged Allianz.

Allianz was founded in Berlin, Germany, in 1890 as Allianz Versicherungs-Aktien-Gesellschaft. As the firm became a leading insurer in Germany, it also looked to extend its reach into other countries to build both the company and the brand. This involvement and investment in foreign markets helped Allianz weather the effects of World War I, Germany's postwar inflation, and the restrictions of the Treaty of Versailles. During the 1920s Allianz acquired a number of companies that enabled the firm to provide new services and serve new markets. Instead of operating these newly acquired businesses as individual companies, Allianz decided to incorporate them into a whole, integrated unit and restructure the company.

Like other German companies, Allianz suffered greatly during and after World War II. Its Berlin headquarters were heavily damaged and because they were located on the east side, the company was forced to relocate its central office after the Soviets took control of that part of the city. It also lost its business in the newly formed country of East Germany. Regardless, during the 1950s and 1960s Allianz focused on building its business in other parts of Germany and eventually became the largest German insurer.

Beginning in the 1970s Allianz shifted its focus to international activities by establishing new companies overseas, buying foreign companies, and diversifying its banking and investment offerings. Like many international insurance companies, Allianz was deeply affected by the September 11, 2001, terrorist attacks against the United States. It was the insurance industry's most severe loss ever, as the damage and loss of lives cost billions of dollars. Through its aviation and property insurance policies to insured clients, Allianz estimated that the covered damages and business interruption cost the firm EUR1.5 billion.

Allianz also grappled with international recessions, banking problems, and economic volatility during the early 2000s. To help solve these issues, it joined other German corporations in helping the troubled Greek banking system during the latter half of the first decade of the 21st century. It also continued its global presence with expansion in Europe and elsewhere. Time after time, Allianz has shown resiliency by continuing and expanding its business and brand despite a host of external factors.

BRAND ELEMENTS

- The logo for Allianz consists of three vertical blue lines encircled by a blue ring. The lines look like a stylized eagle.
- Previous Allianz logos have featured lines that resemble stylized eagles and sometimes rings. They all evoke its first logo, a highly detailed depiction of an eagle.
- Allianz chose its corporate color blue for its connotations to several positive qualities.
- The rounded curved walls and blue lighting of Munich's Allianz Arena echo the blue ring of Allianz's logo.

Allianz's logo consists of three vertical blue lines encircled by a blue ring. The logo's center vertical line is taller than the other two and curves slightly over the logo's first vertical line. Taken as a whole, these lines resemble a bird, as the curved vertical line resembles the head and beak, while the shorter surrounding lines look like its wings.

The circular logo is a modified version of Allianz's previous logos. Previous versions of the logo consisted of three vertical lines inside a stylized eagle silhouette, while a 1977 modification slightly tweaked this logo and added a blue ring to surround it. All these logos harken back to the highly detailed eagle image that Allianz used for its first logo.

When launching the 1977 logo modification, Allianz explained why it chose to use the color blue. The firm noted on its website, "Clear and distinct colors characterize strong and distinguished companies. The corporate color of Allianz is blue." It added that psychologists have determined "that blue is often associated with qualities such as respectability, reliability, discretion, prudence and elegance while also evoking notions of objectiveness, dynamism and modernity."

Allianz recalls visual aspects of its logo in an unconventional way. It sponsors the Allianz Arena, which is where Bayern Munich football (soccer) games and other events are held. The arena has rounded exterior walls with variable lighting that changes the walls different colors, including blue. When the rounded walls are blue, they resemble the blue ring of the Allianz logo. Atop this giant blue ring are the Allianz stylized bird in a ring logo and the word *Allianz*, all in blue. In essence, the arena serves as a giant logo for Allianz.

BRAND IDENTITY

- The cover of Allianz's 2011 annual report has a matchbook that features a cartoon resembling the popular Allianz matchbook cartoons of the 1950s, illustrating Allianz's history and place in popular culture.
- An American advertisement for Allianz instructed people to "Say 'Ah Lee Ahnz'" and acknowledged the company's reputation and experience.
- An Australian advertisement for Allianz asked "What's one word two millions think of for insurance?" and told viewers that the helpful Allianz brand can help customers "Be OK."

The cover of Allianz's 2011 annual report has a matchbook that features a colorful cartoon of a man extinguishing a fire with a hose and an Allianz-stylized eagle logo (an eagle silhouette with the lines but no outer ring) underneath the cartoon. The cartoon resembled Hansjörg Dorschel's cartoons that adorned the matchbook covers that Allianz distributed during the 1950s. By using a cartoon that resembled popular images from its past, Allianz evoked the brand's longtime popularity and its place in popular culture. Because the cartoon depicted a man putting out a fire and was featured on a box of matches, it illustrated the brand's ties to fire insurance and its abilities to help customers "put out fires" and solve their problems.

Besides its use of a stylized eagle as its logo, Allianz has employed further bird imagery in its advertising. An advertisement that described the brand to American audiences featured a colorful drawing of a parrot, the tagline "Say 'Ah Lee Ahnz,'" and information about its insurance operations in the United States. The advertisement helped define the brand by acknowledging the company's reputation and linking its name to its correct pronunciation. The copy of the ad stated "Allianz. The company everybody knows ... but can't pronounce." The ad defined Allianz's identity and intentions by implying that even though the German brand had a difficult name to pronounce for English-speaking Americans, the brand was committed to and skilled at American business.

In an Australian television commercial Allianz again acknowledged this pronunciation issue and reiterated its insurance experience. The commercial depicted an Australian woman calling Allianz to make a claim on her automotive insurance. Overwhelmed with emotions about her ruined car and having trouble pronouncing the insurance company's name, she said, "Ahhh," whereupon an Allianz employee joined her and finished pronouncing the word *Allianz.* The woman again said "Ahhh," but this time, her expression was a sigh of relief. This interaction implied that Allianz can bring relief by working with its customers to solve problems. A voiceover on the advertisement stated that Allianz is a popular Australian insurance brand, asking, "What's one word two millions think of for insurance?" The answer to this question is of course Allianz. At the end of the commercial, the Allianz name and logo appear on the screen with the words "Be OK" in blue. This phrase reminded viewers that Allianz can help customers "Be OK," just as the commercial's Allianz employee helped the harried woman.

BRAND STRATEGY

- Allianz Global Investors uses Twitter to communicate with investors and other investment professionals, gather information, make targeted investments, and advance the Allianz name.
- The phrase "Understand. Act" demonstrates Allianz Global Investors' commitment to learning about its business and its customers and applying this knowledge to its work.
- Allianz uses the Allianz name for insurance and investment products in Germany and abroad.

Besides using print advertisements and television commercials to promote its insurance, Allianz utilizes other forms of media to address its investment offerings. Allianz Global Investors uses social media such as Twitter to allow its investment employees and Allianz investors to communicate with each other. Allianz also employs this social media to gather information to create tailored investments for its clients. These developments simultaneously help to serve customers and advance the Allianz name.

The incorporation of media such as Twitter has helped Allianz Global Investors embody its philosophy: "Understand. Act." The media allow Allianz to learn about its customers and gather information; it helps Allianz to understand. Allianz then uses this information to create investments; it helps Allianz to act. By using a phrase such as "Understand. Act," Allianz demonstrates the brand's commitment to learning about its customers and applying this knowledge to help them. It demonstrates that Allianz takes efforts to better understand its work and reassures customers that they can feel secure investing their money with Allianz.

Allianz's frequent and widespread use of its name promotes its brand. It uses the Allianz name and logo for its various types of insurance and investment products, both in Germany and abroad. For example, Allianz acquired a majority stake in Arab International Insurance in 2000. After a number of name changes, this company now uses the name Allianz Egypt. This consistency solidifies the Allianz brand globally by frequently repeating the Allianz name and logo and reminding people of Allianz's products and services.

Cassidy Morgan of the brand consultancy Interbrand has addressed Allianz's global consistency. A 2012 press release quoted Morgan, who observed that "Allianz now has a unified brand that leverages cost synergies, enhances its global presence, and supports a consistent global brand experience." This consistency has reaped rewards for the brand. In 2012 Allianz reported that its brand value had increased 16 percent from the year before.

BRAND EQUITY

- Brand Finance named Allianz the 77th-best global brand in 2012, with a brand value of US$10.9 billion.
- MPP Consulting assigned Allianz a brand value of US$4.8 billion in 2012, which placed it eighth on MPP's "DeBrand Top 100 German Brands" list.
- In 2010 Allianz was ranked 24th on Eurobrand's "Top 25 Most Valuable European Single Brands" list, with a brand value of EUR7.4 billion.
- In 2012 Allianz was ranked 28th on *Fortune*'s "Global 500" list, with revenues of US$134.2 billion and profits of US$3.5 billion.

In *Fortune*'s "Global 500" list, Allianz has been listed every year since 2009. It ranked 28th on this list in 2012, with revenues of US$134.2 billion and profits of US$3.5 billion. In Brand Finance's "Global 500 2012," Allianz was ranked the 77th-best brand internationally and the third-best brand in Germany. It also had a brand value of US$10.9 billion.

In another ranking, MPP Consulting placed Allianz eighth on its "DeBrand Top 100 German Brands" list, assigning it a value of US$4.8 billion in 2012. Allianz also appeared on the 2010 and 2011 editions of this list. Allianz Leben, Allianz's life insurance arm in Germany, also captured a 17.5 percent share of Germany's life insurance market in 2012.

Allianz also fares well in yet another market: Europe. It placed 24th on Eurobrand's "Top 25 Most Valuable European Single Brands" list in 2010. Eurobrand assigned Allianz a brand value of EUR7.4 billion for the year. The brand also appeared on this list in 2007, 2008, and 2009.

An Allianz website discussed the brand's dominant position in Germany and the European continent. It stated that the Allianz Group is "Germany's largest financial institution based on market capitalisation" and "Europe's largest insurer based on market capitalization."

BRAND AWARENESS

- Thousands of respondents rated Allianz's Dutch brand value and customer performance highly in the 2012 "Top 100 Dutch Customer Performance Index."

- Siegel+Gale's poll of international respondents ranked Allianz highly in the "Global Brand Simplicity Index"; Siegel+Gale noted that simplicity can lead to brand recommendations and financial benefits.
- In 2012 Allianz Leben captured 17.5 percent of the German life insurance market.

Customers rate Allianz highly. In 2012 it appeared on the "Top 100 Dutch Customer Performance Index," a measurement of Dutch service companies' brand value and customer performance. MIcompany, MetrixLab, and the University of Groningen compiled this index after polling thousands of customers.

Other customers give Allianz high marks in an interesting survey. In its "Global Brand Simplicity Index," the multinational brand professional Siegel+Gale measures the simplicity of brands. According to Siegel+Gale, brand simplicity can help promote "financial value" as well as an "ability to innovate" and create "the increased likelihood that global consumers will recommend a brand that offers a simpler experience." Allianz placed 84th on this survey in 2011, which incorporated the responses of more than 6,000 participants from seven countries.

Given this recognition, it is not surprising that Allianz has enjoyed considerable market share. In 2012 its German life insurance arm, Allianz Leben, captured a 17.5 percent share of the German life insurance market. Isaac Abraham noted in the *International Insurance News* in June 2012 that Allianz was "the world's 12th largest financial services group in the world" in 2011.

BRAND OUTLOOK

- In 2013 Allianz participated in second annual Berlin Demography Forum to keep abreast of demographic trends that can affect it and its customers.
- Allianz and other large European insurers reported a combined 10 percent loss in traditional life insurance premiums in 2011.
- Japan's 2011 earthquake and tsunami, the worldwide economic problems of the early 2000s, and growth in China are all international factors that are impacting Allianz.

Because Allianz is an insurance brand, it deals with demography, the study of human statistics, and their relevance to the greater population. Changing demographics can greatly affect brands such as insurance brands, because insurance deals with life changes. To explore such changes, Allianz participated in the second annual Berlin Demography Forum in 2013. Allianz's participation in this forum demonstrates its desire to stay abreast of current trends to better operate its company and serve its customers.

Allianz has had to contend with trends in the insurance market. It was among the large European insurance firms that reported a combined 10 percent loss in traditional life insurance premiums in 2011. This drop in insurance premiums was accompanied by other Allianz losses. In 2011 the firm reported a net income of EUR2.8 billion (US$3.7 billion), down from a net income of EUR5.2 billion (US$7 billion) in 2010. In June 2012 Isaac Abraham noted in the *International Insurance News* that despite these losses, Markus Faulhaber, the chief executive officer of Allianz Leben, reaffirmed his confidence in traditional life insurance products and added that Allianz Leben was working on launching new insurance products.

In other global developments, the devastating earthquake and tsunami that hit Japan in 2011 affected Allianz, because it had to pay substantial claims. These payments and other economic conditions in Japan prompted the company to announce in 2012 that it would stop selling life insurance in the country. In addition, the company faced problems during the recessions and economic problems in Europe, the United States, and Japan during the early 2000s. On a more positive note, Allianz experienced considerable success in the Chinese market and it predicted "continued robust growth" for that market in its 2013 *Global Strategic Outlook*. These experiences illuminate how Allianz has attempted to address various external factors to preserve and build its brand.

FURTHER READING

Abraham, Isaac. "Allianz Life Remains Traditional amid Changing Times." *International Insurance News*, June 22, 2012.

"Allianz." RankingTheBrands.com. Accessed February 12, 2013. http://www.rankingthebrands.com/Brand-detail.aspx?brandID=146.

"Allianz Global, ACTIVE Network Launch Race Registration Insurance." *Insurance Journal*, November 27, 2012.

"Alliance SE." *International Directory of Company Histories*. Ed. Karen Hill. Vol. 119. Detroit, MI: St. James Press, 2011.

Boyle, Charles E. "Allianz Posts $3.73 Bn Net Income." *Insurance Journal*, February 24, 2012.

"Global Brand Simplicity Index." Siegel+Gale, 2013. Accessed February 12, 2013. http://www.siegelgale.com/white_paper/2012-global-brand-simplicity-index/.

Global Strategic Outlook. Allianz Global Investors, January 2013. Accessed February 12, 2013. http://www.allianzglobalinvestors.eu/Documents/AllianzGI_GlobalStrategicOutlook_1Q2013.pdf.

"Increasingly International." Allianz. Accessed February 13, 2013. https://www.allianz.com/v_1342874982000/_resources/history/timeline/timeline_en.html.

"1977: Blue, the Color of Allianz." Allianz. Accessed February 13, 2013. https://www.allianz.com/v_1342874982000/_resources/history/timeline/timeline_en.html.

"Successful Brand Supports Business." Allianz SE, October 2, 2012. Accessed February 13, 2013. https://www.allianz.com/en/press/news/company/brands/news_2012-10-02.html.

AMAZON.COM

AT A GLANCE

Brand Synopsis: The definitive e-commerce brand, Amazon.com is associated with values such as selection, price, and convenience.
Parent Company: Amazon.com, Inc.
410 Terry Avenue North
Seattle, Washington 98109-5210
United States
http://www.amazon.com/
Sector: Consumer Discretionary
Industry Group: Retailing
Performance: *Market share*—60 percent of e-book reader market (2012); 29 percent of U.S. book sales (2012); 15 percent of all U.S. online sales (2012). *Sales*—US$61.2 billion (2012).
Principal Competitors: Barnes & Noble; Costco; eBay; Macy's; Netflix; Target; Tmall; 360Buy; Walmart

BRAND ORIGINS

- Amazon was founded by Jeff Bezos in 1994, launched online in 1995, and quickly became the online destination for buying books.
- By the end of 1999, Amazon had shipped 20 million items to 150 countries, and annual sales had reached US$1.6 billion.
- Amazon entered the e-reader market with the Kindle in 2007, soon becoming a major player in the market.

Founded by former Wall Street executive Jeff Bezos in 1994, Amazon.com started business in July 1995 as an online seller of books at inexpensive prices. The Internet was then in its infancy, and Bezos saw an opportunity to build a business that sold products over the World Wide Web. He started with books because they were inexpensive and there was a large market. He also believed they would be easy to sell over the Internet. With a million titles in its inventory, Amazon.com was instantly popular with consumers, shipping books to all 50 states and 45 countries within a month. Within two months, sales reached US$20,000 per week. Amazon quickly became the number-one book-related site on the web.

From its earliest days as a brand, Amazon strove to be innovative, regularly adding new services and product lines. In 1996 it began the Associates program, which allowed individual website owners to offer books from their sites on Amazon.com in exchange for a commission. There were 30,000 Associate members by early 1998 and 60,000 by late 1998. As Amazon expanded its product lines, it also grew the types of merchandise available from Associates.

In 1997 Amazon became a publicly owned company and delivered its one-millionth order. Sales reached US$147.8 million for the year. To further build the brand, Amazon also established partnerships with America Online and Yahoo so it could be promoted on these high-traffic websites. In 1998 Amazon became the third-largest bookseller in the United States. To increase its product offerings, Amazon acquired the online Internet Movie Database, allowing entrance into the online video sales market, and created Amazon Music, with 125,000 music titles initially available. International expansion also occurred. Though Amazon shipped around the world, the acquisition of Bookpages, an online bookseller based in the United Kingdom, and Telebook, based in Germany, took the brand international, with dedicated local websites Amazon.co.uk and Amazon.co.de, respectively.

Still focusing on market share over profit, Amazon greatly increased its services and offerings. In 1999 it launched Amazon Auctions, an online auction house designed to compete with eBay, and it also rolled out Amazon Toys and Amazon Electronics. It divided its offerings into virtual stores and became the first website to offer free digital downloads. By the end of 1999, Amazon had shipped 20 million items to 150 countries, and annual sales had reached US$1.6 billion. By 2000 it was the leading online shopping site in the world, with 17 million customers in 160 countries and US$2.76 billion in sales. Amazon was living up to its tagline "Earth's Biggest Selection" of products.

To increase both its competitiveness and its audience, in 2001 Amazon began offering a 30 percent discount on books priced at more than US$20 as part of a greater emphasis on price reduction. A customer-friendly service debuting in 2002 was the Super Saver shipping program, which offered free shipping to customers ordering more than US$99 in merchandise. Amazon finally became profitable in 2003, with sales of US$5.2 billion, up 34 percent over 2002, and profits of US$35.3 million. The following year, sales climbed to nearly US$7 billion.

Despite Amazon's vast diversification, in 2004 the brand was still largely known for selling books. That year the brand began working on changing consumer perceptions so that Amazon would be regarded as a website where they could buy anything. Eschewing traditional advertising, Amazon used its own website to underscore its diverse offerings. Amazon Theater offered five short promotional films, featuring Hollywood stars, that highlighted various products for sale on the website.

Sales continued to soar between 2005 and 2008, going from US$8.49 billion in 2005 to US$10.7 billion in 2006, US$14.83 billion in 2007, and US$19.2 billion in 2008. Amazon entered a whole new market, and vastly increased its sales, with the introduction of the Kindle in 2007. The Kindle was an e-book reader, developed by Amazon.com subsidiary Lab126. It was not the first e-reader on the market, but it had the advantage of not requiring a computer to operate. Selling the Kindle also created more demand for Amazon's e-books. The Kindle 2, which was thinner and more robust, came out in 2009, as did an international version. By 2011 Kindle was the most popular e-reader in the world, and its global share of the e-reader market was 59 percent, up by 14 percentage points from 2010.

A worldwide economic downturn that began in 2008 affected the fortunes of many retailers, but Amazon was not among them. In 2009 sales jumped to US$24.5 billion. The brand also hit a new milestone in December 2009 when it sold more digital books than printed titles. By 2010 Amazon had about 10 percent of all online retail sales in North America. Amazon successfully entered the business of streaming movies and television shows with Amazon Prime Instant Video Service in 2011.

To continue its spectacular growth, Amazon also focused on expanding its international operations, especially in China. While Amazon had been in the Chinese market since 2004, when it bought Joyo for US$75 million, it did not rebrand its operation as Amazon China until 2011. Amazon had ten operation centers in China by 2011, and opened two more in 2012. By 2012 Amazon's sales reached US$62 billion annually, and it controlled more than 15 percent of online sales in the United States. At the beginning of 2013, Amazon had 188 million active users around the world.

BRAND ELEMENTS

- As a brand, Amazon used its logos to underscore its values.
- In 1997 the logo was simple black and white text which read "amazon.com," with the tagline "Earth's Biggest Bookstore."
- In 2002 a yellow arrow was added to the logo linking the "a" and the "z" in the brand name to communicate the idea that Amazon sold everything from a to z.

Since its introduction on the Internet in 1995, Amazon.com has had distinctive logos which helped define the brand as it evolved. One of the first logos, used for a few years beginning in 1995, was an abstract "A" with a curvy river or sidewalk in the middle; the logo's color varied from year to year. The Amazon.com name appeared underneath in small caps. This logo symbolized the brand as one dedicated to taking consumers on a journey online and through books. In 1997 the logo was simplified to text, in black on white or white on black, which read "amazon.com," with the straightforward tagline "Earth's Biggest Bookstore" underneath.

In 1998 the brand moved to a logo which retained the use of "amazon.com," but emphasized its new, wider offerings with "Books, Music & More" above the brand name and a yellow curved line underscoring the name along the bottom. Two years later amazon.com remained in black. However, "Books, Music & More" was removed and the curve became a yellow arrow linking the "a" to the "z," thus underscoring the brand's wide variety of items available for sale. A logo introduced in 2002 added a tagline "and you're done," though it was a short-lived addition. To market the brand internationally, Amazon.com used a similar logo for each of its dedicated country websites. One of Amazon's most definitive products, the Kindle, used a logo similar to the parent brand's, with a yellow arrow through text reading "Amazonkindle."

BRAND IDENTITY

- Amazon emphasizes a wide selection of products and low prices.
- To be customer friendly, Amazon regularly expands its offerings and has introduced apps to reach consumers whenever they feel like shopping.
- Since its beginnings, Amazon has been most closely identified with books and related activities.

As a brand, Amazon.com emphasizes a positive customer experience, wide selection, low prices, and convenient shopping. Pricing policies had to be aggressive to keep prices low. Amazon strives to be the most customer-oriented brand worldwide, a website where its customers can find whatever products they want, and discover new ones, online. Amazon is even used as a search engine as consumers start their shopping trip.

In its efforts to be customer friendly, Amazon regularly expands its product lines and services and employs focused marketing to ensure that customers know that items they want or might want are available. The Associates program, in which third-party websites linked to Amazon to sell their products, helped enhance both Amazon's offerings and also the customer's ability to find nearly anything, no matter what the product category, on Amazon. To be convenient for customers and stay current with shopping trends, Amazon.com was not only accessible via the Internet but through shopping apps for various devices. Such an app was introduced for the iPad in 2010, for example, while an Amazon Deals app debuted in 2011.

While Amazon.com's offerings have become as diverse as apparel, streaming videos, and Zippo lighters, the brand is most deeply identified with books, as its one-time tagline "Earth's Biggest Bookstore" proclaimed. In 1995 the online retailer started by selling books, which remained a core product line even into the early 2010s. Amazon's link to the printed word goes beyond selling printed books. In 2007 it introduced the popular e-reader, the Kindle, which became the biggest selling e-reader in the world. In addition to introducing new and improved models of the Kindle, Amazon also sold e-books for the reader, was active in self-publishing, and owned several publishing imprints.

BRAND STRATEGY

- Amazon.com began expanding its product offerings in the late 1990s.
- Amazon offers a number of branded services for consumers and other businesses.
- One of Amazon's most successful products was the Kindle.
- Amazon emphasized international growth in the early 2000s.

From its debut as an online retailer in 1995, Amazon.com has regularly increased the number of products it has for sale, made it easier for customers to receive their items, and added various services to enhance the customer experience. After starting out with books in 1995, Amazon began selling new product lines in the late 1990s and into the early 2000s, including toys, videos, compact discs, and housewares. Amazon's Wheels Store debuted in 2010. Beginning in 1996 with its Associate program, Amazon worked with third-party sellers who offered items, whether new, refurbished, or used, through Amazon.com to complement what the brand sold directly. By 2012 Amazon.com was working with more than two million third-party sellers.

Amazon also offered branded services. Some were related to shipping and customer service. Introduced in 2005, Amazon Prime was a service in which users paid an annual fee of US$79 to receive guaranteed two-day delivery of all Amazon products in stock. Others were product-oriented. Amazon Prime Instant Video Service, which began in 2011, allowed users to instantly stream movies and television programs from its list of thousands. In 2000 Amazon began pursuing the business-to-business sector in earnest by offering various aspects of its e-commerce platform to retailers and individual sellers through services like Checkout by Amazon. In 2006 Amazon Web Services was launched to offer infrastructure to businesses through services like Amazon Elastic Compute Cloud. Amazon also developed self-publishing, online advertising, and marketing and promotional services targeting specific audiences.

One product sold by Amazon that did not carry the Amazon brand was the Kindle, an e-book reader introduced in 2007. While not the first e-reader, it was successful from the first, in part because Amazon was already a purveyor of e-books. The Kindle product was inexpensively priced so that Amazon could gain volume from sales of e-books and related content. Upgraded and international versions of Kindle became available in 2009. Amazon took on the iPad in 175 countries in 2011 when it introduced several tablet versions of the Kindle, including Kindle Fire, Kindle Touch, and Kindle Touch 3G. An updated version of the Kindle Fire, the Kindle Fire HD, debuted in early 2013.

Amazon divided itself into two segments: North America and International. In addition to its home U.S. website, it maintained dedicated websites for certain countries, including the United Kingdom, Germany, Japan, France, Canada, China, Italy, and Spain. Amazon placed an emphasis on growing its international markets, especially China. By 2010, about 48 percent of its sales came from outside of the United States. Its international sales grew by 38 percent in 2011.

BRAND EQUITY

- Amazon.com is the largest e-commerce site in the world.
- Amazon.com controls 15 percent of all online sales in the United States.
- Amazon is considered one of the most valuable brands in the world, regularly increasing in value.

Ever since Amazon.com went live as a website in 1995, it has been an industry leader, first as a bookseller, then as an online retailer. The world's largest e-commerce site, it had US$62 billion in sales in 2012. In the United States, Amazon controlled 15 percent of all online sales and 60 percent of the e-reader market. Amazon is not only a major online retailer, it is also the 56th-largest company in the United States by market capitalization and the 15th-biggest retailer by revenues. In *Forbes* magazine's ranking of *The World's Most Powerful Brands*, Amazon was number 28.

Amazon is also regularly ranked among the most valuable brands in the world, and it climbs in the rankings annually. In Interbrands's *Best Retail Brands 2012* report, there is a ranking of *The Most Valuable Retail Brands 2012*. Amazon.com is number nine with a brand value of US$12.758 billion. It was listed as a top riser in this report, increasing its brand value by 32 percent over 2011. Interbrand also listed the *Best Global Brands for 2012*, ranking Amazon at number 20 with a brand value of US$18.625 billion, a 46 percent increase over 2011.

Similarly, Brand Finance ranked the *Best Retail Brands* for 2012. Amazon was number two. On Brand Finance's *Global 500* for 2012, Amazon was number 10. According to Brand Finance, Amazon's brand value was US$28.665 billion, and its enterprise value was US$94.398 billion for 2012. In "BrandZ Top 100 Most Valuable Global Brands 2012," Amazon was number 18, with a brand value of US$34.077 billion. It also was number two on the *BrandZ* report's list of Movers and Shakers in Retail, after Walmart.

BRAND AWARENESS

- Amazon shipped its products to 180 countries and had 188 million active users by early 2013.
- Amazon had high brand recognition as one of the first major online retailers.
- Amazon regularly ranked highly in surveys of brand loyalty and reputation.

Since its inception, Amazon.com has sought to be an industry-leading e-commerce website, shipping its products to nearly 180 countries and 188 million active users. Successful from the first, Amazon emphasized building positive customer relationships and customer loyalty by regularly expanding its offerings, selling its products at low prices, and ensuring reasonable shipping costs and times. Because of its customer-focused efforts, the Amazon brand has high recognition and strength, not only in the United States but around the world. Amazon has top-of-mind awareness as an online source for books and just about anything else. Customer surveys regularly underscore Amazon's high brand awareness. For example, Brand Keys put together a global ranking of *Brand Keys Customer Loyalty Leaders* for 2012. Amazon ranked fourth. In 2012 the Reputation Institute's *Global RepTrak 100*, a worldwide ranking of brand popularity among consumers, placed Amazon at number 28. The Reputation Institute also ranked Amazon number five in 2012 on its *Global Reputation Pulse-U.S. Top 100.*

BRAND OUTLOOK

- The global market for e-commerce is growing and is expected to reach as high as 20 percent of all retail sales within a few years.
- Amazon.com is well positioned to continue its long-term positive growth.
- Amazon has major competition from Chinese-based Tmall, which could usurp Amazon's place as the number-one global e-commerce retailer.

Consumer use of online shopping is only increasing in the early 2010s, both in the United States and globally. According to Interbrand's *Best Retail Brands 2012*, online sales in the United States reached US$200 billion and comprised 9 percent of total retail sales. E-commerce is also a force in other markets, reaching about ten percent in the United Kingdom and three percent in the Asia Pacific region. It is believed that web-based retailing eventually might reach as high as 20 percent of all retail sales within a few years.

Amazon produced positive growth even during the worldwide economic downturn that began in 2008, and it had developed solid plans to build on its consumer success in the United States, grow internationally, and expand its business-to-business offerings. Amazon.com now expected to continue its upward sales trajectory unabated. While Amazon planned to remain primarily an online operation for the foreseeable future, it reportedly was considering opening a brick-and-mortar store in Seattle to explore whether a physical retail network would be profitable.

Though Amazon acknowledges that there is intense competition among e-retailers and that international growth is costly, the brand is positioned, partly because of its experience and high brand awareness, to remain a global market leader. However, Amazon has competition. Some industry experts believe that Tmall, a Chinese-based online retail platform, could surpass Amazon in 2015 and become the biggest e-commerce site by revenue.

FURTHER READING

Amazon.com. *2011 Annual Report.* Accessed February 7, 2013. http://phx.corporate-ir.net/phoenix.zhtml?c=97664&p=irol-reportsAnnual.

"Amazon.com." *Forbes.* Accessed February 6, 2013. http://www.forbes.com/companies/amazon/.

"Amazon.com, Inc." *International Directory of Company Histories.* Ed. Tina Grant. Vol. 113. Detroit, MI: St. James Press, 2010.

"Best Global Brands 2012." Interbrand. Accessed February 6, 2013. http://www.interbrand.com/en/best-global-brands/2012/Best-Global-Brands-2012.aspx.

"Best Retail Brands 2012." Interbrand. Accessed February 6, 2013. http://www.interbrand.com/en/BestRetailBrands/2012-Best-Retail-Brands.aspx.

Brand Finance. "Amazon.com." *Brandirectory.* Accessed February 6, 2013. http://brandirectory.com/profile/amazoncom.

"BrandZ Top 100 Most Valuable Global Brands 2012." Millward Brown. Accessed February 6, 2013. http://www.millwardbrown.com/brandz/2012/Documents/2012_BrandZ_Top100_Report.pdf

Matthews, Christopher. "E-Commerce: Will Amazon Take over the World?" *Time,* July 16, 2012.

AMERICAN EXPRESS

AT A GLANCE

Brand Synopsis: The world's largest card issuer by purchase volume, American Express is a global leader in financial services.
Parent Company: American Express Company
World Financial Center
New York, New York 10285
United States
http://www.americanexpress.com
Sector: Financials
Industry Group: Diversified Financials
Performance: *Market share*—19.3 percent (2011). *Sales*—US$33.8 billion (2012).
Principal Competitors: Discover Financial Services; MasterCard Incorporated; Visa Inc.

BRAND ORIGINS

- American Express was founded in 1850 as an express shipment company for packages.
- American Express started offering money orders and traveler's checks at the end of the 19th century.
- American Express ventured into the travel business during World War I, taking advantage of its cargo ships.
- The company released its first charge card in 1958.

American Express was an express mail company founded in 1850 in Buffalo, New York, as a joint venture between the express mail companies Wells & Company, Livingston, Fargo & Company, and Wells, Butterfield & Company. At that point the U.S. Postal Service shipped only letters, so additional mail companies were necessary for the shipping of packages. Even though American Express was not a financial company in the beginning, most of its clients were banks.

In 1882 American Express ventured into the financial world by introducing the first money order system. The company furthered its venture in 1891, when it introduced the world's first traveler's check. Both systems were instantly successful; within 10 years the company was selling more than US$6 million in traveler's checks annually. To be successful, American Express began building relationships with European banks that would honor the traveler's checks and money orders. As business grew in Europe, the company opened its first European office in Paris in 1895, followed by an office in London. The company continued its growth into the 20th century and received a contract from the U.S. Immigration Department in 1905 to provide official currency exchanges due to the influx of immigrants into the country.

The company moved into the travel industry during World War I. When approximately 150,000 American travelers became stranded in Europe following the outbreak of war, American Express became high in demand because it could cash the travelers' money orders and checks, allowing them to pay their way home. Meanwhile, American Express continued to operate as a shipment company. In 1915 the company began offering travel accommodations on its cargo ships, which enabled it to make more of a profit off of routes the ships already took. Within the next 10 years the company was operating tours to Europe, South America, the Far East, and the West Indies.

The 1930s brought a few misfortunes upon the company. The company was almost absorbed by Chase National Bank, which had been gradually purchasing American Express shares and by 1929 owned 97 percent of the company. The remaining shareholders refused to sell their shares. In 1933 Congress passed the Glass-Steagall Act, which prohibited banks from engaging in nonbanking activity, and Chase was forced to surrender its shares. During the few years that Chase controlled the company, most corporate activity ceased, which was also at the height of the Great Depression. When World War II broke out, American Express had built its cash reserves back up through its traveler's checks and money orders.

American Express issued its first charge card in 1958. By 1963 the company had over 1 million cardholders and over 85,000 establishments that accepted them. The card was quickly accepted in Europe as well. The company responded by expanding its charge cards to include the American Express Gold Card in 1966. During the 1970s American Express continued its corporate growth by acquiring small companies, which proved to be a financial mistake. By the 1980s the company had sold all of its noncore businesses and honed in on its previous successful ventures: the charge card, money orders, and traveler's checks. During the 1990s the company formed partnerships with airlines, banks, and retailers to encourage more businesses to accept its charge card.

The company has remained strong into the 21st century, despite the corporate headquarters being severely damaged during the terrorist attacks in New York City on September 11, 2001. During the attack, 11 employees were killed and the company was forced to rely on satellite offices to maintain business.

BRAND ELEMENTS

- American Express's name relates to its original enterprise, as an express shipping company.
- American Express has two primary logos: a centurion's head within an ovular shield and a simple blue square with "American Express" highlighted in a bold, white outline.
- American Express has been using the slogan "Don't Leave Home without Them/It" since 1975, relating to both traveler's checks and charge cards.

The American Express brand name has remained unchanged since the company was founded in 1850. The name originally related to the company's founding industry; American Express was a shipping company, shipping packages in the United States where the U.S. Postal Service only worked with letters. Since then, the name has been recognized as a point of reliability; the money orders and traveler's checks that bear the American Express logo indicate money that will be provided immediately. Additionally, the American Express charge cards also emanate immediacy in service.

American Express has had three primary logos in its history. When the company operated in shipments, its logo was a dog lying on top of a trunk with the name "American Express" written across the trunk. The best-known logo for American Express was introduced alongside the release of the charge card in 1958, which featured the head of a Roman centurion inside an ovular shield. Since 1975 the company has also used a blue square with the company's name highlighted in a bold, white outline. The logo was used for its ease of placement, size, and recognizability.

In 1975 American Express introduced the slogan "Don't Leave Home without Them" for its traveler's checks. The concept was to encourage travelers to carry traveler's checks as a form of currency insurance, especially when traveling in foreign countries. The ads featured the Academy Award-winning actor Karl Malden, who represented the company for 25 years. After Malden's departure as the company figurehead, the company maintained the same slogan, but instead began relating it to the card. The company continues its use of celebrities in advertisements, all of whom are featured as cardholders.

BRAND IDENTITY

- American Express traveler's checks and money orders have helped the company market itself as an international brand.
- The American Express charge card is built off of a core of corporate integrity, which is part of the company's "Blue Box Values."
- American Express established Small Business Saturday in 2010 as part of a goodwill campaign to encourage consumers to shop at locally owned businesses on the Saturday following Thanksgiving.

American Express has been offering money orders and traveler's checks since the late 1800s. The company has advertised its travel-friendly operations since the new operations were introduced, building customer loyalty through reliability. One of the key moments to demonstrate the company's dependability was when World War I broke out and thousands of Americans were stranded in Europe. American Express was able to honor and cash traveler's checks to ensure that the American visitors returned back to the United States safely. American Express markets itself as a trustworthy company to ensure brand reliability and gain repeat business.

Additionally, the American Express charge card, introduced by the company in 1958, also encourages brand loyalty by offering reward programs to its cardholders. Unlike the competitors Visa and MasterCard, American Express maintains a reputation for having more exclusive cardholders, typically more affluent customers and business owners. The company describes its corporate integrity as its "Blue Box Values," citing customer commitment, quality, and integrity as the attributes customers will receive by using American Express.

American Express's corporate mission statement is "We work hard every day to make American Express the world's most respected service brand." Through this mission statement, American Express hopes to encourage its customers to know that the company is service-based, meaning that the customer will get the best possible service, and plan, possible. Part of this vision is applied with the encouragement of Small Business Saturday, an American shopping day held the Saturday following Thanksgiving, which is designated to encourage consumers to shop at local businesses. The program was introduced by American Express in 2010 to counter "Black Friday," the Friday following Thanksgiving, which is the busiest shopping day of the year in the United States and typically a day when large businesses and big-box stores receive most of their business. By encouraging consumers to support their local economy, American Express is successfully marketing itself as a service-based company instead of a profit-based company.

BRAND STRATEGY

- American Express was able to expand its money order and traveler's check services internationally by building a rapport with European banks.
- The American Express charge card was introduced in 1958, and by 2012 it had several different tiers of benefits and rewards based on the exclusivity of the card.
- American Express strives to build brand loyalty, which is part of the reason it began pushing consumers to shop at local businesses for Small Business Saturday.

Even though American Express began business as a cargo shipment company in 1850, the company eventually expanded its operations beyond shipments by offering the first money order in 1882. The money orders were successful from the beginning and as the company began establishing relationships with European banks, the money orders were also accepted as international currency. American Express continued its expansion beyond the shipping industry in 1891, when it introduced traveler's checks. With the already established relationship with banks throughout the United States and Europe, American Express was able to offer a way for travelers to carry multiple currencies, cashing the prepaid checks as they entered new destinations and not having to figure out the exact exchange rate between different currencies.

American Express ventured beyond traveler's checks and money orders in 1958, when the company offered its first charge card. The charge card has been the most successful venture the company has taken. Under the charge card, American Express offers several different cards dependent on the cardholder and the cardholder's needs. The standard American Express card is the Zync card, a basic silver with minimum rewards; the subsequent cards, in ascending order for exclusivity, are the Green, Gold, Platinum Centurion, and finally the AmEx Centurion, or American Express Black. The Black card is available to customers through invitation only and the benefits of owning the card are not public knowledge. By offering exclusive credit cards that would otherwise be unattainable, American Express is allowing its customers to have the knowledge that they are holding an exclusive card.

A large part of American Express's corporate strategy as a brand has been building brand loyalty. Besides the longevity and well-known name of the company, American Express still adheres to the vision that the company is entirely service-based, meaning the customer is most important. As part of the effort in demonstrating the goodwill of the company, American Express started a campaign for Small Business Saturday in 2010, a day when consumers are encouraged to shop at local business instead of at larger retail chains. The result for this marketing is twofold: first, American Express is proving generosity to its customers, and second, in supporting smaller businesses, American Express is gaining small business trust and getting more businesses to accept American Express cards.

BRAND EQUITY

- American Express is the world's largest credit card issuer, based on purchase volume.
- In 2012 American Express ranked as the 24th most successful global brand by Interbrand, with competitor Visa appearing at 74th.
- In 2012 American Express's brand value was estimated at US$18.2 by Brand Finance.

As the world's largest card issuer by purchase volume, American Express is a global leader in financial services. American Express was also the first successful American credit card issuer, after it began introducing the charge card in 1958. Unlike Visa, a venture by Bank of America, which issued 60,000 unsolicited credit cards during the first year, American Express holds a reputation of exclusivity, allowing only specific consumers to become cardholders.

According to Interbrand's 2012 ranking of the top 100 brands, American Express ranked 24th with a brand value of US$15.7 billion, whereas Visa came in at 74th, with a value of US$4.9 billion, and MasterCard at 94th, with a value of US$3.9 billion. American Express ranked first among charge cards on the list. American Express saw an increase in popularity in 2012, in part due to Visa's hit in popularity by being the only credit card accepted at the 2012 Olympic Games in London. Brand Finance's "Global 500 2012" ranked American Express 32nd, up from 46th in 2011, and estimated its brand value at US$18.2 billion. Visa ranked 136th in the same list with a brand value of US$7.1 billion.

BRAND AWARENESS

- American Express became well known among consumers for its traveler's checks, which were introduced in 1891 and are still being used in the 21st century.
- The American Express charge card was introduced in 1958 and, unlike competitors Visa and MasterCard, has maintained a reputation for exclusivity.
- Small Business Saturday, a shopping day following Thanksgiving, was encouraged by American Express to help local and small businesses and to build its corporate image as a goodwill company.

American Express has built its company based off of a few insights that enable consumers to know about the company and create brand loyalty. One of the largest and best-known corporate aspects has been the introduction of the traveler's check. Started by American Express in 1891, the traveler's check has become a form of ease and security for travelers worldwide. Unlike cash, traveler's checks are insured by American Express and can be replaced if lost or stolen. One of the most beneficial aspects of the traveler's check is how the check can be cashed in either foreign or domestic countries with either foreign or domestic currency, making purchases overseas easier for the consumer.

The company became well known during the second half of the 20th century for its charge card. The card was originally issued in 1958 and has been continually successful for the company. Unlike the competitors Visa and MasterCard, American Express bears the reputation for exclusivity. When Visa was launched at the end of 1958, Bank of America sent out 60,000 unsolicited credit cards, without an application process. American Express has not done the same, even with it most exclusive card, the AmEx Centurion, which is available to customers only through an invitation. Additionally, the well-known blue and white American Express square is an easy-to-spot logo for the company, standing out against the competitors' colors.

In 2010 American Express sought to make a new name for itself among customers by launching Small Business Saturday, an American shopping day on the Saturday following Thanksgiving. The idea was to encourage customers, who typically shop during the weekend following Thanksgiving, to shop at local and small businesses instead of at big-box retailers. In this attempt, American Express became known as a goodwill company by encouraging shoppers to help the American economy.

BRAND OUTLOOK

- In 2012 American Express's net income increased by only 1.02 percent, down from 6 percent from the previous year.
- In 2012 American Express introduced the Bluebird prepaid debit card to be sold in Wal-Mart stores.
- In 2012 American Express led the credit card market with US$33.8 billion in sales and accounted for 25 percent of credit card spending in the United States.

In 2011 the global credit card industry generated total revenues of US$154.9 billion, of which American Express held a 19.3 percent market share. The profit for American Express has been rocky since the end of the economic recession in 2009. In 2012 the company had a slowdown in spending, but this slowdown was at the rate analysts surveyed by Bloomberg had expected. In spite of the uneven economy, the company's net income increased 1.02 percent in 2012, down from a 6 percent increase the year before. In preparation for potential future losses, the company reported that it was setting aside US$479 million to account for the uneven global economy. Additionally, American Express reported that card member spending increased 8 percent during the fourth quarter of 2012, despite a brief interruption due to the disaster caused by Hurricane Sandy.

Comparatively, in 2012 Visa reported an increase in sales of US$627 million, or 14 percent. Visa held 5.9 percent and MasterCard held 4.3 percent of the global market for credit cards in 2011. In 2012 American Express still led the credit card market with US$33.8 billion in sales, compared with Visa's US$4.2 billion. It also accounted for 25 percent of credit card spending in the United States.

In late 2012 American Express introduced the Bluebird prepaid debit card, which was sold at more than 4,000 Wal-Mart stores. The new card was designed to be less costly to the consumer, as there is no reload fee if it is done within a Wal-Mart location. The card also allows American Express to be exposed to a new demographic of consumers, as it has the largest amounts of credit card purchases in the highest-earning demographic. It also benefits from the partnership with Wal-Mart because it will earn revenue off of the interchange fee each time a card is used.

FURTHER READING

American Express. "Our Story." March 15, 2006. Accessed January 25, 2013. https://secure.cmax.americanexpress.com/Internet/GlobalCareers/Staffing/Shared/Files/our_story_3.pdf.

Anisha. "Breakdown: American Express Card Benefits." NerdWallet. Accessed January 25, 2013. http://www.nerdwallet.com/blog/credit-card-benefits/breakdown-american-express-cards/.

Brand Finance. "Global 500 2012." *Brandirectory*. Accessed January 25, 2013. http://brandfinance.com/images/upload/bf_g500_2012_web_dp.pdf.

Fitzgerald, Kate. "Report: Credit Card Industry Revenue Fell 6% in 2011." *American Banker*, January 3, 2012.

Johnson, Andrew. "AmEx Profit, Revenue Beat Expectations." *Wall Street Journal*, April 18, 2012.

Kopecki, Dawn. "AmEx Profit Meets Estimates as Card-Spending Growth Slows." *Bloomberg News*, October 17, 2012.

"2012 Ranking of the Top 100 Brands." Interbrand. Accessed December 12, 2012. http://www.interbrand.com/en/best-global-brands/best-global-brands-2008/best-global-brands-2011.aspx.

U.S. Government Accountability Office. *Credit Cards: Rising Interchange Fees Have Increased Costs for Merchants, but Options for Reducing Fees Pose Challenges*. November 2009. Accessed January 25, 2013. http://www.gao.gov/new.items/d1045.pdf.

Wack, Kevin. "Visa's Profits Surge on Revenue Growth." *American Banker*, October 31, 2012. Accessed February 12, 2013.

APPLE

AT A GLANCE

Brand Synopsis: Originally just a personal computer brand, Apple is now a lifestyle brand, known for its innovative, integrated products and services.
Parent Company: Apple Inc.
One Infinite Loop
Cupertino, California 95014
United States
http://www.apple.com
Sector: Consumer Discretionary
Industry Group: Consumer Durables & Apparel
Performance: *Sales*—US$156.5 billion (2012).
Principal Competitors: Hewlett-Packard Company; Research in Motion Limited; Samsung Electronics Co., Ltd.

BRAND ORIGINS

- Apple was founded in 1976.
- Apple's "1984" Super Bowl commercial helped to establish key elements of the brand.
- While Apple computers were revered by designers, it enjoyed limited sales in the 1990s.
- The return of Steve Jobs in 1997 began the transformation of the Apple brand.
- Apple became a lifestyle brand in the early 2000s.

The origins of the Apple brand date to 1976 when a pair of college dropouts, 21-year-old Steve Jobs and 26-year-old Steve Wozniak, began selling electronic devices that allowed users to make free long-distance calls. A self-taught electronic engineer, Wozniak began work on a hobbyist computer, and the two partners pooled their money, about US$1,300, to start their own business, called Apple Computer Company. While the origins of the name are not entirely clear, it was certainly coined by Jobs. The first Apple logo, designed by Ronald Wayne, one of the company's little-known founders, featured Sir Isaac Newton with an apple poised to drop on his head. It was soon replaced by a new apple logo designed by Rob Janoff of Regis McKenna Advertising. It featured a rainbow-colored apple with a bite taken out of it. It would serve as the corporate mark for Apple Computer for more than 20 years. McKenna also developed Apple's first advertising campaign, promoting the new computer in consumer magazines.

The Apple I computer was sold through a handful of retail stores in the United States, and was replaced by the Apple II in 1977. The new computer was also sold in Europe, expanding the Apple brand. Apple's reputation for innovation, an important element of the brand, began to grow in 1978 with the introduction of an interface card to connect printers and a minifloppy disk, the fastest and least expensive disk drive on the market at the time. Moreover, the new disk drive allowed for the development of software for the computer and the expansion of the market from hobbyists to general consumers.

Apple went public in late 1980. The company expanded its dealer network around the world, and despite stiff competition from more than 100 companies producing personal computers, Apple was able to remain ahead of the field because of its commitment to innovation. It even challenged IBM in the business market with the 1983 launch of the Lisa computer, which introduced point-and-click computing through the use of a mouse and on-screen graphic images. While Lisa failed to crack the business market, its innovations were adopted by Apple's Macintosh personal computer that Jobs positioned as the "people's computer." It was introduced in spectacular fashion during a Super Bowl commercial that paid homage to George Orwell's *1984*. It was a landmark moment on a number of counts. It established a benchmark for all subsequent Super Bowl ads while laying the foundation for key elements of the Apple brand. The company created an image of the heroic outsider, with which many consumers could identify. Apple also established a tradition of introducing new products with a splash.

The Macintosh carved out a space for Apple in the business market, but it was mainly relegated to designers. The Mac created strong loyalty with its users, but after Jobs left in 1985 Apple struggled for the next dozen years, due in large measure to a succession of new chief executives that provided little continuity. Jobs returned as interim CEO in September 1997, a post that would turn permanent as he revived the company he founded and built Apple into a global powerhouse brand.

Under Jobs, Apple developed a more affordable computer line, the iMac. Sleek and colorful, it helped Apple to build a reputation as a stylish brand. Jobs also abandoned the rainbow apple logo for a new, more modern-looking monochromatic version, helping to reposition the Apple brand. In the new century, Apple unveiled a succession of new groundbreaking products that solidified the company's standing as a consumer electronics innovator. In 2001 the iPod changed the way people listened to their personal music, and the iTunes virtual music stores changed the way music was sold. It was also in 2001 that Apple opened its first retail store, which further supported the brand's identity. Apple next turned its attention to the mobile phone industry and in 2007 introduced the iPhone, setting the standard for the modern smartphone. As it had done with iTunes, Apple also introduced the App Store, where iPhone users could buy and sell software applications for the phone.

While the launch of the iPhone generated a great deal of excitement, there was little notice given to a change in the company name prior to the product's release. "Computer Company" was dropped, leaving just Apple Inc. The modification caused no stir because, by this time, few people saw Apple as a mere computer brand. In fact, Apple had transcended consumer electronics to become a lifestyle brand. Its true power became apparent when Apple introduced the iPad tablet computer in 2010. There was little perceived need for the product, which fell somewhere between a laptop and a smartphone. Nevertheless, it found a ready market and carved out a new computing niche. Even with the death of Jobs in 2011, the Apple brand was well established and now regarded by many as the world's most valuable brand.

BRAND ELEMENTS

- The Apple name is an important brand element.
- The monochromatic Apple logo was adopted in 1998.
- High quality and stylish products are key to the Apple brand.
- Apple retail stores reinforce the brand's identity.
- More than a line of products, Apple is an experiential brand.

The Apple brand is supported by a variety of elements, beginning with the name and logo. Jobs's choice of the word "Apple" as the name of the new computer company he cofounded proved highly effective on a number of levels. It was simple yet evocative. There are many positive associations connected to the fruit, long known for its medicinal virtues. For a computer company touting innovation, the apple was especially apt because it supposedly provided inspiration to Sir Isaac Newton. In fact, the company's first logo depicted the famous moment. It was quickly replaced by the rainbow apple with a missing bite that served the brand well until 1998. The graphic image was updated to a modern chrome image that became an especially important branding element, affixed to the back of Apple products and building brand awareness.

The products themselves are perhaps the most important element of the Apple brand. They are high quality and stylish, making Apple products status symbols to many consumers. Even the sleek packaging reinforces this image. Also key to the design of Apple products is a simple and intuitive user interface. In keeping with high quality and its premium product positioning, Apple products maintain a relatively high price point, a difference with the competition that further defines the brand.

Apple products and services work together seamlessly, serving the everyday needs of users, whether at home or on the road. Apple is essentially an experiential brand, representing a way of life more than a line of products. The Apple way is reflected in, and reinforced by, the Apple retail stores. The décor and fittings are of high quality, including patented floor tiles, crafted wooden tables, and surgical grade aluminum fixtures. Befitting the brand, the customer care is excellent. There are no cash registers to be seen. Sales associates process credit card purchases with the iPhones they carry, further promoting the product and the brand.

Distinctive advertising is also an important part of the Apple brand. The "1984" commercial set a standard for all Super Bowl ads. In the 1990s, Apple further established its image as outsider and iconoclast with its "Think Different Campaign." In the new century, the iPod print ads and television commercials featuring silhouetted characters against bright-colored backgrounds, dancing and listening to iPods, were especially effective in promoting the device as well as the iTunes music store.

BRAND IDENTITY

- Apple products are at the heart of the brand's identity.
- Capability and ease of use are important aspects of the Apple brand.
- Apple products have become a fashion statement.
- Apple identifies closely with its customers.

Apple is a brand that in every aspect of its outward expression espouses a way of life, and in turn it creates a strong connection with its customers. At the heart of Apple's identity since the founding of the company have been the products. They have been consistently innovative, high quality, and premium priced, reflecting the upscale nature of the brand. More than that, Apple products have always been known for their blend of capability and ease of use. Intuitive user interfaces are key. Thus, the simplicity of Apple products removes complexity from the lives of users, an important promise the brand has kept since its founding.

Aside from functionality, Apple styling has evolved from the days of the original boxy Macintosh computers. Apple products have since become known for their sophisticated design. Style is an important part of Apple's identity. As a result, carrying an Apple product has become something of a fashion statement for many people. Style is also reflected in the design of the Apple logo, and the décor of Apple stores.

Ultimately, Apple's identity is its customers. At the heart of the brand is the company's attitude toward product development. Rather than ask customers what they want, Apple leaders, due primarily to the influence of Steve Jobs, assume the role of the customer and ask what they would want as individuals. Designers then worked backward, using technology to meet that desire. As a result, there was a closing of the loop: Apple was the customer, and the customer was Apple.

BRAND STRATEGY

- Initially Apple was both a corporate and product brand.
- For many years, Apple's branding was Mac-oriented.
- The "i" prefix was applied to a number of Apple products in the new millennium, starting with the iPod.
- Apple products work together to create an integrated and harmonious user experience.

Apple's branding strategy has matured over time. When Apple was purely a computer company, the corporate brand and product brand were one in the same. The Lisa computer brand broke the mold in 1983 but fared poorly. A new brand name for a less expensive computer aimed at a wider market was unveiled in spectacular fashion during the 1984 Super Bowl telecast. Playing off of the corporate brand, it was called the Macintosh, a popular apple variety. For most of the next 20 years, Apple's branding efforts centered around the Mac.

Not until the new century did Apple move beyond its Mac identity. Apple now introduced a series of game-changing consumer electronic products, the most notable of which were the iPod, the iPhone, and the iPad. On the service side there was also the iTunes media store. Other Apple products and services also adopted the "i" prefix, such as iBook laptops, iMac computers, iLife and iSight computer peripherals, and such software titles as iDVD, iMovie, iPhoto, and iWork.

A new product naming system, however, was far less important to the success of Apple in the new millennium than was a switch in the focus of the brand. The products were marketed less as individual products and more as representatives of an integrated and harmonious user experience. In or out of the home, there was an Apple product that met the needs of Apple customers, and they all operated under a familiar rubric, serving to reduce the complexity in everyday living. As a result, the success of one Apple product helped to generate sales for other Apple products. The new Apple retail stores also served to nurture the brand and build awareness.

The company's refined branding strategy transformed Apple in an experiential brand, a lifestyle and emotive brand. Consumers identified with Apple, and Apple's brand identity was that of its target customer: passionate, innovative, hopeful, and individualistic. While the devotion of its customers to the brand led to some measure of ridicule from the outside, criticism only served to reinforce the bond. It was a dynamic that, in little more than a decade, elevated Apple from a tired, specialty brand to the world's most valuable brand.

BRAND EQUITY

- One measure of Apple's brand equity is the higher price Apple products are able to command.
- According to Brand Finance, Apple's brand was valued at US$70.6 billion at the end of 2011.
- The Apple brand was valued at US$182.951 billion by Interbrand in 2012.
- *Forbes*'s 2012 valuation of the Apple brand was US$87.1 billion.

- Apple was ranked as the world's most valuable brand in 2012 by Brand Finance, BrandZ, and *Forbes*.

Apple does not compete on the basis of price. Rather, it allows rivals to fight for customers at lower price points. While rival products may measure up to Apple products on a performance level, Apple is still able to command a higher price. It is the difference between the price of Apple and comparable rival products that is the true measure of Apple's brand equity. Perhaps the ultimate reflection of Apple's growing brand equity is the steady increase in annual revenues the company has enjoyed since Apple began its brand ascendancy. Revenues in 2001, at the depth of the tech downturn, stood at US$5.4 billion. In 2011 that number grew to US$108.25 billion.

Several entities have placed a monetary value on the Apple brand. According to brand consultancy Brand Finance plc, the Apple brand was worth US$70.6 billion at the end of 2011. It was a performance that earned Apple the No. 1 spot on Brand Finance's 2012 Global 500 list of the world's most valuable brands. It also culminated a steady rise in the value of the brand. Only five years earlier, in 2007, Apple had been listed at No. 44 on what was then known as the Global 250.

Another branding consultant, Millward Brown, ranked Apple No. 1 on its BrandZ Top 200 Most Valuable Global Brands in both 2011 and 2012. The brand improved its standing in 2012, increasing in value by 19 percent to US$182.951 billion. Apple was also at the head of *Forbes* magazine's 2012 list of the World's Most Powerful Brands. According to *Forbes's* methodology, Apple's brand was valued at US$87.1 billion, representing a 52 percent increase since *Forbes* last compiled the list two years earlier. Branding agency Interbrand, on the other hand, ranked Apple No. 2 on its Best Global Brands 2012, trailing Coca-Cola, but gaining fast.

BRAND AWARENESS

- Consistent use of the Apple logo has helped to build brand awareness.
- Awareness of the Apple brand was mainly limited to designers and other core Mac users in the 1990s.
- Apple stores helped to increase brand awareness.
- Apple's iPod, iPhone, and iPad product enjoy top-of-mind brand awareness.

Apple enjoys excellent brand awareness. The company has been a prominent player in the personal computer industry since the beginning and has used its iconic apple logo to maintain awareness of the brand even during some lean years in the 1990s when designers were the core advocates for the brand. As Apple expanded beyond PCs and laptops in the new century with the introduction of a series of groundbreaking handheld electronics, the brand increased awareness to a wider group of customers. Moreover, the brand grew awareness throughout the world. The company's expanding sales were indicative of increased awareness, improving 20-fold in a matter of 10 years.

Helping to build brand awareness has been Apple's successful advertising campaigns of recent years. The hundreds of Apple stores that have opened since the start of the new century have also served to increase awareness of Apple and reinforce the brand's identity. Also helping to grow awareness are the company's much-anticipated product introductions. The events are well covered by the media and create excitement among consumers, so much so that lines of customers form outside retail stores, waiting for a new Apple product to go on sale.

One of the highest forms of brand awareness, "top-of-mind," develops when a brand becomes so associated with a product that it is virtually a synonym in the minds of consumers. Apple has been able to achieve this goal with a series of products. The iPod is what comes immediately to mind when many consumers think of an mp3 player. The same can said for the iPhone in the smartphone category, or iPads with tablet computers.

BRAND OUTLOOK

- The loss of Steve Jobs brings uncertainty to Apple's future.
- As the world's top brand, Apple has become a target of criticism.
- Emerging markets like India, Russia, and China offer opportunities for growing the Apple brand further.
- The business community presents another opportunity for Apple.

Although Apple enjoyed spectacular growth in the early 2000s, ultimately emerging as the world's most valuable brand according to many, it faced its share of challenges. In October 2011, Steve Jobs passed away. Although he left behind a strong company culture and seasoned executives, he was a master marketer and the man most responsible for the transformation of the Apple brand. While Apple was likely to carry on successfully without him, it was nevertheless a significant loss.

Now regarded as the world's top brand, Apple found itself a ready target for critics. The loyalty of Apple customers became a source of mockery. Samsung exploited that opening in a series of commercials poking fun at the iPhone and by doing so made significant headway in the smartphone market. Apple also stumbled in the fall of 2012 with its Apple Maps iPhone app that proved wholly inadequate. Because Apple was so renowned for its excellent products and services, the matter received a great deal of unflattering publicity.

Nevertheless, Apple enjoyed an enviable perch, and there remained ample opportunities for growing the brand. A number of emerging markets appeared to hold promise. India led the way, followed by Russia, China, and the United Arab Emirates. The move toward cloud storage, offered through Apple's iCloud service, is a logical next step for the company, allowing customers to share content across Apple devices. Such a development would further reinforce the integrated lifestyle already represented by the brand. Perhaps the greatest opportunity for the Apple brand lay in the business sector. Outside of designers, Apple had never enjoyed more success in the commercial world. Now many companies were testing iPhones and iPads, as well as the Macbook Air, for business use. In addition, Apple might very well surprise the world again, unveiling a new product that no one knew they had always wanted.

FURTHER READING

"Apple Inc." *International Directory of Company Histories*. Ed. Derek Jacques and Paula Kepos. Vol. 132. Detroit, MI: St. James Press. 2012.

Badenhausen, Kurt. "Apple Tops List of the World's Most Powerful Brands." *Forbes*, October 2, 2012.

Brand Finance. "Global 500 2012." *Brandirectory*. Accessed January 10, 2013. http://brandirectory.com/league_tables/table/global-500-2012.

Bulik, Beth Snyder. "Marketer of the Decade." *Advertising Age*, October 18, 2010.

Chapman, Mike. "'1984': As Good as It Gets." *Brandweek*, January 31, 2011.

Cuneo, Alice Z. "Apple Transcends as Lifestyle Brand." *Advertising Age*, December 15, 2003.

Elkin, Tobi. "Like the Company, Apple's Familiar Rainbow Logo Undergoes Change." *Brandweek*, June 1, 1998.

———. "Steve Jobs: Return of the King." *Brandweek*, October 12, 1998.

Joseph, Jim. "How Do I Love Thee, Apple?" *Brandweek*, May 24, 2010.

Millward Brown. "BrandZ Top 100 Most Valuable Global Brands 2012." Accessed January 10, 2013. http://www.millwardbrown.com/brandz/Top_100_Global_Brands.aspx.

Mitchell, Alan. "Source of Apple's Success." *Marketing*, April 14, 2010.

"The Only Way Is Apple." *Marketing Week*, June 7, 2012, 20.

ARMANI

AT A GLANCE

Brand Synopsis: One of the most successful luxury retail and design brands in the world, Armani embodies simple sophistication.
Parent Company: Giorgio Armani S.p.A.
Giorgio Armani Spa
Via Borgonuovo, 11
20121 Milano
Italy
http://www.armani.com
Sector: Consumer Discretionary
Industry Group: Consumer Durables & Apparel
Performance: *Market share*—3.7 percent of the global luxury market. *Sales*—US$2.31 billion (2011).
Principal Competitors: Gianni Versace; Dolce & Gabbana; Hugo Boss; Burberry

BRAND ORIGINS

- Giorgio Armani founded his company in 1975 in Milan as a ready-to-wear menswear retailer.
- Armani's clothing was inspired by classic English looks, and the natural fit and subtle colors shocked the world of fashion design.
- Giorgio Armani used local textile companies to manufacture its clothing in order to better oversee the production.
- The company became popular in the United States following successful product placement in films and television shows.

Named for its founder, Giorgio Armani was established in 1975 in Milan, Italy. Armani was born in Piacenza, Italy, in 1934. Before establishing his own business, he worked at the large Italian department store La Rinascente as a window dresser. His work included making frequent trips to England in search of design inspiration. He said: "We used to travel to London for the influences, to see the shops, to learn. I remember seeing some yellow cardigans in a small boutique and bringing them to Il Rinascente and everyone thought I was insane. Yellow cardigans were what the Duke of Windsor was about; they were not something for the average man. The entire idea of such clothing was so outré, so elitist ... very, very English."

After becoming a freelance designer in the early 1970s, Armani partnered with his friend Sergio Galeotti, an architectural draftsman, and launched his own line in 1975. Armani started with a menswear line and quickly expanded to include a successful line for women. His styles featured a more natural fit, with neutral colors. In 1978 Armani signed a deal with Gruppo Finanziario Tessile, an established Italian textile manufacturer. The deal allowed the company to produce ready-to-wear luxury apparel while overseeing all of its own operations. Although they were an instant success in Europe, the firm's designs did not become popular in the United States until the 1980s. Giorgio Armani fashions made their film debut in *American Gigolo*, which starred Richard Gere and inspired a number of celebrities to begin wearing the Italian design.

The 1980s American television show *Miami Vice* also featured Giorgio Armani designs in its costuming.

In the early 1980s, Giorgio Armani signed a deal with the French-owned cosmetics company L'Oréal and launched a line of perfumes. During this period the firm also introduced Armani Junior, Armani Jeans, and Emporio Armani lines of clothing, followed by swimwear, underwear, and accessories. Armani also used his unique style to launch an ad campaign that incorporated television and billboards, media not traditionally used by designers.

Armani clothing became a status symbol among business professionals. The company's "power suits" were in high demand. The business continued to grow, even after the death of CEO Galeotti. Armani proved that he could run the business and design fashion without the help of his friend. Expanding the reach of its brand, Giorgio Armani opened its first restaurant in 1989; soon afterward it purchased the clothing manufacturer Simmit and bought shares in other businesses.

The company faced legal trouble in 1996, pleading guilty to bribing Italian tax officials from 1989 to 1990. The success of the company, however, was not affected by its legal troubles. By 2000 Giorgio Armani designs were being sold in more than 2,000 retail locations around the world, with annual sales of US$2 billion. Expansion into other markets continued, with forays into book publishing, home interiors, jewelry, and hotels. In 2005 Giorgio Armani launched its first haute-couture line, which Armani said he developed in order to challenge himself as a designer.

BRAND ELEMENTS

- Giorgio Armani is named after its founder, who started the company in Milan in 1975.
- Armani is known for its use of subtle colors, sleek cuts, and fine fabrics, used even for everyday wear.
- Armani's fragrance line, launched in the early 1980s, is designed to be diverse enough to offer a scent for anyone.

Armani has many brand elements that make it memorable, most notably its name, which it shares with the company's founder and main designer, Italian-born Giorgio Armani. Armani worked as a freelance fashion designer in the early 1970s and started his own clothing line and company in 1975. The company sells a wide range of products, from ready-to-wear men's and women's fashions to perfume and jewelry. Giorgio Armani also has an array of brands under its umbrella, such as Emporio Armani, Armani Junior, and Armani Jeans.

The best-known elements of Armani clothing design are the black, white, and neutral fabrics and the natural cut that is intended to flatter the figure. These elements, applied to high-end business wear, have made the Armani "power suit" a staple. The simple and sophisticated suit bears a professional look appropriate for any occasion, and it is less bulky and more comfortable than traditional suits. Armani also developed a line of professional wear for women that departed from traditionally flowery and feminine designs and adhered to a sleek cut and more subtle colors. Armani is also known for using fine and expensive fabric in everyday clothing, which increases the quality and longevity of the designs.

Armani is well known for its perfume lines, which include a numerous fragrances in order to appeal to a wide range of consumers. The company began offering fragrances in the early 1980s after signing a deal with French-based cosmetics company L'Oréal. Giorgio Armani's scents include Armani Code, Armani Mania, Acqua Di Gio, Attitude, Armani Eau Pour Homme, Emporio Armani for Him, Sensi, Privé, and Emporio Armani Diamonds, which featured singer Beyoncé Knowles in its advertising.

BRAND IDENTITY

- Armani strives to maintain its image as a designer of sophisticated luxury clothing as well as other products.
- Armani clothing is known for its subtle colors, fine fabrics, and streamlined cut.
- Armani is still owned by its namesake, Italian designer Giorgio Armani, which accounts for its consistency in design and product quality.

Since its founding in 1975 Armani has offered sophisticated ready-to-wear clothing made with fine fabrics. Natural fit and neutral colors have characterized the brand from its inception and continue to do so today. On its website, Armani is self-described as "the embodiment of style as lifestyle, of sophisticated simplicity as a mark of elegance." Armani is synonymous with high-quality luxury and reliable design. In 2012 Armani himself still owned the company and oversaw the production of all products. A majority of the merchandise is produced in-house to ensure superior quality control.

BRAND STRATEGY

- Giorgio Armani offers a wide array of products, from clothing and accessories to hotels and resorts.
- Giorgio Armani takes pride in the fact that 99 percent of his products are available for purchase in stores.
- Armani is known for its creative marketing, which has included the effort to outfit American celebrities in Giorgio Armani fashions.

Although Giorgio Armani started as a menswear company, it quickly expanded to include clothing for women. Its strategy has always emphasized offering a diverse array of luxury goods. Giorgio Armani offers clothing for every member of the family, from men and women to infants and teenagers. Armani Casa is a home line, featuring lamps, furniture, and linens. In the early 1980s, the company signed a deal with French-based cosmetics company L'Oréal to launch its fragrance collection. In 2004 the company signed a deal with Emaar Properties, based in the United Arab Emirates, to build and operate luxury hotels and resorts under the Giorgio Armani name. In 2012 Armani said that accessories would account for more than 40 percent of his firm's overall profit.

Armani has expressed pride in the fact that 99 percent of his runway designs can be found in stores. Instead of making his brand exclusive, Armani strives to deliver what consumers want rather than items that just look good on a model. He has been known to give pep talks to models at runway shows, directing them to walk elegantly and smile and demonstrate how the clothes should be worn. This strategy has succeeded: Armani "power suits," as they have come to be known, are popular among men and women because of their simplicity, subtle colors, and professional appearance.

Armani uses creative marketing to present his brand to consumers. During the 1980s Armani advertised in a way that other designers had not—through television ads and billboards—eschewing the idea of the exclusivity of luxury. Armani was also one of the first designers to exploit the marketing power of celebrities. Starting with the film *American Gigolo*, Armani has enjoyed a secure relationship with Hollywood. Other film credits include *Batman, Pulp Fiction*, and the television show *Miami Vice*. This type of marketing further spread the awareness of Armani designs into the previously untapped American market, and the company continues to employ the strategy: at the 2012 Olympic Games in London, Italy's athletes wore Emporio Armani.

In 2011 Giorgio Armani opened 100 additional stores, 28 of which were in China. Expansion in Asia helped fuel a 23 percent increase in operating profit in 2011.

BRAND EQUITY

- Armani's 2012 brand value was the fourth highest among Italian brands.
- Armani ranked 37th in a global ranking of luxury brands in 2011.
- Although Armani ranked 93rd on Interbrand's list of the top-100 brands in 2011, it was not included in the 2012 list.

In 2012 Armani's brand value ranked fourth among Italian brands, behind Ferrari, Prada, and Gucci. The company reported a 23 percent increase in operating profit in 2011, which was largely attributed to the company's expansion into China. According to the Milan consulting company Pambianco Strategie di Impresa, Armani ranked 37th globally among luxury brands in 2007. Burberry stood at 39th place and Dolce & Gabbana placed 45th.

On Interbrand's 2011 list of the top 100 brands, Armani was ranked 93rd, with a brand value of US$3.79 billion, but the company did not make the list in 2012. Competitor Prada was not ranked in the 2011 list but was ranked 84th in 2012 with a brand value of US$4.27 billion.

BRAND AWARENESS

- Armani was ranked by *Forbes* as the 97th most powerful brand, based on consumer resonance.
- In China, Armani was ranked as the 28th most searched-for luxury brand, based on 150 million customer queries.
- While 12 percent of global Internet customers purchase the Armani brand, 30 percent stated they would buy Armani if money was not an issue.

According to a report released by *Forbes* in 2012, Armani is the 97th most powerful brand in the world, based on the company's resonance with consumers as well as the company's brand values. Of a survey of 21,000 online consumers in 42 countries, one in three consumers stated he would buy Armani products if money were not an issue. A large part of the brand's success has been that Armani not only sells fashion, but it sells an image that customers are willing to pay high prices for.

In China, where the economy is booming, Armani is ranked as the 28th most searched-for luxury brand on Internet search engines. The ranking is based on more than 150 million customer queries on both Baidu, the leading Chinese search engine, and Google. In a similar survey in the United States, Armani was ranked as the 47th most searched-for luxury brand. The ranking is based on more than 470 million queries by American consumers on Bing and Google. As reported by the Nielsen Group, while 12 percent of global Internet consumers purchase Giorgio Armani, 30 percent said they would buy Armani if money were no object.

BRAND OUTLOOK

- Giorgio Armani reported a 23 percent increase in operating profit in 2011, mainly because of its growing operations in China.
- In 2012 Giorgio Armani reported operating more than 500 retail locations globally.
- Giorgio Armani is one of few privately owned luxury retailers; Armani owns 100 percent of his company.

Giorgio Armani reported an operating profit in 2011 of US$354 million, an increase of 23 percent that was mostly attributed to the company's expansion into China. In China the company's profits increased by 45 percent in 2011. In that same year, Giorgio Armani opened an additional 100 stores worldwide. Twenty-eight of the new stores were in China—more than were added in any other country and more than double the number of new stores opened in Europe. The firm has placed increased emphasis on expanding in the burgeoning Asia market.

In 2004 Giorgio Armani signed a deal with Emaar Properties to build hotels and resorts under the Giorgio Armani name. In 2010 a Giorgio Armani hotel opened in the Burj Khalifa skyscraper in Dubai, occupying the first 39 floors of the building. In 2012 Giorgio Armani operated more than 500 retail stores and 13 factories worldwide, employing more than 5,000 workers. It also ran a bar and nightclub in New York City.

Armani remains a member of a small group of Italian designers who have shunned a public share sale. He owns 100 percent of the company. Despite the fact that rival companies such as Prada and Burberry have become public companies in order to boost overall profit, Giorgio Armani remains successful and reported no loss during the economic recession of 2008.

FURTHER READING

ACNielsen. "Giorgio Armani and Gucci—the 'world's most coveted' fashion brands." March 2006. Accessed February 15, 2013. http://no.nielsen.com/news/documents/breakingnews2702.pdf.

Bloomberg News. "Armani, Gucci dominate in survey." *Washington Times*, February 20, 2006. Accessed February 15, 2013. http://www.washingtontimes.com/news/2006/feb/20/20060220-101004-1204r/?page=all.

Bundhun, Rebecca. "Armani No Longer Just Clothing." *National*, December 16, 2011.

Ciancio, Antonella. "Armani Aims to Boost Bags, Shoes Offer." *Chicago Tribune*, September 20, 2012.

Deeny, Godfrey. "Armani Scores 23 Percent Rise in 2011 Profit." *Fashion Wire Daily*, May 24, 2012.

Forden, Sara Gay. "Armani Plans to Maintain Chinese Expansion as Sales Increase." *Bloomberg News*, February 10, 2009.

Galloni, Alessandra. "The Future of Armani." *Wall Street Journal Online*, May 23, 2012.

"Giorgio Armani: A Retrospective." *Studio International*, November 17, 2003. Accessed November 2, 2012. http://www.studio-international.co.uk/reports/armani.asp.

"ItalBrand Top 100 Italian Brands." RankingTheBrands.com. Accessed November 2, 2012. http://www.rankingthebrands.com/The-Brand-Rankings.aspx?rankingID=160&year=316.

"Luxury Sales to Rise in Europe". *Warc*, February 2, 2011. Accessed November 3, 2012. http://www.warc.com/LatestNews/News/Luxury%20sales%20to%20rise%20in%20Europe.news?ID=27851.

Sylvers, Eric. "Armani's Profits Look the Part." *Financial Times*, May 24, 2012.

SyncForce. "Giorgio Armani." *Ranking The Brands.com*, 2012. Accessed February 15, 2013. http://www.rankingthebrands.com/Brand-detail.aspx?brandID=381.

"2011 Ranking of the Top 100 Brands." Interbrand. Accessed October 15, 2012. http://www.interbrand.com/en/best-global-brands/previous-years/best-global-brands-2011.aspx.

"2012 Ranking of the Top 100 Brands." Interbrand. Accessed October 10, 2012. http://www.interbrand.com/en/best-global-brands/2012/Best-Global-Brands-2012.aspx.

ASAHI

AT A GLANCE

Brand Synopsis: A leading beer brand in Japan, Asahi prides itself on a continued quality and social commitment to its employees, business partners, local communities, and consumers.
Parent Company: Asahi Group Holdings, Ltd.
3-7-1 Kyobashi, Chuo-Ku
Tokyo 104-9323
Japan
http://www.asahibeer.co.jp/
Sector: Consumer Staples
Industry Group: Food, Beverage & Tobacco
Performance: *Market share*—37.9 percent (2011). *Sales*—US$19.3 billion (2010).
Principal Competitors: Kirin Brewery Company, Limited; Mercian Corporation; Sapporo Breweries Limited; Suntory Holdings Limited; Takara Holdings Inc.

BRAND ORIGINS

- Asahi Beer was first released to the market in 1892.
- Asahi Breweries was created in 1949 as a result of the break-up of Dai Nippon Brewery.
- Asahi was the first Japanese brewery to have its beer produced overseas; further licensing agreements in foreign markets has been a source of expansion for the company.

The history of Asahi Breweries is linked with that of virtually every other brewery in Japan. Beer had been introduced to Japan during the mid-1800s. The American Commodore Matthew Perry brought several cases of beer to Japan as a gift for the Tokugawa shogunate. The beverage was so well liked that the Japanese government soon decided to establish a brewing industry. After an extensive search for a suitable area, wild hops were found growing on the island of Hokkaido, the northernmost island in the Japanese archipelago. As a result, in 1876 the commissioner general for the development of Hokkaido founded Japan's first brewery in the town of Sapporo. (Coincidentally, the global beer capitols of Munich, Milwaukee, and Sapporo are all located along the 45 degrees north latitude.)

During the late 1880s the government sold its Hokkaido brewery to private interests, and thus the Osaka Beer Brewing Company, the Japan Beer Brewery Company, the Sapporo Brewery, and the Nippon Brewing Company all came into being. In 1888 Hiizu Ikuta was sent to Germany by the Osaka Beer Brewing Company to study brewing at the famous School of Weihenstephen in Bavaria. He returned the following year and was appointed manager and technical chief of the Suita Brewery, one of the individual breweries that was controlled by Osaka. Three years later, in 1892, his creation, Asahi Beer, was released for sale. The following year Osaka was reorganized as Osaka Breweries, Ltd.

In 1906 the Osaka Breweries, the Sapporo Brewery, and the Nippon Brewing Company were amalgamated into the Dai Nippon Brewery Co., Ltd. Asahi, now a separate division of the new company, began producing nonalcoholic beverages as well as beer. Asahi pioneered the soft drink industry in Japan with both Mitsuya Cider and Wilkinson Tansan, a mineral water. Mitsuya Cider was released for sale in 1907, 15 years after Asahi Beer had first been introduced to the market. In 1949, as a result of antimonopoly laws, Dai Nippon Brewery, which had cornered nearly 70 percent of the beer market in Japan, was divided into two parts: Asahi Beer, Ltd., and Nippon Breweries, Ltd. (the latter was eventually renamed as Sapporo Breweries Limited).

Asahi began importing wine and spirits from foreign countries during the early 1970s. In a joint venture with the Nikka Whiskey Distilling Company of Japan, Asahi established Japan International Liquor to import foreign liquors, primarily Scotch whiskeys (Dewars and King George IV). Asahi was also the first Japanese brewery to have its beer produced overseas under license when it concluded a technical assistance agreement with United Breweries of New Guinea, and a brewery was subsequently constructed at Port Moresby. Further notable licensing agreements included the Löwenbräu Company of Germany, Cadbury Schweppes of the United Kingdom, Bass Brewers of the United Kingdom, Foster's Brewing Group of Australia, Canadian Molson Breweries, Miller Brewing of the United States, Tsingtao Brewery of China, and the Australian wine company Lindemann's.

BRAND ELEMENTS

- *Asahi* means "morning sun" in Japanese; a red, rising sun was part of the initial company logo.
- During a logo redesign in 1986, Asahi officials worried that changing the existing logo would alienate customers who had been loyal to company for many years.
- The Asahi Beer Hall, which is located at the company headquarters in Tokyo, has gained architectural prominence.

Asahi means "morning sun" in Japanese. The original logo for Asahi featured the company name in plain brown capital letters, with a red rising sun positioned underneath. In 1986 Asahi commissioned a complete redesign of its logo. Company officials worried that a new logo would alienate loyal, existing consumers, but also hoped that a new logo would rid the company of the image of a stagnant past. They wanted a logo that would invigorate the brand with a conveyance of youth and progress. The logo color was changed from brown to blue to convey a crispness, coolness, and freshness. The company name was retained, with only the first letter capitalized, in a simple Japanese calligraphic font. The red sun was dropped from the image.

The Asahi Beer Hall, which houses a restaurant and bar, has gained architectural prominence. Situated within Asahi's headquarters on the east bank of the Sumida River in Tokyo, Japan, the building is a unique modern structure and one of the most recognizable in Tokyo. Built in the shape of a beer glass, it was designed to complement a nearby office building in the shape of a beer mug. An enormous gold-colored flame is perched at the top, simulating the froth of a beer.

BRAND IDENTITY

- During the 1970s Asahi moved to improve the quality of its products; the company began buying its raw ingredients from growers in other countries rather than rely solely on Japanese growers.
- Asahi was the first brewer in Japan to market beer in cans rather than bottles; the company also moved its beer onto supermarket shelves and convenience stores.
- Asahi uses imagery in its advertising that portrays its brands as being urbane and sophisticated.

As a way to counter slumping sales of the 1970s, Asahi pushed to become more attuned to its customers, with a renewed attention to quality. Asahi abandoned its policy of purchasing most of its wheat and hops from Japanese growers and began buying the best raw materials available, regardless of cost or origin. The company also made moves to ensure the freshness of its beer by having salespeople visit stores to discard of any Asahi Beer that was older than three months.

In Japan most beer was traditionally sold in small liquor stores by the bottle. In 1958 Asahi launched a canned version of Asahi Beer, making it Japan's first canned beer. The company then targeted nontraditional customers by producing more of its beer in cans and packaging it in six-packs and by sending the canned beer into supermarkets and convenience stores. The company also became much more aggressive in its pitches to retailers who sold beer and continued to emphasize the freshness of its product.

Asahi is proud to have consumers view its products as global brands of Japanese origin. Asahi's primary identity comes from owning Japan's number-one beer, Asahi Super Dry, and from the quality of all its products. Asahi uses advertising both at home and around the globe that communicates its market leader position with urbane and sophisticated imagery.

BRAND STRATEGY

- Asahi pioneered the soft drink industry in Japan by introducing Mitsuya Cider; other nonalcoholic beverages followed, including Wilkinson Tansan mineral water, Bireley's Orange, and a variety of waters, sports drinks, teas, and canned coffees.

- Asahi Super Dry was released to the market in 1987 and became a phenomenal hit, leading to the Japanese mania for dry beer.
- Besides its beer brands, Asahi produces lines of low-malt and nonalcoholic beverages.

Asahi pioneered the soft drink industry in Japan with Mitsuya Cider, which was released in 1907. Asahi later added Wilkinson Tansan mineral water and Bireley's Orange, a fruit-flavored soft drink, both released in 1951. Besides Orange, Bireley's is available in Apple, Sarasara Tomato, and a Bottle Breakfast series. Asahi expanded its contemporary line of nonalcoholic beverages to include a variety of waters, sports drinks, teas, and canned coffees.

Asahi conducted a series of market surveys, which revealed that 98 percent of the beer drinkers surveyed wanted Asahi to change the taste of its beer. Asahi subsequently developed and introduced Asahi Draft, a full-bodied beer with a crisp taste. In 1987 Asahi introduced Japan's first dry beer, Asahi Super Dry, which became a blockbuster hit. Super Dry, a cold-filtered draft beer, contained slightly more alcohol than other Japanese beer, but less sugar and was thus lighter; it was also less bitter. The brand became particularly popular among younger drinkers and helped increase Asahi's market share just one year after its introduction.

The company launched Asahi Honnama, a low-malt beer, in 2001. In Japan beer is taxed according to its malt content, so the tax on low-malt beers, known as happoshu, is significantly lower, which results in a retail price about two-thirds that of a regular beer. Happoshu gained increasing popularity and Asahi Honnama enjoyed the same acclaim and sales success as Asahi Super Dry. The company has subsequently released two more happoshu beers: Asahi Aqua Blue and Asahi Style Free, a carbohydrate-free happoshu.

Asahi Gold, a lager, was introduced in 1957 and became the company's flagship beer until it was supplanted by the phenomenal success of Asahi Super Dry. Asahi Gold and Asahi Draft both continue in production. Other beer brands include Asahi Stout; Asahi Z, a dry lager; Asahi Kuronama Black, a black lager; Clear Asahi, a barley-based beer; and Asahi Premium Beer Jukusen, a pilsner beer.

Asahi also produces a line of shochu, an alcoholic beverage that is generally distilled from barley or rice. Shochu has less alcohol by volume than whiskey or vodka, but is stronger than wine or sake. Several of Asahi's shochus were branded "Kanoka," which means "good fragrance" in Japanese; Asahi chose the name to reflect its shochu's delicate fragrance and mellow taste. Two of Asahi's shochus are distilled from sweet potatoes: Satsuma Kokumurasaki and Satsuma Tsukasa.

BRAND EQUITY

- Beer accounts for half of all alcohol consumption in Japan; lager beers are the most popular types of beer.
- Asahi was ranked 642 in the *Forbes* "Global 2000" in 2012.
- Asahi was ranked 354 in the *Fortune* "Global 500" in 2012.

Beer is a popular drink in Japan, accounting for half of all alcohol consumption. The Japanese beer market had total sales of US$34.9 billion in 2010, with lager beer sales generating 74 percent of the market. Asahi Super Dry beer provides the bulk of revenue for the company.

In 2012 Asahi was ranked at number 642 in the *Forbes* "Global 2000," with sales of US$13.2 billion. That same year Asahi was ranked number 354 in the *Fortune* "Global 500," with a brand value of US$3.2 billion.

BRAND AWARENESS

- In 2011 Asahi held a 38 percent market share in Japan, edging out rival Kirin Brewing Company with a 36 percent market share.
- Asahi Super Dry was named the 10th most popular beer in the world in 2011.
- The company exports Asahi Super Dry to more than 80 countries around the world.

Brought to market in 1987, Asahi Super Dry quickly became the most popular beer in Japan. Super Dry is now exported to more than 80 countries and produced under license in Canada, China, the Czech Republic, Russia, Thailand, and the United Kingdom. It is the top-selling Japanese lager in the United Kingdom and South Korea, and in 2011 it was named the 10th most popular beer in the world. That same year Asahi held a 38 percent market share in Japan, which was slightly more than the 36 percent market share that was held by Kirin Brewing Company.

In 2005 Asahi was the leading low-malt beer brewer in Japan, with a 38.8 percent market share. Three years later, in 2008, Asahi was ranked as the 10th-largest beverage firm in the world and the top beer maker in Japan, with a 37.5 percent market share. Asahi was also the third-largest soft drink maker in the Asia-Pacific region, with a 2.6 percent market share. In 2009 Asahi was the third-largest juice maker in Japan, with a 4.5 percent market share, behind only Coca-Cola and Pepsi. By 2010 Asahi was ranked as the seventh-largest consumer beverage company in the world.

BRAND OUTLOOK

- The beer industry in Japan has been stagnating for several years, in part because of a shrinking and aging population.

- Asahi announced in 2012 that it was postponing plans to expand throughout China due to tensions between China and Japan.
- Asahi's nonalcoholic brands may provide opportunities for expansion as consumers seek lower-calorie beverages.

The Japanese beer industry has been stagnant, in part because of the decreasing number of young people and because of changing consumer tastes. In 2011 the northern part of Japan was devastated by an earthquake and tsunami, which forced breweries to shut down temporarily. As people looked to recover from the disaster, there was an inclination to abstain from drinking. Asahi's brewery in Fukushima, near the site of the nuclear facility that was damaged, reopened with radiation detectors installed to ensure product safety.

Asahi's dominant market position with Super Dry gives it the power to attract new customers. However, a large part of its revenues are generated only from Japan. Continuing strategic global partnerships and entering into new accords will give Asahi the opportunity to enhance its existing business. In 2012 Asahi announced that it had reached an agreement with the U.S.-based Brown-Forman Corporation to begin selling several of its brands in Japan, including Early Times and Jack Daniels whiskey.

Also in 2012 Asahi announced that it was postponing its planned expansion in China because of increasing anti-Japanese sentiment in the country. Asahi had hoped to sell Super Dry throughout China; it currently sells its products in Shanghai and Beijing. Tensions between China and Japan escalated after Japan nationalized three of the five disputed East China Sea islands.

Asahi also owns lines of quality nonalcoholic brands that may provide options for the company to diversify even further. More consumers are turning to nonalcoholic beverages for health and wellness reasons, as these drinks are often much lower in calories than alcoholic beverages.

FURTHER READING

"Asian Beer." *Drinks International*, July 30, 2012. Accessed January 3, 2013. http://www.drinksint.com/news/fullstory.php/aid/3157/Asian_beer_.html.

"Asahi Breweries, Ltd." *International Directory of Company Histories*. Ed. Jay P. Pederson. Vol. 52. Detroit, MI: St. James Press, 2003.

"Asahi to Sell Jack Daniel's Whiskey in Japan." *Jiji*, September 19, 2012.

"Interview: Asahi to Postpone Beer Business Expansion in China." *Jiji*, October 5, 2012.

Pinijparakarn, Sucheera. "Asahi Beer Copes with Ad Ban." *Nation*, December 11, 2009.

Shinn, Cheng Herng, and Shunichi Ozasa. "Asahi Holds Onto Lead over Kirin in Japan." *Bloomberg*, January 16, 2012.

"Top 10 Biggest Beer Brands." *Drinks Business*, September 24, 2012. Accessed January 3, 2013. http://www.thedrinksbusiness.com/2012/09/top-10-biggest-beer-brands/11.

Viet. "The Great Japanese Beer (aka Sparkling Water) War." *Tofugu*. Accessed January 3, 2013. http://www.tofugu.com/2012/05/03/the-great-japanese-beer-aka-sparkling-water-war.

ASDA

AT A GLANCE

Brand Synopsis: ASDA's goal is to offer its customers the best possible shopping experience through low prices, high quality, and guaranteed satisfaction.
Parent Company: Wal-Mart Stores, Inc.
ASDA House, Great Wilson Street
Leeds, West Yorkshire LS11 5AD
United Kingdom
http://www.asda.co.uk
Sector: Consumer Discretionary
Industry Group: Consumer Durables & Apparel
Performance: *Market share*—17.9 percent (2012). *Sales*—US$34.9 billion (2011).
Principal Competitors: J Sainsbury plc; Tesco PLC; Sainsbury's Supermarkets Ltd.; Wm Morrison Supermarkets PLC

BRAND ORIGINS

- ASDA's origins go back to 1920, when the Yorkshire dairy farmer J. W. Hindell formed the local partnership Hindell's Dairy Farmers Ltd.
- The first ASDA food stores were built in 1965, promising low prices, high quality, and no frills.
- ASDA was purchased by Wal-Mart Stores, Inc., in July 1999 for US$10.8 billion.
- In 2010 ASDA acquired Netto Foodstores Ltd. and its chain of 193 supermarkets and rebranded them as part of the ASDA supermarket chain.

In 1920 the Yorkshire dairy farmer J. W. Hindell gathered his fellow dairy farmers to form the local partnership Hindell's Dairy Farmers Ltd. When World War I came to its conclusion, the fixed pricing of consumer goods was lifted. As a consequence, many products, including dairy, were purchased from cheaper European markets, which drove down the price of local dairy. Hindell's group opened both wholesale and retail outlets for their own dairy products, selling them directly to the public, eliminating the middleman, and earning higher margins on sales.

Over the next 25 years the company added eight more businesses to its operation, including dairy shops, bakeries, and cafés. By March 1949 the partnership went public under the new name, Associated Dairies and Farm Stores Ltd. By that time the company consisted of 26 farms, three dairies, two bakeries, 42 retail shops, and 1,200 employees. During the next 15 years the conglomerate continued to expand and acquire competitors at a dizzying pace. By 1965 its annual sales had reached US$21.4 million and Associated Dairies decided to use some of that income to form the new subsidiary ASDA Stores Ltd.

The formula was to place warehouse-style food stores at the edge of large towns and sell a limited number of products at very low or even bulk rate prices. The stores were located outside of towns, where land and buildings were less expensive to purchase; thus, low overhead enabled even lower prices on products. However, the isolated locations made the stores dependent on customers having transportation to get to them. As it turned out, the British public was more concerned with lower prices than with loyalty to local vendors, and the ASDA supermarkets became an immediate and huge success. By 1978 there were 60 of the superstores located throughout the northern half of England with further sites being developed in London and throughout the surrounding region. That same year Associated Dairies conducted several large purchases and mergers. In October of that year Associated Dairies Group Ltd. was incorporated as the holding company for all the subsidiaries in the organization.

By the early 1980s the novelty of the low-price, no-frills warehouse superstore was wearing off and ASDA's competition was drawing customers away with eye-catching displays, marketing gimmicks, and greater variety. When John Hardman became the managing director in June 1984, he decided that ASDA needed to make some major changes to stay ahead of the competition. He proposed a five-stage plan that started with giving the stores a consistent and appealing physical makeover, including a soothing green color scheme, dramatic lighting, and eye-catching displays. Next, the company would introduce its own line of "ASDA brand" foods. To improve record-keeping accuracy and inventory control, all stores would be upgraded with electronic point-of-sale registers. A network of nine distribution warehouses would be built to streamline the process of getting products into the stores. Finally, ASDA would aggressively expand into southern England, London in particular, where few superstores had yet been built. All five of these measures were applied and yielded impressive, positive results.

In 1985 ASDA merged with MFI, a low-priced furniture retailer, and Allied Carpets. The partnership turned out to be short-lived and unprofitable and by 1987 MFI was sold for US$718 million. ASDA also sold off Associated Fresh Foods, which was the last of the original dairy companies that started under the Hindell name. In February 1988 the company changed its name to ASDA Group Limited. At that point, it had 117 food superstores. The following year ASDA purchased 62 superstores from rival Gateway for US$1.1 billion.

In July 1999 ASDA was involved in the most significant business transaction in its 80-year existence when it was purchased by Wal-Mart Stores, Inc., for US$10.8 billion. The purchase was extremely beneficial to both companies. Wal-Mart gained a huge foothold in the United Kingdom market, and ASDA instantly more than doubled its international sales. Almost immediately, ASDA adopted many of Wal-Mart's programs and strategies, including Wal-Mart's famous "price roll-back" program, which started price wars among the major supermarket companies in the United Kingdom.

The first ASDA superstore to open with the Wal-Mart name and logo alongside its own was in 2000. At that point ASDA also launched its Smart Price brands, which was similar to Wal-Mart's Great Value and Sam's Choice lines of products. By year-end 2004 ASDA had 265 total stores in operation, with sales increasing 20 percent to US$21.7 billion. In 2006 ASDA introduced a new marketing strategy by incorporating its ASDA Essentials and ASDA Living formats. By 2008 ASDA had grown to 347 stores in the United Kingdom and had introduced an online home shopping service in Ireland. The company also unveiled two new clothing brands for customers over the age of 45: Boston Crew for men and Moda for women. In another landmark transaction, in 2010 ASDA acquired the Danish supermarket chain Netto Foodstores Ltd. from Dansk Supermarked. All Netto stores were converted to the ASDA brand name and operations and have thus far done well. That one acquisition earned ASDA an additional US$660 million in revenues in 2011.

BRAND ELEMENTS

- ASDA made its first appearance in 1965 as a subsidiary of Associated Dairies and was named ASDA Stores Ltd.
- The ASDA name is actually a contraction of Asquith and Dairies.
- The earliest slogan developed by ASDA was "All Together Better," and ran from 1981 to 1984.

ASDA originated in 1920 as Hindell's Farmers Ltd. When the company went public in 1949, it became Associated Dairies and Farm Stores Ltd. The ASDA name made its first appearance in 1965 as a subsidiary of Associated Dairies and was named ASDA Stores Ltd. The ASDA name is actually a contraction of Asquith and Dairies. Asquith was a small chain of three supermarkets that merged with Associated Dairies in 1965. The company has long prided itself in offering its customers low prices, good value, and no frills. This is reflected in its logo, which features the company name in a light green color scheme; the simple design represents value and simplicity and serves to remind customers of the company's agricultural base and its promotion of a clean, fresh image.

ASDA has developed several slogans over the years, and nearly all of them contained the same basic theme of low prices. The earliest slogan developed by the company was "All Together Better" and ran between 1981 and 1984 to advertise the low prices that could be found at ASDA supermarkets. Between 1985 and 1989 the slogan was "One Trip and You're Laughing." From 1994 on the slogans directly focused on low prices. The first of these was "Pocket the Difference" in 1994. Between 1996 and 2001 it was "Permanently Low Prices—Forever." Between 2002 and 2005 ASDA utilized the slogan that its new parent company was well known for: "Always Low Prices." Since 2008 the slogan has been "Saving You Money Every Day." To further reinforce the message of saving money, a longtime standard in ASDA advertisements has been the sound of change jingling as a person taps his or her pocket, signifying that customers will always have extra money in their pocket when they shop at ASDA.

BRAND IDENTITY

- ASDA's "Chosen by You" line of products is based on blind taste tests by the general public.
- ASDA's longest lasting ad campaign has been the series of pocket tapping ads, which first ran in 1977 and have continued for over 30 years.
- In 2012 ASDA won the *Grocer* magazine's Lowest Price Supermarket Award for the 15th consecutive year.

Everything ASDA does is based around the concept of low prices. Whether it is a new marketing scheme, a change in the visual elements of store displays, or an entirely new line of products, it always comes down to this basic concept. In 2012 ASDA won the *Grocer* magazine's Lowest Price Supermarket Award for the 15th consecutive year. The company also reinforces its message through various marketing strategies, such as its price guarantee: "If we're not 10 percent cheaper on your comparable grocery shopping we'll give you the difference." Another successful program has been the "Chosen by You" line of foods, in which all the products in this store-brand category have been "tried, tasted and chosen" by the public through blind taste tests carried out by an independent company. By far, ASDA's most successful and longest lasting ad campaign has been its pocket tapping ads, in which customers tap their pockets to jingle the coins there, signifying that they have saved money by shopping at ASDA. The ads first ran in 1977 and have featured a list of celebrities who have appeared in the ads as "tappers."

BRAND STRATEGY

- In 1989 ASDA purchased 62 superstores from the rival supermarket chain Gateway for US$1.1 billion.
- The 1989 purchase of part of the Gateway superstore chain increased ASDA's total floor space by 50 percent.
- The George line of clothing is named after the fashion tycoon George Davies and earned ASDA over US$2.8 billion in 2005.

From the start, ASDA has maintained a simple, straightforward brand strategy: give the customer the lowest possible prices on high-quality foods and products, and keep the entire process as simple as possible. With the company originating in northern England, the obvious course of expansion was southward. From its humble beginnings in 1920, the company grew through carefully selected partnerships and purchases of rivals, while at the same time building new stores in areas where there was little competition. This strategy was most notable in 1989, when ASDA purchased 62 superstores from the rival supermarket chain Gateway for US$1.1 billion, which effectively increased its total store space by 50 percent. In 2010 this feat was surpassed when ASDA purchased the discount retailer Netto and all its 193 stores located in the United Kingdom.

ASDA has also branched out from the supermarket venue by offering a variety of new products and services. In 1990 it began offering a line of "quality fashion clothing" known as George. The label was named after the fashion tycoon George Davies, who designed the clothing collection. By 2005 the George clothing line alone was worth US$2.8 billion and estimated to be the fourth-largest clothes retailer in the United Kingdom. During the mid-1990s it launched the ASDA Smart Price line of products. These were store-brand food items that were almost always offered at the lowest price, compared with similar name-brand items. This is similar to Wal-Mart's lines of Great Value and Sam's Choice food products and its Equate health and beauty line of products. During the first decade of the 21st century the Smart Price label was expanded to include almost every product category in the store. In October 2003 ASDA launched a new store format that focused on general, nonfood merchandise. The stores were named ASDA Living and stocked a number of products, including clothing, toys, electronics, cookware, and health and beauty items. As a subsequent step to the development of ASDA Living, in 2009 ASDA spun off food sales into its own supermarket division. The following year the Netto supermarkets were folded into this division to strengthen and dramatically expand its territory. ASDA has also developed Internet operations to capture a piece of the online retail market. In 2008 it launched ASDA Direct to sell a wide variety of electrical and electronics products online.

BRAND EQUITY

- By year-end 2011 ASDA had a total of 541 stores and employed over 180,000 people.
- In 2011 alone ASDA hired more than 30,000 new employees.
- In 2011 ASDA's total market value was estimated to be US$21.3 billion.

ASDA is the second-largest supermarket chain in the United Kingdom behind Tesco. As of December 2011, ASDA had a total of 541 stores: 32 supercenters, 309 ASDA Superstores, 27 ASDA Living stores, and 173 ASDA supermarkets (including Netto store conversions). In 2011 the company hired over 30,000 new personnel for a year-end total of over 180,000 employees. For fiscal year 2011 the company recorded revenues of US$31.8 billion, which was an increase of 6.3 percent over the previous year. Of that total, US$660 million was generated by the recently converted Netto supermarkets that ASDA purchased in 2010. As a subsidiary of Wal-Mart, ASDA accounted for 7.6 percent of all Wal-Mart store sales in 2011, and its total market value was estimated to be US$21.3 billion.

BRAND AWARENESS

- In 2012 ASDA won the *Grocer* magazine's Lowest Price Supermarket Award for the 15th consecutive year.
- In 2010 ASDA was named "Britain's Favourite Supermarket of the Year" at the Grocer Gold Awards.
- Between 2011 and 2012 ASDA's market share rose from 17.3 percent to an all-time high of 17.9 percent.

With over 45 years of experience under the ASDA brand and consistently being one of the most popular supermarket chains in the United Kingdom for over three decades, the company has become a ubiquitous presence among British shoppers. Having been purchased by Wal-Mart in 1999 only further solidified its reputation. ASDA has worked hard to make itself synonymous with low prices and great value in the minds of consumers. Its "pocket tap" ads with the sound of jingling coins have been around since 1977. In 2010 ASDA was named "Britain's Favourite Supermarket of the Year" at the Grocer Gold Awards, which is the food industry's version of the Oscars. Customers also know that through the ASDA Price Guarantee, they will always be able to purchase products 10 percent cheaper there than anywhere else. In 2012 ASDA received the *Grocer* magazine's Lowest Price Supermarket Award for the 15th consecutive year. A true indicator of ASDA's success is the fact that even though its competitors, such as Tesco and Morrison's, struggled through the recent global economic downturn, ASDA actually gained in market share, increasing from 17.3 percent in 2011 to 17.9 percent in 2012. Likewise, its profits have been fairly strong, rising 6.3 percent in 2011.

BRAND OUTLOOK

- In 2012 ASDA approved US$800 million to open 25 new stores and three depots that would create approximately 5,000 new jobs.
- In 2010 ASDA announced a five-year goal to open 150 ASDA Living outlet stores by the end of 2015.
- Since 1999, when it was taken over by Wal-Mart, ASDA has been gaining ground on Tesco, the market leader.

In April 2010 ASDA announced an ambitious set of goals for the next five years. The most prominent of these goals was to open 150 ASDA Living outlet stores by the end of 2015. In 2012 ASDA set aside US$800 million to open 25 new stores and three depots, which would create approximately 5,000 new jobs. Of these new stores, the majority would be in England, three in Scotland, and one in Wales. That same year ASDA announced that it will open several George clothing stores on the international market, beginning with two pilot stores in the Middle East, to be handled through a partnership with SandpiperCI.

Since being taken over by Wal-Mart in 1999, ASDA has gained increased ability to drive down product prices at a rate competitors find difficult to keep up with. The result has been that ASDA continues to gain ground on Tesco, the market leader. However, these gains will be slow and irregular, as Britons have cut back on nonessential spending due to overall price increases that have outpaced cost-of-living wage increases. Furthermore, high unemployment levels have continued to dampen consumer confidence. In January 2012 Andrew Godwin of Oxford Economics predicted that the United Kingdom's potential output growth will average only about 1.6 percent through 2016, while its gross domestic product will grow by 2.1 percent through 2016, gradually closing the gap. As of early 2013, the most serious concern was the ongoing European debt crisis, which threatened to trigger another deep recession in the United Kingdom if further defaults occurred. In the near future, low inflation rates will contribute to a 1.5 percent increase in household disposable income for 2013.

FURTHER READING

"ASDA Group Ltd." *International Directory of Company Histories.* Ed. Tina Grant and Miranda H. Ferrara. Vol. 64. Detroit, MI: St. James Press, 2006.

"Asda Set to Invest over £500m in 2012." ASDA. Accessed January 28, 2013. http://your.asda.com/press-centre/asda-set-to-invest-over-500m-in-2012-.

"Asda Slogans." Logopedia. Accessed January 28, 2013. http://logos.wikia.com/wiki/ASDA_Slogans.

"Best Retail Brands 2012." Interbrand. Accessed January 28, 2013. http://www.interbrand.com/Libraries/Branding_Studies/Best_Retail_Brands_2012.sflb.ashx?download=true.

Brand Finance. "Asda Brand Profiles and Valuations." *Brandirectory.* Accessed January 16, 2013. http://brandirectory.com/profile/asda.

Godwin, Andrew. "The UK Economic Outlook." Institute for Fiscal Studies, January 23, 2012. Accessed February 12, 2013. http://www.ifs.org.uk/budgets/gb2012/12chap2.pdf

Thomson, Rebecca. "Analysis: How Can Retailers Raise Brand Awareness?" *RetailWeek*, September 6, 2012.

Walker, Ian. "Tesco, J Sainsbury Christmas Market Share Unchanged from Year Ago." 4-Traders.com, January 15, 2013. Accessed January 28, 2013. http://www.4-traders.com/TESCO-PLC-4000540/news/Tesco-J-Sainsbury-Christmas-Market-Share-Unchanged-From-Year-Ago-15826107/.

Williamson, Mark. "Asda's Profits Boosted by Netto." *Herald* (Edinburgh, Scotland), October 7, 2012.

AT&T

AT A GLANCE

Brand Synopsis: As a direct descendant of the original Bell System, the AT&T brand has always been synonymous with the term *phone company* in the United States—and more than 100 years after its founding it remains just as relevant, ranking as the second-largest mobile phone company in the United States.
Parent Company: AT&T Inc.
208 S. Akard St., Dallas, TX 75202
http://www.att.com/
Sector: Telecommunication Services
Industry Group: Telecommunication Services
Performance: *Market share*—35.1 percent of the U.S. mobile market; 6.8 percent of the global mobile market (2010). *Revenues*—US$127 billion (2010).
Principal Competitors: Verizon Wireless; Sprint Nextel; T-Mobile USA; MetroPCS

BRAND ORIGINS

- Alexander Graham Bell, along with his partners, created Bell Telephone Company in 1877; American Telegraph & Telephone, a subsidiary, was incorporated in 1885.
- AT&T began using a two-way radio for transatlantic telephone service in 1925, allowing international calls for the first time.
- AT&T was split into eight separate companies in 1984 as the result of an antitrust investigation.
- AT&T completely digitized its network in the early 1990s to realize the possibilities of the Internet.

AT&T's corporate history goes all the way back to the invention of the telephone. In 1875 inventor Alexander Graham Bell received financing from Gardiner Hubbard and Thomas Sanders for his work on creating a talking telegraph. He earned patents for his work in 1876 and 1877. In 1877 Bell, along with his partners, created the Bell Telephone Company in New Haven, Connecticut. Within three years all major cities in the United States had telephone exchanges through the American Bell Telephone Company. After acquiring the Western Electric Company manufacturing unit as well as most of its licensees, the collective enterprise became known as the Bell System. The American Telephone and Telegraph Company (AT&T), a subsidiary of Bell, was incorporated in 1885 and was chartered to build and operate the original long-distance telephone network, stretching from New York to Chicago by 1892.

Up until Bell's patent expired in 1894 Bell Telephone was the only company that could legally operate telephone systems in the United States. In 1899 AT&T acquired the assets of Bell, becoming the parent company of the Bell System instead of a subsidiary. After the patent expired independent telephone companies sprouted all across the United States. Within 10 years the number of telephones increased 1,163 percent. The primary difficulty with the new companies was that they were not connected, making it impossible for subscribers to different companies to call each other, a situation not resolved until 1914.

AT&T began manufacturing Western Electric telephone equipment to sell internationally. It sold Western Electric in 1925, however, in an effort to concentrate on the goal of a universal telephone service in the United States. To achieve that goal AT&T began using a two-way radio for its transatlantic telephone service. Although this kind of service would also be used in Hawaii and Tokyo, it was very expensive, with limited capacity; calls were subject to fading and interference. Not until 1956 did the company begin cable service, after laying submarine telephone cable across the Atlantic Ocean. It did the same across the Pacific Ocean in 1964.

During the majority of AT&T's history the company acted as a regulated monopoly. The argument in favor of such an arrangement was that in order for the Bell System to be effective it would have to operate as a monopoly. The U.S. government expressed its agreement via with the Kingsbury Commitment in 1913, but AT&T was required to connect noncompeting independent telephone companies to its network and get rid of its controlling interest in Western Union Telegraph. The company was the subject of an antitrust suit filed in 1949, resulting in regulation by the Department of Justice that restricted AT&T to operating the national telephone system and government work. A subsequent antitrust suit was filed in 1974, resulting in the breakup of the Bell System in 1984. The company was split into AT&T and seven regional Bell operating companies.

Following the divestiture of the Bell System, AT&T was forced to surrender the Bell logo and name as well as US$100 billion in assets. The company now also had competitors in long-distance business, resulting in a market share loss. AT&T quickly recovered, however, due to an increase in call volume. As the boom of computers and the Internet in the 1990s increased the amount of data that passed through the company's network, AT&T's financial strength returned, allowing it to digitize the entire network. In the early 1990s AT&T acquired computer manufacturer NCR and McCaw Cellular and created its AT&T Wireless unit.

AT&T had an internal corporate breakup in 1995 that restructured the company into Lucent Technologies, a systems company; NCR, a computer company; and AT&T, a communication services company. It was the largest voluntary corporate breakup in United States history. After the split AT&T focused its attention on voice and data instead of long distance. As the company adapted to the Internet and wireless market, it split into three networks: data, broadband, and wireless. In 2000 the volume of data traffic exceeded the volume of voice traffic for the first time. AT&T Wireless broke away as an independent company in 2001.

BRAND ELEMENTS

- The AT&T company name was created as a part of the Bell System, the original telephone system in the United States, in 1885.
- The company had used a bell logo as part of the Bell System until the 1984 divestiture, after which it used the now-familiar logo of a globe with the name AT&T.
- AT&T's two recent notable slogans were "Your World. Delivered" (2005) and "Rethink Possible" (2010).

The AT&T name has a long history, dating almost as far back as the invention of the telephone. Alexander Graham Bell, the innovator behind the telephone, created the American Telephone & Telegraph subsidiary in 1885, and the company acted as a portion of the Bell System, the first phone system throughout the United States. The name carried throughout the company's history and was the name that remained after the firm was forced to split apart in 1984. The nature of the company has changed throughout the history of the name—from telephone provider to long distance provider to data provider and, finally, wireless service provider. In 2013 AT&T was primarily a wireless service provider, having split apart the other services into separate companies. The company name is the most recognizable aspect of the brand.

The logo had gone through several changes, but the logo as of 2013 had been the same since the Bell System was shut down in 1984. The previous logo was a well-known black bell image used to represent the Bell System. After the divesture of the Bell System AT&T lost the rights to the previous logo. The new logo was a simple black globe with the name "AT&T" next to it. This design was altered slightly in the 1990s to add the color blue to the globe image.

AT&T has used two well-known slogans in recent years. In 2005, after AT&T had acquired 60 percent of Cingular Wireless and changed the name to AT&T Wireless, it released the slogan "Your World. Delivered." The company introduced the new slogan "Rethink Possible" in April 2010 as part of a rebranding effort to demonstrate the brand itself as a lifestyle, rather than any specific product. The sub-slogan "It's what you do with what we do" was added in 2012.

BRAND IDENTITY

- AT&T is the longest-running telecommunications brand in the United States, with its roots in the original Bell System that invented the telephone.
- AT&T focused its strength on its long-distance service after the divestiture of the Bell System, but as its market share dropped, the company began to embrace data transfer as the business of the future.

- In 2013 AT&T advertised itself as having the largest 4G network in the United States.

AT&T's brand identity has changed several times throughout the course of the company's history. When the brand was a subsidiary of the original Bell System, the company identified itself as a leader in the advancing telephone industry and became part of the monopoly in the United States for telephone service. The company's monopoly had been endorsed by the United States government in order to ensure proper function of telephones. For a brief period in the early 20th century, when competing telephone companies appeared, subscribers of the various companies were able to call subscribers of their companies only. Bell purchased the competitors and maintained the monopoly while making phone service universal throughout the nation.

After the Bell System was divested in 1984, AT&T's identity changed from that of a well-known telephone provider to solely a long-distance provider. The company was forced to change its familiar bell logo, opting for an image of a globe with the company's name. As competition for long-distance service changed and AT&T's market share dwindled, the company altered its identity again. In the early to mid-1990s the rising popularity of personal computers and Internet use resulted in significant increases in data transfer through phone lines, leading AT&T to digitize its phone system to better transfer the data.

The company went through another large identity change in the first decade of the 21st century. As cellular devices became the norm and the use of landlines began to dwindle, AT&T purchased back its shares of AT&T Mobile that had previously been sold to Cingular Wireless, rebirthing AT&T in 2005. With the new direction came a new image intended to focus on AT&T's mobile offerings as a lifestyle. Part of that identity was demonstrated with the slogan "Your World. Delivered." In 2013 AT&T promoted its 4G network coverage, claiming to be "the nation's largest 4G network."

BRAND STRATEGY

- The company has maintained the AT&T brand name since being established as a long-distance provider in 1885.
- After Cingular Wireless acquired AT&T Wireless to become the largest wireless provider in the United States, AT&T Inc. acquired Cingular and rebranded it as "the New AT&T."
- AT&T has a history of transformations, beginning as the first long-distance provider and then reinventing itself as the first digitized phone company and of one of the first mobile providers in the United States.

AT&T has maintained the use of its brand name since the company was founded as the American Telephone & Telegraph Company in 1885. The name is an important part of the brand's image because it is the most recognizable feature. As the company releases new products and services, it has consistently stayed with the brand name AT&T, even though it has not offered telegraph services since Western Union Telegraph was divested in 1913. As the long-distance-service subsidiary of the Bell System, AT&T was commonly associated with Alexander Graham Bell, the well-known inventor of the telephone; however, when the Bell System was divested in 1984 AT&T lost the rights to the Bell name.

In 2001 the company turned its mobile service into a subsidiary called AT&T Wireless Services, Inc. The wireless provider struggled against the competition until it was purchased by Cingular Wireless in 2004, and Cingular became the largest wireless provider in the United States. AT&T later acquired Cingular, however, and Cingular was rebranded in 2005 as "the New AT&T," and the Cingular brand was phased out. Previous Cingular subscribers were immediately transferred to AT&T with no alteration in services.

AT&T has remained a successful brand in part because of its transformations over the years. For example, in the early 1990s, as it recovered from the 1984 divesture, the company turned its attention to the growing data market. Until that time faxes were the primary form of data being transferred through telephone lines. AT&T digitized its network to meet the growing demand for data fueled by the Internet boom.

As of 2013 AT&T offered mobile voice service to more than 225 countries and wireless data coverage in more than 210 countries. Internationally, the majority of AT&T's business is conducted in the Asia-Pacific region.

BRAND EQUITY

- As the exclusive U.S. carrier of Apple's iPhone when it was launched in 2007, AT&T gained subscribers.
- Brand Finance ranked AT&T as the 11th most valuable brand in 2012, coming in one place ahead of competitor Verizon.
- AT&T was not included on Interbrand's list of the 100 best global brands in 2012.

When Apple's iPhone was released in 2007 AT&T became the sole U.S. mobile carrier for the popular device, a deal that remained in place until 2011. The exclusive arrangement resulted in a significant gain in subscribers, but AT&T also faced a backlash when its service sometimes failed to keep up with the increased demand for data that the iPhone engendered.

Brand Finance's "Global 500 2012" ranked AT&T at number 11 and estimated its brand value at US$28.379 billion. U.S. competitor Verizon was right behind AT&T at number 12, with an estimated brand value of US$27.616 billion. Interbrand, however, did not include AT&T on its list of the 100 best global brands in 2012.

BRAND AWARENESS

- AT&T has brand awareness that dates back almost as far as the invention of the telephone.
- The brand has reinvented itself several times, including as a digital data provider and a wireless provider.
- In an agreement with Apple, AT&T became the exclusive U.S. carrier for the iPhone when it was released in 2007.

Part of AT&T's solid brand awareness is the fact that the company has existed almost since the invention of the telephone. Originally a subsidiary of the Bell Telephone Company, AT&T was incorporated as the American Telephone & Telegraph Company in 1885. The name remained associated with the Bell System until the divestiture of 1984. The brand recovered from the breakup, first as a long-distance provider and later as a digital data provider.

AT&T gained more traction after its wireless company reemerged out of Cingular Wireless, creating "the New AT&T." Immediately after the corporate rebranding, Apple entered into an agreement with AT&T, making it the exclusive U.S. carrier for the iPhone. The iPhone was an instant success, in turn bringing success to AT&T because subscribers were required to sign a two-year contract along with the purchase of the phone.

BRAND OUTLOOK

- As of early 2013, 64 percent of AT&T's contract customers owned smartphones, which have a higher-priced contract, resulting in more revenue for the company.
- The end of AT&T's tenure as the exclusive U.S. carrier for Apple's iPhone in 2011 presented a challenge to its success in the mobile market.
- AT&T scouted potential acquisitions of other mobile providers as a way to compete in the ever-tightening wireless market, having acquired Alltel in 2013 while looking to expand into Europe through a merger.

Competition in the wireless market in the United States stiffened considerably after the iPhone became accessible to other carriers in 2011, presenting a challenge to the AT&T brand. As of early 2013, 64 percent of AT&T's contract customers owned smartphones, while competitor Verizon stood at 53 percent, an indicator of how the exclusive iPhone deal had benefited AT&T. (Smartphone-owning contract customers were particularly lucrative for wireless carriers because of the higher prices of smartphone plans.) But whereas AT&T had reported adding 319,000 new contract subscribers in the third quarter of 2011, in the same period of 2012 that number had dropped to 151,000—one-tenth of the 1.5 million new contract customers that Verizon had added in the third quarter of 2012. Still, AT&T sold a record 10 million smartphones in the fourth quarter of 2012, 8 million of which were iPhones.

AT&T announced in early 2013 that it had acquired regional mobile carrier Alltel for US$780 million. Alltel's customer base spanned six states: Georgia, Idaho, Illinois, North Carolina, Ohio, and South Carolina. AT&T acquired Alltell's 585,000 existing subscribers along with wireless facilities, network access, and retail stores. AT&T was also reported to be seeking a merger that would give it access to the European market.

FURTHER READING

AT&T Inc. "The History of AT&T." Accessed January 19, 2013. http://www.corp.att.com/history/.

———. "2011 by the Numbers." Accessed January 20, 2013. http://www.att.com/gen/general?pid=22537.

Brand Finance. "Global 500 2012". *Brandirectory*. Accessed September 3, 2012. http://brandirectory.com/league_tables/table/global-500-2012.

Chen, Brian. "Solid Profit for AT&T Despite a Setback". *New York Times*, October 24, 2012.

Elliott, Stuart. "As Technology Evolves, AT&T Adjusts a Theme." *New York Times*, April 8, 2012.

Gibbs, Colin. "AT&T Plans Major 'Your World. Delivered.' Branding Campaign." *RCR Wireless*, December 29, 2005.

Team, Trefis. "AT&T Earnings Preview: Wireless Growth and Acquisition Plans In Focus." *Forbes*, January 23, 2013.

"2012 North American MPLS/IP VPN Services Market Share Leadership Award". Frost & Sullivan. Accessed January 21, 2013. http://www.att.com/Common/about_us/pdf/frost_sullivan_2012_north_american_ip_vpn_services.pdf.

AUDI

AT A GLANCE

Brand Synopsis: A prominent piece of the most successful multi-brand group in the automotive industry, Audi's brand has evolved over its more than 100-year history to represent luxury vehicles distinguished by quality engineering and cutting-edge design.
Parent Company: Volkswagen Aktiengesellschaft
VHH 11th floor
P.O. Box 1849
D-38436 Wolfsburg
Germany
http://www.vw.com/
Sector: Consumer Discretionary
Industry Group: Automobiles & Components
Performance: *Market share*—Audi is the best-selling luxury car brand in the world (2012). *Sales*—EUR44.10 billion in gross sales (US$56.47 billion) (2011).
Principal Competitors: BMW; Mercedes-Benz; Lexus; Acura

BRAND ORIGINS

- The Audi brand originated in four separate companies at the turn of the 20th century.
- The Audi brand has, from its beginnings, been associated with performance and innovation.
- The Audi brand has been a subsidiary of Volkswagen since 1964.
- During the early part of the 21st century, the Audi brand reclaimed its reputation for innovative design and top performance in the luxury vehicle market.

As represented in its logo of four interlocking rings, Audi is an amalgamation of four motor-vehicle manufacturers: Horch, Audi, DKW, and Wanderer. The first of those, A. Horch & Company, was established in Cologne, Germany, in 1899 by August Horch. In 1910 Horch used the Latin translation of his name (which means "listen" in English), to rename his company Audiwerke Gmb, the forerunner of the Audi brand. Meanwhile, Jörgen Skafte Rasmussen began producing a steam-driven vehicle (the "Dampfkraftwagen," from which the acronym DKW was derived) in 1907 to support the German effort in World War I. The fourth company, Wanderer, began manufacturing vehicles in Germany in 1913. All four businesses merged in 1932 to form Auto Union AG.

From its early days, Audi has been known for innovation, particularly advancements in engineering and safety. In 1921, for example, Audi became the first German car manufacturer to present a production car with left-hand drive in order to provide drivers a safer experience by giving them a better view of oncoming traffic. Other advancements included the first German car with an eight-cylinder engine (1926), the first volume-built car with front-wheel drive (1931), the first race car with a sixteen-cylinder engine and designed with an attention to aerodynamics (1934), and the industry's first crash and rollover tests (1938).

With production of consumer vehicles interrupted by World War II, Auto Union produced vehicles exclusively for military purposes until it was dismantled by the Soviet military after the war. Loans from the Bavarian state government and Marshall Plan aid, however, supported construction of a new car manufacturing plant, and Auto Union began consumer production of motorcycles and delivery vans in 1949 and passenger cars in 1950. After significant growth accompanied by two corporate takeovers, first by Daimler-Benz in 1958 then Volkswagen (its current parent company) in 1964, Auto Union was presented to the world for the first time as the reborn Audi brand in 1965.

Upon its re-emergence in the mid-1960s, Audi started its climb toward the luxury car market, first by producing the upper-midsize Audi 100 in 1968. This model, developed by technical director Dr. Ludwig Kraus, took the Audi brand into the competitive market segment of the upper-midsize class for the first time. The Audi 100 quickly became a best seller and formed the basis for a new Audi model series that ensured the future independence of the Audi brand.

The Audi brand solidified its relationship with modern car buyers when it introduced the Quattro in 1980 and relaunched the 100 in 1982. The Quattro was the industry's first four-wheel-drive luxury sports coupe. Four-wheel drive had previously only been used on trucks and off-road vehicles, and the development signaled Audi's commitment to combining progressive design and performance in luxury vehicles. The new Audi 100 of 1982 also celebrated the brand's commitment to progressive design and, at the time, was praised for its attention to aerodynamics. Over the next decade, Audi cemented its place as an innovator in the premium car market. Some of the brand's noteworthy innovations during this period include the first fully galvanized body (1986), electronically controlled automatic transmission (1988), the turbo diesel engine (1989), and the aluminum space frame (1993).

Although Audi maintained its reputation as an industry innovator during the 1980s, the brand also suffered a significant setback in the U.S. car market. Sales in the United States fell after a series of recalls of Audi 5000 models. The cars were subject to sudden unintended acceleration and were linked to six deaths and more than 700 accidents. A *60 Minutes* report that aired on November 23, 1986, featuring interviews with six people who had sued Audi after reporting unintended acceleration, showed an Audi 5000 malfunctioning when the brake pedal was pushed. Though it was later revealed that *60 Minutes* had engineered the failure, and despite the fact that other reports suggested the deaths were caused by driver error, the damage to Audi's reputation was severe. Audi's U.S. sales, which had reached 74,061 vehicles in 1985, dropped to 12,283 in 1991.

By the mid-1990s, however, Audi had successfully repositioned itself in the U.S. premium car market. In 1995, Audi delivered more than 18,000 vehicles in the United States, a 44 percent improvement in sales figures over 1994. In 1997 the world's first all-aluminum volume production car, the A8, was introduced in the United States, and Audi was recognized as the industry leader in body technology. By 1999, Audi had sold its one millionth car in the United States. In 2006, Audi introduced its first performance sport utility vehicle (SUV), the Q7, to the U.S. market.

During the first decade of the twenty-first century, Audi continued its commitment to technological innovation. New technologies introduced by Audi to the premium car market included its multitronic continuously variable transmission (2002), FSI direct fuel injection (2003), direct shift gearbox (2003), multimedia interface (2004), LED daytime running lights (2006), and Bluetec clean six-liter, twelve-cylinder diesel engine (2007).

From 2002 to 2007, Audi headed the Audi Brand Group, a subdivision of the Volkswagen Group, which consisted of Audi, Lamborghini, and SEAT. The point of this arrangement was to group brands under the larger VW umbrella by type, with the brands in the Audi Brand Group recognized for the production of various types and sizes of performance cars.

In 2012, Audi manufactured nine cars and three SUV models in seven production facilities throughout Europe. Also in 2012, Audi announced it would begin construction of its first production facility in North America. The facility, located in Puebla, Mexico, is scheduled to begin operations in 2016.

BRAND ELEMENTS

- The badge composed of four interlocking silver rings is Audi's most recognizable brand element.
- Audi uses a simple two-character system instead of names to identify its models.
- Audi's corporate tagline is "Progress through Technology."
- Audi's current campaign in the U.S. market features the tagline "Truth in Engineering."

The badge composed of four interlocking silver rings is Audi's most recognizable brand element. The emblem symbolizes the merger in 1932 of four previously independent motor vehicle manufacturers: Audi, DKW, Horch, and Wanderer. These companies formed the foundation on which the present-day Audi is built. Though the emblem is strikingly similar to the six colored interlocking rings that symbolize the Olympics (which prompted the International Olympic Committee to sue Audi in 1995), the four rings remain the brand's dominant mark.

The Audi brand, like fellow European brands BMW and Mercedes-Benz (and, formerly, Saab), takes a distinctive approach to its model numbering system. Unlike American brands, which tend to give names to their car models, Audi uses a two-character system to identify its models. Whether it is the A6 sedan, the TT coupe, or the Q7 sport utility vehicle (SUV), each Audi model takes its unique identity from two simple characters. Much like BMW and Mercedes-Benz, the higher the Audi number is, the more luxurious the model. For example, the A8 is Audi's top-of-the-line full-size premium car, while the A3 is a small family sedan.

Audi is also distinguished by its slogans and taglines. Audi's corporate tagline is "Vorsprung durch Technik," which translates to "Progress through Technology." This tagline is used by the brand worldwide, though it has been augmented by additional taglines, particularly in the U.S. market. In 2002, Audi unveiled a new tagline in the U.S., "Never Follow," intended to capture the brand's spirit of design and innovation. This campaign, according to the automaker, was built on the "five nevers": Never quit. Never do the expected. Never rest on your laurels. Never think great is good enough. Never follow.

In May 2007, Audi introduced the brand's first multimedia advertising campaign since 2002. The campaign was focused on several Audi models, the TT, A4, A6, Q7, and the A6 sedan, and each ad was accompanied by the tagline, "Truth in Engineering." According to Audi, the tagline represents the notion that Audi's design, history, and engineering provide the most authentic, truthful driving experience in the luxury segment.

BRAND IDENTITY

- Although Audi is known for its logo and its history of innovation, it has sought to distinguish itself more clearly from its competitors.
- In 2010, Audi initiated an effort to create a distinctive, easily recognizable sound for its cars.
- Audi is positioned as a luxury car that delivers exceptional performance, style, comfort, and beauty.

Perhaps more than its competitors, the Audi brand has struggled to establish a clear identity with consumers. Whenever a consumer hears of Volkswagen, for example, he or she instantly connects the brand with target audiences of all kinds: car enthusiasts, young drivers, and even recovered hippies. When a consumer hears of Chevy, he or she might be taken back to the fabulous 1950s or to the tracks of NASCAR. With the Audi brand, however, such instant identification does not occur.

Consumers typically know an Audi by its logo of four interlocking rings and its LED daytime running lights, but the company has been working to establish such a clear brand identity that a person would be able to recognize an Audi by its signature sound alone. Audi describes its luxury and performance cars with words such as renowned, outstanding, elite, unique, agile, athletic, efficient, dominating, striking, spirited, and innovative.

The S6 model is promoted as "the sport sedan that provokes a reaction every time you press the accelerator," delivering exceptional performance and beauty. Another model offers "a distinguished, gratifying driving experience" and "a wealth of space and amenities." The flagship model A8 "represents progressive advances in engineering, technology, design and performance. The A8 has moved luxury forward, solidifying our commitment to excellence with a refusal to settle for anything less."

By striving to produce luxury cars with all the latest innovations, Audi is meant to be the brand that promises perfection, meeting the highest standards. These goals are summed up in the company's longtime motto, "progress through technology."

BRAND STRATEGY

- Audi aims to become the premier car brand of the future.
- Audi's "Strategy 2020" gives greater weight to environmental concerns and the trend toward increased urbanization.
- Audi's strategy emphasizes electric vehicles and commitments to emerging markets.

In adopting its "Strategy 2020," the Audi brand focused on the challenges inherent in becoming the premier brand of the future. The strategy gives more weight to issues that have emerged as a result of heightened global environmental awareness, including growing uncertainty about the future availability of fossil fuels and increasing urbanization. For example, Audi has begun investing heavily in marketing its vehicles in metropolitan areas. "We have defined 25 metro areas as the key focus of our business [in the United States]," commented Audi CEO Rupert Stadler in 2008. Stadler indicated that an emphasis will also be placed on electric vehicles as well as emerging markets for luxury vehicles abroad, particularly China, where the brand continues to see major sales successes.

BRAND EQUITY

- Audi has achieved a slow and steady increase in its brand equity over recent years.
- The Audi brand consistently ranks in the top three on the list of "Best Business Brands Germany."
- The Audi brand is competing successfully in the emerging luxury car markets of India, Russia, and China.

Audi has demonstrated a slow and steady increase in its brand equity in recent years. On Interbrand's list of "Best Global Brands," for example, Audi moved up from 65th on the list in 2009 to 59th in 2011 and 55th in 2012. As an auto maker focused on luxury performance vehicles, this steady climb against much more diverse brands suggests that Audi is continuing to hone and refine its products and to strengthen their presence in the luxury and performance car markets. This effort is also reflected in the brand's jump from 82nd to 55th position in the "Consumer Superbrands Official Top 500," published by the Centre for Brand Analysis in 2012 (though Audi's 2012 ranking was down from its high of 35th place in 2011).

In Germany, Audi consistently ranks in the top three on the list of "Best Business Brands Germany," published by Das Deutsche Markenranking, and in the "AutomarxX Brand Ranking" by brand research firm ADAC. Outside of Germany, Audi fares decently, ranking in the middle of the pack for customer service and owner satisfaction in studies by the U.S. firm J. D. Power & Associates. In *Consumer Reports'* survey of car brand perception, Audi placed thirteenth among the twenty auto brands included in the poll.

Audi appears to be competing most successfully in emerging luxury car markets, such as those in India, Russia, and China. International brand communication specialists the Digital Luxury Group, or DLG, ranks Audi first and second on its list of the "Top 50 Most-Searched For Luxury Brands" in China and Russia respectively. Audi's recent performance in these emerging luxury car markets has dramatically affected its brand equity. According to the *Economist,* profits for the Volkswagen group, which includes Audi, more than doubled to a record US$23.8 billion in 2012.

BRAND AWARENESS

- Audi has been involved in auto racing since the 1930s.
- Audi has focused on Formula 1 racing, particularly the 24 Hours of Le Mans, but has no involvement in U.S. racing series.
- Audi remains less visible in popular culture than its parent company, Volkswagen.
- Consumers ranked Audi fifth for performance in 2011 and sixth for design and style in 2012.

Like its parent company Volkswagen, Audi has maintained a significant presence in motorsports. Since the brand's beginnings in the 1930s, Audi has been involved with auto racing, particularly rally, endurance, and touring events abroad. Though the brand has steered clear of the NASCAR and other popular U.S. racing series, Audi has been heavily involved in Formula 1 racing, particularly the 24 Hours of Le Mans. From its earliest roots in racing, Audi has built a worldwide presence in the sport.

While nowhere near as prominent as its parent company, Audi has established a presence in popular culture. In 2005, for example, the Audi A8 was featured in the action thriller *Transporter 2.*

In a 2011 survey by *Consumer Reports,* respondents ranked Audi in fifth place for performance, with a brand perception score of 17 percent. BMW was first (27 percent), Porsche second (21 percent), Ford third (19 percent), and Chevrolet fourth (19 percent). This represented an improvement of 8 percent since 2010, which was attributed to Audi's S model variants and R8 supercar flagship.

In 2012 Toyota bumped Audi out of the top five for performance, while BMW held its lead. However, Audi almost made the top five for design and style that year, missing by only a fraction of a point. In that category Cadillac was first, followed by BMW, Mercedes-Benz, Lexus, and Chevrolet

BRAND OUTLOOK

- In 2010, Audi became the first luxury carmaker to sell one million cars in China.
- Audi has expanded the size of some of its models specifically for the Chinese market.
- Audi plans to expand its line of electric and hybrid vehicles in order to maintain its competitive edge in the luxury car market.

With the effects of the model recalls in the mid-1980s now safely in the past, the outlook for the Audi brand is positive. Audi continues to demonstrate that design strength, technological innovation, imaginative approaches to retail, and rich brand experiences are a winning approach to sustainable, profitable growth in the automotive industry.

As a prime example of the growth that heralds a bright future for the brand, in 2010 Audi became the first luxury carmaker to sell its millionth car in China, and the brand expects unit sales to reach two million by 2013. According to news reports, the brand takes pains to cater to its Chinese customers. To accommodate the demand for big, roomy cars, it stretched its A4 and A6 models for the Chinese market. Its new A8 long version has a spacious rear seat, replete with all of the gadgets and features the most demanding chauffeured executive or government bureaucrat might want. Audi relies heavily on sales to the Chinese government, and this business now accounts for about 20 percent of Audi's total sales in China.

Integrating a wide range of innovations—such as its electric E-Tron system and forthcoming plug-in hybrid technology—into a range of luxury performance cars and sport utility vehicles, Audi is on its way to solidifying its global presence in the fiercely competitive high-end vehicle market. With such an approach, the Audi brand strategy seems well-positioned for future success.

FURTHER READING

Audi AG. "Corporate Strategy." Accessed October 19, 2012. http://www.audiusa.com/com/brand/en/company/investor_relations/audi_at_a_glance/corporate_strategy.html.

Audi USA. "Audi History." Accessed October 13, 2012. http://www.audiusa.com/us/brand/en/about/main/history.html.

"Capturing the Sound of an Audi." *AudiInTheNews.com,* October 12, 2010. Accessed October 19, 2012. http://www.audiinthenews.com/video-capturing-the-sound-of-an-audi/.

Gillies, Mark. "Audi's Growth Strategy Outlined." *Car and Driver,* March 2008. Accessed October 21, 2012. http://www.caranddriver.com/news/audis-growth-strategy-outlined-auto-shows.

Reed, John. "China: Audi Sells a Million." *Financial Times,* October 20, 2010. Accessed October 15, 2012. http://blogs.ft.com/beyond-brics/2010/10/20/audis-millionth-car-sale-shows-china-still-tops/#axzz29fqj4RwB.

Superbrands.com. "Audi." Accessed October 12, 2012. http://www.superbrands.com/za/pdfs/AUDI.pdf.

SyncForce. "Ranking per Brand." Accessed October 10, 2012. http://www.rankingthebrands.com/Brand-detail.aspx?brandID=193.

Welsh, Jonathan. "Audi E-Tron: Will Your Next Luxury Car Be Electric?" *Wall Street Journal,* June 15, 2012. Accessed October 22, 2012. http://blogs.wsj.com/drivers-seat/2012/06/15/audi-e-tron-will-your-next-luxury-car-be-electric/.

AVON

AT A GLANCE

Brand Synopsis: One of the largest personal care product companies in the world, Avon has been empowering women since the 19th century through its successful direct-marketing strategy.
Parent Company: Avon Products Inc.
1345 Avenue of the Americas
New York, New York 10105-0196
United States
http://www.avoncompany.com/
Sector: Consumer Staples
Industry Group: Household & Personal Products
Performance: *Market share*—11.4 percent in direct selling; 3.2 percent in beauty and personal care products. *Sales*—US$11.3 billion (2011).
Principal Competitors: Estee Lauder Companies Inc.; L'Oréal S.A.; Mary Kay Inc.; The Proctor and Gamble Co.; Revlon, Inc.

BRAND ORIGINS

- Avon was founded as the California Perfume Company in 1886.
- By the mid-1970s Avon had become the world's largest cosmetics and toiletries company.
- Avon celebrated its 125th anniversary in 2011 amidst uncertainty about its future.

The company that became known as Avon had its origins in the California Perfume Company, which had been founded in New York City by door-to-door salesman David H. McConnell in 1886. His first product was a perfume set. Believing the best way to market his products was through personal contact, McConnell hired Mrs. P. F. E. Albee to sell his cosmetics to friends and neighbors in her community. She was the first "Avon Lady" and convinced several friends to help sell the popular items, showing the power of recruitment early on.

By the end of the 1890s, the California Perfume Company had distributed its first text-only catalog. By the first decade of the 20th century, it was selling more than 100 products, had begun advertising in leading magazines, had thousands of direct sales representatives, and had published its first color catalog. The California Perfume Company attained national distribution by 1920 and exceeded US$1 million in annual sales. After McConnell visited Stratford-on-Avon, England, he began using the Avon brand name on products in 1928. The official name of the company was changed to Avon Products Inc. in 1939. Avon went public in 1946, and its annual sales reached US$25 million in 1949.

In the post–World War II era, increasing numbers of American women began working outside the home. Jobs as Avon representatives were seen as ideal part-time earnings opportunities for many women. With more representatives, Avon achieved phenomenal growth. In 1954 Avon inaugurated its long-running advertising campaign, "Ding-Dong Avon Calling!" Sales and earnings gains consistently ran in the 17 to 19 percent range during the 1950s, at a time when there were about 100,000 Avon representatives.

Avon's phenomenal growth continued during the 1960s. From 1961 to 1971, the brand's sales experienced double-digit increases and topped US$1 billion in 1972. The brand's sales made Avon the most consistently profitable company in the country. Beginning in the 1950s, Avon had been regularly entering new international markets so successfully that by the mid-1970s Avon had become the world's largest cosmetics and toiletries company.

Yet Avon began struggling during this period because of the effects of high inflation in the United States and lower profit margins. Although the brand was still number one in the mid-1970s, it was not as profitable as it had been during the 1960s and lost market share. In response, Avon adopted new strategies in the 1970s and 1980s, including cutting prices, moving into new product lines like fashion, jewelry, and gifts, and buying businesses such as Tiffany & Company. Avon's profits still declined annually from 1979 to 1984 in part because of its unfocused line of business but also because changes in society affected Avon's old business model. More women began working full-time outside the home, and the company experienced a high turnover rate among representatives.

Although Avon's sales reached US$2.9 billion by the mid-1980s, the company was transformed as its product line was pared down, new items were offered in the growing skin care market, and Avon engaged in more targeted marketing. Deep discounting was eliminated to raise profits and the perception of quality. The brand retained the direct-selling strategy but updated methodology to match the times. A revision of an age-old policy allowed representatives to sell in work environments. During the 1980s Avon also expanded rapidly in Latin America, Asia, and Eastern Europe. By 1990 international sales contributed 56 percent of Avon's product turnover.

By 1994 Avon had 1.7 million sales associates in 100 countries around the world with global sales of US$3.8 billion. Despite continuing innovations, however, Avon's U.S. sales declined so much that it became the number three cosmetics company there. To focus on its core personal care and cosmetics business, Avon shed Tiffany & Co. and other such subsidiaries by the mid-1990s. Still, by 2001 Avon remained the largest direct sales company in the world with 3.4 million sales representatives in 139 countries and sales revenues of US$5.7 billion; 50 percent of all sales took place in workplace settings. By 2004 Avon was selling its products online, through catalogs, at mall kiosks, and in a day spa, and it was working to expand its appeal to a younger demographic.

Avon celebrated its 125th anniversary in 2011 but struggled to meet sales targets and faced a declining global performance. Its reliance on individual sales representatives, even armed with the latest technology, empowered women but seemed to stall its growth momentum despite an increase in revenues to US$11.29 billion in 2011. At the time Avon was serving 300 million customers in more than 100 countries through 6.5 million sales associates. Because of ongoing problems, longtime CEO and chairman Andrea Jung resigned effective in early 2012 and was replaced as CEO by Sherilyn McCoy, who was focused on reinvigorating the direct-selling model.

BRAND ELEMENTS

- The Avon logo includes the company name in black, all capital letters, widely spaced with the tag line "the company for women" running beneath.
- Avon is known for its primarily female direct sales force, in place since the company's founding in 1886.
- The longest and most successful ad campaign for Avon focused on its sales method, "Ding Dong Avon Calling."

The Avon logo includes the company name in black, all capital letters, widely spaced in a thin, geometric, sans-serif font. Beneath it, in bolder type, runs the tagline "the company for women," all lowercase, with *the* in pink and the rest of the phrase in black. The current logo has been in use since 2009 and conveys a bright, modern sensibility, with the traditionally feminine color of the pink *the* emphasizing the message it introduces.

Since its founding in 1886, Avon has been strongly identified with its direct sales agents, commonly known as "Avon Ladies" and later "Avon Representatives." Company founder David H. McConnell, a book salesman, noticed that women were more interested in his perfume samples than in his books and that many had the natural ability to be salespeople. He turned from books to perfume sales and to women as his sales force. Although employment opportunities for women were limited in the late 19th century, McConnell set a tone of support. The values he defined have remained core to Avon's identity as a brand concerned with female empowerment and success. Though some men have been Avon Representatives, the sales force has been overwhelmingly female. Avon Ladies emphasized personal relationships and customer service. The longest and most successful advertising campaign for Avon, "Ding Dong, Avon Calling," ran from 1954 to 1967 and emphasized this personal touch. Although company policies changed over time, this element remained key to Avon's identity.

From the 1880s to the 1980s, Avon Ladies primarily focused on door-to-door sales. Avon Representatives were permitted to sell in workplaces beginning in 1986, and with the advent of the Internet, online tools and sales became available. In the early 21st century Avon Representatives were still Avon's primary means of sale, especially in such international markets as Brazil, China, and

Russia. Avon spends a significant amount of time and money recruiting, training, and supporting its more than 6.5 million representatives.

BRAND IDENTITY

- Avon is identified as "the company for women."
- In 2011 Avon celebrated its 125th anniversary with a 16-city world tour highlighting the company's history and the contributions of women to its success.
- Avon supports such causes as breast cancer research and ending domestic violence.
- Avon has been endorsed by athletes and entertainment celebrities, including Derek Jeter, Catherine Deneuve, and Reese Witherspoon.

In its logo Avon includes the tagline "the company for women" under the brand name. From the first, Avon has focused on women both as its direct sales force and its primary clientele. The largest direct-selling organization in the world and one of the biggest personal care product companies, Avon is closely associated with female empowerment and social issues of special concern to women. In 2011 Avon celebrated its 125th anniversary with the Avon Believe World Tour, a global event celebrating the history of the company and the contributions made by women to Avon and the world. More than 125,000 sales representatives participated in tour events in 16 cities, including Istanbul, London, Mexico City, Moscow, New Delhi, São Paulo, and Shanghai.

Avon has connected its brand with various charitable concerns that underscore its commitment to and concern for women and the issues that are important to them. It is the largest corporate sponsor focused solely on women's issues around the globe. The Avon Foundation was established in 1955, becoming the Avon Foundation for Women in 2009 with a renewed focus on improving women's lives. Since 1992 Avon has supported breast cancer research and awareness with such events as the Breast Cancer Crusade, the Avon Walk for Breast Cancer, and the Avon Walk Around the World for Breast Cancer. In 2004 Avon began supporting initiatives to address domestic violence. Avon launched the "Hello Green Tomorrow" campaign in 2010 to empower women worldwide on environmental issues, with a primary focus on reforestation.

Throughout its history Avon also associated the brand with achievement in sports and the arts. In addition to sponsoring such events as the 1996 Summer Olympic Games in Atlanta, Georgia, Avon sponsored the Avon Running Championship beginning in 1999. Since the 1940s it has developed endorsement agreements with a variety of celebrities, including the American baseball players Joe DiMaggio and Derek Jeter, the Chinese diver Guo Jingjing, the French actress Catherine Deneuve, and the Mexican actress Salma Hayek. In 2007 the American actress Reese Witherspoon became the brand's first global ambassador. She also created a signature fragrance, In Bloom. Singer Fergie had her own signature fragrance, Outspoken by Fergie, which was the brand's most successful perfume launch ever.

BRAND STRATEGY

- Avon product lines comprise three divisions: beauty, fashion, and home.
- Nearly three-quarters (73 percent) of Avon's sales came from beauty products in 2011.
- Avon constantly adjusts its product lines and adds new products to stay current and retain customer appeal.
- A vast majority of Avon's sales come in the international market, where Avon focused much attention on growth.

Primarily selling its products with the assistance of its direct sales representatives, Avon has three product divisions: beauty, fashion, and home. Beauty includes color cosmetics, fragrances, skin care, and personal care; well-known products include Avon Color, ANEW, Skin-So-Soft, and Advance Techniques. Fashion includes jewelry, watches, apparel, footwear, and accessories. Home includes gift and decorative products, house wares, entertainment and leisure products, and children's and nutritional products. In 2011, 73 percent (US$8.1 billion) of Avon's sales came from beauty, 18 percent (US$2 billion) from fashion, and 9 percent (US$1 billion) from home.

To stay current with industry trends and retain customer appeal, Avon regularly adjusts its product lines and introduces new items. For example, ANEW was launched in 1992, making Avon the first company to bring alpha hydroxy acid (AHA) anti-aging technology to the consumer market; ANEW Genics, for women over age 60, debuted in 2011. In 2003 Avon launched mark., a global cosmetics line targeted at women age 24 and younger, and in 2004 it introduced a line of skin care products for men. In 2012 Avon added Satin Satisfaction lip color and True Color eye shadow sets.

Avon began adding international markets in the 1950s, and by the 21st century a vast majority of Avon's sales were generated outside of the United States, with 60 percent coming from fast growing markets alone in 2011. Avon had subsidiaries in 63 countries and marketed its products in 41 other countries and territories through distributorships. In the first decade of the 21st century Avon expanded significantly in Central and Eastern Europe and the Caribbean. International growth was a priority, especially in key markets like Brazil and Russia.

BRAND EQUITY

- Avon's biggest market was Latin America, where it had 45.5 percent of its sales in 2011.
- Avon consistently ranks among the top brands in the world.
- In the *Forbes* ranking of the "World's Most Powerful Brands" in 2012, Avon was number 70.

Avon had US$11.3 billion in revenue in 2011 and was the world's largest direct-selling company. While Avon was an American company, its key markets were outside the United States where the brand focused much energy. In 2011, 18.5 percent of Avon's sales were in North America (US$2.1 billion), 45.5 percent (US$5.1 billion) in Latin America, 13.5 percent (US$1.5 billion) in Western Europe, the Middle East, and Africa, 14 percent (US$1.6 billion) in Central and Eastern Europe, and 8.5 percent (US$.9 billion) in the Asia Pacific region.

Despite struggles to remain relevant in the 21st century, Avon continued to have high brand value and was consistently ranked among the top brands in the world. On the *Forbes* ranking of the "World's Most Powerful Brands" in 2012, Avon was number 70, with a brand value of US$5.2 billion. In the *Brand Finance* ranking of the "Top 50 Cosmetics Brands" in 2012, Avon, with a brand value of US$7.9 billion, was number two, second only to Olay. Avon also made the *Brand Finance* "Global 500" in 2012, ranking number 119. In the "BrandZ Top 100 Most Valuable Global Brands" in 2012, Avon was number 13 among personal care companies, with a brand value of US$2.7 billion. However, it lost 53 percent of its brand value from 2011.

In the annual Interbrand ranking of the "Best Global Brands" in 2012, Avon was ranked number 71 with a brand value of US$5.2 billion. Interbrand also ranked Avon number 37 in its 2012 list of "Best Global Green Brands," a measure of performance on environmental sustainability practices. Avon was ranked number 19 on the Interbrand list of the "Most Valuable U.S. Retail Brands" in 2012, with a brand value of US$5.4 billion.

BRAND AWARENESS

- Avon has 90 percent brand recognition in most major markets around the world.
- Avon has top-of-mind awareness as the leading direct sales company in the world.
- Avon is a highly regarded company, ranking high in surveys of brand power and awareness.

With a high profile from the mid-20th century forward, Avon operated in over 100 countries with 6.5 million registered representatives worldwide in 2011. Despite having almost no presence in stores and relying primarily on individual sales representatives, Avon has 90 percent brand recognition in most major markets around the world and high brand awareness in terms of sales and brand. It has top-of-mind awareness as the leading direct sales company in the world, especially among cosmetics brands, particularly in growth markets like Brazil and Eastern and Central Europe. Surveys and studies regularly show Avon's brand power. On the *CoreBrand* ranking of the 100 best corporate brands in 2011, Avon was number 41. The Reputation Institute's "Global RepTrak 100" for 2012 considered how stakeholders identified companies and how those perceptions affected purchasing power and ranked Avon at number 81. The Reputation Institute also compiled the "Global Reputation Pulse—U.S. Top 100," which focused on consumer trust and admiration of American companies; Avon ranked number 32 in 2012.

BRAND OUTLOOK

- Avon's complicated business structure could have negative long-term effects.
- Avon underwent a major change at the top as CEO Andrea Jung was replaced by Sherilyn McCoy at the beginning of 2012.
- As one of its social responsibility goals, Avon was committed to reducing global paper consumption.

The personal care and cosmetics industries were negatively affected by the worldwide economic downturn that began in 2008, and concepts like brand loyalty, trust, and awareness were important. Consumers continued to spend money to look good but were more value-conscious in their purchases. Despite somewhat flat sales in the second decade of the 21st century, Avon sold four lipsticks every second around the world, demonstrating the brand's global power and value. Yet the website 24/7 Wall St. put Avon as number 10 on its 2012 list of "Ten Brands That Will Disappear Next Year."

The reasons for such a negative outlook were many. Avon had a complicated business structure, which included a large direct sales force and dependence on printed brochures in a digital age. While Avon has managed to keep direct sales and female empowerment relevant by incorporating e-commerce aspects, further adjustment was needed to ensure that sales would continue to grow as people shopped more online. Avon also gained new leadership at the beginning of 2012, when Sherilyn McCoy replaced longtime CEO Andrea Jung. McCoy and new chairman Fred Hassan were expected to capitalize on growing sales in emerging markets such as Latin America and Eastern and Central Europe while overcoming supply problems that emerged in key markets like Brazil in 2011.

Avon was also committed to becoming more transparent on issues of sustainability. In the corporate social responsibility report *The Beauty of Doing Good* (2011) Avon outlined its plan to reduce global paper consumption. Primarily because the company still printed an extraordinary number of brochures, Avon's paper consumption was the major contributor to the brand's large carbon footprint.

FURTHER READING

"Avon Products on the *Forbes* List." *Forbes*, April 2012. Accessed January 20, 2013. http://www.forbes.com/companies/avon-products/.

"Best Global Brands 2012." Interbrand. Accessed January 20, 2013. http://www.interbrand.com/en/best-global-brands/2012/Best-Global-Brands-2012.aspx.

"Best Global Green Brands 2012." Interbrand. Accessed January 20, 2013. http://www.interbrand.com/en/best-global-brands/Best-Global-Green-Brands/2012-Report/BestGlobalGreenBrandsTable-2012.aspx.

"Best Retail Brands 2012." Interbrand. Accessed January 20, 2013. http://www.interbrand.com/en/BestRetailBrands/2012-Best-Retail-Brands.aspx.

"BrandZ Top 100 Most Valuable Global Brands 2012." Millward Brown, May 5, 2012. Accessed January 20, 2013. http://www.millwardbrown.com/brandz/2012/Documents/2012_BrandZ_Top100_Report.pdf.

Dougals, April S. "Avon." *Encyclopedia of Consumer Brands, Vol. 2: Personal Products.* Ed. Janice Jorgensen. Detroit, MI: St. James Press, 1994.

Kowitt, Beth. "Avon: The Rise and Fall of a Beauty Icon." *CNNMoney*, April 11, 2012. Accessed January 20, 2013. http://management.fortune.cnn.com/2012/04/11/avon-andrea-jung-downfall/.

"Ten Brands That Will Disappear in 2013." 24/7 Wall St., June 21, 2012. Accessed January 20, 2013. http://247wallst.com/2012/06/21/247-wall-st-10-brands-that-will-disappear-in-2013/.

AXA

AT A GLANCE

Brand Synopsis: One of the world's most successful insurance companies, AXA is a French-based conglomerate, providing annuities and life, health, and other insurance.
Parent Company: AXA S.A.
25, Avenue Matignon
75008 Paris
France
http://www.axa.com
Sector: Financials
Industry Group: Insurance
Performance: *Market share*—3.3 percent of the global insurance market (2010). *Sales*—US$111.3 billion (2011).
Principal Competitors: Allianz SE; Assicurazioni Generali; ING Groep NV

BRAND ORIGINS

- Mutuelle de l'Assurance contre l'Incendie was founded in the early 19th century in Rouen, in northern France.
- The U.S. insurance company Equitable, which would later become part of the AXA group, was founded in 1859.
- Equitable was an innovator in the insurance market, introducing medical insurance, individual annuities, and home insurance.
- Equitable was the first American company to use its name on a building as a form of marketing.
- In 1991 AXA invested US$1 billion in Equitable, becoming the largest shareholder.

Insurance had become a popular trend in Europe by the turn of the 19th century. Since the time of the Great Fire of London in the mid-17th century, insurance had become more than just a guarantee of cargo. Insurance companies were now able to insure homes and lives. The insurance company now known as AXA S.A. was created through the merger of multiple companies over the course of a century, beginning in 1819. The first of these companies was Compagnie d'Assurance Mutuelle contre l'Incendie, founded at about this time in Rouen, France, as a fire insurance company. At the time of its creation, it was only the second insurance company in France, following Mutuelle ACL, which was founded in 1816. Over the next 165 years, the company merged with more than a dozen other French insurers to become the leader of the AXA group.

In 1859 Henry Hyde, a teller at Mutual Life Insurance of New York, left his position in order to start his own company, the Equitable Life Assurance Society of the United States, a company later acquired by AXA. Hyde was an innovator both in insurance and in technology. Within only 20 short weeks, Hyde had raised the required US$100,000 needed to start his company. In 1866 Hyde was utilizing transatlantic cable technology to communicate with his European agents. In 1868 Hyde introduced the concept of tontines, a form of life insurance where the share of a deceased participant is divided among members of a group. The form became extremely popular and was widely used until the turn of the 20th century. Another of Hyde's ingenious ideas was to use the physical building of his business as a marketing tool. In 1870 construction of Equitable's headquarters was completed, and the company became the first American business to put its name on its building. Measured in surplus, Equitable had become the largest insurance company in the world by 1890.

In the early 20th century, Equitable continued on its innovative path, despite the death of its founder. In 1909 it became the first insurance company to sell home purchase insurance, which remained popular for five decades. Equitable sold the first-ever group plan insurance to the Pantasote Leather company in 1911, followed by Montgomery Ward the next year. The start of the new century also dealt a significant setback, however, as Equitable's headquarters burned to the ground in 1912. By 1915 the building had been rebuilt as the tallest building in the world, further stamping the Equitable brand on the New York skyline.

In 1946 Mutuelle de l'Assurance contre l'Incendie merged its three businesses (fire, life, and accident insurance) into one company called Ancienne Mutuelle. The company established itself internationally in 1955, when it acquired Quebec-based United Provinces, and it went on to merge with and acquire other insurance companies both in Europe and in Canada.

In 1951 Equitable launched the first major medical insurance plan and, in 1968, its first line of individual variable annuity products, thus changing the landscape of the insurance world and making the company more profitable. Meanwhile, Mutuelle de l'Assurance contre l'Incendie acquired Compagnie Parisienne de Garantie in 1978 and became Mutuelles Unies. Mutuelles Unies purchased the Drouot Group in 1982 and changed the company's name to AXA in 1985. In 1991 AXA began the process of acquiring control of Equitable, which enabled AXA to become an insurance provider in the United States.

BRAND ELEMENTS

- The AXA name was chosen in 1985 to ensure that the company's name could be pronounced by speakers of all languages.
- Prior to a rebranding in 2007, AXA had favored happier advertisements that reflected its slogan, "Be Life Confident."
- AXA changed its slogan to "Redefining Standards" as part of an effort to be more honest with consumers.

The name AXA is the most important aspect of its brand. Although the name appears in capital letters, it is not an acronym. In the 1980s, having acquired several other insurance companies, Mutuelles Unies's chairman and CEO, Claude Bébéar, hired an outside consultant to conduct a computer-aided search for a new company name. Bébéar was looking for something that would catch the eye of consumers and that was pronounceable in any language. In 1985 the name AXA was chosen, satisfying Bébéar's goal of an easy-to-pronounce name as well as ensuring that the name would appear at the top of most directories.

AXA went through a rebranding in 2007 and altered its long-standing slogan of "Be Life Confident" to "Redefining Standards." The new slogan was added as a red stripe through its blue logo. With this change came a change in the company's advertising. Instead of showing happy commercials and advertisements featuring actors, the company decided to cease all such "rosy" depictions and began showing people facing real problems in its advertisements. The goal was to be more realistic with consumers and to show that AXA is a reliable company. Prior to the rebranding, AXA's ads had featured an animatronic gorilla, who reminded consumers that it is never too early to start planning for retirement. The gorilla was expected to be completely phased out by 2013.

BRAND IDENTITY

- In 2007 AXA changed its slogan from "Be Life Confident" to "Redefining Standards" to reflect its aim to be more realistic with consumers.
- During its rebranding, AXA altered its marketing to feature less "rosy" scenes and to emphasize instead more lifelike situations.
- AXA has begun altering certain plans based on the input of its clients to make the plans more appealing.

Since the creation of AXA in 1985, the company has striven to become the most-used insurer in the world. In order to achieve this goal, it has bought out large competitors and other insurance companies over the years, most notably Equitable in 1991. With its new identity, AXA defined its three core attributes as "available," "attentive," and "reliable." The slogan used in advertising the company's life insurance until 2007 was "Be Life Confident." In 2007 CEO Claude Brunet led a campaign to reinforce the brand, and a new slogan was adopted in 2008: "Redefining Standards."

AXA's ad campaigns from 2006 to 2012 featured an animatronic gorilla who politely suggested to consumers that it is never too early to think about retirement. The gorilla retired in 2011, after an online vote to determine where he should retire. Even though the gorilla was a new mascot—part of the rebranding effort—it was replaced with the "Redefining Standards" slogan. AXA no longer wanted to be considered just another insurance company. Instead, the company wanted to prove its reliability as an insurer and to build consumer confidence. Also during the rebranding of 2007, AXA, now with an extensive global presence, began tailoring its marketing to specific regions of the world. As people in different cultures are more likely to purchase different kinds of insurance, AXA worked to identify these differences in order to offer products attuned to each market.

During the rebranding of 2007, AXA altered its marketing campaigns, abandoning depictions of nature and happy scenes with actors to try a more realistic approach with its clients. The company's ads began to feature real, difficult situations that were or could have been improved by there being an insurance company on the client's side.

In 2010, under the guidance of new CEO Henri de Castries, AXA began considering the possibility of including unique services in health plans, based on client reviews and input. One of the most significant was the idea of home care following a hospital stay: a nurse would help the client while the client recovered from a hospital treatment. Previously, such patients were required to go to a nursing facility in order to receive care covered by insurance.

BRAND STRATEGY

- AXA has sought to build on the reputation for innovation established by Equitable.
- For the global market, AXA alters its marketing and its insurance plans depending on the location and culture.
- In an effort to avoid alienating clients, AXA has kept the names of many of the companies it has acquired and simply added its name to the existing name.
- AXA uses social media throughout the world to establish contact with younger consumers.

Prior to the creation of AXA in 1985 and the acquisition of Equitable in 1991, Equitable had been a forward-thinking insurance company. From being the first company to put its name on its building in 1870 to initiating the practice of paying death claims immediately in 1881, Equitable established a reputation for innovation and offered services that were appealing to its clients. At the turn of the 20th century, Equitable began training its agents, another practice that was new to the industry. Through its trained agents, Equitable was able to support its marketing message that it was a trustworthy insurer. AXA has continued to build on such innovative ideas.

With the rebranding of AXA in 2007, CEO Brunet wanted to project an image of trustworthiness to consumers. Instead of focusing on a "land of promise," the company would now focus on a "land of proof." The company held a conference for its management, enforcing the concept that brand management means more than changing a logo: it means changing the culture surrounding insurance.

To improve its responsiveness to consumers, AXA altered its marketing to target specific markets. For example, in 2012 AXA worked on launching new health insurance policies in the United States that would offer home care after a client leaves the hospital. Asian clients, however, are less likely to need this service due to cultural differences. Instead, a more common issue in Asia was finding the correct health provider to address a specific need. In Asia, AXA provides a service to guide clients to the correct provider within a reasonable amount of time.

Most of the company's subsidiaries function under the name AXA; however, there are a few exceptions. Due to Equitable's long-standing reputation in the United States, AXA primarily operates in there under the name AXA Equitable Life Insurance Company. Also, after acquiring the life insurance company Sun Life Direct in 2000, AXA kept the name Sun Life but added AXA to it. As for its global brands, AXA applies the location to the name of each group—for example, AXA U.K. or AXA Middle East.

AXA has also established itself at the forefront of social media. Within its first year on the social networking website Facebook, AXA gained half a million followers. Additionally, AXA has multiple Facebook pages in many countries and regions, the goal being to stay current with younger clients and to encourage them to begin planning early for their retirement.

In 2012 AXA had locations in 55 countries worldwide and employed approximately 214,044 workers.

BRAND EQUITY

- AXA is the second-largest insurance conglomerate in the world, after Japan Post Insurance.
- In 2012 Interbrand estimated AXA's brand value to be US$6.7 billion.
- AXA placed 61st on Brand Finance's ranking of the top 500 global brands, with an estimated brand value of US$13.4 billion.

In 2011 AXA was the second-largest insurance conglomerate in the world, behind Japan Post Insurance. The company's revenues reached $111.3 billion in 2011.

According to Interbrand's ranking of the top 100 brands in 2012, AXA placed 58th, with a brand value of US$6.7 billion. Top competitor Allianz SE was ranked 62nd on the same list, with a brand value of US$6.18 billion. Brand Finance's Global 500 2012 ranked AXA 61st overall and estimated its brand value at US$13.4 billion. Allianz placed 77th on the same list, with a brand value of US$10.95 billion.

BRAND AWARENESS

- Although the company has operated for almost two centuries, the relative newness of the AXA brand has affected brand awareness.

- AXA is the dominant insurance provider in France, where it claims about three-quarters of the market.
- The retired AXA Gorilla was the best-known marketing tool that AXA has used since the company was formed in 1985.

AXA's brand awareness has developed differently than that of competing companies because the company is the product of multiple mergers that took place over many years. Though the company has been in business for almost two centuries, the AXA brand itself is relatively new. Nevertheless, the company employs more than 200,000 people at locations in 55 countries. It holds a dominant market share of 74 percent in France, the source of about a quarter of its revenues in 2011.

AXA's most memorable marketing strategy employed an animatronic gorilla starting in 2006. The gorilla was very popular on social media sites, where it even hosted a contest in which people suggested where the gorilla should go when he was retired as a mascot in 2011. Although he still featured on a few marketing items in 2012, the gorilla was to be completely phased out by 2013. AXA did not replace the gorilla with another mascot but instead emphasized its recently adopted slogan, "Redefining Standards."

BRAND OUTLOOK

- Despite the ongoing Eurozone crisis, AXA has continued to perform profitably.
- In 2011 AXA sold AXA Canada to competitor Intact Financial.
- In 2012 AXA continued its global expansion by opening its first branch in India.

In 2011 AXA's brand value fell due to continuing economic turmoil in Europe. Additionally, AXA's revenues were negatively affected by the sale of its Canadian operations to Canada's leading insurer, Intact Financial. Despite these setbacks, AXA still saw an increase in profit for the year. In 2012 AXA continued its global expansion, working with the Bank of India to open its first branch in that country.

In July 2012, AXA's CEO Henri de Castries released AXA's half-year progress report. Despite ongoing economic problems in various parts of the world, AXA remained profitable. Developed countries, where AXA does most of its business, had been more affected by depressed economic conditions. Nevertheless, AXA reported a 4 percent increase in property-casualty revenues and enrolled 600,000 new clients during the first half of 2012.

FURTHER READING

AXA Group. "Half Year 2012 Earnings." Accessed October 11, 2012. http://www.axa.com/lib/axa/uploads/rsp/2012/AXA_Half_Year_Results_2012_Scriptb.pdf.

———. "Our History." Accessed October 10, 2012. http://www.axa-equitable.com/axa/history.html.

Brand Finance. "AXA." *Brandirectory*. Accessed October 10, 2012. http://brandirectory.com/profile/AXA.

———. "Global 500 2012." *Brandirectory*. Accessed October 11, 2012. http://brandfinance.com/images/upload/bf_g500_2012_web_dp.pdf.

Interbrand. "Henri de Castries." Accessed October 11, 2012. http://www.interbrand.com/en/best-global-brands/2012/articles-and-interviews/axa-henri-de-castries.aspx.

———. "2012 Ranking of the Top 100 Brands." Accessed October 11, 2012. http://www.interbrand.com/en/best-global-brands/2012/Best-Global-Brands-2012-Brand-View.aspx.

"Leading Global Insurance Companies." *Statista*. Accessed October 11, 2012. http://www.statista.com/statistics/185746/revenue-of-the-leading-global-insruance-companies/.

Michel, Stefan, and Jean-Pierre Baillot. "Redefining the AXA Brand." *Harvard Business Review*, April 10, 2010.

Plunkett Research, Ltd. "Introduction to the Insurance Industry." Accessed October 11, 2012. http://www.plunkettresearch.com/insurance-risk-management-market-research/industry-trends.

BAE SYSTEMS

AT A GLANCE

Brand Synopsis: Based in the United Kingdom, BAE Systems is one of the world's top defense contractors, offering services that include defense electronics, naval vessels, munitions, land warfare systems, and civil and military aerospace services.
Parent Company: BAE Systems plc
Stirling Square, 6 Carlton Garde
London, England SW1Y 5AD
United Kingdom
http://www.baesystems.com
Sector: Industrials
Industry Group: Capital Goods
Performance: *Market share*—3.2% of aerospace and defense market, worldwide (2010). *Sales*—£19.2 billion (US$29 billion) (2011).
Principal Competitors: European Aeronautic Defence and Space Company EADS N.V.; Boeing Company; Lockheed Martin Corporation; Northrop Grumman Corporation; Raytheon Company; General Dynamics Corporation; Finmeccanica S.p.A.

BRAND ORIGINS

- BAE Systems was officially formed by the 1999 merger of civil and military aircraft manufacturer British Aerospace and defense contractor Marconi Electronic Systems.
- Before the merger British Aerospace was the largest defense contractor in Europe and the United Kingdom's largest exporter. In the first decade of the 21st century BAE Systems acquired multiple U.S. and European defense-related companies.
- In 2010 BAE Systems pled guilty to violations of the Arms Export Control Act (AECA) and the International Traffic in Arms Regulations (ITAR).

BAE Systems was officially formed by the 1999 merger of civil and military aircraft manufacturer British Aerospace and defense contractor Marconi Electronic Systems. However, the company's origins go back much further. After World War II the British government began a huge consolidation of the country's aircraft manufacturers, determining that its national industry would have a better chance of surviving and thriving in the international market if companies in the sector were merged. British Aerospace, for example, was formed by the consolidation of multiple U.K. aircraft manufacturers, several of which had also formed as the result of mergers and acquisitions. Thus, BAE Systems is the successor to many of the United Kingdom's most prominent aircraft, warship, and defense electronics manufacturers.

In 1977 the Aircraft and Shipbuilding Industries Act nationalized large parts of the U.K. aerospace and shipbuilding industries. The newly state-owned companies were placed under the umbrella of one of two corporations, British Aerospace and British Shipbuilders. In 1981 the British government sold a majority of its shares in British Aerospace, and in 1985 it sold all but a £1 "golden share," which would allow the government to block foreign control of the company in the event of a sale or merger.

Although at its peak British Aerospace was the largest defense contractor in Europe and the United Kingdom's largest exporter, the company lacked the resources to manufacture an aircraft suitable for competing in the growing commercial airliner market. In 1979 British Aerospace joined the consortium of European companies in control of Airbus, acquiring a 20 percent share of the airplane manufacturer and offering US$500 million for costs associated with the development of its A310 commercial airliner. In 1983, with the help of a generous line of credit from the U.K. government, British Aerospace was permitted a 26 percent share of Airbus's new A320 model and produced wings for the airliner. The A320 would go on to become the best-selling single-aisle aircraft in the world.

Before it was acquired by British Aerospace, Marconi Electronic Systems (also known as GEC-Marconi) acted as the defense arm of the General Electric Company. The company's history of military products dates back to World War I, when it supplied radios and bulbs for the war efforts. During World War II Marconi Electronic Systems was involved at a much higher level, helping to develop a number of advances in radar technology. The company made several significant defense-related acquisitions during the 20th century and was widely considered one of the world's most important defense contractors between 1945 and 1999.

The 1995 formation of U.S. defense contractor Lockheed Martin and the 1997 merger of U.S. corporations Boeing and McDonnell Douglas forced competing European defense companies to consider consolidation. In 1999 BAE Systems was officially formed by the merger of British Aerospace and Marconi Electronic Systems, creating a U.K. company capable of effectively penetrating the U.S. defense market.

The first decade of the 21st century was a time of expansion, mergers, and restructuring for the newly formed company. The first BAE Systems annual report outlined several key areas of growth, including support services to militaries, further involvement in Airbus, and integrated systems for air, land, and naval applications. A 2004 review identified the company's top goal as expansion and investment in the United States. Over the next few years BAE Systems made a number of strategic U.S. and European acquisitions, divesting many of its commercial aviation interests while ramping up its defense portfolio, which included entering into significant contracts with governments and militaries in the United States, United Kingdom, India, and Saudi Arabia.

Despite initially identifying its involvement in Airbus as an area for growth, in 2006 BAE Systems sold its 20 percent stake in the airliner to the European Aeronautic Defence and Space Company EADS N.V. (commonly referred to as EADS), a corporation formed by the merger of the other three partner companies in the Airbus consortium. The following years were uncertain ones for BAE Systems. In 2010 the company pled guilty to violations of the Arms Export Control Act (AECA) and the International Traffic in Arms Regulations (ITAR), for which it was ordered to pay a record US$400 million in fines. In 2011 BAE Systems began talks with its unions to cut nearly 3,000 jobs. The company's 2012 half-year report showed a 10 percent decline in revenues in the previous six months, signaling what was projected to be a steep reduction in defense-related spending over the coming years.

BRAND ELEMENTS

- BAE Systems has strict guidelines for communication of its brand identity, operating a standalone website outlining meticulous procedures for use of its brand elements.
- The BAE Systems logo is a simple rendering of the company name in white, uppercase letters over a surrounding "Corporate Red" rectangle.
- "Keylines," or horizontal lines used as a pair or as the starting point for an ad illustration, are a central element of BAE Systems' branding.

BAE Systems has strict corporate branding standards, operating a standalone website dedicated to identifying and explaining its brand guidelines, including correct use of its logo, corporate colors, and even its name. For example, the company must always be referred to as "BAE Systems," never "BAE," and when written the two words should always appear on the same line (rather than split over two consecutive lines). Likewise, the guidelines instruct that only the "S" in the word "Systems" should be capitalized in headings or in running text, the only exception being if the surrounding words are also written in capital letters.

The BAE Systems logo is a simple rendering of the company name in white, uppercase letters over a surrounding red rectangle. BAE Systems refers to the background color as "Corporate Red," providing the pantone reference in its guidelines to ensure consistent use. Reversal of the red and white colors is considered unacceptable, although the company provides a black version of the logo for materials on which the red color would be unappealing. A "Corporate Grey" version of the logo is also available for use on brushed steel. BAE Systems offers several approved taglines that can be used underneath the logo, such as "Real Performance. Real Advantage." The company's brand guidelines provide a description of where the logo should be positioned (which depends on the item) and where to position it in reference to a partner logo.

In addition to providing an approved color palette and acceptable typefaces, the BAE Systems brand guidelines identify something called "keylines," which the company considers to be at the heart of its brand identity. Keylines are essentially horizontal lines that can be used as a pair or as the starting point for an illustration or infographic in advertisements. Although their appearance can vary, keylines must always be "a thin, agile, dynamic element, not a thick rule." The company's brand guidelines also identify four levels of imagery acceptable for use in its advertisements: people; thought leaders; customers; and capabilities, products, and services.

BRAND IDENTITY

- In 2000 British Aerospace changed its name to BAE Systems to shed its image as a British aircraft manufacturer.
- BAE Systems strictly regulates its brand and how the brand is presented.
- BAE Systems uses two taglines: "Real Performance. Real Advantage." and "Real Pride. Real Advantage."

In 2000, after acquiring Marconi Electronic Systems, British Aerospace changed its name to BAE Systems to shed its image as a British aircraft manufacturer and more fully embrace its new global identity. By the 21st century, according to the *International Directory of Company Histories,* the firm had already begun divesting its commercial aviation interests. BAE Systems is now considered a global defense, aerospace, and security company, with products and services that cover air, land, and naval forces, as well as advanced electronics, security, and information technology.

BAE Systems feels so strongly about its brand identity and how it wishes to be perceived that it has a website devoted solely to its brand and how it should be presented. The company uses two taglines: "Real Performance. Real Advantage." and "Real Pride. Real Advantage." Both taglines promote the brand as competent, reliable, and the best choice. By strictly regulating how the BAE Systems brand should be presented, from the logo to color choices to photos and font size, the company puts forth a unified and very consistent brand identity.

BRAND STRATEGY

- BAE Systems operates a variety of defense, aerospace, and security branches, and its business is not dependent on any one segment.
- Strategic defense-related acquisitions and contracts with a number of governments and militaries have been key elements of BAE Systems' business strategy in the 21st century.
- BAE Systems sees growth potential in its exports business and in offering information technology and cyber security services.

BAE Systems has a balanced portfolio that is not dependent on a single segment of the aerospace and defense industries. According to its website, the company considers its principal markets to be the United Kingdom, the United States, Australia, India, Saudi Arabia, South Africa, and Sweden.

As it emerged into the 21st century, BAE Systems conducted a large number of acquisitions to strengthen its holdings in the defense industry. The company's 2000 purchase of Lockheed Martin Aerospace Electronic Systems was considered critical to its expansion into the United States. In 2004 BAE Systems acquired the United Kingdom's top manufacturer of armored vehicles, Alvis Vickers, and, in 2005, of the U.S. defense company United Defense Industries (UDI), which became the unit responsible for manufacturing combat vehicles, artillery systems, naval guns, missile launchers, and precision-guided munitions. Further acquisitions during the decade included U.S. military equipment manufacturer Armor Holdings, Australian defense contractor Tenix Defence, U.K. technology consulting firm Detica Group, Danish cyber and intelligence company ETI, Irish financial crime and compliance software developer Norkom Group, and U.S. marine support company Atlantic Marine.

Strategic partnerships with international governments and militaries are also a critical part of the BAE Systems corporate strategy. In the first decade of the 21st century BAE Systems saw significant orders from the United States, the United Kingdom, India, and Saudi Arabia. In 2006 Saudi Arabia signed a contract worth up to £10 billion (US$15 billion) for 72 fighter aircraft to be manufactured by BAE Systems. That same year the company won a £2.5 billion (US$3.8 billion) contract to upgrade aircraft for the aviation branch of the Saudi Arabian armed forces, while a US$227 million contract with the U.S. Army in 2006 saw BAE Systems overhauling 361 U.S. military vehicles for combat. In 2012 BAE Systems won a £328 million (US$496 million) contract to design the United Kingdom's next generation of nuclear-armed submarines.

Meanwhile, the company has steadily increased its presence in India, partnering with Mahindra & Mahindra Limited in 2010 to form New Delhi-based Defence Land Systems, of which BAE Systems holds 26 percent. Besides military and government contracts, exports account for a significant percentage of business, and BAE Systems considers this to be an important source of growth. Additionally, with the increasing threat of cyber-attacks on militaries, governments, and private businesses, BAE Systems has begun to expand into information technology and cyber security.

BRAND EQUITY

- BAE Systems took the 268th spot on Brand Finance's Global 500 2012 list, with a brand value of US$3.9 billion.
- In its home country of England, BAE Systems enjoys greater brand recognition than competing defense and aerospace companies like Raytheon, General Dynamics, and Lockheed Martin.
- In 2012 *Defense News* ranked BAE Systems as the world's third-largest defense contractor based on applicable 2011 revenues.

With a brand value of US$3.9 billion, BAE Systems took the 268th spot on Brand Finance's Global 500 2012 list, a slight drop from its ranking of 257th in 2011. In comparison, competitors Boeing and Airbus were ranked in the 97th and 213th spots, respectively, in 2012. In the 2012 Brand Finance ranking of the top 50 brands in the United Kingdom, BAE Systems was ranked 28th, down three spots from the previous year. Although BAE Systems saw a slight drop in its rankings in 2012, the company has a relatively strong brand. This is especially true in its home country of England, where BAE Systems enjoys greater brand recognition than competing defense and aerospace companies like Raytheon, General Dynamics, and Lockheed Martin.

In 2012 defense industry magazine *Defense News* ranked BAE Systems the world's third-largest defense contractor based on applicable 2011 revenues. The company's defense revenues for that year were placed at US$29.1 million, a 4.2 percent drop from 2010. The leading companies on the 2011 list, Lockheed Martin and Boeing, were the only two among the top dozen to see defense revenue growth from the previous year.

BRAND AWARENESS

- BAE Systems entered the 21st century seeking to identify itself as a distinct, unified company providing global defense, aerospace, and security services.
- BAE Systems has products in use in more than 100 countries and employs more than 100,000 people around the world.
- BAE Systems was the world's third-largest defense contractor in 2011, and it has top-of-mind awareness in the aerospace and defense industries.

The company that would in 1999 become BAE Systems had its roots in the mergers of some of the United Kingdom's most successful aircraft, warship, and defense electronics manufacturers. As a result, the company entered the 21st century seeking to shed the identities of its predecessors and apply a "one company" approach across all parts of the business. Although British Aerospace had been largely perceived as an aircraft manufacturer, upon its formation BAE Systems began divesting its commercial aviation interests and strengthening its portfolio of global defense, aerospace, and security services.

Based in London, BAE Systems now has products in use in more than 100 countries and employs more than 100,000 people around the world. As of 2011 the company was the third-largest defense contractor, playing a significant role in the production of military equipment for many of the world's largest armed forces. With its lucrative contracts with the U.S. and U.K. governments and militaries, BAE Systems enjoys top-of-mind awareness in those countries, as well as in other key markets like India and Saudi Arabia.

For those not involved in the defense industry, BAE Systems may be best known for its role as the subject of multiple corruption investigations. In the 1980s British Aerospace served as the prime contractor for the Al Yamamah arms deal, considered one of the biggest trade controversies of the decade, in which the United Kingdom sold a record amount of arms to Saudi Arabia without conditions in regard to security or human rights. Numerous bribery allegations were made against both the U.K. government and British Aerospace, claiming that the deal had been a result of bribes paid to government officials and Saudi royal family members. The investigation continued into the 21st century, even as British Aerospace transformed into BAE Systems, but despite widespread condemnation by human rights organizations like Amnesty International, the Serious Fraud Office (SFO) discontinued its investigation in 2006. The Al Yamamah deals, valued at up to £20 billion (US$30 billion), continue to account for a large percentage of BAE Systems profits.

BRAND OUTLOOK

- From 2010 to 2011 BAE Systems saw a 4.2 percent drop in defense-related revenue growth, reflecting a steep reduction in U.S. defense spending.
- BAE Systems continues to invest and expand in the United States.
- BAE Systems now sells more to the U.S. Department of Defense than to the U.K. Ministry of Defense.

The defense industry is historically subject to regular ebb and flow, and from 2010 to 2011 BAE Systems saw a 4.2 percent drop in defense-related revenue growth, reflecting a recent trend among defense contractors. According to *Defense News,* competitors Lockheed Martin and Boeing were the only top defense contractors to see defense-related revenue growth in that period. Some analysts believe the 2011 drop in revenues marked the beginning of a steep reduction in U.S. defense spending expected to continue for several years. The deepest cuts were expected to hit in fiscal 2013, when caps on U.S. defense spending, many originating in the Budget Control Act, were projected to cut nearly $50 billion annually from the U.S. defense budget. The reduction of U.S. forces in Afghanistan and the continuing fiscal troubles in Europe as of 2012 were also expected to have a damaging effect on defense spending.

Nevertheless, BAE Systems continues to invest and expand in the United States, and the company now sells more to the U.S. Department of Defense (DOD) than to the U.K. Ministry of Defense (MOD). In 2012 BAE Systems and EADS reached a deadlock in their talks for a merger. However, some analysts predict that BAE Systems will eventually merge with one of North America's major defense contractors to gain an even stronger foothold in that market.

FURTHER READING

"Aircraft." *Encyclopedia of Global Industries.* Ed. Lynn M. Pearce. Detroit: Gale, 2012. *Business Insights: Global.* Accessed November 7, 2012. http://bi.galegroup.com/global/article/GALE%7CI2501600075/cf9c4c028c28412b3ebfd0a558cf237a?u=itsbtrial.

BAE Systems. "Company Strategy 2012." Accessed November 7, 2012. http://asp-gb.secure-zone.net/v2/index.jsp?id=624/1890/4238.

"BAE Systems plc." *International Directory of Company Histories.* Ed. Jay P. Pederson. Vol. 108. Detroit: St. James Press, 2010. *Business Insights: Global.* Accessed November 7, 2012. http://bi.galegroup.com/global/article/GALE%7CI2501313369/0293b6c2ae10eae7f61f4d88515b6496?u=itsbtrial.

"BAE Systems plc." *Notable Corporate Chronologies.* Detroit: Gale, 2013. *Business Insights: Global.* Accessed November 7, 2012. http://bi.galegroup.com/global/article/GALE%7CI2501150175/f2537d1bafe3ca353564967bd0b61827?u=itsbtrial.

Brand Finance. "Global 500 2012." *Brandirectory.* Accessed November 5, 2012. http://brandirectory.com/league_tables/table/global-500-2012.

"EADS in Merger Talks with BAE Systems." *Air Transport World* 49.10 (2012): 9. *Business Source Alumni Edition.* Accessed November 7, 2012.

Fryer-Biggs, Zachary. "Defense News Top 100: Revenue Declines Are Just Beginning as U.S. Budget Cuts Loom." *Defense News,* June 21, 2012. Accessed November 30, 2012. http://www.defensenews.com/article/20120621/DEFREG02/306210005/Defense-News-Top-100-Revenue-Declines-Just-Beginning-U-S-Budget-Cuts-Loom.

"Largest Commercial Jet Makers in Europe, 2008, 2010, 2012." *Market Share Reporter.* Robert S. Lazich and Virgil L. Burton III. Detroit: Gale, 2010. *Business Insights: Global.* Accessed November 7, 2012. http://bi.galegroup.com/global/article/GALE%7CI2502029779/30ec33dc096720b91f78e0c8a052f3bb?u=itsbtrial.

"Top Aerospace and Defense Firms, 2010." *Market Share Reporter.* Detroit: Gale, 2012. *Business Insights: Global.* Accessed November 7, 2012. http://bi.galegroup.com/global/article/GALE%7CI2502041601/338f245f4e53bf377477636f538115ff?u=itsbtrial.

"World's Most Valuable Aerospace and Defense Brands, 2011." *Business Rankings Annual.* Ed. Deborah J. Draper. Detroit: Gale, 2013. *Business Insights: Global.* Accessed November 7, 2012. http://bi.galegroup.com/global/article/GALE%7CI2501282896/a94f1af1334c6a9eac8277bfaf0589d1?u=itsbtrial.

BANK OF CHINA

AT A GLANCE

Brand Synopsis: Bank of China is one of the largest and most prominent international banks in the world, working with governments, businesses, and individuals to provide a host of banking services.
Parent Company: Bank of China Limited
No. 1 Fuxingmen Nei Dajie, Xicheng District
Beijing 100818
People's Republic of China
http://www.boc.cn/index.html
Sector: Financials
Industry Group: Banks
Performance: *Profit*—CNY124.18 billion (US$19.69 billion) (2011).
Principal Competitors: Westpac Banking Corporation; Industrial and Commercial Bank of China; China Construction Bank; Agricultural Bank of China; First Pacific Bank

BRAND ORIGINS

- Along with the Industrial and Commercial Bank of China Limited, the China Construction Bank, and the Agricultural Bank of China, the Bank of China is one of the big four of China's largest banks.
- Sun Yat-sen helped found the Bank of China in 1912.
- The Bank of China has been involved in international trade agreements and loans and was the first Chinese company to issue foreign bonds, including bonds to the United States.
- The Bank of China offers personal financial services, such as savings accounts, investment services, and insurance.

The Bank of China is one of the four largest banks in China. It joins the Industrial and Commercial Bank of China Limited, the China Construction Bank, and the Agricultural Bank of China as members of the "big four," an elite quartet of large government-affiliated banks. Owned by the Chinese government, the Bank of China's ties to the government run deep.

Revolutionary leader Sun Yat-sen helped found the Bank of China in 1912 after the republican revolution in 1911 ousted the Qing dynasty. Through the decades, this bank, the oldest of the big four, has served as a bank for the government. After the Communist Party took control of China in 1949, the Bank of China focused on foreign exchange.

It has also represented China by serving as an intermediary in Chinese trade agreements. In fact, its international work has been quite extensive. It opened its first foreign office in London in 1929. Later, as China began opening to foreign involvement, in 1979 the Bank of China signed the first energy loan agreement between China and Japan. In 1984 it became the first Chinese bank to issue bonds on the foreign market, and in 1994 it was the first Chinese bank to issue bonds to the U.S. market. In 2001 it combined a number of its Hong Kong banks and a credit card subsidiary to create Bank of China (Hong Kong), a major subsidiary. The bank also has branches, banking relationships, and other connections in several countries.

This international work accompanies its domestic work. It offers a multitude of banking and financial services for individuals and businesses in China and for Chinese citizens living abroad. Long known for its loans and monetary services, the Bank of China also provides personal banking and financial services, such as savings accounts, investment services, and insurance.

The Bank of China's involvement in personal banking has resulted in even more firsts. It began offering the first Chinese credit card in 1985 and the first Chinese ATM card in 1987. Known as the Great Wall ATM card, it featured the circular Bank of China logo and a stylized depiction of the Great Wall of China. Similar depictions can be seen in the bank's Great Wall International Euro Credit Card, introduced in 2004 and featuring the round symbol, a drawing of the Great Wall, and a Euro symbol. These images depict the bank, its ties to China, and international finance.

BRAND ELEMENTS

- The Bank of China uses a red, circular symbol with a symmetrical interior design, accompanied by Chinese characters and the words "Bank of China."
- The Bank of China and the rest of China's big four banks feature circular logos, symbols reminiscent of both each other and the Chinese banking industry.
- A 2009 television commercial for the Bank of China uses its red circular symbol multiple times, as well as currency symbols for the yuan and dollar.

The Bank of China's symbol is simple yet evocative. It is a red ring with a symmetrical design in the center, consisting of a vertical red line and a small red square. Accompanying this symbol are Chinese characters and the English words "Bank of China," all in black. The red Bank of China symbol resembles a Chinese coin, a fitting image to represent its field, banking, and its home country, China.

The circular symbol ties the Bank of China to other Chinese banks. The three other members of the China's big four banks all use circular symbols. Two of these banks, Industrial and Commercial Bank of China Limited and Agricultural Bank of China, also feature circles with symmetrical designs in the middle, just like the Bank of China. The Bank of China's symbol thus evokes the Chinese banking industry as a whole.

A 2009 television commercial for Bank of China (Hong Kong) used the company's red logo and showed its bank cards, which also featured the red logos. This commercial also superimposed dollar and yuan symbols over footage of different activities; Hong Kong uses the dollar as currency while China uses the yuan. The commercial showed the cost of living in China and Hong Kong and explained how Bank of China customers could pay for these costs. By using currency signs in its advertising, the Bank of China linked itself to the financial world, reminiscent of how its coin-like logo connects to financial matters.

BRAND IDENTITY

- At over 1,200 feet high, the Bank of China Tower in Hong Kong is one of the world's tallest buildings.
- The Bank of China Tower symbolizes the resources, expertise, problem-solving abilities, connections, and success of Bank of China (Hong Kong).
- The building website noted that the Bank of China Tower's design symbolizes bamboo, as the plant has a multisectioned trunk that is "propelled higher and higher by each new growth."

Prominent architecture mirrors the bank's own prominence. Completed in 1990, its Bank of China Tower in Hong Kong was the tallest structure in Asia until 1992 and is still one of the tallest buildings in the world. Measuring over 1,200 feet high, it was the first building outside the United States to top 1,000 feet. Architects included Pei Cobb Freed & Partners, a firm associated with renowned architect I. M. Pei.

This skyscraper is a symbol. It graphically portrays the Bank of China (Hong Kong) as a bank that has the resources to build something massive, the expertise and talent to solve construction problems and other matters, and the connections needed to attract prominent architects. Its imposing height and impressive façade imply that the Bank of China (Hong Kong) is a powerful, dynamic, successful bank that, by extension, can employ its power, dynamism, and success to help its customers achieve similar prominence.

The Bank of China building represents other things. While it is a modern building that incorporates glass, steel, and lighting elements to evoke urban industrial design, other aspects of its appearance evoke China's agriculture. According to the building's website Emporis, the tower takes its design cues from bamboo, a plant featuring a multisectioned trunk that is "propelled higher and higher by each new growth." As a consequence, added Emporis, the building "is symbolic of strength, vitality and growth." Taking its cue from bamboo, which adds trunk sections as it grows, the bank portrays itself as having a long, successful history and aiming to add to its successes. The use of modern industrial materials to echo an ancient plant also demonstrates how the Bank of China (Hong Kong) operates in both urban and rural areas.

BRAND STRATEGY

- Bank of China's investment banking subsidiary, BOC International Holdings Limited, promoted the Bank of China name to business professionals through cocktail hours at the Real Estate Investment World China 2011.

- In 2012 the Bank of China (Hong Kong) sponsored a Hong Kong art exhibit featuring the work of Chinese artist Zhang Daqian.
- By serving as a partner bank for the 2008 Beijing Summer Olympics and the Paralympics Games, the Bank of China promoted China, Beijing, and itself to millions of people worldwide.

The Bank of China has taken unique measures to publicize its brand. Its investment-banking subsidiary, BOC International Holdings Limited (BOCI), sponsored cocktails at the Real Estate Investment World (REIW) China 2011 in Beijing, China. REIW China is a multiday conference for international professionals in real estate, investment, and other fields. By sponsoring cocktails at REIW China, the Bank of China provided a social setting for conference attendees, potentially helping them conduct business in such settings. It also promoted the Bank of China name to people who could utilize the bank's services.

Other sponsorships have advanced the bank's name. For example, in 2012 the Bank of China (Hong Kong) sponsored the art exhibit *A Testament of Friendship—Zhang Daqian Paintings and Calligraphy from the Collection of You Yi Yang*. This Hong Kong exhibition highlighted the work of Zhang Daqian, a Chinese artist whose work is very popular at auctions. By acknowledging the popularity of this artist and enabling many Hong Kong residents to experience his art, the Bank of China encouraged them to celebrate their heritage and conveyed the bank's support of their culture and history.

Another Bank of China venture with symbolic significance was its affiliation with the 2008 Beijing Summer Olympics and the Paralympics Games. The company provided financial operations as a partner bank for these events, held in the same city as the bank's headquarters. Bank of China's work helped represent China, Beijing, and itself to millions around the world.

BRAND EQUITY

- *Euromoney* magazine called Bank of China the best bond underwriter in China in 2012 due to the bank's Chinese issuances and its 14.6 percent bond market share.
- The Bank of China and the three other banks of China's big four held 58 percent of China's retail deposits in 2011.
- In *Forbes* magazine's 2012 list of largest companies in the world, the Bank of China placed 21st.

Given its myriad activities and international involvement, the Bank of China is a significant presence in different financial markets. From 2011 to early 2012, it performed well in the bond market of its home country. The bank's issuances for that period and its 14.6 percent market share in China's bond market for the first part of 2012 led *Euromoney* magazine to call the bank China's best bond underwriter.

The Bank of China and other members of China's banking big four hold an even larger market share in another financial area. In 2004 the Bank of China, the Industrial and Commercial Bank of China Limited, the China Construction Bank, and the Agricultural Bank of China together accounted for 66 percent of China's retail deposits. These four companies jointly captured 58 percent of this market in 2011.

All four banks have appeared on *Forbes* magazine's list of largest companies in the world, the "Forbes Global 2000." In fact, in 2012, all four banks placed among the top 25, with the Bank of China placing 21st among the world's largest companies. The Bank of China was the fifth-largest Chinese company and the seventh-largest bank worldwide on this list.

BRAND AWARENESS

- World Brand Lab determined that the Bank of China had the 10th-highest brand value of any Chinese company in 2012.
- Bank of China (UK) has forged business relationships with prominent companies like the UK's Rolls-Royce.
- *International Alternative Investment Review* magazine honored the Bank of China in 2011.

Due to its size and business success, the Bank of China is a valuable global brand. Brand analyst and market strategist World Brand Lab, in an extensive study of Chinese brands, has rated the Bank of China's brand value highly. It determined that the Bank of China had the 10th-highest brand value of any Chinese company in 2012.

The bank has taken steps to build awareness in different countries. Bank of China (UK) has forged business relationships with prominent companies, such as the UK's own Rolls-Royce. It has also raised its profile by offering loans and hiring new staff, two practices other banks were reluctant to undertake during the financial crisis of the early 2000s.

The Bank of China's work has brought it international awards. It won an IAIR Award in Milan, Italy, from *International Alternative Investment Review* (IAIR) magazine in 2011. According to a website for the magazine, it gave the bank this award "in recognition of its capacity to support Chinese enterprises abroad and to be the most internationalized bank in China. With much dedication, it has successfully become one of the best trade finance service banks in the world."

BRAND OUTLOOK

- In 2013 Bank of China Aviation purchased additional aircraft for its aircraft leasing and purchasing services.
- Based in Rotterdam, the Netherlands, the Bank of China (Luxembourg) S.A. was the first Chinese financial institution to open in the Netherlands.
- Bank of China ELUOSI opened its first branch in Russia's Far East in 2012.
- The Bank of China works with almost 1,500 banks in more than 170 countries and regions.

Bank of China has expanded some of its other services. In 2013 its subsidiary Bank of China (BOC) Aviation purchased additional aircraft. This purchase reinforced the fleet for the company, which leases aircraft to airlines around the world and offers financing for purchasing plans through BOC Aviation and the Bank of China. Reflecting the multinational nature of its business, the Bank of China owns Singapore-based BOC Aviation, which in turn has offices in Seattle, Washington, the United States, and Dublin, Ireland.

The company has also expanded to other geographic areas in the early 2000s. It entered the Netherlands in 2007, opening in Rotterdam to become the first Chinese financial institution to have a presence in that county. This Rotterdam branch of the Bank of China (Luxembourg) S.A. targets Chinese and Dutch businesspeople, embassy and government workers, and Chinese students, especially those studying in the Netherlands.

The Bank of China extended its business reach through additional developments. A subsidiary, Bank of China (ELUOSI), established a foothold in Russia's Far East region when it opened a branch in Khabarovsk in June 2012, followed by a branch in Vladivostok. The Bank of China also established a business counter in Uganda in 2013, allowing Ugandan and Chinese businesses to work together. According to a Bank of China web page, this venture is one of many international affiliations, which include "correspondent and cooperation relations with nearly 1,500 foreign banks in 179 countries and regions."

FURTHER READING

Bank of China. "About Bank of China (Luxembourg) S.A. Rotterdam Branch." Accessed January 31, 2013. http://www.bankofchina.com/nl/en/aboutus/ab1/201110/t20111023_1567770.html.

———. "Bank of China Awarded 'China's Best Bond Underwriter.'" July 25, 2012. Accessed January 31, 2013. http://www.boc.cn/en/bocinfo/bi1/201208/t20120810_1932035.html.

———. "BOC Set up Chinese Business Counter in Uganda." January 14, 2013. Accessed January 31, 2013. http://www.boc.cn/en/bocinfo/bi1/201301/t20130114_2124638.html.

"Bank of China." *International Directory of Company Histories*. Ed. Tina Grant and Miranda Ferrara. Vol. 63. Detroit, MI: St. James Press, 2004.

"Bank of China: 'It's a Great Honor for Us Receiving IAIR Awards.'" *IAIR*, January 31, 2013. Accessed January 31, 2013. http://www.iairawards.com/bank_of_china_winner.php.

Bank of China Limited. *2011 Annual Report*. Bank of China. Accessed January 31, 2013. http://pic.bankofchina.com/bocappd/report/201204/P020120427343360067816.pdf.

"Bank of China Tower." *Emporis*. Accessed January 31, 2013. http://www.emporis.com/building/bankofchinatower-hongkong-china.

"China's Big Four Banks Losing Market Share." *S. J. Grand*, July 4, 2011. Accessed January 31, 2013. http://www.sjgrand.cn/chinas-big-four-banks-losing-market-share.

DeCarlo, Scott. "Forbes Global 2000." *Forbes*, April 18, 2012. Accessed January 31, 2013. http://www.forbes.com/global2000/list/#p_1_s_a0_All%20industries_All%20countries_All%20states.

"How the Bank of China Stepped out of the Shadows." *Telegraph* (London), October 1, 2009.

BARCLAYS

AT A GLANCE

Brand Synopsis: Despite much criticized business practices, Barclays presents itself as a trustworthy world-class financial institution that understands the needs of its customers.
Parent Company: Barclays plc
1 Churchill Place
London
United Kingdom
http://www.barclays.com
Sector: Financials
Industry Group: Banks
Performance: *Total assets*—US$2.45 trillion (2011).
Principal Competitors: Deutsch Bank AG; HSBC Holdings plc; The Royal Bank of Scotland Group plc

BRAND ORIGINS

- The firm's origins date to 1690.
- An image of an eagle became the firm's trademark in the early 1700s.
- Barclay's became one of the United Kingdom's "big five" banks in 1918.
- Barclay's retooled its brand in 2004.

Barclays is one of the world's oldest banking and financial services brands. It represents London, United Kingdom–based Barclays plc, a global concern with operations throughout Europe, Africa, the Middle East, and the United States. The firm's origins date to 1690 when Quakers John Freame and Thomas Gould went into business as goldsmith-bankers. It wasn't until 1736 that the Barclays name became associated with the business. In that year, James Barclay, who had married Freame's daughter, became a partner with Freame's son, Joseph. Even before Barclay became partner, the bank had adopted the eagle as its corporate symbol, laying a foundation for the Barclay's image.

Other partners joined the firm, including Silvanus Bevan in 1767 and John Henton Tritton in 1782. For about a century, the firm operated as Barclays, Bevan & Tritton. After a change in law in 1879 that permitted joint-stock associations to convert to a limited-liability structure, the modern Barclays began to take shape. Barclays, Bevan & Tritton grew larger through an 1888 merger, and in 1896 it joined with two other large concerns and 17 smaller Quaker-run banks to create Barclay & Company Ltd., a joint-stock association that boasted 182 branches and £26 million in deposits, both impressive numbers for the time.

Barclays continued to grow in the 20th century, completing further acquisitions to become Barclays Bank Ltd. and one of the country's "big five" banks in 1918. The following decade Barclays established an international footprint through the acquisition of banks in Egypt and South Africa. Following World War II, Barclays accelerated its rate of growth. In the 1980s it became the first U.K. bank to gain a listing on both the Tokyo Stock Exchange and the New York Stock Exchange. It was also during this decade that Barclays Capital was formed to pursue investment banking, and in 1985 Barclays UK and Barclays International merged to form Barclays plc. Barclays Global Investors was added to the mix in the 1990s.

Barclays maintained its growth in the new millennium. Because it was involved in a large number of banking and investment sectors around the world, Barclays launched a major revamping of its brand. The firm's famous Eagle trademark was given a facelift, as Barclays fashioned a brand to aid in the further pursuit of its global ambitions.

BRAND ELEMENTS

- Three crowns were added to the Barclays eagle in the 1930s.
- Eagle logo was redesigned in 2004.
- "Fluent in finance" was one of Barclays' better known taglines.

Like many of the world's venerable banking houses, Barclays draws its name from one of the firm's early partners, James Barclay. The name is long attached to the banking industry, and it is that history that provides the Barclays' brand with an image of stability and trustworthiness. These attributes are also reinforced by the consistent use of the eagle as a corporate symbol.

In 1728 the banking partnership of John Freame and Thomas Gould moved to a new location at the sign of the Black Spread Eagle, in keeping with the law that London merchants identify their business with a pictorial sign, since many London residents at the time were unable to read or write. Barclays became so closely associated with the Eagle that in the 1930s the bank secured a Grant of Arms using the symbol. To differentiate the Barclays' eagle from the many other eagles used over the years by royal houses and other business concerns was the addition of three silver crowns. The logo was updated in 1981 and 1999, but it retained the spread wings and three crowns. In 2004, as part of a rebranding effort, the crowns were eliminated and the double-winged eagle was joined by the Barclays name in a new version of the corporate logo. Depending on the purpose, the logo was rendered in varying shades of blue.

Barclays has no long-term association with a particular slogan. The bank has used several advertising taglines in recent years. Two of the better-known phrases are "Fluent in finance" and "It's our business to know your business." In 2010 Barclays relaunched its corporate brand with a campaign anchored by the tagline "Power to Help You Succeed."

BRAND IDENTITY

- Barclay presents itself as a trustworthy world-class financial institution.
- As part of its identity, Barclay implies an understanding of customer needs.
- The Barclays eagle symbol suggests strength and other positive attributes.
- Barclays' taglines assert financial expertise as well as a commitment to meeting customer needs.

Barclays' brand identity, the way the bank presents itself to the world, is of a trustworthy world-class financial institution that understands the needs of its customers and therefore offers the kind of products and services its customers need when they need them. Moreover, Barclays lays claim to a commitment of treating people as individuals and valuing its relationships with them.

The consistent use of the eagle logo reinforces the idea of longevity and stability with many customers. Moreover, the eagle carries a good deal of symbolic value. The eagle has ties to ancient Egypt, the Greek God Zeus, the Roman legions, royal families, and nations. It has been closely aligned with the concepts of strength, courage, foresight, and immortality. All of these positive attributes helped to position Barclays as a strong and reliable brand.

Taglines have provided some help as well in maintaining Barclays' brand identity. Through the use of "Fluent in finance," Barclays asserted that it was a knowledgeable partner for customers. The tagline "It's our business to know your business" implied that not only was Barclays competent, but that it also cared about the needs of its customers. A similar message was inherent in the 2010 tagline, "Power to help you succeed." Such declarations were meant to help create a sense of confidence in the brand and engender loyalty to it.

BRAND STRATEGY

- For many years, Barclays lacked a group marketing director.
- Poorly envisioned ad campaigns in the early 2000s troubled Barclays.
- "House of brands" approach developed spontaneously.
- Barclays returned to a corporate brand strategy only to have the brand tarnished by the Libor scandal.

Barclays has generally pursued a single brand approach, promoting the Barclay name across several sectors. Like other banks of its size, Barclay's branding was far from inspired in the 1990s, due in part to structural limitations. The bank's business was divided among four units—retail financial services, corporate banking, Barclays Capital for investment banking, and Barclays Global Solutions for asset management—yet lacked a group marketing director or a unified marketing department.

Faced with increasing competition from emerging markets, such as banking operations cropping up in supermarkets, Barclays attempted to become more adroit in its branding. The goal was to make Barclays an emotional as well as a rational choice for customers. In March 2000 Barclays launched a major advertising campaign anchored by the tagline, "A big world needs a big bank." This campaign was ill-fated, however, when the following month, Barclays closed 171 branches in a single day, more than half of which were located in rural areas where residents were limited in their banking options. To make matters worse, Barclays received poor publicity over a suggested ATM fee and the revelation that its new chief executive had been paid £1.3 million for just three months work.

After the public relations disaster of the "big bank" campaign, Barclays hired American actor Samuel L. Jackson to deliver commercial monologues on money-related issues, culminating with the tagline, "Money speaks in many languages. Barclays speaks them all." In reviewing the campaign, one critic, marketing consultant Mike Sommers, told *Marketing* that the campaign simply reinforced the perception that Barclays was "arrogant and out of touch," adding that the advertising money would have been better spent on improving and communicating its basic banking service. Barclays next attempted to inject some humor and a bit of warmth in its advertising via a television commercial depicting a man acting erratically and comically after having an allergic reaction from a wasp sting. The man ends up being shot with a tranquilizer dart and arrested, while a voiceover suggested that the odds of changing your bank were similarly outrageous. Viewers found the ad frightening to children and offensive to allergy sufferers, and the ad was banned by the United Kingdom's Advertising Standards Authority. Barclays issued an apology for any offense the ad may have caused.

Some of the Barclays' business units sought to carve out their own sub-brand identities. The movement began with Barclay's Wealth, which felt that it was hampered in its efforts to win the business of high-net worth individuals by its connection to the brand's retail banking massaging. Barclays Commercial soon followed suit in crafting its own brand, as did Barclay's Capital, which assumed the name BarCap.

Barclays CEO Robert Diamond put an end to the "house of brands" approach. In March 2012 the company returned to its emphasis of a single, overarching brand, but that would soon have to shoulder all of the weight of the Libor scandal, which hit the unit that had been known as BarCap. While there was little Barclays could do to put a positive spin on a criminal probe and £290 million in fines, some critics suggested that the bank exacerbated the situation by showing little if any remorse for its conduct. In the end, Diamond lost his post and Barclays sacrificed a measure of brand equity.

BRAND EQUITY

- Brand Finance estimated the value of the Barclays' brand at US$13.552 billion in 2011.
- Barclays was listed number 60 on the Brand Finance's 2012 Global 500 list of the world's most valuable brands.
- Barclays ranked number 12 on Brand Finance's 2012 Banking 500.
- According to Brand Finance, Barclays was the seventh most valuable United Kingdom brand.
- The loss of brand equity from the Libor scandal caused harm to Barclays on multiple levels.

Based on Barclays' 2011 performance, brand consultancy Brand Finance plc estimated the value of the Barclays' brand at US$13.552 billion. This performance afforded Barclays the number 60 position on Brand Finance's Global 500 list of the world's most valuable brands in 2012. Barclays was also listed number 12 on the 2012 Banking 500 and number 7 among all United Kingdom brands. These results represented a diminished showing, however. Following the acquisition of some assets from bankrupted Lehman Brothers in 2008, Barclay's had significantly improved its standing. In 2011 the brand was ranked as the 34th most valuable brand in the world, the 7th most valuable banking brand, and the 6th most valuable United Kingdom brand.

Barclay's 2012 ranking did not reflect the damage caused to the brand by the Libor scandal of that year and would be reflected in the 2013 listings. Recognizing that their continued presence was causing harm to the Barclay's brand, Diamond and chairman Marcus Agius resigned from the bank in July 2012. According to Mark Ritson writing in *MarketingWeek*, Barclays was "now experiencing the opposite of brand building. Where once brand equity was a force for positive, advantageous growth for Barclays, it is now exacting an increasing negative impact on the business from many angles." At the consumer level, Barclays would have to spend more in advertising to attract new customers and retain the ones it already had. A loss in reputation would also have a dampening effect on employee morale. Eroding brand equity would be reflected in the loss of talent and the cost of attracting new employees and retaining old ones.

BRAND AWARENESS

- Because of its long history, the Barclays brand is well known in the United Kingdom.
- The Barclays Center in Brooklyn has raised brand awareness in the United States.
- Controversy during the Libor scandal burdened Barclays with undesirable brand awareness.

Awareness of the Barclays brand is especially high in the United Kingdom where the bank enjoys a long history and for nearly the past century has been recognized as one of the nation's "big five" banks. Barclays also enjoys strong brand awareness in former British Commonwealth countries in which it has done business for many years. The banking brand does not enjoy as much awareness in other markets, but recognition is improving. In the United States, for example, the bank's association with a new high-profile arena in Brooklyn, the Barclays Center, helped to raise general awareness of the brand, especially in the key New York market.

The brand received unwanted recognition, or negative brand awareness, in the Libor scandal. In early 2012 Barclays and several other U.K. banks were fined heftily for the manipulation of Libor and Euribor Rates. These are average rates determined by the submissions of London's major banks. Through coordinated manipulation, Barclays and the others were able to inflate or deflate the rate as a way to profit on trades. The Barclays name and image suffered as a result.

BRAND OUTLOOK

- Despite controversies, Barclays remains one of the world's most valuable bank brands.
- Outside of the United Kingdom, damage to the Barclay's brand has been limited.
- Barclay's faces significant challenges in the years ahead as it attempts to repair the damage done to its brand.

Regardless of the negative publicity it has received from the Libor scandal, or other high-profile missteps in recent years, Barclays remains a highly valuable brand. Moreover, it is a global brand, and outside of the United Kingdom, where the media spotlight does not burn as brightest for the bank, the negative publicity is unlikely to have much of an impact on its business. In the United States, there was little public outcry over Barclays' role in the Libor scandal. There was no clamor, for example to remove the Barclay's name to the new Brooklyn arena, as there had been in Houston a decade earlier when Enron was embroiled in controversy and Enron Field, home of Major League Baseball's Houston Astros, replaced its corporate naming sponsor.

The injury done to the Barclays brand might very well be repaired in the years ahead. The bank, however, faced serious challenges. Mark Ritson in his July 2012 *MarketingWeek* article indicated that "right now almost every existing piece of Barclays' promotional material is being vilified by the British public." He also warned "The bigger the brand, the faster and further it can fall—and the greater the impact when it hits the floor."

FURTHER READING

"Barclays' Charm Offensive." *Marketing*, August 29, 2002.

"Barclays plc." *International Directory of Company Histories*. Ed. Tina Grant. Vol. 64. Detroit, MI: St. James Press, 2006.

"Barclays Reveals Identity to Lead Global Growth." *Marketing*, April 28, 2004.

Bawden, Tom. "Bird on a Wire." *Marketing Week*, September 16, 1999.

Brand Finance. "Global 500 2012." *Brandirectory*. Accessed December 28, 2012. http://brandirectory.com/league_tables/table/global-500-2012.

Clark, Tom, and Jill Treanor. "Reputation of Barclays Takes a Battering after Libor Scandal." *Guardian* (London), September 11, 2012.

Osborne, Hillary. "Barclays Is UK's Most Complained about Bank, New Figures Reveal." *Guardian* (London), February 28, 2012.

Parsons, Russell. "Barclays' Boss Quits 'to Avoid Brand Contagion.'" *Marketing Week*, July 2, 2012.

———. "Barclays Pushes Corporate Brand Launch." *Marketing Week*, September 6, 2010.

Pitcher, Mark. "Why Barclays' Advertising Strategy Is a Big Mistake." *Marketing Week*, April 13, 2000.

Ritson, Mark. "It's An Equitable Brand Life, Barclays." *Marketing Week*, July 12, 2012.

Spanier, Gideon. "Barclays Is a Media Brand but Fails to Think Like One." *London Evening Standard*, July 11, 2012.

BASF

AT A GLANCE

Brand Synopsis: Though its name and advertising tagline enjoy high recognition, consumers have little idea of the product line associated with BASF, whose parent company is the largest chemical producer in the world.
Parent Company: BASF SE
Carl-Bosch-Str. 38
67056 Ludwigshafen
Germany
http://www.basf.com
Sector: Materials
Industry Group: Chemicals
Performance: *Market share*—15 percent (2011). *Sales*—EUR73.497 billion (US$95.2 billion) (2011).
Principal Competitors: Bayer AG; Dow Chemical Company; E.I. du Pont de Nemours and Company; PPG Industries

BRAND ORIGINS

- German jeweler Friedrich Engelhorn founded Badische Analin- und Soda-Fabrik in 1865.
- BASF, Bayer, and other dye companies formed a cartel known as Dreibund in 1904.
- In 1925 BASF merged with Bayer and several hundred other chemical companies to form IG Farben.
- Because of its involvement in Nazi war crimes, IG Farben was disbanded after World War II and BASF reestablished in 1952.

German jeweler Friedrich Engelhorn founded Badische Analin- und Soda-Fabrik (Baden Analine and Soda Factory), a producer of synthetic dyes, in Mannheim, Germany, on April 6, 1865. Because the town council refused to allow a chemical plant in Mannheim, Engelhorn located the manufacturing facility across the Rhine in Ludwigshafen. Production rapidly expanded to include a number of chemicals, including alizarin, a red-orange dye; the company's own methylene blue, which received the first German patent for a coal tar-based dye; a highly concentrated form of sulfuric acid made from a process developed by the company in 1888; and ammonia.

Leaders of German dye and other chemical companies began discussing formation of a cartel to ensure their controlling status in the marketplace, and in 1904 BASF, with Bayer and other firms, established the Dreibund dye cartel. During World War I, cartel members produced mustard gas and explosives for the German military.

In 1925 BASF merged with Bayer and several hundred other German chemical companies to create a syndicate known as Interessen-Gemeinschaft Farbenindustrie AG ("community of interests") or IG Farben. By the early 1930s, IG Farben had become aligned with the rising Nazi Party, and during World War II it benefited from the use of slave labor in concentration camps. After the war, the Allies took control of its operations and tried its board of directors for war crimes. IG Farben was dissolved, and BASF (one of five companies formed from its breakup) was reestablished on January 30, 1952.

BRAND ELEMENTS

- Several early BASF logos used two shields that showed a prancing horse and a lion.
- In 1922 and 1955, BASF adopted logos that showed the company name inside a vertical oval.
- Beginning in 1953 and for several periods thereafter, the company used a simple logotype (a logo consisting of words only).

The first BASF logo, in 1873, consisted of two shields showing a prancing horse and a lion. In 1922 the company replaced this with a vertical oval containing the letters "BA" and "SF" respectively above and below a horizontal line that bisected the oval.

A 1952 logo resurrected the shields, but now the figures were solid black, with the letters "BASF" above them and "1865" below, and a circle surrounded these elements. A year later, BASF introduced a simple logotype with the company name in a varsity-style font like those used on college sweatshirts.

The fifth logo in 1955 returned to the vertical oval, but this time the upper-left and lower-right quadrants were in black, with the "B" and "F" (now in a more distinctive serif font) made up of negative space.

In 1967 the company returned to the simple logotype format, now with the letters "BASF" in a non-serif font appearing in negative space against the backdrop of a black horizontal rectangle. Two years later, the rectangle was gone and the company letters themselves appeared in black.

In 2003 the company adopted a logo that rendered its name in thick black non-serif letters, with a small, light-gray square to the left, and to the left of that a larger square outlined in light gray with negative space in its interior. Below ran the slogan "The Chemical Company."

BRAND IDENTITY

- The squares on the BASF logo, according to the company CEO, "signify a key and a lock, with the key being the company's chemical solutions."
- Adding the phrase "The Chemical Company" to its logo in 2003 was a bold branding initiative on the part of BASF.
- At a time when environmentalists and others were condemning chemical manufacturers, BASF sought to emphasize the image of itself as a chemical company.
- BASF set itself apart from leading rivals such as Dow, DuPont, and Bayer, all of whom deemphasized chemicals as an element in their brand identities.

According to BASF, its logo is "at the heart of our corporate design." The squares on the logo "stand for partnership, cooperation and mutual success," though CEO Jurgen Hambrecht told Claudia Deutsch of the *New York Times* that these "signify a key and a lock, with the key being the company's chemical solutions fitting into the keyhole of customer's needs."

Regarding the phrase that appears on the logo, the company has stated that "along with the claim 'The Chemical Company' we underscore our aim and ambition to stand for chemistry like no other company." In fact its use of that tagline, with its emphasis on the word "chemical," marked a bold new branding initiative when it appeared in 2003. "The fact is, we all run for cover when we hear the word," brand consultant Michael Watras told Deutsch. "BASF is bucking a trend, stepping into uncharted waters, and they could easily draw heat from environmentalists and shareholders alike."

Yet the company made this move for several reasons, including the need to take the initiative away from critics of the chemical industry. "Isn't the intelligent thing to do to engage people and tell them of the benefits chemicals bring to their lives, like BASF has done?" asked Simon Robinson in *ICIS Chemical Business*. "Or is it to let others describe your business?" In the words of BASF corporate communications director Christian Schubert, "The best way to turn around negative attitudes is to speak positively about what you do." The branding initiative also set BASF apart from its leading rivals—Dow, DuPont, and Bayer—all of whom sought to deemphasize chemicals as an element in their brand identities.

BRAND STRATEGY

- Rather than market directly to consumers, BASF primarily sells to businesses and other large entities.
- BASF divides its product line into six segments: Chemicals, Plastics, Performance Products, Functional Solutions, Agricultural Solutions, and Oil & Gas.
- To successfully distinguish itself within the chemical industry, BASF has adopted a strategy of emphasizing innovation and service.

BASF does not market primarily to consumers, a fact emphasized by its long-running tagline, "At BASF, we don't make a lot of the products you buy. We make a lot of the products you buy better." Rather, the firm that touts itself as "The Chemical Company" markets primarily to businesses and other large entities who collectively constitute the customer base for its six segments or divisions: Chemicals, Plastics, Performance Products, Functional Solutions, Agricultural Solutions, and Oil & Gas. Five of these each account for approximately 15 percent to 20 percent of annual revenues each, while Agricultural Solutions represents only about 6 percent.

In formulating a successful marketing strategy, BASF has sought to distinguish itself in an industry for which differentiation can be difficult. Bob Lamons, himself a longtime consultant to chemical companies, explained in *Marketing News* why this is so: not only are chemicals required to meet rigid specifications, meaning that "if your product is 'off-spec,' you're out of the game," but "price isn't even a differentiator because buyers will tell you what you need to charge in order to be 'competitive.'"

Therefore, Lamons concluded, "a better way to differentiate is through personal services like R&D support or onsite field services," adding, "This is why becoming known as an innovative, service-oriented company is the ultimate differentiating strategy." Tony Graetzer of Tucker Hampel Stefanides, BASF's advertising firm, told Lamons, "We have conducted numerous customer satisfaction studies over the years, and one finding is consistently clear. Companies are frequently viewed as equal in product quality, but they are never viewed as equal in the quality of their services."

BRAND EQUITY

- BASF showed dramatically positive growth between 2010 and 2012, according to its ratings by Brandirectory and the Centre for Brand Analysis.
- The company ranked first among chemical firms worldwide in 2008.
- According to a survey published in *Fortune* in March 2011, BASF ranked first among the "World's Most Admired Chemicals Companies" for 2010.

Brandirectory estimated the value of the BASF brand in 2012 at US$5.415 billion, and gave it an AA+ rating. This showed positive growth. Two years earlier, Brandirectory gave BASF a rating of AA, and estimated its value at US$3.497 billion. BASF ranked first among chemical firms worldwide in 2008, with sales of US$70.4 billion as compared to US$57.5 billion for second-place Dow.

According to a survey published in *Fortune* in March 2011, BASF ranked first among the "World's Most Admired Chemicals Companies" for 2010. Conducted among executives, directors, and securities analysts, the survey measured companies on the basis of criteria ranging from innovation to financial soundness to social responsibility. Du Pont, Bayer, Dow, and PPG Industries rounded out the top five. A similar survey in the same issue of *Fortune* ranked BASF eighth among the "Most Admired Companies in Europe" for the preceding year.

Newsweek ranked BASF first on its list of "The World's Greenest Big Basic Materials Companies" for 2010, and placed it 74th on its "Green Ranking Global Top 100" for the year. BASF rose rapidly on the Centre for Brand Analysis "Business Superbrands Official Top 500" list, from number 100 in 2010 to number 56 in 2012. The European Brand Institute ranked BASF 37th on its "Top 100 Brand Corporations Worldwide" list for 2012, and 9th on its "Europe's Most Valuable Brand Corporations" list for 2011.

BRAND AWARENESS

- Consumers often erroneously identify BASF as makers of audio- and videotapes, product lines the company sold off in 1997.
- BASF research found that most consumers recognized the brand's tagline about making products better, yet had little idea what BASF actually does.
- For BASF, the purpose of advertising is not to sell products; it is to sell the brand as a whole.
- Because of the stigma associated with chemical companies—as well as its past with IG Farben and the Nazis—it is important for BASF to speak to the public directly.

BASF advertises to the public in print and electronic formats, using the tagline "We don't make a lot of the products you buy. We make a lot of the products you buy better." Many consumers might wonder why BASF bothers to advertise to the public at all, especially since, as their slogan admits, they make few consumer products. Indeed, they are often erroneously identified as a maker of audio- and videotapes, which they were until 1997 when they sold off that product line.

As the *New York Times'* Claudia Deutsch noted in 2005, "In almost every brand awareness test, its 14-year-old North American commercial tagline ... ranks among the most recognized corporate slogans. The recognition is particularly striking considering that BASF has generally run its commercials on cable business news programs, rather than prime-time sitcoms or other expensive venues." Yet as she went on to note, "Its own research shows that while most people associate BASF with 'the folks who make things better,' many draw a blank when asked how, exactly, BASF improves products." Furthermore, research showed that 30 percent of respondents still believed that BASF made tapes.

Regarding the question of why a business-to-business marketer such as BASF would bother advertising in the first place, communications director Christian Schubert explained that "The company needs the acceptance of its stakeholders, i.e., our business-to-business customers, neighbors of its production sites, government officials and opinion makers from all parts of society in order to effectively operate the business." For BASF, the purpose of advertising is not to sell products; rather, it is to sell the brand as a whole.

Given the stigma attached to chemical companies in a culture heavily influenced by environmental activism, it is important for BASF to reach over the heads of the news media and other gatekeepers and speak to the consuming public directly. This is particularly important for BASF because, in addition to concerns over its practices with regard to the environment—an area in which it has actually won high acclaim—it still bears the stigma of its past association with Nazism.

In 2003 the company launched a massive branding campaign that coincided with the adoption of the phrase "The Chemical Company" on its logo. This was, as Schubert wrote in 2010, "a courageous decision at the time—and even today, as a number of chemical companies continue to consider it safer to not be associated with an industry that still has certain reputational challenges." Nor was Schubert alone in praising the company for this: Simon Robinson in *ICIS Chemical Business* wrote that BASF "has shown it is not afraid of what most of the informed civil society, green groups and environmentalists feel about that word." He went on to say that "If the chemical industry continues to fail to engage with the mainstream media and stays in its bunker of reactivity ... then its image will be defined by those who are anti the industry."

BRAND OUTLOOK

- Adopting a legal form for public limited-liability corporations under the laws of the European Union, BASF AG became BASF SE in January 2008.
- According to company leadership, future growth for BASF will focus on Asia rather than on Europe or North America.
- BASF goals for growth by 2020 would involve sustainable products and emerging markets.

The name BASF long ago ceased to be an acronym, and today is simply the brand and company name. The company itself changed from BASF AG—the latter standing for *Aktiengesellschaft*, or corporation—to BASF SE in January 2008. The new designation stands for *Societas Europaea*, sometimes called "Europe Inc.," a legal form for public limited-liability companies under the laws of the European Union.

But much more than formal changes have been underway for BASF since Jürgen Hambrecht took over as chairman and CEO in 2003, initiating rebranding and reorganization efforts whose effects continued to be felt. In 2005 Hambrecht introduced "Vision 2015," a set of guidelines for growth over the next decade. Future growth, he said, would take place primarily in Asia rather than in Europe or North America, and the company would remain focused in three areas: agricultural products and nutrition; chemicals, plastics, and performance products; and oil and gas. According to Hambrecht, this unique product lineup established a strong distinction between BASF and its competitors.

In December 2011 BASF revealed a 2020 sales goal of EUR115 billion (US$153 billion), an increase of 80 percent from 2010. In order to achieve this, the company would implement a strategy of focusing on more sustainable products and expanding within emerging markets. Nigel Davis of *ICIS Chemical Business* noted such acquisitions as Ciba Specialty Chemicals and Cognis as efforts to "strengthen the customized products part of its portfolio."

However, as Navasha Alperowicz wrote in *Chemical Week*, "BASF may have difficulty achieving its objectives, given the current economic slowdown, analysts say." She quoted one such analyst as saying that "We find BASF's strategy statement and new 2020 targets positive but ambitious for the long run, but we believe their short-term challenges overshadow the positive." In August 2012 BASF reported a 15.5 percent decrease in second-quarter profits as compared with the same period a year earlier. Though the brand enjoyed growth in the agricultural solutions and oil and gas segments, its chemical sales volume declined. According to Kurt Bock, who took over as chairman after Hambrecht's retirement in May 2011, this decline reflected uncertainty in the global economy.

FURTHER READING

Alperowicz, Navasha. "BASF Building a Stronger Brand in Chemicals." *Chemical Week* February 2, 2005.

———. "BASF Outlines 2020 Targets Including 80% Sales Rise." *Chemical Week*, December 5, 2011.

BASF. *Marketing and Corporate Communications: Summary of Corporate Design Policy*. August 2004. Accessed February 11, 2013. http://www.basf.com.ar/pdf/directrices_de_identidad_corporativa.pdf.

"BASF SE." *International Directory of Company Histories*. Ed. Jay P. Pederson. Vol. 108. Detroit, MI: St. James Press, 2010.

Davis, Nigel. "BASF Shifts Strategy." *ICIS Chemical Business*, December 12, 2011.

Deutsch, Claudia. "In an Experiment with Its Image, BASF Will Add the Word Chemical to Its Corporate Name." *New York Times*, October 26, 2004.

Lamons, Bob. "Brand Power Moves BASF Past Commodity." *Marketing News*, March 15, 2004.

Robinson, Simon. "Should BASF Fear Labelling?" *ICIS Chemical Business*, May 15, 2006.

Schubert, Christian. "We Create Chemistry: Implementing BASF's Global Brand in Asia/Pacific." International Association of Business Communicators, July 10, 2010. Accessed February 11, 2013. http://www.iabc.com/cwb/archive/2010/0710/Schubert.htm

Young, Ian. "BASF Reports Lower Earnings, Maintains Full-Year Outlook." *Chemical Week*, July 30, 2012.

BAYER

AT A GLANCE

Brand Synopsis: For more than a century the name Bayer has been virtually synonymous with aspirin, with a reputation that implies purity, dependability, and permanence.
Parent Company: Bayer AG
CHEMPARK Leverkusen
Kaiser-Wilhelm-Allee
D-51368 Leverkusen
Germany
http://www.bayer.com
Sector: Materials; Health Care.
Industry Group: Materials; Pharmaceuticals, Biotechnology & Life Sciences.
Performance: *Sales*—EUR36.5 billion (US$47.3 billion) (2011).
Principal Competitors: BASF; Dow Chemical; DuPont; Johnson & Johnson; GlaxoSmithKline; NBTY Inc.; Pfizer Inc.; Procter & Gamble Co.; Merck and Co.; Novartis; Reckitt Benckiser.

BRAND ORIGINS

- Bayer researchers developed and trademarked the first marketable aspirin pain reliever in the late 1800s.
- The company expanded internationally almost immediately, continuing to innovate in medical and commercial chemicals.
- The United States confiscated Bayer's products and trademark during World War I, though German Bayer continued to operate independently.
- By the end of the 20th century Bayer had re-acquired the U.S. Bayer and become an international leader in pharmaceuticals, agricultural chemicals, and high-tech materials.

While best known today for its aspirin, Bayer's history goes back to the 1863 founding of a dyestuffs factory in Barmen, Germany, near the modern city of Wuppertal. Chemical dye experts Friedrich Bayer and Johan Friedrich Weskott established the factory, which became a site of innovations in the newly evolving chemical industry. The company grew quickly, expanding its employee base from 3 in 1863 to 300 in 1881. Because dyes react in specific ways to organic tissue, Bayer dyes began to be used in medical research. Expansion into the creation of pharmaceuticals was a natural next step, and in 1878 the company launched its scientific research laboratory. One of the Bayer laboratory's early discoveries would prove to be the "drug of the century." For centuries folk healers had used herbs such as willow bark and meadowsweet for pain relief, and scientists had tried to isolate the salicylic acid compounds found in such plants. In 1897 a Bayer researcher named Felix Hoffman succeeded in creating acetylsalicylic acid, a modified version of salicylic acid, which eliminated many of the harsh effects of its predecessors. Testing proved the drug not only relieved sore joints and headache pain but reduced fever as well, and Bayer soon put it on the market, where it became one of the most widely used medications of the era.

World War I devastated the German dyestuffs industry, and at the end of the war Bayer, BASF, and Agfa decided to form a syndicate to regain a position in export markets. This community of interests was called I.G. Farbenindustrie AG. Bayer scientists and research facilities invented polyurethanes and researched cures for such diseases as malaria, discovering the therapeutic effects of sulfa drugs. A U.S. subsidiary was established in New York City in 1895 and began marketing aspirin under the Bayer trademark by 1908. When the United States entered World War I, Bayer's U.S. assets were seized and sold to Sterling Drug, Inc., which sold products under the Bayer name and logo in North America until the 1990s.

The German Bayer profited enormously from the Nazi war effort during the 1930s and 1940s, establishing factories using labor from the Maidanek and Auschwitz death camps. At the conclusion of World War II the Allied military government broke up I.G. Farbenindustrie AG into 12 competitive companies, with Bayer being one of them, newly re-established in 1951. This began a period of increased research, including further development of polyurethane chemistry, new crop-protection and fertilization products, fibers such as the polyacrylonitrile fiber Dralon and the thermoplastic Makrolon, new dyestuffs for synthetic fibers, and many other inventions. New products—such as cardiovascular medicines, dermal antifungals, and broad-spectrum antibiotics—emerged from Bayer's pharmaceutical laboratories and entered the market. These products paved the way for Bayer's continued expansion in its home market of Europe as well as in the United States, where, in spite of having lost many of its patents following World War I, it introduced more than 6,000 new products.

In 1994 the German Bayer A.G. bought back its name from Sterling Drug, by then a division of Eastman Kodak. Acquisitions in the United States, Canada, and Japan continued to drive Bayer's growth through the end of the 20th century. In the 2000s Bayer continued to grow and to introduce new drug therapies as well as innovations in the area of crop science. Today Bayer employs almost 112,000 workers, with 32 percent of them in Germany, where the company is headquartered. The company maintains operations in all major regions of the world. Its divisions include HealthCare, MaterialScience, and CropScience. It markets more than 20 brands in the HealthCare division along with other major brands in MaterialScience and CropScience.

BRAND ELEMENTS

- The word "aspirin" was once a Bayer trademark but is now a generic name.
- The Bayer cross-in-circle logo appears on a wide variety of the company's products.
- The "Science for a Better Life" slogan allows Bayer to tie together its disparate divisions under the rubric of modernity and progress.

Bayer created the brand name "Aspirin" for its new analgesic tablet. Bayer tied the name to its traditional-medicine roots by basing it on spirea, one of the plants used to treat pain, and modernized it by adding –in, a common medicinal suffix of the day. During World Wars I and II Allied nations invalidated German patents and trademarks, opening the door for other manufacturers to call their products aspirin. However, Bayer Aspirin has remained one of the most recognizable pharmaceutical brand names.

In 1904 Bayer registered its trademark in Germany, a cross formed by the word "Bayer" written vertically and horizontally, sharing the letter "Y" and encircled by the company name, Farbenfabriken vorm. Friedr. Bayer & Co. Elberfeld. After the 1925 merger that created I.G. Farbenindustrie, the name was removed and replaced with a simple circle. A pleasingly symmetrical design with its roots in ancient symbology, the cross-in-circle logo has remained the recognizable indicator of Bayer products from aspirin to agricultural chemicals. The enormous version of the logo that illuminates Bayer's headquarters in Leverkusen, Germany, is one of the largest illuminated signs in the world. Some conflicts arose over use of the cross-in-circle trademark between the U.S. Bayer, owned by Sterling Drug, and German Bayer, such as a 1969 case dealing with the marketing of agricultural chemicals in the Philippines.

In the early 2000s Bayer introduced its slogan "Science for a Better Life," an optimistic phrase that encompasses all of the company's divisions, promising increased health through its medications, improved global food supply through its agricultural fertilizers and pest control products, and advanced building methods and reduced energy consumption through its high-tech materials.

BRAND IDENTITY

- Bayer distinguishes itself from other aspirin products through its focus on brand superiority and purity.
- Bayer has acquired subsidiaries that fit in with its corporate image of being professional yet accessible.
- The company has shifted its corporate image to reflect modern values of sustainability and innovation.

The Bayer logo appears on numerous popular over-the-counter (OTC) medications and lawn and garden products. Through decades of carefully targeted advertising, Bayer has created a corporate image of care, tradition, purity, and strength that begins with its aspirin and extends to its other products, particularly in the health care line. While all brands of aspirin contain similar ingredients, Bayer's emphasis on purity works to persuade consumers that they will not only have better results themselves from choosing Bayer products, but they will be better parents if they give Bayer products to their children. Bayer thus confronts the lower prices of generic aspirin with its distinguished corporate identity of experience and its product image of unadulterated power. Bayer's acquisition of Miles Laboratories in 1978 associated the company with additional widely recognized and valued pharmaceutical products such as Flintstones children's vitamins and Alka-Seltzer antacid, as the company hoped to increase its association in the public mind with effective and accessible health care products.

In its other divisions as well, Bayer works to promote public perception of the company as a benevolent innovator whose discoveries will benefit people around the globe. In 2009 the company released its new corporate image film *Elements of Fascination,* which juxtaposes dramatic nature photography, images of children around the world, and scenes of Bayer scientists at work to project a brand identity of playful creativity, world unity, and serious scientific achievement. Bayer hopes to create a public image in tune with a global atmosphere of increasing interest in environmental concerns and sustainable agriculture and manufacturing techniques.

BRAND STRATEGY

- Bayer has worked to create a benign and evolving public image.
- Regaining control over the Bayer brand in the United States was an important step in developing the brand worldwide.
- Bayer has shifted its demographic focus to keep products vital and relevant.
- Bayer has managed a number of competing products by developing distinct sub-brand images.

A powerful brand since the beginning of the 20th century, Bayer has refocused its corporate policies and its public image to reflect the changing values of society. From fairly right-wing roots in post-World War I Germany and active participation in Hitler's Third Reich, the company has transformed its image into one of progressive innovation and compassionate professionalism. Its internal policies earned it a score of 85 out of 100 on the Human Rights Campaign Corporate Equality Index in 2011.

This kindly corporate image has been carefully orchestrated through decades of advertising campaigns. Early Bayer taglines, such as "Best aspirin the world has ever known" in the 1950s and "Pure aspirin, not just part aspirin" in the 1960s, emphasized the unique nature of Bayer aspirin and the wholehearted recommendations of doctors. During the 1980s and 1990s Bayer sidestepped economic recession by streamlining corporate operations and divesting itself of unprofitable subsidiaries. At the same time, the company continued to grow, re-acquiring the right to its brand name and products in the United States and with it all of Sterling Drug's OTC line, boosting its public recognition with such popular and familiar products as Midol pain relievers and NeoSynephrine nasal decongestant.

Bayer has also strategized to maintain brand visibility for changing demographics. As other popular analgesics began to impinge on Bayer Aspirin's market share during the 1980s, Bayer refocused its advertising to highlight the heart benefits of aspirin for older adults. Similarly during the first decade of the 21st century the company reached out to younger audiences by engaging a popular rock star as spokesperson for its Contour glucose meter, thereby imparting an image of hip vitality to an otherwise clinical product.

Though its diverse pharmaceutical holdings have meant that Bayer necessarily produces some medications that compete with other Bayer products, the company has managed this conflict in its health care division by chiefly stressing the Bayer name on its aspirin. For example, while the Bayer logo is featured prominently on its OTC anti-inflammatory drug Aleve, advertisements for the product do not highlight it as a member of the Bayer family but instead build brand recognition for the Aleve name.

BRAND EQUITY

- Bayer's policy of product diversification protects the company from fluctuations in the consumer market.
- Through intensive research and development, Bayer builds brand equity by innovation.
- Through expansion into foreign markets, Bayer is able to maximize brand equity and absorb losses.

Bayer has built brand equity through constant diversification and a focus on research and development. A diverse portfolio of products has given the brand economic stability and flexibility. The 2012 Brand Finance list of the world's top brands valued Bayer's brand at US$3.4 billion and ranked it at 323 globally. A 2011 Portland Investment counsel report commended the company's diversification, stating that Bayer's leading five medications account for only 43 percent of the company's earnings in pharmaceuticals, while other products are responsible for 73 percent of revenue in the larger HealthCare division. The introduction of new products, such as the anticoagulant Xarleto in 2012, is expected to boost the profitability of the Bayer brand. The company hoped to improve its aspirin market share by redefining its brand with such products as its new Advanced Aspirin for pain packaged in bright purple.

In the CropScience division as well, innovation led to the introduction of several new products in 2012, with the expectation of more than a billion dollars in potential sales. However, Bayer executives acknowledged in 2011 that the performance of the MaterialScience division had been disappointing, due in large part to the expense of raw materials and the cost of building and maintaining foreign operations.

While political debate over health care and medical insurance coverage led to some instability in the United States, Bayer's European markets were strong, and Bayer's brand equity in such emerging nations as Russia and China had grown. The Bayer brand has been consistently profitable in European and Asian markets, and *Market Share Reporter* listed the company among the top pesticide makers worldwide and the world's most valuable chemical companies in 2011.

BRAND AWARENESS

- Bayer's aspirin and many of its OTC medications have longevity and "top-of-mind" recognition.
- Bayer has gained strong brand recognition for many of its pharmaceuticals through creative marketing approaches.
- Bayer has used professional conferences and similar venues to raise awareness of its technical products.
- Some of Bayer's health care products have generated negative brand awareness because of their severe side effects.

Bayer's original aspirin product has been familiar for more than a century to consumers internationally, many of whom closely identify the drug with the Bayer brand. Other popular OTC medications such as Aleve, Midol, Alka-Seltzer, and One-a-Day may not be as instantly identified as Bayer products (though all bear the distinctive Bayer logo), but they have immediate brand recognition of their own, cultivated through advertising slogans and promotions. Bayer pharmaceutical products have also entered the public consciousness through news reports. The antibiotic Cipro, for example, received publicity during the early 2000s when an anthrax scare swept the United States. Creative advertising campaigns, such as one for the Contour glucose meter, which promoted juvenile diabetes awareness using pop singer Nick Jonas and fashionable Bayer "dog tags," have also benefited Bayer's brand awareness.

Bayer lawn and garden products do bear the company name and logo and, while not marketed as aggressively as the health care brands, achieve widespread recognition through their placement in popular chain stores such as Lowe's and The Home Depot. Bayer's "Science for a Better Life" campaign aimed to create increased awareness of innovations in agriculture and building. Recognition of the Bayer brand in agricultural chemicals and high-tech building materials is generally limited to professionals in those fields, promoted by such outreach programs as the Green World project in Kenya. Bayer boosts its brand awareness by maximizing its presence at professional conferences such as the 2012 PestWorld conference in Boston, where the company launched its new Harmonix insect spray. Bayer increased consumer awareness of its innovative building materials when it renovated its corporate offices in Robinson Township, Pennsylvania, using the project to showcase its environmentally safe and sustainable products.

Some consumer awareness of the Bayer brand has been negative. For example, the cholesterol medication Baycol, introduced in the late 1990s, and the birth control pill Yaz, released in 2006, both had severe side effects, leading to thousands of lawsuits (and a recall of Baycol) and damaging Bayer's reputation.

BRAND OUTLOOK

- Bayer ranked number two globally in OTC medications and high in other medical markets in 2012.
- The company was at the top of the worldwide crop protection market.
- Bayer was well positioned for growth in the 2010s.

In the 21st century Bayer AG has performed well in the markets in which it competes. According to company statistics, Bayer ranked number two globally in the OTC market; in the medical care business it had the number one fluid injection system and was number four in blood glucose monitors. It ranked fourth in the animal health business. It was number one globally in insecticide and seed treatment sales and second in fungicides. Bayer outperformed the market during the first decade of the 21st century in the OTC and consumer care markets. Sales of Bayer Aspirin, more than 100 years old, grew 10 percent in 2011.

Bayer's pipelines in the health care business and the crop science business were well stocked, allowing the company to continue to grow. It spent EUR3 billion (US$3.83 billion) in overall research and development in 2012. The largest portion of this, EUR2 billion (US$2.63 billion), went to HealthCare, while CropScience received EUR800 million (US$1.05 billion) and MaterialScience spent approximately EUR200 million (US$263 million).

These research-and-development expenditures defined the company's sales targets through 2014. Sales of Bayer HealthCare and Bayer CropScience were expected to reach EUR20 billion (US$26.3 billion) and EUR8 billion (US$1.05 trillion), respectively.

Bayer AG appears to be well positioned to take advantage of current environmental trends, including world population growth, the aging of populations in many countries, and the resulting increases in the need for food and health care. Its diversified portfolio lowers risk and allows for growth.

FURTHER READING

Alperowicz, Natasha. "Bayer Details R&D Spending, Names Innovation Projects." *Chemical Week,* November 19, 2012. *Business Insights: Global.* Accessed February 27, 2013. http://bi.galegroup.com/global/article/GALE%7CA310866529/8a8c92240e99dc1c5082c31bfde47e98?u=itsbtrial.

Alperowicz, Natasha. "Bayer Says BMS Is Core for Now, Eyes Higher Pharma Rank." *Chemical Week,*March 7, 2011. *Business Insights: Global.* Accessed February 27, 2013. http://bi.galegroup.com/global/article/GALE%7CA252191388/e09ea40d5ac56f1894b8fb7ec91fc34c?u=itsbtrial.

"Bayer at JPMorgan Global Healthcare Conference." CQ Transcriptions, LLC, 2012. Accessed February 27, 2013.

"Bayer Sets Sales Targets Through 2014." *Chemical Week,* March 26, 2012. Accessed February 27, 2013. http://bi.galegroup.com/global/article/GALE%7CA285533414/5bfb68ec35dd7b5de0744ffa105df1a3?u=itsbtrial.

"Bayer USA Foundation Awards $500,000 Grant to SySTEMic Innovations." *Agri Marketing* 49.7 (2011): 11. *General OneFile.* Accessed February 27, 2013. http://go.galegroup.com/ps/i.do?id=GALE%7CA270532526&v=2.1&u=itsbtrial&it=r&p=ITOF&sw=w.

Breitstein, Joanna. "Cipro Nation." *Pharmaceutical Executive,* December 1, 2001. Accessed February 27, 2013. http://www.pharmexec.com/pharmexec/article/articleDetail.jsp?id=2755.

Doyle, Kerry. "The Aleve 'Arthritis Pain Relief' Success Story: Taking a Different Approach." Resonant Communications, 2009. Accessed February 27, 2013. http://www.kerrydoyle.com/samples/Aleve-Success_Story-Case_Study.pdf.

Furberg, Curt D., and Bertram Pitt. "Withdrawal of Cerivastatin from the World Market." *Current Controlled Trials in Cardiovascular Medicine* 2.5 (2001). *National Library of Medicine.* Accessed February 27, 2013. http://www.ncbi.nlm.nih.gov/pmc/articles/PMC59524/.

Hein, Kenneth. "Bayer Sued over Cancer Claims." *AdWeek,* October 1, 2009. *General OneFile.* Accessed February 27, 2013. http://go.galegroup.com/ps/i.do?id=GALE%7CA209403979&v=2.1&u=itsbtrial&it=r&p=ITOF&sw=w.

Moore, Mark. "Bayer CropScience: Past, Present, Future." *Farm Industry News.* February 1, 2013. *General OneFile.* Accessed February 27, 2013. http://go.galegroup.com/ps/i.do?id=GALE%7CA317233922&v=2.1&u=itsbtrial&it=r&p=ITOF&sw=w.

Portland Investment Counsel, Inc. "Bayer AG." 2011. Accessed February 27, 2013. http://www.portlandinvestmentcounsel.com/PDFs/ENG/company_briefs/Bayer%20-%20June11.pdf.

Ritchie, Alanna. "Amid Mounting Yaz/Yasmin Lawsuits, Bayer Seeks to Diversify." *DrugWatch,* October 31, 2012. Accessed February 27, 2013. http://www.drugwatch.com/2012/10/31/amid-mounting-yazyasmin-lawsuits-bayer-seeks-to-diversify/.

Wehrspann, Jodie. "Reformulating Bayer." *Farm Industry News,* December 1, 2007. *General OneFile.* Accessed February 27, 2013. http://go.galegroup.com/ps/i.do?id=GALE%7CA171874906&v=2.1&u=itsbtrial&it=r&p=ITOF&sw=w.

BBC

AT A GLANCE

Brand Synopsis: The BBC enjoys an international reputation for quality radio, television, and digital broadcasting and is a symbol of the United Kingdom around the world.
Parent Company: British Broadcasting Corporation
BBC Broadcasting House, Portland Place
London W1A 1AA
United Kingdom
http://www.bbc.co.uk
Sector: Consumer Discretionary
Industry Group: Media
Performance: *Market share*—96 percent of the British population used the BBC's radio, television, or online services at least once per week (2011–12). *Sales*—£5.1 billion (US$6.28 billion) (2012).
Principal Competitors: ITV plc; British Sky Broadcasting Group plc; Virgin Media Inc.

BRAND ORIGINS

- The BBC began as a private corporation in 1922, when its first daily radio service began airing in London.
- In 1927 the BBC became a public corporation established under a Royal Charter.
- By the late 1920s, the BBC had expanded internationally, transmitting experimental radio broadcasts to the Americas and launching its foreign-language services.
- In 1954 the British government passed legislation that broke the BBC's monopoly on broadcast television and introduced the country's first commercial network.
- In the early 21st century, despite large budget cuts and consolidation, the BBC remains one of the world's largest and most recognized broadcasters.

The history of the British Broadcasting Corporation (BBC) dates to 1922, when the company began its first daily radio service in London, broadcasting primarily news along with several music, drama, and talk radio programs. Although originally founded as a private corporation, the BBC in 1927 became a public corporation established under a Royal Charter, through which the company was granted a monopoly on broadcasting in the United Kingdom. In the 1930s the BBC expanded beyond radio and began to experiment with television broadcasts.

The BBC's history as an international broadcaster extends far back into the 20th century as well. By 1923 the company was transmitting experimental radio broadcasts to the Americas, and in 1938 the BBC began broadcasting in Arabic, Portuguese, and Spanish. During World War II, BBC Radio provided foreign-language services to occupied countries, English-language services to British troops, and news and other programming to British citizens at home. The war temporarily halted the BBC's fledgling television services, although television operations continued at the broadcaster's main TV transmitting center, Alexandra Palace, where transmitters helped jam the navigational systems of German planes flying over London. The BBC's television operations resumed in 1946, and in 1948 the company undertook its most technically advanced broadcast yet, airing 68.5 hours of live coverage of the Summer Olympics.

In 1953 the BBC broadcast the coronation of Queen Elizabeth II. The broadcast, watched by more than 20 million people across Europe, was a significant moment in the history of television and was credited with boosting television sales worldwide. In 1954 the British government passed legislation that broke the BBC's monopoly on broadcast television and created the Independent Television Authority (ITA), thereby introducing commercial networks to the United Kingdom for the first time. Despite the loss of its monopoly, the BBC continued on as a semiautonomous public service broadcaster, a status it has maintained in the 21st century.

In 1964 the BBC launched a second television channel, BBC Two, which in 1967 became the first full-color TV service in Europe. BBC One, in comparison, did not begin broadcasting in color until 1969. Numerous television channels, including BBC News and BBC Kids, were added throughout the 20th century, and the BBC's list of radio stations grew extensively as well. In the 1980s, deregulation of the United Kingdom's television and radio markets brought increased competition from cable television, while the 1990s and early 21st century brought new competitors in the form of satellite television providers and digital television services.

In the first decade of the 21st century, the BBC reorganized some of its television and radio channels and launched several new ones, including its first high-definition channel, BBC HD, in 2006. The following year, the company announced plans to make large cuts and consolidations to reduce the size of the company as a whole. Since its founding, the BBC's services in the United Kingdom have been funded by an annual television license fee charged to all British households and organizations that use equipment to receive live television broadcasts. In 2010 it was announced that the BBC's TV license fee would be frozen at its existing rate until 2017, while the cost of running the BBC World Service and BBC Monitoring would be passed from the UK Foreign and Commonwealth Office to the BBC. In 2011 partially in response to those developments, the BBC announced it would be cutting 20 percent of its budget over the following five years, precipitating drastic changes in programming and the loss of an estimated 2,000 jobs.

Despite its recent financial difficulties, the BBC remains one of the most recognized broadcasters in the world, with its radio, television, Internet, and mobile outlets providing news to the United Kingdom and other countries daily. In 2010 the BBC was the largest broadcaster in the world in terms of number of employees.

BRAND ELEMENTS

- The "BBC Blocks" logo, used in its current iteration since 1997, features three squares, each square containing one of the letters in "BBC."
- Many of the BBC's channels and stations use a version of the BBC Blocks logo.
- A version of the BBC Blocks logo is also used for BBC America, as well as programs aired by the American Public Broadcasting Service (PBS).
- The "Greenwich Time Signal," a series of six beeps known as "the pips," has been aired each hour on BBC Radio since 1924.

The official BBC logo consists of three squares (or blocks), each square containing one of the letters in "BBC." All three letters are capitalized and appear in a simple sans-serif typeface. Often referred to as the "BBC Blocks" logo, this logo is also used by many of the various BBC channels and stations, with the specific channel or station designation added above, below, or next to the three blocks. The colors of the blocks and background vary for these logos, although the letters "BBC" always take on the color of the background. For example, the logo for BBC News features the word "News" in white under the three blocks, also in white, while the background and "BBC" are in red. Although the current iteration of the BBC Blocks logo was introduced in 1997, versions of it have been in use since the 1950s.

The BBC's branding is consistent across the Atlantic, as BBC America also uses the BBC Blocks logo, with the word "America" appearing beneath the three squares. This logo appears with BBC programs broadcast by the American Public Broadcasting Service (PBS). BBC Blocks logos are also used by BBC Audiobooks America and by BBC America Shop, a website offering BBC programs, BBC audio recordings, and British-themed items.

The "Greenwich Time Signal" is a sound irrevocably linked with the BBC. This sound features a series of six beeps, known as "the pips," broadcast at one-second intervals, with the sixth beep longer than the rest. Heard at the top of the hour on BBC Radio programs since 1924, this sound originally marked Greenwich Mean Time but now indicates Coordinated Universal Time and can be used to synchronize timepieces.

BRAND IDENTITY

- Thanks to its close ties to the United Kingdom's development in the 20th century, the BBC is widely considered a quintessential English institution.
- London's BBC Broadcasting House features a statue of the Shakespearean character Ariel, a symbol of the BBC's ties to English life and culture.

- Recently, the BBC has been challenged to meet new marketplace demands while maintaining its identity as an established and trustworthy provider of news and entertainment.

Based in London, the BBC is widely considered an English institution and a vital force in the history of the country. For many people, the BBC *is* England. Kim Hjelmgaard, writing in the *Wall Street Journal*, noted that "the BBC is venerated at home and away for the exacting and disciplined way it explains Britain to itself, and to the world. And the world to Britain."

The BBC has emphasized its connection to its home in different ways. Its head office, BBC Broadcasting House, epitomizes these ties. Located in the capital city of London and built in 1932, the building has a long broadcasting history. It also has ties to British history—it has hosted monarchs and it experienced World War II-related bombing damage. Still in use in the 21st century, the structure houses television, radio, online, and news services. Outside, a statue of Ariel, from William Shakespeare's *The Tempest*, adorns the building. Known for his enchanting songs, Ariel is a fitting symbol for a broadcasting company that seeks to create compelling programming.

Like other established media companies, the BBC has had to adjust to the proliferation of news and entertainment outlets brought about by the deregulation of Britain's radio and television markets and the introduction of cable, satellite, and Internet media services. The challenge since the late 20th century has been for the brand to broaden its appeal through increases in the diversity of its own offerings, launching new channels and embracing new technologies, while at the same time maintaining its status as a uniquely English brand and the gold standard of the media industry. It has tuned its international programming, available through such networks as BBC America and services like the BBC World Service, to regional audiences while also carefully aligning the content with the BBC brand through the characteristic attention to quality, objectivity (in news reporting), and the projection generally of an air of impartiality and trustworthiness—valuable assets in the age of globalization. The *BBC Online* website, initially launched in the mid-1990s, has become increasingly important to the brand as a means of reaching ever wider audiences and reinforcing the BBC's identity as a dominant and reliable source of information and high-quality entertainment. Changes to the BBC logo and other emblems have similarly focused on efforts to update the brand's image, conveying a sense of inclusiveness and innovation, without losing sight of its historical preeminence in the media industry and its close connections to the history of the United Kingdom.

In the early 21st century, the BBC has faced continuing budget cuts and aggressive efforts to shrink and streamline the company. In part, these changes were intended to level the playing field of commercial broadcasting in the United Kingdom. The BBC, however, has also pointed to the changes as a new opportunity to refocus the brand and improve the services it offers.

BRAND STRATEGY

- In the 21st century, the BBC has used its website to expand its presence, offering news in more than 20 languages.
- International ventures that extend the BBC name include BBC America, BBC Canada, and the BBC World Service.
- The BBC has exploited new mobile technologies to make its programming available to people who may lack access to television or Internet services.
- Internet users can listen to BBC Radio and watch BBC television programs.

Like many companies, the BBC has used the Internet to expand its presence in the 21st century. The homepage of its corporate website includes a wealth of news in the realms of business, technology, health, sports, and more, reflecting the BBC's history as an important source for the latest news worldwide. The website's homepage also points to the broadcaster's multicultural and international interests, with links to international news in more than 20 languages.

These multicultural websites join other the BBC's other international ventures, such as the television networks BBC America and BBC Canada, which extend the BBC name and programming across the Atlantic. The BBC also operates the BBC World Service, an international radio network that broadcasts all over the world. Such international ventures, some of them in place since the days of the British Empire, reinforce the global presence of the brand via television and radio channels operating under divisions and subsidiaries of the BBC. Thus, whether at home or abroad, the BBC brand represents world-class broadcasting and programming.

The BBC has used technology to advance its brand as well. Internet users can listen to BBC Radio programs, watch BBC television programs (with a license), or watch programs on the website Hulu under the BBC America banner. People using mobile devices can also download BBC applications (apps) to access news or watch BBC programming. These developments have allowed the BBC to transmit its content and promote its name across several media platforms to people around the world.

BRAND EQUITY

- The BBC's various media offerings reach the entire United Kingdom and many other countries, giving it a significant market share among broadcasters.

- The BBC's annual report for 2011–12 noted that the broadcaster reached 96 percent of the British population weekly with its television, radio, or online programming.
- In 2012 Brand Finance named the BBC the 29th most valuable UK brand on its UK Top 50 list.

The BBC's radio and television programming reaches the entire United Kingdom and numerous other countries around the world. Writing for "MarketWatch" in the *Wall Street Journal*, Kim Hjelmgaard noted that "there are few media companies that can boast such enviable market share" as the BBC.

The BBC's annual report for 2011–12 stated that 96 percent of the British population used the BBC's radio, television, or online services at least once per week. The report also stated that 78.8 percent of the British population viewed the BBC One television station at least once per week, while 54.3 percent viewed BBC Two weekly. The report went on to note that 22.3 percent of British radio listeners tuned in to BBC Radio One weekly and that 27.4 percent listened to BBC Radio Two at least once per week. The report also mentioned the BBC's popularity with British Internet users, with 42.5 percent visiting BBC Online at least once weekly.

Its large market share has helped the BBC become a prominent British and international brand. Brand Finance named the BBC the 273rd best brand in the world on its Global 500 list in 2012, with a brand value of US$3.9 billion. Another 2012 Brand Finance list, the UK Top 50, named the BBC the 29th most valuable brand in the United Kingdom.

BRAND AWARENESS

- The BBC enjoys top-of-mind awareness among consumers in the United Kingdom and is known worldwide for the high quality of its news reporting.
- BBC television programs have won recognition in the United Kingdom and the United States, demonstrating the broadcaster's international reputation and appeal.
- In the United Kingdom, the BBC is often referred to as "Auntie" or "the Beeb," reflecting the broadcaster's familiar and historical presence in British lives.

Writing on the digital news website Newsonomics, Ken Doctor compared the BBC brand to the American newspaper the *New York Times*. He described them as "two august, truly global news institutions," adding that the two brands "are immensely powerful, sometimes comically balkanized in their decision-making, too often lumbering in execution, and yet both have made major strides in transitioning their power and work to the digital age."

Besides having top-of-mind awareness in the United Kingdom due to its ubiquitous presence in the country, the BBC enjoys a reputation for high standards and objectivity in its news reporting. The broadcaster has received substantial critical praise throughout its history. The 2012 MediaGuardian Edinburgh International Television Festival granted the BBC several awards, including terrestrial channel of the year for BBC Two, digital channel of the year for BBC Four, and cross-platform innovation of the year for the BBC iPlayer digital application (app).

The BBC has also won accolades for its television dramas and comedies. The 2012 MediaGuardian Edinburgh International Television Festival named the BBC television series *Sherlock* the terrestrial program of the year, while *Sherlock* was also nominated for five Emmy Awards, the American awards honoring television excellence. Several other BBC television shows have been nominated for awards in the United States in recent years, including BBC Two's situation comedy *The Office*, which in 2004 became the first British comedy to win a Golden Globe for best television series in the musical or comedy category. These honors and nominations demonstrate the BBC's international reputation for quality programming.

The BBC is also known by some famous nicknames, including "Auntie Beeb" or "the Beeb." These names illustrate its role in English society as an institution with age and authority but one that is also familiar and regarded with affection by younger generations. The "Auntie Beeb" nickname was popularized by Kenny Everett, a comedian, disc jockey, and television presenter who appeared on a number of television and radio programs broadcast by the BBC. This nickname acknowledged the broadcaster's prominent and familiar role in English life.

BRAND OUTLOOK

- In 2011 the BBC announced that it would cut 20 percent of its budget over the following five years.
- In 2012 allegations of sexual abuse against deceased BBC television presenter Jimmy Savile posed a potential threat to the company's reputation.
- In 2011 the BBC introduced the BBC iPlayer mobile application, which the company hopes will attract more international viewers.

In 2010 the BBC's television license fee was frozen at its existing rate until 2017. At the same time, responsibility for funding the BBC World Service and BBC Monitoring, both of which had been previously funded by the UK Foreign and Commonwealth Office, was transferred to the BBC. Due in part to the license fee freeze and the new financial obligations, the BBC announced in 2011 that it would be cutting 20 percent of its budget over the following five years and that these cuts would involve a drastic change in programming and the loss of an estimated 2,000 jobs. In the BBC's financial statements for 2011–12, the broadcaster listed one of its goals as the delivery of "£700 million [US$861.37 million] of savings to enable the BBC to live within its means following the license fee settlement in 2010."

In 2012 the BBC suffered a blow to its reputation for high standards and accountability when multiple allegations of child sexual abuse were made against BBC presenter and disc jockey Jimmy Savile, who had died the previous year. Throughout Savile's career at the BBC, he had worked primarily with children and teenagers, and several of his accusers alleged that the abuse had taken place on BBC premises. In 2011 the BBC television program *Newsnight* produced a story about the abuse allegations but did not broadcast it, leading to questions about whether the shelving of the episode was part of a larger cover-up. Several BBC employees resigned as a result. It was unclear how the scandal would affect the BBC's long-term reputation.

In more positive recent developments, the BBC has begun harnessing new technologies. In 2011 it introduced a mobile application (app) called the BBC iPlayer, designed to introduce BBC content to viewers in European countries. Users of the app could watch limited BBC programming free of charge or subscribe to a special plan to access additional content.

Millions of British and international viewers turned to the BBC to watch the 2012 Summer Olympics in London. The BBC estimated that 55 million international viewers watched the games at BBC Sport online, while more than 51 million British viewers watched the games on the BBC's television channels and on its Red Button digital television platform. The broadcaster also said that millions of people watched the games on their mobile devices using the BBC's digital services, tuning in to what the company called the "first truly mobile games."

FURTHER READING

BBC. "BBC Sport Breaks Online Records with First Truly Digital Olympics." Accessed November 29, 2012. http://www.bbc.co.uk/mediacentre/latestnews/2012/sport-online-figures.html.

———. "2011/12 BBC Annual Reports and Accounts." Accessed November 29, 2012. http://www.bbc.co.uk/annualreport/2012/.

"BBC Set to Cut 2,000 jobs by 2017." *BBC News*, October 6, 2011.

Brand Finance. "Global 500 2012." *Brandirectory*. Accessed November 26, 2012. http://brandirectory.com/league_tables/table/global-500-2012.

———. "UK Top 50 2012." *Brandirectory*. Accessed November 26, 2012. http://brandirectory.com/league_tables/table/uk-top-50-2012.

"British Broadcasting Corporation Ltd." *International Directory of Company Histories*. Ed. Jay P. Pederson. Vol. 89. Detroit, MI: St. James Press, 2008.

Chignell, Hugh. "The BBC and National Identity in Britain, 1922-53." *Reviews in History*, May 2011. Accessed November 28, 2012. http://www.history.ac.uk/reviews/review/1079.

Doctor, Ken. "BBC's Mark Thompson Jumps out of the Frying Pan and into the New York Times." *Newsonomics*, August 14, 2012.

Hjelmgaard, Kim. "BBC's News Grip, Lauded but Also Absolute." *Wall Street Journal*, August 22, 2011.

Lloyd, Paul Robert. "Graphic Design on UK Terrestrial Television & the Effects of Multi-Channel Growth." Paulrobertlloyd.com, June 2012. Accessed November 27, 2012. http://paulrobertlloyd.com/articles/dissertation/branding_itv_and_bbc/.

BIORÉ

AT A GLANCE

Brand Synopsis: Bioré is an innovative personal care brand, primarily for women, that creates exciting new products such as the Pore Perfect Deep Cleansing Strips.
Parent Company: Kao Group
14-10, Nihonbashi Kayabacho 1-chrome
Chuo-ku, Tokyo 103-8210
Japan
http://www.kao.com/
Sector: Consumer Staples
Industry Group: Household & Personal Products
Performance: *Market share*—3.18 percent among U.S. facial cleanser brands (2011). *Sales*—US$20.7 million (2012).
Principal Competitors: Aveeno; Cetaphil; Clean & Clear; Dove; Garnier; L'Oreal; Neutrogena; Olay; Pond's

BRAND ORIGINS

- Bioré was launched in Japan in 1980 by what became known as the Kao Group.
- Bioré debuted in the United States in 1997 with its Bioré Pore Perfect Deep Cleansing Strips.
- By 2012 Bioré was the number-seven facial cleanser brand in the United States.

Bioré was launched in 1980 as a brand of what is now the Kao Group, a Japan-based company. Kao had been founded in 1887 as Nagase Shoten by Tomiro Nagase. This company sold Western-style sundry goods and introduced its first product, Kao Sekken (a quality toiletry soap), in 1890. This marked the beginning of the toiletries market in Japan. Over the years, Kao introduced other personal and home-care products, including detergents, baby care, cosmetics, and beauty care, as well as healthy foods.

Bioré's first product, Bioré Facial Foam, was a gentle, foaming facial cleanser. At the time, most facial soaps were sold in bar form. Bioré Facial Foam was different in that it was a neutral cleanser that was mild for the skin. The facial wash was targeted at women of all ages in Japan. Bioré and its product soon became available throughout Asia. Four years later, Bioré introduced its Bioré U body wash, its first entry into the body-wash market, and it soon became a best-seller in Japan.

In the late 1990s Bioré moved from Asian into North American and European markets. Kao had acquired the American personal care company, the Andrew Jergens Company, in 1988, and through this subsidiary entered the U.S. market in 1997 with several products. In addition to a hydrating moisturizer and two cleansers (one foaming and one gel), Bioré revolutionized skin care when it introduced Bioré Pore Perfect Deep Cleansing Strips. These strips were placed on the nose to remove dirt and grime from pores, using a special technology called C-Bond. With the tagline "Absolutely Clean," the strips had a target audience of 18- to 34-year-old women.

The award-winning Pore Strips became the number-one-selling skin care product in the United States by the end of 1997, with other Bioré products gaining sales because of the brand momentum created by the strips. In 1997 Bioré became the overall number-five skin-care brand in the United States, while Bioré held 85 percent of the Japanese market for this category. Building on the success of the strip, Bioré introduced the gentler Pore Perfect Face Strip to be used on other parts of the face. By February 1998 U.S. strip sales had reached US$55 million.

Bioré continued to introduce more groundbreaking products over the next few years. In 1998 three new products hit the market: a Mild Daily Cleansing Scrub, Pore Perfect Toner, and, most notably, a Self-Heating Mask. Designed for oily skin, the mask was packaged in individual-use packets and grew warm when applied to the skin, changing color when it was time to be washed off. The Self-Heating Mask was a success, selling at least US$13 million-worth in the United States alone in its first year. By 1998 Bioré was the number-three skin-care brand in the United States, with sales of US$150 million. Men comprised only 20 percent of Bioré users, so Bioré targeted its advertising efforts on women, for example sponsoring the first years of the female-oriented concert tour The Lilith Fair.

Bioré remained an industry leader in 1999 by debuting a number of popular new products, including Pore Perfect Ultra Strip (an extra-strength strip for the nose), Fine Line Gel Patches (an anti-wrinkle patch for the eye area), and Facial Cleansing Cloths (premoistened cloths to clean the face). Bioré again was ahead of the curve with its Facial Cleansing Cloths, targeted at young women who, studies showed, did not have time to wash their faces before going to bed. Also in 1999, Bioré introduced more self-heating products, including the Self-Heating Moisture Mask and Warming Deep Pore Cleanser for daily use. By 1999 Bioré had become a market leader for skincare in the United States.

During the first decade of the 21st century Bioré remained an industry leader in introducing new products. In 2000 it came out with Blemish Fighting Cleanser, which was an extension of Bioré Foaming Cleanser, and Blemish Bomb, designed to fight pimples and prevent acne breakouts with salicylic acid. In 2001 it rolled out Bioré Blemish Double Agent, a gel that helped protect pimples healing under makeup and reduce redness. Because of the success of Bioré, Kao was the number-one household-products maker in Japan in 2000. Also in 2000, Bioré had US$36.9 million in sales in the United States, with a 6 percent market share. Bioré Pore Perfect (then separated from other Bioré products) had sales of US$21.4 million and a 3.4 percent market share on its own. Bioré was ranked third in the United States in sales, while Bioré Pore Perfect was 10th.

In 2002 Bioré introduced Beyond Smooth Daily Facial Moisturizer, which moisturized skin while making facial hair less noticeable, and the brand also revamped its packaging because it had widely diversified its brand offerings. A color-coded system for various skin types was introduced, as well as a larger logo and easier-to-discern product attributes. Two years later, Kao labeled many of its personal care brands "premium." In the United States, this revamping helped refresh the brand, as did some product reformulations and a new tagline, "Beauty Starts Here." By this time, Bioré had become a US$67 million brand. By 2005 the brand was focusing on eliminating the shine created by oily skin, and it introduced a line of Shine Control products, such as Moisturizer, Foaming Cleanser, Cream Cleanser, Clay Mask, and Oil Blotting Sheets that used oil-absorbing ingredients. The tagline for this product launch was "Let Her Shine."

Though Bioré continued to add new products and constantly update the brand, Bioré only had a 3.18 percent market share among facial-cleanser brands in the United States and sank to number seven by 2011. The market leader was Cetaphil, with a 7.06 percent market share. In Japan sales were impacted by the earthquake and tsunami that devastated much of the country in early 2011. The brand put out a new line of facial products in 2011 called Bioré Skin Care Facial Foam, which used groundbreaking Skin Purifying Technology (SPT) developed by Kao. Targeting women in their thirties, the line was first introduced in Asia before entering other global markets. By the time it was introduced in the United States in 2012, Bioré had undergone another relaunch, with new blue and white packaging as well as new formulas and names for certain products. By 2012 Bioré was the number-seven facial cleanser brand in the United States, with annual sales of US$20.7 million. It is number one in this category in Japan and number two in Asia.

BRAND ELEMENTS

- The Bioré name was created by combining the words "bio" and "ore."
- Taglines like "Let Her Shine" emphasize the brand's commitment to self-improvement.
- In 2012 Bioré underwent a relaunch which led to the return to the brand's heritage colors of blue and white, and the adoption of a logo that included a "burst of joy" icon.

As a brand, Bioré was created by what became the Kao Group in 1980. The brand's name was created by combining the words "bio," or life, and "ore," for the concept of gold. The brand's name was also given meaning letter by letter. The B stands for beauty, I for intelligence, O for originality, R for reliability, and E for enrichment.

Many of Bioré's product launches and related taglines underscore the brand's commitment to the values embodied in the letters of its name. When its groundbreaking Bioré Pore Perfect Deep Cleansing Strips entered the market in 1997, it was with the tagline "Absolutely Clean." In

2005, in support of the introduction of Bioré Shine Control products, the tagline stated "Let Her Shine," emphasizing that the products improved the consumer's beauty, allowing her to be herself.

Over the years, Bioré underwent several relaunches as a brand. In 2012 Bioré's products and product lines were revamped, and its packaging was refurbished to reflect its heritage simplicity and the colors of blue and white. The brand's logo now included a blue and white, flower-like "burst of joy" icon, reflecting the positive simplicity of Bioré.

BRAND IDENTITY

- Bioré is linked to the concept of product innovation.
- Groundbreaking products by Bioré include Pore Perfect Deep Cleansing Strips and the Self-Heating Mask.
- In 2011 Bioré launched a loyalty program on Facebook as part of its attempt to reach its target audience of women in their twenties.

From its introduction, Bioré has benefitted from the emphasis Kao, its parent company, has placed on research and development. Bioré is regarded as a transformative brand because it has created new product categories within the personal care market. When Bioré was launched in Japan in 1980, it was with Bioré Facial Foam, a foaming liquid facial wash at a time when most facial washes came in bar form. In 1997 Bioré was launched in the United States, Australia, and other global markets with Bioré Pore Perfect Deep Cleansing Strips. These strips featured a special technology called C-Bond, which removed dirt and grime from nose pores. These strips were unique and became the best-selling personal care item in the U.S. market within months. This led to competitors rushing to put similar products on the market.

Over the years, Bioré refined its strips and added new strips for the face at various strengths, and it has remained closely identified with this product. Other innovative products by Bioré include the Self-Heating Mask introduced in 1998. This mask grew warm and changed color when applied, helping to better dissolve and remove facial dirt and oil. In 2011 Bioré debuted the first products using ground-breaking Skin Purifying Technology (SPT) in Japan. SPT was a cleansing agent which gently removed dirt and excess oil without irritation and left skin feeling smooth. The first Bioré products to use SPT were Bioré Skin Care Facial Foam and Bioré U body cleanser. Aya Takashima served as the face of Bioré Skin Care Facial Foam in Japan.

Though Bioré products are used by women of a variety of ages, beginning in 2010 the brand altered the age component of its brand strategy in the U.S. market as part of the Bioré Restage Project. Because the market for facial cleansers is so competitive, the company decided to reexamine its demographic. It found that women in their twenties tend to have more brand loyalty, and so it decided to focus on them rather than on other age groups. Bioré reached them through digital marketing and online interaction. Because this audience spent more time on Facebook than at the websites of brands they used, Bioré launched Prove It! Facebook Rewards Programming in August 2011. This loyalty program gave rewards for meeting health challenges and answering related trivia questions, as well as for regularly visiting the Facebook page and sharing related content. As a result, the Bioré Facebook page had 200,000 fans by the end of 2011. By 2013 Bioré had over 400,000 likes on Facebook.

BRAND STRATEGY

- Bioré regularly introduced new products and extensions to encourage consumer interest.
- Products such as the Bioré Bright White range were tailored to specific markets.
- Items with new Skin Purifying Technology began rolling out globally in 2012 and were targeted toward local demographics and brand guidelines.

As a leading global personal-care brand, Bioré has regularly added new products and brand extensions since its introduction in 1980 in Japan to keep the brand fresh in the minds of consumers. Its first item was a gentle foaming cleanser, Bioré Facial Foam, and more products were added by 1984, when the brand introduced Bioré U body wash. Bioré went on to add many more products, including various cleansers, facial lotions, makeup removers, astringents, toners, cleansing cloths, and oil-blotting sheets to appeal to its predominantly female users.

A number of Bioré's product introductions sought to address skin problems for consumers in unique ways. When Bioré entered some major developed markets, including the United States and Australia, in 1997, it debuted five products, among them its brand-defining Pore Perfect Deep Cleansing Strips. Additional Bioré items debuted in 1998, including the Self-Heating Mask. In 1999 the Bioré warming line was extended with the debut of the Self-Heating Moisture Mask and Warming Deep Pore Cleanser. Pore strips were regularly refined and introduced in new variations over the years as well. In 2011 Bioré continued to attract consumer attention, and it widened its appeal to women in their thirties by introducing, in Japan, Bioré Skin Care Facial Foam and Bioré U body cleanser, which employed a new Skin Purifying Technology (SPT).

Bioré began moving into markets outside of Japan as early as 1981. While many of its best-known products were available globally, certain items and lines were chosen and tailored to local markets. For example, in 2003 the Bioré Aromatherapy Pore Pack, which cleaned pores and removed blackheads, debuted in Japan, Singapore, and Thailand. This was an extension of the Bioré Bright White range, which was available only to consumers in Southeast Asia. The items in this line featured ingredients such as green tea, yuzu orange rose, and lavender. Items with SPT technology began rolling out globally in 2012, but were targeted toward local demographics and brand guidelines.

BRAND EQUITY

- Bioré had significant market share in the United States in 2011, with 3.18 percent of facial cleansers.
- Bioré was a top-ranked brand in Taiwan.
- By 2011 Bioré was the most valuable cosmetics and personal-care brand in Japan.

A leading global personal care brand, Bioré had significant market share in countries like Japan, Taiwan, and the United States for different products and product lines. By 2011, for example, Bioré was number seven among facial cleanser brands in the United States, with a 3.18 percent market share. In comparison, Cetaphil was number one with 7.06 percent of the market. In 2011 sales in Asia grew, especially in Taiwan, Hong Kong, and Indonesia. Bioré's success helped increase sales of Kao's beauty care products division by 0.8 percent to JPY537.9 billion (US$6.545 billion) in fiscal 2011. This division accounted for about 44 percent of Kao's total sales. Its overall sales for fiscal 2011 were JPY1.216 trillion (US$14.796 billion), despite the impact on Japan of the devastating earthquake and tsunami of March 2011.

Bioré was the most valuable cosmetics and personal-care brand in Japan in 2011, according to Brand Finance. It had a brand value of US$3.014 billion. It was ahead of Shiseido, which had a brand value of US$2.907 billion. In Brand Finance's 2012 ranking of the *Top 50 Cosmetics Companies*, Bioré was ranked ninth, with a brand value of US$3.336 billion. In 2011 Bioré was ranked 10th.

BRAND AWARENESS

- Bioré is a leading skin-care brand in Japan.
- Bioré has high brand-awareness in markets like Japan, the United States, Mexico, China, and Taiwan.
- Effective advertising campaigns with taglines like "Beauty Starts Here" have built brand awareness.

One of the leading skin-care brands in Japan, Bioré is sold in 44 territories around the world, with markets in Europe, Asia, the Middle East, the Caribbean, and the Americas. The brand had strong growth in the United States, Mexico, China, and Japan. Bioré had the highest brand awareness in these countries plus Taiwan. It is a top-ranked brand in Taiwan, Hong Kong, and Indonesia. Bioré worked to build a strong global presence through pioneering products like pore cleaning strips, self-heating masks, and Skin Purifying Technology. Bioré's marketing and advertising efforts underscored the effectiveness of its products. Through successful online and print campaigns, using taglines like "Beauty Starts Here," Bioré has positioned itself as a premium skin care brand among young, female consumers.

BRAND OUTLOOK

- Sales of premium skin-care products began growing in 2011.
- Bioré had been successfully positioned as a premium skin-care brand in 2004.
- Bioré's parent company, the Kao Group, invested heavily in research and development for its brands.

Though the global facial-cleanser market was maturing, sales of premium skin-care products were beginning to grow in 2011. This was expected to continue further into the 2010s. Bioré positioned itself as a premium brand in 2004, after it underwent a rebranding and introduced a number of new products. Bioré continued to market itself as a premium facial-care brand in the 2010s, after undergoing another relaunch. This included offering new products with Skin Purifying Technology. Bioré's parent company, the Kao Group, was committed to research and development activities to come up with new ingredients, products, and technologies for all of its brands. Kao made a commitment in 2009 to becoming an ecologically aware company with the long-term goal of helping achieve a sustainable society.

FURTHER READING

"Bioré." RankingTheBrands.com. Accessed January 30, 2013. http://www.rankingthebrands.com/Brand-detail.aspx?brandID=3254.

"Bioré Embarks on Global Relaunch." *Cosmetics International*, February 10, 2012.

Brand Finance. "Bioré." *Brandirectory*. Accessed January 30, 2013. http://brandirectory.com/profile/Bioré.

Kao Group. *Kao Annual Report 2012*. Accessed February 5, 2013. http://www.kao.com/jp/en/corp_ir/imgs/reports_fy2012e_all.pdf.

Malone, Chris. "Brands Are People, Too." *Forbes*, November 28, 2011.

Nagel, Andrea, and Koji Hirano. "Kao Jazzes up Its Beauty Image." *Women's Wear Daily*, April 16, 2004.

Taylor, Rod. "Bioré: The Nose Knew at Lilith Fair." *Brandweek*, September 15, 1997.

BLACKBERRY

AT A GLANCE

Brand Synopsis: BlackBerry devices epitomize the power of secure mobile wireless communication.
Parent Company: Research in Motion Ltd. (RIM)
295 Phillip Street
Waterloo, ON N2L 3W8
Canada
http://www.rim.net
Sector: Information Technology; Telecommunication Services
Industry Group: Technology Hardware & Equipment; Telecommunication Services
Performance: *Market share*—4.7 percent of smartphones worldwide (2012); 10 percent of smartphones in the United States (2011).
Principal Competitors: Apple Inc.; Motorola, Inc.; Nokia Corporation; Samsung Electronics Co Ltd.

BRAND ORIGINS

- Research in Motion (RIM) was founded in Waterloo, Ontario in 1984.
- In 1996 RIM released the first interactive two-way pager.
- The first BlackBerry device was launched in 1999.
- BlackBerry devices became popular among business users and gradually spread to a wider consumer audience.
- BlackBerry's position has weakened under competition from Apple's iPhone and Android devices.

BlackBerry's parent company, Research in Motion Ltd. (RIM), was founded by Mike Lazaridis in 1984 in Waterloo, Ontario. RIM received contracts to produce electronics equipment for General Motors of Canada, Rogers Cantel Mobile Communications, and Ericsson. In 1992 RIM brought in Jim Balsillie as business manager and co-CEO. In 1996 RIM introduced the RIM 900 Inter@ctive Pager, the first compact two-way paging device, with a full keyboard and small text display.

In 1998 the company released the RIM 950 Pager, whose technological breakthrough was the ability to synchronize e-mail messages almost immediately with the user's home e-mail account. Relaunched under the name BlackBerry in January 1999, the device boasted 164,000 subscribers by February 2000. Service availability spread rapidly across North America, and BlackBerry service began entering European markets as well. Communications achieved during the terrorist attacks against the United States on September 11, 2001, strengthened BlackBerry's reputation for secure, reliable performance, leading to expanded presence in the U.S. military and security markets. RIM continued to release new BlackBerry models despite financial struggles and embroilment in patent litigation; in March 2006 RIM agreed to pay U.S. firm NTP US$612.5 million to settle its patent lawsuits. At this time, RIM held a 70 percent share of the U.S. market for wireless e-mail, with 3.2 million subscribers.

BlackBerry phones faced increasingly intense competition from Apple's iPhone launched in June 2007, and later from devices using Google's Android platform. RIM turned toward the mass consumer market, with initial success, and by spring 2009 BlackBerry posted over 25 million customers. However, service outages and the perception that its products were outmoded sapped BlackBerry's position. As investors put pressure on RIM to change its strategy, in January 2012 Mike Lazaridis and James Balsillie stepped down as co-CEOs, to be replaced by Thorsten Heins. The company staked its future on the long-delayed introduction of its BlackBerry 10 operating system in January 2013.

BRAND ELEMENTS

- The BlackBerry name was devised by the marketing firm Lexicon Branding.
- The BlackBerry logo conveys an impression of speed.
- BlackBerry's e-mail tagline brands mobile e-mail with its name.

After RIM released the RIM 950 Interactive Pager in 1998 with modest success, co-CEO Mike Lazaridis decided that the product needed a more distinctive moniker. The company had come up with PocketLink, but Lazaridis hired U.S. marketing firm Lexicon Branding to brainstorm some snappier names. Some of Lexicon's consultants suggested the name "Strawberry," inspired by the device's tiny keys, but a linguist colleague objected that the name sounded too awkward, and the team soon settled on "BlackBerry."

The BlackBerry word design is written in bold sans serif characters, tilted forwards to convey an impression of speed. An emblem made up of seven seed-like objects appears before the brand name, which is actually a reverse image of four superimposed letter Bs. BlackBerry also boasts a special notification icon for messages, a white asterisk on a red circle, which RIM employees dubbed the "splat." BlackBerry's inclusion of the tagline "Sent from my BlackBerry" at the end of every message effectively branded the whole concept of mobile e-mail with its name.

BRAND IDENTITY

- BlackBerry devices originally were designed to appeal to business users, not the general public.
- BlackBerry symbolized the lifestyle of the business and political elite.
- Celebrity users have provided invaluable publicity for BlackBerry.
- BlackBerry developed a strong rivalry with Apple.
- The spread of BlackBerry Messenger service among young consumers threatened the brand's positioning.

In its early years, BlackBerry's identity was associated with its target market of business users, presenting a forbidding image for much of the public. BlackBerry devices looked large and clunky, with a large screen, a tiny full keyboard and a "thumb dial" that could be operated by the thumb while the user held it in one hand. BlackBerry products and operating systems were typically numbered, often in no apparent order. RIM paid little attention to features that would appeal to mass consumers such as advanced graphic displays, music and video players, and cameras; this actually helped BlackBerry win business from military and government clients. In comparison, rivals such as Palm and Handspring aimed at a broader public with more full-featured and colorful devices.

The word "BlackBerry" soon symbolized not just a product category but also the fast-paced lifestyle of the corporate and political elite, who compulsively fiddled with their devices under the table at meetings or lit up their screens at concerts or in other inappropriate situations. BlackBerry devices were given the punning nickname "CrackBerries" because users found themselves addicted to using them. The American Society of Hand Therapists warned against "BlackBerry Thumb," resulting from prolonged typing with the thumb on the tiny keyboards.

BlackBerry benefited from the influence of celebrity fans such as Oprah Winfrey, who praised BlackBerry on her popular television talk show in November 2005, giving a device to each member of the audience. A web site emerged dedicated to Celebrity BlackBerry Sightings. Perhaps the most notable celebrity advocate was Barack Obama, whose struggle to retain access to his treasured BlackBerry after his Presidential election victory in November 2008 won considerable public sympathy. Doug Shabelman, President of Burns Entertainment, estimated the value of this publicity for the brand at over US$50 million.

BlackBerry developed a rivalry with a powerful, confident competitor, Apple. Launched in June 2007, the Apple iPhone was a sleekly designed portable video and music player and web surfing device with a touchscreen keyboard that attracted millions of consumers. The challenge from Apple accelerated BlackBerry's adoption of a more consumer-friendly style. RIM rolled out BlackBerry devices with more distinctive styling and memorable names, starting in 2006 with the Pearl, followed by the Curve in 2007, and the Gold, Storm, and Bold models in 2008. After Apple introduced the iPad, which sparked the new category of tablet computers, RIM developed its own tablet computer, the BlackBerry PlayBook, released in April 2011.

As many young customers adopted BlackBerry devices to use BlackBerry Messenger (BBM), the brand perception threatened to lose value. One of the pitfalls of this situation emerged in August 2011, when the brand became associated with the use of BBM by urban rioters in Britain to encourage looting. More generally, as prices fell, BlackBerry devices became commoditized, losing their cachet among many of their original users and aspiring customers in Western markets.

BRAND STRATEGY

- BlackBerry's performance during terrorist attacks on September 11, 2001, helped open the U.S. government and military markets.
- RIM introduced more consumer-oriented models from 2006 onward.
- Use of BlackBerry devices has spread widely in developing countries.

RIM staked out a profitable niche for the BlackBerry brand in large organizations and among busy professionals willing to pay a premium for the benefits of synchronized portable e-mail. A crucial event in developing BlackBerry's reputation was unexpected—the terrorist attacks on New York City and Washington, D.C. on September 11, 2001. BlackBerry's proprietary transmission technology kept working when cell phones, landline phones, and other devices failed. U.S. military and security agencies gearing up for war provided another booming market for RIM to target.

By 2006 RIM was gearing up to target mass consumers. The Pearl was an apt name for a tiny, sleekly designed chrome and black device. Its larger successor, the Curve, added a full keyboard and more multimedia features; however, the name puzzled some reviewers and customers, as it had no obvious connection with the product. The Flip folded in on itself like a typical compact cell phone, avoiding some of the "geek" stigma that still dissuaded some consumers from choosing BlackBerry. The BlackBerry Bold 9000, introduced in the US market in November 2008, more directly imitated the iPhone, with its bright screen and more attractive fonts. The BlackBerry PlayBook tablet, released in April 2011, disappointed reviewers as it lacked many basic features such as an e-mail reader, cellular phone connection, or GPS app, suggesting that it had been hastily developed to compete with the Apple iPad.

The company promoted BlackBerry Messenger (BBM) as an alternative to texting, which had especial appeal to young people. Under the BBM label, BlackBerry rolled out services such as BBM Music, a social-oriented music platform. Meanwhile, RIM promoted BlackBerry phones as entry-level devices in developing countries for a potential target market of hundreds of millions of consumers. By 2010 BlackBerry had already become the leading smartphone brand in Latin America and was making strong inroads in many African and Asian countries. However, governments such as those in the United Arab Emirates, Saudi Arabia, and India threatened to ban BlackBerry service unless RIM allowed them to intercept and monitor messages sent over its network.

BRAND EQUITY

- BlackBerry's brand value ranking fell 37 positions to 93rd in 2012 according to Interbrand.
- In 2012 the BlackBerry operating system had a market share of 4.7 percent worldwide in smartphones according to IDC.
- In 2012 BlackBerry continued to rank first or second in developing markets such as Indonesia and Nigeria.

According to Interbrand's *2012 Best Global Brands* report, BlackBerry ranked 93rd with a brand value of US$3.9 billion, down 37 positions and 39 percent from 2011. BlackBerry ranked seventh among electronics brands and according to Interbrand's *2012 Canadian Brands Report* ranked fourth among Canadian brands. In 2012 International Data Corporation (IDC) estimated world market share of the BlackBerry operating system at 4.7 percent, third behind Android at 68.3 percent and Apple's iOS at 18.8 percent. BlackBerry's U.S. share of smartphones had already fallen from 44 percent in 2009 to under 10 percent at year's end 2011.

Even in its home market in Canada, by 2011 the iPhone was shipping more units than BlackBerry: 2.85 million to 2.08 million. Much higher share remained in developing overseas markets. According to IDC, in the Middle East and Africa, 8.3 million BlackBerry devices were shipped in 2011 compared to 2.5 million iPhones; in Latin America, the figures were 10.5 million BlackBerrys and 2.1 million iPhones. In 2012 BlackBerry still ranked second in Indonesia with 37 percent market share of smartphones, just behind Android phones. Meanwhile in Nigeria, Africa's most populous country, BlackBerry enjoyed an estimated 50 percent market share, though it faced increasing competition as demand rapidly grew from a small base.

BRAND AWARENESS

- In the United Kingdom, BlackBerry ranked behind its competitors in 2012 in terms of emotional connection and brand buzz according to Harris Interactive.
- In 2012 BlackBerry ranked below average among mobile phone and tablet computer brands according to the Harris Poll EquiTrend survey.
- In emerging markets such as South Africa, BlackBerry remained the most popular mobile phone brand in 2012.

Regarding brand awareness of BlackBerry in Western markets, a Harris Interactive survey of U.K. consumers conducted in June 2012 indicated that 36 percent of respondents stated that they either use BlackBerry or are very familiar with the brand, behind Nokia at 53 percent and the iPhone at 39 percent; only 1 percent had never heard of the brand. BlackBerry ranked last in emotional connection behind the iPhone, Nokia, Samsung, and Android, with only 7 percent of respondents saying they "love" the brand and 20 percent indicating that they "like" it, and 36 percent responding that they did not know the brand well enough to have an opinion. In the category of "brand buzz," only 21 percent of respondents stated BlackBerry is "ahead/really going places" or "somewhat ahead of the game," well behind the iPhone at 45 percent. More ominously, even among BlackBerry users, 24 percent believed that the brand was "getting left behind" or "really getting left behind."

According to the Harris Poll 2012 EquiTrend survey of brand perceptions, BlackBerry ranked below the category average among mobile phone brands, behind the iPhone, HTC, Samsung, LG, Motorola, and Sharp. The BlackBerry Playbook also ranked below the category average in tablet computers, behind the leading iPad brand as well as Samsung Galaxy, Sony Tablet, Motorola Xoom, and Lenovo ThinkPad. However, brand perception remains strong in emerging markets where BlackBerry retains an aspirational appeal. For example, in South Africa, the Sunday Times Generation Next 2012 Brand Survey named BlackBerry as the "Coolest Brand Overall" among consumers between ages eight and 22, as well as the "Coolest Cellphone" with 36.7 percent of the vote and "Coolest High-Tech Gadget" by a narrow margin with 12.5 percent.

BRAND OUTLOOK

- BlackBerry's market position was declining in 2012.
- In June 2012 RIM shed 5,000 jobs and delayed the introduction of the BlackBerry 10 operating system until January 2013.
- BlackBerry's worldwide share of smartphones will slightly decline through 2016 according to IDC.

By 2012 BlackBerry's position was slipping in the smartphones market, which was increasingly dominated by phones running on Google's Android operating system. In January 2012 RIM cancelled the planned launches of the BlackBerry Colt and Milan handsets and delayed the launch of BlackBerry London. That same month, co-CEOs Mike Lazaridis and Jim Balsillie resigned and were succeeded by company executive Thorsten Heins. In June 2012 the company announced it would terminate 5,000 jobs and delay the introduction of the BlackBerry 10 operating system until 2013. Industry analysts speculated that the company might have to sell off its BBM network or invite a competitor to purchase a stake. Throughout the year, a steady trickle of corporations and U.S. government agencies shifted away from BlackBerry to Apple and Android devices, which were less expensive and now featured relatively robust security. Moreover, BlackBerry was losing its "cool" factor, as young people attracted by the BBM service drifted away from the brand. Still there were nearly 80 million subscribers to BlackBerry service in late 2012.

In late 2012 photographs and prototypes of BlackBerry 10 devices began circulating ahead of the planned launch on January 30, 2013. Company executives held numerous demonstrations and strove to persuade application developers not to desert to other platforms. Under BlackBerry 10's Flow paradigm, applications are designed to be operated easily by thumb, a nod to the habits of veteran users. International Data Corporation (IDC) predicts that BlackBerry's worldwide market share of smartphones will decline to 4.1 percent in 2016, falling behind Windows Phone in the race for third place.

FURTHER READING

Austen, Ian. "A Beloved Gadget Thrives, Even When It Deliberately Passes up the Bells and Whistles." *New York Times*, October 4, 2004.

Brand Buzz, Wave 2. Rochester, NY: Harris Interactive, 2012.

Browning, Jonathan, and Amy Thomson. "BlackBerry's Fall from Executive Suite to London Looters May Bruise Brand." Bloomberg.com, August 9, 2011.

Bulik, Beth Snyder. "It Will Take More Than Marketing to Put BlackBerry Back in Race." *Advertising Age*, February 27, 2012.

Coster, Helen. "RIM Wants BlackBerry to Shed Its Image." *Forbes*, October 26, 2009.

Harmon, Amy. "E-Mail You Can't Outrun." *New York Times*, September 21, 2000.

Hicks, Jesse. "Research, No Motion: How the BlackBerry CEOs Lost an Empire." TheVerge.com, February 21, 2012.

Krill, Paul. "RIM Developer Faithful Find Hope in BlackBerry 10 Revival." InfoWorld.com, September 27, 2012.

Marlowe, Iain, and Josh O'Kane. "RIM's Latest Foe: Fickle Youth." *Globe and Mail* (Toronto), June 26, 2012.

McConnachie, Kathryn. "BlackBerry Still 'Cool' to SA Youth." *ITWeb*, June 4, 2012.

Meier, Barry, and Robert F. Worth. "Emirates to Cut Data Services of BlackBerry." *New York Times*, August 2, 2010.

Miles, Stuart. "BlackBerry Makes Music Social with BBM Music." Pocket-lint.com, August 25, 2011.

Miller, Hugo. "BlackBerry Loses Top Spot to Apple At Home." Bloomberg.com, March 22, 2012.

Pogue, David. "A BlackBerry for Collars of All Colors." *New York Times*, May 10, 2007.

"Research in Motion, Ltd." *International Directory of Company Histories*. Ed. Jay P. Pederson and Tina Grant. Vol. 106. Detroit, MI: St. James Press, 2010.

Romero, Simon. "The Simple BlackBerry Allowed Contact When Phones Failed." *New York Times*, September 20, 2001.

Roose, Kevin. "How the BlackBerry Died: The Five Mistakes That Killed a Once-Great Device." *New York*, July 19, 2012.

Sweeny, Alistair. *BlackBerry Planet: The Story of Research in Motion and the Little Device That Took the World by Storm*. Mississauga, ON: John Wiley & Sons Canada, Ltd., 2009.

2012 Best Global Brands. Interbrand, 2012.

Webster, Paul Christopher, and Iain Marlow. "Where the BlackBerry Still Reigns Supreme." *Globe and Mail* (Toronto), November 30, 2012.

BMW

AT A GLANCE

Brand Synopsis: Known for its timeless slogan "The Ultimate Driving Machine," BMW is globally recognized as a leading brand in auto manufacturing, appealing particularly to lucrative segments of the automotive customer base, from luxury car owners to sports car enthusiasts.
Parent Company: BMW-Hochhaus
Petuelring 130, D-80809 Munich
Germany
www.bmw.de
Sector: Consumer Discretionary
Industry Group: Automobiles & Components
Performance: *Market share*—2.4 percent of the U.S. car market (2011). *Sales*—EUR$68.8 billion worldwide (US$89.2 billion) (2011).
Principal Competitors: Audi; Acura; Mercedes-Benz; Lexus

BRAND ORIGINS

- Bayerische Motoren Werke, or BMW, was incorporated in 1913.
- BMW built its first automobile in 1928.
- The BMW brand is associated with precision engineering, innovative design, and consumer appeal.
- All BMW vehicles—past and present and regardless of nameplate—celebrate chic.

Bayerische Motoren Werke, or BMW, was incorporated in 1913. However, BMW was not fully established as a business entity until 1917, following the restructuring of Rapp Motorenwerke aircraft manufacturing. The company first produced aircraft engines, largely for the German war effort in World War I. When the Treaty of Versailles prohibited BMW's continued production of aircraft products, the company turned its attention to motorcycles. Basing most of its early designs on aircraft, BMW constructed its first motorcycle—the M2 B15—in 1921.

Two years later, the legendary motorcycle designer Max Friz created the 486cc R32, which reached a top speed of 60 mph. Launched in 1923, the R32 is considered to be BMW's first production motorcycle. While it would eventually focus most of its attention on the design and manufacture of automobiles, BMW remained committed to innovation in the motorcycle market, producing BMW and Husqvarna motorcycles. In 2011, for example, its K1600 series was the first BMW motorcycle to be powered by a six-cylinder engine.

BMW built its first automobile in 1928 and was just beginning to establish itself as an auto brand in the 1930s when World War II interrupted this growth. Unlike other German auto manufacturers, such as Daimler-Benz and Volkswagen, BMW struggled to regain its place in the industry following the war. With BMW facing bankruptcy and on the verge of being handed over to its chief competitor, Daimler-Benz, the industrialist Herbert Quandt bought a controlling interest in the company in 1959. Quandt is credited with saving the brand from being relegated to manufacturing axles for Mercedes-Benz. With the launch of its 1930s-inspired car—the 1500—in 1961, BMW began the process of creating a brand known for precision engineering, innovative design, and consumer appeal.

In the 21st century, BMW produces several lines of cars, including the sedans, coupes, hatchbacks, and convertibles of the 1, 3, 5, 6, 7, and 8 series (along with their respective high-performance "M" derivatives); sports cars in the Z line; and "sports activity" (instead of "sport utility") vehicles in the X line. BMW also sells Rolls Royce and Minivehicles. It jettisoned its production of Rover vehicles in 2000 after 10 years of production and management challenges with the British automaker. One thing is true of all vehicles—past and present—in the BMW group, regardless of nameplate: they all celebrate chic.

BRAND ELEMENTS

- BMW's naming system consists of the product line number and the motor type.
- BMW's circular logo is based on the original Rapp Motorenwerke logo.
- The BMW logo is most recognized in the automotive industry for its color pattern rather than its shape or design.

Similar in some ways to its closest competitor, Mercedes-Benz, BMW uses a naming system that consists of the product line number and the motor type. For example, the designation "850" indicates that the car is in the 8 series and the engine is 5.0 liters in size. The addition of a letter or two following the number series gives additional information about the model. For example, an "i" indicates a fuel-injected model and a "t" indicates a touring edition.

BMW maintains that this naming system is clear and logical and can be easily understood around the world. The Z and X series do not quite fit within this system, however. Other than the Z3 (the third in the Z series) and the X5 (named 5 to symbolize its midsize status within the X series), however, the BMW branding strategy is quite simple: no names, just numbers.

Another key element of the BMW brand is its colorful logo. The circular blue and white BMW logo or roundel evolved from the circular Rapp Motorenwerke company logo, and it is the logo most recognized in the automotive industry for its color pattern rather than its symbol or design.

BRAND IDENTITY

- BMW presents itself to consumers, especially men, as a brand built for pleasure and prestige—"The Ultimate Driving Machine."
- BMW is easily recognized by its sleek design, logo, and model-numbering system, all of which are aimed to appeal directly to consumers.
- Even though a higher BMW series carries more prestige, the brand excels at creating customer loyalty and community across all of its lines.

BMW presents itself to consumers, especially men, as a brand built for pleasure and prestige. Whereas safety and security are often identified with Volvo and the rugged outdoors with Subaru, BMW is all about classy, dynamic excitement and quality German engineering. BMWs are seen as beautiful, reliable, powerful, and high-performing automobiles.

A BMW is easily recognized by its sleek and sporty design features, blue-and-white checkered logo, and model-numbering system, all of which are aimed to appeal directly to consumers. The model-numbering system indicates the status of a car within the BMW line. The more powerful and luxurious the car (and the higher the cost), the higher the number. In this way, a top-of-the-line 7 series BMW sedan is clearly and carefully distinguished from an entry-level 3 series sedan.

Even though a higher BMW series brings with it a different level of prestige, the brand excels at creating customer loyalty and community across all of its series through its approach to design and engineering. Each BMW—whether a 3 series or an 8 series, a Z roadster or an X sports activity machine—has the distinct lines of a BMW. Even from a distance, consumers have little difficulty identifying a BMW vehicle. This distinctiveness is complemented by the brand's logo and its slogan, "The Ultimate Driving Machine."

BRAND STRATEGY

- BMW wants to be viewed as always fresh and new, young and active.
- BMW maintains a high-profile branding strategy.
- To keep its products young and fresh, BMW regularly introduces new models for each of its series.

According to StealingShare, an international brand-management company, "BMW's strategy is to keep its products in the introduction and growth stages by periodically introducing new models in each of its product lines. In fact, BMW does not like to have any products in the maturity or decline stage of the product life cycle." BMW wants to be viewed as always fresh and new, young and active. This fountain-of-youth approach allows for perhaps the greatest brand appeal across all demographics. BMW routinely removes products in decline from the market rather than remodel or reinvent them. While many of its competitors, such as Mercedes-Benz, celebrate their past, BMW prefers to focus on the present.

BMW also regularly introduces new models for each of its series. According to StealingShare, the BMW 3 series, for example, will have a new sedan model one year, a new coupe the next year, and a new convertible after that, and so on. Models are not replaced; they are continuously improved. With this approach, BMW stresses better performance, a strategy that is easily communicated to consumers. Improved engineering and technology equals better performance, which means an even better driving experience. This strategy of improving performance is now a large part of the brand's identity and has only continued to increase the brand's relevance, even in a difficult economy for the high-end car market.

BMW maintains a high-profile branding strategy. Examples include buying commercial time during the world's most-watched event, the Super Bowl, and partnering with Hollywood studios. The BMW Z line, for example, was launched in a James Bond movie. BMW finds ways to command consumers' attention while emphasizing its young, sexy, and stylish image.

BRAND EQUITY

- BMW reported revenues of EUR68.8 billion (US$89.2 billion) in 2011.
- The brand value of BMW was calculated at US$21.3 billion for 2012, up from US$16.6 billion in 2010.
- Brand Finance recognized BMW as the most valuable of all German brands in 2012.

BMW reported revenues of EUR68.8 billion (US$89.2 billion) in 2011, up from EUR60.5 billion in 2010.

Brand Finance calculated the brand value of BMW at US$21.3 billion for 2012, up from US$20.2 billion in 2011 and US$16.6 billion in 2010. BMW was number 22 on Brand Finance's "Global 500" list of the world's top brands in 2012, up from number 31 during the international economic recession of 2008. Rival Mercedes-Benz was number 26 on the list in 2012, with a brand value of US$19.8 billion. Toyota outranked both premium brands, coming in at number 15, with a brand value of US$24.5 billion.

BMW placed first on Brand Finance's "Germany 30" list of the most highly valued brands for that country in 2012. Mercedes-Benz was second, and Volkswagen was third. On Milward Brown's "BrandZ Top 100" list of the world's most trusted brands, BMW was number 23, valued at US$24.6 billion. Toyota was number 28, valued at US$21.8 billion.

BRAND AWARENESS

- In a 2012 worldwide survey by the Reputation Institute, consumers named BMW as the most popular brand overall.
- BMW's brand awareness is highest in its home country, Germany, where it rarely ranks outside the top-five brands and often comes in first.
- In the United States, BMW scored in the top 10 in nearly all consumer satisfaction categories.

In a survey of more than 100,000 consumers, the Reputation Institute placed BMW first in its Global RepTrak Top 100 for 2012. BMW was ranked first overall in brand popularity with consumers worldwide, ahead of mega-brands such as Disney, Apple, and Google.

SyncForce, an international brand management firm based in the United States, ranked BMW fourth on its "Top 100 Brands" list. The Dow Jones Sustainability Index listed BMW as the world's most sustainable automotive company for the seventh consecutive year in 2012. BMW was the first and second most-desired brand in Russia and China, respectively, and held the 69th position on *Fortune*'s Top 500. *Forbes* named BMW the most reputable company in June 2012.

BMW's brand awareness is highest in its home country, Germany, where it rarely ranks outside the top-five brands and often comes in first, as in brand surveys conducted in 2012 by Brand Finance and Das Deutsche Markenranking.

In the United States, J.D. Power and *Consumer Reports* ranked BMW in the top 10 in nearly all consumer satisfaction categories. Buyology Inc. listed BMW as the third most-desired brand among men in the United States in 2012.

BRAND OUTLOOK

- BMW is poised to remain one of the most powerful brands in the world.
- BMW is on the leading edge of the design and delivery of e-commerce.
- BWM aspires to remain the sexiest, most prestigious, and most pleasurable car brand.

BMW appears poised to remain one of the most powerful brands in the world by maintaining its tradition of style and luxury while responding to increasing consumer demand for energy-efficient and environmentally friendly products. In July 2011 BMW unveiled two zero-emission, plug-in electric cars: the sporty i8 hybrid super coupe and the i3 urban all-electric car, both planned for production by 2013. In addition, BMW developed a factory in Germany that is run entirely by on-site wind power, installed British Columbia's first commercial wind turbine in one of its dealerships, and built an environmentally friendly factory in China. Innovations such as its "i" series and its "Efficient Dynamics" initiative, which applies green thinking to every stage of product development, earned BMW a spot on Interbrand's "Best Global Green Brands for 2012" list.

BMW is also on the leading edge of innovation in the design and delivery of e-commerce. Its highly interactive website is widely recognized as the standard in the auto industry. On the site, customers can configure a car to their own specifications (selecting interiors, exteriors, engines, packages, and options) and send those specifications to the closest BMW dealer. Innovations such as these demonstrate BMW's ongoing development of its own particular understanding of the desires of consumers.

BMW's famous slogan got a creative boost in 2010 with the addition of the tagline "Sheer Driving Pleasure." The change was a further attempt to position the brand as the sexiest and most prestigious and pleasurable among automakers.

FURTHER READING

"Best Global Green Brands 2012: Top 50 Brands." Accessed September 1, 2012. Interbrand. http://www.interbrand.com/en/best-global-brands/Best-Global-Green-Brands/2012-Report/BestGlobalGreenBrandsTable-2012.aspx.

BMW AG. *BMW Annual Report 2011*. Accessed September 3, 2012. http://annual-report2011.bmwgroup.com/bmwgroup/annual/2011/gb/English/pdf/report2011.pdf.

"BMW Brand Study." StealingShare.com, 2010. Accessed September 9, 2012. http://www.stealingshare.com/content/1148328698453.htm.

"BMW Motorcycle History." Motorcycle.com. Accessed September 13, 2012. http://www.motorcycle.com/manufacturer/history-bmw-motorcycle.html.

"BMW Uncovers Its Brand Essence: Joy." BrandStoke.com, March 2, 2010. Accessed August 30, 2012. http://www.brandstoke.com/2010/03/02/bmw-uncovers-brand-essence-joy/.

Brand Finance. "BMW." *Brandirectory*. Accessed August 29, 2012. http://brandirectory.com/profile/bmw.

Dougherty, Tom. "BMW Is the Ultimate Branding Machine." StealingShare.com, January 9, 2012. Accessed September 8, 2012. http://www.stealingshare.com/blog/?p=3065.

Fich, Nicole. *Brand Management of Luxury Goods*. Santa Cruz, CA: GRIN Verlag, 2011.

Johnson, Richard A. *Six Men Who Built the Modern Auto Industry*. St. Paul, MN: Motorbooks, 2005.

Kapferer, Jean-Noel. *The New Strategic Brand Management: Creating and Sustaining Brand Equity Long Term*. 4th ed. London: Kogan Page, 2008.

Kiley, David. *Driven: Inside BMW, the Most Admired Car Company in the World*. Hoboken, NJ: John Wiley & Sons, 2004.

O'Guinn, Thomas C., Chris T. Allen, and Richard J. Semenik. *Advertising and Integrated Brand Promotion Independence*. Mason, OH: South-Western Cengage Learning, 2011.

Rothacher, Albrecht. *Corporate Cultures and Global Brands*. Hackensack, NJ: World Scientific Publishing Company, 2004.

Schultz, Jonathan. "BMW Officially Announces BMW i Brand." *New York Times*, February 21,2011.

Smith, Jacquelyn. "The World's Most Reputable Companies." *Forbes*, June 7, 2012. Accessed September 6, 2012. http://www.forbes.com/sites/jacquelynsmith/2012/06/07/the-worlds-most-reputable-companies/.

SyncForce. "BMW." Rankingthebrands.com, 2012. Accessed September 10, 2012. http://www.rankingthebrands.com/Brand-detail.aspx?brandID=14.

Vijayenthiran, Viknesh. "BMW Voted Most Valuable Car Brand. Where Does Your Car Rank?" *Christian Science Monitor*, May 23, 2012.

BNP PARIBAS

AT A GLANCE

Brand Synopsis: BNP Paribas, "the bank for a changing world," is one of Europe's most recognized banking brands.
Parent Company: BNP Paribas
16 Blvd. des Italiens
Paris 75009
France
http://www.bnpparibas.com
Sector: Financials
Industry Group: Banks
Performance: *Market share*—The second-largest bank in the world in terms of total assets (2011). *Assets*—US$2.5 trillion (2011).
Principal Competitors: Deutsche Bank; HSBC Holdings; Crédit Agricole; Société Générale

BRAND ORIGINS

- Paribas was created in 1872 from a merger between Banque de Crédit et de Dépôt des Pays-Bas and Banque de Paris.
- BNP (Banque Nationale de Paris) was created from the nationalized banks BNCI and CNEP in 1966, whose merger formed the largest bank in France.
- BNP was privatized in 1993 and immediately gained 2.8 million shareholders.
- In 2000 BNP merged with Paribas, becoming BNP Paribas.

BNP Paribas was created from the merger in 2000 of the Banque Nationale de Paris and Paribas, both French banks with complex histories. In 1863 French entrepreneur Alphonse Pinard, Dutch banker Louis-Raphaël Bischoffsheim, and capitalist Edouard Hentsch began the Banque de Crédit et de Dépôt des Pays-Bas ("Bank of Credit and Deposit of the Netherlands" in English), the predecessor of Paribas. Due to Bischoffsheim's history in both Amsterdam and Paris, the bank opened branches simultaneously in both cities in 1863. The bank continued its expansion through 1870, when branches opened in Brussels, Geneva, and Antwerp. In 1872 Banque de Crédit et de Dépôt des Pays-Bas merged with the three-year-old Banque de Paris, creating the Banque de Paris et des Pays-Bas, commonly known as "Paribas."

At the time of Paribas's founding, a capital market was emerging across Europe. The bank quickly tailored its focus to the issuance of public funds, stocks, and bonds of private companies. The bank also initiated the creation of a securities portfolio as an effort to achieve greater capital gains. Paribas rapidly became a competitor with the largest banks in France, in part because it assumed leadership of an international financial syndicate charged with issuing the second payment on the loan taken to repay Germany after France lost the Franco-Prussian War in 1871.

In 1919 Horace Finaly became CEO of the company, where he left a lasting impression. A specialist in international economics, Finaly initiated transactions in heavy industry, chemicals, and oil in both Europe and the Middle East. Also during the first decades of the 20th century, the Banque Nationale de Crédit (BNC), a newer French bank, was focusing on expansion, commissioning a massive headquarters with imposing facades featuring neo-Egyptian pilasters and an Art Deco interior. Although considered an eyesore at the time, the building later became the headquarters of the Banque Nationale de Paris in 1966 and remained the headquarters of the new bank following the merger of BNP and Paribas in 2000. BNC suffered greatly from the stock market crash of 1929 and was subsequently liquidated, with the Banque Nationale pour le Commerce et l'Industrie (BNCI) emerging from the liquidation.

Following the end of World War II, French minister of finance René Pleven launched a reform of the banking industry in 1945 to aid in the reconstruction of France. This reform led to the nationalization of the four major banks of France: BNCI, CNEP, Crédit Lyonnais, and Société Générale. The shares of these companies were transferred to the French state and the boards of directors dissolved. In 1947 the National Credit Council was created. Before any new branch of a nationalized bank could be opened, the council's approval was required. The council rarely approved expansions, a policy that prompted the nationalized banks to take over regional banks. BNCI was especially successful, acquiring 23 branches in this manner between 1947 and 1966. In 1966 French finance minister Michel Debré merged BNCI and CNEP in an effort to reform and consolidate, creating the Banque Nationale de Paris (BNP).

The last three decades of the 20th century and the beginning of the 21st were times of acquisition and expansion for BNP. The company bought Bank of the West in 1979 and then merged Bank of the West with the French Bank of California, a subsidiary of BNP. The bank further expanded in the 1980s and 1990s following the acquisition of several regional banks in the United States. The largest of these was the consolidation of Bank of the West and the First Hawaiian Bank in 1998, placing them under the umbrella company BancWest. Since 2001 BNP Paribas has owned 100 percent of BancWest. In 1993 BNP was privatized, which made possible the later merger of BNP and Paribas and brought the company 2.8 million shareholders. In 2006 BNP Paribas acquired Italian-owned bank BNL (Banca Nazionale del Lavoro), which had been privatized in 1998. In 2009, following the break-up of Fortis, BNP Paribas purchased BGL (Banque Générale du Luxembourg), an international commercial and investment bank.

BRAND ELEMENTS

- BNP has a history of using short, direct slogans in radio advertising and elsewhere.
- The brand's slogan, "bank for a changing world," is an integral part of the brand's identity, reiterating the bank's forward-thinking philosophy.
- BNP Paribas's logo is a green square with four white stars representing honesty and optimism.

The BNP Paribas brand is best known for its direct, concise slogans. In 1954 BNCI became the first bank to advertise on the radio, and it continued to do so into the 21st century. Since advertisement time on the radio is short, the bank was in need of a catchy slogan. The company's use of this type of marketing began in earnest in 1973 when BNP ran radio advertisements featuring slogans such as "We Want Your Money" ("Votre Argent m'Interesse"). Although some considered the phrase too brash, it proved effective nevertheless and initiated the corporate tradition for direct, effective slogans. In 2012 the tone of abrupt honesty remained an important marker in the company communications as a bank. After the merger of BNP and Paribas, the bank continued to use the same sort of slogans, including "The bank for a changing world" and "Let's tell it like it is."

The brand's name is an integral part of the brand's identity, as the name combines two well-known banks in Europe, maintaining the customer loyalty of both BNP and Paribas, although the brands are now combined. While the original logos of the individual brands were abandoned after the merger, the new brand retained the legacy of the previous brands by focusing on promoting customer faith. The brand's logo as of 2013 promotes the brand's image of optimism with the use of the color green, encouraging customers who lost faith in the banking system to put their trust in the BNP Paribas brand as well as demonstrating that BNP Paribas has all of the experience required in a trustworthy bank, while demonstrating that it can change to meet the needs of its customers.

BNP Paribas's logo features a green square with four white stars and the company's name. This logo was introduced in 2000 when BNP and Paribas merged. The logo features distinctive elements, including the color green, which make the logo stand out. The stars are intended to represent honesty and optimism, while evoking images of Europe and universality, characteristics that the bank wishes to project.

BRAND IDENTITY

- BNP Paribas is "the bank for a changing world," adapting itself to meet the needs and expectations of its customers.
- The company describes itself as a "responsible bank" with a strong tradition of ethical policy and treatment of clients.
- In 2011 BNP Paribas reported that it had provided financial education to more than 70,000 people.

BNP Paribas, a globally active company with a sharp focus on international recognition, positions its brand as the leader in banking and financial services in Europe. The brand endeavors to put the customer first, rigorously working to innovate the banking industry while acclimating to the changing and uneven global economy. The brand's primary slogan, "the bank for a changing world," reiterates a commitment to adapt to the global climate by offering more customer service options, such as the "Mon crédit responsible," feature, where bank customers can ask credit-related questions for free. BNP Paribas seeks to capture market share and win consumers with a portfolio of brands in each region that are appealing to corporations and customers around the world.

BNP Paribas also wishes to convey an image of a company committed to social and economic responsibility. On BNP Paribas's website, the company describes itself as a "responsible bank," citing a strong ethical tradition. Formally launched in 2011, the company's corporate responsibility policy is rooted in four main areas: economic responsibility, social responsibility, civic responsibility, and environmental responsibility. BNP Paribas touts its practice of awarding more loans to young adults and advising clients on how to avoid defaulting on loans. In 2011 BNP Paribas reported that the company had provided financial education for more than 70,000 adults and children.

BRAND STRATEGY

- BNP Paribas grew out of mergers that took place over more than a century, with some dating back to the 1860s.
- BNP Paribas often maintains the original branch name after a corporate takeover to minimize the loss of clients.
- BNP Paribas markets the image of a transparent and trustworthy bank by using short, straightforward slogans.

The modern BNP Paribas is a combination of many different mergers, takeovers, and government changes throughout the company's history. Because of its complex history, BNP Paribas controls many subsidiaries in several different countries. While BNP Paribas operates more than 2,200 branches in France alone, the company also makes use of acquired banks' names and brands. The largest are BNP Paribas Fortis and BancWest. By keeping the original banks' name, BNP Paribas is able to retain clients who may not be familiar with the BNP Paribas brand.

When opening branches outside of France, BNP Paribas often attempts to keep the name of BNP Paribas while integrating it suitably with the new location's branding needs. For example, BNP Paribas Egypt, BGL BNP Paribas, and Geojit BNP Paribas all contain the name of the parent company while still reflecting the local identity of the subsidiary. Alternately, there are many BNP Paribas subsidiaries that have names that do not reflect the brand itself, such as Sahara Bank, Banque de Bretagne, and Banca Nazionale del Lavoro. While maintaining the original names for those subsidiaries does not strengthen the brand familiarity of BNP Paribas, retaining the original name makes it more likely that existing customers will remain with the bank.

BNP Paribas's brand strategy is also supported by the company's emphasis on marketing campaigns that make use of its short and powerful slogans, such as "We Want Your Money," "If Only It Were True," and "Let's Tell It Like It Is." The purpose of these campaigns is to project the image of the company as transparent and straightforward in its business practices, in the hope of encouraging trust and loyalty among clients.

BRAND EQUITY

- BNP Paribas is one of the most profitable banks in the world and the most successful French bank in terms of value.
- In 2012 Brand Finance listed BNP Paribas as the 40th most successful brand, with an estimated brand value of US$16.8 billion.
- In 2001 *Forbes* named BNP Paribas the best French enterprise.

BNP Paribas is one of the most profitable banks in the world, and it ranks first in France in terms of value and number of credits processed. In 2011 BNP Paribas was rated the second-most successful bank in the world, behind Deutsche Bank, with assets of US$2.5 trillion and a capital value of US$33.2 billion.

In its 2012 list of the top 500 global brands, Brand Finance ranked BNP Paribas 40th overall and estimated its brand value at US$16.8 billion. British-owned competitor HSBC was listed as the strongest banking brand in the world by Brand Finance, coming in 13th overall with an estimated brand value of US$27.6 billion. According to the *Forbes Global 2000 2011*, BNP Paribas ranks first among French enterprises, first among banks in the Eurozone, and sixth in the global banking sector. Competitor HSBC is the third-largest bank on the list.

BRAND AWARENESS

- BNP Paribas was found to have high brand awareness in European countries among both individuals and companies.
- BNP Paribas's brand recognition is low outside of Europe.
- In 2010 the company launched a "keep reaching" advertising campaign, promoting the brand positively in an effort to boost global brand awareness.

In a survey conducted by TNS Sofres in 2010 of small and medium enterprises in 12 countries and individuals between the ages 18 and 65 in 14 countries, BNP Paribas was found to be one of Europe's most-recognized banking brands. Prompted by which banks were known by name, awareness among individuals was found to be 92 percent in Belgium, 86 percent in Luxembourg, and 43 percent in Italy. In the United States and Russia, however, the brand is less known, with only 6 percent of Americans and 8 percent of Russians familiar with the brand. For corporations, BNP Paribas had 99 percent awareness in Belgium, 100 percent in Luxembourg, and 89 percent in Italy. The United States and Russia again showed low brand awareness with only 16 percent of businesses in the United States and 22 percent in Russia having knowledge of the bank.

Since BNP Paribas only has top-of-mind awareness in European countries, in 2010 the brand began promoting a "keep reaching" advertising program in order to increase brand awareness in the international banking market. The campaign demonstrates the company's image of "the bank for a changing world," demonstrating the positivity of the brand. Although the company is considered the largest global banking group in the world and has a presence in more than 80 countries, the brand is not recognized commonly among individuals outside of Europe.

BRAND OUTLOOK

- BNP Paribas remained profitable in 2011, despite the ongoing financial crisis in Europe.
- Chinese lenders now account for 29.3 percent of the global banking profit, threatening BNP Paribas's position in the Asian market.
- Standard & Poor's forecasted a negative long-term outlook for BNP Paribas.

A significant recession hit the global economy in 2008. In 2011 the economy remained weak, share prices largely remained low, and Europe struggled with a widespread debt crisis. Despite these challenges, BNP Paribas remained profitable, with a net income of more than US$7.8 billion in 2011. Although this figure represented a decline in profit from 2010, when the company's net profit was US$10.1 billion, BNP Paribas weathered the European debt crisis better than most banks. In 2011 the company hired a new CEO, Michel Pébereau, and began to restructure.

The company's outlook is not completely challenge-free, however. Standard & Poor's gave BNP Paribas an AA– rating with a negative outlook in the long term. In 2011 Chinese lenders accounted for almost a third of the global bank profit, an increase of 4 percent since 2007. Eurozone banks accounted for only 6 percent of the global profit. As of 2012, Chinese banks posed the biggest threat to BNP Paribas's market share.

FURTHER READING

"BNP Paribas: an internationally-renowned brand". *BNP Paribas.* Paris: May 12, 2010. Accessed February 16, 2013. http://www.bnpparibas.co.uk/en/2010/05/12/bnp-paribas-an-internationally-renowned-brand/.

BNP Paribas. "The BNP Paribas Group through the Years." 2012. Accessed October 23, 2012. http://www.bnpparibas.com/en/node/4131/bnp-paribas-group-through-years.

"BNP Paribas." Rebrand. Accessed October 22, 2012. http://www.rebrand.com/notable-bnp-paribas.

"BNP Paribas Securities Services Opens New Offices in Colombia and Chile, Makes Senior Hires." *HITC Business*, March 26, 2012. Accessed October 25, 2012. http://hereisthecity.com/2012/03/26/bnp-paribas-securities-services-opens-new-offices-in-colombia-an/.

Brand Finance. "Global 500 2012." *Brandirectory.* Accessed September 3, 2012. http://brandirectory.com/league_tables/table/global-500-2012.

Brownsell, Alex. "Banking Giant BNP Paribas Looks to Boost Brand Overseas". *Marketing Magazine.* London: November 19, 2010. Accessed February 16, 2013. http://www.marketingmagazine.co.uk/news/1042042/Banking-giant-BNP-Paribas-looks-boost-brand-overseas/.

"China Banks Took 29 Pct of 2011 Global Profit." Reuters, July 2, 2012.

DeCarlo, Scott. "The World's Biggest Companies." *Forbes*, April 19, 2012. Accessed October 25, 2012. http://www.forbes.com/global2000/#p_1_s_a0_All%20industries_All%20countries_All%20states_.

"Keep Reaching: The Global Corporate Advertising Campaign". *BNP Paribas.* Paris: 2010. Accessed February 16, 2013. http://www.bnpparibas.com/en/news-press-room/brand.

"Top Banks in the World." 2012. BankersAccuity. Accessed October 23, 2012. http://www.bankersaccuity.com/resources/bank-rankings/.

BOEING

AT A GLANCE

Brand Synopsis: In order to meet its goal of becoming the largest and best aerospace company in the world, Boeing focuses on innovative designs and a commitment to meet the ever-changing needs of its clients.
Parent Company: Boeing Co.
100 North Riverside
Chicago, IL 60606
United States.
http://www.boeing.com
Sector: Industrials
Industry Group: Capital Goods
Performance: *Market share*—50% of all airline planes in service (2011). *Sales*—US$68.7 billion (2011).
Principal Competitors: European Aeronautic Defence and Space Company EADS N.V.; Airbus S.A.S.; BAE Systems PLC; Aviation Industry Corporation of China; Lockheed Martin Corp.; Northrop Grumman; Raytheon Co.; General Dynamics Corp.

BRAND ORIGINS

- In 1916, William Boeing incorporated Pacific Aero Products Co., which became Boeing Airplane Co. in 1917 and Boeing Co. in 1961.
- In the years prior to World War II, Boeing established itself as the leading manufacturer of airplanes.
- Boeing built the roving vehicle used to explore the moon in the early 1970s on the final three Apollo missions.
- In the 1990s, Boeing acquired the aerospace and defense units of Rockwell International and McDonnell Douglas to become the world's largest aerospace manufacturer.

The history of Boeing follows the same trajectory as the history of the expansion of airplane and space vehicle manufacturing. Founder William Boeing took his first flight in 1910 and became fascinated with aviation. His father's forestry business sent Boeing to the state of Washington, where he met a Navy engineer named Conrad Westerveldt, who shared his fascination with aviation.

Boeing and Westerveldt built a biplane they called the B&W, and Boeing took it on its first flight in May 1916. That same year, Boeing founded Pacific Aero Products Co. (which was renamed Boeing Airplane Co. in 1917), whose first customer, the government of New Zealand, bought two B&W planes for mail delivery and pilot training.

During World War I, Boeing was asked to train flight instructors for the U.S. Army. After the war, when the post office solicited bids for various airmail routes, Boeing submitted a bid and was awarded the contract. The Kelly Airmail Act of 1925 opened the way for private airmail delivery on a much wider scale, and Boeing purchased a number of air transport companies to expand its business; its airline holdings included the original United Air Lines. In 1928 all of these companies were organized under a holding company called Boeing Aircraft and

Transportation Co. A government investigation of collusion in the airmail business in 1934 led Congress to declare that airline companies and airplane manufacturers could not be part of the same business concern. This led to the breakup of three aeronautic conglomerates, including Boeing.

In the years before World War II, Boeing led the way in developing single-wing airplanes and established itself as the leading manufacturer of airplanes. During the war, Boeing produced hundreds of its B-17 "Flying Fortress" aircraft for the U.S. Army and an improved bomber called the B-29 "Super Fortress." In the 1950s, Boeing introduced a new jet, the B-707. At the same time, the company developed a prototype vehicle for manned space travel. Boeing built a lunar roving vehicle for the final three Apollo missions in the early 1970s. In the early 1990s, Boeing served as the prime contractor for the International Space Station.

In addition, the company was also becoming increasingly involved in commercial space projects, most notably Sea Launch, a consortium of which Boeing owned 40 percent, with partners from Russia, Ukraine, and Norway. Boeing complemented its space business by buying the satellite manufacturing operations of Hughes Electronics for US$3.9 billion in 2000. This and several other mergers and acquisitions (of divisions of Rockwell International and McDonnell Douglas, for example) helped Boeing become the largest aerospace manufacturer in the world.

BRAND ELEMENTS

- A 2006 brand audit resulted in a brand-unification effort that emphasized uniformity and a simplified color palette for Boeing's logo.
- Boeing's trademarked logo consists of elements that originated in the logos of Boeing and McDonnell Douglas that were in use before their merger.
- The current Boeing logo features a circle with a Saturn-like ring rotating around it and the company's name in dynamic, Stratotype letters.

Founded in 1916 as Pacific Aero Products Co., Boeing was later known as Boeing Airplane Co. (1917), Boeing Air Transport Co. (1927), and Boeing Aircraft and Transportation Co. (1928), before changing its name to Boeing Co. in 1961.

In 2006, Boeing launched an audit of its brand and determined that the company's message had become lost because of outdated materials and a lack of brand unity. An ensuing overhaul focused on brand unity and modernizing the company's look, reducing costs by ensuring uniformity, and decreasing disorder and confusion in the company's communications. The color palette was simplified and Helvetica was chosen as the company's standard font.

It also important to note the Boeing's current trademarked logo is a melding of the pre-merger logos of Boeing and McDonnell Douglas. The current Boeing symbol, a circle with a Saturn-like ring rotating around it, is actually taken from the McDonnell Douglas logo in use at the time of the merger. A stylized outline of a jet also appears on the lower right edge of the circle. The rightward-slanting, Stratotype letters used in the Boeing name are from company's pre-merger logo.

BRAND IDENTITY

- In 2008 Boeing launched a "one brand, one company" campaign to unify the brand and strengthen its identity.
- Boeing identifies itself as a global aerospace company committed to innovative technology in a full range of capacities: commercial, defense, space, and securities.
- New advertising campaigns were used by Boeing to close the gap between current perceptions of Boeing and its intended brand identity.

The Boeing brand is an incomparable asset for the company. By the early 21st century, the numerous acquisitions and the variety of the company's products had shifted and changed the Boeing brand. In 2008 the company instituted the "one brand, one company" campaign to unify the brand. This effort created a standard across Boeing's companies, simplified its color palette, unified its logo, and clarified the logo's use. According to the company, this rebranding also supported the company's new brand identity: "to the best and best-integrated aerospace company in the world." It wants consumers to know that its products are backed by integrity as well as innovation, plus a commitment to developing efficient, environmentally friendly technologies.

More than just focusing on its abilities to convey its status as a global brand, Boeing wishes to convey its status as a global *aerospace* brand. In order to close the gap between consumers' current perceptions of Boeing as a producer of commercial airliners and its true scope as a global defense, space, and securities firm, Boeing has launched several new advertising campaigns. In recent years Boeing has launched ads that explain the types of innovative products they design, which include, in addition to cleaner and more efficient airplanes, green technologies used to find more efficient energy supplies. Other ads have focused solely on saluting the military for their service as a way to identify the Boeing brand with the defense markets in which it operates.

BRAND STRATEGY

- Boeing's commercial segment focuses on the development of new products like the 787 Dreamliner and the 747-8 Freighter.

- In addition to developing new products, Boeing seeks to increase its operational output to ensure on-time delivery of its airplanes.
- As in the commercial division, Boeing's Defense, Space, and Security division also focuses on the development of new, innovative products like the 702 MP satellite.
- Part of the Boeing strategy is to change with its clients' needs, investing, for example, in new defense technologies for intelligence and surveillance.

Boeing is an international market leader in the design and manufacture of commercial aircraft and defense and space products. With a 2016 goal of being the biggest and best aerospace company, Boeing's most crucial commercial strategies are to develop and sell new, efficient products and to improve upon their delivery times for these products. In 2011 Boeing Commercial Aircraft sold 805 new airplanes, including 150 of its new 737 MAX. Another example of the new product launches Boeing made in 2011 was the certification and first deliveries of the 787 Dreamliner and the 747-8 Freighter. These planes, with new designs that make them safer, faster, and more efficient, marked a new beginning for Boeing's future, as well as its clients' futures, as it positions itself to add value to an industry in need of change.

With new development underway, like the assembly plant for the 787 Dreamliner in South Carolina, Boeing's second key strategy for the commercial segment is to find ways to deliver punctually on its sales contracts. According to the company's 2011 annual report, Boeing will continue to invest in its operations in order to deliver outstanding orders. Over the following three years alone, planned production was targeted to boost commercial airplane output by more than 40 percent. This number is important to Boeing's brand promise of being the biggest and best company because its market keeps expanding. In 2011, Boeing Commercial Airplanes took in revenues that were 11 percent higher than in 2010. With US$355 million worth of undelivered planes, strategies aimed at raising production rates should boost revenues tremendously.

Likewise, strategies for Boeing's Defense, Space, and Security division also rely upon strong sales of existing products and continued production of new products. In 2011, the company achieved milestones that demonstrate the new product development that defines the brand: the introduction of the Block III Apache helicopter and the first deliveries of the 702 MP satellite.

While this development may falter a bit due to declines in the U.S. and European defense budgets, Boeing is also attempting to grow its brands overseas in places like the Middle East and Asia. Additionally Boeing seeks to increase its stake in the use of technology for defense purposes. While the United States and other countries are cutting their budgets, they nevertheless plan to increase spending on intelligence and surveillance. Part of Boeing's strategy will be to make the necessary budget cuts so that the company can invest in acquisitions that lead to competence in these new markets. So far, Boeing has made 11 acquisitions in order to realize the new technology capabilities that its customers demand.

BRAND EQUITY

- Boeing's airplane deliveries increased from 2009 to 2010, boosting the value of the Boeing brand to an estimated US$9.02 million.
- Boeing ranked 97th in *Brandirectory's* Global 500 in 2012; rival Airbus ranked 213th.
- Boeing's continued development of new products also serves as an explanation for its greater brand value in 2012.

With record revenues of US$68.7 billion in 2011, Boeing was ranked 97th on the *Brandirectory* Global 500 list in 2012; its competitor Airbus came in at number 213. According to *Brandirectory*, Boeing recorded a decline in revenues between 2009 and 2010, but that was the same period during which Boeing reported the second-highest net income in the company's history. In 2012, *Brandirectory* gave Boeing its AA rating, valuing the brand at US$9.02 billion, up from its 2010 value of US$7.06 billion. The increase in brand value appeared to coincide with an increase in the number of aircraft delivered by Boeing Commercial Airplanes. That number doubled from 2009 to 2010, and Boeing, according to Brand Finance, anticipated an 11 percent increase in its production of the popular 737 jetliner. Additionally, Boeing's development of several other new aircraft, like the 787 Dreamliner, helped raise both its bottom line and its brand value.

BRAND AWARENESS

- Boeing enjoys high brand recall, especially in the business-to-business arena.
- The 2008 rebranding effort, paired with current ad campaigns, strove to strengthen Boeings brand awareness among consumers.
- Legal disputes between Boeing and Airbus between 2004 and 2012 led to negative publicity.

Boeing enjoys high business-to-business brand awareness with, according to its long-term market forecast, 50 percent placement of all in-service airplanes. However, Boeing has also tried to spread awareness of its brand to the general population through its recent ad campaigns focusing on the military. In addition to expressing gratitude to those who serve, Boeing aims to teach the public about its line of services extending beyond commercial flight.

While Boeing enjoys high brand recall, some of this recognition is the result of negative publicity. From 2004 to 2012, for example, Boeing and its rival Airbus were entangled in a legal dispute before the World Trade Organization (WTO). Each side claimed that the other had gained an unfair advantage through government subsidies or loans of billions of dollars. In December 2011 the WTO found that Airbus had received subsidies from European governments and, several months later, announced that Boeing had received support from the U.S. government. Both sides claimed victory in the dispute. In October 2012 the European Union requested billion-dollar sanctions against Boeing, as the governments moved toward arbitration in an effort to resolve claims that the United States had continued to subsidize Boeing.

BRAND OUTLOOK

- The future of Boeing's brand looks bright due to anticipated growth in passenger numbers and the creation of innovative products to handle this growth.
- The 787 Dreamliner, positioned to help Boeing take a large part of the commercial market, was designed to help airlines save on fuel and maintenance costs.
- Between 2007 and 2012, Boeing increased its commitment to preserving the environment and surpassed its goal of reducing its energy-use footprint by 25 percent.

The future of Boeing's brand looks promising. Although air travel has declined in recent years due to the 2008 economic recession, Boeing's long-term market forecast suggests that passenger demand is expected to grow. According to the report, growth in 2012 was expected to be close to the long-term average rate of 5 percent because "trends that drove above-average passenger growth in 2011 have continued into 2012." These trends included: "economic growth and expanding middle classes in emerging markets; liberalization and new airline business models that stimulate demand; and corporate focus on revenue growth, which bolsters demand for business-class travel." Boeing has positioned itself to take a big piece of this projected growth with innovative new products and a broad range of global consumers.

One example of this can be seen in the release of the 787 Dreamliner. While Airbus was making headlines with its massive new A380 in the early 21st century, Boeing conceived its latest design, the 787 Dreamliner, specifically as an aircraft that could save airlines money. With passenger growth and fuel prices on the rise, the 787 promises to use 20 percent less fuel than a traditional jetliner of similar size, while also lowering maintenance costs 30 percent. Sales of the Dreamliner skyrocketed, and between 2004 and 2007 Boeing took in 700 orders—faster sales than for any other aircraft in history. Boeing also anticipated orders for more than 7,290 airplanes over the next 20 years as older models are retired and fuel-efficiency concerns increase.

In addition to building efficient products, Boeing has also sought to strengthen the future of its brand by improving its corporate citizenship. According to Brand Finance, Boeing established goals for improving the company's environmental footprint 25 percent across various categories between 2007 and 2012. By the end of 2010, Boeing had surpassed its goals, reducing greenhouse gas emissions by 28 percent, energy consumption by almost 33 percent, water intake by 42 percent, and hazardous waste by 44 percent.

FURTHER READING

"Aircraft." *Encyclopedia of American Industries.* Ed. Lynn M. Pearce. Detroit: Gale, 2012. *Business Insights: Global.* Accessed October 25, 2012. http://bi.galegroup.com/global/article/GALE%7CRN2501400411/acce42e8aaa590e2f00aaf8acbcbf41b?u=itsbtrial.

Beirne, Mike. "These Wings Have A Name." *Brandweek* 46.6 (2005): 16-17. *Business Source Alumni Edition.* Accessed October 23, 2012. https://web.ebscohost.com/ehost/detail?sid=687f3159-b1e3-4f8c-8536-2cceda821fad%40sessionmgr110&vid=33&hid=106&bdata=JnNpdGU9ZWhvc3QtbGl2ZQ%3d%3d#db=bah&AN=16202211.

"Boeing and Airbus Spar in London." *Business Travel World* (2008): 6. *Business Source Alumni Edition.* Accessed October 25, 2012. https://web.ebscohost.com/ehost/detail?sid=687f3159-b1e3-4f8c-8536-2cceda821fad%40sessionmgr110&vid=30&hid=106&bdata=JnNpdGU9ZWhvc3QtbGl2ZQ%3d%3d#db=bah&AN=37836371.

"The Boeing Company." *MarketLine Company Profiles Authority.* Accessed October 23, 2012. https://web.ebscohost.com/ehost/pdfviewer/pdfviewer?sid=687f3159-b1e3-4f8c-8536-2cceda821fad%40sessionmgr110&vid=40&hid=106.

"Boeing sees North American market for 7,290 new airplanes over 20 years." *Airline Industry Information,* October 26, 2012. *Business and Company ASAP.* Accessed October 28, 2012. http://go.galegroup.com/ps/retrieve.do?sgHitCountType=None&sort=DA-SORT&inPS=true&prodId=GPS&userGroupName=itsbtrial&tabID=T003&searchId=R5&resultListType=RESULT_LIST&contentSegment=&searchType=BasicSearchForm¤tPosition=1&contentSet=GALE%7CA306479350&&docId=GALE|A306479350&docType=GALE&role=ITOF.

"Boeing WTO Case Continues." *European Report,* October 15, 2012: 322-441. *Business Insights: Global.* Accessed October 28, 2012. http://go.galegroup.com/ps/retrieve.do?sgHitCountType=None&sort=DA-SORT&inPS=true&prodId=GPS&userGroupName=itsbtrial&tabID=T004&searchId=R4&resultListType=RESULT_LIST&contentSegment=&searchType=BasicSearchForm¤tPosition=1&contentSet=GALE%7CA305184738&&docId=GALE|A305184738&docType=GALE&role=ITOF.

Brand Finance. "Global 500 2012." *Brandirectory.* Accessed October 23, 2012. http://brandirectory.com/league_tables/table/global-500-2012.

Burrows, Peter, et al. "Outsourcing Innovation." *Businessweek* March 21, 2005, 84-94. *Business Source Alumni Edition.* Accessed October 23, 2012. https://web.ebscohost.com/ehost/pdfviewer/pdfviewer?vid=26&hid=106&sid=687f3159-b1e3-4f8c-8536-2cceda821fad%40sessionmgr110.

"Business: Fearful Boeing." *Economist,* February 27, 1999, 59-60. *ABI/INFORM Complete; ProQuest Research Library.* Accessed October 24, 2012. http://search.proquest.com/pqrlalumni/docview/224059386/fulltext/13A45066DB96FDD763A/1?accountid=35803.

Donnini, Frank P. "Boeing versus Airbus: The Inside Story of the Greatest International Competition in Business." *Air & Space Power Journal* 24.1 (2010): 112-3. *ABI/INFORM Complete; ProQuest Research Library.* Accessed October 24, 2012. https://web.ebscohost.com/ehost/pdfviewer/pdfviewer?sid=687f3159-b1e3-4f8c-8536-2cceda821fad%40sessionmgr110&vid=17&hid=106.

"EU request for Boeing sanctions referred to WTO arbitration." *Xinhua News Agency,* October 23, 2012. *Business Insights: Global.* Accessed October 28, 2012. http://go.galegroup.com/ps/retrieve.do?sgHitCountType=None&sort=DA-SORT&inPS=true&prodId=GPS&userGroupName=itsbtrial&tabID=T004&searchId=R6&resultListType=RESULT_LIST&contentSegment=&searchType=BasicSearchForm¤tPosition=1&contentSet=GALE%7CA306050486&&docId=GALE|A306050486&docType=GALE&role=ITOF.

Frank, John N. "My Kind of Marketing Town, Chicago Is ..." *Marketing News* 43.14 (2009): 4. *Business Source Alumni Edition.* Accessed October 23, 2012. https://web.ebscohost.com/ehost/pdfviewer/pdfviewer?sid=687f3159-b1e3-4f8c-8536-2cceda821fad%40sessionmgr110&vid=13&hid=106.

Gasbarre, April Dougal, David E. Salamie, and Frederick C. Ingram. "The Boeing Company." *International Directory of Company Histories.* Ed. Jay P. Pederson. Vol. 111. Detroit: St. James Press, 2010. Accessed October 20, 2012. http://go.galegroup.com/ps/retrieve.do?sgHitCountType=None&isETOC=true&inPS=true&prodId=GPS&userGroupName=itsbtrial&resultListType=RELATED_DOCUMENT&searchType=PublicationSearchForm&contentSegment=&docId=GALE|CX2624600014.

Howard, Carrie. "One for All." *Boeing Frontiers.* Accessed October 24, 2012. http://www.boeing.com/news/frontiers/archive/2009/february/mainfeature.pdf.

Kte'pi, Bill. "Boeing." *Encyclopedia of Business in Today's World.* Ed. Charles Wankel. Vol. 1. Thousand Oaks, CA: Sage Publications, 2009, 163-64. http://go.galegroup.com/ps/retrieve.do?sgHitCountType=None&isETOC=true&inPS=true&prodId=GPS&userGroupName=itsbtrial&resultListType=RELATED_DOCUMENT&searchType=PublicationSearchForm&contentSegment=&docId=GALE|CX3201500109.

"Leading Commercial Aircraft Makers, 2010." *Market Share Reporter.* Ed. Robert S. Lazich and Virgil L. Burton III. Detroit: Gale, 2012. *Business Insights: Global.* Accessed October 24, 2012. http://bi.galegroup.com/global/article/GALE%7CI2502038032/19afd6ef9deba44cbaafb2d87e4a0803?u=itsbtrial.

Sprott, David, Sandor Czellar, and Eric Spangenberg. "The Importance of a General Measure of Brand Engagement on Market Behavior: Development and Validation of a Scale." *Journal of Marketing Research* 46.1 (2009): 92-104. *Business Source Alumni Edition.* Accessed October 23, 2012. https://web.ebscohost.com/ehost/pdfviewer/pdfviewer?sid=687f3159-b1e3-4f8c-8536-2cceda821fad%40sessionmgr110&vid=8&hid=106.

Sullivan, Elisabeth A. "Building a Better Brand." *Marketing News* 43.14 (2009): 14-17. *Business Source Alumni Edition.* Accessed October 23, 2012. https://web.ebscohost.com/ehost/pdfviewer/pdfviewer?sid=687f3159-b1e3-4f8c-8536-2cceda821fad%40sessionmgr110&vid=5&hid=106.

BOMBARDIER

AT A GLANCE

Brand Synopsis: Initially known for snowcraft and watercraft, Bombardier now makes planes, trains, and transportation components to contribute to what it calls the evolution of mobility.
Parent Company: Bombardier Inc.
800 René-Lévesque Boulevard West
Montreal, Quebec H3B 1Y8
Canada
http://bombardier.com/
Sector: Industrials
Industry Group: Transportation
Performance: *Sales*—US$17.7 billion (2011).
Principal Competitors: Boeing Commercial Airplanes; CitationShares Holdings, LLC; Delta AirElite Business Jets, Inc.; Embraer S.A.; Flight Options LLC; Gulfstream Aerospace Corporation; NetJets Inc.; Siemens Aktiengesellschaft

BRAND ORIGINS

- In 1937 Joseph-Armand Bombardier received a patent for his seven-passenger B7 snowmobile, which led to the founding of a company known for creating various modes of transportation.
- Bombardier produced snowcraft like the Ski-Doo, watercraft like the Sea-Doo, and personal recreational vehicles. Today, a separate company, Bombardier Recreational Products, makes these products.
- The acquisition of various aircraft companies around the world helped create Bombardier Aerospace, one of the world's leading aircraft manufacturers and a provider of other air services.

Bombardier has a colorful history that started with snowmobiles and other snowcraft as well as personal watercraft and recreation vehicles. Today, Bombardier is known for other transportation products. It is a major manufacturer of air and rail transport products and provides other services and operations for these fields.

The company is named after its founder, Joseph-Armand Bombardier, who was a mechanic and inventor. As a teenager, Bombardier began building vehicles that could navigate the snowy winter roads in his native Quebec, Canada. In 1937 he received a patent for the seven-passenger B7 snowmobile. Orders for the B7 immediately followed, and in 1940 Bombardier built a factory to meet this demand. Other snowcraft followed, in addition to all-terrain vehicles for the mining, oil, agriculture, and forest industries. The company even built military snowcraft that were used in World War II.

In 1959 it began building the Ski-Doo snowmobile. This vehicle became extremely popular with various outdoor workers and recreational riders. Bombardier also built personal watercraft such as the Sea-Doo and all-terrain vehicles. The company no longer makes these types of personal snow, water, and recreational vehicles; instead, Bombardier Recreational Products makes these products.

During the 1970s and 1980s the company began producing rail products, such as railway and subway cars. This part of Bombardier, Bombardier Transportation, today manufactures trains and railway components and provides rail operations all over the world. Befitting this international work, the headquarters of Bombardier Transportation are in Berlin, Germany.

The company's participation in yet another industry intensified in 1986, when it bought the Canadian aircraft producer Canadair. Three years later Bombardier acquired another aircraft company, Northern Ireland's Short Brothers. Bombardier's other significant aircraft acquisitions include the assets of Learjet Corporation (1990) and Canada's de Havilland (1992). These acquisitions have helped build this part of Bombardier, Bombardier Aerospace, into one of the world's leading aircraft manufacturers. Bombardier manufactures products and provides services for customers all over the world.

BRAND ELEMENTS

- The logo for Bombardier is the company name in bold black letters.
- Bombardier conveys its evolution of mobility brand promise in annual reports, advertising, and web pages.
- Bombardier's Flexjet service has a logo featuring a horizontal line with an attached tail fin, echoing the jets of the Flexjet Program.

Bombardier uses a simple logo, consisting of the company name in black capital letters. This simple logo is a departure from earlier company logos, which featured the company name on or near images of wheels or sprockets. The new streamlined logo reflects Bombardier's status as a company that provides a variety of transportation products and services, not just ones involving wheels or sprockets.

While simplifying its logo, Bombardier has also placed increasing emphasis on its brand promise: the evolution of mobility. This phrase is used in materials such as annual reports, advertising, and web pages. Instead of communicating the fact that it is a transportation brand with its wheel or sprocket logo, Bombardier now communicates this through its evolution of mobility brand promise.

Bombardier has not abandoned all brand logos, however. Its Flexjet service, which allows customers to buy or partially buy aircraft or flights, has a logo that consists of a drawing of a long horizontal line with an airplane tail fin sticking out of it. This logo looks one of the jets featured in the Flexjet service and almost appears to move, reiterating the company's interests in mobility.

BRAND IDENTITY

- Bombardier originally made snowcraft and watercraft; its evolution of mobility brand promise reflects these brand changes.
- Bombardier's 2011 annual report featured a cover photograph of plane and train passengers and the tagline "It's all about what's next."
- A Bombardier brochure detailing its manufacture of bogies (wheeled undercarriages of trains and vehicles) featured a striking photograph of bogie wheels on the cover, again linking the brand to transportation production.

Over the years Bombardier has transitioned from creating personal snow- and watercraft to manufacturing airplanes and railway and subway cars. The company's brand promise, the evolution of mobility, encompasses this transition. By using the word *evolution*, this brand promise portrays Bombardier as a progressive company that changes and adapts in its quest to become a better company. The mobility part of the promise describes Bombardier's field of work: transportation. In addition, mobility suggests a company that is moving and can help others move as well.

The company communicated its status as a transportation brand in its 2011 annual report. The cover of this report featured large photographs of people traveling in planes and trains, immediately establishing the fact that Bombardier is involved in aerospace and rail transportation. Reinforcing the travel theme, the cover used Bombardier's evolution of mobility brand promise with the tagline "It's all about what's next."

Other Bombardier written materials convey its transportation work. For example, it produced a brochure describing its manufacture of bogies, which are the wheeled undercarriages of trains and vehicles. The front of the brochure included a dramatic photograph of a bogie that displays its wheels prominently. Because this photograph was on the cover, it immediately showed people what bogies are and that Bombardier manufactures them. To reinforce this connection, the brochure prominently featured the Bombardier logo and the tagline "Our Innovations Keep You Moving."

BRAND STRATEGY

- A 2012 promotional campaign highlighted the services and flexibility of Bombardier's Flexjet Program. Bombardier manages these plans in addition to building and servicing the aircraft for these plans, which allow customers to buy or partially buy aircraft or flights.
- Bombardier's three-pronged corporate strategy is to "create better ways to move the world," to focus on "global growth opportunities," and to enhance its "customer-focused excellence."
- Regardless of the product it is making or the region or client it is serving, Bombardier uses its Bombardier brand name instead of other brand names.

In 2012 Bombardier launched a campaign to promote its Flexjet Program, which allows people to buy private jets.

They can buy these aircraft as individuals or as part of a group in a concept known as fractional ownership. They can also buy individual trips or pay for trips with a debit account. Bombardier manages these plans in addition to building and servicing the aircraft for these plans. The 2012 campaign highlighted these services and flexibility and emphasized images of people instead of just aircraft.

Another Bombardier initiative relates to its interests in transportation. In 2012 the company offered the online Bombardier YouCity competition, which challenged contestants to create new mobility solutions for urban areas. Contestants could work on engineering, business, or urban planning issues and, befitting Bombardier's global interests, could tailor their urban mobility plans to address London; Belo Horizonte, Brazil; or Vientiane, Laos.

Bombardier has a three-pronged corporate strategy. The first part of this strategy is to "create better ways to move the world." The second part of the strategy involves focusing on "global growth opportunities." The third and final part of the strategy explains that the company wants to enhance its "customer-focused excellence." This strategy is meant to enhance the brand name. Regardless, whether it is making planes, trains, or bogies for markets in North America or Asia or for a variety of customers, Bombardier is consistently Bombardier. It does not market entirely new brands, although its brand name sometimes appears on some of its joint products, such as the Lear Jet. The consistent use of the Bombardier name continues to connect the company to its transportation products and services.

BRAND EQUITY

- In 2011 Europe provided 45 percent of Bombardier's revenues, the United States, 24 percent; Asia-Pacific, 15 percent; Canada, 7 percent: and other regions, 9 percent.
- Bombardier earned 50 percent of its 2011 aerospace revenues from business aircraft, 20 percent from commercial aircraft, 18 percent from aircraft services, and 12 percent from other sources.
- In 2012 Bombardier captured approximately one-third of China's market for business jets.
- In 2012 Bombardier had a 24 percent market share for business jets in the Middle East and Turkey.

As befitting an international company, Bombardier earns money from operations around the world. In 2011 Europe provided 45 percent of the company's revenues; the United States, 24 percent; Asia-Pacific, 15 percent; Canada, 7 percent; and other regions, 9 percent. That same year Bombardier reported revenues of US$8.6 billion and was rated to be the third-largest civil aircraft manufacturer in the world. Concerning its rail technology, it had revenues of US$9.8 billion. Bombardier earned 50 percent of its 2011 aerospace revenues from business aircraft, 20 percent from commercial aircraft, 18 percent from aircraft services, and 12 percent from other sources.

As one of the world's largest aircraft and rail providers, Bombardier has significant market share in certain regions. In 2012 it captured approximately one-third of China's market for business jets. That same year Bombardier had a 24 percent market share for business jets in the Middle East and Turkey.

BRAND AWARENESS

- Interbrand named Bombardier the 16th most valuable Canadian brand in 2012.
- In 2012 Brand Finance ranked Bombardier eighth in the top 50 Canadian brands.
- In 2012 Brand Finance ranked Bombardier 245th in its "Global 500 2012."

In its "Best Canadian Brands 2012," Interbrand named Bombardier the 16th most valuable Canadian brand in 2012. The company also made this list in 2010 and 2011. In the 2012 list, Interbrand noted that the company held an "industry-leading position in both aerospace and rail transportation through game-changing developments" and that the evolution of mobility brand promise described "the brand's strong reputation for innovation within the transportation industry."

Similarly, Bombardier placed eighth in the 2012 edition of the "Canada 50," Brand Finance's list of the top Canadian brands. Brand Finance also lists the top brands in the entire world in its annual "Global 500." In 2012 Bombardier placed 245th on the list. It also ranked among the top-500 brands on this list in 2009, 2010, and 2011.

During the late 1990s and early 2000s Bombardier's reputation suffered as customers reported dissatisfaction with its services. Bombardier worked to remedy these problems by improving its services around the world, making parts more available, extending warranties, and bringing its service operations together as a single unit. Bombardier took these measures to serve global customers and to compete with other global companies.

BRAND OUTLOOK

- Anticipating that China's growing companies and increasing number of wealthy individuals will want new aircraft, Bombardier has expanded its operations in the region by hiring more salespeople, support workers, and executives.
- In 2012 Bombardier had more than 8,000 employees and eight production sites in Germany.
- In 2012 Bombardier announced its plans to continue operating and maintaining its people mover system in Spain's Madrid-Baraja Airport and its intention to provide rail technology in Poland.

During the second decade of the 21st century Bombardier is looking to expand its operations in China. In preparation for this expansion, it has hired more salespeople, support workers, and executives for the region. Bombardier has taken these measures due to the increasingly large number of large corporations and wealthy individuals in China. Bombardier anticipates that these companies and individuals will want new aircraft, and it wants to be ready to meet this demand.

The company is heavily involved in other ventures outside of North America. In 2012 Bombardier had more than 8,000 employees and eight production sites in Germany, and it started construction on the Bogie Technical Centre in Siegen, Germany. As the name indicates, the center will focus on bogies, which are undercarriages with wheels for rail vehicles such as trains.

Bombardier announced other international work in 2012. It would continue operating and maintaining its people mover system in Spain's Madrid-Baraja Airport. It also planned to provide rail technology in Poland and extend its work for the public transit system in Toronto, Canada. This work illustrates Bombardier's pledge to provide mobility for people all over the world.

FURTHER READING

"Best Canadian Brands 2012." Interbrand. Accessed January 28, 2013. http://www.interbrand.com/en/Interbrand-offices/Interbrand-Toronto/Best-Canadian-Brands-2012.aspx.

"Bombardier, Inc." *International Directory of Company Histories.* Ed. Jay P. Pederson. Vol. 87. Detroit, MI: St. James Press, 2007.

"Bombardier 2010 Olympics Commercial—Olympic Torch." YouTube, February 26, 2010. Accessed January 29, 2013. http://www.youtube.com/watch?v=P3e_h3LVn90.

Brand Finance. "Global 500 2012." *Brandirectory.* Accessed January 28, 2013. http://brandirectory.com/league_tables/table/global-500-2012.

Epstein, Curt. "Bombardier Claims One-Third Share of Booming China Market." AINonline, March 27, 2012. Accessed January 28, 2013. http://www.ainonline.com/aviation-news/abace-convention-news/2012-03-26/bombardier-claims-one-third-share-booming-china-market-0.

"MEBA2012: Bombardier—the View from the Top." Arabian Aerospace Online News Service, December 12, 2012. Accessed January 28, 2013. http://www.arabianaerospace.aero/meba2012-bombardier-the-view-from-the-top.html.

"New Flexjet Director of Marketing Taking Brand to New Heights." Bombardier, June 4, 2012. Accessed December 31, 2012. http://us.bombardier.com/us/press_release_04062012_1.htm.

Silcoff, Sean. "Bombardier, the Comeback Kid." *Globe and Mail,* August 23, 2012.

BP

AT A GLANCE

Brand Synopsis: Since 2000 BP has promoted an image of environmental responsibility, embracing a "Beyond Petroleum" message, only to have its brand identity undercut in 2010 by history's worst marine oil spill.
Parent Company: BP plc
One St. James Square
London
United Kingdom
http://www.bp.com
Sector: Energy
Industry Group: Energy
Performance: *Market share*—BP is the world's third-largest publicly traded oil company (2012). *Sales*—US$38 billion (2012).
Principal Competitors: Exxon Mobile Corporation; Royal Dutch Shell plc; Chevron Corporation

BRAND ORIGINS

- Company origins date to 1901.
- The BP corporate mark was the result of a 1920 employee design competition.
- The British Petroleum Company name was adopted in 1954.
- The 1998 merger with Amoco Corporation set the stage for oil industry consolidation.
- BP adopted a new global branding strategy in 2000.

One of the world's largest integrated oil companies, BP plc maintains more than one brand. In addition to the flagship BP brand, they include brands for several subsidiaries. BP is an abbreviation for British Petroleum Company, a corporate name that did not exist until 1954. The company's roots actually date to 1901 when Englishman William Knox D'Arcy secured a concession to explore for oil in Iran. In 2008 he struck oil, and the following year he formed Anglo-Persian Oil Company, which would one day become known as British Petroleum, and ultimately BP plc.

The BP brand preceded the British Petroleum name by more than 30 years. In 1920 the company held an employee contest to design the first corporate mark. The winning entry, submitted by a member of the purchasing department, depicted the letters BP within the outline of a shield. Initially there were no designated colors for the mark. It was used throughout the United Kingdom on gas station signage and on the globes that topped gas pumps. Advertising was limited in the 1920s because driving was still very much the pastime of the upper class. As automobiles became more affordable in the 1930s, the BP brand was promoted to the general public.

While the BP brand was taking shape in the United Kingdom, it was also being introduced to other European countries. It was the French operation in 1923 that began applying green and yellow to the corporate mark. The color scheme was soon adopted by the Swiss. In Britain the BP pumps and delivery trucks were painted bright red. Supposedly, rural residents complained that the vivid color marred the scenery, leading to the repainting of the pumps to a more acceptable green. During the 1930s all subsidiaries were required to use a green and yellow BP trademark.

In addition to assuming the British Petroleum name during the post–World War II era, the company expanded globally. The BP brand was extended to Canada in 1953. BP staked a claim in the United States in 1968 when it acquired the East Coast refining and marketing operations of the Atlantic Richfield Company. A year later, an alliance was established with Standard Oil Company of Ohio. In 1987 SOHIO was acquired, resulting in the creation of BP America.

In 1998 BP sparked a period of consolidation in the oil industry when it acquired Amoco Corporation, the United States' fifth-largest oil company, in a US$50 billion transaction. The greatly enlarged company assumed the name BP Amoco plc, and for a time the BP shield was joined by Amoco's well-known torch mark. In 2000 the company unveiled a new global BP brand, including a new mark to replace both the shield and the torch and a new brand image the company felt was suited for the new millennium.

BRAND ELEMENTS

- The BP initials were retained in the 2000 global branding program.
- BP's traditional green and yellow colors were incorporated into a new logo in 2000.
- The Helios of the BP logo is named after the Greek sun god.
- The Helios symbolizes all forms of dynamic energy.
- The "Beyond Petroleum" tagline was meant to convey a commitment to green energy.

There are several elements at the heart of the BP brand. The BP name maintains ties to the company's British Petroleum linage. The initials, presented in lower case, are also included in the company's logo. The primary image was what the company called the Helios. Named after the Greek sun god, the mark is a sunburst of green, yellow, and white. The green and yellow colors had been long associated with the BP brand. In their new configuration when introduced in 2000, the colors were now meant to symbolize dynamic energy in all of its forms and represent BP's commitment to the development of new sustainable forms of energy. The symbol also looked like a blossoming flower, another image in line with BP's sustainable energy positioning.

A promise to become something of a green company was also conveyed in BP's new slogan, "Beyond Petroleum." On the surface it was a playful recast of "British Petroleum," but it also reflected a new brand promise. BP's ability to keep that promise, however, proved problematic.

BRAND IDENTITY

- BP's brand identity and brand image diverged sharply following the 2010 Deepwater Horizon accident.
- The 2000 rebranding initiative positioned BP as an environmentally responsible company.
- Both the BP workforce and the general public were won over by the "Beyond Petroleum" messaging.
- BP's brand positioning proved detrimental following the 2010 Deepwater Horizon accident.

After the public relations nightmare resulting from the 2010 Deepwater Horizon disaster that caused a historic oil spill in the Gulf of Mexico, BP's brand identity, meaning how the company wished to be perceived, diverged greatly from the public perception of the brand. The "Beyond Petroleum" branding campaign launched in July 2000 was crafted as a way to position the BP brand as a leader in cleaner petroleum and renewable energy. On its website, the company boasted, "BP is progressive, responsible, innovative and performance driven. Our logo—the Helios—symbolizes these values." Headlines on BP materials also reflected the brand's new identity. One declared, "It's time to go on a low-carbon diet." Another mused, "Biofuels, solar, hydrogen, natural gas. We think it's important to diversify, too."

These were certainly messages that consumers wanted to hear, as people increasingly exhibited concerns about the fate of the earth's environment. BP employees were also buoyed by the rebranding. According to surveys, they held a positive image of the new brand and believed the company was turning in the right direction. In reality, BP had changed its message, but little else. It remained very much an oil company, devoting only a token amount of funds to the exploration for some form of renewable energy. BP also experienced periodic oil containment incidents, none of which were close in scale to the Deepwater Horizon incident. Until then, BP enjoyed success with its "Beyond Petroleum" tagline. According to branding agency CoreBrand, BP steadily increased its "Brand Power" score following the 2000 rebranding. After Deepwater Horizon, however, the "Beyond Petroleum" messaging became a liability to the brand.

BRAND STRATEGY

- BP's 2000 rebranding effort was supported by consumer advertising that portrayed BP as an environmentally friendly company.
- BP's 2001 "BP on the street" campaign offered sample opinions from residents in several U.S. cities on energy issues.
- In addition to its global corporate brand, BP maintains several subsidiary brands.

- While BP was building its brand around environmental responsibility, it was implicated in a number of environmental disasters.
- The Deepwater Horizon accident forced an immediate change in brand strategy.

BP was a typical oil company brand until the 1998 acquisition of Amoco Corporation. Faced with the consolidation of two prominent brands, BP embarked on a bold new global rebranding of BP. It was broadly conceived, aimed at both consumers and employees. Amoco and old BP gas stations were painted in the new colors, and new signage featuring the Helios symbol was installed. The company's consumer advertising supported a new brand image of an environmentally friendly company.

In 2001 BP launched the "BP on the street" campaign, featuring sample opinions from residents in several U.S. cities debating energy issues. BP then used these opinions to lay claim to a commitment to producing cleaner fuels and other green initiatives. In another example of the new brand positioning, BP began running ads in 2005 with the statement, "We're investing millions to lose our baggage—carbon emissions."

The new BP brand was also designed to excite and unify employees. A major thrust in this regard was a new internal magazine titled *Beyond*. It promoted several themes based on the new brand positioning. BP wished to be seen by its employees as progressive in its approach to doing business, committed to green initiatives, and making innovative use of technology. The magazine also promoted the idea that BP was performance-driven and eager for employees to embrace the new BP brand as a way to meet or exceed financial targets.

While BP polished its corporate and flagship consumer brand, it pursued a branding strategy that included the promotion of several subsidiary brands. They included ARCO, a regional U.S. gas station brand; ARAL, a German gas station brand; ampm, a convenience store chain in the western United States; Castrol motor oil and lubricants; and Wild Bean Café, a coffee house-café chain operating in about 10 countries. In the case of Wild Bean, the BP logo was used to promote the sub-brand.

While BP nurtured its green image in the early 2000s and achieved some level of success, the branding never went beyond the surface. In 2005 a fatal explosion at a BP Texas refinery led to a US$50 million criminal fine. A year later BP had to shut down an operation in Alaska because of leaking wells. In 2007 BP received negative publicity for applying and receiving a permit from the state of Indiana to dump additional levels of toxic discharges into Lake Michigan from its Whiting, Indiana, refinery. In 2009 a group of Colombian farmers sued the company, claiming a BP pipeline contaminated their groundwater and soil and caused other damage. In April and May of 2010 more than 500,000 pounds of chemicals, including a known carcinogen, were released into the air of the Texas City area because of faulty equipment at a BP facility. Two weeks after BP admitted to the chemical release, on April 20, 2010, the offshore drilling rig Deepwater Horizon exploded after a blowout, killing 11 people, and sent crude oil gushing into the Gulf of Mexico in what would become the oil industry's worst oil spill.

BP's branding strategy made an abrupt change. The primary goal now was to limit the damage to the brand. Because BP had laid claim to being an environmentally responsible company, the brand positioning now proved detrimental as it became readily apparent that the company's practices had not changed, just its messaging. The well was finally capped on July 15, 2010, but not before nearly 5 million gallons of oil poured into the Gulf. Even as crews worked to remedy the damage done to Gulf Coast states, BP sought to rebuild its tarnished brand. To help in this regard, BP launched an advertising campaign in late 2011 to promote tourism in the area. The feel-good spots claimed that all the beaches and waters of the area were open and that tourism was bouncing back. It was an overoptimistic assessment that the head of the Louisiana Shrimp Association called "BP propaganda." In truth, it would be many years before the Gulf Coast could recover from the disaster and before BP could restore any lost equity to its brand.

BRAND EQUITY

- The 2010 Deepwater Horizon accident caused deep erosion in BP's brand equity.
- At the end of 2010, Brand Finance estimated BP's brand value at US$8.754 billion.
- BP's brand value improved to US$10.222 billion at the end of 2011.
- BP was ranked No. 82 on Brand Finance's 2012 Global 500.
- Brand Finance listed BP as the 9th most valuable brand in the United Kingdom in 2012.

In spite of the harm caused to BP's reputation by the Deepwater Horizon accident, BP remains a very valuable brand. According to brand consultancy Brand Finance, the value of BP's brand fell 28 percent to US$8.754 billion by the end of 2011. BP ranked No. 104 on Brand Finance's Global 500 list of the world's most valuable brands in 2012. It was also listed as the United Kingdom's 11th most valuable brand. A year earlier, however, BP was No. 55 on the Global 500 and ranked as the United Kingdom's 7th most valuable brand. Due to the strength of BP's holdings and the health of the oil industry, BP's brand value, based largely on financial metrics, rebounded in 2011. It increased to US$10.222 billion, elevating BP to No. 82 on the 2012 Global 500 and No. 9 among the United Kingdom's top brands.

Despite BP's improving brand value, there was no doubt that BP's reputation had been severely compromised around the world. It was not only consumers, but also the morale of BP employees, that were impacted. It was impossible to place a monetary figure on the damage done to the equity of the BP brand in terms of the trust of both consumers and employees.

BRAND AWARENESS

- Traditionally BP enjoyed strong brand awareness in Europe.
- Brand awareness accelerated following the 1998 Amoco acquisition.
- The 2010 Deepwater Horizon accident created a high level of negative brand awareness.

BP enjoys strong brand awareness around the world. The BP trademark and its green and gold colors became well-known in the United Kingdom and Europe from the 1920s onward. The BP brand spread to North America and other parts of the world, and following the acquisition of Amoco in 1998, a revamped BP brand became familiar to a growing number of people. Nearly 22,000 gas stations around the world boast the BP name, affording ample opportunity to spread awareness of the brand. Additionally, BP is a major advertiser, further building brand awareness.

Not all brand awareness is good for business, however. The Deepwater Horizon accident in 2010 exponentially increased awareness of the BP brand. The publicity was, of course, unwanted and almost entirely negative. BP achieved top-of-mind awareness with consumers. Unfortunately for the company, the public equated the brand with environmental irresponsibility, the direct opposite of BP's brand positioning.

BRAND OUTLOOK

- BP's brand outlook appeared so dire in 2010 that there was pressure to use the Amoco brand for U.S. gas stations.
- BP returned to drilling in the Gulf of Mexico a year after the Deepwater Horizon accident.
- The long-term impact of the Deepwater Horizon accident on the BP brand remains to be seen.

In the weeks following the Deepwater Horizon disaster, the outlook for BP's brand appeared dire. In August 2010 there were press reports suggesting that the pressure in the United States was reaching a point at which BP should consider rebranding their U.S. gas stations under the old Amoco brand. A tarnished brand also cost BP in extra fees and margins when it sought funding from bankers to support the cleanup effort in the Gulf. A backlash against the brand might also have an impact on employees. One of the primary reasons for the 2000 rebranding of BP as "Beyond Petroleum," according to Mark Ritson of *Marketing Week*, was to avoid losing talent to "better positioned, more ethical brands." Because of Deepwater Horizon, he argued, BP might very well have to contend with a damaged brand as well as an "increasingly second-rate management team."

Little more than a year after it capped the Deepwater Horizon well, BP received a permit to again drill in the Gulf of Mexico. Ritson expressed concern over BP's decision to continue promoting its environmental credentials. He cited BP as "one example of a growing trend in which brands openly flout ethics, the law or their own well-established positioning—and seem to get away with it with relatively impunity." The long-term prospects for the BP brand, however, remained very much an open question.

FURTHER READING

"BP p.l.c." *International Directory of Company Histories*. Ed. Jay P. Pederson. Vol. 103. Detroit, MI: St. James Press, 2009.

Brand Finance. "Global 500 2012." *Brandirectory*. Accessed January 9, 2013. http://brandirectory.com/league_tables/table/global-500-2012.

Halliday, Jean. "BP Touts Greenness, Then Asks to Dump Ammonia." *Advertising Age*, August 20, 2007.

Melillo, Wendy, and Steve Miller. "Companies Find It's Not Easy Marketing Green." *Brandweek*, July 24, 2006.

Ritson, Mark. "Negative Brand Equity's A Death Sentence." *Marketing Week*, July 15, 2010.

———. "Who Cares about Brand Reputation?" *Marketing Week*, November 20, 2011.

Shayon, Sheila. "BP—Back in Business." *Brandchannel*, November 4, 2011.

Wasserman, Todd. "Branding Experts Say BP Will Get beyond This Crisis." *Brandweek*, May 10, 2010.

BRADESCO

AT A GLANCE

Brand Synopsis: By providing modern banking services to people who might not otherwise have access to them, Banco Bradesco S.A. is an innovative, socially responsible brand that helps customers become upwardly mobile.
Parent Company: Banco Bradesco S.A.
Cidade de Deus, Prédio Novo
Osasco, São Paulo 06029-900
Brazil
http://www.bradesco.com.br
Sector: Financials
Industry Group: Banks
Performance: *Market share*—22 percent of Brazilian branch banking (2011). *Net income*—US$5.4 billion (2011).
Principal Competitors: Banco do Brasil SA; Itaú Unibanco Holding SA; Caixa Econômica Federal; Banco Santander (Brasil), S.A.; HSBC Holdings plc; Banco Votorantim; Banco BTG Pactual SA; Banco Safra S.A.; Banco do Estado do Rio Grande do Sul SA (Banrisul)

BRAND ORIGINS

- Amador Aguiar launched the Bradesco brand in 1943 when he assumed control of Casa Bancária Almeida e Companhia.
- Aguiar changed the firm's name to Banco Brasileiro de Descontos S.A., which was later shortened to Banco Bradesco S.A.
- Unlike most Brazilian banks in the 1940s, Bradesco actively welcomed customers from the middle and lower classes of society.
- Bradesco thrived throughout the second half of the 20th century and was the largest privately owned bank in Brazil from 1951 until 2008.

The Bradesco brand was established by Amador Aguiar, a farmer's son who entered the banking profession as a clerk at Banco Noroeste. In 1943, after nearly two decades as an employee in the industry, Aguiar assumed control of Casa Bancária Almeida e Companhia (Almeida Banking House). The firm had six branches in addition to its headquarters in the city of Marília in São Paulo, Brazil. Aguiar renamed the enterprise Banco Brasileiro de Descontos S.A., which was later shortened to Banco Bradesco S.A.

In an era when most Brazilian banks almost exclusively served customers from the upper classes, Aguiar structured the Bradesco brand to meet the needs of small-business owners, customers with low incomes, and civil servants. The intent was to attract as many clients as possible, from all walks of life. After a few years of rapid growth, the firm moved its headquarters to downtown São Paulo.

During the 1950s deposits at the bank doubled every month as Brazil enjoyed a brisk economic expansion, thanks in part to thriving coffee exports. In 1951, only eight years after its reorganization by Aguiar, Bradesco became Brazil's largest privately operated financial institution, competing with large banks owned by the Brazilian government. In 1953 the company moved its headquarters once again, this time to the community of Osasco, located on the outskirts of São Paulo.

Over the next four decades Brazil experienced military coups, government reforms, and alternating periods of economic turmoil and prosperity. Through it all, Bradesco maintained its position as one of the nation's foremost brands, with a strong reputation for integrity, social responsibility, and innovative technology. The firm acquired numerous banks and other businesses over the years, including telecommunication networks and an automobile financing unit. The company also opened a small number of branch offices and subsidiaries in various cities around the world. Bradesco remained the largest privately owned bank in Brazil until 2008, when it was surpassed by Itaú Unibanco Holding SA, formed by the merger of two of Bradesco's primary rivals, Banco Itaú and Unibanco.

BRAND ELEMENTS

- The Bradesco logo features the brand name in black letters beneath a red square with white graphic elements.
- Bradesco's original brand name was similar in meaning to "dime savings bank," indicating that the bank welcomed customers from the lower and working classes.
- Amador Aguiar, Bradesco's founder, was a pious man who named the site of his corporate headquarters Cidade de Deus ("City of God").
- By offering free essential services to hundreds of thousands of people, the Bradesco Foundation has strengthened the brand's philanthropic image.

Bradesco's logo features a red square with two white, crescent-shaped brush strokes that overlap above two white columns, one slightly shorter and thinner than the other. Beneath this graphic element the word "Bradesco" is rendered in black letters.

The Bradesco brand has long been associated with an altruistic regard for the common people. In fact, even the bank's original name reflected this characteristic. When Amador Aguiar became the proprietor of the bank that would become Banco Bradesco S.A., he called it Banco Brasileiro de Descontos S.A., which translates to "ten conto bank," a reference to an outdated form of currency. The name, which in English would be comparable to "dime savings bank," was meant to appeal to customers who were not in the wealthy upper classes. By encouraging customers to deposit small amounts of money in his bank, Aguiar not only built a large base of clients but also helped people from the lower and working classes (who were at that time largely unwelcome in Brazilian banks) learn to use the modern banking system to improve their financial status.

Aguiar's philanthropic intentions stemmed in large part from his religious beliefs. When Bradesco moved its corporate headquarters to the outskirts of São Paulo, Aguiar named the new location Cidade de Deus ("City of God"), after a book by the Christian theologian St. Augustine. In addition to office buildings, the complex featured housing, recreation facilities, hospitals, and schools for the 9,000 Bradesco employees who worked at its headquarters. The compound's construction and the support provided for its inhabitants fostered the growth of a thriving suburb around Cidade de Deus.

Aguiar's religious beliefs informed Bradesco's corporate culture as well, with piety and company loyalty serving as fundamental requirements for hiring and promotion. The work environment was replete with religious references. The company letterhead, for example, featured Bible verses and the phrase "Nos confiamos em Deus" ("We trust in God"). New hires endorsed a "declaration of principles" that required the setting aside of personal interests in favor of the good of the country and the company.

In 1956 the corporation created the Bradesco Foundation to provide a free education, along with meals and help with medical and dental expenses, to children, teenagers, and adults living in poverty. Besides its goal of reducing illiteracy rates in Brazil, the organization aimed to promote ethical values and a sense of civic duty. By 2011 the Bradesco Foundation was operating 40 schools and serving more than 600,000 students through various outreach efforts. Bradesco's other philanthropic efforts have included the Sustainable Amazon Foundation, which seeks to reduce deforestation and preserve biodiversity in areas of the Amazon, and the Bradesco Sports and Education Program. Bradesco's long history of benevolence toward people, the country of Brazil, and the environment has helped solidify the brand's reputation for social responsibility.

BRAND IDENTITY

- Bradesco has promoted itself as a brand that offers innovative technology and products and unparalleled customer service.
- The slogans "Presença" ("Presence") and "Lado a Lado" ("Side by Side") reminded consumers that Bradesco is always present and working side-by-side with its customers.
- Through its philanthropic efforts and inspirational marketing campaigns, Bradesco has sought to associate itself with sustainable development, social responsibility, and faith in people.

Bradesco markets itself as a friendly brand that excels at innovation in products and services. In 1962 the company became the first in Latin America to use a computer, and later it became the first bank in Brazil to make computer automation part of its daily operations, an unusual move at a time when Brazilian banks were slow to adopt new technology. Also in the 1960s, Bradesco used its computers to introduce daily bank statements, an exclusive and popular service that allowed customers to keep close watch on their accounts. Bradesco launched the first credit card program in Brazil in 1968 and the country's first Internet banking system in 1996. In 2012 the bank introduced the country's first biometric ATMs to one of its branches in São Paulo, allowing users to access their accounts via hand recognition. Bradesco marketed the new technology with the slogan "Segurança Bradesco na Palma da Mão" ("Bradesco Security in the Palm of Your Hand").

Throughout its existence Bradesco has reached out to rural areas and was the first bank to open branches in many remote communities in Brazil. Founder Amador Aguiar made a number of changes to typical banking services to make Bradesco's target clientele, people from the lower and working classes, feel welcome. For example, Bradesco branches offered extended office hours so that coffee growers and ranchers could do their banking before their workday began. To reduce the intimidation factor common to many Brazilian financial institutions at the time, Aguiar moved his managers and loan officers from "cages" at the rear of the bank to more approachable desks near the front doors. In 2011 Bradesco opened more than 1,000 new branch offices throughout Brazil. By bringing banking services to even the most remote communities, Bradesco hoped to help more individuals become upwardly mobile and transform Brazil into a more modern nation.

To promote its customer-focused core identity and multitude of locations across Brazil, Bradesco launched the new marketing slogan "Presença" ("Presence") in 2009, followed in 2010 by the related slogan "Lado a Lado" ("Side by Side"). These initiatives were meant to convey that Bradesco is always present and working side-by-side with its customers. The campaign expressed this idea with various other taglines, including "Presença é Bradesco" ("Presence is Bradesco").

Although Bradesco has grown rapidly, it has maintained its commitment to integrity and virtue by emphasizing sustainable development and a commitment to community. The Bradesco Foundation has provided hundreds of thousands of Brazilians with a free education since the 1950s, and in 2007 Bradesco announced its cofounding of the Sustainable Amazon Foundation, which aims to reduce deforestation and improve the quality of life for those living in the Amazon region. In 2011 the company launched an emotional and inspirational marketing campaign that included a film called "Acreditar" ("Believe") to promote the theme that "living is the best sport." Bradesco planned to continue this marketing campaign for five years following its launch, particularly at the Brazilian sporting events it sponsors and at the 2016 Summer Olympics in Rio de Janeiro.

BRAND STRATEGY

- In 2012 Bradesco was operating in two business segments and eight principal divisions.
- Bradesco has thousands of branch offices, many of them acquisitions that were rebranded into the Bradesco network.
- Early in its history, Bradesco cultivated a positive brand image by processing utility payments and delivering basic supplies to remote communities.
- Diversification has been a hallmark of the Bradesco brand.

As of 2012 Bradesco was operating in two business segments: its banking segment and its insurance, pension plans, and savings bonds segment. Upon its initial reorganization in the 1940s, Bradesco had a central headquarters and six branches. That number expanded steadily over the next several decades, with numerous offices opening throughout Brazil. The firm also acquired other banks and rebranded them into the Bradesco network. Two of the largest of those purchases were INCO-Banco Indústria e Comércio de Santa Catarina, a 105-branch system acquired in 1967, and Banco da Bahia, a 200-branch system acquired in 1973.

During a time of hyperinflation in the early 1980s, Bradesco opened more than one branch per day to accommodate customers who were rapidly transferring funds from one account to another in hopes of finding better yields. After government intervention in 1986 led to the closure of hundreds of branches and the lay-offs of 80,000 employees, Bradesco depended increasingly on automation to enhance productivity, and it outsourced several peripheral businesses. Nevertheless, the corporation continued to acquire banks and add them to the Bradesco line.

Bradesco opened more than a thousand branches in 2011 alone. It was the first private Brazilian bank to establish some kind of presence, ranging from branch offices to ATM machines, in every city in the country. Bradesco Expresso, the company's correspondent bank segment, operates small outlets in supermarkets, drugstores, department stores, and other retail chains across Brazil, providing an even wider presence for the brand and helping smaller Brazilian communities develop socially and economically. In 2011 Bradesco had almost 48,000 "service points" throughout Brazil, part of the firm's strategy to help the customer, the company, and the country grow together.

Early in its history Bradesco diversified by processing utility payments and using its branch offices to supply isolated regions with products from industrialized areas of the country. This strategy endeared the Bradesco brand not only to the rural recipients of medicine, fuel, and other benefits of modernization but also to the industrialists and manufacturers whose sales increased as a result.

Diversified products and services have continued to be a hallmark of the Bradesco brand. Like other top Brazilian financial institutions, Bradesco is well capitalized and has a broad retail network. It also operates the largest insurance company in the region. In 2011 Bradesco was expecting competitive growth in its business lending, mortgage lending, credit card, and insurance divisions.

BRAND EQUITY

- In 2012 Bradesco was one of the largest privately operated Brazilian banks, with US$31.3 billion in tier 1 capital.
- In 2011 Bradesco reported a net income of US$5.4 billion and total assets of US$373.2 billion.
- Brand Finance valued the Bradesco brand at US$15.7 billion in 2012.

In 2012 Bradesco reported on its website that it was one of the largest banks in Brazil not owned by the government and that it operated the most extensive private-sector network of branch offices in the country. The firm also said that it employed about 105,000 people, with 86,000 of those working for the bank itself and the remainder working for affiliated businesses.

According to the company's annual report, Bradesco's 2011 net income was approximately US$5.4 billion, up from about US$4.9 billion in 2010. Total assets were roughly US$373.2 billion in 2011, up from US$312.4 billion in 2010. Bradesco stated on its website that its customer service branches held a market share of 22.2 percent in 2011 and 18.7 percent in 2010.

In 2012 *Banker* magazine ranked Bradesco third on its list of the top four banks in Latin America, listing Bradesco's tier 1 capital at US$31.3 billion. The other three banks on the list were also Brazilian. Itaú Unibanco was in the top spot with US$38.2 billion of tier 1 capital and Banco do Brasil was second with US$32.3 billion.

In 2012 brand valuation consultancy Brand Finance calculated the value of the Bradesco brand at US$15.7 billion, down from US$18.7 billion in 2011, but up substantially from its US$4.1 billion brand value in 2008. In 2012 Bradesco dropped from sixth to eighth place on the Brand Finance Banking 500 list, primarily because of a slowdown in the Brazilian economy.

BRAND AWARENESS

- Bradesco is a trusted brand thanks in part to its longstanding relationship with customers.
- Bradesco served 65 million clients in 2012 and led the Brazilian private banking industry in checking accounts, credit cards, rural loans, and demand deposits.
- Bradesco won various awards in 2012, including honors for its customer service, career opportunities, and investor relations.

Thanks to its longstanding relationship with customers, Bradesco has become a familiar and trusted brand in Brazil. On its website Bradesco reported that it had 65 million clients by 2012 and held more checking accounts, credit cards, rural loans, and demand deposits than any other privately operated Brazilian financial institution.

In 2012 *Consumidor Moderno* magazine gave Bradesco its award for excellence in customer service in the premium bank and credit card categories. At its 2012 Euromoney Awards for Excellence, British magazine *Euromoney* named Bradesco the best Brazilian bank and best Latin American bank. Latin American magazine *Você S/A* named Bradesco one of the best companies in which to launch a career, and Bradesco was named the best company for investor relations in the financial sector category at the *IR* Magazine Awards Brazil 2012.

BRAND OUTLOOK

- The Brazilian economy flourished despite a global financial crisis that affected Europe and the United States starting in 2008.
- In 2012 some analysts predicted that economic turmoil could spread to Brazil and destabilize the currency.
- The Bradesco brand performed particularly well in 2011, with impressive profits and a balanced portfolio.
- Brazil's strong economy has attracted foreign banks that, by 2012, were beginning to pose new challenges for the Bradesco brand.

In 2008 a global financial crisis spread across Europe and the United States, causing widespread market volatility, but Brazilian banks weathered the storm relatively well. This was due in part to the country's prior history of financial turmoil, which had led the Brazilian government to impose strict regulations to prevent catastrophic monetary meltdowns. The *Banker* magazine reported that while more developed countries struggled with fiscal chaos, Brazil enjoyed economic growth that jumped from an average of 3.3 percent between 2000 and 2009 to 7.5 percent in 2010. The flourishing business climate generated enormous wealth and allowed many lower-class workers to become upwardly mobile, boosting the size of the middle class and the use of financial services, which increased profits for banks. Although Brazil predicted its growth would continue with proper management, the economy eventually began to experience a slowdown, and by 2012 some analysts were expressing concerns about a possible credit bubble and destabilization of the currency, according to LatinFinance magazine.

Despite turbulence in the global economy, the Bradesco brand managed particularly well in 2011, maintaining its reputation for impressive profitability ratios and substantial reserve cushions. The company had a healthy portfolio of corporate, individual, and small and medium enterprise (SME) loans and planned to improve its balance of retail banking, corporate finance, and insurance. This diversification of services was expected to give Bradesco an edge over some competitors as credit growth began to slow.

In terms of assets, Bradesco dropped from first place to second among privately owned Brazilian banking institutions after Banco Itaú and Unibanco merged in 2008, according to *Business Rankings Annual*. Taking steps to recapture the lead, Bradesco outbid its primary rivals in 2011 to acquire Banco do Estado do Rio de Janeiro SA from the Rio de Janeiro state government, as reported in *Global Banking News* magazine. However, a 2011 *Bloomberg* article noted that because of Brazil's flourishing economy, Bradesco was beginning to face new competition from foreign banks that, were quickly beginning to establish a presence in the region. However, Bradesco executives quoted in *Euromoney* magazine predicted that Brazilian banks would not feel greatly threatened by foreign competition, since the top local brands had already established strong relationships with their customers.

FURTHER READING

Banco Bradesco S.A. "Bradesco Investor Relations." Accessed October 19, 2012. http://www.bradescori.com.br/site/TUTORIAL_en/abertura.html.

Brand Finance. "Global 500 2012." *Brandirectory*. Accessed October 15, 2012. http://brandirectory.com/league_tables/table/global-500-2012.

———. "Profile: Bradesco." *Brandirectory*. Accessed October 15, 2012. http://brandirectory.com/profile/bradesco.

Brasileiro, Adriana, and Dawn Kopecki. "Brazilian Banks Beat Wall Street as Itau Shows Who Rules." *Bloomberg*, May 5, 2011. Accessed February 15, 2013. http://www.bloomberg.com/news/2011-05-05/brazil-banks-beating-wall-street-as-itau-shows-jpmorgan-who-rules-markets.html.

"Brazil guide: Bradesco—A decade of performance." *Euromoney*, January 2012. Accessed October 14, 2012. http://www.euromoney.com/Article/2963123/Brazil-guide-BradescoA-decade-of-performance.html.

"Brazil's Banco Bradesco acquires BERJ." *Global Banking News*, May 24, 2011. *Highbeam Research*. Accessed February 15, 2013. http://www.highbeam.com/doc/1G1-257139399.html.

Draper, Deborah J. "Largest Brazilian Banks by Capital, 2008." *Business Rankings Annual*. Detroit: Gale, 2011. *Business Insights: Essentials*. Accessed February 15, 2013. http://bi.galegroup.com/essentials/article/GALE%7CI2501274316/cd8f4c064ac2bf2d9e13807f44a44234?u=itsbtrial.

Gasbarre, April D., and Paul Ingati. "Banco Bradesco S.A." *International Directory of Company Histories*. Ed. Drew Johnson. Vol. 116. Detroit, MI: St. James Press, 2011.

"Itaú Muscles out Bradesco in New Issue Squeeze." *Euroweek*, November 19, 2010. Accessed October 14, 2012. http://www.euroweek.com/Article/2718461/Ita-muscles-out-Bradesco-in-new-issue-squeeze.html.

Miller, Ben. "Prudent but Profitable." *LatinFinance*, November 1, 2011. Accessed October 14, 2012. http://www.latinfinance.com/Article/2933366/Banks-and-Bankers/Prudent-but-Profitable.html.

Pavoni, Silvia. "Colombian banks rise in Latam rankings." *Banker*, February 7, 2012. Accessed October 14, 2012. http://www.thebanker.com/Top-1000-World-Banks/Colombian-banks-rise-in-Latam-rankings.

"The 2011 guide to Brazil." *Euromoney*, December 2011. Accessed October 14, 2012. http://www.euromoney.com/Article/2947136/Category/17/ChannelPage/-1/Euromoneys-guide-to-Brazil.html.

BT

AT A GLANCE

Brand Synopsis: The BT Group (BT) is a telecommunications brand that aims for connectivity: it connects customers around the world to its telephone, entertainment, IT, and other services
Parent Company: BT Group plc
BT Centre, 81 Newgate Street
London, EC1A 7AJ
United Kingdom
http://www.btplc.com
Sector: Telecommunication Services; Information Technology
Industry Group: Telecommunication Services; Technology Hardware & Equipment
Performance: *Market share*—47 percent of the United Kingdom consumer lines market (2012); 37 percent of the United Kingdom fiber broadband, DSL, and LLU retail markets (2012). *Sales*—US$30.9 billion (2012).
Principal Competitors: Nippon Telegraph and Telephone Corporation; AT&T Inc.; Verizon Communications Inc.; Siemens AG; Hutchison Whampoa Limited; China Mobile Communications Corp.; France Telecom SA; Telecom Italia SpA; Vodafone Group Plc; Deutsche Telekom AG

BRAND ORIGINS

- The government-owned General Post Office held a monopoly on British telecommunications services beginning in 1912.
- The British Telecommunications Act of 1981 created the British Telecommunications Corporation (British Telecom), a separate government-owned corporation for telecommunications services.
- In the 1980s and 1990s further legislation transformed British Telecom from a government-run corporation to a private corporation.
- British Telecom has traded under the name BT since 1991 and later became part of the BT Group holding company.
- In 2012 approximately 40 percent of BT's revenues came from its BT Global Services division.

BT touts itself as the oldest telecommunications company in the world, with origins dating back more than a century. In 1912 the government of the United Kingdom granted a monopoly on telephone service to the General Post Office, a government department. Nearly 60 years later, the Post Office Act of 1969 removed the General Post Office as a government department. In 1977 it was divided into two separate entities, the Post Office and Post Office Telecommunications.

The British Telecommunications Act of 1981 resulted in further separation. The Post Office kept its postal services, while its telecommunications branch was established as a separate government-owned corporation known as the British Telecommunications Corporation (or British Telecom). Further legislation in the 1980s and 1990s transformed British Telecom from a government-run corporation to a private corporation and allowed for more competitors in the telecommunications market. This history parallels that of other global telecommunications companies, including BT's counterparts AT&T in the United States and the NTT Group in Japan, both of which started as government-controlled corporations before being privatized in the 1980s.

Trading under the BT name since 1991 and later incorporated into the BT Group holding company, BT has a significant presence in the United Kingdom and worldwide. It began focusing heavily on global expansion in the 1980s and 1990s, working with various European, North American, and Asian countries. This expansion has continued into the 21st century and is a vital part of the company's strategy. In 2012 BT had more than 89,000 employees in 50 countries and was operating in 170 countries worldwide. BT Global Services, one of the corporation's four lines of service, accounted for 40 percent of BT's revenues in 2012.

BRAND ELEMENTS

- Adopted in 2003, BT's "connected world" logo consists of a transparent sphere covered with dots of different colors.
- Some of BT's service divisions use the corporate logo alongside their own unique logo.
- The BT Tower, the tallest building in the United Kingdom until 1980, is another visual image BT uses to represent the brand.
- BT has also used the red telephone boxes popularly associated with mid-20th century London to symbolize how its communication services unite people.

In 2003 the logo for BT's Internet division, BTopenworld, became the logo for the entire corporation. Known as the "connected world" logo, the design consists of a transparent sphere (representing a globe) covered with several dots of different colors. The letters "BT" appear in dark blue to the left of the sphere. This logo can be seen on BT's buildings, signs, marketing materials, websites, and company vehicles. BT's Japanese and U.S. counterparts, the NTT Group and AT&T, also use circular or sphere-shaped logos.

While BT's corporate website uses the connected world logo, some of the company's smaller division websites feature their own logo alongside the corporate logo. For example, the website for BT Vision, the corporation's subscription digital TV service, features a purple and white, three-dimensional, upside down triangular shape that overlaps the last part of the words "BT Vision," which are written in black. Other BT logos are simpler. The BT Life logo features the words "BT Life" in magenta, while BT Wholesale's logo features the words "BT wholesale" in blue, using all lowercase letters for the word "wholesale."

BT has also promoted itself by using visual images on a much larger scale. In the 1960s the company built the BT Tower in London. At 581 feet, this communications tower was the tallest building in London and the entire United Kingdom until Tower 42 (originally known as the National Westminster Tower) was completed in 1980. The BT Tower has been featured in a number of movies, television programs, and novels.

Another well-known image used to promote the BT brand is the iconic red telephone box used in the United Kingdom throughout much of the 20th century. The British Post Office had long used variations of these telephone boxes (also known as phone boxes or kiosks), and BT used them as well when it became a telephone service provider. A modified version of one of these boxes appeared in a 1980s BT television commercial explaining how the company and its phones helped unite people and places. Although demand for these payphones is now nearly nonexistent, BT's ties to the phones remain. Under its Adopt a Kiosk program, BT sells the kiosks (without phones) to towns and villages, where they have been repurposed as libraries, art galleries, and storage sites. In 2012, to benefit the charity ChildLine, BT commissioned 80 artists to design full-sized replicas of the telephone boxes, which were displayed in public places throughout London and then sold at auction.

BRAND IDENTITY

- BT's colorful sphere logo is intended to symbolize a "connected world" and communicate the company's international reach.
- The logo for BT Vision, the company's subscription digital TV service, uses an upside down triangular frame shape that represents the "V" in "Vision."
- In 2011 BT Vision launched a rebranding campaign to establish an identity separate from its role as part of the larger telecommunications company BT.

The BT brand puts a large emphasis on connectivity, and its dotted sphere logo is meant to symbolize a "connected world." BT has said that the logo "reflects the wide range of activities that BT now encompasses" and "represents BT as being in-tune with the multi-media age as well as communicating the company's international reach."

BT Vision, the company's subscription digital TV service, also uses a logo with symbolic meanings. The logo's upside down triangular frame shape, besides representing the "V" in "Vision," is intended to resemble the "play" button on many electronic devices, reminding customers that they can use BT Vision to view content and that BT's telecommunication services make that viewing possible.

BT Vision introduced this triangular logo as part of a 2011 rebranding campaign, which was designed to separate the digital TV service somewhat from its parent company in the minds of consumers. As part of this relaunch, BT Vision promoted itself as a company offering premium entertainment. The BT Vision website featured the slogan "Your essential guide to what's on TV" and listed a number of the television programs and movies offered through the service. To watch this content, BT Vision customers use a device that combines the functions of a cable box, an on-demand device, and a digital recorder. Despite BT Vision's intention to establish a distinct identity separate from that of its parent company, both the viewing device and the accompanying remote control feature the BT corporate logo alongside the words "BT Vision."

BRAND STRATEGY

- BT Global Services, one of BT's four lines of business, provides telephone, IT, network, communications, and security services for businesses around the world.
- In 2012 BT sponsored ArtBox, a philanthropic effort in which the company invited artists to decorate replicas of its famous red telephone boxes.
- BT served as the official communications service partner for the 2012 Summer Olympics in London, which helped raise its brand awareness internationally.

BT is organized into four lines of business: BT Global Services, BT Retail, BT Wholesale, and Openreach. Although the brand's identity is rooted in its history as a British company, BT has a large presence in global markets, operating in 170 countries around the world. The BT Global Services division, which accounted for 40 percent of the company's revenues in 2012, provides telephone, IT, network, communications, and security services in countries worldwide.

In 2012 BT drew on the fame of the iconic red telephone boxes used in the United Kingdom throughout much of the 20th century when it helped sponsor an event called ArtBox. Through this initiative, BT commissioned artists to decorate full-size replicas of the original telephone boxes, which were then displayed throughout London. The telephone boxes were eventually auctioned off by Sotheby's to raise funds for ChildLine, a British charity that provides 24-hour counseling services for at-risk children via telephone, text, and e-mail. In addition to highlighting its philanthropic efforts, sponsorship of the ArtBox program emphasized BT's connection to the famed telephone boxes and to telephone service in general.

BT served as the official communications service partner of the 2012 Summer Olympics and the 2012 Summer Paralympics, both of which took place in London. The company's involvement had begun years before, and in 2007 a giant message reading "Back the Bid" was projected on the BT Tower to support London's bid to host the 2012 events. BT's involvement in these high-profile, international events has helped build its brand awareness among consumers around the world.

BRAND EQUITY

- By revenue, BT is the largest telecommunications services wholesaler in Europe.
- In 2012 BT held 47 percent of the UK consumer lines market and a 37 percent share of the DSL, fiber broadband, and LLU retail markets.
- BT's involvement in the UK superfast broadband market has led some British politicians to express concerns about a future BT monopoly.
- In 2012 Brand Finance named BT the 86th top global brand overall, the 13th top telecommunications brand, and the United Kingdom's 10th most valuable brand.

BT holds considerable shares of various telecommunications markets. In terms of revenue, BT is the largest telecommunications services wholesaler in Europe. According to its 2012 annual report, the company held a 47 percent market share of the UK's consumer lines market and a 37 percent market share of the DSL, fiber broadband, and LLU (local loop unbundling) retail markets. The report also noted that BT claimed about 18 percent of total European wholesale revenue in the telecommunications market. Competitors in that field include France Telecom, with a 13 percent market share; Deutsche Telekom at 11 percent; Telecom Italia at 8 percent; and Spain's Telefonica at 7 percent.

BT's 2012 annual report also noted the company's intention to make inroads in the British superfast broadband market. By 2012 BT had installed faster cables and upgraded communication connections for 10 million homes and businesses in the United Kingdom, prompting some British politicians to fear a BT monopoly of that service.

BT's large market share and geographical coverage parallel its success as a brand. In its 2012 ranking of the top 500 global brands, Brand Finance named BT the 86th top brand overall, the 13th top telecommunications company, and the United Kingdom's 10th most valuable brand.

BRAND AWARENESS

- In 2012 Brand Finance argued that BT is better known than its competitors because early government control established strong brand awareness.
- A 2012 brand tracker determined that BT is popular with people who access Facebook, Twitter, and blogs.
- British students ranked BT one of their favorite brands in the 2012 "Youth 100" list.

In its 2012 ranking of the top 500 global brands, Brand Finance made the argument that BT is better known than many of its competitors because it evolved from government control, which helped to establish BT's brand awareness and market share. Brand Finance added that the "brand enjoys very strong awareness across the whole of the UK, also spreading outside of its home markets with BT Global providing IT network services ... across 170 countries."

Other measurements have determined BT's brand awareness. Unruly, a company working with social videos, created a brand tracker to analyze the sponsors of London's 2012 Summer Olympics. Unruly's tracker determined how many "shares" each Olympic sponsor received from people accessing Facebook, Twitter, and Internet blogs. BT finished 12th in a list of 25 sponsors, with 14,499 shares. This measurement demonstrated BT's brand awareness and popularity among social media and Internet users.

BT has also been a popular brand among young people. More than 1,000 students in the United Kingdom discussed their favorite brands in a survey published by The Beans Group in 2012. These 18- to 24-year-olds stated that BT was one of their 100 favorite brands on the "Youth 100" list. This ranking demonstrates that young people know about the BT brand and regard it highly.

BRAND OUTLOOK

- In recent years BT has participated in showcases in India and China and has hired 300 new employees in the Asia Pacific region.
- In 2012 BT expressed its interest in expanding further into Africa, Turkey, and the Middle East.
- A graphic illustrating BT's global involvement was posted on its corporate website in 2012, with case studies showing how BT operates in different geographical regions.
- In 2012 BT's website featured a report stating the company's goal of improving connections with its customers.

BT continues to pursue more global opportunities as it moves further into the 21st century. In recent years the corporation has participated in showcases in the huge markets of China and India, and in 2012 BT hired 300 additional employees in the Asia Pacific region. In 2012 BT also stated its intention to expand further into the Middle East, Turkey, and Africa.

In 2012 BT's corporate website featured a graphic illustrating the company's global involvement, which included case studies describing how BT has operated in various regions of the world. A report posted on its website around the same time discussed BT's intention of becoming "better connected," describing how the company is aiming to improve connections with its customers and make communications more efficient, affordable, accessible, secure, and safe. As it moves into the future, BT continues to promote the value of connectivity and to demonstrate how it can help consumers achieve this connectivity.

FURTHER READING

Brand Finance. "Global 500 2012." *Brandirectory*. Accessed October 18, 2012. http://brandirectory.com/league_tables/table/global-500-2012.

BT Group plc. "2012 Annual Report." Accessed October 18, 2012. http://www.btplc.com/Sharesandperformance/Annualreportandreview/index.cfm.

"BT Unveils New Logo." *BBC News*, April 7, 2003.

Classe, Olive, et al. "BT Group plc." *International Directory of Company Histories*. Ed. Jay P. Pederson. Vol. 114. Detroit, MI: St. James Press, 2010.

Garside, Juliette. "BT 'Monopolising' UK's Superfast Broadband." *Guardian* (London), May 22, 2012.

Jingting, Shen. "Foreign Telecom Companies Eye China Market's Growth Prospects." *China Daily*, September 12, 2012.

O'Reilly, Lara. "BT Vision Overhauls Brand Identity." *Marketing Week*, September 30, 2011.

Sift Media. "BT." Accessed October 20, 2012. http://www.sift.com/client/bt.

"UK Broadband Market Share." *Guardian* (London), July 28, 2011.

BUDWEISER

AT A GLANCE

Brand Synopsis: Known as the "King of Beers," Budweiser is considered to be the national beer brand of the United States and is a symbol of American life around the world.
Parent Company: Anheuser -Busch Companies (a subsidiary of Anheuser-Busch InBev NV/SA)
1 Busch Place
St. Louis, Missouri 63118-1852
United States
http://www.budweiser.com/
Sector: Consumer Staples
Industry Group: Food Beverage & Tobacco
Performance: *Market share*—8.4 percent of the U.S. beer market. *Sales*—38.7 million barrels worldwide.
Principal Competitors: Busch; Coors; Corona; Heineken; Michelob; Miller; Molson; Pabst; Skol; Snow Beer

BRAND ORIGINS

- Budweiser was first sold in the United States in 1876.
- Budweiser became the best-selling beer in the United States in 1957.
- The low-calorie beer that eventually became known as Bud Light was introduced in 1982.
- By 1997 Budweiser accounted for more than half of the beer sold worldwide.
- By 2002 Budweiser was sold in 60 countries worldwide and was still the best-selling beer in the world.

Budweiser began in St. Louis, Missouri, in the mid-19th century. In 1860 Eberhard Anheuser bought a failing brewery, and his son-in-law, Adolphus Busch, joined the company in 1864. It was Busch and the restaurateur Carl Conrad who created Budweiser. They fashioned a beer that was similar to the pilsners brewed in their native Bohemia in central Europe.

Budweiser was first sold in 1876, initially only in Missouri. The brand soon benefited from innovations in food safety such as pasteurization and refrigerated railroad cars, which had recently been invented. Busch used such cars to distribute Budweiser nationally, and by the 1880s Anheuser was supplying beer to every state in the union. Budweiser was its brewery's leading brand, and by the 1890s its advertisements touted it as one of the most popular beers in the United States.

Though Budweiser continued to be a leading American beer during the early 20th century, Prohibition temporarily brought an end to sales. Between 1919 and 1933 near-beer Budweiser, its alcohol content reduced to meet legal requirements, was produced to retain market share during Prohibition. When Prohibition ended, Budweiser was brewed again, though public tastes had changed to favor sweet over the generally more bitter commercial beers. The recipe for Budweiser, unlike that of other beers, was not modified, however, and it remained a best seller.

Because Budweiser's parent company decided to focus on the war effort, Budweiser was not distributed on the Pacific coast during World War II, and the demand often exceeded supply between 1935 and 1950. Still, by 1957 Budweiser had become the most popular beer by sales in the United States. The brand maintained its dominance in part through advertising campaigns that kept it in the public eye, such as the 1969 ads that featured the slogan, "This Bud's for You."

Budweiser faced challenges during the mid-1970s when a competitor, Miller Brewing Company, introduced a low-calorie beer, Miller Light. Budweiser temporarily lost its place as the best-selling beer in the United States. In response, Anheuser-Busch debuted its own low-calorie beer, which came to be known as Bud Light, in 1982. During the 1980s Budweiser also entered the international market, expanding first to England, Japan, and Canada. International sales became increasingly important late in the decade, as Americans began consuming less alcohol and younger consumers favored beers produced by smaller, often local breweries. To counter these developments, new products were introduced as part of the Budweiser brand, including Bud Dry and Bud Ice Draft. Budweiser's international presence continued to grow, and investments were made in memorable ad campaigns.

Even though Budweiser was the number-one selling beer in the United States in 1993, claiming 24 percent of the market, domestic sales soon began to stagnate. The brand retained its international momentum, however. By 1993 Budweiser was available in 21 European countries, and it soon was being exported to new markets such as China and Argentina. In 1997 Budweiser accounted for more than half of the beer sold worldwide.

To address declining U.S. sales, new advertising campaigns were developed to appeal to young consumers and to retain loyal Budweiser drinkers. Popular campaigns featuring talking frogs and Louie the Lizard appeared during the mid-1990s. During the first decade of the 21st century Budweiser continued to produce award-winning ads, including the "Wassup?" and "True" campaigns.

Nevertheless, these efforts did not stem the long-term decline in Budweiser's sales. In 2001 Bud Light replaced Budweiser as the best-selling beer in the United States. Even though by 2002 only one in every five alcoholic drinks consumed in the United States was a Budweiser, Budweiser was by then sold in 60 countries worldwide and remained the best-selling beer in the world. In addition, although Budweiser's domestic sales continued to slide, it remained the second best-selling beer after Bud Light.

In 2008 Anheuser-Bush, Budweiser's parent company, was acquired by the Belgian-based InBev for US$52 billion and was renamed Anheuser-Busch InBev. The new owner made a concerted effort to sell Budweiser in new international markets such as the Dominican Republic, Italy, India, and Vietnam to capitalize on its popularity and to secure long-term sales. Budweiser also continued to introduce new products to increase its presence in the United States. These included Budweiser American Ale, Bud Light Lime, and Bud Light Golden Wheat. While sponsorships of Major League Baseball, the National Football League, the National Basketball Association, and auto racing had long been a staple of Budweiser's marketing strategy, the company moved into branded musical festival sponsorships in 2011 and 2012. It also contracted with the rap mogul Jay-Z to represent the brand in the hope of reviving U.S. sales.

BRAND ELEMENTS

- Budweiser's iconic Clydesdales were introduced in 1933 at the end of Prohibition.
- The recipe for Budweiser has remained unchanged since its introduction in 1876.
- In 2011 Budweiser redesigned its label and cans to emphasize the brand's history and global outlook.

When Budweiser was introduced in 1876, it was something different because it was a light pilsner. Its distinctive taste has essentially remained the same because of the consistent use of its original brewing recipe. To reach new markets, Budweiser has introduced variations over the years to enhance its appeal in certain markets. Budweiser & Clamato Chelada and Bud Light & Clamato Chelada, for example, were brought out in 2008 to appeal to the Latin American market.

Since the days of Adolphus Busch, Budweiser has been marketed as the "King of Beers." Over the years, the brand has also been associated with definitive taglines such as "This Bud's for You," "Nothing Beats a Bud," and "Proud to Be a Bud." Such taglines helped Budweiser grow its market share.

In 1933, at the end of Prohibition, Budweiser acquired its most potent symbol: a team of Clydesdale horses. The owner of Anheuser-Busch, Adolphus Busch Jr., sent the team to deliver cases of beer to Governor Al Smith of New York and President Franklin D. Roosevelt. Thereafter, the popular Clydesdales represented Budweiser in numerous ad campaigns and public appearances. A 2012 ad campaign featuring the Clydesdales promoted both beer and optimism in a time of economic turmoil.

Packaging has been as important as the Clydesdales to Budweiser. For many years, brown Budweiser bottles have borne a distinctive blue, white, and red label. While the first Budweiser cans introduced in 1936 were yellow, later versions had a similar tricolor look. In 2011, to reinforce Budweiser as a brand, a new visual identity for cans and labels was introduced that employed mostly red and white and emphasized a bow-tie shape on the label, with the Budweiser crown above. This new look included the Budweiser motto "King of Beers," which appears below the bow-tie shape. This major change drew on Budweiser's past while creating a new look for its global future.

BRAND IDENTITY

- Budweiser debuted its own YouTube-like channel, BudTV, in 2007.
- In 2012 Budweiser sponsored the "Budweiser Made in America" concert festival, featuring the rapper Jay-Z, which targeted urban audiences.
- In 2012 Budweiser was the official beer sponsor of the FIFA World Cup.

Budweiser was one of the first beers to be sold nationwide in the United States. As it entered the international market during the 1980s, Budweiser was marketed as a representation of American life. Playing off the American flag, the Budweiser bottle labels and cans have featured some combination of red, white, and blue for much of the 20th and early 21st centuries. When the Budweiser label and cans were redesigned in 2011, the goal was to emphasize Budweiser as a global brand. The change was accompanied by a new campaign with the tagline "Grab Some Buds."

Emphasizing both All-American and masculine brand values, Budweiser has long been identified with sporting events, which it uses as venues to reach its target consumer base: adult beer drinkers. The brand has debuted some of its most memorable ad campaigns during the National Football League's Super Bowl. For example, the Bud Bowl series of commercials began in 1989 during the contest, and the Budweiser frogs appeared for the first time during the 1995 telecast of the championship.

Budweiser has also sponsored the U.S. Olympic team and hockey, bowling, boxing, and horse racing events. Budweiser is the long-time official beer of Major League Baseball and the National Basketball Association, while Bud Light is the official beer sponsor of the National Football League. To strengthen its international presence, Budweiser began sponsoring soccer during the late 1990s. In 2011 Budweiser and Budweiser Chelada became the official beer cosponsors of Major League Soccer in the United States, while Budweiser was the official beer sponsor of the 2012 FIFA World Cup.

During the early 21st century Budweiser moved into new types of sponsorships, such as music festivals, to expand its worldwide appeal. In 2012 the rapper Jay-Z curated the "Budweiser Made in America" concert festival, which targeted urban audiences.

In 2007 Budweiser launched its own television network, BudTV, in an innovative effort to promote the brand, but the network shut down in 2009. Budweiser has also begun to focus more on social media and interactive media marketing, including the introduction of the Budweiser Ice Cold and Track Your Bud apps. In 2012 Budweiser sponsored a sports-themed reality TV series *Bud United Presents: The Big Time.*

BRAND STRATEGY

- To adapt to changing consumer tastes, Budweiser began introducing new products in 1982, starting with Bud Light.
- Worldwide, Budweiser's sales increased 3.1 percent by volume in 2011.
- By 2012 the number of competing Budweiser sub-brands had been reduced significantly in the United States.

For the first century of its existence, Budweiser was its brand's only product. After entering the light beer market during the early 1980s with Bud Light, Budweiser again introduced new beers during the early 1990s to adapt to changes in the American beer market. Bud Dry, Bud Ice, and Bud Ice Light debuted during the early to mid-1990s. Beginning in 2008 Budweiser again introduced new beers to meet changing consumer tastes. These included Budweiser American Ale, Bud Light Golden Wheat, Budweiser Select 55, and Bud Light Select. Such products led to a greater overall market share for Budweiser for a time but also meant that Budweiser products competed against each other. By 2012 the number of competing sub-brands in the U.S. market had been reduced to five for both Budweiser and Bud Light.

As the American beer market became more fragmented during the 1980s, Budweiser began looking abroad to expand its sales. The effort included licensing agreements, joint ventures, and marketing campaigns that targeted international markets. Budweiser initiated its international strategy in Japan and England, and had extended its reach to 60 countries by 1992. The expansion continued into the 21st century as Budweiser entered the markets in Russia, China, Vietnam, and Brazil. To support this international strategy, Budweiser launched a new global visual identity in 2011. The results paid off as Budweiser's sales rose 3.1 percent by volume worldwide for the year.

BRAND EQUITY

- In 2011 about 44 percent of Budweiser's sales came from outside of the United States.
- Budweiser lost market share in the United States in 2012, becoming the third-ranked beer behind Bud Light and Coors.
- Budweiser was the 48th most valuable brand and the second most valuable beer brand in 2012, according to BrandZ™.
- Interbrand's "Best Global Brands of 2012" ranked Budweiser at number 31.

For many years, Budweiser was the best-selling beer in the United States and the world. By 2011 about 44 percent of the brand's sales came from outside the United States. Budweiser's long-term goal was to be the first truly global beer brand, though it was already considered the most valuable beer brand in the world. In 2011 Bud Light, the number-one beer in the United States, held 19.1 percent of the market. Budweiser was third, behind Coors Light, with an 8.4 percent market share. Bud Light and Budweiser were also dominant brands in the Canadian market in 2011.

According to BrandZ™'s "Top 100 Most Valuable Global Brands 2012," Budweiser was the 48th most valuable brand in the world, with a brand value of US$15.88 billion. On the BrandZ™ list of the top beer brands, Bud Light regained its number-one ranking, with a brand value of US$8.37 billion. Budweiser was number two at US$7.51 billion, having lost 15 percent of its brand value over the previous year. Interbrand's "Best Global Brands of 2012" ranked Budweiser 31st among the best brands, with a brand value of US$11.87 billion.

BRAND AWARENESS

- Budweiser's top-of-mind awareness has persisted despite declining domestic sales.
- In 2011 Budweiser was the number-one beer brand in Canada.
- In 2011 Budweiser experienced substantial global growth as targeted marketing brought it increased international exposure.

A best-selling beer for much of its history, Budweiser is as synonymous with beer as Coca-Cola is with cola drinks. For years, the Budweiser brand has had top-of-mind awareness among alcoholic beverages, far exceeding any other beer brand. Even though the Budweiser brand name is synonymous with the American way of life, its sales and market have generally been on the decline for several decades in the United States. However, Anheuser-Busch InBev has made a concerted effort to grow the brand by adding new markets and sponsoring events such as the World Cup to raise awareness of the brand in emerging markets. As a result, in 2011 Budweiser experienced global growth, performed particularly well in countries such as China and Great Britain, and made headway in new markets like Russia as well. Budweiser was also the number-one beer brand in Canada in 2011.

BRAND OUTLOOK

- Domestic shipments of Bud Light and Budweiser declined between 2009 and 2011.
- Anheuser-Busch InBev is committed to making Budweiser the first truly global brand of beer.
- Budweiser has agreed to be the official beer sponsor of three FIFA World Cups, beginning in 2012.

Since the 1980s the market for beer in the United States has been undergoing a transformation, a trend that accelerated in the first decades of the 21st century. Tastes and habits of beer drinkers have been changing, moving away from not only full-calorie beers like Budweiser but also beers produced by national and international companies like Anheuser-Busch InBev. The preference for craft beers, microbrews, and beers produced by local breweries has been growing.

Beer sales and volume were up in the United States in 2011, but the growth did not come from sales of beers like Budweiser brand products. Domestic shipments of Bud Light and Budweiser declined for the year. Though Bud Light was the best-selling beer in the United States in the period between 2009 and 2011, for example, shipments numbered 41.3 million barrels in 2009 but only 39.85 million in 2011. In the same period, Budweiser tumbled from 20 million barrels in 2009 to 17.7 million barrels in 2011, the year it fell behind Coors Light.

To counter this trend, Anheuser-Busch InBev has implemented several changes, including the introduction of new Budweiser brands—such as Budweiser American Ale and Budweiser Select 55—designed to attract new consumers. The brand is also using social media and interactive marketing to create a sense of community and connection among Budweiser drinkers. In addition to these changes, Budweiser has also committed to supporting communities, the environment, and former members of the military in the United States.

Most importantly, after InBev acquired Anheuser Busch in 2008, the company made a concerted effort to grow the Budweiser brand internationally by testing new markets, which has led to increasing international sales. The company wanted to make Budweiser the first real global brand of beer and focused on the premium market segment as part of its long-term strategy. To support this ongoing expansion, plans were made to construct new or upgrade existing breweries and related facilities in such markets as China, Brazil, Argentina, and Paraguay. Beginning in 2012, Budweiser will be the official beer sponsor for at least three FIFA World Cup soccer tournaments, in which at least 80 countries participate.

FURTHER READING

"Anheuser-Busch Companies, Inc." *Encyclopedia of Major Marketing Campaigns*. Vol. 2. Detroit, MI: Gale, 2007.

"Anheuser-Busch Company, Inc." *International Directory of Company Histories*. Ed. Thomas Derdak. Vol. 1. Chicago, IL: St. James Press, 1988.

"Anheuser-Busch InBev." *International Directory of Company Histories*. Ed. Tina Grant. Vol. 100. Detroit, MI: St. James Press, 2009.

Anheuser-Busch InBev. "2011 Annual Report." Accessed October 27, 2012. http://www.ab-inbev.com/go/media/annual_report_2011.

"Best Global Brands 2012." Interbrand. Accessed October 27, 2012. http://www.interbrand.com/en/best-global-brands/2012/Budweiser.

Carey, Charles W., Jr. "Busch, Adolphus." *American Inventors, Entrepreneurs and Business Visionaries*. Ed. Ian C. Friedman. Rev. ed. New York: Facts On File, 2011.

"Coors Light Overtakes Budweiser as No. 2 Beer in the U.S." *Los Angeles Times*, January 11, 2012.

Groden, Louise L. "Budweiser." *Encyclopedia of Consumer Brands*. Ed. Janice Jorgensen. Vol. 1. Detroit, MI: St. James Press, 1994.

Haig, Matt. "Budweiser: The Targeted Brand." *Brand Royalty: How the World's Top 100 Brands Thrive and Survive*. London: Kogan Page, 2004.

Logan, Tim. "Hips Hops? The King of Beers Tries to Be Cool Again." *St. Louis Post-Dispatch*, August 26, 2012.

Millward Brown. "BrandZ™ Top 100 Most Valuable Global Brands 2012: Beer." Accessed November 7, 2012. http://www.millwardbrown.com/BrandZ/Top_100_Global_Brands/Categories/Beer.aspx.

BURBERRY

AT A GLANCE

Brand Synopsis: With a history of offering high-end luxury, Burberry mixes practical outerwear with sex appeal and British tradition.
Parent Company: Burberry Group plc
Horseferry House, Horseferry Road
London, SW1P 2AW
United Kingdom
http://www.burberry.com
Sector: Consumer Discretionary
Industry Group: Retailing
Performance: *Market share*—1 percent of the global luxury market (2010). *Sales*—EUR2 billion worldwide (2010).
Principal Competitors: Giorgio Armani S.p.A.#x0003B; Benetton Group S.p.A.#x0003B; Arcadia Group Limited

BRAND ORIGINS

- Thomas Burberry, a dressmaker, opened the first Burberry store in 1856 at the age of 21.
- Burberry merged with Great Universal Stores in 1955.
- In 1999 Burberry sought to change its target market, pursuing an image of sexy British luxury.
- Burberry had more than 500 store locations worldwide as of 2012.

In 1856 Thomas Burberry, a trained dressmaker, opened the first Burberry shop in Basingstoke, England, at the age of 21. Although Burberry's background was in dressmaking, he began making and selling outerwear, and this niche became the business's primary focus in the 19th century. In 1879 Burberry created gabardine, a tightly woven, waterproof fabric designed for use in coats that would protect the wearer from rain. Burberry patented gabardine in 1888. The fabric is typically made using a twill weave and is therefore more comfortable to wear than rubberized outerwear. Gabardine was popularized in the early 20th century by polar explorers Roald Amundsen and Ernest Shackleton in their separate expeditions to Antarctica. British mountaineer George Mallory wore a jacket made of gabardine during his fatal attempt to climb Mount Everest in 1924.

In 1891 Burberry opened its first store in London and began marketing gabardine. This location remained Burberry's headquarters until the beginning of the 21st century, when the headquarters were relocated to Westminster. In 1895 Burberry released the innovative Tielocken coat design, which was the predecessor of its famous trench coat, created during World War I. The introduction of officer coats into its line further established Burberry in the niche of outdoor attire. To ensure that his company maintained this reputation, Thomas Burberry had well-known British officers promote his coats by wearing them. Two of these notable officers were Lord Herbert Kitchener, known for his part in conquering the Sudan in the 19th century, and Lord Robert Baden-Powell, a British lieutenant general and founder of the Scout Movement. In addition to its well-known coat, Burberry began producing outdoor supplies made of the gabardine material, including tents that were popular with explorers.

In 1901 Burberry unveiled its logo of a knight jousting on horseback, which is still used today. The word *prorsum* (Latin for "forward") appears on the knight's banner. The logo was also trademarked in 1901. The knight is commonly featured on all Burberry correspondence, marketing materials, and signage.

In 1914, at the start of World War I, Burberry was commissioned by the UK war office to adapt the Tielocken coat to make it suitable for combat. What Burberry created was the renowned and still-popular "trench coat," designed to handle the elements encountered in the trenches of World War I. After the war, the coat became popular with civilians, and it remains so today. Burberry also began to fashion ski suits after the war and created aviator suits to be worn in open-air airplanes.

In 1920 Burberry introduced the now-familiar tartan pattern to the lining and exterior of its trench coats. Around this same time, Burberry greatcoats became regulation attire for officers of the king's household and its guards, a boost to the company's regal reputation. In the 1930s, Burberry's ski suits and other outerwear went commercial and became popular among the masses.

Burberry remained an independent business until 1955, when it was acquired by British-controlled Great Universal Stores (now GUS plc). The merger did not affect Burberry's marketing or operations. In 1959 Burberry began pursuing the high-end retail market by introducing its Blueblood line of coats and marketing the brand's reputation for luxurious attire by referring to the line in advertisements as "weatherproof luxury." Burberry did not lose sight of its association with durable weatherproof outerwear, however. Burberry was the outfitter of choice for Robert Swan during his expedition to the South Pole in 1985–86, when he and his team completed the longest unassisted march in history, walking 900 miles.

Burberry experienced a "proletarian drift" between the 1970s and 1990s, a time when its fashionable coats became associated with football hooligans and the casual subculture. As a result, Burberry revamped its advertising and marketing in 1999, releasing an advertising campaign featuring British model Kate Moss wearing nothing but a Burberry coat.

Burberry established itself as a global brand in 1909, opening a store in Paris, its first international location. As of 2012, Burberry had more than 500 store locations in 50 countries.

BRAND ELEMENTS

- In 1888 Thomas Burberry patented his waterproof gabardine fabric, which is still used in many of Burberry's outdoor fashions.
- In 1901 Burberry began using a logo featuring a jousting knight.
- After World War I, the Burberry trench coat, originally designed for British soldiers, became popular among civilians.
- Burberry revamped its marketing strategy in 1999, with a great focus on its British heritage.

In 1879 Thomas Burberry created a waterproof fabric called gabardine. The fabric, unlike its rubberized equivalent, is created from tightly woven wool that is waterproofed before being spun. Burberry patented the fabric in 1888, and gabardine became an integral part of Burberry's image and products. Because of Burberry's success at creating weatherproofed but comfortable outerwear, famous British explorers and aviators began wearing and recommending its products. During World War I, Burberry created the "trench coat" in response to a request from the British War Office for a coat that would protect soldiers from the elements.

After World War I, Burberry successfully marketed the trench coat for civilian wear, and it remains one of the most popular designs sold by the company. In the early 1920s, Burberry introduced "Burberry tartan," a check pattern that was originally used to line the trench coats but was later used as a pattern for outer fabrics, as well. The tartan pattern, which became available in a variety of colors, was still being used in Burberry attire as of 2012.

In 1901 Burberry released its iconic logo of a jousting knight on horseback with the Latin word *prorsum*, which means "forward," on his banner. As of 2012, the logo was still being used on all Burberry marketing materials and signage.

A large part of Burberry's modern image, which was revamped in 1999, has to do with its British heritage. Relying heavily on British models, Burberry attempts to keep fresh in the mind of consumers the fact that the company is a British brand and a fixture in British history. In 2010 Burberry launched a campaign called Burberry Acoustic. The campaign features British singers and songwriters in videos on the Burberry website. The same artists also perform at Burberry runway shows. In 1999 Burberry began marketing its looks in a more provocative manner: its campaign that year featured famous British model Kate Moss wearing only a Burberry coat.

BRAND IDENTITY

- In 1999 Burberry went through a marketing overhaul that led to expanded product lines.
- Burberry reported a 7 percent increase in revenues between 2009 and 2010.
- Burberry uses its British heritage as a brand identifier.

In 1999, Burberry rebranded itself from being just the originator of the trench coat and weatherproof outerwear by releasing an advertising campaign featuring British model Kate Moss wearing nothing but a Burberry coat. A shift in image, Burberry began pushing its brand as sexy, young, and chic, while reminding consumers that it is historically British. According to the Burberry 2011/2012 Financial Report, the company wants to continue to maintain its image as a symbol of British heritage and practical outerwear while also marketing itself as sexy luxury. In order to successfully project that image, the Burberry brand only markets its merchandise with British models.

Burberry saw success with its marketing during the first decade of the 21st century. In 2010 the brand reported a 7 percent increase in sales from the previous year, with revenues of EUR2 billion. Burberry has remained at the forefront of new style trends and technology, keeping its products focused on young adults. In 2010 Burberry launched Burberry Acoustic, a group of British singers and songwriters featured in videos on the company website. In recent years, Burberry has emphasized its British heritage in all its marketing campaigns, heightening consumer awareness of the brand's identity with British culture and history.

BRAND STRATEGY

- Burberry was acquired by Great Universal Stores in 1955.
- In the late 1950s, Burberry launched the Blueblood line, pursuing a reputation for outfitting noble and socially prominent people.
- Burberry went through an extensive rebranding in 1999, redefining itself as a sexy luxury brand.
- Burberry maintains a steady presence in the Asian market, offering separate brands to accommodate different cultural tastes.

The Burberry brand has gone through several brand identity changes since Great Universal Stores took over the company in 1955. Following the takeover, Burberry began to hone in on its target market of wealthy consumers by marketing its products as high-end fashion. In the late 1950s, Burberry released the Blueblood line of jackets. Associating the line with "blue blood," or the aristocracy, Burberry promoted its products as befitting people of noble background or social prominence. This reputation lasted only a couple of decades, until the casual subculture emerged in the 1970s. The decade marked the beginning of Burberry's "proletarian shift," meaning that its products were being purchased by a market opposite the one the brand had targeted.

Burberry sought to transform its image a second time in 1999 in order to counteract the association of the Burberry trench coat with football hooligans and ruffians known as "chavs." With this second image shift, Burberry promoted its products as sexy, young, and chic. In Burberry's new advertising campaigns, British model Kate Moss appeared nude except for a Burberry trench coat. At the same time, Burberry began to assert its British heritage and use British models exclusively in its advertising campaigns. Burberry has since released Burberry Acoustic, a social-media-focused promotional campaign featuring British musical acts.

After the brand transformation at the turn of the last century, Burberry began offering four separate brands under the Burberry name: Burberry Prorsum (high-end luxury fashion), Burberry London (trendy work fashion), Burberry Brit (weekend wear), and Burberry Sport (sportswear, including ski suits). Burberry also uses the brand names Burberry Black Label and Burberry Blue Label for its Japanese and Korean markets. The different labels are designed to make luxury fashion accessible to various income levels.

After the rebranding of 1999, Burberry also expanded the range of products it sells. Burberry launched a line of perfumes and handbags and began selling makeup in 2010 under the brand name Burberry Beauty. The expansion of its product lines allowed Burberry to dip into previously untapped markets and helped the company float during the global recession that began in 2008.

In 2006 Burberry began selling its products online in the United States and the United Kingdom, allowing Burberry to become easily accessible to people who do not live near a Burberry retail location. Burberry markets the same products globally, with the exception of Asia. In Japan and South Korea, Burberry markets certain fashions based on what is popular in the Asian market.

Burberry was floated on the London Stock Exchange in 2002, and the remaining stocks were placed on the exchange in 2005 by GUS plc (formerly Great Universal Stores). In 2008 Burberry was dramatically affected by the global economic recession: shares lost 56 percent of their value, and sales fell to EUR1 billion during 2009. Over the next few years, however, Burberry's shares increased in value by more than 159 percent, making the company more profitable than ever. Part of this success is attributable to the company's ability to stay ahead of trends in both fashion and social media.

BRAND EQUITY

- Burberry's brand value grew an estimated 21 percent in 2012.
- In 2011 Interbrand ranked Burberry as the 95th most successful global brand.
- In 2012 Burberry ranked 371st in Brand Finance's "Global 500," with an estimated brand value of US$3 billion.

In 2012 Burberry ranked 20th in the BrandZ Top 100 Most Valuable Global Brands, with a growth in brand value of 21 percent. Burberry's web presence and the new diversity of the brand have led to greater success. Burberry has recovered from its 2008 low, with an estimated 159 percent increase in share value.

Burberry ranked 95th in leading brand consultancy Interbrand's 2011 ranking of the top 100 brands, with a brand value of US$3.7 billion. In comparison, competitor Giorgio Armani ranked 93rd, with a US$3.8 billion brand value. In the same poll, Burberry ranked seventh in the luxury category, trailing Giorgio Armani. In 2012 Brand Finance ranked Burberry 371st overall in its "Global 500" and estimated its brand value at US$3 billion. In the same list, competitor Louis Vuitton ranked 202nd, while Giorgio Armani was not listed.

BRAND AWARENESS

- According to a survey performed by *Marketing Week*, Burberry is the 84th most sought-after brand in the U.K.
- During a study conducted in a shopping mall in China, only 57 percent of the consumers recognized the Burberry brand.
- Burberry has been featured in popular media, with the brand name being used as lyrics in hip-hop music.

According to *Marketing Week*'s ranking of the U.K.'s 100 most desired brands, Burberry was ranked 84th in 2011. The ranking was based on respectability, attractiveness, and whether consumers would want to use the brand in the future. *Arcada* put out a study in 2012 after surveying consumers in China regarding the reasons consumers wish to purchase Burberry products. Of the consumers surveyed, 22.22 percent stated they purchased Burberry due to the high brand fame and 20.99 percent stated they valued the excellent quality of the brand. In the same study conducted on the average shopper in a shopping mall or center, only 57 percent of consumers recognized the Burberry brand. The Burberry brand was ranked by DLG and Luxury Society as the 16th most-searched luxury brand in web engines in the United States. In a similar ranking, Burberry was listed as the 22nd most-searched luxury brand in China, based on more than 150 million consumer queries.

In the hip-hop culture in the United States, many famous musicians began including the names of luxury brands in their songs in the early 2000s. The Burberry brand was ranked 5th in Agenda Inc.'s 2003 brand rankings of most mentions in songs with 42 mentions. Famous musicians, such as 50 Cent, mentioned the Burberry brand directly in their song lyrics. While Burberry was reported as being unhappy with the association, the brand still progressed as a mark of luxury among hip-hop artists.

BRAND OUTLOOK

- Burberry continues to market its historic image as a British brand by focusing on its trench coats, logo, and tartan print.
- Since the rebranding of 1999 and the expansion of its product lines, Burberry has gained access to more markets and taken on more competitors.
- As of 2012, Asia was Burberry's most profitable market.

As stated in the Burberry 2011/2012 Annual Report, the company will continue to focus on maintaining its image as both a cutting-edge and historic brand. In 2009 Burberry experienced a large loss of profits during the global recession, with retail sales falling to EUR1 billion and operating profit dropping to 15 percent, down 5 percent from 2008. By 2011, however, Burberry had seen an increase in profits, with retail sales increasing 20 percent to EUR1.6 billion.

With the rebranding of 1999 and the expansion of its lines to include products other than apparel, Burberry has seen the ranks of its competitors increase. While Burberry previously competed primarily with Italian brand Giorgio Armani in luxury apparel sales, the introduction of handbags brought Burberry into competition with the U.S. brand Coach. Burberry has also been targeting the Asian market with the introduction of its Burberry Blue Label and Burberry Black Label, which market to the tastes of Japanese and South Korean consumers. As of 2012, these endeavors had proved fruitful, as Burberry reported EUR1.1 billion in Asian sales for 2011, which accounted for 37 percent of total sales. In comparison, Burberry's sales in Europe in 2011 made up 32 percent of total sales.

FURTHER READING

Agenda Inc. "American Brandstand 2004." *Brand Channel.* Accessed February 15, 2013. http://www.brandchannel.com/images/papers/245_brandstand04_final.pdf.

Brand Finance. "Global 500 2012." *Brandirectory.* Accessed September 3, 2012. http://brandirectory.com/league_tables/table/global-500-2012.

———. "Global 500 2012, The Annual Report." *Brandirectory.* Accessed September 6, 2012. http://brandfinance.com/images/upload/bf_g500_2012_web_dp.pdf.

Burberry Group plc. "Heritage." Accessed September 16, 2012. http://uk.burberry.com.

———. "Annual Report 2011/2012." Accessed September 20, 2012. http://www.burberryplc.com/documents/full_annual_report/burberry_ar_final_web_with-urls_indexed.pdf.

"Burberry Unveils Huge New Store." *Sky News*, September 17, 2012. Accessed September 18, 2012. http://www.skynews.com.au/finance/article.aspx?id=795761.

Enright, Allison. "U.K. Online Apparel Sales to Grow 60% by 2015." *Industry Statistics*, April 15, 2011. Accessed September 18, 2012. http://www.internetretailer.com/2011/04/15/uk-online-apparel-sales-grow-60-2015.

"Global Luxury Sales to Increase in 2010." *Warc*, April 19, 2010. Accessed September 20, 2012. http://www.warc.com/LatestNews/News/ArchiveNews.news?ID=26585.

Kennedy, Lesley. "Burberry to Introduce Burberry Acoustic during Live Online Menswear Show." *Huffington Post*, June 18, 2010.

Kollewe, Julia. "Burberry Warning on Profits Wipes £1Bn off Stock Market Value." *Guardian* (London), September 11, 2012.

"Luxury Sales to Rise in Europe." *Warc*, February 4, 2011. Accessed September 20, 2012. http://www.warc.com/LatestNews/News/Luxury%20sales%20to%20rise%20in%20Europe.news?ID=27851.

Millward Brown. "BrandZ Top 100 Most Valuable Global Brands 2012." Accessed September 27, 2012. http://www.millwardbrown.com/BrandZ/Top_100_Global_Brands.aspx.

Petcu, Oliver. "Burberry: Success Story or Cautionary Tale?" *Luxury Society*, February 8, 2011. Accessed September 17, 2012. http://luxurysociety.com/articles/2011/ 02/burberry-success-story-or-cautionary-tale.

"Product Mentions in Rap Music." *Hip Hop*, 2004. Accessed February 15, 2013. http://www.uic.edu/orgs/kbc/hiphop/mentions.htm.

Syncforce. "Burberry." *Ranking The Brands.com*, 2012. Accessed February 15, 2013. http://www.rankingthebrands.com/Brand-detail.aspx?brandID=375.

"2011 Ranking of the Top 100 Brands." Interbrand. Accessed July 3, 2012. http://www.interbrand.com/en/best-global-brands/best-global-brands-2008/best-global-brands-2011.aspx.

Wu, Youran and Ning Wang. "Market Feasibility of Burberry and Gucci in Zhang Jiagang City, P.R China." *Arcada*, 2012. Accessed February 15, 2013. https://publications.theseus.fi/bitstream/handle/10024/42379/Market%20Feasibility%20of%20Burberry%20and%20Gucci%20in%20Zhang%20Jiagang%20City%20%20P%20R%20China.pdf?sequence=1.

CADBURY

AT A GLANCE

Brand Synopsis: With its royal colors and dairy-farm associations, the Cadbury brand straddles the line between premium and mass market chocolate.
Parent Company: Mondelez International, Inc.
3 Parkway North
Deerfield, Illinois 60015
United States
http://www.mondelezinternational.com
Sector: Consumer Staples
Industry Group: Food, Beverage & Tobacco
Performance: *Sales*—US$35 billion (parent company) (2012).
Principal Competitors: Nestle S.A.; The Hershey Company; Kellogg's Company; Frito-Lay North America, Inc.

BRAND ORIGINS

- John Cadbury established the Cadbury brand in England through the sale of hot cocoa in 1824.
- Queen Victoria issued royal warrant to Cadbury Brothers, which became the official confectioner to the Crown.
- Cadbury began exporting to other British Empire countries in 1881.
- Cadbury's milk chocolate bar, Cadbury's Dairy Milk, was introduced in 1905.
- Cadbury and Schweppes merged in 1969.

The Cadbury brand has been associated with chocolate since 1824 when John Cadbury began selling hot cocoa in his grocery shop in Birmingham, England. It was a luxury item at the time that his wealthy customers loved, so much so that seven years later he moved to a larger location and began manufacturing his own cocoa products. Working with his brother, Cadbury developed a wholesale business that received a great boost in 1853 when the company, Cadbury Brothers, received a royal warrant to be the chocolate supplier to Queen Victoria. The royal household was supplied with free chocolate, and Cadbury was able to promote itself as the confectioner to the Crown, the regal connection becoming a lasting element of Cadbury's brand image.

In the short-term the Queen made out better than the confectioner, as the Cadbury partnership was dissolved in 1860. Cadbury's sons took over the business and continued to struggle until 1866 when developed a way to produce cocoa essence, resulting in better drinking cocoa and cocoa butter that could be processed into creamy eating chocolate. In 1868 Cadbury Brothers introduced their own lines of chocolate candy, supported by the advertising slogan: "Absolutely Pure—Therefore the Best." The company also promoted its products, which soon included chocolate creams, with decorated boxes, some of which featured the paintings of partner Richard Cadbury, a talented artist. Not only did the company break the lock on the British chocolate trade held by French confectioners, Cadbury was able to take advantage of the breadth of the British Empire to enter new markets. In 1881 Cadbury began exporting chocolate to Australia, and within the next few years, the Cadbury brand was introduced into other British Empire countries (New Zealand, South Africa, India, and the West Indies) as well as North and South America.

In 1905 Cadbury introduced a new recipe for milk chocolate using full-cream that it branded Cadbury's Dairy Milk. It became the most popular molded chocolate product in the history of the United Kingdom and served as the basic ingredient for several new Cadbury products. Initially, Dairy Milk chocolate bars were packaged in a pale mauve wrapper with red script. In 1920 a purple and gold wrapper was adopted. In time, these distinctive colors became an important element in the Cadbury brand.

At the heart of the Cadbury brand was high quality chocolate. No matter what chocolate confection was attached to the Cadbury name, consumers were promised a superior product. The brand's image was diluted somewhat after the 1969 merger between Cadbury and beverage manufacturer Schweppes. Through the end of century, Cadbury Schweppes added several high-profile beverage brands, including Canada Dry, Dr. Pepper, Seven Up, and Snapple. The Trebor and Bassett's candy brands were added as well, followed in the early 2000s by the addition of chewing gum brands, including Trident. Cadbury Schweppes decided to bring more focus to its operations, and in 2008 the beverage assets were spun off as public company called Dr. Pepper Snapple Group. Recast as Cadbury plc, the venerable confectioner looked to regain its position as a pure candy brand, one that management hoped to promote on a more global basis.

BRAND ELEMENTS

- "Absolutely Pure—Therefore the Best" was the brand's first advertising slogan.
- Purple and gold colors were first used in 1915.
- Cadbury script logo initially displayed on delivery trucks in 1921.
- "Glass and a half" image introduced in a 1928 ad campaign.
- High quality chocolate is the most important element of the Cadbury Master Brand.

While several products bearing the Cadbury name are promoted as unique, the Cadbury Master Brand includes a set of elements that apply to all of the company's product lines, including chocolates, candies, and chocolate beverages. The high quality of pure chocolate is one such element. Trust is another. For more than a century, Cadbury has nurtured a reputation as a brand the consumer can trust. The company's first advertising slogan for its milk chocolate, "Absolutely Pure—Therefore the Best," laid the foundation for Cadbury's reputation.

Another enduring and important element of the Cadbury Master Brand is the distinctive script used to render its signature and serve as the corporate logo. The first Cadbury logo was commissioned by William Cadbury in 1905. It featured a stylized cocoa tree with the Cadbury name intertwined. It was used consistently from 1911 to 1939 and for a short time after World War II. The contemporary logo was based on the signature of William Cadbury and first appeared on Cadbury delivery trucks in 1921. The signature was simplified over the years, and finally in 1952 it was employed across major brands to become an important part of the Cadbury Master Brand.

The Cadbury colors play a further role in distinguishing the Cadbury Master Brand in the marketplace. Purple and gold pay tribute to the brand's long association with royalty. The colors were first used in 1915 in the packaging for a new product, Milk Tray, an assortment of reasonably priced chocolates. Other chocolate assortments were expensive and positioned as a product limited to special occasions. They featured fancy packaging to support the high price point. In contrast, Milk Tray adopted less elaborate packaging to appeal to a wider, everyday market, but through its colors, the product retained some of the elegance customers associated with chocolate assortments. In 1920 Dairy Milk began using the colors in its packaging, and within a few years deep purple and gold were adopted as the official corporate colors. In 2008, Cadbury received a United Kingdom trademark for the particular shade of purple used in its logo.

The Cadbury corporate logo also included trademarked language and other images. A 1928 advertising campaign for Dairy Milk made the claim of a "Glass and a Half of Full Cream Milk in every half pound." To illustrate the point, a drawing of two glasses of milk, one full and one half-full, was included. The image later became part of the Dairy Milk wrapper, and in the 1960s, the drawing was incorporated into the Cadbury corporate logo, as was the line "The first name in chocolate." Nevertheless, it was the chocolate itself that was arguably the most important element in the Cadbury Master Brand.

BRAND IDENTITY

- Cadbury equates itself with chocolate.
- Trustworthiness is a key to Cadbury's appeal to families.
- Television commercials reinforced playful, exciting aspects of the Cadbury Master Brand.

Cadbury has positioned itself over its long history to bring certain associations to the minds of consumers, but at the heart of the brand's identity is a simple declaration: "Cadbury is chocolate." Not only is chocolate the core business of the company, the company wants consumers to equate chocolate to Cadbury. In other words, Cadbury and chocolate are synonymous, and other companies selling chocolate are just that: sellers of chocolate. The consistent use of the Cadbury script logo and other imagery, along with the purple and gold colors, over a long period of time help to solidify this connection.

An important condition to making such an expansive claim is the trustworthiness of the brand. Cadbury declared the quality of its products in its earliest advertising slogan: "Absolutely Pure—Therefore the Best." The "glass and a half" phrase and image also reinforced the idea that Cadbury products were wholesome and reliable. Given that a large portion of Cadbury's customers are parents and their children are the consumers, trustworthiness is a promise that the brand makes explicitly and is a core message it attempts to convey. Moreover, the Cadbury Brand through its imagery and advertising makes another promise: Cadbury products are delicious.

More than just offering consumers a stamp of approval regarding the quality and taste of its products, Cadbury seeks to identify its brand to positive emotions, largely centered on the family, such as friendliness, togetherness, and wholesome fun. Aligning itself to such feelings is especially important because of the brand's interrupted relationship with many of its customers. The consumption of chocolate and other confections taper off as children become adolescents, and several years will pass before these consumers have children of their own and become key purchasers of candy. Hence, maintaining a deep emotional bond between the brand and consumers is a key to building a long-term relationship between Cadbury and its customers.

Doing much of the heavy lifting of creating the friendliness and fun-loving aspect of the Cadbury brand has been the company's television advertising. It was one of just 24 brands to advertise on Great Britain's ITV when it began commercial broadcasting in 1955. Many of the Cadbury-branded products would be promoted on television, including Dairy Milk, Milk Tray, Flake, and Roses. In 1959 the Flake girl was created to demonstrate how the chocolate bar was too good to be shared. The light-hearted approach proved so successful that the Flake girl became a staple of British television for the next 45 years, albeit increasingly suggestive in nature. Another humorous long-running Cadbury advertising concept that reinforced the fun-loving, as well as adventurous, spirit of the brand was the Milk Tray stuntman who overcame incredible obstacles to deliver a box of chocolates to his lady love.

BRAND STRATEGY

- Individual brands were promoted through much of the 20th century.
- Megabrand strategy adopted in 1952.
- To promote family-values association with brand, Cadbury sponsored Save the Children.
- Cadbury World theme park opened in 1990 to become major tourist attraction.
- Cadbury Land brand created for children's market.

Through the first half of the 20th century, Cadbury promoted its individual product brands, including Dairy Milk, Milk Tray, and Crème Eggs (cream-filled chocolate Easter eggs introduced in 1923). It was a branding approach that Cadbury's principal competitors, Mars and Nestle, also embraced. Each product, in essence, operated as a unique brand, so that it was not necessary for consumers to understand which manufacturers were responsible for which products. Nevertheless, Cadbury began to take steps to create a consistent corporate image, most notably the Cadbury Tree logo registered in 1911. The image adorned assortment boxes, was imprinted on aluminum foil candy bar wrappers, and appeared on promotional items and in catalogs.

The Cadbury script logo proved even more important, transforming in style while finding its way from delivery trucks to packaging over the years. Finally, in 1952 the Cadbury script was prominently displayed on all of the products. Crème Eggs were now promoted as Cadbury's Crème Eggs, Dairy Milk became Cadbury Dairy Milk, and so on, as Cadbury adopted a Master Brand strategy. Three years later, Cadbury began advertising on British commercial television and the Cadbury Master Brand gained increasing prominence. The Cadbury name would be attached to a variety of new products, such as Crunchie, a honeycomb bar covered with milk chocolate, Wispa, a textured chocolate bar; Twirl, two strips of Flake dipped in Dairy Milk; Spira, a pair of hollow twists of Dairy Milk chocolate; and Strollers, a bagged assortment of caramel, raisin, and biscuit centers covered in milk chocolate.

In the 1990s many of the Cadbury products received updated packaging. The purple and gold colors were incorporated to reinforce the Cadbury Master Brand. It was also during this time that market research revealed that the Cadbury name was closely linked to family values in the United Kingdom. As a way to further that association, the company sponsored a program to raise money for the Save the Children Fund and pursued other philanthropic activities. Also to reinforce the Cadbury Master Brand, the company converted its Birmingham factory into Cadbury's World, a company museum-theme park that became a major tourist attraction. Later in the 1990s, Cadbury rebranded its chocolate lines that primarily targeted children (Buttons, Fudge, Curly Wurly, Chomp, Wildlife, Taz, and Freddo) under the Cadbury Land banner. To appeal to children, each product was assigned a cartoon character whose personality reflected the brand. Television advertising also continued to play an important role in maintaining the brand's identity with the British public. In 1996 Cadbury became the first sponsor of ITV's "Coronation Street," which would become the country's most popular soap opera, in what was the most expensive TV sponsorship in the history of British television.

Cadbury's branding efforts proved especially effective in the United Kingdom and other former countries of the British Empire. In the United States, Cadbury sold its confectionery operations to Hershey Foods as a franchise, allowing the U.S. giant to use its large distribution network and marketing clout to sell Cadbury-branded products in that market. (At home Cadbury acquired the Bassett and Trebor businesses in 1989, adding well-known English confectionery brands.) Elsewhere in the world, however, the Cadbury brand was not especially well known, despite Cadbury products being sold in 190 countries. It wasn't until 1997 that the company finally hired an international marketing director. Cadbury now took steps to pursue a global megabrand strategy. According to *Marketing Week*, "All brands use the same chocolate and the idea is that consumers will recognize new products as simply different delivery mechanisms. So Cadbury can simultaneously build master brand loyalty and drive up sales with new products."

At least in the United Kingdom, brand loyalty allowed the company in the new century to launch several product brand extensions, including ice cream and cake products. Cadbury also continued to tinker with its master brand strategy. The "Your happiness loves Cadbury" television advertising campaign did not prove effective mid-decade, leading to a modified approach: "Choose Cadbury, choose happiness." While the company may have struggled to draw emotional connections to the brand, or raise awareness of the brand in non-British heritage countries, there was no doubt that in its home market, at least, that when the word "chocolate" was uttered, the Cadbury name came to mind.

BRAND EQUITY

- Cadbury sold to Kraft Foods in 2010 for US$19 billion.
- Cadbury brand valued at US$3.55 billion in 2012, according to Brand Finance.
- Cadbury listed number 306 on 2012 Brand Finance Global 500.
- Among British brands, Cadbury ranked number 31 by Brand Finance.

Assigning a valuation to a brand is a difficult proposition, but in the case of Cadbury the value of the business as a whole can be quantified to a degree because in early 2010, Kraft Foods agreed to pay £8.5 a share, or about US$19 billion, for Cadbury. Some analysts, however, argued that the company was in fact worth £10 a share. It was a transaction that was not especially well received by the British public. A study cited by *Marketing Week*, indicated that the feeling of the British public toward the Cadbury brand had been adversely impacted by the sale, indicating that the brand might be weakening.

According to Brand Finance, a brand evaluation consultancy, Cadbury's brand value had been on the rise, increasing from US$3.26 billion in 2011 to US$3.55 billion in 2012. It was a performance that improved Cadbury's standing in Brand Finance's list of the 50 most valuable brands of British origins, moving from number 34 to number 31. Cadbury also ranked number 306 on the Brand Finance Global 500.

BRAND AWARENESS

- Cadbury is especially well known in the United Kingdom and former British Empire countries.
- Cadbury Land brand achieved high brand awareness with children in a short period of time.
- Cadbury has been rated as one of the United Kingdom's most trusted brands.

With a history approaching two centuries and a consistent presence on television since commercial broadcasting began, the Cadbury brand is well entrenched in the United Kingdom, where it enjoys strong top-of-mind awareness. Its name closely linked to chocolate with British consumers. The company has also been very successful in making children aware of the Cadbury brand. Shortly after the Cadbury Land label was launched, for example, a company marketing study indicated that the new brand was recognized by 83 percent of children. Moreover, the percentage of children who named Cadbury when asked "who makes the best chocolate for kids?" increased from 47 percent to 67 percent just one year after the Cadbury Land introduction.

Cadbury also scored well on brand loyalty. In a study conducted by Taylor Nelson Sofres in the early 2000s, 85 percent of consumers said that Cadbury consistently delivered on its promises in advertising. In 2009 a Readers Digest survey recognized Cadbury as the most trusted chocolate brand in the United Kingdom, Not only did Cadbury enjoy a 53 percent winning margin in its category, it received more support from consumers than any other winning brand. In addition, Cadbury enjoyed strong brand recognition in countries with ties to the former British Empire, where Cadbury products had been exported for many years. In the United States, where the brand was supported by the marketing prowess of Hershey, and later Kraft, Cadbury also enjoyed excellent brand awareness. The company's strong Easter egg business was especially helpful in bringing the Cadbury brand to the mind of American consumers year round. In other parts of the world, however, brand awareness of Cadbury lagged further behind.

BRAND OUTLOOK

- "Eyebrows" campaign featuring children with dancing eyebrows reflects more whimsical side to Cadbury brand.
- Cadbury worked with Fairtrade Foundation to receive certification and demonstrate social responsibility.
- Parent company adopted newly coined name, Mondelez, in 2012.

Although many United Kingdom consumers were not pleased that the ownership of the Cadbury brand passed out of British hands, their long-standing ties to Cadbury were strong and would likely remain so in the years ahead. Rather than depend solely on nostalgia, however, Cadbury continued to keep up with the changing tastes and beliefs of its customers. The company took steps to connect consumers with the brand through offbeat marketing, such as its "Eyebrows" campaign that featured children with dancing eyebrows. In the new century, Cadbury also introduced new healthier products, such as a low-sugar version of Dairy Milk. In 2009 the company sought to establish a socially responsible side to the brand by agreeing to work with the Fairtrade Foundation to make sure that the cocoa used to make its chocolate came from third world sources that have been Fairtrade certified.

Having been acquired by Kraft, Cadbury in 2012 found itself part of a corporate spin-off along with other Kraft snack brands around the world that created a new company called Mondelez International, Inc. A newly coined word, Mondelez, was supposed to evoke the idea of "delicious products." Whether Mondelez would ever establish its own identity and become a brand recognized, trusted, and even beloved by consumers around the world was a question yet to be answered. Cadbury, on the other hand, had long since established itself on these terms with a wide swath of consumers in many countries. There was every reason to expect that with the global backing of Mondelez, Cadbury would become recognized in corners of the world where it has not yet penetrated in the years to come.

FURTHER READING

Brand Finance. "Global 500 2012." *Brandirectory*. Accessed July 3, 2012.

"British Brands: The Top 50 British Brands." *Marketing Week*, July 29, 2010.

"Cadbury plc." *International Directory of Company Histories*. Ed. Jay P. Pederson. Vol. 105. Detroit, MI: St. James Press, 2010.

"Cadbury in Global Rebranding Drive." *Marketing*, December 2, 1999.

Conley, Clare. "Cadbury Seeks Global Fusion." *Marketing Week*, November 6, 1997.

"50 Years of Fame: Brandfame—Cadbury." *Marketing*, September 21, 2005.

"Great British Brands: Cadbury." *Marketing*, August 1, 2002.

"Trusted Brands Survey: Case Study—Cadbury." *Marketing Week*, March 26, 2009.

CANON

AT A GLANCE

Brand Synopsis: Known primarily for its cameras and printers, the Canon brand also appears on products like scanners, imaging equipment, and medical diagnostic equipment.
Parent Company: Canon Inc.
30-2, Shimomaruko 3-chome
Ohta-ku, Tokyo, 146-8501
Japan
http://www.canon.com
Sector: Electronics; Consumer Durables & Apparel; Office/Business Equipment
Industry Group: Consumer Discretionary; Information Technology
Performance: *Market share*—19 percent of the world market for digital cameras in both 2009 and 2010. *Sales*—JPY3.6 trillion ($US45.9 billion) (2011).
Principal Competitors: Xerox Corporation/Fuji Xerox Corporation; Hewlett-Packard Company (HP); Lexmark International, Inc.; Ricoh Company, Ltd.; Seiko Epson Corporation; Toshiba Corporation; Sharp Corporation; Konica Minolta Holdings, Inc.; Sony Corporation; Fuji Photo Film Co., Ltd.; Olympus Corporation; Nikon Corporation; Casio Computer Co., Ltd.; Matsushita Electric Industrial Co., Ltd.; Eastman Kodak Company; Sigma Corporation; Pentax Corporation; Victor Company of Japan Ltd.; ASML Holding N.V.

BRAND ORIGINS

- The Precision Optical Instruments Laboratory was the predecessor to Canon. In 1934 it produced a trial camera named the Kwanon, after the Buddhist goddess of mercy.
- Allied occupying forces used Canon cameras and equipment after World War II. Foreign correspondents in the Korean War also used Canon products. These users took Canon products back home and foreshadowed Canon's export success.
- Canon greatly expanded its product line starting in the 1960s, offering still and movie cameras, copiers and printers, computers, calculators, camcorders, storage equipment, and other products.
- In 2011 Canon had 198,307 employees worldwide: 70,346 in Japan; 86,017 in Asia and regions of Oceania; 22,739 in Europe, the Middle East, and Africa; and 19,205 in the Americas.
- The Canon Foundation, based in the Netherlands, promotes educational and cultural relationships between Japan and Europe.

In 1934 Japanese doctor Takeshi Mitarai and his friends developed a camera that used 35 millimeter film for their company, Precision Optical Instruments Laboratory. They called this trial camera the Kwanon after the Buddhist goddess of mercy. The company would later change its name Precision Optical Industry, Co., Ltd., in 1937. A few years later, in 1940, the company developed an indirect X-ray camera, which helped prevent the transmission of tuberculosis in Japan. The company's name was changed to Canon in 1947.

Like other Japanese businesses, Precision Optical Industry suffered during World War II, as the Japanese economy focused on supporting the military, not businesses. After the war, limited resources and money further hurt the company, but Takeshi Mitarai convinced the Allied occupying forces to stock Canon products. The Allied forces later took Canon products home, foreshadowing Canon's later success as an exporter. The Korean War also helped Canon's fortunes, as war correspondents discovered that the photographic equipment of Japanese companies like Canon was as good as the German equipment they usually used. This popularity outside of Japan was reflected in Canon's establishment of a New York branch in 1955 and of Canon Europa (now Canon Europe) in Europe in 1957.

Throughout Canon's expansion during the middle of the 20th century the company was also expanding its product line. Canon manufactured still cameras, movie cameras, and television cameras, as well as equipment for those products. The company made calculators and products for electronic recording, and in 1965 it began selling copiers, a product line that would prove to be very successful for the company. The 1970s brought Canon printers and computers, the 1980s brought video camcorders and word processors, and the 1990s and 2000s saw the boom of digital cameras and copiers. These products and other Canon products incorporated technological advances and established Canon's reputation for innovation.

Canon's growth and innovation was reflected across the globe. In 2011 Canon reported 198,307 employees worldwide: 70,346 in Japan; 86,017 in Asia and regions of Oceania; 22,739 in Europe, the Middle East, and Africa; and 19,205 in the Americas. In other international developments, the company created the Netherlands-based Canon Foundation to promote educational and cultural relationships between Japan and Europe in 1987. This organization reflects the company's multinational presence.

BRAND ELEMENTS

- An early Precision Optical Instruments Laboratory logo featured the words Camera Kwanon in a stylized font accompanied by a drawing of the Buddhist goddess Kwanon.
- Looking for a name for the international market, the Precision Optical Instruments Laboratory chose Canon for its various meanings and its resemblance to the name Kwanon.
- The Canon logo uses the word Canon in a red in a stylized font that resembles calligraphy.
- Precision Optical Instruments Laboratory changed its name a number of times, including changes to Precision Optical Industry Co., Ltd. in 1937, Canon Camera Co., Inc. in 1947, and Canon, Inc. in 1969.

The name Canon relates to Kwanon, the trial camera produced by Precision Optical Instruments Laboratory. Kwanon can also be spelled different ways, including Guanyin, Guan Yin, Kuan Yin, and Kwan-yin. Searching for a name it could use internationally, Precision Optical chose Canon because the word sounded similar to Kwanon and because "canon" has a number of meanings. Canon's website notes that canon can mean "scriptures, criterion and standard. The trademark was therefore worthy of a company involved with precision equipment, where accuracy is fundamentally important."

The Canon logo is the name Canon in red in a stylized font that somewhat resembles calligraphy. This logo follows the logo used in the early days of the company, which featured the words Camera Kwanon in a stylized font accompanied by a drawing of the Buddhist goddess Kwanon. In 1935 Precision Optical registered the name Canon as a trademark. This Canon logo used a stylized font, which underwent refinement in 1953 and again in 1956, when it took the form still used today. Precision Optical Instruments Laboratory also changed its name a number of times in its history, including changes to Precision Optical Industry Co., Ltd. in 1937, Canon Camera Co., Inc. in 1947, and Canon, Inc. in 1969.

BRAND IDENTITY

- Canon India's Canon Image Square stores educate customers about products like digital cameras and printers.
- Print advertisements have demonstrated Canon products and their features by using images in ways that emphasize Canon's devotion to capturing images.
- In Canon's 2011 annual report, the cover image of a mother and child using a Canon camera demonstrated how the brand can appeal to emotions and unite people.

In its Canon Image Square stores in India, Canon uses its brand elements and products to reinforce its brand identity. These stores employ consistent designs that reinforce the company's brand image, using the Canon name logo repeatedly as well as red-and-white color schemes that reflect the colors of the logo. Employees at the stores educate customers about the digital cameras and printers on sale at the stores, and so potential buyers can see the products and how they work. These stores clearly emphasize the identity of the brand, display the brand's products, and explain how the brand's products work.

Some Canon print advertisements have highlighted the brand's interest in capturing images. One such advertisement featured photographs of Canon cameras, which capture images in the form of photographs. The ad drew attention to the large viewfinders on these Canon cameras, which show photographers an image before they photograph it. The advertisement then showed someone using a Canon camera and viewfinder to take a picture. The advertisement itself consisted of a number of photographs, thus demonstrating the brand's identity as a specialist in the capture of images.

The cover of the company's 2011 annual report featured a photograph of a woman and a child looking at an image on the viewfinder of a Canon camera. As is apparent from the photograph, the image on the camera made the woman smile and the child laugh, and thus the scene portrayed Canon as a brand that can appeal to people's emotions. In addition, the woman and child in the photograph appeared to be a mother and her child, and so the scene could also be interpreted as suggesting that Canon is a brand that can bring families together by offering ways to record and share their experiences.

BRAND STRATEGY

- Discussing what it calls "the power of image," Canon has unified its communications and created a stable brand strategy for its Europe, Middle East, and Africa (EMEA) region, an area with more than 110 countries.
- The "power of image" strategy capitalizes on Canon's interests in photography, digital imaging, printing, and copying.
- The "You Can" brand platform and the "Make Photography New Again" advertising campaign both address how people can use Canon products for creative projects.
- Canon's "Long Live Imagination" promotional campaign featured a contest, Project Imagin8tion, where photographs formed the inspiration of a short film called *When You Find Me.*
- Another Canon advertising campaign featured a series of commercials and print advertisements starring American actor Jack Klugman in the 1980s.

In 2009 Canon adopted a new brand strategy for the regions of Europe, the Middle East, and Africa (EMEA), an area that encompasses more than 110 countries. This strategy attempted to unify the company's advertising and internal and external communications, and also aimed to create a stable visual identity. This strategy addressed the company's belief in what it called "the power of image," referring to the company's interests in fields such as photography, digital imaging, printing, and copying.

This power of image strategy joined the company's "You Can" brand platform in Europe, a platform emphasizing creative uses of the company's technology. Creative uses of Canon products are also featured in Canon's "Make Photography New Again," an advertising campaign for Canon cameras launched in Europe in 2008. Canon also encouraged photographic creativity in its campaign "Long Live Imagination," which began in 2011.

"Long Live Imagination" featured a contest, Project Imagin8tion, in which users submitted Canon photographs related to movie themes. American director, producer, and actor Ron Howard selected eight winning photographs from Project Imagin8tion to incorporate in a short film called *When You Find Me.* Ron Howard's daughter, actor and director Bryce Dallas Howard, directed this film. Canon and Ron Howard continued their involvement in the Project Imagin8tion project in 2012. This promotion joined other Canon promotions using prominent American entertainment figures. In the 1980s, American actor Jack Klugman appeared in television commercials and print advertisements for Canon copiers, showcasing Canon's initiative to incorporate people from creative fields and the promotion of the creative process into the company's advertising campaigns.

BRAND EQUITY

- Canon is the largest camera manufacturer in the world.
- Canon captured 19 percent of the world market for digital cameras in both 2009 and 2010.
- In other markets, Canon held an 18.8 percent share of the hardcopy peripheral product market in 2010. Hardcopy peripheral products are printers, digital copiers, and multifunction printers.
- In Interbrand's ranking of the best global brands, Canon ranked 30th in 2012.
- Brand Finance listed Canon the 93rd best global brand in 2012. Canon has made Brand Finance's "Global 500" list of the best global brands every year since 2007.

Canon is the largest camera manufacturer in the world. American market research firm IDC reports that Canon captured 19 percent of the world market for digital cameras in both 2009 and 2010. Nikon and Sony finished second and third in this digital camera market for both 2009 and 2010. IDC also reports that Canon holds significant shares of other markets. For example, IDC reported that Canon held 18.8 percent of the international hardcopy peripherals market in 2010, behind industry leader Hewlett-Packard's 42.5 percent. Hardcopy peripheral products are printers, digital copiers, and multifunction printers.

Interbrand ranked the Canon brand highly. In its "Best Global Brands 2012," it named Canon the 30th best brand in the world, with a brand value of around US$12 billion. Brand Finance considered Canon to be the 93rd best international brand in its ranking "Global 500 2012" and determined Canon's brand value to be about US$9.3 billion. Canon has placed in the top 150 companies in Brand Finance's list of 500 top global companies every year since 2007.

BRAND AWARENESS

- In 2011 Online Market Intelligence asked Russian consumers to name top-of-mind awareness for certain brands. These consumers cited Canon first for photography equipment and named Canon the 15th-best overall brand.
- In the Reputation Institute's "Global RepTrak 100" surveys, consumers gave Canon the eighth best reputation in the world in 2011 and the ninth best in 2012.
- Canon has partnered with the National Center for Missing & Exploited Children to help find missing children, using photographs to find children by donating equipment to law enforcement agencies.
- In Europe, Canon has partnered with the Red Cross to support children and education.

Canon's presence in international markets can be seen in a number of polls. In 2011 Online Market Intelligence (OMI) asked Russian consumers which brands they associated with the word love, in essence, asking them for top-of-mind awareness. When asked about photography equipment, these Russian consumers named the Canon brand. These poll respondents also ranked Canon as the 15th-best brand overall.

Other consumers have given Canon a favorable reputation as well. International consumers ranked Canon the company with the eighth-best reputation in the world in 2011 and the ninth-best reputation in 2012 in the Reputation Institute's "Global RepTrak 100" surveys. This poll found that 55 percent of consumers would be likely to recommend Canon (and the poll's other top companies) to other consumers.

Canon U.S.A. has increased awareness of its company and of social issues by partnering with the National Center for Missing & Exploited Children (NCMEC) to help find missing children. Canon created the campaign Canon4Kids, which promotes the use of photographs to find missing children. As part of this campaign, the company donated photographic and imaging products to law enforcement agencies and NCMEC. This campaign simultaneously involves Canon in community interests and informs the public about Canon's products and how they can be used. In Europe, Canon has partnered with the Red Cross to support children and education. By involving itself in these campaigns, Canon has involved itself in communities around the world and has raised awareness about its brand.

BRAND OUTLOOK

- Canon has partnered with the Dutch printer company Oce and the American technology company Hewlett-Packard to produce printers.
- Products like the C300 digital camera for filmmakers, with its small size and interchangeable lenses, exemplify Canon's development of new products.
- In the United States, Canon earned the third-most patents of any company in 2011, behind IBM and Samsung.

In 2011 Canon finished its acquisition of the Dutch company Oce, a printer manufacturer. Oce is now known as a Canon Group Company. This partnership recalls Canon's longstanding alliance with Hewlett-Packard to produce printers, a link that was forged in the 1980s. These partnerships have strengthened Canon's position in the international printer market. The company is also seeking to expand its presence in emerging markets via such ventures as its Canon Image Stores in India, which not only sell Canon products but educate consumers in how to use them.

In addition to expanding its international activities, Canon continues to develop more products. In late 2011 and early 2012, it released the C300, a digital single-lens reflex camera for filmmakers. This camera is notable for its small size and the fact that filmmakers can use other Canon camera lenses on the camera, epitomizing Canon's continuing commitment to innovation. Canon earned more than 2,800 patents in 2011 alone, coming in third for the most patents filed in 2011 (following IBM and Samsung).

FURTHER READING

Bedigian, Louis. "Did Canon Just Steal the Future of Filmmaking?" Benzinga Insights. *Forbes*, November 7, 2011. Accessed October 6, 2012. http://www.forbes.com/sites/benzingainsights/2011/11/07/did-canon-just-steal-the-future-of-filmmaking/2/.

Brand Finance. "Global 500 2012." *Brandirectory*. Accessed October 1, 2012. http://brandirectory.com/league_tables/table/global-500-2012.

Canon. "Canon Europe Announces New Brand Strategy in EMEA." June 10, 2009. Accessed October 5, 2012. http://www.canon.co.uk/About_Us/Press_Centre/Press_Releases/Corporate_News/Canon_Europe_announces_new_brand_strategy_in_EMEA.asp.

"Canon, Inc." *International Directory of Company Histories*. Ed. Jay P. Pederson. Vol. 79. Detroit, MI: St. James Press, 2006.

Interbrand. "Best Global Brands 2012." Accessed October 4, 2012. http://www.interbrand.com/en/best-global-brands/2012/Best-Global-Brands-2012-Brand-View.aspx.

Online Market Intelligence. "Our Products, Your Technology: Russians Love Global Technological Brands." *Online Market Intelligence*, January 11, 2012. Accessed October 4, 2012. http://www.omirussia.ru/en/analytics/press_releases/2012/01/news134.html.

Reputation Institute. "New Study: Reputation Is Impacted More by What You Stand for Than What You Sell." Global RepTrak 100, June 7, 2012. Accessed October 5, 2012. http://www.reputationinstitute.com.

CAPGEMINI

AT A GLANCE

Brand Synopsis: Capgemini provides global offerings in technology and outsourcing with the goal of creating "a collaborative business experience."
Parent Company: Cap Gemini Sogeti Group
Place de l'Étoile
11 rue de Tilsitt
75017 Paris
France
http://www.capgemini.com
Sector: Information Technology
Industry Group: Software & Services
Performance: *Market share*—1.8 percent of the global consulting service market (2009). *Sales*—US$10.72 billion (2011).
Principal Competitors: Accenture PLC; IBM Global Services; HP Enterprise Group

BRAND ORIGINS

- Capgemini was formed in 1975 as the result of a merger of Sogeti and CAP, followed by the acquisition of Gemini Computer Systems.
- By 1975 Cap Gemini Sogeti was present in 21 countries across Europe, and in Morocco, Iran, and Lebanon.
- In the early 1990s the group acquired SCS in Germany, Hoskyns in the UK, and the U.S.-based United Research Corporation and The Mac Group.
- Capgemini made alliances in the 1990s with partners like Microsoft, Oracle, and Sun Microsystems and became a leading expert in SAP global enterprise software.
- In 2003 Capgemini's new business structure focused on five units: North America, Central and Southern Europe, Northern Europe and Asia Pacific, Outsourcing Europe, and Sogeti.

Founded in 1967, the company Sogeti provided IT services and technical support to computer users via branch offices in Geneva. By 1972, 14 branches had been established in France and Switzerland. Each branch employed approximately 30 computer specialists, a workforce that has increased 19-fold since the branches were opened. Sogeti at this time offered services in the areas of facility management, business consulting, data processing, and corporate training, and by 1973 it was among the leading IT providers in France. In 1974 Serge Kampf, a shareholder in the custom software company CAP, proposed a merger between the two companies. The resulting organization, Cap Sogeti, soon became the leading IT provider in France. In the following year, the Cap Gemini Sogeti Group was formed after the acquisition of the American company Gemini Computer Systems.

As businesses began to automate during the late 1970s and early 1980s, the demand for IT grew. By 1975 Cap Gemini Sogeti was present in 21 countries across Europe, as well as Morocco, Iran, and Lebanon. In order to advance further globally, the group shifted its sight to industrialized countries with high-growth potential for investment. A series of acquisitions across Europe led the company to open a branch in Washington, D.C. In 1989 the brand was listed on the Paris Bourse, where it was among the CAC 40 of the top French listed companies. The 1990s brought changes for the group. Following the acquisition of SCS in Germany and Hoskyns in the UK, the group also bought the U.S.-based United Research Corporation and The Mac Group, both of which resulted in the growth of the Cap Gemini Sogeti's management consulting service. Due to economic factors at the end of 1991, Cap Gemini Sogeti experienced a downturn in revenues that signaled the need for a large-scale corporate renovation. The resulting changes saw the introduction of the brand's seven strategic business areas, which combined country divisions and sector specializations. The Capgemini Group University, a training center for the group's 10,000 managers and employees, was opened in 1991. Taking advantage of the increased interest in IT services, Capgemini made alliances with partners like Microsoft, Oracle, and Sun Microsystems and became a leading expert in implementing SAP global enterprise software. In 1999 the group was named European company of the year.

With the acquisition of Ernst & Young Consulting in 2000, the group's global position was strengthened, only to be followed by a decline in global business beginning in 2001. By 2003 the group had implemented a new structure that focused on five business units: North America, Central and Southern Europe, Northern Europe and Asia Pacific, Outsourcing Europe, and Sogeti. The group's strategic priorities involved outsourcing its primary development track, creation and development of production capacities in low-wage countries, and engaging in more local professional services. Capgemini also developed Rightshore, an IT approach that relied on offshore capabilities (particularly in India, after the group's acquisition of Kanbay, a Chicago-based IT services firm with a strong presence in India) and nearshore resources in countries such as Poland and Spain.

BRAND ELEMENTS

- Capgemini's branding slogan is "People matter, results count."
- Capgemini's visual advertisements in the 2000s have included cartoon illustrations provided by Herge and Neal Adams.
- In 2004 the brand officially became Capgemini, retaining the the spade and the blue palate of the logo introduced in the 1990s.

Capgemini's characteristic slogan is the line "People matter, results count." The brand's Collaborative Business Experience message represents its ability to bridge IT and business needs. Several advertising campaigns centered upon the Collaborative Business Experience idea that were released in the early 21st century combined the tagline "Together. Free our energies" with cartoon illustrations provided by Hergé (*The Adventures of Tintin*) and Neal Adams.

The Capgemini logo features the spade (chosen for the symbol carrying the highest value in the game of bridge) and was designed by Serge Kampf as early as 1992. In 1996 the characteristic blue color palate was introduced to represent the Group's information technology and management consulting services. In 2004 the brand officially became Capgemini, but retained the spade graphic and blue palate. In recognition of its connection to Capgemini, Sogeti also features the spade logo, but with an orange palate.

BRAND IDENTITY

- Also known in the IT industry as the Group, Capgemini combines human expertise with up-to-date technology in order to cater to create business-specific solutions.
- Capgemini is defined in part by the Collaborative Business Experience, which includes targeting value, mitigation of risk, optimization of capabilities, and alignment of the client organization.
- Capgemini's Collaborative Business Experience is founded upon the desire to "listen, rather than talk" to clients.

Also known in the IT industry as the Group, Capgemini combines human expertise with cutting-edge technology to meet individual client objectives and create business-specific solutions. The Group's diverse workforce allows the brand to grow in the global marketplace and provide culturally specific solutions to businesses.

Capgemini is defined in part by its Collaborative Business Experience, which is the central philosophy of the Group. Capgemini provides its clients with a tailored strategy and aids in implementation through four "dimensions of collaboration": targeting value (isolating the client's goal and establishing targets to meet the objective), mitigation of risk (determining the stakes of a client initiative), optimization of capabilities (the two-way transfer of knowledge during the project that ensures that Capgemini devotes to the client the maximum level of expertise), and alignment of the organization (identifying possible inhibitors of client success).

Capgemini's Collaborative Business Experience is founded upon the company's desire to "listen, rather than talk" to its clients, which puts power in the hands of Capgemini customers. To demonstrate the significance of collaboration to the Capgemini philosophy, the brand regularly advertises "Client Success Stories" to show how the collaborative methodology helps organizations accelerate their performance through innovation.

BRAND STRATEGY

- Capgemini uses a cross-disciplinary approach in solution services, integrating expertise across the four main service lines: consulting, technology, outsourcing, and Sogeti.
- In 2011 Capgemini conducted a study examining how companies benefit from digital technologies and the best practices involved in implementation.
- In 2011 the brand announced new collaborations to provide software integration for clients in aerospace, defense, transportation, automotive, and energy.
- In 2012 Capgemini released its first publication in the PointZero series, which described the brand's plans to integrate security and connectivity with software development.
- In 2012 the brand was recognized for its "completeness of vision" and "ability to execute" by the technology research firm Gartner Inc.

Capgemini uses a cross-disciplinary approach in solution services, integrating expertise across the four main service lines: consulting, technology, outsourcing, and Sogeti's local professional services. Cloud computing technology has also played a major role in Capgemini's business services; its specialized IT infrastructure allows Capgemini to offer cloud services to suit specific client needs. Capgemini's decision to focus on digital technology in 2011 resulted in a three-year research collaboration with the MIT Center for Digital Business. Capgemini's study focused on digital transformation, examining how companies benefit from digital technologies and the best practices involved in implementation.

In 2010 Capgemini executed an analysis and design project for Vodafone Netherlands and worked with teams across primary care trusts in the United Kingdom to develop a method of accelerating and embedding change (called a "hothouse") for the healthcare organization NHS West Sussex. Capgemini uses such partnerships and strategic alliances to increase its brand awareness and supplement its technological capabilities and solutions. Capgemini also develops industry-specific services to diversify its portfolio. In 2011, for example, the brand announced its sixth alliance with EMC, an IT service provider, and Dassault Systèmes to provide PLM (product lifecycle management) software integration for clients in the aerospace, defense, transportation, automotive, and energy industries. Capgemini also partnered with PolarLake to provide enterprise data management solutions to clients in financial services.

In 2012 Capgemini released its first publication in the PointZero series, which describes Capgemini and Sogeti's collaborative vision for maintenance of business applications. The publication promoted the Group's plans to integrate security and connectivity with software development. In the same year, the brand's "completeness of vision" and "ability to execute" earned it a place in the leader's quadrant in the most recent "Magic Quadrant for CRM Service Providers, Worldwide," a report published by the technology research firm Gartner Inc.

BRAND EQUITY

- In 2011 Capgemini had an estimated brand value of US$3.27 billion and a market share of 1.8 percent.
- In 2011 Capgemini was ranked 80th among the top 100 French brands and 327th among the top 500 global brands.
- Capgemini's income comes from each of the brand's global services: Consulting, Local Professional Services, Outsourcing, and System Integration.

In 2011 Capgemini had an estimated brand value of US$3.27 billion and a 1.8 percent share of the global consulting service market. In the same year, Capgemini placed fifth in the Computable 100, a ranking of the top IT companies in the Netherlands. Freebrand ranked Capgemini 80th among the top 100 French brands, and the brand was ranked 327th among the top 500 global brands. Capgemini reported profits for 2011 of US$389 million, and the company's assets were valued at US$11.01 billion. Capgemini's income comes from each of the brand's global services: Consulting (6 percent), Local Professional Services (16 percent), Outsourcing (36 percent), and System Integration (42 percent).

BRAND AWARENESS

- Capgemini is one of the top global service providers in China.
- Historically, Capgemini has enjoyed its strongest brand awareness in Europe.
- The acquisition of and formation of alliances with well-known U.S.-based companies has boosted Capgemini's brand awareness in the United States in the 21st century.

While Capgemini has enjoyed strong brand awareness in Europe, it is not as well known outside the region. In the late 1990s, however, the company initiated a series of acquisitions, alliances, and expansions that analysts have speculated will boost awareness of the Capgemini brand worldwide. The acquisition of such well-known U.S.-based companies as Ernst & Young and Vengroff Williams and Associates strengthened Capgemini's position in the management consultancy and finance and accounting markets, respectively, and won the brand important exposure in the United States. A similar approach in China led to Capgemini's being recognized as one of the top 10 global service providers in that country.

BRAND OUTLOOK

- In 2012 Capgemini set a goal to generate two-thirds of its revenue from fast-growth, high-margin strategic offers by 2015.
- Capgemini planned to focus its offers portfolio through the identification of new and high-value market segments, as well as investments and relationships with strategic partners.
- The brand's aim was to expand its portfolio during 2012 by increasing its emphasis on business analytics, the analysis of past business practices.

In 2012 Capgemini set a goal of generating two-thirds of its revenue from fast-growth, high-margin strategic offers by 2015 (compared with the one-third generated in 2011). To meet this goal, Capgemini planned to focus its offers portfolio through the identification of new market segments ripe for innovation and investment; investments and relationships with strategic partners for the purpose of developing new offers in niches with fast growth; enhancing team skills in sectors with high value and achieving a managed slowdown in activity in declining markets; and a greater focus on offers that integrate intellectual property. The brand's primary aim was to expand its portfolio during 2012 by increasing its emphasis on business analytics, the analysis of past business practices, which entails the management of big data (data sets too large to analyze using traditional tools and methods).

FURTHER READING

Bakalove, Elitsa. "Capgemini Will Continue to Battle Lingering Market Uncertainty in Europe, Constraining the Firm's Growth to Low-to mid-Single Digits during 2012." *Technology Business Research Inc.*, February 16, 2012. Accessed November 5, 2012. http://www.tbri.com/news/commentary_pgView.cfm?commentary=1555.

Capgemini. "2011 Registration Document: Annual Financial Report." Accessed November 5, 2012. http://www.capgemini.com/m/en/ext/investor/assets/2011_Financial_Report.pdf.

"Capgemini BPO Eyes 20 Per Cent Growth: Hubert Giraud, CEO, Capgemini." *Economic Times*, October 30, 2012.

"Capgemini Collects Vengroff Williams to Slip into Third Spot for Global Finance & Accounting BPO." *Horses for Sources*, November 15, 2011. Accessed November 6, 2012. http://www.horsesforsources.com/capgemini-vwa-11-15-11.

"Capgemini Furthers Brand on 'People' Platform." *Forbes*, October 12, 2012.

Flinders, Karl. "Are Capgemini's Consultancy Prices on a Slippery Slope?" *ComputerWeekly*, November 9, 2012. Accessed November 9, 2012. http://www.computerweekly.com/blogs/inside-outsourcing/2012/11/are-capgeminis-consultancy-prices-on-a-slippery-slope.html.

———. "Capgemini Will be a Mainly Offshore Based Supplier by 2015." *ComputerWeekly*, November 8, 2012. Accessed November 9, 2012. http://www.computerweekly.com/blogs/inside-outsourcing/2012/11/capgemini-will-be-a-mainly-offshore-based-supplier-by-2015.html.

Von Uechtritz, Michael. "Market Share Analysis: Top 10 Consulting Providers' Revenue, Growth and Market Share, Worldwide and Regional, 2009." Deloitte, April 30, 2010. Accessed January 18, 2013. http://www.deloitte.com/assets/Dcom-Global/Local%20Assets/Documents/Press/deloitte_vol2_article3.pdf.

CARREFOUR

AT A GLANCE

Brand Synopsis: As a mass retailing brand, Carrefour cares about helping customers and consumers to enjoy better quality lives every day.
Parent Company: Carrefour SA
33 Avenue Emile Zola
92100 Boulogne Billancourt
France
http://www.carrefour.com
Sector: Consumer Discretionary
Industry Group: Retailing
Performance: *Market share*—US$100 million (2012).
Principal Competitors: Groupe Auchan S.A.; METRO AG; Wal-Mart Stores, Inc.

BRAND ORIGINS

- Carrefour was established in Annecy, France, in 1959.
- Carrefour's first hyperstore opened in 1963.
- A public stock offering in 1970 accelerated international expansion.
- Carrefour exited the US market in 1993.
- The Promodes merger in 2000 made Carrefour the world's second-largest retailer.

The French retailing brand Carrefour took shape in Annecy, France, in 1959. Cofounders Marcel Fournier and Louis Defforey were businessmen interested in operating large supermarkets, a shopping format that had emerged during the post–World War II era and was replacing the country's traditional family-run grocery stores. At the same time, French consumers were becoming disgruntled with the country's large department stores that were both inconveniently located and expensive. It was a familiar situation for Fournier, who ran a department store. The partners, along with 10 stockholders, launched Carrefour and acquired a building already under construction that had a planned supermarket on the ground floor.

The first Carrefour store opened in June 1960 and was an immediate success. It became even more popular after it began offering discounted gasoline. Carrefour then entered the Paris market in 1963. The new store was large by French standards, combining a supermarket and a department store. It was dubbed a "hypermarket" by the press. Like the store in Annecy, it was also highly popular, especially with younger shoppers and suburbanites. Because of high inflation, discount pricing was a key factor in its success. Carrefour also became known as an innovative brand, introducing new ways to weigh, price, wrap, and refrigerate products.

Carrefour opened new and larger hypermarkets in other French cities in the 1960s and moved its headquarters to Paris. The company then began to expand internationally, supported by a public offering of stock in 1970. Hypermarkets also increased the range of products they carried. The pace of growth outside of France quickened in the late 1970s. By 1985 the Carrefour brand was established in ten countries spread across three continents. Three years later, the chain, now consisting of 65 hypermarkets in France and about one hundred fifteen units in Europe and South America, entered the coveted US market, opening a 330,000-square-foot hypermarket near Philadelphia, Pennsylvania. A second store opened in the region in 1991. While the brand enjoyed success elsewhere, as new stores opened in new countries in the early 1990s, Carrefour failed to crack the US market. The two Philadelphia hypermarket stores closed in 1993.

Despite the setback in the United States, the Carrefour brand was taken to other parts of the world. In 1996 the first Carrefour hypermarket opened in Seoul, South Korea, and more than two dozen stores soon followed in the Asian market. The company also grew through external means at the turn of the new century. Comptoirs Modernes SA was acquired, adding 790 supermarkets. Next, Carrefour merged with a major hypermarket competitor, Promodes SA, a deal that received regulatory approval in early 2000, creating the largest European retailer. With more than 8,000 stores in 26 countries generating about US$65 billion in annual sales, Carrefour became the world's second-largest retailer, trailing only Wal-Mart Stores, Inc.

Prior to the Promodes merger, Carrefour had devoted little attention to building a brand image, preferring instead to focus on advertising its products. The company now found itself with a wide array of brands covering several categories, including food, beauty, general merchandise, consumer electronics, and apparel. In addition to the hypermarket format, Carrefour also operated supermarkets, convenience stores, and cash-and-carry outlets. Almost by necessity Carrefour began to craft a brand management strategy. Over the course of the next decade, amid an extended sales slump, Carrefour slowly developed a brand and the means to communicate it to a worldwide customer base.

BRAND ELEMENTS

- Carrefour name was drawn from the French transliteration of the Greek word for marketplace, *agora*.
- Carrefour logo comprises two parts: the word "Carrefour" and a "C" symbol.
- Logo colors for signage are red and blue.
- *Avec Carrefour je positive!* served as the slogan for 15 years.
- Single-brand strategy was supported by revamped private-label program.

Cofounder Marcel Fournier provided Carrefour with its name, drawing on the French transliteration of the Greek word for marketplace, *agora*. The word "Carrefour," which the company refers to as its logotype, is also incorporated into the brand's logo. Joining it is a "C" device symbol, formed in the white space between two abstract shapes and rendered in different colors, depending on the application. For store fascias and external signage, for example, the logo employs red and blue. The two parts are also used to create banner logos for "Carrefour market," "Carrefour express," and "Carrefour city." Graduated versions of the logo are used in a variety of colors for packaging, shopping bags, in-store signage, and communications. In addition the "C" device is used by itself for packaging and other applications.

Carrefour has used a number of taglines or slogans over the years. In France, from 1988 until 2003 the brand relied on the slogan *Avec Carrefour je positive!* ("With Carrefour, I positive"), which was combined with the C device of the logo. The company tried other approaches over the next few years, but in 2009 it introduced *Le positif est de retour* ("Positive is back!"). A year later the message was "Positively every day." In 2012 Carrefour tried a different tack: *Les pris bas ... La confiance en plus*, or "Low in price ... but high in trust." Other slogans would be used in other markets as well, often making use of the word "positive" or emphasizing low prices and convenient locations.

Carrefour-labeled products are another important element of the Carrefour brand. In 2005 Carrefour began placing greater emphasis on premium private-label products. The revamped products combined low prices with high quality. The packaging was also colorful, and it prominently displayed the Carrefour logo. All told, the products helped to support a single-brand strategy for Carrefour as it attempted to bring focus to the plethora of brands it inherited through the acquisitions of the previous few years.

BRAND IDENTITY

- Care for customers is at the heart of Carrefour's brand identity.
- High-quality products and low prices are tangible evidence of the Carrefour brand promise.
- The Carrefour brand seeks to demonstrate to customers and consumers that it is committed, positive, and caring.
- To make Carrefour a "lovemark" is the ultimate branding goal.

In its brand book, Carrefour states the goal it hopes to achieve through its branding strategy: "Our dream is to be recognized and loved for helping our customers and consumers enjoy better quality lives every day." At the heart of the brand is the promise that Carrefour cares about its customers. Thus, the company emphasizes high-quality, low-price products and services, and it makes the shopping experience convenient as well as simple and enjoyable. The large number of stores and the multiformat approach—hypermarkets, supermarkets, convenience stores, and cash & carry outlets—allow Carrefour to serve its customers whenever, wherever, and however desired.

There are three key values that Carrefour hopes to convey to customers. First, the retailer is committed to the well-being of its customers and employees, the communities in which it does business, and the planet. For customers that means Carrefour is dedicated to finding new products and services to improve their quality of life. Second, Carrefour focuses on the word "positive," something the retailer's marketers have attempted to connect to the brand. In a retailing context, a positive attitude means an energetic and enthusiastic approach to serving customers, again developing products and services to make the lives of customers better. Finally, Carrefour seeks to be associated with the idea of caring. The brand promise is that Carrefour cares for its customers and consumers, welcoming them into their stores and listening to their concerns. Moreover, Carrefour wants to be seen as caring for the communities in which its customers live. Ultimately the goal has been to create an emotional bond with people, to transform the Carrefour brand into a "lovemark," according to the company's brand guide.

BRAND STRATEGY

- Carrefour initially spread to other countries through partnerships.
- Carrefour introduced unbranded, generic products in 1975.
- Through acquisitions, Carrefour inherited an uncoordinated group of brands.
- A brand-development team was formed in 2005 to revamp the private-label program.

Carrefour was true to the meaning of its name, *marketplace*, by launching the hypermarket concept in the early 1960s. Although the retailer did little in the way of brand building, Carrefour became known for its wide variety of products and reasonable prices. It was a message that was especially well-received by French consumers because of inflation, and in the 1960s the brand easily spread across France, supplanting the traditional retailing model of family-owned grocery stores.

Through partnerships in other countries, Carrefour spread to Belgium, Switzerland, the United Kingdom, and Italy. Eventually Carrefour bought out its partners to become the sole owners of their international outposts. In addition to Europe, Carrefour was successful in the 1970s in planting its brand in South America, specifically in Brazil and Argentina. In 1975 Carrefour introduced private-label products. These so-called *Products libres*, known elsewhere as generic products, were sold in white packaging and did little to grow the Carrefour brand. It wasn't until a decade later that the Carrefour name was attached to private-label products. However, because it was not prominently displayed, this created little brand equity.

An attempt to crack the US market proved unsuccessful by the early 1990s, due in no small measure to the dominance of Wal-Mart, whose own retail model in time emulated Carrefour's hypermarket approach. Worldwide, Carrefour became Wal-Mart's chief rival, especially after two major acquisitions at the turn of the century vastly expanded the size of Carrefour. While Carrefour hoped to enjoy economies of scale with almost 9,000 stores in the fold, those savings did not materialize to the level expected. Moreover the company faced a branding nightmare.

Carrefour inherited a host of uncoordinated brands across a variety of sectors. Promodes stores had to be closed temporarily after the chain's acquisition in order to adopt the Carrefour name. Carrefour also implemented a brand-management strategy to improve the sagging image of hyperstores, which consumers regarded as cold and distant. Instead of focusing on products, Carrefour paid more attention to its brand and devoted greater attention to market surveys to learn more about its customers—what they buy as well as what they wanted to buy.

Carrefour's brand-building efforts took another major step in 2005, when it formed a brand-development team, which included eight brand managers divided among food, nonfood, and services. The goal was to create a private-label program that would not only drive sales but grow the Carrefour brand. Research indicated that shoppers expected not only prices that were low, but also products that were socially responsible. With this in mind, the company created three product categories: Carrefour for Everyday for staples; Carrefour Agir for organic and ethical products; and Carrefour Selection for premium products. Within the Everyday brand were subcategories: Carrefour Baby, Carrefour Kids, and Carrefour Lite. New packaging was also designed to reinforce the image of the new private-label products. Over the course of 3 years, Carrefour repositioned more than 15,000 products.

To highlight the new, branded products, Carrefour conducted sales and promotional events, including in-store campaigns. Advertising was done on television, in print, and with billboards. Carrefour also improved store layouts and merchandising concepts to improve the shopping experience and help fulfill the brand promise of caring for customers. Basket sizes, for example, were enlarged. Shopping time was also reduced. It was all part of a single-brand approach to making Carrefour a consistent global brand. While the retailer enjoyed some success, it still did not perform very well, due to the difficult economic conditions that prevailed at the end of the first decade in the new century.

BRAND EQUITY

- Brand Finance estimated Carrefour's brand value at US$8.812 billion in 2012.

- Carrefour fell from No. 50 in 2008 to No. 101 in 2012 on Interbrand's top 500 global brands.
- Carrefour is France's most valuable retail brand.

A long-term association with the hypermarket concept affords Carrefour considerable brand equity, as does a global footprint that provides geographical diversification and gives Carrefour a competitive edge over smaller rivals. With four formats, Carrefour is able to serve a diverse customer base as well. The company generated US$117 billion in total sales in 2011. While that represented a 1.1 percent increase from 2010, sales were still down during a period of poor economic conditions after they had peaked at US$120.9 billion in 2008.

Brand Finance Plc, a brand evaluation consultancy, estimated in 2012 that Carrefour's brand value was US$8.812 billion, representing more than a US$3 billion loss in value over the previous year. In 2008 Brand Finance had listed Carrefour No. 50 on its list of the top 500 global brands. In 2012 Carrefour fell to the No. 101 position. Given poor the economic conditions, it was not a surprising development. Interbrand noted that "Carrefour's brand value and enterprise value will largely rise and fall in line with global markets." In France, on the other hand, Carrefour remained the top retail brand in 2012, according to Interbrand, posting more than three times the sales of its closest challenger.

BRAND AWARENESS

- Carrefour enjoys long association with the hypermarket concept.
- Carrefour enjoys strong brand-awareness in Europe, especially in France.
- Carrefour is well-known in selected Latin American and Asian countries.

The Carrefour brand is well-known around the world. At the end of 2010, the company operated nearly 16,000 stores in four formats on three continents. In addition to strong brand awareness in France, Carrefour is well-known in other European countries in which it operates, including Belgium, Bulgaria, Cyprus, Greece, Italy, Poland, Portugal, Romania, Turkey, and Spain. Carrefour is also known in three Latin American countries: Argentina, Brazil, and Colombia. In the Asian region, Carrefour operates in China, Indonesia, Malaysia, Singapore, Taiwan, and Thailand. While Carrefour has been closely associated with the hypermarket concept, especially in its home country, the view of the brand has changed in recent years. The broad array of Carrefour-labeled products that have been introduced has helped to improve general awareness.

BRAND OUTLOOK

- Global economic conditions hindered growth.
- Asian market offers growth opportunities.
- Emerging markets include India, Russia, and the United Arab Emirates.

With a downturn in market conditions during the latter half of the first decade of the 21st century, Carrefour, like many retailers, experienced a significant decrease in sales. The *New York Times* offered a blunt assessment of the company at the start of 2009 when a new chief executive was installed: "Market share had slipped at home, shareholders were uneasy and the group had lost focus on core clients, while pursuing a haphazard international expansion." To get the business and the brand back on track, Carrefour further emphasized the focus on customers.

The company also initiated a reset on core European markets. According to the *New York Times*, "That meant focusing on the rebranding and refurbishing stores, automating checkout lanes at hypermarkets, introducing recession-friendly value brands, overhauling the information technology systems and better leveraging its huge buying power to improve price competitiveness." While Carrefour had to contend with poor global economic conditions and growing competition, there were also opportunities to extend the brand further in Asian markets, which in 2010 only contributed 8 percent of the company's total revenues. There were also the emerging markets of India, Russia, and the United Arab Emirates that the company hoped would prove fertile ground for the Carrefour brand.

FURTHER READING

Brand Finance. "Global 500 2012." *Brandirectory*. Accessed July 3, 2012. http://brandirectory.com/league_tables/table/global-500-2012.

"Carrefour SA." *International Directory of Company Histories*. Ed. Jay P. Pederson. Vol. 137. Detroit, MI: St. James Press, 2012.

"France: Carrefour Extends 'Single Brand' Strategy." just-food.com, June 5, 2008. Accessed December 15, 2012. http://www.just-food.com/news/carrefour-extends-single-brand-strategy_id102644.aspx

Hayes, Thomas C. "The Hypermarket: 5 Acres of Store." *New York Times*, February 4, 1988.

Kapferer, Jean-Noel. "Competition of Brands—or of Business Models?" *Advertising Age*, February 26, 2007.

Kapner, Suzanne. "Two Big European Retailers Contrast in Strategy and Profit." *New York Times*, August 31, 2001.

"Most Valuable French Retail Brands, 2012." *Business Rankings Annual*. Ed. Deborah J. Draper. Detroit, MI: Gale, 2013.

Saltmarsh, Matthew. "Carrefour Chief Pursued Strategy to Strengthen Home Market." *New York Times*, June 3, 2010.

CARTIER

AT A GLANCE

Brand Synopsis: Considered to be the "king of jewelers and the jeweler of kings," the Cartier brand is synonymous with luxury.
Parent Company: Richemont
50, chemin de la Chênaie, CP30
1293 Bellevue, Geneva
Switzerland
http://www.cartier.us
Sector: Consumer Discretionary
Industry Group: Retailing
Performance: Cartier is the world's largest jewelry retailer based on sales. Cartier's sales make up about 90 percent of Richemont's jewelry business, which grossed EUR 4.6 billion in the fiscal year ending in 2012. Cartier's sales alone constitute 2.8 percent of the global jewelry market, slightly ahead of competitor Tiffany & Co.'s 2.1 percent share. Cartier also owns a significant share of the luxury watch market, although a 2012 study of consumers' Internet searches for watch brands indicated that Rolex and Omega continue to hold an edge over Cartier.
Principal Competitors: Bulgari; Tiffany & Co.; Rolex; Omega

BRAND ORIGINS

- Cartier was founded in 1847, when Louis-François Cartier took over a master jeweler's business in Paris.
- Louis-François Cartier's grandsons opened locations in New York and London.
- Cartier created the first ladies' wristwatch in 1888 and popularized a men's wristwatch with a leather band in the early 1900s.
- After changing ownership several times, Cartier was taken over by the Swiss-based Richemont group in the 1990s.

In 1847 a young man named Louis-François Cartier took over the workshop of master jeweler Adolphe Picard on Rue Montorgueil in Paris. From the beginning, Cartier sold only the finest gems and metals available. It catered to nobles as early as 1856, when Princess Mathilde, a niece of Napoleon I, made her first purchase from the company. Not long afterward, Napoleon III's wife, Empress Eugénie, also became a client, giving Cartier a royal reputation.

At the end of the 19th century, Louis-François Cartier's three grandsons, Louis, Pierre, and Jacques, took control of the company. Although their father, Alfred, was still overseeing the production of jewelry, the sons took Cartier in another direction. Under their management, Cartier became a global company, with Jacques opening a store in London and Pierre opening another in New York. Louis retained control of the Paris location.

Cartier made a new name for itself in 1888, when it debuted the first ladies' bracelet watch. The male counterpart, a substitution for the pocket watch, was created in 1904 at the request of Alberto Santos-Dumont, a pilot who found that looking at a pocket watch during flights was impractical. The "Santos" watch is still made today. Although Swiss manufacturer Patek Philippe has been credited with inventing the wristwatch,

Cartier popularized this alternative to the standard pocket watch. The firm also was the first to place the wristwatch on a leather band.

At the turn of the 20th century, Cartier launched another revolution in timepieces with its "mystery clocks." The clocks had a completely invisible mechanism, making their operation a mystery to casual observers. At that time, Cartier signed an exclusive contract with Edmond Jaeger, a French watchmaker, to supply extraordinarily thin mechanisms for Cartier timepieces.

Meanwhile, Cartier continued to deal in fine jewelry. In the early 20th century, the firm bought and sold the famous Hope Diamond, one of the largest known blue diamonds. It also introduced a line of multicolored, Art Deco jewelry called "Tutti Frutti."

In 1904 Cartier became the official purveyor to King Edward VII of the United Kingdom and to King Alfonso XIII of Spain. Solidifying its reputation as the "jeweler of kings," Cartier later supplied jewelry to several other monarchies, including those of Siam, Egypt, and Albania.

Cartier Paris was sold in 1972 to a group of investors led by Joseph Kanoui. The company soon adopted the slogan "*Les Must de Cartier*," meaning that Cartier products were "must-haves," and debuted a new line of products. In 1979, Cartier's Paris, London, and New York interests were combined to create Cartier Monde.

In 1984, Cartier created the *Fondation Cartier pour l'art contemporain* (Cartier Foundation for Contemporary Art) as a means to collaborate with living artists and to promote contemporary art. An exhibition of Cartier pieces opened in Paris in 1989. It later traveled to museums throughout the world. In the 1990s the Swiss-based, South African-owned Richemont group gained a controlling interest in Cartier.

BRAND ELEMENTS

- The name Cartier is the most important element for the brand; it is the element most recognized by consumers.
- The brand's logo is simple, emphasizing the Cartier name while also utilizing the famous red found in the packaging for Cartier's products.
- Every Cartier product is sold in a red leather box with gold lace, a significant part of the consumer experience of Cartier.
- The slogan "The Jeweler of Kings" has been the brand's longest-running slogan, emphasizing the brand's history of working with royalty.

The Cartier name is the most important element associated with the Cartier brand. While the name originated with the company's founder, Louis-François Cartier, who started the company in 1847, the brand name has evolved to become synonymous with luxury. Given the brand's history of providing jewelry to monarchs around the world, the name Cartier has come to represent more of a coveted experience, rather than merely a jewelry company.

The brand's logo is simple: the name Cartier is imprinted in a simple, white cursive type on a ruby red background. Instead of using an image to represent the Cartier brand, the company uses only the name; such simplicity suggests the brand's high consumer awareness. The red used in the company logo is also a signature element of the brand's identity. Cartier's ruby red leather boxes belie the delicate treasures that lie inside. Gold lace frequently borders the outside of the box, and the boxes are lined with either black velvet or white silk to further set off the jewels inside.

While the company has used several different slogans for the brand throughout its history, the slogan that has been used most consistently is "The Jeweler of Kings." The slogan dates back to the original Cartier's service to the emperors of France during the 19th century and, subsequently, to monarchs throughout the world. In using the slogan today, Cartier is reminding customers that the brand is the highest form of luxury, the source of jewels for kings and queens around the world.

BRAND IDENTITY

- Cartier is not only a high-end international jeweler; it is also a historical and cultural icon.
- Cartier represents the highest standards of excellence in quality and customer service.
- Cartier stands for socially responsible business practices, such as refusing to deal in conflict diamonds.

Since the 1800s Cartier has been a premier high-end jeweler in Europe. In the late 1800s and early 1900s, while gaining success in timepiece design and sales, Cartier became a leading international jeweler. In an effort to set itself apart from more recent competitors, Cartier positions itself as a European staple. It defines itself, according to a public statement, as "a historical and cultural institution, an icon of its time." By endowing itself with such significance, the Cartier brand tells consumers that purchasing a Cartier product is akin to partaking of a priceless heritage.

In addition to heritage, the brand Cartier connotes excellent quality and customer service, along with social responsibility. Guaranteeing all of its products, Cartier agrees to repair any piece made since the company's founding in 1847. Moreover, Cartier describes itself as a "responsible jeweler." It refuses to deal in conflict diamonds, which are diamonds mined and sold by insurgent forces in war-torn countries. It also refuses to deal with gem or metal suppliers who engage in human rights abuses or cause environmental damage.

BRAND STRATEGY

- Brand consistency is a key component of Cartier's marketing strategy.
- Cartier introduced timepieces to its product line in 1888.
- "*Les Must de Cartier*" represented a broadening of the Cartier brand to include less-exclusive products.
- Cartier has been an international company since the turn of the 20th century, with its flagship locations in Paris, London, and New York.

Since its founding in 1847, Cartier has gone through very few identity changes. This consistency is a part of the company's current marketing strategy, which promotes the idea that buying Cartier jewelry is like buying an elegant slice of history. The company has always had a high-end clientele, starting with Princess Mathilde, a niece of Napoleon I. Many other aristocrats and monarchs of Europe have appointed Cartier as their premier jeweler. The only major addition to the brand's jewelry line has been its timepieces, starting with its innovative bracelet watch for women in 1888 and its popular leather-banded wristwatch for men in 1904.

The brand's name and reputation have remained constant through changes in the company's ownership. In the 1970s, for example, Cartier introduced the less-exclusive, "must-have" product line called "*Les Must de Cartier*" to appeal to a broader base of consumers. It also began using new designers in an attempt to refresh its image. Yet, throughout this period, Cartier continued to sell unique fine jewelry and watches. It also began exhibiting its jewelry and timepieces in museums as timeless works of art.

In 2012, Cartier had more than 300 locations around the world, primarily in major cities. Its international efforts began in the early 20th century, when Cartier expanded from Paris to London and New York. Those three flagship stores placed Cartier at the head of the international jewelry market and helped it to become the purveyor to several monarchs throughout the world.

BRAND EQUITY

- Cartier has a long history of selling to royalty and dealing in prestigious jewels.
- In 2011, Interbrand ranked Cartier 70th out of 100 global brands, three places above competitor Tiffany & Co.
- According to Brand Finance in 2012, Cartier ranked 357th out of 500 global brands.

Cartier is considered one of the oldest jewelry companies in the world as well as one of the most prestigious. Having been associated with royalty since its beginning, Cartier symbolizes luxury and elegance. In 1910 Cartier New York acquired and sold the infamous Hope Diamond, bolstering its reputation as a high-end jeweler.

According to Interbrand's "2011 Ranking of the Top 100 Brands," Cartier ranked 70th, with a brand value of $4.8 billion, whereas Tiffany & Co. ranked 73rd, with a $4.5 billion brand value. According to the same poll, Cartier ranked third in the luxury sector, closely followed by Tiffany & Co.

Brand Finance's "Global 500 2012" ranked Cartier 357th overall and estimated its brand value to be $3.2 billion. Tiffany & Co. ranked 384th overall. In 2012, Cartier's return on equity was calculated to be 18.6 percent, similar to Tiffany & Co.'s 18.4 percent.

BRAND AWARENESS

- Cartier has carefully chosen the symbols associated with the brand, which are memorable for their elegance and luxury.
- As of 2012 Cartier has over 300 store locations in 125 countries, with flagship stores in Paris, London, and New York.
- Cartier has maintained its reputation as the "king of jewelers" for more than a century and a half.

Cartier has carefully selected its store locations and the symbols associated with the brand in order to highlight its traditions and historic role. The brand's connections to royalty, the red leather of its packaging, and the sleekness of its panther emblem all call to mind elegance and luxury. The Cartier brand dates back to 1847, and the only major change in the brand has been the addition of the design, creation, and sales of unique timepieces. Cartier's entry into the international market at the turn of the 20th century vastly extended the brand's reach, which by 2012 encompassed 300 stores in 125 countries. Cartier's advertising reminds consumers that purchasing Cartier is tantamount to investing in European history. Thus, every consumer can be a king, since Cartier is the "king of jewelers."

The originality of Cartier's jewelry as well as the constant change in its designs is also appealing to consumers, as it is unlikely that two friends or family members will acquire the same piece of jewelry. Additionally, Cartier's unique and innovative timepieces, such as the "mystery clock" and "Santos" watch, have extended the brand's appeal and placed it at the forefront of timepiece sales.

BRAND OUTLOOK

- Richemont reported about a 30 percent increase in sales from 2011 to 2012.
- The Cartier brand has not been greatly affected by the global economic downturn.
- Asian markets are likely to offer the brand substantial opportunities for growth.

Cartier accounted for approximately 60 percent of the profits of its parent company, Richemont. According to Morgan Stanley, the economic downturn of the early 21st century has not significantly affected Cartier's sales, as its average consumer is in a high income bracket. In 2012 Richemont reported a 30 percent increase in sales from the previous year.

Approximately 18 percent of Cartier's sales come from the United States, and about 47 percent come from the European market. Markets in Asia, particularly Japan, account for a growing portion of the remainder. Cartier's dominant position stems partly from its success in Asia and in major cities around the world. At the turn of the 21st century, Cartier was among the first luxury brands to tap into the booming Chinese and Russian markets. Even as other luxury brands, such as Louis Vuitton, have entered the jewelry and watch business, they have not affected the sales and reputation of the Cartier brand.

FURTHER READING

Bottelli, Paola. "Cartier the Queen of Profits." *Luxury 24*, February 2008. Accessed September 11, 2012. http://www.luxury24.ilsole24ore.com/ModaStili/2008/02/cartier-analisi-english-version_1.php.

Brand Finance. "Global 500 2012." *Brandirectory*. Accessed September 3, 2012. http://brandirectory.com/league_tables/table/global-500-2012.

Brand Finance. "Global 500 2012: The Annual Report." *Brandirectory*. Accessed September 6, 2012. http://brandfinance.com/images/upload/bf_g500_2012_web_dp.pdf.

Business of Fashion Team. "BoF Daily Digest." *The Business of Fashion*, April 29, 2009. Accessed September 10, 2012. http://www.businessoffashion.com/2009/04/bof-daily-digest-pradas-profit-falls-cartier-cuts-hours-gap-teams-with-asos-missonis-london-store-ballantynes-new-chairman.html.

Cartier. "Cartier: Corporate Responsibility." Accessed September 12, 2012. http://www.cartier.us/#/tell-me/excellence/commitment:/tell-me/excellence/commitment/cartier-responsible-jeweler/our-commitments.

Cartier. "Cartier Through Time." Accessed September 7, 2012. http://www.cartier.us/#/tell-me/through-time.

"Cartier Faces Fresh Competition." *BBC News*, November 11, 2004. Accessed September 10, 2012. http://news.bbc.co.uk/2/hi/business/4002007.stm.

Donovan, Kate. "Richemont Results Boosted by Record Jewellery and Watch Sales." *Retail Jeweller*, June 27, 2011. Accessed September 10, 2012. http://www.retail-jeweller.com/in-business/richemont-results-boosted-by-record-jewellery-and-watch-sales/5026663.article.

Interbrand. "2011 Ranking of the Top 100 Brands." Accessed July 3, 2012. http://www.interbrand.com/en/best-global-brands/best-global-brands-2008/best-global-brands-2011.aspx.

Krups, Donald. "Cartier Engagement Rings." *Live Journal*, August 27, 2010. Accessed September 11, 2012. http://donaldsrings.livejournal.com/23613.html.

Luxury Education Foundation. "Cartier: Digital Innovation in the Bridal Category." Accessed September 10, 2012. http://www.luxuryeducationfoundation.org/programs/master-class/116.

"Omega Is Gaining on Rolex in Worldwide Market Share." *eRelyx*, March 8, 2012. Accessed September 10, 2012. http://www.erelyx.com/blog/article/tag/cartier-market-share.

Revill, John. "Cartier Watches the Luxury Market." *Wall Street Journal*, March 25, 2012. Accessed September 9, 2012. http://online.wsj.com/article/SB10001424052702303812904577291470421859842.html.

Tiffany & Co. "Shareholder Information." Accessed September 12, 2012. http://investor.tiffany.com/financials-keyRatios.cfm.

CATERPILLAR

AT A GLANCE

Brand Synopsis: As the world's largest manufacturer of construction and mining equipment, Caterpillar has been a staple in large machinery since the company was founded in 1925.
Parent Company: Caterpillar Inc.
100 North East Adams Street
Peoria, Illinois 61629
United States
http://www.caterpillar.com
Sector: Industrials
Industry Group: Capital Goods
Performance: *Market share*—18.3 percent worldwide (2011). *Sales*—US$60.1 billion (2011).
Principal Competitors: AB Volvo; CNH Global N.V.; Hitachi Construction Machinery Co., Ltd.; Komatsu Ltd.; Kubota Corporation

BRAND ORIGINS

- Benjamin Holt came up with the original design for Caterpillar after developing a solution for tractors driving over sand; he patented the practical continuous track in 1907 and called the device Caterpillar after the way it crawled.
- In 1925 the Holt Manufacturing Company merged with the C.L. Best Tractor Company; the new company was named Caterpillar Tractor Company.
- Having gained notoriety during World War II, Caterpillar was in demand with the postwar boom in construction.
- Caterpillar became multinational during the 1950s, expanding to countries all over the globe.

Benjamin Holt, an inventor of manufacturing equipment, had an epiphany in 1904 regarding the wheels and movements of steam tractors. Previously, tractors commonly got stuck in sand and soft dirt because of their heavy weight. After attempts of making the tractors wider and increasing the size of the wheels, Holt decided to bolt planks to chains in place of wheels, giving better traction to the heavy machines. It is said that Holt named the device "Caterpillar" due to the way that the machine crawled. This innovation was one that became associated with Holt's devices, and the continuous track was patented by Holt in 1907, followed by the trademark of the name Caterpillar in 1910.

Prior to World War I Holt had shipped about a thousand of his tractors to Europe for farming and agriculture. However, during the war the tractors were used to haul war equipment and as artillery tractors with a gun turret mounted on them. The British military later modeled its tank design after the Holt tractor, although a British firm built them. While Holt's tractors were in Europe, the company's primary competitor, C.L. Best Gas Tractor Company, was dominating the farm industry in the United States. Having received government grants during the war, Best became the main tractor supplier for farmers.

Even though both Holt and Best did well during the war, following the end of the hostilities only Best managed to witness strong sales. Because there was no longer a high demand for large tractors in Europe, the Holt Manufacturing Company went into debt. Benjamin Holt died in 1920, and his company went through a massive restructuring, during which the company's product line shifted from large tractors to small tractors. In 1925 the Caterpillar Tractor Company was founded following the merger of the Holt Manufacturing Company and the C.L. Best Tractor Company.

The merger was immediately successful, with Best's brand popularity and Holt's innovative design leading to strong profits for the newly formed company. During its first year of business Caterpillar reported US$13 million in sales. By 1929 its sales jumped to US$52.8 million. Despite the Great Depression, Caterpillar continued to grow, adopting the diesel engine to replace gasoline. The company was again useful during World War II, aiding in the construction of numerous projects for the U.S. military and federal government. Due to the company's notoriety during the war as well as the postwar construction boom, the company experienced rapid growth, leading to its launch into other countries during the 1950s. Caterpillar machines helped construct a 10.5-mile-long superhighway through the Andes Mountains, allowing for access to areas never before possible. In 1953 India purchased Caterpillar machines to develop the country's roads. Caterpillar machines were also used in Antarctica during the late 1950s by the U.S. military as part of Operation Deep Freeze I, a multinational science mission.

Caterpillar maintained its multinational expansion by aiding projects in Canada, France, New Zealand, South Africa, Thailand, among others. The company continued to grow by acquiring smaller companies and by developing new machines. In 1965 Caterpillar established its forklift line after acquiring Mentor, a company based in Ohio. Following the acquisition of the solar and turbomach divisions of the International Harvester Company in 1981, Caterpillar ventured into industrial gas turbines.

In 1999 CAT expanded into Russia for the first time, building the first electrical substation since the dissolution of the communist government in 1991. Additionally, CAT began production in China in 2009, manufacturing medium wheel loaders and motorgraders for use in the Asian market. As of 2012, the corporate headquarters in California managed facility construction.

BRAND ELEMENTS

- Benjamin Holt patented the practical continuous track on his tractors in 1907 and trademarked the name Caterpillar in 1910; the company has since trademarked its nickname CAT.
- Caterpillar machines are made in the color Caterpillar Yellow, a trademarked golden yellow, which is also used in the company's logo.
- The most commonly used slogan for the company is "Earthmoving solutions for today's challenges," eluding to the fact that Caterpillar machines move earth.

Caterpillar was the first company to use the practical continuous track around the axle of its tractors. The design was created by Benjamin Holt in 1904, after he was looking for a solution to his tractors getting stuck in soft and sandy earth. He patented this design in 1907.

The shortened version of Caterpillar Inc.'s name, CAT, is more commonly associated with the company. Benjamin Holt named his continuous track tractor Caterpillar after a bystander had commented on it crawling like a caterpillar. The name was trademarked by Holt in 1910, but did not become the company's name until Holt Manufacturing merged with the C.L. Best Tractor Company in 1925.

CAT machines are also noted for their golden yellow, or trademarked Caterpillar Yellow. The color is also contained within the CAT logo, which is featured with either the company's complete name or the abbreviated version of the company's name. It is a simple logo, with the company name featured in block black or white letters with a small Caterpillar Yellow triangle under the letters "CAT." The shortened version of the logo is "CAT" with the yellow triangle underneath. The triangle is meant to signify a hill and how the CAT machines are easily able to ascend and descend hills.

The corporate slogan used by CAT is "Earthmoving solutions for today's challenges," making a jest at the concept that the company manufactures machines that move earth.

BRAND IDENTITY

- Caterpillar guarantees that its name is synonymous with the word *trustworthy* by ensuring that all its products are manufactured with the quality the brand is known for.
- Caterpillar maintains more than 8,000 employees in its research and development department to stay on the forefront of technology, especially as the brand's famous trademarks are mimicked by its competitor Komatsu Ltd.
- Caterpillar relates to its customers by promising that its products will not negatively affect the economy and maintaining positive practices of global sustainability.

As the premier manufacturer for construction and mining equipment, Caterpillar has built its name as a staple in the construction industry. On its website, Caterpillar states that "one thing that will never change is our commitment to maintaining the highest ethical standards. Our reputation is one of our greatest assets," making the Caterpillar name synonymous with the word *trustworthy*. To emphasize the brand's reliability to its customers, the company maintains a Worldwide Code of Conduct, started in 1974, to ensure that products made at any location in the world will meet the expectation of the brand's high reputation.

Additionally, Caterpillar aims to keep its brand as the global standard for innovation with a research and development department that employs more than 8,000 engineers and technical experts. The goal is to constantly improve the company's already successful products and to stay ahead of its competitor Komatsu Ltd., which has mimicked Caterpillar's trademarked gold and the design that made the Caterpillar brand famous, the continuous track on the axel of its tractors. Despite the company's age and the threat of competition, Caterpillar stays on top of technology by using virtual tools, predictive analysis, and quality and manufacturing systems to create more cost-effective products.

As global awareness for the environment becomes more popularized in the 21st century, Caterpillar wants to relate its brand with the change in perspective among its customers through three primary elements. The first is "Vision," targeting less impact on the environment; the second is "Mission," enabling economic growth through energy and infrastructure development; and the third is "Strategy," providing products and services that efficiently use natural resources without negatively impacting the environment or the global economy. Due to the growing demand for more sustainable companies, Caterpillar has developed a sustainability approach. A large portion of the company's machines use diesel and natural gas and, in response to growing concern of greenhouses gases, Caterpillar has made a pledge to reduce its emissions by a minimum of 25 percent and to use alternative or renewable sources to meet 20 percent of the company's energy needs by 2020, further proving to its customers that the brand not only produces trustworthy products but is also environmentally responsible.

BRAND STRATEGY

- Caterpillar had been on the forefront of new technology even before the company was founded in 1925; Holt patented his continuous track for tractors in 1907.
- As part of the company's efforts for growth, Caterpillar has been acquiring smaller companies since the 1950s, enabling it to benefit from other machine types.
- Caterpillar has been a multinational company since 1951, when it began acquiring other manufacturers to grow the company and expand its product line.

Caterpillar's strategy since its formation in 1925 has been to be an innovator in the construction industry by staying on the forefront of technology. Benjamin Holt began that corporate tradition with his invention of the continuous track on his tractors in 1904. The idea was a solution to the ongoing problem of driving heavy machinery on soft ground; Holt patented his design in 1907. Since then, Caterpillar has worked on developing machines that are innovative, bringing farmers and workers the tools they desire. For example, during World War I Europe required large Caterpillar tractors to carry and use heavy military artillery. After the war, however, smaller tractors were in demand on farms throughout the United States and Europe. As of 2012, Caterpillar maintained its tradition of staying on top of innovation. It has a research and development department with over 8,000 employees, made up of engineers and technical experts.

During the second half of the 20th century Caterpillar began acquiring other construction companies and manufacturers as an effort to grow the company and expand its product line. By 2012 Caterpillar had acquired over 35 companies. Companies such as Towmotor Corporation, a forklift manufacturer, the solar and turbomach divisions of the International Harvester Company, a maker of industrial gas turbines, and Barber-Greene Co. Inc., a paving products manufacturer, have helped expand Caterpillar's products and business and keep the company ahead of competitors.

Caterpillar has been a multinational corporation since the 1950s and has since expanded all around the globe, in both developing and developed countries. While countries such as India and Brazil were still growing, Caterpillar was the preferred tractor and machine company used to build roadways and structures. The company continued its expansion later in the 20th century, venturing into Russia after the fall of the communist rule and, more recently, built a manufacturing plant in China in 2009 to compete with its main competitor Komatsu Ltd., a Japanese manufacturer of construction and mining equipment.

BRAND EQUITY

- Caterpillar is ranked by KHL Group's "2011 Yellow Table" as the most successful construction equipment manufacturer in the world.
- In 2012 Interbrand ranked Caterpillar at number 61 among the top-100 brands, with a brand value of US$6.3 billion.
- In 2012 Brand Finance ranked Caterpillar 111th out of the top-500 global companies, with a brand value of US$8.3 billion.

According to the KHL Group's "2011 Yellow Table," Caterpillar is the most successful construction equipment manufacturer in the world, holding 18.3 percent of the global market. Komatsu Ltd., its closest competitor, is ranked second on the list, holding 11.7 percent of the global market. Additionally, Caterpillar's total shareholder returns are in the top 25 percent of the S&P 500.

In "2012 Ranking of the Top 100 Brands," Interbrand indicates that Caterpillar was ranked 61st with a brand value of US$6.3 billion in 2012. Brand Finance's "Global 500 2012" ranked Caterpillar 111th overall in 2012 and estimated its brand value at US$8.3 billion. Komatsu was ranked 459th in the same list, with a brand value of US$2.6 billion.

BRAND AWARENESS

- Caterpillar has been successful with branding; its nickname CAT has become the commonly used word for tractors.
- Caterpillar's signature Caterpillar Yellow has become the assumed color for construction equipment, with even toys mimicking it.
- In 2011 Caterpillar held 18.3 percent of the global market and 50 percent of the U.S. market.

Caterpillar, or CAT as it has become colloquially known, remains the best top-of-mind construction equipment manufacturer in the world. The word *CAT* has become associated with farm tractors in general, not adhering to any specific brand, although the Caterpillar Yellow is also a staple for construction equipment. The gold color has become such a representation for construction equipment that even the typical construction toy comes in the famous color. CAT itself does have its own toy line as well; however, even toys not made by the company are featured in its signature color.

Part of CAT's success with brand awareness dates back to Benjamin Holt's innovation of the practical continuous track used on tractors. The concept was a solution to the difficulties of heavy machines getting stuck in soft earth. Patented by Holt, the concept became the desired design for tractors and has since become essential for heavy machinery, including agriculture machines.

According to KHL's "2011 Yellow Table," Caterpillar is the most successful manufacturer of construction equipment in the world, holding 18.3 percent of the global market. Its main competitor Komatsu Ltd. is listed second, holding 11.7 percent of the global market. In regard to revenue, Caterpillar has a hold on the U.S. market, with 50 percent in market share, with its closest domestic competitor Deere & Co. at less than 27 percent. Customer loyalty plays a large role in Caterpillar's continued success as the brand has built its reputation for quality since the company was founded in the early 20th century.

BRAND OUTLOOK

- In spite of an increase in competition from Asian manufacturers, Caterpillar maintained an 18.3 percent global market share in 2011.
- In the domestic market the Caterpillar brand is synonymous with tractors and construction equipment, due to its high brand awareness and loyalty.
- To quell the competition from Asian manufacturers and thus decrease threats to its global success, Caterpillar is increasing its production in China.

Despite growing competition from Asian manufacturers, the Caterpillar brand had an 18.3 percent global market share in 2011. Even though Asian manufacturers are increasing their production, Caterpillar is still the world's best-known manufacturer of tractors and other large farming and mining equipment. Additionally, Caterpillar held 50 percent of its domestic market share in 2012. Given that the brand was started in the United States and its gold trademarked color has become synonymous with tractors and construction equipment, the brand continues to maintain a loyal customer base.

However, in 2012 the brand suffered in the Asian market due to an increase in competition that mimicked Caterpillar's brand designs and colors. The company said in a statement that even though it has not had profit-loss, the demand is not growing as fast as expected, leaving Caterpillar dealers with too much inventory. To prevent future threats to the brand's global dominance, Caterpillar has begun expanding production in China, which is becoming more of a manufacturing environment. It is hoped that this increased production in China will still the competition by facilitating the accessibility of the brand's products and therefore maintain its brand awareness and reputation.

FURTHER READING

Brand Finance. "Global 500 2012." *Brandirectory*. Accessed January 29, 2013. http://brandfinance.com/images/upload/bf_g500_2012_web_dp.pdf.

Cancino, Alejandra. "Caterpillar Sees 3Q Profit Jump 49 percent but Demand Slows." *Chicago Tribune*, October 22, 2012.

"Caterpillar: A Long and Storied History of Heavy Equipment Innovation." Cleveland Brothers. Accessed January 29, 2013. http://www.clevelandbrothers.com/caterpillar-history.php.

"Caterpillar, Inc. Becomes an Ethical Role Model." Daniels Fund Ethics Initiative, 2011. Accessed February 12, 2013. http://danielsethics.mgt.unm.edu/pdf/Caterpillar percent20Case.pdf.

Date Singh, Shruti. "Diggers Pile up Unsold as Caterpillar Adds Capacity." *Bloomberg News*, December 21, 2012.

"2012 Ranking of the Top 100 Brands." Interbrand. Accessed January 29, 2013. http://www.interbrand.com/en/best-global-brands/best-global-brands-2008/best-global-brands-2011.aspx.

"The 2011 Yellow Table." KHL Group. Accessed December 20, 2012. http://www.khl.com.

Williams, Jake, Tom Piazzi, and Martin Zhang. "Caterpillar Inc." Krause Fund Research, April 17, 2012. Accessed February 12, 2013. http://tippie.uiowa.edu/krause/spring2012/cat_sp12.pdf.

CHEVROLET

AT A GLANCE

Brand Synopsis: Part of one of the most diverse multibrand groups in the automotive industry, Chevrolet focuses on the values and aspirations of the middle and working classes by providing a unique blend of high style, versatility, economy, and value.
Parent Company: General Motors Company
300 Renaissance Center
Detroit, Michigan 48265
United States
http://www.gm.com/
Sector: Consumer Discretionary
Industry Group: Automobiles & Components
Performance: *Market share*—37 percent of the U.S. sports car sector (2011); 28 percent of the U.S. luxury sports car sector (2011). *Sales*—4.8 million vehicles sold worldwide (2011).
Principal Competitors: Ford Motor Company; Toyota Motor Corporation; Honda Motor Co., Ltd.

BRAND ORIGINS

- The Chevrolet Motor Company was formed in 1911 by William Durant and Louis Chevrolet.
- Chevrolet introduced its first car in 1912 and its first pickup truck in 1917.
- Chevrolet became a division of General Motors Company (GM) in 1918.
- Chevrolet flourished in the 1950s, releasing several cars that would become cultural icons.
- Chevrolet's car sales declined throughout the 1980s and 1990s, and the automaker's pickup trucks began to account for a larger percentage of overall sales.
- In 2011 two Chevrolet vehicles, the Cruze and the Silverado, were among the top 10 best-selling vehicles in the United States.

The Chevrolet Motor Company (Chevrolet) was formed in 1911 as a cooperative venture between Louis Chevrolet, a Belgian-born race-car driver, and William Durant, an entrepreneur and founder of General Motors Company (GM). Durant had been ousted from GM's management in 1910.

Chevrolet introduced its first car, the Classic Six, in 1912. Priced at $2,500, the high-end Classic Six failed to earn a profit, so Durant encouraged Chevrolet to design a high-style yet affordable car to challenge the dominant car on the market at the time, the Ford Model T. In 1915 the Chevrolet Series 490 was released. Named for its $490 price tag, the Series 490 was an immediate success, establishing Chevrolet as a manufacturer of quality, affordable cars. Durant bought his partner's share of Chevrolet in 1915, and the company was soon so profitable that Durant used his Chevrolet stock to repurchase a controlling interest in GM. In 1918 Chevrolet joined GM as the corporation's low-priced brand, with Durant becoming GM's new president. By 1927 Chevrolet was outselling the Ford Model T in the United States.

Chevrolet introduced its first pickup truck in 1917, and the manufacture of trucks remains an integral part of the brand's identity today. The automaker introduced the industry's first six-cylinder engine in 1929, leading to a significant jump in the brand's performance and value. The six-cylinder engine was also integral to Chevrolet's 1935 introduction of the Suburban station wagon, a model still sold today as a sport-utility vehicle. The Chevrolet Suburban is the longest continuously used automotive nameplate in the United States.

The 1950s were prosperous years for Chevrolet. The automaker incorporated several mechanical advancements into its cars, such as automatic transmissions, power windows and brakes, and eight-cylinder engines. Chevrolet cars of the period also incorporated stylistic innovations like rear tail fins and long, low body structures. Using these advancements and innovations, Chevrolet produced several cars in the 1950s that would become cultural icons, including the Bel Air, the Impala, and the Corvette.

In the 1960s Chevrolet introduced more popular models, such as the Camaro, the Nova, and the Chevelle. The 1970s saw the introduction of the Malibu and the Monte Carlo. During this time Chevrolet continued to advance its pickup truck line, introducing the popular Chevrolet C/10 stepside pickup truck in 1976. In the 1980s sales of the brand's cars began to falter, with pickup trucks beginning to account for a larger percentage of total sales. Although Chevrolet continued to have success in the truck and sport-utility vehicle markets throughout the 1990s and the first decade of the 21st century, overall sales continued to decline, culminating in the U.S. government's bailout of GM in 2009. Nevertheless, Chevrolet has shown signs of bouncing back, and in 2011 two of its models, the Cruze and the Silverado, were among the top 10 best-selling vehicles in the United States.

BRAND ELEMENTS

- Chevrolet continues to use the logo that was introduced in 1913.
- Known as the "bow-tie logo," the Chevrolet logo features a simple cross shape in a gold metallic color.
- In the 21st century, Chevrolet has emphasized the use of typography to set its brand apart.

In 1913 Chevrolet cofounder William Durant introduced the company's iconic logo, which is still used today. Known as the "bow-tie logo," the design features a simple cross shape in a golden metallic color. When the Chevrolet name appears beneath the logo, it is written in black, all-capital letters. There is some dispute over the inspiration for Chevrolet's logo, with some suggesting that Durant was inspired by wallpaper in a French hotel and others claiming his inspiration was a newspaper ad or even the Swiss flag. Regardless of its origin, the bow-tie logo has been an immediately identifiable symbol of the brand for a century.

In the 21st century Chevrolet has employed the use of typography to set its brand apart, choosing specific fonts that the company uses across all communication materials. From 2006 until 2012, a font called Klavika Condensed was used. In 2012 Chevrolet began using two simple and easily readable fonts, Louis Sans and Durant Serif, named after the company's founders.

BRAND IDENTITY

- Initially, Chevrolet sought to establish a brand identity that combined stylishness with affordability.
- In the minds of many Americans, the Chevrolet brand is closely linked with the prosperity of the 1950s.
- Chevrolet continues to redesign and reintroduce such previously popular models as the Camaro.
- Since the 1980s Chevrolet's line of pickup trucks has become an increasingly important aspect of its brand identity.

Chevrolet built its initial brand identity in the early 20th century on a foundation that merged high style with affordability, marketing its cars using the values and prospects for upward mobility that appealed to middle-class and working-class Americans. Chevrolet's advertising slogan from the Great Depression era, "The Great American Value," is an example of how the brand sought to identify itself with economy and value. Chevrolet's slogan of the 1980s, "The Heartbeat of America," remains a significant marker of the brand's identity today, with more recent incarnations of the slogan including "An American Revolution," "America's Best Trucks," and "Chevy Runs Deep."

For many Americans, Chevrolet remains intricately linked with the 1950s, a decade of prosperity in the United States. Rock 'n' roll, the race to space, and the evolution and expansion of suburbia influenced not only the culture of the times but also the design and manufacture of Chevrolet vehicles. Interstate highways were connecting all points of the country, and the automaker's advertising encouraged consumers to "See the USA in a Chevrolet."

The success of those iconic models from the 1950s and 1960s still provides the foundation of the Chevrolet brand. Despite struggling through the economic recession of the first decade of the 21st century, Chevrolet continues to redesign and reintroduce its once-popular models, including the Camaro, which was relaunched in 2009 after a seven-year hiatus from the market.

Chevrolet's pickup trucks have also become an integral part of its brand identity, particularly since the 1980s, when the company's pickup trucks began outselling its cars. Accompanied by the Bob Seger song of the same name, the popular "Like a Rock" advertising campaign used for Chevrolet trucks from 1991 to 2004 touted the Chevrolet Silverado as "the most dependable, longest lasting truck on the road." In 2011 the Silverado was the second best-selling vehicle in the United States, behind only the Ford F-series pickup.

BRAND STRATEGY

- In 2012 Chevrolet was still recovering from the recent economic recession in the United States, a period when sales plummeted for the automaker.
- In a move *CNN Money* called one of the "Dumbest Moments in Business," GM in 2010 said it would stop referring to Chevrolet as "Chevy."
- Chevrolet's brand strategy as of 2012 appeared to be moving toward a focus on environmentally friendly and fuel-efficient vehicles, such as its plug-in electric model called the Volt.

In 2012 Chevrolet was still recovering from the U.S. economic downturn that had begun in 2007. The U.S. government had been forced to bail out General Motors Company (GM) during the recession after sales of GM's vehicles, including those from Chevrolet, plummeted.

In 2010 GM announced that it would no longer refer to Chevrolet as "Chevy," a move *CNN Money* included on its list of the "Dumbest Moments in Business." Consumers had been referring to Chevrolet by this shortened name since the company's inception, and critics condemned the decision as an unproductive attempt by the brand to distance itself from its declining consumer following at the time. However, some brand strategists have suggested that the move was necessary. Chevrolet's sales were continuing to spiral downward, and according to brand blogger Tom Dougherty, the name "Chevy" was beginning to sound "old-fashioned and quaint." Considering that Chevrolet eventually resumed its use of "Chevy," however, it is safe to assume that the automaker took the criticism to heart.

Rather than aiming for a complete brand overhaul, in 2012 Chevrolet appeared to be focusing on its rebound from poor performance, which the brand refers to as its "growing momentum." In recent years Chevrolet has begun introducing new cars across a range of markets that emphasize the company's commitment to the environment, including its well-received plug-in electric car, the Volt. Vehicles powered by ethanol, natural gas, electricity, and hydrogen are now a core part of Chevrolet's brand identity.

BRAND EQUITY

- Chevrolet's brand performance fell off significantly in the early years of the 21st century.
- Although Chevrolet struggled during the U.S. economic recession that began in 2007, 2012 sales figures suggested that the automaker was on the rebound.
- In 2011 Chevrolet performed well in the sports car and luxury sports car sectors of the U.S. car market.
- In 2012 Chevrolet ranked high on surveys of consumers' brand perceptions and quality of customer service.

Chevrolet's brand performance fell off significantly in the early part of the 21st century. In 2012 *Brandirectory* ranked Chevrolet 211th on its list of the top 500 brands. Just five years earlier, in 2007, the automaker had held the 65th spot on the same list. Similarly, Chevrolet's brand value in 2012 stood at US$4.8 billion, a significant drop from the company's US$6.2 billion brand value just three years earlier.

Although Chevrolet struggled mightily during and after the 2007–09 economic recession in the United States, evidence suggests that the automaker is on the rebound. For example, SyncForce ranked Chevrolet 51st on its "Ranking the Brands" Top 100 list in 2012, up from 68th in 2011 and 78th in 2010. Additionally, sales reached an all-time high for the brand in 2011, with 4.8 million vehicles sold around the world. Sales in the United States were up 13 percent at the close of the 2011 sales year, and several international markets also saw double-digit increases, including Vietnam (79 percent), Russia (49 percent), Turkey (30 percent), and Germany (21 percent).

Chevrolet has also performed well recently in the sports car and luxury sports car sectors of the U.S. car market. In 2011 the Camaro and the Corvette accounted for one out of every three sports cars sold in the United States. That same year Chevrolet held a 37 percent share of the U.S. sports car sector, selling close to 90,000 Camaros that year and surpassing its nearest competitor, the Ford Mustang, by more than 18,000 units. Also in 2011 Chevrolet held an almost 28 percent share of the U.S. luxury sports car segment, selling 13,164 Corvettes, the only domestic car in the segment.

Chevrolet's recent momentum is also evident in improved perceptions of its brand image. In 2012 *Consumer Reports* ranked Chevrolet in the fourth spot for the third year in a row in its "Best Car Brand Perception" category. In 2012 J.D. Power and Associates gave Chevrolet high rankings for customer service, and Harris Interactive ranked Chevrolet fourth on its "Best Full Line Automotive Brands" list.

BRAND AWARENESS

- Chevrolet has strengthened awareness of the brand in the United States through its sponsorship of the popular NASCAR series.
- According to *Consumer Reports*, Chevrolet's brand awareness among American consumers was 75 percent in 2011 and 76 percent in 2012.
- In 2012 Chevrolet became the official car sponsor of two of the world's most popular professional soccer teams, expanding the brand's presence in international markets.

- In 2011 Chevrolet's brand awareness in Europe, where it held a 2.5 percent market share, was estimated to be 4 to 5 percent.

In its annual Car Brand Perception Survey of consumers in the United States, *Consumer Reports* ranked Chevrolet second for two years in a row, with a brand awareness of 75 percent in 2011 and 76 percent in 2012. Ford placed first in both years, with a brand awareness of 87 percent in 2012. Toyota was third, with 70 percent brand awareness, in 2012.

The survey also asked consumers to rate cars across seven categories. In 2012 this produced a combined brand-perception score of 92 for Chevrolet, in fourth place behind Toyota (131), Ford (121), and Honda (94). For the third year in a row, Chevrolet ranked among the top five brands for quality, value, performance, and environmental friendliness. Chevrolet also placed in the top five for design in 2010 and 2012.

In Europe, Chevrolet held an overall market share of about 2.5 percent and a brand awareness of 4 percent to 5 percent in 2011, according to Ward's Automotive Group, an industry analyst organization. Wayne Brannon, president of Chevrolet Europe, told WardAuto that he expected brand awareness to increase throughout Europe with the launch of new models such as the Chevy Malibu D-car.

To publicize the brand, Chevrolet replaced Audi in 2012 as the official car sponsor of two of the world's most popular soccer teams: Manchester United and Liverpool. Chevrolet also sponsors racing events around the world, including the FIA World Touring Car Championship, the National Association for Stock Car Auto Racing (NASCAR) series, the American Le Mans Series, and the 24 Hours of Le Mans.

BRAND OUTLOOK

- Chevrolet responded to the 2007–09 recession and the U.S. government bailout by focusing on becoming more environmentally responsible.
- In 2011 Chevrolet made a commitment to reduce carbon dioxide emissions by up to 8 million metric tons over the next decade.
- Chevrolet's electric-powered Volt and its "Ecologic" strategy seem to point to a positive outlook for the Chevrolet brand in the years to come.

After automobile sales plummeted during the recession of 2007–09, the U.S. government bailed out Chevrolet's parent company, General Motors Company (GM), in 2009. Despite significant losses, Chevrolet appears to be a brand on the rebound. A major contributor to its improving success is the manufacturer's commitment to the environment, which grew in large part from Chevrolet's response to the economic downturn and resulting government bailout. Chevrolet has committed to developing more fuel-efficient cars and trucks to compete with those of foreign automakers. In late 2010 Chevrolet began production of the plug-in electric Volt (and the Volt's European version, the Opel/Vauxhall Ampera), which was subsequently named 2012 North American Car of the Year, European Car of the Year, and World Green Car of the Year.

In 2011 Chevrolet made a commitment to reduce carbon dioxide emissions by up to 8 million metric tons over the coming decade. Besides reducing its carbon footprint, Chevrolet plans to reduce its environmental impact in four ways: using more environmentally responsible manufacturing processes, improving the fuel efficiency of its vehicles, designing more alternative-energy vehicles, and improving the postconsumer recyclability of its vehicles. The brand's "Ecologic" initiative demonstrates its attention to environmental responsibility and is a marker of its positive outlook.

By integrating a wide range of innovations in fuel-efficient, low-emissions mobility solutions, Chevrolet has already witnessed some of what may be its future success. The Volt, for example, gets an estimated 94 miles per gallon in electric mode and 40 miles per gallon on the highway in gas mode. A strong echo of the brand's success in the 1950s, 1960s, and 1970s, the Volt appears to have reminded consumers that Chevrolet is not simply a U.S. automaker of a bygone era but a brand for value-minded and environmentally aware consumers around the world. Chevrolet's Volt and its "Ecologic" strategy seem to suggest a positive outlook for the brand as it moves further into the 21st century.

FURTHER READING

Bartlett, Jeff. "2012 Car Brand Perception Survey: Consumers name their top 20 brands." *Consumer Reports*, January 24, 2012. Accessed February 15, 2013. http://news.consumerreports.org/cars/2012/01/2012-car-brand-perception-survey-consumers-name-their-top-20-brands.html.

———. "2012 Car Brand Perception Survey: Ford leads all brands in awareness." *Consumer Reports*, January 26, 2012. Accessed February 15, 2013. http://news.consumerreports.org/cars/2012/01/2012-car-brand-perception-survey-ford-leads-all-brands-in-awareness.html.

Brand Finance. "Chevrolet." *Brandirectory*, 2012. Accessed October 1, 2012. http://brandirectory.com/profile/chevrolet.

Buss, Dale. "Chevrolet Hoping Brand Catches up with Products." *Edmunds AutoObserver*, November 3, 2011. Accessed September 29, 2012. http://www.autoobserver.com/2011/11/chevrolet-hoping-brand-catches-up-with-products.html.

———. "GM's 'Essential Brand Elements' Gets Dealer Pushback." BrandChannel.com, March 5, 2012. Accessed September 28, 2012. http://www.brandchannel.com/home/post/2012/03/15/GM-Dealer-Pushback-031512.aspx.

Chevrolet. "History and Heritage." Accessed September 29, 2012. http://www.chevrolet.com/culture/article/history-and-heritage.html.

"Chevrolet." RankingTheBrands.com. Accessed September 30, 2012. http://www.rankingthebrands.com/Brand-detail.aspx?brandID=319.

"Chevrolet Ranks as Top Performance Brand in U.S." ConceptCarz.com, n.d. Accessed September 29, 2012. http://www.conceptcarz.com/articles/article.aspx?articleID=241.

Dougherty, Tom. "Maybe It's Not So Dumb: Chevy to Chevrolet." *StealingShare*, June 4, 2012. Accessed September 30, 2012. http://www.stealingshare.com/blog/?p=3680.

Job, Ann. "Chevrolet Camaro: A *Transformers* Movie Star." *MSN Autos*, n.d. Accessed October 2, 2012. http://editorial.autos.msn.com/article.aspx?cp-documentid=435766.

Keegan, Matt. "Chevrolet Brand Outlook: 2012 and Beyond." *Auto Trends Magazine*, August 8, 2011. Accessed September 28, 2012. http://www.autotrends.org/2011/08/08/chevrolet-brand-outlook-2012-and-beyond.

CHEVRON

AT A GLANCE

Brand Synopsis: Chevron strives to be the global energy brand most admired for its people, partnership, and performance.
Parent Company: Chevron Corporation
6001 Bollinger Canyon Road
San Ramon, California 94583-2324
United States
http://www.chevron.com
Sector: Energy
Industry Group: Energy
Performance: *Sales*—US$244.4 billion (2011).
Principal Competitors: Royal Dutch Shell; BP; Exxon Mobil Corp.; PetroChina Company, Ltd.

BRAND ORIGINS

- In 1876 Frederick Taylor and Demetrius Scofield struck oil in California, beginning the business venture that led to the creation of Chevron.
- In 1911 Standard Oil of California (Socal) formed in the wake of several mergers and acquisitions.
- With the creation of Caltex, Socal was able to produce and market Middle Eastern oil from the 1930s through the 1960s.
- Socal changed its name to Chevron Corporation in 1984.
- Chevron expanded its exploration and marketing capabilities by merging with the Gulf Oil Corporation in 1984 and Texaco in 2000.

As employees of the oil company California Star in 1876, Frederick Taylor and Demetrius Scofield were pioneers in the quest for black gold. Shortly after their success, Pacific Coast Oil Co. purchased California Star and the earliest ancestor of Chevron was born. The company's immediate success put California on the map as an oil-producing state and demonstrated the spirit and grit that would define the company. Pacific Coast built a large exploration and production company but could not compete with other marketers in downstream operations. Consequently, it allowed Standard Oil of Iowa, a subsidiary of Standard Oil of New Jersey, to acquire the company. This merger gave Standard Oil more access to crude oil and Pacific Coast Oil more access to marketing savvy and financial backing. By 1906 the two companies completed their integration by becoming Standard Oil Company (California), a company that successfully marketed gasoline and lubricants and that developed the world's first service station in Seattle.

After several mergers and a forced split from its parent company, Standard Oil (California) became known as Socal (Standard Oil Company of California) in 1911. The company continued its pioneering work in California, searching for natural gas, expanding pipelines and service stations, and taking both its marketing and exploration overseas. In 1930, through the acquisition of the Gulf Company, Socal got the rights to dig in Bahrain, where they struck oil for the first time in the Middle East. This oil strike marked the beginning of a long relationship with the Middle East, particularly Saudi Arabia, and the beginning of a relationship with the Texas Company, later Texaco. The latter connection led to the formation in 1936 of the California Texas Oil Company (Caltex), a joint venture between Socal and Texaco whose purpose was to produce, refine, and market Middle Eastern oil worldwide.

After World War II Socal expanded its explorations for oil throughout the world. It also expanded its line of domestic products, offering several new gasolines and motor oils under the brand name Chevron. Socal also began manufacturing and marketing petrochemicals under the name Oronite Chemical Co. In the 1970s, however, the company suffered from the political changes that drove up oil prices, the nationalization of assets in foreign lands, and drilling restrictions. In response to these changes, Socal restructured its business, cutting jobs and developing a new domestic presence under the name Chevron USA. While trying to create a stronger national presence by exploring other energy means in the United States and to identify itself with its most successful brand, Socal changed its name to the Chevron Corporation in 1984. In the same year, it bought the Gulf Oil Corporation, thereby doubling its U.S. oil reserves and making it one of the integrated oil and gas giants.

With the 1990s came a new focus on risk management, cost-cutting efficiency, and environmental responsibility. The company once again turned its attention to overseas exploration and marketing. At the end of the decade, with a new mergers and acquisitions department, Chevron began searching for new companies that would complement its own. After several years of negotiations, Chevron and Texaco merged, creating the second-largest oil company in the U.S. The next 10 years would lead to exceptional financial success, growing expansion in both upstream and downstream activities, and continuing efforts to improve the company's records for safety and environmental responsibility.

BRAND ELEMENTS

- While the company name has changed over time, Chevron's logo has changed only minimally, reflecting consistency within the firm.
- Chevron's logo includes red and blue chevrons, symbolizing both the company's grit and pioneering spirit and its commanding market position.
- Chevron's tagline, "The Chevron Way," encompasses its vision and core values.

Because the Chevron Corporation has a long history of mergers and acquisitions, its logo has evolved over time. The current logo, which has been used since Socal changed its name to Chevron in the 1980s, consists of Chevron's name in blue letters set above red and blue chevrons made from the image of folded ribbons. The chevrons repeat the same pattern used in the initial Standard Oil logo of the early 1900s and contribute to a sense of consistency within the company. While the company has changed, it has retained its commanding position in the market, symbolized by the military-like chevrons. Similarly, Chevron's tagline, "The Chevron Way," also evokes the continuing pioneering spirit of the company. As much a part of the branding as the logo, the tagline represents the company's vision and such core values as integrity and ingenuity. These brand elements outline the company's fundamental purpose: to provide the energy needed to fuel human progress.

BRAND IDENTITY

- Chevron's branding has focused closely on the company's mission and core values.
- "The Chevron Way" promotes the brand's pursuit of the best people, performance, and partnerships.
- Advertising campaigns in 2007 and 2011 demonstrated Chevron's company values and willingness to engage with the communities in which they operate.

Chevron's fundamental purpose is to provide the energy needed to fuel human progress. A large part of Chevron's branding is aimed at helping employees, shareholders, and partners understand how the company strives to do this responsibly: by seeking the best people, performance, and partnerships. Under "The Chevron Way," the company outlines how it will achieve these goals through its mission and core values. The mission is to provide sustainable energy throughout the world, while at the same time building a reputable firm and healthy partnerships. The values, which include integrity, diversity, and ingenuity, ensure that clients can depend on quality service and ethical behavior. By linking these core values to its motto, Chevron reminds the public of the brand's essence each time the brand is encountered.

Linking the brand to the company's values has also been the purpose of Chevron's recent global advertising campaigns. A 2007 campaign titled "The Power of Human Energy" aimed to foster people's engagement with energy issues and to highlight Chevron's efforts to bring additional energy supplies to the marketplace, according to *Convenience Store News*. Chevron understands that most people associate oil companies with the price of gasoline, and it wants the brand to be about more than oil. The company wants the public and future partners to see it as a group of people working hard to pioneer new technology, new energy, and an awareness of global responsibility. The second campaign, "We Agree," was launched in 2010. According to *Entertainment Close-Up*, Chevron has said about the campaign, "We hear what people say about oil companies—that they should develop renewables, support communities, create jobs and protect the environment—and the fact is, we agree." This campaign demonstrates Chevron's values as a company and the greater value they provide in meeting the world's demand for energy. Identifying the brand as one that strives to find common ground with people is essential for the company's future success in a market where environmental awareness and corporate responsibility are key.

BRAND STRATEGY

- Chevron spends most of its capital on upstream activities to provide both traditional and new sources of energy.
- Chevron has spent the past 25 years restructuring its company to bring more products under the Chevron brand.
- Attention to products and services under the Chevron brand, like HDAX and Extra Mile, exemplifies the company's commitment to growing the brand.

Chevron's goal of becoming a leader in exploration, production, and new technologies is at the forefront of their brand strategy. According to *Pipeline & Gas Journal*, Chevron invested US$32.7 billion in its activities in 2012, with approximately 87 percent of that amount directed to upstream activities around the world. Downstream investments made up 11 percent of the total capital expenditure. Some of the downstream investments consisted of unifying products under the Chevron name. This strategy began in the 1970s when Socal restructured its domestic business under the name Chevron. Since then, the company has twice changed its corporate name to reflect the popular brand. Today, the trend continues as the company strives to bring more products under the Chevron name. For example, according to *Entertainment Close-Up*, Chevron announced in 2012 that it had begun consolidation of its gas engine oils under the Chevron HDAX brand. Not only will this strategy align its engine oils with the Chevron brand, but it will also eliminate product line complexity and focus on only the best products from around the globe.

Creating a more efficient system, as was done with HDAX engine oils, has also been a major brand strategy for Chevron since the early nineties. A good example of this can be seen in the company's pulling of the Texaco brand. Since 2009, Chevron has pulled its Texaco brand out of 14 northeastern states. According to *National Petroleum News*, Chevron is not working aggressively to expand the Texaco brand because it sees Chevron as its growth brand. Instead, the company has put capital into its Extra Mile service station line under the Chevron brand. According to *Convenience Store News* in 2007, "Chevron Corp.'s Extra Mile brand is growing. The company will increase its franchised store count from 271 to 400 by the end of next year, adding at least 60 new locations this year alone, and is expanding its offerings inside the stores as well." Chevron sees this strategy as its most promising in the convenience store category.

BRAND EQUITY

- Chevron's increasing financial success, with revenues of US$244 billion in 2011, has led to increases in its brand value as well.
- In 2012 Chevron's brand value increased 9 percent to US$17.5 billion, placing it 37th on Brand Finance's Global 500 report.
- Chevron continues to expand its global upstream activities, particularly in deepwater drilling and natural gas exploration.
- Although successful, Chevron's exploration activities have led to allegations of environmental irresponsibility and pollution.

With its outstanding revenues, upwards of US$244 billion in 2011, and expanded global exploration and production activities, Chevron's brand value increased by 9 percent in 2012. In its Global 500 2012 report, *Brand Finance* ranked Chevron 37th, up from 44th place in 2011, with a brand value of US$17.5 billion. Always striving to live by its tagline, "The Chevron Way," the company maintained the health of its brand by using its financial gains to reinvest in technology and new energies. Recently, for example, the company increased its deepwater drilling by purchasing exploration blocks off the southern coast of China and continued its exploration for natural gas through the acquisition of Atlas Energy and its shale formations.

While the company's pioneering strategies have clearly worked to improve their business and the value of the Chevron brand, its methods have been challenged. Chevron has faced numerous allegations of noncompliance with the core values found in "The Chevron Way" mission. From criticism about new technologies like "fracking" to complaints about pollution in Puerto Rico and Ecuador, Chevron has not always maintained its values without some tarnish. The brand, however, has not suffered major consequences as a result of these allegations.

BRAND AWARENESS

- Chevron is one of the most recognized brands in the oil and gas industry.
- Brand awareness for the Chevron brand is difficult to measure as it markets many products under three separate brand names.
- Chevron has been accused of hypocrisy in its response to oil contamination and pollution in recent years.

Chevron Corporation is one of the top integrated oil companies in the world. While Chevron, which ranks second domestically behind Exxon Mobil, is certainly a brand that consumers recognize, its level of recognition is difficult to measure. Because Chevron markets products under three major brands, Chevron, Texaco, and Caltex, it is sometimes difficult for consumers to know which products are associated with each brand. While Texaco is a popular brand in the southern United States, Chevron's Extra Mile service stations are most popular in the West. The Caltex brand, which dates back to the 1930s union between Texaco and Socal to drill for oil in the Middle East, still dominates brand recognition in Asia, the Middle East, and Africa. According to *brandchannel*, as with most integrated oil companies, by the time Chevron's product gets to the pump, its association with the brand is so diluted that top-of-mind awareness is unlikely, especially given that consumers are more interested in the price than the brand.

While levels of brand recall may be difficult to quantify, Chevron has been receiving additional attention that it will not want to mention in its portfolio. Several recent headlines addressing oil contamination in Puerto Rico and pollution in the Amazon may prove damaging to its brand image. Traditionally, Chevron has been recognized for its attention to safety and environmental awareness. However, according to *Brand Finance*, Chevron has been accused of hypocrisy in its response to these allegations by pushing its "We Agree" advertising campaign, which promotes an image of Chevron as a model corporate citizen, while critics allege that the company is doing little to change its damaging drilling practices.

BRAND OUTLOOK

- The future of Chevron includes growing its business and stock value, contributing to global economic expansion, and building stronger communities.
- Chevron will focus on investing large amounts of capital in exploration and production to ensure the success of its business and brand.
- Corporate citizenship within the communities where it operates is Chevron's way to both give back to the world and strengthen its brand's reputation.

According to its annual report for 2011, Chevron's future goals are to grow its business, contribute to global economic expansion, build stronger communities, and create enduring value for stockholders. There are two main ways Chevron seeks to meet these goals: investing in exploration and production and increasing its corporate citizenship. A report in *Pipeline & Gas Journal* suggests that the former is well under way: "over the next three years, 28 projects with a Chevron share of capital of more than US$250 million each are scheduled to start production. Additionally, over the next three years, the company expects to make final investment decisions on 12 more projects." These types of investments are important because they help build business and ensure the brand's value in an ever-growing and competitive market. In 2011 for example, Chevron's return on capital employed was 21.6 percent, a gain that led in turn to increases in upstream development and downstream products. Moreover, investments in exploration support the global effort to identify new energy sources. According to Chevron's website, forecasters predict that the world's energy demand could increase as much as 50 percent in the next 30 years. While Chevron continues to produce traditional energy sources, some of their exploratory investments are aimed at finding next-generation renewables, such as biofuels, solar power, and wind power, to meet increasing energy needs without draining the planet of its non-renewable resources. Developing these sources successfully, ahead of the competition, will ensure brand success.

In addition to investing in exploration, Chevron is also investing in people to help support economic expansion and sustainable communities. Because the public is becoming more socially conscious, they look to large firms to behave similarly, and Chevron is taking this stance seriously. According to its website, Chevron has built partnerships with governments, nonprofit organizations, and aid agencies to help strengthen and improve the communities where they operate. These partnerships are focused on three areas of support: health, education, and economic development. For example, Chevron fights AIDS with the *Global Fund to Fight AIDS, Tuberculosis, and Malaria* in Africa and Asia; supports science, math, and engineering programs like a robotics class in California; and helps finance young entrepreneurs in places where funding is limited. With initiatives like this, Chevron hopes to help communities prosper and increase its brand's performance.

FURTHER READING

Brand Finance. "Global 500 2012." *Brandirectory*. Accessed October 10, 2012. http://brandirectory.com/profile/chevron.

Chevron Corporation. *2011 Annual Report*. Accessed October 10, 2012. http://www.chevron.com/annualreport/2011/documents/pdf/Chevron2011AnnualReport.pdf#page=31.

"Chevron Launches 'Human Energy' Campaign." *Convenience Store News*, October 1, 2007.

"Chevron Launches New Global Advertising Campaign." *Entertainment Close-up*, October 22, 2010.

"Chevron Reports on Prosperous 2011, Future Growth." *Pipeline & Gas Journal*, July 2012, 45.

"Chevron to Bring Together Gas Engine Oils under HDAX Brand." *Entertainment Close-up*, July 12, 2012.

Lofstock, John. "Image Is Everything." *Convenience Store Decisions*, October 2006, 6.

Mastroberte, Tammy. "Poised for Growth." *Convenience Store News*, May 1, 2012.

Reid, Keith. "Brand Update: Chevron: Taking a Look at Chevron's Downstream Focus in the Current Economy." *National Petroleum News*, September 2011.

Silverstein, Barry. "Pumping Energy into Gasoline Branding." *brandchannel*, October 1, 2007. Accessed October 17, 2012. http://www.brandchannel.com/features_effect.asp?pf_id=388.

CHINA MOBILE

AT A GLANCE

Brand Synopsis: China Mobile is the corporate brand of China Mobile Limited, the world's largest provider of mobile telecommunications services. The company also uses three primary service brands: GoTone, M-Zone, and Easyown.
Parent Company: China Mobile Limited
60th Floor, The Center
Hong Kong
http://www.chinamobileltd.com
Sector: Telecommunication Services
Industry Group: Telecommunication Services
Performance: *Market share*—75 percent in China (2012). *Sales*—US$82.9 billion (2011).
Principal Competitors: China Unicom (Hong Kong) Limited; China Telecom Corporation Limited; Hutchison Telecommunications Hong Kong Holdings Limited

BRAND ORIGINS

- The reorganization of China's telecommunications industry in 1997 resulted in the creation of China Telecom (Hong Kong) Limited to pursue the mobile sector.
- China Telecom (Hong Kong) introduced the China Mobile brand in 1999.
- China Telecom (Hong Kong) was renamed China Mobile Communication Corporation in 2000.
- In 2006 China Mobile Communication Corporation shortened its name to China Mobile Limited.
- Besides its corporate brand, China Mobile created the GoTone, M-Zone, and Easyown sub-brands.

China Mobile is the corporate brand of the Hong Kong–based China Mobile Limited, which is China's—and the world's—largest mobile telecommunications service provider. The origins of the company date to November 1987, when the Chinese province of Guangdong established a commercial mobile telephone network using the total access communication system protocol. Operating initially as the Guangzhou Exchange, it was China's first cellular telecommunications exchange. The company adopted the Guangdong Mobile name in 1988. Because its home province was located on the coast of the South China Sea and near the entrepreneurial Hong Kong, the company, as the only player in the mobile market in China, prospered during the country's economic boom in the mid-1990s. Guangdong Mobile introduced digital mobile telephone service in 1995, relying on the new global system for mobile communications technology. Two years later the company had more than 1.2 million subscribers.

By the late 1990s, however, Guangdong Mobile was no longer unchallenged in the Chinese market. Mobile telephone networks had been established in other provinces. One of the largest operated in the Zhejiang province. Realizing the advantages that came with having a national mobile telephone operator, the Chinese government replaced the Ministry of Posts and Telecommunication in 1997, which provided telecommunications service through its China Telecom operational arm, with a new body, the Ministry of Information Industry. Its mission was to reorganize the country's inefficient state-run telecommunications sector. China Telecom was divided into three parts: fixed-line, mobile, and satellite. To pursue the mobile sector, a new company called China Telecom (Hong Kong) Limited was established in September 1997. (In that year, Hong Kong was reunified with China.) The new company included the Guangdong and Zhejiang operations. The following month the company was taken public, raising US$4.2 billion in an initial stock offering while gaining a listing on both the Stock Exchange of Hong Kong Limited and the New York Stock Exchange.

China Telecom (Hong Kong) used some of its cash to begin acquiring other provincial operators, including the mobile telephony provider in Jiangsu in June 1998. The following year China Telecom (Hong Kong) acquired Fujian Mobile Communication Company Limited, Henan Mobile Communication Company Limited, and Hainan Mobile Communication Company Limited. In 1999 all of the China Telecom (Hong Kong) subsidiaries began using China Mobile as their brand, which was heavily promoted and quickly superseded the subsidiary names in the minds of consumers.

The next step in the restructuring of China's telecommunications industry took place in June 2000, when China Telecom (Hong Kong) was given more authority in running its own affairs, although the Ministry of Information Industry continued to act as an industry regulator and offered "macro control and guidance." To be aligned with its emerging brand and better reflect its mission, China Telecom (Hong Kong) was renamed China Mobile Communication Corporation. Six years later, in 2006, the corporate name was shortened to China Mobile Limited. A host of smaller mobile telephone operators were acquired in the next few years, as China Mobile became the dominant brand in the country. To serve different parts of the market, the company created three sub-brands: GoTone, M-Zone, and Easyown.

BRAND ELEMENTS

- An image of clasped hands is used in the China Mobile corporate logo.
- The GoTone sub-brand logo emulates the colors of the corporate brand.
- The M-Zone logo is more stylish than the China Mobile and GoTone logos.
- The Easyown logo makes use of a cartoon figure.
- China Mobile's 3G business has its own logo and tagline.

The China Mobile corporate brand and service brands are defined by a variety of elements. The China Mobile name, rendered both in English and in Chinese characters, is at the heart of the corporate brand. The all-caps word mark is also combined with an image to create the brand's logo. Either located to the side of the word mark, or located above it, is a stylized depiction of clasped hands that also appear like an English *S*. The logo is primarily colored in different shades of blue but sometimes also appears in black. The corporate brand includes a tagline that roughly translates into English as "A mobile information expert that communicates from the heart."

Each of the three sub-brands is made up by its own unique brand elements. The flagship brand is GoTone. As is the case with the corporate brand, GoTone's word mark is coupled with the equivalent Chinese characters. The logo shares the same shades of blue that are used in the China Mobile logo and combines the word mark with an image: a swirling arrow within an oval. The brand's translated tagline is "Be a winner in life."

A second tier sub-brand is M-Zone. It is geared to a younger, more fashion-oriented market. As a result, its word mark and logo have more flair. The Chinese characters are given a three-dimensional look and the font used to depict the English version is unusual and appears to be drawn by hand. Moreover, the colors deviate from the corporate brand: "M-Zone" is presented in orange, while the Chinese characters are yellow with black highlights. The brand uses its own tagline, which can be translated as "I call the shots on my own turf."

The final sub-brand, Easyown, diverges even further from the corporate brand. The colors of the logo are green, which represents the divine land, and yellow, which is symbolic of the sun. The logo also incorporates a smiling cartoon figure mascot in mid-stride to reflect mobility. Also part of the logo is a brand tagline, roughly translated as "Easy for me."

China Mobile introduced third-generation (3G) service later than providers in other countries, and to promote it, the company created the G3 brand and a separate logo for the business. The logo includes a black letter *G* that appears as if created by a traditional Chinese ink painting brush stroke and is reminiscent of the old Chinese word *Tai Chi*, meaning "supreme ultimate force." The number three is colored red and depicted in Chinese seal form so that it resembles the sun rising in the East, which is indicative of a promising future. China Mobile's 3G business is also supported by a tagline that is roughly translated as "G3, leading the new life of 3G times."

BRAND IDENTITY

- At the heart of China Mobile's corporate identity are the concepts of reliability and sincerity.
- China Mobile's clasped hands logo reinforces the brand's commitment to community.
- China Mobile's sub-brands have their own distinct identities.

China Mobile has crafted a corporate brand identity as well as individual identities for its sub-brands. At the corporate level, China Mobile presents itself as a proficient and reliable provider, the best in the market, while also being sincere and committed to being a good corporate citizen. This portrayal of the brand is supported by the logo with its image of clasped hands. According to the company, the logo "reflects the Company's continuing resolve to improve its mobile communications services, bringing ever closer together our customers, the Company and people everywhere. Reaching out from the Heart." Further reinforcement is provided by the slogan "A mobile information expert that communicates from the heart."

Each of China Mobile's sub-brands have established their own identities, which have been crafted to appeal to different types of customers. GoTone, China Mobile's highest tier of service, embraces the slogan message "Be a winner in life." It is an identity of the powerful individual who caters to high-end customers. Targeting a younger demographic, the M-Zone brand has a brand personality that is embodied in the slogan "I call the shots on my turf." The bright, brash logo supports this idea of individuality, as does the flexibility the service plan provides to customers. The Easyown brand is used for China Mobile's pay-as-you-go service. It assumes a fun, friendly, and relaxed persona, as reflected in the brand's cartoon mascot. The brand identity is also supported by the logo, which includes the "Easy for me" brand slogan.

BRAND STRATEGY

- China Mobile's brand strategy includes the use of a corporate brand and service brands.
- The ZONG service brand was created for a subsidiary in Pakistan.
- The G3 and Ophone brands were created as circumstances dictated.

China Mobile primarily pursues a bifurcated brand strategy. At the top level is the China Mobile corporate brand. This overarching brand is applied to subsidiaries and business units. In 2007 China Mobile expanded beyond its home market by acquiring Paktel Ltd., a mobile telephone service provider in Pakistan. This deal followed a failed attempt to acquire Paktel's parent company, the Luxembourg-based Millicom International Cellular SA, a move that would have taken China Mobile into other Asian markets, as well as into Latin America and Africa. China Mobile extended its corporate brand to the new Pakistan operation, renaming it China Mobile Pakistan. It also introduced the ZONG brand for its mobile service in Pakistan.

The use of service brands is the second plank of China Mobile's brand strategy. While ZONG is devoted to an entire market, China Mobile created three sub-brands for use in China to pursue different parts of the market. Hence, GoTone is designed to appeal to high-end customers, those older than 25 and able to afford the higher monthly subscription cost of China Mobile's premium mobile service. The M-Zone service brand targets younger customers. The service can be modified to better serve the needs and desires of this demographic, and the brand is crafted to appeal to the sensibilities of this market. The third service brand, Easyown, offers a low-end value proposition, relying on prepaid SIM cards. Its easy-going brand identity is also created to reflect this no-contract, no obligation service.

Besides its corporate brand and service brands, China Mobile creates other brands as the need arises. For many years the company relied on second-generation mobile communication technology and was slow to introduce a third-generation (3G) service. When it did, China Mobile created the new logo G3, which was essentially a new brand. After China Mobile was unsuccessful in bringing the iPhone to China in 2009, the company introduced the Ophone brand, which was its own version of the Apple smartphone based on the Android operating system. However, the Ophone failed to take hold in the market because not enough handset vendors supported it.

BRAND EQUITY

- China Mobile had a brand value of US$23.3 billion at the end of 2012, according to Brand Finance.
- In 2013 China Mobile ranked 20th on Brand Finance's "Global 500" list of the world's most valuable brands.
- Millward Brown listed China Mobile number 10 on its "BrandZ Top 100 Brand Ranking" for 2012.
- In 2011 and 2012 WPP ranked China Mobile as the most valuable brand among state-owned Chinese enterprises.

The brand equity of China Mobile and its service brands is most clearly demonstrated by the higher prices the company is able to charge compared to its rivals. By definition, brand equity is the difference in price between a branded product or service and a generic equivalent. Because China Mobile competes against other brands, there is no generic equivalent to serve as a true measure of its brand equity. Nevertheless, leading brand consultancies and trade publications have developed models to assign monetary values to brands for comparison purposes, based on quantifiable metrics, such as sales and market capitalization. According to the brand consultancy Brand Finance, China Mobile had a brand value of US$23.3 billion at the end of 2012. As a result, it was ranked 20th on Brand Finance's "Global 500" list of the world's most valuable brands in 2013. Brand Finance also ranked China Mobile sixth in the "Top 500 Telecom" brands in 2012, and first in the "China 100" brands in 2011.

Another brand consultancy, Millward Brown, listed China Mobile number 10 on its 2012 "BrandZ Top 100 Brand Ranking," with a value of US$47 billion. The European Brand Institute estimated the worth of the China Mobile brand at US$44 billion, placing it number 11 on its "Top 100 Brand Corporations Worldwide" rankings in 2012. Among state-owned Chinese enterprises, China Mobile was China's most valuable brand in both 2011 and 2012, as determined by WPP, the world's largest advertising group.

BRAND AWARENESS

- China Mobile's high brand awareness is reflected in its high number of subscribers.
- China Mobile dominates its market with a 75 percent share.
- Outside of China, China Mobile is a well-known brand with investors.

China Mobile and its service brands enjoy strong brand awareness in China. The company's customer base is massive at more than 700 million. Its market share is just as impressive. In 2012 it controlled more than 75 percent of the market, compared to China Unicom (Hong Kong) Limited, with 15.7 percent, and China Telecom Corporation Limited, with 9 percent. That discrepancy not only reflects strong brand awareness but also builds on it.

Exactly how well known the China Mobile brands are and whether they achieve top-of-mind status are difficult to determine. One study conducted by Chinese academics that used China Mobile's GoTone service brand as part of a study on brand equity does offer some insights. The researchers contacted 967 mobile phone users in Hainan province and discovered that 574 were GoTone subscribers. Using a seven-point scale, the researchers calculated GoTone's brand awareness at 5.44, which they characterized as a relatively high level.

Outside of China, there is little general awareness of the China Mobile brand. The same cannot be said of the investor class. China Mobile's stock is listed on the New York Stock Exchange and has steadily risen in value since its premiere. On Wall Street and elsewhere in the business community, China Mobile is a well-known and respected brand.

BRAND OUTLOOK

- Only half of China's 1.3 billion people have mobile phones, creating an opportunity for further growth for China Mobile.
- China Mobile may extend its brand to new product and service categories.
- China Mobile may expand into new countries.

For a company with more than 700 million subscribers, China Mobile still has a great deal of room to grow its brands. First, the Chinese market is immense with a population of more than 1.3 billion, and approximately half of the people do not yet have mobile telephones. This represents a pool of potential China Mobile customers that is double the size of the U.S. population. As a result, China Mobile is anything but a mature brand.

There are other growth opportunities for China Mobile in its home market as well. Despite the failure of its Ophone, China Mobile is very likely to begin offering its own branded handsets. In 2011 the company acquired Topssion, a mobile phone handset and devices distributor, laying the foundation for greater inroads in the handset business. In addition, China Mobile could extend its brand or create new service brands in the Internet sector. In 2012 China Mobile tested a cloud service that was branded as McLoud. There is no shortage of other digital services and products that China Mobile could pursue in the years ahead.

The global telecommunications services market is expected to enjoy rapid expansion. China Mobile might very well introduce its brand in other countries to enjoy even further growth. The company already has a foothold in Pakistan and has the potential to enter other markets. However, there is no lack of competition for China Mobile. Besides China Telecom Corporation Limited and China Unicom (Hong Kong) Limited, China Mobile has to contend with potential newcomers and competitors in other market sectors in which it wishes to operate. Nevertheless, there is good reason to believe that that the China Mobile corporate brand, along with its service brands, has not yet reached its potential.

FURTHER READING

Betts, Paul, and Kathrin Hille. "China Mobile Trudges Slowly along Lonely 3G Path." *Financial Times*, May 27, 2009.

"China Mobile, Branding Itself in Individual Services Area." Lab Brand, November 18, 2008. Accessed February 27, 2013. http://www.labbrand.com/brand-source/china-mobile-branding-itself-individual-services-area.

"China Mobile Ltd." *International Directory of Company Histories*. Ed. Jay P. Pederson. Vol. 108. Detroit, MI: St. James Press, 2010.

"China Mobile Makes Landmark Acquisition." *Business Daily Update*, February 16, 2007.

"China Mobile to Offer Cloud Storage Service." *Business Daily Update*, August 22, 2012.

"China Mobile Stabilizes, Set for Growth." *South China Morning Post*, February 21, 2013.

"China Mobile Tops Value List." *People's Daily Online*, December 5, 2012.

Kan, Michael. "China Mobile to Brand Own Handsets, as It Waits for iPhone." *Computerworld*, December 5, 2012.

CHINA UNICOM

AT A GLANCE

Brand Synopsis: China Unicom, the country's second largest mobile service provider, is a global brand centered on passion, innovation, and setting the latest trends in telecommunications.
Parent Company: China United Network Communications Group Co., Ltd.
No. 21 Financial Street, Xicheng District
Beijing 100140
China
http://www.chinaunicom.com
Sector: Telecommunication services
Industry Group: Telecommunication services
Performance: *Market share*—20% of domestic market (2011). *Sales*—CNY 209.15 billion (US$33.3 billion) (2011).
Principal Competitors: China Telecom Corporation Limited; China Mobile Communications Corporation; China Netcom Limited; China Mobile Group Shanghai Company Limited

BRAND ORIGINS

- China Unicom began as a government-owned company intended to break the monopoly in the domestic telecommunications industry.
- China Unicom Limited was incorporated in Hong Kong in 2000.
- In 2002 the brand launched a public listing on the Shanghai Stock Exchange.
- In December 2002 China Unicom completed the acquisition of GSM mobile communications services in nine autonomous regions.
- China Unicom merged with China Network Communications Group Corporation ("Netcom Group") in 2009.

In 1994, the central committee of the Communist Party of China incorporated China Unicom as a state-owned enterprise with the goal of breaking the monopoly in the domestic telecommunications industry. China Unicom set out to build a nationwide mobile communications network and a cutting-edge unified multi-service network platform. Beginning in 1999, China Unicom collaborated with Cisco Systems in order to compete more effectively and moved into the long-distance voice business via IP technology, mobile data, and eventually a convergence solution that leveraged both voice and data capabilities.

China Unicom Telecommunications Corporation Limited was incorporated in Hong Kong in 2000 and listed on the New York Stock Exchange and the Hong Kong Stock Exchange the same year, with the IPO raising US$5.65 billion. The following year the brand was included as a constituent stock of the Hang Seng Index. In 2002 China Unicom launched a public listing on the Shanghai Stock Exchange, becoming the first telecom services operator in China to be listed in Hong Kong, New York, and Shanghai. In December of the same year, the company completed the acquisition of GSM mobile communications services in nine autonomous regions in China, including Jilin, and completed the sale of the interests in Guoxin Paging to Unicom group (the brand's parent company).

In 2006 the brand issued an aggregate principal amount of US$1 billion convertible bond to SK Telecom Co. Ltd. of Korea, and the companies entered into a strategic alliance. The following year China Unicom acquired its cellular services and GSM network assets in Guizhou Province from the parent company and finished the listing of operations in the People's Republic of China. In 2008 the brand gave its CDMA business to China Telecom and merged with China Netcom Group Corporation Limited. With this merger the brand was officially renamed China Unicom Limited. The company publicly announced proposed acquisitions of assets and businesses by its core company and the lease (from Unicom Group) of telecommunication networks across 21 provinces in Southern China.

The brand merged with China Network Communications Group Corporation ("Netcom Group") in 2009. Also in 2009 a subsidiary of the brand, China United Network Communications Corporation Limited, was granted approval to operate 3G digital business with Wideband Code Division Multiple Access technology nationwide in China and officially launched 3G services in October. In the same month China Unicom entered into an alliance with Telefónica. In 2011 this alliance would be enhanced by both parties, thus increasing their shareholdings.

In 2010 China Unicom celebrated the 10th anniversary of its listing on the New York Stock Exchange and the Stock Exchange of Hong Kong, and its 3G users exceeded 10 million. By 2011 China Unicom was engaged in GSM and WCDMA cellular service in 31 provinces, municipalities, and autonomous regions in China and total subscribers were 372 million.

BRAND ELEMENTS

- China Unicom's logo consists of a red endless knot and the Chinese characters for "China Unicom," accompanied by the name in English.
- China Unicom's logo was inspired by the Lucky Buddha Knot and signifies order, brisk operation, and a self-perpetuating, eternal business.
- China continued to use the color red in its logo recreation in 2006 because of its strong visual impact in advertising.
- The website features photographs with the repeated motif of an open doorway standing in an outdoor location to suggest innovation.

China Unicom's logo is composed of a red endless knot and the Chinese characters that represent "China Unicom," as well as the name in English. The knot was inspired by the ancient Chinese Buddhist graphics "Pan Zhang" and the "Lucky Buddha Knot." It represents China Unicom's status as a modern telecommunication brand characterized by order, brisk operation, and a self-perpetuating, eternal business. Red, the color of the Chinese national flag, signifies passion and energy and remained part of the China Unicom logo through the revision of the logo in 2006 because of its strong visual impact. The two red "I"s in the name represent two people communicating, recalling the spirit of the brand: "Let everyone get connected as they wish."

Another brand element is the striking visual motif that appears in several photographs on the China Unicom website. The motif is a doorframe (sometimes with an open door) standing on a beach, before an ocean, or out in a field. Several photographs using this motif show people who have either moved through the doorway or are about to do so. This suggests a portal into the future, emphasizing the company's desire to innovate. Other photographs using the motif draw attention to various services offered by China Unicom. For example, one image emphasizes personal communication by showing a mother and child playing "telephone" through the doorway—talking to each other by using tin cans connected by string. Another emphasizes business communications by showing a distant meeting of two people with a laptop, framed by the doorway in the foreground.

BRAND IDENTITY

- In 2006 China Unicom launched a new corporate brand logo and new business strategy.
- In 2009 China Unicom rolled out a video whose theme was "Innovation Changes the World" to promote it as a cutting-edge leader in telecommunications.
- China Unicom is the second-largest Chinese telecommunications carrier.
- China Unicom is committed to becoming a world-leading broadband communications and information service provider.

In 2006 China Unicom launched a new corporate brand logo and with it, a new business strategy to symbolize the new era of telecommunications that the brand was preparing to enter. This new era would bridge the space between the consistency and continuity of the old brand with a new internationalized image of passion, innovation, and trendiness.

"Innovation Changes the World" was the theme of a 2009 video promoting China Unicom as the only truly integrated telecommunications service provider in China, able to provide fixed voice, cellular, data, and paging services. The video focused on the company's emphasis on cutting-edge improvements and commitment to deliver the best services for consumers.

China Unicom, currently the second-largest Chinese telecommunications carrier, is committed to becoming a world-leading broadband communications and information service provider. The company intends to take a leadership role in the expansion of 3G services while improving its overall competitiveness. It wants to promote the growth of mobile broadband Internet services and to roll out broadband multimedia services to accelerate its transformation into an information service provider.

BRAND STRATEGY

- In 2009 China Unicom partnered with Apple Inc. to introduce the iPhone in Beijing.
- In 2011 China Unicom launched the WO+ system with the intent of boosting subscriber usage.
- In 2011 China Unicom promoted sales through e-channels and experienced increased sales in its online store.
- China Unicom accelerated 3G network building by completing the 3G HSPA+ upgrade in 56 cities, maintaining its leading edge in 3G technology.

China Unicom raised awareness of the brand significantly in 2009 by partnering with Apple Inc. to introduce the iPhone in Beijing. Despite the lack of the sell-out Apple had hoped for, China Unicom achieved its goal of increasing its brand's exposure.

In 2011 China Unicom pursued another strategy by launching the WO+ system with the intent of increasing product aggregation, channel sales, and refined operations, all of which would increase subscriber usage. The logo for the 3G business consisted of the frequently used Chinese exclamation "wo-" and the accompanying homophonic character. The logo was color-coded to reach three distinct target markets: young people, businesses, and families. China Unicom was one of three mobile service providers in the country that offered 3G services.

In another 2011 strategy, China Unicom promoted sales through e-channels and experienced increased sales in their online store: turnover for the online store was CNY 23.07 billion (US$3.7 billion) for the year, an increase of 86 percent from the previous year. The brand focused on marketing such products as music, reading material, and applications and experienced increases in subscriber usage in these categories. The brand accelerated 3G network building through continued improvement of the GSM networks and the establishment of more 3G base stations. China Unicom completed the 3G HSPA+ upgrade in 56 cities, maintaining its leading edge in 3G technology.

BRAND EQUITY

- In 2012 the brand won "China's Most Promising Companies 2011" award from the *Asset.*
- In 2012 Brand Finance ranked China Unicom at number 13 in its top 50 global telecom brands.
- In 2011 China Unicom's revenue totaled CNY 209.15 billion (US$33.3 billion), and the brand claimed a market share of 20 percent.
- In 2011 China Unicom's mobile subscribers numbered 199.66 million, an increase of 19.3 percent from the previous year.

Interbrand added China Unicom to its list of the top Chinese brands in 2007. In 2011 China Unicom was ranked 17th in the Top 500 Telecom Brands, 10th in the China 100, and 154th in the Global 500. In 2012 the brand also won "China's Most Promising Companies 2011" award from the *Asset,* which acknowledges the most promising Chinese corporations based on financial performance, growth strategies, and competitiveness. In the same year, Brand Finance released a study titled "2012 Top 50 Global Telecom Brands," which ranked China Unicom at number 13. Brand Finance estimated China Unicom's brand value at US$7.9 billion in 2012.

In 2011 China Unicom's revenue totaled CNY 209.15 billion (US$33.3 billion), and capital expenditure was CNY 76.66 billion (US$12.2 billion). China Unicom recorded CNY 4.23 billion (US$672 million) in profits in the year 2011 and a market share of 20 percent. Operating cash flow of the brand was CNY 66.49 billion (US$10.6 billion), an increase of 0.2 percent from the previous year.

The year 2011 was a time of growth for the brand. Service revenue exceeded the industry average by 3.4 percent. China Unicom's mobile subscribers numbered 199.66 million, an increase of 19.3 percent from the previous year. 3G data usage accounts for 20 percent of China Unicom's total mobile subscribers.

BRAND AWARENESS

- In 2009 China Unicom launched the official Chinese version of Apple Inc.'s iPhone, which resulted in increased brand exposure.
- The additions of 3G subscribers had a net value of CNY 40.02 million (US$6.4 million) in sales in 2011.
- China Unicom lagged far behind its rival China Mobile in its share of the market for smartphones.

In 2009 China Unicom launched the official Chinese version of Apple Inc.'s iPhone. Despite an unenthusiastic public reception, China Unicom nevertheless managed to raise its brand awareness via the extensive media coverage of the deal between the companies. The 3G business is responsible for a large portion of the brand's revenue growth, and the WO+ advertising campaign of 2001 led to increases in both the number of subscribers and levels of subscriber usage. The net value of additions to of 3G subscribers was CNY 40.02 million (US$6.4 million) in 2011, accounting for 20 percent of China Unicom's mobile subscription revenues.

In terms of the market share for smartphones, China Unicom has lagged far behind its largest rival. In early

2012, China Mobile's market share was about 66 percent, compared to 20 percent for China Unicom—a difference of more than three to one. However, the gap between the two brands was smaller in the subcategory of 3G phones. China Mobile's share in that category was only twice as large as China Unicom's, showing that China Unicom was more competitive in the newer technology.

BRAND OUTLOOK

- In 2011 the growth of China Unicom's revenue accelerated, with revenues reaching CNY 209.15 billion (US$33.3 billion) for the year.
- China Unicom seeks to further improve its quality of service through the acquisition of a mobile license.
- Chinese demand for telecommunications is expected to rise, which suggests a bright future for China Unicom.

In 2011 the growth of China Unicom's revenue accelerated, and revenues increased by 22 percent over the previous year, totaling CNY 209.15 billion (US$33.3 billion). Due to an increase of 2,293 percent in mobile data usage compared with 2010, the revenue from the mobile non-voice service experienced rapid growth and accounted for 37.2 percent of the total mobile service revenue.

China Unicom intends to enter a new stage of brand development, increasing the company's core competitiveness and input/output ratio. The brand seeks to further improve its quality of service through the acquisition of a mobile license and by participating in the Connect the Villages Project, a nationwide campaign to share information technology with disadvantaged communities.

According to the CIA's *World Factbook,* China's GDP has increased more than tenfold since 1978. By 2012, it had the world's second-largest economy in terms of purchasing power parity. As China continues to industrialize and the Chinese middle class continues to grow, the Chinese demand for telecommunications will rise sharply. If China Unicom can continue to pursue innovations in technology and improvements in customer service, it will be poised to take advantage of that demand.

FURTHER READING

"China to Surpass 1 Billion Mobile Connections in May 2012." *Wireless Intelligence,* n.d. Accessed October 22, 2012. https://wirelessintelligence.com/analysis/2011/07/china-to-surpass-1-billion-mobile-connections-in-may-2012/.

China Unicom. "China Unicom Annual 2011." Accessed October 24, 2012. http://www.chinaunicom.com.hk/files/doc/report/a2011/a2011en.pdf.

Cisco Systems. "China Unicom's Strategy of 'Chayihua' Sets Them Apart in the Marketplace." *Success Story: China Unicom.* Accessed October 23, 2012. http://www.cisco.com/web/about/ac79/docs/success/china_unicom.pdf.

DeWoskin, Kenneth. "The WTO and the Telecommunications Sector in China." *China Quarterly* 167 (2001): 630-54.

Harwit, Eric. "China's Telecommunications Industry: Development Patterns and Policies." *Pacific Affairs* 71.2 (1998): 175-93.

Labbrand. "China Unicom Launches Logo for 3G Business." *BrandSource,* March 19, 2009. Accessed October 22, 2012. http://www.labbrand.com/brand-source/china-unicom-launches-logo-3g-business.

———. "Insights on Branding in China and Abroad: China Unicom Brand Benefits from iPhone Launch." *BrandSource,* November 6, 2009. Accessed October 23, 2012. http://www.labbrand.com/brand-source/china-unicom-brand-benefits-iphone-launch.

Madden, Normandy. "Interbrand Ranks Chinese Brands." *Ad Age China,* December 19, 2007. Accessed October 23, 2012. http://adage.com/china/article/china-news/interbrand-ranks-chinese-brands/122599/.

Sung-Cheol Lee, Kark-Bum Lee, and Ji-Yeon Ryu. "Technology Transfer of Foreign Direct Investment in China." *Geography* 88.4 (2003): 289-99.

Wilson, Ernest J., III, and Adam Segal. "Trends in China's Transition toward a Knowledge Economy." *Asian Survey* 45.6 (2005): 886-906. Accessed October 26, 2012. http://www.ernestjwilson.com/uploads/TRENDS.PDF.

CHIPOTLE

AT A GLANCE

Brand Synopsis: Chipotle is a fast-growing chain of quick service Mexican restaurants that emphasizes fresh food and a responsible corporate philosophy.
Parent Company: Chipotle Mexican Grill Inc.
1401 Wynkoop St., Suite 500
Denver, Colorado 80202-1729
United States
http://www.chipotle.com
Sector: Consumer Discretionary
Industry Group: Consumer Services
Performance: *Market share*—Chipotle is the second-largest chain of quick service Mexican restaurants in the United States in terms of sales. *Sales*—US$2.27 billion (2011).
Principal Competitors: Fresh Enterprises, Inc.; Rubio's Restaurants, Inc.; Moe's Southwest Grill, LLC; Qdoba Restaurant Corporation; El Pollo Loco, Inc.

BRAND ORIGINS

- Steve Ells founded the first Chipotle Mexican Grill in Denver, Colorado, in 1993.
- McDonald's Corporation began taking ownership of Chipotle in 1998.
- Chipotle claims that it provides "food with integrity" and that its restaurants take people, animals, and the environment into consideration.
- Chipotle opened in Canada in 2008, in England in 2010, and in France in 2012 and now has more than 1,110 locations.
- In 2011 Chipotle began opening ShopHouse restaurants, which offer Asian cuisines from a number of regions.

Freshness, integrity, and flavor are three adjectives associated with the Chipotle brand. Chipotle has aimed to provide all three qualities and has built a hugely successful brand in the process.

Trained at the Culinary Institute of America, Steve Ells had been interested in all kinds of food his entire life. While working at a high-end San Francisco restaurant, Ells became fascinated by the city's taquerias, which served made-to-order tacos and burritos. He combined this customization with gourmet ingredients and an emphasis on freshness at the first Chipotle Mexican Grill, which opened in Denver, Colorado, in 1993, in a former Dolly Madison Ice Cream shop.

Chipotle was an innovator in the quick service restaurant field. These restaurants were more upscale than fast food restaurants but offered faster service than casual dining establishments. Other Chipotles began opening in 1995, and even more opened after the McDonald's Corporation began buying into the chain in 1998. In addition to other forms of assistance, McDonald's helped Chipotle find locations and access suppliers.

In addition to its business expansion, Chipotle developed a philosophy of corporate responsibility. It claims that it provides "food with integrity" and that the company takes people, animals, and the environment into consideration in its operations. Chipotle supports sustainable agricultural practices, recycling efforts, charitable involvement, and participation in community activities.

A successful American chain since the 1990s, Chipotle opened its first international location in Toronto in 2008. A location in London followed in 2010, and the first Chipotle opened in Paris in 2012. Chipotle now has more than 1,110 locations. With regard to employees, the Chipotle website states that, of new managers appointed in 2011, "97 percent ... were promoted from hourly positions within Chipotle."

The company began opening ShopHouse restaurants in 2011. These restaurants offer Asian cuisines from a number of regions. ShopHouse restaurants are similar to Chipotles in that both are quick service restaurants offering ethnic food and minimalist (and environmentally friendly) design. ShopHouse is another example of Chipotle's commitment to expansion and to its food and corporate philosophies.

BRAND ELEMENTS

- A drawing of a chipotle, a smoked or dried jalapeño pepper, forms the center of Chipotle's logo. The words Chipotle Mexican Grill appear in a circle with this chipotle drawing to complete the logo.
- Chipotle's food packaging emphasizes the recyclability of the materials.
- Chipotle's restaurants often use simple, exposed elements such as wood, steel, and concrete, in both American and international locations.

A chipotle is a smoked or dried jalapeño pepper. Fittingly, a drawing of a chipotle pepper appears at the center of the restaurant's logo. The words "Chipotle Mexican Grill" appear in a circle around the chipotle image to complete the logo. This logo appears in its restaurants and on its website. Also available in Spanish, the website discusses Chipotle's environmental and agricultural initiatives in addition to the usual restaurant website information, including menus, the company's history, investor information, and other data.

Paralleling Chipotle's embrace of the environment and a quest for simplicity, its restaurants often use simple, exposed construction materials such as wood, steel, and concrete. Even its Paris location uses these elements in a minimalist design. The restaurants use brown paper bags bearing whimsical writings and designs for its food items. The napkins are a similar brown color and have messages printed on them stating that they are made of recycled materials and have not been bleached. The company's website also uses similar shades of brown, as well as a simple design.

BRAND IDENTITY

- Using a visible food preparation station for made-to-order food demonstrates Chipotle's commitment to freshness.
- By using free range meat without genetic modifications or growth hormones and taking other measures, Chipotle demonstrates its social commitments.
- Chipotle seeks to educate customers about the benefits of its responsible agricultural practices.

In addition to its visual elements, the Chipotle brand is associated with other traits. The chain has worked to present its food in different ways. It has touted the freshness of its food since the restaurant's early days. Even in its original Denver location, Chipotle had a food preparation station in the front of the restaurant where customers could order their food according to their own specifications. This process enabled customers to see the ingredients being used and witness their food being prepared. It ensured that the resulting meals were fresh.

Its food is not only fresh, says Chipotle, but it appeals to diners' social consciences. In concert with its commitment to freshness, Chipotle has practiced corporate responsibility for some time. In 2000 it started using free range pork for its carnitas, a type of seasoned meat. These changes resulted in a more expensive product, but the change did not harm Chipotle's sales or drive away customers. Chipotle began using organic ingredients, stopped using ingredients that had been genetically modified or that contained growth hormones, and used naturally raised meats like chicken and beef. For every two restaurants Chipotle opens, the chain adds another farmer to the Niman Ranch, a network of meat-producing ranchers and farmers who treat their animals in humane ways.

The restaurant's link to responsible agricultural practices also spans continents. Bags from its Paris location feature drawings of food and farm animals. A cow in one such drawing is shown saying the word "cultiver" in a dialogue bubble. *Cultiver* is the French word for cultivate. Interestingly, the French term *se cultiver* means to become enlightened, much as the English word "cultivate" can mean both to grow and to refine. These dual meanings point to the restaurant's support of humane farming and its interest in educating people about such matters.

BRAND STRATEGY

- In 2011 Chipotle opened 150 restaurants, and it planned to open 155 to 165 more in 2012.
- In 2012 Chipotle released an animated short film as a television commercial that encouraged viewers to "Cultivate a Better World."
- Chipotle utilizes social media sites like Facebook and Twitter and word-of-mouth promotion.
- By posting, viewing, and voting on Facebook and Twitter photographs, people have participated in Chipotle's Boorito costume contest on Halloween.

People have gotten to know the Chipotle brand through increasing exposure to the restaurants themselves.

Chipotle has opened several stores in the 2000s. In 2011 alone, it opened 12 in the first quarter, 39 in the second, 32 in the third, and 67 in the fourth quarter, for a total of 150 restaurants. This complements the 155 to 165 new Chipotles the company planned to open in 2012.

Chipotle does not employ a lot of traditional advertising. One notable exception was a commercial that appeared during the telecast of the 2012 Grammy Awards. This commercial was an animated short film depicting a farmer who adopted new agricultural practices, which included letting his animals live outdoors and planting trees. The end of this commercial featured the farmer loading products onto a Chipotle truck and a sign featuring the slogan "Cultivate a Better World" and Chipotle's web address. Critics gave the advertisement high marks, and the spot won awards at the Cannes Lions International Festival of Creativity.

The chain also uses social media sites like Facebook and Twitter to promote the Chipotle brand. American brand manager and analyst Expion conducted a 2011 poll to determine how restaurant chains interact with social media. It found that Chipotle representatives responded to 83 percent of the Facebook posts related to the company, the highest rate of response in the quick service and fast casual restaurant category. It also found that these Chipotle representatives supplied an answer within 1 hour and 37 minutes, one of the fastest response times in the poll. According to Chipotle spokesperson Chris Arnold, Chipotle responds to Facebook posts as part of the company's tradition of using word-of-mouth promotion.

In 2012 Chipotle used the social media site Twitter to announce that customers who visited the restaurants in Halloween costumes could buy burritos for US$2.00, with profits from the sale going to different farming charities. During parts of October and November 2011 and 2012, customers could also use Twitter or a Chipotle Facebook site to send pictures of themselves in costume at Chipotle restaurants as part of the Boorito contest. Twitter and Facebook users then voted on the winners, who could receive prizes such as money and burrito parties hosted at Chipotle. The restaurant also offers a special app (application) that allows Apple technology users to order food from Chipotle restaurants.

BRAND EQUITY

- More than 27 percent of Chipotle's restaurants "are located in the ten [American] states with the highest median incomes," according to Helix Investment Management.
- In the second quarter of 2012 Chipotle reported a 61 percent jump in net income from the previous year.
- In 2012 the business magazine *Fast Company* named Chipotle the 34th most innovative company in the world and the 2nd most innovative food company in the world.

The geographical concentration of Chipotle restaurants has fueled the chain's growth. In January 2012 more than 27 percent of its restaurants were "located in the ten [American] states with the highest median incomes," according to representatives from Helix Investment Management. Helix added that the American economic recession of the 2000s would not affect these more affluent customers. The firm added that these customers are also willing and able to pay premium prices for Chipotle's items because they perceive these items to be quality products.

These geographic and demographic factors have earned Chipotle financial rewards, even in rough economic times. In the second quarter of 2012, Chipotle reported a 61 percent jump in net income from the previous year. It reported net income of US$214.9 million in 2011, up from around US$179.98 million in 2010.

This economic success has led to customer respect. Chipotle was named the 34th most innovative company in the world and the 2nd most innovative food company in the world in a poll by business media publication *Fast Company* in 2012.

BRAND AWARENESS

- Customer awareness of the Chipotle brand, Chipotle's opening of additional restaurants, and the chain's loyal patrons contributed to Chipotle's healthy revenues in 2011.
- A 2012 Goldman Sachs poll found that Chipotle had a national brand awareness of 55 percent.
- October 2012 photographs of American presidential candidate Mitt Romney and a Chipotle manager, Marty Arps, generated publicity for the Chipotle brand.

Rising costs in the food industry impacted restaurants in 2011, but Chipotle still performed well. Writing in *Forbes* magazine, the Trefis Team attributed the chain's healthy 2011 revenues to a number of factors. These factors included Chipotle's opening of several new restaurants, the restaurants' loyal patrons, and customer awareness of the Chipotle brand.

Polling 2,000 respondents about restaurants, in 2012 Goldman Sachs found that Chipotle had a national brand awareness of 55 percent and was a strong brand overall. This survey reported that the chain was the highest ranked quick service restaurant.

An October 2012 visit to a Chipotle restaurant by American presidential candidate Mitt Romney inadvertently raised the chain's profile. At a Chipotle location in Denver, Romney posed for pictures with Chipotle employees, one of whom, manager Marty Arps, sported a wide-eyed facial expression in the photographs. A number of television programs and Internet sites used the photos of Romney and Arps in their news reports, generating a fair amount of publicity for Chipotle in the process.

BRAND OUTLOOK

- Taco Bell's Cantina menu, launched in August 2012, offered more expensive menu items that were similar to Chipotle's offerings.
- By selling lunch bags manufactured from recycled materials and donating the profits to an educational organization in 2012, Chipotle continued its environmental and social commitments.
- Chipotle's 2012 social initiatives included its agreement to support the Coalition of Immokalee Workers' Fair Food Program.

In 2012 Chipotle faced competition from the Mexican fast food market leader, Taco Bell. In August of that year, Taco Bell launched its Cantina menu. This upscale menu featured more expensive items than the chain's other offerings, items much like those found on Chipotle's menu, such as rice with cilantro; salads with meat, vegetables, and beans; and burritos with rice, meat, beans, and vegetables. These similar offerings from a competitor point to the success of Chipotle and the popularity of its food.

The company has continued its focus on environmental efforts. In 2012 Chipotle's online store sold lunch bags that were made from recycled billboard materials. Customers who purchased these bags before a certain date could receive free food from Chipotle. The chain also donated profits from the repurposed bags' sales to Chipotle Cultivate Foundation, which supports farming, sustainable agricultural efforts, and food-related education.

In addition, the company has continued its social commitments. In October 2012 the company agreed to comply with the Fair Food Program of the Coalition of Immokalee Workers (CIW). The Fair Food Program provides better working conditions, higher pay, labor education, and conflict resolution measures for Florida workers in the tomato industry. These examples show how Chipotle continues to link its brand with various environmental and social efforts.

FURTHER READING

Brandau, Mark. "Speed Matters When It Comes to Facebook." *Nation's Restaurant News*, May 18, 2011.

Chipotle Mexican Grill. Accessed November 8, 2012. http://www.chipotle.com/en-US/Default.aspx.

Helix Investment Management. "Chipotle: Wait for a Better Entry Point to Buy a Company with Outstanding Fundamentals." *Seeking Alpha*, January 17, 2012. Accessed November 8, 2012. http://seekingalpha.com/article/320040-chipotle-wait-for-a-better-entry-point-to-buy-a-company-with-outstanding-fundamentals.

Klamm, Dan. "How Chipotle Uses Social Media to Cultivate a Better World." *Mashable*, March 21, 2012. Accessed November 8, 2012. http://mashable.com/2012/03/21/chipotle-social-media/.

Salamie, David E. "Chipotle Mexican Grill, Inc." *International Directory of Company Histories*. Ed. Jay P. Pederson and Miranda H. Ferrara. Vol. 67. Detroit, MI: St. James Press, 2005.

Salzman, Avi. "Good News for Chipotle, Darden in Goldman Restaurant Survey." *Barron's*, July 13, 2012.

Trefis Team. "Chipotle Charging More for Chow but Food Costs Bite." *Forbes*, July 26, 2011.

"The World's Most Innovative Companies." *Fast Company*. Accessed November 7, 2012. http://www.fastcompany.com/most-innovative-companies/2012/chipotle.

CHIQUITA

AT A GLANCE

Brand Synopsis: Identified with its premier product, the banana, Chiquita is recognized by its blue sticker and remembered for its fruit-hatted mascot.
Parent Company: Chiquita Brands International
550 S. Caldwell St.
Charlotte, North Carolina 28202
United States
http://www.chiquita.com
Sector: Consumer Staples
Industry Group: Food, Beverage & Tobacco
Performance: *Market share*—39 percent of the U.S. banana market and 2.8 percent of the global fruits and vegetable market (2011). *Sales*—US$3.14 billion (2011).
Principal Competitors: Dole Food Company; Fresh Del Monte Produce; Fyffes plc.

BRAND ORIGINS

- United Fruit Company was created in 1899 after the Boston Fruit Company merged with Minor C. Keith's railroad and plantation businesses.
- The Chiquita name and image were introduced in 1944.
- The company formally changed its name to Chiquita Brands International in 1990, taking advantage of its global brand awareness.

While building a national railroad in Costa Rica during the 1870s, American businessman Minor C. Keith began to acquire banana plantations along the route. In 1899 Keith merged his holdings with those of the Boston Fruit Company, which was founded by Lorenzo Dow Baker to ship bananas to New Jersey from Jamaica. The new firm was named the United Fruit Company. That same year, United Fruit established the Fruit Dispatch Company to distribute bananas throughout the United States.

United Fruit began using refrigerated vessels to transport produce, which revolutionized the produce import industry. By 1910 the company was experimenting with hybridizing bananas in an attempt to develop a disease-resistant variety. Despite these efforts, in 1935 sigatoka disease, a leaf fungus, arrived in the American tropics and damaged the company's crops.

During World War II all production was halted because the company's ships had been requisitioned by England and the United States for use in the war effort. When the war ended and business resumed, United Fruit established Chiquita as its brand name and introduced the Miss Chiquita character and her jingle. The Chiquita name was registered as a trademark in 1947.

By 1955 Chiquita's thriving operation was processing more than 2.7 billion pounds of fruit per year. In 1963 a new branding campaign introduced the blue Chiquita sticker with the slogan "This seal outside means the best inside." In the mid-1960s Chiquita expanded its importing business to Europe.

In 1970 Chiquita merged with AMK Corporation, which operated the John Morrell meat business, and changed its name to United Brands Company. United

Brands introduced a new slogan in 1989: "Chiquita. Quite possibly, the world's perfect food." In 1990 the company officially changed its name to Chiquita Brands International to take advantage of the global recognition of the Chiquita brand. The meat operation was sold in 1995, and Chiquita returned to the business it knew best: bananas and other produce. Chiquita opened the world's largest banana processing plant in Costa Rica in 1998. Three years later the company filed for Chapter 11 bankruptcy protection. Chiquita tried to regain its financial footing in the early 2000s. By 2011 it had reported four consecutive profitable years, but the numbers were still disappointing enough to cost CEO Fernando Aguirre his position in 2012.

BRAND ELEMENTS

- Chiquita started using its well-known blue stickers on its produce in 1963, a practice that continues to the present day.
- The company started using the brand name Chiquita near the end of World War II as part of a rebranding process.
- Since the mid-1990s Chiquita has positioned its products as an important part of a healthy lifestyle.

The Chiquita brand is best known by the blue stickers that are placed on its fruit. Introduced in 1963, the sticker has gone through a few image changes, but the color and size of the sticker have remained constant. The original Chiquita brand image was that of a female character in the shape of a banana and wearing a hat topped with fruit. That image was updated in 1998 to show Miss Chiquita as a woman wearing a fruit hat. Bananas remain the Chiquita product that consumers recognize most.

The company's name has its origins in a corporate rebranding that began near the end of World War II. The Chiquita brand name and the Miss Chiquita character were introduced in 1944. The word "chiquita" is Spanish for "little girl." The company name remained United Fruit Company, however. A formal change to Chiquita Brands International took place in 1990.

Chiquita has used several slogans since the brand was introduced. One of the longest-running slogans appeared alongside the introduction of the famous blue sticker in 1963: "This seal outside means the best inside." The slogan was altered in 1989 to "Chiquita. Quite possibly, the world's perfect fruit." As consumers in the United States became more health conscious in the late 20th century, Chiquita responded by promoting its fruits and vegetables as part of a balanced diet. In particular, the company positioned bananas as a heart-healthy food choice beginning in the mid-1990s. Continuing with that theme in 2012, Chiquita's corporate slogan then was "Improving world nutrition, because taste is not the only thing we care about."

BRAND IDENTITY

- During the mid-1940s United Fruit created the Chiquita brand and the banana mascot wearing a hat topped with fruit.
- The name Chiquita was introduced after World War II as part the United Fruit Company's first large-scale attempt to brand themselves as a source of fresh fruit, particularly bananas.
- Chiquita was certified by the American Heart Association in 1997, which furthered Chiquita's efforts to position itself as a healthy food company and bananas as a heart-healthy food.

While the brand identity of Chiquita has gone through various changes throughout the company's history, the company has always identified itself with fresh food, specifically with bananas. The United Fruit Company did little advertising or marketing before World War II, yet it succeeded and grew, expanding to multiple countries. During World War II, however, distribution for the company ceased because the British and American militaries had requisitioned all of the company's ships for the war effort. When the ships became available again near the end of the war, United Fruit began a comprehensive branding effort. Offering a fresh and contemporary image, the company created the Chiquita brand as well as a fun mascot, the banana, wearing a hat topped with fruit. That image remains largely intact today.

In addition to identifying itself as a reliable source of fresh fruit, Chiquita has further identified its products as healthy choices to coincide with the push towards healthy eating. Since the late 1990s, Chiquita has positioned bananas in particular as a heart-healthy fruit, going so far as to be certified by the American Heart Association in 1997. The company slogan used in 2012 was "Improving world nutrition, because taste is not the only thing we care about," emphasizing how Chiquita's products can help consumers enjoy a healthy lifestyle.

BRAND STRATEGY

- Chiquita made a name for itself with its fun mascot wearing a hat piled high with fruit.
- Global expansion has been a primary goal since the company was founded.
- Chiquita's ventures beyond the banana business include the acquisition of salad packager Fresh Express and teaming with France-based Danone to produce a line of beverages.
- Chiquita is still best known for its bananas.

The primary strategy for Chiquita has been spreading its products globally. Under the name United Fruit Company, it became one of the first large international fruit import/export businesses. Through the use of innovative technology, United Fruit was able to expand its business.

At the turn of the 20th century, the company was transporting its goods in ships that had been painted white in order to reflect the tropical sun and prevent the produce from spoiling as it traveled between countries. Refrigerated ships, first used in the early 20th century and improved over the years, allowed produce in transit to stay fresh longer than it ever had before. It was with all of this quality-assurance technology in mind that Chiquita introduced its famous blue sticker in 1963 along with the slogan "This seal outside means the best inside."

The company has attempted a few ventures beyond the banana business throughout its history. It merged with the John Morrell meat business in 1970 to extend its reach beyond fruits and vegetables. That lasted until 1995, when Chiquita sold the meats operation. Other ventures include the acquisition in 2005 of Fresh Express, the top seller of packaged salads in the United States. Fresh Express held a 40 percent retail market share and generated approximately US$1 billion in revenues. In 2010 Chiquita entered into a joint beverage venture with the French food company Danone, a world leader in dairy products.

In 1998 Chiquita opened the world's largest banana processing plant in Costa Rica, but the firm was forced to file for Chapter 11 bankruptcy protection just three years later. It placed the blame for its financial woes in part on stringent tariffs levied by the European Union. Overall, Chiquita has done best with its original business, selling bananas.

BRAND EQUITY

- Chiquita is the world's largest importer of bananas and holds 39 percent of the U.S. banana market.
- Chiquita does not deal in the same quantities of produce as its top competitor, Del Monte, and its profits are smaller than Del Monte's.
- Although it does not appear on Interbrand's or Brand Finance's list of most valuable brands, Chiquita is known as the premier banana brand.

Chiquita is the world's largest importer of bananas and holds 39 percent of the banana market in the United States. Top competitor Del Monte is the world's most successful fruit and vegetable company. Del Monte brought in annual net revenues of US$3.67 billion in 2011, compared to Chiquita's US$3.14 billion, but Chiquita also had higher overhead costs, and its overall profit was less than that of Del Monte. Chiquita also does not deal in the same quantity of produce that Del Monte does.

The Chiquita brand name has been the most valuable asset of the company since it was trademarked in the late 1940s. Chiquita is known as the premier banana brand. Chiquita does not, however, appear on the Interbrand's or Brand Finance's list of the world's most valuable brands.

BRAND AWARENESS

- Chiquita is best known for its bananas and for the blue stickers placed on them.
- Chiquita has used its high brand awareness to co-market with other companies, while at the same time increasing its own brand recall.
- The recent emphasis on healthier eating has given Chiquita opportunities to promote its produce and its brand in new markets overseas.

Chiquita began as the United Fruit Company in 1899. Its first product was bananas, and bananas remain the product that consumers most closely associate with the Chiquita brand. This lasting brand awareness has been aided by the familiar blue sticker bearing the Chiquita name. In fact, in a special multimedia campaign to promote both the Chiquita brand and the animated movie *Rio* (2011) domestically, marketers took advantage of the well-known sticker. In addition to an interactive Chiquita website with games, videos, and healthy recipes, the marketers placed a *Rio*-themed sticker on millions of Chiquita bananas to further generate awareness for the brand and the movie. According to a press release from PR Newswire, "within just six-week's time the media campaign had generated over 400 million impressions and over half a million unique visits to the microsite, vastly exceeding expectations." This success was due, in large part, to the familiarity of the Chiquita logo and the easily recognized blue sticker.

Globally, Chiquita also enjoys very high top-of-mind recall. Because Chiquita positions itself as a brand that offers consumers healthy foods, it is looking to expand its healthy food in a business-to-consumer (B2C) manner. According to an article by *just-food.com*, Chiquita is looking to do this by selling dried passion fruits in the regions where it has the highest brand recognition. According to the article, places like Scandinavia, Germany, Austria, Belgium, Holland, Italy, and Greece have a brand awareness of about 98 percent. Chiquita hopes to take advantage of the brand's momentum and springboard into new markets.

BRAND OUTLOOK

- Chiquita Brands International filed for Chapter 11 bankruptcy protection in 2001 and was able to restructure itself by 2002.
- Chiquita has continued to engage in ventures with other companies as a means of tapping new markets.
- Chiquita's most recent marketing efforts have positioned the brand as a healthy choice at a time when consumers have become more aware of nutrition.

Chiquita weathered some financial difficulties in the early years of the 21st century. In 2001 it filed for Chapter 11 bankruptcy protection because of outstanding debts. By 2002 Chiquita had restructured its debt, and in 2011 it reported a profit of US$57 million, an improvement over losses as great as US$47 million in previous years. Despite the brand's renewed profitability, earnings in 2012 were still disappointing, and CEO Fernando Aguirre was forced to step down.

The company has attempted to branch out beyond its well-known produce business. In 2005 it acquired Fresh Express, a packaged fruit and vegetable company known best for its salads. As of 2012, the deal had not gone well: salad sales had fallen 93 percent as capital expenditures increased. In 2010 Chiquita started a joint venture with Danone, the France-based global leader in dairy products, to create a beverage line.

Chiquita's most recent marketing efforts have promoted the health benefits of eating fruits and vegetables and have positioned Chiquita's products as good choices for a healthy lifestyle. Consumers' continued interest in establishing healthier lifestyles and eating habits suggests that Chiquita is likely to remain a popular brand in the produce business in the coming years.

FURTHER READING

Askew, Katy. "Just the Answer: Wouter Van Cauwenbergh, Chiquita Brands." *Just-food.com*, November 20, 2012. Accessed February 13, 2013. http://www.just-food.com/interview/wouter-van-cauwenbergh-chiquita-brands_id121267.aspx.

Chiquita Brands International. "The Chiquita Story". Accessed November 25, 2012. http://www.chiquita.com/Our-Company/The-Chiquita-Story.aspx.

"Chiquita Brands International." *Seeking Alpha*. Accessed November 24, 2012. http://seekingalpha.com/symbol/cqb/description.

"Fruit & Vegetable Markets in the US: Market Research Report." *IBISWorld*, August 2012. Accessed November 23, 2012. http://www.ibisworld.com/industry/default.aspx?indid=1045.

"Global Fruits & Vegetables Processing: Market Report." *IBISWorld*, June 2012. Accessed November 23, 2012. http://www.ibisworld.com/industry/global/global-fruit-vegetables-processing.html.

Portillo, Ely. "Surprise: Chiquita Brands CEO is on the way out." *Charlotte Observer*, August 8, 2012.

PR Newswire. "Chiquita Brands' Rio Multi-Channel Media Campaign Achieves Record Results." *Reuters*, June 29, 2011. Accessed February 13, 2013. http://www.reuters.com/article/2011/06/29/idUS124893+29-Jun-2011+PRN20110629.

Robinson, Matt, and Charles Mead. "Chiquita Slips on Salad as Cash Dwindles." *Bloomberg*, August 22, 2012.

CHRISTIAN DIOR

AT A GLANCE

Brand Synopsis: One of the most coveted and top-selling luxury brands in the world, Christian Dior is a consummate brand of glamour, elegance, and prestige.
Parent Company: Christian Dior S.A.
30, avenue Montaigne
Paris, 75008
France
www.dior-finance.com
Sector: Consumer Discretionary
Industry Group: Consumer Durables & Apparel
Performance: *Sales*—EUR24.63 billion (US$33.32 billion) (2011).
Principal Competitors: Chanel S.A.; Compagnie Financière Richemont S.A.; Gucci Group N.V.; Hermès International S.A.; Prada Holding N.V.

BRAND ORIGINS

- Christian Dior established his couture house in 1946 with financial backing from wealthy Frenchman Marcel Boussac.
- Christian Dior's first collection debuted in 1947; dubbed the "New Look," the designs emphasized and flattered the feminine figure.
- Within two years of its founding, the Christian Dior brand accounted for 75 percent of Paris fashion exports.

Christian Dior was born in 1905. As heir to a family fortune built on fertilizer and chemicals, Dior had little ambition to finish college, instead whiling away his 20s in Paris bars in the company of poets and artists. Dior dabbled in art, and in 1928 launched a gallery financed with a large gift from his father. However, heavy borrowing and the Great Depression combined to bankrupt the family business in the early 1930s, and Dior's family was forced to sell homes, furniture, jewelry, and other heirlooms.

Dior moved in with a friend in Paris and decided to use his artistic talents in the fashion industry. Beginning in the mid-1930s he designed on a freelance basis, selling drawings of hats and gowns to magazines and couture houses. He snared a full-time position with Robert Piguet's fashion design house in 1938, but was soon drafted into service for World War II. He returned to occupied Paris in 1941 and found work as a design assistant with the couture house of Lucien Lélong, designing custom-made dresses, suits, and ball gowns for some of the wealthiest women in the world.

In 1946 French fabric maven Marcel Boussac, then the nation's wealthiest man, offered to back Dior's launch of his own maison de couture. Christian Dior Ltd. started out that year with 85 employees, capital of FRF6 million, and "unlimited credit." In exchange for his creative genius, Dior negotiated a generous salary; a significant, though not controlling, stake in the firm; legal status as its leader; and one-third of pretax profits. It was quite an unusual arrangement, given Boussac's legendary need for control.

The designer introduced his first and most famous line, dubbed the "New Look" by Carmel Snow of *Harper's Bazaar*, in 1947. The collection was a striking refutation of the war's deprivation: Whereas rationing restricted the amount of fabric used in a dress or skirt, Dior used an extravagant 20 yards of only the finest fabrics in his long, wide skirts. With help from elaborate undergarments, the dresses emphasized the feminine figure, from the tiniest of waists to peplum- or tulle-enhanced hips and tight-fitting bodices, often with deep décolletage. The line was an immediate and nearly complete success, garnering a clientele ranging from European royalty to Hollywood stars.

Women who could not afford haute couture copied it at home. Soon enough, and to Dior's chagrin, knock-off artists did the "dirty work" for them. Eventually, the maison fought fire with fire, establishing a ready-to-wear line of somewhat less-expensive versions of the couture line. In 1948 the first Dior boutique with the ready-to-wear line opened in New York City.

In 1949 alone, Christian Dior fashions constituted 75 percent of Paris fashion exports, and 5 percent of all French export revenues. Dior opened a New York outlet before the end of the year and established London operations in 1952. From the outset, fully half of the company's sales were made in the United States. By the end of 1953, the company had operations in Mexico, Canada, Cuba, and Italy.

After Dior's parent company, Boussac, declared bankruptcy, a group of investors led by builder and real estate developer Bernard Arnault acquired it in 1984. Under Arnault, the Dior brand became the cornerstone of one of the world's largest and most important fashion companies. The new leader formed Christian Dior S.A. as a holding company for the fashion house, then used the holding company as a vehicle to purchase a controlling stake in Moët Hennessy Louis Vuitton (LVMH) in 1990. In 1995 Christian Dior Couture became a wholly owned subsidiary of Christian Dior S.A.

BRAND ELEMENTS

- The Christian Dior logo is a prestigious trademark, symbolizing the luxury, refinement and style of the brand.
- Small variations on the Dior logo over the years inform the buyer from which collection the item is from, what year it was created, and where it was manufactured.
- The Christian Dior logo is a wordmark, a text-only logo that is a visual symbol of the brand.

The Christian Dior logo is a prestigious trademark, symbolizing some of the world's most coveted apparel and accessories. The elegant wordmark is presented in all black lettering, representative of the style and refinement of the brand. The Dior logo is distinctive in its simplicity and has become synonymous with luxury and style.

Over the years, Christian Dior has used multiple variations on its logo. While each iteration remains stylistically similar, each variation apprises the buyer from which collection the item is from, what year it was created, and where it was manufactured.

BRAND IDENTITY

- Christian Dior died unexpectedly from a heart attack in 1957 at age 57.
- Christian Dior's young assistant, Yves Saint Laurent, was promoted to lead designer after Dior's death, but left the brand when he was drafted into the armed services in 1960.
- The popularity of Christian Dior's early designs made him a virtual global dictator of fashion.

Christian Dior's untimely death in 1957 left the house in chaos. The company considered shuttering the worldwide operations, but neither Dior's licensees nor the French fashion industry, which owed 50 percent of its export volume to the House of Dior, would consider it. The challenge to the house would be to find a new lead designer who could guide and promote the brand without completely altering its identity and status.

Yves Saint Laurent, a 22-year-old assistant whom Dior had hired just two years previously, was promoted to lead designer. The young designer's 1958 floaty trapeze-dress line was successful, but his 1960 "bohemian" look met heavy criticism from the press, especially the influential fashion industry magazine *Women's Wear Daily*. When Saint Laurent was drafted into the armed services that year, Marc Bohan succeeded him as lead designer. Bohan, another protégé of Dior, had been hired to head the London outlet shortly before the founder's death. Bohan would go on to serve Dior until 1989. *Contemporary Fashion*'s Rebecca Arnold credited Bohan with keeping the House of Dior "at the forefront of fashion while still producing wearable, elegant clothes."

In 1989 Italian designer Gianfranco Ferré was hired to succeed Bohan as the maison's artistic director. Ferré broke from the romantic and flirtatious traditions set by Dior and Bohan, opting instead to continue in his own well-established vein with a collection described in *Contemporary Fashion* as "refined, sober and strict."

In 1996 British designer John Galliano was appointed to succeed Ferré as Dior's creative head. Galliano was instrumental in reviving Dior's image—stirring up continued controversy with such events as a "homeless show," featuring models dressed in newspapers and paper bags, and an "S&M show." The resulting uproar helped stimulate the Dior brand, sending sales soaring.

Christian Dior stayed with the "New Look" for seven years, becoming a virtual global dictator of hem lines and lengths in the process. He understood that women were craving glamour and he delivered a return to luxury.

Subsequent designers have made their mark on the brand, shaping and transforming it with each collection.

The Dior brand continues to invoke a sense of splendor and indulgence. A mix of modernity and heritage, with a sophisticated style, creativity, femininity, and inventiveness, imbues the brand and brings with it a devoted audience. The Dior brand represents enduring luxury throughout generations.

BRAND STRATEGY

- A licensing program begun in 1950 as a marketing ploy put the Christian Dior name on hundreds of accessories; licensing of Dior products would eventually become more restrictive to protect the integrity of the brand.
- Christian Dior "J'adore" perfume, created in 1999, is one of the best-selling fragrances of all time.
- A small afterthought in original Dior collections, purses and handbags would become some of the most desired and iconic pieces in the brand's collections.

A licensing program begun in 1950 put the Christian Dior name on a slew of accessories, including ties, hosiery, furs, hats, gloves, handbags, jewelry, lingerie, and scarves. While denounced by Dior's colleagues as a cheapening of the high-fashion industry's image, this licensing scheme would become a cornerstone of the company's long-term success and be copied by other fashion houses. As brand integrity became harder to maintain, the company eventually opted for quality and exclusivity over quantity and accessibility, tightly controlling any remaining licenses.

Parfums Christian Dior was launched in 1947, with the immensely successful "Miss Dior"; "J'adore" perfume, introduced in 1999, is one of the best-selling fragrances of all time. Dior lipstick was introduced in 1955 and would eventually expand to include a full line of beauty and skin care products. Shoes were added to the Dior design portfolio in 1953 and Baby Dior was established in 1967. A small afterthought in original Dior collections, purses and handbags would become some of the most desired and iconic pieces in the brand's collections.

Christian Dior Couture had built its fame on women's fashions. In 2001, however, the company gambled that it could become equally famous in the area of men's fashion, launching Dior Homme. Although Dior had licensed the production of men's clothing for decades (introducing men's ties in 1950), customers tended to be older. New designs for Dior Homme involved sleek tailoring, led by trim suits and skinny jeans. The line was becoming a major player among a younger audience, creating a new expression of masculinity. In 2003 Dior phased out its traditional menswear line.

BRAND EQUITY

- In 2012 Christian Dior had a brand value of EUR10.6 billion according to Brand Institute.
- Christian Dior ranked at number 322 in *Fortune's* "Global 500" and 2012 and at number 210 in the "Forbes 2000" and 2011.
- Christian Dior consistently ranks near the top of lists of Europe's most valuable brands.

Brand Institute ranked Christian Dior at number 91 in its "2012 Top 100 Brand Corporations Worldwide" with a brand value of EUR10.6 billion. The same brand valuation by Eurobrand placed Christian Dior at 32nd in "Europe's Most Valuable Brand Corporations" in 2011. *Brand Finance* placed Christian Dior's 2012 brand value at US$2.54 billion.

Fortune ranked the brand at number 322 in its "Global 500 2012," with revenues of US$34.24 billion. In 2011 *Forbes* ranked the company at number 210 in its annual "Forbes 2000," with a market value of US$28.3 billion. *Forbes* also rated Christian Dior 88th in its "World's Most Innovative Companies, 2011," and first in its "World's Largest Apparel and Accessories Companies Overall, 2011."

The *Financial Times* ranked Christian Dior fourth in its ranking of "Europe's Most Valuable Personal Goods Companies, 2011," and seventh in its "World's Most Valuable Personal Goods Companies, 2011," according the company a market value of US$25.62 billion. Christian Dior also ranked 1st in the "Largest Consumer Products Companies in Europe, 2010," with sales of US$25.38 billion. The *Financial Times* also ranked Dior third, behind only luxury brands Porsche and Hermes, in its ranking of the "World's Top Brands by Brand Momentum, 2007."

BRAND AWARENESS

- Christian Dior is one of the most coveted luxury brands worldwide, with exclusive boutiques in over 35 countries.
- Christian Dior has emerged as one of the top luxury brands in both China and Russia.
- Celebrities become living advertisements and raise brand awareness every time they are photographed wearing Christian Dior clothing.

Christian Dior operates more than 235 boutiques in over 35 countries, including China, Australia, the United States, Hong Kong, Singapore, Switzerland, Italy, Thailand, Spain, South Korea, and India; Japan alone has 26 boutiques. Celebrities, royalty, and the affluent regularly grace red carpets around the world draped in Christian Dior couture. Such a significant global presence dramatically increases awareness of the brand. As representative of its brand recognition, in 2012 Christian Dior was the eighth most searched for luxury brand in China and the 14th in Russia. In 2009 Dior was the second leading fragrance brand in China, behind only Chanel.

BRAND OUTLOOK

- One of the brand's greatest strengths is its name; Christian Dior is one of the most recognizable luxury brand names in the world and is synonymous with exceptional craftsmanship.
- A growing number of millionaires around the globe fuel profits for the brand, even as a range of countries struggle with an economic recession.
- Counterfeit merchandise is a continuing threat to the Christian Dior brand; the company has employees devoted to searching the internet for illegal use of the trademark.

In the highly competitive upscale market of luxury products, Christian Dior's greatest strength is its name; Dior is one of the most recognizable brands in the luxury market. Consumers equate the Dior name with a distinguished craftsmanship that is reflected in artistic design and exceptional textiles and leathers. Christian Dior's strong brand equity provides the company with an edge over its competitors. Coupled with its wide market presence, the brand continues to rise to the top of the luxury market.

Even as the world reeled from a major recession, the Dior brand chose to go more upscale. In 2008 it introduced the Dior mobile phone, priced at US$5,400. In 2009 Dior introduced the Trente bag, named after the company's address at 30 avenue Montaigne, with a price tag of US$2,300. Its Lady Dior bags, which now started at US$1,400 and never sold at a discount, posted double-digit gains. Dior's revenue explosion reflected the increasing demand for luxury items by the growing number of millionaires around the world.

John Galliano was fired from Dior in 2011 amid scandal over anti-Semitic remarks the designer made in a Paris bar. In 2012 Raf Simons was named creative director for the house. At runway shows in Paris in 2013, the designer was lauded for his newest collections, with many critics entrusting Simons to rejuvenate the brand the way Christian Dior did with his New Look back in 1947. The allure of the Dior brand coupled with the talent of the designers is key to the house remaining a leader in the luxury market.

Counterfeit merchandise is a continuing threat to the Christian Dior brand. Clothing, leather goods, fragrances, accessories, and cosmetics sold by counterfeiters introduce low-quality merchandise bearing the Dior logo into the marketplace. The inferior products not only harm company profits but also, perhaps more importantly, the allure of the brand and the confidence of consumers in its products. Christian Dior actively pursues threats in these areas, winning pivotal trademark lawsuits against eBay and other companies.

FURTHER READING

Christian Dior. "Annual Report." April 30, 2012. Accessed February 8, 2013. http://www.dior-finance.com/en/pdf/20121005-Rapport-annuel-au-30-avril-2012.pdf.

"Christian Dior S.A." *International Directory of Company Histories*. Ed. Tina Grant. Vol. 110. Detroit, MI: St. James Press, 2010.

Claridge, Peter. "Move over Burberry, Dior Becomes the Top Luxury Brand on Social Media." *Unmetric*, November 7, 2012. Accessed February 8, 2013. http://blog.unmetric.com/2012/11/move-over-burberry-dior-becomes-the-top-luxury-brand-on-social-media.

Diderich, Joelle, and Cynthia Martens. "Italian, French Fashion Industries Fight Back against Counterfeits." *Women's Wear Daily*, May 23, 2012.

"Dior Notes 2012 Rebound in US Luxury Market." *Chicago Tribune*, January 21, 2013.

Horyn, Cathy. "Galliano Case Tests Dior Brand's Future." *New York Times*, March 1, 2011.

Leviste, Larry. "Raf Simons Rises to the Challenge at Dior." *Philippine Daily Inquirer*, January 25, 2013.

Menkes, Suzy. "Battle of the Champions." *New York Times*, September 26, 2012.

CHRYSLER

AT A GLANCE

Brand Synopsis: As a leading automotive brand, Chrysler provides consumers with luxury "Imported from Detroit."
Parent Company: Chrysler Group L.L.C.
PO Box 21-8004
Auburn Hills, Michigan 48321-8004
United States
http://www.chryslergroupllc.com
Sector: Consumer Discretionary
Industry Group: Automobiles & Components
Performance: *Market share*—11.4 percent (2012). *Sales*—US$55.0 billion (2011).
Principal Competitors: Hyundai Motor Company Ltd.; Renault S.A.; AB Volvo; Ford Motor Co.; Volkswagen AG; General Motors Co.; Nissan Motor Company Ltd.

BRAND ORIGINS

- Chrysler Corporation was established by Walter Percy Chrysler in 1920.
- The introduction of the minivan in 1984 and the acquisition three years later of American Motors Corporation and its Jeep brand positioned Chrysler for resurgence in the 1990s.
- Daimler-Benz and Chrysler merged in November 1998, forming DaimlerChrysler AG.
- Daimler sold 80.1 percent of Chrysler to Cerberus Capital Management in August of 2007 for US$7.4 billion.
- Fiat gained majority control of Chrysler in 2011 during its post-bankruptcy restructuring.

The story of the Chrysler Corporation began in 1920, when the company's founder, Walter Percy Chrysler, resigned his position as president of Buick and vice president of General Motors (GM) over policy differences with GM's founder, William C. Durant. Chrysler was soon asked by a group of New York bankers to restore the Maxwell Motor Corporation to solvency. In the process, he designed a new Maxwell model, the Chrysler Six. First exhibited in 1924, the car was an immediate success, and before year's end the company sold 32,000 cars at a profit of more than US$4 million. In 1925 Chrysler renamed the company Chrysler Corporation.

By 1927 the Chrysler Corporation had become the fifth largest company in the industry. Dodge became a division of Chrysler in July 1928. Overnight, the size of the company increased fivefold. Soon thereafter, Chrysler introduced the low-priced Plymouth and the DeSoto.

Under Walter Chrysler's leadership the company survived the Great Depression far better than most in the industry and remained on sound financial standing until well into the 1940s. During the early 1950s poor financial performance prompted the company to develop international markets for its cars. Additionally, management was centralized, and the role of the engineering department was redefined.

When these reforms proved ineffective, the company eventually consolidated its Chrysler and Plymouth car divisions and closed some unproductive plants. Sales were enhanced by improving the quality of the Chrysler automobile, introducing the best warranty the industry had yet seen, and instituting a more aggressive marketing policy.

Complex and highly charged negotiations eventually saved Chrysler from bankruptcy in 1978. The federal government agreed to guarantee loans up to US$1.5 billion, provided Chrysler raised US$2 billion on its own. Politicians could not justify such a massive bailout, however, without changes in Chrysler's management. The charismatic Lee Iacocca took over, presiding over Chrysler's comeback. The Chrysler Loan Guarantee Bill passed the U.S. Congress on December 27, 1979, and guaranteed US$1.2 billion in loans to Chrysler.

In August 1983 Chrysler was able to pay off the government loan guarantees seven years early. Chrysler's road to recovery was a difficult one, demanding the closure of several plants and the reduction of the company's workforce. Two key developments in the 1980s helped form the foundation for a 1990s resurgence. These were the introduction of the minivan in 1984 and the acquisition three years later of American Motors Corporation and its Jeep brand for US$1.2 billion.

Daimler-Benz and Chrysler merged in November 1998, creating DaimlerChrysler AG in a US$37 billion deal. Daimler sold 80.1 percent of Chrysler to Cerberus Capital Management in August 2007 for US$7.4 billion. Financial difficulties, exacerbated by the economic recession, resulted in Chrysler receiving roughly US$6.6 billion in government financing in 2009. Italian car maker Fiat gained majority control of the company in 2011 during a post-bankruptcy restructuring of Chrysler, and once again the company was foreign-owned.

BRAND ELEMENTS

- The Chrysler brand has been associated with several different logos since 1924, including an early medallion-like logo that was used through the mid-1950s.
- The iconic Pentastar design, which would become synonymous with the Chrysler brand, was created in 1961 by Lippincott & Margulies Inc.
- In 2011 Chrysler's award-winning "Born of Fire" Super Bowl commercial introduced the "Imported from Detroit" tagline.

The Chrysler brand has been associated with several different logos since 1924, when the Chrysler Six was represented by a ribbon-style logo adorned with two thunderbolt-like "Z"s that honored engineer Fred Zeder. This was temporarily replaced by the image of an oak tree with the tagline, "From Many Roots, Standardized Quality." Ultimately a medallion-like logo was adopted, of which different iterations would be used through the mid-1950s.

The movement toward sleeker, futuristic automotive designs resulted in the development of the Forward Look in 1955 by Chrysler's Virgil Exner. This new look included a logo featuring two sideways chevrons. Within two years, the symbol appeared on television advertisements, in printed collateral, and on vehicles.

The image that would ultimately become synonymous with the Chrysler brand was created in 1961. The Pentastar design, created by Lippincott & Margulies Inc., was chosen from a sea of 800 potential logos to represent all of the company's brands. The symbol consisted of five independent triangles separated by a five-pointed star, comprising a pentagon shape.

Although some associated the five-pointed star with Chrysler's five company divisions at the time, this was not the intent of the logo. According to an August 6, 2007, Chrysler Corporation news release, "Townsend wanted a symbol with a strong, classic look that would be instantly recognizable, but was universal—without written words—allowing it to be used in all countries and across many cultures." Lippincott & Margulies executive Robert Stanley is credited with creating the logo and Pentastar name.

In addition to appearing on vehicle hood-ornaments and corporate stationery, a two-story-high glass version of the Pentastar was created to adorn Chrysler's Auburn Hills, Michigan, headquarters in 1996. Chrysler revived its medallion logo that year, and following the creation of DaimlerChrysler, a pair of silver wings was added to the design. This effectively replaced the Pentastar. However, in 2007 Chrysler reintroduced a modernized, 3-D version of the iconic Pentastar design.

In 2011 Chrysler's award-winning "Born of Fire" Super Bowl commercial, which featured Detroit rapper Eminem, introduced the "Imported from Detroit" tagline. The phrase communicated the fact that the Chrysler brand delivers domestically produced luxury. In conjunction with the commercial, the patriotic tagline appealed to consumers by evoking images of attitude and hard work.

BRAND IDENTITY

- The availability of domestically produced luxury to the majority is a key element of Chrysler's brand identity.
- Chrysler's patriotic "Imported from Detroit" tagline has appealed to consumers by evoking images of attitude and hard work.
- Chrysler's "Imported from Detroit" tagline was introduced in conjunction with its award-winning 2011 "Born of Fire" Super Bowl commercial.

In a June 15, 2012, Benzinga.com news release, Chrysler describes its brand the following way: "The spirit of hard work and the belief that luxury shouldn't be a luxury. Earning your place without forgetting where you're from. Luxury and quality conceived and developed domestically. That's what the Chrysler brand and its vehicles are all about."

All of these elements were introduced in Chrysler's award-winning 2011 "Born of Fire" Super Bowl commercial. Featuring Detroit rapper Eminem, the commercial introduced the brand's "Imported from Detroit" tagline. The phrase communicated the fact that the Chrysler brand delivers domestically produced luxury to the majority, not just to those with the means to purchase exotic or luxury vehicles. In conjunction with the commercial, the patriotic tagline appealed to consumers by evoking images of attitude and hard work.

In the September 10, 2012, issue of *just-auto.com*, Chrysler Brand Head Saad Chehab elaborated on Chrysler's brand identity: "Chrysler is and will continue to be distinctly American, and part of what it means to be American is to keep fighting, to never give up. There's always more to be done, Chrysler will continue fighting, and defining American luxury. That's what it means to be 'Imported from Detroit.'"

BRAND STRATEGY

- After Chrysler lost much of its luster with consumers, a powerful brand strategy that tapped directly into the patriotic spirit of consumers resulted in Chrysler's resurgence in the United States, where it generates the vast majority of its sales.
- A turning point for the Chrysler brand was its award-winning 2011 "Born of Fire" Super Bowl commercial, which featured Detroit rapper Eminem and introduced the brand's "Imported from Detroit" tagline.
- The Chrysler brand has made tremendous progress in Mexico, Chrysler Group's second-largest international market behind Canada.

By 2009 Chrysler's image had lost much of its luster with consumers. As *New York Times* writer Bill Vlasic explained in an April 27, 2012, article, "consumers shunned its tired portfolio of mediocre cars and gas-guzzling trucks and sport utility vehicles." Chrysler's resurgence from bankruptcy under the ownership of Fiat has been fueled by product improvements, including better fuel efficiency and reliability, as well as more luxurious features. However, a powerful brand strategy has played an equally important role in Chrysler's success.

After falling 36 percent in 2009, Chrysler Group's share of the U.S. new-vehicle market soared 26 percent under the watch of marketing head Olivier Francois, reaching an 11.4 percent market share by the end of 2012. The turnaround was driven by a brand strategy that tapped directly into the patriotic spirit of consumers in the United States, where Chrysler generates the vast majority of its sales. Francois reinvigorated an iconic brand while also restoring faith in Detroit, which many perceived in a negative light.

The turning point for the Chrysler brand was its award-winning 2011 "Born of Fire" Super Bowl commercial. Featuring Detroit rapper Eminem, the commercial introduced the brand's "Imported from Detroit" tagline. The phrase communicated the fact that the Chrysler brand delivers domestically produced luxury to the majority, not just to those with the means to purchase exotic or luxury vehicles. In conjunction with the commercial, the patriotic tagline appealed to consumers by evoking images of attitude and hard work. In the December 3, 2012, issue of *Automotive News*, automotive consultant Steve Wilhite commented: "[Francois] did a wonderful job of telling better stories, bigger stories and more powerful stories that resonate with America in a very important way, changing the trajectory of how people conversed about the brand."

Chrysler kept the patriotic momentum from "Born of Fire" going with additional captivating Super Bowl ads that created tremendous buzz, especially in social media. Following a 2012 ad featuring actor Clint Eastwood, in 2013 Chrysler unveiled a commercial for the 2013 RAM 1500 pickup truck that featured the essay, "So God Made a Farmer," from the late radio commentator, Paul Harvey. In addition, a spot named "Whole Again" lifted up the Jeep brand while paying tribute to the U.S. military.

In a February 5, 2013, *Detroit News* article, Chrysler Ram Truck Division President Fred Diaz reflected on how the company had utilized the Super Bowl to connect the brand with consumers: "When you look at the first spot we did—'Imported from Detroit' with Eminem—that was all about helping the city of Detroit. The following year, with Clint Eastwood, it was about motivating America and America's will to not give up despite all the tough times that we've been through with the economy. Now, it's all about cause marketing and giving back, because we don't forget where we were and where we've come from."

Beyond the United States, the Chrysler brand has made tremendous progress in Mexico, Chrysler Group's second-largest international market behind Canada. In 2012 the company's sales increased 7 percent over the previous year. This was accomplished through targeted marketing campaigns and the introduction of popular vehicle features. For example, the Chrysler Town & Country became the first minivan in the Mexican market to offer a Blu-ray entertainment system. Greater focus on safety features resulted in 12 Chrysler vehicles receiving Safety Pick status from the Insurance Institute for Highway Safety.

BRAND EQUITY

- *Automotive News* reported that Chrysler ranked 13th among the 20 best-selling car brands in 2012.
- In 2012 the Chrysler Town & Country minivan received the Polk Automotive Loyalty Award for the 11th consecutive year, reflecting strong levels of brand loyalty.
- The financial value of the Chrysler brand is enhanced by a significant body of related intellectual property, and research and development expenditures which totaled US$1.67 billion in 2011 alone.

Chrysler's strong brand equity is evident in its high placement in a number of leading rankings. For example, in 2012 *Automotive News* reported that Chrysler ranked 13th among the 20 best-selling car brands, propelled by a 39 percent sales increase. This was a significant improvement from the previous year, when the company ranked 17th. It also was in 2012 that Chrysler's Dodge/Ram brand was included on *focus2move's* ranking of the world's leading 25 car brands.

Chrysler has benefited from strong levels of brand loyalty. In 2012 the Chrysler Town & Country minivan received the Polk Automotive Loyalty Award for the 11th consecutive year, which was a testament to its good standing with consumers, especially families with younger children. The achievement was reflected in the Test of Ownership advertising campaign, developed by Wieden + Kennedy.

The financial value of the Chrysler brand is enhanced by the significant body of related intellectual property, including patents and trademarks pertaining to automotive designs and technologies, that Chrysler has produced. In 2011 alone Chrysler devoted US$1.67 billion to research and development. This was an increase from US$1.5 billion in 2010 and US$1.1 billion in 2009.

BRAND AWARENESS

- Chrysler was among the best overall car brands in the 2013 Car Brand Perception Survey conducted by the Consumer Reports National Research Center.
- Between late 2009 and mid-2012 the Chrysler brand saw its overall loyalty rate double, according to data from R.L. Polk.
- All Chrysler Group brands achieved better year-over-year performance in J.D. Power and Associates' 2012 U.S. Automotive Performance, Execution and Layout study.

The Chrysler brand has long benefited from strong levels of top-of-mind awareness. In 2013 Chrysler was among the best overall car brands in the 2013 Car Brand Perception Survey conducted by the Consumer Reports National Research Center. The results measured consumer perception in the categories of environmentally friendly/green, design/style, safety, value, quality, and technology/innovation.

Between late 2009 and mid-2012 the Chrysler brand saw its overall loyalty rate increase significantly. The percentage of Chrysler owners who purchased an additional Chrysler vehicle doubled, climbing from 15 percent to 30 percent, according to data from R.L. Polk. This increase in loyalty was also evident with specific models, such as the Chrysler Town & Country minivan. In 2012 the vehicle received the Polk Automotive Loyalty Award for the 11th consecutive year.

Another measure of the awareness surrounding the Chrysler brand was its performance in J.D. Power and Associates' 2012 U.S. Automotive Performance, Execution, and Layout (APEAL) study. The study evaluated consumer gratification with new vehicles, via measurements of more than 80 different attributes. All Chrysler Group brands achieved better scores over the previous year. The study acknowledged consumer awareness of Chrysler's improvement in several areas, including performance, quality, and design.

BRAND OUTLOOK

- Chrysler's domestic market share totaled 11.4 percent in 2012, up two points from 2010, while the market share of Ford and General Motors remained flat that year.
- The tagline, "Imported from Detroit," held new meaning as Chrysler Group was gearing up to expand its brands internationally, including the development of an entry-level Jeep for foreign markets.
- In 2013 some analysts were concerned that Chrysler's new product plans were somewhat sparse, posing potential problems as competition intensified from domestic and Japanese competitors.

The Chrysler brand was on strong footing in early 2013. While General Motors saw its 2012 sales increase 3.7 percent, and Ford achieved a 4.7 percent increase, Chrysler Group's domestic sales rose 20.6 percent. That year Chrysler Group's earnings soared to US$1.7 billion.

By 2012 Chrysler's domestic market share totaled 11.4 percent, up two points from 2010. By comparison, the market share of Ford and General Motors remained flat in 2012. Although Fiat had stepped in to rescue Chrysler Group from its financial troubles, by 2013 it was the Chrysler family of brands that was helping Fiat maintain financial health as that company faced poor sales and overcapacity in Europe.

The tagline, "Imported from Detroit," held new meaning as Chrysler Group was gearing up to expand its brands internationally. One component of this strategy was the development of an affordable, entry-level Jeep for the international market. In support of this, Chrysler was laying the groundwork to produce Jeeps in China and also at an underused Fiat facility in Italy.

Despite these positive factors, some analysts were concerned that Chrysler's new product pipeline was somewhat sparse. Fiat's ability to provide the financial resources necessary to develop new Chrysler products was limited by its own need to withstand challenging conditions in the European market and to continue developing vehicles under nameplates such as Alpha Romeo. As the company's competitors scrambled to catch up, some analysts argued that a lack of new products could have a negative impact. In addition to domestic competition, Japanese automakers such as Honda and Toyota were expected to turn up the heat after recovering from the tsunami and earthquake that disrupted their operations during 2011.

FURTHER READING

"DaimlerChrysler AG." *International Directory of Company Histories*. Ed. Tina Grant and Miranda H. Ferrara. Vol. 64. Detroit, MI: St. James Press, 2006.

"'The Dark Knight Rises' and Chrysler Present: Imported from Gotham City." Benzinga.com, June 15, 2012.

Halpert, Julie. "A Turnaround Born of Fire; How Frenchman Olivier Francois Restored Motor City Pride at Bankrupt Chrysler with Ad Campaigns That Resonated across America." *Automotive News*, December 3, 2012.

Hoffman, Bryce G. "Chrysler Super Bowl Ads Again Create Big Buzz." *Detroit News*, February 5, 2013.

"Pentastar Returns as Symbol for the New Chrysler." Chrysler.com, August 6, 2007. Accessed February 3, 2013. http://media.chrysler.com.

"US: Chrysler Brand—Offering Ultra Exotic Features to the Masses." *just-auto.com*, September 10, 2012.

Vlasic, Bill. "In Unlikely Comeback, Chrysler Is Outgaining Bigger Detroit Rivals." *New York Times*, January 15, 2013.

———. "With New Vehicles and a Comeback Story, Chrysler Is Soaring." *New York Times*, April 27, 2012.

CISCO

AT A GLANCE

Brand Synopsis: A provider of networking technologies, Cisco distinguishes itself by making the company's role in facilitating human communications central to its brand identity.
Parent Company: Cisco Systems, Inc.
170 West Tasman Dr.
San Jose, California 95134
United States
http://www.cisco.com
Sector: Information Technology
Industry Group: Technology Hardware & Equipment
Performance: *Market share*—Ethernet switches, 65.1 percent; 10-gigabit Ethernet switching equipment, 69.4 percent worldwide (2012). *Sales*—US$46.1 billion (2012).
Principal Competitors: Alcatel-Lucent; Aruba Networks; Brocade Communications Systems; Hewlett-Packard; Huawei Technologies; IBM; Juniper Networks

BRAND ORIGINS

- Cisco Systems was created by Stanford University employees who developed technologies to connect computers on campus.
- With the advent of venture capital funding, Cisco Systems underwent significant management changes in the late 1980s.
- After becoming a publicly traded company in 1990, Cisco continued to grow, eventually becoming the world's leading networking firm.

Cisco Systems—originally spelled with a lowercase "c"—was formed to commercialize technologies developed at Stanford University to support the school's campus-wide computer network. Designed by Leonard Bosack and Sandy Lerner, the network was created to allow computers to communicate with each other despite being in separate offices and to enable computers to share resources without needing to exchange physical storage media such as floppy disks. Bosack and Lerner initially designed and built routers, testing the hardware in their house before using it on campus. The project also integrated Stanford's various local networks into a single network. Ultimately, it would connect 5,000 computers across a 16-square-mile campus.

The multiprotocol router Bosack and Lerner developed with two colleagues could work with many different types of computers. This was different from networking solutions available at the time, when hardware and software were not interchangeable and a single vendor's networking hardware could only run using that same company's software.

As word spread about the development of the Stanford network, Bosack and Lerner were frequently asked to share their networking expertise; however, Stanford University did not want to license the technology. Lerner and Bosack quit their jobs and launched Cisco from their home in 1984. The name is a truncation of "San Francisco." The company sold its first router in 1986. In its first month, Cisco was awarded contracts worth more than US$200,000. Stanford University demanded

US$11 million in licensing fees but reportedly settled for a tenth of that amount along with free product and tech support in perpetuity. Lerner and Bosack hired friends and neighbors in return for deferred salaries or stock options. Among its first customers were organizations such as Rutgers University and HP Labs. The couple financed Cisco by mortgaging their home and accruing credit card debt.

"At that point I think we were—Cisco was doing, I think, a quarter million, maybe 350,000 a month without a professional sales staff and without an official conventionally recognized marketing campaign," said Bosack. "So it wasn't a bad business just right then. And so I think just for the novelty of it, the folks at Sequoia [Capital] listened to us."

With the arrival of venture capital funding in late 1987, management changes in the company became rampant. John Morgridge was hired as chief executive officer. Continued discord with Morgridge forced Lerner to leave in August 1990. Bosack soon followed. The couple reportedly sold the two-thirds stake they had in Cisco, worth approximately US$170 million. (According to *Forbes.com*, Bosack and Lerner made approximately US$112 million and donated roughly three-quarters of their wealth to philanthropic causes, including the Bosack/Kruger Foundation, which they founded in 1990.)

Ralph Gorin, hand-selected by Bosack as his replacement at Stanford, said Cisco created "a very clever way to sell software by the simple expedient of concealing the software inside hardware.... They also had the benefit of being in an environment that was on the cutting edge of applying networking on a large scale."

Cisco became a public company in 1990. The next year, John Chambers joined the firm as its chief executive officer. At the time its sales were roughly US$70 million. Cisco grew into one of the most popular technology stocks of the decade. In 2011 it was the world's leading network technology provider, with revenues exceeding US$43 billion for the fiscal year.

BRAND ELEMENTS

- The Cisco Systems name was simplified to Cisco in 2006.
- The company's bridge logo represents the connections its technologies help customers make.
- Cisco's brand concept has continued to subtly evolve in order to reflect the possibilities inherent in adopting new communications technologies.

Although Cisco founders Leonard Bosack and Sandy Lerner knew what their fledgling technology company's business was from the outset, a brand identity was slow to develop. Not until they made a trip to Sacramento to register their business did it occur to them that San Francisco and its Golden Gate Bridge encapsulated and conveyed that ideal well. The lowercased "cisco" was used as the company's name, and the bridge became its logo.

The company's bridge logo has undergone gradual transformations. The original logo of a bridge enclosed in a box was designed in-house. The logo was redesigned in 1996 and then altered again by Joe Finocchiaro and Jerry Kuyper in 2006 as part of the larger "Welcome to the Human Network" marketing campaign and corporate rebranding initiative. At this time, Cisco Systems became known as simply Cisco. The designers sought to retain the bridge symbol but were tasked with making the logo easier to reproduce and to align with the new branding, which was intended to extend the corporate brand into the consumer market and portray the company as a conduit to "the gateway of possibilities."

The company was rebranded in 2011 with a new slogan: "Together we are the human network." Autumn Truong, Cisco's senior manager of global marketing and corporate communications, explained that, although the wording change was subtle, the new slogan better described the "significant role in bringing these human connections together" that video plays in communication. Truong said that the rebranding campaign communicated "a broader, more human vision of what the network can offer—a richer, deeper experience of being together."

The bridge continues to be central in the corporate logo and is an important brand-image concept for Cisco, representing the connections its technologies help customers make.

BRAND IDENTITY

- Despite any transformations in Cisco's message, the Golden Gate Bridge remains central to its brand identity.
- In 2000 Cisco began increasing its mass media advertising, including event sponsorships, to reinforce and build its brand.
- When brand repositioning has been necessary, Cisco has gradually changed its message and identity to carefully reinforce and build its brand.

Cisco sells hardware, software, and services. It has long been challenged with communicating its brand such that it differentiates its products from competitors' networking offerings. The company created its brand identity around San Francisco and a Golden Gate Bridge-based logo, the latter of which conveys an image of Cisco as a conduit to "the gateway of possibilities." Despite changes in and the evolution of the company and the networking technology market, the bridge remains Cisco's central brand-image concept.

The market in which Cisco participates is fluid; the technologies available for networking and communication continue to change and converge. In such conditions, Cisco's competitors can include resellers, distributors, and even previous strategic partners. In 2006, for example, the company needed to reposition its identity to adequately reflect its move into video and network-collaboration technologies, which included purchasing Scientific-Atlanta, a specialist in set-top boxes and video systems integration. Cisco sought to change its branding slowly over time, being mindful to maintain its reputation among enterprise users while courting new users. One means it employed to reinforce this new direction was philanthropic in nature, centered on the idea of building a better world with technology. Cisco employed a 2006 marketing campaign with the tagline of the "Human Network" to achieve this transition. In addition, the emergence and adoption of technology standards, such as Internet protocol version 6 (IPv6), have required the company to introduce new ideas gradually to its consumers while reinforcing the concepts and values on which the brand is based.

BRAND STRATEGY

- Cisco's strategy is to stay relevant to all of its customers and to create technologies that help them stay connected.
- Cisco has used several rebranding efforts, like the 2012 "Tomorrow Starts Here" campaign, to refocus its brand identity on its core values of innovation, inspiration, and thought leadership.
- Cisco focuses most of its business strategy on researching and developing relevant technologies that drive its business.
- At the 2012 Olympics in London, Cisco House, which showcased Cisco's technology, helped connect the brand with consumers in global markets.

Striving to stay consistent with its brand identity of providing technologies to connect users, Cisco has stated that as it expanded, it sought to make its brand "relevant to diverse audiences across all media, connecting with authority and authenticity to its customers, worldwide." Cisco wanted to appropriately convey its corporate values, which include innovation, inspiration, and thought leadership, as well as the company's goal of "changing the way we work, live, play, and learn." To achieve these purposes, Cisco has used various marketing campaigns, continued research and development for appropriate technologies, and sought to spread the brand globally.

An extensive rebranding across various media in 2006 was meant to improve the brand's alignment with its core values. This included a redesign of its website and social media presence as well as the launch of its "Human Network" ad campaign. As clients' needs have grown, Cisco, staying true to its values, has continued to broaden its image. Another corporate rebranding effort in December 2012 was launched around a new tagline, "Tomorrow Starts Here," promoting an "Internet of Everything" concept. The global marketing efforts included a Twitter hashtag campaign.

In addition to marketing, Cisco has sought to strengthen its brand identity by focusing on the latest technological developments. John T. Chambers, Cisco chairman and chief executive officer, stated in the company's 2012 annual report that the business has five "foundational priorities." The primary priority is "leadership in the core business," which it defines as network routing, switching, and services. It is also focused on developing and providing technologies for data center operations, collaboration, video, and "architectures for business transformation." Chambers added that "driving innovation and sustainable differentiation" are "the lifeblood of Cisco." To that end, and to meet its customers' needs for better, novel networking and communications products and services, Cisco has frequently ventured outside the company to acquire a portion or all of another firm. It has also established joint-development agreements to create products, and it has resold other firms' products. The company continues to connect people by providing whatever services they need to build strong networks.

Part of Cisco's strategy to innovate and inspire is to make sure that its products are marketable on a global level. A good example of this is Cisco's sponsorship of the 2012 Summer Olympic Games. In order to demonstrate its dedication to customers in the United Kingdom and increase its brand awareness, the company hosted more than 11,000 customers at Cisco House, a showcase for its technology in East London that was open for five months, and it worked with NBC to provide online coverage of the games. This effort was built upon a five-year strategy designed to improve Britain's network infrastructure and support math and science education in schools. Once the Olympic flame was doused in London, Cisco sought to replicate its successes by making similar investments in Brazil in preparation for the 2014 World Cup and 2016 Olympics in Rio de Janeiro.

BRAND EQUITY

- Cisco achieved a boost in equity in 2009 when it was added to the Dow Jones Industrial Index.
- Cisco was ranked 14th among the top international brands from 2009 through 2012.
- The range of Cisco professional certifications helps reinforce its brand equity among IT professionals.

Although it is a business-to-business brand, Cisco continually works to insure that consumers worldwide are as aware of the brand as IT professionals are. The company spent US$87 million on advertising in 2007. The following year its brand value was estimated at US$14.8 billion.

Cisco achieved a brand equity boost when it was added in 2009 to the Dow Jones Industrial Average, an index of 30 United States companies that serves as a gauge of the nation's economic temperature. The company was named Interbrand's 14th most valuable global brand in 2009, a ranking it held through 2012. The company's brand value increased 7 percent to US$27.20 billion in 2012. Interbrand stated that the Cisco brand was being challenged by Huawei, a Chinese firm deemed a "strong and nimble" competitor.

The *Motley Fool* reported that, despite a decline in market capitalization since 2000, "the company's overall position is much stronger, even though it has faced tough competition from Alcatel-Lucent and Juniper Networks, as well as from Huawei." The *Motley Fool* also said that Cisco's professional certifications "help enhance its brand standing in the eyes of its target market," adding that this could be a platform for future brand modernization.

BRAND AWARENESS

- Cisco used an "ingredient brand" print advertising campaign during the Internet boom to reinforce brand awareness among consumers.
- The company launched its first television advertising in 1998.
- Cisco uses mass-market advertising to support brand awareness and attract new customers.

Although Cisco never sought to be a consumer brand, in 1997 the company aimed to cultivate awareness of itself as a so-called "ingredient brand" with the "Cisco Powered Networks" campaign. An ingredient brand is one that consumers perceive as adding value to another product or service. The Cisco ingredient awareness campaign launched with full-page ads in the *Wall Street Journal* and *Financial Times* designed to help consumers associate the company name and its bridge logo with home networking. The campaign linked the brand with service providers and reinforced Cisco's reputation for reliability, quality, and dependability among IT professionals. Cisco was ranked tenth among the leading global firms in the hardware market in 2009 with US$29.51 million in revenue, according to *Market Share Reporter*.

Raising brand awareness through mass-market advertising became increasingly important to organizations engaged in business-to-business markets at the turn of the century. Cisco determined that the most effective means of reaching its users during the Internet boom was to launch a mass marketing campaign. In 1998 Cisco debuted its first international television advertising campaign aimed at consumers. The "Empowering the Internet Generation" campaign included branding advertisements in print and online media as well as the televised ads.

BRAND OUTLOOK

- Cisco seeks a consistent brand image across media platforms.
- The company is challenged by a perception that it is only in the business-to-business market, although it is not a consumer brand.
- Cisco continues to make heavy investments in global marketing.

Cisco has embraced a wide range of media to cultivate relationships with customers and communicate a consistent brand message. It uses a broad mix of social media engagement and community involvement to reinforce its messages.

Marilyn Mersereau, Cisco's senior vice president of corporate marketing, explained in 2010 that the key is "making sure that the brand and business are aligned. Ideally, we want every business decision to consider the brand-related implications. Expansion into new markets, acquisitions and new products and solutions all take into account how we continue to build on the strength of the Cisco brand."

In 2012 Cisco's Blair Christie told *Marketing Week* that the company intends to increase its global marketing, particularly in key markets outside the United States such as Brazil, China, Germany, and the United Kingdom. A continual challenge, said Christie, is getting past the public perception that Cisco is solely a business-to-business firm to explain its solutions and services to consumers. Yet, said Christie, Cisco is "not a consumer brand and nor should we be."

Cisco sought to replicate its marketing and brand awareness successes of the 2012 London Olympics by making similar investments in Brazil in preparation for the 2014 World Cup and 2016 Olympics in Rio de Janeiro. The company sought to differentiate its offerings in emerging markets for cloud networking and virtualization.

FURTHER READING

"Global - Networking Equipment." *Datamonitor Industry Market Research*. Datamonitor, 2007.

Mathieson, Clive. "Marketing Battle Hots Up; IT Plus." *Times* (London), December 1, 1999.

Menefee, Craig. "Cisco readies consumer ad campaign." *Computer Dealer News*, September 1, 1998.

PBS. "Serving the Suits: Adult Supervision." *Nerds 2.0.1*. Accessed October 9, 2012. http://www.pbs.org/opb/nerds2.0.1/serving_suits/cisco.html.

Tajnai, Carolyn. "Cisco Systems Spotlight." *Wellspring of Innovation*. Stanford University. Accessed October 9, 2012. http://www.stanford.edu/group/wellspring/cisco_spotlight.html.

"Top Hardware Firms Worldwide, 2009." *Market Share Reporter*. Ed. Robert S. Lazich and Virgil L. Burton III. Detroit, MI: Gale, 2012.

CITI

AT A GLANCE

Brand Synopsis: Citi is the corporate brand of Citigroup Inc., including the Citibank retail banking division. Citi represents the parent company as a reliable and innovative firm that is capable of serving the current and future needs of its clients and customers.
Parent Company: Citigroup Inc.
399 Park Avenue
New York, New York 10022
United States
http://www.citigroup.com
Sector: Financials
Industry Group: Banks
Performance: *Revenues*—US$59.3 billion (2012). *Assets*—US$1.8 trillion (2011).
Principal Competitors: Bank of American Corporation; Barclays PLC; HSBC Holdings plc; JPMorgan Chase & Co.

BRAND ORIGINS

- The origins of the Citi brand date to 1791 and the founding of First Bank of the United States.
- During post-Civil War era, "Citibank" was coined as a wire code address.
- In 1976 First National City Bank was formally renamed Citibank.
- Citigroup was formed in 1998 following a merger with Travelers Group Inc.
- Citigroup adopted "Citi" as its global brand name in 2007.

Citi is the corporate brand for Citigroup Inc., one of the world's largest financial services companies. Citi's roots reach back to the founding of the United States, to 1791 and the opening of the First Bank of the United States, which acted as a central bank for the young country. After the bank's 20-year charter expired, the New York branch was reorganized as the City Bank of New York in 1812. It operated as a state bank until it received a national charter in 1865. Thereafter known as National City Bank of New York, it once again played a national role by distributing a new national currency and acting as an agent for government sales. It was during this post-Civil War period that the wire code address "Citibank" was adopted and became the bank's informal name.

By the end of the 1920s Citibank was the United States' largest bank, and through affiliates it was also one of the largest securities and trust firms. When the stock market crash of 1929 ushered in the Great Depression of the 1930s and created numerous bank failures, Citibank was able to use its size to remain in business. However, the passage of the Glass-Steagall Act of 1933 forced it to separate its commercial and investment banking operations. A somewhat smaller Citibank emerged, but it remained one of the country's largest banks.

Citibank's official name was changed to First National City Bank in 1962. Six years later it pioneered the idea of forming a bank holding company as a way to skirt federal regulations on its activities. The one-bank holding company took the name of First National City Corporation. The name was changed to Citicorp in 1974, and two years later First National City Bank finally formalized its common name, becoming Citibank, N.A. Soon "Citi" would be used as a prefix for product brands, such as Citi Cards for credit cards and Citi Teller for automated teller machines.

During the 1990s restrictions that had been imposed by the Glass-Steagall Act were lifted, resulting in a rash of large bank mergers and banks becoming involved in a wider range of financial services. In 1998 Citicorp merged with Travelers Group Inc., a major insurance company, to create Citigroup Inc. The Travelers' iconic red umbrella symbol was incorporated into the Citibank logo, but the insurance assets failed to provide the kind of synergy that bank officials had hoped for, and Travelers Property and Casualty was sold in 2002. The life insurance and annuities underwriting businesses were retained, but three years later these operations were sold to MetLife. The only asset that remained was the Travelers' umbrella trademark, and that would finally be sold back to a revamped Travelers firm in 2007. In the meantime, Citigroup's branding had become a jumble, with the "Citi" prefix used inconsistently, and logos lacking uniformity. In January 2007, after a 14-month review, Citigroup unified the company under one global brand name: Citi.

BRAND ELEMENTS

- The use of Citi as a brand prefix began during the 1970s.
- The red arc in the Citi logo is a vestige of the merger with Travelers Group Inc.
- "The City never sleeps" tagline was created during the 1970s to promote automated teller machines.
- The "Citi never sleeps" tagline was adopted as part of the corporate brand in 2008.

The primary elements of the Citi brand are its name, logo, and tagline. The Citibank name has a long history and predates its formal adoption, and the use of "Citi" as a brand-prefix for products and services dates to the 1970s. As a result, the Citi brand, despite the relatively few years it has served as Citigroup's global brand, enjoys the kind of strong familiarity that is normally associated with a brand of greater longevity. Citi is especially well known in the New York City area, where Citibank branches promote the name. Additionally, Citi has the naming rights to the Citi Field, the home stadium of the New York Mets of Major League Baseball. Not only does the signage at the stadium, both externally and internally, promote the Citi brand to New Yorkers but also televised Mets games and media accounts of the games create exposure for the Citi brand.

More important than the Citi name to the brand building potential of signage is the logo that incorporates the name. The Citi name is presented in lowercased letters, generally in blue but in some cases in gray. A red arc emanates from the top of the *t* and spans the letter *i* on either side. It creates an umbrella image, a vestige of the previous relationship with Travelers. The connection between Travelers and the umbrella dates to 1870, when it was first used in a newspaper advertisement. The signature red color was introduced during the late 1950s. It was such a well-known image that Citigroup embraced it following the Citicorp and Travelers Group Inc. merger, but with the divestment of Citigroup's insurance assets, the umbrella lost much of its relevance. The umbrella symbolized protection, a service associated with insurance but not generally with banking. Even though Citigroup sold back the umbrella trademark to Travelers, it retained the red arc in its logo, which in its new context suggests unity among Citigroup units.

The "Citi never sleeps" tagline is another important brand element. The original tagline, "The Citi never sleeps," was crafted during the early 1970s by Bob Wilvers, a copywriter at the Wells Rich Green advertising agency. At the time, the slogan was used to promote a new automated teller machine (ATM) service to the public and proclaim that basic banking could now be done 24 hours a day at Citibank. Given that New York was known as the city that never sleeps, it was a clever play on words. In time, ATMs ceased to be a novelty, and the tagline was retired during the early 1990s despite its popularity. It was succeeded by "Where money lives" and "Live richly," neither of which enjoyed the same success despite massive advertising support.

When Citigroup conducted a brand review in the early 2000s, some consideration was given to the revival of the old catchphrase. In the end, management elected to go with "Let's get it done." It was meant to be a call to action for employees to help turnaround the firm and an invitation to customers to make greater use of its services. Despite testing well with focus groups, the phrase proved to be less than inspiring, due in part to the implicit suggestion that it was about time that the bank stop procrastinating and do something. In the spring of 2008, Citigroup dusted off the old tagline and shortened it slightly to "Citi never sleeps."

BRAND IDENTITY

- Citi's brand identity is that of a reliable innovative firm dedicated to meeting the needs of its clients and customers.
- The "Citi Never Sleeps" tagline reinforces the brand identity of a hardworking firm that will not rest until its customers' goals are met.
- Negative publicity over the years has undermined Citi's brand identity.

As crafted by its marketers and reinforced by the elements of the Citi brand, Citigroup portrays itself as a reliable yet innovative firm that is dedicated to serving the needs of its clients and customers, today and in the future. The venerability of the brand is supported by the Citi name, which as part of Citibank has been well known for many years, especially to New Yorkers. The Citi logo does not have the same kind of longevity, but it is widely seen in bank branch signage, at Citi Field, and in advertisements. Sheer ubiquity of the logo suggests the strength of the firm represented by it. The tagline, "Citi Never Sleeps," not only makes the promise that Citigroup is hardworking in general but also that the firm will not rest until it helps customers meet their personal goals.

Citi's brand identity is promoted internally through Citigroup's stated mission: "Citi works tirelessly to serve individuals, communities, institutions and nations. With 200 years of experience meeting the world's toughest challenges and seizing its greatest opportunities, we strive to create the best outcomes for our clients and customers with financial solutions that are simple, creative and responsible." The brand is meant to embody this purpose, so that there is no daylight between the actions of the company it represents and the brand promise. In a sense, the company will ideally become the brand.

However, Citigroup's reputation has not always matched its brand identity. It was embroiled in the Enron, WorldCom, and Global Crossing scandals at the turn of the millennium, and in 2008 it received US$45 billion in federal aid from the Troubled Asset Relief Program (TARP) to help it survive the subprime mortgage crisis. Citigroup later paid US$75 million to settle civil charges that it misled investors about high-risk mortgages. It also had to contend with the adverse attention from the New York attorney general Andrew Cuomo, who accused Citigroup of paying hundreds of millions of dollars in bonuses to about 1,000 employees out of the TARP money it had received. In 2013 Citigroup was one of 10 large banks that agreed to reimburse customers US$8.5 billion for using documents that were either defective or fraudulent to pursue mortgage foreclosures. None of these very public matters reflected well on Citigroup and, as a result, its brand identity was undermined.

BRAND STRATEGY

- Citigroup initiated a brand review in 2005.
- According to the new branding strategy unveiled in 2007, the color of the Citi logo arc was to have a different color, depending on the division.
- Most Citigroup businesses use "Citi" as a separate prefix, with the exception of Citibank, CitiMortgage, and CitiFinancial.

Even before the creation of Citigroup through the 1998 merger of Citicorp and Travelers Group Inc., the management of the Citi brand had become disjointed. The situation only grew worse following the merger. Citibank pursued its own branding strategy; the Citi prefix was attached to different business units without a coherent rationale or a formal approval process. "The result, in the eyes of some," wrote Eric Dash in a January 15, 2007, *New York Times* article, "was a mishmash of logos and titles that appeared disconnected, while many Wall Street clients, Main Street customers and even Citigroup employees simply referred to the different parts of the conglomerate as Citi." In late 2005 a review of the bank's brand was initiated. When it was completed 14 months later, Citigroup was rebranded "Citi."

As part of the rebranding, the Travelers umbrella trademark was sold. The only remnant of the merger that remained was the arc within the Citi logo that created an umbrella image. The original rebranding plan called for the arc to have a different color depending on the use. Citi's corporate and investment banks were to use a black arc, the consumer business division a blue arc, and the wealth management division a red arc. In the end, Citigroup decided to maintain consistency and the red arc was used for all divisions.

For the most part, the Citi brand was not fused to a division name, with the exception of Citibank, CitiMortgage, and CitiFinancial, all of which had long been known by these names. Other businesses that employed the new usage of Citi included Citi Cards, Citi Private Bank, Citi Capital Advisors, Citi Institutional Clients Group, Citi Investment Research, and Citi Microfinance. Unaffected by the change was the Smith Barney brokerage arm, which was a joint venture with Morgan Stanley and was eventually acquired in full by Morgan Stanley. There were a few other notable exceptions: OneMain Financial, a consumer loan company that Citigroup felt would enjoy better success by forging its own identity; the Women & Co. financial strategies company, created to serve the particular needs of women; and Banamex, a major Mexican commercial bank that Citigroup acquired in 2001 and was a well-established brand in its own market.

BRAND EQUITY

- Brand Finance estimated the Citi brand was worth US$21.7 billion at the end of 2012.
- According to Brand Finance, Citi was number 29 on its 2012 "Global 500" list.
- Brand Finance listed Citi as the world's fifth most valuable bank brand in 2013.
- According to Interbrand, Citibank was the world 50th most valuable brand in 2012.
- Citibank was number 82 on Millward Brown's "BrandZ Top 100 Brand Ranking."

While it is impossible to determine Citi's brand equity precisely, Citi is undoubtedly one of the world's most valuable banking brands and one of the most valuable brands in general. According to the brand consultancy Brand Finance, which estimates the monetary value of brands for comparison purposes, Citi was worth US$21.7 billion at the end of 2012. As a result, Brand Finance considered it to be the fifth most valuable bank brand in 2013, trailing only Wells Fargo, Chase, HSBC, and Bank of America. In Brand Finance's 2012 "Global 500" list of the world's most valuable brands, Citi was listed number 29. Even though these were strong rankings, they were a far cry from Citi's place a few years earlier. In 2007 Brand Finance considered Citi to be the world's top banking brand and overall the world's third most valuable brand, this despite the Enron, WorldCom, and Global Crossing scandals earlier in the decade. The financial losses Citigroup suffered from the subprime mortgage crisis and the loss of face by being rescued by the federal government led to an unavoidable loss of brand equity.

Another brand consultancy, Interbrand, estimated the value of the Citibank brand (rather than the Citi corporate brand) at US$7.6 billion in 2012. It was a performance that made Citibank the 50th most valuable brand in 2012, according to Interbrand's methodology. The Millward Brown branding agency assigned a value of US$9.8 billion for Citibank in 2012. As a result, Citibank placed number 82 on Millward Brown's "BrandZ Top 100 Brand Ranking."

BRAND AWARENESS

- Citi's brand awareness is supported by 1,300 Citibank branches in 16 states.
- Citibank has enjoyed success in building brand awareness in China.
- Negative brand awareness has hurt Citi's standing.

Citi enjoys strong brand awareness, due in large part to the long use of the Citibank name and the scope of Citigroup's global operations. Citigroup does business in more than 160 countries and jurisdictions, serving about 200 million customer accounts. Helping to bring exposure to the Citi brand are more than 1,300 Citibank branches in 16 states. While a large number, it falls short of the 5,600 branches maintained by Bank of America in 36 states or the 6,600 branches by Wells Fargo in 41 states. In terms of automated teller machines (ATMs), Citibank maintains 3,200, but again it is outstripped by Wells Fargo's 12,000 ATMs and Bank of America's 16,000 ATMs. Citibank enjoys its strongest brand awareness in the New York City area, but in many respects it was upstaged by another area bank with deep roots, Chase, which maintained about 5,500 branches and 15,000 ATMs in 26 states.

In the United States, general awareness of the Citi brand is not as strong outside of the New York City area, although with institutional and high net worth individuals who are key to the success of Citigroup, awareness is considerably higher. The same can also be said outside the United States, but Citi is making inroads in emerging markets. Citibank has enjoyed particular success in China. *Asian Banker* awarded Citibank with the Best Brand Building Award in China for 2011. According to the editorial copy that announced the award, the trade publication noted that "Citibank has built significant mind share and increased its brand relevance amongst consumers in China."

The naming rights to the New York Mets' new stadium, Citi Field, also helped build awareness of the Citi brand. As was the case with other dealings of Citigroup, the US$400 million sponsorship deal created some negative publicity in light of the Troubled Asset Relief Program funds the firm received. Because of concerns that taxpayer funds were being used to finance the deal, two members of Congress wrote the U.S. secretary of the treasury requesting that the deal be dissolved. Even though nothing came of the request, it was the kind of brand awareness that Citigroup needed to avoid, especially because earlier an order for a new US$50 million executive jet for the bank was forced to be canceled. Such news stories brought undesired attention to the Citi brand and were likely one of the reasons, along with poor customer satisfaction scores, that Citigroup ranked fifth on the *Investment News* list of "The 10 Most Hated" companies in the United States in 2013.

BRAND OUTLOOK

- Citigroup has not recovered from the financial crisis as well as its peers.
- Citi hopes to become more of a premium aspirational brand in the years ahead.
- Citibank wants to become known as the world's digital bank.

In the aftermath of the financial crisis, Citigroup has failed to see its stock recoup losses to the same degree as its peers. Citi's branding strategy may have played a role in this shortcoming. According to Jez Frampton in a September 22, 2008, *Advertising Age* article, the strategy of bringing a group of businesses together under a corporate brand "can be a double-edged sword. While in the good times everyone appears to benefit, in bad times any negative impacts will be felt across the board."

Growing the Citi brand will be a key factor in the recovery of Citibank's stock price and future expansion. Playing to the benefit of Citigroup is its geographic reach and the potential to build on the firm's strengths around the world. Also of importance is an emphasis on digital technology. A new brand officer, Dermot Boden, was hired as well. He told *Marketing Week* in a December 20, 2012, article that he wanted Citi to be considered "a premium, aspirational brand; a brand that is building towards being the world's digital bank." To achieve that end, he said that Citigroup will need to develop new services and technologies that consumers do not even realize they need yet. More than that, Citigroup will have to redress the negative associations to the Citi name if it is to enjoy the full benefit of a global corporate brand.

FURTHER READING

"Citibank China Wins Best Brand-Building Award." *Daily the Pak Banker* (Lahore, Pakistan), June 3, 2011.

"Citigroup Inc." *International Directory of Company Histories.* Ed. Thomas Derdak. Vol. 137. Detroit, MI: St. James Press, 2012.

"Coke Top Brand in the World." *Mirror* (London), February 2, 2007.

Cone, Steve. "Citi Awakes from Slumber." *Adweek*, June 9, 2008.

Dash, Eric. "Citi's New Slogan Is Said to Be Second Choice." *New York Times*, May 12, 2008.

———. "Citigroup Goes Global in Ad Effort." *New York Times*, April 28, 2007.

———. "Just 'Citi' As the Brand, and a Folded Umbrella." *New York Times*, January 15, 2007.

———. "What's Red, Familiar, Ubiquitous and May Be on Its Way Out?" *New York Times*, June 20, 2006.

"Foundations in Place to Build a Better Citi." *Marketing Week*, December 20, 2012.

Frampton, Jez. "Wall Street's Angst Is Now Main Street's." *Advertising Age*, September 22, 2008.

Quinn, James. "Citigroup Examines Striking out $400m Sponsorship Deal with New York Mets." *Daily Telegraph* (London), February 4, 2009.

CITROËN

AT A GLANCE

Brand Synopsis: A French automotive brand, Citroën has a long history of innovation and emphasizes its "Créative Technologie."
Parent Company: PSA Peugeot Citroën Group
75 Avenue de la Grande Armee
Paris 75116
France
http://www.psa-peugeot-Citroën.com/en
Sector: Consumer Discretionary
Industry Group: Automobiles & Components
Performance: *Market share*—13.5 percent of the French market (2003). *Performance*—US$73.913 billion (parent company PSA Peugeot Citroën Group) (2011).
Principal Competitors: Audi; BMW; Mercedes-Benz; Opel; Porsche; Renault; Toyota; Volkswagen

BRAND ORIGINS

- Citroën was founded by French industrialist Andre-Gustave Citroën in 1919.
- One of the brand's most popular models, the 2CV, was introduced in 1948.
- PSA Peugeot Citroën, struggling badly in the wake of the global economic recession that began in 2008, received assistance from the French government.

Citroën was launched in 1919 by French industrialist André-Gustave Citroën. His company was one of the first manufacturers of automobiles. By the end of 1919, his namesake cars were being produced at a rate of 30 a day in a former World War I munitions factory.

André-Gustave Citroën put an emphasis on brand building. His first car, the Type A, was a three-seater that was the first car to be mass-produced in Europe and designed with the intention of reaching the popular market. Ads for the Type A were placed in the French press before the car was actually produced, making the industrialist a pioneer in prelaunch advertising. He continued to advertise his cars, though he could not meet consumer demand.

The Citroën brand soon became well-known in Europe because of its association with motor racing, compelling a vast increase in sales and production. In 1920 a Citroën won the fuel-economy grand prix at Le Mans. In 1921 the company began producing three types of half-trucks, and in 1922–23 the model powered by the B2 engine became the first motorized vehicle to cross the Sahara. To build on this publicity, Citroën began exporting in 1921, shipping 3,000 cars abroad that year. By 1924 Citroën had subsidiaries in Brussels, Amsterdam, Cologne, Milan, Geneva, and Copenhagen, and it exported 17,000 cars.

During the 1920s Citroën regularly introduced new models, including its first budget model, the 5 HP, and the economical, easy-to-drive 5VH Type C, both in 1922. In 1924, the same year it incorporated as Automobiles Citroën, the company introduced the B10, the first all-steel automobile in Europe. Some of the brand's advertising during the 1920s emphasized that automobiles could offer consumers freedom to travel inexpensively, while other ads focused on various features of the cars or on the prestige that came with owning a Citroën.

By 1928 Citroën was producing 1,000 vehicles per day and had 14 distributors in France and North Africa. Its overseas sales accounted for 45 percent of all French auto industry exports. However, the brand struggled during the Great Depression. Though it was still introducing new models, Citroën went bankrupt and was acquired by its primary creditor, Michelin, in 1934. Though Citroën had developed what would become one of its signature cars, the 2CV, in 1936, the onset of World War II in 1939 delayed its release.

During the war, Citroën was essentially in limbo, with production ceasing from 1943 to 1945. Small-scale production resumed in 1945, and in 1948 the 2CV finally made its debut. The economical compact was the least expensive French car on the market for many years. Three million were built between 1949 and 1984. During the 1950s and 1960s, Citroën continued to introduce new models and regained its place as one of the leading French car makers. The popular DS model debuted in the mid-1950s, while the top-of-range Ami 6 was introduced in the 1960s.

While Citroën found success with model launches like the SM, a luxury coupe, in 1970, the brand was deeply impacted by the global oil-crisis which started in 1973 when the Organization of Petroleum Exporting Countries suddenly and drastically increased the price of oil. In 1974 Michelin and the Peugeot Group began merging Automobiles Citroën with Automobiles Peugeot, the leading French car company. Peugeot took over 38.2 percent of Citroën in 1974 and increased its share to 90 percent in 1976, forming PSA Peugeot Citroën.

Under new ownership, Citroën retained its brand identity, and by the early 1980s, when the brand was struggling again, emphasized brand promotion. A new identity campaign changed Citroën's colors from blue and yellow to red and white, while ads featured a herd of horses running in the formation of the double chevron that formed the Citroën logo. After several years of multimillion-dollar losses, Citroën became profitable again in 1986 and found success exporting to markets such as Portugal, Spain, and Great Britain. New models, like the luxury XM (1988) and the family-car ZX (1991), were introduced, while the last 2CV was produced in 1990.

By 1993 Citroëns were being sold in 85 countries. The ad campaigns featured slogans like "Discover What Citroën Can Do For You" (1993) and "Nothing moves you like a Citroën" (mid-1990s). In 1998 the brand introduced a new model, the Xsara Picasso, which was a compact minivan named after the artist. Sales continued to rise through the first years of the 21st century, based on strong demand for the Picasso and another new model, the C5.

Citroën sold 1.14 million cars in 2001 and became profitable again. In 2002 the brand debuted the C3 model, the successor to the iconic 2CV, and in 2003, the larger C6. By 2003 Citroën was the number-four automaker in France, with 13.5 percent of the market, and its parent company's sales reached US$68.3 billion. By 2006 PSA Peugeot Citroën was second-largest automaker in Europe by sales.

Citroën began a design renaissance in 2009, which led to the introduction of a number of premium cars under the DS banner, including the high-end DS3. Also in 2009 the brand celebrated its ninetieth birthday with the launch of a new logo and the slogan, "Créative Technologie." Yet the brand struggled as consumer demand fell in the wake of the worldwide economic downturn that began in 2008. PSA Peugeot-Citroën was in serious trouble by 2009. The French government gave Citroën's parent company a credit line of US$3.9 billion because the company could not secure credit from private sources.

Citroën sales in Europe continued to be sluggish, though in 2011 Citroën remained the number-13 car brand in the world, making gains in China and other markets. (PSA Peugeot Citroën had adopted the goal of making half of its sales income outside of Europe.) By 2012 the company was in a downward spiral, with billions of dollars in losses. Late that year, the French government announced a rescue deal for PSA Peugeot Citroën, which included a restructuring plan and partnerships with automakers such as General Motors, itself the beneficiary of a U.S. government assistance program.

BRAND ELEMENTS

- The Citroën logo was inspired by the teeth of a gear.
- The Citroën logo has been modified several times, including an overhaul in 2009.
- The slogan "Créative Technologie" was adopted in 2009 to define Citroën after ninety years in business.

The Citroën brand is deeply linked to its unique logo, a double chevron. The origins of the logo lay in the background of brand founder André-Gustave Citroën. His uncle held a patent on a gear mechanism that had double-helical teeth in a chevron-like pattern and was used in factories in Poland. The teeth helped the gears work smoothly together. When Citroën founded the Citroën Gear Company in 1913, he used the same type of gears, and when he established his automotive company six years later, he adopted the double-chevron design as its logo.

Initially, the logo was two very simple chevron lines. Over the years, the logo was occasionally modified, such as in 1932 when the C4G and C6G were announced. These cars eliminated vibrations by placing their engines on soft mounts. To reflect the improvement, a flying swan was placed between the double chevrons. After a new brand identity was launched in 2009, the logo was modified to become more space age in appearance, with rounder edges and a puffier look. During the same transition, Citroën adopted a slogan that would define the brand through the early 2010s. "Créative Technologie" emphasizes the brand's commitment to bold yet attractive car design and to the latest in car technology.

BRAND IDENTITY

- Citroën has defined itself as a quintessentially French brand that offers both freedom and advanced technology to its customers.
- Citroën was an early adopter of the celebrity endorsement, beginning with aviation pioneer Charles Lindbergh.
- Citroën has also built its brand through sponsorships of road events like early motorized expeditions across Africa and road rallies.

From its founding in 1919, Citroën has been a prestigious and definitive brand of French-made automobiles. In the 1920s the brand educated French consumers on the benefits of car ownership, claiming that automobiles like Citroëns were a form of transportation that was practical and economical, but that also could bring happiness. It used such taglines as "Both breadwinner and joy-bringer" and "Flee the city and savor the pleasures of a trip to the country." The brand continued to associate itself with freedom of movement in the 1980s and 1990s with its 1984 commercial "Citroën Sauvages." It included an image of horses running across the desert while forming Citroën's double chevron logo. In the mid-1990s the car maker used the tagline, "Nothing moves you like a Citroën." By the first decade of the 21st century Citroën put a greater emphasis on the brand's incorporation of impressive automotive technology, as promoted in the 2005 tagline "Alive with technology" and the brand slogan adopted in 2009, "Créative Technologie."

Though Citroëns are sold in approximately 85 countries, the brand has also underscored its identity as a French automotive company and its association with major 20th and 21st century celebrities. To bring attention to the brand in 1925, André-Gustave Citroën paid for the right to put the Citroën brand name on the Eiffel Tower. "Citroën" appeared in lighted letters along 30 meters on one side of the Tower, bringing wide attention to the brand for nine years. Two years later, in 1927, Citroën linked its brand to Charles Lindbergh, who claimed to have used the lighted name to guide him toward his landing Paris at the end of his transatlantic flight. An early proponent of celebrity marketing, Citroën continued to link its brand identity with well-known figures, such as model Claudia Schiffer. By buying the rights to the name Picasso from the late artist's estate, Citroën created a new type of celebrity identity, calling several models of cars Picassos and using Picasso imagery in its advertising.

When Citroën was building its brand identity in the early 1920s, it began using sponsorships of automotive-related events to demonstrate the power, strength, and technological advancement of its cars. In addition to sponsoring and providing vehicles for the first motorized expeditions across the Sahara Desert in 1922, Citroën allowed its vehicles to participate in other high-profile expeditions in Africa, Asia, and North America. Beginning in the 1950s, Citroën entered or provided cars for various road rallies and circuit races, winning events like the Tour of Corsica and the 1971 Moroccan Rally. In the 1990s the Citroën team won numerous Paris-Dakar rallies and related World Championships. Victories in rally events continued into the early 2000s, including a seventh World Manufacturers title in 2011.

BRAND STRATEGY

- Citroën has regularly introduced new models under its brand name.
- Most Citroën cars have been given coded alphanumerical names, with the Picasso being the most notable exception.
- Citroën has done well in China and other markets outside of France for years.

When Citroën was founded in 1919, it had one model of automobile, the Type A. It was a three-seater that was the first car in Europe to be sold fully equipped with an electric starter, lighting, hood, and spare tire. The Type A was also the first car designed in Europe with the intention of reaching the popular market. Citroën would continually expand its line of cars, keeping up to date with, if not defining, the latest in automotive design and technology. Some early models, like the 5CV Type C introduced in 1922, helped make the automobile more popular because this car was inexpensive and it was easy to drive. Two years later, the B10 debuted as the first car with an all-steel body. Citroën entered the bus market in 1931, launched the aerodynamic 7A in 1934, and brought out the inexpensive and extremely popular 2CV in 1948. Ten years later it introduced the very practical, two-wheel-drive 2CV Sahara, which proved useful in desert areas.

While the Picasso, introduced in the late 1990s, was an exception, nearly all Citroën cars have featured coded alphanumeric names, including the successor to the 2CV, the C3, introduced in 2002. After a rebranding in 2009, Citroën introduced a modern version of the classic DS line of premium cars. In 2013 Citroën announced that a new version of the C4 Picasso, using the EMP2 platform and producing lower emissions, would be available in showrooms in 2014.

Though Citroën is a definitive French brand, Citroën cars are available in at least 85 countries. André-Gustave Citroën himself saw the importance of exporting and began selling his cars in other countries as early as 1921. Citroën's international reach expanded over the course of the 20th century and has proven a major source of the brand's sales and its strength as a brand. In 2011 Citroën's parent company, PSA Peugeot Citroën, set a goal of selling half of its cars outside of Europe, where sales had gone stagnant in the wake of the worldwide economic downturn. Between 2008 and 2011, Citroën saw its sales outside of Europe increase by 10 percent, with China becoming an especially important international market.

BRAND EQUITY

- Citroën was ranked number 13 among car brands in 2011.
- Citroën's sales were deeply affected by the economic recession that began in 2008, though sales increased outside of Europe.
- Citroën maintained a high brand value of US$4.175 billion in 2012, according to Brand Finance.

By 2011 Citroën was the number-13 car company in the world. Its fortunes have been mixed, especially in the last quarter of the 20th century and the first years of the 21st. However the brand has a loyal following, particularly in its native France, the United Kingdom, and China. Citroën's sales have been deeply affected by the economic recession that began in 2008 and hit Europe particularly hard. However Citroën's sales outside of Europe grew by 10 percent between 2008 and 2011, and it still has a relatively high brand value. In 2012 Brand Finance's *Global 500* ranked Citroën at 246th, with a brand value of US$4.175 billion and an enterprise value of US$16.409 billion.

BRAND AWARENESS

- Citroën started building brand awareness right from its launch in 1919.
- Placing the Citroën name in lights on the Eiffel Tower from 1925 to 1934 heightened brand awareness for years after.
- Citroën's cars, like the highly acclaimed original DS, have also increased brand awareness.

Ever since its founding in 1919, Citroën has worked to build awareness of its brand as one of the first major automobile manufacturers in Europe and one of the earliest to promote cars as desirable and practical for a wide variety of consumers. From the first, the automaker's founder, André-Gustave Citroën, invested in prelaunch advertising for his cars and eye-catching stunts like placing the Citroën name in lights on the Eiffel Tower for nine years. Many of the brand's cars have been memorable, with models like the original Citroën DS considered a landmark in French car history. Car designers have named it one of the most beautiful cars ever made. Citroën continued to bring global brand recognition to itself by buying the rights to use the name Picasso on a line of cars in the late 1990s. Though the fee was high, the deal gave Citroën the right to associate its cars with the work of one of the world's most admired artists. The Xsara Picasso debuted in 1998 and sold a million units in its first year, beating projections. Surveys underscore Citroën's position. ADAC's *AutomarxX Brand Ranking*, which considers the performance, image, market strength, and satisfaction of auto brands globally, ranked Citroën number 19 in 2012. In 2009 Citroën was number 84 on the Brand Republic News list of *The 100 Most Mentioned Brands on Twitter*.

BRAND OUTLOOK

- European markets for cars were sluggish after the onset of an economic downturn in 2008.
- Citroën's parent company, PSA Peugeot Citroën, needed major interventions from the French government in 2009 and 2012.
- Citroën's sales have grown outside of Europe, especially in China.

Globally, most car brands saw their value decline significantly between 2011 and 2012, a general trend that began with the onset of the global economic recession in 2008. Most European car brands, like European brands in general, lost value in that continent's troubled economy. Car sales slowed in most countries, except Germany, during the economic crisis. Citroën was severely impacted, with its parent company, PSA Peugeot Citroën, requiring major interventions from the French government in 2009 and 2012 to stay afloat. This situation has made Citroën's long-term future uncertain in Europe. However, the brand has taken advantage of the fact that the auto industry has become more global, with China emerging as the world's largest car market. Citroëns are sold in at least 85 countries, and the brand has done well in China, where it regularly introduces new models. With its investments in building the brand in growing, non-European markets, Citroën was poised to remain viable and relevant in the 21st century.

FURTHER READING

"Automobiles Citroën." *International Directory of Company Histories*. Ed. Paula Kepos. Vol. 7. Detroit, MI: St. James Press, 1993.

Brand Finance. "Citroën." *Brandirectory*. Accessed February 12, 2013. http://brandirectory.com/profile/citron.

"Citroën." *Advertising Age*, September 15, 2003.

"Citroën." RankingTheBrands.com. Accessed February 12, 2013. http://www.rankingthebrands.com/Brand-detail.aspx?brandID=205.

"Citroën Reveals Details of New Technospace Concept Vehicle." *Auto Business News*, February 11, 2013.

"Global Ambitions; PSA Has Big Plans for Booming Markets Such as China, but Wants to Be Green and Premium Too." *Automotive News Europe*, June 22, 2011.

Hennessy, Kathryn, and Beth Landis Hester. "Great Marques—The Citroën Story." *Car: The Definitive Visual History of the Automobile*. New York: DK Publishing, 2011.

Scoltock, James. "Inside Knowledge: Citroën Is Aiming for a Return to the Premium Segment, Starting with Its Compact DS3." *Automotive Engineer*, September 2009.

COACH

AT A GLANCE

Brand Synopsis: Coach luxury goods made from leather and other materials are known for their quality and classic design.
Parent Company: Coach, Inc.
516 West 34th Street
New York, New York 10001-1394
United States
http://www.coach.com
Sector: Consumer Goods, Consumer Discretionary, Consumer Durables and Apparel
Industry Group: Textile: Apparel, Footwear, and Accessories
Performance: *Sales*—US$4.2 billion (2011). *Gross profit*—US$3 billion (2011).
Principal Competitors: Fifth and Pacific Companies, Inc.; Dooney & Bourke, Inc.; Gucci Group NV; Prada SpA; Kenneth Cole Productions, Inc.; Jones Group, Inc.; Hermès International SCA; LVMH Moët Hennessy Louis Vuitton SA; PreVu, Inc.; Ralph Lauren Corporation; Etienne Aigner AG

BRAND ORIGINS

- Coach began as a small leather goods workshop in New York City in 1941.
- Although Coach began as a wallet and billfold maker, it gained fame by making handbags.
- Bonnie Cashin designed brightly colored handbags and accessories for Coach in the 1960s and 1970s.
- Coach has shifted from being a manufacturer to being a designer and marketer of goods.
- Consumers can buy Coach goods in the company's stores, in boutique areas of other stores, and online.
- Coach has a large presence in Asian markets.

Coach, Inc., began as a small wallet maker in New York City and grew to become a company with an international presence. It has stressed quality manufacturing, stylish design, and a respect for tradition.

In 1941 Coach was established as a small workshop in New York City. Coach employee Miles Cahn helped to develop a treatment process that made leather soft and supple but strong, much like the leather in a baseball glove. Coach workers initially used their leatherworking skills to make items like wallets and billfolds, but Cahn's wife, Lillian, another Coach employee, suggested that the company produce other products as well. One of those products, the handbag, would become the mainstay of the Coach brand. Handbags (also known as purses, pocketbooks, or simply bags) account for the bulk of Coach's business. According to Coach's 2011 Annual Report, handbags accounted for 63 percent of its net sales in the 2011 fiscal year. This report notes that accessories—such as wallets, small leather goods, cosmetic cases, and other goods—made up 27 percent of its sales that year, while the remaining 10 percent of its sales came from such products as messenger and tote bags, shoes, jewelry, and clothing items.

Bonnie Cashin designed some handbags and accessories for Coach in the 1960s and 1970s. Cashin's Coach designs utilized bright colors and included a handbag shaped like a bucket. Her designs highlighted the fashion-forward aspects of a company that has tried to balance contemporary fashion with timeless tradition. Coach now focuses more on designing and marketing than manufacturing, and its products are made outside of New York City by its contractors and partners. This shift from manufacturer to marketer was not the company's only major transition as a business. The Sara Lee Corporation bought Coach in 1985 and controlled the business until Coach regained its status as an independent company in 2000.

In 1999 Coach began selling its goods on its website. By that time, the company had already started intensifying its focus on international markets. In the 1980s, it began setting up Coach boutiques in stores in England and Japan. Coach opened stores in Russia in 2008 and in China in 2012 and has established retail spaces on cruise ships. Coach's presence in Asia is a testament to its popularity there and its growth as a global brand.

BRAND ELEMENTS

- The Coach logo as of 2012 features the image of a coach, a driver, and horses, along with the words "COACH" and "EST. 1941." Variations of the logo are similar, often including the words but not the image.
- Coach uses the recognizable "C" from its logo as the "Signature C" pattern on some of its goods.
- Hangtags appear on several Coach bags. These hangtags are so famous that the tags, rather than the products, appear in some Coach advertising campaigns.
- Manufacturing information appears on the Coach creed patches that are attached to Coach products.

The logo for Coach connotes style, elegance, and luxury, with a nod to the past. The logo is a drawing of a coach and driver with a pair of horses. Underneath the drawing, a rectangular lozenge shape contains the word "COACH" in ornate capital letters, with "EST. 1941" beneath in smaller capital letters. The word "COACH" on the label is in a specially designed typeface, while the "EST. 1941" is in a plainer font. A variant of the logo places the drawing of the coach, driver, and horses above a rectangular lozenge containing the words "COACH LEATHERWARE," while the "EST. 1941" is located outside of and beneath the lozenge shape.

Older logos feature the word "COACH" in ornate capital letters and the word "LEATHERWARE" in a smaller, plainer font beneath. This logo does not have a rectangular lozenge surrounding the words, nor does it feature the coach drawing. If the Coach logo is printed, it is often black and white. Sometimes the logo is stamped onto leather or made of metal and thus takes on the color of the material. According to Famous Logos, a website focusing on the logo design industry, "The Coach logo is probably the most memorable logo in the leatherware industry." The "C" of the logo, known as the "Signature C," is so recognizable that it is used to form a repeating pattern on some of Coach's products.

Coach brands its products in other prominent ways. Many of its handbags feature attached hanging tags known as hangtags. Originally created to identify the materials used to make a particular Coach item, hangtags are now considered a way of identifying an item as a Coach product. These hangtags are so tied to the Coach brand that the company chose the shape of the tags, rather than actual Coach products, to animate a series of short films used to promote Coach on its corporate website and other sites on the Internet. In addition, the company has inserted patches containing the Coach creed in its products. This creed is a statement that tells a buyer what materials were used to make the item and where the item was made.

BRAND IDENTITY

- The logo of Coach, with its image of a horse-drawn carriage, evokes tradition and luxury.
- Coach's advertising campaigns connect the brand with tradition, success, and American history.
- Although its advertising evokes American traditions, Coach is also a popular international brand, especially in Japan.
- The popularity of Coach products has led to the production of counterfeit Coach goods and to Coach's efforts to stop such counterfeiting.

Coach's logo of a horse-drawn carriage draws upon history and tradition. Similarly, the company uses history and timelessness to promote a number of its products. Its website describes the company as "defining classic American style" and features a number of the company's products, including handbags described as Coach Classics (featuring a conservative, classic style) and the Legacy Collection (featuring styling reminiscent of older Coach pieces). Advertising campaigns for Coach have used the famous Coach lozenge logo with the tagline "An American Legacy." Other advertisements for the brand have depicted the descendants of famous people alongside Coach products, thus linking Coach with American history, tradition, and success.

Although its advertising often focuses on American tradition, Coach is quite popular with international consumers, particularly in Japan. Large numbers of foreign tourists visit Coach's flagship store in New York City every year, which prompted the company to open Coach stores and boutiques abroad beginning in the 1980s. According to Trefis, an online financial community, Japan's high living standards and Coach's position as a moderately priced luxury brand have helped drive the company's success in the country.

The brand's success has encouraged imitators eager to duplicate Coach's products. The brand has taken measures to stop the manufacture of counterfeit Coach goods and has taken companies to court with the charge of copying Coach designs. The company website contains a list of stores and websites that sell authentic Coach goods, along with a list of Internet sites that have sold counterfeit items. The website also provides a phone number and e-mail address where people can report suspected counterfeiting.

BRAND STRATEGY

- Coach offers variations on its classic products and new product lines to attract returning and new customers.
- Expansion in Japan has been extremely profitable for Coach, generating a significant percentage of its revenue.
- Product repairs and monograms are some of the services Coach offers its customers.
- The successful Coach factory outlet stores offer Coach merchandise at reduced prices.

Although Coach respects tradition, it has embraced change as well. Coach has needed to adapt to remain competitive. The brand is known for quality and classic styling, but the company has recognized that these qualities make it difficult to market additional Coach products to past customers, because those customers may feel that their existing Coach products are still functional and stylish. To entice old as well as new customers, Coach now offers variations on its products, including new colors, and offers more product types, such as jewelry, eyewear, home accessories, fragrances, and wearable accessories like socks, scarves, and suspenders.

Coach has also changed where it does business. In 2001 Coach partnered with Japan's Sumitomo Corporation to form Coach Japan, although Coach bought Sumitomo's share of the company in 2005. Coach has opened numerous stores and boutiques in Japan. This expansion has paid off for the brand, as Coach Japan was generating more than 18 percent of the company's total revenue by the fiscal year 2003.

Customer service has been another hallmark of the Coach brand. For a shipping-and-handling fee of US$20, U.S. and Canadian customers can send most Coach items to the company for repairs. In addition, men who purchase Coach leather goods online can get free monograms on those items.

Coach has also tried to accommodate customers who are unable or unwilling to pay full price for its items. It operates a number of Coach factory outlet stores featuring less expensive Coach merchandise. These factory stores have been extraordinarily successful. Writing for Reuters, Phil Wahba noted that despite Coach's "image as a high-end brand, Coach's factory outlets, where it sells handbags and wallets for up to 50 percent less than at its stores, generate twice as much business as its full-service stores by some estimates."

BRAND EQUITY

- Coach ranks among the largest 2,000 global companies, according to *Forbes* magazine.
- Coach has been named a prominent retail brand and international brand by several reputable publications.
- Consumers have made Coach the leader in the U.S. luxury handbag market.

Growth in U.S. and international markets has landed Coach a spot on the "World's Biggest Public Companies," a 2012 *Forbes* magazine ranking of the 2,000 largest international companies. *Forbes* places Coach as number 985 on the 2012 list, with US$4.5 billion in sales and US$1 billion in profit.

Its global presence has placed Coach at number 360 on the "2012 Global 500," a ranking of the top 500 global brands by brand valuation consultancy Brand Finance. In yet another ranking of brands, Coach placed seventh on the list of "2012 Best Retail Brands" from Interbrand, another leading global branding consultancy. Coach also ranked 36th in *STORES* magazine's "2012 100 Hot Retailers" list and 227th in its "2011 Top 250 Global Retailers" list.

Coach is popular not only with business analysts but also with buyers. Coach "has dominated the U.S. luxury handbag market for more than a decade and powered through the recession," wrote Cotten Timberlake of *Bloomberg*.

BRAND AWARENESS

- A poll of wealthy consumers found that those consumers recognized and bought the Coach brand more often than its competitors.
- Other polls found that Coach was the most popular Internet search for luxury handbags and was also one of the most frequently searched luxury brands on the Internet.
- Coach has listed shares on the Hong Kong Stock Exchange to raise awareness of the company in Asian markets.

Coach is a recognizable brand as well as a popular one. In a 2007 survey analyzing the luxury handbag market, the Luxury Institute found that Coach had the greatest "mind-share" among the wealthy consumers questioned in the survey, meaning that survey participants were more familiar with Coach than with any other brand. These same survey respondents gave Coach the largest market share in its industry, meaning that they had purchased more products from Coach than from its competitors in the previous year.

Similarly, the Digital Luxury Group and the Luxury Society conducted surveys that studied consumers' Internet searches. They found that Coach was the number one luxury handbag brand identified in these searches. Their 2011 survey revealed that, among American consumers seeking any type of luxury product, Coach was the third most frequently searched brand, trailing only the automotive companies BMW and Audi.

In 2011 Coach tried to capitalize on its international success by listing shares of the company on the Hong Kong Stock Exchange. Because Coach retained its listing on the New York Stock Exchange, the Hong Kong listing was not intended to raise money but to raise awareness of the company in Asian markets.

BRAND OUTLOOK

- Coach is making efforts to tap into the huge Chinese market.
- By launching its Global Business Integrity Program, Coach hopes to clarify its ethical and legal responsibilities to its workers, partners, and affiliates.
- Coach has committed to moving its headquarters to Hudson Yards, a developing area in Manhattan.

Coach hopes to build on its international success by tapping into one of the largest markets of all, China. Just as improving Japanese economic standards spurred Coach's popularity in Japan, the rising standard of living and other improving economic conditions in China have helped Coach sell more in that country. Coach planned to open a number of its stores in China in 2012 to complement the Coach boutiques currently located in existing Chinese stores.

With this expansion in mind, Coach launched the Global Business Integrity Program, a program detailing the company's ethical and legal responsibilities with regard to its workers, partners, and various affiliates. It has established a phone number and e-mail address that employees and others can use if they want to report infractions of the company's ethical policies.

Coach has also shown a commitment to its home country. In 2011 it committed to moving its corporate headquarters to Hudson Yards in New York City. Hudson Yards is the center of a large redevelopment project that focuses on establishing new office and retail space, apartments, and other types of buildings on the far west side of Manhattan. Along with its international aspirations, Coach has maintained its New York roots.

FURTHER READING

"Best Retail Brands 2012." Interbrand. Accessed September 10, 2012. http://www.interbrand.com/en/BestRetailBrands/2012-Best-Retail-Brands.aspx#page-wrap.

Brand Finance. "Global 500 2012." *Brandirectory*. Accessed September 10, 2012. http://brandirectory.com/league_tables/table/global-500-2012.

Coach, Inc. "2011 Annual Report." Accessed September 12, 2012. http://phx.corporate-ir.net/External.File?item=UGFyZW50SUQ9NDQyMzM2fENoaWxkSUQ9NDY0NzA4fFR5cGU9MQ==&t=1.

"Coach, Inc." *International Directory of Company Histories*. Ed. Jay P. Pederson. Vol. 99. Detroit, MI: St. James Press, 2009.

"Coach Is the Most Competitive Brand in the Highly Profitable Luxury Handbags Category." *Fashion Trendsetter*, May 2007. Accessed September 12, 2012. http://www.fashiontrendsetter.com/content/press/2007/Luxury-Institute-Survey.html.

"Could Coach Replicate Its Japanese Market Success in China?" *Trefis*, January 21, 2011. Accessed September 11, 2012. http://www.trefis.com/stock/coh/articles/36137/could-coach-replicate-its-japanese-market-success-in-china/2011-01-21.

DeCarlo, Scott, editor. "The World's Biggest Public Companies." *Forbes*, April 18, 2012. Accessed September 25, 2012. http://www.forbes.com/global2000/.

Doran, Sophie. "The Most Searched for Handbag Brands in the World." *Luxury Society*, June 27, 2012. Accessed September 12, 2012. http://luxurysociety.com/articles/2012/06/the-most-searched-for-handbag-brands-in-the-world.

Doran, Sophie. "The Top 50 Most Searched for Luxury Brands in the United States." *Luxury Society*, February 24, 2012. Accessed September 12, 2012. http://luxurysociety.com/articles/2012/02/the-top-50-most-searched-for-luxury-brands-in-the-united-states.

Famous Logos. "Coach Logo." Accessed September 11, 2012. http://www.famouslogos.us/coach-logo/.

Timberlake, Cotten. "Michael Kors Brand Takes on Coach in U.S. Luxury Market." *Bloomberg*, March 16, 2012.

"2011 Top 250 Global Retailers." *STORES*, January 2012. Accessed September 11, 2012. http://www.stores.org/2011/Top-250-List.

"2012 100 Hot Retailers." *STORES*, August 2012. Accessed September 11, 2012. http://www.stores.org/2012/Hot-100-Retailers.

Wahba, Phil. "Coach Pays Price for Ditching Coupons; Shares Slump." Reuters, August 1, 2012.

COCA-COLA

AT A GLANCE

Brand Synopsis: As the leading global soft drink brand, Coca-Cola is focused on "passionately refreshing a thirsty world."
Parent Company: The Coca-Cola Company
One Coca-Cola Plaza
Atlanta, Georgia 30313
United States
http://www.thecoca-colacompany.com
Sector: Consumer Staples
Industry Group: Food, Beverage & Tobacco
Performance: *Revenues*—US$46.5 billion (2011).
Principal Competitors: PepsiCo, Inc.; Dr Pepper Snapple Group Inc.; Monster Beverage Corp.; Nestle SA; Kraft Foods Inc.; Dean Foods Company

BRAND ORIGINS

- Dr. John Styth Pemberton invented Coca-Cola in 1886.
- World War II played a key role in introducing Coca-Cola to the world.
- Advertising was used to market Coca-Cola to African Americans and other minorities beginning in the 1950s.
- During the 1970s Coca-Cola was introduced in Russia and China.
- In 1985 Coca-Cola's 99-year-old recipe was reformulated, creating New Coke, but within a year the old Coke was brought back as Coca-Cola Classic.

In 1886 an Atlanta pharmacist named Dr. John Styth Pemberton invented Coca-Cola when he concocted a mixture of sugar, water, and extracts of the coca leaf and the kola nut. He added caffeine to the resulting syrup so that it could be marketed as a headache remedy. Through his research Pemberton arrived at the conclusion that this medication was capable of relieving indigestion and exhaustion in addition to being refreshing and exhilarating. The first newspaper advertisement for Coca-Cola appeared exactly three weeks after the first batch of syrup was produced, and the famous trademark, white Spenserian script on a red background, made its debut at about the same time.

By 1891 a successful druggist named Asa G. Candler had purchased Coca-Cola for a mere US$2,300. Candler improved Pemberton's formula with the help of a chemist, a pharmacist, and a prescriptionist. Responding to complaints about the presence of minute amounts of cocaine in the Coca-Cola syrup, in 1901 Candler devised the means to remove all traces of the substance. By 1905 the syrup was completely free of cocaine.

The one-millionth gallon of Coca-Cola syrup was sold in 1904. In 1916 the now universally recognized, uniquely contoured Coke bottle was invented. Through the 1920s and 1930s, developments such as the six-pack, which encouraged shoppers to purchase the drink for home consumption, coin-operated vending machines in the workplace, and the beverage cooler expanded the domestic market considerably.

During World War II, at the request of General Dwight Eisenhower, Coca-Cola plants were set up near the fighting fronts in North Africa and eventually throughout Europe to help increase the morale of American soldiers. Thus Coca-Cola was introduced to the world. By 1944 the Coca-Cola company had sold one billion gallons of syrup, by 1953 two billion gallons had been sold, and by 1969 the company had sold six billion gallons.

Radio advertising began in 1927, and by the mid-20th century Coca-Cola's advertising was aimed at all Americans. By early 1950 African Americans were featured in advertisements, and by the mid-1950s there was an increase in advertising targeted at other minority groups. Advertisements never reflected the problems of the world, only the good and happy life.

During the 1950s Coca-Cola experienced its greatest period of European expansion. Throughout the decade new Coca-Cola plants opened at a rate of approximately 15 to 20 per year throughout the world. During the 1970s, Coca-Cola was introduced in Russia and China.

An important development took place in 1985 when, based on information gathered from blind taste-tests, a decision was made to reformulate Coke's 99-year-old recipe in the hope of combating Pepsi's growing popularity. The change to New Coke was not enthusiastically greeted by the American public. Company leadership apparently did not understand the public's emotional attachment to the name "Coca-Cola" and all that it stood for: stability, memories, and the idea of a "golden America." Within less than a year the company brought back the old Coke, calling it Coca-Cola Classic. New Coke was universally considered the biggest consumer-product blunder of the 1980s, but it was also viewed in a longer-term perspective as a positive thing, because of the massive amount of free publicity that the Coke brand received from the debacle.

BRAND ELEMENTS

- Coca-Cola's famous trademark, white Spenserian script on a red background, made its debut shortly after the first batch of syrup was produced in 1886.
- Coca-Cola is available in a number of different variations.
- Since 1916 Coca-Cola has been packaged in a universally recognized, uniquely contoured bottle.
- Coca-Cola has been particularly effective at adapting its brand to international markets.

Although there were at least 10 different variations of the brand in 2012, the original Coca-Cola was developed in 1886 when Dr. John Styth Pemberton concocted a formula consisting of sugar, water, caffeine, and extracts of the coca leaf and the kola nut. The formula was modified in 1905 to remove traces of cocaine. In 1985 Coca-Cola's 99-year-old recipe was reformulated, creating New Coke. Within less than a year the old Coke was brought back as Coca-Cola Classic. At the time of Coca-Cola's 125th anniversary in 2011, the record of the secret formula was relocated from the company's headquarters to the The World of Coca-Cola museum in Atlanta.

Coca-Cola's famous trademark, white Spenserian script on a red background, made its debut shortly after the first batch of syrup was produced. The brand has been communicated through a number of memorable slogans. These include "It's the Real Thing," "Always Coca-Cola," and "Coke is it!" In 2009 the company rolled out its "Open Happiness" campaign, which captured the heart of the brand's identity.

Since 1916 Coca-Cola has been packaged in the universally recognized, uniquely contoured Coke bottle, the diameter of which is widest in the midsection. The bottle was designed by Earl R. Dean of the Indiana-based Root Glass Company. He was said to have designed the bottle to reflect the gourd-shaped outline of the coca pod. An article in the April 29, 2012, issue of the *Jakarta Post* indicated that global research has found Coca-Cola's contour bottle to be the world's second-most-recognizable form, after the egg. The contour bottle has been modified several times, including the introduction of different sizes in the 1950s; a lower-weight, more impact-resistant ultra-glass contour bottle in 2000; and an aluminum contour bottle named the Magnificent 5 in 2005.

Coca-Cola has been particularly effective at adapting its brand to international markets. For example, during the 1920s the company discovered that to be successful in England, Coca-Cola could not be marketed with the same pomp as in other markets. Time was taken to understand the nuances of British attitudes and business customs prior to the launch of television advertising during the 1950s.

BRAND IDENTITY

- Throughout its history, optimism and happiness have been key elements of Coca-Cola's brand identity.
- The Coca-Cola brand has demonstrated the ability to make an emotional connection with society at key moments in history.
- In 2009 Coca-Cola unveiled its "Open Happiness" campaign, which captured the heart of its brand identity.

Throughout Coca-Cola's history, optimism and happiness have been key elements of its brand identity. The brand has demonstrated the ability to make an emotional connection with society at key moments in history. During the mid-20th century Coca-Cola's advertising to minorities emphasized the best and happiest moments of life. In

1971 the brand's well-known "Hilltop" advertising campaign communicated a sense of optimism following the Vietnam War.

In 2009 Coca-Cola unveiled its "Open Happiness" campaign, which captured the heart of its brand identity. In the Coca-Cola Company's *2011 Annual Review*, Chairman and CEO Muhtar Kent discussed how the brand occupies "a unique place in the hearts of people worldwide." The company has capitalized on this by "creating memorable moments of connection and fun" for its customers. The company concludes that it provides affordable luxury to its customers by selling "moments of happiness, for cents at a time, more than 1.7 billion times a day in more than 200 countries."

BRAND STRATEGY

- By 2011 Coca-Cola had reorganized its marketing teams to make them less localized and was focused on finding common elements shared by consumers globally.
- Market fragmentation has prompted Coca-Cola to adopt a brand strategy that encompasses a variety of different tactics, some of which are unconventional.
- The appeal of Coca-Cola has been maximized through the introduction of multiple variations of the original brand.
- Social media is a key component of Coca-Cola's brand strategy, and by 2011 it had developed the leading consumer product page on Facebook.
- In 2012 Coca-Cola ranked 33rd on *License!*'s ranking of the world's top 125 global licensors.

Traditional advertising is an important aspect of Coca-Cola's strategy. Citing data from the *Wall Street Journal*, in October 2011 *DM News* reported that Coca-Cola's soda-related advertising totaled US$253 million in 2010, compared to PepsiCo's US$153 million. Even so, both companies had reduced their advertising spending from only five years before (US$377 million and US$348 million, respectively). Fragmentation has created a marketplace that prevents Coca-Cola from relying on a single mass media campaign to reach the majority of consumers. In 2012 this was made evident by a brand strategy that encompassed a variety of different tactics, some of which were more conventional than others.

By 2011 Coca-Cola's global strategy was focusing on the elimination of so-called geographic silos, according to the May 11, 2011, issue of *Marketing*. In this regard, the company had reorganized its marketing teams to make them less localized. An emphasis was placed on finding common elements shared by consumers everywhere, regardless of geography. One catalyst for this strategy was the 2008 Olympic Games in Beijing. The *Marketing* article referred to the company's international "Open Happiness" campaign, which was "designed to extend beyond country borders and the realms of traditional media."

Coca-Cola Music is one example of the brand's use of nontraditional approaches to connect with consumers. Described in the company's *2011 Annual Review* as an "integrated music platform, focused on teen recruitment," the initiative involved providing fans with opportunities to interact with well-known artists. One example involved providing fans with a means to upload footage for use in a music video from the band, One Night Only.

Another unconventional brand strategy was Coca-Cola's "Where Will Happiness Strike Next?" project. Launched in about 40 markets worldwide, this initiative involved the use of special teams who created roughly 100 "films and brand experiences centered on surprising moments of authentic happiness," according to Coca-Cola's *2011 Annual Review*. This unique approach was highly successful, resulting in more than 285 off-line and online impressions throughout the world.

The appeal of Coca-Cola has been maximized through the introduction of multiple variations of the original brand. In 2012 these included Coca-Cola Black Cherry Vanilla, Coca-Cola Black, Coca-Cola C2, Coca-Cola Citra, Coca-Cola Light/Diet Coke, Coca-Cola with Lemon, Coca-Cola with Lime, Coca-Cola with Raspberry, and Coca-Cola Zero. Customers gained unprecedented options for enjoying Coca-Cola following the introduction of the Coca-Cola Freestyle fountain. Introduced to the US markets in 2011, the new dispenser offered the ability to make custom blends of Coca-Cola beverages at quick-serve restaurants and other venues.

Social media is another key component of Coca-Cola's strategy. The brand has achieved tremendous success on Facebook, where it maintains the social network's leading consumer product page. By late 2011 the brand had amassed roughly 34 million Facebook fans, a figure that was growing approximately 3 percent monthly.

Product licensing provides Coca-Cola with other opportunities to connect with consumers in new ways. In 2012 the brand ranked 33rd on *License!*'s ranking of the world's top 125 global licensors. In this area, Coca-Cola worked with leaders in the categories of sports, fashion, and technology to connect with approximately 500 million consumers who purchase licensed merchandise every year. Coca-Cola benefited from additional licensing opportunities in 2012 in connection with its 125th anniversary.

BRAND EQUITY

- In 2011 the Coca-Cola brand was valued at US$71.9 billion, an increase of 2 percent over the previous year.

- Interbrand ranked Coca-Cola as the leader on its 100 Best Global Brands ranking for the 12th consecutive year in 2011.
- In 2012 Coca-Cola was ranked as the leading soft drink brand, and sixth overall, on Millward Brown Optimor's 2012 BrandZ Top 100 ranking.
- Coca-Cola was a billion-dollar brand in 18 countries in 2011.

In 2011 the Coca-Cola brand was valued at US$71.9 billion, an increase of 2 percent over the previous year. That year Interbrand ranked Coca-Cola as the leader on its 100 Best Global Brands ranking for the 12th consecutive year. In 2012 Coca-Cola ranked sixth on Millward Brown Optimor's 2012 BrandZ Top 100 ranking. However, it was the soft drink category leader, ahead of Pepsi (67) and Red Bull (80). Coca-Cola's brand equity is geographically dispersed, which is evidenced by its status as a billion-dollar brand in 18 countries.

Citing figures from Euromonitor, *Market Share Reporter* indicated that Coca-Cola was the leading soft drink manufacturer worldwide in 2010, with a 42 percent market share. This compared to competitors PepsiCo (29 percent) and Dr Pepper Snapple Group (17 percent). By 2011 The Coca-Cola Co.'s beverages were available in more than 200 countries worldwide. Customers enjoyed about 1.7 billion servings of the company's drinks, including Coca-Cola, every day.

BRAND AWARENESS

- By the time of its 125th anniversary in 2011, the Coca-Cola brand was universally recognized in virtually all corners of the world and had attained an iconic status.
- Coca-Cola had amassed about 34 million friends on Facebook by late 2011 and maintained the social network's leading consumer product page.
- According to a Harris Interactive poll, Coca-Cola was ranked by consumers as the leading soft drink brand in 2012.

In 2011 Coca-Cola celebrated its 125th anniversary. By this time the brand was universally recognized in virtually all corners of the world and had attained an iconic status. As *Marketing* explained in its May 11, 2011, issue: "The word 'icon' is overused in branding, but Coca-Cola is among the more deserving of the description. ... Coke is one of the greatest branding success stories in history."

Compared to the second half of the first decade of the 21st century, leading beverage companies have scaled back the portion of their advertising budgets devoted specifically to soft drinks. However, in 2011 the Coca-Cola Co. promoted awareness of its beverage brands with a generous advertising budget. That year overall advertising expenses totaled US$3.26 billion, up from US$2.92 billion in 2010 and US$2.79 billion in 2009.

Social media is another means of measuring Coca-Cola's brand awareness. By late 2011 it had amassed about 34 million friends on Facebook, where it maintained the social network's leading consumer product page. At that time Coca-Cola's Facebook fan base was achieving a monthly growth rate of about 3 percent. Citing the results of a study from Covario Inc., the *North County Times* (Escondido, CA) indicated that the typical Coca-Cola Facebook post generates about 1,750 likes from fans. The study revealed that the most engaging brand postings typically obtain at least 1,500 likes.

In its April 27, 2012, issue, *just-drinks* shared the results of a Harris Interactive poll that measured the health of approximately 1,500 US brands. Results were gleaned from approximately 38,500 respondents. Among the attributes measured by the research was the public's familiarity with a particular brand. When rating the leading soft drink brand of the year, 72.30 percent of consumers chose Coca-Cola, compared to Pepsi-Cola (70.07 percent), Sprite (68.05 percent), 7UP (67.32 percent), and Dr Pepper (66.08 percent).

BRAND OUTLOOK

- Coca-Cola's 2020 Vision includes a goal to at least double the number of beverage servings to more than 3 billion per day by 2020.
- One major challenge for Coca-Cola was the fact that fewer Americans were consuming soda in 2012.
- The Coca-Cola Co.'s beverage portfolio had grown to include more than 800 low-calorie beverages by 2011.

In its *2011 Annual Review* the Coca-Cola Co.'s "2020 Vision" statement outlined the company's strategy for the coming decade. The statement's goals included at least doubling the number of beverage servings to more than 3 billion per day and becoming the leader in a number of nonalcoholic, ready-to-drink beverage categories and markets. The company also revealed plans to more than double the revenues generated by the Coca-Cola system, which includes Coca-Cola Co. and its approximately 300 bottling partners.

One major challenge that Coca-Cola and other beverage manufacturers faced was the fact that fewer Americans were consuming soda in 2012. Citing figures from *Beverage Digest*, in 2011 the *Atlanta Journal-Constitution* reported that US per capita soft-drink consumption had declined to 1988 levels. Rising levels of health consciousness, as well as concerns over childhood obesity, were potential roadblocks to increasing volume. In 2011 the City of Boston revealed plans to eliminate sugary drinks on city property. The following year New York City Mayor Michael Bloomberg proposed a ban on single-serve soft drinks larger than 16 ounces, a move that some industry observers feared could establish a national precedent.

Boding well for the Coca-Cola Co. was a beverage portfolio that had grown to include more than 800 low-calorie beverages by 2011. These included Coca-Cola Zero, a no-calorie version of the flagship brand that was introduced in one of the most successful product launches in the company's history. In 2009 alone more than 600 million cases of Coca-Cola Zero were sold worldwide, and by the following year the beverage was available in more than 130 countries. In 2011 the Coca-Cola Co. added more than 100 no- or low-calorie beverages to its product range.

FURTHER READING

"Classic Bottle Gives Added Contours to Brand Identity." *Jakarta Post*, April 29, 2012.

The Coca-Cola Co. "Passionately Refreshing a Thirsty World: 2011 Annual Review." Accessed October 1, 2012. http://www.thecoca-colacompany.com/ourcompany/ar/company-highlights.html.

"The Coca-Cola Company." *International Directory of Company Histories*. Ed. Jay P. Pederson. Vol. 67. Detroit, MI: St. James Press, 2005. *Business and Company Resource Center*. Accessed October 1, 2012.

"Coca-Cola and PepsiCo Face New Headwinds as New York Bans Sale of Oversized Sodas and Sugary Drinks." *Internet Wire*, June 5, 2012.

Fikes, Bradley J. "Coca-Cola Tops Brands on Facebook, Says Covario." *North County Times* (Escondido, CA), October 22, 2011.

Le Barile Krause, Reinhardt. "Taking a Hard Line on Soft Drinks; Drink Makers Respond to Health-Savvy Markets with New Products and an Overseas Push." *Investor's Business Daily*, July 2, 2012.

Lisanti, Tony. "Top 125 Global Licensors: This Exclusive Report Ranks the World's Largest Licensors." *License!*, May 2012.

"Making Coke's Brand Fizz." *Marketing*, May 11, 2011.

McWilliams, Jeremiah. "'World's Best Brand' Plans to Get Better with Age: But It Won't Be Easy as Competition Stiffens." *Atlanta Journal-Constitution*, May 1, 2011.

Slack, Eric. "A True Classic Anywhere: No Other Beverage Brand Has as Hefty a Worldwide Resonance, Built on a Platform of Thinking Globally and Acting Locally, than Coca-Cola, and It Continues to Be One of the World's Best Brands." *Retail Merchandiser*, September–October 2011.

Washkuch, Frank. "Battle of the Brands: Cola Giants Scurry to Attract Younger Consumers in Decades-Long Turf War." *DM News*, October 1, 2011.

Wehring, Olly. "Just the Facts—The 2012 Harris Poll EquiTrend." *just-drinks*, April 27, 2012.

COLES

AT A GLANCE

Brand Synopsis: With millions of transactions every week, Coles operates under a number of brands and is the second-largest supermarket chain in Australia.
Parent Company: Wesfarmers Limited
Wesfarmers House, 11th Floor
40 The Esplanade
Perth 6000, Western Australia
Australia
http://www.coles.com.au/
Sector: Consumer Staples
Industry Group: Food & Staples Retailing
Performance: *Market share*—Coles and its main competitor, Woolworths Limited, account for almost 80 percent of all food retail in Australia. *Sales*—US$45.77 billion (2011).
Principal Competitors: Woolworths Limited; Foodland Associated Limited; ALDI Group; Metcash Limited

BRAND ORIGINS

- George and James Coles opened the first Coles variety store in the suburban Melbourne town of Collingwood, Victoria, Australia, in 1914.
- The 1950s and 1960s saw the Coles family acquire stores, including supermarkets, which they operated as Coles New World stores throughout Australia and Tasmania.
- From 1986 to 2006 Coles was associated with the Myer department store chain and other stores and known as Coles Myer Limited.
- The Coles Group Limited is part of Wesfarmers, a business group comprising a host of retailers and other businesses.

George (G. J.) and James (Jim) Coles opened a variety store in the suburban Melbourne town of Collingwood, Victoria, Australia, in 1914. Nearly 100 years later, there were more than 700 Coles supermarkets and other Coles stores throughout Australia, all part of the retailing group Coles Group Limited.

The Coles brothers' variety stores were 3d., 6d., and 1/- variety stores. This meant the stores sold items for 3d. (threepence), 6d. (sixpence), and one shilling (1/-). The stores were known for their slogan "Nothing over 2/6," or nothing over two shillings and sixpence. Australia used these units of currency before it adopted dollars and cents as its units of currency.

The Coles family opened variety stores throughout Australia and Tasmania. It also acquired a number of other Australian retail businesses, including supermarkets. It began opening supermarkets in the late 1950s and 1960s under the Coles New World name. This supermarket chain became known simply as Coles in 1991. It operated a number of supermarkets under the Bi-Lo name but stopped using the name in the early 2000s. Similarly, Coles once operated a number of Kmart discount stores in Australia, but the parent company of Coles, Wesfarmers, created a separate Kmart division in 2007.

Coles has been linked to a number of other retailers. From 1986 to 2006 Coles was associated with the Myer department store chain and other stores and known as Coles Myer Limited. Beginning in November 2006 Coles became part of Coles Group Limited. In addition to supermarkets, this group contains the chain Coles Express (gas stations and convenience stores) and the alcohol retailers Liquorland, Vintage Cellars, and First Choice Liquor. Online customers can shop at the Coles.com or Coles Music sites. Coles offers the flybuys loyalty program and a MasterCard credit card and also has nonretail businesses, such as hotels and car insurance and home insurance enterprises.

The Coles Group Limited is a member of the Wesfarmers group of businesses. Wesfarmers contains all of the aforementioned Coles businesses as well as the Australian Kmart chain; the Australian discount chain Target (not related to the American discount retailer); office supply and home improvement retailers; insurance and banking companies; and companies specializing in chemicals, energy, safety and industrial products and services, and other business interests. These multiple and diverse interests have made Coles and Wesfarmers huge presences in Australian retailing.

BRAND ELEMENTS

- The Coles logo consists of the word Coles in lowercase red letters.
- Coles' private store brands include Coles Create & Cook brand, Coles Finest, and Coles Simply Less.
- Environmentally conscious Coles brands include Coles Green Choice (environmentally friendly cleaning products) and Coles Organic (organic food).
- Coles claims that almost 90 percent of Coles private brand foods and beverages and many of its Coles Organic foods are from Australia.

The Coles logo is extremely simple: the word Coles in lowercase red letters. This logo and the color red appear on different signs inside and outside of Coles stores and on shopping trolleys (carts), employee uniforms, websites, and materials associated with the brand, such as press releases.

As with other supermarkets throughout the world, Coles sells a number of its own store brands. The Coles brand consists of food and beverages, almost 90 percent of which, according the company, are made in Australia, as well as cleaning products and baby products. The Coles Create & Cook brand includes ingredients (such as sauces, pastes, and seasonings) and recipes used to make meal preparation easier. Coles Finest includes gourmet food products, Coles Smart Buy (also known as $mart Buy) consists of a wide variety of reasonably priced items, and Coles Simply Less features products for health-conscious consumers.

Other Coles private brands target environmentally conscious consumers. Coles Green Choice consists of environmentally friendly cleaning products. Coles promotes these goods as being environmentally responsible as well as cheaper than the average eco-friendly cleaner. The Coles Organic brand features organic foods. Many of these organic foods are from Australia and stand as yet another example of the store's commitment to Australian producers and their products.

BRAND IDENTITY

- The Coles website includes the trademarked slogan "Coles: Helping Australia Grow."
- The Coles website states that many of its foods and beverages are from Australia and includes information about these products.
- Several Coles products demonstrate their Australian origins with badges marked "Australian Made" or "Australian Grown."
- The 2012 Coles advertising slogan emphasized the chain's commitment to freshness: "There's no freshness like Coles freshness."

Coles focuses a lot of attention on its home country. Its website says that "For more than 90 years, Coles has been a highly regarded and much loved part of Australian life." In fact, Coles frequently reminds people that it is an Australian brand, that it sells Australian products, and that it serves the Australian people. That, in sum, is its brand identity.

Evidence of Coles's Australian identity can be found on its website. The Coles website includes the trademarked slogan "Coles: Helping Australia Grow." It offers information and videos about Coles products from Australia, including the fact that it acquires 100 percent of its fresh meat, fresh salmon, mangoes, and fresh milk for drinking, and 96 percent of its fresh vegetables and fruit from Australia. Several Coles products feature badges with kangaroos that say "Australian Made" or "Australian Grown." Kangaroos, of course, are native Australian animals and heavily associated with the country. By using kangaroos on its labels, Coles further identifies with its home country. This focus on Australian products also means a focus on freshness. In 2012 Coles emphasized the freshness of its food when it began using the advertising slogan "There's no freshness like Coles freshness."

The store's interest in Australia can also be seen in its charitable and community endeavors. Part of the proceeds from the sales of its private brand Coles Green Choice go to Clean Up Australia, which, as its name indicates, is an organization working to clean up and improve Australia's environment. By affiliating with Clean Up Australia, Coles demonstrates its interest in the environment. It also reinforces its status as an Australian company working for Australians, a company that works with its fellow Australians to improve their shared country.

BRAND STRATEGY

- Coles offers a variety of stores and store brands under the Coles name and other names.
- Joseph Mimran's Mix Apparel clothing and accessories line began appearing in Coles stores in 2011, raising awareness for Coles and its unique offerings.
- In 2010 Coles established a tie-in with the popular television program *MasterChef Australia*, which brought the chain increased visibility.

Coles has used its own brand name and other brand names in various applications, from store names to store brands. The Coles name appears on its supermarkets, its Coles Express gas stations and convenience stores, and the online Coles.com or Coles Music, although it does not use the Coles name for its Liquorland, Vintage Cellars, and First Choice Liquor stores. Coles supermarkets use the Coles name for its variety of store brands: Coles Create & Cook, Coles Smart Buy (or Coles $mart Buy), Coles Simply Less, and Coles Green Choice. The frequent name repetition portrays Coles as a retailer with a wide variety of offerings. Even Coles entities that do not use the Coles name reinforce Coles's position as a prominent retailer.

In recent years, Coles has partnered with professionals and television programs to raise awareness of its brands. It began offering the Mix Apparel clothing and accessories line by Canadian designer Joseph Mimran in Coles stores in 2011. In 2010 Coles established a tie-in with the television program *MasterChef Australia*, the Australian version of a popular cooking competition program that has aired in several countries. Its stores began using the slogan "To cook like a MasterChef cooks, shop where a MasterChef shops" and featured recipe cards relating to recipes used on the program. Coles hired celebrity chef Curtis Stone, a frequent guest on *MasterChef Australia*, to represent the company in advertisements and online. Two years later, in 2012, Stone continued to represent the brand, linking Coles to food, cooking, and creative culinary endeavors.

BRAND EQUITY

- Coles's association with the television program *MasterChef Australia* has led to dramatic increases in the sales of products used as ingredients on the show.
- Coles and another Australian chain, Woolworths Limited, accounted for 75 percent to 80 percent of all food retailing in Australia in 2012.
- Coles and Woolworths together captured more than half of Australia's beef market in August 2012.

Its association with *MasterChef Australia* has reaped benefits for Coles. When *MasterChef Australia* featured a recipe for beef stroganoff, beef sales at Coles rose 30 percent overnight. Coles has also experienced dramatic sales increases for other products used in other *MasterChef Australia* recipes.

Coles Group Limited and another Australian chain of supermarkets and other stores, Woolworths Limited, dominate Australian retail. These two corporations accounted for 75 to 80 percent of all food retailing in Australia in 2012. A study published in 2011 reported that Coles and Woolworths accounted for almost 40 percent of all retail spending in Australia. Some critics have alleged that the companies hold too much market share and have accused them of operating as a duopoly. These charges have led some customers to boycott the chains.

Both Coles and Woolworths control large portions of various markets. For example, both control large percentages of Australia's beef market. In August 2012 Coles held 26.4 percent share of that market and Woolworths stores' claimed a 30.3 percent market share.

BRAND AWARENESS

- In 2011 and 2012 Coles and Woolworths engaged in price wars, fighting to offer the lowest prices for items like milk and bread.
- The 2011 and 2012 price wars between Coles and Woolworths generated a great deal of publicity and raised awareness for both chains.
- In 2011 Coles aired a television commercial for its hormone-free beef; within a week of the airing, the company reported an 85 percent brand awareness for the beef.

Woolworths Limited and Coles Group Limited are the two largest supermarket chains in Australia and together dominate the country's retail food market. Neither appears to be satisfied with this success. Instead, they have taken actions to gain even more sales, customers, and publicity. In 2011 and 2012 Coles and Woolworths engaged in price wars. In 2011 they fought "milk wars" to provide the lowest prices for milk, bread, and laundry detergent. In 2012 they both lowered prices on fresh vegetables and fruits. Various news outlets publicized the stores' actions, raising awareness for Coles and Woolworths as well as their products.

Brand awareness for Coles also soared because of a divisive but memorable advertising campaign in 2011. A television commercial for Coles hormone-free beef featured a new version of Australian singer Normie Rowe's 1960s hit "Shakin' All Over." The commercial also featured Coles spokesperson Curtis Stone, who had previously appeared in various promotions for Coles food. In a poll conducted after the commercial was broadcast, significant numbers of Australians admitted that the ad helped them feel more positively about Coles. Others, however, reported that the ad made them feel more negatively about the chain. These strong opinions garnered an 85 percent brand awareness for Coles hormone-free beef a week after the commercial aired.

BRAND OUTLOOK

- In 2012 Coles announced plans to open new stores and renovate old ones.
- Coles captured a 31 percent share of Australia's grocery market in 2011, second only to Woolworths's 41.1 percent share.
- Since 2010, Coles's Down Down price-cutting campaign has improved sales volumes, market share, and revenue.

In 2012 Coles announced its plans to open a number of new stores and renovate older stores. This concerned owners of smaller, independent grocery store chains. They worried that the numbers and sizes of Coles and Woolworths stores could add to the two chains' already dominant position in Australian food retailing. Coles and Woolworths already accounted for 75 to 80 percent of all Australian grocery spending in 2012.

According to a 2012 report, Coles estimated that it held a 31 percent share of the Australian grocery market in 2011, second only to Woolworths's 41.1 percent share. These findings discussed that newer entries to Australia's grocery market, such as German-based ALDI, had taken market share from independent Australian grocers in recent years.

Since 2010, Coles has reduced prices as part of its Down Down campaign. The reduced prices have encouraged shoppers to buy more, thus improving Coles's sales volume, market share, and revenue. A 2012 report noted that sales volume for a type of Coles brand milk improved 333.38 percent by 2012. In 2013, Coles continued its Down Down campaign, publicizing its cost cutting on a number of products. This move continues Coles's roles as a brand committed to value and a highly visible retailer.

FURTHER READING

Carney, Matthew. "Coles, Woolies 'Deliberately Killing Competition.'" ABC News, August 14, 2012.

"Coles Group Limited." *International Directory of Company Histories*. Ed. Jay P. Pederson. Vol. 85. Detroit, MI: St. James Press, 2007.

Condon, Jon. "Woolworths Lifts Retail Beef Market Share, at Coles Expense." *Beef Central*, October 5, 2012. Accessed November 10, 2012. http://www.beefcentral.com/p/news/article/2244.

Deloitte Access Economics. "Analysis of the Grocery Industry: Coles Supermarkets Australia." October, 2012. Accessed February 21, 2013. http://www.coles.com.au/Portals/0/content/pdf/Shareholders/Grocery%20Industry%20Report.pdf.

"Lampooned Normie Rowe Remix Leads to Record Beef Sales for Coles." *mUmBRELLA*, February 3, 2012. Accessed November 10, 2012. http://mumbrella.com.au/lampooned-normie-rowe-remix-leads-to-record-beef-sales-for-coles-72740.

Pallant, Jason. "Can Coles (Fly) Buy Shopper Loyalty?" *Conversation*, April 24, 2012. Accessed November 9, 2012. http://theconversation.edu.au/can-coles-fly-buy-shopper-loyalty-6640.

Sinclair, Lara. "MasterChef Sparks Coles Sales Surge." *Australian*, June 21, 2010.

Viellaris, Renee, and Nick Gardner. "Coles and Woolworths Receive Almost 40 Per Cent of Australian Retail Spending." *Sunday Mail* (Sydney, Australia), April 24, 2011.

COLGATE

AT A GLANCE

Brand Synopsis: The leading oral-care company in the world, Colgate is associated with trusted, quality, often market-defining toothpastes, toothbrushes, and related products.
Parent Company: Colgate Palmolive
300 Park Avenue
New York, New York 10022
United States
http://www.colgatepalmolive.com/
Sector: Consumer Staples
Industry Group: Household & Personal Products
Performance: *Market share*—45 percent of the global toothpaste market (2011); 36.6 percent of the U.S. toothpaste market (2011); 32.8 percent of the global manual toothbrush market (2011).
Principal Competitors: Aim; Aquafresh; Arm & Hammer; Close-Up; Crest; Mentadent; Oral-B; Pepsodent; Sensodyne

BRAND ORIGINS

- Colgate began as a soap company in 1806 in New York City.
- Colgate introduced its first toothpaste in 1873.
- The introduction of Colgate Total in 1997 restored the brand's number-one position in the toothpaste market globally and in the United States.

Colgate's origins stretch back to 1806 when William Colgate started his own business manufacturing laundry and hand soaps. Over the next few decades, his soaps stood out for their quality and affordability, and he added starch and candles to his product line. In 1873 Colgate introduced its own brand of aromatic toothpaste, sold in jars. Formulated with a mild abrasive (slightly heavier than chalk), a detergent, and mint extracts, Colgate entered the market as an entirely new concept in dental care, a palatable dentifrice, marketed as Colgate Dental Cream.

A better-tasting alternative to chalky, soapy-tasting competitors, Colgate was introduced as a major brand, though few people used toothpaste at the time, in part because it was considered a luxury item. In the late 19th century the technology for tubes was imported into the United States and soon further improved Colgate's fortunes. In 1896 Colgate introduced toothpaste in tubes. The brand became the toothpaste market-leader, and the tube technology became the norm in the United States.

In 1908 the brand developed its own unique rectangular nozzle opening on the tube that extruded the toothpaste as a more usable flat bar in 1908. Colgate Dental Cream then became Colgate Ribbon Dental Cream. For years, Colgate ads featured the slogan "Comes out a ribbon; lies flat on the brush." Though the Colgate company had more than 800 products by 1906, it was primarily known for its toothpaste because of innovations like the tube and the nozzle.

Colgate also realized that ingraining the habit of toothbrushing in children would help build the brand. Colgate distributed two million free tubes of toothpaste, and several thousand toothbrushes, to schools in 1911 and 1912, when tooth brushing was still only sporadically practiced. Colgate also included literature aimed at parents. This marketing effort effectively instilled habitual brushing in American society and improved the reputation of Colgate. Similar programs for children are still part of Colgate's marketing efforts.

As Colgate was building its brand, it went international for the first time in 1914, when moved into the Canadian market. During the 1920s Colgate began spreading into various markets in Europe, Asia, Latin America, and Africa, something that would continue in the 20th century. In 1928 Colgate & Company, as it had been known since 1857, merged with Palmolive-Peet Company, which also began as a soap company. Originally the Colgate-Palmolive-Peet Company, it became the Colgate-Palmolive Company in 1953. By the 1950s, Colgate had slogans like "It Cleans Your Breath While It Cleans Your Teeth," and was recognized as both a global and U.S. market leader.

In 1955, after the introduction of Procter & Gamble's Crest, which contained decay-fighting stannous fluoride, Colgate's market share began to fall. After Crest was endorsed by the American Dental Association (ADA), Colgate lost its number-one status to Crest. In response, a reformulated Colgate toothpaste with monofluorophosphate was put on the market in 1968. New ads proclaimed that Colgate was "unsurpassed" in cavity protection. Colgate's new toothpaste gained ADA recognition in 1969, which stemmed the loss of market share to Crest.

Also in the 1960s, Colgate introduced its first brand extension, a mouthwash called Colgate 100. While Colgate remained a secondary brand to Crest throughout the 1970s, the brand took advantage of new market trends by introducing its first gel toothpaste in 1981, first toothpaste in a pump in 1984, and first tartar control toothpaste in 1986, among many other products.

By 1994 Colgate had a 22.5 percent market share in the United States and was the second-best-selling toothpaste brand after Crest, on sales of US$225 million. Colgate was able to regain its number-one position, both globally and in the United States, in the years after the introduction of Colgate Total in 1997. It was the first toothpaste to fight cavities, tartar, and gingivitis, and eventually became the brand's best-selling toothpaste.

Colgate continued to build its brand through product introduction, with a significant number of new products launched every year in the oral care market. By 2004 Colgate was struggling again, as Proctor & Gamble, including Crest, seemed ready to overtake Colgate. Colgate then launched a four-year restructuring plan. The plan led to an increase in market share, including 35.3 percent of the U.S. market in 2005 and 36 percent by 2008. By 2009 Colgate-Palmolive revenues were over US$15 billion, and there was a greater focus and investment in emerging markets such as India. By 2012 Colgate-Palmolive revenues had reached US$16.73 billion, with 43 percent coming from its oral care division, primarily the Colgate brand.

BRAND ELEMENTS

- The Colgate name has been associated with quality since the brand's founding in 1806.
- Colgate's packaging, logo, and advertising underscore the brand's simple, straightforward values.
- Colgate's logo is the Colgate name in streamlined white letters on a red background, reflecting its core values.

From the company's founding, the Colgate name has been associated with quality. When William Colgate started his soap company in 1806, his products stood out because they were of a higher quality than was generally available at the time. Over the next few decades, Colgate improved the quality of its soaps but kept them affordable. In the 1840s, Colgate also introduced scented soaps, which proved extremely popular, and in the 1860s the first milled, perfumed toilet soaps. When Colgate toothpaste, sold in jars, entered the market in 1873, it successfully followed the same business model as Colgate soaps and eventually became the primary focus of the brand.

Colgate's packaging, logo, and advertising reflected the brand's simple, straightforward values. When Colgate toothpaste was first packaged in tubes in 1896, it was in all-tin tubes on which was pasted a pinkish-tan paper label with maroon lettering. The tube was packaged in a bronze-colored cardboard box that featured a signed guarantee from Samuel Colgate, then the head of the company, and a testimonial from a professor of dental surgery, one of the first scientific endorsements on a product.

Colgate's color scheme was changed radically in 1933. Company leader S. Bayard Colgate oversaw the creation of an all-white tube with a thick scarlet band printed across it. Within that band, the name Colgate was printed in streamlined white letters. This enduring modern design has remained basically unchanged ever since, though red replaced scarlet on the Colgate logo and packaging. Throughout the 20th and into the 21st century, Colgate's advertisements have been similarly focused on promoting the brand with honest statements about the product's purpose. In 2012 the tagline for Colgate Total Advanced Whitening was "Advanced whitening, plus 12-hour germ fighting protection."

BRAND IDENTITY

- Colgate has emphasized low-key, informative advertising since its introduction.
- Colgate currently defines itself through many media, including television, radio, and print advertisements and also digital campaigns, including social media.

- The "Colgate Bright Smiles, Bright Futures" program effectively markets the brand's oral care products while educating and helping children globally.

In the late 19th century, many toothpaste brands made wild claims about the medicinal qualities of their products, including the ability to cure pyorrhea and acid mouth, firm the gums, and fill cavities. Colgate never made such claims in its advertisements, but instead emphasized that toothpastes could not perform such fantastic feats. By being honest with the public, Colgate soon built a strong trust-equity with consumers.

The greatest health claim made by Colgate in its early days was that its toothpaste was a safe cleansing agent that was refreshing, pleasant tasting, and economical. This trend of being low-key, honest, and simple in its advertising claims continued for decades. In the early 1950s, for example, one ad campaign for Colgate claimed "It Cleans Your Breath While It Cleans Your Teeth." Such advertisements helped make Colgate the leading toothpaste brand in the world.

Over the years, Colgate has improved its products and developed new ones intended to make teeth more resistant to decay, provide fresher breath, and combat gum disease. Many advertisements focused on Colgate's superior qualities and emphasized its seal of approval from the American Dental Association (ADA), gained in 1969. Colgate also then claimed it was unsurpassed in cavity protection. Other ads proclaimed "Colgate. Because your smile was meant to last a lifetime" and "Colgate—the world's biggest smile." By 2012 the brand's straightforward and informational taglines included "Advanced whitening, plus 12-hour germ fighting protection" for Colgate Total Advanced Whitening and "A healthier whole mouth clean for sensitive teeth and gums" for Colgate 360° Sensitive. Such messages were also emphasized in integrated marketing campaigns, through television, radio, and print ads, as well as in-store and digital outlets, including social media.

From its earliest days, Colgate was concerned with corporate citizenship, and it remained highly ranked globally in this area in the 21st century. To promote its product and improve Americans' dental health, in 2011 Colgate began distributing millions of free tubes of toothpaste to children through their schools, with related literature for their parents. This practice continued with the "Colgate Bright Smiles, Bright Futures" campaign. In addition to toothbrushes, toothpaste, and dental information, needy children receive free dental screenings and education. By 2012, 650 million children were reached in 80 countries.

BRAND STRATEGY

- Colgate, an innovative brand, introduced Colgate Total in 1997.
- Every year Colgate introduced or improved hundreds of products and brand extensions globally.
- Beginning in 2005, Colgate focused on growing international markets in Latin America and Asia.

Since the early 20th century, Colgate has identified itself as an innovative brand, an industry leader in product development. Colgate was one of the first to introduce toothpaste in tubes in 1900. Years later, in 1997, it put Colgate Total on the market. It was the first toothpaste to be an all-in-one solution for cavities, tartar, and gingivitis, and helped Colgate regain its number-one position globally and in the United States.

Colgate also regularly introduced brand extensions and new products, as well as improving its existing products. Colgate presented its first brand extension, a mouthwash called Colgate 100 in the 1960s. Colgate also added new toothpastes, dental floss, whitening systems, and professional products with prescription-strength doses for dentist offices. In addition, Colgate responded to industry trends by introducing a fluoride version in 1968, a gel version in 1981, a pump-packed toothpaste in 1984, tartar control toothpastes in 1986, a baking soda formula in 1992, and numerous whitening and sensitivity-relief toothpastes in the first years of the 21st century.

New products were introduced in 2011 and 2012, including Colgate Sensitive Pro-Relief toothpaste and the Colgate Optic White whitening system. To appeal to children, Colgate had products with such popular characters as Dora the Explorer, Barbie, and Sponge Bob Square Pants. In 2013 the brand introduced One Direction themed oral care products in the United States, including toothpastes and power and manual toothbrushes.

By 2012 Colgate was selling its products in over 220 countries worldwide. While the brand had been available internationally since 1914, its strongest sales were in developed markets in North America and Europe. Beginning in 2005, Colgate invested more and more in international markets, especially emerging ones, first in Latin America, then, in 2009, Asian markets such as India and China. By 2012 Colgate's products dominated the Indian oral-care market.

BRAND EQUITY

- Colgate is the number-one toothpaste and manual toothpaste brand in the world.
- *Forbes* lists Colgate as number 44 among the world's most valuable brands.
- In BrandZ's ranking of the best personal care brands in 2012, Colgate was number two.

Colgate is the number-one dental care brand in the world and in the United States, and has been since the late 1990s. Globally Colgate has 45 percent of the global toothpaste market and 32.8 percent of the global manual toothbrush market. In many studies of brand value, Colgate is often considered as part of its parent company, Colgate-Palmolive, which sold not only oral care but also other personal care, home care, and pet nutrition products. About 43 percent of Colgate-Palmolive's sales in 2011 were from oral care products, mostly Colgate-branded. In 2011 sales for Colgate-Palmolive were US$16.7 billion, up from US$15.6 billion in 2010, with about 75 percent coming from international markets.

Colgate is regularly found to be one of the most valuable brands in the world. In 2012 Colgate-Palmolive was number 44, with a brand value of US$7.5 billion on *Forbes* list of *The World's Most Powerful Brands. Forbes* also ranked Colgate-Palmolive as number 37 on its list of *Innovative Companies.* In Interbrand's *Best Global Brands 2012,* Colgate was ranked 47. Its 2012 brand value was US$7.643 billion, up 7 percent from 2011. In "BrandZ Top 100 Most Valuable Brands 2012," Colgate was ranked 51st in 2012. Its 2012 brand value was US$14.948 billion. On BrandZ's select ranking of the best personal care brands, Colgate was number two, second only to Gillette and ahead of Crest, which ranked ninth. In the 2012 Brandirectory *Global 500,* Colgate had a brand value of US$4.415 billion and an enterprise value of US$20.018 billion, and it was ranked 234.

BRAND AWARENESS

- Colgate has built its brand awareness since the late 19th century.
- In India, Colgate has high brand awareness and was listed as one of the most trusted brands by Indian consumers between 2010 and 2012.
- Colgate ranks in the top ten of TrustR, the BrandZ measure of brands that inspire consumer trust.

Since introducing its first toothpaste in 1873, Colgate has carefully built its brand name, first in the United States, and then internationally, beginning in 1914. Using effective advertising and long-running campaigns, such as efforts to educate children about the importance of dental health, Colgate has built global consumer trust and loyalty. In North America, Colgate is a household name with a reputation for trustworthiness. While good dental care was considered a priority primarily in developed economies until the mid-1990s, Colgate focused on developing markets beginning in 2004 in Latin America, then in Asia beginning in 2009. Because of its marketing efforts in India, Colgate was listed as the most trusted brand of any kind by Indian consumers in 2010, 2011, and 2012.

Consumer surveys confirm Colgate's position as a respected brand with high awareness. In *TrustR,* BrandZ's global ranking of brands that inspire consumer trust and recommendation, Colgate ranks in the top ten. In the *2012 Global RepTrack 100,* a study produced by the Reputation Institute that considers how consumers perceive companies and how it affects the choices they make, Colgate was ranked 13th. Colgate also registered on the Reputation Institute's *Global Reputation Pulse—Top 100,* which considers the reputation of the largest American companies among consumers. Colgate was ranked 14th.

BRAND OUTLOOK

- Colgate has a history of long-term, steady growth, trends that are expected to continue.
- Colgate's largest growth areas are in international markets, especially in developing countries.
- In 2011 Colgate-Palmolive introduced a four-year "Sustainability Strategy."

The global market for oral-care products is growing in the early 21st century, and it was not deeply impacted by the worldwide economic downturn that began in 2008. With a long history of strong performance, Colgate has had steady, high, long-term earnings, and it posted double-digit growth in emerging markets in the early 2010s. These trends are expected to continue. In India, a developing economy, the brand is number one, with more than half of the oral-care market and few competitors. Colgate has invested in more global advertising and has a clearly defined strategy for growing market share around the world.

Colgate also invested in sustainability through its parent company, Colgate-Palmolive. In 2011 Colgate introduced its "Sustainability Strategy," to be implemented over the next four years. The strategy was divided into People, Performance, and Planet. In addition to promoting healthier lives for its employees and committing to contributing to the community, Colgate-Palmolive outlined ways it would increase its products' sustainability profile, including reducing the environmental impact of products and packages by 20 percent, with more use of sustainable and recycled materials. The company also set goals of reducing energy consumption and carbon emissions associated with manufacture and distribution of products by 20 percent and decreasing waste sent to landfills by 15 percent.

FURTHER READING

"Best Global Brands 2012." Interbrand. Accessed January 26, 2013. http://www.interbrand.com/en/best-global-brands/2012/Best-Global-Brands-2012.aspx.

Brand Finance. "Colgate." *Brandirectory.* Accessed January 26, 2013. http://brandirectory.com/profile/colgate.

"BrandZ Top 100 Most Valuable Brands 2012." Millward Brown. Accessed January 26, 2013. http://www.millwardbrown.com/brandz/2012/Documents/2012_BrandZ_Top100_Report.pdf.

"Colgate-Palmolive." *Forbes.* Accessed on January 26, 2013. http://www.forbes.com/companies/colgate-palmolive/.

"Colgate-Palmolive." RankingTheBrands.com. Accessed January 26, 2013. http://www.rankingthebrands.com/Brand-detail.aspx?brandID=38.

Colgate-Palmolive Company. *2011 Annual Report.* Accessed January 26, 2013. http://www.colgate.com/us/en/annual-reports/2011/.

"Colgate: The Total Brand." *Brand Royalty.* Ed. Matt Haig. London: Kogan Page, 2004.

Frederickson, Tom. "Restructuring Gives Colgate Fresh Sparkle; Company Is a Solid Buy as Its Market Share and Margins Both Rise." *Crain's New York Business,* November 13, 2006.

Simley, John. "Colgate." *Encyclopedia of Consumer Brands, Vol. 2: Personal Products.* Ed. Janice Jorgensen. Detroit, MI: St. James Press, 1994.

"William Colgate." *Business Leader Profiles for Students.* Ed. Sheila Dow and Jaime E. Noce. Vol. 2. Detroit, MI: Gale, 2002.

COMCAST

AT A GLANCE

Brand Synopsis: Comcast's promise to continually push the boundaries of innovation and technology is reflected in its status as the largest cable provider in the United States.

Parent Company: One Comcast Center
Philadelphia, Pennsylvania 19103
United States
http://www.comcast.com

Sector: Consumer Discretionary

Industry Group: Media

Performance: Market share—32 percent among U.S. cable television providers (2011). *Sales*—US$55.8 billion (2011).

Principal Competitors: DIRECTV; DISH Network Corporation; Time Warner Cable Inc.; Verizon Communications Inc.; AT&T Inc.

BRAND ORIGINS

- In 1963 Ralph Roberts bought American Cable Systems, a community antenna television (CATV) service based in Tupelo, Mississippi.
- Comcast is an amalgamation of the words "communication" and "broadcast."
- Comcast began offering cable services in London in 1983.
- Comcast entered the cellular telephone market in 1988 with the purchase of American Cellular Network Corporation.

Comcast began in the early 1960s as American Cable Systems, Inc., a small cable operation serving Tupelo, Mississippi. At the time, American Cable Systems was one of only a few community antenna television (CATV) services in the nation. The CATV business was predicated on the fact that rural areas were underserved by commercial television stations, which catered to large metropolitan areas. Without CATV's huge antennas that pulled in distant signals, consumers in rural areas had little use for television. Although they were required to pay for CATV, customers considered the benefits worth the cost.

In 1963 Ralph J. Roberts and his brother Joe learned that the owner of American Cable Systems, Jerrold Electronics Company, wished to sell the CATV concern. The two brothers had just sold their interest in Pioneer Industries, a men's accessories business in Philadelphia, and were looking to invest the proceeds in a new industry. After some research, they enlisted the help of a young accountant named Julian Brodsky, who had helped them liquidate Pioneer Industries, and Daniel Aaron, a former systems director at Jerrold Electronics, to help them evaluate the opportunity. The four agreed that while the system carried only five channels and served only 1,500 customers, the investment had great potential. Ralph Roberts bought American Cable Systems and later asked Brodsky and Aaron to join him in managing the company.

Growth within Tupelo was difficult, and in 1964 the company purchased additional franchises within Mississippi. While these acquisitions succeeded in increasing subscribership, they failed to have much effect on penetration, as there remained an insufficient number of subscribers to deliver a high return given the cost of setting up a local system. Roberts turned his attention to the larger potential market of Philadelphia. In 1966 he acquired franchises in the suburbs of Philadelphia and other local communities.

Having decided that the name American Cable Systems sounded too generic for his growing company, Roberts decided in 1969 to change its name. In an effort to build a more technological identity, he took portions of the words "communication" and "broadcast" to create the company's new name, Comcast Corporation, and reincorporated the business in Pennsylvania. Now boasting 40,000 customers but hampered by a continued stagnation in subscriber penetration rates, Comcast needed funds to finance further expansion. In 1972 Roberts decided to take the company public, offering shares on the over-the-counter market.

Cable by this time had become much more than an antenna service. For several years cable operators had been including local access and special programming channels, as well as programming from large independent stations. In 1977 the government relaxed many of the restrictions that had been in place on cable services. As the cable industry was allowed to mature, additional cable-only stations were added, making the service viable within metropolitan areas that were well served by broadcasters.

While continuing to expand within the United States, Comcast began to develop its global market. In 1983, in partnership with Ladbrokes, a British gambling and entertainment enterprise, Comcast won a license to establish a cable television system in the residential suburbs of London. Most cable licenses in the United States had been taken, and those that remained were expensive or only marginally profitable. The industry was still in its infancy in the United Kingdom, however, and British viewers would appreciate cable's selection, as Britain had only about five stations at that time, offering mostly government-supported programming.

In 1988 Comcast made a strategic move when it purchased American Cellular Network Corporation, or Amcell, a cellular telephone business serving New Jersey. Government legislation had previously prevented competition in landline services, and so this was the first time that cable companies and telephone companies were competing with one another in the cellular telephone business. Also for the first time, a cable company was able to offer telephone customers an alternative to the telephone company.

BRAND ELEMENTS

- Comcast changed its logo in 1999, about the same time that the company began to focus more intently on expanding its cable and high-speed communications business.
- In 2010 Comcast rebranded its cable, Internet, and telephone services, choosing the name XFINITY.
- The XFINITY name appears in all capital letters in text but in lowercase letters in the new logo.

From 1969 to 1999 the Comcast logo was futuristic looking, with thick black-and-white uppercase lettering and a block-letter "C." The company rebranded and updated the logo in 1999, with the new logo featuring a red, crescent-shaped "C" next to the all lowercase lettering of "comcast." Around this same time, Comcast began to focus more intently on expanding its cable and high-speed communications business.

In 2010 Comcast rebranded its cable, Internet, and telephone services to XFINITY. In text, the new brand name is written in all capital letters, but in logo format, the name is presented in lowercase letters. The XFINITY logo is in shades of red, with the dots over the "i's" omitted and the lower right leg of the "x" extended.

BRAND IDENTITY

- Comcast has invested billions of dollars upgrading and building infrastructure for its Internet, cable, and voice systems to keep the brand current with cutting-edge technology.
- In 2010 Comcast changed the name of its consumer services to XFINITY to revitalize the Comcast brand.
- Comcast's business services continued to operate under the Comcast name.

In the early 1960s American Cable Systems offered cutting-edge technology with its antenna systems for television. Over the years, under its new brand name of Comcast, the company evolved into an industry titan, with billions of dollars invested in upgrading and building infrastructure for its Internet, cable, and voice systems with the goal of keeping the brand at the forefront of technology.

As part of its effort to strengthen its brand image, Comcast changed the name of its consumer services to XFINITY in 2010; its business services would continue to use the Comcast name. With the name change, Comcast hoped to realign the brand and improve customer satisfaction with enhanced technology, a multitude of content choices, and cross-platform features. Although critics claimed that the name change was simply a way to gloss over the myriad of customer service problems plaguing the company, Comcast pledged its commitment to improving customer service, endeavoring to change customers' perceptions of the company.

BRAND STRATEGY

- Through a complex mix of acquisitions, mergers, and joint ventures Comcast has evolved into one of the world's leading media, entertainment, and communications brands.

- As a means of brand extension, Comcast established the sports and entertainment company, Comcast Spectacor, and the Comcast Sportsnet cable channel.
- In 2011 Comcast acquired a majority stake in NBC Universal, allowing the company to broadcast its news and entertainment content to a global audience.

With approximately 24 million subscribers, Comcast is the largest cable provider in the United States. Growth for the brand comes through a complex mix of acquisitions, mergers, and joint ventures as well as organic growth from the addition of new subscribers. As part of its brand strategy, Comcast has developed systems to not only deliver third-party programming to its customers, but also produce and deliver its own branded content to customers of competing television services.

As a method of brand extension, in 1996 Comcast entered into a venture with sports company, Spectacor, which owned the Philadelphia Flyers National Hockey League (NHL) team, two sports arenas in Philadelphia, and the Philadelphia 76ers National Basketball Association (NBA) team. The new venture, now branded Comcast Spectacor, allowed Comcast to establish Comcast SportsNet, a 24-hour branded regional cable sports channel, which featured telecasts of major league sports programming. Comcast also continued to invest in acquisitions of national cable channels, including The Golf Channel, E! Entertainment, Outdoor Life Network, and G4.

In 2011 Comcast acquired a 51 percent stake in NBC Universal Media, LLC (NBC Universal) through a joint venture with General Electric Co. The joint venture gave Comcast a controlling interest in a vast array of media and entertainment around the world, including NBC News, MSNBC, NBC's broadcast stations and regional sports channels, Spanish-language channel Telemundo, and NBC cable channels including Bravo and USA Network. NBC Universal also owns CNBC, a financial cable channel shown across the United States, Europe, the Middle East, and Africa; the company also operates cable channels in the United Kingdom through NBC Universal Global Networks. Through the acquisition, Comcast also gained majority control over NBC Universal's motion picture companies, television production companies, and theme parks.

BRAND EQUITY

- In 2011 Comcast was the world's largest broadcasting and cable company, according to *Forbes*.
- In 2011 Comcast was the world's second most valuable media company, behind only the Walt Disney Company.
- Comcast consistently ranks among the top 100 global brands, with a 2012 brand value between US$9 billion and US$12 billion.

According to *Forbes*, in 2011 Comcast was the world's largest broadcasting and cable company, beating out the Walt Disney Company and New York–based News Corporation for the top spot. Comcast was the world's second most valuable media company in 2011, with the Walt Disney Company in the top spot. The *Financial Times* ranked Comcast second in its 2011 ranking of the world's most valuable media companies, with a market value of US$67.4 billion.

In Brand Finance's Global 500 2012, Comcast ranked 68th, with a brand value of US$12.5 billion. The European Brand Institute of Vienna ranked Comcast 75th, with a brand value of US$8.7 billion, in its 2012 Top 100 Brand Corporations Worldwide.

BRAND AWARENESS

- Comcast's 2011 acquisition of NBC Universal has allowed Comcast to reach new customers across the globe.
- NBC Universal's divisions include cable television channels, production companies, theme parks, and more.
- Comcast launched a media campaign clarifying its new XFINITY brand during the 2010 Winter Olympics and again during the 2012 Summer Olympics.

Comcast's acquisition of NBCUniversal Media, LLC (NBC Universal) in 2011 gave Comcast a new way to reach consumers throughout the world. CNBC Europe, wholly owned by NBC Universal, is broadcast in Europe, the Middle East, and Africa, and is watched by an estimated 3.1 million viewers every week. CNBC Asia, also owned by NBC Universal, broadcasts throughout Asia, with programming originating from Hong Kong, Singapore, and Sydney, Australia.

Its majority ownership of NBC Universal gives Comcast the rights to all Hallmark channels outside the United States, plus the British channels Movies 24 and KidsCo. NBC Universal owns the television production company Carnival Films, based in London, and Geneon Universal Entertainment, based in Tokyo. NBC Universal also owns or licenses Universal Studios theme parks in the United States, Japan, and Singapore.

Comcast has faced an ongoing struggle since rebranding its cable, Internet, and telephone division under the XFINITY name in 2010. Consumers were left baffled as to how the new brand's services differed from those offered previously under the Comcast name. Comcast launched a media campaign explaining its new XFINITY brand during the 2010 Winter Olympics. Faced with continuing customer confusion, the company initiated a new marketing campaign during the 2012 Summer Olympics aimed at expanding customer understanding and improving perception of the brand.

BRAND OUTLOOK

- Even during the worldwide economic downturn, Comcast remained hugely profitable, increasing revenue 47 percent from 2010 to 2011.
- Comcast can depend on its majority ownership of NBC Universal as a source of global expansion and revenue.
- Comcast's solid subscriber base will allow it to generate the revenue needed to continue to enhance technology and services for its customers.

Even during the 2008–2012 global recession, Comcast managed to remain highly profitable and continued to see steady earnings growth. Revenue increased 47 percent from 2010 to 2011. Much of this growth was driven by an increase in the company's subscriber base, as well as by price increases. In 2011 Comcast held a 32 percent market share of cable television providers in the United States. Its closest competitor was Time Warner Cable Inc., with a 14 percent market share. According to the Comcast 2011 Annual Review, 1.4 million new customers were added in 2011, for a total of 22.3 million cable customers, 18.1 million high-speed Internet customers, and 9.3 million digital voice customers. Of those cable customers, 37 percent purchased a bundle of all three services, reflecting the diversity of the company's revenue streams.

By all accounts, NBC Universal Media, LLC (NBC Universal) will continue to be a source of strength for Comcast. NBC Universal's cable channels continue to draw large numbers of viewers and a healthy revenue stream. Universal Pictures and Focus Features, both divisions of NBC Universal, released a number of hit movies in the United States and abroad in 2011 and 2012.

Comcast's colossal subscriber base for its cable, voice, and Internet services, coupled with its successful acquisition of NBC Universal that brought in millions of additional customers, should give Comcast an edge over potential competition and drive growth for the brand for years to come.

FURTHER READING

"Can Comcast Increase Pay TV Market Share?" *Forbes*, February 9, 2011.

Krippendorff, Kaihan. "Why Comcast Will Crush Netflix." *Fast Company*, March 1, 2012. Accessed October 12, 2012. http://www.fastcompany.com/1822129/why-comcast-will-crush-netflix.

Ramachandran, Shalini. "Xfinity? Comcast Sets out to Explain Bundled Service: Marketing Campaign Aims to Better Explain Comcast's TV-Phone-Web Service." *Wall Street Journal*, July 27, 2012.

Simley, John, David E. Salamie, and Stephen Meyer. "Comcast Corporation." *International Directory of Company Histories*. Ed. Derek Jacques and Paula Kepos. Vol. 112. Detroit, MI: St. James Press, 2010.

Spector, Dina, Gus Lubin, and Vivian Giang. "The 15 Most Disliked Companies in America." *Business Insider*, June 29, 2012.

"Top Cable Television Providers, 2011." *Market Share Reporter*. Detroit, MI: Gale, 2012.

"2011 Annual Review." Comcast Corporation. Accessed October 12, 2012. http://www.comcast.com/2011annualreview/?SCRedirect=true.

"World's Largest Broadcasting and Cable Companies Overall, 2011." *Business Rankings Annual*. Ed. Deborah J. Draper. Detroit, MI: Gale, 2013.

"World's Most Valuable Media Companies, 2011." *Business Rankings Annual*. Ed. Deborah J. Draper. Detroit, MI: Gale, 2013.

THE CO-OPERATIVE GROUP

AT A GLANCE

Brand Synopsis: The largest consumer cooperative in the world, The Co-operative Group is a British brand devoted to serving its members in every aspect of their lives with a diverse group of businesses that includes farming, food retailing, banking, and funeral services.
Parent Company: Co-operative Group Ltd.
New Century House
Manchester M60 4ES
United Kingdom
http://www.co-operative.coop/
Sector: Consumer Staples; Financials; Industrials
Industry Group: Food & Staples Retailing; Diversified Financials; Commercial Services & Supplies
Performance: *Market share*—90 percent of cooperative business in the United Kingdom (2011). *Sales*—£13.3 billion (US$21.4 billion) (2011).
Principal Competitors: ALDI Group; ASDA Group Ltd.; Bongrain SA; Booker Cash & Carry Ltd.; The Boots Company; Friesland Coberco Dairy Foods Holding N.V.; J Sainsbury plc; John Lewis Partnership plc; Marks and Spencer plc; Safeway plc; Somerfield plc; Tesco plc; Koninklijke Wessanen N.V.

BRAND ORIGINS

- The Co-operative Group grew out of a co-operative founded in 1844 by the Rochdale Society of Equitable Pioneers.
- In 1863 the Rochdale group and other cooperatives in the region formed the North of England Co-operative Wholesale Industrial and Provident Society.
- Expanding geographically, the North of England Co-operative became known as The Co-operative Wholesale Society, or CWS, by 1872.
- The CWS and later The Co-operative Group were involved in food retailing and farming, banking and insurance services, and funeral and burial services.
- In 2001 The Co-operative Group took its present name and combined its building service subsidiaries to form Synchro.

The Co-operative Group includes food and convenience stores, pharmacies, funeral services, travel agencies, and banks. It also runs the largest farming operation in the United Kingdom and operates in several other types of business as well. Although The Co-operative Group's roster of businesses may initially seem unusual, its history and goals help unite this disparate group of companies under one central brand.

In 1844 a shop opened in Rochdale, England, near Manchester, called the Rochdale Society of Equitable Pioneers. This shop catered to poorer customers and strove to use honest business practices. The shop's customers participated as members of a cooperative: they voted on the operations of the business and received dividends, or "divis", based on the shop's profits. The Rochdale shop was part of the larger cooperative movement that was growing in popularity across the country at the time. Much as people did during the company's modest beginnings, customers today can sign up as members of The Co-operative Group and receive points for their purchases. Customers receive a share of the company's profits based on these points and are also eligible for special offers.

Both the Rochdale shop and the cooperative movement proved successful. In 1863 cooperatives throughout Yorkshire and Lancashire, including the Rochdale group, banded together to form the North of England Co-operative Wholesale Industrial and Provident Society. Expanding beyond northern England, the organization became the Co-operative Wholesale Society (CWS) in 1872. Because these cooperatives sold food, they established farms from which to source fresh foodstuffs. In addition to food retailing and farming, the cooperatives provided banking and insurance services as well as funeral and burial services. The Co-operative Group continues to operate successfully in these areas. It has also added more businesses, including travel, pharmacy, insurance, and legal services, and it sells a wide array of goods, including work clothes, appliances, and cars.

In the wake of mergers and a company-wide reorganization, the CWS became known as The Co-operative Group in 2001. Also in 2001 the company combined its building services subsidiaries to create a new subsidiary, Synchro. In addition to conducting its own business, The Co-operative Group has merged with struggling cooperatives in order to assist them. These actions exemplify The Co-operative Group's commitment to its own businesses and the cooperative movement as a whole, securing its prominent position in the worldwide cooperative movement.

BRAND ELEMENTS

- The Co-operative Group's slogan is "good for everyone."
- The Co-operative Food's slogan is "good with food," and The Co-operative Bank's is "good with money."
- The Co-operative Group uses a consistent logo design for its different companies.

At the corporate level, The Co-operative Group uses the slogan "good for everyone." The slogans of its subsidiaries echo this slogan. The food stores assert that they are "good with food" while the bank proclaims that it is "good with money."

The company logos exhibit a similar simplicity. The Co-operative Group uses the phrase "The co-operative" (with only an initial capital letter) in blue font on its website. For its subsidiaries, it uses the "The co-operative" logo and adds the name of the specific subsidiary, such as The co-operative food, The co-operative bank, The co-operative funeral care, and The co-operative travel.

BRAND IDENTITY

- The branding of the cover of The Co-operative Group's ethical plan depicts the company's farming business and its interests in nature and the environment.
- In 2012 The Co-operative Group began using a new tagline, "Here for you for life," meant to reflect the cooperative, caring image of the brand.
- The Co-operative Group brand focuses on supporting global causes, including the fair trade movement, which seeks to establish fair trade in developing countries.

Publications by The Co-operative Group have incorporated certain slogans and images to emphasize and reinforce the brand. For example, the company issued the report *Setting Our Sights: Our Ethical Plan for 2012-14 (and beyond ...)*, the cover of which featured The Co-operative Group name and familiar "good for everyone" slogan in the brand's usual fonts. The cover also featured a large, colorful photograph of sheep in a field. The sheep and the field reminded readers that The Co-operative Group is the largest farming operation in the United Kingdom and thus depicts the brand's business activities and prominent success in its field. By featuring nature-themed imagery on the cover, The Co-operative Group also portrayed itself as a brand interested in the environment, an image reinforced by the fact that the report discussed the company's ethical interests.

The Co-operative Group's identity is not just about its visual images. The company prides itself on its cooperative status. Members share in the profits, have a say in the corporation, and can serve as representatives for other members. This interest in people is also reflected in The Co-operative Membership Community Fund. As the name indicates, this organization helps fund community initiatives. Profits from customer purchases finance this fund, and members can also contribute to this fund by donating their share of the group's profits. The Co-operative Group also supports global causes. In the 1990s, for example, the company began supporting the fair trade movement, which promotes and supports fair trade practices in developing countries.

In 2012 The Co-operative Group began using a new tagline, "Here for you for life," which reflected the cooperative, caring image promoted by the brand. By informing customers that The Co-operative Group was "here for you," it reassured people that the brand could help them, even support them, since the phrase "I am here for you" is used as a sign of support. The "for life" section of the tagline is a reminder of The Co-operative Group's many business branches and of the fact that members can employ these businesses in practically every aspect of their lives. It also reminded customers that they may remain members of The Co-operative Group for the duration of their lives, since The Co-operative Group offers services that span from birth (insurance and retail services) to death (funeral services).

BRAND STRATEGY

- The Co-operative Group's consistent use of visual elements and slogans unifies its extremely diverse businesses and creates a consistent, unified brand.
- The Co-operative Group Farms store brand evokes farming, fresh food, and member benefits and extends The Co-operative Group's predominant brand.
- Participation in the United Nations' International Year of Cooperatives 2012 gave The Co-operative Group' brand international exposure.

Although The Co-operative Group offers several businesses in an extremely diverse range of fields, it presents its brand consistently across all of its businesses. It uses the same font for logos across all Co-operative logos. It modifies the "good for … " phrase to describe its individual businesses in order to echo The Co-operative Group's "good for everyone" slogan. The consistent use of brand elements unifies otherwise separate parts of an extremely diverse company.

The brand's consistency also extends to individual products. The Co-operative Group members can buy produce and other food products from The Co-operative Group Farms brand. Labels for the food include the familiar "The Co-operative" logo in its usual typeface and add the word "Farms." By combining its usual logo with the word "Farms" and placing these designations on produce and other food, The Co-operative Group repeats its name and reinforces its visual imagery while aligning the brand with food and farming. The labels remind customers that The Co-operative Group is a large farming business in addition to a food retailer, providing its members with such benefits as produce fresh from the farm. The labels used by the brand communicate that The Co-operative Group and its brands are successful, involved in many operations, and ultimately beneficial to members.

In 2012 The Co-operative Group participated in international efforts to promote its brand as a cooperative. That year it served as a sponsor of the International Year of Cooperatives 2012, an initiative by the United Nations intending to raise global awareness of cooperatives. With this work The Co-operative Group advanced its own brand name and promoted cooperatives in general. It portrayed itself as a brand that is committed to educating people and participating in larger movements. By participating in this initiative, The Co-operative Group also introduced its brand to new people and to new regions, since the initiative was an international effort by the United Nations, an institution with a global presence.

BRAND EQUITY

- In 2011 The Co-operative Group held about a 90 percent market share for cooperative business in the United Kingdom.
- The Co-operative Group runs the largest farming operation and owns the most convenience stores in the United Kingdom.
- The Co-operative Pharmacy is the third-largest in the United Kingdom, and The Co-operative Food is the country's fifth-largest food retailer.
- The Co-operative Group and Dignity Caring Funeral Services together held an estimated 25 percent share of the funeral services market in the early 2000s.
- Brand Finance named The Co-operative Group one of the largest brands in the United Kingdom and the world.

The Co-operative Group is the world's largest consumer-based cooperative. It leads United Kingdom businesses in a number of categories. It is the largest farming business, provider of funeral services, and convenience store chain in the United Kingdom. With its banks and insurance concerns, it ranks among the United Kingdom's largest finance companies, and it is the country's third-largest pharmacy chain (and the largest pharmacy chain in Wales), and the fifth-largest food retailer. The Co-operative Group controls about 4,800 retail units and employs more than 106,000 individuals. In 2011 it paid £142 million (US$229 million) in dividends to its more than 7 million members.

The company's success and diversity enable it to dominate in multiple markets. In the United Kingdom, The Co-operative Group held a market share of about 90 percent for cooperative business in 2011. In 2012 the company's various banks and financial operations represented approximately 7 percent of the bank accounts in the United Kingdom. Its 2012 share of the United Kingdom's food retail market was estimated at around 6.5 percent. As for the funeral services market, The Co-operative Group and Dignity Caring Funeral Services together held an estimated 25 percent market share in the early 2000s.

The success of its various businesses has made The Co-operative Group a lucrative international brand. Brand Finance ranked The Co-operative Group 174th among the top 500 global brands in both 2011 and 2012, with a 2012 brand value of approximately US$5.4 billion. Brand Finance also determined the company to be the 21st-largest brand in the United Kingdom in 2012.

BRAND AWARENESS

- Many people associate the entire cooperative movement with The Co-operative Group.
- British consumers have named The Co-operative Group one of the most trusted companies and have associated it with the fair treatment of employees and suppliers.

- In 2010 business analysts attributed The Co-operative Bank's 140,000 new accounts to the company's good reputation amidst problems in the financial industry.

The Co-operative Group's history, size, and presence in a number of industries have made it a prominent company. Annie Warren, an employee of the *Co-operative News*, stated that when she began working for the paper, she associated cooperatives mostly with The Co-operative Group.

Consumers rank The Co-operative Group highly. In a 2006 poll by AccountAbility and the National Consumer Council, British consumers named The Co-operative Group one of the most trusted companies in the United Kingdom. The respondents also associated The Co-operative Group with the fair treatment of employees and suppliers.

Business analysts noted that this positive reputation has driven the growth of The Co-operative Group's banking business. In 2010 the company reported that it had acquired 140,000 new banking customers (an increase in new accounts of 38 percent). Many of these customers were previously members of other banks, and this increase came at a time of worldwide financial uncertainty.

BRAND OUTLOOK

- The 2008 acquisition of the Somerfield supermarket chain increased The Co-operative Group's size but brought it lingering problems.
- The Co-operative Group's participation in the 2009 climate awareness march The Wave demonstrated the brand's commitment to its customers and to the future.
- The focus on balance and a unified brand strategy moving forward were the brand's strong points as it moved into the 21st century.

The Co-operative Group bought the British chain of Somerfield supermarkets in 2008, and the acquisition yielded mixed results. After the sale, the supermarkets, which began using The Co-operative Group name, experienced declining sales. Customer complaints also rose and The Co-operative Group faced problems incorporating Somerfield employees and data into The Co-operative Group's operations. The brand did experience some positive results with the acquisition of Somerfield in the form of the removal of some retailing competition and an increase in the size of its own retailing business.

The Co-operative Group focused on acknowledging certain global events towards the end of the first decade of the 21st century, specifically those that aligned with the brand's image as a socially responsible entity that cares for its employees, members, and the environment. The Co-operative Group transported about 2,500 of its members and their families to London on December 5, 2009 to join in The Wave, a march related to the United Nations' Summit on Climate Change. The members' involvement and the use of company logos and slogans in this effort drew attention to The Co-operative Group as a brand. The cooperative's involvement reinforced its interest in environmental preservation. It also reflected the brand's longtime interests in its members by helping them participate in The Wave march by offering transportation, demonstrating that The Co-operative Group's awareness of issues that its members care about as well as awareness and engagement in global events remained at the forefront of the company's brand strategy.

As the brand entered the second decade of the 21st century, the outlook for the brand was solid. "We have learned a great deal about being not only ethically driven, but commercially focused," said Len Wardle, chair of The Co-Operative Group, in 2011. The internal confidence of the company regarding the brand's future stems largely from this balance between ethics and commercialism, as well as from the unified brand strategy employed by all Co-operative Group businesses.

FURTHER READING

Balkan, Donna. "What's in a Brand? The Amazing Success of The Co-operative Group." *Co-operative News*, November 16, 2011. Accessed October 14, 2012. http://www.thenews.coop/blog/what%E2%80%99s-brand-amazing-success-co-operative-group.

Brand Finance. "Global 500 2012." *Brandirectory*. Accessed October 11, 2012. http://brandirectory.com/league_tables/table/global-500-2012.

Co-operative Group Limited. *The Co-operative/Good for Everyone*. Accessed October 11, 2012. http://www.co-operative.coop/.

"Co-operative Group (CWS) Ltd." *International Directory of Company Histories*. Ed. Tina Grant. Vol. 51. Detroit, MI: St. James Press, 2003.

Forstater, Maya, and Jeannette Oelschlaegel, with Maria Sillanpää. "What Assures Consumers?" London: AccountAbility and the National Consumer Council, July 2006. Accessed October 11, 2012. http://www.accountability.org/images/content/0/5/052/What%20Assures%20consumers.pdf.

Jones, Rupert. "Co-operative Bank: How Does It Compare?" *Guardian* (London), July 19, 2012.

Kollewe, Jill. "Co-op Profits Surge as Customers Desert UK's Bigger Banks." *Guardian* (London), March 18, 2010.

Lawson, Alex. "The Co-operative Food: Steve Murrells' to Do List." *Retail Week*, July 16, 2012.

"The UK Funeral Industry." UK Funerals Online. Accessed October 11, 2012. http://www.uk-funerals.co.uk/funeral-industry.html.

Warren, Annie. "How Co-operatives Can Promote Themselves More Successfully." Co-operatives and Mutuals Hub. *Guardian* (London), September 28, 2012.

CORONA EXTRA

AT A GLANCE

Brand Synopsis: The number-one imported beer in the United States, Corona Extra is a Mexican-made beer with strong international appeal and an image linked to relaxation.
Parent Company: Grupo Modelo, S.A.B. de C.V. (a partially owned subsidiary of Anheuser-Busch InBev)
Piso 4
México, D.F. 01210
Mexico
http://www.gmodelo.mx/
Sector: Consumer Staples
Industry Group: Food, Beverage & Tobacco
Performance: *Market share*—3.4 percent in the United States (2011); *Sales*—27.9 million barrels worldwide (2010); 7.24 million barrels in the United States (2011).
Principal Competitors: Budweiser; Bud Light; Carta Blanca; Sol; Dos Equis; Heineken; Stella Artois; Tecate

BRAND ORIGINS

- Corona Extra was created in Mexico in 1925.
- The beer first became available in the United States in 1976.
- In 1997 Corona Extra became the best-selling imported beer in the United States.

Corona Extra is a lager beer manufactured by Grupo Modelo, originally called Cerveceria Modelo (Modelo Brewery) when it was founded in Mexico City, Mexico, in 1925 by Pablo Diez, a Spanish immigrant. Among the first beers he brewed was Corona Extra. By 1935 it was the best selling beer in Mexico. Corona Extra was marketed as a high quality product and a brand associated with sociability. Corona continued to be innovative, and in 1940 it became the first bottled beer with the label printed directly on the bottle.

Sold in only Mexico for several decades, Corona moved into the draft beer market in 1967 after the company's manufacturing process was modernized. Over the years, Corona developed a reputation as a cheaply made beer that was favored by workers in Mexico. Yet the brand was also linked with the beauty of that country. In 1970 Corona began its "Bellezas Naturales" campaign, which publicized Mexico's most beautiful natural sights.

In 1976 the first Corona Extras were exported to the United States, and the brand began being regularly exported to the U.S. market in 1981. Initially just 150,000 cases were exported, and Corona was priced higher than major domestic beers, though not as high as many European brands. At first Corona Extra was sold only in the Southwest, but the brand soon made extensive inroads into other markets.

By the mid-1980s U.S. sales exploded. Though Corona sold less than a million cases in 1984, in 1985 five million cases were exported, accounting for more than 50 percent of all beer exported from Mexico. By 1986 Corona sold 13.5 million cases and became the second-best-selling import in America. By 1987 it was available in more than 30 states and sold more than 22 million cases. Most of the growth in popularity came via word of mouth among yuppies.

The record sales underwent a drastic reversal in the United States between 1988 and 1991. There were several reasons for the decrease. There were false rumors in 1987, started by a competing distributor, that Modelo brewery workers urinated in the beer. Corona's sales were also impacted by new products on the American beer market, such as dry beer and light beers.

In response, Corona introduced Corona Light, its entry in the low calorie beer market, in the United States in 1989. It sold one million cases that year. Modelo also pursued new international markets, and by the early 1990s, Corona Extra was being sold in 55 countries in Latin America, Europe, Asia, and the Pacific Rim.

In 1992 Corona's parent company became Grupo Modelo (Modelo Brewing Group). By this time, Grupo Modelo was producing nearly 70 percent of all the beer exported to Mexico and half the beer consumed in Mexico. Sales in the United States soon rebounded, and 1992 saw an increase to 12.8 million cases of Corona Extra. By this time, Grupo Modelo had become the tenth largest brewer in the world, with US$1.5 billion in sales and annual production of 2.1 billion liters, almost half of which was Corona Extra.

Sales of Corona continued to grow throughout the 1990s and the early 2000s. By 1994 Corona Extra controlled about 10.5 percent of the imported beer market in the United States. By 1997 it toppled Heineken as the best-selling import in the United States. Corona Extra was exported to more and more countries, and by 1999 the brand had an ad campaign which emphasized this fact.

Corona's sales deeply affected the sales of leading American beers, like Budweiser, over the years. Yet Anheuser-Busch had bought 18 percent of Grupo Modelo in 1993. In 2012 Anheuser-Busch InBev announced plans to complete the purchase of Modelo in early fiscal 2013 for US$20.1 billion, as long as the transaction passed the muster of U.S. regulators. When the acquisition is completed, Anheuser-Busch InBev will have control of many of the best-selling beers in the world, including Corona Extra and Corona Light.

BRAND ELEMENTS

- Bottles of Corona Extra and Corona Light are always clear, not dark.
- Corona Extra has had its label directly printed on it since 1940.
- Corona Extra and Corona Light are mild lagers served with lime in the United States.

Corona Extra is packaged in a recognizable bottle that is essentially unchanged in its basic elements from the brand's introduction in 1925. Though dark bottles are better for beer because they better preserve the flavor, Corona has been packaged in a clear bottle since 1926 so that consumers can see the beer and its fine ingredients. Some of the brand's success has been linked to the clear bottle. In 1940 Corona Extra became the first bottle with the label printed directly on the bottle. When Corona Light was introduced in 1989, it was first packaged with just the outline of the label and its elements in white to emphasize the light, low calorie qualities of the beer.

On its labels and other packaging, Corona Extra and Corona Light employ a distinctive color scheme associated with the brand, using the colors blue, gold, and white. A crown is also featured, as "corona" means crown in Spanish. Two griffins, which are legendary creatures often seen as representing the king of the beasts, are found on packaging of Corona's products as well.

Inside the bottles of Corona Extra and Corona Light is a beer that is a mild, golden type of lager. One reason for the brand's initial success in the United States was its mild, light-tasting, soft flavor. Corona tasted like a typical, popular domestic American beer, but still looked and was marketed like an import. Its taste conformed to American preferences, which were shared by consumers in other countries. Corona is often served with a lime wedged in its neck in the United States, a trend started in 1981. The popularity of this practice inspired competing lagers like Bud Light to produce a beer with added lime taste, Bud Light Lime.

BRAND IDENTITY

- Corona is identified with the beach, relaxation, and tranquility.
- Corona's first sports sponsorship came in 1955 when it helped build a stadium for a soccer team.
- Corona has sponsored sports like beach volleyball, pro surfing, and pro tennis in recent years.

Corona is a source of Mexican pride, the best-selling beer there since 1935. Coming from an emerging market, exported and popular in the developed world, Corona is seen as a global symbol of Mexico. As Corona moved into the U.S. market in late 1970s and 1980s, the brand became identified with the beach, relaxation, and a tranquil attitude towards life. Though other advertising strategies have been employed over the years, these concepts have remained core to Corona's identity, not only in Mexico and the United States, but in markets worldwide. Campaigns like 2004's "Miles Away from Ordinary" and 2011's "Find Your Beach" employed the idea of the beach, and of Corona as the beer to take consumers there.

Sponsorships have been key to promoting Corona. In Mexico the brand sponsored radio soap operas and concerts like the Caravana Corona from the early 1950s to the early 1970s. To attract young consumers, Corona worked with Sony Music on the Corona Music project. In 2011 Corona sponsored a tour by country artist Kenny Chesney.

In 1955 Corona partnered with Nemesio Diez to build a stadium for the Diablos Rojos soccer team, marking the beginning of its sports sponsorships. In 2009 and 2010 Corona sponsored beach volleyball in the United States. In Australia in 2011 Corona sponsored the Quicksilver Pro world surfing tour. To further increase Corona's global presence, in 2011 Corona also sponsored men's tennis through 12 professional tournaments, including those in key markets like Japan and China.

BRAND STRATEGY

- Corona Light was introduced in the United States in 1989.
- Corona Extra is the best-selling import in the United States, Canada, and Australia.
- Corona Extra is sold in 180 countries, while Corona Light is sold in 11.

Corona Extra was the only product of the Corona brand from 1925 to 1989. To address declining sales because of the increasing fragmentation of the beer market, including the popularity of new low-calorie beers, Corona Light was introduced in 1989. Initially only available in the United States, it sold a record one million cases there that year. Corona Light was still not available in Mexico as of 2007, and by the end of 2011 it was only distributed in 11 countries.

In contrast to Corona Light, Corona Extra was distributed in 180 countries by the end of 2011. In addition to being the best-selling imported beer in the United States since 1997, Corona Extra is a top selling import in Australia, Canada, and the United Kingdom. In Australia it is the number-one premium imported beer, with 10 percent growth between 2010 and 2011 and a market share of 38 percent among imports.

The exporting of Corona Extra to new markets as it sought to increase sales began in the late 1980s and early 1990s, primarily in Europe, Latin America, and the Pacific Rim. There were some challenges. Spain, France, Hungary, and certain Latin American countries already had trademarked products using the name Corona. In Spain and Hungary, the brand had to alter its name to Coronita.

Corona Extra has continued to expand to new markets through the second decade of the 21st century. Emerging markets in Africa and Asia have been a particular focus. In Asia, Corona Extra is sold in 30 countries and is the number-one premium import in five of them. Around the globe, Corona is positioned differently, depending on the market, but it always emphasizes a carefree lifestyle embraced by younger consumers.

BRAND EQUITY

- Corona is the fourth-most-profitable beer brand in the world, though its value seems to be declining overall.
- In 2012 Interbrand's ranking of that year's Best Global Brands put Corona at 89.
- According to Brand Finance's *Brandirectory*, Corona's brand value declined from US$4.568 billion in 2010 to US$2.886 billion in 2012.

Corona is the fourth-most-profitable beer brand in the world, with high brand value not only in its dominant markets in Mexico and the United States, but in many markets around the world. In 2012 Interbrand's list of that year's Best Global Brands ranked Corona number 89. Its brand value was US$4.061 billion, an increase of only 3 percent. This resulted in a drop of three places from 2011. In 2010 Interbrand ranked Corona at number 85.

According to Brand Z's Top 100 Most Valuable Global Brands 2012 report, Corona ranked fourth among the Top 8 Latin American brands, with a brand value of US$5.114 billion. Although it suffered a 6 percent drop in brand value from 2011, it moved up a spot on the list. In the same report's rankings of beer brands, Corona also ranked fourth, with a 6 percent loss in value. The reasons for this change included a shrinking beer market and a decrease in consumer spending by its core market.

In 2012 Brand Finance's *Brandirectory: The Definitive Online Encyclopedia of Brands* stated that Corona's brand value was US$2.886 billion with an enterprise value of US$10.854 billion. Corona was ranked 393rd in Brand Finance's Global 500 for 2012. While Corona still had a high brand value, it was much higher two years earlier, according to Brand Finance. In 2010 Brand Finance's rankings of the Best Global Brands ranked Corona 187 with a brand value of US$4.568 billion and an enterprise value of US$17.091 billion.

BRAND AWARENESS

- Corona has high brand awareness worldwide.
- In 2010 Corona was number nine on a list of the brands with most appeal to the Dutch.
- Its 2010 campaign "Win a Beach Getaway" resulted in a 13 percent increase in brand awareness.

Though Corona has been sold in the United States for little more than three decades and other global markets for even less time, the brand has achieved high awareness, with consumers linking it to Mexico, the beach, and relaxation. Available in Mexico in 1925, it is a source of Mexican pride as the national beer, and it is particularly well known in North America and Latin America. Various surveys have emphasized the high brand awareness of Corona worldwide. In 2009 Corona was voted the favorite beer of 2.5 million people surveyed on Facebook. In 2010 Corona was number nine on a list of the brands with most appeal to the Dutch conducted by BR-ND Positioneringsgroep en MetrixLab. When Yomego ranked the top 50 brands in social media, Corona came in at number 49 in 2011. One reason for the brand's success was its effective advertising campaigns, including those on social media. In its 2010 "Win a Beach Getaway" contest, the brand used a mobile advertising campaign, among other devices, to promote Corona and the contest. As a result, Corona experienced a 49 percent increase in purchase intent and a 13 percent hike in brand awareness.

BRAND OUTLOOK

- The worldwide economic recession that began in 2008 impacted beer sales, including Corona's.
- In 2011 Corona Extra had the largest increase by volume of any Grupo Modelo brand.
- In the early 21st century Grupo Modelo invested in renewable energy resources to produce its products, including Corona.

While Corona remains strong as a brand, it had slower growth in the second decade of the 21st century, especially in the United States. There, the beer industry was affected by the economic recession, the reduced spending power of its primary customers who were young men of drinking age, and changing consumption patterns for beer and other alcohols. European markets were also impacted by a decrease in consumption of beer and the ongoing economic difficulties.

Despite these handicaps, Corona Extra had the largest increase in volume of the brands sold by Grupo Modelo in 2011. And there was continued growth in Australia, Europe, Asia, Latin America, and the Caribbean. Demand was expected to increase overall in 2013 as the world economy continued to recover, despite the rise of craft beer, greater competition, and consolidation in the beer industry. The forthcoming sale to Anheuser-Busch InBev could affect Corona's fortunes, not only in the United States but in many global markets.

In the United States, Corona was popular among Latinos. The expected growth of the Hispanic market over the coming decades was likely to result in increased sales for Corona, as long as the brand was marketed to them in a meaningful manner. To increase its share of the Spanish market, Corona used environmental concerns and its link to beach culture. The brand also developed a "Save the Beach" campaign to highlight the poor condition of many beaches worldwide. Through extensive public relations and media activities, the brand gained volume growth and market share in Spain.

Corona's producer, Grupo Modelo, made a particular effort in its breweries to invest in renewable energy sources, which provided about 11 percent of the energy in 2011. The manufacturer used biomass, primarily as fuel. It had plans to add wind power and biogas in related wastewater treatment plants.

FURTHER READING

"Best Global Brands 2012." Interbrand. Accessed December 26, 2012. http://www.interbrand.com/en/best-global-brands/2012/Corona.

Brand Finance. "Corona." *Brandirectory*. Accessed December 26, 2012. http://brandirectory.com/profile/corona.

"BrandZ Top 100 Most Valuable Global Brands 2012." Millward Brown. Accessed December 26, 2012. http://www.millwardbrown.com/brandz/2012/Documents/2012_BrandZ_Top100_Report.pdf.

"Corona Wide Open Brings Beach Volleyball Festivals to Eight U.S. Markets." *PR Newswire*, March 11, 2009.

De la Merced, Michael J. "No. 1 Brewer Nears Deal for Modelo." *New York Times*, June 25, 2012.

Grupo Modelo. *2011 Annual Report: Objectives Shaped into Results*. Accessed December 26, 2012. http://m.gmodelo.mx/download/Informe_anual_2011_eng.pdf

Olson, Elizabeth. "Corona Light Sets Sights on a Younger Party Crowd." *New York Times*, August 2, 2010.

Pfeifer, Marinne. "Greystripe Boost Corona Brand Metrics According to comScore." Examiner.com, September 24, 2010. Accessed December 29, 2012. http://www.examiner.com/article/greystripe-boost-corona-brand-metrics-according-to-comscore.

Reid, Scott. "Mexican Wave for Brewing Giant Anheuser-Busch InBev As It Snaps up Corona." *Scotsman* (Edinburgh, Scotland), June 30, 2012.

Riggs, Thomas. "Corona." *Encyclopedia of Global Brands, Volume 1: Consumable Products*. Ed. Janice Jorgensen. Detroit, MI: St. James Press, 1994.

COSTCO

AT A GLANCE

Brand Synopsis: Costco signifies no-frills, members-only warehouse shopping for bulk groceries, household items, and other, sometimes surprising, consumer goods.
Parent Company: Costco Wholesale Corporation
999 Lake Drive
Issaquah, Washington 98027
United States
http://www.costco.com
Sector: Consumer Staples
Industry Group: Food & Drug Retailing
Performance: *Market share*—50 percent of the U.S. warehouse club market (2009). *Sales*—US$99.1 billion (2012).
Principal Competitors: Sam's Club; BJ's Wholesale Club, Inc.; Meijer, Inc.; Carrefour; Tesco

BRAND ORIGINS

- A former employee of Price Club, another wholesale warehouse club, helped found Costco in 1983.
- Price Club and Costco both operated in large warehouses, employed a limited number of salespeople, and advertised only when opening new locations.
- Price Club and Costco shared common retail practices, such as buying items directly from manufacturers and offering a limited number of products sold in bulk.
- The warehouse club industry boomed in the 1980s and 1990s, and Price Club and Costco opened new locations outside their West Coast bases.
- Price Club and Costco merged in 1993 to create PriceCostco, Inc., later known as Costco Wholesale Corporation.

As is true of a number of large corporations, the history of Costco Wholesale Corporation is really the story of multiple companies. Price Club opened in 1976 in San Diego, California, and other locations followed. Price Club was a wholesale membership club, which meant that members paid annual membership fees to shop at its warehouses. For those fees, shoppers could buy at wholesale prices. The fees also helped to offset Price Club's overhead operating expenses, which were already low for several reasons. For example, its large warehouses were located in industrial areas, not in areas with high real estate costs. Also, it employed fewer salespeople than typical retail stores, and it advertised only when the company opened a new warehouse.

Price Club kept its prices low through its retail practices. It bought its goods in bulk directly from their manufacturers. This practice meant that Price Club received discounts for buying large amounts and that the company did not have to deal with distributors. Its customers could buy different kinds of items in bulk, but they had fewer items to choose from, which reduced inventory costs.

James D. Sinegal and Jeffrey H. Brotman opened the first Costco in Seattle, Washington, in 1983. Sinegal had worked at Price Company, Price Club's parent company, and he brought many of Price Club's retail practices to

Costco. Europe's hypermarkets were another inspiration for Costco. A hypermarket combines a department store and a grocery store under a single roof. The European hypermarket chain Carrefour opened its first store in France in 1963.

In the 1980s and early 1990s Price Club and Costco expanded beyond their initial locations on the West Coast to areas throughout the United States. As the warehouse club industry boomed, new competitors emerged. Retail giant Walmart (Wal-Mart Stores, Inc.) created Sam's Club, which became a chief competitor. The growing presence of Sam's Club in the industry helped to prompt the merger of Costco and Price Club in 1993. The new company initially used the name PriceCostco, Inc. It later reincorporated and changed its name once again, to Costco Wholesale Corporation.

Since the merger, Costco has experimented with other retail concepts. It sold home furnishings through its Costco Home stores, a venture that ended in 2009. Costco's Internet site, Costco.com, debuted in 1998. This site allows existing members to purchase Costco's products and to renew their memberships. The site also enables nonmembers to join Costco.

BRAND ELEMENTS

- Costco's logo features COSTCO in large red capital letters above WHOLESALE in smaller blue capital letters, preceded by three horizontal lines in the same shade of blue.
- Visual elements of Costco locations include large undecorated warehouse spaces with products on high shelves or in stacks.
- Signs are largely absent in Costco stores, sometimes frustrating consumers, but Costco executives liken shopping there to a "treasure hunt."
- Bulk items are a signature of Costco.
- Costco leads the United States in sales of toilet paper, meat, and wine.

Costco is a company that prides itself on the low prices it offers consumers, and so its name, which draws attention to this low-cost approach, is an important asset. The Costco logo is a registered trademark. It consists of red capital letters spelling out COSTCO atop three horizontal blue lines, which lead to smaller blue capital letters that spell out WHOLESALE.

Like the simple Costco logo, Costco's warehouses reflect the no-frills identity of the brand. The corporation's warehouses are large buildings, averaging about 145,000 square feet, although Costco warehouses range from 73,000 to 205,000 square feet. They feature merchandise in stacks or on high shelves. The warehouses are largely undecorated and do not even feature many signs. While the lack of signage has frustrated some customers, Costco marketing executive Robin Ross claims, "There is a treasure hunt aspect to shopping at the store. Costco wants you to walk around and browse. It's a unique experience."

This unique experience extends to the goods sold by Costco. Its bulk offerings echo the large size of its warehouses. Costco shoppers can buy such items as a 12-pound pail of honey, a liter of shampoo, and a package of 96 rolls of toilet paper. Not surprisingly, Costco sells more toilet paper than any other retailer in the United States. It also sells more meat and wine than any other U.S. retailer.

BRAND IDENTITY

- Costco's brand is defined by the array of products it sells under a single roof, including bulk items and regular merchandise.
- Under its private label Kirkland, Costco markets a wide variety of inexpensive products, including food, apparel, personal care items, health products, travel goods, and housewares.
- The Costco brand encompasses more-expensive designer and high-end products.
- Costco warehouses sell a surprisingly wide range of products and services, from groceries and fast-food meals to insurance plans and coffins.

Costco's brand is defined by the wide variety of products it sells under a single roof. Costco offers a combination of bulk items and regular merchandise. It also offers different price points within the same warehouse. For example, it carries a wide range of inexpensive items under its private Kirkland label. The Kirkland name appears on products as varied as bottled water, groceries, cookware, boots, pain relievers, mattresses, luggage, baby care items, and hearing aids.

Costco also offers name-brand products, some with high-end designer labels. Since the corporation does not advertise, these unexpected offerings have helped to entice shoppers to visit more frequently. Costco and Costco.com also sell a limited number of expensive items, including pieces of jewelry that cost more than US$100,000.

A vast assortment of other products and services complete the brand's identification with one-stop shopping. Costco warehouses feature grocery sections with fresh produce, meat, seafood, and bakery items; sections offering health and beauty goods; pharmacies; optical centers; hearing-aid centers; tire centers; photo-processing centers; florists; and gas stations. At some locations, shoppers may even purchase insurance plans, wedding dresses, and coffins. While shopping, members can snack on free food samples or purchase a meal at the Costco food court. In the United States, Costco's food courts sell millions of hot dogs a year as part of a US$1.50 value meal.

BRAND STRATEGY

- Only about 4,000 different items appear in a Costco warehouse store at a time, promoting the idea of exclusivity.
- Costco offers three elite types of membership: Business, Gold Star, and Executive.
- Business owners make up a significant customer base for Costco, which actively recruits new candidates for Business Memberships.
- The success of the Costco brand relies on members' word-of-mouth advertising.

The Costco brand connotes exclusivity at a reasonable price. Costco is known for offering large container sizes or multiple items in a single package, but its warehouses feature fewer brand options than other stores. While customers may be able to buy a large quantity of one product, they cannot buy many different types of that product. The warehouses also limit the number of goods they offer at a time to about 4,000 unique items.

This exclusivity extends to its customers. After all, Costco is a membership club. With the exception of a few goods (e.g., alcohol in some states and items that may be purchased with the Costco Cash Card), customers must pay fees before purchasing Costco products. The brand encompasses three elite types of membership.

Costco's Business Membership is open to business owners, farmers, and nonprofit or government organizations. Business owners have long constituted a customer base for Costco, which originally allowed only business owners to shop at its warehouses. This type of membership is still important to the brand, and Costco employees actively work to register businesses and organizations as Costco members.

Individuals may purchase a Gold Star Membership, which entitles members to more than one membership card for their household. Customers with Costco's Executive Membership receive a reward for most of their purchases and have access to special services and other perks.

Since Costco does not advertise, it relies on members to do its advertising by word of mouth. Typically earning more than the average American, Costco members shop the warehouse stores for the low prices as well as the possibility that they may find special things to purchase. Members also benefit from Costco's generous return policy. In addition, customers with the Business Membership can resell their Costco purchases to their own customers.

BRAND EQUITY

- *Forbes* magazine ranks Costco as one of the top 2,000 international companies and as one of its top brands.
- According to Brand Finance, Costco has one of the best international brand values, ranking 125th out of 500 global companies.
- Interbrand ranks Costco as the 15th-best U.S. retail brand.
- Costco and its top-three competitors generate more than 90 percent of the revenue of the warehouse club and superstore industry.

Loyal members have made Costco a successful domestic and international brand. After becoming a public company in 1985, Costco quickly grew into one of the largest companies in the world. In 2004 Costco made *Forbes* magazine's initial "Global 2000" list, a ranking of the world's largest public companies. In the 2012 list, Costco Wholesale Corporation ranks 238th. Moreover, a *Forbes* list of top brands in 2011 lists Costco as number 28, while Walmart is number 60.

In "Global 500 2012," a list of the most successful international companies, Brand Finance ranks Costco 125th, with a brand value of US$7.6 billion. On that same list, Costco's competitor Sam's Club is ranked 75th, with a brand value of US$11.5 billion. Another listing of brands, Interbrand's "2012 Best Retail Brands" ranks Costco as the 15th-best U.S. retail brand, with a value of US$6.4 billion. Sam's Club places eighth on the same list, with a value of US$12.9 billion.

Costco, Sam's Club, BJ's Wholesale Club, and Meijer dominate the industry of warehouse clubs and superstores. According to *Research and Markets*, this field consists of about 12 companies with roughly 4,000 stores. However, the top-four companies generate more than 90 percent of the industry's revenue. With more than 550 U.S. and international stores and 66.5 million members, Costco competes closely with Sam's Club, which boasts almost 600 locations and more than 47 million members in the United States, Puerto Rico, Mexico, Brazil, and China. BJ's Wholesale Club, Inc., runs about 200 stores in the eastern United States. Meijer, Inc., operates a chain of superstores in Michigan, Ohio, Indiana, Illinois, and Kentucky.

BRAND AWARENESS

- Some commentators have likened Costco members to the followers of a cult.
- Television programs have registered Costco's popularity by depicting characters who are enthusiastic about warehouse stores.
- *Forbes* magazine named Costco one of "America's Most Reputable Companies" in 2012.
- *Fortune* magazine has repeatedly named Costco one of its most admired companies.
- The 2012 U.S. presidential race featured a candidate talking about Costco and Costco executives participating in politics.

With 66.5 million members, Costco is a well-known retailer to American and international consumers. Most members remain loyal: almost 90 percent of American members renew their memberships, as do 86 percent of members in other countries. As early as 1999, Costco's popularity prompted Shelly Branch to write an article for *Forbes* magazine about the "cult of Costco." Branch noted how the corporation's lack of advertising created a "secretive, clubby aspect." She further observed that some members visit Costco quite frequently and spend a lot of money there. Some even feel compelled to lie about how often they visit and how much they spend.

By the early 21st century the Costco brand had infiltrated U.S. popular culture. In 2009 the television comedy *Modern Family* featured its regular characters shopping there. A 2003 episode of another television comedy, *The Bernie Mac Show*, parodied Costco and its Kirkland label by showing its characters shopping at the fictional warehouse club Cost Depot, which sold products under the "Craigland" label. Characters on both programs are initially reluctant to shop at warehouse clubs. As the episodes progress, however, these characters enthusiastically embrace shopping at the stores and buy bulk amounts of goods.

In the real world, Costco members are equally as enthusiastic. On *Forbes* magazine's 2012 "America's Most Reputable Companies" list, Costco Wholesale placed 31st, while BJ's Wholesale Club ranked 52nd. Moreover, *Fortune* named Costco as one of its most admired companies every year from 2006 to 2012.

In 2012 Costco even figured in the U.S. presidential campaigns. In an August 2012 television interview, Republican candidate Mitt Romney and his wife, Ann, praised Costco and its goods. The following month, Costco cofounder James D. Sinegal addressed the Democratic National Convention in support of the Democratic candidate, President Barack Obama. Sinegal also hosted fund-raisers for Obama.

BRAND OUTLOOK

- In 2012 Costco was considering expansion to additional European markets, such as France and Spain.
- Costco offers better pay and health insurance benefits than many of its competitors.
- Costco's attractive wages and benefits have contributed to low employee turnover as well as concerns about shareholders' profits.

Originating on the U.S. West Coast, Costco has made itself into a multinational corporation. Financial reporters note that Costco's global growth and its affluent customer base are two reasons to have confidence in the brand. Craig Jelinek, who replaced cofounder James D. Sinegal as chief executive officer in 2012, has stated that the company may expand to additional global markets, such as Paris and Madrid.

The company's labor policies have drawn mixed reviews from business commentators, however. The corporation pays higher-than-average wages, compared to companies in the same field. It also has offered health insurance to its employees. These practices have boosted employees' morale and contributed to Costco's low rate of employee turnover, but some commentators have argued that Costco's focus on its employees has reduced profits for its shareholders. They claim that Costco executives have treated Costco as a private company rather than the public company that it is.

The differing perceptions of Costco among its workers and shareholders constitute just one of the brand's contradictions. The no-frills approach that has been embraced by affluent customers, the offering of bulk goods alongside designer items, and massive sales of such disparate goods as wine and hot dogs also capture the paradox of the Costco brand.

FURTHER READING

"Best Retail Brands 2012." Interbrand. Accessed September 8, 2012. http://www.interbrand.com/en/BestRetailBrands/2012-Best-Retail-Brands.aspx.

Branch, Shelly. "Inside the Cult of Costco." *Fortune*, September 6, 1999.

Brand Finance. "Global 500 2012." *Brandirectory*, n.d. Accessed September 8, 2012. http://brandirectory.com/league_tables/table/global-500-2012.

Costco Wholesale Australia. "Company Overview." Accessed September 8, 2012. http://www.costco.com.au/About/AboutCostco.shtml.

"Costco Wholesale Corporation." *International Directory of Company Histories*. Ed. Jay P. Pederson. Vol. 105. Detroit, MI: St. James Press, 2010.

DeCarlo, Scott, ed. "The World's Biggest Public Companies." *Forbes*, April 18, 2012. Accessed September 8, 2012. http://www.forbes.com/global2000.

"Forbes Top Brands." *Forbes*. Accessed September 10, 2012. http://www.forbes.com/lists/2011/forbes-top-brands/list.html.

Smith, Jacquelyn. "America's Most Reputable Companies." *Forbes*, April 4, 2012.

"2011 Report on the $360 Billion US Warehouse Clubs & Superstores Industry." *Research and Markets*, August 2012. Accessed September 8, 2012. http://www.researchandmarkets.com/research/a55392/warehouse_clubs.

Zimmerman, Ann. "Costco's Dilemma: Be Kind to Its Workers, or Wall Street?" *Wall Street Journal*, March 26, 2004.

CREDIT SUISSE

AT A GLANCE

Brand Synopsis: A leader in global finance, Credit Suisse strives to create a premium client-centered brand and to become the most admired bank in the world.
Parent Company: Credit Suisse Group AG
Paradeplatz 8
8070 Zurich
Switzerland
https://www.credit-suisse.com
Sector: Financials
Industry Group: Diversified Financials
Performance: *Market share*—Ranked first in European Equities Trading, first in European cash trading (2011 and 2012), and first in cash trading in the United States (2009 and 2010) by Greenwich Associates. *Sales*—Net revenues of CHF$25.4 billion (US$27.2 billion) (2011).
Principal Competitors: J.P. Morgan Chase; Morgan Stanley; Bank of America; Goldman Sachs; Citigroup; UBS; Deutsche Bank

BRAND ORIGINS

- In 1856, Alfred Escher founded Schweizerische Kreditanstalt in Switzerland as a means to fund the Swiss railroad and to further Swiss industrialization.
- Credit Suisse expanded its business overseas to New York in 1940, paving the way for future mergers and acquisitions, such as the acquisition of First Boston in 1988.
- Fully integrated by 2006, Credit Suisse established itself as a global bank by creating robust alliances and strategically acquiring new firms.

Alfred Escher founded Credit Suisse under the name Schweizerische Kreditanstalt (Swiss Credit Institution) in 1856. Heavily involved in politics and the industrialization of Switzerland, Escher originally planned that the new bank was to finance the privatization and expansion of the Swiss railroad and to build business in Switzerland. The new bank was a bigger success than anticipated. The initial stock was issued with a value of three million francs, and within just three days, the total value of subscriptions amounted to 218 million francs. By 1871, with the exception of one year of losses, the bank had grown into the largest financial institution in Switzerland.

The bank continued to grow through the turn of the 20th century, opening branches throughout Switzerland and other European countries. Credit Suisse also began offering individual consumers savings accounts and credit cards. By 1940, Credit Suisse had opened its first overseas branch in New York. Although foreign trading subsided during World War II, Credit Suisse emerged from the war with goals of expanding its services at home as well as to fund reconstruction efforts at home and abroad. In the 1960s, Credit Suisse began a relationship with White, Weld & Co., a leading American investment bank. This relationship led to a partnership with the American investment bank First Boston in the 1970s after White, Weld & Co. was acquired by Merrill Lynch. During this time, Credit Suisse also began to acquire other banks and services, setting itself up as a global presence with offices on every continent, with the exception of Antarctica.

The late 1980s were difficult years for Credit Suisse, defined as they were by challenging economic times and loss of market share and profitability at First Boston. During the next 20 years, however, Credit Suisse made significant overhauls to operations, taking over First Boston in its entirety and forming a coalition of international investment banks under the name Credit Suisse First Boston. This restructuring, along with further acquisitions throughout the 1990s and two major restructurings of the company's U.S. and Swiss operations, helped to stabilize the institution's securities trading and market share. Credit Suisse emerged in 2006 as a global, integrated bank offering three distinct services under one roof: private banking, investment banking, and asset management.

BRAND ELEMENTS

- The business history of Credit Suisse is mirrored in the many changes to its logo during the past 150 years.
- In 2006, Credit Suisse restructured its business entities to create one integrated, global bank.
- The 2006 logo underscores the importance of a fully integrated bank, while calling attention to its rich history and prestige.

While the Credit Suisse logo has changed many times throughout the institution's 150-year history, the brand's focus on growth and experience has not. Most of the changes to the company's logo were attributed to mergers and acquisitions. No logo is therefore more important than the logo released in 2006 when Credit Suisse merged CS First Boston, its global investment banking branch, and Credit Suisse Group, its Swiss holdings, into one integrated, global bank. The merger brought together the firm's three main services of investment banking, private banking, and asset management, and the 2006 logo underscores the importance of this integration.

The logo displays the firm's name, set in capital letters, followed by two overlapping triangular, sail-like images in the upper right-hand corner. The logo blends elements from both the Credit Suisse and First Boston logos in order to capture the spirit of the fully integrated bank. According to the Credit Suisse website, the classic serif typeface represents "the discretion and prestige associated with [the firm's] long history," and the sail-like symbol echoes the firm's "pioneering spirit" and business heritage.

BRAND IDENTITY

- Credit Suisse presents itself as a premium brand, one that is devoted to the interests of its clients.
- Credit Suisse offers clients a complete list of resources and financial services performed by highly trained professionals.
- Credit Suisse's website and its 2011 advertising campaign showcasing its elite clients demonstrate the company's client-centered approach and the premium quality of its service.

According to Credit Suisse's website, the Credit Suisse brand is an expression of the firm's client-focused business approach and aim to become the world's most admired bank. To accomplish these goals, the firm has aligned itself as a premium brand, one that is responsive to its clients and offers them the best services to achieve their financial goals. Building from the 2006 merging of CS First Boston and Credit Suisse Group, today's Credit Suisse offers clients the ability to take care of all their financial needs within one banking institution. Every outward expression of the Credit Suisse brand, including the firm's logo and website, its list of services, and its association with tennis star Roger Federer in his capacity as the company's ambassador, is aimed toward the elite echelons of society.

Nothing speaks more directly to this branding effort than the client-centered advertising campaign that began in September 2011 and the company's website. The ads, which have aired in Europe, Asia, and the United States, showcase a number of Credit Suisse clients, like Swiss chocolate manufacturer Lindt, depicting different aspects of their businesses. According to *M2 Communications*, the campaign departed "from traditional financial advertising, in that rather than putting the bank at the heart of the story, with the services it provides for clients, the new work showcases client stories and gives the bank a supporting role to that client's successes or ambition." The new ads demonstrate Credit Suisse's commitment to its customers and to providing services of premium quality. Similarly, the Credit Suisse website showcases the company's partnerships with many elite institutions. Rather than emphasizing the bank's services to those institutions, the site also focuses primarily on the institutions' successes, with the bank standing by as a supporting system.

BRAND STRATEGY

- Credit Suisse spent much of 2011 revising its business plan, building capital in accordance with new regulations, and sharpening its client-centered model.
- Brady Dougan, CEO of Credit Suisse, made significant progress in deepening the firm's commitment to transparency.
- The Global Education Initiative and the Microfinance Capacity Building Initiative are demonstrative of Credit Suisse's corporate citizenship.

After the 2008 credit crisis and a disappointing 2011, Credit Suisse focused much of its energy on re-strategizing for the future. Much of 2011 was devoted to building capital to satisfy new government restrictions, strengthening the bank's infrastructure by downsizing and cutting risk-weighted assets, and sharpening its client-centered model. According to its annual report, Credit Suisse agreed that reform of the banking industry is inevitable and necessary and indicated that the above-mentioned changes were made in order to capitalize on new markets in the future, while other competitors would only be beginning the reform process.

Additionally, Credit Suisse made singular efforts to increase the transparency of its operations during this time. In the annual report's "Message from the Chief Officer and CEO," Brady Dougan outlined four goals that the company would strive to achieve: value-added service, long-term value of equity for shareholders and employees, a reputable firm, and greater social responsibility. While these goals were not unlike those of his competitors, Brady Dougan's attitude toward accomplishing these goals was different. In his letter he wrote, "While every decision that we make and every action that we take do not end up perfectly accomplishing these goals, we can assure you that this is our aspiration. ... Achieving this aspiration has been very demanding over the past five years. We think we have done many things right during this challenging period, but certainly not everything." His attitude, representative of the firm's effort to achieve greater transparency, demonstrated Credit Suisse's willingness to accept responsibility for actions that contributed to the public's distrust in the banking industry.

As a further effort to regain the public's trust, Credit Suisse made many commitments to increase its social responsibility throughout the world. In addition to donations made to the Roger Federer Foundation, a charity seeking to improve educational opportunities for impoverished people in Switzerland and several African countries, two examples of corporate citizenship initiatives outlined in Credit Suisse's *2011 Corporate Responsibility Report* are the Global Education Initiative and the Microfinance Capacity Building Initiative. The former program provides 45,000 disadvantaged young people of school age with a solid education, while the latter aims to help those at the base of the income pyramid by promoting financial inclusion. Such programs reflect Credit Suisse's position that all people and companies should give back to their communities as a way to help the world progress.

BRAND EQUITY

- Credit Suisse lost revenue in 2011 due to economic hardships, client inactivity, and restructuring required by new regulations.
- Credit Suisse's brand value fell to CHF$3.8 billion in 2011, and it dropped to 95th place on Interbrand's list of the top 100 global brands.
- To improve its brand value and its revenues, Credit Suisse adopted a more client-focused model and increased its corporate citizenship efforts in 2012.

By its own account, Credit Suisse did not perform in accordance with its aspirations in 2011. While the bank still brought in revenues of CHF$25.4 billion, and a net income of CHF$2 billion, those numbers were down from 2010. According to the bank's annual report, these losses were due to the European sovereign debt crisis, new industry regulations that led the firm to focus on building capital, and the decline in client investment activity. Consequently, the brand lost value in 2012. According to Brand Finance's *Banking 500* report, Credit Suisse ranked 22nd among the world's banks, down from 15th place in 2011, with a brand value of CHF$8.3 billion (US$8.9 billion). The report suggested that several investigations by the U.S. Justice Department and the firm's inability to match analysts' forecasts also figured in the decline.

While losses were typical for banks after the onset of the 2008 global credit crisis, Credit Suisse took transparent steps to combat the resulting negative publicity. According to Interbrand, which in 2011 ranked Credit Suisse down 95th in its list of the top 100 global brands, with a brand value of CHF$3.8 billion, "the bank's ability to hold steady is impressive. The brand has retained relevance through its continued transition to a more client-focused model, ... corporate citizenship effort, use of social media channels, and a multi-year talent and cultural-building effort." These efforts seem to be working, for Credit Suisse is the only representative of the Swiss banking tradition among the world's elite banking brands. It is the firm's hope that these strategies, visible in both its partnership with Roger Federer and its strong marketing campaign, will increase both its revenues and its brand value in the years to come.

BRAND AWARENESS

- Top-of-mind awareness for the brand Credit Suisse probably exists only among the elite levels of society.
- Credit Suisse maintains its brand awareness among the elite by marketing itself as a client-focused, prestigious brand that empowers customers to make sound financial decisions.
- Credit Suisse has controlled its reputation in part by making its story public and its brand highly transparent.

Credit Suisse is easily identifiable as one of the world's oldest financial institutions, specifically in the Swiss banking tradition. However, it most likely does not enjoy top-of-mind awareness among most consumers. Known for being a fully integrated bank that offers its clients help with investments, mortgages, and other financial matters, the brand is best known to those able to take advantage of its premium services. Rather than trying to spread awareness of Credit Suisse throughout the public sector, the firm has focused its attention on the elite. With an advertising campaign centered upon a number of these wealthy clients and by sponsoring elite sports events and cultural programs and engaging in philanthropy, Credit Suisse has become known as a firm that helps its wealthy clients achieve their dreams.

Consequently, Credit Suisse takes good care to maintain its reputation. Unlike many of its competitors (Goldman Sachs, for example), who operate more inconspicuously, Credit Suisse makes an effort to publicize its story. With an expansive website explaining everything from the company's services and branding to the history of its logo and advertising campaigns, Credit Suisse readily presents the public with most of the information about which people might inquire. In fact, there is even mention of moments in its history when the bank's actions were less than pure. This transparency, an aspect of Credit Suisse's client-centered model, appeals to potential clients who might be suspicious of the banking industry and to current employees and shareholders, who have a vested interest in the firm.

BRAND OUTLOOK

- While 2011 was a difficult year for Credit Suisse, the institution projected a hopeful outlook by focusing on an internal review and restructuring.
- Credit Suisse primed the brand for future success by limiting its risks, communicating with regulators, and building its capital.
- Credit Suisse's 2011 and 2012 advertising campaigns focused on the bank's client-centered business model and their elite clientele.
- Sponsorship of important cultural institutions demonstrates Credit Suisse's focus on its wealthy customer base, as well as its ability to maintain long-lasting and beneficial relationships.

Although at first glance the year 2011 appears to have been quite dismal for Credit Suisse, with declines in revenues and brand value, the restructuring that took place in that year hold out promise for a strong future. According to its 2011 annual report, Credit Suisse has taken significant actions that will enable the company to excel in the reformed banking environment, making it possible for the bank to offer the best services to its clients, attractive returns to its shareholders, and a good workplace for its employees. Some of these actions included opening the lines of communication with governments and regulators to try to solve the problems within the global banking industry, continuing to build capital and liquidity, making difficult job cuts as fairly as possible, and reducing risk-weighted assets in investment banking.

In addition, Credit Suisse also invested money in its corporate advertising campaign and "The Roger Federer World Tour 2012" campaign, both of which offered direct commentaries on the brand's client-focused business model and its ability to adeptly help its clients achieve financial success. The global marketing campaign has furthered the company's attempts to prepare for future success with its elite clientele, people who are already wealthy and who are interested in culture and the arts. To that end, Credit Suisse continues to support the arts via several sponsorships, including a sponsorship of the New York Philharmonic. On its website, Credit Suisse says that "when it comes to choosing our sponsorship partners, one factor above all is decisive: In keeping with its premium brand, Credit Suisse only works with people and institutions of the highest class." In this way, Credit Suisse strives to ensure that its partnerships are long-lasting and mutually beneficial and to demonstrate its ability to collaborate, to be supportive, and to develop meaningful relationships, which are all attributes that will be crucial to maintaining a premium brand in the years to come.

FURTHER READING

Brand Finance. "Banking 500 2012." *Brandirectory*, 2012. Accessed October 1, 2012. http://brandirectory.com/league_tables/table/banking-500-2012.

Credit Suisse AG. "Credit Suisse advances to #2 prime broker worldwide in 2012 benchmark survey of industry assets." *Sacramento Bee*, October 2, 2012. Accessed October 4, 2012. http://www.sacbee.com/2012/10/02/4874480/credit-suisse-advances-to-2-prime.html.

Credit Suisse Group AG. *2011 Annual Report.* Accessed October 2, 2012. https://www.credit-suisse.com/publications/annualreporting/doc/2011/csg_ar_2011_en.pdf.

Credit Suisse Group AG. *2011 Corporate Responsibility Report.* Accessed October 7, 2012. https://www.credit-suisse.com/publications/annualreporting/doc/2011/csg_crr_2011_en.pdf.

"Euro RSCG London launches new global advertising campaign for Credit Suisse." *M2 Communications*, September 28, 2011. *General OneFile.* Accessed October 3, 2012. http://go.galegroup.com/ps/i.do?id=GALE%7CA268203822&v=2.1&u=itsbtrial&it=r&p=GPS&sw=w.

Interbrand. *2011 Ranking of the Top 100 Brands.* Accessed October 2, 2012. http://www.interbrand.com/en/best-global-brands/best-global-brands-2008/best-global-brands-2011.aspx.

Macaskill, Jon. "Credit Suisse scheme promotes counterparty accountability." *Euromoney*, March 2012. *General OneFile.* Accessed October 4, 2012. http://go.galegroup.com/ps/i.do?id=GALE%7CA286080543&v=2.1&u=itsbtrial&it=r&p=GPS&sw=w.

"Mergers & Acquisitions revenue—Asia Pacific 2011." *Euroweek*, January 27, 2012. *General OneFile.* Accessed October 1, 2012. http://go.galegroup.com/ps/i.do?id=GALE%7CA281627495&v=2.1&u=itsbtrial&it=r&p=GPS&sw=w.

CVS

AT A GLANCE

Brand Synopsis: One of the leading pharmacy retail chains in the United States, CVS provides consumers with integrated health care solutions that are both effective and affordable.
Parent Company: CVS Caremark Corporation
One CVS Drive
Woonsocket, Rhode Island 02895
United States
www.cvscaremark.com
Sector: Consumer Staples
Industry Group: Food and Staples Retailing
Performance: *Market share*—18 percent in the United States (2011); 3 percent worldwide (2008). *Sales*—US$107.1 billion (2011).
Principal Competitors: The Kroger Co.; Rite Aid Corp.; Walgreens Co.; Wal-Mart Stores, Inc.

BRAND ORIGINS

- The first CVS store opened in Lowell, Massachusetts, in 1963.
- In 1969 the CVS drugstore chain was purchased by the Melville Shoe Corporation.
- In 1995 the Melville Corporation changed its name to CVS Corporation and divested itself of all business holdings except the pharmacy chain CVS.
- By 2012 CVS operated more than 7,000 drugstores in 41 states and Puerto Rico.

The history of CVS is intertwined with that of the Melville Corporation, which traces its roots to 1892, when Frank Melville, a shoe salesman, took over the three stores owned by his employer, who had left town under a cloud of debt. Melville parlayed the three shops in New York into a small but thriving chain. In 1909 he brought his son, John Ward Melville (who was known as Ward), into the family business.

While serving in the army during World War I, Ward Melville struck up a profitable friendship with J. Franklin McElwain, a New Hampshire shoe manufacturer. Together they devised a method to mass-produce shoes and distribute them at low prices through a chain of stores, which they named Thom McAn. They opened the first Thom McAn store in New York in 1922, offering a few simple styles of men's shoes at the fixed price of US$3.99. Despite the lack of variety, the discounting scheme was an immediate success, and new stores were opened all over the Northeast. The duo incorporated their new company as the Melville Shoe Corporation.

Melville Shoe, along with many other businesses, suffered during the Great Depression. The company weathered the storm with careful management, prudent expansion, and financial innovation. Melville made a public stock offering in 1936, taking its place on the New York Stock Exchange. Throughout the 1930s, Melville continued to open additional outlets. By 1939 the company operated 650 Thom McAn stores and also marketed its products through its smaller John Ward and Frank

Tod shoe store chains. Within 30 years, Melville was the nation's largest shoe retailer, operating more than 1,400 stores. In 1969 Melville bought three companies: the Consumer Value Stores (CVS) chain of drug retail outlets; Mark Steven, Inc., a firm that distributed products to CVS; and Retail Store Management, Inc.

Founded by brothers Sid and Stanley Goldstein and Ralph Hoagland, the first CVS store opened in Lowell, Massachusetts, in 1963 as a discount health and beauty aid store in which customers bagged their own merchandise. The CVS name was first used in 1964, by which time the trio were running a 17-store chain. A key development occurred in 1968 when pharmacy departments were added to CVS outlets, prompting the company's eventual emergence as a leading drugstore chain. At the time of its acquisition by Melville in 1969, the CVS chain consisted of 40 stores.

In 1995 Melville announced a sweeping restructuring through which it planned to spin or sell off several of its businesses (which now included shoes, furniture, toys, apparel, and linens) to focus primarily on its most profitable unit, the CVS drugstore chain. In 1996 Melville moved its corporate headquarters from Rye, New York, to the headquarters of CVS in Woonsocket, Rhode Island. Two months later, Melville changed its name to CVS Corporation.

In 2007 CVS acquired the pharmacy benefit management company, Caremark Rx, and renamed the company CVS Caremark Corporation. The merger created the largest integrated pharmacy services company in the United States, with interests in pharmacies, prescription benefits management, health clinics, and health and beauty retailing. By 2012 CVS/pharmacy operated more than 7,000 drugstores in 41 states and Puerto Rico.

BRAND ELEMENTS

- CVS logos portray a feeling of simplicity, compatible with CVS's mission to provide health care solutions that are both effective and easy.
- Both the CVS Caremark logo and the CVS/pharmacy logo are in all red, bold letters.
- CVS advertising slogans include "For All the Ways You Care," "Expect Something Extra," and "Life to the Fullest."

All CVS logos portray a feeling of simplicity consistent with the CVS desire to provide consumers with solutions that are both effective and easy. The CVS Caremark corporate logo is an integration of the former CVS and Caremark Rx logos. CVS is printed in bold lettering and is positioned above and flush to the right of Caremark. Caremark is printed in all capital letters, with the right leg of the second *R* extended with a slash to form an *X*. The logo is printed in red on a white background.

The CVS/pharmacy logo features the bold CVS in all capital letters with pharmacy in bold, lowercase letters on the same line. The two words are printed in red and separated by a slash mark. CVS MinuteClinic uses the name in blue, lowercase letters with "Minute" positioned on top and "Clinic" below and one letter to the left. A red and blue health care "cross" is positioned to the left of the lettering. CVS has employed the slogans "For All the Ways You Care," "Expect Something Extra," and "Life to the Fullest."

BRAND IDENTITY

- CVS emphasizes customer service, convenience, and low prices in its retail outlets and pharmacy services.
- CVS encourages customer loyalty through its ExtraCare program that offers cash rewards and discounts to return visitors.
- CVS seeks to provide integrated health management by offering easy access and convenient solutions to customers.

CVS emphasizes customer service, convenience, and low prices in its retail outlets and pharmacy services. Through its CVS ExtraCare customer loyalty program, it offers cash rewards and discounts to encourage return visits. The ExtraCare ExtraBucks program pays customers 2 percent back on purchases in the form of a coupon printed at the bottom of the store receipt. It also rewards customers with US$1.00 to spend on store merchandise for every two prescriptions purchased. ExtraCare customers also receive surface and electronic mailings with additional offers and coupons. According to the company, ExtraCare had 67 million active card holders in 2011.

CVS promotes itself as a partner in health management, and the company uses social media to further engage with its customers and help customers connect with each other. Through Facebook and Twitter, CVS notifies consumers of special sales and exclusive coupon offers. The CVS Facebook site also hosts health chats with pharmacists and other experts. These efforts support the CVS goals of integrating health management and providing easy access and convenient solutions to customers.

BRAND STRATEGY

- CVS was the first pharmacy chain to offer customers the convenience of ordering prescriptions and general merchandise online for pickup in the store.
- MinuteClinics inside CVS/pharmacy stores offer customers convenient access to health care for a variety of basic and routine needs.
- CVS markets a number of private-label brands of grocery, home goods, and cosmetics for budget-minded customers.

Since its inception CVS has developed new products and services that combine convenience and affordability. In 1999 it became the first pharmacy chain to offer customers the convenience of ordering prescriptions and general merchandise online for pickup in the store. In 2006 CVS expanded its role in customer care with the addition of MinuteClinic, a provider of walk-in health clinics found in retail stores. Located within CVS/pharmacy stores, CVS MinuteClinics are staffed by physician assistants and nurse practitioners who treat common illnesses, minor wounds, and sprains, and provide vaccinations, wellness exams, and lab testing. MinuteClinics provide CVS a way to attract and retain customers by delivering services that reduce health care costs and result in positive outcomes.

CVS also attracted budget-minded customers by offering an array of products under its exclusive private label brands. Introduced in 1995, the Gold Emblem line was one of the first private brand food lines adopted by a major drugstore chain. With more than 200 products in the line, offerings include crackers, chocolate, candy, nuts, popcorn, drinks, canned vegetables, and potato chips. Earth Essentials is a CVS store brand launched in 2008 of natural and environmentally friendly products. The products, which are designed to completely biodegrade, include napkins, toilet paper, and paper towels made with recycled fibers. In 2011 CVS launched its Just the Basics store brand line. Just the Basics offers value-priced items, including household goods, baby care, beauty products, and personal items. CVS offers a 100 percent satisfaction guarantee on the line, assuring customers that the collection offers the highest value for the lowest prices. In December 2012 CVS introduced a new home goods brand, Total Home. Total Home will replace both the CVS Pharmacy and Round the House brands of home goods, including items such as sandwich and storage bags, toilet paper, napkins, and laundry detergent. Other CVS proprietary brands include Essence of Beauty, Life Fitness, Nuance Salma Hayek cosmetics, Skin Effects by Dr. Jeffrey Dover, and 24.7 beauty products.

In addition to serving retail customers, CVS entered the business-to-business market with CVS Caremark Pharmacy Services, the company's pharmacy benefit management program, offering its services to more than 2,000 health plans. Services include processing and paying prescription drug claims, maintaining lists of drugs covered by particular health plans, and negotiating prices and rebates with drug manufacturers.

BRAND EQUITY

- In 2011 CVS was the leading pharmacy by number of prescriptions filled, with over US$56 billion in sales and a 20.7 percent market share.
- *Fortune* ranked CVS at number 90 in the 2012 "Global 500" and first in the "Top *Fortune 500* Food and Drug Stores" in 2011.
- In 2012 *Fortune* accorded CVS Caremark a brand value of US$9.4 billion.

In 2009 the total value of prescription drugs sold was more than US$300 billion. Chain drugstores accounted for 35 percent of those sales. The *Wall Street Journal* reported that CVS Caremark was the leading U.S. pharmacy by prescription revenue in 2011, with prescription sales of US$56.6 billion, translating to a 20.7 percent market share. In contrast, Walgreens had prescription revenue of US$45.1 billion and a 16.5 percent market share.

In 2011 *Fortune* ranked CVS Caremark first in the "Top *Fortune* 500 Food and Drug Stores," with US$107.8 billion in revenue. The *Financial Times* ranked CVS second of the "World's Most Valuable Food and Drug Retailers" in 2011, with a market value of US$46.89 billion, behind only British retailer Tesco. *Forbes* ranked CVS first in their "World's Largest Drug Retailers Overall," 2011, as part of "*Forbes* 2000."

CVS was ranked at number 90 in the 2012 *Fortune* "Global 500," with a brand value of US$9.4 billion, moving up from number 98 in the 2011 rankings with a brand value of US$9.3 billion. Interbrand ranked CVS/pharmacy fourth of the "Most Valuable U.S. Retail Brands" in 2012 with a brand value of US$17.3 billion.

BRAND AWARENESS

- In 2008 CVS held a 3 percent market share worldwide, tied with Walgreens and ahead of Rite Aid.
- In 2009 CVS trailed only Walgreens and Walmart in leading U.S. retailers of health and beauty products.
- CVS was ranked second of pharmacy benefit managers with a 17.3 percent market share in 2011.

CVS is one of the best-known pharmacy retailers in the United States and operates more than 7,000 stores in 41 states and Puerto Rico. With convenient locations, low prices, and an array of health products and services, it is popular with consumers and has more than 67 million registered participants in its ExtraCare customer loyalty program. In 2009 CVS was ranked third, behind Walgreens and Walmart, of leading retailers of health and beauty products, with sales of US$8.1 billion. In 2010 CVS was ranked second of top drugstores, with sales of US$39.8 billion, and in 2011 the company was ranked seventh of top retailers in the United States, with retail sales of US$59.6 billion. CVS Caremark was also ranked second of leading pharmacy benefit managers with a 17.3 percent market share in 2011.

According to Datamonitor, in 2008 CVS held a 3 percent market share worldwide, tied with Walgreens at 3 percent market share and ahead of Rite Aid with a 1.6 percent market share. In 2010 the *Financial Times* ranked CVS second in online retailers with a 2.7 percent market share.

BRAND OUTLOOK

- CVS gained new pharmacy prescription customers during tense negotiations between its rivals Walgreens and Express Scripts.
- An aging population that relies heavily on prescription medications will help to increase the CVS customer base.
- CVS is well positioned to meet customers' needs for both discretionary and nondiscretionary items.

CVS benefited from a negotiations impasse between its chief retail pharmacy rival, Walgreens, and Express Scripts, its primary competitor in pharmacy benefits management. Scores of pharmacy prescription customers transferred their business from Walgreens to CVS. Even after Walgreens finally reached an agreement with Express Scripts, CVS expected to retain 60 percent of those customers who had defected. CVS executives said they would be focusing on customer outreach, advertising, and promotions to retain customers.

CVS fills an estimated 900 million prescriptions annually, making it the largest pharmacy chain by prescriptions filled. Consequently, the company wields a great deal of purchasing power, and is able to negotiate lower prices, passing those savings on to consumers. An aging population and a growing market for generic drugs should help to increase the CVS customer base.

Analysts remained upbeat about the future of CVS. CVS meets customers' needs for both discretionary and nondiscretionary needs, selling such basic items as toothpaste, toilet paper, and light bulbs, essentials such as medicines and other health care items, as well as elective items such as cosmetics, candy, and toys.

CVS continues to expand its pharmacy markets through acquisition. However, nearly all of CVS's revenue comes from within the United States. Walgreens has begun to forge international relationships, and such moves could block CVS from successfully gaining entry into foreign markets.

FURTHER READING

Bias, William. "5 Takeaways from Walgreens' Last Earnings Call." *Motley Fool*, January 4, 2013. Accessed January 11, 2013. http://beta.fool.com/stockdissector/2013/01/04/5-takeaways-walgreens-last-earnings-call/20606.

Freeman, Chris. "Exclusive: CVS Breaks Down New Private Label Plans." *Private Label Buyer*, January 2, 2013. Accessed January 11, 2013. http://www.privatelabelbuyer.com/articles/87080-exclusive-cvs-breaks-down-new-private-label-plans.

Gross, Daniel, David E. Salamie, and Mary Tradii. "CVS Caremark Corporation." *International Directory of Company Histories*. Ed. Jay P. Pederson. Vol. 108. Detroit, MI: St. James Press, 2010.

Kell, John. "CVS Lifts Outlook on Healthy Pharmacy and Store Sales." *Wall Street Journal*, August 7, 2012. Accessed January 11, 2013. http://online.wsj.com/article/SB10000872396390443792604577574741151251720.html.

Lazich, Robert S., and Virgil L. Burton III. "Leading Drug Stores Worldwide, 2008." *Market Share Reporter*. 2011 ed. Detroit, MI: Gale, 2011.

Marcial, Gene. "CVS Caremark Is the Perfect Stock for 2013." *Forbes*, December 11, 2012. Accessed January 11, 2013. http://www.forbes.com/sites/genemarcial/2012/12/11/cvs-caremark-is-the-perfect-stock-for-2013.

Neff, Jack. "From CVS to Costco, Retailers Put the Screws to Brands: Coke, Energizer Ditched in Price Fight, CVS Bills to Make Up Profit Deficit." *Advertising Age*, November 30, 2009. Accessed January 11, 2013. http://adage.com/article/news/cvs-costco-retailers-put-screws-brands/140756.

Redman, Russell. "CVS Rolls out Just the Basics Store Brand." *Chain Drug Review*, February 23, 2011. Accessed January 11, 2013. http://chaindrugreview.com/front-page/newsbreaks/cvs-rolls-out-just-the-basics-store-brand.

DAEWOO INTERNATIONAL

AT A GLANCE

Brand Synopsis: Based in the Republic of Korea (South Korea) but active all over the world, Daewoo International serves as a cornerstone for the expansion of Korea's exports and overseas resource development through its marketing know-how and dedication to international trading and investment.
Parent Company: POSCO
84-11 Namdaemunno 5-ga
C.P.O. Box 2810
Jung-gu, Seoul (100-753)
Korea
http://www.daewoo.com/english/index.jsp
Sector: Energy; Materials; Industrials
Industry Group: Energy; Materials; Capital Goods
Performance: *Sales*—KRW19.5 trillion (US$17.9 billion) (2011).
Principal Competitors: Hyundai Corporation; Mitsui & Co., Ltd.

BRAND ORIGINS

- The Daewoo Group dissolved to form Daewoo International, the Daewoo Corporation, and Daewoo Engineering & Construction Company, Ltd. (Daewoo E&C).
- Daewoo began as a textile producer and exporter and was still operating in the textile industry in 2012.
- Prior to its breakup, the Daewoo Group was involved in several industries: mechanical and electrical engineering, shipbuilding, petrochemicals, and construction.
- Daewoo International also makes automotive parts, as well as consumer electronics, including microwaves and televisions.
- Daewoo International has more than 100 overseas offices and subsidiaries and conducts business with thousands of companies in hundreds of countries.

Daewoo International is one of three large companies—with the Daewoo Corporation and Daewoo Engineering & Construction Company, Ltd. (Daewoo E&C)—that emerged in the early 2000s after the breakup of the Daewoo Group.

Daewoo began in the 1960s, as the Republic of Korea (South Korea) rebuilt itself following the Korean War. It opened a factory to produce textiles and began exporting textiles and other products. Daewoo International is still heavily involved in the textile industry, maintaining textile plants in its home country and all over the world. In the decades following the company's founding, Daewoo continued to trade and entered the fields of mechanical and electrical engineering, shipbuilding, petrochemicals, and construction. The company also manufactured electronics and other consumer products, such as televisions and microwaves.

The company's activities in these fields led to many international business ventures. In the 1980s, Daewoo participated in a number of production and trading projects with the United States and Europe. One notable example was Daewoo's debut in the automotive industry.

In 1986 Daewoo launched Daewoo Motor, a 50/50 partnership with U.S. automaker General Motors. This was a true international venture. The company partnered with General Motors to produce Pontiac and Oldsmobile cars for multiple markets. Daewoo used the Opel automobile as a model for some of these cars. Opel is a German subsidiary of General Motors. Daewoo International continues to make automotive parts, but Daewoo Motor no longer exists. General Motors bought increasingly larger stakes in the company, and the company was known as GM Korea in 2012.

Throughout its history, Daewoo has had a complicated relationship with the South Korean government. Government programs had encouraged and partly financed the company, and the government passed legislation to protect the company's products from imports. However, other government programs favored smaller companies, forcing Daewoo to close some of its subsidiaries. The Daewoo Group was a "chaebol," a Korean term for a conglomerate that consists of a diversified parent company and related smaller subsidiary companies. New South Korean president Kim Dae-jung wanted to break up chaebols like the Daewoo Group in the late 1990s. Daewoo, facing this government pressure, as well as massive debt due to overseas expansion and a multinational financial crisis, agreed to restructure as the company entered the 21st century.

Daewoo International emerged from this restructuring in 2001. It is a large, multifaceted company. The company has more than 100 overseas offices and subsidiaries and conducts business with thousands of companies in hundreds of countries. Some of its business activities include importing materials and exporting steel products, importing and exporting machinery and petrochemicals, and operating in the mining, oil, and natural gas industries. The company is involved in the operation of power plants, produces and exports textiles and automotive parts, and runs the Daewoo Department Store in Changwon, South Korea.

In 2010 another Republic of Korea company, POSCO, bought a majority interest (around 68 percent) in Daewoo International. POSCO is one of the world's largest steelmakers and one of South Korea's largest companies. This move linked the global Daewoo International to another large international company.

BRAND ELEMENTS

- The name Daewoo means "great universe."
- The Daewoo International logo is a blue oval with white lines in the center that fan out as they rise to the top.
- Pictures of globes and world maps on Daewoo International's website reflect the company's global interests.

The name Daewoo means "great universe." Daewoo International's website reflects this celestial theme. It features a human figure and a globe floating among clouds in a sky. This home page design contains examples of the company's repeated references to its international presence. In addition to the globe, the page features a world map with arrows emerging from the company's home base of the Republic of Korea to represent its global reach.

The Daewoo International logo is a blue oval with six vertical white lines that begin in the center of the lower half of the oval and fan out as they rise to its top. The words "Daewoo International" appear in capital blue letters either under or to the right of this oval. This logo appears on several company websites, sometimes more than once on the same page. The oval logo, which is reminiscent of a globe, emphasizes Daewoo's international character, while the flaring lines convey a sense of movement and growth.

In addition to the logo, company websites also feature faint silhouettes of the world's continents, further emphasizing Daewoo's international focus. Daewoo International's Business Activity websites feature globes that show the regions of eastern Asia and Australia. Multiple rings with highlighted dots circle these globes, apparently indicating the sites of company business.

BRAND IDENTITY

- Daewoo International defines itself as a "company dedicated to international trading and investment" and as a "cornerstone for the expansion of Korea's exports and overseas resource development."
- Daewoo International's website emphasizes the company's global business interests, providing links to parent company POSCO and to online trading sites.
- An introductory movie about Daewoo International, viewable on the company's website, is available in Japanese, Chinese, Russian, Spanish, or English.
- The Code of Corporate Conduct and Ethics, issued by Daewoo International Myanmar E&P in 2007, described the company's social and environmental responsibilities.

Daewoo International defines itself as a "company dedicated to international trading and investment" and as a "cornerstone for the expansion of Korea's exports and overseas resource development through international marketing know-how accumulated through [a] global network of international experts in trading, procurement of high quality commodities ... and abundant domestic and international sales bases." In pursuit of these goals, Daewoo bases its corporate culture on three main qualities: creativity, the spirit of challenge, and trust and reliability.

The "Company Profile" section of its website identifies the following core competencies for Daewoo International: 1. a group of trading experts, 2. a global network,

3. a stable business portfolio, 4. brand value and reliability, and 5. information-technology based real-time enterprise. Daewoo International also prides itself on having diverse business models in such areas as international trade, project organizing, investments in manufacturing and production, and the development of energy and mineral resources abroad.

Daewoo International's focus on global business interests is stressed on its website. Tabs on these web pages allow Internet users to easily choose whether they want to read the websites in Korean or English. Another tab links to POSCO, Daewoo International's parent company, itself a Korean company with substantial business in other Asian countries and across the globe. Yet another website link leads Internet users to an online trading site. This trading site lists the business groups that make up Daewoo International, reinforcing the company's brand while providing a place to conduct business transactions.

To educate online visitors about Daewoo International, the website links to an introductory movie about the company. Internet users can watch this movie in a number of languages: Japanese, Chinese, Russian, Spanish, or English. These choices spotlight once again the company's multinational business interests.

A subsidiary of Daewoo International, Daewoo International Myanmar E&P, addressed its multinational business interests by issuing a Code of Corporate Conduct and Ethics in 2007. This code detailed Daewoo International's responsibilities, including its treatment of its employees and the environment. The code also described how the company planned to relate to the countries and communities hosting its businesses.

BRAND STRATEGY

- In Arakan State, Myanmar, Daewoo International is the majority operator of the Shwe Gas Project.
- Daewoo International and Korea Resources Corporation (Kores) both own a percentage of a coal mine in Narrabri, New South Wales, Australia.
- Daewoo International and the Kenya Electricity Generating Company (KenGen) plan to build East Africa's largest power plant in Kilifi County, Kenya.
- Daewoo International established the Migrants' Help-call Center to assist workers of different cultures and migrant workers.
- In 2011 Daewoo International signed a deal to sponsor the Republic of Korea's bobsleigh and skeleton team for eight years.

One of Daewoo International's key goals is to become a "top global company," and it is pursuing strategies to accomplish that goal. Like a number of other international companies, Daewoo International now operates in Myanmar. Daewoo is the majority operator of Shwe Gas Project in the country's Arakan State. The expansion of Daewoo's interests in Myanmar has not come without complications. Protests have accompanied this project, as residents in Arakan have asked the company for rights to the electricity the project generates.

Despite such disputes, Daewoo International continues to operate and expand internationally. In September 2011 it began shipping coal extracted from a mine in Narrabri, New South Wales, Australia. Daewoo International and Korea Resources Corporation (Kores) both own a percentage of the mine. Because of this project, Daewoo International planned to expand its business at its office in Sydney, Australia.

The company is active in Africa as well. In November 2012 Daewoo International joined the Kenya Electricity Generating Company (KenGen) in plans to build a US$1.3 billion coal-fueled power plant in Kilifi County, Kenya. This plant would be the largest power plant in East Africa.

Daewoo International operates multicultural corporate responsibility programs that reflect its international focus. As a part of its corporate responsibility effort, Daewoo established the Migrants' Help-call Center, which provides assistance to migrant workers and workers from different cultures. The company provides services in several different languages through the Migrants' Help-call Center. These efforts combine with other Daewoo initiatives, including employee volunteer programs, to further the brand's desired image as a conscientious global company.

Alongside its Migrants' Help-call Center initiative, Daewoo International has made other efforts to portray the brand positively and globally. In 2011 the company signed a deal to sponsor the Republic of Korea's bobsleigh and skeleton team for eight years. This decision provided funding for training and equipment, and boosted Daewoo's public profile as well. Social networking sites such as Facebook have featured photographs of team members wearing Daewoo's name and logo prominently on team clothing. By signing the sponsorship deal in 2011, Daewoo insured that its name would be featured at a number of international events, including the 2014 Winter Olympics and the 2018 Winter Olympics, which will be held in Pyeongchang, South Korea.

BRAND EQUITY

- In 2010 Daewoo International's Daewoo Textile Fergana produced 20.29 percent of the textiles for Uzbekistan's textile market.
- Giant steelmaker POSCO's affiliation with Daewoo International may help Daewoo attain and sustain prominence in the steel industry.
- Brand Finance ranked the Daewoo brand 250th in its Global 500 list of the top international brands in 2012 with a value of US$2.15 billion.

In 2011 Daewoo reported revenues of KRW19.5 trillion (US$17.9 billion), and a net income of KRW210.7 billion (US$196.2 million). Daewoo International's global affiliates are a major part of Daewoo International's success. They have helped the company grow additional business. For example, the company owns Daewoo Textile Fergana, a textile plant in Fergana, Uzbekistan. In 2010 this plant produced 20.29 percent of the textiles for Uzbekistan's textile market. Daewoo International is also involved with products closer to home. Its majority shareholder, POSCO, is the largest steelmaker in the Republic of Korea and one of the five largest steelmakers in the world. Some business analysts believe Daewoo's work with POSCO and other businesses may lead to Daewoo International's increased prominence in the steel industry, and brand analysts continue to note Daewoo's international prominence. Due, in part, to their international presence, in Brand Finance's 2012 Global 500 list of the top international brands, the Daewoo brand ranked 250th with a value of US$2.15 billion.

BRAND AWARENESS

- On a Daewoo International website, the company claims that its brand has "high recognition in international markets."
- Other Daewoo brands contribute to Daewoo International's brand awareness; for example, the company's foray into automotive manufacturing helped publicize its name.
- In a poll published in 2000, American college students rated Daewoo the fourth-most popular Korean brand.

Daewoo's history and international presence has helped make Daewoo International a strong brand. The company claims that the brand has "high recognition in international markets." The company also claims that its work in establishing these markets helps smaller companies compete in these markets as well.

The global brand awareness that Daewoo International enjoys is partially due to the recognition of subsidiary Daewoo brands, such as Daewoo Electronics. Daewoo International's former role as an automotive manufacturer put the company's name prominently in front of the public as well. Since the company still manufactures automotive parts and components, it is a recognizable brand that still has ties to the industry.

Academics have also studied Daewoo's brand strength. Two business professors polled a number of American college students about Korean, Chinese, and Japanese brands. The results of this poll, published in 2000, indicated that Daewoo was the fourth-most popular Korean brand among these Midwestern college students.

BRAND OUTLOOK

- Daewoo International welcomes challenges as opportunities for continued growth.
- Daewoo International seeks to adapt to changing business conditions and emerge with new ideas for the future.
- Daewoo International continues to operate and expand internationally, building upon its expertise in trading and its global network.
- Daewoo's stable business portfolio, with six divisions covering diverse industries, allows it to create synergies that increase its profitability and growth potential.
- Being seen as a responsible member of society can only enhance Daewoo's potential for future success.

Daewoo International welcomes challenges as opportunities for continued growth, an attitude that will be essential for its future success. With an emphasis on creativity and innovation, Daewoo International seeks to adapt to changing business conditions and emerge with new ideas for the future.

Daewoo International continues to operate and expand internationally, building upon its expertise in trading and its global network. By pursuing partnerships such as the one with POSCO, it reinforces and expands its existing core competences, activities essential for future growth. Its strengths in information technology and real-time management also position it to succeed at the global level. Further, the company's stable business portfolio, with six divisions covering a wide diversity of industries, allows it to create synergies that increase the profitability and growth potential of the entire company.

Daewoo International also contributes to society at both the global and local levels. Its efforts include disaster relief, NGO support, establishment of sister relationships, sponsorship of academic and cultural events, and employee volunteer activities. The leadership of Daewoo International sees these actions as going beyond the basics of ethical business practices and contributing to the welfare of the communities in which the company operates. Being seen as a responsible member of those communities can only add to the brand's future success.

FURTHER READING

Brand Finance. "Global 500 2012." *Brandirectory*. Accessed November 26, 2012. http://brandirectory.com/league_tables/table/global-500-2012.

Chang, Sungmin. "J. P. Morgan: Daewoo International: E&P Assets Will Start to Deliver." J.P. Morgan, September 17, 2012. Accessed November 26, 2012. https://docs.google.com/.

Choe, Sang T., and Hyun Jeong Cho. "The Effect of Knowledge of Asian Brands on the Purchase Decisions of Young

American Consumers on Products from China, Japan, and South Korea." *Advances in Competitiveness Research*, 2000. Accessed November 26, 2012. http://www.freepatentsonline.com/article/Advances-in-Competitiveness-Research/78630768.html.

Chung-un, Cho. "Daewoo International Makes Inroad into Australian Mining." *Korea Herald*, September 28, 2011.

"Daewoo Group." *International Directory of Company Histories*. Ed. Jay P. Pederson. Vol. 57. Detroit, MI: St. James Press, 2004.

Daewoo International Corporation. "Core Competencies & Profit Models." 2005. Accessed November 25, 2012. http://www.daewoo.com/english/introduce/model.jsp?nav=1_4_0.

Daewoo International Myanmar E&P. "Code of Corporate Conduct and Ethics." November 2007. Accessed November 26, 2012. http://www.daewoo.com/english/introduce/images/Code%20of%20Corporate%20Conduct%20And%20Ethics.pdf.

Lee, Joyce. "Daewoo International Signs Deal to Build $1.3 Bln Kenyan Power Station." Reuters, November 18, 2012.

DAIMLER

AT A GLANCE

Brand Synopsis: Though it is parent to one of the most valuable brand names in the world, Mercedes-Benz, the Daimler brand is far less well-known, a consequence of the company founder's actions more than a century ago.
Parent Company: Daimler AG
Mercedesstrasse 137
Stuttgart
Germany
http://www.daimler.com
Sector: Consumer Discretionary
Industry Group: Automobiles & Components
Performance: *Market share*—2 percent (2010). *Sales*—EUR106.54 billion (US$138 billion) (2011).
Principal Competitors: Bayerische Motoren Werke AG; Fiat S.p.A.; Ford Motor Company; General Motors Company; Volkswagen AG

BRAND ORIGINS

- Daimler originated from two companies founded by three German engineer-entrepreneurs in the early 1880s.
- In 1926 the Daimler and Benz companies merged to form Daimler-Benz AG, which would remain in existence until 1998.
- A US$37 billion merger established DaimlerChrysler AG in November 1998.
- Lack of cohesion between Daimler and Chrysler led to a split, which resulted in the creation of Daimler AG in 2007.

In 1882 Gottlieb Daimler and Wilhelm Maybach founded Daimler-Motoren-Gesellschaft (DMG) in Stuttgart, and in 1883 Carl Benz established Benz & Companies in Mannheim. Four decades later, in 1924, the two companies agreed to coordinate design and production. Daimler had begun producing automobiles under the Mercedes name in 1901, and in 1926, as the two companies merged to form Daimler-Benz AG, the car took on what would become one of the world's most famous brand names: Mercedes-Benz.

The company and its leading brand weathered the Nazi era—Hitler was a Mercedes enthusiast—and the war, as well as the difficult recovery period that followed. By the mid-1950s it had emerged as a major international carmaker, and it prospered for the next three decades. During the late 1980s and the 1990s, however, Daimler-Benz went through a period of financial ups and downs as well as several efforts to restructure the company.

In November 1998 it joined forces with Chrysler Corporation to create DaimlerChrysler AG in a US$37 billion deal. Initially the merger seemed like a good fit, but a series of factors both global and local—the economic downturn after the September 2001 terrorist attacks and lack of cohesion between the two corporate partners—hampered its success. In 2007 DaimlerChrysler became Daimler AG.

BRAND ELEMENTS

- According to Daimler, the badge on its 1895 Riemenwagen is "the oldest surviving trademark on a car body."
- Like the DaimlerChrysler logo, the Daimler symbol is a simple logotype using a serif font.
- The Daimler logotype was designed to resemble writing created using an old-fashioned pointed dip pen.

Daimler's online history of the Mercedes-Benz brand reports that "the oldest surviving trademark on a car body is the badge which Daimler affixed to its Riemenwagen in 1895." This extraordinarily ornate logo eventually gave way to the Mercedes-Benz star, one of the most famous brand symbols in the world. On the other hand, the Daimler logo—like its name—is not nearly as well-known.

DaimlerChrylser AG had an extremely simple logotype that used a serif font similar to Times Roman, with small caps such that the "D" and the "C" stood above the other letters in the name. After the 2007 breakup that created Daimler AG, the company turned to branding consultancy Schindler Parent Identity (later renamed Realgestalt GmbH), which created a new logo in collaboration with pan-European design collective Underware. The Daimler AG symbol is also a simple logotype using a serif font, but the capital letters are all the same size, and are rendered in a Prussian blue shade.

According to a statement from Realgestalt, the Daimler logo "stands for a company that is forward-looking, innovative and modern," yet also "aware of its origins and grand tradition." The font "imitates writing created using a pointed dip pen," which "imparts a sense of elegance, classiness and style to the brand." The serifs of the font are rounded and have "asymmetrical corners," intended to suggest "drive and character."

BRAND IDENTITY

- The 2007 change from DaimlerChrysler AG to Daimler AG required a massive rebranding effort, "Project Name-Change."
- Daimler AG adopted its name in 2007 amid opposition from some shareholders who called for a return to Daimler-Benz or simply Benz.
- Confusion over Daimler's brand identity influenced the decision to adopt the Mercedes brand name.

The 2007 change from DaimlerChrysler AG to Daimler AG required a massive rebranding effort that included the replacement of letterhead, signage, online materials, and other items of corporate symbolism. Nicknamed "Project Name-Change," this undertaking involved some 200 people overseen by a 15-person task force, and cost approximately US$71 million.

Initially even the company's name had been a point of contention. According to John Reed in *Financial Times*, some shareholders proposed a return to Daimler-Benz or simply Benz. Carl Benz's descendants felt slighted, as did residents of the Mannheim area where his company originated. One shareholder pointed out that the name was shorter than Daimler and had half as many syllables, while another maintained that Daimler's name had suffered "serious image damage" because of its "contamination with the name of a U.S. corporation that was often in danger of insolvency." The new company's management, however, responded that the Daimler name "evokes a high degree of confidence in the expertise of the corporation as a globally respected manufacturer." They also pointed out that removing Benz from the company name would avoid confusion with the Mercedes-Benz brand name.

This concern to avoid ambiguity is perhaps fitting for a corporation whose own name has been associated with several companies and brands. In addition to the firm established by Gottlieb Daimler and its direct descendants, there was a prominent subsidiary, Austro-Daimler (1899–1934), whose most famous employee was future carmaker Ferdinand Porsche; and a completely separate British firm, the Daimler Company (pronounced "DAME-lur" instead of "DIME-lur"), which did business throughout the 20th century.

The Mercedes-Benz brand name came about in part because of concerns regarding the fact that Gottlieb Daimler had licensed his company's name for use in other countries. Investor Emil Jellinek, who ran into legal problems attempting to market Daimler cars in France, suggested that the company name its brand after his daughter Adrienne, whose nickname was Mercédès. By then Daimler management had become aware of the licensing problem. Therefore in 1901 the automaker began using the Mercedes brand, which became Mercedes-Benz after the 1926 merger with Benz & Companies. (It is interesting to note that Adolf Hitler's favorite car was named after a Jewish girl—who, like him, was born in Austria in 1889.)

BRAND STRATEGY

- As of 2013, Daimler AG controlled the rights to 22 brands, and (thanks to a partnership with the Renault–Nissan Alliance) had an interest in nine more.
- The corporate structure of Daimler AG, whose five divisions all bear either the Daimler or the Mercedes-Benz name, reflects the importance of its flagship brand.
- Among Daimler's other brands are Smart microcars, Freightliner and Western Star trucks, Setra vans, and ultra-luxurious Maybach cars (discontinued in 2013).

As of 2013, Daimler AG controlled the rights to 22 brands, and—thanks to an April 2010 agreement whereby it purchased a 3.9 percent mutual share in the Renault–Nissan Alliance—had an interest in nine more. By far the most important of these brands, however, was its oldest: Mercedes-Benz.

The corporate structure of Daimler AG, whose five divisions all bear either the Daimler or the Mercedes-Benz name, reflects the importance of its flagship brand. The Mercedes-Benz Cars division includes not only Mercedes-Benz but Smart and Maybach. Smart is a brand of microcars established in 1994 and initially backed by Volkswagen AG until Daimler-Benz took over in October 1998, just before the Chrysler merger. Maybach is an ultra-luxury competitor of Rolls-Royce that was discontinued in 2013.

Mercedes-Benz trucks, at some points a more important source of profit than Mercedes cars, fall under the Daimler Trucks division. Other brands include Thomas Built, an American company whose roots go back to 1916; Freightliner, an American firm established in 1942; Western Star, founded in the United States and Canada in 1967; BharatBenz, an Indian subsidiary created by Daimler AG in 2008; and Mitsubishi Fuso, a former Mitsubishi subsidiary in which Daimler gained a 90 percent interest during the first decade of the 21st century.

Daimler Buses consists of Mercedes-Benz and Setra vehicles, the latter products of a German manufacturer established in 1951 and acquired by Daimler in 1995. Daimler's other two divisions are Mercedes-Benz Vans and Daimler Financial Services, which provides financing for Daimler AG vehicle sales worldwide.

BRAND EQUITY

- The 1998 merger with Chrysler began amid high hopes, but ultimately Daimler divested its holdings in order to preserve its brand equity.
- The company's revenues dropped dramatically between 2002 and 2005, but a slow recovery began after the 2007 DaimlerChrysler breakup.
- Mercedes-Benz ranked 11th on the Interbrand "Best Global Brands" for 2012, whereas Chrysler did not even make the top 100 list.

Daimler divested itself of its Chrysler holdings for a number of reasons, not least of which was the need to improve its brand equity. The 1998 merger had begun amid high hopes, and was lauded as "a marriage made in heaven." But by the time it was over, nine years later, members of the German media were using a very different metaphor, referring to Chrysler as the *ungeliebte US-Tochter* or "unloved American daughter." Daimler had seen its market capitalization drop from US$47 billion in 1998 to US$37 billion five years later, with Chrysler losing over US$600 million in 2003 alone.

"Our earnings will now be more sustainable," CEO Dieter Zetsche told shareholders at the time of the breakup in 2007, "as we will no longer be so strongly dependent on the volatile North American volume market." Just a few years later, a glance at the company's revenue figures for the preceding decade appeared to validate the decision. Income had dropped by more than 35 percent from 2002 to 2005, and only began to really improve in 2007—the year of the breakup. The company went through another slump due to the global recession, hitting a 10-year low in 2009, but by the end of the 2011 fiscal year its revenues were nearly 5 percent higher than in 2007.

Despite the fact that the Daimler name is not exactly a household word, at least outside of Germany, the company owns one of the most famous brands in the world. Mercedes-Benz ranked second among automotive brands, behind only Toyota, on the Interbrand list of "Best Global Brands" for 2012. With a brand value estimated at more than US$30 billion, up 10 percent from the year before, Mercedes ranked 11th overall. Chrysler, by contrast, did not even make the top 100 list. Daimler AG, at more than US$75 billion, also ranked second only to Toyota (over US$139 billion) on the *Financial Times* 2011 ranking of the "World's Most Valuable Automobile and Parts Companies."

BRAND AWARENESS

- Daimler's advertising budget is dwarfed by that of carmakers such as General Motors or its former partner Chrysler.
- Though Daimler owns one of the world's most well-known brands, Mercedes, the Daimler brand itself enjoys very little name recognition.
- Company founder Gottlieb Daimler's penchant for licensing his name all over Europe served to dilute the value of the Daimler brand name.

Daimler's advertising budget is dwarfed by those of other major car companies. Reckoned as a percentage of total sales, its advertising outlay for 2009 placed Daimler seventh among automakers at 1.5 percent. By contrast, frontrunner General Motors invested 4.5 percent of its sales income in advertising. In the first nine months of 2008, Daimler spent US$257 million on advertising, which, though a hefty sum, was dwarfed by GM's more than US$1.5 billion. Cerebrus Capital, which had bought Chrysler from Daimler, came in fifth with US$709 billion, and Daimler ranked ninth among automakers worldwide.

It could be argued that Daimler does not need to spend as much money on advertising as its competitors, given the fact that it owns one of the world's most well-known brands, Mercedes-Benz. The Daimler brand, however, enjoys very little name recognition. Neither Daimler AG nor its predecessors has marketed a car under the Daimler brand name for more than a century—a fact that goes back to the company founder's penchant for licensing the name all over Europe, thus diluting the value.

For most of the 20th century, in fact, there were two completely separate companies named Daimler: the more famous German firm (pronounced "DIME-lur") and Britain's Daimler Company, whose name is pronounced "DAME-lur." In 1891 engineer and inventor Frederick Simms acquired the British patent rights to the Daimler engine. He formed a company in 1896 and soon began marketing cars to Britain's elite, including the royal family. The company changed hands several times over the decades until 1960, when Jaguar acquired the Daimler name. Ford Motor Company took over Jaguar in 1989, and production of cars under the Daimler brand dwindled, ceasing altogether in 2002. (The company did release a Daimler Super Eight, similar to the Jaguar XJ, in 2005.)

In 2007 Daimler AG paid Ford US$20 million to use the Daimler name in British territory. Ford subsequently sold its Jaguar holdings to India's Tata Group, which in July 2008 signed an agreement with Daimler whereby Tata retained the right to build Daimler cars while granting the German automaker the use of the Daimler trade name. According to a spokesman for Jaguar, "The extended usage agreement does not affect either company's existing right to use the Daimler name for a product."

BRAND OUTLOOK

- In 2012 Daimler revealed plans to begin building trucks in southern India—a move that would put it into competition with the Tata Group, owners of the British Daimler.
- Daimler in 2011 announced that the Maybach luxury car, introduced by the company's cofounder in 1909, would come to an end in 2013.
- In a bid to regain market leadership for its Smart car, Daimler launched a mass-produced, fully electric model, and expanded the Smart lineup.
- CEO Dieter Zetsche presented a strategy, "Mercedes-Benz 2020," to regain market leadership for Daimler's flagship brand by the beginning of the next decade.

Soon after purchasing the British Daimler in 2008, the Tata Group—a corporation several decades older than Daimler AG and almost as large, in terms of revenue—announced plans to revive its brand name and signature vehicle. The resurrected Daimler would have been a direct competitor to Daimler AG's own Maybach, but it failed to materialize. Instead, the field of competition between Daimler AG and Tata moved to India, where Daimler had a half-century relationship with Tata Motors. In March 2010 Daimler sold its shares in the company, and in April 2012 it announced that it would build a truck factory in southern India.

Maybach came to an end with a November 2011 announcement that Daimler would discontinue the brand in 2013. The car had its origins in 1907, when Wilhelm Maybach left the company he had cofounded with Gottlieb Daimler and started his own manufacturing firm two years later. It ceased to operate after World War II. Daimler-Benz purchased it in 1960, but it remained dormant for four decades. In 2002, after BMW and Volkswagen had purchased Rolls Royce and Bentley respectively, Daimler relaunched the Maybach. Sales, however, proved spotty even by the standards of its rarefied market segment: in January 2012, for instance, only 5 were sold in the United States as compared with 30 Rolls Royces and 118 Bentleys.

In the world of the 2010s, the low-cost (if not exactly sexy) Smart car seemed to offer much more of a future than the Maybach. However, Daimler faced challenges in this arena as well. Though it had led the microcar wave in the 1990s, the Smart car had since been edged out by competitors such as the BMW Mini, which offered several different models in contrast to the Smart car's one-model lineup. In 2012 Daimler sought to regain leadership by introducing a mass-produced fully electric model, and by expanding the lineup with several other models.

As for Daimler's flagship brand, Mercedes-Benz had in recent years lost market share to competitors BMW and Audi, but in 2011 Daimler CEO Dieter Zetsche presented a strategy to regain the lead by the beginning of the next decade. Among the provisions of "Mercedes-Benz 2020" were plans to expand its range of models and improve vehicle features.

FURTHER READING

Adler, Dennis. *Daimler & Benz, the Complete History: The Birth and Evolution of the Mercedes-Benz.* Foreword by Sir Stirling Moss. New York: Collins, 2006.

Daimler AG. *Annual Report 2011: Innovation and Growth.* Stuttgart, Germany: Daimler, 2012.

"Daimler AG." *International Directory of Company Histories.* Ed. Drew D. Johnson. Vol. 135. Detroit, MI: St. James Press, 2012.

"Daimler Logo." Realgestalt.de. Accessed February 6, 2013. http://www.realgestalt.de/en/projects/daimler-logo-2/.

Hawranek, Dietmar. "Daimler Struggles to Regain Its Spark." Trans. Paul Cohen. *Der Spiegel,* September 28, 2012. Accessed February 6, 2013. http://www.spiegel.de/international/business/mercedes-falling-behind-competitors-despite-strategy-changes-a-858260.html.

"The History behind the Mercedes Brand." Daimler. Accessed February 6, 2013. http://www.daimler.com/dccom/0-5-1279050-1-1279432-1-0-0-0-0-0-17180-0-0-0-0-0-0-0-0.html.

McHugh, David. "DaimlerChrysler Changes its Name to Daimler." *Washington Post*, October 4, 2007. Accessed February 6, 2013.

Reed, John. "Logo Marks Sign of Times as Daimler Goes Solo." *Financial Times*, October 4, 2007.

Spinks, Jez. "Maybach Axed: Daimler Kills off Its Rolls-Royce Rival." Caradvice.com.au, November 28, 2011. Accessed February 6, 2013. http://www.caradvice.com.au/148783/maybach-axed-daimler-kills-off-its-rolls-royce-rival/.

Tschampa, Dorothee. "Daimler Pins Smart Recovery on Electric at Lowest Price." *Bloomberg*, September 12, 2012. Accessed February 6, 2013. http://www.bloomberg.com/news/2012-09-12/daimler-pins-smart-recovery-on-electric-at-lowest-price.html

DANONE

AT A GLANCE

Brand Synopsis: Danone exemplifies the attributes of health and nutrition, along with appealing taste in dairy products, bottled water, and baby food.
Parent Company: Groupe Danone
17 Boulevard Haussmann
Paris 75009
France
http://www.danone.com
Sector: Consumer Staples
Industry Group: Food, Beverage & Tobacco
Performance: *Market share*—23.4 percent of yogurt and 11.7 percent of bottled water worldwide (2010); 25.6 percent of yogurt in the United States (2012). *Sales*—US$23.8 billion (2011).
Principal Competitors: Agro Farma, Inc.; General Mills, Inc.; Kraft Foods Inc.; Muller Quaker Dairy Inc.; Yoplait USA Inc.

BRAND ORIGINS

- Danone was founded by Isaac Carasso in Barcelona, Spain, in 1919.
- Dannon Milk Products, Inc., was established in New York in 1942.
- Gervaise Danone merged with BSN in 1973.
- In 1994 the company changed its name to Groupe Danone and focused on health-oriented, packaged food categories.

In 1919 Isaac Carasso founded a company to manufacture yogurt in Barcelona, Spain, which he named Danone after the nickname of his son Daniel. Daniel Carasso founded a branch in France in 1929. He fled Europe during World War II and founded Dannon Milk Products, Inc., in 1942 in New York City. After returning to Europe at war's end, Daniel sold his share of the American company to his partners, Joe and Juan Metzger, who expanded production and widened Dannon's consumer base. Beatrice Foods, Inc., purchased Dannon Milk Products in 1959 and further accelerated the company's growth.

The French Danone company, known as Gervais Danone after a 1967 merger with the cheese manufacturer Gervais, extended its portfolio and became France's largest food company. In 1973 French manufacturer BSN merged with Gervais Danone, forming BSN-Gervais Danone. In 1981 the company purchased the American Dannon firm for US$84.3 million; 11 years later it acquired a majority stake in Danone Spain, reunifying brand ownership. In 1994 the company changed its name to Groupe Danone, to reflect its most popular brand as it expanded into newly openened markets in Eastern Europe and Asia. Groupe Danone focused its holdings on dairy products, baby food, and bottled water and sold off many of its other units to pursue a consistent health and wellness positioning. Groupe Danone is represented in the United States by Dannon Company, Inc., along with Dannon Waters of America, whose products are marketed and distributed by Coca-Cola.

BRAND ELEMENTS

- The Danone brand was named after the son of founder Isaac Carasso.
- Danone's brand extensions are color-coded to enable easier identification.
- Danone's taglines underline the products' health claims.

The brand was named "Danone" by Isaac Carasso after the nickname of his son Daniel. In the United States, the basic Dannon product-logo has changed relatively little since the brand's introduction in 1942. In the mid-1990s Groupe Danone adopted a new global logo depicting a young boy (evoking the original "Danone") looking up at a star against a blue background. At the same time the American Dannon logo was redesigned to resemble more closely the European Danone logo, placing the name within a chevron against a navy blue background over a red crescent. To make its products stand out in crowded dairy aisles, Danone uses color-coded packaging: dark green for Activia, red for Danimals, purple for Dannon Light & Fit, blue for DanUp, and yellow for DanActive, with the brand extension name often in much larger print than the Dannon logo. Danimals containers also display cartoon characters that reinforce the products' identification with fun for children.

Danone's brand taglines often convey messages about health and wellness. Activia's general motto "Active on the inside and it shows" conveys the link between consumption and good health. Dannon's U.S. promotional taglines convey strong health and wellness claims even after receiving governmental orders to tone down health claims: DanActive containers state "Helps protect the immune system" and Activia containers state "Helps regulate the digestive system." In France the Danette brand of creamy dairy desserts soared in popularity, thanks to its slogan "We all get up for Danette," which was turned into a ubiquitous commercial jingle in the 1970s and 1980s.

BRAND IDENTITY

- Danone is associated primarily with health and longevity, as well as sweetness and texture.
- Yogurt consumption is historically identified more with women than men; however, Danone's marketing targets both men and women for various products.
- Danone seeks to identify its brands with sustainability and ethical business practices.

The brand identity of Danone has been linked with healthy living since its launch. Isaac Carosso developed and marketed Danone yogurt in Spain as a kind of medicinal product, initially distributed through pharmacies. Many Danone/Dannon brand extensions still focus on a health and wellness appeal. Danone Actimel and Activia were pioneering probiotic products, which means they include health-promoting microorganisms. The Danonino brand (sold as Danino in Canada and Petít Gervais in France) is designed for children; available in about 35 countries, it is formulated to combat specific local nutritional deficiencies. Taillefine (a French term for "slim waist") is a no-fat range aimed at younger women. Danacol is a dairy-based drink fortified with plant sterols that are demonstrated to lower blood cholesterol. Danimals is a product line of children's yogurt and drinks marketed in the U.S. and Canada. Meanwhile, other Danone products such as Danette, Danissimo, Dany, and Fantasia emphasize indulgence rather than health.

Historically, yogurt consumption has often been associated with women, who made up an estimated 61 percent of Dannon's U.S. customer base in 2001. On one hand, Dannon has sought to appeal mainly to men. For example in 2001 it aired a U.S. commercial for its Fruit on the Bottom line showing construction workers eating yogurt and grooving to the beat of a soulful song. On the other hand, Groupe Danone markets Activia primarily to women, citing research findings that most women suffer from intestinal distress but do little about it. Women are also chief targets of children's lines, which appeal to industry players because they attract both boys and girls, promising yogurt a larger and more gender-balanced consumer base.

Groupe Danone has long nurtured a reputation for promoting health, sustainability, and a collegial relationship with employees, insisting that businesses have a responsibility to aid society as well as to earn profits. This reputation boosts the brand's appeal among many consumers but also threatens to recoil against it when controversies erupt. For example when Groupe Danone announced plans in 2001 to let go a number of employees in a restructuring plan, polling suggested that French consumers would boycott the company's products if the plan went ahead. The activities of Danone Vitapole, the company's research center in France, and the numerous Dannon Institutes worldwide, which sponsor research and award prizes to nutritional researchers, accentuate the brand's association with nutrition. The Grameen Danone project, founded in 2006 in Bangladesh in collaboration with Nobel laureate Muhammad Yunus, seeks to develop a "social business" model that is both profitable and beneficial to society, coincidentally expanding Danone's presence in developing markets.

BRAND STRATEGY

- Danone and Dannon originally focused on creating demand and expanding the market for yogurt.
- Starting in the late 1980s, Danone expanded to many international markets.

- In the 1980s and 1990s, General Mills's Yoplait brand challenged Dannon for U.S. market leadership.
- Danone popularized probiotic yogurt through the Actimel and Activia brands.
- In the United States, Dannon is striving to compete in the fast-growing Greek-style yogurt category with market leader Chobani.

After the launch of Danone in Spain in 1919 and its gradual spread to other countries, Danone France and Danone Spain (and their U.S. counterpart Dannon) focused on extending distribution and winning public acceptance for yogurt, promoting it as a healthy and invigorating snack. To combat many consumers' perception of traditional yogurt as sour and plain, Danone France introduced Dany yogurt with fruit in 1937 and Danone Fruité in 1953. In the United States, the Dannon brand also appealed to consumers' sweet tooth, introducing Fruit on the Bottom yogurt in 1947. Dannon reinforced its healthy positioning in a 1970s advertising campaign that featured elderly persons eating yogurt in then-Soviet Georgia, a land with a reputation for longevity.

After its acquisition by BSN-Gervais Danone in 1983, Dannon deemphasized health claims and launched numerous brand extensions to compete with products such as Yoplait, an imported brand with a richer consistency distributed by General Mills. Starting in the late 1980s, the Danone brand was launched in newly opened markets such as China and the former Soviet bloc. In 1994 the parent company adopted the name Groupe Danone to emphasize its strongest brand. In Asian countries such as China and Thailand that lacked a strong tradition of dairy consumption, the company launched cookies under the Danone brand, as well as dairy products. Danone entered the market in India in 1993, launching packaged yogurt and milk-based beverages for a small but growing, affluent, urban-consumer base. Already a leading bottled-water producer in Europe, Groupe Danone launched Dannon Natural Spring Water in the United States in 1996, Danone Activ (a product with added calcium) in the United Kingdom in 2000, and Danone Aqua, produced by an Indonesian joint venture, which became the country's leading bottled-water brand.

In 1987 Danone launched the Bio line, the first probiotic yogurt products with high content of microorganisms that supposedly improve digestion and bolster the immune system. It was followed in 1994 by Actimel. In the United States, Danone relaunched Actimel in 2004 under the name DanActive. In 2006 under European Union pressure, Danone changed the Bio brand name to Activia in France and Spain, simultaneously introducing the brand in dozens of other markets, targeting women suffering from digestive problems. The Activia brand is offered in many distinctive local varieties, such as Activia Kefir in Russia, Activia Laban in Saudi Arabia, and a hawthorn-flavored variety in China, as well as indulgent and dessert variants. Danone's probiotics sales have done well, despite tight restrictions on product-health claims in the European Union and the United States, where Dannon was forced to pay fines of US$21 million in a 2010 settlement with the Federal Trade Commission and 39 state attorneys general. In the United States, Dannon has raced to catch up with the Greek yogurt boom, launching Dannon Greek in 2010 and relaunching it as Dannon Oikos Greek in 2011, which settled into second place behind Chobani.

BRAND EQUITY

- Danone ranked as the 52nd-most-valuable brand in the world in 2012 according to Interbrand.
- Danone was the world's second-leading dairy producer in 2011 according to Rabobank.
- In April 2012 Dannon was the second-leading yogurt brand in the United States, close behind its longtime rival Yoplait.

Interbrand ranked Danone as the 52nd-most-valuable brand in the world in 2012 and the seventh-most-valuable brand in fast-moving consumer goods, with a brand value of US$7.5 billion. Danone also ranked ninth in Interbrand's *2012 Best Global Green Brands.* Rabobank data showed Danone as the second-leading dairy producer worldwide, behind only Nestlé with sales of US$18.8 billion in 2011. Euromonitor International ranked Danone as the world's leading company in yogurt with a 23.4 percent value share in 2010, trailed distantly by Yoplait's 6.2 percent. In bottled water, Danone ranked first internationally in 2010 with an 11.7 percent share, edging out Nestlé and Coca-Cola.

For the year ending in March 2012, *Dairy Foods* ranked Dannon as the second-leading dairy brand in the U.S. market, with a 25.6 percent value share, close behind Yoplait at 27.1 percent. This was despite Dannon's having a much lower volume share (18.3 percent) than Yoplait, perhaps reflecting Dannon's greater reliance on Greek yogurt and other specialty products sold at higher unit prices. In the category of Greek-style yogurt, *Advertising Age* ranked Dannon as second as of April 2012, with a 19.7 percent value share (a strong increase from 15.2 percent in 2011), still well behind Chobani's 47.3 percent share.

BRAND AWARENESS

- Danone and its Actimel and Activia lines remain top-of-mind brands in traditional yogurt and probiotics.

- Activia shows high brand-awareness in markets such as the United States, France, and Germany.
- Danone has a strong ethical positioning among consumers.

Throughout Western Europe, Danone (Dannon in the United States) originally defined the yogurt category and remains a top-of-mind brand in traditional yogurt, along with Actimel and Activia in probiotics. A biannual survey conducted by GfK of consumers in 25 countries measured 48 percent brand recognition of Danone in 2006, up four percentage points from 2000. According to research firm Millward Brown, Activia reached as high as 80 percent "aided awareness" six months after its U.S. launch in 1986. In France, the EU-mandated transition from the Bio brand to Activia in 2006 resulted in a decrease in aided awareness from 89 percent to 62 percent by the end of the year, even though the brand's sales actually increased. Meanwhile, in Germany, from 2006 to 2008, brand awareness of Activia increased from 43 percent to 60 percent and "sympathy" from 12 percent to 30 percent, whereas product use increased from 7 percent to 13 percent as it attained market leadership in the "thick yogurt" segment. Chobani remains the top-of-mind brand in the expanding Greek yogurt segment in the United States, but the Dannon Oikos Greek line is gaining a strong presence. Another strength for Danone is its ethical positioning among consumers: a 2007 study conducted by GfK ranked Danone as the most ethically perceived brand in France and as the fourth most in Spain.

BRAND OUTLOOK

- Relatively low per-capita consumption points to continued growth potential in the United States and other outlying markets.
- In East Asia Danone is temporarily deemphasizing dairy production.
- Dannon continues to develop more eco-friendly production to strengthen its environmental positioning.

As per capita consumption of yogurt in Danone's core Western European markets remains much higher than in the United States and other outlying markets, the company anticipates continued strong, worldwide growth opportunities, despite economic uncertainty and fluctuating raw material costs. In the United States, Dannon hopes to be able to finally retake the retail lead from Yoplait, even as both brands suffer under the assault of Greek yogurt champion Chobani and PepsiCo prepares its market entry through the joint venture Muller Quaker Dairy. By contrast, in frozen yogurt the United States accounts for over half of global consumption. Danone sought to strengthen its position in that market with the purchase of YoCream in 2010, though U.S. sales are expected to decrease slightly through 2015, according to Euromonitor International. Emerging markets, especially in Asia and Latin America, will remain another focus of brand growth as fiscal year 2011 marked the first time that emerging economies accounted for more than half of Groupe Danone's revenues. However, Danone dairy products have struggled in East Asian markets that lack a strong tradition of dairy consumption. Danone has decided to focus on developing baby food in China and Indonesia and nurturing steady, long-term growth in dairy.

In keeping with the Groupe Danone motto, "Today, for tomorrow," the company is continuing to develop more eco-friendly production processes to save money as well as improve its environmental positioning. From 2004 through 2011, the company reduced its usage of packaging by an estimated 15 percent, for example by changing from plastic tops to peel-off foil. The 2011 Dannon Sustainable Development Overview stated that since 2008 the company had reduced its carbon footprint by over 29 percent and its water consumption by over 30 percent, and had improved its recycling rate from 75 percent in 2010 to 93 percent in 2011. In 2011 Danone held the highest score among food producers in the Dow Jones Sustainability Index.

FURTHER READING

"Best Global Brands 2012." Interbrand. Accessed January 23, 2013. http://www.interbrand.com/en/best-global-brands/2012/Best-Global-Brands-2012.aspx.

Bouckley, Ben. "'We Are Quite Nothing in Asian Dairy,' Danone CEO Admits." *Dairy Reporter*, February 17, 2012.

Buss, Dale. "Can Activia Survive FTC Punch to the Gut?" BrandChannel, December 16, 2010. Accessed September 15, 2012. http://www.brandchannel.com/home/post/2010/12/16/Can-Activia-Survive-Its-Punch-to-the-Gut.aspx.

de Mesa, Alycia. "Your Product Name: Name or Shame?" Brandchannel, August 2, 2004. Accessed January 20, 2013. http://www.brandchannel.com/features_effect.asp?pf_id=218.

Facenda, Jessica L. "Marketer of the Year: Andreas Ostermayr." *Brandweek*, October 8, 2007.

Fannin, Rebecca. "Dannon's Culture Coup." *Marketing and Media Decisions*, November 1986.

"Groupe Danone." *International Directory of Company Histories*. Ed. Jay P. Pederson. Vol. 93. Detroit, MI: St. James Press, 2008.

Kapner, Suzanne. "Campaigns for Several Products Are Shifting Their Focus from 'Women Only' to Include 'Real Men.'" *New York Times*, August 31, 2001.

Karolefski, John. "Dannon: Cultured." Brandchannel, April 14, 2003. Accessed September 20, 2012. http://www.brandchannel.com/features_profile.asp?pr_id=120.

Lingle, Rich. "Dannon: A Culture of Innovation in Yogurt Packaging." *Food & Beverage Packaging*, May 2011, 28.

Pollack, Judann. "Dannon Mulls New Logo, Switch to Parent's Name: Danone Groupe Push for Global Branding May Bring Change for US' Top Yogurt." *Advertising Age*, December 9, 1996.

"Sales Sour for Cultured Dairy Foods." *Dairy Foods*, May 2012. Accessed September 23, 2012.

Schultz, E. J. "Dannon's Greek Yogurt Oikos Has Sights Set on No. 1 Chobani." *Advertising Age*, September 26, 2011.

———. "Who's Winning the Greek-Yogurt 'Revolution'?" *Advertising Age*, June 6, 2012.

Szalai, Ildiko. "Danone Further Strengthens Its Emerging Market Position via Merger and Acquisition Activity." *Euromonitor Global Market Research Blog*. Accessed September 15, 2012. http://blog.euromonitor.com/2010/12/danone-further-strengthens-its-emerging-market-position-via-merger-and-acquisition-activity.html.

Thompson, Stephanie. "Dannon Triples Yogurt Spending to $12 Million." *Advertising Age*, April 3, 2000.

Watin-Augouard, Jean. "Danone, nouvelle Déméter pour la planète." *Prodimarques*, no. 21, January 1998.

DELL

AT A GLANCE

Brand Synopsis: A leading provider of computer-related technology, services, and support, Dell gives both consumers and businesses "The power to do more."
Parent Company: Dell Inc.
One Dell Way
Round Rock, Texas 78682
United States
http://www.dell.com
Sector: Information Technology
Industry Group: Technology Hardware & Equipment
Performance: *Market share*—8 percent of the computer hardware manufacturing market worldwide (2011); 12.6 percent of the personal computer manufacturing market worldwide (2011); 13.9 percent of the server manufacturing market worldwide (2011). *Sales*—US$62.7 billion (2011).
Principal Competitors: Acer Incorporated; Apple Inc.; Fujitsu Limited; Hewlett-Packard Company; Lenovo Group Limited; Samsung Electronics Co., Ltd.; Sony Corporation; Toshiba Corporation

BRAND ORIGINS

- Dell was founded in Michael Dell's dorm room in 1984.
- Within a few years, Dell was a leading personal computer producer both in the United States and globally.
- In 2013 Michael Dell announced plans to take Dell private and radically change its focus on information technology solutions and software.

Dell began when its founder, Michael Dell, started rebuilding and selling IBM clone personal computers (PCs) from his dorm room at the University of Texas in 1984. He eventually named his company PCs Limited and dropped out of school to focus on his growing business. By 1985 Dell's company had developed its first computer, the Turbo PC. It was advertised in national computer magazines and sold directly to consumers. PCs Unlimited grossed US$6 million during its first year. In 1987 the company changed its name to Dell Computer Corporation and expanded internationally to the United Kingdom.

Even though Dell's business model was dismissed by the industry during its early years, Dell found success by custom building computers and selling them without a retail presence at lower prices than other companies. Dell went public in 1988. That same year the company reported gross revenues of US$257.8 million and had established units in Canada and West Germany. To improve the brand's image and assure its customers that its lack of retail was an asset, Dell's first major advertising campaign, 1989's "Dell Direct," emphasized its direct sales approach and educated consumers about Dell's customer support services, money-back guarantees, and custom-made superior products. By 1990 Dell had sales of US$546 million, of which 40 percent were corporate sales, and was the sixth largest PC maker in the United States.

During the early 1990s Dell continued to expand by adding various types of operations in Europe and Central America, including Ireland, Italy, Finland, and Mexico. By 1993, 36 percent of its sales were international. Dell also became the first PC manufacturer to offer applications software installation as a free standard service option. In addition, Dell entered the laptop market in 1992, when it began producing its first full-color notebook. The following year Dell introduced the low-cost Dimensions by Dell PCs and reported sales of US$2 billion.

One reason for Dell's continued success during the mid-1990s was its successful use of the Internet to fill customers' orders quickly and inexpensively. By 1997 Dell was the largest seller of PCs in the United States, a spot that it held for the next five years. By 1998 Dell had 9 percent of the world PC market and was the number-two PC maker globally.

Beginning in the late 1990s Dell moved into new products and services, in part because many rivals were discounting their PCs. Dell began selling workstations, servers, storage systems, and Dellnet, an Internet access service for customers. By 1998 Dell had revenues of US$12 billion, of which 16 percent were from server sales. In 1999 Dell had US$25.3 billion in annual sales with PCs and notebooks accounting for 80 percent of its sales. Even though Dell was repositioning itself to be more than just a PC manufacturer, it was still the largest seller of PCs in the world and the largest seller via the Internet in 2001.

Despite these numbers and some initial success repositioning itself as an information technology (IT) firm, Dell struggled after the turn of the 21st century. Its sales growth eased and the overall PC market slowed. In 2002 Dell had its first-ever yearly decline in sales, from US$31.9 billion in 2001 to US$31.2 billion in 2002. To increase its still important PC and laptop sales, Dell shifted its advertising approach to appeal to high school and college students and their parents with its "Dude, you're getting a Dell" campaign. Even though the ads became cultural touchstones, they were phased out in 2003 because they did not seem to affect sales.

Dell sales did rebound in 2003, reaching US$40 billion, then US$50 billion in 2004. One reason for Dell's recovery was its continued emphasis on growing its non-PC businesses such as servers and the introduction of many new products, including consumer electronics. When Michael Dell temporarily ceded the chief executive officer (CEO) position between 2004 and 2007, the brand's image was negatively affected by two major recalls, serious complaints about customer service and questions about financial reporting. In 2006 Dell also lost its position as the number-one PC maker in the world to the Hewlett-Packard Company.

When Michael Dell returned as CEO in 2007, he implemented Dell 2.0 to revamp the company and meet the needs of consumers while regaining control of the marketplace. One of the biggest changes was Dell's move away from its struggling direct-sales model. Besides selling its PCs at Wal-Mart and Best Buy, the brand opened retail stores in major markets such as the United Kingdom and China. Between 2007 and 2009 Dell remained the second-largest computer manufacturer. However, Dell was especially affected by the global economic recession that began in 2008.

Dell continued to introduce new PC and laptop models as well as other products, but the brand heavily invested in expanding its storage, systems management, cloud computing, software, networking, security, and IT services. Dell believed its future would be in customer-focused IT solutions and software, primarily for businesses, so it began laying the groundwork to move away from PCs. Even though sales reached US$62.1 billion in 2011, Dell had a declining stock value and concerned investors. Because Michael Dell desired to radically change his company's focus, he announced in 2013 plans to take Dell private.

BRAND ELEMENTS

- As a brand, Dell is deeply linked to Michael Dell, its founder and namesake.
- Michael Dell's vision and drive have defined Dell as a brand.
- The Dell logo consists of the company name with all the letters capitalized and upright, except for the *E*, which is leaning backward.
- The tagline "The power to do more" has been used by Dell since 2009.

Dell is deeply identified with its founder, Michael Dell, who gave his name to the company and brand. Even though he originally called his company PCs Unlimited during the mid-1980s, he chose to rename it Dell Computer Corporation in 1987 and later Dell Inc. in 2003. Except for three years, Michael Dell has been the chief executive officer of Dell and has directed its development, image, and focus. Because of his vision, Dell is regarded as a pioneering technology outfit, first as a successful direct seller of personal computers and second as a brand that has deftly shifted focus to related products such as information technology services.

Even the Dell logo reflects Michael Dell's broad vision to affect the world. Consisting of the company name, the logo has all the letters capitalized and upright, except for the *E*, which is leaning backward. The position of the tilting *E* symbolizes the way that Dell wants the world to be turned on its ear by the company's brand name. The Dell logo is often placed in a circle, which makes the logo into something similar to badge, and can be found on many of the company's laptops and computers. The logo was often rendered in a distinct shade of blue on Dell's website, shipping packages, and certain products, although more polished black, white, and gray and gray and white versions existed and were primarily used for its business-related operations. In 2010 Dell overhauled the logo's color to a specially created shade of blue called Dell Blue, with a secondary Dell Gray for business products.

By 2013 the Dell logo was rendered on the company's website with its latest tagline "The power to do more" underneath. This tagline, introduced in 2009, was one of many that defined the brand. "The power to do more" reflected a change in the company's direction beyond consumer and business-focused hardware and software solutions. Other Dell taglines were memorable expressions of the Dell brand and its focus during its brief history. The taglines "Dell Direct" in 1989 and "Be Direct" in 1998 simply explained that Dell confidently sold its products directly, while "Compaq Compare" during the early 1990s demonstrated that Dells were comparable to Compaq, which was then the top-rated computer maker in the United States. "Easy as Dell," used from about 2001 to 2009, assured consumers that buying a Dell computer online was a hassle-free process. The more personal focused "Dell4Me" during the late 1990s, "Dude, you're getting a Dell" in the early 2000s, and "Dell, Purely You" in 2007 ensured that consumers realized their Dells were built just for them and created excitement about their new computers.

BRAND IDENTITY

- From the first, Dell was an innovative brand because of its sales model, a fact that was underscored in related advertising campaigns.
- Dell continues its direct-sell identity by selling returned or refurbished personal computers via Twitter.
- "The power to do more" campaign, which began in 2009, reflected a shift in Dell's focus and identity as primarily concerned with computer hardware to information technology services.

A key part of the Dell brand story is the fact that Michael Dell began rebuilding and customizing personal computers from his dorm room at the University of Texas during the mid-1980s. Even though Dell soon moved into a corporate environment in the suburbs of Austin, Texas, the brand was still viewed as rebellious and innovative because Dell computers were sold directly from the company and not available in stores, which was an uncommon business practice among computer makers at the time. Dells were also custom built for consumers and had extensive customer support services, making the brand especially customer-friendly. In addition, Dell quickly adapted to e-commerce as another way to sell its computers.

In 1989 Dell's first major advertising campaign, "Dell Direct," focused on the brand's direct sales approach and custom-made superior products while educating consumers about customer support services. A similar campaign, "Be Direct," also emphasized the advantages of Dell's direct-to-customer business philosophy in 1998, while "Dell4Me" during the late 1990s emphasized both the personal touch of custom-built machines and Dell's ability to help consumers get the most out of the technology they purchased. Even though Dell had moved away from solely relying on direct sales by 2007, the brand continued to be inventive by using the Twitter feed @DellOutlet to sell returned or refurbished personal computers.

In 1996 Dell started investing in business-related products such as work stations and servers. By the latter half of the first decade of the 21st century the brand found itself struggling in a changing computer-related marketplace, so Dell decided to put greater emphasis on systems management, cloud computing, software, networking, security, and information technology services. Even though Dell continued to manufacture and sell a wide variety of consumer products, such as computers, laptops, and smartphones, its identity was being defined by taglines such as "The power to do more," which was first used in 2009. This global brand platform helped increase awareness of the changes in Dell while emphasizing that it remained a powerful brand for home or business.

Only one memorable Dell advertising campaign rose to pop-culture icon status: "Dude, you're getting a Dell." Starring a teenaged, stoner-type character named Steven who was relentlessly upbeat about Dell personal computers, the ads ran from about 2001 until early 2003. The Steven character was intended to broaden the company's appeal by targeting first-time teenage buyers and their parents. The company reasoned that these customers might be intimated by the task of purchasing a computer that was not available in stores. Steven helped to make Dell seem far less daunting by bridging the gap between the computer company and its customers. The ad campaign did not particularly increase sales, but it did lead to Steven fan sites, fan mail sent to Dell, and a catchphrase that was indelibly stuck to the brand.

BRAND STRATEGY

- Dell primarily sells its products and services under the Dell brand name.
- When Dell buys other companies, there can be cobranding as when it acquired Alienware in 2006.
- By 2011 Dell was particularly strong in China and was introducing certain products there before any other market.

Dell began by selling low-cost IBM clones via direct marketing under various models and usually Dell-branded names during the mid-1980s. Michael Dell originally sold his merchandise to readers of computer magazines who were sophisticated enough to recognize high-quality merchandise at low prices. Over the years, Dell continued to refine and improve its personal computers by offering models at various price points and targeting various audiences, especially after the introduction of its first notebooks/laptops during the early 1990s. For example, low-cost Dimensions by Dell PCs came on the market in 1993. In 2006 Dell bought Alienware, a computer hardware company that focused on computers for gaming, and sold its products under the cobrand name Alienware/Dell.

As the market for personal computers began to ease in the early 2000s, Dell started selling branded consumer products such as flat-screen televisions, cameras, and digital music players. In 2002 Dell introduced its Axim line of personal digital assistants, while in 2009 it introduced its first smartphone, the Mini 3i, in China as part of its partnership with China Mobile. By that time Dell put an ever-increasing emphasis on information technology solutions and services, primarily for businesses. It had begun moving in this direction in 1996, when it entered the market for servers, then added storage systems and Internet services such as web hosting and wireless Internet access for its markets worldwide. By 2012 Dell's business-related offerings included software, networking, security, and consulting and were primarily branded under the deal name. For example, one of its cloud-related solutions was the Dell Virtual Integrated Systems. In 2013 Michael Dell announced his intentions to make his namesake company private to further refocus Dell as a company and a brand.

Despite these changes, Dell remains committed to computer hardware products for both businesses and consumers, including personal computers and laptops. As a global company with significant markets on every continent, Dell was particularly strong in the United States, China, and India. By 2011 Dell was placing an increasing emphasis on China, its second-largest market after the United States. Dell chose to debut its tablet, the Streak 10 Pro, there in 2011 before any other market in the world. Dell's international strategy includes opening retail outlets in markets such as China and India.

BRAND EQUITY

- In 2011 Dell was the second-largest personal computer maker globally, with 12.6 percent of the market.
- In 2012 *Forbes* ranked Dell 41st among the "World's Most Powerful Brands" and estimated its brand value at US$8.4 billion.
- In 2012 Brand Finance ranked Dell at number 72 in its "Global 500" list, with a brand value of US$11.6 billion and an enterprise value of US$22.5 billion.

By the latter half of the first decade of the 21st century Dell was struggling in the economic recession that gripped the world and was feeling the effects of a shrinking market for personal computers and laptops. Even though Dell's brand value has suffered from these events, it remains a global leader in personal computers and has gained market share and sales in the area of information technology solutions and services. In 2011 Dell was the top computer hardware marker globally with 8 percent of the market. Dell was also the second-largest personal computer maker globally, after the Hewlett-Packard Company, with 12.6 percent of the market. Dell also controlled 13.9 percent of the market among server markers worldwide.

In spite of the market struggles that Dell faced during the early 2000s and its transformation toward new products and services, its brand value was still high. In 2012 *Forbes* ranked Dell at 41st in its "World's Most Powerful Brands" list, with a brand value of US$8.4 billion. Interbrand's ranking of the "Best Global Brands" in 2012 placed Dell at 49th, with a brand value of US$7.6 billion. In the report "BrandZ Top 100 Most Valuable Global Brands 2012," Dell was number 18 on the ranking of "Technology Movers and Shakers," with a brand value of US$6.6 billion. In 2012 Brand Finance's "Global 500" ranked Dell 72nd, with a brand value of US$11.6 billion and an enterprise value of US$22.5 billion.

BRAND AWARENESS

- Since its founding, Dell has built high brand awareness both in the United States and globally through its business model and memorable advertising.
- In 2012 Dell was number 50 on the Reputation Institute's "Global RepTrak 100."
- In 2012 Dell was ranked 36th on the Harris Interactive's "Reputations of the Most Visible Companies" list.

Since its emergence in the late 1980s as a leading producer and seller of personal computers, Dell has built high brand awareness among consumers in part because of its original direct-selling method and custom-made products. From the first, Dell has offered a customer-focused business model, whether those customers are consumers or businesses. Even though its target audience has evolved over years, memorable advertising campaigns such as "Dude, you're getting a Dell" and "The power to do more" have defined Dell as a brand that customers should know and want.

In many of its international markets, especially China and India, Dell has high brand awareness because of its successful efforts to build market share and its extensive international operations network. Studies and surveys confirm Dell's lofty stature. For example, in the Reputation Institute's "Global RepTrak 100," which ranks a brand's global popularity and reputation, Dell was number 50 in 2012. Likewise, Harris Interactive's ranking of "Reputations of the Most Visible Companies" placed Dell at number 36 in 2012.

BRAND OUTLOOK

- The computer industry is being transformed because of new products and the evolution of computer use.
- In 2013 Michael Dell announced that the company was going private so that it could focus on information technology solutions and services; many investors believed this move was quite risky.
- Dell is an environmental leader and recycled 192 million pounds of e-waste in 2012 alone.

The computer industry, for both consumers and businesses, is being transformed by developments such as cloud computing, the growing market for tablets, the widespread adoption of smartphones, and ever more sophisticated information technology (IT) solutions for businesses. Even though the market for computer hardware is still viable and expected to grow in the early 2000s, Dell is putting a greater emphasis on IT solutions and services for businesses over computer sales because the brand's growth has slowed, and both its profits and stock prices have dropped. Dell's investment in IT services and solutions could be as transformative and groundbreaking as Dell's changes to the personal computing industry. While Dell remains in the personal computer market and is an industry leader according to some calculations, computer sales will eventually become secondary to Dell as it refocuses its business under the guidance of Michael Dell and as a private company. Investors had been concerned about Dell for several years, and this move to reorganize as a private entity is considered to be risky.

Even though Dell's future is uncertain, the brand's reputation for being a leader on environmental issues is secure. Interbrand's ranking of the "Best Global Green Brands 2012" placed Dell at number seven. Dell is highly ranked because of its many environmental initiatives, including a 2009 ban on the export of e-waste to developing countries. In fiscal 2012 Dell recycled 192 million pounds of e-waste globally.

FURTHER READING

"Best Global Brands 2012." Interbrand. Accessed February 9, 2013. http://www.interbrand.com/en/best-global-brands/2012/Best-Global-Brands-2012.aspx.

Brand Finance. "Dell." *Brandirectory*. Accessed February 10, 2013. http://brandirectory.com/profile/dell.

"BrandZ Top 100 Most Valuable Global Brands 2012." Millward Brown. Accessed February 9, 2013. http://www.millwardbrown.com/brandz/2012/Documents/2012_BrandZ_Top100_Report.pdf.

"Dell." RankingTheBrands.com. Accessed February 9, 2013. http://www.rankingthebrands.com/Brand-detail.aspx?brandID=18.

"Dell, Inc." *International Directory of Company Histories*. Ed. Margaret Mazurkiewicz. Vol. 143. Detroit, MI: St. James Press, 2013.

"Dell, Michael," *Gale Encyclopedia of E-Commerce*. Ed. Laurie J. Fundukian. Vol. 1. Detroit, MI: Gale, 2012.

Ladendorf, Kirk. "Dell's Big Bet: Computer Company Founder Gambling He Can Shake up Industry Again." Statesman.com, February 9, 2013. Accessed February 10, 2013. http://www.statesman.com/news/business/dells-big-betwith-buyout-plan-founder-of-computer-/nWKym/.

Mancini, Candice. "Dell Inc." *Encyclopedia of Major Marketing Campaigns*. Ed. Thomas Riggs. Vol. 2. Detroit, MI: Gale, 2007.

"World's Most Powerful Brands: Dell." *Forbes*. Accessed February 9, 2013. http://www.forbes.com/companies/dell/.

DELOITTE

AT A GLANCE

Brand Synopsis: Projecting stability, transparency, and other qualities that are important for a financial services firm, Deloitte provides services such as audit, consulting, investment, and tax services.
Parent Company: Deloitte Touche Tohmatsu Limited
Global Office
30 Rockefeller Plaza
New York, New York 10112
United States
http://www.deloitte.com/view/en_GX/global/index.htm
Sector: Industrials
Industry Group: Commercial & Professional Services
Performance: *Market share*—6.1 percent worldwide (2011). *Sales*—US$31.3 billion (2012).
Principal Competitors: PricewaterhouseCoopers International Limited; Ernst & Young Global Limited; KPMG International Cooperative

BRAND ORIGINS

- In 1989 the merger of Deloitte, Haskins and Sells with Touche Ross and its affiliated company Tohmatsu Avoiki & Sanwa created Deloitte Touche Tohmatsu Limited.
- In 2011 Deloitte consisted of 47 of independent companies in more than 150 countries.
- In 2012 Deloitte employed more than 193,000 employees.

Deloitte is not a single corporation with individual divisions. Instead, it is a partnership of separate companies that operate around the world. Different companies have created the company's full name, Deloitte Touche Tohmatsu Limited. In 1989 Deloitte, Haskins and Sells merged with Touche Ross and its affiliated company Tohmatsu Avoiki & Sanwa to form Deloitte Touche Tohmatsu Limited.

According to its website, Deloitte's member companies provide "audit, consulting, financial advisory, risk management, and tax services" for its clients who span the globe. In 2011 there were 47 of these independent companies in more than 150 countries. In 2012 this amounted to more than 193,000 employees who were affiliated with Deloitte.

These member companies have long histories of their own. William Welch Deloitte developed bookkeeping systems in England during the 1800s that helped businesses such as railroad companies deal with capital stock and depreciation. Tax legislation changes in England and the United States and the changing nature of business helped firms such as Deloitte thrive. Besides accounting services, Deloitte provided investment and consulting services.

Another English company, Touche Ross, started in 1899. Known earlier as George A. Touche & Co., the company originally offered services for investment trust companies. Directorships, receiverships, mergers, and reconstruction helped the company expand its operations to Canada, the United States, Europe, Japan, and other places. This multinationalism would be a hallmark of Deloitte Touche Tohmatsu Limited.

Another hallmark of Deloitte would be its consulting services. The company founded Deloitte Consulting in 1995. It provides business consulting for clients all around the world. These consulting services, along with its other services, have made Deloitte one of the four preeminent accounting firms in the world.

BRAND ELEMENTS

- The Deloitte logo is the name Deloitte in block letters followed by a period of a different color. The word *Deloitte* is frequently in white or blue, while the period is often a light green.
- The simple Deloitte logo conveys an all-business image that is easy to read, familiar, and timeless.
- Deloitte's frequent use of the colors blue and green identifies itself and helps portray it as stable and consistent.

The Deloitte logo is simply the name Deloitte in block letters followed by a period of a different color. The word *Deloitte* is frequently in white with a blue background or blue with a white background, while the period is often a light green.

The Deloitte logo is a simple, almost no-frills image. This simplicity is fitting. It projects an all-business image, a perception that the company is too busy with its work to spend large amounts of time and expense on an elaborate logo, money and time that could be better used in serving its clients. The simple, legible block font is easy to read, familiar, and timeless. The logo's appearance is fitting for a company that wants to promote a stable, reassuring image, especially since it operates in the sensitive and often-changing field of finance.

Deloitte frequently uses the colors blue and green to identify itself. These colors appear on its signs, written materials, advertising, and websites. These two colors identify the company and reiterate its visual elements; their repeated use also portrays the company as stable and consistent.

BRAND IDENTITY

- In 2012 Deloitte released the transparency report *Committed to Quality*, which described the company's transparency and honesty. It featured transparent images and detailed information to convey the company's transparency and trustworthiness.
- Beginning in 2009 Deloitte began using the green dot from its logo in a promotional campaign that highlights the brand's usefulness and flexibility.
- The organization, accessibility, and information provided in Deloitte's 2011 annual report communicate the value the brand places on these qualities.

To convey its trustworthiness, Deloitte issued in 2012 the transparency report *Committed to Quality*. This report included detailed information about the company and its commitment to transparency. It also contained visual images that reinforced this concept of transparency. The cover featured a transparent cube, while illustrations within the report included a clear lightbulb and a giant light board with different images.

Deloitte uses its brand elements to help describe its usefulness and flexibility. Since 2009 it has used the Green Dot campaign to promote itself. Named for the green dot that follows its logo, this international advertising campaign has featured the green dot as the sun, a doorknob, or scientific equipment in various pictures. Because the dot represents Deloitte as part of its logo, these advertisements imply that Deloitte can similarly serve various roles.

The green dot also appears on Deloitte-produced materials such as annual reports. For example, Deloitte's 2011 annual report incorporates the blue and green brand colors in addition to the dot. When combined with the report's distinct sections and a good balance of text and financial data, all of these elements help convey that Deloitte is a brand that values organization, accessibility, and information.

BRAND STRATEGY

- Deloitte operates mobility programs in which employees work on international assignments that focus on taxes, auditing, and other financial topics in countries such as China, India, and Taiwan.
- During the London 2012 Summer Olympics Deloitte assisted in the planning and operating of the games.
- Deloitte provides support for the home care services and other support services for the TUNAJALI "We Care" program, which assists Tanzanians who have HIV and AIDS.

Mobility programs are one way that Deloitte extends its brand. In these mobility programs, Deloitte employees work on international assignments that focus on taxes, auditing, and other financial topics. Some of the countries that have participated in the mobility programs include China, India, and Taiwan. More than 4,400 Deloitte employees participated in these programs in 2011, 16.5 percent more than had participated in 2010.

Deloitte participates in other international ventures. One of these ventures was the London 2012 Summer Olympics. Deloitte and its employees helped by providing food and accommodations for the athletes, finding equipment, designing structures, practicing hypothetical situations, and even helping carry the Olympic torch in the relay.

Another of Deloitte's international efforts is its participation as a partner of the TUNAJALI "We Care" program. This program provides medical care for residents of Tanzania who are infected with HIV and helps mobilize other organizations in the fight against HIV and AIDS. Deloitte offers support for the program's home care services and other support services. This effort is another illustration of the company's respect for people all around the world and the international reach of its services.

BRAND EQUITY

- In 2012 Brand Finance estimated that Deloitte's brand value was US$9.7 billion.
- Brand Finance named Deloitte the 89th best global company and the 11th most valuable British brand, both in 2012.
- Intangible Business called Deloitte the second-best British accounting brand in 2006, citing its newly shortened name, communication skills, and the high fees it is able to charge.

This international presence has helped make Deloitte a valuable brand. In 2012 Brand Finance estimated Deloitte's brand value was US$9.7 billion, which was a sizable jump from the previous year's brand value of US$7.8 billion. Among the world's top brands, Deloitte was ranked as 89th by Brand Finance in 2012. In another ranking, Brand Finance determined that Deloitte was the 11th most valuable British brand in 2012.

In 2006 the British branding professional Intangible Business indicated that Deloitte was the second-best brand in the United Kingdom after PricewaterhouseCoopers International Limited. Intangible Business said Deloitte's communication and newly streamlined name helped increase its brand value. It also noted that the company was able to charge higher fees than its competitors, which is an indicator of its brand value.

BRAND AWARENESS

- In 2011 Gartner, Inc., determined that Deloitte was the world's largest business consulting company for the second straight year, based on the combined revenues of its companies; Deloitte captured a 6.1 percent share of the global business consulting market.
- The four largest international accounting firms are known as the Big Four: Deloitte, PricewaterhouseCoopers International Limited, Ernst & Young Global Limited, and KPMG International Cooperative.
- Vault Career Intelligence's annual survey on accounting firms ranked Deloitte the second most prestigious accounting company and the best firm in terms of diversity in 2012.
- In 2012 Deloitte appeared on *Working Mother* magazine's annual list of the best companies for multicultural women for the seventh consecutive year.

Deloitte is a prominent international company. According to the American firm Gartner, Inc., Deloitte was the world's largest business consulting company in 2011, the second straight year it held that distinction. Gartner determined this ranking by combining the revenues for all the firms that make up Deloitte. These calculations determined that Deloitte captured a 6.1 percent share of the global business consulting market in 2011.

Deloitte is one of the Big Four, the four largest international accounting firms: Deloitte, PricewaterhouseCoopers International Limited, Ernst & Young Global Limited, and KPMG International Cooperative. This is such a common designation in the accounting field that the term *Big Four* is commonly used to describe these companies.

Deloitte appears with other members of the Big Four in an annual survey about accounting companies. This survey is conducted by Vault Career Intelligence, which provides information for professionals and students. In 2012 Vault's survey ranked Deloitte the second most prestigious accounting company. The survey also ranked Deloitte the best accounting company in terms of diversity. This ranking demonstrates how Deloitte's high earnings have been accompanied by a good reputation. It also demonstrates how the company has succeeded in its pledge to find "strength from cultural diversity."

Other reports echo these findings. Every year the magazine *Working Mother* publishes its list of the best companies for multicultural women. In 2012 Deloitte appeared on this list for the seventh consecutive year. The magazine cited the company's Emerging Leaders Development Program for minority managers and its other programs and initiatives.

BRAND OUTLOOK

- In 2011 Deloitte reported revenues of US$14.3 billion in the Americas, US$10.3 billion in Europe, the Middle East, and Africa, and US$4.3 billion in Asia Pacific.
- In 2012 Deloitte's revenues increased 7.9 percent in the Americas, 6.4 percent in Europe, the Middle East, and Africa, and 16.3 percent in Asia Pacific.
- During the 2011–12 academic year over 40,000 Deloitte employees from 70 countries attended Deloitte University, Deloitte's education and development center in Texas.

- In 2010 Deloitte firms experienced a 20 percent jump in earnings in India and South Korea, an 8 percent increase in China, and sizable revenue growth in Brazil, South Africa, and the Middle East.
- Deloitte plans to employ more than 250,000 employees at Deloitte companies by 2015.

Other financial figures point to Deloitte's widespread business. In 2011 the company reported revenues of US$14.3 billion in the Americas, US$10.3 billion in Europe, the Middle East, and Africa, and US$4.3 billion in Asia Pacific. In 2012 Deloitte's reported revenues increased 7.9 percent in the Americas and 6.4 percent in Europe, the Middle East, and Africa. In Asia Pacific Deloitte reported an increase of 16.3 percent in revenues; one country, India, reported a 19 percent jump in local currency. China and other companies in the region also reported double digit increases.

Deloitte looks to promote its brand through education. In 2011 it opened Deloitte University, an education and development center, outside of Dallas, Texas. During the 2011–12 academic year more than 40,000 Deloitte employees from 70 countries attended the university. The company also sponsors the Deloitte University Press, which publishes business documents and periodicals about a variety of business topics. These efforts position Deloitte as a company that offers business services and that can teach other companies how to improve their own services.

Like a number of other companies, Deloitte hopes to succeed in several different markets around the world, including a number of emerging markets. Its 2010 revenues point to various growth areas. In that year Deloitte firms experienced a 20 percent jump in earnings in India and South Korea, an 8 percent increase in China, and sizable revenue growth in Brazil, South Africa, and the Middle East.

Deloitte hopes to build the company along with its earnings. It has experienced earnings increases and growth in emerging markets with growing populations and economic power. To serve these regions and handle this increased business, it announced its intention to employ more than 250,000 employees at Deloitte companies by 2015. To help accomplish this, it hired 51,000 employees during the 2012 fiscal year, which combined for a total of over 193,000 global employees in that year.

FURTHER READING

"About Deloitte." Deloitte, 2012. Accessed December 21, 2012. http://www.deloitte.com/view/en_GX/global/about/index.htm.

Brand Finance. "Global 500 2012." *Brandirectory*. Accessed February 12, 2013. http://brandirectory.com/profile/deutsche-bank.

"Deloitte Announces Revenue Results of US$31.3 Billion." Deloitte, September 19, 2012. Accessed January 31, 2013. http://www.deloitte.com/2012revenues.

"Deloitte Plans to Hire 250,000 Worldwide in Next 5 Years." *AccountingToday*, September 13, 2010.

"Deloitte Touche Tohmatsu International." *International Directory of Company Histories*. Ed. Tina Grant. Vol. 29. Detroit, MI: St. James Press, 2000.

Deloitte 2011 Annual Review. Deloitte, November 2011. Accessed January 31, 2013. https://www.deloitte.com/view/en_GX/global/about/9de6f47b02563310VgnVCM2000001b56f00aRCRD.htm.

Loosvelt, Derek. "PwC Named Most Prestigious Accounting Firm." Vault Blogs, April 18, 2012. Accessed January 31, 2013. http://blogs.vault.com/blog/workplace-issues/pwc-named-most-prestigious-accounting-firm/.

Maddox, Kate. "Deloitte Introduces Second Phase of 'Green Dot' Campaign." *B2B*, November 1, 2010. Accessed February 11, 2013. http://www.btobonline.com/apps/pbcs.dll/article?AID=/20101101/FREE/101109996/1506/rollout_archive&template=printart.

Starr, Rob. "Deloitte: Leader in Business Consulting Worldwide for Second Year." Big4.com, July 5, 2012. Accessed January 31, 2013. http://www.big4.com/deloitte/deloitte-leader-in-business-consulting-worldwide-for-second-year/.

"The UKs Most Valuable Accountancy Firm Brands." Intangible Business, 2006. Accessed February 12, 2013. http://www.intangiblebusiness.com/Reports/The-UKs-Most-Valuable-Accountancy-Firm-Brands~377.html.

"Vision, Values, and Strategy." Deloitte. Accessed January 31, 2013. https://www.deloitte.com/view/en_GX/global/about/overview/vision-and-strategy/index.htm.

DELTA

AT A GLANCE

Brand Synopsis: Delta Air Lines understands the challenges of contemporary air travel and continually strives to improve the experience of its passengers.
Parent Company: Delta Air Lines, Inc.
1030 Delta Boulevard
Atlanta, Georgia 30320
United States
http://www.delta.com
Sector: Industrials
Industry Group: Transportation
Performance: *Market share*—16.3 percent in the United States (2011). *Sales*—US$36.7 billion (2012).
Principal Competitors: AMR Corporation; United Continental Holdings Inc.; Deutsch Lufthansa AG.

BRAND ORIGINS

- Delta began as a crop-dusting service.
- The Delta Air Service name was adopted in 1928.
- For many years, Delta was known as "The Airline of the South."
- Delta Air Lines name was adopted in 1967.
- Delta grew as an international carrier in the 1990s.

The Delta brand has a rich history that runs parallel to the commercial development of the airplane. US Department of Agriculture employee and former World War I pilot Collet Everman Woolman gave birth to the company by developing a means of dealing with a boll weevil infestation that was destroying cotton crops in Louisiana. He perfected a way to spread insecticide by air, which led in 1924 to the creation of the world's first crop-dusting service, Huff Daland Dusters. In 1928 Woolman quit his government post and raised the money needed to acquire Huff Daland Dusters, renaming it Delta Air Service. The Delta name, suggested by a company secretary, referred to the Mississippi Delta. It was a choice that clearly connected the new brand to the American South.

Woolman quickly diversified his business by winning airmail contracts, followed in 1929 by the launch of passenger air service between Dallas and Jackson, Mississippi. Delta increased the visibility of its brand in 1930 when it was awarded its first mail contract from the US government. It wasn't until the post–World War II era that Delta grew into a national concern, focused on passenger service, and began to truly shape its brand. In 1953 Delta merged with Chicago and Southern Air Lines to gain scale, followed by a 1967 merger with Delaware Airlines. Since 1941 the company had been known as Delta Air Corporation, but it was now renamed Delta Air Lines. The Southern carrier then increased its national recognition through the 1972 acquisition of Northeast Airlines. Delta became an international carrier in 1991 by acquiring the assets of Pan American World Airways, including a German hub and dozens of routes between American cities and Europe.

Due to the gradual evolution of flight and Delta's growth as a company, the essence of the Delta brand evolved over time as well. One of the earliest slogans, "The Airline of the South," reflected the brand's early regional ties. What was little more than a geographic distinction grew to an association between Delta and the values represented by the South. This shift was reflected in the slogan used in the late 1950s, "Hospitality and Service from the Heart." The South was the heartland, and Delta's commitment to hospitality and customer comfort was heartfelt by implication. Later the company touted the "Delta spirit" and made other commitments to customer care that became the core of the Delta brand.

BRAND ELEMENTS

- The Delta triangle is known as the widget.
- Different shades of red provide dimension to the Delta triangle.
- The Delta aircraft tail livery rotates the widget to appear like a plane taking off.
- "Keep Climbing" slogan has been in use since 2010.

At the heart of the Delta brand is its name. What was originally a reference to the Mississippi Delta and a simple declaration of operational territory has become a blank slate for a carrier brand that serves a global market. The Delta name, rendered in upper-case block letters, also serves as the logotype centerpiece of the corporate logo. To the left of the logotype is the corporate symbol, or the widget, as it is known internally. It is a stylized triangle, a "delta," comprised of two parts. The upper half of the triangle is shaped like the swept-back delta wing of an aircraft. Separated by a band of white space is a triangle at the base of the symbol. Different shades of red are used to provide dimension, creating the image of an aircraft out of the triangular shape. To the right of the Delta name in the corporate signature is the carrier's Skyteam logo, which is used in all customer-visible communications.

The widget and logotype are employed in combination in a variety of ways. They are used as part of subbrands for subsidiary businesses Delta Shuttle and Delta Cargo, for the Delta Skymiles frequent flyer program, and for other programs and services offered by the airline. The widget and logotype are emblazoned on the body of Delta aircraft, which becomes itself a significant brand element. The distinctive tail livery uses the red widget, rotated to represent an aircraft taking off and accented by a deep shade of blue. The widget and logotype are also used throughout the cabin of the aircraft, the uniforms of attendants, written materials, napkins, and the like. Another brand element is *Sky Magazine*, the official magazine of Delta Air Lines. It is provided on flights and sold in bookstores throughout the United States to provide greater exposure to the Delta brand

Since its founding, Delta has used 19 logos. The carrier has also used a number of memorable slogans, including "We love to fly" and "We love to fly and it shows." In 2010 the carrier adopted a new slogan, "Keep Climbing." In some uses, the slogan is joined to the corporate logo, generally positioned above and to the right.

BRAND IDENTITY

- Delta Air Lines provides employees with a brand book to help maintain a consistent brand identity.
- The Delta brand claims to understand the modern-day frustration of air travel.
- Intelligent and witty communications imply that Delta "gets it."
- The "Keep Climbing" slogan inspires passengers to excel while promising the airline will continue to improve its service.

Through a brand book it provides to employees, Delta Air Lines makes clear the image of the Delta brand it wishes to convey. The carrier wants to be seen as a passenger's sympathetic partner, someone who understands the modern-day frustrations of air travel and doesn't pretend things are otherwise. In keeping with that spirit, the carrier's advertisements and other communications attempt to be fresh, intelligent, and witty, again stressing the idea that Delta "gets it." Other attributes the brand attempts to communicate are confidence, reassuring passengers that Delta was the right carrier to choose; honesty and respect, a promise that the carrier will be a good partner for passengers; humanity, reflecting a concern for passengers that goes beyond a mere business transaction; and modernity, a promise that Delta Air Lines will offer best-in-class service in the airline industry.

The "Keep Climbing" slogan embodies much of Delta's brand promise. On the surface, the phrase alludes to air flight, a simple connection between the brand and its industry. More importantly, the declarative statement is both inspirational and aspirational. The passenger is urged to strive for excellence. For the business passenger, the climb might be to the top of the corporate ladder. The slogan also suggests that Delta Air Lines is a partner in the climb. The implied promise is that the airline will continue to improve its service to help passengers in their personal climb and will never rest. Thus Delta Air Lines will be forever relevant to its passengers, because it is a carrier that respects them and their time and uses technology to provide helpful service amenities as a way to serve as a valuable partner.

BRAND STRATEGY

- Delta's first slogan, introduced in 1929, was "Speed, Comfort and Safety."
- Delta emphasized service, competence, and reliability in the 1950s and 1960s.
- The "On top of the world" campaign of the 1990s was considered too ethereal by Delta executives.

- Bankruptcy led to relaunch of the Delta brand in 2007.
- An inspirational brand book was distributed to Delta employees as part of the 2007 relaunch.

Delta's brand strategy has changed over the years, in large part due to the growth of the company and changes in air travel. The carrier's initial slogan, coined in 1929, was "Speed, Comfort and Safety." It was a brand promise relevant for the age. Air travel was reserved for the affluent, who had to be assured of both comfort and safety at a time when flight was considered dangerous by many. Speed was a key selling point, primarily because that was the only clear advantage that the airplane held over the train. Delta also associated its brand with the American South, laying claim to being the region's most reliable carrier.

In the 1950s and 1960s, Delta emphasized service, competence, and reliability, using such slogans as "Delta: Best thing that ever happened to air travel" and "Delta is ready when you are." The brand attempted to draw more of a personal connection to passengers in the 1970s and 1980s. The "Delta is my airline" slogan was unveiled in 1974. Passengers were told "Airlines are the same: Only people make the difference" in 1980. In the final years of the century, Delta created a positive, adventurous brand spirit with such taglines as "We love to fly" and "We love to fly and it shows." The advertising, accentuated with inspirational music, glorified the journey as much as it promoted the Delta brand. The carrier's "On top of the world" campaign of the 1990s featured images of dolphins and floating balloons accompanied by new age music. It was deemed too ethereal by management and dropped in favor of a more utilitarian brand image, essentially a promise to shorten the waiting lines and not lose passenger luggage.

The new century brought a host of challenges to the airline industry, due in no small measure to the terrorist attacks of September 11, 2001, that adversely impacted air travel. In the early 2000s Delta adopted the upbeat slogan "Good goes around." In 2005 Delta filed for Chapter 11 bankruptcy protection. As part of its emergence from bankruptcy, Delta reviewed the state of its brand and concluded that it had become inconsistent and muddled.

In the spring of 2007, a new Delta brand identity was revealed. While honoring the carrier's heritage, the brand now offered a more modern look and a focus on the customer experience. New aircraft livery and Delta terminal signage were introduced to support the new brand strategy. To further emphasize the commitment to an improved passenger experience, Delta also launched its Sky Priority program, offering exclusive amenities to key customer groups, and the Delta Sky Club, a new in-airport club for select passengers. The airline also upgraded gate areas and in-flight entertainment options. To engage Delta employees in the new branding effort, an inspirational brand book was distributed. Moreover, Delta issued guidelines to the communications staff and marketing agencies in order to create a consistent brand image. Changes continued in 2010 when the "Keep Climbing" slogan was adopted to reinforce Delta's promise to continually find ways to improve the travel experience.

BRAND EQUITY

- Brand Finance Plc assigned a brand value of US$3.013 billion to Delta in 2012.
- Delta was ranked No. 378 on the Brand Finance Global 500 in 2012.
- Delta was the most valuable North American Airline brand in 2012, according to Heardable, Inc.

As an internationally recognized brand, Delta Air Lines enjoys strong brand equity. This plays an important part in the more than US$35 billion in annual revenues the carrier generates. Using a proprietary methodology, brand evaluation consultancy Brand Finance Plc placed a value of US$3.013 billion on the Delta Air Lines brand in 2012. Brand Finance also assigned it an AA Brand Rating. The brand value accounted for 16.9 percent of Delta's enterprise value of US$17.785 billion.

In 2011 Brand Finance listed Delta as the world's fourth most valuable airline brand. It was also ranked No. 345 on the Brand Finance Global 500 list of the world's most valuable brands. The following year, however, Delta slipped to No. 378. According to the methodology of another brand consultancy, Heardable Inc., Delta was the top airline brand in North America in 2012.

BRAND AWARENESS

- Delta's brand awareness is greatest in the American South.
- The acquisition of Pan Am assets helped to elevate Delta's brand awareness in the 1990s.
- The 2010 merger with Northwest Airlines expanded the number of destinations, further increasing brand awareness.
- New mobile applications helped to greatly improve brand awareness among business travelers.

Delta is one of the world's most recognizable airline brands. An important factor in Delta's brand awareness is the carrier's long history, stretching back to its days as a crop-dusting service and mail delivery operator. Because of its roots in the American South, the Delta brand is even better known in that part of the country, where the connection to the Mississippi Delta offers greater resonance. Through acquisitions, Delta was able to expand to all corners of the United States and increase brand awareness throughout the country.

The Delta name was introduced to a global marketplace in the 1990s through the acquisition of Pan American World Airways' assets. With the addition of a hub in Germany and dozens of routes between American cities and Europe, Delta increased the exposure of its brand, especially among European travelers. In 2010 Delta completed a merger with Northwest Airlines to emerge as one of the world's largest commercial air carriers. Now flying to about 350 destinations in more than 60 countries and serving more than 160 million customers each year, Delta has spread global awareness of its brand even further.

With the introduction of its "Keep Climbing" slogan in 2010, Delta also introduced an aggressive new campaign to build brand awareness among business travelers through mobile devices. Among this key, targeted group, Delta doubled brand awareness and brand favorability, as well as increasing its awareness of the carrier's business elite services.

BRAND OUTLOOK

- Helping to promote the brand was a new international concourse that opened in Atlanta in 2012.
- Improvements to international business-class benefits promised to enhance the Delta brand internationally.
- Acceptance of an open-skies policy in many parts of the world was expected to open up new destinations.

The successful revamping of its brand in 2007 and the subsequent merger with Northwest Airlines have laid the foundation for continued growth of the Delta brand. Helping to promote the brand was a new international concourse that opened in Atlanta in 2012. The following year Delta was scheduled to open an expanded, state-of-the-art facility at Terminal 4 at John F. Kennedy International Airport. Improvements to international business-class benefits also promised to enhance the Delta brand internationally. Delta offered new flat-bed seats for long flights, an improved menu, and an on-demand entertainment system that included a library of 250 movies, 50 hours of HBO programming, 100 television programs, and video games.

Also boding well for the growth of the brand was the acceptance of an open-skies policy in many parts of the world that should open up new destinations. Moreover, the travel and tourism industry was expected to enjoy steady growth. This should help Delta to strengthen its brand around the world in the years to come.

FURTHER READING

Brand Finance. "Global 500 2012." *Brandirectory*. Accessed November 12, 2012. http://brandirectory.com/league_tables/table/global-500-2012.

"Delta Air Lines, Inc." *International Directory of Company Histories*. Ed. Tina Grant. Vol. 92. Detroit, MI: St. James Press, 2008.

"Delta Drops Ad Theme 'On top of the World.'" *Advertising Age*, April 12, 1999.

Goetzl, David. "Delta's New $100 Mil Push Signals Shift in Branding." *Advertising Age*, March 13, 2000.

"Image Is (Nearly) Everything." *Air Transport World*, May 1995.

Stevens, Shannon. "Bumping up Delta." *Brandweek*, December 15, 1997.

DEUTSCHE BANK

AT A GLANCE

Brand Synopsis: Deutsche Bank is the largest bank in Germany and one of the largest in the world; it has been a major presence in international finance since the 1870s.
Parent Company: Deutsche Bank AG
Theodor-Heuss-Allee 70
Frankfurt am Main, 60486
Germany
https://www.db.com/index_e.htm
Sector: Financials
Industry Group: Banks
Performance: *Market share*—5.6 percent of the investment market worldwide (2012). *Net income*—EUR665 million (US$862 million) (2012).
Principal Competitors: Commerzbank AG; UBS AG; Citigroup Inc.

BRAND ORIGINS

- Deutsche Bank means German bank, although the bank has a long international history.
- Founded in Berlin in the 1870s, Deutsche Bank had international offices by 1873.
- Following World Wars I and II, Deutsche Bank rebuilt its international presence.
- Germany's biggest bank, Deutsche Bank operates the telephone bank Deutsche Bank 24.

Although Deutsche Bank means "German bank," the bank also has a long history of international work. Founded in Berlin in 1870, Deutsche Bank started its international work early, opening offices in Shanghai, Yokohama, and London by 1873, in addition to branches in Bremen and Hamburg. During these early years, the bank acquired other banks and was heavily involved in the finances of the electrical and railroad industries in Germany and abroad. Its success enabled it to make loans to governments.

After this early success, World War I, World War II, and the bank's affiliation with the Nazi Party hit the bank hard. It reorganized, relocated its headquarters to Frankfurt, and signed up new account holders on its way to becoming Germany's biggest bank.

Deutsche Bank also rebuilt its international presence. It opened its first American branch office in New York in 1979 and acquired companies from North America, Great Britain, and elsewhere. It consolidated its Asian operations, opened more Asian branches, and founded Deutsche Bank North America. This would later be followed by Deutsche Bank Middle East & North Africa, Deutsche Bank Malaysia, and Deutsche Bank Argentina, to name a few.

The bank expanded its domestic services and continued its frequent use of the Deutsche Bank name when it created Deutsche Bank 24, Germany's first full-service telephone bank. Its international operations continued, though. During the world financial crisis of the early 2000s, Deutsche Bank adapted by reorganizing and continuing its focus on international operations. In the early 2000s, then, Deutsche Bank resembled the bank it was in the 1870s, a bank with local and international interests.

BRAND ELEMENTS

- German artist Anton Stankowski won a contest to create Deutsche Bank's logo in 1972.
- Deutsche Bank's slash-in-a-square logo appears as signage, on the Internet, on its materials, and as decorative elements at its banks.
- Deutsche Bank's Frankfurt headquarters reinforces the use of its logo by featuring it in a BrandSpace.

Deutsche Bank uses what it calls a "slash in a square" as its brand logo. This image is a blue box outline with a blue forward slash in the center. It chose this logo in 1972 after it commissioned designs from several graphic artists. German graphic artist, painter, and photographer Anton Stankowski produced the winning design, the slash-in-a-square logo. The involvement of several participants in this selection process was a collaborative effort, reflecting Deutsche Bank's belief in working cooperatively with current and potential customers.

Deutsche Bank frequently uses the slash-in-a-square logo and elements from it. Large versions appear on and in buildings as signs for the bank, while other versions appear on the Internet and other media. Deutsche Bank buildings, websites, and promotional materials use the logo's colors and shapes to reinforce the bank's visual image. Its branches frequently use blue lighting elements and other blue design features, such as slanted, blue room dividers that echo the logo's blue color and slash shape.

To further reinforce the company's ties to this logo, it established a BrandSpace at its Frankfurt headquarters in 2011. This space displayed the logo in various ways. Visitors can use their bodies to form an interactive logo or they can view an elaborate 10-foot-high logo that incorporates lights and several moving parts.

BRAND IDENTITY

- According to Deutsche Bank, the slash in its logo "stands for consistent growth and dynamic development," while its "square-shaped frame can be interpreted as a sign of security."
- According to Deutsche Bank, its entire logo portrays "growth in a stable environment."
- Deutsche Bank's use of a forward slash ties the company's identity in to the age of the Internet.
- Deutsche Bank frequently uses the slogan, "Passion to Perform," which captures the bank's enthusiasm and success.

The bank's slash-in-a-square logo symbolizes several concepts. According to Deutsche Bank, it chose this "simple yet striking" logo to easily identify itself and provide a "consistent frame of reference." It has created this consistency by using the slogan multiple times in different formats. Deutsche Bank added that the "'slash' stands for consistent growth and dynamic development," while its "square-shaped frame can be interpreted as a sign of security," together portraying "growth in a stable environment."

In the Internet age, the bank's use of a forward slash has taken on additional meanings. Web addresses frequently use forward slashes, as in "http://www..." Deutsche Bank's slash-in-a-square symbol thus evokes the bank's interest in modernity and technology as well as its access to information and its connections to others, important qualities for a bank to possess. Although the bank began using this image in 1972, before the widespread use or even knowledge of the Internet, now the bank's use of a symbolic forward slash helps the bank to appear particularly forward-thinking, alert, and aware, other important traits for a bank to possess.

The bank uses the logo prominently when it advertises in different markets. For example, print advertisements for Deutsche Bank in India, Australia, and Sweden incorporated this logo. These advertisements also incorporated the bank's slogan, "Passion to Perform," which captured the bank's enthusiasm and success. The company has used this slogan so frequently that the slogan and the familiar blue box have identified the company since 2010; the company does not use the Deutsche Bank name as part of its logo.

BRAND STRATEGY

- Describing its brand, Deutsche Bank noted that "we are here to perform—in business and beyond. We do this with a unique mix of passion and precision."
- Deutsche Bank has allied its logo and "Passion to Perform" slogan with different products and banks in various countries.
- To protect its brand and brand components, Deutsche Bank has issued brand books describing how people can treat its brand.

According to The Financial Brand.com, Deutsche Bank has described its commitment to its brand in this way: "We are here to perform—in business and beyond. We do this with a unique mix of passion and precision." This statement describes its brand while echoing its "Passion to Perform" slogan.

While doing this work, Deutsche Bank reminds customers about its presence. It uses the Deutsche Bank logo and "Passion to Perform" slogan for its various products in several different countries. Websites for its banks in different countries feature its ubiquitous box logo, so even if Internet users cannot understand the different languages used on the sites, they can readily identify them as Deutsche Bank websites. Deutsche Bank has made its strong brand identity even stronger by consistent reinforcement of its logo and slogan.

The bank, then, relies heavily on its brand and individual brand components. It has taken steps to preserve the distinctiveness of this brand. To safeguard its logo and elements, Deutsche Bank has issued brand books that delineate how people can use the logos, typefaces, and other elements associated with the bank.

BRAND EQUITY

- In 2012 Deutsche Bank led both the United States and the world in market share for fixed-income investments.
- Deutsche Bank held the second-highest market share for fixed-income investments in both Europe and Asia.
- Deutsche Bank was the worldwide banking leader in insurance company and central bank business in 2012.
- Despite worldwide financial problems in the early 2000s, Deutsche Bank captured a 5.6 percent share of the global investment market in 2012, up from 4.3 percent in 2008.
- Brand Finance determined Deutsche Bank's brand value to be US$14.573 billion in 2013.

Deutsche Bank's international work has garnered considerable market share. It reported that it was the world's leading bank in 2012 for fixed-income investments, investments that pay predetermined, regular dividends. It captured 10.7 percent of this global market in 2012. That year it also captured 12.2 percent of the U.S. fixed-income investment market, leading that market as well.

Deutsche Bank fixed-income investments performed well in other regions in 2012. It captured the second-highest market share for this market in Europe and in Asia excluding Japan, where it held the fifth-highest share. It also led the world in other banking areas, serving as the global leader in business with insurance companies and central banks in 2012. The bank also received favorable rankings in 2012 for its individual products, according to financial services consultant and researcher Greenwich Associates.

It has even managed to hold and build market share during rough economic periods. In 2008 it held 4.3 percent of the global investment market. Around this time, several countries experienced severe, prolonged economic problems. Despite these developments, Deutsche Bank captured a 5.6 percent share of the global investment market in 2012.

International recognition and high brand value have accompanied this strong market share. Brand Finance determined Deutsche Bank's brand value to be US$14.573 billion. From 2008 through 2013 it was rated among the top twenty banks on the "Banking 500," Brand Finance's list of top global banking brands. The bank performed well on another Brand Finance list, the "Germany 30." This list ranked Deutsche Bank the fourth best German company in 2011 and the fifth best in 2012.

BRAND AWARENESS

- According to The Financial Brand.com in 2011, Deutsche Bank's "logo is more popular today [in Germany] than those of branding giants Apple and Nike."
- In 2011 Deutsche Bank had 80,528 "likes" on Facebook.
- Private and business banking clients of Spain's Deutsche Bank España gave the bank the best quality-of-service ratings from 2009 through 2012.

Deutsche Bank's promotional work, which includes the frequent repetition of its logo and slogan, has been successful. Consumers know the brand and its elements well. According to a 2011 piece posted on *The Financial Brand.com*, "the bank's logo is more popular today [in Germany] than those of branding giants Apple and Nike."

Another article in *The Financial Brand.com* describes another measure of the bank's popularity. In 2011 it noted that Deutsche Bank had 80,528 "likes" on Facebook, making it the world's 12th-most-popular bank on the social media site.

Customers have also given the bank high rankings. Private and business banking clients of Spain's Deutsche Bank España gave the bank the best quality-of-service ratings for four straight years, 2009 through 2012. Deutsche Bank España led a number of banking categories in the 2012 survey, including treatment of clients.

BRAND OUTLOOK

- In the early 2000s Deutsche Bank was involved in a number of financial scandals and lawsuits.
- Deutsche Bank received an Islamic finance license in 2010 to better address clients' needs in Muslim areas.
- Deutsche Bank has a "passion to perform" for different people around the world.

The lingering worldwide economic recession of the early 2000s may have had a less serious impact on Deutsche Bank than a series of scandals and lawsuits in that period. In 2012 and 2013 it was accused of money laundering and fixing international interest rates. Around that time it was also accused of tax fraud relating to trading in emissions certificates and was mired in prolonged legal proceedings relating to the bankruptcy of a German media group. These problems resulted in financial uncertainty for Deutsche Bank, but it has taken corrective measures to restore its business and reputation.

Deutsche Bank has also taken steps to assert itself in Islamic countries for future growth. It earned an international Islamic finance license in 2010. Islamic finance employs principles based on ethics, justice, and morality related to Mohammed's teachings and Islamic practice. Participation in this type of finance acknowledges different clients and markets and represents Deutsche Bank's "passion to perform" for different people around the world.

FURTHER READING

Brand Finance. "Deutsche Bank." *Brandirectory*, 2013. Accessed February 3, 2013. http://brandirectory.com/profile/deutsche-bank.

Comfort, Nicholas, and Annette Weisbach. "Deutsche Bank Beating UBS in Investment Bank Revival Sign." *Bloomberg*, October 29, 2012.

Deutsche Bank. "Brand History: The Development of the Deutsche Bank Logo." Deutsche Bank Group Communications, 2011. Accessed February 2, 2013. https://www.db.com/en/media/Logo_History.pdf.

Deutsche Bank AG. "Deutsche Bank Recognised as World's No. 1 Fixed Income Bank." January 14, 2013. Accessed February 2, 2013. https://www.db.com/medien/en/content/4238_4276.htm.

———. "Deutsche Bank Tops Once Again the Quality of Service Ranking in Spain." February 5, 2013. Accessed February 11, 2013. https://www.db.com/en/content/company/headlines_deutsche-bank-tops-once-again-the-quality-of-service-ranking-in-spain.htm.

"Deutsche Bank AG." *International Directory of Company Histories.* Ed. Jay P. Pederson. Vol. 114. Detroit, MI: St. James Press, 2010.

"Euromoney Awards for Excellence 2012: Best Global Investment Bank." Deutsche Bank Corporate Banking & Securities, 2012. Accessed February 2, 2013. http://cbs.db.com/new/docs/Euromoney_Awards_for_Excellence_Re_DB_low_res.pdf.

"Peek Inside: Deutsche Bank's BrandSpace, Strategy & Standards." TheFinancialBrand.com, April 29, 2011. Accessed February 11, 2013. http://thefinancialbrand.com/18206/deutsche-bank-brand-space-strategy-graphics-standards/.

"The Top 35 Banks on Facebook." TheFinancialBrand.com, September 1, 2011. Accessed February 11, 2013. http://thefinancialbrand.com/19526/the-top-35-banks-on-facebook/.

DHL

AT A GLANCE

Brand Synopsis: With its easily recognizable yellow delivery trucks, DHL is a global powerhouse in international shipping.
Parent Company: Deutsche Post AG
Charles-de-Gaulle-Strasse 20
Bonn 53113
Germany
http://www.dp-dhl.com
Sector: Industrials
Industry Group: Transportation
Performance: *Market share*—DHL is the largest logistics company in the world (2011). *Sales*—US$76.3 billion (2011).
Principal Competitors: FedEx Corporation; United Postal Service (USPS); United Parcel Service, Inc. (UPS)

BRAND ORIGINS

- DHL was founded as an air-courier company in 1969 by shipping executives Adrian Dalsey, Larry Hillblom, and Robert Lynn.
- In the mid-1990s DHL bought its own cargo fleet, debuted its website, and saw revenues grow by 23 percent.
- In 1998 Deutsche Post AG, a German postal service, bought a 25 percent stake in DHL International.
- In 1998 Deutsche Post acquired Danzas Group, a Swiss logistics company, initiating DHL's shift into worldwide logistics.
- In 2009 DHL ceased domestic pickup and delivery service in the United States, choosing instead to focus on its more lucrative international services.

The original DHL company was founded in 1969 by Adrian Dalsey, Larry Hillblom, and Robert Lynn, three shipping executives looking for a way to increase turnaround speed for ships at port. Their solution was to begin an air-courier company, using the first letters of their last names to form the acronym DHL. The first delivery system linked California and Hawaii and quickly expanded into flying routes in the Middle East as the brand developed its international service. In 1972 Korean entrepreneur Po Chung was recruited, and with his assistance, the sister company DHL International Ltd. was established. From this point onward, the brand operated as two separate companies: DHL Airways (based in Redwood City, California) and DHL International (headquartered in Brussels, Belgium).

In the 1980s the brand experienced stiff competition from FedEx and UPS. To increase its influence in the United States, DHL opened major airport hubs in Salt Lake City, Utah, and Cincinnati, Ohio, and bought three Boeing 727s and seven Learjets. By 1983 DHL was using helicopters to expedite documents in New York and Texas. Around that time, DHL entered into a strategic agreement with Hilton International Company, through which DHL would collect documents from 49 Hilton Hotels for international delivery.

To compete with FedEx and UPS, which had by then gone international, DHL entered into a partnership to deliver documents for Western Union in 1985. The following year DHL International entered into its first joint venture in the People's Republic of China. Despite a decline in market share in 1987, DHL revenues in 1988 were recorded as being between US$1.2 billion and US$1.5 billion. At that time, DHL controlled 98 percent of all outbound shipments from Eastern Europe and 91 percent of the packages shipped to the region from the West.

To continue boosting its brand presence in the United States, DHL created several U.S. advertising campaigns in 1989 and 1990, one of which employed Gary Larson, creator of "The Far Side" comic strip, to draw cartoons for the brand. In 1990 DHL International sold off parts of its business to several international corporations. By 1994 the brand's 25-year anniversary, DHL controlled 52 percent of the Asian express shipment market, and the brand was in the process of expanding into 16 new cities in China, India, and Vietnam, with more facilities planned for Bangkok, Tokyo, Auckland, and Sydney. The following year, the company debuted its website and saw its revenues grow by 23 percent to US$3.8 billion. In 1996 DHL bought its own cargo fleet to gain more control over its future growth.

In 1998 Deutsche Post AG, a German postal service, bought a 25 percent stake in DHL International and took control of DHL's distribution in Europe. This provided DHL with funds for further expansion and greater access to Germany. DHL continued to develop its services by moving into freight transport, and in 1998 Deutsche Post acquired Danzas Group, a Swiss logistics company, which began DHL's shift into worldwide logistics. The following year, DHL entered into an alliance with the United States Postal Service (USPS) and established a new agreement with Deutsche Post that increased its stake in DHL.

In 2002 Deutsche Post took full ownership of DHL, merging Danzas Group into the brand and changing the DHL worldwide network to a Deutsche Post subsidiary. Other Deutsche Post business units and subsidiaries were then absorbed into the DHL brand. In 2004 the company launched China Domestic, the first domestic express service in mainland China run by an international provider. This was followed by a joint venture with the express and logistics unit of New Zealand Post. In 2008 DHL moved its European hub to Leipzig, Germany, a more central position for providing timely service to the European Union.

In 2003 Deutsche Post acquired the U.S. delivery service Airborne and combined it with DHL, signaling the company's intentions to ramp up domestic competition with FedEx and UPS. The following year, DHL spent US$1.2 billion to upgrade its shipping operations in the United States. However, due to economic uncertainty and its consistently small market share among US overnight delivery companies, DHL in 2009 announced it would cease all domestic pickup and delivery service in the United States. DHL has since continued to focus on strengthening its already large international presence.

BRAND ELEMENTS

- The DHL brand is widely recognized for its bold yellow and red corporate colors, used for the company's trucks, planes, packaging, and logo.
- The DHL logo features "DHL" in red letters on a yellow background, with horizontal red lines appearing on either side of the brand name.
- DHL marketing slogans in the 21st century have included "Competition. Great for you. Bad for them." and "Excellence. Simply delivered."

The DHL brand is widely recognized for its bold yellow and red corporate colors, which are used on all of the company's packaging, marketing materials, delivery trucks, and planes. The DHL logo also uses these colors, with "DHL" appearing in bold, slanted, red letters on a yellow background. Three horizontal red lines appear to the right and left of "DHL," ostensibly representing movement and the brand's promise of swift delivery. DHL introduced its yellow and red color scheme and logo as part of a rebranding effort in 2002.

Before it abandoned its U.S. delivery and pickup service in 2009, DHL had been ramping up its marketing efforts in the United States, attempting to challenge its top two competitors in the country, FedEx and UPS. In 2005 DHL launched a marketing campaign with a pitch reading, "Competition. Great for you. Bad for them." Unlike the many brands that avoid mentioning their competitors by name, DHL ran television ads showing its delivery drivers outmaneuvering FedEx and UPS drivers.

In 2010 DHL began a global marketing campaign with a tagline reading, "Excellence. Simply delivered." The campaign, which included print and digital media ads displayed around the world, was aimed at supporting DHL's new corporate strategy of simplifying services in its logistics business and delivering sustainable solutions.

BRAND IDENTITY

- DHL is the world's leading logistics company and a top international mail provider.
- DHL wants to be perceived as a trustworthy brand.
- DHL offers services and delivery to countries worldwide.

DHL is the world's leading logistics company and a top international mail provider, offering a diversified portfolio of products and solutions. The DHL brand is united around three core brand positioning elements: personal commitment, proactive solutions, and local strength worldwide. With these elements in mind, the brand strives to generate a feeling of trust and confidence in its customers, take the initiative on a personal and organizational level, and provide a worldwide network while maintaining a strong presence at a local level.

DHL wishes to be seen as the brand that is at the heart of businesses worldwide. The brand's 'International specialists' campaign illustrated this part of DHL's personality using the image of a variety of business events being made possible through the "speed of yellow."

BRAND STRATEGY

- Since 2009 when DHL shuttered its pickup and delivery service in the United States, the brand has focused on expanding its international services and market share.
- Although already operating hubs in Hong Kong, Bangkok, and Singapore, In 2012 DHL began operating a new North Asian hub in Shanghai. DHL's "Strategy 2015" aims to make DHL the "logistics company for the world."
- In 2011 DHL CEO Frank Appel announced that the brand planned to take advantage of opportunities in the e-commerce sector.

Since shutting down its U.S. delivery and pickup service in 2009, DHL has focused on expanding its already prominent international presence. The company maintains a multihub system in the Asia Pacific region that allows the brand to serve countries such as China, India, and South Korea, countries that have helped drive the global economy in recent years. Although it has existing hubs in Hong Kong, Bangkok, and Singapore, DHL began operating a new North Asian hub in Shanghai in 2012, employing a team of 600 for the purpose of round-the-clock quality control of all shipments in the air and on the ground. Additionally, DHL plans to invest US$750 million in its German parcel network in 2012 and 2013.

DHL's "Strategy 2015," announced by the brand in 2009, involves objectives designed to maintain the brand's status as the primary postal service for Germany while making DHL the "logistics company for the world" by leveraging the global strength of its logistics business. The strategy also includes the goals of continuing to operate profitably in the mail division and of adding further communications services to enhance the brand's portfolio. DHL's Express, Supply Chain, and Global Forwarding and Freight divisions provide opportunities for the brand to take advantage of growth in the logistics industry.

In 2011 DHL CEO Frank Appel announced that the brand sees great potential in the growing e-commerce sector. A Deutsche Post study titled "Shopping 4.0" found that one in three Germans shopped online at least three times during a six-month period. The study also suggested that the rising use of smartphones and social media would provide a boost to the e-commerce sector.

DHL's divisions offer services and delivery to countries worldwide. Because it is not a U.S. company, DHL is able to ship to countries under trade embargoes or sanctions imposed by the United States, including Cuba, Iran, and North Korea. When DHL discontinued its air and ground operations in the United States in 2009, it lost its ability to make deliveries between U.S. airports. As a result, DHL formed an agreement with the United States Postal Service (USPS) that allowed DHL to deliver small packages to American customers through the USPS network.

BRAND EQUITY

- DHL is the global leader in the logistics industry, operating an international network comprising more than 220 countries and territories and approximately 275,000 employees.
- In 2011 DHL's brand value increased 34 percent over the previous year, from US$7.3 billion to US$9.8 billion.
- In 2011 Brand Finance ranked DHL 91st on its Global 500 list, and *Fortune* magazine ranked Deutsche Post 98th on its Global 500 list in 2012.

DHL has showed a measurable brand value increase since 2010, when the consulting company Senior Brand Brokers calculated DHL's value to be EUR 12,692 million, putting the brand again in sixth place in a ranking of the most valuable German brands. By the following year this value had risen 34 percent. In 2011 DHL was committed to bringing the brand's awareness to over 90 percent.

In 2011 DHL was ranked 91st on the Brand Finance Global 500 list, while in 2012 *Fortune* magazine placed parent company Deutsche Post 98th in its Global 500 rankings, down slightly from the 93rd spot in 2011. Also in 2012 DHL was ranked 10th on Brand Finance's German Top 30, 16th on Business Superbrand's Official Top 500, and 54th on Global Brand's Simplicity Index.

BRAND AWARENESS

- DHL's brand awareness was 60 percent in 2010.
- In 2011 DHL became the first training kit sponsor of Manchester United Football Club.
- DHL has served as the logistics partner for international fashion and cultural events, including the 2012 Mercedes-Benz Fashion Week in Berlin.

According to online marketing magazine BtoBOnline.com, DHL enjoyed a brand awareness of 60 percent in

2010. This was a significant increase compared to earlier years and was boosted by DHL's first advertising campaign in two decades. The combination of the campaign and the brand's ubiquitous yellow delivery trucks sent brand awareness from 11 percent to 60 percent in two years.

In 2011, having partnered with Manchester United and Formula One, DHL saw an all-time high in terms of brand recall, broke record association numbers, and saw business directly impacted in South Africa. DHL has also raised its brand awareness by sponsoring international fashion and cultural events. In 2012 DHL served as the official logistics partner for the 2012 Mercedes-Benz Fashion Week in Berlin, arranging distribution of runway designs to global distributors, covering exclusive Vivienne Westwood events, and offering the DHL Express Fashion Export Scholarship to emerging fashion designers. Additionally, DHL organizes the logistics for Leipzig Gewandhaus Orchestra events, including their performance for Pope Benedict XVI's birthday celebration in 2012.

BRAND OUTLOOK

- With more than 275,000 employees in more than 220 countries, DHL is focused on growing and sustaining its diverse network of global services. DHL sees great potential in the e-commerce sector, as well as in the emerging markets of Brazil, Russia, India, China, and Mexico.
- A 2010 report from parent company Deutsche Post acknowledged that the logistics industry will be integral in reducing carbon emissions.
- DHL has said it considers sustainability a key aspect of its corporate strategy.

With more than 275,000 employees in more than 220 countries, DHL is focused on growing and sustaining its diverse network of global services. As it moves further into the 21st century, the company aims to maintain its position as the world's leading logistics provider and strengthen its position as an international market leader in sea and air express mail delivery services.

In 2011 DHL CEO Frank Appel announced that the brand sees great potential in the growing e-commerce sector, particularly with the increasing popularity of smartphones and social networking. Although it already has a significant presence worldwide, parent company Deutsche Post considers Brazil, Russia, India, China, and Mexico to be emerging markets for the brand. As of 2012, DHL had not announced any intention of reentering the U.S. pickup and delivery market.

Like many other international brands, Deutsche Post has expressed a strong interest in becoming a more environmentally sustainable corporation. In 2010 the company unveiled a 150-page report on green business trends, which stated that the logistics industry will be central to comprehensive carbon reduction efforts in most sectors. A press release concerning the study reiterated that DHL and its parent corporation consider sustainability, particularly the reduction of carbon emissions, to be a central aspect of their corporate strategy.

FURTHER READING

Bole, Kristin. "DHL Gets Its Wings: Plans to Buy Own Jets in Asia Marks Change in Strategy." *San Francisco Business Times*, May 10, 1996.

Brady, Diane. "Delivery Giants Race to Set up Hubs for Overnight Service to Asian Cities." *Wall Street Journal*, August 7, 1997.

"Clal Trading Sells Shigur Express to DHL." *Israel Business Today*, February 28, 1997.

"DHL Plans to Spend $1.2 Billion in Challenge of FedEx and UPS." *Wall Street Journal*, June 25, 2004.

"DHL Worldwide Express." *International Directory of Company Histories*. Ed. Jay P. Pederson. Vol. 24. Detroit, MI: St. James Press, 1999.

Low, Elizabeth. "DHL Starts Global Push." *Adweek*, April 27, 2010. Accessed November 29, 2012. http://www.adweek.com/news/advertising-branding/dhl-starts-global-push-102181.

Michel, Matt. "Your Brand Awareness Is Higher Than You Think." *Contracting Business*, April 30, 2010. Accessed February 20, 2013. http://contractingbusiness.com/archive/your-brand-awareness-higher-you-think.

"Package Delivery Battle Hinges on DHL Ruling." *Wall Street Journal*, May 13, 2003.

Silverstein, Barry. "Delivering Overnight Brands." *BrandChannel*, December 3, 2007. Accessed November 29, 2012. http://www.brandchannel.com/features_effect.asp?pf_id=398.

"Sustainability Is Key for Future Success of the Logistics Industry." Deutsche Post AG, October 3, 2010. Accessed November 29, 2012. http://www.dp-dhl.com/en/media_relations/press_releases/2010/nachhaltigkeit_schluessel_des_erfolgs_fuer_logistik.html.

"U.S. Ruling Delivers Victory to Deutsche Post and DHL." *Wall Street Journal Europe*, May 14, 2001.

DIRECTV

AT A GLANCE

Brand Synopsis: DIRECTV prides itself on providing the greatest variety and quality of programming of any digital television entertainment provider through innovation and industry-leading technology.
Parent Company: DIRECTV
2230 East Imperial Highway
El Segundo, California 90245
United States
http://www.directv.com
Sector: Consumer Discretionary
Industry Group: Media
Performance: *Market share*—20 percent in the United States and 31 percent in Latin America of the market for digital pay-TV entertainment service providers (2011). *Sales*—US$27.2 billion (2011).
Principal Competitors: Comcast Corporation; DISH-Network Corporation; Time Warner Cable Inc.; Cox Communications, Inc. (subsidiary of Cox Enterprises); Verizon Communications Inc.; Charter Communications, Inc.; AT&T Inc.

BRAND ORIGINS

- DIRECTV launched its first satellite in 1993.
- In 1996 DIRECTV took on its first major partner when AT&T purchased a 2.5 percent share of the company.
- In 2003 Rupert Murdoch purchased a 34 percent share of DIRECTV's parent company, Hughes Electronics Corporation, for US$6.6 billion.
- In 2011 DIRECTV had its best year ever, with a record 3.7 million new subscribers and US$27.2 billion in revenues.

The history of DIRECTV extends back to 1985, when Hughes Electronics Corporation, a division of General Motors Company (GM), saw potential in direct broadcast satellite services and began intense research to improve the quality of satellite signals. This research and the resulting development of digital compression would become a game-changer in satellite television technology. Satellite television service up to this point had posed little if any threat to cable television, as the picture quality for satellite-transmitted television signals was noticeably inferior to that of cable, while satellite television's programming options were not nearly as robust. The new digital compression technology changed all that, increasing satellite broadcast capacity more than eight-fold and producing a picture quality far superior to what had been available previously via satellite. In 1990 Hughes Electronics Corporation allocated US$750 million to fund a new start-up it named DIRECTV.

In 1993 DIRECTV signed distribution agreements with Turner Broadcasting, USA Network, the Sci-Fi Channel, the Family Channel, MTV, and others. The company attacked the cable industry in the two areas that previously had been glaring weaknesses for satellite television: image quality and programming. No longer inferior in either area, DIRECTV boasted a sharper image than cable TV and also offered a greater variety of programming. By December 1993, DIRECTV had launched its first satellite, five times more powerful than any existing satellite and able to transmit up to eight times as many video signals. DIRECTV signed agreements with Sears, Best Buy, Circuit City, and other stores to begin selling its equipment to customers by the fall of 1994. At the rate of US$30 per month per subscriber, DIRECTV estimated that it would break even with the sale of around 3 million subscriptions.

DIRECTV experienced a milestone year in 1996. The company took on its first major partner when AT&T paid US$137.5 million for a 2.5 percent take in the company. One million new subscribers signed up that same year. In late 1997, DIRECTV reached the point of hypothetical profitability, with 3 million subscribers, but the year ended with financial losses. Seeking to attract more new subscribers, DIRECTV lowered the price of its dish and set-top box package to US$199, a below-market price that consequently added to the company's losses.

Meanwhile, the cable TV industry was beginning to catch on to the benefits of digital compression technology, and DIRECTV was frantically trying to capture as much market share as possible before it lost its early advantage over competitors. In January 1999, Hughes Electronics Corporation purchased United States Satellite Broadcasting (USSB), a major partner of DIRECTV, and PrimeStar, DIRECTV's closest competitor. In March 1999 the company launched a promotional campaign offering new subscribers free installation and free service for the first three months. By year's end, DIRECTV's total number of subscribers topped 7 million.

In 2002 competitor Comcast merged with AT&T's cable and Internet divisions, and in 2003 media mogul Rupert Murdoch paid US$6.6 billion for a 34 percent share of Hughes Electronics Corporation, giving him control of DIRECTV. This purchase gave DIRECTV access to a huge pool of additional resources through Murdoch's News Corporation enterprises. The name of DIRECTV's parent company was changed from Hughes Electronics Corporation to the DirecTV Group, Inc., and ownership was passed from News Corporation to one of its subsidiaries, Fox Entertainment Group, Inc. DIRECTV's new owners immediately sought to make the company more focused and cost-effective by eliminating anything not directly related to satellite broadcasting.

Over the next few years, DIRECTV's subscriber base grew at a tremendous rate, but the company continued to lose money due to its strategy of accepting short-term losses by offering free equipment and services upfront in order to gain new subscribers. That strategy ultimately appears to have paid off, however. DIRECTV's 2011 annual report stated that 2011 was the company's best year ever, with US$27.2 billion in revenues and a record-setting 3.7 million new customers in the United States and Latin America. In 2011, DIRECTV owned 12 satellites, with plans to launch two more in 2014 and 2015.

BRAND ELEMENTS

- The DIRECTV name, which was first used in 1990, is a contraction of the term "direct broadcast satellite television."
- The DIRECTV logo has remained relatively unchanged since it was developed in1994.
- The white, sweeping curved shape in the company logo is what DIRECTV calls a "cyclone treatment" and is used in all DIRECTV visual advertising.

The DIRECTV name, which was first used in 1990, is a combination of the words "direct" and "TV" and a contraction of the term "direct broadcast satellite television." The company logo features a white, sweeping curve (which DIRECTV calls a "cyclone treatment") on a two-toned blue background. The curve is a representation of the letter "D" but can also represent satellites orbiting in space or the curve of the familiar DIRECTV satellite dish. This logo has remained relatively unchanged since 1994, though starting in 2004 it began to take on a more three-dimensional appearance in many DIRECTV ads and brochures.

As emphasized in DIRECTV's brand guidelines, the curved shape in the logo is used as the basis of all visual advertising, with both the shape and the color blue giving the company a consistent branded look that's easily distinguishable in the marketplace. The shape is generally used as a framing device, either along the bottom or right side of an ad.

Taglines for the company have included "Don't just watch TV. DIRECTV" and "Good TV. Better TV. DIRECTV." In certain ads and television commercials, these taglines have been expanded into "There is good TV. There is better TV. Then there is DIRECTV."

BRAND IDENTITY

- DIRECTV promotes itself as the brand to "experience" rather than the brand to "watch."
- DIRECTV offers exclusive programming.
- Providing the newest technologies is one of DIRECT's goals.

DIRECTV's brand identity is based on its ongoing pursuit of cutting-edge technology and innovation in order to provide customers with the best possible viewing experience. DIRECTV does not consider itself a company which, like some of its competitors, offers customers programming to "watch." DIRECTV's goal is to offer customers an "experience" in every sense of the word. The company tried to accomplish this through award-winning sound technology, more high-definition channels than any other provider, and unique services that set it apart from the rest.

DIRECTV's philosophy, which involves providing customers with the best possible viewing experience through constant research, development, and application of the newest technologies and widest varieties of standard and exclusive programming, has also been a mainstay throughout the company's existence. In recent years DIRECTV has upgraded its set-top boxes with new and more powerful add-ons, including features that allow screening in multiple rooms of a home, the recording of multiple channels, and the viewing of channels in high definition.

DIRECTV also seeks to be considered unique and thus offers exclusive programming by signing contracts with content creators. The company's premium sports packages are the best example of this. These packages include NFL Sunday Ticket, through which DIRECTV has exclusive rights to broadcast all National Football League (NFL) regular season games to fans who would otherwise be unable to watch those games on their local stations.

BRAND STRATEGY

- Fewer than five years after selling its first subscription, DIRECTV purchased its largest satellite TV competitor, PrimeStar, for US$1.8 billion.
- Rupert Murdoch purchased Hughes Electronics Corporation in 2003, thereby gaining ownership of DIRECTV.
- In order to streamline its operations, DIRECTV sold off all interests not related to satellite TV between 2004 and 2007.

DIRECTV grew quickly and by 1999 was able to purchase its largest satellite TV competitor, PrimeStar, for US$1.8 billion. By the time Rupert Murdoch purchased Hughes Electronics Corporation in 2003, giving him ownership of DIRECTV, the satellite TV provider had developed into a massive technology conglomerate, with many resources and services but without a strong focus. In February 2004, DIRECTV announced that it would streamline its operations by selling off all interests not primarily involved in satellite television operations. Some of its larger selloffs included a controlling interest in PanAmSat, sold for US$3.5 billion, and Hughes Network Solutions, sold for US$257 million. The company's share in satellite launch services, set-top box manufacturing, and XM Satellite Radio was also sold off, after which its payroll was cut by 50 percent. The recouped money was used to purchase two satellite companies, Pegasus Communications and the National Rural Telecommunications Cooperative.

In 2004 DIRECTV began restructuring its holdings in Mexico and South America. It dropped its Mexican market but retained a 41 percent ownership in Sky Mexico. In 2007 DIRECTV eliminated its market in Brazil and migrated the customers to Sky Brazil, an affiliate in which DIRECTV owned a 74 percent stake.

DIRECTV has begun investing in the expansion of the variety and quality of its programming. In 2012 the provider was offering more than 200 high-definition (HD) channels, the most extensive collection of HD movies in 1080p resolution in the industry, and three dedicated 3-D channels for customers who own 3-D-capable televisions. DIRECTV has also been making inroads in offering alternative-format services on tablet devices and smartphones.

The biggest obstacle DIRECTV must overcome in the process of expanding the brand is found in the cable television sector, which services 58 percent of the total subscription-based television market. The solution to gaining market share is to continue streamlining the overall operation such as the restructuring of Latin American holdings, as well as offering the highest quality technology at competitive pricing. Whereas other providers simply offer a menu of standard options available to their total customer base, DIRECTV focuses on designing a great deal of flexibility into their services so that customers may create a personally tailored package. A key factor in DIRECTV's continued success and growth has been their strong association with the National Football League and their brand. DIRECTV has been the exclusive provider of NFL Sunday Ticket since 1994.

BRAND EQUITY

- *Business Rankings Annual* placed DIRECTV third on its 2012 list of the fastest-growing companies, which were ranked by profit growth from 2005 to 2010.
- In 2011 DIRECTV saw the largest customer gain in its history, with 3.7 million new subscribers added in the United States and Latin America.
- In 2011 DIRECTV had total revenues of US$27.2 billion in the global market, making it the leader among satellite TV providers worldwide.

In 2012 *Business Rankings Annual*, published by Gale, placed DIRECTV third on its list of the fastest-growing companies, which were ranked by five-year profit growth from 2005 to 2010. DIRECTV's profits grew by 57.1 percent during that time period. In comparison, Apple Inc. was first on the list, with 57.8 percent growth, and Tech Data Corporation was second, with 57.5 percent. In 2012 DIRECTV appeared to be continuing this growth. The company's 2011 annual report states that in 2011 it experienced its largest customer gain in its history, with 3.7 million new subscribers added in the United States and Latin America. In addition, earnings per share increased by more than 50 percent in 2011 due to a higher operating profit and an ongoing stock repurchase program.

For the fiscal year ending on December 31, 2011, DIRECTV had total revenues of US$27.23 billion, with net profits of US$2.64 billion. This breaks down to a domestic market share of 20 percent based on 19.9 million subscribers and revenues of $21.9 billion, while the Latin American market share is 31 percent, with 11.9 million subscribers and revenues totaling $5.1 billion. The company has a workforce of 25,500 full-time and employees.

BRAND AWARENESS

- DIRECTV has maintained a relatively consistent brand concept since its launch in 1994.
- DIRECTV has won awards for being #1 in customer satisfaction in 2007 and again in 2012.
- DIRECTV has an extensive online presence with websites, as well as Facebook, Twitter, Youtube, G +1 and many other social media accounts.

DIRECTV has literally been a household name since June 1994 when the satellite service began broadcasting. Aside from its 20 million customers in the U.S. and 12 million in Latin America, the DIRECTV brand is well known throughout both regions through aggressive marketing via television commercials, magazine, billboard and Internet advertising. The brand is also strongly recognizable to the general public as it has remained consistent with the brand logo and messaging for nearly 20 years now.

Another way in which people recognize DIRECTV is through their two-decade association with professional sports. DIRECTV has been the exclusive provider of NFL Sunday Ticket since 1994 and in 2007 began advertising their brand at major league baseball games with the unveiling of the DIRECTV blimp. The company also has an extensive online presence with websites, as well as Facebook, Twitter, Youtube, G +1, and many other social media accounts. In 2007 DirecTV received the J.D. Power Award for being #1 in customer satisfaction and repeated again with a similar award in 2012 from the American Customer Satisfaction Index.

BRAND OUTLOOK

- DIRECTV prepared for its number of U.S. subscribers to surpass 20 million in 2012.
- DIRECTV will be adding two new satellites to its fleet, one to be launched in 2014 and the other in 2015.
- Nomad is a DIRECTV product that enables subscribers to transfer DVR-recorded content to a tablet, smartphone, or other mobile device.

DIRECTV expected to reach a milestone in 2012 as it prepared to surpass 20 million subscribers in the United States. To keep up with its expanding and evolving customer base, DIRECTV will be adding two new satellites to its fleet, one scheduled to be launched in 2014 and the other in 2015.

Because modern technology gives customers a vast array of entertainment and information choices, DIRECTV plans to begin adding new products and services that go beyond the home television. One such product, called Nomad, enables subscribers to transfer DVR-recorded content to a tablet or other mobile device. DIRECTV is also addressing the ubiquity of Internet usage by offering more DIRECTV movie titles for download and creating applications (apps) for a variety of devices, including tablets, smartphones, and traditional computers. To continue its expansion into communications markets, DIRECTV is also seeking to expand alliances with companies such as AT&T, CenturyLink, and Verizon.

Despite the global recession that has continued to adversely affect economies at every level, DIRECTV and the subscription television market in general have done fairly well. Moving forward, DIRECTV has some positive economic indicators that signal a bright future for the company. According to industry estimates, the Latin American market is gaining momentum in pay-TV growth that is expected to last at least until 2015. During this four-year period total subscriptions are predicted to grow by 74 percent. The overall global pay-TV market is expected to grow between 5 and 8 percent per year by 2015 and presents a tremendous opportunity for DIRECTV to expand into the European and Asian markets.

FURTHER READING

DIRECTV. "Brand Toolbox 5.0." Accessed October 17, 2012. http://directv.sites.depot.vitrue.com/images/Brand%20 Book/5.0_BrandToolbox_HRez.pdf.

———. "DIRECTV 2011 Annual Report." Accessed October 17, 2012.http://files.shareholder.com/downloads/DTV/2126602952x 0x554314/10371236-905D-4AC2-B42A-36E4FBD4F1E7/ Directv_2011_Annual_Report_Updated_As_Printing.pdf.

"DirecTV—A Look at the Latest HD DVRs, Set-Top Boxes, and the 'Nomad.'" *DTVUSAForum*, October 21, 2012. Accessed October 21, 2012. http://www.dtvusaforum.com/blogs/ dtvusaforum-staff/221-directv-look-latest-hd-dvrs-set-top-boxes-nomad.html.

Glassner, Joanna. "DirecTV Buys PrimeStar." *Wired*, January 22, 1999. Accessed October 17, 2012. http://www.wired.com/ techbiz/media/news/1999/01/17479.

Global Data. "The DIRECTV Group, Inc. (DTV)—Financial and Strategic Analysis Review." MarketResearch.com, August 31, 2010. Accessed October 17, 2012. http://www.marketresearch.com/ GlobalData-v3648/DIRECTV-Group-DTV-Financial-Strategic-2797254.

Krause, Reinhardt. "DirecTV Mulls Brazil Deal, May Roil Stock Buyback." *Investor's Business Daily*, October 22, 2011.

Manly, Lorne. "From the Mind of a TV Producer, Satellite Television in a Portable Box." *New York Times*, January 8, 2007.

MarketLine. "DIRECTV Company Profile." *Datamonitor*, September 25, 2012. Accessed October 17, 2012. http://www.datamonitor.com/store/Product/directv? productid=8769D6A3-25E0-402E-A55B-19832D67A0D5.

"Murdoch's DirecTV Purchase 'Approved.'" BBC News, February 9, 2001.

Stettner, Morey."DirecTV Leadership Development Program Is a Big Hit." *Investor's Business Daily*, October 19, 2011.

DISNEY

AT A GLANCE

Brand Synopsis: Synonymous with family values and entertainment, the Disney brand is built on a heritage of creative animated films for children.
Parent Company: The Walt Disney Company
500 S. Buena Vista Street
Burbank, California 91521
United States
http://www.thewaltdisneycompany.com
Sector: Consumer Discretionary
Industry Group: Media: Broadcasting, Entertainment; Travel: Travel and Tourism; Leisure: Recreational Services
Performance: *Market share*—12.2 percent in the United States (2011). *Sales*—US$40.9 billion (2011). *Total assets*—US$72.1 billion (2011).
Principal Competitors: Time Warner; Viacom; Vivendi; NBC Universal; Sony Pictures Entertainment

BRAND ORIGINS

- Disney was the pioneer in developing feature-length animated films.
- Disney exploited its animated celebrities in merchandise, television, and theme parks
- Disney dramatically expanded and diversified into other entertainment products during the 1990s.
- Following the ouster of former CEO Michael Eisner in 2005, the company attempted to revive the original core values of the brand.

The Disney Brothers Cartoon Studios were established in Hollywood, California, in 1923: Walt Disney did the drawing, and his brother Roy managed the finances. The first success of the company was the character Mickey Mouse, who appeared in the synchronized-sound short *Steamboat Willie* in 1928. Following on the great success of *Snow White and the Seven Dwarfs*, a full-length feature cartoon of 1937, the company built the Walt Disney Studios in Burbank, and Walt Disney Productions went public in 1940. The company continued to create feature-length animated films that introduced such well-loved characters as Donald Duck, Dumbo, and Bambi. In the 1950s, Disney produced its first live-action feature film and moved into television (in an alliance with the ABC Network). The company opened its first theme park, Disneyland, in 1955. It continued to produce memorable animated features while increasing its television programming, which included such shows as *The Mickey Mouse Club* and *Davy Crockett*, and its production of live-action films. More theme parks began operating in the 1970s and 1980s, including Walt Disney World and EPCOT in Florida, and the first theme parks were opened outside the United States.

Disney began as a producer of creative content, at first leaving its distribution and marketing to other entities, but in the late 20th century the company formed its own film distribution organization and television channels. Disney merchandise was once sold in numerous retail outlets, but during the 1980s and 1990s, the company developed its own global network of Disney branded stores. Under the leadership of Michael Eisner (1984–2004), the company embarked on an ambitious expansion, enhanced its reputation for creativity with some blockbuster feature films, and aggressively pushed the Disney brand onto new digital platforms with the rise of the Internet. In 1996 Disney merged with Capital Cities/ABC, which brought it into a group of several high-profile television networks, including ABC, ESPN, and A&E. The management team of Eisner and Jeffrey Katzenberg aimed to make the 1990s "the Disney decade" with a global expansion of theme parks and the establishment of several new Disney franchises based on hugely successful films like *The Lion King* (1994) and *Toy Story* (1995).

Some of these decisions shifted the brand far from the core values promoted by Walt Disney. In 1993 Disney acquired Miramax Films, a leader in independent film production with a reputation for confrontational films featuring excessive violence and explicit sex scenes.

Some well-documented missteps, including problems establishing the Euro Disney Resort (now Disneyland Paris), also took the shine off the brand and opened the company to both internal and external criticism. In 2004 Roy E. Disney, Walt's nephew, led a shareholder revolt that eventually ousted Eisner in 2005. Disney promised a return to the values that originally characterized the brand: creativity and quality were to reinvigorate a "rapacious and soulless company." Robert Iger replaced Michael Eisner as CEO, and Roy E. Disney returned to the company as consultant and director.

At the heart of Disney's reputation for innovation and creativity were its feature-length animated films. In the 1990s the dramatic development of digital technology changed the way that cartoons were made and viewed, and Disney responded by releasing its first three-dimensional animated film in 2005 and taking full control of the highly innovative Pixar animation studio in 2006. Disney has moved away from Walt Disney's policy of producing all its characters in-house by exploiting those created by Pixar and by acquiring Marvel Entertainment, with its store of well-known cartoon characters, in 2009.

BRAND ELEMENTS

- Walt Disney's signature was the basis of the company's first brand identifier.
- The brand is associated visually with its many famous cartoon characters.
- Blockbuster hits have provided a steady stream of new characters to associate with the brand.

Like many family owned businesses in the early 20th century, Disney Brothers used its family name as its brand, and true to its identity as a creative company, the Disney name was styled in a flowing cursive hand, in just the way Walt might have signed his name at the bottom of a drawing. This element remains central to the brand today, yet it was soon overtaken by Disney's first successful cartoon character, Mickey Mouse, who remains the global trademark of the company. Mickey Mouse's appearance has changed over the years, becoming more human and less mouse-like, but he is still the face of the company, beloved and recognized by children all over the world. Each blockbuster feature cartoon has added more characters, from Snow White to Buzz Lightyear, to represent the brand.

The establishment of Disneyland provided another widely recognized symbol of the company. The image of the "Sleeping Beauty" castle has been updated and applied to a range of Disney products.

BRAND IDENTITY

- According to Roy E. Disney, the Disney brand is an American icon.
- The history and heritage of the brand are central to its identity.
- In the 21st century Disney has sought to realign itself with family values.
- Creativity and innovation are highly valued elements of the brand's identity.

In a speech to shareholders in 2004, Roy E. Disney claimed that the Disney brand was "an authentic American icon," something that had real meaning for several generations of Americans, as well as millions of other consumers. The values and aspirations of his uncle Walt have prevailed in the brand identity of the company he founded: creativity, quality, and authenticity. Today's Disney Company is far different from the original animation studio of the 1920s, and although Roy E. Disney has not been completely successful in bringing the company back to the financial success or core values of its founder, the Disney Company still enjoys an enviable reputation as a master storyteller whose products, in the words of Walt Disney, speak to the child in all of us.

A business that deals in images and fantasies has a head start in creating a brand identity because its products—animated cartoons, television shows, and theme parks—do the work of establishing that identity. Mickey Mouse plays the twin roles of film star and brand mark.

The Disney Company has constantly affirmed that the core of its identity is to be found in innovation and in supporting the creative people it employs. From the very beginnings of the company, when Walt Disney took a chance on the new technology of talking pictures, innovation and creativity have been key components of its image. The company stresses the quality of its people as well as its products in its promotion of the brand. The public face of Disney might be the characters of its cartoons and television shows, but behind them are a mass of well-publicized employees, from the artists who create the cartoons to the greeters at the theme parks.

Very few of Disney's competitors have corporate histories that stretch back to the beginning of the 20th century or that are as well known to consumers. Disney has exploited this heritage of quality and authenticity in support of the brand. The company has been very successful in marketing images and values of the 19th century—the "good old days" of America that are celebrated in its theme parks and television programming—and this has given rise to the perception that the company has an even longer history. In realizing an idealized American past, Disney has strengthened its heritage and developed the iconic status of characters such as Mickey Mouse and Davy Crockett. In the production and marketing of fantasies, Disney has managed to appropriate legends and images from other times and places and make them part of the brand. The "Sleeping Beauty" castle that is the centerpiece of Disneyland was based on a castle built by King Ludwig of Bavaria, and that 19th-century German structure has, as a result, become part of American popular culture. Possibly no one has realized the power of fantasy more than Walt Disney, and the company that he founded has managed to continually incorporate its characters and stories into its brand identity. Winnie the Pooh, for example, is now associated with the Disney brand, despite a long career in literature before his appearance in Disney's animated feature. Each hit movie has generated more characters that speak for the brand, such as Buzz Lightyear from *Toy Story*.

BRAND STRATEGY

- Disney seeks to maintain its reputation as the family's storyteller.
- Disney's expansion into other media has helped build its brand.
- The Disney brand is only applied to businesses that fit its core values.

Part of Disney's brand strategy is to do whatever it must to protect its image as the family storyteller. The history of Disney has been a history of brand extension, as the company has pursued a strategy of acquisition and diversification. Some of the acquisitions have been beneficial to the brand. Pixar, for example, not only cemented Disney's position as a major producer of feature cartoons, it also enhanced the company's reputation for innovation and creativity. ESPN, the leading sports media brand, brought with it a reputation of quality programming that also enhances the Disney brand. The company has protected the brand by carefully distancing the Disney name from subsidiaries that do not adhere to its family values, such as Miramax, and by forming other companies to front activities and products that do not fit the brand identity. Films with more adult content, for example, have been released under the Touchstone Pictures banner.

There is a perpetual conflict within a brand that was built on a strong sense of its heritage but that is also dependent on a reputation for innovation and creativity. Disney has managed to walk this fine line as it forms new entertainment businesses and finds new platforms for its creative content. The benefit of having cartoon characters represent the company is that they are not fixed in time or in context: Mickey and Minnie have moved effortlessly onto smartphone apps and cruise ships.

BRAND EQUITY

- Disney is often ranked among the top-10 global brands.
- In 2011 Disney ranked ninth among Interbrand's list of the top global brands, with a valuation of US$35 billion.
- In 2012 Disney was ranked 50th in Brand Finance's "Global 500," with a valuation of US$15 billion.

Disney started the 21st century ranked among the top-10 global brands. A 2002 *Business Week*/Interbrand study estimated that the brand contributed 68 percent of the company's market capitalization. In 2011 Interbrand placed Disney at number nine in its list of top global brands with a valuation of US$35 billion. The company was ranked 47th in the *Brandirectory* Global 500 in 2011 but slipped to 50th place in 2012 with a valuation of US$15 billion.

BRAND AWARENESS

- Disney reaches out to consumers at a very early age.
- Its diversified businesses help spread recognition of the brand.
- Disney is perceived as a source of fun and affirmation.

The Disney brand has become ubiquitous as it has aggressively moved into new entertainment media and new products while protecting its heritage of family values and animated celebrities. Those famous characters first appeared on toys for children but can now be found on soap, cashmere sweaters, and wedding gowns since Disney has extended the marketing of its merchandise to affluent adults. A truly global brand that dominates family entertainment, tourism, and media networks, Disney enjoys an enviable level of brand awareness.

Disney cartoons are always full of humor, and Disneyland was conceived as "the happiest place on earth." The cartoons, films, television programming, and tourist destinations cement the brand's association in the minds of consumers with joy and affirmation. This message reaches viewers at a tender age, initiating an association with the company that can last well into middle age. Baby Boomers remember the cartoons, *The Mickey Mouse Club*, and family visits to Disneyland with affection and nostalgia. Disney is thus part of a collective memory that continues to preserve the vision of its founder decades after his death.

BRAND OUTLOOK

- Disney is reliant on the development of new blockbuster franchises.
- Disney is well-positioned to exploit new media technologies.
- Future growth of the brand is anticipated in Asian markets.

Disney entertainment is locked into the blockbuster imperative, which builds franchises based on hit films. While the rewards are great when a film is successful, failure can also generate huge losses: the science fiction film *John Carter* (2012) lost about US$165 million for Disney. The company has a strong library of franchise films that it continues to exploit via sequels, but the future growth of the company depends upon the creation of more blockbusters.

Disney's theme parks have outperformed rivals during a global economic downturn, and it is secure in its top position and market share in the industry. Disney is also well-positioned with regard to emerging media, and although its Internet and Interactive Media Groups are not profitable yet, they have the potential to be profit centers in the future.

Much of the future growth of the company is seen in the emerging entertainment markets in India and China. Disney has established a foothold in these markets, and its theme parks have achieved considerable success. Unlike live-action feature films, animated films can easily reach a global audience, and the focus on developing markets outside the United States bodes well for a company that relies heavily on animation.

FURTHER READING

Barnes, Brooks. "Disney, by Design" *New York Times*, November 5, 2008.

Brand Finance. "Best Global Brands 2012." *Brandirectory*. Accessed September 8, 2012. http://brandirectory.com/league_tables/table/global-500-2012.

Lindemann, Jan. "Brand Valuation." *Brands and Branding*. New York: Interbrand/Economist, 2004. Accessed September 8, 2012. http://www.brandchannel.com/images/papers/financial_value.pdf.

SlideShare. "Sales/Profit Forecast for Walt Disney." Accessed September 9, 2012. http://www.slideshare.net/lokeshg90/walt-disney-annual-report-analysis.

"2011 Ranking of the Top 100 Brands." Interbrand. Accessed September 8, 2012. http://www.interbrand.com/en/best-global-brands/best-global-brands-methodology/Overview.aspx.

Walt Disney Company. *Annual Report 2011*. Accessed September 7, 2012. http://cdn.media.ir.thewaltdisneycompany.com/2011/annual/WDC-10kwrap-2011.pdf.

DFM

AT A GLANCE

Brand Synopsis: Dongfeng Motor Corporation (DFM) means superior quality, safety, and economy through a process of learning and applying that knowledge to surpass the competition.
Parent Company: Dongfeng Motor Corporation
29 Baiye Road
Wuhan, Hubei
China
http://www.dfmc.com.cn/
Sector: Consumer Discretionary
Industry Group: Automobiles & Components
Performance: *Market share*—11.7 percent (2011). *Sales*—US$21.66 billion (2011).
Principal Competitors: Chang'an Automobile (Group) Co., Ltd.; China FAW Group Corporation; Shanghai Automotive Industry Corporation (Group)

BRAND ORIGINS

- DFM began as the Second Automobile Works in 1969, founded under Mao Zedong as a state-owned corporation.
- Although completed in 1969, no significant production came from DFM until 1983, when 30,000 vehicles were produced.
- In 2007 DFM produced 1.1 million vehicles for revenues worth RMB12.8 billion (US$2.1 billion), meeting production goals three years ahead of schedule.
- In 2010 DFM sold 2.7 million vehicles, making it the second best-selling vehicle manufacturer in China.

Founded under Mao Zedong, Dongfeng Motor Corporation began as the Second Automobile Works (SAW) in 1969. The company was given this name because of its primary competitor back then, First Automobile Works (FAW), which is now known as China FAW Group Corporation. Mao decided to build SAW's factory complex in Hubei Province in central China because he believed it would be more secure if China were ever invaded. For many years SAW simply functioned as a support complex to the work that was being completed at FAW. There was no significant production coming from the plant until 1983, when 30,000 vehicles were produced. At about this time SAW was removed from the direct administrative control of the central government, which gave the organization greater freedom in pursuing projects. The first of these was a joint venture with the Cummins Engine Company, which supplied SAW with diesel engines for cargo trucks. This venture allowed SAW to increase its manufacturing volume, so much so that by 1986 it was producing over 100,000 trucks annually.

In 1992 SAW changed its name to Dongfeng Motor Corporation (DFM). Shortly thereafter, the company decided to add light passenger cars to its manufacturing output. The first passenger vehicle to roll off the assembly line was the Fukang DC7140. The result of a joint venture with the French car manufacturer Peugeot S.A., this was a variation on the Citroën ZX. The successful production brought more joint ventures, particularly with major partners such as Honda Motor Co., Ltd. and Nissan Motor Co., Ltd. By 1993 production had increased to 220,000 vehicles with profits of RMB1.49 billion (US$240 million).

In 2001 China entered into the World Trade Organization. DFM benefitted greatly by this development because it opened up possibilities for new international joint ventures. Buoyed by these possibilities, the company crafted a five-year plan that established several goals, including attaining an 18 percent market share by 2005 and reaching an annual production of 1 million units by 2010. The first step toward achieving these goals was to create new joint ventures with current partners.

In 2003 contracts were established with Honda and Peugeot to build a total of 200,000 new vehicles. The company also began negotiations with Kia Motors Corporation and the Yueda Automotive Group that resulted in a total demand for 400,000 new vehicles annually. In July 2003 DFM partnered with Nissan in a joint venture to form the subsidiary Dongfeng Motor Company, Ltd. (DFL), with 50 percent ownership on each side. All new passenger vehicles that came from the plant would have the Nissan brand name, while the commercial vehicles produced would have the Dongfeng brand name. The DFL venture was the largest automotive joint venture in China, and by 2005 it helped propel DFM to being the third-largest automotive manufacturer in China.

In December 2005 the Dongfeng Motor Group Corporation, another subsidiary of DFM, debuted on the Hong Kong Stock Exchange with an initial public offering of 2.5 billion shares priced at US$0.22 per share. In early 2006 construction was completed on a large expansion to the Dongfeng Wuhan plant. The joint venture with Honda would require a dramatic increase in production from 30,000 vehicles annually to 120,000. Another important development in 2005 was the formation of the Dongfeng Peugeot Auto Finance Company. Only 2.4 percent of all Chinese owned a vehicle, so the potential sales market was enormous, especially if something could be done to make purchasing a new vehicle easier. By July 2006 the new company began offering wholesale financing to car dealers, first in Beijing and then nationwide. The financing plan applied only to Dongfeng Peugeot and Citroën vehicles and was backed by the Bank of China.

DFM was growing dramatically because of all the joint ventures it had developed over the years. In 2005 DFM's sales increased 39.4 percent, in 2006 they increased 27.9 percent, and in 2007 they increased 21.9 percent. The growth in sales enabled the company to achieve its 2010 goal of producing over a million vehicles per year three years ahead of schedule. In 2007 DFM produced 1.1 million vehicles for revenues worth RMB12.8 billion (US$2.1 billion) and profits of RMB677.8 million (US$108.8 million). Well over half of the vehicles produced were from the joint venture with Nissan, with over 610,000 units produced. In September 2007 Dongfeng Passenger Vehicle Company, another joint venture with Nissan, began building a new factory for the production of midlevel and luxury sedans. That same year DFM set new targets for 2010, which included a new production goal of 1.6 million vehicles within the next three years. One way it would achieve this goal was through the production of hybrid vehicles, which were becoming increasingly popular. DFM began applying hybrid technology to all of its vehicle types, even trucks and buses. The company also developed several models of hybrid sedans for future testing. In late 2007 DFM and Nissan agreed on yet another joint venture to produce 3.0 liter engines at a recently completed factory in Zhenghou. The factory would build 120,000 of the engines per year as well as light business vehicles.

In late 2008 the global financial crisis hit, causing among other things a significant decrease in the demand for new vehicles of all types. Nearly all of DFM's joint ventures with Nissan, AB Volvo, Renault S.A., and others were adversely impacted. The only production lines not affected were those of Dongfeng Honda, which continued to meet production goals and demand. Through consolidation and restructuring, DFM managed to sell 1.9 million vehicles by the end of 2009. In 2010 DFM sold 2.7 million vehicles, making it the second best-selling vehicle manufacturer in China. In October 2012 Dongfeng acquired a 70 percent stake in the Swedish engineering company T Engineering AB to gain one of the world's best and most knowledgeable teams on vehicle and powertrain electronic controls. The purchase also created potential business opportunities for the company on the international auto market. What was significant about this purchase was that it was DFM's first business foray outside of China.

BRAND ELEMENTS

- In 1992 Second Automobile Works was renamed Dongfeng Motor Corporation (DFM); in Chinese, *dongfeng* means "east wind."
- DFM works closely with world-class auto manufacturers such as Nissan Motor Co., Ltd., Honda Motor Co., Ltd., Kia Motors Corporation, and Peugeot S.A.
- DFM's corporate philosophy is reflected in the slogan "Learn, innovate, surpass."

Dongfeng began in 1969 as the Second Automobile Works. It was given that name because there was already a First Automobile Works. It was not until 1992 that the company name was changed to Dongfeng Motor Corporation (DFM); in Chinese, *dongfeng* means "east wind."

The specific origin and reason for the name are not clear, other than the observation that the Dongfeng company complex is located in the eastern portion of China.

The corporate logo consists of two red *V*s, one upright and one upside down, that are spinning clockwise around one another inside a red circle. This logo is based on the company's name. It is usually placed either to the right of or above the company name, which is spelled in black or red capitalized letters.

DFM has never invested much effort into promoting its own brands. Most of the work the company does is in joint ventures with world-class auto companies, such as Nissan Motor Co., Ltd., Honda Motor Co., Ltd., Kia Motors Corporation, and Peugeot S.A., to manufacture vehicles. These are all massive corporations that already spend millions of dollars each year to promote their own brand names. Even so, DFM does have three specific slogans that represent the company: its official ideology is based on the slogan "Care for every single person and vehicle"; its corporate philosophy is reflected in the slogan "Learn, innovate, surpass"; and its corporate spirit is based on the slogan "Realize the value, shift the future."

BRAND IDENTITY

- DFM has built its brand reputation over the past 30 years by working with some of the elite names in the automotive industry, including Nissan Motor Co., Kia Motors Corporation, Honda Motor Co., AB Volvo, and Peugeot S.A.
- DFM has taken a leadership role in producing and advancing clean-energy vehicles in China through joint ventures with long-time partners Honda and Nissan.
- All of DFM's new clean-energy vehicles meet or exceed the stringent new emissions standards that were recently established by the Chinese government.

Dongfeng Motor Corporation (DFM) does not attempt to directly promote its own brand identity. For the past 30 years the company has worked hard to build a reputation, as the old adage goes, to be judged by the company it keeps. Since 1983 DFM has created multiple joint ventures with some of the biggest international automotive companies in the world, including Nissan Motor Co., Kia Motors Corporation, Peugeot S.A., Renault S.A., AB Volvo, and Honda Motor Co. As long as these titans of the auto industry keep partnering with DFM in joint ventures to help build vehicles, DFM's brand image will continue to thrive.

DFM's primary focus in not on the consumer end of the market but rather on the manufacturing end. When these joint-ventured vehicles are manufactured, they display the brand of the foreign manufacturer, such as Nissan, Honda, or Kia. When it comes time to sell the vehicles, these same foreign manufacturers also take on the lion's share of marketing them to consumers. DFM still makes its money on the sale of the vehicles, but the more well-known brand names are what promote them.

Over the last few years DFM has made significant strides in hybrid and electric vehicle technologies, thanks in large part to its venture partners Honda and Nissan. DFM was one of the very first companies in China to begin producing alternate-fuel vehicles and has recently decided to commit a significant portion of its resources to what it sees as the future of automotive technology. It now strives to be recognized as a leader and promoter of clean-energy vehicles. Recently, the Chinese government established strict emissions laws that took effect in 2013. Due to DFM's foresight and initiative, its new hybrid and electric vehicles will be fully compliant with the new laws.

BRAND STRATEGY

- DFM has experienced explosive growth over the past 30 years by partnering with other vehicle manufacturers in joint ventures rather than directly competing against them.
- DFM had a goal of producing 1 million vehicles annually by 2010, and ended up surpassing that goal in 2007, three years ahead of schedule.
- In 2011 DFM manufactured 3.1 million passenger vehicles and trucks.

Dongfeng Motor Corporation (DFM) exists among a multitude of major vehicle manufacturers around the world in an industry that is both crowded and competitive. It could have attempted to make a name for itself by developing its own line of vehicles and then fighting for some sort of brand recognition, spending untold millions of dollars in the process. Instead, DFM has utilized over the past 30 years a simple yet very effective brand strategy. Rather than developing and promoting its own brand, it partners with globally recognized auto manufacturers to help them build their vehicles better and more inexpensively than they could have done on their own.

Since its first joint venture with the Cummins Engine Company, which supplied DFM with diesel engines for cargo trucks, production has gone up almost exponentially. That first joint venture produced 30,000 commercial trucks. By 1986 the company was producing over 100,000 trucks annually. Then came the first joint venture with Peugeot S.A., which resulted in the Fukang DC7140, a variation of Peugeot's Citroën ZX passenger vehicle. The success of this venture led to partnerships with Nissan Motor Co., Kia Motors Corporation, and Honda Motor Co. By 1993 total production was up to 220,000 vehicles annually. DFM set a goal to produce 1 million vehicles by 2010 and because of its joint ventures it produced 1.1 million vehicles by 2007. In 2011 DFM had a total production of 3.1 million units, and this success was achieved during a global recession.

Currently, DFM is shifting its manufacturing emphasis to hybrid, electric, and other clean-energy vehicles. DFM produces a popular commercial bus under its own brand name, the Dongfeng EQ6110 hybrid electric city bus, that operates at 30 percent better fuel efficiency than regular city buses, while also dramatically lowering emissions. At the Fifth International Clean Vehicle Technology Exhibition in 2011 it unveiled a new fully electric microcar under its own brand name, the Dongfeng Fengshen E30 EV. The vehicle is designed for urban driving with a top speed of 80 kilometers per hour and a range of 110 to 180 kilometers per charge.

BRAND EQUITY

- In 2011 DongFeng Motor Corporation generated a total of US$21.66 billion in revenues.
- DFM is the second-largest vehicle manufacturer in China and had an 11.7 percent market share in 2011.
- In 2012 *Forbes* "Global 2000" list ranked DFM 437th in sales, 369th in profits, 1117th in assets, 565th in market value, and 450th overall.

In 2011 Dongfeng Motor Corporation (DFM) generated a total of US$21.7 billion in revenues on the manufacture and sale of 3.1 million vehicles that were produced at the company's many factories throughout China. Its gross profits were US$4.2 billion, and its net profits were US$1.6 billion. DFM is the second-largest vehicle manufacturer in China and had an 11.7 percent market share in 2011. As of December 31, 2011, the company had 102,219 full-time employees. According to the *Forbes* "Global 2000" list of world's largest companies, DFM ranked 437th in sales, 369th in profits, 1117th in assets, 565th in market value, and 450th overall in 2012.

BRAND AWARENESS

- DFM is the second-largest vehicle manufacturer in China and the number-one manufacturer of Chinese trucks and farm vehicles.
- As a major manufacturer of mass transit buses, DFM is the most-recognized brand in China for public transportation.
- DFM is leading the way in manufacturing clean-energy vehicles to alleviate some of the serious pollution problems in China's major cities.

Within China, Dongfeng Motor Corporation (DFM) is a popular and well-recognized name. DFM is the second-largest vehicle manufacturer in the country and has dozens of large factories located throughout the nation. DFM is also the number-one manufacturer of Chinese trucks and farm vehicles, such as tractors, backhoes, and loaders. So, in China at least, DFM is as popular and well known as, for instance, the Ford Motor Company is in the United States.

When discussing brand awareness in China, however, the answer is more complicated than it would be in other nations. Even though Chinese vehicle manufacturers produce their own brands of vehicles for sale domestically, the majority of most of their production comes from contracts and joint ventures with foreign corporations. For instance, if one were to look at a list of the 10 largest passenger car manufacturers in China, there would be no clear brand names except for Toyota. This is because the list is made up of "manufacturers" and not "brands." The top-10 manufacturers in China make up 86 percent of the total domestic market. The other 14 percent is made up of about 110 smaller manufacturers. The reason brand awareness becomes confusing is because General Motors (GM) may be a brand sold in China, but the vehicles may be manufactured by four of the top-10 manufacturers. As such, there may be a choice of a Shanghai GM, an FAW GM, and a Dongfeng GM. Vehicles sold domestically will usually have both the manufacturer and brand names, while those for export will only show the brand name.

The area in which DFM truly makes its name recognizable by the public is in the production and sales of commercial vehicles. Whereas passenger autos manufactured by DFM primarily sport the foreign brand DFM is partnering with, there is no confusion in the commercial vehicle sector. DFM places its own brand name on the majority of trucks, city buses, and farm vehicles that it manufactures and sells. The brand name is recognized by virtually any company in China that operates trucks, by any member of the general public who uses mass transit, and by anyone in the farming sector, who will undoubtedly be operating DFM farming equipment.

In the near future, DFM will also be widely known throughout China's metropolitan areas for its own brand of clean-energy passenger vehicles. The company is currently working on a variety of makes, models, and engines that will be sold extensively to consumers living in large cities, which as of 2013 have enacted major emissions regulations for all new vehicles. All of DFM's new clean-energy vehicles will conform to these stringent regulations.

BRAND OUTLOOK

- In 2007 DFM set a goal to produce 1.6 million vehicles per year by the end of 2010 but three years later it had actually produced 2.7 million vehicles.
- For 2013 DFM signed a major new joint venture with the German automaker Volkswagen to produce

the Touareg hybrid vehicle and two new fully electric vehicles.

- DFM has set a goal to produce 100,000 hybrid vehicles and 50,000 purely electric vehicles by 2015, and over 800,000 clean-energy vehicles by 2020.

Between 2007 and 2011 DFM grew tremendously in terms of its annual production. In 2007 the company manufactured a total of 1.1 million vehicles, a goal that was achieved three years ahead of schedule. It set a new goal for 2010 of 1.6 million vehicles and ended up producing over 2.7 million. For 2011 the figure was over 3 million vehicles. That same year DFM was the second-largest automaker in China, with revenues of US$21.7 billion, ahead of China FAW Group Corporation, with US$18.9 billion, and behind Shanghai Automotive Industry Corporation, with US$33.6 billion.

The China Association of Automobile Manufacturers (CAAM) notes that auto sales for the first half of 2012 grew by 2.9 percent in comparison to a 3.4 percent increase over the same period in 2011. Overall, China's gross domestic product slowed to 7.6 percent in the second quarter of 2012, marking the lowest quarterly expansion for the country in three years. Factors affecting this slowdown include decreased foreign demands due to the global recession, increased government controls on various sectors, and a structural shift toward domestic demand to compensate for external decreases. Despite all this, CAAM predicts that sales of passenger cars will increase by 11 percent for 2013, while commercial vehicle sales will decrease by 3 percent. Even though these are generally positive numbers, they are still lower than in previous years. Overall, the slowdown in the auto sales market signals the slowing of China's overall economy.

The outlook for DFM generally looks positive. The company has shown strong growth over the last four years, despite the global recession. DFM has gotten an early jump on its Chinese competitors by establishing long-term joint ventures with both Honda Motor Co., Ltd., and Nissan Motor Co., Ltd., to produce a variety of hybrid vehicles. The company also formed a new joint venture with the German automaker Volkswagen, which will introduce its own hybrid vehicle, the Touareg, and two all-electric vehicles, the Golf and Lavida, in China all in 2013. Recently, DFM announced a goal to produce 100,000 hybrid vehicles and 50,000 all-electric vehicles by 2015 and over 800,000 clean-energy vehicles by 2020. It has allocated CNY3 billion (US$482 million) to put this plan into motion.

FURTHER READING

"China's Auto Sales Expected to Hit 20m in 2012." Chinadaily.com.cn, July 27, 2012. Accessed February 12, 2013. http://www.chinadaily.com.cn/bizchina/2012-07/27/content_15622925.htm.

"DongFeng." Yahoo.com. Accessed February 12, 2013. http://finance.yahoo.com/q?s=0489.HK&ql=1.

Dongfeng Motor Corporation. "Corporate Profile." Accessed February 12, 2013. http://www.dfmc.com.cn/info/managerAddress_en.aspx.

———. "General Manager's Address." Accessed February 12, 2013. http://www.dfmc.com.cn/info/managerAddress_en.aspx.

———. *2011 Annual Report*. Accessed February 12, 2013. http://quote.morningstar.com/stock-filing/Annual-Report/2011/12/31/t.aspx?t=XHKG:00489&ft=&d=e4cc76685ffba10fb74edae0e903f57b.

"Dongfeng Motor Corporation." *International Directory of Company Histories*. Ed. Jay P. Pederson. Vol. 105. Detroit, MI: St. James Press, 2010.

"Global 2000 List: DongFeng Motor." *Forbes*. Accessed February 12, 2013. http://www.forbes.com/companies/dongfeng-motor/.

Ning, W. E. "Dongfeng Sets up R&D Center in Sweden." CarNewsChina.com, October 18, 2012. Accessed February 12, 2013. http://www.carnewschina.com/2012/10/18/dongfeng-sets-up-rd-center-in-sweden/.

Schmitt, Bertel. "China Car Market 101: Who Makes All Those 18 Million Cars?" The Truth about Cars, January 19, 2011. Accessed February 12, 2013. http://www.thetruthaboutcars.com/2011/01/china-car-market-101-who-makes-all-those-18-million-cars/.

DOVE

AT A GLANCE

Brand Synopsis: A leading personal care brand, Dove emphasizes quality, purity, personal beauty, and self-acceptance.
Parent Company: Unilever
Unilever House
Springfield Drive
Leatherhead, KT22 7GR
United Kingdom
http://www.unilever.com/
Sector: Consumer Staples
Industry Group: Household & Personal Products
Performance: *Market share*—3.4 percent of the U.S. mens' body wash market (2011); 4 percent of the U.S. nondeodorant bar soap market.
Principal Competitors: Dial; Garnier; Ivory; Olay; Neutrogena; Nivea; Pantene

BRAND ORIGINS

- Dove was introduced in the 1950s.
- Since 1957 Dove has called itself a beauty bar, not a soap, and emphasized its mild and nondrying qualities.
- The "Campaign for Real Beauty" helped build Dove sales after its introduction in 2003.

A company with a long history in the soap industry, Lever Brothers Company introduced the Dove Beauty Bar in the 1950s and launched the Dove brand. Lever Brothers had its origins in 19th-century England. William Hesketh Lever formed Lever Brothers in England in 1855 with his brother James. Lever Brothers became the world's largest soap seller and, after a merger with a Dutch company, became Unilever in 1930.

During World War II, a formula similar to the later Dove Original Beauty Bar was developed as a nonirritating skin-cleanser to treat the burned and the wounded. After the war, consumers sought soaps that were gentler to the skin. American scientists refined the formula and commercialized the Original Dove Beauty Bar. Originally launched in the 1950s in the United Kingdom as a moisturizing soap, it was repositioned as early as 1957 as a "beauty bar."

From the first, Dove focused on female consumers and emphasized that clinical research supported its moisturizing claims. Early advertisements emphasized that Dove was milder on the skin than all other leading brands. Such ads featured the tagline, "Soap dries your skin, but Dove *creams* your skin while you wash."

Original Dove became available nationwide in the United States in the 1960s. Similar bar skin-cleansers gained a 15 percent to 20 percent share of the market within a few years of introduction in the United States, but Ivory soon emerged as the market leader. With focused marketing and continued emphasis in 1970s on the fact that dermatological tests showed that Dove was less irritating and drying than ordinary soaps, the brand gained market share both in the United States and around the world.

In the 1980s, Dove became the number-one physician-recommended cleansing bar in the world, helping Unilever to become dominant globally. In 1983 Dove finally unseated long-time soap market-leader Ivory. Dove gained nearly a 12 percent market share in 1984, but then lost the top spot to Dial. In 1989, however, Dove retook the top spot on the strength of a consumer movement toward upscale moisturizing products. New products were introduced in this time period, including White Unscented Dove Beauty Bar in the 1980s and Original and Unscented Liquid Dove Beauty Wash in 1990.

By 1991 the beauty segment accounted for 32 percent of total bar-soap dollar sales, and Dove passed Procter & Gamble in toilet soap revenue, becoming the number-one brand in the US$1.5 billion bar-soap category. Unilever cultivated the growth of the Dove brand by repositioning the product intelligently and capitalizing on the brand's image as a nondrying beauty bar. In the early 1990s, Lever advertised Dove as the number-one dermatologist-recommended cleanser.

Sales increased greatly in the early to mid-1990s through effective brand-building and market expansion. In 1992 the Dove Beauty Bar was launched as a new brand in Europe, supported by a brand strategy created to communicate a high quality, functional identity via major advertising and promotions. In the United States in the mid-1990s, Dove was the number-one-selling toilet soap, with a 16.5 percent market share and sales of US$235 million.

Beginning in 1995 and on into the early 21st century, Dove expanded its line of skin cleansers and later added personal care products. Sales reached about US$1 billion dollars in 1999, and were growing about 20 percent annually. By 2001 Dove was selling hair care products and antiperspirants/deodorants, and it added firming lotions and lifting creams by 2004 as well.

In 2003 the Dove brand launched one of the biggest advertising efforts in Unilever's history: the "Campaign for Real Beauty." It did not just promote Dove brands but sought to redefine what was beautiful, beyond the models who normally helped sell such products. The campaign's ads featured real women of various sizes in their undergarments. Spreading to at least ten countries, the "Campaign for Real Beauty" helped increase sales by 13 percent to 25 percent, and the brand gained at least US$1.2 billion in value. By 2005 Dove was largest cleansing-brand in the world, sold in 80 countries.

Building on the success created by the "Campaign for Real Beauty," Dove continued to add new products for women, including anti-aging and toning brands. By 2010 it had added products for men, under the Dove Men+Care name, including body and facial washes and deodorants/antiperspirants. While sales in the United States grew rapidly, at 9.8 percent in 2011, there was more focus on emerging markets in Asia and Latin America. Sales of Dove exceeded EUR3 billion in 2011.

BRAND ELEMENTS

- The Dove Beauty Bar was a pioneering product, the first cleansing beauty-bar with moisturizing cream.
- The Dove Beauty Bar forms the core of the brand.
- The Dove logo consists of the Dove name in italics and a semi-abstract silhouette of a dove underneath.

Developed in the mid-1950s, Original Dove Beauty Bar, still on the market today as the Dove Beauty Bar, was the first cleansing beauty bar containing moisturizing cream. Originally developed for people with burns and wounds during World War II, the Dove formulation contains two principal ingredients: an ester of vegetable-oil fatty acids to provide cleansing and lathering properties in hard or soft water and a substance commonly used in cleansing creams to provide mildness and moisturizing benefits. Unilever developed a special production process that made it cost-effective to mass-produce the mild, esterified cleansing agent in Dove.

The Dove Beauty Bar, then, is composed primarily of synthetic detergents and fillers. The active ingredient is a relatively mild surfactant that is combined with a high level of stearic acid, presumably providing the "1/4 moisturizing cream" often mentioned in advertising. This bar and formulation formed the core of the Dove brand.

Since the introduction of the Original Dove Beauty Bar, the brand's products and advertisements have featured the Dove logo. The Dove name is often presented in blue in a special, italic-style font with a small, semi-abstract silhouette of a tan dove underneath. The color scheme changes for various products and lines. Dove Men+Care often features white lettering and a gray dove. The Dove name and symbol honor Dove's origins as a gentle cleanser for World War II burn and wound victims. The dove, or peace pigeon, is also seen as a representation of the brand's purity and mildness.

BRAND IDENTITY

- The qualities of the Dove Beauty Bar defined the brand for decades.
- The "Campaign for Real Beauty" positioned Dove as an advocate brand.
- Dove moved away from its image as a feminine brand with its line for men, Dove Men+Care.

Though Dove's identity has changed over the years, the core product of the brand, the Original Dove Beauty Bar, has been successfully marketed as a nondrying, moisturizing, mild, dermatologist-recommended cleanser. From the 1970s until the 1990s, Dove's advertising emphasized that endorsement from medical doctors. Advertisements included taglines like "Dove creams your skin while you wash" and "For softer, smoother skin switch to Dove." Later, an emphasis on the Beauty Bar's moisturizing qualities led

Unilever to use the slogan "Dove is 1/4 moisturizing cream." It was modified to "Dove contains 1/4 moisturizing cream. It won't dry your face like soap." The new claim emphasized that skin care went beyond simple cleaning.

As Dove added more products to its brand line, beginning in the mid-1990s and especially after 2000, it continued to market itself as a brand that was effective and of high quality. In 2003 the brand redefined itself with its US$100 million, groundbreaking "Campaign for Real Beauty." Dove assured its users that all women, of all ages, shapes, and sizes were beautiful, and the campaign demonstrated that Dove did not buy into the standards for beauty set by professional models and fashion magazines. The ads for the campaign featured real women of various sizes showing their bodies.

As part of this five-year campaign, Dove had a related website on which the concept of beauty was examined in polls and online forums. There was also a related philanthropic effort, done in conjunction with the Girl Scouts, to fund a program called "Uniquely Me!" to improve self-esteem in girls aged 8 to 17. In 2010 the "Campaign for Real Beauty" was turned into a kind of social movement, the "Dove Movement for Self-Esteem," aimed at the next generation and continuing Dove's image as an advocate brand.

By 2013 Dove ads for its body cleansers returned to describing how Dove stood out from its competitors. These ads, many for reformulated Dove beauty bars and washes, featured such taglines as "Soap Strips Your Skin. Dove Is Different" and "Your Body Wash Might Be Harsher Than You Think." The brand also had a dedicated YouTube Channel providing information on products and presenting promotions like "Dove Body Language" and "Dove: Litmus Test."

When Dove introduced its line for men, Dove Men+Care, in 2010, the brand had to overcome the fact that Dove was identified as feminine. To attract male consumers, Dove Men+Care hired sports-related personalities to appear in advertisements. In 2011 Dove Men+Care ads in the United States focused on the concept of a "Journey to Comfort," focusing on families and featuring ESPN commentator Kirk Herbstreit and former NBA star Magic Johnson, among others. In 2012 in Canada, two former professional hockey athletes were hired as brand ambassadors.

BRAND STRATEGY

- The first Dove brand extension was the White Unscented Dove Beauty Bar in the 1980s.
- In 2010 Dove debuted a line of personal care products for men, Dove Men+Care.
- International markets have been key to Dove's success in the early 21st century.

From the 1950s to 1980s, the Original Dove Beauty Bar was Dove's only product. The brand introduced White Unscented Dove Beauty Bar in the 1980s and Original and Unscented Liquid Dove Beauty Wash in 1990. By the mid-1990s, Unilever introduced Dove Dishwashing Liquid, though it was later taken off the market. Dove began adding to its product line in earnest in the mid-1990s through the early 2010s, to become not just a beauty-bar brand but one that was a major player in the beauty and personal care category. These extensions included body lotions, firming lotions, hair care products (including various shampoos, conditioners, treatments, and style products), and deodorants/antiperspirants.

Other lines with the Dove name were more specialized. In 2006 the brand lent its name to a line of beauty products, Dove Spa, in the United Kingdom. Developed with a spa operator, Dove Spa was put on the market in conjunction with the opening of a Dove-branded spa in Surrey, England, and featured 39 products. In 2010 Dove debuted a line of products for men, Dove Men+Care, and added to it over the next few years. Dove Men+Care included body and facial wash, body and facial bar soaps, antiperspirants/deodorants, and hair care products.

Though Dove began in the United Kingdom in the 1950s, it expanded to the United States in the 1960s and other international markets soon after. Over the years, Dove focused on international markets as part of a greater Unilever strategy to pursue growth. In 2012 emerging markets had sales growth of 11.4 percent for Unilever and accounted for 55 percent of Unilever's revenues. While efforts like "Campaign for Beauty" were international in scope, Dove created advertising and marketing efforts specifically for emerging markets. For example, Dove was a relatively small brand in China until a creative campaign called "Better Than Milk" in 2010 helped propel Dove into a greater market share for its body wash.

BRAND EQUITY

- Dove is positioned as a valuable global brand and a leading brand of personal care items.
- Dove was a part of Unilever's personal care division, which saw significant growth in 2011.
- Dove had a high brand value, ranked number four on BrandZ's list of movers and shakers in personal care for 2012.

Sales of the Dove brand exceeded EUR3 billion globally in 2011, driven by the successful introduction of new products and lines like Dove Men+Care. That year, the personal care division of Unilever, which included Dove, had sales growth of 8.2 percent, with total sales of EUR15.5 billion. Globally, Dove had significant market share in a number of categories, including skin cleansing and deodorants/antiperspirants.

Dove had a high brand value. According to the "BrandZ Top 100 Most Valuable Global Brands 2012," Dove was number four on its list of movers and shakers in personal care products, with a brand value of US$4.696 billion, an increase of 23 percent over 2011. In Brand Finance's *Global 500* for 2012, a ranking of leading global brands, Dove was ranked 199. It had a brand value of US$5.045 billion and an enterprise value of US$10.250 billion. Brand Finance also ranked Dove number seven on its list of *Top 50 Cosmetics Brands* and number 22 on its list of *UK Most Valuable Brands* for 2012.

BRAND AWARENESS

- Initially, the Original Dove Beauty Bar and the Dove brand were niche items.
- By the late 20th century, Dove had high brand value and awareness because of effective marketing campaigns.
- In 2012 Dove ranked number four in surveys of the most desired brands for both men and women in the United States.

When Dove was introduced in the late 1950s, it was a niche item with limited visibility, until the brand began advertising extensively in key markets such as the United States in the 1960s. Through its marketing efforts over the years, Dove assured consumers that its primary product, the Dove Beauty Bar, was quite different from the soaps on the market because of its moisturizing properties. Dove built on this brand awareness through the last decades of the 20th century, positioning itself well for expansion into new lines, such as hair care, body lotions, antiperspirants/deodorants, and items for men. Dove was seen as having a high value, and came to be seen as a premium brand. Dove's groundbreaking "Campaign for Beauty," which began in 2003 and lasted until approximately 2010, also brought widespread attention to the brand beyond its products, becuase it emphasized that all women are beautiful just as they are. Consumer studies emphasize Dove's widespread appeal. In 2012 Buyology ranked the *Most Desired Brands in the U.S.: Men* and the *Most Desired Brands in the U.S.: Women*; Dove ranked number four in both lists.

BRAND OUTLOOK

- Consumers continued to spend money on high-quality personal care items like Dove, during the worldwide economic recession that began in 2008.
- In the early 2010s, Dove focused on growing its share in emerging markets and in the men's personal-care category.
- The Dove Self-Esteem Program gave the brand a positive identity, reached millions of girls, and was expected to contribute to the brand's long-term growth.

Despite the global economic downturn that began in 2008 and had not fully abated by the early 2010s, consumers still valued personal grooming, though the buying of private-label items increased in times of economic distress. Consumers wanted items that were effective, and brands like Dove stayed strong. Dove's sales continued to increase in the early 21st century as the brand understood and took advantage of emerging markets like China and the growing men's market, especially in developed economies like the United States. Emerging markets grew in double digits for Unilever, at 11.5 percent in 2011 and 11.4 percent in 2012.

Dove's strong advertising campaigns and use of online and social media helped build the brand, and these measures were expected to contribute to continued success in the 2010s. The Dove Self-Esteem Program was also expected to reap long-term benefits for the brand. The program provided tools and resources to build girls' self-esteem and address their appearance-related anxieties. This program began in 2005 as "Uniquely Me!," and between 2005 and 2011, over 8.5 million girls participated. In 2011 the Dove Self Esteem Program had one million participants in 26 countries. For 2015, the brand had set a goal of reaching a total of 15 million girls.

FURTHER READING

Brand Finance. "Dove." *Brandirectory*. Accessed January 27, 2013. http://www.rankingthebrands.com/Brand-detail.aspx?brandID=1015.

"BrandZ Top 100 Most Valuable Global Brands 2012." Millward Brown. Accessed January 27, 2013. http://www.millwardbrown.com/brandz/2012/Documents/2012_BrandZ_Top100_Report.pdf.

"Dove." RankingTheBrands.com. Accessed January 27, 2013. http://www.rankingthebrands.com/Brand-detail.aspx?brandID=1015.

"Dove Spreads Its Wings." *Grocer*, April 22, 2006.

Kolstad, Jonathan, and Judson Knight. "Unilver PLC." *Encyclopedia of Major Marketing Campaigns*. Vol. 2. Detroit, MI: Gale, 2007.

Maxfield, Doris Morris. "Dove." *Encyclopedia of Consumer Brands, Vol. 2: Personal Products*. Ed. Janice Jorgensen. Detroit, MI: St. James Press.

Neff, Jack. "Dove's Second Act Generates Strong Sales." *Advertising Age*, November 28, 2011.

Newman, Andrew Adam. "Dove Shows Athletes off the Court." *New York Times*, March 6, 2011.

Unilever. *Annual Report and Accounts 2011*. Accessed January 27, 2013. http://www.unilever.co.uk/Images/Unilever_AR11_tcm28-283849.pdf

DR PEPPER

AT A GLANCE

Brand Synopsis: As America's oldest soft drink, Dr Pepper differentiates itself from the competition with a flavor that is "Always One of a Kind" in comparison to traditional colas.
Parent Company: Dr Pepper Snapple Group, Inc.
5301 Legacy Dr.
Plano, Texas 75024
United States
http://www.drpeppersnapple.com
Sector: Consumer Staples
Industry Group: Food, Beverage & Tobacco
Performance: *Sales*—US$5.9 billion (2011).
Principal Competitors: Coca-Cola Company; PepsiCo Inc.

BRAND ORIGINS

- In 1885 a pharmacist in Waco, Texas, named Charles C. Alderton invented Dr Pepper in Morrison's Old Corner Drug Store.
- During the 1970s Dr Pepper was promoted through its memorable and long-running "Be a Pepper" campaign.
- Dr Pepper Snapple Group was formed in 2008 when Cadbury Schweppes spun off Cadbury Schweppes Americas Beverages.
- In 2010 Dr Pepper celebrated its 125th anniversary.

Dr Pepper was invented in Waco, Texas, at Morrison's Old Corner Drug Store. In 1885 a young pharmacist who worked for Morrison's, Charles C. Alderton, experimented on his own soft drink. He mixed phosphorescent water, fruit juice, sugar, and other ingredients to produce a new soft drink. With Morrison's approval, Alderton offered the drink to the store's customers. One of them jokingly called the concoction "Dr. Pepper's drink." This was a reference to Dr. Charles Pepper, the disapproving father of a woman Morrison had been courting. The hope was that Pepper might be flattered.

The name and the soft drink, with its tart yet sweet flavor, became popular locally, and in 1887 Morrison offered beverage chemist Robert S. Lazenby the opportunity to participate in its marketing and development. After sampling "Dr. Pepper's drink," Lazenby agreed to go into partnership with Morrison to produce the beverage at his Circle A Ginger Ale Company, also in Waco. Alderton, the drink's inventor, dissociated himself from Dr Pepper, opting instead to turn his talents to the pharmaceutical trade.

The new product, "Dr. Pepper's Phos-Ferrates," was available only in soda fountains until 1891, when the manufacturers began bottling the beverage. With Lazenby handling the business end, Dr Pepper became a top seller in and around Texas. Expansion was inevitable, and Lazenby found an excellent marketing opportunity in the 1904 World's Fair, where samples were offered to some of the approximately 20 million attendees. Dr Pepper's success encouraged Lazenby and Morrison, who founded the Artesian Manufacturing and Bottling Company, which would eventually be renamed the Dr Pepper Company. By 1923 headquarters were moved from Waco to Dallas, Texas.

Although its unique flavor was a distinguishing factor, Dr Pepper was not marketed simply as a refreshment during its first decades, but was instead promoted as a health drink. The postwar period saw the baby boom, which produced an unprecedented number of soft drink consumers. In its marketing efforts, Dr Pepper sought to appeal to this lucrative market. Dr Pepper became a regular sponsor of the hit teen show "American Bandstand," and during the 1970s was marketed through the long-running "Be a Pepper" campaign. Later advertising efforts avoided the so-called cola wars of the 1980s, focusing instead on what made Dr Pepper different. Dr Pepper ads declared the soft drink was "just what the doctor ordered," while Diet Dr Pepper was "the taste you've been looking for."

During the 1990s Dr Pepper was supported by significant levels of advertising spending. For example, in 1993 the brand was supported by a US$60 million broadcast advertising budget, which then was the largest to date. In 1998 the brand achieved a growth rate of 6 percent, outclassing overall industry growth by a factor of two. During the 21st century's first decade the company unveiled a number of memorable advertising campaigns, including advertisements featuring well-known musicians like Garth Brooks. A special milestone was reached in 2010 when Dr Pepper celebrated its 125th anniversary.

BRAND ELEMENTS

- Dr Pepper's formula consists of a blend of 23 different flavors.
- The Dr Pepper brand is available in a number of different variations.
- Dr Pepper has its own unique bottle design.
- Dr Pepper's marketing slogan has been tailored specifically for the Hispanic market through the use of the word *inconfundible*, or "unmistakable."

Dr Pepper's original formula, developed in 1885 by pharmacist Charles C. Alderton, was a mixture of phosphorescent water, fruit juice, sugar, and other ingredients first known as "Dr. Pepper's Phos-Ferrates." Although its unique flavor was a distinguishing factor, Dr Pepper was mainly promoted as a health drink. The beverage was labelled "Dr. Pepper" until the 1950s, at which time the period was deleted.

Dr Pepper's formula consists of a blend of 23 different flavors. The brand is available in a number of different variations. These include Regular, Diet, Cherry, Cherry Vanilla, Diet Cherry Chocolate, Berries & Cream, and a low-calorie iteration for males named Dr Pepper TEN.

During the early-to-mid-20th century Dr Pepper was packaged in glass bottles featuring a white circle crossed by a burgundy band that featured the brand's name. Labels included the numbers 10, 2, and 4, in order to promote the beverage's ability to provide a pick-me-up during those times of the day. In 2012 Dr Pepper's packaging was burgundy in color, featuring the company logo. The logo displayed the brand name in white type on an angled, burgundy oval, which also included the subhead, "Est. 1885." Dr Pepper has its own unique bottle design. The proprietary 20-ounce Angle Bottle was developed for Dr Pepper in 1996 and adopted by the majority of bottlers the following year.

Dr Pepper Snapple Group (DPS) generates nearly 90 percent of its sales in the United States. However, Mexico and the Caribbean represent 7 percent of sales and the Hispanic market is an important part of the company's growth strategy. DPS has used its unique flavor as a key element in promotions to the Hispanic market. According to a 2005 *Advertising Age* article, Dr Pepper's marketing slogan has been tailored specifically for the Hispanic market through the use of the word *inconfundible*, or "unmistakable."

BRAND IDENTITY

- Dr Pepper has long been known for its unique brand position in the soft drink market, as well as for its loyal customer base.
- The uniqueness of the Dr Pepper brand has been promoted with a variety of slogans, including the 2012 "Always One of a Kind" campaign.
- One important element of Dr Pepper's identity is its position as the United States' oldest major soft drink.

Dr Pepper has long been known for its unique brand position in the soft drink market, as well as for its loyal customer base. The brand has promoted its unique identity to consumers with a variety of slogans, including the well-known "I'm a Pepper," which was introduced in 1977, and 2012's "Always One of a Kind." Another important element of the brand's identity is its position as the United States' oldest major soft drink.

In its May 2010 issue, *Beverage Industry* reported how Dr Pepper's growth over the previous two decades had hinged upon the brand's ability to stay in touch with customers. Dr Pepper Snapple Group Executive Vice President of Marketing Jim Trebilcock explained: "The way we make it relevant is by staying close to our loyal Dr Pepper drinkers, but also being very keen on understanding why consumers are drinking Dr Pepper either not at all or infrequently. We then put together programs and messaging to be able to attract new users into the category."

BRAND STRATEGY

- Dr Pepper has benefited from a long and successful brand strategy, resulting in 4 percent annual growth between 1990 and 2010.
- Beyond traditional advertising, the Dr Pepper brand strategy involves tactics such as sponsorship marketing, social media, and product licensing.

- DPS has a long heritage of building the Dr Pepper brand among Hispanic consumers.
- Dr Pepper TEN, a 10-calorie drink for male consumers, was launched in 2011.

Dr Pepper has benefited from a long and successful brand strategy. Between 1990 and 2010 the brand grew at an annual rate of 4 percent. Despite difficult market conditions, stiff competition, and the fact that overall soft drink consumption was declining, the brand remained strong in 2012. For example, during the first half of the year alone Dr Pepper achieved 1 percent growth, or 1 million cases.

Dr Pepper's brand strategy has concentrated on increasing utilization by loyal customers and finding ways to remove utilization barriers for the brand's lighter users. These objectives are accomplished via several different tactics, including traditional advertising. DPS expenditures for television, print, and radio ads (for Dr Pepper and the company's other brands) have grown steadily, reaching US$409 million in 2009, US$445 million in 2010, and US$460 million in 2011.

Beyond traditional advertising, sponsorships and entertainment-related initiatives also have been used to grow the Dr Pepper brand. For example, in 2009 the company sponsored a party deck on the upper concourse of the new Dallas Cowboys Stadium called the Dr Pepper Starbar. In 2012 Dr Pepper entered into a seven-year agreement with the Chicago Bears. The deal, which was worth an estimated US$3 million, was the first of its kind for Dr Pepper and one of the National Football League's largest. It saw Dr Pepper replace Coca-Cola as the exclusive nonalcoholic drink-provider at the team's stadium, Soldier Field.

Social media is another key component of Dr Pepper's brand strategy. In 2012 Facebook unveiled new brand pages designed specifically for companies. In addition to having its own Dr Pepper brand page, DPS was given the opportunity to pilot test a new type of Facebook ad. This ensured that roughly 80 percent of Dr Pepper's 11 million Facebook fans saw the posts made on its new brand page.

It also was in 2012 that Dr Pepper won a Marketing Society Award for Excellence in connection with its online game, The Pepperhood, which could be played through Facebook, as well as the Web and mobile devices. The game allowed DPS to establish stronger connections between the brand and 16- to 18-year-old boys. Research conducted by Facebook and Nielsen revealed that approximately 2.3 million consumers were more likely to buy Dr Pepper as a result of the game, which involved the delivery of approximately 25,700 coupons.

Product licensing provides Dr Pepper with other opportunities to connect with consumers in new ways. In 2012 DPS ranked 71st on *License!*'s ranking of the world's top 125 global licensors. Examples of nonbeverage product licenses include Lip Smackers Dr Pepper–flavored lip balm and Jelly Belly gourmet jelly beans, as well as various forms of branded apparel.

Ethnic marketing is another key element of the Dr Pepper brand strategy. In particular, DPS has a long heritage of building the Dr Pepper brand among Hispanic consumers. In 1987 the brand became a major sponsor of the Hispanic Heritage Awards. By 2005 a Hispanic marketing manager had been hired to develop strategies focusing on both acculturated English-speaking Hispanics and nonacculturated Hispanics who had been in the United States for less than five years. In 2010 DPS Executive Vice President of Marketing Jim Trebilcock told *Beverage Industry* that the company saw long-term growth opportunities within the Hispanic market. This was evidenced by DPS's sponsorship of the Latin GRAMMY Awards in 2011.

Strategic growth of the Dr Pepper brand has also occurred through the introduction of new products. An excellent example of this is Dr Pepper TEN, a 10-calorie drink introduced in 2011 that is intended exclusively for male consumers. Dr Pepper TEN was developed to meet the needs of male consumers who wanted a lower-calorie option, yet were dissatisfied with diet drinks. In addition to using masculine packaging, Dr Pepper TEN was promoted with a marketing campaign that touted, "It's Not for Women." Prior to a nationwide launch of Dr Pepper TEN, pilot-testing in select markets resulted in a 6 percent volume increase for the entire Dr Pepper product range.

BRAND EQUITY

- DPS was the third-leading soft drink manufacturer worldwide in 2010, with 17 percent market share.
- As the United States' oldest major soft drink brand, Dr Pepper has significant brand equity.
- According to DPS, in 2011 Dr Pepper was the leading brand in its flavor category, and the nation's second-leading flavored carbonated soft drink.

Citing figures from Euromonitor, *Market Share Reporter* indicated that DPS was the third-leading soft drink manufacturer worldwide in 2010, with 17 percent market share. This compared to industry leader Coca-Cola (42 percent) and second-place PepsiCo (29 percent). According to *Investor's Business Daily*, in 2011 Coca-Cola, PepsiCo, and DPS collectively accounted for 88 percent of retail beverage sales in the United States. That year DPS reported that Coca-Cola and PepsiCo held a combined 62 percent of the U.S. liquid-refreshment beverage market.

Unlike Coke and Pepsi, Dr Pepper was not included in Interbrand's ranking of the top 100 global brands in 2011. However, as the United States' oldest major soft drink brand, Dr Pepper still has significant value. According to

DPS, in 2011 Dr Pepper was the leading brand in its flavor category, and the nation's second-leading flavored carbonated soft drink.

Dr Pepper's brand equity also is reflected in the areas of advertising spending and intellectual property. In 2011 DPS had a trademark portfolio that included some 2,400 applications and registrations. DPS's advertising expenditures totaled US$460 million in 2011, up from US$445 million in 2010 and US$409 million in 2009. Although these figures are not specific to Dr Pepper, as DPS's flagship brand it is believed to account for a significant share of these expenditures.

BRAND AWARENESS

- The Dr Pepper brand dates back more than 125 years.
- According to a 2012 Harris Interactive poll, Dr Pepper was ranked by consumers as the fifth-leading soft drink brand of the year.
- In 2005 DPS discovered that acculturated, English-speaking Hispanics consumed 62 percent more Dr Pepper than the overall market.
- In 2012 building and maintaining awareness in the Hispanic market continued to be a priority for DPS.

The Dr Pepper brand dates back more than 125 years. During that time the brand has capitalized on its unique attributes and amassed a loyal following. DPS supports Dr Pepper and its other brands with a steadily increasing advertising budget, which totaled US$460 million in 2011.

In its April 27, 2012, issue, *just-drinks* shared the results of a Harris Interactive poll that attempted to measure the degree to which consumers were connected with approximately 1,500 U.S. brands. Results were gleaned from approximately 38,500 respondents. Using attributes such as purchase consideration, familiarity, and quality, the highest percentage scores represented the strongest consumer-brand bonds. Within the soft drink category, the Dr Pepper brand ranked fifth (66.08 percent), behind 7UP (67.32 percent), Sprite (68.05 percent), Pepsi-Cola (70.07 percent), and first-place Coca-Cola (72.30 percent).

During the early 21st century, DPS devoted significant resources to build the Dr Pepper brand among Hispanic consumers, who generally prefer fruit-flavored beverages more than non-Hispanics do. According to the June 20, 2005, issue of *Advertising Age*, at that time the company discovered that acculturated, English-speaking Hispanics consumed 62 percent more Dr Pepper than the overall market. In 2012 building and maintaining awareness in the Hispanic market continued to be a priority for DPS.

BRAND OUTLOOK

- DPS views its smaller size as a competitive advantage, allowing the company to be quicker and more nimble.
- In 2011 alone DPS invested US$15 million in research and development initiatives, boding well for innovative new variations of the Dr Pepper brand.
- One major challenge faced by DPS and other beverage manufacturers was the fact that fewer Americans were consuming soda in 2012.

In its 2011 annual report, DPS indicated that the company's smaller size was a competitive advantage, allowing it to be quicker and more nimble. In particular, DPS felt this would be beneficial at the local level, as the company and its sales force worked to drive retail sales. Chairman Wayne Sanders and President and CEO Larry Young indicated that DPS would continue to devote strong marketing support to the company's brands, with a focus on increasing awareness, conducting product trials, and eliminating barriers to product purchases.

In addition, DPS indicated that it would continue to strengthen its understanding of consumers, as part of an effort to further hone its retail strategy. In 2011 alone DPS invested US$15 million in research and development initiatives. This was a positive reflection of the company's ability to continue developing innovative new variations of the Dr Pepper brand.

One major challenge that DPS and other beverage manufacturers faced was the fact that fewer Americans were consuming soda in 2012. Rising health consciousness in general and concerns over childhood obesity were potential roadblocks to increasing the consumption. In 2012 New York City Mayor Michael Bloomberg proposed a ban on single-serve soft drinks larger than 16 ounces within the city. Some industry observers suggested that this could establish a national precedent.

The fact that DPS planned to devote at least half of its new products to the health and wellness category by 2015 boded well for the company's ability to contend with declining soda consumption. However, products such as Dr Pepper TEN also gave consumers new options for enjoying the brand while remaining health-conscious. In addition to Dr Pepper, DPS planned to implement TEN-style variations of other soft drinks in its portfolio.

FURTHER READING

"Dr Pepper Engages Consumers in 125th Anniversary Celebration." *Beverage Industry*, February 2010.

"Dr Pepper Introduces the 10 Hardest-Working Calories in the Beverage Business: Dr Pepper TEN." *Marketing Business Weekly*, October 30, 2011.

Dr Pepper Snapple Group Inc. "Dr Pepper Snapple Group Annual Report 2011." Accessed September 26, 2012. http://www.drpeppersnapplegroup.com/annualreport/2011/DPSG%202011%20Annual%20Report%20for%20Web.pdf.

"Dr Pepper Snapple Group, Inc." *International Directory of Company Histories*. Ed. Drew D. Johnson. Vol. 124. Detroit, MI: St. James Press, 2011.

Fuhrman, Elizabeth. "Dr Pepper 125 Years of 23 Satisfying Flavors: Marketing, Flavors and Expanding Availability Push Brand Forward." *Beverage Industry*, May 2010.

Krause, Reinhardt. "Taking a Hard Line on Soft Drinks." *Investor's Business Daily*, July 2, 2012.

Morton, Andy. "Just on Call—DPSG Sees No Sign of a Slowdown." *just-drinks*, July 27, 2012.

Quinton, Brian. "Dr Pepper Builds Share among Hispanics." *Promo*, October 1, 2007.

Robinson-Jacobs, Karen. "Dr Pepper, Pepsi Drain Business from Coke." *Dallas Morning News*, April 18, 2012.

Wehring, Olly. "Just the Facts—The 2012 Harris Poll EquiTrend." *just-drinks*, April 27, 2012.

Wentz, Laurel. "Getting Hispanics to Be a Pepper, Too." *Advertising Age*, June 20, 2005.

EBAY

AT A GLANCE

Brand Synopsis: Known by the slogan "Whatever it is, you can get it on eBay," eBay is the world's go-to website for online one-stop shopping.
Parent Company: eBay Inc.
2145 Hamilton Avenue
San Jose, California 95125
United States
http://www.ebay.com
Sector: Information Technology
Industry Group: Software & Services
Performance: *Market share*—2.8 percent (2011). *Sales*—US$14.1 billion (2012).
Principal Competitors: Amazon.com, Inc.; Google Inc.; Overstock.com, Inc.; Wal-Mart Stores, Inc.

BRAND ORIGINS

- In 1995 Pierre Omidyar launched the website AuctionWeb as an experiment; the website and company were renamed eBay in 1997.
- eBay went public in 1998, with its share price closing at US$53.50 on the first day of trading.
- eBay purchased the e-commerce payment processor PayPal in 2002.

The software developer Pierre Omidyar launched AuctionWeb on Labor Day weekend 1995 as part of his personal website containing information about the Ebola virus. Omidyar had done it as an experiment to see if there was any interest for an auction-oriented online marketplace. As part of his experiment, Omidyar posted a broken laser pointer for sale and, to his surprise, the pointer sold to a collector. The company continued to grow and by the end of January 1997 it was hosting over 2 million auctions, which was an improvement over 1996's 250,000 for the entire year. The increase in auctions was in part due to the company's first third-party licensing deal with Electronic Travel Auction, which allowed AuctionWeb to sell plane tickets and other travel accommodations.

In September 1997 the company changed its name from AuctionWeb to eBay. Omidyar had intended to name the company echobay to coincide with his consulting firm Echo Bay Technology Group; however, he discovered that the name was registered to another company. Instead, he shortened the name to eBay. That same year Benchmark Capital invested US$6.7 million in the company to help it expand within the growing market. eBay went public on September 21, 1998, and the target share price of US$18 was outdone as the price went to US$53.50 per share on the first day.

The company continued to expand as it sold products from collectibles to new items. In 2002 eBay purchased IBazar, a European-equivalent company, which enabled eBay to corner the European market. That same year eBay acquired the e-commerce payment processor PayPal, after the eBay community made it clear that it preferred PayPal over any other method of transaction. The purchase enabled eBay to become more efficient in processing payments at the completion of the auctions.

By 2008 eBay had successfully become a global e-commerce company with hundreds of millions of registered users. In 2010 eBay announced its acquisition of brandsforfriends.de, a German shopping club, as part of an effort to expand the company into fashion retail.

BRAND ELEMENTS

- The name eBay was released as a shortened version of the founder Pierre Omidyar's consulting company Echo Bay Technology Group.
- eBay's logo consists of the company name in lowercased letters and printed in primary colors on a white background.
- In 2012 eBay's slogan was "When it's on your mind, it's on eBay."

The company's original name, AuctionWeb, was changed to eBay in 1997. The name eBay was a shortened version of the founder Pierre Omidyar's consulting company Echo Bay Technology Group. The name of the company is the largest identifier for the brand, because that is what is typed into online search engines to access the site. Additionally, the subsidiaries PayPal and Bill Me Later, both e-commerce payment service providers, are known independently of eBay, although both can be accessed through the shopping website and utilized for payment. PayPal was an independent company until 2002, when it was acquired by eBay. eBay acquired Bill Me Later in 2008. Both payment companies are utilized by multiple online retailers, such as Wal-Mart, the U.S. Postal Service, and Hotels.com.

The logo for eBay is the company name listed in all lowercased letters in red, blue, yellow, and green. The company utilized the same logo between 1995 and 2012, featuring the letters of the name in playful positions. In September 2012 the company launched a revision of the logo by placing the letters in a thinner and evenly laid out typeset, resulting in a more elegant design. The colors of the company have remained consistent, with the company name on a white background.

eBay has used several slogans since 1995. From the oldest to the newest, eBay's slogans have been "World's online market place," "Connecting buyers and sellers globally," "What ever it is, you can get it on eBay," "Buy it, sell it, love it," "Buy it new, buy it now," and "When it's on your mind, it's on eBay." When the slogan "Buy it new, buy it now" was launched in 2011, it was met with controversy. Loyal users of the service had become upset at the idea that the company was now targeting new items as opposed to the used items it had previously marketed. The change in marketing was in part to help the company better compete with Amazon.com. The slogan has since been changed to "When it's on your mind, it's on eBay."

BRAND IDENTITY

- eBay built its corporate model on the premise that people are naturally honest and that sellers and buyers will be honest with each other during auctions.
- Pierre Omidyar founded eBay as a place to compete against large retailers by connecting buyers and sellers who would not have had contact otherwise.
- Part of eBay's image is offering flexible selling options, which will result in more customer satisfaction.

When Pierre Omidyar, the founder of eBay, started his online auction marketplace in 1995, he intended to connect people who own items they no longer want with people who are looking to buy those items. On eBay's website, the company states that it was founded "on a simple idea: People are basically good." By taking larger businesses out of the question, people all over the United States were able to contact others they otherwise would not have known about.

In its 2011 annual report, eBay reiterates that the purpose of the brand is to offer a platform to bring buyers and sellers together through an easy-to-use website that is available all around the world at any time. At the heart of the brand is the promise that eBay cares about its customers' needs and will offer a multitude of services to meet those needs. By allowing different kinds of sellers and items while offering both auction-styled and "Buy It Now" options, eBay helps customers of all needs find an item at a price that suits them. The brand goes further by offering not only new items but also collectibles and other used goods that consumers may be searching for.

There are four key values that eBay aims to convey to its customers. First, the brand is trustworthy and reliable with its customer services and proves this trust through security measures to make the buyers more comfortable with their purchases. Second, eBay offers an array of variety and choice to the shopping experience with over 50,000 shopping categories. Third, the brand makes its products available virtually anytime and anywhere through its applications on mobile devices. Lastly, eBay hopes to portray the brand's financial flexibility by offering a wide variety of selling and payment options to make its website more user-friendly.

BRAND STRATEGY

- eBay's foundation is based on the online auctioning of new and used items, linking sellers directly to customers.
- After the company went through a rebranding in 2002, it began offering the "Buy It Now" option to sellers and buyers, letting sellers place an item for a set price.
- eBay acquired the online payment processing company PayPal in 2002 and Bill Me Later in 2008.

The largest aspect of eBay's strategy has been to offer services that are not available elsewhere and to do it well.

The original corporate model supported the company as an online auction marketplace by connecting buyers and sellers directly. This remained the large part of eBay's model for many years. By offering items in an auction format, eBay was able to compete with big retailers without having to maintain any on-hand stock and with much fewer employees. The other large advantage was the items put up for auction could either be used or new, adding a new place for collectors to find items.

eBay went through a corporate rebranding in 2002. In that year it purchased IBazar, a European-equivalent company, and began offering the "Buy It Now" option to sellers. The option enables sellers to set a fixed price for an item so that customers can buy an item straight away instead of going into an auction format. For buyers, it is a guarantee that they will win the item, instead of going through a potential bidding war with other buyers. Another aspect of this feature is that it makes eBay more competitive with Amazon.com, the world's largest online retailer. By offering products at a set price and through eBay stores, eBay is able to compete with its rival.

eBay has acquired several subsidiaries in its short history. Its most important acquisition was the company PayPal, an e-commerce payment processor. Even though eBay had utilized the company for several years, it finally acquired PayPal in 2002, after noting that it was the preferred payment method for users. PayPal expanded further when it acquired Bill Me Later, an online payment company that offers transactional credit.

BRAND EQUITY

- eBay is the second-largest online retailer in the world, falling behind Amazon.com.
- In 2012 Brand Finance ranked eBay as the 98th most valuable brand in the world, with a value of US$8.9 billion.
- In 2012 Interbrand ranked eBay as 36th among the top-100 brands, with a value of US$10.9 billion.

eBay is the second-largest online retailer in the world, behind Amazon.com, that does not otherwise have a retail location. Wal-Mart is the largest retailer with an online presence; however, only 2 percent of its US$447 billion in revenues comes from online sales.

According to Brand Finance's "Global 500," in 2012 eBay was ranked 98th, with a brand value of US$8.9 billion. In contrast, Amazon was ranked 10th, with a brand value of US$28.7 billion, and Google was ranked second, with a value of US$47.5 billion. Among the top-100 brands in 2012, Interbrand ranked eBay at 36th, with a value of US$10.9 billion. Amazon was listed 20th, with a value of US$18.6 billion, compared with Google's US$69.7 billion, coming in fourth on the same list.

BRAND AWARENESS

- eBay has established itself as a used-goods online retailer through its customer-to-customer format and remained known for that business format in 2012.
- eBay's customer brand loyalty stems from the history of the company as an established online retailer that survived the dot-com bubble burst.
- In 2011 the total value of goods sold on eBay was US$68.6 billion.

eBay has a strong strategic awareness advantage over Amazon.com. Even though Amazon sells used goods in addition to new items, eBay has established itself as the premier online retailer for collectors and seekers of used goods as well as for bargain hunters wanting to take advantage of eBay's auctions. In 2012 the top-of-mind awareness for eBay was that it offers used goods.

Additionally, with almost 260 million searches a day, eBay's auction format stands as the best-known and trusted online auction site, overshadowing any potential competitor. For example, the auction competitor Overstock.com has received bad press for its auction setup not being private and is reported to average only 10 million visitors a month. Part of eBay's customer loyalty stems from the legacy of the company, having established itself at the beginning of the dot-com bubble and surviving after the bubble burst. The total value of goods sold on eBay in 2011 was US$68.6 billion, which equates to approximately US$2,100 every second.

BRAND OUTLOOK

- eBay's sales figures increased from US$9.2 billion in 2010 to US$11.6 billion in 2011.
- Even though eBay continues to compete with Amazon.com by offering new items at fixed prices, it is still the go-to website for used and hard-to-find items with 260 million searches daily.
- On Cyber Monday 2012 eBay's shares rose 4.9 percent to US$51.40.

eBay's sales have been steadily increasing, from US$9.2 billion in 2010 to US$11.6 billion in 2011. On Cyber Monday 2012, the Monday following Thanksgiving in the United States when online retailers offer sales, eBay's shares climbed 4.9 percent, closing at US$51.40 at the end of the day. Its stock hit an intraday high of US$51.78, the highest since 2005. Likewise, PayPal reported that its amount of mobile transactions tripled on Cyber Monday 2012 from the same period in 2011.

The company continues to compete with Amazon.com by offering new items at fixed prices. However, during the Christmas shopping season, which is the highest revenue time of year for retailers, eBay is still relied on by customers for out-of-stock and hard-to-find items. As of 2012, 70 percent of listings on eBay were new items with over 350 million listings posted at a time. In the online auction market, eBay is still the dominant website, boasting 260 million searches on average daily. For auction sites, eBay's competitors pale in comparison, with Overstock.com, the next-largest auction site, only reporting 10 million visitors a month. In its "Top Ten Reviews" of online auction sites, TechMediaNetwork ranked eBay first, citing excellent custom selling options, as well as brand exposure and customer loyalty.

FURTHER READING

Brand Finance. "Global 500 2012." *Brandirectory*. Accessed February 4, 2013. http://brandirectory.com/league_tables/table/global-500-2012.

eBay Inc. "2011 Annual Report." Accessed February 18, 2013. http://files.shareholder.com/downloads/ebay/2327321934x0xS1065088-12-6/1065088/filing.pdf.

"EBayInc." EdgarOnline, January 31, 2012. Accessed February 4, 2013. http://files.shareholder.com/downloads/ebay/2224724598x0xS1065088-12-6/1065088/filing.pdf.

Hines, Alice. "EBay's 'Buy It New' Rebranding Angers Devoted Used Goods Sellers." *Daily Finance*, November 2, 2011. Accessed February 4, 2013. http://www.dailyfinance.com/2011/11/02/ebays-buy-it-new-rebranding-angers-devoted-used-goods-sellers/.

"Online Sales Jump on Cyber Monday, eBay Shines." Reuters, November 27, 2012.

"TopTenReviews: eBay." TechMediaNetwork. Accessed February 18, 2013. http://online-auction-sites.toptenreviews.com/ebay-review.html.

"2012 Ranking of the Top 100 Brands." Interbrand. Accessed February 4, 2013. http://www.interbrand.com/en/best-global-brands/best-global-brands-2008/best-global-brands-2011.aspx.

Vit, Armin. "eBay Settles for Lowest Bid." Underconsideration.com, September 14, 2012. Accessed February 17, 2013. http://www.underconsideration.com/brandnew/archives/ebay_settles_for_lowest_bid.php.

Welch, David. "Wal-Mart Gears up Online as Customers Defect to Amazon." *Bloomberg BusinessWeek*, March 20, 2012.

Wolverton, Troy. "eBay Prices Going, Going…Staying Put." CNet, June 24, 2002. Accessed February 4, 2013. http://news.cnet.com/eBay-prices-going,-going…staying-put/2100-1017_3-938860.html.

ECOLAB

AT A GLANCE

Brand Synopsis: Ecolab bills itself as a global leader in water, hygiene, and energy technologies.
Parent Company: Ecolab Inc.
370 North Wabasha Street
Saint Paul, Minnesota 55102-1390
United States
http://www.ecolab.com
Sector: Health Care
Industry Group: Pharmaceuticals & Biotechnology & Life Sciences
Performance: *Market share*—10 percent of the global market. *Sales*— US$6.8 billion (2011).
Principle Competitors: ABM Industries Incorporated; ARAMARK Corporation; Chemed Corporation; Colin Service Systems, Inc.; CPAC, Inc.; Healthcare Services Group, Inc.; ISS A/S; Katy Industries, Inc.; National Service Industries, Inc.; Rollins, Inc.; The ServiceMaster Company; SYSCO Corporation; The Tranzonic Companies; Unicco Service Company; Unilever PLC/ Unilever N.V.

BRAND ORIGINS

- Ecolab began as a company named Economics Laboratory, which sold its first products in the 1920s.
- Economics Laboratory purchased the Magnus Company in the early 1950s, giving the brand access to additional industrial markets.
- By 1956 the brand had opened its first overseas operation in Sweden.
- In 1986 the company changed its name to Ecolab Inc., and its subsequent acquisitions helped the company diversify in the consumer market.
- In the late 1990s and early 2000s Ecolab established a successful pattern of acquisition and growth that would make the brand an industry leader.

Originally named Economics Laboratory, the brand that would become Ecolab sold its first key products (Soilax, a detergent for dishwashers) in the 1920s. The brand's product offerings grew through the 1950s to include specialty cleaning products for restaurants and dairies. The purchase of the Magnus Company in the early 1950s gave Economics Laboratory access to industrial markets such as paper, metalworking, petrochemical processing, and transportation, and by 1956 the brand had begun its international expansion project by opening its first overseas operation in Sweden. In 1973 Economics Laboratory became a public corporation and was divided into five business sectors.

In the early 1970s, Economics Laboratory's market strategy was focused on offering services to supplement specialty chemical products, and profit margins declined during management changes in the latter part of the decade. Economic Laboratory continued its strategy for growth by hiring new staff and acquiring Apollo Technologies (a manufacturer of chemicals and pollution-control equipment). This subsidiary was successful until the early 1980s, when the Clean Air Act depleted the industrial sector it served.

In 1983 the position of chairman and CEO of Economic Laboratory was assumed by Pierson M. Grieve, who shut down the Apollo subsidiary in order to halt the operation's drain on Economic Laboratory's profits. Grieves also formed a plan to develop products internally in order to compete with the Sunlight brand, released by the Lever Brothers, and The Diversey Corporation owned by Molson Companies Ltd. Economics Laboratory's acquisition of Lystads and Foussard Associates in the late 1980s helped broaden the company's customer base and diversified the company in the consumer market. In 1986 the brand changed its name to Ecolab Inc. The acquisition of Gibson Chemical Industries Limited in 1997 was made in the hope of gaining access to the Asia-Pacific regional market.

In 1987 Ecolab purchased ChemLawn, a lawn care servicer that would prove to be a drain on the brand's revenue and an ill fit in the context of a growing environmental movement in the industry. ChemLawn was sold in the early 1990s, and Ecolab concentrated on the global expansion of its core business, enjoying growth in sales and the increased output of new products throughout the 1990s and early 2000s. After acquiring Huntington Laboratories, Chemidyne Marketing, Blue Coral Systems, and Grace-Lee Products, Ecolab established a successful pattern of acquisition and growth that would result in the brand becoming the industry leader in the 21st century.

BRAND ELEMENTS

- Ecolab's mission is represented by the tagline "Circle the Customer, Circle the Globe."
- The Ecolab brand's blue logotext appears with the slogan "Everywhere It Matters,"
- The brand's font is in bold capital letters in an aqua blue color.

Ecolab's business strategy is represented by the tagline "Circle the Customer, Circle the Globe." This, and the slogan "Everywhere It Matters," which often appears underneath the blue ECOLAB logotext, communicates Ecolab's desire to become the global provider of food and water safety products and services. The blue pallete recalls the brand's values of sustainability and clean solutions for businesses.

The company's logo, too, conveys Ecolab's focus on making the world cleaner, safer, and healthier. The logo is in blocky, bold capital letters in a bright blue color that is reminiscent of water. The block letters have a sense of weight and strength.

BRAND IDENTITY

- Ecolab's purpose is to contribute to a cleaner, safer world through the protection of vital resources.
- Ecolab prides itself on working with purpose, reaching goals, and finding innovative solutions to problems.
- Ecolab's business principles focus on economic growth, environmental stewardship, safe processes, and enhancing the lives of customers and their communities.

Ecolab wants to be viewed as a company driven to make the world cleaner, safer, and healthier through the protection of vital resources. Ecolab products and services prevent disease and infection and perpetuate the living of healthy lives. Ecolab's research contributes to food safety and water and energy solutions. Innovation is central to Ecolab's core businesses and to the development of new technologies and efficient solutions. Ecolab employs 1,300 scientists and 22,500 field experts, and it owns 13 RD&E centers around the world.

Ecolab's business principles are related to economic growth; environmental stewardship (which includes the conservation of natural resources and the support of sustainable products and technologies); safe processes that ensure the well-being of customers, communities, and employees; and the enhancement of Ecolab's customers and their communities. Ecolab prides itself on working with a purpose, setting and reaching goals, and finding innovative solutions to problems. The brand values teamwork and finding inspiration in sustainability and making a difference in communities.

BRAND STRATEGY

- In 1980 Ecolab introduced the business model that would solidify its position as the industry leader in the 21st century.
- In 1991 Ecolab entered a joint venture with Henkel KGaA, a move which eventually made Henkel-Ecolab the industry leader in Europe.
- In the 1990s, Ecolab expanded its range of products and services by acquiring Huntington Laboratories, Chemidyne Marketing, Grace-Lee Products Incorporated, and Gibson Chemical Industries.
- In 1999 Ecolab acquired Blue Coral Systems and began moving into the repair of commercial kitchen equipment with the purchase of GCS Service Incorporated.

The business model that brought Ecolab to prominence in the 21st century markets was introduced in the late 1980s and characterized by the tagline "Circle the Customer – Circle the Globe." The strategy was focused on worldwide growth, which began in earnest as Ecolab used various distribution and licensing agreements to set up operations and expand its core business into the Asia-Pacific region, Latin America, Africa, and the Middle East and broadened the range of products and services it offers its customers.

In 1991 Ecolab entered a joint venture with Henkel KGaA, a partnership which eventually made Henkel-Ecolab the industry leader in Europe. By 1994, 22 percent of Ecolab's net sales were generated outside the United States. In the same year, Ecolab expanded its range of products for the institutional, industrial, and hospitality markets by acquiring Kay Chemical, a leader in cleaning and sanitization for fast-food restaurants.

In 1990 Ecolab continued to expand its product and service offerings by acquiring Huntington Laboratories, suppliers of janitorial products to the health and education markets. Further acquisitions during the decade included the Chemidyne Marketing division of Chemidyne Corp., Grace-Lee Products Incorporated, and Gibson Chemical Industries, a maker and marketer of cleaning products for the institutional, healthcare, and industrial markets in Australia and New Zealand. In 1999 Ecolab acquired Blue Coral Systems and began moving into the repair of commercial kitchen equipment with the purchase of GCS Service Incorporated. During this time, Ecolab was also expanding its core business to include car wash equipment and repair services.

The brand's "Circle the Globe" strategy emphasizes Ecolab's goal to become a worldwide leader by gradually entering the Asia-Pacific regions, Latin America, Africa, and the Middle East. The "Circle the Customer" strategy involves maximizing investment in Ecolab's core business by broadening the range of products and services it offers to its customers.

BRAND EQUITY

- In 2011 Ecolab reported net sales of US$6.8 billion and total assets of US$18.2 billion.
- Ecolab was named one of *CRO* magazine's 100 Best Corporate Citizens.
- Ecolab was placed on *Forbes* magazine's America's Best Big Companies Honor Roll.

Ecolab is the global leader in premium commercial cleaning, sanitizing, food safety, and infection prevention products and services. In 2011 Ecolab reported net sales of US$6.8 billion, an increase of 12 percent from the previous year. The brand serves customers in 160 countries globally and has 40,000 employees.

Ecolab provides products and services to many of the world's most recognizable brands. It has the distinction of being named one of *CRO* magazine's 100 Best Corporate Citizens, one of *Ethisphere* magazine's World's Most Ethical Companies, and the brand has also been placed on *Forbes* magazine's America's Best Big Companies Honor Roll.

BRAND AWARENESS

- *Forbes* ranked Ecolab 28th on its World's Most Innovative Companies list.
- In 2012–13 Ecolab was recognized by the Dow Jones Sustainability World Index.
- Ecolab company Nalco was recognized by *Pulp & Paper International* magazine as a preferred supplier in the paper industry.

Ecolab was added to the Dow Jones Sustainability World Index, as well as the DJSI North America Index, based on the brand's commendable sustainability initiatives. Ecolab was one of 41 companies, out of a total of 340 companies, that was listed in the 2012–13 World Index, and the recognition boosted Ecolab's brand recognition and leading position as a world-class provider of sanitization and food-safety products and services. Ecolab was also named 28th on the World's Most Innovative Companies list by *Forbes* in 2012.

In 2012, the Ecolab company Nalco was selected as a preferred supplier for the paper industry by readers of *Pulp & Paper International* magazine, a leading industry trade publication. Ecolab was also acknowledged in the Bloomberg Businessweek 50 and the list of 40 Best Companies for Leaders (on which the brand placed 28th).

BRAND OUTLOOK

- Entering 2012 the total market Ecolab served exceeded US$100 million in value.
- In 2011 Ecolab announced its merger with Nalco, the world's foremost provider of water management products and services.
- Ecolab pursued the merger with Nalco in response to global population growth and predictions that demand for fresh water will exceed supply by 2025.

Announced in 2011, Ecolab's merger with Nalco, the world's foremost provider of water management products and services, was a major move forward for the brand. In response to the growing global population and the World Bank's prediction that demand for fresh water would exceed supply by 2025, the merger with Nalco was pursued in an effort to transform Ecolab into a global leader in water and energy technologies and services. Ecolab will be able to use Nalco's broad range of technologies and expertise to protect vital resources.

The two companies aim to create total water processing solutions, continue building Ecolab's healthcare platform, position the Energy division to gather oil and gas markets in North America, and maintain the best technologies at affordable costs. At the beginning of 2012 the total market Ecolab served exceeded US$100 million in value.

FURTHER READING

Byrne, Harlan S. "Ecolab Inc.: Controversial Acquisition Is Poised for a Move." *Barron's*, October 15, 1990.

"Cleaning-Products Company Set to Acquire Kay Chemical." *Wall Street Journal*, November 4, 1994.

Ecolab. "Annual Report 2011." Accessed December 4, 2012. http://www.ecolab.com/media-center/publications/~/media/Ecolab/Ecolab%20Site/Page%20Content/Documents/Our%20Company/Publications/Annual%20Report/2011CompleteAnnualReport.ashx.

"Ecolab Inc." *International Directory of Company Histories*. Ed. Jay P. Pederson. Vol. 34. Detroit, MI: St. James Press, 2000.

"Ecolab Selling ChemLawn Subsidiary after Five Years of Trying to Turn It Around." *Minneapolis Star Tribune*, March 3, 1992.

Harvilicz, Helena. "Ecolab Makes a Name for Itself by Diversifying Its Operations." *Chemical Market Reporter*, August 16, 1999.

Kaufman, Jonathan. "Heavy Duty: For Latter-Day CEO, 'All in a Day's Work' Often Means Just That." *Wall Street Journal*, May 3, 1999.

Lanners, Fred T., Jr., *Products and Services for a Cleaner World: The Story of Economics Laboratory, Inc.* New York: Newcomen Society in North America, 1981.

Miller, James P. "Ecolab Decision to Shed Lawn-Care Unit Cheered by Investors." *Wall Street Journal*, March 3, 1992.

Peterson, Susan E. "Confident Departure: Retiring Executive Sandy Grieve Turned Ecolab from Trouble to Road to Recovery." *Minneapolis Star Tribune*, December 25, 1995.

ELI LILLY

AT A GLANCE

Brand Synopsis: Over its long history, the pharmaceutical brand Eli Lilly has sought to be known for reliable and innovative medicine.
Parent Company: Eli Lilly and Company
Lilly Corporate Center
Indianapolis, Indiana 46285
United States
http://www.lilly.com
Sector: Health Care
Industry Group: Pharmaceuticals, Biotechnology & Life Sciences
Performance: *Market share*—3.10% worldwide (2012). *Sales*—US$24.29 billion (2011).
Principal Competitors: Pfizer; GlaxoSmithKline; Roche Holding Ltd.; Akzo Nobel; Novartis; Bristol-Meyers Squibb; Merck; Johnson & Johnson

BRAND ORIGINS

- Colonel Eli Lilly founded his pharmaceutical company following his poor experiences with medicine during the American Civil War.
- Lilly's company was immediately successful because of innovations in flavoring and coating medicine.
- Lilly made a name for itself by releasing new and effective medications, including mass-production of the first antibiotic, penicillin.
- Lilly has also profited from expanding beyond pharmaceuticals into the manufacture of medical instruments.

Colonel Eli Lilly, an American Civil War veteran and pharmaceutical chemist, started his research-based company in 1876. During the war, Lilly had seen ineffective and poorly prepared medicine used in the direst of circumstances. Lilly decided that he would commit himself to creating more beneficial and effective medicine. He listed three missions when founding his company: he would manufacture only the highest-quality pharmaceuticals, he would only dispense medicines that would be recommended by physicians and not side-show salesman, and all his medicine would be based on the newest science available. Lilly's first innovation was to coat capsules and pills in gelatin to allow for easier swallowing.

Lilly's business was immediately successful, bringing in US$4,470 in the first year alone and US$48,000 only three years later. Lilly was so successful that he hired his brother James to oversee sales and other family members to take care of other jobs in the business. However, Lilly was still concerned that the medicine his company was producing was not as adequately supported by research and testing as it could be. In 1886 Lilly hired his first full-time chemist to work entirely in research. By hiring a research chemist, Lilly was able not only to ensure that his medicine lived up to advertisement, but also to begin creating new and more effective medicines. The company also began adding fruit flavors and candy coatings to make medicine more palatable during this time of innovation and expansion.

Following Lilly's death from cancer at the end of the 19th century, the company passed down to his son, Josiah, and later to his grandsons, who maintained Lilly's corporate vision and practices. The company made history in 1923, when it released Iletin, the world's first commercially available insulin product. Prior to this innovation, diabetes was considered a terminal illness with no effective treatment options. Additionally, Eli Lilly and Company continued its research and later introduced a treatment for pernicious anemia, for which two of the collaborators in developing the treatment received a Nobel Prize.

Eli Lilly, the grandson of Colonel Eli Lilly, was named the company president in 1932. He expanded the company overseas, opening the first location in England in 1934. During World War II, Lilly began producing blood plasma and Merthiolate, an antiseptic used to prevent infections from injections. By 1943 Eli Lilly became the first company to mass-produce penicillin, a relatively new medicine at the time and the world's first antibiotic.

The company went public in 1952 and, for the first time in company history, began operating under a president who was not related to the Lilly family. Also during the 1950s, Lilly continued its research with antibiotics, releasing vancomycin, a strong antibiotic still used in 2012 to fight drug-resistant infections, and later patenting and releasing erythromycin, another antibiotic that can be used as an alternative in treating patients allergic to penicillin. The company continued its work with antibiotics into the 1960s, launching a new class of antibiotics called cephalosporins, which includes Keflex and Kefzol. Additionally, during this period, Lilly released vincristine and vinblastine, anticancer drugs derived from the rosy periwinkle plant.

Lilly continued to introduce pharmaceutical breakthroughs throughout the remainder of the 20th century, launching such innovative drugs as Humulin, Ceclor, Prozac, and Cialis. The company also continued to expand. In 1971 Lilly purchased the cosmetic company Elizabeth Arden for US$38 million and sold it in 1987 to Fabergé for US$657 million, resulting in a great profit. Also during the 1980s, Lilly entered into the medical instruments industry by purchasing IVAC Corp., a manufacturer of intravenous monitoring systems, and by purchasing Cardiac Pacemakers.

BRAND ELEMENTS

- The company's name originated with Colonel Eli Lilly, the founder of the company.
- The corporate logo features "Lilly" written simply in a red, cursive script, which leverages the history of the company's well-known name.
- Lilly's slogan is "Answers that Matter," which signals that the company provides effective solutions for the treatment of medical conditions.

Eli Lilly and Company is named after its founder, Colonel Eli Lilly, who started the company in 1876, following the American Civil War. Lilly was a pharmaceutical chemist. The company maintained its name as company leadership was handed down through generations of the Lilly family. The company welcomed the first president who was not a Lilly in the 1950s, but the company has continued to use the original Lilly name. The Lilly company is known for producing high-quality, effective medications as well as for its innovative research. When he founded the company, Col. Lilly drafted a mission statement that included goals to manufacture the best medication, to make use of cutting-edge scientific advancements, and to ensure that his company's medicine was only available through the recommendation of a physician. The company has generally upheld Col. Lilly's original company format and his mission, experiencing only one major legal problem in its history, which was related to the antipsychotic medication Zyprexa.

The Lilly corporate logo emphasizes the Lilly name in a simple, straightforward fashion, displaying the name "Lilly" in red, cursive writing. Since the enduring company name is the most important aspect of the Lilly brand, the company uses the name to its advantage. Additionally, the company has patented many innovative and well-known medications—such as Prozac, Cialis, and Cymbalta—whose names have remained highly recognizable even after some began to be sold as generic drugs. The company makes use of the slogan "Answers that Matter," indicating that the company provides pharmaceuticals that are effective for the conditions they treat.

BRAND IDENTITY

- Eli Lilly markets itself as a reliable pharmaceutical company, using the slogan "Answers that Matter."
- From its inception, Eli Lilly has sought to be seen as a state-of-the-art operation that took advantage of the most current science.
- Eli Lilly's brand image was damaged in 2009 when the company plead guilty to representing the antipsychotic drug Zyprexa.

Eli Lilly markets itself as a reliable pharmaceutical company, using the slogan "Answers that Matter" to indicate that the company provides effective treatment for medical conditions that come from research-based medicines. Part of Colonel Lilly's original mission statement when founding the company in 1876 was the objective that the company should prove itself as a state-of-the-art operation that took advantage of the most current science. Col. Lilly founded his company following his negative experiences with ineffective medicine during the American Civil War, with the aim to provide medication that was more palatable, effective, and available. Since that time, the Lilly company has pioneered many new medications and treatments, including mass-produced penicillin and Humulin, the first diabetes treatment to mimic human insulin. Despite its efforts to maintain its image as an effective and scrupulous pharmaceutical company, Lilly has encountered challenges to this image among consumers and within its industry. In 2009 Lilly received the largest criminal fine in U.S. history for misrepresenting the antipsychotic drug Zyprexa as treatment for dementia and for failing to disclose the link between the medication and diabetes. The company was forced to pay approximately US$1.4 billion in damages, including the criminal fine of US$515 million. In addition to fiscal ramifications, the company's image as a provider of reliable and effective medication was also damaged.

BRAND STRATEGY

- The central aspect of Lilly's brand strategy has been to release innovative and effective medications backed by cutting-edge clinical research.
- Lilly has made forays into expanding its brand, including such purchases as the cosmetic company Elizabeth Arden, medical supplier IVAC, and Cardiac Pacemakers.
- After using its 40 percent stake in Dow Chemical to help finance agrochemical research, Lilly sold the shares in the late 1990s.
- In 2012 Lilly began collaborating with the Chinese-based pharmaceutical company Novast in order to produce generic medications bearing the Lilly name.

Eli Lilly's strategy for its brand has largely been the same since the company was founded in 1876. The company creates medicine based on the latest scientific research. Under this model, Lilly has produced a variety of innovative medications and methods, including the practice of candy-coating medicine to make it easier to swallow. Lilly is known for developing some of the first treatments for diabetes, as well as antibiotics effective for consumers with penicillin allergies. By staying on the cutting edge in the pharmaceutical market, Lilly enjoys the brand awareness of a global market leader.

Lilly has attempted a small number of brand expansions into other industries. The company purchased the cosmetic manufacturer Elizabeth Arden in 1971, selling it in 1987 to Fabergé for US$657 million. Additionally, Lilly purchased IVAC Corp, a producer of intravenous monitoring systems and other medical instruments, in the 1980s, expanding the company's product base further outside of pharmaceuticals. Lilly also acquired the medical supply company Cardiac Pacemakers.

The company also purchased 40 percent of Dow Chemical's shares, which it used in part to develop its agrochemical research. Lilly sold its shares in Dow Chemical in 1997 for US$1.6 billion. The following year, Lilly entered into a venture with Icos Corporation, a biochemical company, in order to research and develop the drug known as Cialis, a treatment for erectile dysfunction.

In 2012 Lilly, as part of its goal of expanding into the booming economy in China, entered into collaboration with Novast, a specialist in generic medications. In working with Novast, Lilly aimed to profit from China's burgeoning economy while also lending the well-known Lilly brand name to generic, more affordable medications. Although this collaboration began in 2012, Lilly had already taken steps towards expansion into Asia several years earlier, under the capital unit Lilly Asian Ventures.

BRAND EQUITY

- Eli Lilly was ranked 119th in the 2012 Fortune 500 list.
- In 2012 Eli Lilly was the 10th most successful pharmaceutical brand in the world, according to *Pharm Exec*'s annual review.
- Eli Lilly ranked 8th on *Forbes*'s list of Best Drug Companies.

Eli Lilly was ranked 119th in the 2012 Fortune 500 list. According to *Pharm Exec*'s 2012 annual review, Eli Lilly is the 10th most successful pharmaceutical company in the world, behind such competitors as Pfizer, which is ranked 1st, and Bristol-Meyers, ranked 9th. On the *Forbes* list of Best Drug Companies, Lilly placed 8th, with Pfizer in 4th place and Bristol-Meyers 6th. Instead of revenue, the *Forbes* list is based upon the number of new medications and treatments developed by each company.

BRAND AWARENESS

- Among consumers, Eli Lilly and Company is better known for the name-brand drugs it produces than for its own brand name.
- A number of medications developed by Lilly, including Cialis and Prozac, are highly familiar to consumers.
- The company has been associated with some brands that have strong brand awareness among consumers, such as Elizabeth Arden and Dow Chemical.

Although the Lilly brand has staying power rooted in its long history, it is primarily known for the name-brand prescriptions that it has created and patented. Innovative and popular drugs such as the erectile dysfunction aid Cialis, the antidepressant Prozac, and the now infamous antipsychotic Zyprexa represent both the positive and the negative aspects of the company's brand awareness among consumers. The simple, text-based logo the company uses also reinforces the company's brand, though it does not necessarily link directly to Lilly's emphasis on research.

Although physicians are familiar with the names of pharmaceutical manufacturers, end consumers are less aware of the company names associated with specific medications and more aware of the name of the drug itself.

Other brands that Eli Lilly has been associated with have had greater brand awareness than Lilly itself. Elizabeth Arden, for example, is a well-known cosmetic company, and Lilly owned the company for 16 years, between 1971 and 1987. Also, Lilly at one time owned shares in the prominent multinational chemical company Dow Chemical, before selling the stock in the late 1990s.

BRAND OUTLOOK

- In 2009 Eli Lilly and Company received the largest criminal fine in U.S. history because of its inaccurate marketing of the drug Zyprexa.
- Lilly faces potential future financial troubles as patents on its brand-name drugs expire and they become available to makers of generic drugs.
- To reduce losses caused by patent expirations, Lilly has signed a deal with the China-based company Novast to manufacture and distribute generic medications.
- In 2012 Lilly was working on a treatment for Alzheimer's disease, which would bring great financial gain were the drug to prove successful during trials.

In January 2009 Eli Lilly was ordered to pay US$1.4 billion in damages, including the largest individual corporate criminal fine in history (approximately US$515 million), after the company was found to have inaccurately marketed its antipsychotic medication Zyprexa. The company had been listing the drug as a treatment for dementia, even though the company's research had not proven the drug's effectiveness in this regard. Additionally, the company did not disclose the link between the medication and the onset of diabetes in patients taking it. The fine taxed the company financially and tarnished Lilly's previously pristine brand image.

In addition to the lawsuit, Eli Lilly and Company, along with many other pharmaceutical companies, has faced challenges when brand-name drug patents have expired. Such expirations allow other companies to make generic versions of the drugs and often lead to profit losses. In the fourth quarter of 2011, Lilly experienced a 27 percent decline in profits after Zyprexa went generic in October. Lilly's best-selling drug, Cymbalta, will lose its patent protection in December 2013. In 2012, as an attempt to temper the losses sustained as a result of patent expirations, Lilly signed a deal with the China-based pharmaceutical company Novast to manufacture generic medications bearing the Lilly name.

In the early 21st century, to both stay relevant and boost revenue, Lilly has continued to innovate in the field of pharmaceutical research. For example, the company began work on a new treatment for Alzheimer's disease, tentatively named Solanezumab. Lilly was forced to abandon its research and start over, however, when the drug trials proved unsuccessful. Competitor Pfizer was also developing a new Alzheimer's medication. With both companies subject to the pressures generated by expiring patents, the competition to produce an effective drug quickly was intense. In 2012 the *Wall Street Journal* speculated that if Lilly were successful in the drug trials for Solanezumab, the company could generate US$23 billion in sales by 2020. To combat both the negative publicity from the 2009 lawsuit and the monetary losses that occurred from patent expirations, Lilly needed to keep developing medicines that were revolutionary and effective.

FURTHER READING

Brand Finance. "Global 500 2012." *Brandirectory*. Accessed September 6, 2012. http://brandfinance.com/images/upload/bf_g500_2012_web_dp.pdf.

Eli Lilly and Company. "Annual Report". Accessed November 29, 2012. http://files.shareholder.com/downloads/LLY/2194959350x0x548541/E8FFDA89-5EC1-4D08-AB37-CD85F4C0863D/English.PDF.

———. "Eli Lilly and Company Enters Companion Animal Health Market." January 15, 2007. Accessed December 1, 2012. http://newsroom.lilly.com/releasedetail.cfm?releaseid=225647.

———. "Lilly Expands Strategic Partnership with Chinese Manufacturer Novast to Serve Chinese Patients with High-Quality Branded Generic Medicines." June 12, 2012. Accessed December 2, 2012. http://newsroom.lilly.com/releasedetail.cfm?releaseid=682259.

"Fitch Says Patent Cliff Causes Eli Lilly Revenue to Tumble." Reuters, October 24, 2012.

"Fortune 500." *CNN Money*, May 21, 2012. Accessed December 9, 2012. http://money.cnn.com/magazines/fortune/fortune500/2012/full_list/101_200.html.

Gray, Nicole. "Changing Landscapes." PharmExec.com, May 2006. Accessed December 1, 2012. http://www.pharmexec.com/pharmexec/data/articlestandard//pharmexec/272006/354138/article.pdf.

Herper, Matthew. "The Best Drug Companies of the Past 15 Years." *Forbes*, February 9, 2012.

———. "The Best Drug Companies of 2020." *Forbes*, June 30, 2011.

Loftus, Peter. "Pfizer, Lilly Profits Fall as Drugs Lose Patents". *Wall Street Journal*, February 1, 2012.

"2011 Ranking of the Top 100 Brands." Interbrand. Accessed July 3, 2012. http://www.interbrand.com/en/best-global-brands/best-global-brands-2008/best-global-brands-2011.aspx.

EMIRATES AIRLINES

AT A GLANCE

Brand Synopsis: One of the fastest growing and most profitable airlines in the world, Dubai-based Emirates Airlines associates itself with luxury, numerous destinations, and high-profile sponsorships of sports teams and events.
Parent Company: Emirates Group
PO Box 688
Emirates Group Headquarters Building
Al Maktoum Street
Dubai
United Arab Emirates
http://www.emirates.com
Sector: Industrials
Industry Group: Airlines
Performance: *Market share*—4.52 percent of global cargo airline market (2007). *Sales*—US$16.7425 billion (2012).
Principal Competitors: Air New Zealand; All Nippon Airways; Cathay Pacific; Etihad Airways; Korean Air; Qatar Airways; Singapore Airlines; Thai Airways International; Virgin Atlantic Airways

BRAND ORIGINS

- Emirates Airlines was established in 1985 by the government of Dubai through its Emirates Group.
- Emirates has regularly added new destinations since its founding.
- By 2010 Emirates was the most profitable airline in the world.

Emirates Airlines was founded in 1985, launched at the behest of Sheikh Mohammed, who eventually became the ruler of the United Arab Emirates (UAE). He established Emirates Airlines after a dispute with Bahrainian airline Gulf Air over issues such as the amount of direct service provided outside the Persian Gulf and the airline's unwillingness to implement promotional fares. Sheikh Mohammed also wanted to ensure that Dubai would not be dependent on other air carriers. Emirates has been state-owned through the Emirates Group since its inception, though the Dubai government only invested in its start-up, does not provide any protectionism, and treats it as an independent business entity.

When Emirates started operations, its fleet had several leased Boeing 737s and Airbus A300s and flew to only three destinations: Bombay (Mumbai), New Delhi, and Karachi. By the end of 1986, it added stops in Cairo, Colombo, Sri Lanka, and Dacca, Bangladesh. Emirates became profitable by 1987 and remained so continuously into the early 21st century. By 1989 Emirates began flying to Saudi Arabia. It grew rapidly over the next decade, with revenues increasing at about 20 percent annually, beginning in the mid-1990s. Through this period, Emirates added many new routes and airplanes.

In 1997, however, Emirates decided to rein in expansion, adding only a few new destinations and just two airplanes. Instead it focused on opening the Emirates

Group Training College, a state-of-the-art training facility for the airline, and on the 1998 rollout of its logistics service, the Emirates SkyNet information network, which allowed shippers to track their cargo online. By this time, Emirates was not only a commercial passenger airline, but it also offered cargo services. In 1998 Emirates was the number-three airline group in Africa and the Middle East, with revenues of US$1.315 billion. Also that year, Emirates added service to poorly served areas of Pakistan.

Though Emirates was expanding its destinations on its way to becoming a globally recognized brand, it was also invested in promoting Dubai worldwide. In the late 1990s, Emirates offered a promotion to ensure that customers would consider Dubai a year-round destination, despite the extremely hot summers. In 1999 its "Summer Surprises" campaign promoted visiting Dubai during the summer months and buying a three-day stopover package. The campaign's tagline claimed, "Dubai. ... The Perfect Holiday Blend."

By 2001 Emirates was especially focused on being seen as an international brand, and it began sponsoring European soccer to build the brand and gain a higher global profile. To that end, the airline signed a £24 million (US$35 million) jersey-sponsorship deal with Chelsea, the west London soccer club. At the time, it was one of the largest-ever sponsorships in British soccer. Over the years Emirates added more high-profile sponsorships in soccer and expanded the program to rugby, tennis, Formula One racing, horse racing, and golf, as well as the cultural realms of film, literature, jazz festivals, and symphony orchestras.

As Emirates was building an international reputation, it was also becoming a major airline in terms of size and revenues. In 2001 it placed the largest airplane order in aviation history at the time, purchasing 58 Airbus and Boeing planes for US$15 billion. By 2002 Emirates was the top airline in Africa and the Middle East, based on operating profit. Emirates focused on charitable concerns in 2003 by founding the Emirates Airline Foundation, a nonprofit focused on helping underprivileged children.

Between 2006 and 2011, Emirates grew an average of 20 percent per year as it added more destinations and successfully promoted itself in markets on five continents. By 2006 it was the second-most-profitable airline in the world and was sponsoring 345 different events. By 2007 Emirates was considered one of the most successful brands in Dubai and was the number-12 global airline by passengers transported. With profits skyrocketing, Emirates was the only profitable airline in the Middle East, and it set a goal of becoming the largest airline in the world by 2015. To that end, it signed a contract in 2007 for 142 new planes in a deal worth an estimated US$34.9 billion.

Though Emirates was a leading airline in financial terms, it wanted to be considered an environmentally friendly one as well. In 2008 it launched the world's first cross-polar "green" flight, going from Dubai to San Francisco. By flying over the North Pole, the flight saved about 2000 gallons of fuel and 30,000 pounds of carbon emissions. By 2009 Emirates was flying to 100 destinations in 60 countries, and it accounted for about 40 percent of all flight movements in and out of Dubai. It served 27 million passengers that year, up 21 percent from 2008, despite a global economic crisis. Emirates also added more connections and flights to Africa, selecting Angola as its 17th African destination.

By 2010 Emirates was the world's most profitable airline, with revenues of US$11.8 billion and an operating profit of US$970.9 million. Between 2011 and early 2013, Emirates added at least 15 new destinations, in part because of its sports sponsorships in major European hubs. In 2011 alone, Emirates added three European destinations: Geneva, Copenhagen, and St. Petersburg. That year its fleet of more than 150 aircraft made 1100 weekly flights to 110 cities in 65 countries.

In 2012 Emirates focused on increasing its presence in North America, adding its sixth and seventh U.S. gateways (Seattle and Dallas) and a sponsorship of the U.S. Tennis Open. Other new destinations established that year included Rio de Janeiro, Buenos Aires, Dublin, Lusaka, Harare, Ho Chi Minh City, Barcelona, and Lisbon. By 2012 Emirates had a record income of US$17 billion, based on more than 2500 passenger flights per week from its hub at Dubai International Airport to 123 destinations in 73 countries on 190 planes.

BRAND ELEMENTS

- Emirates Airlines adopted its distinctive logo, which featured the brand's name in both Arabic and English, in 1985.
- Emirates often celebrates its link to Dubai.
- The "Hello Tomorrow" theme song represented Emirates's values and reflected its position as an international brand.

Since it was founded in 1985, Emirates Airlines has been represented by a unique, immediately recognizable logo. It consists of the Emirates name written in Arabic calligraphy, with the name Emirates in English underneath in an elegant typeface. This logo brings together the airline's roots in Dubai and its place as an international brand. While the Emirates logo originally appeared only in gold, it appeared in both gold and red versions after a 1999 update of the typography.

Emirates has had numerous memorable taglines, which often promote and define not only the airline but its home city of Dubai as well. Such taglines include

"Dubai ... The Perfect Holiday Blend," "Over 100 Destinations," and "Change Your View." In the 2010s Emirates had the "Hello Tomorrow" campaign which included its own theme song, also known as "Hello Tomorrow." The song is intended to echo steps along a customer's journey, reminding listeners of the potential of life and the possibilities of the future. The "Hello Tomorrow" theme was also created to appeal to a global audience by showing international influences and touching on the concept that we can be brought together, while setting a tone and mood in Emirates's communications as a brand.

BRAND IDENTITY

- Though Emirates Airlines originally positioned itself purely as a travel brand, it later changed focus to become a global lifestyle brand.
- Emirates's sponsorships were key to its global lifestyle brand-identity.
- Emirates emphasized that it was a luxury airline brand with impressive and extensive first-class amenities.

When Emirates Airlines was founded in 1985, it was primarily marketed as a travel brand, focused on serving customers as they used the airline to reach destinations for work, pleasure, or family. While Emirates did operate a cargo service, it added numerous travel-related services through such divisions as Emirates Holidays. Emirates expanded into more and more travel markets around the world. By the turn of the 21st century, Emirates was changing its focus to become more of a global lifestyle brand.

To fully reposition itself as an international brand, Emirates began sponsoring a number of high-profile sporting and cultural events. The airline believed such sponsorships were vital in brand building because this created a connection to their customers and opened up a closer relationship. Some of the first sponsorships came in Dubai and UAE. The first Emirates-sponsored event was the first powerboat race ever held in Dubai, in 1987. As Emirates expanded its reach as an airline, it began adding sports sponsorships that reflected the local interests of its markets, including Australian rules football, cricket, sailing (sponsoring Emirates's Team New Zealand), horse racing, rugby, golf (as a partner of the 2010 Ryder Cup), Formula 1 racing, and tennis (official airline of the U.S. Open beginning in 2012).

Emirates has made a particular investment in soccer, especially in Europe, and has made the sport a key tool in its quest to be regarded as an international brand while soccer, especially English football, was becoming increasingly global in its appeal. Emirates's first sponsorship deal with English football was a £24 million (US$35 million) jersey-sponsorship arrangement with Chelsea, the west London soccer club, in 2001. Emirates then signed a jersey sponsorship and stadium-naming-rights deal with the London-based Arsenal in 2004, renewing it in 2012. This resulted in significant advertising for Emirates as Arsenal sold an average of 800,000 jerseys between 2007 and 2012. Other noteworthy soccer sponsorships included AC Milan and, beginning in 2013, Paris Saint-Germain. In addition, Emirates was a sponsor of the FIFA World Cup Finals in 2010 and 2014.

The concept of luxury is also important to Emirates as a brand, and it has become more important to its identity over time. Emirates separated itself from its competitors with the luxurious amenities it offered to travelers. For example, first-class flights on its A380 Airbus include private cubicles with vanity desk, personal mini bar, big movie screen, flat bed, and a shower spa treatment. A bar/lounge area and in-flight nanny services are also offered.

BRAND STRATEGY

- Emirates has continually expanded its destinations and its fleet of aircraft.
- Emirates sometimes linked its sponsorships to destination expansion.
- Emirates also offered branded services related to tourism, cargo, travel technology, and airline education.

When Emirates Airlines began in 1985, its purpose was to address Dubai's need for a dedicated airline carrier. Though the airline began with a handful of leased planes and three destinations (Bombay (Mumbai), New Delhi, and Karachi), it soon began buying its own aircraft and expanded to Cairo, Colombo, Dacca, and Saudi Arabia by the end of the 1980s. Throughout the 1990s and early 2000s, Emirates regularly added new destinations. By 2012 it serviced 120 destinations in 110 cities and 65 countries on every continent. Emirates was the only airline to offer worlwide, nonstop service from one hub.

Emirates's expansion efforts were sometimes linked to its sponsorships, as when it entered San Francisco and became the Official Airline of the San Francisco Symphony. Other destinations, especially in the Middle East, Asia, and Africa, were added because they had been poorly served by other carriers. All of its flights were serviced under the Emirates name.

Emirates also offered related services, including Emirates SkyCargo, the airline's shipping service, and EmQuest, a travel technology distribution company. In addition, Emirates Engineering provides aircraft maintenance and engineering support, while Emirates Aviation College trains pilots and other airline professionals. As part of its quest to fully service its customers as a global lifestyle brand, Emirates operates a number of destination and leisure-management units, including Emirates Holidays, Emirates Torus, and Arabian Adventures.

BRAND EQUITY

- Emirates is the most profitable airline in the world.
- Emirates posted a record profit of US$17 billion in 2012.
- Brand Finance places Emirates at number 288 on its *Global 500* with a brand value of US$3.700 billion for 2012.

The world's most profitable airline, Emirates is gaining in market share since it became the number-12 airline in the world by passengers transported in 2007. One of the few profitable airlines in the Middle East and one of the few worldwide airlines that remained profitable during the international economic recession that began in 2008, Emirates posted sales of US$16.743 billion in 2012. It also posted double-digit percentage growth in many years.

Because of its success, Emirates Airlines has become a highly valuable brand, and its value is only increasing. In 2012 Brand Finance placed Emirates at number 288 on its *Global 500*, with a brand value of US$3.700 billion. The previous year, Emirates was 290th on the *Global 500* and had a brand value of US$3.622 billion. In 2011 Brand Finance also offered a ranking of the *Top 20 Airline Brands*, placing Emirates at number three. In 2010, Emirates was number 207 on the *Global 500* with a brand value of US$3.518 billion. That year Emirates was number two on Brand Finance's *Top 20 Airline Brands* and number one in its 2010 ranking of the best brands in the Middle East.

BRAND AWARENESS

- Emirates has made a concerted effort to build brand awareness since its inception in 1985.
- Brand awareness for the airline has been increased through its sponsorships, including European soccer.
- Emirates as a brand is highly valued by business professionals, ranking 68th in the *Business Superbrands Official 500* in 2009.

Since its founding in 1985, Emirates Airlines first built brand awareness in markets in the Middle East and Asia, then globally as it repositioned itself as a global lifestyle brand. It is a leading airline in the Middle East and one of the top airlines in the world. Flying to 65 countries on 6 continents, Emirates has used its sponsorships to increase awareness of its brand and connect with its passengers. These sponsorships have included numerous soccer teams and events in Europe, the Middle East, and Asia. Jersey-sponsorship deals with the London-based Arsenal and Paris Saint-Germain teams meant that Emirates had a presence in two of the busiest travel centers in Europe. In 2009 Emirates was ranked number five on *Sport + Market's European Football Sponsor Brands Top 20*, underscoring the effectiveness of its sponsorships. Emirates was also highly valued by business professionals. In the Centre for Brand Analysis's *Business Superbrands Official 500*, a ranking of brand popularity, Emirates ranked 68 in 2009. Overall, Emirates is regularly considered one of the best airline brands in the world. The Skytrax World Airline Awards list of the *Top 10 World's Best Airlines* ranked Emirates fifth in 2009, eighth in 2010, tenth in 2011, and eighth again in 2012.

BRAND OUTLOOK

- Though the airline industry as a whole was struggling in the early 2010s, Emirates was enjoying great success as the fastest-growing and most profitable airline in the world.
- Emirates has set a goal of becoming the biggest airline in the world by 2015.
- Emirates has implemented an effective sustainability program which has improved fuel efficiency and reduced the rate of carbon dioxide emissions.

The airline industry as a whole is struggling because of economic uncertainties, high and rising fuel costs, and sinking profits. It is believed that profits for the industry as a whole sank by nearly US$5 billion in just one year, from 2011 to 2012. There are bright spots, such as greater demand and profitability in Asia. Middle Eastern airlines on the whole, however, have seen profitability decline because of heavy exposure to European air traffic. Though Emirates has been affected by soaring fuel costs, it has impressive forward momentum as the most profitable airline in the world in the early 2010s and the fastest growing airline in the world. It is positioned for continued growth and has set a goal of becoming the biggest airline in the world by 2015. Emirates also has one of the youngest fleets of planes and is regularly ranked one of the best airline brands in the world, two factors that point to positive growth in the future.

Because the airline industry consumes vast amounts of fuel and creates significant pollution, Emirates has established a sustainability program that includes using less paper, maximizing fuel efficiency, and using fewer vehicles in its ground services. Though its total fuel consumption increased by 9.4 percent in 2010–11, its fuel efficiency improved by 1 percent and its total carbon dioxide emissions were reduced by 9.4 percent in 2011–12.

FURTHER READING

Balancing Our Performance: The Emirates Group 2011–2012 Environmental Report. Accessed February 12, 2013. http://www.emirates.com/english/images/2011_12%20Emirates%20Environment%20Report%20secured_tcm233-888462.

pdf?intcid=EN_Environmental_Report_185_tcm233-889856.

Brand Finance. "Emirates." *Brandirectory*. Accessed February 11, 2013. http://brandirectory.com/profile/emirates-airlines.

"Emirates." *RankingTheBrands.com*. Accessed February 11, 2013. http://www.rankingthebrands.com/Brand-detail.aspx?brandID=1744.

"Emirates Airline." *Air Transport World*, February 1, 2011.

"Emirates Airline and USTA Enter Partnership for US Open and US Open Series." *Food & Beverage Close-Up*, February 21, 2012.

"Kingdom Is a High-Potential Market for Emirates." *Arab News*, June 13, 2012.

Melville, Adrian. "Why Is European Soccer Having Such a Big Impact on the Airline Industry?" *Forbes*, February 7, 2013.

Tomlinson, Hugh. "Tim Clark: President, Emirates Airline: While Other Carriers in the Region Struggle, Dubai-Based Emirates Is on Track to Become the World's Biggest Airline." *Middle East Economic Digest*, November 23, 2007.

Vandyk, Anthony. "New Emirates Airline Causes Stir in Middle East." *Air Transport World*, April 1986.

E.ON

AT A GLANCE

Brand Synopsis: One of the world's largest energy companies, E.ON strives to provide cleaner, better energy products, as well as greater value and performance.
Parent Company: E.ON AG
E.ON-Platz 1
40479 Dusseldorf
Germany
http://www.eon.com
Sector: Utilities
Industry Group: Utilities
Performance: *Market share*—2.30 percent in terms of revenues in Europe (2008). *Sales*—US$157.28 billion (2012).
Principal Competitors: BASF AG; RWE AG

BRAND ORIGINS

- In June 2000 two German companies, VIAG AG and VEBA AG, merged to form E.ON AG, the largest energy company in Europe.
- E.ON's first goal in becoming a profitable energy-focused company was to sell off its unprofitable non-energy related holdings.
- In 2006 E.ON contracted to purchase natural gas from the Russian energy giant Gazprom over the next 30 years.

E.ON was formed in June 2000 from the merger of two German energy industry giants, VIAG AG and VEBA AG. Both companies had been in business since the 1920s. VIAG specialized in aluminum, electricity, and nitrogen, while VEBA was a coal and petroleum company. During the 1990s, both companies began to lose a great deal of money through over-diversification, and they felt that the best solution was to combine their resources and focus strictly on the energy market. The merger, worth EUR13.4 billion (US$17.4 billion), would create the single largest energy company in Europe and was estimated to save the reorganized companies about EUR1.6 billion (US$2.08 billion) per year by 2002. Though the merger was not official until June 2000, the new company became operational in January, and the E.ON name was first announced in April. One of the first orders of business was to streamline the company by getting rid of unnecessary baggage. The non-energy interests were worth more than EUR31 billion (US$40.25 billion) collectively. They included holdings in aluminum, electronics, logistics, packaging, and telecommunications. By selling off these unprofitable divisions, E.ON increased its profit potential but also, perhaps more importantly, raised a huge amount of capital with which it purchased other energy companies, adding to its own reach and market dominance.

In July 2002 E.ON made two important purchases. The first was the acquisition of the British utility Powergen and its U.S. subsidiary, LG&E Energy, for a total of EUR8.2 billion (US$10.65 billion). The second purchase was EUR4.1 billion (US$5.32 billion) for a 40 percent ownership of Ruhrgas, a publicly held company owned by ExxonMobil, Shell, and Preussag. Within a year, E.ON would own Ruhrgas outright, thus establishing a foothold in the huge gas market, with access to 20 European nations. This acquisition was followed up in 2004 with the purchase of a second British energy utility, Midlands Electric. This single acquisition gained E.ON nearly 5 million new customers and made it the second largest electric utility in England. During the last few months of 2004, E.ON acquired majority ownership of power companies in Norway, Bulgaria, and Hungary.

The frantic pace of expansion continued into 2005 with majority purchases of companies in Romania, England, the Netherlands, Italy, Sweden, and Russia, as well as more buyouts of competitors in Germany. E.ON was also getting actively involved in offshore drilling. E.ON Ruhrgas purchased a 30 percent stake in the Njord oil and gas field in the Norwegian Sea. Reserves were estimated to include 10 billion cubic meters of natural gas and 50 billion barrels of oil. E.ON also acquired UK-based Caledonia Oil and Gas Limited, with fifteen large gas fields in the British North Sea. In December 2005 E.ON struck a joint venture with Russian energy giant Gazprom and Germany's BASF to build a 900-kilometer-long pipeline from the Baltic Sea gas fields to a hub in Vyborg, Russia. This was followed up in 2006 with a deal in which E.ON Ruhrgas purchased 400 billion cubic meters of natural gas from Gazprom through 2036.

By this time, business was going extremely well for E.ON, and, true to its stated commitment to both customers and employees alike, the company transferred EUR5.4 billion (US$7.01 billion) to its company pension reserves, ensuring the financial security of employee pensions. E.ON also initiated several new large ventures to develop and support environmentally friendly technologies. By December 2007 it was already one of the world's largest wind-farm operators, with a capacity of more than 900 megawatts. Additional acquisitions boosted this capacity to more than 3,500 megawatts by 2012. Because of these types of environmental efforts, in December 2011 E.ON Climate & Renewables was awarded the "Global Energy Award" for "Green Energy Generator of the Year" as the best developer of offshore wind farms.

BRAND ELEMENTS

- The E.ON brand name was first released to the public in April 2000.
- The E.ON logo is purposely asymmetrical and almost childlike in its simplicity, projecting a lively, playful image of the company.
- The red color of the E.ON logo represents vitality and dynamism.

The E.ON brand name was created in April 2000 with the merger of two huge German conglomerates, VIAG AG (founded in 1923) and VEBA AG (founded in 1929). The "E" in E.ON stands for the words "electricity" and "energy." These words are similar in English, German, French, Spanish, Italian, and many other languages. The word "ON" is meant to represent not only the obvious meaning of having power turned on but also the optimistic symbolism of moving on or forward into the future. The company name is further enhanced by the monumental implications of the words "eon" and "aeon."

The logo consists simply of the brand name in red lowercase letters. Occasionally, the letters are shown in white on a red background. The font used for the E.ON logotype is lively, almost playful. The E.ON logotype is asymmetrical, almost childlike in its simple scrawl. Even the color was purposely selected to separate the organization from its competitors. Rather than a bright blue, which is traditionally associated with the energy sector, E.ON chose to make its logo red, to represent vitality and dynamism.

BRAND IDENTITY

- The E.ON brand identity represents a company that is both successful and reliable.
- Few large companies, especially ones in the energy industry, take the environment as seriously as E.ON does.
- E.ON has been active in exploring a variety of alternative energy options, including the development of large wind farms.

Since its formation, E.ON has worked aggressively to achieve a global reputation as a successful and reliable energy company. For its customers, the key to a positive brand identity has been affordable prices for services, consistent and reliable delivery of those services as close as possible to 100 percent of the time, and fast, effective, and efficient response to problems. For the company's shareholders, the key points are success, growth, innovation, and profitability.

Additionally, E.ON hopes to identity itself as a responsible company. In recent years environmental issues have become an extremely serious concern, and few industries are as closely linked to environmental issues as the energy industry is. E.ON has been exploring a variety of alternative energy options, including the development of a large wind farm off the coast of Cornwall, England, in 2008. Finally, the more than 85,000 people employed by E.ON want to work for a company that is stable, reliable, and conducive to personal growth, high standards, and teamwork. The E.ON brand is not just about selling a product. It is also about being there for the millions of people who depend upon it.

BRAND STRATEGY

- When E.ON purchased UK-based Midlands Electricity in 2004, the acquisition added 4.8 million new customers to E.ON's base.
- In 2007 the E.ON Energy Research Center developed a process that may remove up to 90 percent of carbon dioxide from conventional power plant emissions.
- E.ON is the world's largest wind-farm operator, with generating capacity of more than 3,500 megawatts.

Since its inception in 2000, E.ON's primary goal has been to transform itself from a European company with multiple operations into a global presence in the field of energy. This process was begun almost immediately and continued at a rapid pace for several years. The merger of VEBA and VIAG, which were already the second- and third-largest energy companies in Europe, created Europe's single largest energy company. To focus its efforts on the energy markets further, the new company systematically sold off EUR31billion (about US$29 billion at the time) worth of nonenergy businesses. These included holdings in electronics, logistics, packaging, telecommunications, and aluminum.

E.ON made two major acquisitions in July 2002. The first was a deal to purchase 100 percent of UK-based Powergen and its U.S. subsidiary, LG&E Energy, for EUR8.2 billion (US$10.65 billion). The Kentucky subsidiary gave E.ON new growth opportunities in the U.S., the largest energy market in the world. Later that same month, E.ON purchased a 40 percent stake in Ruhrgas for EUR4.1 billion (US$5.32 billion). Within a year, E.ON bought the company outright. The purchase of Ruhrgas opened up markets for E.ON in more than 20 European countries. In 2004 E.ON added another UK-based power company to its portfolio with the purchase of Midlands Electricity, with 4.8 million customers. During 2004 and 2005 E.ON purchased majority shares in power companies in England, Hungary, Romania, Italy, the Netherlands, Norway, Sweden, and the Russian Federation. In August 2006 E.ON Ruhrgas concluded negotiations with Russian energy giant Gazprom to purchase 400 billion cubic meters of natural gas through 2036.

E.ON's other major goal was to be the world leader in supporting and developing environmentally friendly energy technologies. To back up this claim, in October 2006 E.ON launched an industry-wide technology initiative to foster research and development of energy technologies. Next, in April 2007 E.ON opened the E.ON Energy Research Center in western Germany and committed EUR40 million (US$51.93 billion) in research funds over the next 10 years. The research center's focus was to be on energy efficiency and climate protection. Their first project was to test a process which may capture up to 90 percent of carbon dioxide from conventional power plant emissions. In December 2007 E.ON acquired wind-farm operators Airtricity Inc. and Airtricity Holding Ltd. E.ON now has more than 3,500 megawatts of wind-power capacity, making it one of the world's largest wind-farm operators. In 2008 it began three large-scale projects that more than doubled that capacity by adding large wind-farms in Denmark, England, and Texas. In 2011 E.ON, in partnership with Abengoa Solar, powered up two massive solar thermal power plants near Seville, Spain. The solar concentrators were made up of 121,000 mirrors covering an area the size of 300 soccer fields. The facility is capable of generating over 100 megawatts of electricity.

BRAND EQUITY

- According to the 2012 *Forbes* Global 2000 list of leading companies, E.ON ranked 409th overall and first among global electric utility companies.
- E.ON's total assets as of December 2011 were estimated at EUR152.74 billion (US$198.30 billion), with a market value of EUR37.86 billion (US$49.15 billion).
- Between 2010 and 2011 E.ON's sales increased 22 percent.

According to the 2012 *Forbes* Global 2000 list of leading companies, E.ON ranked 409th overall and first among global electric utility companies, based on revenues of EUR121.28 billion (US$157.3 billion). E.ON's total assets as of December 2011 were estimated at EUR152.74 billion (US$198.30 billion), with a market value of EUR37.86 billion (US$49.15 billion). Sales from 2010 to 2011 increased a respectable 22 percent, as the company continued to invest and expand into new territories and markets. According to the online encyclopedia *Branddirectory,* the E.ON brand ranked 88th in the world in 2012, and its brand value was US$9.7 billion.

BRAND AWARENESS

- E.ON's predecessors, VEBA and VIAG, were powerful conglomerates in the revitalization of the post–World War I German economy.
- As of 2012, E.ON had more than 26 million customers in over 30 countries around the world.
- Since 2006 E.ON has invested more than EUR25 billion (US$32.85 billion) to modernize older power plants and build more efficient new ones.
- Because of rapid expansion, brand awareness has been low in new markets. The company is combatting this through advertising, telemarketing, and corporate sponsorship.

Though E.ON has only been in existence since 2000, it has quickly managed to position itself as the proverbial 800-pound gorilla in the room. Its origins date back to the 1920s, when its parent companies, VEBA AG and

VIAG AG, were formed to supply and support the revitalization of Germany's post–World War I infrastructure through a wide variety of industrial operations as well as administrative and financial enterprises. These two companies formed a significant part of the backbone of the German economy and the development of the Reich as a fearsome military power. By the end of the 20th century, these two companies had grown to be the second- and third-largest energy companies in Europe, and their merger formed the single largest power utility company on the continent.

As of 2012, E.ON had more than 26 million customers in more than 30 countries around the world, and it continued its expansion not only into new territories but also into new energy alternatives. E.ON has become a world leader in wind and solar power and has made great strides in research aimed at making power plants more efficient and less harmful to the environment. It is estimated that between 2006 and 2009 alone E.ON invested approximately EUR25.3 billion (US$32.85 billion) to modernize older power plants and build new ones that operated with as much as 59 percent greater efficiency and generated cleaner energy.

Because of its rapid expansion, E.ON has had relatively low brand awareness in many of the new markets it entered, such as the Netherlands and the Czech Republic. Advertising and telemarketing campaigns raised awareness of the brand in those cases. In Britain, awareness of the E.ON brand increased because the company sponsored the FA Cup, a competition in English football, for several years.

BRAND OUTLOOK

- A positive factor in E.ON's brand outlook is the insatiable global appetite for energy and the increasing demand for renewable energy.
- In 2012 E.ON applied for and received designation as a "European Company" or a "Societas Europaea" (SE).
- E.ON has designated EUR4 billion (US$.19 billion) for investment in its Russian subsidiaries alone in 2012.
- In 2012 E.ON pledged EUR7 billion (US$9.09 billion) for the construction of three very large offshore wind farms.
- E.ON has set a goal to build one new offshore wind farm every 18 months.

A positive factor in E.ON's brand outlook is the insatiable global appetite for energy. The need for energy will continue to grow as more and more countries develop their economies. According to *International Energy Outlook 2011,* published by the U.S. Energy Information Administration, global energy consumption is expected to nearly double between the years 2000 and 2035, from 406 quadrillion Btu to 770 quadrillion Btu. To meet this ballooning need, many countries are trying to increase their use of renewable energy, in which E.ON is a market leader. For example, in 2009, the Council of the European Union passed the EU Renewable Energy Directive, setting the goal that the European Union would get 20 percent of its total energy needs from renewables by the year 2020.

E.ON is positioning itself to help meet that goal. According to E.ON's 2011 annual report, the company will continue to focus on "expanding our operations in renewables, generation outside Europe, and decentralized energy solutions." One of the most notable transitions will be the goal of transforming E.ON into a "European Company" or a "Societas Europaea" (SE), as it is more formally known. This new corporate designation, based on European Community Law, will allow E.ON to operate more flexibly throughout Europe and to be governed by Community Law, which is directly applicable in all member states of the European Community.

E.ON is also looking at expansion possibilities in Brazil, Russia, India, and China over the next few years. Its investment in its Russian subsidiaries alone was earmarked for EUR4 billion (US$5.19 billion) in 2012. E.ON has also continued its dedicated investments in the expansion of renewable energy. The company approved EUR7 billion (US$9.09 billion) over the next five years for, among other things, the construction of offshore wind farms at Amrumbank West, in the German part of the North Sea; Humber Gateway, off the coast of Yorkshire, England; and Karehamn, in the Baltic Sea of Sweden. For the future, E.ON has established a goal to commission a new offshore wind farm every 18 months.

FURTHER READING

Brand Finance. "Best Global Brands: E.ON." *Brandirectory.* Accessed November 15, 2012. http://brandirectory.com/profile/eon.

"E.ON AG." *International Directory of Company Histories.* Ed. Karen Hill. Vol. 128. Detroit, MI: St. James Press, 2012.

E.ON AG. "2011 Annual Report." Accessed November 15, 2012. http://www.eon.com/en/about-us/publications/annual-report.html.

"E.ON: Company Overview." *Encyclopedia of Business in Today's World.* Ed. Robert N. Stacy. Vol.2. Thousand Oaks, CA: Sage Publications, 2009.

E.ON Hungaria Group. "The Origin of the E.ON Brand." Accessed November 15, 2012. http://www.eon-hungaria.com/en/corporate/brand/origin.

Moulson, Geir. "German Utility E.ON Lowers 2013 Outlook." *Sun Herald* (Biloxi-Gulfport, MS), November 13, 2012.

Stromsta, Karl-Erik. "EON's Recipe for Success—Renewables plus Russian Gas." RechargeNews.com, August 13, 2012. Accessed November 15, 2012. http://www.rechargenews.com/business_area/finance/article319718.ece.

ERICSSON

AT A GLANCE

Brand Synopsis: Active in more than 90 percent of the world's countries, Ericsson is a leading global provider of telecommunications equipment.
Parent Company: Telefonaktiebolaget LM Ericsson
Torshamnsgatan 23
Kista
Stockholm 164 83
Sweden
http://www.ericsson.com
Sector: Information Technology
Industry Group: Technology Hardware & Equipment
Performance: *Market share*—38 percent in mobile network equipment (2012); 43 percent in the world's 100 largest cities (2012). *Sales*—SEK227.8 billion (US$35.5 billion) (2012).
Principal Competitors: Alcatel-Lucent SA; Cisco Systems Inc.; Ruckus Wireless Inc.

BRAND ORIGINS

- Swedish inventor Lars Magnus Ericsson founded the company in 1876 as a telegraph repair shop.
- Ericsson expanded into international markets during the late 1890s, beginning with Britain and Russia.
- In 2012 Ericsson employed nearly 110,000 people worldwide, of which about 18,000 worked in the home country of Sweden.

The history of Telefonaktiebolaget LM Ericsson dates to the beginning of the telecommunications era in the late 19th century. Its founder, Lars Magnus Ericsson, was an inventor and innovator whose designs supported the development of communications networks in his native Sweden. Ericsson began as a metal smith and engraver during his youth and then worked for a company that manufactured telegraph equipment. He started his own telegraph repair shop in Stockholm in 1876. Two years later he began making telephone equipment and began supplying his products to the only telecommunications company in Sweden at the time. As new companies entered the Swedish telephone market, Ericsson expanded and refined his designs. In 1878 the Ericsson company began manufacturing unique telephones, rather than simply improving those it purchased from Bell Telephone Company and Siemens. In 1918 Ericsson merged with the independent telephone company Stockholms Allmänna Telefonaktiebolag to become Allmänna Telefonaktiebolaget LM Ericsson.

Ericsson expanded into international markets during the late 1890s, establishing factories in Britain and Russia in order to procure contracts in those countries. The company also began operations in China, Mexico, South Africa, and South America. The United States was largely impenetrable at the time because the market was dominated by Bell Telephone Company. Lars Ericsson retired in 1901 and relinquished financial interest in the company in 1903.

A series of equity investors assumed control of the company, which was renamed Telefon AB LM Ericsson in 1925. Mismanagement and fraud led the company into an era of weak financial performance during the mid-20th century. It was saved from bankruptcy through a combination of bank and government assistance. Marcus Wallenberg Jr., with the backing of his family's financial institutions, was able to turn the company around. The Wallenberg family, through its investment company, Investor AB, has controlled the company since 1960.

From 2001 to 2011 Ericsson participated in a joint venture with Sony to codevelop handsets. The collaboration was initially successful with a line of phones offering enhanced music and photography capabilities under the Walkman and Cybershot brand names. However, the advent of the Apple iPhone caused difficulties in gaining market share, and Sony took full control in late 2011. Sony continued to market the Android-based smartphones under the Sony Ericsson brand name.

As of 2012 the company employed almost 110,000 people throughout the world, with about 18,000 located in the home country of Sweden. It is listed on the NASDAQ OMX Stockholm and the NASDAQ New York. Ericsson provides telecommunications network equipment and services with products designed for the enterprise, cable, mobile platform, and power module markets. The company holds 30,000 patents and applies for an average of 16 per day.

BRAND ELEMENTS

- Ericsson's logo includes the company name centered beneath three upward sloping, thick lines, which represent a stylized *E.*
- Ericsson's current logo has been in use since 2009.
- Blue is the primary color used by Ericsson, with custom fonts based on Garamond 3 and Neue Helvetica.

Ericsson uses blue as its primary color for brand identification. Its logo has changed many times throughout the years, with most versions including either the surname or initials of the company's founder, L. M. Ericsson. The current logo, representing a stylized *E,* dates from a design introduced in 1982, which featured the company name followed by three upward sloping, thick lines with rounded ends. Beginning in 2009 the logo was presented as the company name centered beneath the three upward sloping lines or simply as the three upward sloping lines without accompanying text. The custom typefaces used by the company, Ericsson Roman and Ericsson Sans, are based on Garamond 3 and Neue Helvetica.

BRAND IDENTITY

- Ericsson focuses on using "innovation to empower people, business and society."
- Ericsson envisions a networked society in which everything that can benefit from connection does so.
- Ericsson was named the most admired company in Sweden in 2012 by *Fortune* magazine.

The Ericsson brand is closely associated with innovation in communications and connectivity. Through improved communications technologies, Ericsson promotes new ways for individuals and businesses to interact, participate, and collaborate with each other. For example, in 2012 Ericsson announced that it was joining forces with the Volvo Car Group in a project to advance automotive Internet capabilities, allowing drivers and passengers access to cloud-enabled services and applications in real time.

The brand focuses on the ability of communications technologies to enhance people's lives by making access to services and government more convenient, by improving education, and by helping to address such global concerns as poverty and climate change. The company states on its website, "At Ericsson we use innovation to empower people, business and society. We envisage a Networked Society that is sustainable, and where everything that can benefit from a connection will have one." Ericsson is primarily known within the global communications industry for its networking technology; it is a leading provider of long-term evolution wireless technology for mobile networks, for example. The company prides itself on providing end-to-end communications products and services for voice, messaging, and multimedia applications.

Ericsson was rated the most admired company in Sweden in 2012 by *Fortune* magazine. In addition it has won numerous industry awards, including being named the leading optical transport firm, the leading DSL vendor, and the top telecom infrastructure equipment maker worldwide.

BRAND STRATEGY

- Ericsson's brand strategy includes advancing its concept of a networked society.
- Ericsson seeks to be the prime driver in an "all-communicating world."
- Ericsson's guiding principles are customer intimacy, continuous process improvements and innovation, and scale in delivery and technical solutions.

Ericsson emphasizes its "Networked Society" vision, in which it hopes to network virtually everything anyone touches during the course of a day. Through its continuous research and development it positions itself to play a leading role in offering end-to-end solutions for network carriers, utilizing all major mobile communications standards. Its website states, "Our vision is to be the prime driver in an all-communicating world."

Already a leader in the telecommunications and information communications technology industries, Ericsson has a truly global presence, with operations in 180 countries around the world. It does business with all major telecom operators worldwide and invests billions of dollars in research and development to maintain its technology dominance. As mobile communications has become the dominant method of communicating in the 21st century, Ericsson has focused on this area of equipment supply. It has continued to modernize its carriers' networks and has increased its market share in Europe. It continues to leverage its global presence and scale of operations in order to support its guiding principles of customer intimacy, continuous process improvements and innovation, and scale in delivery and technical solutions.

Ericsson's sponsorships are focused on bringing people and cultures closer together, creating an understanding and acceptances of differences, and helping to reduce social prejudice. It aims to provide solutions that make communications affordable for everyone as well as easily accessible.

BRAND EQUITY

- The Ericsson brand is a leader in the global business-to-business telecommunications market.
- In 2012 Ericsson maintained a 43 percent market share in the world's 100 largest cities.
- Ericsson has over 90 patent license agreements and is a net receiver of royalties in its patent portfolio.

Ericsson is a leader in the global business-to-business telecommunications market. It retains about 38 percent market share in mobile network equipment and a 43 percent share in the world's 100 largest cities, according to its internal data. It is also a leader among communications developers, licensing its technology through more than 90 patent license agreements, and is a net receiver of royalties in its patent portfolio.

On *Fortune's* "Global 500" for 2011, Ericsson is ranked 339th, with revenues of US$28.2 billion. In 2012 *Forbes* listed Ericsson as the 66th most powerful brand in the world and ranked it number 239 on the "Global 2000" list, with sales of US$32.4 billion. In 2012 the international market research firm Infiniti Research Limited named Ericsson among the top companies in the carrier WiFi equipment market for the years 2011 through 2015.

BRAND AWARENESS

- Ericsson's brand awareness is high among telecom operators worldwide.
- Ericsson operates in more than 90 percent of the world's countries and sells to all the major telecom services providers.
- Ericsson increases its brand awareness through creative projects and sponsorships that foster connectivity and social improvement.

As a company that largely sells to other companies, Ericsson is best-known to its corporate customers, and awareness of Ericsson among its direct market—telecom carriers—is extraordinarily high. As it operates in more than 90 percent of the countries around the world, it is very well known among the major telecommunications services providers across the globe.

To strengthen brand awareness outside its core business-to-business marketplace, Ericsson uses creative projects that support its core principles of connectivity and social improvement. In 2012 it served as a founding partner in the Picture Today Inspire Tomorrow photography project led by the Swedish nonprofit foundation Expressions of Humankind. Published by Aday.org, the project invited people throughout the world to use photography to document their lives on a single day, May 15, 2012. Both amateur and professional photographers from 165 countries submitted 100,000 photos, which were compiled into a digital exhibit available online and in book form.

The company also sponsored the Volvo Ocean Race, which is billed as the world's toughest around-the-world sailing challenge. In its home country, Ericsson sponsors the Swedish Sports Organization for the Disabled and the Swedish Paralympic Committee; Nobel Media, which develops and manages the media associated with the awarding of Nobel Prizes; as well as a theater company that features actors with developmental disabilities. In 2009 Ericsson increased its brand awareness by acquiring the naming rights to the Stockholm Globe, a sports and entertainment area now known as the Ericsson Globe, the largest spherical building in the world.

BRAND OUTLOOK

- The outlook for Ericsson's equipment sales is favorable as mobile data is a rapidly growing market segment.
- Ericsson maintains a research lab that tracks consumer trends that might impact the company.
- Huawei of China surpassed Ericsson as the world's leading telecom equipment provider by revenues in 2012, but Ericsson shipped more units.

Ericsson is a leading supplier to an industry that is expanding rapidly. The company predicts a 10-fold increase in global mobile data traffic by 2016. As this growth occurs, mobile operators will be called on to increase capacity, which will benefit Ericsson and other equipment providers. However, expansion may depend on spectrum availability, which is controlled by governments, not vendors. As of 2012, Ericsson was second only to Huawei of China among the world's largest telecom infrastructure manufacturers when ranked by revenue. Ericsson was the largest cellular infrastructure maker in the world, with Huawei having larger handset and enterprise businesses. When ranked by units shipped, however, Ericsson claimed the top position.

Ericsson's revenues from its operations in the Middle East and Africa were increasing in 2012, even as revenues from the rest of the world experienced limited or no growth. A contributing factor to the regional gain is Ericsson's work in Iran supporting the network expansion of the country's largest mobile telecom operator and its continued support of another Iranian mobile carrier despite Western sanctions against Iran. Financially, Ericsson saw a steep revenue drop in the fourth quarter of 2011, which continued into 2012. In an effort to reduce costs as it faced further revenue declines, the company eliminated more than 1,500 jobs in Sweden in late 2012.

To counteract decreasing revenues, the company sought to generate new ways to connect with its consumers. For example, a network gateway was announced late in 2012 that would allow for differentiated and personalized services. This is designed to increase the demand and adoption of cloud and video services in homes; it will also decrease network operators' operational costs, all the while giving the company opportunities to sell additional equipment. Ericsson's Consumer Lab is a market-sensing organization that annually releases hot consumer trends. This keeps Ericsson's name in front of consumers as well as giving it an advantage in anticipating trends that will call for new or different telecom equipment that can be sold to operators.

With its leading position in an expanding sector and long-term contracts with many of the world's leading telecom operators, Ericsson should continue to comprise a high-value brand in the telecommunications industry. It is far ahead of the firm that once dominated the U.S. industry—what is now Alcatel-Lucent—and it experiences wider distribution of its equipment than does Huawei. The company seems well positioned for future growth.

FURTHER READING

"Ericsson Releases 10 Hot Consumer Trends for 2013." *Telecom Tiger,* December 19, 2012. Accessed February 6, 2013. http://www.telecomtiger.com/fullstory.aspx?storyid=16447.

"Ericsson Unveils Broadband Network Gateway for Connected Homes." *Telecom Tiger,* October 17, 2012. Accessed February 6, 2013. http://www.telecomtiger.com/fullstory.aspx?storyid=15935.

Field, Roger. "Ericsson Maintains Growth in MEA Region." *CommsMEA,* October 28, 2012. Accessed February 6, 2013. http://www.commsmea.com/12768-ericsson-maintains-growth-in-mea-region/#.URLQw_JfTDs.

Fitchard, Kevin. "Huawei Knocks off Ericsson as World's Biggest Telecom Vendor." *Gigaom,* July 24, 2012. Accessed February 6, 2013. http://gigaom.com/2012/07/24/huawei-knocks-off-ericsson-as-worlds-biggest-telecom-vendor/.

Grundberg, Sven. "Sony Buys Ericsson Stake in Handset Joint Venture." *Wall Street Journal,* October 28, 2011.

McBride, Stephen. "Ericsson to Cut 1,500 Jobs." *CommsMEA,* November 10, 2012. Accessed February 6, 2013. http://www.commsmea.com/12797-ericsson-to-cut-1500-jobs/#.URLRVvJfTDs

"Sweden Supports Iranian Telecom." *Pakistan & Gulf Economist,* December 2, 2012.

"World's Most Admired Companies." *Fortune,* March 19, 2012. Accessed February 1, 2013. http://money.cnn.com/magazines/fortune/most-admired/2012/intl/Sweden.html.

EXXONMOBIL

AT A GLANCE

Brand Synopsis: The ExxonMobil corporate brand portrays Exxon Mobil Corporation as the world's premiere energy company, while the Exxon, Esso, and Mobil brands are used to market fuels, services, and lubricants.
Parent Company: Exxon Mobil Corporation
5959 Las Colinas Boulevard
Irving, Texas 75039
United States
http://www.exxon.mobil.com
Sector: Energy
Industry Group: Energy
Performance: *Sales*—US$467 billion (2011).
Principal Competitors: BP p.l.c.; Chevron Corporation; Royal Dutch Shell plc

BRAND ORIGINS

- Exxon Mobil Corporation grew out of the 1911 breakup of Standard Oil Company.
- The Esso brand was introduced by Standard Oil of New Jersey.
- The Exxon brand replaced Esso and Enco in 1972.
- The Mobil brand was trademarked by Vacuum Oil Company in 1899.
- The ExxonMobil corporate brand was created following the acquisition of Mobil Oil Company by Exxon Corporation.

ExxonMobil is the corporate brand of Exxon Mobil Corporation, which also markets fuels and lubricants under the Exxon, Esso, and Mobil Brands. All of the brands trace their heritage to The Standard Oil Company, incorporated in 1870 by John D. Rockefeller and partners. It was a vertically integrated behemoth that controlled everything from the forests that produced the wood to make the barrels, to the warehouses that stored the oil refined by the company. To circumvent antimonopoly laws, it was reorganized in 1882, creating the United States' first trust. Standard Oil fended off attempts to force its breakup until 1911, when, after years of court battles, the U.S. Supreme Court upheld a lower court's ruling that Standard Oil violated the Sherman Antitrust Act and ordered the dismemberment of the trust.

Kerosene had been the original flagship product of Standard Oil. Gasoline was little more than a nettlesome byproduct until it was discovered that it proved to be an ideal fuel for the internal combustion engine used to power the new automobiles. Esso, Exxon, and Mobil would all become major gasoline brands that grew out of the Standard Oil breakup. Esso was controlled by the new, smaller version of Standard Oil of New Jersey, but the brand could only be used in a limited number of states and overseas. Elsewhere, Standard Oil offered the Humble brand. Subsidiary Humble Oil & Refining Company introduced the Enco brand, an abbreviation for ENergy COmpany, in select states in 1960. In 1972 Standard Oil of New Jersey changed its name to Exxon Corporation. Esso and Enco were replaced by a single brand, Exxon, for use in the United States, but Esso continued to be used in other parts of the world.

The Mobil brand was created by Standard Oil Company of New York, or Socony, another one of the companies that resulted from the 1911 dissolution of Standard Oil. The company initially used Socony as its brand name, but added the Mobil and Mobilgas brands through the 1931 merger with Vacuum Oil. Mobil had been trademarked by Vacuum in 1899. Socony-Vaccum changed its name in 1955 to Socony Mobil Oil Company. The Mobilgas brand name was shortened to Mobil in 1963, and three years later the corporate name was trimmed as well, becoming Mobil Oil Company.

Exxon and Mobil charted independent courses until the late 1990s. An oil glut created record low prices for crude, prompting a wave of consolidation in the oil industry, as companies hoped to achieve economies of scale to better control costs. It was against this backdrop that Exxon agreed to acquire Mobil for about US$75 billion in December 1998. In order to pass regulatory muster, about 2,400 Exxon and Mobil gas stations had to be divested, but the deal was ultimately completed, resulting in the creation of the Exxon Mobil Corporation. The company elected to retain both the Exxon and Mobil brands, which had accumulated a great deal of brand equity over the years, and used ExxonMobil as its corporate brand.

BRAND ELEMENTS

- The Esso name is a phonetic rendering of Standard Oil's initials: "S.O."
- Esso's "Put a Tiger in your Tank" is one of corporate America's most successful slogans.
- Both Esso and Exxon make use of a cartoon tiger as a brand element.
- The winged horse Pegasus has been a long-time image associated with the Mobil brand.
- The ExxonMobil corporate brand is mostly used in corporate communications.

Exxon Mobil's corporate brand and product brands are comprised of several elements, some of them brand-specific and others shared between brands. The Esso name reflects the parent company's Standard Oil heritage. It is a phonetic rendering of Standard Oil's initials: "S.O." The logo features "Esso" in red letters and enclosed within a blue oval. The "E" is distinctive, looking like a backward "3."

Esso is associated with one of the most recognizable slogans in American corporate history: "Put a Tiger in your Tank." The phrase was coined in 1959 as a way to increase fuel sales by suggesting Esso gasoline would provide superior performance. It drew on the perception of the tiger as being strong, energetic, and fast. In 1964 the McCann-Erickson advertising agency created a cartoon tiger to accompany the slogan in print ads. It proved to be a winning combination, as demonstrated by soaring sales. The "Esso Tiger" was used around the world to promote the brand.

After Standard Oil of New Jersey changed its name to Exxon Corporation in 1972, the Exxon brand was created. Originally, the company planned to follow the four-letter tradition of Esso and Enco by using Exon. Supposedly this spelling was rejected to avoid an association with a politician of the same name, Nebraska Governor J. James Exon. Thus, an additional "x" was added to create Exxon. In the rendering of the name, it shares the same red color for lettering and transforms the blue oval of the Esso logo into a thick blue strip below the Exxon name. Both were presented against a white background and enclosed within a rectangular box. The two X's in Exxon were combined to lend a distinctive look. Exxon would also make use of the tiger as a brand element. It was presented in dozens of guises, from close-ups to full-bodied poses.

Mobil possesses its own brand elements. The logo uses red and blue lettering: The O is red, while the remaining four letters are blue. Red is also used in the rendering of Mobil's iconic corporate symbol of Pegasus, the winged horse of mythology. Over the years, Pegasus has been used in innumerable ways to support the Mobil brand, including signage, gas pump globes, advertisements, and promotional items.

The ExxonMobil corporate brand fuses the Exxon and Mobil wordmarks. In some cases, the two logos are stacked on top of one another, but mostly the wordmarks are presented entirely in red, fused together side by side. The logo is primarily used in corporate communications. The ExxonMobil brand also employs a unique slogan: "Taking on the World's Toughest Energy Challenges."

BRAND IDENTITY

- ExxonMobil is a Big Oil brand that projects an identity dissimilar to its image with many people.
- ExxonMobil's identity is that of a cutting-edge, environmentally responsible energy provider.
- Esso, Exxon, and Mobil offer similar identities as safe and reliable brands.

As the world's largest integrated oil company, as well as the number-one company on the Fortune 500, Exxon Mobil is Big Oil personified. The company counteracts what is essentially a negative image by crafting positive identities for its corporate and product brands. The overarching ExxonMobil brand presents Exxon Mobil Corporation as the world's premiere energy company, a cutting-edge concern that is highly competent and environmentally responsible while supplying the energy needs of the world. This portrayal of the brand is supported by the tagline "Taking on the World's Toughest Energy Challenges." The emphasis is on energy rather than oil, deflecting attention from the connection of fossil fuel to global warming and Exxon Mobil's environmental record. Moreover, ExxonMobil implies that it is willing and able to meet the world's energy needs. The corporate brand identity is also supported by the logo. The connected X's are meant to symbolize reliability but also suggest unity of purpose.

The Exxon Mobil product-brands share similar individual identities within the corporate brand. The Esso brand has been long associated with its tiger mascot, and many consumers still recall the tagline "Put a tiger in your tank." These elements were initially used as a way to differentiate Esso from other brands of gasoline, staking the claim that Esso was a high-performance brand. Over the years, consumers came to view gasoline as a commodity, with price more a factor in their buying decision than brand. Nevertheless, the tiger mascot continues to project an identity of a powerful and effective brand, while at the same time being warm and friendly. The long and consistent use of the distinctive Esso logo also supports the idea of reliability. Exxon's brand identity is essentially the same as Esso. It is also known for the use of the tiger mascot. The major difference is that Exxon is a more forward-looking brand, an identity in keeping with its more modern wordmark.

Offering essentially the same fuels, lubricants, and services, Mobil presents a brand identity that is very similar to Esso and Exxon. For many years, the brand's identity was tied to Pegasus, a symbol that suggested travel and freedom. Later, while Esso was laying claim to fuel effectiveness, Mobil tried to differentiate itself in the market as a clean-burning gasoline. In advertisements, the red "O" in an otherwise blue wordmark was depicted as a washing machine. While this image no longer resonates with consumers, Mobil continues to promote its clean fuels as a way to protect engines and increase mileage. Mobil is also well known for its motor oils, which it claims promote long engine life. All of these elements support Mobil's identity as a safe and reliable brand.

BRAND STRATEGY

- Exxon Mobil's multifaceted brand strategy operates at both the corporate and product levels.
- The Exxon Valdez accident had a lasting impact on the corporate-branding efforts of Exxon Mobil.
- Esso, Exxon, and Mobil are essentially used in the same way to market fuel.
- Mobil is positioned as a higher-quality lubricant brand than Exxon or Esso.
- In 26 countries the "On The Run" convenience store brand is used.

Exxon Mobil employs a multifaceted brand strategy that operates at both the corporate and the product levels. The ExxonMobil brand is used to promote Exxon Mobil's macro-interests. In some cases, that has meant damage control. Before the Exxon and Mobil combination, Exxon Corporation had to contend with the Exxon Valdez oil spill in Alaska in 1989. That experience would have a lasting impact on the company's corporate branding efforts after the acquisition of Mobil. Writing in a September 27, 2006, article in *Marketing*, Mark Ritson maintained that ExxonMobil had masterminded one of the most impressive global communications campaigns in the history of public relations, but he added that "the company's success in obfuscating the issues in its response to global warming must surely rank as one of the most shameful exercises in corporate self-interest."

In 2004 Exxon Mobil launched a corporate social responsibility campaign to sand off some of the rough edges of its public image, highlighting the company's pursuit of energy conservation and alternatives to fossil fuels. It wasn't until 2006, however, that Exxon Mobil, after years of challenging the science behind global warming, finally acknowledged a link to fossil fuels. It came a decade after BP had become the first major oil company to make the concession. BP went on to position itself as "beyond petroleum," and laid claims to being something of a "Green" company. ExxonMobil, in contrast, was seen as pursing an outdated brand strategy, which in the words of Ritson was "synonymous with spin, superficiality and even shadowy manipulation of truth."

Exxon Mobil also learned the impact that environmental disasters could have on its corporate brand. In 2006 the company was digging an exploratory well in the Gulf of Mexico that after 500 days of drilling reached a record depth of about 30,000 feet. Although seismic reports suggested that just 2,000 feet further down was a massive reservoir of oil, the company decided the well had become too risky. It was abandoned, and the company wrote off US$187 million. In the same waters four years later, BP's offshore drilling rig Deepwater Horizon exploded after a blowout, killing 11 people and sending crude oil gushing into the Gulf of Mexico in what would become the oil industry's worst oil spill. BP had ignored some of the same warning signs that had prompted Exxon Mobil to give up on its deep-water well. The violation of its brand promise gravely hurt BP. While perceived as less environmentally friendly than BP, the ExxonMobil brand gained in respect for the parent company's prudent conduct. Exxon Mobil was not shy about highlighting the differences between it and BP. The company quickly launched a blog called "Perspectives" to provide commentary on the BP spill that promoted its brand at the expense of its rival.

Separate brand strategies are employed with Exxon, Mobil, and Esso. All three are used to sell fuels, whether for the automotive, marine, or fuel markets. With lubricants there is some differentiation. Mobil had established a great deal of value in its motor-oil brand before the Exxon and Mobil combination. Mobil now serves the high-end performance segment, while Exxon and Esso are positioned as reliable and efficient but are placed in a lower tier. Exxon, Esso, and Mobil are also employed in fuel marketing, lending their names to service stations, airports, and marine ports around the world. An unattended retail format, Esso Express, is found in France and Belgium. In addition Exxon Mobil operates the "On The Run" convenience-store brand, used in conjunction with the Esso brand, in 26 countries.

BRAND EQUITY

- Mobil had a higher brand equity in the lubricant sector than Exxon and Esso.
- Brand Finance assigned a US$16.419 billion value to ExxonMobil at the end of 2011.
- ExxonMobil was ranked 43rd on the 2012 Brand Finance Global 500.
- ExxonMobil was listed 34th on its 2012 "BrandZ Top 100 Brand Ranking."
- ExxonMobil ranked number 55 on the 2012 top-100 CoreBrand Brand Power Ranking.

While a big-oil brand like ExxonMobil is not especially loved, there is no doubt that it enjoys significant brand equity. As fuel brands, Exxon, Esso, and Mobil offer less brand equity than in an earlier time when consumers were more loyal to a particular gasoline brand. Contemporary consumers see little difference between fuel products, and in fact fuels have become engineered to perform so well with modern engines that there is no significant difference. Price is the key factor, not brand, in the fuel category. The same cannot be said for lubricants, however. Mobil is a well-respected motor oil brand and accordingly has a higher brand equity in this sector than do Exxon or Esso.

Determining the true brand equity of ExxonMobil, or any brand, is always difficult. Using their own methodologies, some brand consultancies and business publications have attempted to place a monetary value on brands as a way to objectively compare them. According to one consultancy, Brand Finance, ExxonMobil was worth US$16.419 billion at the end of 2011. It was a value that ranked ExxonMobil 43rd on the 2012 Brand Finance Global 500 list of the world's most valuable brands. Branding agency Millward Brown assigned a value of US$18.315 billion to ExxonMobil in slotting it at 34th on its 2012 "BrandZ Top 100 Brand Ranking." Another agency, CoreBrand, placed ExxonMobil at 55th on its 2012 Top 100 CoreBrand Brand Power Ranking. In the annual listing presented by the European Brand Institute, ExxonMobil was the 46th-most-valuable brand, worth EUR16.141 billion.

BRAND AWARENESS

- ExxonMobil has high brand awareness, but not all of it is positive.
- As a target of Greenpeace, ExxonMobil received undesirable brand recognition.
- Longevity and advertising have created strong brand recognition for ExxonMobil.
- The Exxon, Esso, and Mobil brands are used in 42,000 retail outlets in 118 countries.

ExxonMobil enjoyed very high brand awareness, as did its subbrands Exxon, Esso, and Mobil. Not all of the awareness brought positive associations to the company, however. Exxon Mobil's size and aggressive campaign to thwart environmental protection measures brought recognition but also made ExxonMobil an unsympathetic brand in the eyes of many and a target of environmental activists. In the early 2000s Greenpeace launched a pan-European campaign called "Stop Esso" and encouraged motorists to buy fuel from other retailers. Greenpeace even created a fake Exxon Mobil 2002 annual report that satirized the company's environmental record. It was seen by many as a matter of turnaround being fair play, because in 1998 ExxonMobil released a report that raised doubts about climate change. Designed to look like it had been issued by the National Academy of Sciences, the report was widely circulated in Washington, D.C., and was taken seriously by politicians as well as members of the media until the Academy denounced the ruse.

Exxon Mobil's product brands are well known as well. Mobil and Esso have been in use for many decades, and even the more recently created Exxon has been around since 1972. Awareness has been greatly aided by large advertising budgets devoted to promoting the brands over an extended period of time. Awareness is also supported by the signage of Exxon Mobil's fuel marketing business. All told, the three brands are divided among 42,000 service stations, 700 airports, and 300 marine parts operating in 118 countries.

BRAND OUTLOOK

- Little emotional bond exists between ExxonMobil and its customers, who view the relationship as purely transactional.
- Exxon Mobil is well positioned to enjoy success in the near term because of its size and diversified operations.
- From a long-term perspective, Exxon Mobile is in an untenable position and needs to extend its brands to new forms of energy.

ExxonMobil is not a beloved brand, albeit it is respected in many quarters for the size and strength of its corporate parent. Nor are the Esso, Exxon, and Mobil product brands held in the same high regard as they were before the days of oil shortages and the specter of global warming, when the tiger and Pegasus mascots created a warm, emotional appeal with their respective brands. There is little if any emotional bond between customers and ExxonMobil or its sub-brands. It is purely a transaction relationship, engendering little more than pump-and-pay loyalty. For some, these are even hated brands. Nevertheless, they remain very valuable and powerful, a truth not likely to change in the immediate future.

Exxon Mobil is well positioned to enjoy success in the near term because of its size and diversified operations. Compared to 2010 levels, energy demand is expected to grow 30 percent by 2040. The company has an extensive portfolio of major oil and gas projects that it can exploit to meet this need. It also possesses unconventional assets, such as oil sands and acid/sour gas. The future is not free of challenges, however. Exxon Mobil sells a product of which there is only a finite supply. In time there will be no choice but to move to other forms of energy, including renewable sources. Higher taxes on gasoline might be imposed to wean the population off of fossil fuels, a move that could hurt big oil companies like Exxon Mobil. From a long-term perspective, Exxon Mobile is in an untenable position. Whether it can extend its brands to new forms of energy is a question yet to be answered.

FURTHER READING

"Business Powerbrands Flex Marketing Muscle." *Marketing Week*, September 8, 2011.

Dennis, Anita. "Exxon and Mobil and ExxonMobil. And Tosco?" *New York Times*, December 12, 1999.

Embrey, Alison. "Battle of the Brands." *Convenience Store News*, June 14, 2004.

"Esso Faces Critics with Global Ethics Campaign." *Marketing*, May 19, 2004.

"Exxon Mobil Corporation." *International Directory of Company Histories*. Ed. Jay P. Pederson and Miranda H. Ferrara. Vol. 67. Detroit, MI: St. James Press, 2005.

Linnett, Richard, and Laura Petrecca. "ExxonMobil Units Review $100 Million Media Acc't." *Advertising Age*, October 9, 2000.

Mouawad, Jad. "New Culture of Caution at Exxon after Valdez." *New York Times*, July 12, 2010.

Ritson, Mark. "Exxon Vision Is Perilously Short-Term." *Marketing*, September 27, 2006.

Snyder, Adam. "In the Court of Public Opinion, Exxon Is Not the Only One on Trial." *Adweek's Marketing Week*, March 5, 1990.

Wieners, Brad. "Grab a Tiger by Its Tail: ExxonMobil Feels the Heat." *New York Observer*, June 30, 2003.

FACEBOOK

AT A GLANCE

Brand Synopsis: Already an iconic brand in its short history, Facebook is the world's most popular social network and provides connectivity by linking people and various websites.
Parent Company: Facebook, Inc.
1601 Willow Road
Menlo Park, California 94025
United States
https://www.facebook.com/
Sector: Information Technology
Industry Group: Software & Services
Performance: *Sales*—US$3.7 billion (2011).
Principal Competitors: craigslist, inc.; Friendster, Inc.; Google Inc.; Linkedin Corporation; Microsoft Corporation; Myspace Inc.; Twitter, Inc. United Online, Inc.; Yahoo! Inc.; YouTube, LLC

BRAND ORIGINS

- The Harvard University undergraduates Mark Zuckerberg and Dustin Maskovitz and the former classmate Adam D'Angelo started Facebook in February 2004 as thefacebook.com.
- Originally, Facebook was limited to college and high school students and corporate employees. Later, anyone with a legitimate e-mail address could join.
- Even though its social network, information, games, and other content are free for members, Facebook earns money by accepting advertisements on its site.

The Harvard University undergraduates Mark Zuckerberg and Dustin Maskovitz and the former schoolmate Adam D'Angelo founded Facebook while still young adults. Facebook is now the most popular social networking site and one of the most famous brands overall in the world.

Founded in February 2004 as thefacebook.com, the site was where Harvard students could post their personal information and photographs; later, students at other colleges began posting their own information. The site began accepting advertising, a practice that would eventually generate huge profits for the company and make Facebook a valuable international brand.

The site registered as a corporation in July 2004 and attracted outside investors. It continued to grow as its membership extended to more college students, then to high school students, and eventually to employees of corporations. Developers created Internet applications for Facebook, and the site allowed users to share links for articles and videos from a variety of sources. Besides communicating with other users, Facebook users could access information and entertainment options, from news to games, all for no charge.

New members continued to join Facebook, which broadened its membership to people with legitimate e-mail addresses, not just to people with academic or corporate affiliations. By 2007 the site had more than 20 million registered users. As its membership grew, so did its outside funding, advertising revenues, and recognition.

This growth continues, as the site is a popular, profitable, and recognizable global brand.

BRAND ELEMENTS

- The logo for Facebook is the company name in lowercase block letters, usually in white letters with a blue background.
- The lowercase *f* from the Facebook logo appears on the website's drop-down menus and tabs. It also appears in a blue box as a badge on other websites and serves as a link to the Facebook website.
- Facebook features a Follow button, once known as the Subscribe button. This button allows Facebook users to follow other users.
- Facebook employs a Like button that enables users to indicate whether they like, approve, or agree with something.

Befitting its status as a highly visual medium, Facebook has a number of distinctive visual elements. Its logo is the word *Facebook* in lowercase block letters. This lowercase logo is usually in white letters in front of a blue background.

Facebook repeats elements of this lowercase logo and uses these elements with other brand identifiers. For example, the initial lowercase *f* from the Facebook logo appears as part of the website's drop-down menus and tabs identifying the site. This lowercase *f* also appears within a blue box on other websites. These lowercase Facebook f badges serve as links to the Facebook website.

The social media site frequently uses other elements to publicize itself. Its Follow button, once known as the Subscribe button, is a rectangle with the word *Follow* accompanied by the Facebook f badge. Facebook users who use the Follow button can follow other users, even if they are not Facebook friends with them. This is yet another instance of Facebook repeating the use of its visual f badge and constantly referencing itself, given that the Follow button is on a Facebook page and references other Facebook sites.

Another popular Facebook visual image is the Like button. This button is a drawing of a hand with a raised thumb and uses Facebook's signature colors of blue and white. Known as the thumbs-up position, this hand gesture in American culture means a person likes, approves, or agrees with something. Facebook users click on the Like button to signal that they like, approve, or agree with another person's post. This button is another multipromotional Facebook tool, because clicking on the names that are listed next to the Like button brings an Internet user to the Facebook page of the people who posted the Like button. The Like button's thumbs-up symbol has transcended Facebook and is used to signify the approval of things outside of the Internet and even appears on merchandise.

BRAND IDENTITY

- A 2012 Facebook commercial said the brand was like chairs, doorbells, airplanes, bridges, and dance floors because they all connect people.
- Facebook's YouTube channel contains Facebook Stories that users can share and comment on, reinforcing Facebook's role as a unifying force.
- People connect to others on Facebook by "friending" them; Facebook uses silhouettes of people to signify these friends.

A 2012 commercial for Facebook described what the brand does. It stated that Facebook is similar to items such as chairs, doorbells, airplanes, bridges, and dance floors because they all connect people. This minute-and-a-half commercial also featured multiple groups of people in different international settings, further reinforcing the connectivity theme.

The advertisement used the tagline "The things that connect us." This tagline is featured prominently on Facebook's YouTube channel. The channel also contains Facebook Stories, which are short videos that have been posted by Internet users. When other Internet users watch these videos and post comments about them, they are participating in a communal activity. Facebook's YouTube channel, then, is a forum for the brand to communicate with and unite people.

The brand emphasizes this connection in other ways. People connect to other people on Facebook by "friending" each other. Facebook depicts these friends by using stylized silhouettes of people. Even though Facebook is an Internet-based brand, its advertisements, YouTube channel, terminology, and logos all emphasize people instead of technology.

BRAND STRATEGY

- Facebook's own web pages promote itself. They feature the lowercase f badge, the Like button (which links to other Facebook pages), and various Facebook posts. These posts often have links to other Facebook pages.
- Images and information about Facebook and its employees appear on Facebook's own pages. These pages explain what Facebook is and how users can use it.
- The cofounder Mark Zuckerberg is a symbol of Facebook, appearing in interviews, on television programs, and even as a character in *The Social Network*, a 2010 movie about the creation of Facebook.

Facebook promotes itself by offering the Like button and the lowercase f badge, which links to its website. Its own Facebook pages also promote itself. These pages feature the lowercase f badge, the Like button (which links to other Facebook pages), and various Facebook posts. These posts demonstrate how users can utilize Facebook. For example, Facebook has created links to its Global Disaster Relief on Facebook page. This page describes global disasters and provides links to organizations that work to relieve these disasters. This page also contains posts from other Facebook users with links to their own Facebook pages.

Facebook's own pages also feature images and information about the brand and its employees, such as photographs of a Mark Zuckerberg television interview. These pages help explain what Facebook is and how users can use it. They also promote the company and reinforce elements of its brand.

The cofounder Mark Zuckerberg is a visible living embodiment of Facebook. He has appeared in a number of interviews in a variety of media and even guest starred in an episode of *Saturday Night Live*, a popular comedy and musical show in the United States. The episode was hosted by the actor Jesse Eisenberg, who portrayed Zuckerberg in *The Social Network*, a 2010 movie about the creation of Facebook. Like the lowercase f badge and the thumbs-up Like button, Zuckerberg is a visual symbol of Facebook.

BRAND EQUITY

- In 2012 *Forbes* magazine indicated that Facebook is among the 100 most powerful brands in the world.
- According to the international brand professional Landor Associates, Facebook was the leading breakaway brand in 2011 and 2012.
- In 2012 the brand research firm General Sentiment named Facebook the most valuable global brand.

In 2012 *Forbes* magazine stated that Facebook is among the 100 most powerful brands in the world. Facebook was also the leading breakaway brand in 2011 and 2012, according to the international brand professional Landor Associates. The firm noted that breakaway brands excel in connection, convenience, and confidence and indicated that between 2008 and 2011 Facebook experienced a 206 percent growth in brand strength.

Interbrand ranked Facebook 69th among the best global brands in 2012, with a brand value of US$5.4 billion. That same year Facebook was ranked 19th in BrandZ's "Top 100 Brands" list, with a brand value of US$33.2 billion.

In an October 2012 report, the brand research firm General Sentiment named Facebook the most valuable global brand. Interestingly, it argued that publicity about Facebook, even negative publicity, helped the site gain prominence in 2012. Discussing this report in *Forbes*, Jeff Bercovici cited Facebook's "sheer brand ubiquity."

BRAND AWARENESS

- In 2012 Twitter tested a system that allowed its users to use a Like button instead of its Favorite button to mark something they liked.
- Published in 2012, a survey of Facebook advertisers reported that their two biggest reasons for buying Facebook ads were to build their brand awareness and sentiment and to direct users to their own websites.
- A survey published by Pingdom in 2012 found that 43 percent of American teenagers cited Facebook as the favorite media site.
- A study published in 2011 found that social network users spent 95 percent of their time on Facebook. A *comScore* study said that Facebook had a 90.4 percent market share in Turkey and a 81.7 percent share in the United Kingdom in 2010.

The movie *The Social Network* is testament to Facebook's brand awareness. The fact that a Hollywood film studio invested millions of dollars to make a movie about the creation of the website and that millions of people paid to see the movie demonstrates how many people find Facebook interesting and illustrates the fame of the Facebook brand. The movie also earned critical recognition, nominations, and awards, which further publicized the movie and Facebook.

Competitors are aware of Facebook and its features. In 2012 Twitter tested a system that allowed its users to use a Like button instead of its Favorite button to mark something they liked. The Technorati contributor Adi Gaskell wrote in October 2012 that Twitter's use of the Like button appeared "to be borrowed directly from arch rival Facebook."

Advertisers hope to capitalize on Facebook's brand awareness to improve their own brand awareness. In an article that was published by *WebProNews* in July 2012, Josh Wolford reported on a survey of Facebook advertisers that was conducted in 2012 by *Advertising Age* and Citigroup. The survey indicated that advertisers' two biggest reasons for buying Facebook ads were to build their brand awareness and sentiment and to direct users to their own websites. These advertisers believed that Facebook itself had high brand awareness and Internet popularity; they hoped that these factors would help boost their own brand recognition and Internet presence.

Teenagers in particular are big Facebook fans. Published in 2012, a survey by Pingdom found that 43 percent of American teenagers cited Facebook as their favorite social media site. Another 28 percent rated Twitter as their favorite and 12 percent liked Instagram the best. This popularity among young users could bode well for the brand's future.

Other studies have chronicled Americans' use of Facebook. A study published in 2011 found that social network users spent 95 percent of their time on Facebook. According to Jennifer Moire of AllFacebook, this means that "social networking really means time spent on Facebook." A separate study published in 2012 found that Internet users spent one of every seven minutes online at Facebook. The site's presence in other countries is also high. For example, it reached 90.4 percent of Turkish homes and 81.7 percent of homes in the United Kingdom that used social media in 2010, according to *comScore*.

BRAND OUTLOOK

- Facebook's highly anticipated initial public offering of stock was held in May 2012. The offering soon led to criticism due to technical glitches that plagued the trading and resulted in negative publicity for both Facebook and NASDAQ, the exchange where it traded.
- In 2011 Facebook launched Facebook for Every Phone (for feature phones), Facebook for iPad, Facebook applications, and other items.
- Facebook reported sales of US$3.7 billion and US$1 billion in profit in 2011.
- In 2012 Facebook reported more than 1 billion monthly users.
- Facebook began experimenting with charging users who wanted to send messages in late 2012.

In May 2012 Facebook sold stock in an initial public offering on NASDAQ. This highly anticipated and widely publicized offering also received widespread criticism, as technical glitches plagued the trading and resulted in confusion, trading problems, and even lawsuits. These glitches also brought negative publicity for Facebook and NASDAQ.

More positive developments for the social network include its forays into other devices and media. In 2011 it launched Facebook for Every Phone (for feature phones), Facebook for iPad, Facebook applications, and other items. In addition, Internet users can access Facebook Live, a streaming channel that offers live videos. These features connect people in various ways while promoting Facebook.

Facebook announced in 2012 that it topped more than 1 billion monthly users. Approximately 189 million of these monthly users were from the United States and Canada, 253 million were from Europe, 277 million were from Asia, and 288 million were from other regions.

Besides its user popularity, the brand is also a profitable one. In 2011 the site reported sales of US$3.7 billion and US$1 billion in profit. These profits are expected to grow as the site sells more advertising revenue. In late 2012 it began experimenting with charging Facebook users for sending messages, which is another way the company may earn additional revenue in the future.

FURTHER READING

Badenhausen, Kurt. "Apple Tops List of the World's Most Powerful Brands." *Forbes*, October 2, 2012.

Bercovici, Jeff. "Facebook Haters Help Make It World's Most Valuable Brand." *Forbes*, October 16, 2012.

Bergesen, Mich, and Stephanie Simon. "Facebook Maintains Hold as Leading 'Breakaway Brand' for 2012." *Forbes*, September 4, 2012.

Blythe, David. "Facebook Builds Brand Identity." uPublish.info, December 1, 2010. Accessed February 12, 2013. http://www.upublish.info/Article/Facebook-Builds-Brand-Identity/408846

Elowitz, Ben. "UNBALANCED: Facebook Captures 14 Percent of Our Online Attention but Only 4 Percent of Ad Spending Online." *Business Insider*, June 27, 2012.

"Facebook, Inc." *International Directory of Company Histories*. Ed. Tina Grant. Vol. 90. Detroit, MI: St. James Press, 2008.

"Facebook Is Nr.1 Market Share in 15 of 18 European Markets." *comScore*, March 2, 2011. Accessed February 12, 2013. http://www.comscoredatamine.com/2011/03/facebook-is-nr-1-social-network-in-15-of-18-european-markets/

"Facebook vs Twitter vs Instagram: What Do Teens Prefer?" *mobileYouth Idea Factory*, November 14, 2012. Accessed February 12, 2013.

Gaskell, Adi. "Is Twitter Building a 'Like' Button?" Technorati, October 23, 2012. Accessed February 1, 2013. http://technorati.com/social-media/article/is-twitter-building-a-like-button1/.

Moire, Jennifer. "INFOGRAPHIC: Facebook Has 95 percent Market Share in U.S." AllFacebook, December 21, 2011. Accessed February 1, 2013. http://allfacebook.com/facebook-market-share_b71620.

Olanoff, Drew. "Facebook Announces Monthly Active Users Were at 1.01 Billion as of September 30th, an Increase of 26 percent Year-over-Year." TechCrunch, October 23, 2012. Accessed February 1, 2013. http://techcrunch.com/2012/10/23/facebook-announces-monthly-active-users-were-at-1-01-billion-as-of-september-30th/.

Wolford, Josh. "Brand Awareness Is the Top Goal for Facebook Ads, Say Marketers." *WebProNews*, July 9, 2012. Accessed February 1, 2013. http://www.webpronews.com/brand-awareness-is-the-top-goal-for-facebook-ads-say-marketers-2012-07.

FALABELLA

AT A GLANCE

Brand Synopsis: Based in South America, Falabella is a department store chain that focuses on affordable quality products and accessible department stores.
Parent Company: S.A.C.I. Falabella
Calle Rosas 1665
Casilla, Santiago 1737
Chile
http://www.falabella.com
Sector: Consumer Discretionary
Industry Group: Consumer Durables & Apparel
Performance: *Market share*—43 percent of the domestic market; 7 percent of department stores globally (2011). *Sales*—US$2.8 billion (2011).
Principal Competitors: Cencosud; Wal-Mart de México y Centroamérica

BRAND ORIGINS

- The company was named for its founder, Salvatore Falabella, and opened in 1889 as a tailor shop.
- Under the guidance of Alberto Solari in 1937, Falabella began selling family clothing.
- In 1990 Falabella began investing with the Mall Plaza Group.
- In the late 1990s Falabella became a public company, went international, and diversified into travel, banking, insurance, and other businesses.

Salvatore Falabella, an Italian immigrant, founded Falabella in 1889 in Santiago, Chile. It was the first large tailoring shop in Chile. In 1937 Alberto Solari, who was married to Falabella's granddaughter, joined the family business. Under Solari's guidance, the store began to sell family clothing, giving a boost to the company's image and profits. Following a rebranding in 1937, Falabella began to explore other outlets for products, transforming Falabella from a tailoring shop to a store selling clothing for the entire family.

In 1958 Falabella further increased the size and variety of products offered in its store and rebranded itself again, this time as a full-service department store selling not only clothing, but also home products. The shift towards a more comprehensive retail structure benefited the company, and Falabella capitalized on this success until the early 1970s, when the company was requisitioned by the state. During the presidency of Salvador Allende (1970–73), the Marxist government enacted price caps and only allowed nationalized companies to continue to operate. The loyal employees of Falabella were said to have refused entry to the company's new administrators. According to former Falabella vice president Juan Cúneo Salari, business for Falabella was so slow during the 1970s that, with limited stock and even more limited consumer traffic in the store, employees sometimes passed the time by playing chess.

As an attempt to regain customer confidence, Falabella released its own credit card in 1980. In order to offset the expense of extending credit, Falabella negotiated with its suppliers to extend the company a 60-day credit, enabling Falabella to then pass along the credit to the end consumer. In 1983 Falabella moved its location to a larger space in Parque Arauco, where it opened its doors to a more affluent clientele.

Also in the early 1980s, Falabella was forced into further change with the death of their company president, Arnaldo Falabella, and the retirement of Alberto Solari, Arnaldo's son-in-law and architect of many previous successes in the company. As a result of these changes, the Falabella family decided to sell their stock, the majority of which was purchased by a group of investors. Under the new management, the company began to focus on such goals as expansion through internationalization, inclusion within shopping malls, and further retail diversity.

In 1990 Falabella invested with the Mall Plaza Group, opening Mall Plaza Vespucio. The mall was the first of its kind in South America to specifically focus on catering to the middle class. The Mall Plaza Group subsequently opened six more mall locations, with Falabella holding a half-share of each. Falabella became an international company in 1993, when it opened its first location in Argentina. The company was able to expand into Peru in 1995, when it acquired the Peruvian division of the U.S. company Sears, called Saga.

By 1996 Falabella's annual sales had reached US$500 million, with 13 stores in Chile. By the end of 1996 Falabella owned 22 stores and had begun exploring projects in real estate and financial services. That same year, the company issued an IPO on the Chilean Stock Exchange. With the success of its expansion, Falabella took on additional commercial ventures in 1997, establishing a partnership with U.S. company Home Depot and creating a travel agency and insurance brokerage. In 1998 Falabella continued its expansion and opened Banco Falabella, a bank focusing on small businesses, mortgages, and auto loans. Falabella opened its first location in Buenos Aires in 1999 and also purchased shares of the largest drugstore chain in Chile, Farmacias Ahumada S.A. In 2012 Falabella was the largest department store chain in Chile, with over 250 locations in South America and 27 shopping malls.

BRAND ELEMENTS

- The logo consists only of the Falabella name in light green, lowercase, italic type.
- Alternate versions of the logo include white letters on a green background and a shortened version as letterhead for documents.
- Falabella's simple, graphical logo is used across Falabella's multiple business ventures as well as its websites.

Falabella's name comes from the founder of the company, Salvatore Falabella, an Italian immigrant. Given its involvement in many different industries, Falabella has become a widely recognized brand across South America. The company's logo, consisting solely of typographical elements, is simple and easily recognizable. The logo consists of the word "Falabella" in a lowercase, italic script in light green. The Falabella logo is used both on the company's storefronts and on company websites. An alternate logo gives the name in white letters on a green background. A smaller version of the logo, consisting of the letter *f* followed by a period, in the same light green italic script, is used as letterhead in documents such as the company's annual report.

Falabella uses separate names for some of its other ventures. These include Banco Falabella, which was established in 1998. The bank offered home, auto, and small business loans. The same light green that appears in the Falabella logo is used in the names of the company's other ventures to create brand unity.

BRAND IDENTITY

- Falabella has committed to pursuing sustainability in all of its businesses.
- The company's main goal is to provide products consumers want at reasonable prices.
- Falabella operates across various consumer sectors, reinforcing the widespread influence of its brand.

Given that Falabella has a wide range of franchises, its brand has several facets. Overall, the company aims to provide quality products at convenient prices. Since the company has a presence in four countries, it tailors its franchises to each location and adjusts product lines accordingly. In the online research journal of Wharton School, Luis Alfredo Lagos of the marketing firm Cadem Research International describes Falabella's approach this way: "The chain has a permanent program of contacting consumers, getting to know them in depth, and then adapting their supply of products. This doesn't take place by chance; it is not a question of whether someone has good taste in clothing, for example." Thus Falabella has made a name for itself as a store that listens to its customers rather than trying to change their taste and habits. By operating on several platforms and in several markets, such as malls, department stores, banks, and pharmacies, Falabella has succeeded in making the brand name known in many market segments.

As a result, Falabella is South America's second most successful department store chain, after Cencosud. In Falabella's 2011 annual report, the company emphasized the importance of environmental sustainability. It was not only the first retailer in South America to feature environmentally friendly retail stores and to be certified by Leadership in Energy and Environmental Design (LEED) but was also the first retail giant to consistently measure its carbon footprint. This dedication set Falabella apart from its biggest competitors, Cencosud and Wal-Mart.

BRAND STRATEGY

- Falabella converted from a clothing-only retailer into a full-service department store in 1958.
- In the 1990s Falabella focused on the expansion and diversification of its brand, opening shopping malls, grocery stores, and pharmacies.
- The company went international in 1993, when it opened its first location in Argentina.
- In the early 2000s Falabella merged successfully with several competing companies, increasing its market share in the process.

Starting with the rebranding of 1937, Falabella has gone through many image changes since the company's inception. When Alberto Solari joined the company in 1937, his innovative ideas transformed the company from a men's tailor shop into a clothing store for the entire family. In 1958 the second rebranding of Falabella, by which it became Chile's first department store, was also a successful move. The idea for this change sprang from the growth of the global market, with stores like Sears opening locations in South America, for example. Altering its product lines, Falabella began to compete with such international companies.

The most substantial changes to the company's brand strategy occurred from the 1980s, when the Falabella family passed control of the company to new investors, who pursued a more modern and expansive image. The first innovation was to introduce store credit, which enticed consumers to return. Falabella experienced financial struggles in the 1970s, making the introduction of credit for its customers in the early 1980s difficult; however, the company's suppliers also extended credit to Falabella, which enabled the plan to succeed. In 1983 Falabella moved its location in Santiago to the upscale area of Parque Arauco in order to attract a more affluent clientele.

In the 1990s Falabella's management created a model for expansion and diversification of the brand, including internationalization, investing in real estate, and an expansion into banking. The company also developed its first shopping mall, the first step in its plan for large-scale property expansion. Following a merger with the Mall Plaza Group, the company went international in 1993, when it opened its first department store in Argentina and, later, Peru. The expansion continued in 1997, when Falabella opened its first travel agency and signed an agreement with Home Depot, bringing the U.S.-based home improvement store to Chile. The diversification continued to accelerate as the Falabella Bank was opened in 1998 and the pharmacy chain Farmacias Ahumada was acquired in 1999.

By 2001 Falabella had purchased all shares of Home Depot Chile, and it changed the name to Home Store. The following year, Falabella opened its first hypermarket in Peru, under the name Tottus. In 2003 Home Store took over its primary competitor, Sodimac, and expanded its presence to Argentina, Peru, and Colombia. Sodimac was not the only competitor to merge with the retail giant. Falabella took over competitors in many different markets during its expansion plan, including San Francisco Supermarkets in 2005, the Imperial Mall in 2007, and the Mall Calama in 2010. As one of the most successful companies in Chile, Falabella has excelled in absorbing the competition and expanding both its brand awareness and market share.

BRAND EQUITY

- Falabella is the second-largest retailer in Chile.
- In 2012 Falabella was ranked 434th among the 500 most successful global brands, with competitor Wal-Mart taking fifth place.
- In 2012 Falabella's brand value was estimated at US$2.67 billion.

Falabella is Chile's largest department store chain. In 2012, it was ranked the third most valuable brand in Latin America in *BrandZ Top 100 Most Valuable Global Brands 2012,* published by Millward Brown, who estimated Falabella's brand value at US$5.2 billion. Falabella is Chile's second-largest retailer behind Cencosud and had 28 percent of Chile' domestic market share according to Latin American Retail Connection. Although Cencosud also operates supermarkets and malls, Falabella has a larger presence in Latin America and invests in even more diverse affiliates, including clubs and jumbo hypermarkets. Falabella was voted company of the year by the Chilean business magazine *Capital* in 2001. That year also marked a deep recession in Argentina, but the five Falabella locations in the country reported profits.

According to Brand Finance's *Global 500 2012*, Falabella ranked 434th overall, with an estimated brand value of US$2.67 billion. Competitor Cencosud was not ranked on this list. However, competitor Wal-Mart came in 5th, with a brand value of US$38.3 billion.

BRAND AWARENESS

- Falabella's department store brand, created in 1958, was still strong in 2012.
- In the 1990s Falabella began a large diversification project, making the company's services and products accessible to more consumers through different retail outlets.
- Countries where the Falabella brand has thrived include Chile, Argentina, Colombia, and Peru.

Although it began as a tailor shop, the department store model has been both the longest-lasting and best-known model associated with the Falabella brand. In 2012 there were more than 200 Falabella department store locations in South America. Because the company has diversified dramatically since 1990, the consumer awareness of Falabella is high in Chile, Argentina, Colombia, and Peru. In Peru, the affiliated hypermarket Tottus is even better known and more successful than the department store. Additionally, upon the acquisition of Home Depot Chile, the expansion of the Falabella brand enabled it to reach an entirely new clientele. Since Falabella has continuously expanded its business and ventured into new areas of consumerism, the South American market is saturated with the brand. In 2011 Funding Universe reported that Falabella controlled a 43 percent market share among department stores in Chile.

BRAND OUTLOOK

- Falabella has continued to thrive in recent years, even during economic downturns.
- In 2011 Falabella held 43 percent of the Chilean market share for department stores.
- In 2012 Falabella partnered with Marriott International to build its first hotel, thus extending the brand to the hospitality industry.

Since the diversification and expansion activities initiated in 1990, Falabella has continued to do well, having grown from one department store to encompass more than 200 locations in South America. The company thrived even during an economic downturn in Chile in 2001. In 2011 Falabella held 43 percent of the department store market share in Chile, up from 25 percent in 2005. The diversification of the company brand has enabled Falabella to thrive in different markets. In 2012 Falabella entered into a deal with Marriott International, with the goal of extending its brand to include hotels. The partners' first hotel is set to open in 2014 in Santiago.

Additionally, as shown in Falabella's 2011 annual report, the company has begun rebranding itself as an environmentally sustainable company. In this effort, Falabella has been keeping track of its carbon footprint in all retail locations, the first South American department store chain to do so. These efforts, as well as the company's commitment to its employees and shareholders, position it to have a successful future.

FURTHER READING

Bird Picó, María. "King of Commerce." *Shopping Centers Today*, September 2005. Accessed September 23, 2012. http://www.icsc.org/srch/sct/sct0905/retail_chile.php.

Brand Finance. "Global 500 2012." *Brandirectory*. Accessed September 3, 2012. http://brandirectory.com/league_tables/table/global-500-2012.

"Chain Stores in Peru." *AnaPeruana*, March 12, 2009. Accessed September 26, 2012. http://www.anaperuana.com/2009/03/12/chain-stores-in-peru/.

"Chile Retail Report Q2 2012." *Business Monitor International*, March 13, 2012.

Falabella. "History Timeline." Accessed September 23, 2012. http://www.falabella.com/falabella-cl/static/staticContentWithHeader.jsp?title=Inversionistas-EN-Grupo-Falabella.

"Falabella arribará a México en 2012." *Diario Financiero*, March 19, 2012. Accessed September 26, 2012. http://eleconomista.com.mx/industria-global/2012/03/19/falabella-arribara-mexico-2012.

"S.A.C.I. Falabella." *International Directory of Company Histories*. Ed. Jay Pederson. Vol.69. Detroit, MI: St. James Press, 2005.

Webber, Jude. "Chile's Falabella: Coming to NYSE?" *Beyondbrics*, March 20, 2012. Accessed September 25, 2012. http://blogs.ft.com/beyond-brics/2012/03/20/chiles-falabella-coming-soon-to-nyse/#axzz27Y85r5G3.

FANTA

AT A GLANCE

Brand Synopsis: A truly global brand, the many fruit flavors of Fanta appeal primarily to youth and young adults as a fun, free spirited, and bright soda.
Parent Company: The Coca-Cola Company
1 Coca-Cola Plaza
Atlanta, Georgia 30312-2499
United States
http://www.coca-colacompany.com/
Sector: Consumer Staples
Industry Group: Food, Beverage & Tobacco
Performance: *Market share*—1.9 percent in the United States (2011). *Sales*—US$12 billion worldwide (2010); 2 billion cases worldwide (2012).
Principal Competitors: Pepsi; Mountain Dew; Dr. Pepper; Tango; Sunkist; Crush; Welch's; Mirinda; Slice

BRAND ORIGINS

- Fanta was created in Nazi Germany to address the lack of availability of Coca-Cola.
- Fanta was reintroduced in Europe in 1955.
- In 1960 Fanta first became available in the United States.
- Fanta began being aggressively marketed in the early 21st century.

Fanta was originally introduced in 1940 in Nazi Germany. It was created by Max Keith, the head of Coca-Cola in Germany, after the United States entered World War II and the Coca-Cola syrup became unavailable. Keith's formula included what was left over from apples used to make cider, surplus fruit from Italy, and saccharin. Fanta was a big seller during the war years in Germany.

After World War II ended and the German Coca-Cola operation again became part of the international parent company, Fanta was discontinued for nearly a decade. Though Coca-Cola had only made its signature product to this point, Pepsi was having success by introducing new flavored beverages during the 1950s. In response, Coca-Cola looked to Fanta and reintroduced the beverage in Europe in 1955. Keith's formulation was discarded, and the first Fanta was an orange soda. Over the next few years, Fanta expanded globally to Africa, Latin America, and Asia, and more flavors were added.

Coca-Cola brought Fanta in the United States in 1960, as part of a larger strategy to introduce new products to the market. Orange Fanta had not become available in the United States before then because Coca-Cola did not want to undercut sales of its primary cola brand. In the United States there was little marketing support and sales of Fanta were poor until the mid-1980s. In 1986 Coca-Cola stopped selling Fanta on a nationwide basis, though it was available in select markets with large immigrant populations from countries where Fanta had strong sales.

By the 1990s Fanta continued to have low sales volumes in the United States, minimal advertising support globally, and little attention from Coca-Cola executives.

Yet in 1995 Fanta sales grew by 8 percent. By 1996 Fanta was selling one billion cases annually, mostly abroad, and was the number-five brand in the world. Its biggest markets were Germany, Brazil, Mexico, Japan, Thailand, and Spain.

In the mid-1990s Coca-Cola began to capitalize on the surprising popularity of Fanta with a global advertising campaign, "High Voltage Taste," which was aimed at teenagers. In the United States, however, Fanta still had relatively limited availability. It was mostly sold through fountain dispensers because Coca-Cola had decided earlier in the decade to focus on Minute Maid branded carbonated juice drinks.

At the beginning of the 21st century, Coca-Cola adopted a new strategy for Fanta in the United States. In 2001 Fanta became available in new markets with a significant Hispanic, primarily Mexican-American, population that was familiar with the beverage. These locations included Texas, Arizona, Southern California, and Atlanta.

As a result, case sales in the United States exploded from 24.4 million in 2000 to 42.2 million in 2001, and Fanta became The Coca-Cola Company's number-two brand worldwide, with US$1.4 billion in case sales globally. Building on this success, Coca-Cola again made Fanta available nationwide in the United States in 2002. While there were 70 variations of Fanta sold in 180 countries, only orange, pineapple, strawberry, grape, and berry were available in the United States.

There was still only limited advertising support for Fanta until the first decade of the 21st century. By 2009 Fanta was sold in 187 countries and was world market leader in orange and grape soft drinks. Because of brand growth, Fanta overtook Diet Dr. Pepper to become number nine among sodas in the United States in 2011, part of a larger positive trend in worldwide momentum for the brand.

BRAND ELEMENTS

- Fanta is associated with concepts like fun, playfulness, and fruity flavors.
- Fanta was known for numerous fruity variants that were modified to reflect local tastes.
- In 2002 the Fantanas made their debut.

Fanta is a German word meaning fantasy or imagination, and the Fanta logo and product are linked with these ideas as well as with fun, flavorfulness, and playfulness. The puffy Fanta logo, in use since the late 20th century, is a distinctive shade of blue, often with a green leaf or other fruit-related symbol linked to the "t." The logo reflects the brand's core ideas of being bright, bubbly, and fruity.

Since its reintroduction in Europe in 1955, Fanta has been known for its bold flavors and lack of caffeine. Including at least 70 varieties, nearly every fruit grown is available as a Fanta flavor somewhere in the world. The brand's formulas were not sacred however, unlike Coca-Cola's or Pepsi's. The brand constantly changed its flavors and formulas to reflect local tastes. Fanta conducted research to ensure that the brand's many flavors matched consumers' changing tastes. In the first years of the 21st century, some types of Fanta began to be manufactured with 100 percent natural flavors and colors to address consumer demand for more healthy products. Fanta Orange is the biggest seller in the United States and many other countries.

In 2002 Fanta launched a memorable marketing push featuring the Fantanas, four girls who symbolized the Fanta brand, primarily in the United States. Each member of the girl group represented a Fanta flavor, whether orange, pineapple, strawberry, or grape, and wore an appropriately colored variation of the group's outfit. Fun was at the core both of the ads featuring the Fantanas as well as of the Fantanas themselves. The Fantanas were also multiethnic, multiracial, and multinational, reflecting the brand's transculturalism and the increased global awareness of its target teen audience. In the ads featuring the catchy jingle "Wanta Fanta?," the Fantanas left their home base, the tropical Fantana Island, to bring Fantas to distressed teenagers and young adults. The Fantanas became brand ambassadors who made personal appearances. Though Fanta initially ended the campaign in 2006, the Fantanas were revived in 2009 and 2010 with an interactive contest to choose the Pineapple Fantana.

BRAND IDENTITY

- Fanta focused its marketing on teens and their parents.
- The globally unified campaign "More Fanta. Less Serious." began in the early 21st century.
- Fanta reaches its target teen audience online, especially through Facebook, Twitter, and YouTube.

Fanta is the second oldest brand owned by The Coca-Cola Company, and is its second most popular outside of the United States. The brand sells well in many countries around the world and is especially popular in tropical areas like Mexico and Brazil. Fanta focuses its advertising and marketing primarily on young children and teenagers, and their parents. Because of the global popularity of the brand, much of its marketing and advertising is geared toward teens. It is the biggest noncola soft drink chosen by youth worldwide. In the Unites States alone, two-thirds of its sales came from teenagers by 2012. Youth appeal is key to the brand's identity.

In 2007 Fanta launched its biggest global advertising campaign to date. It focused on the idea of play, because research showed that teenagers were being pressured to grow up and to give up having fun. The campaign relied on intense images and graphics with limited language, so that the campaign could appeal to teens around the globe. Fanta Play and the tag line "Fanta. Play On." were used in various markets until 2011. By this time, Fanta was using another global campaign, "More Fanta. Less Serious," or sometimes just "Less Serious." It was the largest and most unified campaign ever for Fanta.

Like Fanta Play, "Less Serious" focused on teens and their parents and worked to bring a sense of play and fun into their lives. Used in 90 percent of global markets by mid-2011, the campaign featured a number of vibrant, animated, multicultural characters who have fun, cool, sometimes mischievous lives. Each of them stood for a different type of play and reflected the diversity in the world of teenagers. In 2011 in China, as part of "Less Serious," the brand had the "9th Class" campaign which used the fact that Chinese school children had eight long school lessons during the day which could then be followed by Fanta fun time.

While the "Less Serious" campaign employed traditional television ads, billboards, posters, store signs, and print ads, Fanta also promoted it online and via social media. Media included mobile ringtones, websites, digital banners, and Facebook, forms favored by its target audience. This underscored the brand's grasp of how teens spend their time. On Facebook, Fanta had a related game app, "Lost in Time." In the United States, Fanta had a partnership with Jenga mobile gaming application to target new teen customers. Extremely active on Facebook and Twitter, Fanta had at least six million followers by early 2013. On Twitter's "@FantaFun" the brand interacted daily with its followers. The brand also had its own dedicated channel on YouTube.

BRAND STRATEGY

- Fanta regularly introduced variants in markets worldwide.
- In 2009 a 100 percent natural, reformulated Fanta Orange hit the market in the United States.
- In 2012 the midcalorie Fanta Select was test-marketed in the United States.

Fanta targets youth and their parents in markets around the world with its many bold flavors. The brand continuously introduced new variants in various markets and adjusted them to local tastes to maintain top appeal. Fanta Blackcurrant, for example, became available in Nigeria in 2000 and the United Arab Emirates in 2002. In 2009 Fanta Portello Grape and Fanta Cream Soda were launched in Sri Lanka. In 2011 Fanta began introducing some flavors not previously available in the United States, including Fanta Toronja.

In 2009 a reformulated Fanta Orange became available in the United States. Along with this flavor came a revamp of Fanta's packaging and graphics to make them more vibrant and colorful. Fanta Orange was made with 100 percent natural flavors. Other variants, including Fanta Apple and Fanta Grapefruit, were also reformulated with 100 percent natural flavors. These changes were made to address consumer demand for healthier products.

In some countries, Fanta produced diet versions of selected variants. Fanta Light had been available by the turn of the 21st century, and in 2005 no-added-sugar Fanta Z was introduced in the United Kingdom to replace Fanta Light. In the United States, this version was known as Fanta Zero, and it hit the market in 2008. In 2012 midcalorie versions of Fanta were test marketed in certain markets in the United States. Called Fanta Select, it only had 70 calories. Fanta Select was created in response to a larger trend toward midcalorie, healthier sodas.

By 2010 Fanta was the second-best-selling soda in most of Africa, behind only Coca-Cola. It was also a strong seller in Europe and Latin America, where Brazil was the largest consumer market for Fanta. The Coca-Cola Company consciously tried to expand the Fanta brand in Asia in the late 20th and early 21st centuries. In addition to mounting focused campaigns in China, Fanta launched in India in 1995 and was reformulated several times for the market over the years. In 2007, for example, Fanta Orange was redone so that it tasted like the oranges available in India. By 2011 Fanta was the fourth-largest-selling soft drink in that country.

BRAND EQUITY

- Fanta is the second-most-popular carbonated soft drink in the world, with growing sales.
- Fanta saw an increase in market share in the United States between 2010 and 2011.
- Fanta was ranked fifth on the list of movers and shakers in the soft drink category in "BrandZ Top 100 Most Valuable Global Brands 2012" report.

Globally, Fanta is the second-most-popular carbonated soft drink in the world, and the second largest brand for The Coca-Cola Company outside of the United States, after Coke. Popular largely by word-of-mouth for years, Fanta benefited from successful advertising campaigns in the first decades of the 21st century that capitalized on its youth appeal. This led to increases in sales and market share in the United States at a time when carbonated soft drinks were becoming less popular.

Fanta has a high brand equity. According to Brand Finance's *Brandirectory*, Fanta has a brand value of US$2.792 billion in 2012, a brand rating of AA+, and an enterprise value of US$12.628 billion. It ranked 408th in Brand Finance's *Global 500* for 2012, after being not ranked in 2011. According to "BrandZ Top 100 Most

Valuable Global Brands 2012" report, Fanta was ranked fifth on its list of "movers and shakers" in the soft drink category, after Coca-Cola, Diet Coke, Pepsi, and Red Bull. Fanta's brand value was US$3.998 billion, a decrease of 8 percent. Its brand momentum, which measures prospects of future earnings, was five on a scale of one to ten.

BRAND AWARENESS

- Fanta was consumed over 130 million times daily worldwide.
- Fanta has high brand awareness in Latin America, Europe, the Middle East, and North America.
- Fanta has high brand loyalty among teens in various countries.

Consumed in excess of 130 million times per day globally, Fanta has high brand awareness, especially in Latin America, Europe, the Middle East, and North America. In the mid-1990s, when there was little advertising support for the brand, Fanta was number seven in terms of logo recognition, ahead of such iconic logos as Levi's. It has high brand loyalty among teens, and Fanta actively cultivates its youth appeal. In 2011 Fanta was number 100 on the Smarty Pants ranking of Kids' Top 100 Most Loved Brands in the United States. The UK Kid Brand Index for 2011 ranked Fanta at number 37. This ranking showed what children aged 7 to 15 thought of leading brands.

Support by consumers of all ages in various countries ensured that Fanta would remain a highly regarded, well-known brand. In 2009 it was number 59 in Je Zuster's ranking of the Dutch Top 100 Best Brand Awareness. Two years later, Fanta was ranked 45th on the Dutch Brand 100, compiled by the Symphony IRI Group. This is a ranking of the revenue of the biggest brands sold in Dutch supermarkets. Fanta was ranked 28th in 2009 and 45th in 2010. In 2012 Fanta was number six on the DeBrand Top 100 German Brands list.

BRAND OUTLOOK

- Fanta saw a 3 percent increase in sales in 2011 in the United States and was expected to continue to grow.
- Despite a decrease in carbonated soft drink consumption, Fanta sales have increased globally.
- Growth in the Hispanic population in the United States is expected to help future sales of Fanta.

The carbonated soft drink market, both in the United States and worldwide, faced challenges because of concerns about obesity, worries about a link between carbonated soft drinks and poor health, and competition from energy drinks, bottled water, teas, and private label soft drinks. A decrease in soda consumption began in 1999, and the decline worsened beginning in 2005. The Coca Cola Company agreed not to sell sodas in elementary schools and middle schools, beginning in 2006, and no sugary sodas in high schools. Despite negative trends, Fanta saw an increase in sales and seemed to have positive long-term-growth prospects. Its 3 percent growth was the largest of the top ten carbonated soft drink brands in the United States in 2011. One reason for Fanta's growth, at least in the United States, was the fact that its target teen audience was less concerned with health than were older consumers. The growth of the Hispanic population in the United States could also help the brand, which was popular in Latin America. Fanta invested more in Asian markets like China and India to build its already impressive global growth.

FURTHER READING

Brand Finance. "Fanta." *Brandirectory.* Accessed January 10, 2013. http://brandirectory.com/profile/fanta.

"BrandZ Top 100 Most Valuable Global Brands 2012." Millward Brown. Accessed January 10, 2013. http://www.millwardbrown.com/brandz/2012/Documents/2012_BrandZ_Top100_Report.pdf.

Elliott, Stuart. "Now, Hit 'Play' If You Want a Fanta." *New York Times,* April 5, 2011.

"Fanta," RankingTheBrands.com. Accessed January 10, 2013. http://www.rankingthebrands.com/Brand-detail.aspx?brandID=631.

McWilliams, Jeremiah. "Coke Has Thirst for More Than Cola." *Atlanta-Journal Constitution,* November 7, 2010.

Palmer, Brian. "Why Do Foreigners Like Fanta So Much?" *Slate Magazine,* August 5, 2010.

"Special Issue: U.S. Beverage Results for 2011." *Beverage-Digest,* March 20, 2012. Accessed January 10, 2013. http://www.beverage-digest.com/pdf/top-10_2012.pdf.

Walker, Rob. "The Fanta Clause." *Slate Magazine,* July 22, 2002.

Zmuda, Natalie. "Coca-Cola Pumps up Fanta Ad Support across 190 Countries." *AdvertisingAge,* March 29, 2011.

FEDEX

AT A GLANCE

Brand Synopsis: Synonymous with shipping, FedEx is the second-largest delivery service in the world and provides a host of business solutions, including global delivery and document services.
Parent Company: FedEx Corporation
942 South Shady Grove Road
Memphis, Tennessee 38120
United States
http://www.fedex.com/
Sector: Industrials
Industry Group: Transportation
Performance: *Sales*—US$42.68 billion (2012).
Principal Competitors: DHL International GmbH; United Parcel Service, Inc.; United States Postal Service

BRAND ORIGINS

- A Yale University term paper by founder Frederick W. "Fred" Smith outlined plans for an air freight company that offered overnight delivery services.
- Smith started Federal Express in 1971.
- Using its own private aircraft fleet meant that Federal Express could ship packages quickly, since it did not have to rely on commercial airlines' regulations or schedules.
- In 1989 Federal Express expanded internationally by acquiring the Flying Tiger Line.
- Federal Express became FedEx in the 1990s.

Federal Express, now known as FedEx, had its origins in a Yale University term paper by former Marine pilot Frederick W. "Fred" Smith. Smith described his plans for an air freight company that offered overnight delivery services. This company would concentrate on speed, access smaller cities, contain a central hub to allow the company to control its services, and own its own fleet of aircraft so it would not have to deal with commercial airlines' schedules and regulations.

This academic theory became a business reality in 1971 when Smith formed the Federal Express Corporation. Federal Express's central hub was Memphis. The company began serving 25 cities in 1973. Federal Express used its planes to pick up packages from these airports nightly, fly the packages back to Memphis, sort the packages, and resend the packages to other airports.

Building a private aircraft fleet created high start-up costs and initial debt for the company, but having its own fleet helped it ship packages more quickly than if it had to rely on commercial airlines. The company soon began turning a profit. It also began capturing significant market share, becoming well known for its overnight delivery service. Deregulation of the airline industry in 1977 meant Federal Express could carry larger payloads, and it invested in bigger airplanes to accomplish this.

In 1989 Federal Express acquired other aircraft when it bought Tiger International, Inc., and its cargo airline, Flying Tiger Line. This acquisition expanded the company's international presence, as Flying Tiger had landing rights at airports in Europe, Japan, Southeast Asia, and South America. Other efforts outside the United States included the creation of a division in the 1990s to handle the company's Latin American and Caribbean business and expansion of its business in regions like China and Europe.

In the 1990s Federal Express modified its brand logo and its name, adopting the shorter "FedEx" as its new name. It also provided new services. It bought Kinko's, a chain of document and printing service stores, in the early 2000s and changed the name to FedEx Office in 2008. This is just one FedEx division. Others include FedEx Express, FedEx Ground, FedEx Global Logistics, FedEx Custom Critical and FedEx Services, FedEx Trade Networks, and the FedEx SupplyChain. FedEx also operates at OfficeMax office supply stores, has drop boxes at locations such as office buildings and banks, and works with the United States Postal Service (USPS) to deliver mail and packages. These divisions and services help FedEx customers conduct business all over the world.

BRAND ELEMENTS

- The current FedEx logo features the word "FedEx" in block letters, with the *Fed* in purple and the *Ex* in different colors to represent different company divisions.
- The FedEx logo appears on items being shipped, vehicles doing the shipping, and places that can help customers do this shipping.
- The FedEx logo appears frequently on the company's web pages, reinforcing the company's shipping capabilities.

The current FedEx logo features the word "FedEx" in block letters, with *Fed* in purple and *Ex* in different colors to represent different parts of the company. The "Ex" part of the logo features a white space between the *E* and *x* that resembles an arrow. This arrow represents speed and movement and is an appropriate symbol for a company that aims to ship goods quickly.

The large, block-letter FedEx logo appears prominently on its corps of delivery trucks and vans, freight trucks, airplanes, envelopes, boxes, FedEx drop boxes (spots used to drop off items needing delivery), and branches of its FedEx Office printing, shipping, and office services chain. This logo thus appears on items being shipped, vehicles doing the shipping, and places that can help customers do this shipping. All of this reinforces FedEx's reputation as a shipping company and as a company that gets things done.

This logo appears multiple times on the company's web pages. These pages allow users to do several things. Customers can order shipping supplies, create shipments, schedule pickups or find FedEx Office branches, track their orders, and handle their shipping documents, invoices, and other information. These functions again reinforce the company's shipping capabilities and illustrate how its business activities can help customers conduct their own business.

BRAND IDENTITY

- During the 1980s Federal Express commercials featured fast-talking actor John Moschitta and the tagline "When it absolutely, positively has to be there overnight."
- The tagline "When it absolutely, positively has to be there overnight" acknowledged customer needs and how FedEx would satisfy them.
- A 2008 catalog illustrated FedEx Office's customer knowledge and job expertise by showing its employees, customers, and finished products.
- In 1994 Federal Express rebranded itself as FedEx and introduced a new logo with an arrow that represents speed.

Business activity, accomplishment, and speedy shipping were topics explored in a famous FedEx advertising campaign from the 1980s. This campaign featured commercials with actor John Moschitta as a fast-talking business executive conducting several business deals quickly during the course of the commercials, which featured the tagline "When it absolutely, positively has to be there overnight."

With this tagline, FedEx portrayed itself as a company that recognized its customers' needs—they needed packages delivered quickly. It promised that FedEx would satisfy these needs in a definitive fashion by "absolutely, positively" delivering the packages quickly. The tagline positioned FedEx as a customer-focused brand.

Its commitment to customers can also been seen in a catalog. A 2008 catalog by FedEx Office depicted the signs and graphics it sold by illustrating some of its products and services in those areas. It described its customer service just as graphically. The cover of the catalog does not highlight FedEx-produced signs or products. Instead, the cover shows a photograph of a FedEx Office employee holding a banner and interacting with another person, presumably a customer. Just inside the cover is another photograph of a FedEx Office employee interacting with a customer. This employee appeared to be holding a sign.

Situated in prominent locations (the catalog's cover and early pages), these catalog pictures highlighted FedEx's willingness to communicate with its customers. By showing FedEx employees with completed products (the banner and the sign), the pictures demonstrate how this customer knowledge and job expertise can produce successful projects for all FedEx customers.

In 1994 Federal Express rebranded itself as FedEx. Federal Express's founder, chief executive officer, and president Frederick W. "Fred" Smith wanted a logo he could see on company trucks from five blocks away. The company conducted extensive work to create this brand and logo, including work with focus groups. The result was the new, shorter name FedEx, a name meant to convey speed. The arrow in the logo also indicates speed. This new name and logo in different colors meet Smith's visibility requirements, according to marketing and branding expert Susan Gunelius, who praised the new FedEx logo as "simple, clean, bold, and flexible."

BRAND STRATEGY

- The company's three-part brand strategy involves knowing your company (FedEx's reliability); proving this quality (being reliable); and communicating reliability plus information about the company.
- FedEx paid for naming rights for the NFL football stadium FedExField in Maryland and the NBA basketball arena FedExForum in Tennessee.
- FedEx has sponsored tennis's ATP World Tour and the French Open, is affiliated with the ERC, and was a longtime sponsor of college football's Orange Bowl.

Monica Skipper, a brand strategy leader at FedEx, said that the company's three-part brand strategy can be applied to different businesses. According to Skipper, the first part involves knowing your company. Skipper maintained that FedEx is all about reliability and that proving its reliability forms the second step of FedEx's brand strategy. Communicating reliability plus information about the company is FedEx's third step. Skipper noted that businesses can tailor messages to reach different audiences, but they should not be afraid to repeat themselves.

Another way that FedEx has promoted its name is by sponsoring a variety of sporting events and facilities featuring its name. It paid for the rights to use its name on FedExField, in Landover, Maryland, home to the National Football League's Washington Redskins, and FedExForum in Memphis, Tennessee, home to the National Basketball Association's Memphis Grizzlies. For over 20 years, it also sponsored the Orange Bowl, a college football bowl game in Florida.

FedEx also serves as a sponsor and carrier of tennis's ATP World Tour and the French Open (also known as Roland Garros, after a French, World War I aviator) and as a carrier for the European Rugby Cup (ERC). Its tennis and rugby affiliations have promoted the FedEx name to sports fans all over the globe.

BRAND EQUITY

- A 2008 article reported that FedEx had a 31 percent share of the market for overnight package deliveries.
- In 2010 FedEx, UPS, Germany's DHL, and TNT Express of the Netherlands held a combined 70 percent share of the world's small-package market.
- Brand Finance named FedEx the world's second-most-valuable brand in transportation in 2012, behind UPS.

A 2008 article reported that FedEx had a 31 percent share of the market for overnight package deliveries, the USPS had a 32 percent share, and the UPS had a 25 percent share. A few years later, Ben Comston wrote in 2010 that FedEx continued to hold considerable market share. Comston noted that FedEx and three other delivery services, UPS, Germany's DHL, and TNT Express of the Netherlands, held a combined 70 percent share of the world's small package market. He added that DHL has a greater presence abroad, so that the United States essentially has two small-parcel carriers: FedEx and UPS. Comston argued that this market dominance constituted an oligopoly.

FedEx is also a valuable brand around the world. Brand Finance ranked the company the world's second-most-valuable brand in transportation in 2012, behind UPS. In its annual "Global 500" list, Brand Finance has ranked FedEx one of the 100 most valuable brands in the world every year since 2008. It placed 83rd on this list in 2012, with a brand value of more than US$10 billion.

BRAND AWARENESS

- In a 2010 poll, American businesspeople named FedEx the seventh-most-recognizable American brand and FedEx Office the 16th-most-recognizable brand.
- The FedEx name has become so connected with speedy delivery services that "to FedEx" something means to use a delivery system to send something quickly. Brand Finance has ranked FedEx one of the 100 most valuable brands in the world every year since 2008 in its annual "Global 500" list. In 2012 FedEx placed 83rd on this list.
- Consumers named FedEx the world's 39th most reputable company in 2012 in the Reputation Institute's "Global RepTrak 100."

Due to FedEx's ubiquity, American businesspeople are well acquainted with FedEx and its various divisions. Americans at small or medium-sized businesses named FedEx the seventh-most-recognizable American brand in a poll conducted by *American City Business Journals*, published in 2010. FedEx Office placed 16th on this list. The 2009 version of the *American City Business Journals* list ranked FedEx 10th and FedEx Office 31st.

To many consumers, FedEx is synonymous with shipping. According to marketing service company Marketing

Excellence Inc., "to FedEx" something has become a common usage meaning a delivery system that sends packages quickly. FedEx has been so successful and recognizable that its name has become a verb.

FedEx also has a good reputation, according to the Reputation Institute. It polled more than 100,000 consumers in several countries for the 2012 edition of its annual "Global RepTrak 100," its ranking of the world's most reputable companies. These consumers named FedEx the 39th most reputable company in the world in 2012. It placed 46th in 2011's "Global RepTrak 100," so FedEx has maintained a consistently positive reputation.

BRAND OUTLOOK

- In 2012 FedEx began offering the FedEx SameDay service to deliver packages the same day in the same city.
- China allowed FedEx to operate without partners in 2012.
- FedEx is addressing the changing nature of global businesses.

Long known for offering overnight delivery services, FedEx began offering even faster services in 2012. That year it began FedEx SameDay in certain markets in the United States. In this service, customers order small shipments from online retailers, and if the deliveries are in the same city, FedEx can deliver the shipments that same day.

The company also has major operations outside of the United States. In China, it once operated with several regional partners. In 2012 the country allowed FedEx to operate without partners. This permission, coupled with the China's large and growing pool of online shoppers who utilize delivery services to obtain their goods, gives FedEx reason to hope it can build a substantial market in China.

Online sales provided a big boon to FedEx during the end-of-the-year holiday season in 2012. That holiday season set online sales records, with totals of more than US$29 billion by December 17, 2012, more than a full week before Christmas. FedEx services that handle these online sales include FedEx Home Delivery as well as FedEx SmartPost, a service that can handle the shipping needs of small businesses. By focusing on these delivery services for online customers and retailers, FedEx is addressing the changing nature of global business.

FURTHER READING

Brand Finance. "FedEx." *Brandirectory*. Accessed December 19, 2012. http://brandirectory.com/profile/fedex.

Comston, Ben. "The Small Parcel Oligopoly." *Seeking Alpha*, September 20, 2010. Accessed December 19, 2012. http://seekingalpha.com/article/225976-the-small-parcel-oligopoly.

FedEx. "FedEx Ground Celebrates Record-Setting Holiday Shopping Season with Opening Bell Ringing at the NYSE." FedEx Newsroom, December 17, 2012. Accessed December 20, 2012. http://news.van.fedex.com/fedex-ground-celebrates-record-setting-holiday-shopping-season-opening-bell-ringing-nyse.

"FedEx Corporation." *International Directory of Company Histories*. Ed. Derek Jacques and Paula Kepos. Vol. 109. Detroit, MI: St. James Press, 2010.

Gunelius, Susan. "Branding the Right Way—Rebranding FedEx." Ask Your Target Market. Accessed December 19, 2012. http://aytm.com/blog/research-junction/rebranding-fedex/.

Marketing Excellence Inc. "Branding and Brand Equity: Not Only Creates Value but Is Valuable." *In Pursuit of Excellence ... Marketing Excellence*, 2011. Accessed December 18, 2012. http://marketing4excellence.blogspot.com/2008/01/branding-and-brand-equity-not-only.html.

Shult, Kevin. "Battle of the Brands: UPS vs. FedEx." *DailyFinance*, May 5, 2008. Accessed December 19, 2012. http://www.bloggingstocks.com/2008/05/05/battle-of-the-brands-ups-vs-fedex/.

Skipper, Monica. "Be It before You Say It: The Essence of Branding." American Express Open Forum, March 14, 2011. Accessed December 19, 2012. https://www.openforum.com/idea-hub/topics/the-world/article/be-it-before-you-say-it-the-essence-of-branding-monica-skipper-marketing-manager-fedex-global-brand/.

Sullivan, Sean. "Trying to Put FedEx in a Box." *Seeking Alpha*, September 12, 2012. Accessed December 19, 2012. http://seekingalpha.com/article/863281-trying-to-put-fedex-in-a-box.

"Survey: FedEx in Top 10 for Brand Awareness." *Memphis Business Journal*, April 12, 2010.

FERRARI

AT A GLANCE

Brand Synopsis: Though few consumers can afford its luxury automobiles, Ferrari and its prancing horse logo are a fixture in the popular imagination, thanks in part to a merchandising effort that capitalizes on the brand's mystique.
Parent Company: Ferrari S.p.A.
Via Abetone Inferiore, 4
Maranello, Modena 41053
Italy
http://www.ferrari.com
Sector: Consumer Discretionary
Industry Group: Automobiles & Components
Performance: *Market share*—Less than 1 percent (2011). *Sales*—EUR2.25 billion (US$2.91 billion) (2011).
Principal Competitors: BMW; Lamborghini; Mercedes-Benz; Porsche; Rolls Royce

BRAND ORIGINS

- Enzo Ferrari decided to become a race-car driver while watching the 1908 Circuit de Bologna at age 10.
- In 1929 Enzo established an auto racing team known as *Scuderia Ferrari*, or "Ferrari Stable."
- In 1946 Enzo Ferrari's company, Auto Avio, produced the first Ferrari vehicle, the 125 C.
- Fiat purchased a 50 percent interest in Ferrari in 1969, and it increased its share to 90 percent after Enzo's death in 1988.

Enzo Ferrari first decided to become a race-car driver while watching the 1908 Circuit de Bologna when he was just 10 years old. After World War I, during which he served as an artilleryman before almost meeting his death in the influenza outbreak of 1918, he went to work for a small Italian carmaker and began racing automobiles. His successes attracted the attention of automobile manufacturer Alfa Romeo, which in 1920 recruited him to direct its racing team.

In 1929 Enzo established a team known as *Scuderia Ferrari*, or "Ferrari Stable." He continued to race until 1932, after which he devoted himself to managing racing events. In 1940 he split from Alfa Romeo to form a company called Auto Avio Construzioni, which supplied racing parts to other teams, but auto racing soon came to a standstill when Italy entered World War II. During the war Enzo relocated from his hometown of Modena to Maranello, where Auto Avio produced the first Ferrari vehicle, the 125 C, in 1946.

In 1960 Auto Avio became a joint stock firm and, in 1965, renamed itself Ferrari S.p.A. Esercizio Fabbriche Automobili e Corce. Ford Motor Company expressed an interest in buying Ferrari during the early 1960s, but the deal fell apart. In 1969 Fiat purchased a 50 percent interest. When Enzo died in 1988, Fiat increased its stake to 90 percent, and in the following year, the firm changed its name to Ferrari S.p.A. In 1997 Fiat sold Ferrari a 50 percent stake in another premium sports car brand, Maserati, and two years later Ferrari purchased the remaining half.

BRAND ELEMENTS

- The Ferrari logo depicts a prancing horse, an old heraldic symbol that likewise appears on the logo of Ferrari's rival, Porsche.
- Ferrari's use of the prancing horse logo dates to June 17, 1923, when Enzo Ferrari won an auto race in Ravenna, Italy.
- The airplane flown by Francesco Baracca, Italy's greatest flying ace during World War I, sported the prancing horse symbol.
- Baracca's mother, the countess Paolina, encouraged Enzo Ferrari to adopt the prancing horse logo as his own.

The Ferrari logo depicts a prancing horse, or *cavallino rampante*, in black with white highlights against a canary-yellow background on a shield bordered in black. Above the horse are horizontal stripes of green, white, and red (the Italian national colors), and below it is the name *Ferrari* in black. The upper horizontal arm of the initial letter is elongated in such a way that it cantilevers over the others, ending just before the dot atop the *i*.

The prancing horse is an old heraldic symbol that appears, for instance, in the coat of arms for the German city of Stuttgart. Stuttgart is home to Ferrari competitor Porsche, which likewise uses the symbol in its logo. In fact the name of Stuttgart derives from a German term meaning "stud farm," which in Italian is *scuderia*, as in Scuderia Ferrari, the racing team established by Enzo Ferrari in 1929.

Ferrari's use of the logo dates to June 17, 1923, when Enzo won an auto race in the Italian city of Ravenna. Though not an important race, the win attracted the attention of the Countess Paolina Baracca, whose son Francesco had been Italy's greatest World War I flying ace. Baracca's plane bore a prancing horse symbol, and the countess suggested that Enzo adopt it as his own.

Baracca's crest had depicted the horse in red, with a background in the shape of a cloud. Its tail pointed downward, whereas Ferrari's points up. Ferrari reportedly changed the horse's color to black as a symbol of mourning for Francesco Baracca, who died in the war, while the canary color is the color of his hometown, Modena.

BRAND IDENTITY

- Ferrari's cars are beyond the reach of most buyers: the 458 Italia, for example, cost US$332,032 in 2011.
- The paint alone on a Ferrari costs more than many cars.
- Of 1.1 million cars and trucks sold in the United States in October 2012, just 160 were Ferraris.
- A key element of Ferrari's identity is exclusivity, and therefore they always make and sell fewer cars than the market demands.

Ferrari's identity is closely tied to its mystique, its air of exclusivity, and the fact that its products remain far beyond the reach of all but a very privileged segment of society. In 2011, for example, the 458 Italia carried what Michael Austin of *Car and Driver* called an "eye-popping" price tag of US$332,032. By comparison, a Honda Civic in 2011 had a manufacturer's suggested retail price of US$16,605. The paint alone on the Ferrari cost US$28,000, yet according to Austin, "Judging by the long waiting list for a 458 (the full production run is essentially sold out), potential owners don't seem to mind Ferrari's pricing."

The fact that Ferrari had virtually sold out its production run points to another aspect of the brand's mystique: the scarcity of its product. Of almost 1.1 million cars and trucks sold in the United States during the month of October 2012, just 160 were Ferraris. Much of the public might perceive Mercedes-Benz or BMW as luxury brands, but with sales in the neighborhood of 26,000 each for the month, they seem almost common compared to Ferrari. Only Rolls-Royce and the ultra-exclusive Maybach sold fewer units during the period.

Not only are all of Ferrari's cars produced by hand at its campus in Maranello, but they are custom-made: thus, whereas a Ford or Toyota assembly line might turn out hundreds of vehicles in a day, the Ferrari plant produces between 10 and 12. "We have a business model that we always sell less than the market demands," Ferrari's Stefano Lai told David Cushnan of *SportsPro*. "We have a waiting list, so if you want a Ferrari you have to desire it."

BRAND STRATEGY

- Ferrari is not simply a car; rather, it is an entire world, with its own complexities and intricacies that are meant to evoke passion in the customer.
- Since the beginning, Ferrari has produced an astounding variety of models, but its production runs are typically very small.
- As its main business strategy, Ferrari continues to research and make the best possible vehicles, but merchandising and fan play also help promote the brand today.

Ferrari is not simply a car. Rather, it is an entire world, with its own complexities and intricacies, and like prize horses, its vehicles earn their reputation on the racetrack. The very first model to bear the Ferrari name was the 125 C. This car marked the beginning of a brand strategy that still exists today: a machine built for one thing and one thing only—passion. Ferrari builds cars that evoke a passion for speed, a passion for engines, and a passion for racing. According to Vertygo Team, a marketing strategy consultancy, Ferrari's marketing has survived the test of time even though it is based only on "passion and excitement because it goes through to every racing sport lover all around the world."

This passion continues today in every car that Ferrari builds. In fact, *GQ* magazine named Ferrari's F12berlinetta the 2013 "Supercar of the Year," gloating that it is "the fastest, most powerful Ferrari production car ever. If its body looks too complex to be straightforwardly sinfully sexy, then bear in mind that all those scoops and ducts hustle air and bully physics more effectively than anything this side of an F1 car. And it's a V12." This need for speed is still the element that sells cars and makes racing fans and car lovers dream about owning a Ferrari.

In addition to passion, the 125 C represented the establishment of a number of other strategies that Ferrari still uses today, including both limited production runs and proven performance in the field of competition. Prior to Fiat's purchase of a 50 percent stake in 1969, Ferrari produced an astounding variety of models, many in very small quantities. Some were intended only as racecars, not street vehicles. After the Fiat deal, production runs, though minuscule by the standards of most automakers, typically exceeded 1,000. Today, due to the price of the vehicles and the continued aim of the company to build desire for its vehicle, Ferrari still produces only limited numbers of its vehicles.

While continued investment in research and development in building high quality machines—like its first hybrid model, the 2010 California HELE (High Emotion Low Emissions)—forms a large part of Ferrari's business strategy, the company has also begun to promote its cars through merchandising. Clothing, jewelry, and other merchandise reportedly contribute to revenues that may account for as much as 30 percent of Ferrari's profits, according to Ben Oliver of *Automobile* magazine. There is even a Ferrari World theme park in Abu Dhabi where Ferrari aficionados can enjoy more than 20 rides, look at cars, and buy Ferrari merchandise.

BRAND EQUITY

- Observing that "Ferrari success cannot be measured in terms of revenues," one marketing analyst described it as the world's most valuable brand.
- Morgan Stanley reportedly valued Ferrari at US$4 billion, more than parent company Fiat, which produces about 330 times as many cars.
- A good portion of Ferrari's profits come from sources other than the sale of automobiles, including customization, various client experience opportunities, and merchandise.
- Only a few people can afford a Ferrari, but millions buy Ferrari merchandise.

Interbrand ranked Ferrari 99th on its list of the best global brands in 2012, with an estimated brand value of US$3.77 billion, an increase of 5 percent from the year before. However, in the words of marketing analysts Vertygo Team, "Ferrari success cannot be measured in terms of revenues and sales, or in terms of market capitalization. Ferrari never made an [initial public offering of stock] and is not even quoted in any stock exchange market," yet "[p] ossibly the Ferrari brand is worth more than ... any other brand."

According to Ben Oliver of *Automobile* magazine in 2011, Morgan Stanley valued parent company Fiat, which produced about 2 million cars for a profit of US$800 million, at US$3.9 billion. In contrast, Ferrari, which produced about 6,000 cars at a profit of US$400 million, actually had a higher value at US$4 billion. As Oliver wrote, "That's partly due to the bankers' belief that Ferrari's profits will grow, but it's also partly due to what one called the 'magic dust' of the brand."

A good deal of Ferrari's profits comes from sources other than the sale of automobiles as such. Oliver estimated that the average client spends about US$25,000 customizing his or her purchase. Furthermore, they pay much more for such experiences as the opportunity to "play at being a factory test driver with the FXX and 599XX programs, do a season's racing in an F430 Challenge, ... learn to drive better on a Pilota course," and so on.

But even these ancillary sources of revenue pale in comparison to the sale of licensed materials ranging from clothing and jewelry to computer equipment, all of which contribute to a revenue stream that may account for as much as 30 percent of Ferrari's profits. There is even a Ferrari World theme park in the oil-rich Persian Gulf sheikhdom of Abu Dhabi. The fact that people all over the world, consumers who could never afford an actual Ferrari automobile, collectively pay millions of dollars every year for Ferrari-licensed merchandise is perhaps the ultimate tribute to the value of the brand.

BRAND AWARENESS

- Ferrari does not advertise and never has, yet it is among the most widely known automobile brands in the world.
- Though few consumers can afford its cars, the Ferrari logo is nearly as familiar as that of McDonald's or Apple.
- Instead of Ferrari paying advertisers to promote its product, consumers actually pay Ferrari for the privilege of advertising it.
- Ferrari merchandise includes everything from clothing to electronic equipment.

Where Ferrari is concerned, the usual expectations regarding brand performance do not apply, and this is especially true with regard to brand awareness. Ferrari does not advertise and never has, yet it is among the most widely known automobile brands in the world. Its prancing horse logo is nearly as familiar as the symbols of McDonald's and Apple, even though those companies' products are accessible to the average consumer in a way that Ferrari's are not. Nevertheless, a piece of the Ferrari mystique lies within the reach of middle-class consumers.

Most brands pay advertisers to promote their product, but Ferrari is one of those rare examples of a brand so admired that consumers actually pay for the privilege of advertising it. Ferrari merchandise includes clothing, eyewear, watches, fragrances, jewelry, pens and pencils, bicycles, cell phones, laptop computers, and other electronic goods. Then there is Ferrari World, a theme park in Abu Dhabi on the Persian Gulf built at a reported cost of US$40 billion. Opened in November 2010, it is the world's largest indoor amusement park and features the world's fastest roller coaster, the Formula Rossa, capable of reaching 149 mph (240 kph).

Such goods and services are directed toward a different market than Ferrari's automobiles, Ben Oliver noted in *Automobile* magazine: "clients buy cars, fans buy coffee mugs, and Ferrari's marketing effort makes a clear distinction between the two." The opening of Ferrari World marked something of a departure, however. Enzo Ferrari "was famously dismissive of those who bought his road cars, regarding them as dupes who paid for his racing," and this attitude had carried over to the company's marketing, which Oliver compared to "pretty girls ... playing hard to get." The opening of a Ferrari theme park, Oliver suggested, posed "the risk ... that by being a little less aloof and a little more ubiquitous, Ferrari might tarnish that famous brand and make us want its cars a little less."

BRAND OUTLOOK

- Neither the ubiquity of its trademark nor the more obvious threat of a global recession seems to have diminished Ferrari's prospects.
- Despite rumors that Ferrari would spin off its merchandising arm and begin issuing stock, neither had happened by late 2012.
- Though European and American sales remain strong, Ferrari is looking increasingly toward the emerging markets of China, the Middle East, and India.

Neither the ubiquity of the Ferrari trademark, which Ben Oliver in *Automobile* magazine suggested might spawn consumer backlash, nor the more obvious threat of a global recession seemed to dim the prospects of the Italian luxury sports car manufacturer. In 2011, for instance, Ferrari posted record sales revenues of EUR2.25 billion (US$2.91 billion), an increase of more than 17 percent over the previous year, and posted a profit of EUR312.4 million ($404.5 million) on sales that included 7,195 cars, along with numerous automobile personalization services and experiences, and of course the highly popular Ferrari merchandise.

Despite a spring 2010 announcement that it would spin off the merchandising arm, Ferrari has maintained close control over this important segment. A rumored IPO, or initial public offering of Ferrari stock, has likewise failed to materialize. The company has continued to invest heavily in research and development, as well as improvements to its Maranello facility. In 2010 it introduced its first hybrid model, the California HELE (High Emotion Low Emissions), which was scheduled to appear in dealerships by 2015.

The North American market accounted for about one-quarter of Ferrari's sales in 2011, and Europe accounted for a large portion of the remainder. China, where the company sold 777 vehicles in 2011, also gained importance as a market, as did the Middle East. On May 26, 2011, Ferrari solidified its presence in another important emerging market when it opened a dealership in New Delhi, India.

FURTHER READING

Alderman, Liz. "'Sex on Wheels?' Now It's 'Room for Groceries,' Too." *New York Times*, May 15, 2011.

Austin, Michael. "2011 Ferrari 458 Italia vs. 2011 McLaren MP4-12C, 2011 Porsche 911 GT2 RS: Chariots of the Gods: Three Exotics Ready to Take You to Supercar Paradise—Fast." *Car and Driver*, September 2011.

Cushnan, David. "Ferrari: The Magic Brand." SportsProMedia. Accessed November 9, 2012. http://www.sportspromedia.com/notes_and_insights/ferrari_the_magic_brand/.

"Ferrari S.p.A." *International Directory of Company Histories*. Ed. Jay P. Pederson. Vol. 36. Detroit, MI: St. James Press, 2001.

Mahalingam, Eugene. "The Ferrari Brandname Has Not Only Survived, but Thrived without Conventional Advertising." *Star* (Petaling Jaya, Malaysia), April 16, 2011.

Oliver, Ben. "The World of Ferrari." *Automobile*, March 2011.

Vertygo Team. "Ferrari Marketing Strategy and Communications." Accessed November 9, 2012. http://www.vertygoteam.com/ferrari_marketing_strategy.php.

"What's Moving: U.S. Auto Sales." *Wall Street Journal*, November 1, 2012.

FIAT

AT A GLANCE

Brand Synopsis: The largest and most diverse auto manufacturer in Italy, Fiat enters the 21st century striving to expand significantly around the globe, most notably in the United States.
Parent Company: Fiat S.p.A.
Via Nizza, 250
Torino 10126
Italy
http://www.fiatspa.com
Sector: Consumer Discretionary
Industry Group: Automobiles & Components
Performance: *Market share*—31.2 percent in Italy (2010); 8.78 percent of European light vehicle market (2010). *Sales*—EUR59.6 billion (US$77.02 billion) (2011).
Principal Competitors: Ford Motor Company; Toyota Motor Corporation; Honda Motor Co., Ltd.; Kia Motors Corporation; Hyundai Motor Company

BRAND ORIGINS

- Fiat was founded in 1899 in Turin, Italy, and the company opened its first factory in 1900.
- Fiat's achievements in fuel economy and compact size in the 1930s would become hallmarks of the brand for generations to come.
- Fiat grew significantly throughout the 1950s, and many historians believe its success was a leading factor in Italy's economic recovery following World War II.
- By 1993 the brands owned by Fiat included Fiat, Lancia, Autobianchi, Abarth, Ferrari, Alfa Romeo, and Maserati.
- In 2009 Fiat acquired a controlling interest in Chrysler, which significantly increased Fiat's presence in the United States.

Fiat was founded in 1899 in Turin, Italy, by Giovanni Agnelli and other investors. The company opened its first factory in 1900 in Corso Dante, producing 24 cars in its first year. With immediate success in the emerging automobile industry, Fiat expanded within its first decade to North America, establishing the Fiat Automobile Company in the United States in 1908. Almost as quickly, Fiat expanded its manufacturing efforts to include commercial vehicles, marine engines, trucks, and trams.

In addition to securing several patents for its mechanical innovations, Fiat began construction of its Lingotto factory, the largest in Europe, which occupied five floors and had a futuristic test track on the roof. Completed in 1922, the factory soon became the emblem of the Italian automotive industry. After opening its first subsidiary in Russia, Fiat soon expanded its activities to include the steel, railway, electricity, and public transportation industries.

At the outbreak of World War I, the company shifted its production to focus entirely on supplying the Italian army. The postwar crisis in Europe brought transformation and uncertainty to the brand, but by 1923 growth had resumed, and Fiat launched several new car models, including the Fiat 509, the first car with four seats. In an attempt to curb costs and strengthen overall production, Fiat developed its first financial services division, invested heavily in mass production systems, and even developed some of the first employee services, such as health care, in the automobile industry.

During the years of Benito Mussolini's regime in the 1930s, Fiat rescaled its plans for a strong international presence and concentrated instead on the domestic market. In doing so, Fiat launched two of its most successful cars, the Balilla, recognized for its low consumption of fuel, and the Topolino, the smallest utilitarian car in the world at the time. These achievements in fuel economy and compact size would become hallmarks of the Fiat brand for generations to come.

During World War II, Fiat drastically reduced its production of cars and increased its construction of commercial vehicles. Following the war, U.S. subsidies from the Marshall Plan helped fund the reconstruction of Italy's destroyed manufacturing plants, and this led to a period of research and innovation for Fiat. The company grew significantly throughout the 1950s. In 1951 Fiat installed innovative heating and ventilation systems in its cars and developed the first Italian jet aircraft. The company designed its first diesel vehicle in 1953 and its first station wagon in 1957. Many historians believe Fiat's success during this time period was a leading factor in Italy's postwar economic recovery and growth.

Fiat also returned to its earlier interest in global expansion after the war, constructing manufacturing plants abroad and honing its mass production model. When the auto industry was forced to cope with the oil crisis in the early 1970s, Fiat worked on the design for its "Robogate" system, a flexible robotized system for assembling bodywork. By 1979 Fiat had grown to the point that its booming auto division, which included the brands Fiat, Lancia, Autobianchi, Abarth, and Ferrari, was separated from the larger corporate entity. Five years later, Fiat acquired Alfa Romeo and added the brand to its auto division. In 1993 Fiat added Maserati, another Italian brand, to its auto brand lineup.

In the 1980s, Fiat models such as the Panda, the Uno, and the Tipo were recognized for their utilitarian style on the outside and their radical innovations and technological solutions on the inside, which included advanced electronics, superior materials, and clean engine design. Several new models were introduced throughout the 1990s, with many vehicles winning awards for their attention to innovation. Its success during this period even led Fiat to enter a challenger into the booming SUV market in 1995.

Meanwhile, Fiat continued to escalate its expansion into international markets, attaining a worldwide presence. The brand was one of the first auto manufacturers to focus on developing markets such as Brazil. The Fiat brand found success throughout the 1990s by continuing to promote what had become its mantra: utilitarian vehicles rich in avant-garde technological solutions delivered at affordable prices.

The 21st century has seen the passing, in 2003, of Gianni Agnelli (the grandson of founder Giovanni Agnelli), who led the company for almost 50 years, and the 2009 acquisition of a controlling interest in U.S. automaker Chrysler, which exponentially increased Fiat's presence in the United States. The company has also announced plans to partner with Japanese auto manufacturer Mazda to redesign models under the Mazda and Alfa Romeo brands in yet another move that suggests Fiat is continuing its transformation from an Italian automaker into a significant global vehicle manufacturer.

BRAND ELEMENTS

- The original Fiat logo, an oval on a blue background surrounding the name in capital letters, was adopted in 1904.
- A laurel wreath was added to the logo in the 1920s to celebrate Fiat's successful participation in competitive auto racing.
- Fiat believes its current logo suggests "advanced technology, Italian design, dynamism and individualism."

The original Fiat logo, an oval on a blue background surrounding the word "FIAT" in capital letters, was adopted in 1904. In 1925 the logo became circular, with the Fiat name appearing in red on a white background. A laurel wreath was also added around the outside of the logo to celebrate Fiat's victorious participation in competitive auto racing. In 1932 another version of the logo was created, with the new design taking the form of a shield, a symbol considered more fitting for the radiator grilles on Fiat's new models at the time. Although slight changes were made to its design, this logo was used on Fiat cars until the late 1960s.

In 1968 Fiat adopted a new logo featuring four blue rhombuses encasing the four letters in the brand's name. This logo would become the main identifying element for the Fiat brand for the remainder of the 20th century. In 1999, to celebrate the brand's 100th anniversary, Fiat returned to the logo of the late 1920s, with a blue background, chrome plating, and a stylish laurel wreath. In 2007 the logo changed once again, this time taking on the red color and shield shape of the logo adopted in 1932. According to the Fiat website, this latest logo features "formal, three-dimensional characteristics, in terms of form and color, that suggest advanced technology, Italian design, dynamism and individualism."

BRAND IDENTITY

- Fiat, after a long absence from the U.S. market, is in the process of reestablishing itself with American consumers.
- Fiat is attempting to shed its ultra-compact, ultra-cheap image and create an identity that merges high style with affordability.
- To raise consumer awareness of the brand and build a new identity, Fiat has enlisted celebrities to appear in its advertising.
- Fiat representatives report that customer awareness of the brand since its U.S. marketing relaunch in 2011 has risen to nearly 50 percent of consumers.

Largely absent from the U.S. auto market for the latter portion of the 20th century and the first decade of the 21st century, Fiat was in the process of establishing an updated and improved identity with American consumers. With the help of advertising executives from its U.S. subsidiary, Chrysler, Fiat is attempting to shed its ultra-compact, ultra-cheap image and create an identity that merges high style with affordability.

As Tom Dougherty, brand researcher and CEO of the U.S. brand services firm Stealing Share, wrote on his blog, "When I think about the Fiat from the [19]70s, I remember very stylish designs like its Spyder.... However, for the most part, I am filled with memories of my own family's dalliance into the Italian brand. It was, how do I say? Not good." Indeed, many Americans still associate Fiat with the mechanical problems that plagued its cars during that period.

Perhaps due in part to this negative perception, Fiat failed to reach its sales goal by thousands of units during its 2011 relaunch in the U.S. market. The Fiat brand has since turned to Chrysler for help with its makeover in the United States. In order to raise consumer awareness of the brand and build an entirely new identity, Fiat has enlisted celebrities like Jennifer Lopez and Charlie Sheen, as well as Romanian model Catrinel Menghia, to represent the brand in its commercials and advertisements. It remains to be seen whether these new marketing efforts will achieve the desired effect. However, according to Fiat representatives, customer awareness of the brand since 2011 has grown from the single digits to nearly 50 percent of consumers.

BRAND STRATEGY

- Fiat appears to be returning to its original mission of building attractive, exciting cars that are accessible and affordable.
- In 2003 Fiat saw success with the release of its new Panda, which was named 2004 European Car of the Year.
- In 2009 Fiat acquired a controlling interest in U.S. automaker Chrysler, making Fiat the world's sixth largest automotive group.
- In 2012 Fiat announced a collaboration with Japanese auto manufacturer Mazda to redesign models under the Mazda and Alfa Romeo brand names.
- Fiat has shown some interest in entering the "green" automobile market, most notably with the compact, solar-powered Phylla concept vehicle.

In addition to its efforts to grow globally, Fiat appears to be returning to its original mission: to build cars with attractive styling and exciting engines that are accessible and affordable.

In 2003 Gianni Agnelli, the grandson of Fiat founder Giovanni Agnelli, passed away after almost half a century at the helm of the company. Despite the loss of its longtime leader, Fiat continued to focus on technological research, design quality, and the continuous and rapid overhaul of its vehicles. In 2003 the brand reclaimed its position as a leader in the super-compact segment with the new Fiat Panda, named 2004 European Car of the Year and celebrated for its high-tech, intelligent solutions designed to simplify operation.

After failed attempts to partner with Ford Motor Company and to acquire pieces of General Motors Company (GM), Fiat successfully acquired a controlling interest in Chrysler, along with Dodge and Jeep, in April 2009. According to published reports, the acquisition made Fiat the world's sixth largest automotive group and was projected to increase the brand's production from about 2.1 million units in 2010 to more than 6 million by 2014.

In 2012 Fiat was manufacturing cars under several brand names, including Fiat, Alfa Romeo, Ferrari, Lancia, and Maserati. The company announced it would be collaborating with Japanese auto manufacturer Mazda to redesign models under both the Mazda and Alfa Romeo brand names. This move was yet another sign that the brand intends to continue to build its reputation as an international automaker.

Fiat has also shown signs in the 21st century of its intention to enter the "green" automobile market. In 2008 the brand unveiled its Phylla concept vehicle, a compact, solar-powered car designed to be driven in urban areas. The Phylla was scheduled to be introduced to market in 2010, but as of 2012 it remained a concept-only vehicle.

BRAND EQUITY

- Despite Fiat's significant growth in recent years, the brand has yet to significantly impact brand ratings.
- Fiat's status in comparison to other brands may have been affected by its long absence from the U.S. market.
- In recent years the Fiat brand has struggled to be recognized as a top brand in Italy and throughout Europe.

- In 2012 Fiat seemed to be attracting the attention of consumers, brand researchers, and the media in the United States and abroad.

According to Brand Finance, Fiat's brand value in 2012 was around US$4.4 billion, a slight decrease from its estimated value in 2011. Probably as a result of its acquisition of a controlling interest in Chrysler, Fiat's brand value increased 25 percent from 2009 to 2010, jumping from US$3.3 billion to US$4.4 billion.

In addition to a brand value that has remained largely stagnant, another indicator of concern is the brand's steady decline on recent Brand Finance Global 500 lists, often considered the definitive ranking of brands around the world. After reaching the 185th spot in 2008, Fiat saw its ranking slip to 196th in 2010, 224th in 2011, and 239th in 2012. In 2012, of the 27 auto brands on Brand Finance's list, Fiat was ranked 15th.

Similarly, Fiat fell 40 positions, from 55th to 95th, on SyncForce's 2009 Top 100 Brands list, and then fell off the list entirely. As of 2012 the brand had been unable to reclaim a spot on the list, which some researchers suggest is a result of uncertainty surrounding the impact that the acquisition of Chrysler will have on the Fiat brand.

Fiat has also struggled to be recognized as a top brand in its home country of Italy and throughout Europe. In 2012 ADAC, a respected brand researcher in Germany, ranked Fiat 30th out of 33 automakers on its AutoMarxX brand study, which uses such criteria as brand image, market strength, customer satisfaction, product strength, environmental performance, and safety. In 2011 the European Brand Institute ranked Fiat 38th in its Europe's Most Valuable Brands study, which evaluated companies based on their impact on the European economy.

Despite these less-than-stellar rankings, some signs suggest that Fiat is starting to capture the attention of consumers, brand researchers, and the popular media in the United States and elsewhere. In 2012 Fiat was recognized by Pied Piper, a U.S. brand researcher, as the seventh best automaker in terms of its "prospect satisfaction index" (PSI), a benchmark of the U.S. auto industry that measures how automobile brand dealerships treat car shoppers. In 2012 Fiat appeared for the first time on *Newsweek's* Green Ranking Global Top 100 list, attaining the 82nd position. This list ranks the most environmentally responsible companies among the largest publicly traded companies in developed and emerging markets.

BRAND AWARENESS

- Fiat sought to increase its international brand awareness by becoming the official vehicle sponsor of the 2006 Winter Olympics in Turin, Italy.
- In 2011 Fiat had a presence on the popular U.S. television show *American Idol*, and it advertised during the 2012 Super Bowl.
- Fiat's 2009 acquisition of a controlling interest in U.S. automaker Chrysler has dramatically increased its presence in the United States.
- In 2011 Fiat expanded on its new presence in the United States by launching a marketing campaign featuring popular entertainer Jennifer Lopez.
- In 2012 Fiat estimated that its brand awareness in the United States had grown from the single digits to nearly 50 percent of consumers.

Despite waning sales in Europe, Fiat has sought to increase its presence in the United States and around the world. In 2006, for example, Fiat's cars were the official vehicles of the 2006 Winter Olympics in Turin, Italy. In 2011 the Fiat brand had a presence on the popular U.S. television show *American Idol*, and the following year Fiat launched a Super Bowl advertisement featuring actor Charlie Sheen.

Thanks to its 2009 acquisition of a controlling interest in U.S. automaker Chrysler, Fiat has seen a dramatically increased presence in the United States after a 27-year absence from that market. With the acquisition, Fiat also launched a new marketing campaign to increase awareness among U.S. consumers. A 2011 Fiat campaign featuring popular singer and entertainer Jennifer Lopez was part of the brand's long-term plan to build a new identity for itself in the U.S. market. Lopez's "Papi" music video, which features the Fiat 500 convertible, had been viewed more than 60 million times on YouTube as of November 2012. According to Fiat representatives, customer awareness of the brand since its 2011 marketing launch in the United States has grown from the single digits to nearly 50 percent of U.S. consumers.

BRAND OUTLOOK

- Despite Fiat's 2009 acquisition of a controlling interest in Chrysler, its future as a brand remains uncertain.
- Stagnant brand values and slow sales in the United States and Europe suggest the Fiat brand may have reached a plateau.
- New marketing efforts in the United States and an increased presence in emerging markets may help Fiat recover from declines in brand value and sales.

It is difficult to make a safe prediction about Fiat's future as a brand. While Fiat's investment in U.S. automaker Chrysler stands to reap dividends in the U.S. car market, the volatility of the domestic and European car markets, combined with Fiat's smaller brand footprint globally, suggests that the brand has reached a plateau.

A stagnant brand value, slow sales of Fiat cars in the United States, and recent sales declines in Europe are concerning. In August 2012, for example, Fiat sales fell 34 percent in Italy and 15 percent in Germany, despite an overall market decline of only 5 percent in Germany.

In 2012 the brand ramped up its marketing efforts in the United States despite sluggish sales, and it attempted to establish a presence in emerging markets. Although Fiat's future success as a global automaker is uncertain, those two moves combined may help the brand recover from its recent stagnant ratings and declining sales.

FURTHER READING

Brand Finance. "Fiat." *Brandirectory*. Accessed October 28, 2012. http://brandirectory.com/profile/fiat.

Dougherty, Tom. "Fiat: Let's Hope They Don't Make Cars Like It Used To." StealingShare.com, June 11, 2009. Accessed October 28, 2012. http://www.stealingshare.com/blog/?p=476.

Felipe, Juan. "Fiat Group's World." CarIndustryAnalysis.com, September 12, 2012. Accessed October 28, 2012. http://carindustryanalysis.wordpress.com/2012/09/12/quick-outlook-at-fiat-group-results-in-europe-august-2012/.

Fiat. "The Fiat Brand." Accessed October 29, 2012. http://www.fiat.com.

"Fiat." RankingtheBrands.com. Accessed October 30, 2012. http://www.rankingthebrands.com/Brand-detail.aspx?brandID=159.

Gross, Daniel. "The Italian Job." *Newsweek*, August 13, 2012.

Natarajan, Prana Tharthiharan. "Fiat-Chrysler Merger: Birth of a New Auto Giant." *Frost & Sullivan*, August 3, 2011. Accessed October 29, 2012. http://www.frost.com/sublib/display-market-insight-top.do?id=239447224.

Wayland, Michael. "Why Chrysler Morphed Fiat's Image from J-Lo to Charlie Sheen." *Michigan Live*, March 21, 2012. Accessed October 29, 2012. http://www.mlive.com/auto/index.ssf/2012/03/why_did_chrysler_switch_gears.html.

FIFA

AT A GLANCE

Brand Synopsis: The FIFA brand seeks to portray itself as the champion of football, promising to use the sport as a way to improve the world.
Parent Company: Fédération Internationale de Football Association
Fifa House, Hitzigweg 11
Zurich
Switzerland
http://www.fifa.com
Sector: Consumer Discretionary
Industry Group: Media
Performance: *Sales*—US$1 billion (2012).
Principal Competitors: The National Basketball Association; National Football League; The R&A

BRAND ORIGINS

- Football (soccer) became an organized sport in England in 1863.
- FIFA was organized in Paris in 1904.
- FIFA organized its first Olympics in 1924.
- The first World Cup tournament was held in Uruguay in 1930.
- FIFA did not begin to aggressively market itself or the World Cup until the 1970s.

FIFA is the acronym and brand of the Fédération Internationale de Football Association. Also known in English as the International Federation of Association Football, it is the international governing body of association football, the sport called soccer in the United States. Organized football has its roots in the United Kingdom, where in 1863 football and rugby diverged and the Football Association was established. The sport took a major step forward in popularity in 1871 when the Association created a challenge cup competition for its member clubs. It was the world's first football competition, laying the foundation for future tournaments in the sport.

Organized football spread to Denmark and the Netherlands in 1889 and made its way to New Zealand in 1891 and Argentina in 1893. Football was introduced to neighboring countries on both continents. By the early 1900s it became apparent to many people involved in the sport that an international governing body was needed to ensure there were uniform rules and to serve other organizational purposes. Thus, in May 1904 seven national associations met in Paris to form the Fédération Internationale de Football Association. Notably absent was Great Britain, making it difficult for FIFA to organize a true international tournament without British countries. Even after Great Britain joined in 1905, FIFA was overshadowed by the Football Association, which became the organizer for Olympic football tournaments for the 1908 and 1912 Olympics.

It was not until 1924, after the world recovered from World War I, that FIFA was entrusted with organizing Olympic football in 1924. Over the years, FIFA officials discussed the idea of hosting a world championship tournament, but it wasn't until the organization's success at the Olympics that FIFA members agreed to stage such an event. It would be called the World Cup, and it became the most important element of the FIFA brand.

Where to hold the inaugural event became a contentious issue, however. Because Uruguay had won the previous two Olympic competitions, the first World Cup was held in Uruguay in 1930. European teams showed no interest in making the long journey to South America, but some arm-twisting by FIFA president M. Jules Rimet resulted in four European countries participating in the first World Cup, which the host country won.

The modern format of the World Cup began to take shape in 1934, when the tournament was held in Italy. Because of greater interest, qualification games had to be held to determine the 16 participants. Additionally, the games were spread throughout the host country. Boycotting the event was defending champion Uruguay, still upset over the lack of European support for its tournament. When the 1938 World Cup was awarded to take place in France, other South American countries grew incensed as well, having been led to believe that the tournament would alternate between South America and Europe. Among South American countries, only Brazil participated in 1938. The dispute was just one of many that would pit national football associations against FIFA in the years ahead.

The Second World War interrupted the growth of FIFA and the World Cup. It wasn't until 1950, at which point there were 70 member nations in FIFA, that the World Cup resumed. The modern shape of the organization and the tournament continued to grow during the postwar years. Continental federations were formed to provide further structure to the international game. The televising of the World Cup, beginning in 1958, resulted in the growing popularity of the event. By 1970 the World Cup enjoyed the largest viewership of any televised event. Despite the success of its signature tournament, however, FIFA was on the verge of bankruptcy. It was in 1974, with the election of Joao Havelange as its president, that FIFA began to aggressively market its brand. A seminal sponsorship deal with Coca-Cola laid the foundation for further opportunities, while also providing the funds FIFA needed to promote football in Third World countries and launch youth tournaments. In the process, FIFA became a powerful entity, its leaders pampered and feted by nations eager, sometimes desperate, to host a World Cup or FIFA-sponsored event. The result was an extremely powerful brand, but an environment ripe for corruption.

BRAND ELEMENTS

- The first FIFA corporate mark featured a globe with only half of the world.
- In 1928 a second globe depicting the Western Hemisphere was included in the FIFA corporate mark.
- The current FIFA slogan, "For the Game. For the World," was adopted in 2007.
- FIFA modernized its logo in 2009.
- The World Cup tournament is FIFA's most important brand element.

There are several elements key to the FIFA corporate brand, including the corporate mark, which has evolved over the years. The first symbol used to represent FIFA was a global representation of the Earth, minus the Western Hemisphere, indicative of a Eurocentric attitude that would not wear well with South American members. It was not until 1928 that a second globe depicting the Western Hemisphere was added. Instead of longitude and latitude lines, the globes in the 1978 version of the corporate mark incorporated the pentagonal lines of a football. The FIFA name was also placed below the twin globes. In 1996 a slogan was added to the logo: "For the good of the game." In 2007 the slogan was changed to "For the Game. For the World." It was meant to represent the organization's mission. The globes were finally dropped in 2009. The word "FIFA" in large block letters now dominated the image, with the slogan presented in much smaller type. The wordmark was extremely valuable to the FIFA brand, because it was associated with any event it organized and every item endorsed by FIFA. Given the sheer volume of signage, communications, and FIFA-endorsed merchandise, the wordmark received vast exposure around the world.

For the 1994 World Cup, FIFA introduced an anthem that became a significant brand element. Initially the anthem was only played before FIFA-sanctioned matches and tournaments. In 2007 an abbreviated version of the anthem became required playing during the broadcast of FIFA-sponsored games. Not only was the anthem used to open and close broadcasts, it was also employed as a segue between commercial breaks.

The most important element of the FIFA brand is the World Cup. Each event has its own logo and endorsed merchandise, but the FIFA name is closely attached to all of it. The World Cup has also been represented by a mascot since the 1966 tournament. Hosted in England, the competition made use of a lion as mascot. Over the years, a variety of characters, as well as inanimate objects like a Mexican hot pepper and a Spanish orange, have served as World Cup mascots. As FIFA became more marketing oriented, the mascot was sure to tout the FIFA brand.

BRAND IDENTITY

- The FIFA slogan, "For the Game. For the World," reflects the organization's stated mission: "Develop the game, touch the world, build a better future."
- FIFA equates itself with football.
- FIFA's identity has been marred by a bribery scandal and other accusations of corruption among its executive committee.

FIFA's brand identity, the image FIFA wishes to convey to the world, is not necessarily what is perceived by the international football community and the world in general. The FIFA slogan, "For the Game. For the World," reflects the organization's stated mission: "Develop the game, touch the world, build a better future." FIFA wants to be seen as the honest advocate for football, making constant improvements to the sport for the benefit of everyone. More than that, FIFA wants to be seen as a force for ultimate good, using football to have a positive impact on the world.

At a more fundamental level, FIFA equates itself with football. FIFA makes sure that it is always aligned to anything football-related that it controls. In its own communications, images of the game are always linked to the FIFA name. In text-only material, whenever FIFA is mentioned, the word "football" will be close by. The logical assertion is unmistakable: wherever there is football there is FIFA, and wherever there is FIFA there is football. In turn, the positive emotions generated by football in its passionate followers are meant to be transferred to the FIFA brand.

FIFA's image with the public is not quite what the organization desires, however. While tapping into the marketing potential of the World Cup made FIFA financially secure, allowing it to expand the sport to all corners of the world as well as open up the game to women players, the money that flowed in with the game led to corruption. After a book published in 2006 accused FIFA officials of engaging in cash-for-contracts behavior, the British Broadcasting Service broadcast its own expose. Following the controversial awarding of the 2018 and 2022 World Cups to Russia and Qatar, respectively, a British parliamentary inquiry in 2011 led to accusations that six top FIFA officials participated in a bribery scandal. FIFA now faced a media firestorm about the conduct of its 24-member executive committee, which according to a *New York Times* profile formed "an elite all-men's club, reaping annual salaries and bonuses of up to US$300,000 in addition to their various perks." Some FIFA officials were forced to resign, but FIFA president Sepp Blatter was reelected in 2011 and downplayed the scandal. Nevertheless, the reputation of FIFA was greatly tarnished and the identity of the brand severely compromised.

BRAND STRATEGY

- FIFA's branding efforts were negligible until the 1970s.
- Coca-Cola played an important role in FIFA's adoption of a more sophisticated branding strategy.
- A family-of-sponsors approach was adopted in the mid-1980s.
- A brand promise was first introduced in 1996.
- FIFA launched a revamped branding strategy in 2007.

For most of its history, FIFA did little in the way of brand building, emphasizing, rather, the organization's signature event, the World Cup. Monetizing of the event was limited until the early 1970s, when perimeter advertising began to appear. It was Coca-Cola, the world's preeminent brand manager, that created a true sponsorship package with the World Cup at the 1978 event in Argentina. In the mid-1980s FIFA finally established a modern sponsorship program that included a family of about a dozen noncompeting brands, including Coca-Cola, Gillette, Budweiser, Snickers, Duracell, and Fuji. All of these major consumer brands worked together to elevate FIFA's competition brand, the World Cup, as well as the corporate brand.

In 1996 FIFA introduced a slogan, "For the Good of the Game," which for the first time established a brand promise. In the new century, FIFA's branding efforts grew more sophisticated. The organization adopted a portfolio strategy for managing its brands in 2001, creating a more integrated brand identity for its properties. In 2007 FIFA introduced a new brand identity, reflected in the new slogan "For the Game. For the World." The revamped branding approach was first employed for the 2007 Women's World Cup in China.

With a new slogan came a new brand claim. FIFA no longer limited itself to acting for the good of football. It now promised to help improve the world through football. On the more mundane level of commerce, FIFA also created a new three-tier sponsorship model. FIFA refined its branding strategy further with the introduction of a simplified corporate mark. The twin globes of earlier incarnations had been replaced by a pair of footballs in 1998 and were now completely eliminated. All that remained was "FIFA" and the slogan. While FIFA's stated mission may have been to promote international football as a way to change the world for the better, the new corporate mark promoted the FIFA organization more than it did the sport that the organization represented. In effect, the corporate brand was claiming dominance over the competition brand, a reversal of the longstanding relationship between the World Cup and FIFA.

BRAND EQUITY

- *Forbes* estimates a US$147 million brand value for the FIFA World Cup.
- According to *Forbes*, the FIFA World Cup is the world's third-most-valuable brand.
- The equity of the FIFA brand has been adversely impacted by scandal.

While this may be difficult to quantify, there is no doubt that FIFA enjoys strong brand equity. How much of that equity is tied to the brand equity of the World Cup is difficult to determine. According to *Forbes*, the FIFA World Cup is the world's third-most-valuable sports brand. Estimated to be worth US$147 million, it trailed only the Summer Olympics, with a brand value of US$230 million, and American football's Super Bowl, with a brand value of US$425 million. Another indication of the brand equity of the World Cup is the eagerness of many of the world's top brands to be associated with it. Marketing opportunities for FIFA have escalated rapidly over the years, with no end in sight.

While FIFA's competition brand, the World Cup, is thriving, the same cannot be said for the corporate brand. Because of the immense popularity of international football, it is difficult to estimate the drag created by the adverse impact of scandal connected to the corporate brand. FIFA hugs the World Cup and the game of football closely, insisting it is unified with them as one brand. The sad fact is, however, that FIFA as an organization is reviled in many quarters of both football and society, no matter how beloved the game and tournament it promotes. And the brand value has suffered.

BRAND AWARENESS

- With a long history and worldwide reach, FIFA is ensured of strong brand awareness.
- The two-year regional World Cup qualifying process builds brand awareness and excitement for the quadrennial event.
- A collective audience of about 30 billion watched the 2010 World Cup.

As the international governing body of football, the world's most popular sport, FIFA has ample opportunity to build awareness of both its corporate and competition brands. The century-old organization has always been present in the life of football supporters, and it dominates national and regional governing bodies. Moreover, FIFA is involved in all levels of the game in all parts of the world. It organizes a variety of youth tournaments. Since 1991 FIFA has also organized the Women's World Cup, and it also hosts under-17 and under-20 world cups for women.

While FIFA's youth tournaments and Women's World Cup are popular in their own right, it is the men's World Cup that creates the greatest awareness of the FIFA brand. Leading up to the quadrennial competition, 200 national teams participate in six regional qualifying tournaments that establish the field of 32 countries that will vie for the World Cup. These preliminary games are stretched out over two years, maximizing exposure to the FIFA brand in all parts of the world over an extended period of time. These preliminary rounds build excitement for the World Cup itself. In the 2010 World Cup held in South Africa, about three million people attended games. That number was insignificant compared to the collective television audience, which was estimated at 30 billion for the month-long event.

BRAND OUTLOOK

- The World Cup continues to grow in popularity.
- The United States represents the last major market to grow international football.
- Women present a large market in which to grow the FIFA brand.
- To avoid brand erosion caused by scandal, FIFA will likely be forced to embrace reform.

The brand outlook of FIFA is a very mixed bag. The competition brand has never been more popular and is likely to sustain its growth. The only significant market where international football does not enjoy immense popularity is the United States. Even there, however, there are large youth participation, a professional league that is gaining a following, and a growing Hispanic population with deep ties to the sport. Games from all of the major domestic leagues in the world are also available on American television, as are World Cup qualifying games and international "friendly matches" of both the US men's and women's national teams. Football as a participatory sport is popular with American women. The game has benefited from legislation in the 1970s that prohibited sex discrimination in academics or athletics, resulting in increased funding for women's soccer programs in high schools and colleges. The result, in effect, was a soccer youth development program for US women, creating an international football powerhouse that spurred growth in other countries where the women's game had previously been neglected. Thus there exists ample opportunity to increase awareness of FIFA with the female portion of the world's population in the years ahead.

The outlook for FIFA's corporate brand, on the other hand, is not as bright. Its executive committee has become embroiled in controversy. There was no doubt that such negative publicity was taking its toll on the FIFA brand, and might very well damage the reputation of the game itself. Regional organizations like the European Club Association, representing 200 professional clubs on the continent, were beginning to voice their disapproval of the way FIFA was conducting its affairs. In all likelihood, FIFA will have to embrace serious reform to prevent further erosion of its brand.

FURTHER READING

Branch, John, and Jeré Longman. "Soccer Leader Wins Vote, Immune to Scandal." *New York Times*, June 1, 2011.

Carvajal, Doreen. "For FIFA Executives, Luxury and Favors." *New York Times*, July 17, 2011.

Carvajal, Doreen, and Stephen Castle. "European Soccer Clubs Challenging FIFA." *New York Times*, July 29, 2011.

"Fédération Internationale de Football Association History." *International Directory of Company Histories*. Ed. Jay P. Pederson. Vol. 27. Detroit, MI: St. James Press, 1999.

"FIFA Places Focus on Social Development." *Marketing*, June 6, 2007.

Longman, Jeré. "Accusations Are Replaced by Anger at FIFA." *New York Times*, May 30, 2011.

———. "Six from FIFA Are Accused in Bribery Case." *New York Times*, May 10, 2011.

Siddle, Richard. "The Main Attraction." *Super Marketing*, May 8, 1998.

FNAC

AT A GLANCE

Brand Synopsis: The FNAC brand represents top-quality products at competitive prices.
Parent Company: Pinault Printemps-redoute International SA
Ivry-sur-Seine
France
http://www.fnac.com/
Sector: Consumer Discretionary
Industry Group: Retailing
Performance: *Sales*—EUR4.16 billion (US$5.52 billion) (2011).
Principal Competitors: Amazon.com, Inc.; Carrefour SA; DirectGroup Bertelsmann GmbH

BRAND ORIGINS

- In July 1954 André Essel and Max Théret opened the Federation Nationale d' Achats des Cadres (FNAC) in Paris.
- FNAC began as a members-only shopping club that offered discounted photographic equipment.
- In 1974 FNAC attracted national attention when it began selling books 80 percent below the list price, a move that outraged publishers, writers, and other booksellers.
- In 1994 Pinault Printemps-redoute International SA acquired FNAC and has owned it ever since.

In July 1954 André Essel and Max Théret opened in Paris the Federation Nationale d' Achats des Cadres (FNAC; National Shopping Federation for Managers), a members-only shopping club that offered discounted photographic equipment. Both men were members of a militant, leftwing group known as the Young Socialists, and part of their motivation in opening the shop was to offer discount pricing to the common worker. The shop quickly gained popularity due to the special services it offered. Its salespeople were trained in their product categories, purchases were guaranteed for a full year, and all products were tested before being added to the store's inventory, with results and comparisons published in the free magazine *Contact*. FNAC also began a blacklist of items that it believed were unfit to be sold to its customers. By the end of its first full year in business, FNAC had earned over FFR500,000 (US$100,000).

In 1957 the store began selling a variety of electronics, including televisions, radios, and records. The members-only policy was abandoned in 1966 and a second store was opened to take advantage of the expanded customer base. By 1969 FNAC was operating with 580 employees. The business was doing well and ready to expand but needed additional financing to do so. In 1972 the owners sold 40 percent of their stock to the insurance firm Union Des Assurances, which in turn sold 16 percent of its shares to the investment bank Banque de Paris et des Pays Bas, later known as Banque Paribas. That same year the stores made US$70 million in sales and had net profits of US$2.2 million.

In 1974 FNAC attracted national attention when it began selling its books at 80 percent below list price.

Publishers, writers, and other booksellers were outraged by the move, and the controversy continued until 1982, when the so-called anti-FNAC law was signed, limiting discounts on books to a maximum of 5 percent. In 1980 FNAC was listed on the Paris Stock Exchange. By that that point its sales had reached FFR2.2 billion (US$440 million). In 1981 the first FNAC store opened in Brussels, Belgium. Two years later, in 1983, Essel retired from the business and Théret, who was worth over a billion francs, went on to purchase a newspaper to support his socialist cause. Not only did he lose almost his entire fortune to the failing newspaper but also he was convicted for participating in an insider trading scandal and sent off to prison in 1988.

Jean-Louis Periat took over as head of FNAC in 1987 and announced a FFR1.5 billion (US$300 million) plan to open 15 new stores. Part of the reason for this major move was due to a feud between FNAC and the upstart Virgin Records. In 1988 the new company opened a Virgin megastore in Paris. FNAC responded by drastically cutting prices and spending FFR130 million (US$24 million) to open its own megastore near the Virgin store. In 1991 the company opened the first of an anticipated chain called FNAC Music, but because the business never gained more than 2 percent of the Parisian market share it was shut down three years later. In 1994 Pinault Printemps-redoute International SA acquired a majority stake in FNAC, and within a year it officially became the new owner and has remained so ever since.

In 1996 FNAC reported revenues of FFR10 billion (US$2 billion) and net earnings of FFR200 million (US$40million). In 1999 FNAC acquired the online bookseller Alize and expanded into the Asian market by opening a store in Taiwan. By that point FNAC had nearly 100 stores in five countries. In 2001 FNAC opened a new store in Rio de Janeiro, Brazil. Within three years it had opened six stores in Brazil and was planning to open several more in Spain and Portugal. In 2004 the European Commission okayed a joint venture between FNAC and the Greece-based Marinopoulos Brothers S.A. to sell cultural and entertainment-related products. Eight stores were built in Greece and Cyprus over the next five years. In June 2007 FNAC decided to take on Apple's iTunes Store by establishing a music downloads site in Belgium. As of December 2011, FNAC was operating 154 stores with 14,082 full-time employees in eight countries around the world.

BRAND ELEMENTS

- When FNAC was started in 1954, the owners attracted customers by building a reputation based on excellent products at competitive prices.
- FNAC's logo consists of an angled orange box with the company name in lowercased white letters.
- FNAC'slogo is simple; this simplicity implies that people can find products of excellent quality and value and purchase them at the most competitive price at FNAC, the store with the orange box.

When André Essel and Max Théret started FNAC in 1954, they had a very basic brand concept. There was no flashy advertising, no clever slogans or logos, and no colors, shapes, or sounds. Their basic brand element was a reputation for excellent products at low prices. Today's FNAC has a basic logo that consists of an angled orange box with the company name in lowercased white letters. The message the company is broadcasting through this logo is simply that if people want products of excellent quality and value and if they want to purchase them at the most competitive prices, then they know where to go: the store with the orange box. This almost subliminal form of branding does not rely on clever slogans, ads, or television commercials. Regardless, FNAC has successfully won over millions of customers with this simple message.

BRAND IDENTITY

- All FNAC employees are rigorously trained to know specific areas and products to better assist and educate customers.
- In 2002 FNAC developed a set of policies designed to guide businesses in how to treat independent labels and their artists fairly and favorably.
- In 2003 FNAC began a five-year project to combat illiteracy among school-children.

FNAC is a company that sells products in the categories of entertainment, technology, and culture. This includes items such as books, music, films, gaming devices, televisions, appliances, and designer brand items. After nearly 60 years in business, the company still continues to offer a high standard of quality service that was initially developed in 1954 by its founders. The company has built a reputation from the start by training all employees in specific areas to maximize their ability to both assist and inform customers. Furthermore, many of the items that are sold in FNAC stores are first thoroughly tested at independent testing centers. The items that fail the rigors of close scrutiny end up on FNAC's blacklist, which lists products that the company will not sell.

However, FNAC is not just interested in selling merchandise. It also wants to take a strong public stance against exclusion, racism, and censorship. In 2002 it made a commitment to defending the diversity of music by publishing the manifesto "Manifeste pour la diversité musicale," which was followed by a new set of policies designed to guide businesses in how to treat independent labels and their artists fairly and favorably. In 2003 FNAC began a five-year project to combat illiteracy among school children. FNAC does not want to be known just for its marketing and financial talents. It wants to be seen as a company that has a conscience and that wants to leverage its strengths to instill positive changes in the world.

BRAND STRATEGY

- In 2011 FNAC began a five-year strategic plan to create new education-based products for its younger customers.
- In 2011 FNAC began unveiling a new "Kids World" area in select stores in France, offering a wide range of educational games and toys for children.
- In a joint venture with Kobo, an e-book reader company, FNAC launched the Kobo by FNAC in 2011. The e-book reader is designed specifically with FNAC customers in mind.

In 2011 FNAC developed a five-year strategic plan that would focus on creating educational products for children. One of the first of these was the "Kids World" area, set up in select stores in France, that offered a wide variety of educational games and toys. The company also planned to test market an in-store telephony section in 10stores. The new section would offer information, sales, and service for the constantly expanding and evolving smartphone market. In a joint venture with Kobo, an e-book reader company, FNAC launched the e-book reader Kobo by FNAC in 2011. The device can access a catalog of over 2 million books and other items, including 200,000 titles in French.

One program that FNAC has resurrected is the special club membership. For a nominal fee, FNAC club members receive additional benefits, such as more and better discounts, rewards for frequent purchases, a free subscription to the company's membership magazine *Contact*, and exclusive invitations to special sales and events. FNAC has over 600,000 club members out of a general customer base of 12 million per year. FNAC also has a customer loyalty program that awards points each time the card is presented for euros spent in the store or online.

BRAND EQUITY

- In 2012 FNAC had 154 stores, including 91 in France and 63 in seven other countries.
- As of December 31, 2011, FNAC had total revenues of EUR12.2 billion (US$16.3 billion) and net profits totaling EUR1.1 billion (US$1.4 billion).
- In 2012, 72.6 percent of FNAC's revenues were generated within France.

As of 2012, FNAC had over 150 stores, including 91 in France and 63 in seven other countries, as well as the online virtual store FNAC.com. The seven countries were: Belgium, Brazil, Italy, Morocco, Portugal, Spain, and Switzerland. The company is operated by more than 14,000 full-time employees and as of December 31, 2011, it had total revenues of EUR12.2 billion (US$16.3 billion) and net profits of EUR1.1 billion (US$1.4 billion). Approximately 72.6 percent of the total revenues were generated within France, which was a 3.5 percent increase from the previous year. In 2012 FNAC's parent company, Pinault Printemps-redoute International SA, was listed on the *Forbes* "Global 2000" list with a market capitalization of US$22.7 billion and had an overall "Global 2000" ranking of number 362. As a subsidiary of Pinault Printemps-redoute International, FNAC is not listed on any of the *Forbes* lists or any stock market indexes.

BRAND AWARENESS

- Based on visitor numbers, FNAC.com is the number-one online retailer in France .
- Even though Carrefour SA has 4,600 stores in France compared with FNAC's 91, FNAC is still the top book and music retailer in France due to a focus on quality products and customer service.
- FNAC's 154 stores have an annual patronage of 12 million customers.

Founded by two socialist idealists in 1954, FNAC has been around for nearly 60 years. With over 150 stores, 91 of which are located in France, FNAC is the country's leading retailer for books, music, and electronic equipment. It is a company that specializes in products for the mind, and the French have come to strongly associate these types of products with the company name. Even though FNAC has less than 100 stores in its home country, as opposed to retailers such as Carrefour SA, which has over 4,600 in France alone, FNAC is still the number-one seller of books and music in the country and FNAC.com is the top e-commerce site based on visitor numbers. What it lacks in size, it makes up for in longevity, product quality, and customer service, and these are features that its 12 million annual customers recognize and respond to. Customers enjoy being catered to by salespeople who are trained to be extremely knowledgeable in their area. Customers also appreciate the efforts FNAC makes to support the artistic community and education, through annual programs such as book fairs, grants, and anti-illiteracy campaigns. Since 2001 the company has also presented the annual award "Le prix du roman FNAC," whose winners are chosen by an independent panel of booksellers and loyal store customers.

BRAND OUTLOOK

- Between 2012 and 2017 FNAC plans to open smaller stores, rather than relying on the traditional large stores in fewer locations.
- FNAC is currently developing new strategies to compensate for the intense competition from e-commerce sites and brands.
- FNAC's annual revenues dropped from EUR4.6 billion (US$6.1 billion) in December 2008 to EUR4.2 billion (US$5.5 billion) in December 2011.

Between 2012 and 2017 FNAC will continue to develop its brand through new product lines and services and more stores throughout France and around the globe. One of the major plans for the near future is to open more, smaller stores that can be placed in midsized cities and towns. The company believes this will be a more effective model of business rather than opening large stores, which have to be placed in large cities, where competition for consumers' attention is considerably greater. Furthermore, the company plans to further integrate its physical stores with its website by increasing reciprocal promotion of each other and by offering new options for evaluating, purchasing, and even returning products.

In terms of economics, there has been a moderate yet noticeable downturn in consumer spending since the economic recession first occurred in late 2008. Over the period from December 2008 to December 2011 FNAC's annual revenues dropped from EUR4.6 billion (US$6.1 billion) to EUR4.2 billion (US$5.5 billion). Another concern for the company is loss of revenue due to the lower pricing available through competitors' stores and e-commerce sites. Even though FNAC is a large international company, it does not begin to compare with the likes of direct competitors such as Carrefour SA, with its 9,700 stores and reported revenues of US$26.9 billion in 2011. DirectGroup Bertelsmann had 800 stores and reported revenues of US$20.4 billion. Concerning online e-commerce, FNAC is dwarfed by the online retail behemoth Amazon.com, which had revenues totaling US$61.1 billion in 2011. Because of these issues, FNAC's future efforts will focus on broader operations, such as expanding business through smaller stores in more locations, rather than through large stores in fewer locations. FNAC is also placing great confidence in its Kobo e-book reader and its new "Kids World" area that offers educational toys and games.

FURTHER READING

"Best Retail Brands of 2012." Interbrand. Accessed February 13, 2013. http://www.interbrand.com/Libraries/Branding_Studies/Best_Retail_Brands_2012.sflb.ashx?download=true.

Brand Finance. "Best Global Brands: FNAC." *Brandirectory.* Accessed February 13, 2013. http://brandirectory.com/profile/fnac.

"FNAC." *International Directory of Company Histories.* Ed. Tina Grant and Jay P. Pederson. Vol. 21. Detroit, MI: St. James Press, 1998.

"FNAC." *Notable Corporate Chronologies.* Detroit, MI: Gale, 2009.

"Forbes Global 2000 List: PPR." Forbes.com.Accessed February 13, 2013. http://www.forbes.com/companies/ppr/.

Pinault Printemps-redoute International SA. *PPR 2011 Annual Report.* Accessed February 13, 2013. http://www.ppr.com/sites/default/files/publications/PPR_AnnualReport_2011.pdf.

"Yahoo Financials: PPR." Yahoo.com.Accessed February 13, 2013. http://finance.yahoo.com/q?s=PP.PA&ql=1.

FORD

AT A GLANCE

Brand Synopsis: Ford is an iconic American brand of automobiles built upon a promise of innovation, high quality, powerful performance, style, comfort, and safety.
Parent Company: Ford Motor Company
One American Road
Dearborn, Michigan 48126-2798
United States
http://www.ford.com
Sector: Consumer Discretionary
Industry Group: Automobiles and Components
Performance: *Market share*—14.7 percent of the global auto market (2012); 16.5 percent of the U.S. market (2011). *Sales*—US$136.3 billion (2011).
Principal Competitors: Chrysler Group LLC; General Motors Company; Honda Motor Company, Ltd.; Toyota Motor Corporation

BRAND ORIGINS

- After several failed ventures, Henry Ford established Ford Motor Company in 1903.
- Ford revolutionized the automobile industry by using assembly-line mass production techniques to produce the Model T.
- Despite phenomenal success over the past hundred years, the brand floundered in the early 21st century.
- The company has adopted a "brand-defining One Ford philosophy" to distinguish Ford vehicles from a multitude of competitors worldwide.

The Ford brand grew from humble beginnings. Inventor and entrepreneur Henry Ford established the Detroit Automobile Company in 1899, and after it dissolved, incorporated the Henry Ford Company in 1901. The latter would become the Cadillac Motor Company, but by then Ford had established Ford Motor Company. Within three months of its founding in 1903, the firm showed profits of nearly US$37,000. The extraordinary popularity of the Model T automobile (launched in 1908) and the Model A (launched in 1928) helped Ford quickly become one of the top brands in America.

Henry Ford's strong leadership and innovations in production were an important part of the brand's early success. Before 1908 automobiles had been manufactured one at a time, but beginning with the Model T, Ford employed assembly-line mass production techniques that made it possible to build some 18,000 units in the company's first year. The strategy was so effective that businesses around the globe followed Ford's example, changing the way industries operated.

Over the years Ford marketed many of the most successful lines of cars, trucks, and sport utility vehicles in the world. Nevertheless, by 2005 the business was floundering financially due to factors such as high operating costs, increasing competition, and soaring gasoline prices. The company was restructured, some of its product lines were divested or discontinued, and new brands were launched, including futuristic hybrid cars that could run on fuels other than gasoline. In recent years Ford has invested substantially in the research and development of alternative fuels for automobiles.

Since 2008, operations in North and South America, Europe, and Asia have been standardized through the "One Ford Global Product Development System" to ensure that vehicles bearing the Ford brand name would have a typical look, feel, sound, way of handling, and general characteristic design that the company called a "global DNA." This "brand-defining One Ford philosophy" was intended to distinguish Ford vehicles from the brand's numerous competitors worldwide and to help the company produce new models for the global market at an affordable cost. In 2012 the company launched what it called the first in a wave of truly global vehicles designed to appeal to drivers on all continents.

BRAND ELEMENTS

- The Ford logo features the name "Ford" in white against a background of dark blue within a horizontal oval shape.
- An early incarnation of the classic logo in 1912 used just the name "Ford" in a flamboyant script against an oval-shaped background.
- The logo that appeared on the new Model A vehicles in 1928 was the first to include a dark blue background.
- Among Ford's best-known advertising slogans are "Have you driven a Ford lately?" and "Quality Is Job One."
- The Ford brand possesses an element rare among even the largest and most venerable corporations: a legendary founder.

The Ford logo features the name "Ford" in white against a background of dark blue within a horizontal oval shape. The flamboyant cursive lettering of the name is in a font known simply as "Ford script," while the shade of blue is designated as "Pantone 294C." The oval has a white border just inside the rim, making the oval's outer edge blue like the interior. Adopted in 2003 the "Centennial Oval" is a latter-day incarnation of a design that first appeared in 1928.

Ford's earliest logo was an ornate one, bristling with stylized curlicues. The company experimented with trademarks until in 1912, when Ford adopted an early incarnation of what became the classic logo, with just the name "Ford" in a flamboyant script (most notable for its capital *F*) set in a horizontal oval shape. The new Model A vehicles in 1928 were the first cars to feature a logo with the dark blue background that became a permanent feature of the Ford trademark. Several slight adjustments followed in the years leading up to the company's 100th anniversary in 2003, when it introduced its "Centennial Oval."

Among Ford's best-known advertising slogans are "Quality Is Job One" and "Have you driven a Ford lately?" The Ford brand also possesses an element rare among even the largest and most venerable corporations: a legendary founder who ranks among the most influential figures in history. Henry Ford built his first vehicle, the Quadricycle, in 1896, and revolutionized automobile design before turning to a variety of sometimes controversial interests later in life. He made such an impact that fictional characterizations of him or his legacy appear in the literary classics *Brave New World*, by Aldous Huxley (1932), and *Ragtime*, by E. L. Doctorow (1975).

BRAND IDENTITY

- Ford is positioned as the brand that offers "power-packed performance and stylish comfort."
- Ford emphasizes its history of innovation and promises to deliver the same creativity and quality in the future.
- J. Walter Thompson has handled much of Ford's advertising, but Wells Rich Greene created the famous "Quality Is Job One" tagline.

Ford positions itself as the brand that offers "power-packed performance and stylish comfort," excellent fuel economy, driving convenience and safety, and state-of-the-art technology. Ford describes its cars as advanced yet simple to use, comfortable, adventurous, and modern, while its trucks are "tough and durable from the inside out." The company emphasizes its long history of innovation within the automobile industry and promises to deliver the same level of quality into the future.

As befits a brand well into its second century, Ford has been known for a variety of advertising slogans over the years. Many were the creation of the firm J. Walter Thompson, which began working with the company in December 1943. The agency produced such slogans as "There's a Ford in your future" (1945), "The fine car at half the fine-car price" (1956), "Ford ... has a better idea" (1968), "Built Ford tough" (1977), and "Have you driven a Ford lately?" (1983). One of the company's most iconic taglines, "Quality Is Job One" (1981), was the work of another firm, Wells Rich Greene.

BRAND STRATEGY

- The Ford brand first rose to preeminence with its extraordinarily popular Model T and Model A cars.
- The release of the Edsel in 1958 was a colossal marketing failure.
- The F-150 pickup has been the United States' best-selling vehicle every year since its introduction in 1984.
- Ford's most successful models of cars include Mercury, Thunderbird, Taurus, Explorer, Escape, Escort, and Mustang.

- In the 21st century the company was restructured to focus on global marketing of its core Ford and Lincoln brands.

Over the years, Ford has produced extraordinarily popular American automobiles. The brand first rose to preeminence with the Model T, a staggering 15 million of which were sold between 1908 and 1927 to become one of the most successful cars in history. The acquisition of the Lincoln brand in 1922 took Ford into the luxury market, while the Model A, launched in 1928, replicated the Model T's success on a smaller scale. In 1938 Ford launched a third major brand: Mercury. In 1948 the company introduced its enormously successful F-series of pickup trucks, and in 1955 the stylish Thunderbird debuted.

One of history's greatest marketing failures occurred in 1958 when the Edsel, named after the company founder's late son, was introduced. The car sold poorly, and Ford lost millions as a result. However, the brand bounced back, partly through diversifying (in 1959 the Ford Credit Corporation was established), and partly through sales of the highly successful Mustang sports car, introduced in 1964. By 1965 Ford was selling 2 million units worldwide annually. In 1968 Ford of Europe, which had been established the previous year, introduced the compact Escort, which made its North American debut in 1981.

Ford prospered in the 1980s as its F-150 pickup, which it rolled out in 1984, began a three-decade run as America's best-selling vehicle. By 1992 the Taurus had replaced the Honda Accord as the top-selling car in America, and in the 1990s the Explorer, Escape, and Lincoln Navigator helped Ford establish dominance in the sport utility vehicle (SUV) market.

Between 1989 and 2000 the company's brand platforms expanded rapidly with the acquisition of the prestigious Swedish brand Volvo and the British brands Jaguar, Aston Martin, and Land Rover. Ford fell on hard financial times in the early 21st century, however, leading to talk of "brand fatigue." The company would ultimately return to basics, as well as to profitability, by divesting itself of its British and Swedish brands, discontinuing the Mercury line of cars, and adopting a restructuring program known as "The Way Forward." In 2012 Ford held just two brand platforms, Lincoln and Ford itself, but was promoting those aggressively in a worldwide marketing effort under the brand-defining slogan, "One Ford."

BRAND EQUITY

- With an estimated brand value of $7.96 million, Ford ranked 45th on Interbrand's 2012 list of best global brands.
- Ford was the only U.S. carmaker to earn a place on the Interbrand list.
- In 2010 Ford ranked second only to General Motors for total units produced worldwide.
- Ford's total estimated value of $56.4 billion was fifth among global automobile and parts companies in 2011.
- In terms of gross revenues, Ford was the third-largest manufacturer in the world in 2009.

Ford ranked 45th on Interbrand's 2012 list of the top global brands, with an estimated brand value of US$7.96 billion, an increase of 6 percent over 2011. This figure put it in sixth place among automotive brands, behind Toyota, Mercedes-Benz, and BMW (all valued in the range of US$30 billion); Honda, worth twice as much as Ford; and Volkswagen, with a value of more than US$9 billion.

It is important to note that several of the high-ranking brands belonged to companies with production figures, overhead, and total value much smaller than Ford's. In 2010 Ford ranked second only to General Motors (GM) in total production, with some 1.9 million units, compared to GM's 2.2 million. Following Ford in the top five were Toyota, Honda, and Chrysler. Neither GM nor Chrysler, however, even came close to Interbrand's top-100 list for 2010 or the two years after that.

With a total value estimated at more than US$56.4 billion, Ford ranked fifth among the world's most valuable automobile and parts companies in 2011, and third (behind Toyota and GM) among the world's largest manufacturers by gross revenues in any sector for 2009. It placed first on the list of most valuable U.S. automobile and parts companies for 2011, well ahead of GM, Johnson Controls, Harley-Davidson, and others. (Chrysler did not make the top 8 list.) Additionally, Ford ranked sixth (behind Honda and ahead of Toyota) on *Fortune*'s 2010 list of most admired motor vehicle companies.

BRAND AWARENESS

- At the time of its 2003 centennial, Ford ranked sixth among U.S. advertisers.
- With 87 percent awareness among consumers polled, Ford ranked first in *Consumer Reports*' 2012 Car Brand Perception Survey.
- Henry Ford's political and social views frequently provoked negative publicity for the Ford brand during his lifetime.
- Ford experienced further negative publicity with the failures of the Edsel in the 1950s and the Pinto in the 1970s.
- Extremely popular vehicles such as the Model T and the F-150 pickup have earned Ford long-term positive awareness among consumers.

Ford has long been one of the world's leading advertisers. In 1952 for instance, it introduced that year's line of cars and trucks with full-page ads in more than 6,000 newspapers and spots on more than 1,000 radio stations, and in 1969 it spent what was then the massive sum of more than US$90 million on TV advertising. By the time of its 2003 centennial, Ford ranked sixth among U.S. advertisers with an annual budget of US$2.2 billion. Network television expenditures exceeded US$450 million in 2008, placing Ford in fifth place among U.S. advertisers (GM ranked third). With 87 percent awareness among consumers polled, Ford ranked first in *Consumer Reports'* 2012 Car Brand Perception Survey, followed by Chevrolet and Toyota with 76 percent and 70 percent, respectively.

Ford has also gained attention for negative reasons, not least its founder's controversial views. In 1932 Henry Ford sparked a massive worker protest when he stated that the unemployed were not trying hard enough to find work, even as he was assisting Josef Stalin's communist regime by building a plant in Russia. Many of the plant's employees, including American citizens, died in Stalin's Great Terror. Additionally, Ford's anti-Semitism was legendary, and he proved such a friend of the Nazis that he received the Grand Cross of the German Eagle (the highest honor Nazi Germany was able to bestow on a foreigner) in 1938.

The company has also confronted negative publicity related to its vehicles. Despite an extensive research and promotional effort, the Edsel, introduced in 1958, suffered from a number of basic design and marketing flaws. By the time production ceased in 1960, the company had lost some US$350 million (close to US$3 billion today), and the name "Edsel" had become a synonym for failure. In the 1970s, the Pinto subcompact ran into trouble in Brazil when it turned out that the name means "tiny male genitals" in Portuguese slang. More serious problems followed when defects in the Pinto's manufacturing were blamed for several hundred deaths, evoking a furor that intensified when *Mother Jones* magazine published information indicating that Ford executives knew of the problems but kept quiet about them.

However, Ford has always bounced back from such problems, thanks in part to the overall success of its vehicles, beginning with the Model T. In addition to the extraordinarily popular Mustang, F-150, Escort, and Taurus, Ford's sport utility vehicles (SUVs) reshaped American life in the 1990s. The Explorer, launched in 1991, was instrumental in transforming SUVs from a niche product to a mainstream one, and the 1998 introduction of the Lincoln Navigator helped carve out a new luxury segment in the SUV market. In 2004 the Escape became the first gasoline–electric hybrid sport utility, which further influenced ideas about SUVs by introducing the concept of fuel efficiency.

BRAND OUTLOOK

- In the early 21st century, Ford fell on such hard times that it had to mortgage the rights to its blue oval logo.
- Unlike competitors GM and Chrysler, Ford did not go bankrupt or seek a federal bailout in the wake of the 2008 financial crisis.
- "The Way Forward," a blueprint for recovery adopted in 2006, returned the company to profitability in 2009.
- Ford's future includes expansion to emerging geographic markets and the development of additional fuel-efficient vehicles.

With its longevity and prominence, Ford has gone through a number of difficult periods, only to rebound each time. The company experienced one such setback at the beginning of the 21st century, when it became so overburdened with debt that in December 2006 it mortgaged all of its assets, including the blue oval trademark, in order to raise US$23.4 billion in cash from a bank syndicate. More challenges followed with the global economic downturn in 2008, which forced competitors GM and Chrysler into bankruptcy. Ford remained solvent, however, and, unlike GM and Chrysler, did not seek a bailout from the federal government.

In the meantime, Ford began implementing "The Way Forward," a blueprint for recovery introduced in January 2006. In addition to plant closings and layoffs, The Way Forward called for the replacement of several long-standing products (such as the Lincoln Town Car), closure or divestment of several product lines, and an emphasis on production of compacts, crossover SUVs, and hybrid vehicles. The Way Forward set a goal of returning the company to profitability by 2010, but in fact Ford showed a profit in 2009, and margins grew in the following years even as the company reduced its debt. Ford regained ownership of its trademark in May 2012.

As Ford looks toward the future, it plans to open plants in China, India, and other regions where car sales are likely to grow at a much faster pace than in more established markets. The company has established a goal of using just nine core platforms to produce 85 percent of its global volume by 2013, which will allow it to cut costs by using a reduced number of suppliers and by selling the same vehicle in a number of geographic markets. It is also increasing production of hybrid models, and the company is expected to hold a 12 percent market share of electric vehicles, with only Toyota claiming a larger share, by 2015.

FURTHER READING

Autoevolution. "Ford Brand History." Accessed October 4, 2012. http://www.autoevolution.com/ford/history/.

Bartlett, Jeff. "2012 Car Brand Perception Survey: Ford Leads All Brands in Awareness." *Consumer Reports*, January 26, 2012.

"Ford Brand Ranking." RankingTheBrands.com. Accessed October 4, 2012. http://www.rankingthebrands.com/Brand-detail.aspx?brandID=178.

"Ford 100: 100 Years, 100 Stories." *Automotive News*, June 16, 2003.

"Ford Motor Co." *Advertising Age*, September 15, 2003.

"Ford Motor Company." *International Directory of Company Histories*. Ed. Tina Grant and Miranda H. Ferrara. Vol. 64. Detroit, MI: St. James Press, 2006.

Halliday, Jean. "Ford: Moving On." *MediaWeek*, May 24, 2010.

Ritson, Mark. "Why Ford's Brand Focus Is Best in the Business." *MarketingWeek*, August 5, 2010.

"2012 Ranking of the Best Global Brands." Interbrand. Accessed October 4, 2012. http://www.interbrand.com/en/best-global-brands/2012/Best-Global-Brands-2012.aspx.

FUJIFILM

AT A GLANCE

Brand Synopsis: Fujifilm's products, which include cameras, films, medical and industrial equipment, and storage devices, demonstrate that it is a brand devoted to the capture of images and information.
Parent Company: Fujifilm Holdings Corporation
7-3, Akasaka 9-chome
Minato-ku, Tokyo 107-0052
Japan
http://www.fujifilm.com/
Sector: Consumer Discretionary; Information Technology
Industry Group: Consumer Durables & Apparel; Technology Hardware & Equipment
Performance: *Market share*—4.2 percent of digital camera market, worldwide (2011). *Sales*—JPY2.2 trillion (US$19.2 billion) (2011).
Principal Competitors: Eastman Kodak Company; Agfa-Gevaert N.V.; Canon Inc.; Ricoh Company, Ltd.; Konica Minolta Holdings, Inc.; Olympus Corporation; Sony Corporation; Nikon Corporation; Hewlett-Packard Company

BRAND ORIGINS

- Japanese manufacturer Dainippon Celluloid Company spun off an independent company in 1934, Fuji Photo Film Co., Ltd.
- Fuji Photo Film Co. introduced film for amateur photographers in the 1950s.
- Eastman Kodak and Fuji Photo Film Co. waged a long battle for control of the photographic industry.
- In the 1970s, 1980s, and 1990s, Fuji Photo Film expanded geographically and diversified its product output to include industrial, medical, and digital products.

Fujifilm Corporation began as an offshoot of Japanese film manufacturer Dainippon Celluloid Company (later known as Daicel Chemical Industries, Ltd.). Created in 1934, this offshoot, known as Fuji Photo Film Co., Ltd., manufactured motion picture film, dry plates, and photographic paper. It struggled to improve its quality and build its brand reputation as it fought against cheaper and better imports.

After continued research and work, the independent company produced its first film in 1936 and later developed motion picture negative film. The company's technical expertise in developing the difficult negative film impressed Japanese studios. In 1938 the company opened its second factory. World War II halted the company's research and civilian production, and the company's factories sustained bomb damage during the war.

When Japan's civilian trade resumed in 1947, Fuji began exporting its cameras and binoculars throughout Asia and South America, and it exported motion picture film to India beginning in 1949. It began producing color film in 1948 and manufactured X-ray film as well.

In the 1950s, Fuji Photo Film Co. began producing film for amateur photographers. The company would dominate this market in Japan for years and come to hold a significant percentage of the world market. In 1962 Fuji Photo Film Co. and the Anglo-American company Rank Xerox joined forces to form Fuji Xerox Co., Ltd. This company also captures images and information with such products as printers, scanners, multifunction devices (printer/scanner/copiers), and software. The Fujifilm Corporation, Fuji Xerox, and Toyama Chemical are all members of Fujifilm Holdings Corporation.

The company continued its global expansion in the 1950s and 1960s. It exported to North and Central America and Asia and established its North American office, Fuji Photo Film U.S.A., Inc. (now known as FUJIFILM U.S.A., Inc.), in New York state in 1965. It strove to improve quality and compatibility of its products. By 1969 all of its films, photo paper, and chemicals were fully compatible with devices manufactured overseas. This compatibility was crucial as Fuji battled with Eastman Kodak for the market in photographic materials and equipment.

By the 1970s, Kodak led the market among amateur photographers, but Fuji's improvements in film speed and color made it a favorite among professional photographers and more serious amateurs. Fuji continued its geographic expansion in the 1970s and 1980s, especially in the United States and Europe. It also developed products for medical imaging and heavy industry. It was the first company outside the United States to manufacture videotapes. In 1986 it introduced its disposable camera in Japan and later became the first company to bring this product to the United States.

In the 1990s the company continued its interest in film and photography. It opened a number of photofinishing laboratories, which competed with rival Kodak, and launched products like smaller camcorders. It also began selling its digital products. This move would be crucial to the company's later survival, since digital cameras would greatly reduce the need for the company's film. The company also continued to develop products for medicine and heavy industry. This diversification would also help the company during the digital transition. Now known as Fujifilm Corporation, the company and its affiliates have more than 35,000 employees around the world.

BRAND ELEMENTS

- The Fujifilm logo consists of the company in black capital letters, except for the "I" in Fuji, which features a red point on top.
- The former Fujifilm logo consisted of the word Fuji in a red box resembling a box of camera film.
- The logo of Fuji Xerox displays the company name in red and a large white-and-gray X that wraps around a red sphere.

The Fujifilm logo consists of the name of the company in capital letters. These letters are all black except for the I in Fuji, which features a red pointed shape for its top half and a black line as its bottom half. The Fujifilm logo appears on Fujifilm's products, buildings, advertising, company-affiliated materials, and other items. It appears multiple times on its websites, which also incorporate Fujifilm's corporate color, green, a color used throughout Fujifilm's history.

The black and red Fujifilm text logo is a departure from its longtime logo, which consisted of the word Fuji in a red box resembling a box of camera film. This box logo appeared within a larger green box displaying the word Fujifilm in white. The company used to make much of its income from photographic film for consumer cameras, but the rise of the digital camera changed the industry and Fujifilm's business.

The logo of another Fujifilm Group company, Fuji Xerox, consists of the company name in red accompanied by a large white-and-gray X that wraps around a red sphere. The red text color echoes the dash of red in the Fujifilm logo, while the X echoes the first and last letter in Xerox.

BRAND IDENTITY

- Fujifilm says that its logo red "I" shape represents its "commitment to advanced technologies" and "its determination for continuous innovation."
- After adopting its new logo, Fujifilm retained its green corporate color, thus acknowledging its brand's visual history.
- Fujifilm used an airship (blimp) to signify its global reach and to help whale photographers, which illustrated its helpfulness and commitment to photography.
- Fujifilm has trademarked the phrase Image Intelligence, symbolizing its interest in image capture and its position as a brand intelligent enough to perform this work.

Fujifilm wanted to convey an image of a dependable and reliable yet innovative brand. A Fujifilm website states that the pointed red shape in the "I" in the Fujifilm logo is symbolic. It represents the company's "commitment to advanced technologies. The dash of red expresses its determination for continuous innovation." Although this logo replaced other Fujifilm logos, Fujifilm still used its longtime green corporate color. With this decision, Fujifilm noted that it was "inheriting its established brand assets." Fujifilm thus did not create a total change in the brand's visual identity. Finally, Fujifilm noted that it intended to use its logo on its "products, advertising media, facilities, and office supplies." This repetition would help solidify the new trademark and help to create a consistent look for the brand.

A blimp, or airship, served as a major symbol for Fujifilm for years. This airship featured the brand's old logo that looked like a red film box as well as its corporate green color. More than just a huge floating advertisement for Fujifilm, the airship symbolized different things. Since it flew over several countries and participated in international events, it represented the brand's multinational presence. It illustrated that Fujifilm could travel as smoothly and as far as its airship. In Florida in 2005, the Fujifilm airship helped move scientists who researched and filmed whales and also helped photographers film whales in Cape Cod. These endeavors promoted Fujifilm as a brand interested in the environment and in helping people. By associating with such visible photographic endeavors, it also reminded people that Fujifilm is a brand that produced films, cameras, and other image capturing products.

Given Fujifilm's interest in capturing images, it is not surprising that it has trademarked the phrase Image Intelligence. This phrase captures the Fujifilm brand's interest in image capture. It also portrays Fujifilm as an intelligent, experienced brand, a brand savvy enough to provide innovations that capture the best images in photographic, printing, and medical imaging processes.

BRAND STRATEGY

- The Internet site YouTube and Fujifilm Canada's website have featured *The Fuji Guys*, a series of videos featuring discussions of Fujifilm products.
- Fujifilm's high-profile sponsorships have supported an airship, the World Cup in soccer, North American fishing tours, and German soccer teams.
- Reflecting its interest in the environment, Fujifilm has posted annual sustainability reports in Japanese, Chinese, and English on its websites.

Fujifilm's North American branch launched a brand campaign in 2012. This mostly print campaign featured its medical imaging products. By highlighting these products, Fujifilm demonstrated that it produces much more than cameras and films. The advertisements demonstrated how the company has diversified and featured the headline "Just when you thought you knew us" and the slogan "Expect innovation." The company also used the "Expect innovation" slogan—and the Fujifilm green brand color—on a number of Fujifilm North American social media sites.

The Internet site YouTube and Fujifilm Canada's website have hosted another Fujifilm promotion, *The Fuji Guys*, a series of videos in which two men discuss and demonstrate Fujifilm products. The YouTube pages include consumer comments and questions about the products, providing a forum for current customers, potential customers, and company representatives.

Throughout its history, Fujifilm has sponsored an international blimp, the massively popular World Cup soccer event, North American fishing tours, and the German soccer teams Bayer 04 Leverkusen and TSG 1899 Hoffenheim. These involvements are examples of the company's global interests.

Fujifilm's websites demonstrate another company interest: the environment. The company has posted annual sustainability reports since 2007 on its websites. Internet users can download the most recent copies of this sustainability report in Japanese, Chinese, and English.

BRAND EQUITY

- In 2000 consumer photographic film accounted for 60 percent of Fujifilm's sales, but digital camera sales caused this figure to drop dramatically.
- For a particular type of optical film used in liquid crystal display (LCD) screens, Fujifilm has a 100 percent market share.
- Fujifilm India held a 7 percent share of the country's digital camera market in 2012.

A 2012 article in the *Economist* discusses Fujifilm's market share and the changing nature of its business. It noted that digital photography had a huge impact on the consumer photographic film market, as film sales accounted for 60 percent of Fujifilm's profits in 2000 but were reduced to "practically nothing" in the years following. Prior to the development of the digital camera, Fujifilm and American company Kodak had "lucrative near-monopolies of their home markets" in Japan and the United States.

The *Economist* article added that despite the decline of the market for consumer camera film, Fujifilm continues to prosper due to its diversification and adaptability. It produces optical films for liquid crystal display (LCD) screens. For one type of these films, Fujifilm has a 100 percent market share.

In India, Fujifilm India held a 7 percent share of the country's digital camera market in 2012. Employees said the company was trying to claim an incrementally larger market share in each fiscal period. To do this, it planned to expand to developing regions of India and to strengthen its operations in developed areas of the country.

BRAND AWARENESS

- In 2012 *digit!* and *Photo Presse* magazines gave Fujifilm a photokina STAR 2012 award for its X E-1 interchangeable lens camera.
- International consulting and analysis company Frost & Sullivan gave Fujifilm two awards for its mammography machines in 2012.

- VARINDIA's *Brand Book 2012* named Fujifilm India one of the best brands in India, noting that "Fujifilm as a brand needs no recognition."

Fujifilm's products have won honors. In 2012 *digit!* and *Photo Presse* magazines gave Fujifilm a photokina STAR 2012 award for its X E-1, a camera with interchangeable lenses. Held every two years, photokina is a fair for the imaging field. Since the fair, which took place in Cologne, Germany, also exhibited various photography and imaging products, this prize demonstrated Fujifilm's prominence in the imaging industry.

Fujifilm's business products have also garnered awards. In 2012 it won two awards for its mammography machines, devices used to screen for breast cancer. International consulting and analysis company Frost & Sullivan granted these awards, once again indicating Fujifilm's global presence.

Analysts in other countries have rated Fujifilm highly. VARINDIA's *Brand Book 2012*, which discussed the most trusted companies in India, named Fujifilm India one of the best brands in that country. The *Brand Book* noted that "Fujifilm as a brand needs no recognition since it was one of the pioneers of the camera and imaging business. Over a period of time they expanded and created sub-brands in order to strengthen distinct identities for each business. However, Fujifilm was always careful about the Master Brand and was always promoting Fujifilm along with all sub-brands." This description documents Fujifilm's marketing skill, business success, and brand strength.

BRAND OUTLOOK

- Fujifilm still sells film, but for motion picture cameras and for use in such devices as liquid crystal display (LCD) screens.
- A 2013 report questioned whether the changes in photography, international regulations, and a strong yen could hurt Fujifilm's outlook.
- In 2012 Fujifilm developed a new magnetic tape media made with new materials that offer improved storage options.

Analysts have often commented on the rise of digital cameras and the subsequent decline of consumer film sales. Fujifilm has experienced both of these phenomena firsthand. It sells less consumer camera film than before, but it now sells digital cameras. It still sells film, though primarily for motion picture cameras and for use in other industries. For example, it produces optical films for liquid crystal display (LCD) screens. This ability to adapt and innovate has helped Fujifilm stay competitive.

A 2013 report also mentioned how Fujifilm has grappled with the changes to traditional photography. This report also worried that international regulations could hurt business, as could the value of Japan's currency, since a strong yen would mean lower profits for Fujifilm. Fujifilm itself downgraded its estimated earnings, estimating its 2013 net income to be JPY45 billion (US$482 million) instead of its previously stated JPY50 billion. Regardless of these issues, the 2013 report had confidence in Fujifilm's ability to perform and recommended it to investors.

Fujifilm's innovation continues as it develops new products. In 2012 it announced that it had developed a new magnetic tape. This highly compressed tape for storing electronic data incorporated new materials to optimize storage options. This new product is another example of Fujifilm's innovative approach to capturing information.

FURTHER READING

Baar, Aaron. "Fujifilm's First Brand Campaign Talks Tech." *Marketing Daily*, March 22, 2012.

Fujifilm. "Corporate History." Accessed December 3, 2012. http://www.fujifilm.com/about/history/corporate_history/.

———. "FUJIFILM LTO Ultrium6 Data Cartridge." November 22, 2012. Accessed December 2, 2012. http://www.fujifilm.com/news/n121122.html.

———. "Fujifilm Unveils New Corporate Brand Logo, Aims to Strengthen Corporate Brand in Accordance with New Group Management Structure." Accessed November 30, 2012. http://www.fujifilm.com/news/n060712.html.

"Fujifilm Downgraded to Underperform." *Zacks Equity Research*, February 6, 2013. Accessed February 14, 2013. http://finance.yahoo.com/news/fujifilm-downgraded-underperform-174844640.html.

Greve, Henrich. "Kodak versus Fujifilm." *INSEAD Blog*, January 23, 2012. Accessed December 2, 2012. http://blog.insead.edu/2012/01/kodak-versus-fujifilm/.

"The Last Kodak Moment?" *Economist*, January 14, 2012.

Pandit, Priy. "Fujifilm Aims at 10 Per Cent Market Share by 2013." EFYTimes.com, September 21, 2012. Accessed November 30, 2012. http://efytimes.com/e1/fullnews.asp?edid=91138.

VARINDIA. "Fujifilm India." *Brand Book*, 2012. Accessed December 2, 2012. http://www.brandbook.varindia.com/c_fujifilm.htm.

Walsh, Ray, and David E. Salamie. "Fuji Photo Film Co., Ltd." *International Directory of Company Histories*. Ed. Jay P. Pederson. Vol. 79. Detroit, MI: St. James Press, 2006.

FUJITSU

AT A GLANCE

Brand Synopsis: Though its logo uses the infinity symbol, Fujitsu has long found itself overshadowed by industry leaders IBM and Hewlett-Packard, and by the early 21st century it had begun to move away from computer hardware to technology services.
Parent Company: Fujitsu Limited
Shiodome City Center
1-5-2 Higashi-Shimbashi
Minato-ku, Tokyo 105-7123
Japan
http://www.fujitsu.com/global/
Sector: Information Technology
Industry Group: Software & Services; Technology Hardware & Equipment
Performance: *Market share*—3 percent (2010). *Sales*—JPY4.468 trillion (US$54.483 billion) (2012).
Principal Competitors: Accenture Ltd.; Apple Inc.; Computer Sciences Corporation; Dell Inc.; Hewlett-Packard Company; International Business Machines Corporation; Oracle Corporation; Panasonic Corporation; Sharp Corporation

BRAND ORIGINS

- A 1923 joint venture between Furukawa Electric of Japan and the German firm Siemens created Fuji Electric.
- Fuji Electric established Fuji Tsushinki Seizo in 1935.
- The company developed Japan's first commercial computer in 1954.
- Fuji Tsushinki Seizo became Fujitsu in 1967.

A 1923 joint venture between Japan's Furukawa Electric Company and Germany's Siemens created Fuji Electric Company, which on June 20, 1935, established Fuji Tsushinki Seizo, or Fuji Telecommunications Equipment Manufacturing. The new company became involved in telephone and radio communications, which in prewar Japan remained in an archaic state. After World War II, the Japanese Ministry of Communications created Nippon Telephone and Telegraph (NTT), a public utility that became one of Fuji Tsushinki's key customers.

Fuji Tsushinki manufactured the first Japanese commercial computer, the FACOM 100, in 1954, and followed this with the FACOM 222 in 1961. IBM meanwhile introduced the first transistorized computer in 1959, which posed a serious challenge to Japan's nascent computer industry. The national government responded with a number of measures that included restrictions on foreign imports and subsidies to local manufacturers. By then seven Japanese companies had entered the computer business, and six formed research alliances with US companies. IBM offered to form an alliance with Fuji Tsushinki, but the company remained the sole holdout. Fuji Tsushinki also distinguished itself from the others, which had interests in a number of areas, by devoting itself entirely to communications and computers.

As part of FONTAC, a government-sponsored program that also involved Hitachi and NEC, Fuji Tsushinki worked on a product to compete with IBM's 1401 computer. The initiative failed in that regard, but it did pave the way for the Japanese Electronic Computer Company (JECC), a joint venture of seven firms that succeeded in increasing domestic computer sales by more than 200 percent. In part through help from JECC, Fuji Tsushinki in 1965 introduced the most advanced Japanese computer to date, the FACOM 230. In 1967 the company changed its name to Fujitsu Ltd.

BRAND ELEMENTS

- Fuji Tsushinki's first logo reflects its origins as a joint venture of Fuji Electric and Siemens.
- In 1962 Fuji Tsushinki adopted a logo that used the Japanese name for Fujitsu Limited, along with the English words "Communications and Electronics."
- The 1972 Fujitsu logo, in red, white, and blue, was the company's first to use color.
- Notable features in Fujitsu's fourth logo are the "J," whose arc hangs below the other letters, and the infinity symbol atop it and the "I."

The first Fuji Tsushinki logo, adopted at the time of its establishment in 1935, consisted of a circle surrounding the letters "f" and "S" superimposed on one another. The letters, of a rounded non-serif font drawn in a thick, black line like the one that outlines the circle, refer to the company's parents: Fuji Electric Ltd. and Siemens.

By 1962 the company had begun informally referring to itself as Fujitsu Limited, or "Fujitsu Kabushiki Kaisha." This name now appeared in large, black Japanese characters surrounded by a horizontal rectangle with the English words "Communications and Electronics" along the bottom.

A third logo, introduced in 1972, retained the Japanese characters, now rendered in red. These appeared in a wide horizontal band of negative or white space bordered top and bottom by light blue stripes.

Fujitsu in 1989 adopted a logo that remained in use a quarter-century later. The logotype, in a color designated as "Fujitsu Red," is in all-caps serif type. The most notable feature is the "J," whose arc hangs below the other letters. At its top, forming the dot on this letter and the "I" next to it, is a version of the infinity symbol (like a numeral 8 on its side), but rather than being horizontal, this one tilts to the lower left and has loops of unequal size.

BRAND IDENTITY

- Contrary to popular belief, the corporate name "Fuji" does not directly refer to Japan's highest mountain.
- The name "Fuji" in Fuji Electric and Fujitsu is a portmanteau representing corporate parents Furukawa and Siemens.
- The loops of the infinity symbol in the Fujitsu logo represent the Earth and Sun.
- Fujitsu mandates use of only four principal colors in its corporate symbolism: "Fujitsu Red" and authorized variants, Black, White, and PANTONE® Warm Gray 9C.
- Any representation of the Fujitsu brand must meet criteria explicitly laid out by the corporation.

As noted by Fujitsu on a web page devoted to the history of its symbols, "The evolution of the corporate logo illustrates the background of each age and the history of Fujitsu." Thus the 1935 logo represented its origins as a joint venture of Fuji Electric and Siemens.

In fact, contrary to popular belief, the name "Fuji" itself does not directly refer to Japan's highest mountain. Though fortuitous, this reference is in fact coincidental to the principal meaning of the name as a portmanteau representing the two companies that created Fuji Electric: "Fu" for Furukawa and "Ji" for Siemens ("based on the German pronunciation," according to Fujitsu).

By the time of the second logo, Fujitsu had organized itself into two divisions, Computer Manufacturing and Electronics Manufacturing, represented by the English words at the bottom of the logo. The 1972 version uses red to symbolize passion, blue for peace, and white for purity, according to Fujitsu, which also explained the infinity symbol in the 1989 logo. The smaller of the two loops symbolizes the Earth and the larger the Sun, while the symbol itself "represents the wide open universe and infinite possibility."

Fujitsu provides strict guidelines for the use of its symbols and its colors. These include "Fujitsu Red" (simply 100 percent Magenta according to the CMYK color system) and permissible variants, most notably PANTONE® Red 032C; Black and White (defined as 100 percent K and 0 percent K respectively on the CMYK scale respectively); and PANTONE® Warm Gray 9C.

In an online statement regarding its brand identity, Fujitsu notes that "Every successful brand is centered on one common idea and this is presented homogeneously both internally and externally." The company lists four criteria that all visual representations of its brand must meet: to make the brand "visible, recognizable and memorable"; to symbolize it in a positive way; to represent the coherence of the company's structure; and, for employees, to help them identify both with the company as a whole and with their specific departments.

BRAND STRATEGY

- Two themes of Fujitsu's early history came together in 1970, when the Japanese government directed its efforts to compete with IBM.
- The company has formed relationships with several overseas firms, most notably Amdahl Corporation, that ultimately became part of Fujitsu.

- Fujitsu's areas of focus over the years have included telecommunications, electronics, and computers.
- By the early 21st century, Technology Solutions, including System Platforms and Services, accounted for two-thirds of Fujitsu's net sales.

The early part of Fujitsu's history was characterized by government support on the one hand, and fierce competition with IBM on the other. These two strands came together in 1970 when, under international pressure, the Japanese government announced its intention to lower restrictions against computer imports by 1975. To develop a hedge against the coming onslaught from IBM and its 370 line of computers, the Ministry for Trade and Industry (MITI) directed Fujitsu and its Japanese archrival Hitachi to develop a competitive line dubbed the M series.

Fujitsu in turn formed a partnership with the US Amdahl Corporation, whose own stated goal was to develop a 370 competitor. The relationship helped propel Fujitsu to a lead over IBM in the Japanese computer market, and in 1997 Fujitsu made Amdahl, based in Sunnyvale, California, a wholly owned subsidiary. Fujitsu continued to pursue relationships with overseas companies, most notably British mainframe manufacturer International Computers Ltd. (ICL) and California's HAL Computer Systems, both of which became subsidiaries; as well as Ross Technology, based in Austin, Texas, closed down and absorbed into the parent firm.

Begun as a telecommunications and electronics company, Fujitsu divided itself into electronics and computers divisions in the mid-20th century. By the early 1980s, three areas had emerged: computers, telecommunications, and electronic devices. The first of these accounted for about two-thirds of the company's business.

In the early 21st century, Fujitsu divided its products and services into three main groups. Technology Solutions, which accounted for about two-thirds of net sales, was in turn divided into System Platforms and Services. Ubiquitous Solutions, which represented about one-quarter of Fujitsu's business, included PCs/Mobile Phones and Mobilewear (car audio and navigation systems, mobile communication equipment, and automotive electronics). The remainder, about one-twelfth of net sales, fell under the heading of Device Solutions, including LSI (large-scale integration) and Electronics Components (semiconductor packages, batteries, structural components, optical transceiver modules, and printed circuit boards.)

BRAND EQUITY

- According to Brandirectory, Fujitsu's brand value declined slightly from about US$5.5 billion in 2010 to just under US$5.35 billion in 2012.
- Fujitsu held a slightly more than 3 percent share of the highly segmented IT service and consulting market in 2010.
- Among computer and office equipment companies worldwide in 2008, Fujitsu ranked third after Hewlett-Packard and Dell with about US$4.7 billion in revenues.

Brand Finance online-rating-source Brandirectory estimated Fujitsu's brand value at just under US$5.35 billion in 2012, down from US$5.635 billion in 2011. Its brand rating of AA- for those years also constituted a small decline from 2010, when it had an AA brand rating with an estimated brand value slightly less than US$5.5 billion.

According to *Market Share Reporter*, Fujitsu held slightly more than a 3 percent share among information technology (IT) service and consulting firms worldwide in 2009 and 2010, behind IBM and Hewlett-Packard, with about 7 percent and 4.5 percent respectively. Various companies represented the vast majority (slightly more than 80 percent) of the market not held by the top five companies, which also included Accenture and Computer Sciences Corporation (CSC).

Among IT outsourcing firms worldwide in 2011, Fujitsu again ranked third, with a 4.5 percent market share as compared to nearly 11 percent for IBM and just over 6 percent for Hewlett-Packard. Fujitsu held almost a 4.5 percent share among server makers worldwide in 2010, according to *Market Share Reporter*. This placed it well behind Hewlett-Packard and IBM, both of which had around 31 percent; Dell, with nearly 15 percent; and Oracle at more than 6 percent. Among cell-phone makers in Japan for 2012, its market share was nearly 12 percent, more than half that of Sharp and almost as much as Panasonic's.

Fujitsu ranked third among computer and office equipment companies worldwide for 2008, with about US$46.7 billion in revenues as compared with nearly US$118.4 billion for Hewlett-Packard and US$61.1 billion for Dell. Among computer hardware companies overall in 2010, Fujitsu ranked fourth after Hewlett-Packard, Apple, and Dell in terms of combined revenue, profit, asset, and market capitalization figures, according to *Forbes*.

BRAND AWARENESS

- In conjunction with the adoption of its "infinity" logo in 1989, Fujitsu began using the slogan "The possibilities are infinite."
- The company's 75th anniversary in 2010 saw the introduction of a new slogan, "Shaping tomorrow with you."
- Fujitsu's environmental record has won it recognition from Greenpeace and *Newsweek*.

In conjunction with the adoption of its "infinity" logo in 1989, Fujitsu began using the slogan "The possibilities are infinite." The company's 75th anniversary in 2010 saw the introduction of a new slogan, "Shaping tomorrow with you." Discussing this tagline in *Market Leader*, Fujitsu strategy director for international business Vincent Rousselet noted that "before investing strongly in any substantial media campaign," the company used it as a way of reassuring its 175,000 employees that, even in uncertain economic times, they would continue to have jobs.

As Fujitsu prepared to launch its tablets and smartphones outside the Asian market for the first time in 2012, Lara O'Reilly of *Marketing Week* discussed the accompanying promotional strategy with product marketing director James Maynard, who described the use of the infinity sign as "our standardized branding for mobile." As to the business metrics Fujitsu would use for evaluating the campaign's success, Maynard answered that "Brand awareness is important for any launch in the consumer space. Sales volume plays less of a part for us as it's more about sustainability.… If we set a volume target it will be forever held up for us to try and beat it, but it's not the core focus of the business."

Fujitsu has earned recognition from Greenpeace, which in 2010 put Fujitsu at 13th place on its "Guide to Greener Electronics" ranking and in 2012 ranked it third among 21 leading IT companies for "leadership in the fight to stop climate change." *Newsweek* ranked it 17th on its "Green Ranking Global 100" for 2012. Fujitsu ranked 22nd on the Interbrand list of "Japan's Best Global Brands" for 2012.

BRAND OUTLOOK

- A number of factors, most notably global economic instability, thwarted Fujitsu's ambitious plans for large-scale expansion outside Japan in 2012.
- Fujitsu had a goal of increasing its cloud computing business to account for 30 percent of revenues by 2015.
- According to vice chairman Satoru Hayashi, Fujitsu's ability to meet future goals depended to a large extent on its ability to rebrand itself.
- In February 2013 Fujitsu announced projected losses of US$1 billion by the end of the fiscal year.

In November 2011 Fujitsu "made some bold announcements around a new service-oriented focus and its desire to grow outside of Japan," according to Penny Jones of Datacenter Dynamics. Unfortunately, thanks to a number of factors, most notably global economic instability, the year that followed did not turn out as planned. Company leadership had hoped to see 40 percent of sales coming from outside Japan, but "Much of this hinges on [Fujitsu's] ability to rebrand," Jones wrote, "creating a new company image focused on services and solutions, as opposed to hardware."

The company had a goal of increasing its cloud computing business to account for 30 percent of revenues by 2015; but in order to do this, Jones wrote, "the company needs to get its rebranding message heard." Fujitsu vice chairman Satoru Hayashi expressed the situation thus: "In Japan we have been in the IT business for more than 77 years, so most companies know us. Outside of Japan we are starting to build our brand, but we have a different history in each region." Hayashi also observed that "Creating a brand is time-consuming—you can [do it fast] if you have deep pockets, but we are primarily in the B2B business, so we have to receive the conviction from the customers."

As the 2013 fiscal year began to take shape, Fujitsu looked ahead to greater challenges, in February 2013 announcing that it expected a loss of US$1 billion. In response, it would cut approximately 3 percent of its workforce, or about 5,000 jobs, according to Hiroyuki Kachi in the *Wall Street Journal*. The company also planned a number of adjustments that Kachi described collectively as a "decision to back away from manufacturing semiconductors," referring to this as "another indication of Japan's lost competitiveness in an industry it once dominated." Kachi went on to say that these moves indicated "a general pullback from manufacturing for Fujitsu, which has shifted its focus in recent years from producing electronics hardware to providing technology services to corporate customers."

FURTHER READING

Fujitsu Limited. *Fujitsu Limited Annual Report 2012: Moving ahead, Realizing Our Vision.* Tokyo: Fujitsu, 2012.

"Fujitsu Limited." *International Directory of Company Histories.* Ed. Jay P. Pederson. Vol. 103. Detroit, MI: St. James Press, 2009.

"Fujitsu Logo History." Fujitsu. Accessed February 10, 2013. http://www.fujitsu.com/global/about/plus/logo/transition/

"Fujitsu Statement on Brand Identity." Accessed February 10, 2013. http://www.brand-workroom.com/en/news/do/detail/id/2.html

Jones, Penny. "Fujitsu—Expanding the Cloud Brand." Datacenter Dynamics, January 16, 2013. Accessed February 10, 2013. http://www.datacenterdynamics.com/focus/archive/2013/01/fujitsu-%E2%80%93-expanding-cloud-brand.

Kachi, Hiroyuki. "Fujitsu Warns Loss Will Total $1 Billion." *Wall Street Journal*, February 7, 2013.

O'Reilly, Lara. "Q&A: Fujitsu Product Marketing Director James Maynard." *Marketing Week*, March 1, 2012.

Rousselet, Vincent. "The Pursuit of Happiness." *Market Leader*, October 3, 2012.

Wakabayashi, Daisuke. "Japan's Dimwitted Smartphones: Electronics Makers Sony and Sharp Play Catch-Up to Apple's iPhone; 'The Golden Age of TV Is Over.'" *Wall Street Journal*, August 16, 2012.

GAP

AT A GLANCE

Brand Synopsis: Gap is an international clothing brand known for iconic, casual designs that are appropriate for adults of any age group.
Parent Company: Gap, Inc.
2 Folsom St.
San Francisco, California 94105
United States
http://www.gapinc.com
Sector: Consumer Discretionary
Industry Group: Retailing
Performance: *Market share*—2.59 percent worldwide (2011); 2.39 percent in the United States (2012). *Sales*—US$14.5 billion worldwide (2011); US$5.7 billion in the United States (2012).
Principal Competitors: Abercrombie & Fitch; American Eagle Outfitters; J. Crew; H&M

BRAND ORIGINS

- Started in 1969, The Gap was originally a retailer for the increasingly popular Levi Strauss blue jeans.
- The company began offering clothing under its own label in 1973 and made it the primary merchandise by the early 1980s.
- The Gap purchased Banana Republic in 1983.
- GapKids and babyGap have been continually successful for the company since opening in 1986.
- Old Navy was created in 1994 as a low-cost retailer in order to expand the company's consumer base.

Doris and Donald Fisher opened the first Gap store in San Francisco in 1969 as a jeans retailer. As blue jeans, traditionally made by Levi Strauss for laborers and outdoorsmen, became popular among American youths, the demand dramatically increased. Donald Fisher noted this trend when he was unable to find a pair of jeans in his size in a department store. Together with his wife, Doris, Fisher opened the first store near San Francisco State University, selling both Levi Strauss blue jeans and LP records. Due to a lack of marketing, the business venture nearly failed, but after the placement of ads in local newspapers, the store's stock quickly sold out. The Fishers named their store "The Gap" in order to lure younger consumers by playing off the contemporary issue of the Generation Gap.

The business grew quickly, despite the Fishers' lack of retail experience, due to its selection of jeans and low prices. They quickly added new outlets in San Francisco and soon business grew more due to the name recognition and previous success. The stores continued to sell primarily Levis and were painted with bright colors and played rock music to appeal to younger consumers. New stores were located within shopping malls. Within two years after opening, The Gap's sales were an estimated US$2.5 million annually and the Fishers converted it into a public corporation. The company's continued success was due to maintaining low prices, keeping stores well-stocked, offering a wide range of colors and sizes for t-shirts, jeans, and jackets, and, most importantly, selling items as long as they were popular. By 1973 The Gap began marketing several labels of its own, in addition to continuing to offer Levis.

In The Gap's initial public offering in 1976 the shares initially sold well, but there was a large loss, which led to class-action suits from the stock purchasers against The Gap. In spite of the company's trouble, it continued to add between 50 and 80 stores annually, pushing its sales up to US$307 million by 1980. As Levis began to be sold at other retailers and the stores' original clientele outgrew the company's initial image, The Gap went through a massive rebranding in the early 1980s. Under the supervision of a new president, Mickey Drexler, The Gap began marketing only its own line of clothing. The design of the clothes was also altered to appeal to consumers who wanted to look young without appearing rebellious. The layout of the stores was also altered, and they were given more neutral colors. Although the rebranding was costly, it was evident within a year that it had been successful. Soon The Gap began acquiring other retail chains, the most noteworthy being Banana Republic, which had been started in 1979 by Melvyn and Patricia Ziegler. The store originally sold safari and travel apparel and maintained a catalogue business.

In a new venture, The Gap launched GapKids in 1986, featuring comfortable clothes for the children of parents who shopped at The Gap. The venture was an immediate success, just as Banana Republic had been. GapKids continued to do well, even leading into babyGap in 1990, but Banana Republic became a corporate liability and struggled with a rebrand. However, by the mid-1990s Banana Republic had introduced new products and began to turn around as an upscale retailer, featuring more cutting-edge designs. During the same period, the company aimed to attract consumers who were less willing to spend money on clothes and launched the Old Navy division. Old Navy offered clothing that was priced 20 percent to 30 percent less than The Gap's clothing.

In the early 2000s The Gap again saw a dip in sales as new competitors appeared in the market, but after another rebranding in 2002, the company was able to bounce back. As of 2013, Gap Inc. had five major divisions: The Gap, Banana Republic, Old Navy, Piperlime, and Athleta, within over 3,000 stores in over 90 countries.

BRAND ELEMENTS

- The Gap name has been used for the company since it was founded in 1969.
- The Gap has used the blue box logo since the early 1980s, and the one attempt to change it in 2010 was met with controversy.
- The Gap's five major divisions each employ an individual logo that is unique and distinct from The Gap's logo.

The Gap's name is a large part of the corporate brand. The company was named for the Generation Gap, a term that came into play during the 1960s as a reference to the differences between youths and their parents. The Fishers decided on the name to appeal to their target audience: youths who wanted to become part of the trend of blue jeans as the new casual wear. The company has continued the use of the original name, despite a massive rebranding in the 1980s. The company has acquired and developed new divisions, each taking on an original name, with the exception of GapKids and babyGap. The other divisions, Banana Republic, Old Navy, Piperlime, and Athleta, do not contain name similarities to their parent company, but instead maintain their own name and branding.

The company's logo has maintained simplicity since it was first introduced as part of the company's rebranding in the early 1980s. The previous logo was black and white, with a playful design. The second and current logo is simple: a navy blue box with the name "Gap" in white capital letters. Gap released another new logo in 2010, but this one was considered to be a fiasco and was discarded within a week of the launch. Ever since, Gap has stayed with the well-known 1980s logo. The five major divisions of Gap all have different logo schemes. Old Navy's logo contains a dark blue oval with white capital lettering as well, not dissimilar to Gap's. Banana Republic's logo consists of the initials "BR" with the *B* inverted. The design is simple and elegant. Piperlime and Athleta's logos are of similar shape and size, with both containing simple circles. Piperlime's logo is a bright green lime-slice, while Athleta's is a white pinwheel within a purple circle. The Gap name has been trademarked by the company since 1972. Although the company had originally trademarked the name for retail clothing store services, the trademark was expanded later in the 1970s to encompass all the company's businesses.

BRAND IDENTITY

- Gap's identity is intertwined with bridging the consumer age gap between young and old by offering timeless, casual styles.
- The company uses television campaigns to emphasize the brand's broad demographic through timeless music and dance.
- The brand's simple and sleek slogan demonstrates the casual nature of the brand.

Gap's brand identity is intertwined with its original slogan, "For every generation, there's a gap," referring to the widely recognized generation gap between young adults and their parents. The slogan was so immersed in the brand image of the company that it adopted the name of "The Gap." While the original identity of the brand exploited the generation gap by appealing to young people, the contemporary brand instead bridges that gap by appealling to adults of all ages. In order to successfully relate to its customers, the brand offers classically designed casual apparel to fit the lifestyle of all of its customers.

Gap has been successful at marketing its brand image through a series of campaigns on television, showing 20-somethings dancing or singing while wearing Gap brand apparel. The goal of the marketing is to demonstrate that the brand is appropriate for fun or casual wear just about anywhere. The advertisements are commonly accompanied by familiar songs from a wide array of genres and generations to appeal to a broad demographic of customers. Gap's clothing is simple, casual, and suitable to be marketed across multiple age groups.

Even Gap's logo adheres to the company's brand. By maintaining a clean, basic design, Gap's logo demonstrates the simple style of its merchandise. The logo also is appealing to the wide demographic of the brand's customer base by not utilizing playful or extreme styles or colors, instead emphasizing the casualness of the brand. Gap's logo has been utilized since the early 1980s and has become synonymous with the brand's identity of classic, casual merchandise.

BRAND STRATEGY

- Gap stores have similar layout and design and offer the same merchandise.
- The company has aimed to expand across the Asian market.
- The Gap has been recognized by Ethisphere for attempting to assure safe and healthy working conditions in its overseas operations.

Gap's original store concept was to offer merchandise that was popular among young consumers, but not available to a mass market in a wide array of sizes. After the company's original consumer base began to age and Levi Strauss began selling its jeans through other stores, Gap was forced to rebrand in order to survive. Stores began to sell clothing that was casual and fun without being rebellious, as Gap began appealing to the older consumers who had previously shopped at the stores. Additionally, Gap began marketing only clothing that had a Gap label, which gave further exposure to the brand. The company also revamped the atmosphere of the stores, replacing the bright lights and colors with neutral colors, softer lighting, and quieter music. The company maintains the same ambience and design for each store, which has brought both criticism and praise. The company has maintained the same image for Gap stores since the rebranding in the early 1980s and has expanded the concept internationally. Since 2010 Gap has targeted the Asian market as a point of expansion, offering the same clothing and store designs. The venture has proven effective, and by 2013 approximately 12 percent of the company's sales were international.

The company has also continued its growth through acquiring or creating other companies. Banana Republic, previously a safari-themed clothing store, was purchased in 1983 and rebranded in the 1990s to depict luxurious and cutting-edge fashion. Gap started the Old Navy division in 1994 to appeal to lower-income families as well as low-income young adults. Originally the Old Navy stores were going to be called Gap Warehouse, but the decision was made to present the stores as something independent of Gap, with the hope of drawing an untapped market. The company further expanded through the creation of Piperlime, an online retailer, in 2006. In contrast to Gap stores, Piperlime offers merchandise in non-Gap brands. Gap launched another division, Athleta, in 2009. This division is designed to offer athletic apparel for women.

The company has had many critics due to the fabrication of its clothing in Asia, with reports of unsafe working conditions, creating unwanted publicity. Having used overseas labor since the 1970s, Gap is not new to negative attention regarding sweatshops. In order to avoid surges in negative media coverage, Gap has responded to every accusation with action, going so far as to pull merchandise produced under inhuman conditions. It has also begun monitoring its overseas factories more closely to ensure safe workplace practices. As a result of these actions, Gap has been recognized as one of the world's most ethical companies by Ethisphere since 2007, allowing consumers to have more confidence in the ethics of the brand.

BRAND EQUITY

- The company has stated that it will close 189 store locations in the United States by the end of 2013 as the company focuses its attention on Asia.
- Brand Finance ranked Gap as the 426th-most-valuable brand in 2011, but the brand did not make the 2012 rankings.
- Interbrand ranked Gap as the 100th-most-valuable brand in 2012, with competitor H&M ranked 23rd.

Gap had reported that it aimed to close 189 locations, or 21 percent of all Gap stores, within the United States by the end of 2013. The goal is to expand further into the Asian market as competition increases in the U.S. market. Gap's chief executive officer, Glenn Murphy, stated that the company is aiming to reach the top-10 apparel markets worldwide.

Brand Finance's *Global 500 2011* ranked Gap 426th overall and estimated its brand value at US$2.589 billion. However, the brand was not listed in the 2012 ranking. Prime competitor H&M was ranked 89th in the 2011 list, with a value of US$9.875 billion, but dropped on the 2012 ranking to 105th, with a value of US$8.596 billion. Gap made Interbrand's *Best Global Brands 2012*, ranked as the 100th-most-valuable brand at US$3.731 billion. H&M came in at 23rd on the same list.

BRAND AWARENESS

- Gap has a guaranteed customer base, with Americans spending 8.3 percent of their clothing money on jeans.
- More than 60 percent of Gap sales come from denim jeans.
- The Gap has 100 percent brand awareness in the United States, with 50 percent reporting they wore the brand at least occasionally.

Of the company's multiple brand extensions, the Gap brand is the best-known among consumers. Having become established as a prime marketer of denim jeans, the company has a guaranteed customer base, with Americans spending 8.3 percent of their clothing money on jeans. The brand is known by its casual, timeless designs. It is the standard for simple apparel. Due to the company's history of making and selling jeans and t-shirts, the brand is still a go-to for consumers looking for jeans. In 2012 Gap, Inc., reported that over 60 percent of the brand's sales came from denims. The consumer staple is so important to the brand's image that the company even lays out the store to make shopping for jeans more appealing to consumers and places the jeans close to the fitting rooms.

Among clothing specialty retailers, Gap has the largest scale and strongest brand awareness, though it also has the lowest operating margin and the highest debt ratio. According to market research, the Gap has 100 percent brand awareness in the United States and over 70 percent of U.S. apparel consumers have reported being in a Gap or Old Navy store within the previous six months. Fifty percent of all apparel consumers have reported owning and wearing Gap or Old Navy merchandise.

BRAND OUTLOOK

- Gap launched the new brand Athleta in 2009 to help the company gain market share.
- The company is closing 189 U.S. retail locations as it expands into the Asian market.
- The company looked to ramp up its flagging sales and market share in North America by increasing appeal for the Gap, Old Navy, and Banana Republic brands.

Although Gap sales have been continually sliding since 2000 due to an increase in competition and an uneven economy, the company has launched new initiatives to gain market share. The brand Athleta, launched in 2009, has plans to reach 50 stores in 2013 under the marketing campaign "Power to the She." The brand features athletic apparel for women, but is still directed at Gap brand's primary market of ages 25 to 35.

The company also has announced that it will have closed 189 U.S. retail locations between 2011 and 2013 as it expands its efforts to China. As the Chinese economy becomes more of a player within the global marketplace, competitors, such as J. Crew, are responding by opening locations in that booming country. China's economy is quickly outpacing the U.S. economy, growing 8.9 percent within the last three months of 2011, compared to only 2.8 percent for the same period in the United States. J. Crew opened its first Chinese location in Hong Kong in 2012, with plans to expand to Beijing soon after. That same year H&M, Gap's Swedish competitor, opened its 100th store location in China. In order to keep pace with competitors, the Gap brand is expanding beyond the single store location it opened in China in 2010, aiming to have 35 store locations by the end of 2013. Gap is also expanding its online presence, in an effort to regain the European market. Apart from improving international and online sales, the company is also looking to ramp up its flagging sales and market share in North America by increasing brand appeal for the Gap, Old Navy, and Banana Republic brands.

FURTHER READING

D'Innocenzio, Anne. "Gap Closing about Fifth of U.S. Stores, Expanding in China." *USA Today*, October 13, 2011.

Gap Inc. "Gap Inc. Recognized as One of World's Most Ethical Companies for Fourth Year in a Row." March 22, 2010. Accessed February 13, 2013. http://www.gapinc.com/content/gapinc/html/media/pressrelease/2010/med_pr_WME201003222010.html.

"The Gap, Inc." *International Directory of Company Histories*. Ed. Tina Grant. Vol. 55. Detroit, MI: St. James Press, 2003.

"The Gap Pushes Its Way into China, after Closing Shops at Home." *Huffington Post*, February 15, 2012. Accessed February 13, 2013. http://www.huffingtonpost.com/2012/02/15/the-gap-china_n_1278898.html.

Golodryga, Bianna. "The Gap: Inside America's Favorite Stores." *ABCNews*, March 31, 2010. Accessed February 13, 2013. http://abcnews.go.com/GMA/YourMoney/gap-good-morning-america-inside-americas-favorite-stores/story?id=10240516.

Hiratani, Kozo, Tokuya Ikeguchi, Banche Serngadichaivit, and Pornprom Vongpivat. "Analysis of The Gap, Inc." Valanium Associates, December 3, 2001. Accessed February 13, 2013. http://web.mit.edu/wysockip/www/535/MIT2001/Gap3.pdf.

H&M Group. "H&M Hennes & Mauritz AB Full-Year Report." Accessed February 2, 2013. http://feed.ne.cision.com/wpyfs/00/00/00/00/00/13/7F/61/wkr0005.pdf.

Santoli, Michael. "Can The Gap Come Back?" *Barron's*, December 26, 2011.

"2012 Ranking of the Top 100 Brands." Interbrand. Accessed February 2, 2013. http://www.interbrand.com/en/best-global-brands/2012/Best-Global-Brands-2012-Brand-View.aspx.

Wellington, Elizabeth. "Nothing Blue about Jeans Sales: They're Hot, in Color." Philadelphia Inquirer, March 21, 2012.

GAZPROM

AT A GLANCE

Brand Synopsis: Gazprom, with a focus on efficiency, reliability, and safety, hopes to establish itself as a leader among global energy companies.
Parent Company: OAO Gazprom
16 Nametkina St., V-420
Moscow, 117997
Russian Federation
http://www.gazprom.com
Sector: Energy
Industry Group: Energy
Performance: *Market Share*—domestic gas output, 78%; global gas output, 15%, global liquid natural gas output, 5% (2011). *Sales*—RR $4.74 trillion (US$150.36 billion) (2011).
Principal Competitors: Royal Dutch Shell; BP; Exxon Mobile Corp.; Chevron; PetroChina; Petronas; SINOPEC; Total

BRAND ORIGINS

- Gazprom is a descendent of Russia's state-run gas ministry; it was privatized in 1993 as a Russian joint-stock company.
- After the fall of communism, the tight cash flow throughout the former U.S.S.R. made the first decade of Gazprom's operations difficult.
- Gazprom, with the cooperation of other international oil companies, has spent the past decade developing its rich natural gas fields.
- Scandal and managerial distrust have been a long-time reputational concern for Gazprom.

Gazprom is the descendent of the state-run Soviet Gas Ministry. While the company is now private, its history and connection with the government are strong. In the late 1940s and early 1950s, the Soviet government began exploiting the country's vast natural gas resources, building a system of pipelines and facilities that stretched across the U.S.S.R. After striking huge amounts of natural gas in Siberia, Russia began to export gas to countries like Germany and Finland in the 1970s. This was the beginning of a global business. In the 1980s Russia extended a pipeline to the border of Germany. During these years, however, Gazprom was never a financial success.

While the entity Gazprom was set up by the Soviet government just before its demise in 1989, the company as it is known today became privatized soon after the breakup of the U.S.S.R. In 1993 the Russian joint stock company (RAO) Gazprom was officially formed, with the government retaining a 40 percent share and close political connections to the company. The first few years were rough for the newly formed entity as most of Russia and the surrounding countries were in debt and cash flow was tight. Without payments coming in, and amidst the economic crash in Russia, the company struggled. It could not afford to make advances in exploration or fix deteriorating infrastructures without a new strategy. In the second half of the decade, the company began forming partnerships with other international companies, such as Royal Dutch Shell, Fortum of Finland, and Eli of Italy, to build pipelines, develop new gas fields, and, ultimately, regain control of its finances. Additionally, the company restructured as an open joint stock company, renamed OAO Gazprom, and began to see some progress. These projects, as well as contracts to supply gas to Finland, Turkey, and other foreign countries, helped bring Gazprom a more promising future.

At the turn of the century, Gazprom, while financially more stable, was marked by scandals, political abuse, and the misuse of assets by upper management. Although the company restructured its upper management in 2000, political strife and scandal still troubled the company. However, the international cooperation that the company built throughout the late 1990s and early 2000s led to gas capacities and increasing infrastructures that could not be ignored by foreign investors. Despite the scandals surrounding the Gazprom name, by 2003 the company achieved record revenues and net profits and saw its share prices skyrocket. During recent years, Gazprom sold off non-core assets and focused on building its natural gas production and transmission infrastructure. While political scandal and connections with the Russian government, which now owns 50.2 percent of shares, are still a troublesome aspect of the company's reputation, its command of the world's gas output remains fiercely competitive.

BRAND ELEMENTS

- Gazprom's logo, exhibiting a flame and blue color, identifies its large market share in the gas industry.
- Gasprom's large Russian market share stems from its monopoly in the domestic gas industry.
- Gazprom's strength is demonstrated by the 2009 example of a local government in Siberia placing a giant Gazprom logo atop a mountain peak.

Gazprom's logo, a capital G with a flame above it and the word Gazprom printed next to it, identifies the company by bringing to mind its major business: gas supply and transmission. While Gazprom also deals in oil, other hydrocarbons, and electricity, the blue color of the logo symbolizes its large market share in the gas industry, as natural gas is often referred to as "blue fuel." Gazprom's hold over the market is in large part due to its connections to the Russian Federation. Although the firm is privatized, the Federation continues to hold more than 50 percent of the company's shares. Gazprom's monopoly in Russia has contributed to the company's ability to continue its widespread exploitation of the region's gas reserves. In fact, in 2009, a region in Siberia where Gazprom has mined large amounts of natural gas planned an expedition to the top of an 11,200-foot (3,410-meter) mountain peak to erect a giant Gazprom logo on top, according to *America's Intelligence Wire*. This logo, according to the article, is for Western consumers, more associated with acrimonious disputes, and symbolizes Russia's blunt-edged energy clout; but for many Russians, the logo is emblematic of Russia's resurgence in the global economy.

BRAND IDENTITY

- Gazprom's mission is to build a brand that can ensure a reliable, efficient, and balanced energy supply for its customers.
- Focusing on consumers' future energy needs by analyzing market trends is one way Gazprom plans to fulfill its mission.
- Providing energy in an environmentally responsible manner is an integral part of Gazprom's brand.

According to its 2011 annual report, Gazprom's main goal is to identify its brand as one that is reliable, efficient, and safe. Gazprom delivers on this promise by the way in which they supply customers with natural gas, other energy resources, and their derivatives. The company aims to be consumer-oriented, planning exploration and production around the long-term needs of its clients. According to the annual report, international agencies predict that "gas consumption will grow to a 25% share in the global energy balance. By 2030 the global demand for gas is expected to grow by 50% as compared with the 2010 level. And the gas consumption is expected to grow in all target markets of Gazprom." While they will continue to explore other energy resources in response to customers' needs, Gazprom's main focus will continue to be gas, as Gazprom's top-priority Russian market was expected to see increased demand. Being able to fulfill this demand is central to Gazprom's mission and its identity as a reliable brand.

Moreover, the brand aims to deliver these energy resources to its consumers in an environmentally responsible manner. According to its website, Gazprom recognizes that its business activities affect millions of people, and the company is careful to recognize that safety is just as important as efficiency. Gazprom was one of the first Russian companies to adopt an environmental policy in 1995. This policy adheres to both Russian and international standards and tries to strike a balance between building global business and maintaining harmony with the environment for current and future generations. To achieve this, the company invests millions every year in protecting the water, ecosystems, and atmosphere affected by Gazprom's operations. Additionally, the company strives to use new technology to conserve energy in its operations and to develop alternative fuels, like compressed natural gas for natural gas vehicles. Its goal is to prevent unnecessary environmental harm.

BRAND STRATEGY

- Gazprom's main brand strategy is to become the strongest company in the world's energy sector.
- Gazprom will implement its strategy by ensuring its energy supply, diversifying its products, and expanding to new markets.
- Reaching new markets also helps Gazprom bring a better quality of life to people in Russia and around the world.

Gazprom strives to be the strongest company in the world's energy sector. According to its 2011 annual report, "this strategy is the only appropriate one in the current economic environment as only robust, vertically-integrated global companies are able to win the competition in the global energy market." Gazprom's ability to be the best is, in part, based upon three key goals: ensuring its supply, diversifying its products, and entering new markets. To ensure its supply, Gazprom continues to invest in exploration and production, and in 2011 geological exploration led to record-high increases in accessible gas reserves.

While the company has always produced pipeline gas, it now produces liquefied natural gas (LNG) and alternative fuels like compressed natural gas, thus diversifying its offerings. In fact in 2011 Gazprom sold 2.3 million tons of LNG to the Americas and the Asia-Pacific region.

These products are, as seen in the LNG example above, taking Gazprom to new international markets, which is its third goal, and contributing to a bigger share of the gas market overall. Some new markets occur within Gazprom's domestic sector as well. Trying to build a larger customer base, while at the same time improving the quality of life for many Russians, is important to Gazprom. Bringing gas to the rural areas of eastern Russia, while at the same time creating sustainable markets for the future of Gazprom's business, is one way the company achieves both objectives.

To help with the transportation of its products, the company has taken on many new projects like the Nord Stream and the South Stream that will connect the Russian and the European transportation systems, as well as the building of new infrastructures that will allow the company to deliver gas to more customers in eastern Russia.

BRAND EQUITY

- Gazprom's financial success has grown significantly, earning them the top spot in the most-profitable category of *Fortune* magazine's 2012 Global 500 report.
- Gazprom owns the world's largest natural gas reserves, which has contributed to the company's rising brand value.
- Brand Finance's Global 500 report placed Gazprom at number 150 in 2012, with a brand value of US$6.4 billion.

While Gazprom's early financial earnings were not always promising, the past five years have been markedly more successful. Gazprom's continued strategy of joining other major international oil and gas companies to expand its exploration and production has helped the company attract more investors and has, consequently, led to increased profits. In fact, in 2011 Gazprom topped *Fortune* magazine's Global 500 list in the most-profitable category with net profits of US$44.5 billion, more than competitor Exxon Mobile's US$41 billion. High profits, in addition to owning the world's largest natural gas reserves, have also resulted in an increase in brand value in the 2010s. While measuring the brand value of a company so closely tied to the government can be difficult, Gazprom has found a place in *Brandirectory's* Global 500 list for several years. In 2012 Gazprom landed at number 150 on the list with a brand value of US$6.4 billion.

BRAND AWARENESS

- Gazprom's monopoly in the Russian gas industry and its close connections with the Russian Federation bring it top-of-mind brand awareness.
- While the relationship that Gazprom shares with Russia's government is mutually beneficial, its international reputation has suffered because of it.
- Gazprom's long history of scandal includes the European Commission's 2012 accusations that the company violated antitrust laws.

Gazprom's domination of the gas industry and its monopoly in Russia due to its connection to the Russian Federation ensure its top-of-mind brand awareness both in Russia and in international communities. The government's connection to the company is something the country appears to support. For example, according to *America's Intelligence Wire* in 2009, leaders in the remote Russian region of Altai wanted to name one of the region's tallest mountains in honor of Gazprom.

Gazprom's tight-knit relationship with the Russian Federation, however, can be a double-edged sword because other countries are wary of the company's political clout. Gazprom has been the subject of political scandal for years. Most recently, according to the *New York Times,* in September 2012 the European Commission accused Gazprom of violating E.U. antitrust laws by restricting European buyers' rights to sell gas to one another and by unfairly raising prices by linking gas prices to oil prices. While Gazprom denied the allegations and said it has the status of a "strategic organization in Russia," its connections with the government have always made investors wary. In fact, part of Gazprom's business strategy since the turn of the century has been to attract more investors by focusing on transparency and restructuring its management. Judging from the increases in both sales and brand value, these strategies seem to be helping to keep reputational issues at bay.

BRAND OUTLOOK

- The future of Gazprom depends on its ability to increase oil production and to maintain its top position in the gas industry.
- Gazprom's close ties to the Russian Federation will ensure the future of the brand.
- The Druzhba-Sochi gas pipeline for the 2014 Olympics exemplifies the mutually beneficial projects engaged in by Russia's government and Gazprom.

Gazprom feels that the success of its brand depends upon the firm's ability to establish itself as a leader in the energy business. According to the 2011 annual report, the company hopes to achieve this position in the future by increasing oil production, increasing operating efficiency of power generating entities, and, most importantly, retaining its leading position in the global gas industry. According to Gazprom's analysis, maintaining this position means retaining its share in the domestic market (currently more than 70 percent), meeting one-third of the European demand for gas, obtaining 10 to 15 percent of the Northeast Asian market, and producing up to 15 percent of the global LNG volume in the distant future.

This task, while seemingly difficult, will come with some assistance for Gazprom. Given its close ties to the Russian Federation, the future of Gazprom's brand appears to be quite secure. In fact, according to the *Moscow Times,* critics suggest that the line between government finances and the budgets of companies like Gazprom is becoming more blurred. Consequently, Gazprom's monopoly will continue to get boosts from the government as long as it is beneficial to the Federation. One example of this can be seen in Gazprom's involvement with the building of Russia's 2014 Winter Olympics infrastructure. According to the company's website, its interests are in bringing sustained gas supplies to the sports venues and, subsequently, to homes on the Black Sea coast. However, critics paint a muddier picture. According to the *Moscow Times,* "Only part of the company's spending on the Olympics is going to finance projects linked to its core business. According to the estimate by BNP Paribas, 31.5 billion rubles will be spent on the Druzhba-Sochi gas pipeline, with the rest going to build ski resorts and other facilities not related to the gas industry." The benefit to the government is quite obvious; but there is also a benefit beyond the additional market the new pipeline will bring to Gazprom: Russia's gas producers bear a lower tax burden than oil producers. The government, according to the *Moscow Times,* considers this a fair trade-off. These types of politically motivated arrangements will continue to support Gazprom in meeting the goals it envisions for the future of its brand, but they may also make international cooperation difficult.

FURTHER READING

Brand Finance. "Global 500 2012." *Brandirectory. Accessed* November 7, 2012. http://brandirectory.com/profile/Gazprom.

Filatova, Irina. "Report: State Role in Economy to Grow." *Moscow Times,* Nov. 7, 2012, 5008. Accessed November 12, 2012. http://www.themoscowtimes.com/business/article/report-state-role-in-economy-to-grow/471069.html.

Gazprom. "Annual Report 2011." Accessed November 9, 2012. http://www.gazprom.com/f/posts/51/402390/annual-report-2011-eng.pdf.

"Gazprom is king of the hill in Russian region." *America's Intelligence Wire* June 23, 2009. *General OneFile.* Accessed November 10, 2012. http://go.galegroup.com/ps/i.do?id=GALE%7CA202292963&v=2.1&u=itsbtrial&it=r&p=GPS&sw=w.

"Global 500 2012." *Fortune/CNN Money,* 2012. Accessed November 5, 2012. http://money.cnn.com/magazines/fortune/global500/.

Kanter, James. "Gazprom Objects to European Antitrust Inquiry." *New York Times* September 5, 2012. Accessed November 11, 2012. http://www.nytimes.com/2012/09/06/business/global/gazprom-objects-to-european-antitrust-inquiry.html?_r=0.

Lorenz, Sarah Ruth, and Christina M. Stansell. "OAO Gazprom." *International Directory of Company Histories.* Ed. Tina Grant. Vol. 107. Detroit: St. James Press, 2010. *Gale Virtual Reference Library.* Accessed November 7, 2012. http://go.galegroup.com/ps/i.do?id=GALE%7CCX2283800076&v=2.1&u=itsbtrial&it=r&p=GVR.

"QA: interview with B.D. Yurlov: vice chairman of the Management Committee, OAO Gazprom." *Institutional Investor International Edition* Nov. 2003: 55+. *General OneFile.* Accessed November 11, 2012. http://go.galegroup.com/ps/i.do?id=GALE%7CA133412618&v=2.1&u=itsbtrial&it=r&p=GPS&sw=w.

GDF SUEZ

AT A GLANCE

Brand Synopsis: A leading brand that strives to help the world progress responsibly, GDF SUEZ is the world's largest utility company.
Parent Company: GDF SUEZ Group
22 rue du Docteur Lancereaux
Paris 75392 Cedex 08
France
http://www.gdfsuez.com
Sector: Utilities
Industry Group: Utilities
Performance: *Market share*—87 percent of the residential market and 63 percent of the business market in France (2012); 2.9 percent worldwide (2008). *Sales*—EUR90.7 billion (US$126.1 billion) (2011).
Principal Competitors: E.On AG; RWE AG; National Grid Transco; Centrica; OAO Gazprom

BRAND ORIGINS

- In 1946 Gaz de France (GDF) was formed as a state-run energy company with a monopoly on gas distribution in France.
- In the mid-20th century GDF imported gas to keep up with French demand, thus beginning its global effort to explore new technologies and energy sources.
- In 1991 and 2000 the French government passed laws to allow the company to profit from its gas sales and to denationalize utilities.
- After much negotiation and compromise, GDF and Suez merged to form the 10th-largest electricity provider in the world.

GDF SUEZ's current operations are the result of a 2007 merger of the government-run energy firm Gaz de France (GDF) with utility giant Suez Group. Initially, GDF was formed as a result of the nationalization of utilities by the French government in 1946. By the 1960s, the company held a virtual monopoly on France's gas services. However, GDF did not profit greatly from the endeavor because France's socialist economy kept prices low. As France's need for more gas exceeded its own supply, GDF began importing gas from Algeria and Belgium, thus initiating its global business. Throughout the 1960s, GDF continued to invest in new technologies, pioneering gas liquefaction plants and underground storage. Additionally, in response to changing oil prices and increasing demand during the 1970s, France developed its nuclear power program and required its energy companies to limit supply ratios from each source to less than 5 percent. To accomplish this, GDF signed additional contracts to import natural gas from Russia, Algeria, and Belgium for the next 20 years.

As the company experienced increased competition from France's electric company, EDF, and nuclear power, it began to develop new ways to prosper. By joining other firms in exporting gas and marketing its product as a plentiful, flexible, powerful, and clean source of energy, the company increased its market share. However, governmental control still diminished the company's ability to profit or compete effectively. In 1991 a law was passed allowing GDF to profit from its distribution efforts and to adjust its prices based on the changing market. Additionally, the denationalization of France's utility companies in 2000 allowed GDF to compete in the international market for the first time in 50 years. During the 10 years between these two milestones, GDF began to acquire new companies, build new production plants, and take interest in new utilities. GDF became a major utility provider to Italy, Germany, and Mexico and was able to start new endeavors domestically as restrictions were slowly lifted in France. Continuing to invest in its expansion, GDF bought several companies with exploration and production capabilities during this time to diversify its offerings.

As a way for the French government to profit and for the company to pursue further privatization, GDF offered an IPO in 2005. While results were positive, the company continued to seek new ways to expand its products. In 2006 GDF began to discuss a merger with energy giant Suez. Many citizens, members of parliament, and trade unions heavily opposed the merger, fearing that such a powerful union would impede healthy competition. Although it took much negotiation, a diversification of Suez holdings, and a reduction in the French government's share of GDF to 33 percent, the merger finally took place in 2007. With the consolidation, GDF SUEZ became the 10-largest electricity provider in the world and the fifth-leading supplier in Europe.

BRAND ELEMENTS

- GDF SUEZ's logo is composed of blended elements from both Suez's and Gaz de France's pre-merger logos.
- GDF SUEZ's logo and tagline emphasize the powerful union of Suez and Gaz de France and its commitment to provide the world with energy.
- The "By People For People" slogan and campaign highlight GDF SUEZ's position as a socially responsible company and reinforces the company's core values.

The GDF SUEZ corporate brand is identified by its logo and tagline "By People For People". The logo, which displays the company name in a capitalized font underlined by a curved, teal green line, is a blend of elements from GDF SUEZ's parent companies' logos before the 2007 merger. The logo's font came from the Suez logo and the teal green color and shape came from the Gaz de France logo. The blended elements symbolize the corporate merger and GDF SUEZ's willingness to move forward as a unified company seeking to bring energy to France and its global markets. Similarly, GDF SUEZ's tagline "By People For People" reasserts the company's desire to work hard to bring diverse communities the best product available. According to their website, GDF SUEZ's 2011 advertising campaign was designed to propel this philosophy, highlighting GDF SUEZ's commitment as a socially responsible company and underscoring its four values: drive, commitment, daring, and cohesion.

BRAND IDENTITY

- GDF SUEZ's brand identity is built upon principles of civic service and responsibility.
- The "By People For People" marketing campaign has promoted GDF SUEZ's service and the positive impact it has on the world.
- GDF SUEZ has invested EUR11 billion (US$14.28 billion) in ensuring that they can meet energy demand responsibly and efficiently.
- GDF SUEZ believes that corporate responsibility goes beyond the environment and has built a brand known for corporate citizenship and partnership.

GDF SUEZ prides itself on being a socially responsible brand that delivers quality products both safely and efficiently. Following the 2007 merger between Gaz de France (GDF) and Suez, the new company, with its background as a state-run gas company, sought to further identify itself as a civic company whose main goal was to serve the people. According to its website, GDF SUEZ's "aim is to develop a close and high-quality relationship with its customers. … The group's desire is to build a brand that is unique and unequalled, serving humanity." In this way, GDF SUEZ's 2011 advertising campaign, "By People For People" demonstrated how its actions, both in the utilities sector and in the social sector, helped serve the world. The campaign's television spots have focused on the demonstration of how everyday events are linked together by energy provided by GDF SUEZ.

For GDF SUEZ, the brand's focus on "positive" energy is realized through its efforts to be responsible. Another large part of the company's brand identity centers on providing sustainable development in the utility and social sectors. To do this, the company has invested EUR11 billion (US$14.28 billion) in exploration and production over the course of 2011–13, according to the company's website. GDF SUEZ hopes to meet energy demand by using current resources wisely while incorporating new alternative supplies like wind power, solar power, hydroelectricity, and biomass. Additionally, the company continues to investigate ways to combat the negative effects of climate change. Lastly, GDF SUEZ takes corporate responsibility beyond the environment—the company seeks to build a brand identified as one that is responsible for the human race. By helping children in need, providing the world's disadvantaged with water and power, and mentoring young entrepreneurs, GDF SUEZ strives to keep the world moving in a positive direction.

BRAND STRATEGY

- GDF SUEZ began restructuring its brand architecture in 2011 in order to realign its individual brands with the corporate brand GDF SUEZ.
- Using its advertising slogan "By People For People," the company has aligned its four values to its corporate brand.
- GDF SUEZ hopes that the reorganization of its individual brands will lead to top-of-mind awareness for its corporate brand.

Since Gaz de France (GDF) merged with Suez in 2007, the company has seen large growth both domestically and globally. In 2012 the company's major brand strategy was to rebuild the architecture of the company's brand names, both in France and across global markets, under the single corporate brand of GDF SUEZ. According to the company website, where the company operated the Gaz de France DolceVita brand for individual customers in France in the past, GDF SUEZ now operates the GDF SUEZ DolceVita brand. Similarly, what used to be Gaz de France Provalys and Energies Communes (the line extension supplying utilities for businesses, professionals, and public authorities in France) now operates under the name GDF SUEZ Energies France. The company not only rebranded in France but abroad as well, realigning individual brands under the corporate brand of GDF SUEZ.

The purpose of this rebranding strategy is twofold. First, the corporate brand and its tagline "By People For People" assert the group's four values: drive, commitment, daring, and cohesion. By aligning all brands under the corporate umbrella, each subsidiary identifies itself with these values and each market comes to expect the same quality service represented by these values. Second, by tying the company's individual brands to the corporate brand, GDF SUEZ hopes to increase the brand's spontaneous awareness threshold, achieving the top-of-mind awareness that comes with being the world's number-one utilities provider.

BRAND EQUITY

- While revenues continued to rise, GDF SUEZ's net profits fell in 2011 to EUR2.7 billion (US$3.51 billion) due to unusual weather.
- In 2012 GDF SUEZ's brand value increased 29 percent to US$16.6 billion, making it the world's most valuable brand in the utilities sector.
- Successful advertising and a consolidation of all brands under the corporate brand have helped GDF SUEZ achieve high brand valuation.

While GDF SUEZ made revenues of EUR90.7 billion (US$126.1 billion) in 2011, the company did experience a decline in net profit of 24 percent, to EUR2.7 billion (US$3.51 billion) in the same year. According to *Brandirectory*, these numbers seem to be a result of unusual weather conditions that affected European demand for natural gas in 2011, in addition to unusually strong results from the previous year, which skewed the percentage change for 2011. The company's increasing investments in global sources of renewable energy in countries such as Brazil and Germany and the investments made in GDF SUEZ by China Investment Corp. were expected to help the company bring in strong revenues in 2012.

GDF SUEZ's brand value increased 29 percent to US$16.6 billion in 2012. Brand Finance's Global 500 report listed GDF SUEZ in first place globally in the utilities sector and in the 42nd spot overall. The 2011 advertising campaign, "By People For People," has helped market the corporate brand as one responsible for bringing safe energy to diverse communities all over the world. The company's focus on aligning its consumer brands under the direction of the corporate brand, with its focus on environmental issues and consumer trust, has paid off in terms of the value of the brand.

BRAND AWARENESS

- Gaz de France's history as a state-run gas company has provided GDF SUEZ with top-of-mind recall in its domestic market.
- In order to increase its global brand awareness, GDF SUEZ realigned its individual brands with the corporate brand beginning in 2007.
- The GDF SUEZ corporate brand is marketed as an umbrella brand offering reputable energy to diverse communities throughout the world.

GDF SUEZ is highly rated in the utilities sector, both domestically and globally. Because the company Gaz de France was essentially the only natural gas provider in France in the 50 years leading up to 2000, GDF SUEZ's domestic brand awareness is top-of-mind. Nevertheless, as the company expanded after its 2007 merger with SUEZ Group, the new firm GDF SUEZ spent much of the next two years realigning its multinational brands with its corporate brand. According to the company website, GDF SUEZ feels that to improve its global brand awareness threshold, all GDF SUEZ brands must carry the corporate name. In this manner, the company seeks to unite all of its markets under one roof, from individuals planning a new home to governments fueling cities. Under the new architecture, each branch carries the same corporate identity and offers the same reputable service but is able to do so in a customizable way. For example, according to

NYSE Magazine, GDF SUEZ's diversity allows it to offer almost 4,000 megawatts of power production capacity in the desert of Saudi Arabia while at the same time coupling those electrical plants with desalination plants because the country needs water as well as energy. By linking the diversity and the quality of its product to its corporate brand, GDF SUEZ is able to ensure that, even though they may receive a variety of services, customers recognize that the brand is the same.

BRAND OUTLOOK

- GDF SUEZ has been ranked the second-most admired company for its innovation, a trait essential in the search for sustainable energy.
- A number of investments in exploration and production totaling billions of dollars demonstrate GDF SUEZ's commitment to finding sustainable energy from renewable resources.
- Admirable efforts in corporate citizenship and environmental awareness should help ensure the longevity and reputability of the GDF SUEZ brand.

In 2012, which the United Nations declared "The International Year of Sustainable Energy for All," the outlook for GDF SUEZ is bright. Ranked by *Fortune* magazine as the second-most admired company for its innovative practices, GDF SUEZ has made the development of sustainable energy the heart of its vision and its branding. A number of recent investments put GDF SUEZ at the forefront of this global endeavor. In 2011, for example, the company acquired 70 percent of the United Kingdom's International Power PLC, improving its production of independent power. The company's investment in the massive Jirau hydroelectric dam on the Madeira River system in Brazil and its newly formed relationship with China Investment Corporation, which invested in GDF SUEZ's exploration and production arm, also demonstrate the company's focus on exploiting renewable energy avenues. These types of investments will "boost installed capacity by 33 gigawatts to 150 gigawatts by 2016 and its renewables capacity to 50 percent over 2009 levels by 2015, largely owing to increases in hydro and wind power," according to *NYSE Magazine*.

Moreover, GDF SUEZ's continued focus on safety, corporate citizenship, and environmental awareness has boosted both its business and brand. *Fortune* has also rated the company as the most admired firm for its efforts in social responsibility, a trait that is important to stakeholders and the general public alike. With successful business growth, in addition to a commitment to helping the world progress socially, GDF SUEZ is positioned to remain a top utilities supplier, both in France and throughout the world.

FURTHER READING

Brand Finance. "Global 500 2012." *Brandirectory*. Accessed October 20, 2012. http://brandirectory.com/profile/gdf-suez.

GDF SUEZ. *2011 Annual Report*. GDF SUEZ Group, 2011. Accessed October 22, 2012. http://www.gdfsuez.com/wp-content/uploads/2012/08/POD_GDFSUEZ_RA11_EN_REV01_bd.pdf.

McLaughlin, John. "Power to transform." *NYSE Magazine*. Accessed October 24, 2012. http://www.nysemagazine.com/gdfsuez.

Protat, Florence, M. L. Cohen, and Stephen Meyer. "GDF SUEZ." *International Directory of Company Histories*. Ed. Derek Jacques and Paula Kepos. Vol. 109. Detroit, MI: St. James Press, 2010.

"Top Environmental and Facilities Service Firms Worldwide, 2008." *Market Share Reporter*. Ed. Robert S. Lazich and Virgil L. Burton III. Detroit, MI: Gale, 2011.

"World's Most Admired Companies" *Fortune*, March 19, 2012. Accessed October 24, 2012. http://money.cnn.com/magazines/fortune/most-admired/2012/snapshots/10337.html.

"World's Most Valuable Gas, Water, and Multiutilities Companies, 2011." *Business Rankings Annual*. Ed. Deborah J. Draper. Detroit, MI: Gale, 2012.

GE

AT A GLANCE

Brand Synopsis: Through its electrical work, consumer products, and other diverse efforts, General Electric is a brand that, in its words, brings "good things to life" and exemplifies "imagination at work."
Parent Company: General Electric
3135 Easton Turnpike
Fairfield, Connecticut 06828
United States
http://www.ge.com/
Sector: Consumer Discretionary; Utilities; Health Care; Financials
Industry Group: Consumer Durables & Apparel; Utilities; Health Care Equipment & Services; Diversified Financials; Media
Performance: *Sales*—US$147.3 billion (2011).
Principal Competitors: Agilent Technologies, Inc.; Bank of America Corp.; CBS Corp.

BRAND ORIGINS

- Inventor Thomas Edison's Edison General Electric Company merged with Elihu Thomson and Edwin Houston's Thomson-Houston Electric Company to form the General Electric Company in 1892.
- The early General Electric provided electrified railway systems, motors for factories, power transmission lines, generators, transmission equipment, electrical locomotives, lightbulbs, and a few consumer appliances.
- GE helped found the Radio Corporation of America (RCA), left the company in 1930, and later bought RCA in 1986, which meant that GE acquired RCA's National Broadcasting Company.
- GE provides electrical products, equipment, and services for homes and businesses, operates water processes, offers products and services for the rail industry, manufactures health care equipment, provides software for different fields, and is involved in the oil and gas industries.

General Electric traces its origins back to famous American inventor Thomas Edison. By 1889 Edison had consolidated a number of his electricity-related companies to form the Edison General Electric Company. This company merged with Elihu Thomson and Edwin Houston's Thomson-Houston Electric Company to form the General Electric Company in 1892.

Also known as GE, the fledgling company was involved in all aspects of the electrical industry, providing electrified railway systems, motors for factories, power-transmission lines, generators, transmission equipment, electrical locomotives, and lightbulbs. GE owned utility companies until government antitrust action in 1924 forced it to divest itself of those interests. It also produced consumer appliances, beginning with electric toasters in 1905. This division has proved extremely successful for GE, bringing it profits and recognition.

Other early GE consumer products included radio parts. To develop radio technology, GE helped create the Radio Corporation of America (RCA) with AT&T and Westinghouse. GE left RCA in 1930 but later bought the company in 1986. Because RCA was affiliated with the

U.S. television network the National Broadcasting Company (NBC), this purchase immersed GE in the world of media. GE would eventually own 49 percent of NBC, later known as NBCUniversal, to Comcast Corporation's 51 percent share. NBCUniversal encompasses NBC and cable stations, film studios such as Universal Studios, digital media, theme parks, other entertainment companies, and international interests. One of NBC's television programs referenced and satirized GE's diverse operations. The NBC show *30 Rock* featured a character, Jack Donaghy, who was GE's vice president of East Coast television and microwave programming.

In addition to its consumer products and media interests, GE is also involved in a wide variety of industries in several countries. GE still provides electrical products, equipment, and services for homes and businesses. It operates water processes, offers products and services for the rail industry, manufactures health care equipment, provides many kinds of software, and is involved in the oil and gas industries. GE Aviation makes aircraft engines, while GE Capital provides financing in more than 50 countries. GE also has extensive research and development operations all around the world. These wide-ranging operations have built GE into the huge and diverse company that it is today.

BRAND ELEMENTS

- Used since 1900, the GE logo is an ornate circle with an interconnected cursive *G* and cursive *E*.
- The ornate circular GE logo appears on a large number of GE products and is a long-standing visual representation of the company.
- GE appliance brands include GE Café professional appliances, the GE Profile designer line, the luxury GE Monogram line, and the GE and Hotpoint brands.

An ornate circle with an interconnected cursive *G* and cursive *E* form the symbol for GE. The company has used this symbol since 1900. Prior to that, it used a more ornate intertwined cursive *G* and *E* without a circle around them. The circular GE logo has thus been a consistent visual representation of the GE brand for over a century.

The circular GE logo appears on a large number of GE products. The ornate GE circle symbol notably appears on its lightbulbs. This logo appearance identifies the lightbulbs as GE products, reinforces GE's long association with lighting and electrical equipment, and reminds consumers of the company's long history.

GE offers multiple brands for other consumer products. Its appliance brands include GE Café appliances for restaurants and professional kitchens, the GE Profile line highlighting design, the GE Monogram line of high-end appliances, and appliances sold under the GE and Hotpoint brands. The GE logo appears on all of these brands except for Hotpoint. The logo also appears prominently on other GE product lines, such as turboprop engines, medical equipment, and even the fronts of locomotives.

BRAND IDENTITY

- "We bring good things to life" was GE's long-time slogan from the 1970s until the early 2000s.
- Introduced in the early 2000s, "Imagination at work" is another GE slogan.
- By featuring GE's employees, factories, and products, *The GE Show* illustrated GE's productivity, skill, and size.

"We bring good things to life" was GE's longtime slogan. It was introduced in the 1970s. The slogan appeared in a number of television commercials and print advertisements until the early 2000s. "Imagination at work," another GE slogan, was launched in the early 2000s. This slogan promotes the creativity and productivity of the company and seems to be a paraphrase of the earlier slogan. "Imagination at work" could be construed as the process of "bring[ing] good things to life," reinforcing the earlier slogan's implication that the company was able to imagine wonderful things and then create them. The second slogan also refers to the company's ability to create ideas and produce tangible results. Both slogans stress GE's technical creativity and manufacturing productivity.

GE vividly illustrated its technical and manufacturing prowess in *The GE Show*, an online program posted on its website. One episode of *The GE Show*, "Factory Flyovers," showed GE employees working on different products in different factories and included related facts about the factories and products. This episode depicted GE employees and the GE brand as productive. It showed what GE did. The show also helped to clarify GE's work. The clarification was useful because GE operates in so many diverse fields and sometimes works on projects that can be difficult to explain.

In addition, the GE factories and products pictured in *The GE Show* episode were often massively large, like the factories GE needed for building its locomotives. The episode dramatically portrayed GE as a huge company with the technical and manufacturing capacity to make huge things. *The GE Show* therefore connected the GE brand to skill and size in addition to productivity.

BRAND STRATEGY

- The slogans "We bring good things to life" and "Imagination at work" and Internet pictures of the electrical industry and other industries all illustrate GE's commitment to creation, industry, and productivity.

- GE's websites emphasize its solutions in several areas, including the environment, emphasizing its activity and interest in environmental efforts.
- In 2008 GE began a Chinese campaign to personify GE and build brand awareness, especially during Beijing's 2008 Summer Olympics.

"We bring good things to life" and "Imagination at work" are more than just advertising slogans. They are part of GE's brand strategy. Its websites emphasize the company's work and efforts. Web pages emphasizing individual GE products and services include detailed information. They also include multiple pictures. These pictures feature industrial and technical items, often in the electrical industry. The pictures illustrate current GE products and services. They refer to the company's past accomplishments in electricity. They also refer to industry, manufacturing, and producing in general, and they cast GE as a company that creates and produces.

According to GE, this productivity and activity translate into practical applications and solutions. These solutions appear prominently on its websites. Like its products-and-services websites, the solutions pages include extensive lists of solutions and links to pages with more details. These pages often include photographs of heavy industry and electrical equipment, again echoing the products and services pages. These lists and photographs also feature information and images about ecological and environmental topics. Some of the environmental topics include advanced water recycling, gas engines—biogas solutions, gas engines—CO_2 fertilization for greenhouses, gas turbines—flexible fuel solutions, smart grid, sustainability, waste to value, and other solutions that incorporate environmentally friendly processes. These solutions reinforce GE's reputation for productivity and promote its environmental efforts.

It has also built brand awareness in other countries. In 2008 it began a campaign in China that introduced the characters Li Wang and Bang Li, who personified GE. The brand used designer Li Wang to demonstrate GE's practical applications for everyday life and scientist Bang Li to represent the research, science, and technology behind GE's innovations. GE launched this campaign and other activities to capitalize on the hosting of the Summer Olympics in Beijing, China, and the subsequent attention that accompanies these events. This campaign once again portrays GE as an innovator and manufacturer.

BRAND EQUITY

- A report published by market research publisher IBISWorld stated that GE held 17.1 percent of the U.S. household appliance market in 2011.
- Interbrand named GE the world's sixth-best brand in 2012, with a brand value of US$43.682 billion.
- *Forbes* magazine called GE the world's eighth-most powerful brand, with a US$33.7 billion brand value in 2012.
- The European Brand Institute in Vienna, Austria, determined GE to be the world's 15th-best brand in 2012, with a brand value of EUR32.168 billion.

According to some marketing professionals, the diversity of GE has helped it build brand equity. "The equity of the GE (General Electric) brand is so strong and trusted by consumers it has allowed GE to successfully compete in areas that have nothing to do with light bulbs or electronics—like financial services and construction equipment leasing," wrote social marketer TwinEngine. This equity, according to TwinEngine, means that customers recognize GE's established name and are more willing to purchase from GE than from less established brands.

GE's brand awareness has translated into sales and market share. A report published by market research publisher IBISWorld stated that GE held 17.1 percent of the market for household appliances in the United States in 2011. It had the third-highest market share in this report, trailing only the Whirlpool Corporation and AB Electrolux.

In addition to this success in the American market, the brand is also a successful global brand. In its "Best Global Brands 2012," Interbrand named GE the world's sixth-best brand, with a brand value of US$43.682 billion in 2012. In a similar list, *Forbes* magazine called GE the world's eighth-most powerful brand, with a US$33.7 billion brand value in 2012.

Other regions of the other world have also ranked the GE brand highly. The European Brand Institute, based in Vienna, Austria, determined GE to be the 15th-best brand in the world in 2012 and valued the brand to be worth EUR32.168 billion. It appeared 14th on this same list in 2011 with a similar brand value of EUR31.972 billion, demonstrating the brand's consistency as well as its value.

BRAND AWARENESS

- GE introduced its "We bring good things to life" slogan in the 1970s to update American consumers' perceptions about its brand and provide a slogan that could cover its diverse products and services.
- Published in 2012, a poll conducted by Lifestory Research found that prospective American home buyers had top-of-mind awareness for only three appliance brands: GE, Kenmore, and Whirlpool.
- A poll by Lifestory Research published in 2012 found that consumers ranked GE tops among appliance manufacturers.

GE introduced its "We bring good things to life" slogan in the 1970s to change perceptions about its brand. Brand research and developer and advertising/marketing/public relations agency Baer Performance Marketing noted that American consumers of the 1970s believed GE to be dependable and believed that GE consumers were "unsophisticated, low-income, and older." Due to these perceptions, GE wanted to update its brand, "gain product loyalty," and construct a "single message that could be applied to all of GE's various product lines and services," in the words of Baer Performance Marketing. This message was the slogan "We bring good things to life."

Decades later, consumers had strong opinions about the GE brand. Thousands of prospective U.S. home buyers participated in a poll published in 2012. This poll, conducted by market research firm Lifestory Research, demonstrated the fame of the GE brand. Poll respondents had top-of-mind awareness for only three appliance brands: GE, Kenmore, and Whirlpool. This means that GE, Kenmore, and Whirlpool were the only brands customers could readily recall, without prompting, when asked to name appliance brands.

This survey also questioned consumers about "brand awareness, perceptions of quality, importance of product-class brand and overall impression of the brand manufacturer," according to Lifestory Research. In a list of more than 20 appliance brands, GE finished first in this line of questioning. The allure of GE and other brands is so strong that these survey respondents admitted that they would be more likely to buy houses equipped with GE and other prestigious appliance brands than with other appliance brands.

BRAND OUTLOOK

- The Energy Independence and Security Act of 2007 phased out the use of incandescent lightbulbs by 2014, prompting GE and other manufacturers to sell fluorescent, LED, and halogen lightbulbs.
- In 2011 GE Global Research announced that it had developed data storage discs that can store up to 500 gigabytes of data.
- Petroleum Company of Trinidad & Tobago Limited hired GE Power & Water in 2012 to design and operate water treatment processes for an oil refinery.

The early 2000s have brought a shift in the nature of GE's consumer products. Incandescent lightbulbs, formerly a major product for GE, are no longer a product for GE or any manufacturer. The Energy Independence and Security Act of 2007 called for the adoption of fluorescent, LED (light-emitting diode), and halogen lightbulbs to replace incandescent lightbulbs. The act called for bulbs of different wattages to be phased out in different stages by 2014. As a consequence, GE now sells fluorescent and LED lightbulbs instead of incandescent ones.

The company has developed other products as well. In 2011 GE Global Research announced that it had developed data storage discs that can store up to 500GB (500 gigabytes) of information. This is equivalent to the storage capacity of 20 Blu-ray discs or 100 standard DVDs. The company was also developing micro-holographic discs that would store 1 terabyte (1,000 gigabytes).

GE's efforts in other fields demonstrate its commitment to different countries and its varied operations. Petroleum Company of Trinidad & Tobago Limited (Petrotrin) hired GE Power & Water in 2012 to design and operate filtration and reverse osmosis water processes for a temporary water treatment plant. This water treatment plant would provide steam and cooling water for oil refinery processes in Pointe-a-Pierre, Trinidad and Tobago, in the West Indies. This venture is another sign of GE's diverse business and its global commitments.

FURTHER READING

"Flashback Friday—'We Bring Good Things to Life.'" *Baer Performance Marketing*, January 27, 2012. Accessed December 7, 2012. http://www.baerpm.com/blog/?p=284.

GE. *2011 Annual Report*. Accessed December 7, 2012. http://www.ge.com/ar2011/index.html#!section=ge-2011-annual-report.

"GE Breaks out a New Brand Awareness Campaign for China." GE Information Technology Leadership Program, December 9, 2008. Accessed December 9, 2012. http://www.itlpblog.com/blog/2008/12/9/ge-breaks-out-a-new-brand-awareness-campaign-for-china.html.

"General Electric Company." *International Directory of Company Histories*. Ed. Jay P. Pederson. Vol. 137. Detroit, MI: St. James Press, 2012.

Jing, Wang. "The New Idea Factories." *CKGSB Knowledge*, September 26, 2012. Accessed December 9, 2012. http://knowledge.ckgsb.edu.cn/2012/09/26/china/the-new-idea-factories/.

"Market Share of Household Appliance Companies in the U.S. in 2011." Statista, 2012. Accessed December 9, 2012. http://www.statista.com/statistics/219721/market-share-of-wireless-telecommunication-carriers-in-the-us/.

"New-Home Shoppers Say Appliance Brands Can Influence Purchase Decision; GE Favored Due to Name Recognition." Lifestory Research, September 19, 2012. Accessed December 7, 2012. http://www.lifestoryresearch.com/2012/09/lifestory-research-reports-new-home-shoppers-say-appliance-brands-can-influence-purchase-decision-ge-favored-due-to-name-recognition/.

Solomon, Kate. "GE Unveils 500GB Disc That Can Hold 20 Blu-Rays." *TechRadar*, July 25, 2011. Accessed December 9, 2012. http://www.techradar.com/us/news/computing-components/storage/ge-unveils-500gb-disc-that-can-hold-20-blu-rays-982843.

Trabish, Herman K. "GE Still Dominates US Wind Manufacturing but New Faces Are Emerging." Greentech Media, May 1, 2012. Accessed January 29, 2013. http://www.greentechmedia.com/articles/read/ge-still-dominates-u.s.-wind-making-but-new-faces-are-emerging.

TwinEngine. "Brand Equity ... What's It Made of?" The H Agency, September 19, 2008. Accessed December 7, 2012. http://thehagency.com/2008/09/brand-equity-what%E2%80%99s-it-made-of/.

GENERALI GROUP

AT A GLANCE

Brand Synopsis: Since 1831 the name Generali has been linked to insurance; today, the Generali Group is the largest insurer in Italy and one of the largest in the world, with insurance and other financial interests in Italy and several other countries.
Parent Company: Assicurazioni Generali S.p.A.
P.za Duca degli Abruzzi 2
34132 Trieste
Italy
http://www.generali.com/Generali-Group/home/
Sector: Financials
Industry Group: Insurance
Performance: *Sales*—US$112.6 billion (2012).
Principal Competitors: Allianz SE; AXA; ING Groep N.V.; Zurich Financial Services; Milano Assicurazioni S.p.A.

BRAND ORIGINS

- Giuseppe Lazzaro Morpurgo and others founded insurance company Assicurazioni Generali Austro-Italiche in Trieste in late 1831.
- War and territorial struggles affected Assicurazioni Generali's physical operations but usually not its financial profits.
- Assicurazioni Generali's first non-Italian subsidiary opened in Vienna, Austria, in 1882.
- In the 1960s Assicurazioni Generali partnered with global companies like Aetna Life & Casualty to provide more underwriting funds.
- In 1998 Assicurazioni Generali founded Generali Global to serve its international clients.

The Generali Group and its parent company Assicurazioni Generali have a long, rich history. The Assicurazioni Generali dates back to 1831, when the site of its central office, Trieste, was part of Austria. Trieste was later part of the Austro-Hungarian Empire and other ruling interests. Today it is part of Italy's autonomous Friuli-Venezia Giulia region.

Luckily, the company's corporate history is less complicated than Trieste's and Italy's political histories. Giuseppe Lazzaro Morpurgo and other entrepreneurs founded the Assicurazioni Generali Austro-Italiche in Trieste in late 1831. This company strove to use its extensive capital to provide all types of insurance. Changes in government and in political and business policies complicated these efforts in the following decades. During this time, regions of Italy fought for control and sought to expel Austria from the region. From the 1830s to the 1860s, Assicurazioni Generali opened and closed a number of offices in regions that would later become part of Italy, which unified in 1871.

As political matters stabilized, Assicurazioni Generali's business improved. The company's first non-Italian subsidiary was the Erste Allgemeine Unfall und Schadensversicherung, opened in Vienna, Austria, in 1882, and Assicurazioni Generali opened other companies throughout Europe, beginning in the 1880s. Generali's overseas business today includes operations in around 40 countries with more than 60,000 employees.

Politics intervened in Italy once again during World War I, as the war interrupted communication among Generali offices and forced the temporary relocation of some offices. In 1916 the Italian government even issued proclamations allowing the company to continue in business. Despite these setbacks and further political change with the rise of fascist Italian dictator Benito Mussolini, the company thrived financially. Financial crises in the 1870s and again in the 1920s and 1930s did not affect the company significantly. After World War I it expanded by founding or investing in international companies.

World War II, however, had a major effect on Generali. Clients in Allied countries canceled or altered their operations with Generali, which they associated with Axis power Italy. As a result, Generali lost much of its business in Central and Eastern Europe. Trieste once again shifted hands, prompting the temporary movement of some company operations. Germany occupied Trieste in 1943, and the former Yugoslavia and Italy controlled portions of the region until its designation as autonomous in the 1960s.

Following the political tumult, the company began rebuilding after the war, acquiring Providencia in Argentina in 1948. It continued international expansion in the Americas, rebuilding its American business and expanding throughout Europe. In the 1960s it began joining other global insurers, like the U.S. company Aetna Life & Casualty, to provide more underwriting funds. In a more negative note, worldwide economic setbacks in the 1970s and the early 1980s affected Generali, and it had to exit a few countries that, as a protective economic measure, nationalized their banks.

After these difficult times, the company founded Genagricola, which began to operate the company's agricultural interests in the 1980s. In that decade and beyond, it expanded its business in Japan and various European countries, especially in areas affiliated with the former Soviet Union. In 1998 it founded Generali Global to serve Generali's international clients. The corporation also has multinational banks, asset management services, and other services, in addition to its insurance interests. These holdings have solidified the company's global operations and reputation.

BRAND ELEMENTS

- A winged lion with a book has long been a logo for the Generali Group and Assicurazioni Generali.
- A historic, one- or two-headed eagle has served as an Assicurazioni Generali symbol.
- Generali's winged lion and eagle symbols are so connected with the company that only wings appear on the cover of its 2011 Annual Report.

Assicurazioni Generali and the Generali Group have used different versions of a winged lion with a book for many years. This symbol is reminiscent of the winged lion and book used to symbolize both Venice and its patron saint, St. Mark. Assicurazioni Generali established its Italian headquarters in Venice in 1832. The Italian head office is now in Mogliano Veneto, Italy. The winged-lion-and-book logo thus has historical and geographic connections. In addition, the logo's use of a powerful animal and a book connotes the company's strength and knowledge.

An eagle (often two-headed) has also appeared as an Assicurazioni Generali symbol since the company's early decades. It issued plaques that featured the two-headed eagle in the 1830s and 1840s. In the 19th century the Hapsburg family, which often used a two-headed eagle or else lions as part of its coat of arms, ruled Assicurazioni Generali's home of Trieste. Trieste was then part of Austria and the Austrian flag still uses an eagle. Once again, Assicurazioni Generali and the Generali Group use symbolism to refer to its geographic origins.

The winged lion and eagle logos are so closely associated with the company that large wings appear across the cover of Assicurazioni Generali's 2011 Annual Report. The image is just white and gray wings, with no lions or eagles, over a red background (echoing the normal red of the company logo). The company also refers to its winged lion logo in "The Years of the Lion," an online report about the history of the company.

BRAND IDENTITY

- The Generali Group's 1984 advertising campaign "Generali: un libro aperto," or "Generali, an open book," referred to its winged lion and book symbols and the company's financial transparency.
- Generali Vietnam Life used the phrase "GVL soars—2013" to recall Generali's eagle logo, describe the brand's success, and portray its employees as goal-oriented and ambitious.
- The online report "The Years of the Lion" indicates that Generali respects its history while working for the present and the future.

Because the Generali Group logo features a winged lion with a book, the company has used this book imagery in its promotions. Launched in 1984, its first mass media advertising campaign was known as "Generali: un libro aperto," or "Generali, an open book." Used in print advertisements, this phrase reminds people of the Generali Group logo while touting its transparency and honesty. These qualities are crucial for a company dealing with insurance and financial matters and can reassure current and potential customers.

"GVL soars—2013" was another Generali-generated phrase that recalled its logo. Generali Vietnam Life (GVL) used this phrase as part of a 2013 campaign that highlighted the agency's workers and their future goals.

By saying that "GVL soars," the phrase recalled Generali's eagle logo, a bird famous for its own soaring. The phrase portrayed Generali employees as goal-oriented with high-soaring ambitions.

By using the word *soars* in 2013, "GVL soars" recalled Generali's eagle logo and the brand's work and success. These recollections helped to create an identity for GVL, which began operating in 2011, while simultaneously reinforcing the Generali brand's ties to its successful past and ambitious future plans.

Generali has also defined itself in relation to its past and future in other ways. In the online report "The Years of the Lion," it claims "Assicurazioni Generali: A Journey That Started in 1831." It asserts that for the brand, "success has never been a point of arrival, but rather a stage along the path of constant growth" and summarizes that "the history of Assicurazioni Generali is but the result of the interaction between two forces: the value of tradition and the drive towards innovation." According to "The Years of the Lion," Generali is a brand that respects its past achievements, focuses on its present tasks, and works toward future growth.

BRAND STRATEGY

- Generali's international business included a joint venture in Hungary in 1989.
- Generali joined with India's Future Group to form Future Generali in 2007.
- In 2009 Generali Thailand placed its winged lion with a book image, the Generali Thailand logo, and other company imagery on mass transit Skytrains in Bangkok.

The Generali Group has grown by entering into joint ventures or merging with companies in several countries. Some of these businesses include Generali's joint venture in Hungary in 1989, making the company the first Western insurer in that country. In 1997 Generali acquired Israeli financier and insurer the Migdal Group and also some German and French companies. (It sold Migdal in 2012.) In Asia, Generali joined with the China National Petroleum Corporation to form the Generali China Life Insurance Company Co., Ltd., in 2002.

Generali joined with India's Future Group to form the Indian company Future Generali in 2007. The Future Group is a diversified business that includes Indian shopping malls, hypermarkets, and other retail establishments. This partnership has opened Mallassurance stores, Future Group branches that sell insurance inside shopping malls in India. This practice demonstrates the Generali Group's eagerness to reach new customers in new venues in addition to new countries.

Another international Generali Group company, Generali Thailand, began a brand awareness campaign in 2009. In this campaign, Generali's winged-lion-with-a-book image and the Generali Thailand logo appeared on BTS Skytrains, part of the mass transit system in Bangkok, Thailand. The trains also feature other Generali images, including a doctored photograph of a lion with wings and information about Generali Thailand in the Thai language. The company estimated that around 440,000 customers viewed these Generali advertisements on the Skytrains.

BRAND EQUITY

- Partially owned by the Generali Group, the Czech Republic's Česká pojišťovna held a 23.5 percent share of the Czech insurance market.
- Hungary's Generali-Providencia Biztosító Rt., holds a 17 percent market share of Hungary's insurance market.
- In Italy the Generali Group posted a 16.4 percent share of the life insurance market and a 19.3 percent share of the non-life insurance market in 2011.
- Credit-rating company A.M. Best named Assicurazioni Generali the world's seventh-largest insurance company and the fourth-largest European company based on 2010 nonbanking assets.
- *Fortune* ranked Assicurazioni Generali 48th in its 2012 "Global 500" list.

With business interests in a number of companies in several countries, the Generali Group competes in a number of markets. The Generali Group holds a 51 percent share of the Czech Republic's Česká pojišťovna (Czech Insurance Company). PPF Holding has the other 49 percent. In 2011 Česká pojišťovna held a 23.5 percent share of the Czech insurance market and led the Czech Republic in the areas of property and casualty insurance, life insurance, and pension funds. Another Generali Group company, Hungary's Generali-Providencia Biztosító Rt., holds a 17 percent share of Hungary's insurance market and is the second-largest insurance company in that country.

Not surprisingly, the Generali Group has captured substantial market share in its home country. In Italy the Generali Group posted a 16.4 percent share of the life insurance market in 2011. It also posted a 19.3 percent share of the non-life insurance market in Italy in 2011. These percentages have made the Generali Group Italy's largest insurance company, with about 10.5 million clients and 50,000 people working on Generali's behalf. This size and strength prompted Reuters correspondents Lisa Jucca and Gianluca Semeraro to call the company a "Trieste-based financial heavyweight."

The Generali Group and India's Future Group created Future Generali in 2007, which quickly built market share. In September 2010 Future Generali accounted for

1.3 percent of the insurance market in India. This share is another illustration of the Generali Group's geographically widespread success.

The Generali Group's brand strategies and market share have made it one of the largest insurance companies in the world. Credit rating company A.M. Best named Assicurazioni Generali the world's seventh-largest insurance company, based on 2010 nonbanking assets. It was the fourth-largest European company on this list.

Assicurazioni Generali is a major insurance company and a very large company overall. In *Fortune* magazine's "Global 500," an annual list of the world's largest corporations in all fields, it ranked Assicurazioni Generali 48th in 2012. It was also the third-largest Italian corporation on that 2012 list, based on revenues. The company ranked first among Italian companies on the 2005, 2006, and 2010 versions of the "Global 500" and in Italy's top three every year from 2005 through 2012.

BRAND AWARENESS

- Generali's 1.6 million banking customers in Italy, Austria, Germany, and Switzerland made 9,698 complaints in 2011.
- Generali stated that increases in insurance customer complaints showed its eagerness "to listen and sort out ... problems and inefficiencies."
- *Newsweek* named the Generali Group the world's 12th greenest company in 2012.

The Generali Group's websites have described its large number of clients in different areas of businesses. These websites also discussed customer complaints against Generali. For example, Generali had 9,698 complaints among 1.6 million banking customers in Italy, Austria, Germany, and Switzerland in 2011.

Generali had also had 43.5 million insurance customers in Italy, Austria, Germany, Switzerland, the Czech Republic, France, Spain, and Israel in 2011. These customers made 150,163 complaints, more than the previous year. Generali explained that "the increase in complaints should not be put down to clients being less satisfied, but rather to companies being more willing to listen and sort out the problems and inefficiencies identified by clients." Generali has thus acknowledged and addressed how its customers have perceived it.

Others have recognized Generali for its environmental record. In 2012 *Newsweek* named the Generali Group to "The World's Greenest Companies," its annual list of the world's most ecologically minded companies. The Generali Group placed 12th on this 2012 list, with a green score of 80.1. It placed 30th on this list in 2011 with a green score of 74.1. *Newsweek* determined the green score by measuring how large companies impact the environment and manage their environment actions as well as studying their disclosures about their environmental practices. *Newsweek* thus determined Generali to be ecologically responsible and mindful of the world around it.

BRAND OUTLOOK

- In 2012 Assicurazioni Generali/the Generali Group experienced declining profits and stock market performances and lost money due to European government bond losses, bad weather, and an Italian earthquake.
- Assicurazioni Generali shareholders fired chief executive officer Giovanni Perissinotto in June 2012.
- New CEO Mario Greco and others conducted a strategic review of Assicurazioni Generali/the Generali Group in 2012.

The year 2012 was a time of transition for Assicurazioni Generali/the Generali Group. In 2012 the company experienced declining profits and weak stock market performances. It sustained considerable financial losses on Greek government bonds during the European fiscal crisis in 2012 and also lost money due to bad weather in Europe and an earthquake in Italy.

Assicurazioni Generali shareholders fired chief executive officer (CEO) Giovanni Perissinotto in June 2012. His replacement, Mario Greco, previously from the insurance business in Switzerland, had worked in other countries, including Germany and the United States, and had earned a graduate degree from a U.S. university. This international training and experience parallels the international nature of Generali's business.

New CEO Greco and others started a strategic review of the company in 2012. This review concerned Assicurazioni Generali's products, its asset portfolio, and competition with other companies. It also addressed its geographic influence, including international participation with other companies. In December 2012 Generali announced that the company would consolidate its Italian insurance and banking companies into a new company, Assicurazioni Generali Italia. It also planned to consolidate its ten Italian companies into three: Generali, Alleanza, and Genertel. And it planned to analyze its interests in other regions as well. Analysts had developed greater financial confidence in the company by late 2012, partly because of Generali's sale of the Israeli company the Migdal Group at that time.

FURTHER READING

A.M. Best Company, Inc. "Top Insurers Ranked by Assets, Net Premiums." *Best Week*, January 2012. Accessed December 15, 2012. www.ambest.com/bestweek/marketreports/BW_WorldsLargest.pdf.

"Assicurazioni Generali S.p.A." *International Directory of Company Histories*. Ed. Jay P. Pederson. Vol. 103. Detroit, MI: St. James Press, 2009.

"Ciao, Giovanni." *Economist*, June 9, 2012.

"Future Generali Targets 2% Market Share by This Fiscal End." *Economic Times*, September 2, 2010.

Generali Asia. *Generali Asia News … Letter*. March 2009. Accessed December 15, 2012. http://www.generaliasia.com/uploads/files/newsletters/2009/Generali-Newletter(Mar09)_2forwebop.pdf.

"Generali Group." *2011 Annual Report*. Accessed December 15, 2012. http://www.generali.com/Generali-Group/Investor-Relations/on-line-report/.

Generali Group. "Business Sectors." October 7, 2012. Accessed February 17, 2013. http://www.generali.com/Generali-Group/Sustainability/clients-and-consumers/business-sectors/.

———. "The Years of the Lion." July 7, 2011. Accessed December 15, 2012. http://www.generali.com/Generali-Group/Media-Relations/corporate-magazines/latest-corporate-publications/sezionePop/7582.html.

"Global 500." *Fortune*, July 23, 2012. Accessed December 17, 2012. http://money.cnn.com/magazines/fortune/global500/2012/countries/Italy.html.

Jucca, Lisa, and Gianluca Semeraro. "Generali to Present New Strategic Review in January." Reuters, November 9, 2012.

Semeraro, Gianluca, and Stephen Jewkes. "UPDATE 3-Generali to Spend 300 Mln Euros on Domestic Restructure." Reuters, December 14, 2012.

"The World's Greenest Companies." *Newsweek*, October 22, 2012.

GENERAL MILLS

AT A GLANCE

Brand Synopsis: As one of the world's leading producers of nutritious, conveniently packaged foods, General Mills is the brand that "nourishes lives."
Parent Company: General Mills, Inc.
Number One General Mills Boulevard
Minneapolis, MN 55426-1347
United States
http://www.generalmills.com
Sector: Consumer Staples
Industry Group: Food, Beverage & Tobacco
Performance: *Market share*—granola bars, 39.3 percent; cake/cupcake/pie mixes, 38.1 percent; ready-to-eat wet soup, 37.3 percent; cereal, 30.55 percent; corn snacks other than tortilla chips, 11.4 percent; canned vegetables, 11 percent; breakfast/cereal/snack bars, 8.8 percent; flour milling, 5.2 percent (2011). *Sales*—US$16.7 billion (2012).
Principal Competitors: Kellogg Company; Post Holdings, Inc.; Ralcorp Holdings, Inc.; Kraft Foods Inc.; ConAgra Foods, Inc; Campbell Soup Company; Groupe Danone; Nestlé S.A; PepsiCo.

BRAND ORIGINS

- The General Mills brand developed from a flour mill founded in 1866 by Cadwallader Washburn in Minneapolis, Minnesota.
- In 1928 the business merged with 27 other mills to form General Mills, Inc., the world's largest flour-milling brand.
- Although the company has made attempts at diversifying widely, the brand's core business is cereals, baking mixes, dinner mixes, and other packaged food.

The General Mills brand traces its beginning back to 1866, when Cadwallader Washburn opened the Minneapolis Milling Company, the first flour mill in Minneapolis, Minnesota. Three years later a primary competitor, the Pillsbury Flour Mills Company (forerunner of the Pillsbury Company), was founded nearby. Washburn devised a technique for milling Midwestern wheat into a higher grade of flour—the best available in the United States. When Pillsbury adopted the same technique, Minneapolis became the country's flour-milling center. By 1928 the firm had 5,800 employees and annual sales of $123 million. In that year the business merged with 27 other mills operating in 16 states to form General Mills, Inc., the largest flour-milling brand in the world.

During the 1930s the General Mills brand began an expansion that eventually included ready-to-eat cereals, baking mixes and other packaged food, canned food, ice cream and assorted frozen desserts, snacks, and restaurant chains. The firm also tried diversifying into a wide variety of unrelated products—86 acquisitions into new industries between 1950 and 1986, including toys, jewelry, clothing, chemicals, and appliances—but by 1995 the company refocused the brand on its core business of packaged foods.

Along the way the corporation acquired well-known businesses such as Morton Foods, Inc. (1964); Gorton's, which sold frozen seafood (1968); the Tom Huston Peanut Co. (1968); the Red Lobster restaurant chain (1970); Small Planet Foods, Inc. (2000); and the Pillsbury Company (2001). At that point General Mills was the third largest U.S. food company, behind Kraft and ConAgra Foods.

The company had begun exporting products in 1877 but focused primarily on the United States throughout the 20th century. During the 1950s General Mills began marketing cereal and baking mixes in Canada and flour in Venezuela, Guatemala, and Mexico. Soon the conglomerate purchased the European companies Smiths Food Group Ltd., Tragasol, and Biscuiterie Nantaise, in addition to snack food companies in Latin America and Japan. Since 1991 the brand has been partnered with several other large corporations to sell products globally.

In the 40 years from 1976 to 2006 the firm's sales increased from US$2.6 billion to US$11.6 billion. By 2012 General Mills was one of the world's largest food companies, operating in more than 100 countries and employing 34,500 people.

BRAND ELEMENTS

- The firm was initially called the Minneapolis Milling Company, then the Washburn Crosby Company, and finally General Mills, Inc.
- Betty Crocker was a fictitious spokeswoman created to help the company teach housewives how to use its products.
- The brand logo is a large capital "G" above the name "General Mills" in capital letters.
- General Mills' cereal lines are known as "Big G cereals."
- General Mills products are sometimes made and packaged differently for sale in markets outside the United States.

When the business was founded in 1866 it was called the Minneapolis Milling Company. In 1877 John Crosby became a partner, and the enterprise was renamed the Washburn Crosby Company. In 1928 the firm merged with a number of other major flour-milling companies to form General Mills, Inc.

The brand's famous, fictional Betty Crocker spokeswoman was created in 1921 as a way for the firm to answer questions from housewives who wanted to learn about baking. The name "Betty" was selected because it sounded friendly. "Crocker" was the surname of a former company executive. In addition to sponsoring nationwide cooking schools, the company aired a long-running radio show called *The Betty Crocker Cooking School of the Air* and operated Betty Crocker Kitchens, where home economists tested more than 50,000 recipes annually. Many of those were compiled into Betty Crocker cookbooks, which sold millions of copies and have been in publication for more than 50 years.

The brand logo is a large capital "G" in a bold cursive font above the name "General Mills" in all capital letters. The company's various cereal lines are collectively known as "Big G cereals," which include Cheerios, Chex, Cocoa Puffs, Kix, Lucky Charms, Total, Trix, and Wheaties.

As the brand has expanded globally, the packaging and contents have sometimes been altered. For example, Cheerios cereal is made of oats and sold in a bright yellow box in the United States. In Europe the product is made of oats, corn, wheat, and rice and packaged in a white box. Because General Mills markets products in partnership with other companies in some countries, the General Mills logo is not always featured on the packaging; Cheerios is sold under the Nestlé brand in the United Kingdom and under the Uncle Toby's brand in Australia. In some international markets where cereal is not a traditional breakfast food, General Mills brands such as Cheerios have been sold as part of a kit that includes a plastic bowl, spoon, and cereal in a pouch. This was intended to help customers learn how to eat cereal.

BRAND IDENTITY

- General Mills is promoted as a quality brand that makes life healthier, easier, and more pleasant.
- The brand's promise is to "nourish lives" by offering wholesome, appealing food that is simple to prepare.
- General Mills calls Wheaties cereal "the Breakfast of Champions" and refers to itself as "the Company of Champions."

Since its inception General Mills has been positioned as a quality brand that helps people lead healthier, easier, and richer lives. The company's first branded product, Gold Medal flour, earned its name by winning medals at the International Millers' Exhibition in 1880, and it remains the top-selling flour in the United States. Products such as Bisquick baking mix, Betty Crocker dessert mixes, and Hamburger Helper dinner mixes were innovations that helped housewives prepare appetizing meals more easily. General Mills cereals and yogurt have been promoted as quick, nutritious meals that provide energy and help people manage their weight. In keeping with the company's stated mission of "nourishing lives," the entire line of Big G cereals was converted to whole grains in 2005 to accommodate consumer demand for wholesome foods.

Wheaties, "the Breakfast of Champions," has long been associated with healthy athletes whose photographs appeared on the cereal box. Building on that image, General Mills refers to itself as "the Company of Champions." The corporation has expressed a resolve to maintain strong core values, to "do the right thing, all the time," to strive for superior performance, and to confirm the trust of consumers worldwide who expect the General Mills brand to deliver safe, high-quality food.

BRAND STRATEGY

- General Mills went from flour milling to creating other food products, then to numerous other industries, and finally back to packaged foods.
- Ready-to-eat cereals are the products most commonly associated with the General Mills brand.
- General Mills markets certain products globally through partnerships with other large food companies.

General Mills began as a flour-milling brand, expanded into other food products, ventured into numerous unrelated industries, and then returned to its core business of packaged food.

During World War II the corporation's factories were restructured to produce dehydrated food, medicinal alcohol, sandbags, and equipment for the navy. After the war customers wanted products that were quicker and easier to use. As sales of flour dropped and demand increased for packaged food such as cake mixes, the General Mills brand widened to include other product lines.

When the original flour mill merged with others to form General Mills in 1928, the company's strongest products were Gold Medal flour, Softasilk cake flour (introduced in 1923), and Wheaties cereal (1924). Other successful brands followed, including Bisquick, the first baking mix (1931); Kix cereal (1937); Cheerios (1941); Betty Crocker cake mixes (1947); Trix cereal (1954); Hamburger Helper dinner mixes (1970); Nature Valley granola bars (1975); Yoplait yogurt (U.S. rights purchased in 1977); and Pop Secret microwave popcorn (1985).

Over the years the General Mills brand was most commonly associated with ready-to-eat cereals, but the firm also tried marketing products such as animal feeds, electronics, appliances, toys and games (Kenner Products, Parker Brothers, Rainbow Crafts), jewelry, clothing (many brands, including Lacoste, Eddie Bauer, Talbots, and FootJoy), and furniture (Pennsylvania House, Kittinger). By the late 1970s General Mills was the largest toy manufacturer in the world. The corporation also operated the Red Lobster, Olive Garden, and China Coast restaurant chains.

By 1995 the conglomerate had sold or spun off these disparate businesses and refocused the General Mills brand on packaged food. In 1997 the company paid US$570 million for the branded ready-to-eat cereal and snack mix businesses of Ralcorp Holdings, Inc., including the Chex brand. This put the General Mills brand in second place in the U.S. ready-to-eat cereal market behind Kellogg, and within two years General Mills rose to first place. In 2000 the firm acquired an organic food company, Small Planet Foods, Inc. The next year General Mills paid US$10.4 billion for the Pillsbury Company, which included well-known brands such as Green Giant vegetables, Progresso soups, Old El Paso Mexican foods, and Totino's and Jeno's frozen pizzas.

In addition to its grocery business General Mills operates a bakery and foodservice unit that sells products to convenience stores; vending machine operators; and educational, hospitality, and health care institutions.

Expanding globally, General Mills owned Snack Ventures Europe from 1992 until 2005 in partnership with the Frito-Lay unit of Pepsico, Inc. General Mills markets ice cream in Japan via a joint partnership with Häagen-Dazs and cereal via Cereal Partners Worldwide, a joint venture with Nestlé S.A. General Mills also handles a few local brands, including Jus-Rol pastries in the United Kingdom, Latina pasta in Australia, and La Salteña pastas and tapas in Argentina.

BRAND EQUITY

- The General Mills brand was valued at US$3.5 billion in October 2012, according to *Forbes* magazine.
- The company market value of General Mills was US$25.32 billion in March 2012, according to *Fortune* magazine.
- In FY2011 General Mills had net sales of US$16.66 billion, the third largest revenues in the consumer food products industry.

Forbes magazine estimated the brand value of General Mills at US$3.5 billion in October 2012. *Fortune* estimated the company's market value at US$25.32 billion in March 2012 and ranked General Mills at number 181 among the top 500 corporations in the United States, down from 166 in the previous year. In the consumer food products industry *Fortune* listed PepsiCo in first place with revenues of US$66.5 billion in 2011, Kraft Foods second with US$54.37 billion, General Mills third, and Kellogg fourth with US$13.2 billion.

On its list of the most valuable U.S. food production companies in 2011, *Business Rankings Annual* placed General Mills third, valued at US$23.3 billion. Kraft Foods was first at US$54.9 billion, Monsanto was second at US$38.8 billion, Archer Daniels Midland was fourth at US$22.9 billion, and Kellogg was fifth at US$19.8 billion. Globally *Business Rankings Annual* placed Nestlé S.A. first, valued at US$199.4 billion. Unilever was second at US$87.3 billion, Kraft was third, General Mills seventh, and Kellogg ninth.

For fiscal year 2011 (which ended on May 27, 2012) General Mills had net sales of US$16.66 billion, up from US$14.88 billion in 2010. Of that, US$2.4 billion was derived from sales of Big G cereals in the United States, which amounted to a 30.55 percent market share, close behind Kellogg's 33.22 percent and well ahead of third-place Post Cereals at 11.12 percent. General Mills dominated some food categories in 2011 (first in granola bars with 39.3 percent of the U.S. market and first in cake/cupcake/pie mixes with a 38.1 percent market share) but had only 5.2 percent of the market for flour milling.

BRAND AWARENESS

- General Mills placed second in a 2011 consumer survey of the top 100 U.S. corporate brands.
- *Forbes* magazine named General Mills the most reputable company in the United States in 2012.
- *Fortune* magazine has repeatedly included General Mills on its annual list of the most admired companies in the world.

In a 2011 consumer survey of the top 100 corporate brands in the United States, General Mills placed second, Kraft Foods was fourth, and Kellogg was seventh. Respondents based their ratings on attributes such as honesty, trustworthiness, innovation, and dedication to making communities better places.

On *Forbes* magazine's list of the most reputable companies in the United States General Mills ranked first in 2012, up from 15th in 2011. *Fortune* magazine recognized General Mills on its list of the most admired companies in the United States from 2006 through 2008 and on its list of the world's most admired companies from 2009 through 2012. Harris Interactive's national corporate reputation survey placed General Mills in fourth place in 2008 and ninth in 2011. In recent years General Mills has increased its brand awareness substantially through online social networking sites. Many of the company's subsidiary brands had their own pages on Facebook, where the Betty Crocker and Pillsbury brands had each accumulated more than two million "likes." Six other brands had half a million. At YouTube more than 55,000 people had viewed videos on the main page for General Mills, while 29,000 had subscribed to BettyCrockerTV and 1,700 had subscribed to the Pillsbury channel. At Twitter General Mills had 9,600 followers.

BRAND OUTLOOK

- Due to global economic recession, General Mills expected a low single-digit growth in net sales.
- General Mills will continue to pursue global expansion for its brand.
- Several recent international acquisitions were expected to increase General Mills' presence around the world.

In light of a worldwide economic recession and inflation the General Mills brand was expected to experience single-digit annual growth in net sales, with slow improvement if the economy begins to recover. The corporation plans to increase marketing efforts in countries where demand is growing rapidly for certain types of food products.

After acquiring a controlling interest in French-based Yoplait in 2012, the company planned to expand the Yoplait brand globally. General Mills also acquired Parampara's spice and sauce mixes, which are made in India and marketed mostly in that country; the corporation intended to export these to the United States, Canada, and Japan. A third venture, the purchase of the Brazilian food company Yoki, had more than doubled General Mills' sales in Latin America.

FURTHER READING

"General Mills Inc." *CNN Money.* Accessed December 18, 2012. http://money.cnn.com/quote/financials/financials.html?symb=GIS.

"General Mills Inc." *Notable Corporate Chronologies.* Detroit: Gale, 2011. *Business Insights: Global.* Accessed December 23, 2012. http://bi.galegroup.com/global/article/GALE%7CI2501150758/677657e5160180874f7d9979047aa4b3?u=itsbtrial.

"General Mills Takes Aim at Drug Channel." *Chain Drug Review,* June 25, 2012. *General OneFile.* Accessed December 22, 2012. http://go.galegroup.com/ps/i.do?id=GALE%7CA294901031&v=2.1&u=itsbtrial&it=r&p=ITOF&sw=w.

"General Mills Weathers Tough Inflation in Third-Quarter 2012, but Benefits from New Brands; Global Growth, an Industrial Info News Alert. *Internet Wire,* March 22, 2012. *Business and Company ASAP.* Accessed December 21, 2012.

Harlin, Kevin. "General Mills Buying Back into Hot Brazilian Market." *Investor's Business Daily,* February 13, 2012. *Business and Company ASAP.* Accessed December 21, 2012.

Lapowsky, Issie. "A General Mills Brand Guru on the Art of Selling Food." *Inc.,* May 1, 2012. Accessed December 22, 2012. http://www.inc.com/magazine/201205/design-makeover-healthy-pantry.html.

Russell, Michelle. "The Verdict from Wall Street: Analysts React to General Mills FY Results." just-food.com, June 28, 2012. Accessed December 22, 2012. http://www.just-food.com/news/analysts-react-to-general-mills-fy-results_id119619.aspx.

Schultz, E. J. "Cereal Marketers Race for Global Bowl Domination; As China, India and Brazil Wake Up to American-Style Breakfasts, Kellogg, PepsiCo Look to Spread Their Grains." *Advertising Age,* August 20, 2012. Accessed December 22, 2012. http://adage.com/article/news/cereal-marketers-race-global-bowl-domination/236738/.

Schultz, E. J. "Kellogg Plans British Invasion, Introduces Crunchy Nut to U.S.; No. 1 Cereal Player Imports $154 Million Brand As It Looks for Innovation in Stale Category—and to Put Distance between It and a Gaining General Mills." *Advertising Age,* November 1, 2010. Accessed December 21, 2012. http://adage.com/article/news/kellogg-introduces-u-k-crunchy-nut-breakfast-cereal-u-s/146812/.

"Winners List; Breakfast Foods — Ready-to-Eat Cereal." *Progressive Grocer,* November 1, 2012. Accessed December 21, 2012. http://www.progressivegrocer.com/inprint/article/id5207/winners-list/.

GENERAL MOTORS

AT A GLANCE

Brand Synopsis: One of the "Big Three" automakers in the United States, General Motors is a century-old brand reinventing itself with a renewed dedication to producing the world's best vehicles in terms of safety, quality, innovation, and customer satisfaction.
Parent Company: General Motors Company
300 Renaissance Center
Detroit, Michigan 48265
United States
http://www.gm.com/
Sector: Consumer Discretionary
Industry Group: Automobiles & Components
Performance: *Market share*—in 2011 GM was the world's largest automaker by vehicle unit sales. *Sales*—US$150 million (2011).
Principal Competitors: Ford; Toyota; Honda

BRAND ORIGINS

- William "Billy" Durant founded General Motors on September 16, 1908.
- GM focused on design and innovation, encouraging every consumer to see his or her car as an expression of style and character.
- Environmental concerns, higher fuel prices, and foreign competition prompted dramatic changes at GM during the 1960s and 1970s.
- In response to the bankruptcy filing and federal bailout in 2009, GM shed its Pontiac, Saturn, Hummer, and Saab brands.
- The GM of 2012 is a smaller, leaner company than its predecessor, particularly in the domestic auto market.

General Motors (GM) was founded by William "Billy" Durant on September 16, 1908. Durant was a manufacturer of horse-drawn vehicles before entering the automobile industry. At its inception, General Motors owned the Buick Motor Company brand, but it would soon acquire more than 20 other brands, including Oldsmobile, Cadillac, Pontiac (formerly Oakland), and Chevrolet in the United States, along with Opel and Vauxhall overseas.

GM focused on innovation and design throughout the brand's early years. Following World War II, during which GM donated 100 percent of its production operations and more than US$12 billion in materials to the war effort, the baby boom brought with it an enthusiasm for vehicle design and product consumption that would dominate the manufacturing of cars for decades. Mechanical innovations, like independent front-wheel suspension and uni-body construction, as well as a series of creative designs, ushered in a succession of consumer cars now considered classics: the Buick Roadmaster, the Chevy BelAir, the Cadillac El Dorado, and the Chevy Corvette.

Environmental concerns, increases in fuel prices, and dramatic market changes resulting from foreign competition led to significant changes for GM during the 1960s and 1970s. Forced to design fuel-efficient and environmentally friendly vehicles, GM started to overhaul its brand. While the company did launch vehicles with engines that could run on unleaded gasoline as early as 1971 and introduced the emissions-reducing catalytic converter in 1974 (a technology still in use throughout the auto industry), changes at GM came slowly and met with some resistance.

As GM's domestic brand dominance dwindled significantly over the last quarter of the 20th century, the company's response was to grow globally. The company continued its efforts to reinvent itself domestically, introducing the Saturn brand in 1985, for example, with its famous tagline "A Different Kind of Car Company" and the promise of "no-haggle pricing," the company's major production expansion abroad helped GM sell more than three million cars internationally by 1995.

While the GM brand benefited domestically from a truck boom in the 1990s that saw millions of Americans purchase sport utility vehicles (SUVs) for their family transportation, ever-increasing competition from Japanese, German, and Korean brands continued to weaken the GM brand across nearly all vehicle types and consumer demographics. Still, GM increased its efforts to grow its brand, especially globally, though with mixed success. Partnerships in Japan and Korea, expansion into Brazil and China, and the acquisition of Saab and Hummer were all part of the brand's global strategy during this time. The creation of Daewoo in 2002 furnished GM with a new organization specializing in the engineering and manufacture of smaller cars and proved an important boost to GM as a global brand.

In the early 21st century, further efforts to bolster the brand included reducing and consolidating brands under the GM umbrella, as well as innovations in flex-fuel vehicles and hybrid and electric vehicles. However, production and legacy costs combined with fierce competition from other brands, a deepening recession in the United States, and a global credit crisis to weaken the brand to the point that GM filed for bankruptcy on June 1, 2009. Having been bailed out by the federal government, GM relaunched on July 10, 2009.

As a result of the bankruptcy filing and federal bailout, GM's plan for corporate restructuring included shedding its Pontiac, Saturn, Hummer, and Saab brands; abandoning more than 2,000 of its 6,000 U.S. dealerships; and, in the process, eliminating 100,000 jobs. Following the drastic changes that accompanied the restructuring, GM had to remake and rebuild its brand identity. The company has done so largely by taking a back seat to its surviving brands of Buick, Cadillac, Chevrolet, and GMC trucks, with much of its current identity tied to its top brand, Chevy.

The GM of 2012 is a smaller, leaner company than its predecessor, particularly in the context of the domestic auto market. Besides its four surviving domestic brands, GM continues to enhance its OnStar brand of vehicle monitoring and owner assistance. The brand also continues to grow rapidly in the expanding global auto market, with more than 70 percent of its sales now occurring outside the United States under the brands Baojun (China), Holden (Australia), Jiefang (China), Opel (Germany), Vauxhall (United Kingdom), and Wuling (China).

BRAND ELEMENTS

- The GM logo features the initials "GM" surrounded in blue.
- Model-specific logos on GM's cars are typically more prominent than GM's own brand marks.
- In August 2009, GM decided to remove its own "Mark of Excellence" logo from cars sold under its various brands.

While not nearly as bold as Chevy's bow-tie, Cadillac's crest, and Buick's triple shield, the GM logo, with the initials "GM" surrounded in blue, is easily recognizable as a representation of the brand. The logo's history is not well documented, though some trace its first appearance back to the 1964 World's Fair.

Since GM has always been more of a parent brand than a brand attached to cars seen on the street, the logos for individual models have often taken center stage in the company's marketing efforts, instead of the "GM" logo itself. These model-specific logos are often coupled with the tiny subscript "General Motors Corporation" or the somewhat more prominent "Mark of Excellence" logo used in GM's ads beginning in the 1960s. Probably in response to its bankruptcy and the subsequent image-rebuilding campaign, GM decided in August of 2009 to remove its "Mark of Excellence" logo from any product under its umbrella, thus encouraging consumers to see the GM brand separately from the brands of the cars under the GM umbrella that they desired to purchase.

BRAND IDENTITY

- GM's brand identity is based on innovation, variety, and excellence.
- The GM brand was built on a philosophy of offering a wide range of vehicles for many types of consumers.
- GM has a customer-driven culture that encourages people to love their cars and feel loyal to the brand.
- The brands under the GM umbrella, including Chevrolet, Cadillac, and Buick, are more prominent than the GM brand itself.

As the largest and most diverse car manufacturer in the United States throughout the 20th century, GM offered a wide range of vehicles suited to many types of consumers. The GM brand was built on the philosophy of "a car for every purse and purpose." To move the automobile beyond being merely a mode of transportation, GM focused in its early years on design and innovation, encouraging every type of consumer to see a car as an expression of style and character.

In the 21st century GM has continued to emphasize a customer-driven culture that encourages people to love their cars and feel loyal to the brand. The company describes its automobiles with words such as "passion" and "pride." The GM brand is intended to "create that special bond that can only happen between a driver and their vehicle." GM promises to make safety, quality, and reliability its top priorities, and to design stylish, fuel-efficient vehicles that feature the latest technology.

GM strives to offer automobiles in a range of prices that people can afford, with a higher residual value than some competing brands. For investors, the company has been attempting to transform GM into a brand with integrity, built on a strong financial foundation that shareholders can trust despite the company's declaration of bankruptcy in 2009.

GM has a strong identity as a corporate brand, although in the public eye it has often taken a back seat to the enduringly popular brands under its umbrella, such as Chevrolet, Cadillac, and Buick. That fact has become part of the marketing strategy for "the new General Motors" since 2009 as the firm has worked to rebuild its brand image. Instead of promoting GM to the public, the company has focused primarily on creating a distinct personality and customer loyalty for each of its subsidiary brands.

BRAND STRATEGY

- "A car for every purse and purpose" paid off during GM's best years, when it controlled more than half of the U.S. car market.
- In 2009 GM claimed only 22 percent of the domestic car market.
- Due to its loss of domestic market share, GM's strategy since the turn of the 21st century has been about brand focus.
- In 2006 GM sold off a controlling share of its financial services division, GMAC, and since 2004 has shed other brands under its umbrella.
- With just the four brands of Buick, Cadillac, Chevrolet, and GMC trucks, GM's domestic brand strategy has focused on building up its top brand, Chevy.

GM's brand strategy has remained fairly constant since Durant founded the brand in 1908. According to a *New York Times* report from 2009, Durant and GM developed the company's brand strategy, "a car for every purse and purpose," as early as 1920 in an attempt to retain buyers from the purchase of their first car to the purchase of their last. This strategy paid off during GM's best years, when the company controlled more than half the American car market. This market share declined in the 2000s, however, to the point where GM held only 22 percent of the domestic car market in 2009, with more than half of its share dominated by a single division, Chevrolet.

Due to its loss of market share, GM has tried since the turn of the 21st century to make its brand more focused. While its extensive brand list was an asset throughout the 20th century, increased competition from more focused brands, particularly those from Japan (most notably Honda and Toyota), forced the parent company to rethink its overall strategy as well as its domestic brand lineup. "The more brands a carmaker has," wrote *New York Times* reporter Micheline Maynard in 2009, "the more it must spread money around to develop vehicles and market them."

During the last decades of the 20th century, when competition in the domestic market became increasingly fierce, a multibrand strategy became less and less viable, leading to an overall decline in the GM brand, as well as the brands in its lineup. In 2004 GM started shedding brands, with Oldsmobile the first to be cut. With the buyout of Oldsmobile dealers costing more than US$1 billion, GM realized that focusing its brand in order to match its competitors would be a long and expensive campaign.

In 2006 GM sold off a controlling share of 51 percent of its financial services division, GMAC. GM has also shed other brands under its umbrella both to achieve greater brand focus and to boost financial stability: Saab was sold to a Swedish automaker in 2009, the Saturn brand was closed down in 2009, and the Pontiac and Hummer lines were retired in 2010.

With just the four domestic brands of Buick, Cadillac, Chevrolet, and GMC trucks, as well as a group of several small yet expanding foreign brands, GM's domestic brand strategy in 2012 focused on building up its top brand, Chevy, which was expected to buoy other GM brands. On the global market, GM has invested heavily in developing its brand in China and in 2012 had three Chinese brands in its lineup.

BRAND EQUITY

- The GM brand seems to have recovered to some extent since it was bailed out with taxpayer dollars in 2009.
- GM was ranked fifth in the *Fortune* 500 list of top U.S. corporations in 2012.
- In 2012 *Fortune* magazine ranked GM in 19th place among the world's top brands, but Brand Finance ranked GM 270th.
- GM's brand value was US$3.9 billion in 2012, almost double its value of US$1.9 billion in 2009.

By 2012 General Motors seemed to be recovering to some extent from the challenges it had faced before and after its federal bailout in 2009, when it had posted the third-highest losses across all brands. *Fortune* magazine ranked GM fifth in 2012 on its well-known *Fortune* 500 list of top U.S. corporations, behind three oil companies and megaretailer Wal-Mart and four spots ahead of Ford, its closest domestic competitor. GM's 2012 ranking was up three spots from 2011 on the same list. GM performed nearly as well globally, ranking 19th on the *Fortune* 500 list of top companies worldwide in 2012.

However, on Brand Finance's "Global 500" list of the top brands in the world, GM placed 270th in 2012, with a brand value of US$3.9 billion. That was an improvement over 2010 and 2011, when GM was not included on the list at all. In 2009 GM had ranked 356th with a brand value of US$1.9 billion.

In comparison, Toyota was in 15th place on the "Global 500" in 2012, with a brand value of US$24.5 billion. Ford was 36th with US$17.6 billion, Honda was 55th with US$15.0 billion, Chevrolet (a division of General Motors) was in 211th place with a brand value of US$4.8 billion, and GMC (another General Motors division) was in 352nd place with US$3.2 billion.

BRAND AWARENESS

- Consumers tend to be much more aware of the company's subsidiary brands instead of the GM brand itself.
- Rivals Ford, Toyota, and Honda have a substantially higher brand awareness than GM.
- Consumer awareness of GM's subsidiary brands helps build a general awareness of the GM brand.

When consumers are asked to name a brand of automobile, they tend to mention a subsidiary instead of GM itself. For example, in a 2012 car brand perception survey conducted by *Consumer Reports,* respondents often named Chevrolet (76 percent), Cadillac (38 percent), GMC (33 percent), and Buick (32 percent). GM itself was not among the brands with a consumer awareness of at least 30 percent. In contrast, respondents frequently mentioned GM's primary rivals Ford (87 percent), Toyota (70 percent), and Honda (57 percent).

Other brands under the GM umbrella contribute to a general awareness of the GM brand, however. In the *Consumer Reports* survey, Chevrolet ranked fourth for overall brand perception, with a score of 92 across seven categories (safety, quality, value, performance, environmentally friendly/green, design/style, and technology/innovation). Cadillac was eighth with a score of 63. Toyota was first with 131, Ford was second with 121, and Honda was third with 94.

BRAND OUTLOOK

- The GM brand is still recovering from its 2009 corporate bankruptcy filing.
- GM experienced an upward trend in sales in 2010 and 2011.
- Developing more fuel-efficient vehicles in order to compete with foreign automakers may be the best move for GM in the 21st century.

"Things seemed to have been messy lately for GM," wrote Dale Buss, a regular contributor to the online brand research site BrandChannel.com. According to Buss, problems with finalizing its marketing strategy and frequent turnover among the brand's executives have prevented GM from returning the company's stock price to the level at which the federal government will be able to sell off its remaining stake in the company without incurring heavy losses.

Such analyses of the GM brand suggest that it was still recovering in 2012 from the company's bankruptcy filing in 2009. It is difficult to predict what the future of the brand holds, given the now richly competitive global auto and truck market. Developing more fuel-efficient cars and trucks in order to compete with foreign automakers may be an area in which the GM brand will regain brand solidity and growth in the coming years. In late 2010 GM began production of its plug-in electric vehicles, the Chevy Volt and the Opel/Vauxhall Ampera, which were named the 2012 North American Car of the Year and European Car of the Year, respectively. In September 2012 sales of GM cars continued the upward trend established in 2010 and 2011. Integrating a wide range of innovations into fuel-efficient, low-emission vehicles, combined with realistic expectations domestically and expanded investments abroad, could be a strategy that will extend the brand's life far into the future.

FURTHER READING

Bartlett, Jeff. "2012 Car Brand Perception Survey: Ford Leads All Brands in Awareness." *Consumer Reports,* January 26, 2012. Accessed February 13, 2013. http://news.consumerreports.org/cars/2012/01/2012-car-brand- perception-survey-ford-leads-all-brands-in-awareness.html.

Brand Finance. "General Motors." *Brandirectory.* Accessed October 10, 2012. http://brandirectory.com/profile/general-motors.

———. "GMC." *Brandirectory.* Accessed October 10, 2012. http://brandirectory.com/profile/gmc.

Buss, Dale. "GM Revived and 'Just Getting Started'." BrandChannel.com, October 2, 2012. Accessed October 11, 2012. http://www.brandchannel.com/home/post/2012/10/02/GM-Brands-100212.aspx.

———. "New GM Marketing Boss: 'GM Is Not a Brand.'" *Edmunds Auto Observer,* August 30, 2010. Accessed February 22, 2013. http://www.edmunds.com/autoobserver-archive/2010/08/new-gm-marketing-boss-gm-is-not-a-brand.html.

General Motors. "Company: History and Heritage." Accessed October 5, 2012. http://www.gm.com/company/historyAndHeritage.html.

Healey, James R. "GM Sells Majority of Financing Unit." *USA Today*, April 7, 2006. Accessed October 8, 2012. http://usatoday30.usatoday.com/money/autos/2006-04-03-gm-deal_x.htm.

Isidore, Chris. "GM Bankruptcy: End of an Era." *CNN Money*, 2 June 2009. Accessed October 9, 2012. http://money.cnn.com/2009/06/01/news/companies/gm_bankruptcy/.

Maynard, Micheline. "A Painful Departure for GM Brands." *New York Times*, February 17, 2009. Accessed October 11, 2012. http://www.nytimes.com/2009/02/18/business/18brands.html?_r=0.

SyncForce. "General Motors." RankingtheBrands.com. Accessed October 6, 2012. http://rankingthebrands.com/Brand-detail.aspx?brandID=477.

SyncForce. "GMC." RankingtheBrands.com. Accessed October 6, 2012. http://rankingthebrands.com/Brand-detail.aspx?brandID=451.

Woodyard, Chris. "General Motors to Remove Its 'Mark of Excellence' Logos from New Cars." *USA Today*, August 26, 2009.

GEORGE WESTON

AT A GLANCE

Brand Synopsis: George Weston Ltd. aims to be the leading food product innovator and provider in North America.
Parent Company: George Weston Ltd.
22 St. Clair Avenue East
Toronto, Ontario M4T 2S7
Canada
http://www.weston.ca
Sector: Consumer Staples
Industry Group: Food & Staples Retailing
Performance: *Market share*—The Loblaw division was the sixth-largest grocery retailer in North America in terms of sales (2011). *Sales*—Loblaw division US$31.2 billion, Weston Foods division US$1.8 billion (2011).
Principal Competitors: Maple Leaf Foods Inc.; METRO Inc.; Sobeys Inc.; Canada Safeway Ltd.; Wal-Mart Canada Corporation

BRAND ORIGINS

- George Weston Limited was founded by a Toronto bread salesman in 1882.
- Between 1940 and 1950 George Weston Ltd. bought shares of Loblaw Groceterias and acquired William Neilson, National Tea, and other companies.
- In 1978 Loblaw launched the No Name and President's Choice labels.
- In 1986 George Weston consolidated its food production operations under Weston Foods Ltd.
- Wal-Mart became George Weston Limited's primary competitor in the early 2000s.

In 1882 George Weston, a Toronto bread salesman, started Weston's Bread, and by the end of the century, it was known throughout the city. Over the next six decades, George Weston and his son merged their company with other major Toronto bakers to form the Canadian Bread Company, which was then incorporated as George Weston Limited. Under Garfield Weston's leadership, Weston Bakeries expanded across Canada and into the United States. Its acquisition in the late 1930s of McCormick's Ltd. and Inter-City Western Bakeries Ltd. gave Weston the facilities and resources to offer 370 products, including breads, cakes, biscuits, and candy.

In 1943 the company diversified into paper products, opening a mill in Hull, Quebec, and the acquisition of Western Grocers a year later marked Weston's debut in food distribution. Between 1940 and 1950, the company acquired Loblaw Groceterias shares; William Neilson (a major Canadian chocolate manufacturer); National Grocers of Ontario; National Tea; Kelly, Douglas and Company (a British Columbia wholesaler); and the Zehrmart grocery store chain. In the 1960s the company diversified into fish processing.

A son of Garfield Weston, W. Galen Weston, became president of the company in 1970, and the management halted growth plans in order to reorganize the brand's activities and shift its focus back to food. Weston's grocery operations were consolidated under Loblaw Companies Limited, and National Tea, which was losing US$36 million in sales in 1973, sold 75 percent of its stores. In 1978 Loblaw launched the No Name and President's Choice labels to join the market of private label grocery products with the aim of competing with name-brand goods. Weston entered a bidding war for control of Hudson's Bay Company in 1979 but lost. It instead acquired Stroehmann Brothers Company, an American operation.

In 1986 George Weston Limited consolidated its food processing operations under a subsidiary called Weston Foods Ltd. Weston Bakeries was by this time Canada's largest baker of fresh bread and cake products, and the Stroehmann brand was one of the largest wholesale bakeries in the United States. The financial crisis of the early 1990s coincided with Weston's decision to refocus on food and to unload unprofitable operations like National Tea and Neilson Cadbury. A tighter assemblage of products resulted in revenue growth, and George Weston began once more acquiring operations in their core areas, including Maplehurst Bakeries, which it purchased from Quaker Oats Company in 1998. The Loblaw segment grew simultaneously, as Weston planned to refurbish more than 100 stores in Canada. Looking to the future, Weston made plans for Loblaw to expand its nonfood products and offer general merchandise and financial services. In the new millennium, George Weston's greatest challenge has been competition with Wal-Mart, which forced the Loblaw segment to retool its operations significantly in response to its encroaching Canadian rivals.

BRAND ELEMENTS

- George Weston is represented by a formal gray logotext reading "Weston."
- George Weston Ltd. subsidiary brand logos that receive considerable visibility include the Weston Bakery logotext, the primary-colored balls of the Wonder Bread logo, and the rusing sun symbol of Country Harvest.
- As part of a reevaluation strategy "To Make Loblaw the Best Again," Weston implemented the campaign slogan "Simplify, Innovate, Grow."

The George Weston Ltd. brand is represented by a formal gray logo-text reading "Weston." The George Weston Ltd. subsidiary brand logos received more visibility than the parent company brand logo; among the more well known images owned by George Weston Lt. include the signature white font of the Weston Bakery brand, the vibrant red text and primary-colored balls of the Wonder Bread logo, the rising sun image and wholesome, naturalistic color pallet of the Country Harvest logo, the use of the Italian flag in the advertisements for D'Italiano products, and the cursive President's Choice logotext. George Weston products are characterized by bright, primary-colored packaging and iconic symbols.

Among the better known slogans owned by George Weston are the taglines for Wonder Bread ("Helps build strong bodies twelve ways") and President's Choice ("Worth switching supermarkets for"). The Loblaw brand also became associated with the tagline "Simplify, Innovate, Grow."

BRAND IDENTITY

- In 2007 Loblaw decided to simplify its operations in order to better compete with rivals, particularly Wal-Mart.
- George Weston describes its brand vision as focused on growth, innovation, and flexibility.
- The brand believes success lies in the continual satisfaction of customer demand through innovative new products.
- George Weston's mission is to be recognized in North America for providing the best products and exceeding customer expectations.

George Weston's ultimate mission is to be recognized in North America for providing the best products and exceeding customer expectations. As such its brand vision is focused on growth, innovation, and flexibility. The brand looks for long-term, stable growth in Weston's operating segments, accepting prudent operating risks through capital investment. The brand believes the way to be successful is to continuously deliver on what their customers desire, and to this end George Weston Ltd. encourages innovation and the constant creation of new products.

George Weston's biggest competitor since the turn of the century has been the wholesale retailer Wal-Mart. In 2007 Galen Weston, the chairman of George Weston Limited, declared, "We're not afraid of Wal-Mart. ... We have to make sure we are in fighting fit fashion, and we're not there yet." The company hoped customers would consider George Weston a viable option to Wal-Mart, and to accomplish this it began to simplify and streamline its operations.

BRAND STRATEGY

- George Weston's brand strategy emphasizes innovation, cost management, and process improvement aimed at growing its various controlled brands.
- The increase in Loblaw's operating income in 2011 was due to ongoing labor, supply chain, and cost efficiencies, and improved control label profitability.
- Loblaw's plans for 2012 involved exceeding customer expectations with an improved in-store service experience and competitive prices.

- In the early 2000s Loblaw renovated its stores, introducing a new urban format.

Weston's long-term operating strategies involve maintenance of customer alignment, a focus on brand development and the introduction of new products, optimizing plant and distribution systems (including capital investments), and strategically positioning facilities to support brand growth. An emphasis on innovation, cost management, and process improvement is central to Weston's brand growth and customer satisfaction. In 2012 the Loblaw segment of George Weston aimed to exceed customer expectations with an improved in-store service experience and competitive prices, to achieve milestones in the implementation of its IT system, and to capitalize on its established control brands. George Weston Limited's overall financial strategies include maintaining a strong balance sheet, maintaining liquidity and access to capital markets, and minimizing the risks of operating and financing activities. The acquisition of Keystone and ACE in 2011 boosted sales 8.5 percent and 6.4 percent in their respective markets.

The increase in Loblaw's operating income (US$1.4 billion, up 0.8 percent from 2010) was due to the continued implementation of labor, supply chain, and cost efficiencies; improved control label profitability; and the growth of Loblaw's franchises. Such improvements were offset by continued investment in Loblaw, the growth of Loblaw's Financial Services segment, the start-up costs of launching the Joe Fresh brand in the United States, and investments in information technology. Nevertheless, Loblaw has reaped the benefits of realigning its retail segment into conventional and discount structures. It renovated its stores and introduced a new urban format represented by the brand Joe Fresh, President's Choice Financial, and the flagship Loblaw's store at Maple Leaf Gardens. The results were improved sales in the second half of 2011.

BRAND EQUITY

- Brand Finance estimated George Weston's brand value as US$3.1 million in 2012.
- Weston Foods' sales were US$1.8 billion in 2011, up 1.7 percent from 2010 despite global financial scarcity.
- George Weston was included on Witiger's list of the Biggest Canadian Companies at No. 5 in 2010.

In 2012 Brand Finance estimated George Weston's brand value as US$3.1 million and ranked it 367th in its "Global 500" list. The previous year it was ranked 350th. It was included on Witiger's list of the Biggest Canadian Companies at No. 5 in 2010. Weston Foods' sales in 2011 increased 9.1 percent, and general sales rose 1.7 percent despite rising costs of fuel and raw materials, suggesting to the brand's management that brand loyalty remained strong among consumers.

George Weston Ltd. is a leading fresh and frozen baking company in Canada and has numerous frozen baking and biscuit manufacturing operations in the United States. Through its many brands and distributors George Weston Ltd. is considered a staple of Canadian consumer life, and the Loblaw distributor is Canada's largest grocery chain. The brand has a broad product and brand portfolio.

BRAND AWARENESS

- In 2011 George Weston pursued licensing partnerships with Mrs. Fields Famous Brands, in line with its strategy of establishing licensing partnerships to increase brand awareness.
- Recognition of the George Weston brand itself is minimal.
- Brand recognition is carried mainly by the smaller brand subsidiaries such as Wonder Bread and Weston Bakeries.
- George Weston Ltd. is notably missing from Interbrand's Top Global Brands and Best Canadian Brands.

George Weston relies on establishing licensing partnerships with other companies in order to grow brand awareness; in line with this strategy the brand was compelled in 2011 to enter several licensing partnerships, including one with Mrs. Fields Famous Brands. Despite these efforts, recognition of the George Weston brand itself is low, and most awareness is carried by the subsidiary brands. For instance, the brand recognition displayed by Wonder Bread prompted George Weston to consider launching a "Wonder Milk" line under the Nielsen subsidiary in 1997 to capitalize on customers' recollection of the Wonder Bread packaging. George Weston Ltd. is notably missing from Interbrand's Top Global Brands and Best Canadian Brands.

BRAND OUTLOOK

- Weston Foods' sales for 2011 increased 9.1 percent due to higher pricing in key product areas.
- In the second quarter annual report for 2012, George Weston Limited's adjusted basic net earnings per common share were down US$0.28 to US$1.06.
- George Weston anticipates growth in its urban-format Joe Fresh stores and in sales of luxury food products.

In 2011 Loblaw opened 11 free-standing Joe Fresh stores and nine new Nofrills stores. Weston Foods' sales for 2011 increased 9.1 percent from the previous year due to higher pricing in key product areas. Frozen bakery and biscuit sales grew thanks to product innovation, including the introduction of the Première Fournée de Weston line of artisan-inspired breads.

For 2012 George Weston Limited expected adjusted basic net earnings per common share to be down due to the incremental costs at Loblaw. Weston Foods projected modest sales growth and higher commodity and input costs for the first half of 2012, along with a continuing effort to reduce costs through improved efficiencies. In the second quarter annual report for 2012, George Weston Limited's adjusted basic net earnings per common share were US$1.06, down US$0.28.

FURTHER READING

Bertin, Oliver. "Acquisition Boosts Weston Bottom Line." *Globe and Mail*, February 22, 2002.

Bourette, Susan, and Dave Ebner. "Weston to Bolster Existing Operations: Much of US$800 Million to Be Spent on Eastern Businesses and Small U.S. Acquisitions." *Globe and Mail*, May 11, 1999.

Brand Finance. "Global 500 2012." *Brandirectory*. Accessed February 21, 2013. http://brandirectory.com/league_tables/table/global-500-2012.

Datamonitor. "George Weston Limited." Accessed September 27, 2012. http://www.datamonitor.com/store/Product/george_weston_limited?productid=5C1201B6-55CE-4A3A-81A8-AABAB6E795AD.

Davies, Charles. *Bread Men: How the Westons Built an International Empire*. Toronto: Key Porter, 1987.

George Weston Ltd. "2011 Complete Annual Report." Accessed September 25, 2012. http://www.weston.ca/en/pdf_en/gwl_2012q2_en.pdf.

———. "2012 Second Quarter Report." Accessed September 25, 2012. http://www.weston.ca/en/pdf_en/gwl_2011ar_en.pdf.

"George Weston Ltd." *International Directory of Company Histories*. Ed. Tina Grant. Vol. 88. Detroit, MI: St. James Press, 2008.

"Loblaw Executive Chairman Galen G. Weston and Ontario Environment Minister Laurel Broten Encourage Ontarians to Go Green and Reduce Use of Plastic Bags." Canada Newswire, May 9, 2007.

"Weston Expects Loblaws to Rise." *Calgary Herald*, May 17, 2007.

GILLETTE

AT A GLANCE

Brand Synopsis: With a focus on research and innovation, Gillette has become the world's leading brand for shaving and personal care products.
Parent Company: Procter & Gamble Company
One Procter & Gamble Plaza
Cincinnati, Ohio 45202
United States
http://www.pg.com
Sector: Consumer Staples
Industry Group: Household & Personal Products
Performance: *Market share*—70 percent of global razor blades and razors market (2012).
Principal Competitors: Schick (subsidiary of Energizer Holdings); Société Bic (Bic); Noxzema (subsidiary of Unilever); Remington (subsidiary of Spectrum Brands); Braun (subsidiary of Procter & Gamble Company)

BRAND ORIGINS

- The first safety razor was invented by King C. Gillette and was patented in 1904.
- Gillette began to expand into the global market in 1905, and by 1923 international sales accounted for 30 percent of Gillette's business.
- Gillette's sponsorship of sporting events, under the name "Cavalcade of Sports," became a successful way to promote the brand on radio and television.
- In 2005 Procter & Gamble Company acquired Gillette for US$57 billion.
- With its ongoing research and innovations, Gillette remains a leader in shaving and personal care products.

King C. Gillette invented the first safety razor with replaceable blades when he grew tired of a straight-edge razor that needed constant sharpening. The American Safety Razor Company, established in 1903, soon became the Gillette Safety Razor Company. Gillette received a patent for the new razor in 1904. With the help of advertising, the company sold more than 90,000 razors and 120,000 blades in its second year. Gillette's credo was "There is a better way to shave, and we will find it."

Expansion was rapid. In 1905 Gillette opened a branch in London, and soon after, factories were established in France, Canada, Germany, and other cities in England. By 1923, 30 percent of Gillette's sales were attributable to the global market.

During World War I the company supplied razors and blades to U.S. troops. By the end of the 1920s Gillette was providing shaving supplies to members of the royal families of the United Kingdom and Sweden.

Gillette faced several setbacks in the late 1920s. A dispute over patents led to a merger between Gillette and Auto Strop Safety Razor Company. Questionable financial records caused public confidence in Gillette to fall, along with its stock. Reorganization of the company led to the manufacture of the popular Gillette Blue Blade, but profits were low during the Great Depression of the 1930s.

In 1938 Joseph P. Spang Jr. became president of Gillette. Spang purchased radio broadcast rights to the 1939 World

Series, the annual championship series of Major League Baseball. The resulting sales were more than four times what the company had expected. This success inspired Gillette to sponsor more sporting events, grouping these events under the name "Gillette Cavalcade of Sports," which became a lucrative venue for advertising on radio and television.

Gillette once again supplied razors and blades to the U.S. military during World War II. In the profitable post-war era, Spang expanded the company's shaving line with a "brushless" shaving cream, its first product without a razor or blade.

Between the 1960s and 1980s diversification through acquisition and domestic competition led to fluctuations in Gillette's success. The highs included the company's development of the Trac II twin-blade shaving system, Good News disposable razors, and the Atra, the first razor with a pivoting head. The lows included competition with Eversharp, the maker of Schick razor blades; a price war with the Bic Corporation over disposable cigarette lighters; and an antitrust suit denying Gillette's acquisition of the German company Braun. During the 1970s, environmental concerns about fluorocarbons in aerosol cans negatively affected Gillette's sales of personal care products. In response, Gillette developed nonaerosol pumps and roll-ons for its line of deodorant and hair spray.

In 1989 Gillette avoided a takeover by Revlon and Coniston Partners when Warren Buffett, chairman and CEO of Berkshire Hathaway, bought US$600 million of Gillette convertible preferred shares. Also in 1989 Gillette released the Sensor for men, a razor with thinner blades mounted on springs. The company released the women's version, the Lady Sensor, in 1992. The Sensor and Lady Sensor garnered more than US$500 million in sales for Gillette. This success continued with the 1993 launch of the Sensor Excel for men, which was sold in Japan, England, and the United States. The Sensor Excel for women was released in 1996. In the 1990s, Gillette also released a line of men's toiletries and acquired the companies Parker Pen Holdings, Ltd. and Duracell International, Inc.

In 1998 Gillette debuted the Mach 3 shaving system, the first triple-blade pivoting razor. The Mach 3 was protected by 35 patents, and its launch cost US$35 billion. Consequently, the company set a high price for the Mach 3's replacement cartridges, hoping existing customers would be enticed by the new model's enhanced performance and trade up. Nevertheless, the cost of introducing the Mach 3 to market caused a drop in profits. During the 2001 recession in the United States, sales decreased in both domestic and foreign markets. In 2003 Gillette accused Schick-Wilkinson Sword, maker of the four-blade Quattro shaving system, of patent infringement, a charge that was rejected in court. By 2004 Gillette had regained its strong footing in the market, with the Mach 3 and the Venus (the women's version of the Mach 3) helping to boost profits by 43 percent.

In 2005 Procter & Gamble Company acquired Gillette for US$57 billion. Gillette continued to research new and improved ways of shaving, introducing the Gillette Fusion, the first in a line of five-bladed razors, in 2006. The Gillette Fusion has a five-bladed "shaving surface" on the front and a single blade on the back for precision trimming. Gillette has since released several updated versions of the Fusion. Meanwhile, the Gillette Venus for women has also developed into a five-bladed razor featuring built-in shave gel bars to provide moisture.

BRAND ELEMENTS

- Gillette's products for men are labeled with a bold font and various logos using strong shapes and colors.
- "How're Ya Fixed for Blades?" was one of Gillette's first advertising jingles.
- In 1989 the company introduced the memorable jingle "Gillette, the best a man can get."
- The Gillette Venus razor for women is designed with sensuous curves and promises to "Reveal the Goddess in You."

Gillette is a brand that is constantly evolving. The company's original logo was a horizontal diamond, with the word "Gillette" centered and pierced by an arrow. In 2012 Gillette's products for men featured a logo using a bold, italic font. The basic logo is a capital "G" placed at an angle. The logo for the Gillette Fusion five-bladed razor is meant to suggest science and technology. An orange square contains the blue word "Fusion," with a burst of white coming from the "O." The packaging for Gillette's men's products has featured color combinations that include blue and gray; blue, orange, white, and black; and black and green.

During the 1952 World Series Gillette introduced a jingle that encouraged men to look and be "sharp" when they shave. Gillette television ads featured a character named Sharpie the Parrot singing "How're Ya Fixed for Blades?" In 1989 advertising for the Atra razor featured the jingle "Gillette, the best a man can get." This ad, which also featured images of men playing football, getting married, and holding newborn babies, struck a chord with U.S. audiences and is still recognized by many consumers.

The Gillette Venus razor for women is packaged in pastels with images of curvy scrolls, water, and tropical sunsets. The word mark is sensuous, with a distinctive "V." In 2012 the Venus spokesperson, actress and entertainer Jennifer Lopez, sang a sultry jingle in advertisements, while the razor's tagline urged women to "Reveal the Goddess in You."

BRAND IDENTITY

- Gillette has sponsored international sporting events and partnered with top-tier athletes in its effort to appeal to male customers.
- Gillette's advertising has also appealed to men's sense of style by featuring well-known actors and musicians.
- Advertising for the Gillette Venus suggests that all women can have "goddess legs" if they use the Venus razor.

Gillette identifies itself as an innovative brand that helps men (and women) be the best they can be. Sports have played an important role in achieving this brand promise. The company's sports marketing has evolved from radio ads during the 1939 World Series to sponsorship of international events, such as the FIFA World Cup and rugby and cricket tournaments. Gillette advertisements have featured athletes who appeal to men's drive to be on top of their game, such as tennis player Roger Federer, soccer player Thierry Henry, and golfer Tiger Woods. More recent spokespeople have included Clay Matthews, a National Football League (NFL) linebacker, and Olympic swimmer Ryan Lochte, who joined Gillette in the "Get Started Campaign," which donated US$25,000 to the pool where Lochte learned to swim. Another way Gillette identifies its brand as helping people achieve their best is by appealing to their sense of style. For men, the "Masters of Style" advertising campaign featured well-known actors and musicians shaving with the Gillette Fusion ProGlide Styler. For women, the Gillette Venus encourages them to use the razor and Gillette's Satin Care shave gel to be "Smooth. Sexy. Satin." The Gillette Venus spokesperson as of 2012, actress and entertainer Jennifer Lopez, is portrayed as accomplished and beautiful in ads that convey the message that all women can have "goddess legs" if they use Gillette Venus razors. In the accompanying advertising campaign, women are asked to share their "goddess stories." For each story, the brand donates one dollar to the Venus Goddess Fund for Education, which "helps women across the world reach their full potential." Gillette has earmarked US$50,000 from the same fund for the Step Up Women's Network in the United States, which connects professional women with underserved teen girls, and US$15,000 for Canada's CARE International, a humanitarian organization that works to help women and girls living in poverty.

BRAND STRATEGY

- In preparation for the Mach 3's global release, Gillette used universal advertising and designs to save time and money.
- The merger between Procter & Gamble and Gillette provided opportunities for the latter to gain shelf space and save on advertising and production.
- A series of Gillette-sponsored events at MADE Fashion Week in 2012 shone a spotlight on the role men's grooming plays in fashion and style.

Gillette's main brand strategy is to continue to bring innovative products to market. One good example is the launch of the Mach 3. Gillette's "Global Strategy Gillette" describes the events that led up to the global launch of the Mach 3, the first triple-blade pivoting razor, which cost the brand US$35 billion to bring to market. Gillette translated its advertising message for the Mach 3 into 30 languages. To keep production simple, only the language varied on the packaging, while colors, typefaces, and design elements were universal. The same television ad, featuring models representing diverse cultures, was shown in every country where the product was advertised. By streamlining its marketing of the Mach 3, Gillette was able to create a recognizable look for its new product in a short amount of time.

Additionally, the 2005 merger between Procter & Gamble Company and Gillette was a way for Gillette to gain the funds to continue bolstering its brand. The merger benefited both companies financially. Kurt Barnard, a retail analyst, told *CNN Money*, "They each had a lot of economic power before, but with the marriage they'll have a lot more." *CNN Money* also noted that Procter & Gamble Company would be "opening doors for Gillette in markets such as China and Japan."

Gillette's success is due at least in part to its ability to anticipate the needs of consumers worldwide and bring those products to market. The Gillette Guard, for example, was developed to accord with the shaving habits of men in India, where there's a need for an affordable, simple razor that can be used with minimal light and water. The fact that the Gillette Guard requires 80 percent fewer parts was a bonus.

Additional strategies for the brand include moving into new markets. In 2012 Gillette's website announced that the company would be sponsoring several events spotlighting menswear designers at MADE Fashion Week. This move signaled that Gillette is making an effort to involve itself in men's fashion, which some might consider a natural progression given the brand's significance in the men's grooming industry.

BRAND EQUITY

- In 2012 Gillette ranked 121st on *Brandirectory*'s list of the top-500 global brands and 16th on Interbrand's list of the top-100 global brands.
- In 2012 Gillette's competitors were not included in the *Brandirectory* or Interbrand rankings of top global brands, reflecting Gillette's lead in the market.
- In 2011 Gillette led the U.S. and European markets in volume market shares.

In 2012 Gillette was ranked 121st on *Brandirectory*'s list of the top-500 global brands, with a brand value of US$7.8

billion. Gillette ranked 16th on Interbrand's 2012 list of the top-100 global brands, with a US$24 billion brand value in the "Fast Moving Consumer Goods" sector.

In a report published by Gillette competitor Société Bic (Bic) titled "2011 Group Presentation for Investors," a chart compared the volume market share of Gillette, Schick, and Bic. In the United States, Gillette held the second highest volume market share at 23 percent, compared to Bic's 31 percent and Schick's 21 percent. In the European market, Gillette was in the top spot at 34 percent, compared to Bic's 29 percent and Schick's 27 percent. The report's value market share figures showed Gillette as the clear leader, with market shares of 34 percent in the United States and 41 percent in Europe.

Nielsen data from May 2010 identified the Gillette Venus as the leading women's shaver. Procter & Gamble's global value share in the "Female Blades & Razors" sector was 53.2 percent.

BRAND AWARENESS

- By 1999 the Mach 3 was the number one razor on the market in the United States and several European countries.
- Before its merger with Procter & Gamble in 2005, Gillette products were sold in more than 200 countries.
- Gillette promotes its products through social media and its websites, maintaining top-of-mind presence among international and U.S. consumers.

Gillette has been a household name for more than a century. By 1999 the Mach 3 was the number one razor on the market in Germany, Italy, Spain, England, and the United States. Men in India prefer the Gillette Guard razor to double-edged razors seven to one.

Before the 2005 merger with Procter & Gamble, the *International Directory of Company Histories* reported that Gillette products were sold in more than 200 countries, with more than 60 percent of sales occurring outside the United States. In 2012 Procter & Gamble sold Gillette products in 180 countries around the world.

Gillette maintains a lively presence on Facebook, Twitter, and YouTube. Gillette's corporate website, as well as websites for Gillette India Limited and the Gillette Venus, shares the company's latest innovations, news about sponsored events, and information about how to use its products. Despite the merger with Procter & Gamble, Gillette has maintained its top-of-mind presence among consumers worldwide.

BRAND OUTLOOK

- Procter & Gamble's goal in 2012 was to revive Gillette's innovativeness and consumer awareness.
- In 2011 Gillette was planning to introduce products in more than 40 new countries over the following two years.
- Gillette hopes to convince men in India to switch from their traditional use of double-edge blades to more modern shaving systems.

Robert A. McDonald, chairman of the board and CEO of Procter & Gamble, has identified the Gillette Fusion ProGlide, the Gillette Prestobarba 3 (sold in Latin America), and the Gillette Venus Embrace among the corporation's leadership brands. Since Gillette merged with Procter & Gamble, the turnaround of innovative products has slowed. The company plans to "restart innovation where it has been lacking, to ensure our brands are sufficient to generate consumer awareness, trial, and loyalty." McDonald has stressed the importance of making new investments in Gillette to improve productivity and cost.

According to brand consultancy Interbrand, emerging markets are part of Gillette's growth strategy. In 2011 Gillette was planning to introduce products in more than 40 new countries over the following two years. Gillette has also noted growth opportunities in India, with the chance to introduce more men in that country to more modern and convenient shaving systems.

FURTHER READING

Brand Finance. "Global 500 2012." *Brandirectory*. Accessed September 15, 2012. http://brandirectory.com/league_tables/table/global-500-2012.

Caslin, Yvette. "Andre 3000 Stars in Gillette Ad, Exec Damon Jones Is behind the Campaign." RollingOut.com, March 2, 2012. Accessed September 19, 2012. http://rollingout.com/business/marketing-branding/andre-3000-stars-in-gillette-ad-exec-damon-jones-is-behind-the-campaign/.

"Gillette." *International Directory of Company Histories*. Ed. Tina Grant and Miranda H. Ferrara. Vol. 68. Detroit, MI: St. James Press, 2005.

"Gillette Venus Delivers Category Leading Investment for 2010." TalkingRetail.com, January 2010. Accessed September 19, 2012. http://www.talkingretail.com/products/product-news/gillette-venus-delivers-category-leading-investment-for-2010.

Govindarajan, Vijay. "P&G Innovates on Razor-Thin Margins." *Harvard Business Review*, April 16, 2012.

Indran, N. R. "Gillette India Limited Annual Results Delivers Strong Growth." APNNEWS, August 27, 2011.

Isidore, Chris. "P&G to Buy Gillette for $57B." *CNN Money*, January 28, 2005. Accessed September 18, 2012. http://money.cnn.com/2005/01/28/news/fortune500/pg_gillette/.

Procter & Gamble Company. "2012 Annual Report." Accessed September 21, 2012. http://annualreport.pg.com/annualreport2012/index.shtml.

Solomont, E. B. "Schick Cuts into Gillette's Market Share." *St. Louis Business Journal*, April 20, 2012.

"2011 Ranking of the Top 100 Brands." Interbrand. Accessed September 15, 2012. http://www.interbrand.com/en/best-global-brands/best-global-brands-2008/best-global-brands-2011.aspx.

GLAXOSMITHKLINE

AT A GLANCE

Brand Synopsis: The GlaxoSmithKline brand, a world leader in pharmaceuticals, vaccines, and consumer healthcare products, stresses its commitment to research and development and to delivering innovative products all over the world.
Parent Company: GlaxoSmithKline PLC
980 Great West Road, Brentford
Middlesex TW8 9GS
United Kingdom
www.gsk.com
Sector: Healthcare
Industry Group: Pharmaceuticals, Biotechnology & Life Sciences
Performance: *Market share*—4.70% of drug market, worldwide (2010). *Sales*—US$44 billion (2011).
Principal Competitors: Abbott Laboratories; Amgen Inc.; AstraZeneca PLC; Biogen Idec Inc.; Bristol-Myers Squibb Co.; Eli Lilly and Co.; Genentech Inc.; Genzyme Corp.; Gilead Sciences Inc.; Johnson and Johnson; Life Technologies Corp.; Merck Serono GmbH; MedImmune Ltd.; Novartis Inc.; Pfizer Inc.; Roche Holding AG; Sanofi Aventis; Teva Pharmaceutical Industries Ltd.; Sandoz Ltd.; Watson Pharmaceuticals Inc.; King Pharmaceuticals Inc.; Ranbaxy Laboratories Ltd.; Mylan Inc.

BRAND ORIGINS

- GlaxoSmithKline has been responsible for the development of many top-selling drugs, such as Ventolin, Zantac, and Zofran.
- In 1988 Glaxo held the number two position among international pharmaceutical companies.
- SmithKline Beecham and Glaxo Wellcome merged to become GlaxoSmithKline in 2000.

GlaxoSmithKline has its roots in a number of companies. In 1873 Joseph Nathan & Co., an importer and exporter of patent medicines, was founded in New Zealand, and three years later the firm opened an office in London. After acquiring the rights to a milk-drying process in 1909, the company moved into the baby food business under the name Glaxo. By the beginning of World War II Glaxo was also producing penicillin, anesthetics, and vitamin supplements. After the war Glaxo acquired several companies and spearheaded the development of cortisone and corticosteroids.

In 1969 Glaxo created Ventolin, an asthma drug that would soon lead the international market. By 1988 the popularity of drugs such as Zantac, with its 53 percent market share, had lifted Glaxo to the number two position in the world among pharmaceutical companies. By the early 1990s Glaxo had factories in 30 countries, and its products were purchased in 150 countries, with Zantac becoming the world's best-selling drug. In 1995 Glaxo launched a US$14.9 billion takeover bid for Wellcome PLC, creating Glaxo Wellcome. The new company shed 7,500 employees from its workforce and became the world's number one prescription drug company.

In 1847 an herbalist named Thomas Beecham began selling his own Beecham's Pills, a laxative, in and around the town of Wigan, England. He eventually established a mail-order business. Beecham's son Joseph took over the business and expanded it internationally, using pioneering advertising techniques. In 1924 the firm was sold to financier Philip Hill, who proceeded to expand the business and the company's line of products, especially in the area of antibiotics. Just as Glaxo had, Beecham started acquiring other businesses. In 1989 it merged with SmithKline Beckman and became SmithKline Beecham, posting US$6.9 billion in annual sales.

In 2000 Glaxo Wellcome and SmithKline Beecham merged to create GlaxoSmithKline. The company underwent a research-and-development restructuring, and the yield included a 41 percent increase in clinical trials and plans for introducing five new drugs in 2007. In 2004 the U.S. Internal Revenue Service asserted that GlaxoSmithKline had underpaid its taxes from 1989 to 1996 and billed the company US$2.7 billion; the following year another bill of US$1.9 billion was issued for underpayment of taxes from 1997 to 2000. In 2006 the company agreed to pay about $3.4 billion in fines.

By 2008 GlaxoSmithKline employed 25,000 people in the United States, but that same year it announced that it was cutting 1,800 jobs. In July 2012 the U.S. government accused the pharmaceutical company of "promoting its best-selling antidepressants for unapproved uses and failing to report safety data about a top diabetes drug" and of "improper marketing of a half-dozen other drugs," according to the *New York Times*. GlaxoSmithKline pleaded guilty and agreed to pay US$3 billion in fines. The settlement surpassed any previous settlement with a pharmaceutical company.

BRAND ELEMENTS

- In 2000 GlaxoSmithKline introduced its glowing orange and gray logo with the newly formed company's letters and name.
- The new logo was intended to convey a "contemporary and approachable look and feel," according to its designer.
- After the 2000 merger the brand elements of a number of GlaxoSmithKline consumer products were redesigned as well.

When Glaxo Wellcome and SmithKline Beecham merged to create GlaxoSmithKline, the new company adopted a new logo designed by London branding consultants FutureBrand. The logo featured a glowing orange color palette with "gsk" in lowercase. To the right of the orange triangular element is "GlaxoSmithKline" in gray letters in Frutiger font. FutureBrand's creative director told *Creative Review* in 2001 that the new look was intended "to give the identity a contemporary and approachable look and feel." The merger resulted in more GlaxoSmithKline products that sported the company's logo, and some of the consumer products have had their brand elements redesigned in recent years as well.

BRAND IDENTITY

- GlaxoSmithKline has stated that its mission is "to improve the quality of human life by enabling people to do more, feel better and live longer."
- GlaxoSmithKline has focused on discovering and developing treatments for HIV/AIDS, malaria, and tuberculosis as a part of its focus on global R&D.
- GlaxoSmithKline provided the official drug testing laboratory for the 2012 London Olympics as a way of promoting its image as an innovative research firm.

GlaxoSmithKline's mission is "to improve the quality of human life by enabling people to do more, feel better, and live longer." Consequently the identity of the GlaxoSmithKline brand focuses on the innovative research and development needed to create products that can deliver this promise. While the company has maintained this identity for some time, it has refocused its image to promote its global reach. For example, much of its R&D is focused on discovering and developing treatments for HIV/AIDS, malaria, and tuberculosis. Moreover, with more than 12,500 people working on the R&D for innovative vaccines, the company's vaccines are used in immunization campaigns in 182 countries.

As a way to promote its brand's focus on scientific research, GlaxoSmithKline became the official drug-testing laboratory for the London Olympic Games in 2012. Its anti-doping research was used at the games in screening all athletes who participated. The company's first U.K. brand campaign ran during the Olympics to promote awareness of the global scope of the brand.

While the company has made tremendous strides in achieving its promises, its altruistic global image was tarnished by a transfer-pricing dispute with the U.S. government. Other setbacks included reprimands in 2012 for, as *MarketLine* explained, "introducing misbranded drugs, Paxil and Wellbutrin" and for not reporting safety data to the U.S. Food and Drug Administration about the diabetes drug Avandia. These cases ended in a settlement in which GlaxoSmithKline paid US$3 billion in fines—the largest settlement on record involving a pharmaceutical company.

BRAND STRATEGY

- GlaxoSmithKline spent £4 billion (US$6.05 billion) on research and development in 2011 with a focus on "scientific opportunities in different disease areas" and advances toward cures.

- The company's brand strategy focuses on investing in the globalization of its products and streamlining its operations to more effectively add and sell its products.
- Centralization of development and marketing for some of GlaxoSmithKline's large global brands boosted growth from 3 percent in 2007 to 12 percent in 2008.

According to its 2011 annual report, GlaxoSmithKline's main business strategy was "to improve R&D returns and productivity." The company, which spent £4 billion (US$6.05 billion) on research and development in 2011 with a focus on "scientific opportunities in different disease areas" and advances toward cures, claimed it was one of the few healthcare companies developing treatments for the World Health Organization's three priority diseases: HIV/AIDS, malaria, and tuberculosis.

The report noted that the company had three strategic focal points on which to create returns on their research and development: "to grow a diversified global business, to deliver more products of value, and to simplify the operating model." GlaxoSmithKline made a move in 2008 to start growing markets outside of the United States and Europe. According to the 2011 annual report, those newer markets yielded 38 percent of the company's total sales. As of the end of 2011 GlaxoSmithKline had developed 74 global manufacturing and research-and-development sites situated in the United Kingdom, the United States, Spain, Belgium, and China.

An example of the way GlaxoSmithKline seeks to simplify its operations can be found in the centralization of some of the company's major brands. In 2004 GlaxoSmithKline Consumer Healthcare took a novel approach by centralizing marketing and research and development for several of its larger global brands, such as Lucozade, Aquafresh, Sensodyne, Panadol, and Horlicks. According to a report in *Business Strategy Review,* the centralized effort was called the Future Group, a team of about 150 people that focused on "global brand innovation and brand equity." The consolidation led to measurable results, including a jump in growth from 3 percent in 2007 to 12 percent in 2008. The Future Group, the report said, allowed GlaxoSmithKline to "strike exactly the right balance between the central creation of big brands, global plans and strategic initiatives—and local activation of those plans." Local GlaxoSmithKline marketers then activated any plans the Future Group devised.

BRAND EQUITY

- In 2012 GlaxoSmithKline ranked 455th in Brand Finance's Global 500, a drop from the brand's rankings of 426 in 2011 and 141 in 2008.
- GlaxoSmithKline held the 38th spot in Brand Finance's list of the top 50 U.K. brands.
- In 2012 GlaxoSmithKline's strongest growth area was respiratory products.

In 2012 Brand Finance placed GlaxoSmithKline's brand value at $2.59 billion, which landed the firm at number 455 on the Global 500, a drop from 426 in 2011 and 141 in 2008. In its home country it held the 38th spot among the top 50 U.K. brands. The brand has potential to gain traction as more of its patent-protected medicines have come to market. According to *MarketLine Company Profiles Authority,* respiratory products represented the strongest growth area in GlaxoSmithKline's prescription portfolio in 2012, and the company's vaccines portfolio was "one of the largest in the world."

BRAND AWARENESS

- GlaxoSmithKline spent US$31.3 million to be the official drug tester for the 2012 Olympics.
- GlaxoSmithKline hired ad agency WPP in 2012 for a 2013 campaign designed to demonstrate "the power of GSK's impact around the world."
- GlaxoSmithKline bought two generic-brand drug plants in 2009 to increase its share in emerging markets.

While many of its products, which use different brand names, enjoy top-of-mind recall by consumers, the company brand, GlaxoSmithKline, may not always enjoy high brand awareness. The company has made several new efforts to increase consumer recognition of the brand.

GlaxoSmithKline spent US$31.3 million to be the official drug-testing laboratory for the 2012 Olympic Games in London. With the tag line "The crowd is my only drug," the campaign focused on the company's role in anti-doping measures at the games, reportedly the most extensive program in Olympic history.

Additionally, at the end of 2012 GlaxoSmithKline retained ad agency WPP "to develop and leverage the brand across its entire portfolio." According to *Advertising Age,* WPP was hired for a 2013 campaign designed to "handle a new global corporate branding and communications brief aimed at demonstrating the power of GSK's impact around the world." GlaxoSmithKline's research to find a cure for malaria, which was thought to be close at hand, "is thought to have been a factor in the decision to develop a corporate campaign."

Although GlaxoSmithKline is interested in developing its brand name, in 2009 it also purchased generic-brand manufacturers in South Africa and India. As patents expire, brand-name drugs move to the generic market, and in many countries outside of the United States, patients must pay out of pocket for medicines.

According to the *New York Times,* "company-branded generics can charge more for the promise of quality." This allows the company to continue to establish its brand awareness and utilize its existing distribution channels.

BRAND OUTLOOK

- GlaxoSmithKline's research and development gives the brand a positive outlook, with opportunities to capitalize on a number of drugs in late-stage development.
- In 2006 GlaxoSmithKline agreed to pay about US$3.4 billion in fines to the U.S. government because of a transfer-pricing dispute.
- In 2012 GlaxoSmithKline acquired its partner in the development of the drug Benlysta, Human Genome Sciences.

GlaxoSmithKline's brand outlook is strong, thanks to its research-and-development capabilities. However, the company also has had two significant fines to pay the U.S. government. In 2004 the Internal Revenue Service asserted that GlaxoSmithKline had engaged in transfer pricing and had underpaid its taxes from 1989 to 2000, and it billed the company almost US$4.7 billion. In 2006 GlaxoSmithKline agreed to pay about $3.4 billion in fines. In July 2012 GlaxoSmithKline pleaded guilty and agreed to pay the U.S. government an additional $3 billion in fines. According to the *New York Times,* the government accused the pharmaceutical company of "promoting its best-selling antidepressants for unapproved uses and failing to report safety data about a top diabetes drug" and for the "improper marketing of a half-dozen other drugs." This settlement surpassed any previous settlement with a pharmaceutical company.

The brand took another hit when sales of its best-selling diabetes drug, Avandia, were restricted in the United States and Europe. The loss of Avandia, according to the company's 2011 annual report, resulted in a decline in sales of metabolic pharmaceuticals of 47 percent. One opportunity that emerged in 2012 was GlaxoSmithKline's friendly acquisition of Human Genome Sciences, its partner in producing the drug Benlysta. The deal included ownership of Human Genome Sciences' late-stage drug developments.

GlaxoSmithKline continued to make strides with its restructuring, which began in 2007. During 2011 the company realized an annual savings of US$962 million and expected to save approximately US$4.5 billion by 2014, *MarketLine* reported. GlaxoSmithKline's entry into emerging markets was expected to expand and improve healthcare in those markets, while also providing a new source of revenue. To position itself to take advantage of some emerging markets, GlaxoSmithKline acquired an interest in a Chinese joint venture.

FURTHER READING

Birkinshaw, Julian, and Peter Robbins. "Ideas at Work: Sparkling Innovation." *Business Strategy Review* 21.2: 7-11.

Brand Finance. "Global 500 2012." *Brandirectory.* Accessed December 10, 2012. http://brandirectory.com/profile/glaxosmithkline.

GlaxoSmithKline. "Annual Report 2011." Accessed December 10, 2012. http://www.gsk.com/content/dam/gsk/globals/documents/pdf/GSK-Annual-Report-2011.pdf.

"GlaxoSmithKline." *Notable Corporate Chronologies.* Detroit: Gale, 2009. *Business Insights: Global.* Accessed December 10, 2012. http://bi.galegroup.com/global/article/GALE%7CI2501150779/5f30dfe09b9c8ae269d37e6d1609599f?u=itsbtrial.

"GlaxoSmithKline." *A Website about Corporate Identity,* August 1, 2001. Accessed December 10, 2012. http://hansstol.totaldesign.nl/en/gsk.html.

"GlaxoSmithKline Logo." *Creative Review* Feb. 2001: 8. *General OneFile.* Accessed December 24, 2012. http://go.galegroup.com/ps/retrieve.do?sgHitCountType=None&sort=DA-SORT&inPS=true&prodId=GPS&userGroupName=itsbtrial&tabID=T003&searchId=R1&resultListType=RESULT_LIST&contentSegment=&searchType=BasicSearchForm¤tPosition=91&contentSet=GALE%7CA70651643&&docId=GALE|A70651643&docType=GALE&role=ITOF.

"GlaxoSmithKline PLC." *International Directory of Company Histories.* Ed. Karen Hill. Vol. 119. Detroit: St. James Press, 2011. *Business Insights: Global.* Accessed December 10, 2012. http://bi.galegroup.com/global/article/GALE%7CI2501314491/4c779ffb07c1fa5bd2cbb85738ab7bc4?u=itsbtrial.

"GlaxoSmithKline PLC." *MarketLine Company Profiles Authority. EBSCO Host.* Accessed December 11, 2012. http://search.ebscohost.com/login.aspx?direct=true&db=dmhco&AN=52C96BD1-36D1-4755-AD65-EADEE10E8840&site=ehost-live.

Hall, Emma. "GlaxoSmithKline Taps WPP for Global Branding Effort." *Ad Age,* December 4, 2012. Accessed December 10, 2012. http://adage.com/article/agency-news/glaxosmithkline-taps-wpp-global-branding-effort/238610/.

Singer, Natasha. "Drug Firms Apply Brand to Generics." *New York Times,* February 2, 2010. Accessed December 10, 2012. https://www.nytimes.com/2010/02/16/business/16generic.html.

Thomas, Katie, and Michael S. Schmidt. "Glaxo Agrees to Pay $3 Billion in Fraud Settlement." *New York Times,* July 2, 2012. Accessed December 10, 2012. http://www.nytimes.com/2012/07/03/business/glaxosmithkline-agrees-to-pay-3-billion-in-fraud-settlement.html?pagewanted=all.

GOLDMAN SACHS

AT A GLANCE

Brand Synopsis: A leader in global finance, Goldman Sachs strives to deliver quality services, creative solutions, and healthy returns in order to help the world progress.
Parent Company: Goldman Sachs Group, Inc.
200 West Street, 29th Floor
New York, New York 10282
United States
http://www.goldmansachs.com
Sector: Financials
Industry Group: Diversified Financials
Performance: *Market share*—10 percent in the Americas and 7.4 percent in Europe and Asia for common stock offerings, mergers, and acquisitions (2011). *Sales*—US$28.8 billion (2011).
Principal Competitors: J.P. Morgan Chase; Morgan Stanley; Bank of America; American Express; Citigroup

BRAND ORIGINS

- In 1869 Marcus Goldman began a small, family owned business that would become Goldman, Sachs & Co. in 1885.
- Goldman Sachs has set records for its work in initial public offerings, mergers, and acquisitions, and it continues to enjoy a leading global position in that area.
- Even though Goldman Sachs survived, and in some ways even benefited from, the global credit crisis in 2008, the company's reputation suffered.

In 1869 a German immigrant named Marcus Goldman began trading promissory notes in New York City. By 1885 the business had grown into the general partnership Goldman, Sachs & Co., with Goldman's son, Henry, and son-in-law Samuel Sachs joining the firm. Goldman Sachs's interests and services soon began to grow both domestically and globally. With clients like Sears Roebuck, Cluett Peabody, and Rice-Stix Dry Goods, the company was on its way to greatness. By 1896 its business had expanded to include international commercial finance, foreign and domestic exchange services, currency arbitrage, loans, and finance management. Additionally, the firm joined the New York Stock Exchange and began helping other companies manage their initial public offerings (IPOs), which still form a crucial part of its business today.

Setting records with Ford's IPO in 1956 and with the highest single block trade for Alcan Aluminum in 1967, Goldman Sachs continued to grow in influence throughout the 1970s. The 1980s and 1990s, however, were challenging for the company. Facing a volatile stock market and the retirement of many of its partners, the company had to seek new sources of capital. During this time, Goldman Sachs ramped up its international business, restructured internally, began acquiring other firms and commercial buildings, and finally, after 127 years as a partnership, went public in 1999. The firm named a sole chairman and CEO and changed its name to the Goldman Sachs Group, Inc.

Since the turn of the 21st century Goldman Sachs has built a reputation as the industry leader in mergers and acquisitions and IPOs. The 2008 global credit crisis dealt a significant blow to the company, however. Even though it was one of the few big financial firms to survive and even benefit from the collapse, taking full advantage of the rescue funds from the U.S. government and powerful connections on Capitol Hill, the company's reputation was damaged. In recent years the company has initiated several marketing campaigns to regain customer trust and build new business.

BRAND ELEMENTS

- The Goldman Sachs logo, a blue square with the words Goldman Sachs written in white letters, is demonstrative of the brand's understated image.
- Goldman Sachs's corporate headquarters further demonstrates its brand's use of simplicity to underscore the effectiveness of a superior firm.
- The continued success of Goldman Sachs, seen both in its revenue and leading global position, is strongly linked to its branding.

Goldman Sachs's brand image, including its logo, corporate buildings, and advertising campaigns, is defined mostly by its understatement. The company's logo, a plain blue square with the words Goldman Sachs top-justified in white letters, is relatively lackluster. The limited visual display works, however, because it underscores the seriousness of the firm itself and allows its 14 business principles (see Brand Identity below) to be at the forefront of its branding. Perhaps, more interestingly, the logo also portrays the company as being fairly inconspicuous.

According to an article in the *New Yorker*, the corporate office in lower Manhattan might be the best example of this lack of ostentation. The building is fairly plain and sober on the outside but exhibits cutting-edge design on the inside, boasting artsy cafeterias and conference rooms. The juxtaposition of the office's inside and outside parallels the firm's relationship with the public: the outside conceals the complicated activity of the inside. When the consumer sees these brand images, the simple logo and the unassuming building, his perception is focused on the company as a whole and its reputation as a firm, rather than the complicated, often poorly understood financial products and services it offers. This is the exact goal that the brand pursues in its images and promotions. Even in times of economic crisis and public distrust, the firm continues to profit at industry-leading levels, both globally and domestically, which experts like Mark Ritson attribute to its successful branding.

BRAND IDENTITY

- The heart of the Goldman Sachs brand lies within its 14 business principles, which emphasize superior service and knowledge, trust, and creativity.
- Goldman Sachs's ability to follow its business code and respond to the market allowed them to survive the economic crisis of 2008.
- Part of the success of the Goldman Sachs brand can be attributed to the understated manner in which its power is displayed.

Goldman Sachs strives to uphold a reputation built upon quality service, creativity, and healthy returns to its customers. Nothing is more crucial to the company's image than the 14 business principles stated on their website and included in every annual report since the 1970s. Emphasizing professional quality and customer service, such virtues as "Our clients' interests always come first," "The dedication of our people to the firm and the intense effort they give their jobs are greater than one finds in most other organizations," and "Integrity and honesty are at the heart of our business" are meant to inspire trust and confidence in clients. According to branding expert Mark Ritson, these business principles stress the "'unusual effort' Goldman Sachs puts into recruiting the very best people in the business, the 'pioneering' nature of the firm, and a recognition 'that the world of finance will not stand still, and that complacency can lead to extinction.'" In fact, it was these attributes that enabled Goldman Sachs to survive the economic crisis of 2008, which destroyed many of its competitors. Their ability to bet against subprime mortgages during the crisis what set them apart from other companies. The commitment to their principles did in fact ensure the success of the company and its brand.

In addition to the values built into Goldman Sachs's business principles, the brand also derives uniqueness from its understatement. Even though many people are aware of the brand's industry-leading position, it is not because of strenuous promotions. One of the reasons Goldman Sachs has escaped failure during recent economic crises is its ability to be silent and stealthy. Like its simple logo, an excellent illustration of the brand's understated power is the company's headquarters. According to the *New Yorker*, the building is modern but not cutting-edge, it is neither cheap nor extravagant, and it is efficient without being solely functional. It is, like the firm itself, powerful yet inconspicuous and suggests that the success of Goldman Sachs stands on its record and service alone.

BRAND STRATEGY

- In recent years Goldman Sachs has focused on rebuilding its reputation and its commitment to its 14 business principles.
- In 2010 Goldman Sachs launched an advertising campaign designed to educate the public and connect with ordinary people.
- Part of the brand's strategy has been to launch initiatives like *10,000 Women* to help improve the reputation of Goldman Sachs.

In 2010, still trying to overcome the public outcry over the 2008 financial crisis, a large part of Goldman Sachs' brand strategy included ways to rebuild its reputation and to refocus attention on its 14 business principles. To accomplish this, according to the *New York Times*, the company launched a campaign aimed at the general public rather than future clients. Bearing the tagline "progress is everyone's business," this campaign provided people with a better understanding of Goldman Sachs's reliance on its principles and on the kinds of services offered to clients. In 2012 Goldman Sachs tried to promote itself as a brand that is helpful to all people, one that sought to heal those hurt by a sluggish economy rather than take advantage of those who were not financially savvy.

Besides advertising, Goldman Sachs has also started programs that help small businesses as a way to connect better with the general population. To try to combat negative publicity, like a scathing op-ed in the *New York Times* by a retiring Goldman Sachs executive who bashed the company for being greedy, the company needed to realign the reality of its brand with the vision it promoted. Known previously for working with large commercial companies and governments, Goldman Sachs, itself a large company that has continued to flourish in difficult economic times, has lacked a strong connection with small business consumers. To strengthen that connection, Goldman Sachs is extending its services in a way that truly aids in the client's success rather than just the bank's success. According to *Special Events Magazine*, a Goldman Sachs initiative called *10,000 Women* takes small-business owners through several business courses and provides one-on-one mentoring and pro bono legal advice from Goldman Sachs professionals. The program is designed to help women and their small businesses grow, create jobs, build stronger neighborhoods, and, of course, improve the public's perception of Goldman Sachs. This strategy is designed to bring in new clients who appreciate a brand that cares about more than just making money.

BRAND EQUITY

- In 2011 Goldman Sachs continued to lead the financial industry in revenues, mergers and acquisitions, and initial public offerings.
- While Goldman Sachs remains a leader in the banking industry, its brand value has declined because of questions about its reputation and public distrust stemming from its response to the 2008 financial crisis.
- Goldman Sachs planned to regain customers' trust through a series of advertising campaigns, company initiatives, and a focus on its history of successful service.

Goldman Sachs, one of the world's most successful financial institutions, remains in the number-one position globally in initial public offerings and mergers and acquisitions with a 10 percent market share in the Americas and 7.4 percent share in Europe and Asia, according to *Euroweek*. The firm continues to take in noteworthy revenues, US$28.8 billion in 2011, when economic crises continued to affect the global economy. This success has come at a price, however. While Goldman Sachs still appears on most lists of the top global brands, its total brand value has decreased since 2008.

According to Interbrand's 2011 ranking of the top-100 global brands, Goldman Sachs took the number 38 spot, down one spot from 2010, with a brand value of US$9.09 billion. Brand Finance's "Banking 500 2012" report showed Goldman Sachs's fall to be greater. Brand Finance estimated that the value of the brand declined 30 percent, from a 2011 value of US$13.4 billion to a 2012 value of US$9.3 billion. This places the firm's brand value behind that of competitors J.P. Morgan and Bank of America. The decline occurred for several reasons: first, bad press from the 2008 financial crisis brought Goldman Sachs under strict scrutiny; moreover, the firm's enormous profits at a time when many other businesses were failing and its connections to the federal government fueled public distrust; and, finally, the negative attention Goldman Sachs received from the Occupy Wallstreet movement deepened the public's distrust. In response, Goldman Sachs launched a national advertising campaign designed to strengthen its original, iconic brand image. With a recovering economy, its successful track record, and a renewed focus on trust, the brand hopes to return to its former glory in the future.

BRAND AWARENESS

- Goldman Sachs is recognized as a successful firm that offers a complete selection of financial services prepared by highly skilled employees.
- Goldman Sachs's ethics have been called into question since the 2008 financial crisis, resulting in declines in both brand value and public opinion of the brand.
- While the public's trust in Goldman Sachs is low, the firm's high revenues and leading global position call into question the fiscal impact of public opinion.

Goldman Sachs is easily identifiable as one of the world's most successful financial brands. It generates large revenues, offers generous returns to clients, and assumes only a responsible amount of risk. Since the 2008 financial crisis, however, the manner in which the firm achieved its success has been called into question. Even though criticism of Goldman Sachs runs the gamut from a description of the company as a "blood sucking squid" published in *Rolling Stone* to *Barron's* labeling of the company as the "exemplar of Wall Street's hamstrung, postcrisis fate," there is a general consensus that the firm did not survive the banking crisis without resorting to some questionable behavior. In fact the brand's awareness, which is top-of-mind to most, may come, in part, due to the negative publicity that the firm has received of late.

While Goldman Sachs's brand value definitely suffered because of doubts about the company's ethical conduct, how much that matters remains a topic of debate as revenues and general success still place the brand at the top of industry rankings. According to *Marketing Week*, "Goldman was found to be behaving in direct opposition to its stated brand values ... but suffered almost no reputational repercussions of any kind. The employees involved kept their high salaried jobs, the CEO defended their actions in front of Congress, and Goldman ended the year with profits of US$5.2 billion." As the numbers suggest, the awareness of the brand, whether based upon positive or negative recall, has led to overwhelming success—success that seems to undermine the public's dissatisfaction with the brand and the banking industry in general.

BRAND OUTLOOK

- Goldman Sachs continues to rebuild its reputation with better initiatives, more transparent marketing, and a reaffirmation of its 14 business principles.
- Goldman Sachs should rebound over the next few years as the global economy and client activity levels improve.
- With weaker competitors leaving the business, Goldman Sachs is in position to take a larger percentage of the market share.

Even though Goldman Sachs has lost value both in terms of its brand image and its revenues because of its part in the 2008 global crisis, 2012 and beyond look brighter. With a focus on better initiatives, a reaffirmation of its 14 business principles, and a more transparent marketing approach, Goldman Sachs hopes to recover its reputation.

With the global economy slowly rebounding and client activity slowly increasing, Goldman Sachs may begin to see an upswing in its business as well. According to *Barron's*, "the negative perception of Goldman is far more dour than the reality justifies. The company maintains an abiding leadership position in most of its activities, and is financially sturdier ... than it was a half-decade ago. Based on the likely outlook for capital-markets activity and Goldman's ability to continue growing its book value, it is easy to conclude that the shares could rise at least 25% within a year." Moreover, if weaker competitors (those who cannot compete with Goldman's global reach and full range of service) exit the business as anticipated, the firm will also see an increase in market share by the end of 2013.

FURTHER READING

Brand Finance. "Banking 500 2012." *Brandirectory*, 2012. Accessed September 26, 2012. http://brandfinance.com/images/upload/best_global_banking_brands_2012_dp.pdf.

Goldberger, Paul. "Shadow Building." *New Yorker*, May 17, 2010.

Goldman Sachs Group, Inc. *2011 Annual Report*. Accessed September 27, 2012. http://www.goldmansachs.com/investor-relations/financials/current/annual-reports/2011-annual-report.html.

"Goldman Sachs Small-Business Program Helps Event Planner Grow Her Company." *Special Events Magazine*, May 8, 2012. *General OneFile*. Accessed September 28, 2012. http://go.galegroup.com/ps/i.do?id=GALE%7CA289044249&v=2.1&u=itsbtrial&it=r&p=GPS&sw=w.

Kaplan, Thomas. "Goldman Tries Image Rehab through Advertising." *New York Times*, September 30, 2010.

"Mark Ritson on Branding: Goldman's Is an Unwitting Exemplar." *Marketing*, March 26, 2008.

"Mergers & Acquisitions Revenue: Asia Pacific 2011." *Euroweek*, January 27, 2012.

Santoli, Michael. "Built to Win." *Barron's*, September 29, 2012.

"2011 Ranking of the Top 100 Brands." Interbrand. Accessed September 7, 2012. http://www.interbrand.com/en/best-global-brands/best-global-brands-2008/best-global-brands-2011.aspx.

"Who Cares about Brand Reputation?" *Marketing Week*, November 10, 2011.

GOOGLE

AT A GLANCE

Brand Synopsis: One of the world's most valuable brands, Google provides the world's most popular search engine and has diversified into manufacturing and retail.
Parent Company: Google, Inc.
1600 Amphitheatre Parkway
Mountain View, California 94043
United States
http://www.google.com
Sector: Information Technology
Industry Group: Software & Services
Performance: *Market share*—88.8 percent worldwide (2013); 86.3 percent in the United States (2013). *Sales*—US$37.9 billion (2011).
Principal Competitors: Baidu, Inc.; Facebook, Inc.; Microsoft Corporation; Yahoo! Inc.

BRAND ORIGINS

- Google was founded by Stanford graduate students Larry Page and Sergei Brin in 1998.
- Google rapidly became the leading brand of search engine.
- Google has introduced many innovative, branded services, helping to reshape the information economy.

In the mid-1990s Sergey Brin and Larry Page, graduate students in computer science at Stanford University, began working on a new kind of search engine that ranked websites by the number of links to them in order to more effectively find information in the rapidly expanding World Wide Web. Brin and Page left school to devote themselves to their business, which took the name "Google" as a pun on the fanciful term "googol," referring to the number 10 to the 100th power. In 1998 Google, Inc., was incorporated in Menlo Park, California. The company moved to Palo Alto in February 1999, and that June it secured US$25 million in equity funding from two leading venture capital firms. The rapidly growing company soon moved yet again, to Mountain View, setting up a headquarters which it dubbed the Googleplex.

Glowing press reviews and word-of-mouth praise boosted the Google brand. In addition to licensing its web searching to AOL/Netscape and other leading websites, Google developed an advertising program targeted to particular keywords, as well as AdWords, a self-service advertising program for small businesses. In May 2001 Google appointed Dr. Eric E. Schmidt as chair of the board and later as CEO. Google's IPO in August 2004 raised US$16.7 billion. Google's ambitions spread beyond conventional web searching, as a wide array of Google brand extensions were launched. In 2004 the company began offering the free Gmail service and Google SMS mobile message service. February 2005 saw the rollout of Google Maps and Google Earth, which offered unprecedented geographical detail to web users. The purchase of YouTube in 2006 added the Internet's largest video library to Google's arsenal.

Now one of the world's most valuable corporations, Google was stirring controversy with its expanding reach. For example, its Google Books initiative to scan and share public domain books was criticized for violating copyright laws. Google expanded its platform of services, first introducing in September 2008 the Chrome webbrowser, which took on Microsoft's Internet Explorer, and then the Android mobile operating system, which challenged Apple's iPhone. With huge cash reserves on hand, Google bought up dozens of innovative firms, nearly 60 in 2011 alone. Though its reputation has been somewhat tarnished, Google is still widely identified with free access to information.

BRAND ELEMENTS

- The name "Google" was a punning variation on "googol," which represents a very large number.
- The simple and colorful Google logo has changed little since its introduction.
- Google's "Doodles" playfully celebrate holidays, birthdays, and special events.

Cofounder Larry Page coined the name "Google" as a variation on the word "googol," which represents the number 10 to the 100th power. The name symbolizes Google's ambition to make available vast amounts of information, and yet sounds playful as well. Page's partner Sergey Brin designed the Google logo, with large, bold letters in primary colors against a plain white background. It has remained little changed since its introduction in 1998. Google spokesperson Cindy McCaffrey explained to BrandChannel in 2001, "With its colorful rounded edges, it's approachable and friendly but also serious about what it does."

The basic Google search page includes a search box and two buttons titled "Google search" and "I'm Feeling Lucky." The trademarked "I'm Feeling Lucky" button brings up Google's highest-ranked response to the search query. The phrase "Powered by Google" appears on numerous websites that license Google's search engine. Another distinctive feature of the Google brand is the "Doodles," a series of fancifully reworked Google logos that commemorate national holidays, birthdays of renowned persons, and sporting events like the FIFA World Cup and the Olympics.

BRAND IDENTITY

- Google's search engine developed a plain, no-nonsense image.
- Yahoo! and Microsoft's Bing have become Google's chief competitors.
- Google faces pressure to provide information to government investigators.
- Google closed its Chinese site in 2010 to avoid cooperating with government censorship.

Google staked out the identity of being the fastest, most comprehensive search engine for serious users, with no bells and whistles. Google was not the first popular, branded search engine; in the early days of the web, Yahoo!, AltaVista, Lycos, GoTo.com, and Northern Lights loomed large. The Google home page presented users with a mostly blank screen and one search box, whereas competing search providers loaded their home pages with e-mail, topic boards, banner ads, and other features that distracted users and slowed down searches. However, the Google search engine did not stand for all work and no play: it incorporated fun elements, such as the "Doodles," playfully decorated logos that celebrate holidays and other significant events.

Yahoo! and Microsoft emerged as Google's chief rivals. Microsoft belatedly launched its first search engine, MSN Search, in 2005 but made little headway despite extensive advertising. Yahoo! successfully resisted Microsoft's 2008 bid to purchase it in order to create a strong competitor to Google. In 2009 Microsoft rolled out the Bing search engine. Unable to match Google's emotional connection with consumers, Microsoft's campaign hinted that searching was not helping consumers as effectively as it could. Meanwhile, Google directly challenged Microsoft's dominant Office Suite with Google Apps, in which programs and data are stored outside of users' computers in the "cloud."

The word "Google" soon became a synonym for Internet search, as Internet users and also reporters referred to "googling" information on the web. Adopting the informal motto "Don't Be Evil," Google traded on its image as a creative and ethically motivated company. Google found that image hard to maintain, at times, as it became a lightning rod for criticism about the Internet's expanding role in society and the company's drive to reorganize large sectors of the economy. However, Google could take comfort from the fact that many of its competitors (such as Microsoft and Facebook) faced intense attacks along similar lines.

On one hand, the brand image of Google is dependent upon public trust in the impartiality of search information and the privacy of user data. On the other hand, the company seeks to maximize advertising revenue, raising suspicions about manipulation of search results, and it has faced pressure from governments to cooperate with requests for information about searches and users, ostensibly to help combat terrorism and Internet pornography. In 2006 Google scored a partial victory in U.S. federal court against the Justice Department's request for a complete database of user searches for one week, but official pressure continued. At the same time Google set up a Chinese portal that submitted to government censorship. Not only did Google sully its reputation, but it made little headway against established domestic Chinese search firms, especially the dominant Baidu.com. The company's decision to close down its Chinese portal in March 2010 won widespread approval in the West, at the price of a shrinking share for Google in a booming market.

BRAND STRATEGY

- Google's prosperity relies on its brand image.
- In its early years, Google conducted no advertising campaigns, but then it switched and became a major advertiser.
- Google has launched many brand extensions, with varying success.
- The Google+ social network is growing, but its long-term influence remains uncertain.

Scarcely a decade after its founding, Google had become one of the world's most valuable corporations while relying almost solely on its brand image. This is particularly remarkable because Google seemed to make little conscious effort to develop its brand. Cofounders Larry Page and Sergey Brin trusted that the Google search engine would succeed by giving the fastest, most comprehensive results. Page and Brin relied on media publicity and word-of-mouth praise among users to grow the brand. The rags-to-riches legend of Google being started by a couple of students in a garage also appealed to many consumers and journalists. Tales of life in the luxurious yet quirky environment of the Googleplex, the company's headquarters in Menlo Park, California, further tickled the public's fancy.

For several years Google conducted no systematic advertising campaigns on its own behalf. However, in 2007 Google established an in-house advertising agency, Google Creative Lab, and began ramping up its ad spending tremendously, developing its first billboard and TV advertising. This advertising was devoted mainly to promoting brand extensions such as Google Maps and the Google Chrome browser, rather than to promoting the Google search engine itself. By 2010 Google had even purchased a commercial during the Super Bowl, the most expensive and widely watched American advertising platform.

With huge reserves of cash accumulated from its dominance of search-based advertising, Google launched an ambitious series of brand extensions, most of them related to the core brand identity of providing people with information of all kinds. Some of these extensions became category leaders: for example, Google Earth and Google Maps attracted millions of users by showing large swaths of the earth in unprecedented detail. However, many other extensions struggled or failed. A series of unsuccessful attempts to develop social media platforms culminated in Google Buzz, which at its launch in February 2010 automatically publicized members' e-mail links, drawing unwelcome attention from users and government regulators. The following year saw the introduction of Google+, a kind of social layer covering a variety of services, giving Google access to more personalized information about users than it could acquire from searches alone. By December 2012 Google+ claimed over 500 million members and 135 million active participants. Although many celebrities and leading corporations had accounts, Google+ was still struggling to match the momentum of Facebook, Twitter, or the upstart Pinterest. Google TV was also a disappointment after its launch in October 2010, because it lacked sufficient access to network shows, and users complained that the service was difficult to set up.

BRAND EQUITY

- Interbrand ranked Google as the world's fourth-most-valuable brand in 2012.
- Google ranks among the world's most reputable companies, according to the Reputation Institute.
- Google has a dominant share of searches worldwide, except in East Asia and Russia.

According to Interbrand's *Best Global Brands 2012* report, Google ranked fourth in the world with a brand value of US$69.7 billion, up 26 percent from 2011, and it ranked a close second behind Apple in the technology sector. Meanwhile *Forbes* ranked Google as the world's fifth-most-powerful brand, with a value of US$37.6 billion and brand revenue of US$36.5 billion. Google ranked seventh in consumer perception. In addition, according to the Global RepTrak survey by the Reputation Institute, Google ranked as the world's most reputable company in 2010 and 2011, before falling to sixth in 2012 while still remaining close behind leader BMW.

According to Internet consulting firm Karma Snack, Google enjoyed a global search-engine share of 88.8 percent as of January 2013, and an 86.3 percent share in the United States. Meanwhile, according to comScore, in November 2012 Google searches accounted for a record-high 67 percent of U.S. search traffic, based on measuring explicit core searches (a metric that requires intent to search by the user). Google was well ahead of Microsoft searches and Yahoo searches, with their 16.2 percent and 12.1 percent shares, respectively. Google is actually less dominant in the United States than it is in many international markets, particularly in Europe and South America, where its measured share is often over 90 percent. However, after it stopped supporting its Chinese portal in 2010, Google would fall to fourth place in China, according to CNZZ, with a 4.72 percent share as of October 2012, trailing Baidu with its 72.97 percent share. Yahoo! still has a majority share in Japan and Taiwan, while the South Korean market is dominated by domestic search engines Naver and Daum. In Russia, Google continues to trail domestic search engine Yandex.

BRAND AWARENESS

- Google became one of the world's most popular brands within a few years after its launch.
- The name Google has become nearly synonymous with web search.
- Google enjoys widespread familiarity and strong emotional connection in most Western markets.

Google became one of the world's most popular and trusted brands with remarkable speed. By 2003, just five years after the brand's launch, an Interbrand survey ranked Google as international "brand of the year," and the Brand Keys Customer Loyalty Index cited Google as the second-most-trusted brand among consumers. Google has come to enjoy nearly universal brand awareness in most Western markets, the name often serving as a synonym for web search. For example, according to a Harris Interactive survey of consumers in the United Kingdom conducted in May 2012, 97 percent of respondents stated that they were at least "somewhat familiar" with Google, and 77 percent actually used Google. Google also enjoyed a strong emotional connection, with 20 percent of respondents stating that they "love this brand" and another 49 percent that they "like" it. Google garnered the strongest "Brand Buzz," with 45 percent of respondents stating that the brand is either "ahead/really going places" or "somewhat ahead of the game."

BRAND OUTLOOK

- The Google brand is diversifying into manufacturing and retail.
- Google campaigns in favor of the free flow of information over the Internet.
- Privacy concerns threaten Google's image.
- Google is set to remain the leading international brand in Internet search.

The Google brand is set to continue extending its dominance to the mobile sector, and it also looks to diversify further into manufacturing and retail with the introduction of Chromebooks laptop computers and the opening of the first temporary Google store in London in September 2011. Google continues actively campaigning for the free flow of information. It joined the Open Internet Coalition, advocated "net neutrality," and attacked the proposed Stop Online Piracy Act in the United States in late 2011 and threats of tighter control over the Internet by the United Nations. Google further identified the brand with global citizenship by giving its first Global Impact Awards in December 2012, providing US$23 million to seven enterprises that were using cutting-edge technology to attack major social crises.

Accusations that Google manipulated browser protocols to enable secret tracking of searches and the January 2012 announcement of impending changes to Google's privacy settings to require data sharing across all Google services have shaken many consumers' confidence in the privacy of their searches. Privacy-oriented search engines such as Startpage and DuckDuckGo hope to take advantage of the public's privacy concerns. In another threat to its image, Google came under fire in 2013 in connection with its cell-phone apps store for allegedly giving app sellers the names and email addresses of apps purchasers. Recurring accusations by competitors and consumer activists that Google is abusing its market position pose another threat to the brand. In early 2013 Google settled with the U.S. Federal Trade Commission, agreeing to open specific search features to competing platforms while avoiding any antitrust sanctions. Google still faces scrutiny in the European Union, which has a tradition of tighter regulations on competition and privacy. Google searching is seeing increased competition from social networks, most particularly Facebook's Graph Search, which was introduced in January 2013. Graph Search works through users' social contacts, aiming to spark interactions among friends as well as providing answers. This contrasts with Google's philosophy of providing the strongest search results for all users. Despite these threats, Google's overall international leadership of web search seems secure.

FURTHER READING

"Google, Inc." *International Directory of Company Histories*. Ed. Jay P. Pederson. Vol. 101. Detroit, MI: St. James Press, 2009.

Helft, Miguel, and David Barboza. "Google Shuts China Site in Dispute over Censorship." *New York Times*, March 22, 2010.

Johnson, Bradley. "How Google Became a $2 Billion Global Advertiser." *Advertising Age*, June 25, 2012.

Learmonth, Michael. "As Seen on TV: Why Anti-marketer Google Has Embraced Marketing." *Advertising Age*, November 7, 2011.

Madden, Normandy. "Google Is Clearly King of Search—Except in China: Baidu Commands about 70 percent of Market and US Giants Can't Dent Its Share." *Advertising Age*, January 22, 2007.

Morrissey, Brian, and Mike Shields. "Google: Too Many Moving Parts? How the Search Giant Has Struggled to Expand into Other Businesses." *Adweek*, April 12, 2010.

Newton, Casey. "What Should Google Do about Facebook Graph Search?" CNET, January 18, 2013. Accessed January 19, 2013. http://news.cnet.com/8301-1023_3-57564611-93/what-should-google-do-about-facebook-graph-search/.

Rusch, Robin D. "Google: The Infinite Quest." Brandchannel, August 13, 2001. Accessed February 14, 2013. http://www.brandchannel.com/features_profile.asp?pr_id=30.

Sterling, Greg. "FTC Closes Google Antitrust Case: 'Law Protects Competition Not Competitors,' Says Not Enough Evidence to 'Prove Search Bias.'" *Search Engine Land*, January 3, 2013. Accessed January 10, 2013. http://searchengineland.com/ftc-law-protects-competition-not-competitors-says-not-enough-evidence-to-prove-search-bias-144119.

"2012 Best Global Brands." Interbrand. Accessed January 1, 2013. http://www.interbrand.com/en/best-global-brands/2012/Best-Global-Brands-2012.aspx.

GOYA

AT A GLANCE

Brand Synopsis: Founded in New York in the 1930s, Goya developed into the largest Hispanic-owned food company in the United States by catering to regional Latin American and Caribbean tastes.
Parent Company: Goya Foods Inc.
100 Seaview Drive
Secaucus, New Jersey 07096
United States
http://www.goya.com/english/
Sector: Consumer Staples
Industry Group: Food, Beverage & Tobacco
Performance: *Market share*—12.3 percent of canned beans (except green) in the United States (2011). *Sales*—US$1.26 billion (est., 2008).
Principal Competitors: C&F Foods, Inc.; ConAgra Foods, Inc.; Grupo Jumex S.A. de C.V.; Jugos del Valle S.A. de C.V.; Ruiz Foods, Inc.; Vitarroz Food Inc.

BRAND ORIGINS

- Prudencio Unanue founded Goya Foods in 1936, buying the name from a Spanish company for US$1.00.
- Goya Foods products are sold in both small Hispanic bodegas and large supermarkets.
- Goya Foods is a vertically integrated company, allowing the company to control all aspects of manufacturing, packaging, and distribution.

Goya Foods Inc. was founded in New York City in 1936. Its founder, Prudencio Unanue, had left Spain as a youth in 1902 for Puerto Rico, where he established a small food business. He later moved to the metropolitan New York area and became a food broker for products imported from Spain. When the Spanish Civil War broke out in 1936, food shipments were cut off, and Unanue found himself out of work. He obtained a shipment of Moroccan sardines from a Spanish company and with his wife, Carolina, packaged them in a small Manhattan warehouse, selling to grocery stores. For the sales price of US$1.00, Unanue bought the Goya brand name of the sardines and also gave the Goya name to olives and olive oil that he imported and sold.

Although Unanue formed Unanue, Inc., in Manhattan in 1935, Goya Foods celebrates its anniversary based on the 1936 date Unanue registered the Goya brand and acquired the Seville Packing Company. The immediate precursor of Goya Foods was Unanue & Sons, Inc., formed in 1946. It was renamed Goya Foods Inc. in 1961.

Business picked up dramatically with the heavy influx of Puerto Ricans to New York City in the years immediately after World War II. Unanue established two canneries in Bayamon, Puerto Rico, to produce the foods the newcomers could not buy in supermarkets, such as beef-tripe stew, tropical juices, *pasteles* (meat-filled pasties), *gandules* (pigeon peas), and some 25 varieties of beans. Goya salesmen went to the small Puerto Rican-owned grocery stores called bodegas to take orders for these goods.

Vertically integrated Goya had its own fleet of trucks, offering retailers direct, next-day delivery from the warehouses. Its sales representatives dealt directly with the retailers rather than through wholesalers or brokers, making weekly visits to all its accounts and selling Goya's goods to the smallest bodegas at the same prices it did to supermarkets.

By 1969 Goya Foods was selling to food stores in the Midwest as well as along the East Coast from Boston to Miami, servicing thousands of accounts through Spanish-speaking salespeople. The company's main packaging facilities were in Brooklyn. The largest U.S. distributor of Latin foods, Goya estimated that 80 percent of its customers were ethnic Puerto Ricans or Cubans. In addition, Latin American migration northward was on the rise, swelling Goya's potential customer base.

BRAND ELEMENTS

- Goya formed its own advertising agency, Inter-Americas Advertising, to promote the company's products.
- Goya advertises its products in both Spanish and English.
- The navy blue label of its logo and the tagline "If it's Goya, it has to be good," have become synonymous with Goya Foods.

According to one of the founder's grandsons, other companies were selling foods to New York's Hispanics, but "the one thing that [Goya] did that was different was advertise, something unheard of in the '50s." Because management could not find an advertising agency suitable to the company's needs, Goya formed its own: Inter-Americas Advertising.

Goya also began an English-language television campaign intended to raise its market share by titillating the palates of non-Hispanic Americans. In one ad Hispanics touted kidney beans and black-eyed peas to Anglo friends. A new push in 1984, emphasizing foods that were both healthy and inexpensive, was aimed partly at the children and grandchildren of Hispanic immigrants. Much of Goya advertising was intended to evoke nostalgia and a desire to fulfill longings through food.

In the 21st century Goya advertising includes television and radio promotions as well as print ads in both English and Spanish. Goya also advertises on a variety of food-oriented websites and promotes its products through integrated sweepstakes and sponsorships. Advertising also helps to drive consumers to the company's website, which features authentic Latino recipes, coupons, product information, nutritional information, chef videos, and the Goya eStore, with online shopping.

In an effort to reach out to non-Hispanic customers, Goya recast its labels in 1997 to include the English as well as Spanish name of each product on the front, instead of the back, as had been done previously. The change also was an acknowledgment that Hispanics in the United States were becoming more assimilated, citing a survey that showed 35 percent considered themselves primarily English speakers.

The design of the company logo was tweaked around 1998. The distinctive, rounded font was retained, but the Goya name was moved onto a blue rectangle with a yellow border on the bottom. Marketing campaigns over the years have included the slogans "Goya oh boy-a!" in the 1970s and "Go Goya." The iconic tagline, "If it's Goya, it has to be good," is said to have been written by the company's founder. Both the tagline and the navy blue label have become synonymous with the brand and can evoke instant nostalgia in both Latinos and Anglos alike.

BRAND IDENTITY

- Goya Foods is the largest Hispanic-owned food company in the United States.
- Goya is the first Hispanic company to have an exhibition at the Smithsonian's National Museum of American History.
- Goya is active in Hispanic neighborhoods through sponsorships of community celebrations, festivals, and sports teams, as well as food donations to charities and relief agencies.

As the largest Hispanic-owned food company in the United States, Goya Foods recognizes that for many Latin cultures, food is a representation of ethnic identity, each with its own tastes and traditions. Goya understands how food and family intersect in the lives of its customers, earning the company a global reputation as a trusted and respected brand.

Goya began welcoming Hispanic immigrants to the United States with foods and flavors from their homelands more than 75 years ago. The company has reached out to succeeding generations by introducing new flavors and cooking options that are consistent with their heritage. Goya Foods provides consumers across the United States, the Caribbean, and Europe with a range of authentic Latin foods adapted to the regional variations in Hispanic tastes and preferences.

Goya's place as a cultural icon crystallized in 1999 when the Smithsonian's National Museum of American History launched the Goya Foods Inc. Collection, documenting the history of the company from its founding in the 1930s to the present. The Goya Collection allows patrons to learn not only about the growth of a Latino-owned business but to see how Latino culture has enriched American history.

In 2012 Goya joined with U.S. First Lady Michelle Obama in an initiative called MiPlato, the Spanish-language version of MyPlate, a nutrition guideline published by the U.S. Department of Agriculture. Together with Mrs. Obama's Let's Move! fitness campaign, MiPlato aims to curb obesity and improve health within the Hispanic community.

Goya Foods has been active in community service and support throughout its history. The company has donated hundreds of thousands of pounds of food and meals to aid victims of hurricanes, floods, and earthquakes, as well as to food-relief charities. Goya also sponsors a myriad of scholarships, sports teams, parades, festivals, and dance and theater troupes in Hispanic communities.

BRAND STRATEGY

- Goya became a bestseller among immigrants from Puerto Rico and the Dominican Republic with Caribbean-oriented products ranging from preserves and soups to red-palm oil, mango paste, and specialty beverages.
- Early Goya sales representatives continually updated information about the ethnic mix of neighborhoods to better serve their customers' regional taste preferences.
- Goya Foods sells over 1,500 different products, with manufacturing and distribution centers in the United States, Puerto Rico, the Dominican Republic, and Spain.

Goya used personalized customer service and technology to develop and maintain loyalty among the retailers that carried its products. Goya's early salesmen, always clad in suits and ties, carried pocket-sized computers to feed orders into the company's data-processing system. In addition, the sales force updated the company on a community's ethnic composition, so that Goya could match its product offerings to changing immigrant tastes.

Goya became a bestseller among immigrants from Puerto Rico and the Dominican Republic with Caribbean-oriented products ranging from preserves, stews, and soups to more specialized items including African red-palm oil, Cuban mango paste, Jamaican ginger beer, and malta—a nonalcoholic, noncarbonated licorice tasting beverage composed of grain, malt, and hops.

For the rapidly growing Colombian community, Goya added soda crackers and a block chocolate used in making hot beverages. Frozen products included *empanadillas* (beef-filled turnovers), *rellenos de papas* (potato balls stuffed with spices and meat), tamales, squid, codfish croquettes, paella, and tropical vegetables such as pigeon peas, yautia, and yucca. Nectar drinks and a line of frozen cocktail mixes were crossover items aimed at Anglos as well as Hispanics. Soon, *tostones* (fried green plantains) from Honduras, *nopalitos* (sliced cactus) from Mexico, and *harina pan,* a Venezuelan corn flour used to make *arepas,* somewhat similar to English muffins, were all a part of the Goya product line.

Beans reflected the company's multinational product mix. Cubans, Mexicans, and Nicaraguans called them *frijoles,* but in Puerto Rico and the Dominican Republic they were *habichuelas,* and in Argentina, Paraguay, and Uruguay they were called *porotos.* Cubans in Miami wanted black beans, dry in 14-ounce packages. Puerto Ricans in New York preferred pink beans in water-packed cans. Nicaraguans looked for red beans. Mexicans, who wanted their beans refried, bought dry beans in sacks of four or 10 pounds.

Today Goya Foods sells over 1,500 different products, with manufacturing and distribution centers in the United States, Puerto Rico, the Dominican Republic, and Spain. Food lines encompass a wide variety of products, divided into categories of beans (over 38 varieties), rice, condiments, beverages, frozen foods, reduced-sodium, and organic. Goya regional specialties include foods from the Caribbean, Mexico, and Central and South America. Goya also offers a wide range of Latin pantry staples, including flours, pastas, snacks, cookies, chocolates, cooking oils, and tomatoes. Canned staples include yucca, tuna, seafood, vegetables, fruits, meats, and artichoke hearts.

BRAND EQUITY

- *Forbes* estimated Goya's revenues at US$1.26 billion, placing the company third on its list of "America's Largest Private Diversified Food Companies."
- Goya Foods held a 12.3 percent market share of canned beans (except green) in 2011.
- A broad array of Goya food products earned top spots in rankings for best brands, including beans, seasonings, marinades, and olive oil.

Goya Foods is the largest Hispanic-owned food company in the United States. A privately held company, it does not disclose financial information to the public. In 2007 *Forbes* ranked Goya third on its list of "America's Largest Private Diversified Food Companies," with estimated revenues of US$1.26 billion. In 2008 *Forbes* placed Goya at number 377 of "America's Largest Private Companies" with revenues of US$1.26 billion.

Malta Goya was ranked fifth of the top brands of nonalcoholic beer in 2001, 2002, and 2003 and sixth in 2006. In 2010 Goya was ranked sixth of top Mexican food items, with a 3.34 percent market share. In 2011 Goya held a 12.3 percent market share of canned beans (except green), trailing only Bush's Best beans. In the 2012 Harris Poll EquiTrend study, Goya Coco Water was named the "Coconut Water Brand of the Year."

Between 2010 and 2012, Goya Foods consistently had products placed in the top rankings for seasoning brands, dry dinner brands, bouillon, broth, or stock brands, top meat sauce or marinades, top olive oil brands, frozen soup brands, frozen fruit brands, plain frozen vegetables, rice brands, top frozen bread or pastry, and top bean brands.

BRAND AWARENESS

- Goya enjoys high brand awareness among consumers of prepared Hispanic foods.
- Marketing surveys ranked Goya the top brand in Puerto Rico for the years 2008 through 2012.
- Goya brand awareness is bolstered by its memorable slogan, "Si es Goya, tiene que ser bueno," or "If it's Goya, it has to be good."

With its decades of history and reputation for authenticity, Goya enjoys high brand awareness among consumers of Hispanic foods in the United States. Larry Lucas and Jorge Aguilar of *Brandchannel.com* wrote in 2009 that "When you think about prepared Hispanic foods, Goya is the brand that most likely comes to mind." Among Hispanic consumers outside the United States, Goya has also developed high brand awareness. According to a survey conducted by the Sales and Marketing Executive Association (SME), Goya was the top food brand in Puerto Rico in 2012. In the SME survey, Goya was the top choice in such categories as the brand that works the most for Puerto Rico in terms of social responsibility, the brand that best represents Puerto Rico, the most loved brand, the most prestigious brand, and the brand that gives the most value for the money. The SME also found that the most memorable slogan and jingle in survey participants' minds is Goya's, "Si es Goya, tiene que ser bueno," or "If it's Goya, it has to be good." Goya has been the top brand in Puerto Rico since 2008.

BRAND OUTLOOK

- Goya bases its product offerings on the belief that people want to eat authentic, great tasting food.
- Goya increased offerings of foods from Central and South America as demographics changed in its core communities and consumers became more adventurous in the kitchen.
- Company salespeople continually assess the ethnic mix of the neighborhoods they serve, allowing the company to tailor product offerings to regional tastes.

Goya Foods believes that today's marketplace is not much different from that of 50 years ago; people still want to eat authentic, great tasting food. What has changed, however, is that people live in a more complex and busy world. Goya addresses this lifestyle change through its lines of frozen products and heat-and-serve offerings that can be prepared with limited time. Additionally, Goya launches hundreds of new products each year to cater to changing tastes and health concerns, such as low-sodium beans and seasoning blends.

Goya increases its position in the marketplace by responding to food trends among consumers. For example, it increased offerings of foods from countries in Central and South America as demographics changed in its core communities and as Anglo consumers became more adventurous in the kitchen. Goya's wide variety of products gives the company a unique position to help customers explore new foods. The broad scope of Latin American cuisine represented in Goya's product line ensures that the company remains stable through changing food trends.

A burgeoning Hispanic population in the United States in the 21st century will continue to expand Goya's consumer base. Other mainstream food companies have begun to launch their own lines of Hispanic foods, but Goya's position as the dominant market leader should hold steady. The company's focus on authenticity and quality has allowed it to build a loyal following among immigrants and succeeding generations. Additionally, Goya salespeople continually assess the ethnic mix of the neighborhoods they serve, allowing the company to tailor product offerings to specific regional tastes and changing lifestyle trends.

FURTHER READING

De Lollis, Barbara. "CEO Profile: At Goya, It's All in la Familia." *USA Today,* March 24, 2008. Accessed January 18, 2013. http://usatoday30.usatoday.com/money/companies/management/2008-03-23-bob-unanue-goya-foods_N.htm.

"First Lady Michelle Obama Joins Goya Foods in Announcing 'Mi Plato' Resources for Families." The White House, January 26, 2012. Accessed January 18, 2013. http://www.whitehouse.gov/the-press-office/2012/01/26/first-lady-michelle-obama-joins-goya-foods-announcing-mi-plato-resources.

"Goya Foods: 75 Years of Providing Latino Food Staples to Hispanic Families across the Country." *Huffington Post,* May 16, 2012. Accessed January 18, 2013. http://www.huffingtonpost.com/2012/05/16/goya-foods_n_1520703.html.

"Goya Sponsoring New York Yankees." *Progressive Grocer,* April 16, 2007. Accessed January 18, 2013. http://www.progressivegrocer.com/top-stories/headlines/industry-intelligence/id16662/goya-sponsoring-new-york-yankees.

Halasz, Robert, and Frederick C. Ingram. "Goya Foods Inc." *International Directory of Company Histories.* Ed. Jay P. Pederson. Vol. 91. Detroit, MI: St. James Press, 2008.

Lucas, Larry, and Jorge Aguilar. "Goya Is Big, But Not Great (Yet)." *Brandchannel.com,* February 16, 2009. Accessed February 8, 2013. http://www.brandchannel.com/brand_speak.asp?bs_id=212

Martí, José Ricardo. "Goya Holds Spot as Top-Ranked Brand." *Caribbean Business,* June 27, 2012. Accessed January 18, 2013. http://www.caribbeanbusinesspr.com/news03.php?nt_id=73382&ct_id=1.

Vega, Tanzina. "Goya Aims to Expand the Neighborhood." *New York Times,* September 23, 2012. Accessed January 18, 2013. http://www.nytimes.com/2010/09/24/business/media/24adco.html?_r=0.

GREEN MOUNTAIN COFFEE

AT A GLANCE

Brand Synopsis: Through the years, Green Mountain has maintained that its goals of providing rich, high-quality coffee and creating positive and sustainable changes for both people and the environment are inseparable.
Parent Company: Green Mountain Coffee Roasters, Inc.
33 Coffee Lane
Waterbury, Vermont 05676
United States
http://www.greenmountaincoffee.com
Sector: Consumer Staples
Industry Group: Food, Beverage & Tobacco
Performance: *Market share*—1.9 percent share of the U.S. whole-bean coffee market (2011). *Sales*—US$2.7 billion (2011).
Principal Competitors: Starbucks Corporation; Kraft Foods; The Folgers Coffee Company; Sara Lee Food and Beverage

BRAND ORIGINS

- Robert Stiller bought Green Mountain Coffee with profits earned through the sale of a company that made rolling papers for cigarettes.
- Green Mountain Coffee makes its specialty coffees using high-end arabica beans rather than the lower-quality robusta beans.
- Green Mountain broadened its customer base through placements in gas stations, supermarkets, and high-end restaurants, eventually expanding into workplaces throughout the United States.

In 1971 Green Mountain's founder Robert Stiller helped launch E-Z Wider, a maker of rolling papers for cigarettes. E-Z Wider offered smokers wider papers so that they would not have to lick and splice two papers together to make larger cigarettes. As the 1970s came to a close, Stiller and his partner Burton Rubin sold the company to English tobacconist Rizla for US$6.2 million. Stiller's venture into the coffee business began when he was vacationing at a Vermont ski resort and found a cup of Green Mountain coffee so good that he eventually bought the small company that produced the coffee. At the time, Green Mountain was a modest specialty coffee store (established in 1981) that sold to the public and a few restaurants. Stiller bought out the owners of Green Mountain for US$200,000. Stiller served as the company's president and CEO until 2007, when he retired and was succeeded by Lawrence Blanford.

At the beginning of Stiller's tenure as Green Mountain Coffee's leader, he swiftly discovered that competition in the specialty coffee industry was stiffer than in cigarette papers. Green Mountain struggled for four years, competing at the highest end of the market by producing coffee made from prized arabica beans (versus the lower-quality robusta variety). Although the company made a profit on retail sales, Stiller had a hard time convincing restaurants to pay premium prices for the company's arabica beans.

Free samples, distributed through charitable organizations such as the Kiwanis Club, helped spark demand.

Advertising in gourmet magazines helped build a mail order business. Promotions continued with high-end products like muesli cereal. Stiller convinced a doubtful Mobil convenience store owner to let him sell coffee there, where Green Mountain would compete with a Dunkin' Donuts across the street. Stiller took this partnership to the next level, positioning Green Mountain coffee in Mobil Corporation's 1,000 stores nationwide. Green Mountain also transitioned from selling cups of fresh coffee at a supermarket chain into shelf placement at this time.

With 2,400 wholesale accounts, Green Mountain had sales of approximately US$10 million in 1993. The holding company Green Mountain Coffee Roasters, Inc., was formed and an initial public offering was completed. Green Mountain was now selling 80 varieties of coffee and roasting 25 different types of arabica beans. A partnership with a large New England food service distributor, Jordan's Food Corporation, helped solidify Green Mountain's position among high-end restaurants and institutions.

With a fiercely loyal and expanding customer base, Green Mountain began selling its coffee in supermarkets, Amtrak trains, and the L.L. Bean catalog, and at Weight Watchers International, and on airlines, including Delta Airlines. In 1997 the company signed on as exclusive supplier to The Coffee Station, owner of the largest specialty coffee stores in the United States, and it entered the American workplace through deals with office supplier Staples and Poland Spring Natural Spring Water.

Green Mountain began exporting to Canada and Taiwan in 1994, eventually forming GMCR Canada to oversee operations there. Green Mountain buys its coffee beans from more than 60 countries in Asia, Africa, and South America.

BRAND ELEMENTS

- The slogan "Brewing a Better World" is used by Green Mountain to reflect its dedication to stewardship and corporate responsibility.
- Green Mountain's campaign to educate consumers on the meaning of fair trade certification uses the tagline "Great coffee, good vibes, pass it on."
- The Green Mountain logo features a green oval and white lettering, with a coffee bean replacing the "o" in "Mountain."

In 1997, with a push into catalogs and office break rooms, Green Mountain updated its packaging, using the slogan "Sip and relax—you're on Green Mountain time." Later taglines included "Green Mountain Coffee: A Revelation in Every Cup." Green Mountain also uses "Brewing a Better World" in reference to its dedication to corporate responsibility.

In 2012 Green Mountain launched a new marketing campaign highlighting the relationship the company maintains with coffee bean growers through fair trade certifications. The campaign features the tagline "Great coffee, good vibes, pass it on" and seeks to educate consumers on what it means for coffee to be certified as fair trade. On Green Mountain's Facebook page and on YouTube, videos show several celebrities visiting fair trade coffee farms in Columbia and Sumatra and document first-hand what a fair trade certification means to farmers, their families, and their communities.

The Green Mountain Coffee Roasters logo features a green oval with the company's name centered in white lettering. The "o" in "Mountain" is replaced with a brown coffee bean.

BRAND IDENTITY

- Passionate dedication to social and environmental responsibility has been part of Green Mountain's core values since its inception.
- Like other producers of coffee certified as fair trade, Green Mountain must conform to labor and environmental standards.
- By 2011 Green Mountain had become the largest purchaser of fair trade coffee in the world.

Passionate commitment to both social and environmental responsibilities is at the core of Green Mountain Coffee Roasters' brand identity. Because Green Mountain desires consumers to view the brand as socially and environmentally reliable, it partners with supply-chain communities to improve nutrition, enhance food security, and support environmental programs in regions where Green Mountain buys raw ingredients. The company also supports local communities through grants, in-kind donations of products and equipment, and monetary charitable donations, and the company also works to protect the environment and reduce its environmental footprint in communities where production plants are located. All Green Mountain employees are actively encouraged to donate time to nonprofit and community-based organizations. Green Mountain allocates 5 percent of its pretax profits (about US$15.2 million in 2011) to charitable and nonprofit ventures that are socially and environmentally responsible.

To emphasize the brand's commitment to sustainable practices, Green Mountain partnered with Fair Trade USA to certify portions of its coffee business as fair trade. Producers of fair trade coffee must conform to labor and environmental standards, including sustainable farming practices and minimum prices paid for beans. A premium is added to the base price that reverts back to the farmers and their communities. Green Mountain Coffee is the largest purchaser of fair trade coffee in the world, importing more than 50 million pounds in 2011.

BRAND STRATEGY

- Green Mountain is the exclusive roaster, seller, and distributor of Newman's Own Organics coffee, which is sold in more than 600 McDonald's restaurants.
- Tully's, Van Houtte, and Timothy's World Coffee are all brands acquired by Green Mountain Coffee in the early 21st century.
- In 2006 Green Mountain purchased Keurig, Inc., a manufacturer of single-cup brewing systems that exclusively use coffee packaged in K-Cups.

In 2002 Green Mountain Coffee Roasters signed an agreement to be the exclusive roaster, seller, and distributor of Newman's Own Organics fair trade coffees. By 2006 Newman's Own Organics Blend coffee was sold in more than 600 McDonald's restaurants. In 2009 Green Mountain purchased the Seattle-based Tully's coffee brand and wholesale coffee business as well as the wholesale business of Canada-based Timothy's World Coffee. Green Mountain also bought Diedrich Coffee, owner of Coffee People and Gloria Jean's Coffee, in 2009. Green Mountain acquired the Canadian coffee services company, Van Houtte, in 2010. Tully's, Timothy's World Coffee, and Van Houtte have continued as brands under the Green Mountain umbrella.

In 2006 Green Mountain purchased Keurig, Inc., a manufacturer of brewing systems designed to quickly brew a single cup of coffee, hot chocolate, tea, or other hot beverage. The Keurig system used K-Cups, specialized one-serving cups used exclusively with the Keurig machine. Keurig sells more than 25 owned and nonowned brands and more than 200 varieties of coffee, cocoa, teas, and other hot beverages in its K-Cups, including such brands as Dunkin' Donuts, Folgers, Twinings, Millstone, Newman's Own Organics, Starbucks, Swiss Miss, Gloria Jean's, and Celestial Seasonings. Keurig brewing systems transformed traditional coffee brewing and are widely used in homes, offices, and hotels.

Green Mountain focuses on providing variety for consumers by selling more than 135 varieties of whole-bean and ground coffee, including light roasts, medium and blended roasts, dark roasts, fair trade certified, and organic coffees, as well as hot cocoa and teas. These products are available bagged or in K-Cups for the Keurig brewing systems. Green Mountain also sells coffees through its website, as well as various Internet retailers and wholesale customers. Keurig brewing machines and K-Cups are widely available through stores and Internet retailers, including Amazon, Walmart, Costco, Target, Macy's, and various supermarket chains.

BRAND EQUITY

- Green Mountain Coffee was ranked 361st on Fortune's Global 500 list, with a brand value of US$3.1 billion.
- In 2011 Green Mountain held roughly a 2 percent share of the markets in whole-bean coffees, ground coffees, and bagged teas.
- In 2012 Green Mountain-owned Keurig was ranked second among breakaway brands, behind only Facebook.

Green Mountain Coffee Roasters made its debut on *Fortune*'s Global 500 list in 2012, ranked 361st with a brand value of US$3.1 billion. Green Mountain also ranked ninth in the World's Most Valuable Beverage Brands list of 2011, the only coffee brand in the top 10.

In 2011 Green Mountain held a 1.9 percent share of the whole-bean coffee market, a 2.9 percent share of the ground coffee market, and a 1.2 percent share of the market in bagged tea. In 2008 Green Mountain held a 3 percent share of the specialty coffee market. In 2012 Green Mountain-owned Keurig was ranked second among breakaway brands, or brands that show the greatest increase in brand strength.

BRAND AWARENESS

- Green Mountain Coffee was named the coffee brand of the year in 2012, having beaten out Starbucks, Folgers, and Dunkin' Donuts for the honor.
- Green Mountain's Keurig division held a 76.6 percent share of the market for single-cup coffee makers in 2011.
- Sales of Keurig brewing systems contributed to a 63 percent surge in Green Mountain's revenues between 2009 and 2012.

Coffee is the second-most widely traded commodity in the world. The United States is the largest consumer of coffee: Americans drink 400 million cups of coffee per day, or about 146 billion cups of coffee annually. Coffee represents 75 percent of all caffeine consumed in the United States.

A 2012 Harris Poll EquiTrend study crowned Green Mountain Coffee as the coffee brand of the year, ahead of such brands as Starbucks, Dunkin' Donuts, Eight O'Clock, Folgers, and Seattle's Best. The Harris Poll also named Keurig the brand of the year in its "coffee maker" category.

In 2010 *CNN Money* ranked Green Mountain the second fastest-growing company, citing the Keurig brewing system as the reason revenues at Green Mountain had surged 63 percent since 2009. Green Mountain shipped more than one billion K-Cups in 2008, and K-Cups were ranked eighth among the top new food products of 2010, with sales of US$62 million. Virtually unchallenged, Green Mountain held a 76.6 percent share of the market for single-cup coffee makers with its Keurig brewing systems in 2011.

Green Mountain has about 2 million Facebook fans and is ranked 99th in the *Internet Retailer Top 500 Guide*. Green Mountain endeavors to engage its online consumers with its brand by publishing daily content and by offering promotions, such as free samples, and a range of sweepstakes. Most of the company's customer service has migrated from call centers to social networking sites. Customer feedback on Facebook has also helped drive marketing decisions within the company.

BRAND OUTLOOK

- Patents protecting the Keurig single-cup brewing systems expired in 2012, leaving the company vulnerable to competition.
- Keurig has introduced a new brewing system that uses recyclable Vue Packs and is working on an espresso-based brewing platform.
- Green Mountain strives to educate consumers on what it means to buy fair trade coffee, believing that consumers are an integral part of the company's mission.

Single-cup coffee brewing was a global market worth US$8 billion in 2011. Green Mountain Coffee Roasters has dominated the market in recent years, with 89 percent of its revenues coming from Keurig, largely because of patents protecting Keurig and the K-Cup containers. In 2012, however, the patents expired, leaving Keurig vulnerable to competition. Seeking to assure investors of its dominance and innovation, Keurig introduced a new brewer that uses Vue Packs, which accept a wider range of mug sizes. Unlike K-Cups, Vue Packs can also be emptied and recycled after use. Green Mountain has also begun working on a new espresso-based brewing platform for a brand extension.

Green Mountain roasts arabica beans from various regions around the world to produce its coffees. Many of these regions are prone to political instability that could threaten the company's supply of beans and lead to the discontinuation or substitution of different coffee types. Such scenarios could also lead to loss of revenue and customer dissatisfaction.

Despite such risks, Green Mountain aspires to highlight its position as a corporate citizen in a global marketplace. Most consumers understand what it means to buy organic, and while Europeans tend to be more knowledgeable of the concept of fair trade, Americans generally have less of an understanding of fair trade's defining properties and impact on the global economy. As it continues to educate consumers in the United States, Green Mountain believes that it will be able to build a demand for sustainable products and thereby expand its sales base.

FURTHER READING

"Coffee, Roasted." *Encyclopedia of Global Industries*. Ed. Lynn M. Pearce. Detroit, MI: Gale, 2013.

"Green Mountain Coffee & Environmental Responsibility." *Sustainable Environmental Technologies*. Accessed November 30, 2012. http://www.dutchsustainablecommunities.com/267-green-mountain-coffee-environmental-responsibility.html.

Green Mountain Coffee Roasters, Inc. "Fiscal 2011 Annual Report." Accessed November 30, 2012. http://files.shareholder.com/downloads/GMCR/2189727515x0x540307/C799E76F-7E06-418D-9BB2-B105A85EE3EA/GMCR_AnnualReport_2011.pdf.

Ingram, Frederick C., and Christina M. Stansell. "Green Mountain Coffee Roasters, Inc." *International Directory of Company Histories*. Ed. Tina Grant. Vol. 107. Detroit, MI: St. James Press, 2010.

"100 Fastest Growing Companies: The World's Supercharged Performers." *CNN Money*, September 6, 2010. Accessed November 30, 2012. http://money.cnn.com/magazines/fortune/fortunefastestgrowing/2010/snapshots/2.html.

Sparks, Daniel. "Over-caffeinated Growth Expectations at Green Mountain Coffee." *Motley Fool*, September 26, 2012.

"World's Most Valuable Beverages Brands, 2011." *Business Rankings Annual*. Ed. Deborah J. Draper. Detroit, MI: Gale, 2013.

GRUPO BIMBO

AT A GLANCE

Brand Synopsis: One of the leading bakery brands in the world, Grupo Bimbo is known for its diversity of products and many umbrella brands.
Parent Company: Grupo Bimbo, S.A.B. de C.V.
Prolongación Paseo de la Reforma No. 1000, Colonia
Peña Blanca Santa Fe, Delegación
Álvaro Obregón
México, D.F. 01210
Mexico
http://www.grupobimbo.com/
Sector: Consumer Staples
Industry Group: Food, Beverage & Tobacco
Performance: *Market share*—16.5 percent of bread in the United States. *Revenues*—MXN133.7 billion (2011).
Principal Competitors: Gruma SAB de C.V.; Grupo Corvi S.A. de C.V.; Nestle; Unilever; Kraft Foods Group

BRAND ORIGINS

- What became Grupo Bimbo was founded in 1945.
- Bimbo entered the American market in 1984.
- In 1990 Bimbo began selling corn tortillas in the Mexican market under the Milpa Real and Lonchion brand names.
- Bimbo bought the U.S. bakery operations of Sara Lee in 2010.

Grupo Bimbo was founded in 1945 as Panificadora Bimbo by Lorenzo Servitje Sendra, members of his family, and business partners in Mexico City. Initially baking only four types of bread, the brand operated solely in Mexico City for a decade. By 1948 Bimbo sold white, toasted, rye, and sweet bread, plus buns and pound cakes. It added donuts in 1952. In the mid-1950s Bimbo began launching umbrella brands for specific products with Keikito, a brand of cupcakes. Keikito's name was later changed to the better known Marinela in 1957.

In 1964 Bimbo began expanding by acquiring other brand names. That year the company acquired the rights for the Sunbeam brand of bread in Mexico. Because of such changes, the company's name was changed to Grupo Industrial Bimbo. By the early 1970s, Bimbo was operating in much of Mexico, and new products were added, beginning with sweets and chocolates after the acquisition of a small chocolates plant. In 1973 Bimbo entered into the jams and marmalades market with the Carmel line. In 1974 Bimbo launched the Sunday brand of round pound cakes and then the Tía Rosa brand for sweet breads and, beginning in 1976, tortillinas.

Though Bimbo went public in 1980, an economic crisis in Mexico limited the brand's expansion until the late 1980s. Despite this economic situation, Bimbo moved outside of Mexico for the first time in 1984 when it began selling products in a few markets in the United States. The first products shipped there were cakes produced under the Sunday label. By 1988 Bimbo was producing bread and sponge cake under the names Bimbo, Sunbeam, and Tía Rosa; cakes and cookies under the name Miranela; sweets and chocolates under the

Ricolino name; snacks under the Barcel name; and jams under the name Carmel.

Bimbo moved into many new markets in the late 1980s and the 1990s. In 1989 it began becoming truly international after buying a bread bakery in Guatemala. It soon purchased bread bakeries and was distributing to countries like Chile, Venezuela, El Salvador, and Costa Rica. In 1994 Bimbo began producing and selling products in Argentina. In addition to spreading to more cities and markets in the United States, Bimbo also began operating in Europe. After doing contract work for Park Lane, a German confectioner, Bimbo bought the company in 1998.

By the early 1990s Bimbo was the dominant player in the Mexican bread market. In 1993 its Marinela division had about a 20 percent market share of cookies, pastries, and baked snacks. Not content to rest on its success, Bimbo continued product expansion. In 1990 it began selling corn tortillas in the Mexican market under the Milpa Real and Lonchion names, though the market for such products was still relatively small. In 1993 Bimbo entered the tortilla market in the United States, a move that proved to be quite lucrative.

After Bimbo reorganized its operations in the mid-1990s, Daniel Servitje took over as chief executive officer in 1997, replacing his father, the company's founder. That year, Bimbo was Mexico's largest bakery and food company, with sales of over US$2 billion. In 1998 Bimbo acquired the American bakery Mrs. Baird's, then the largest family owned bakery in the United States, and formed Bimbo Bakeries USA to manage its new American business.

In 1999, when the company held 90 percent of the Mexican bread market, it changed its name to Grupo Bimbo. By 2000 Bimbo was distributing and marketing over 700 products in 15 countries and was the world's third largest bread maker. It was the largest baking company in Mexico and the third biggest in world.

International and brand expansion continued in the first years of the 2000s. Because of local bakery acquisitions, Bimbo moved into the Brazilian market in 2001 and the Chinese market in 2006. In 2002 Bimbo bought the rights to manufacture and sell Entenmann's, Thomas's, and Boboli brands in the Western United States from the Canadian-based bakery company George Weston Ltd. Bimbo purchased all the George Weston U.S. bakery operations in 2008. Expansion in Mexico continued as well, to build on Bimbo's 85 percent penetration of the Mexican market. Bimbo entered the candy industry by buying three Mexican confectionary businesses in 2004.

Bimbo made another major acquisition in 2010, purchasing the struggling U.S. bakery operations of Sara Lee, which gave Bimbo rights to use their name for baked goods everywhere but in Australia and New Zealand. (The acquisition excluded cheesecakes, other frozen desserts, and meat products under the Sara Lee brand.) In 2011 Bimbo bought Sara Lee's operations in Spain and Portugal, helping to expand the brand's presence there. In 2013 Bimbo began negotiations for pieces of the bankrupt Hostess Brands, the U.S.-based producer of Twinkies and other products.

BRAND ELEMENTS

- The Bimbo name has no meaning in Spanish and was created by combining the words Bambi and bingo.
- Grupo Bimbo trademarked "Say 'Beembo!'" to help American consumers separate the brand name from its colloquial meaning.
- The Bimbo bear symbolizes whiteness, softness, neatness, and tenderness.

In 1999 Grupo Industrial Bimbo changed its name to just Grupo Bimbo. The alteration was made to emphasize its focus on baked goods, especially Bimbo bread. Grupo Bimbo is often known simply as Bimbo, pronounced "beem-bo." Bimbo has no meaning in Spanish, but was created as a combination of Bambi, from the Disney animated movie, and the game of bingo. In the United States, bimbo refers to a woman, often attractive but unintelligent, who is perceived as sexually promiscuous. Grupo Bimbo trademarked the phrase "Say 'Beembo!'" to ensure both that its name was pronounced correctly and that consumers did not associate the brand name with its meaning in American English.

Bimbo is also the name of the brand's logo, adopted when the company was founded in 1945. The logo is a little white bear with a white apron and a baker's hat with a red B. The white bear cub was based on an image in a Christmas card received by one of Bimbo's original partners. Bimbo the bear is white to represent the whiteness of the brand's bread. The bear also symbolizes tenderness, neatness, and softness. The Bimbo bear appears not only on the company's Bimbo-branded bread but also on donuts and certain other products.

BRAND IDENTITY

- The Bimbo brand was an unknown giant outside of Mexico for several decades after its founding.
- By the 1990s, the brand began better defining itself to become an international company.
- In 2011 Bimbo became an official major sponsor of the MLS to increase attention on the company in the United States.

For many years, Grupo Bimbo was a relative giant in the commercial baking industry, almost secretive in its identity outside of Mexico during the first four decades of its existence. It focused on expanding its offerings, first in Mexico, then in North America and the rest of Latin America. Along the way, Bimbo created more umbrella brands for its various product types, which made the Bimbo brand name appear to be secondary on most products, except for items like certain breads and donuts.

By 1990 the brand's perspective changed and Bimbo wanted to be the largest baking company in the United States and an international, and internationally known, baking company. Therefore it sought to define itself more clearly. Because of its origins in Mexico, Bimbo was popular in Hispanic markets in the United States, beginning in the 1990s. But it still does not specifically target U.S. Hispanic consumers. After the acquisition of Sara Lee's U.S. bakery business in 2010, Bimbo made a more concerted effort to raise awareness of its brand in the United States, having becoming the dominant bakery company in that country.

To this end, Bimbo signed a four-year, US$12 million deal in 2011 to become a major sponsor of Major League Soccer (MLS) and specifically of the Philadelphia Union team. The red, white, and blue Bimbo name appeared on the front of the Union players' jerseys. This was part of a bigger push to promote the Bimbo brand in the United States. To address the somewhat negative connotation of the Bimbo name in English, the brand created humorous billboard and radio ads with the tagline "It's Beem-bo, B-I-M-B-O" to teach consumers to pronounce the name correctly.

Soccer has been important to Bimbo's identity in Mexico as well. There, the brand has built its identity through television advertising and sponsoring big sporting events, such as World Cup soccer. In Mexico, Bimbo sponsors a number of soccer club teams, including Chivas Guadalajara, the most popular team in Mexico by 2011, as well as two other teams in the Primera Division. Bimbo also sponsors a soccer team in Costa Rica, Deportivo Saprissa.

BRAND STRATEGY

- Bimbo operates in 19 countries and sells 8,000 to 10,000 products under 103 brand names.
- Bimbo launches its own brand and product lines, but also enters new product lines by acquisition.
- To grow geographically, Bimbo buys smaller bakery operations.

Grupo Bimbo produces, distributes, and sells a variety of baked goods, including bread, pastries, cakes, cookies, candy, chocolates, salty snacks and crackers, and tortillas. The company sells between 8,000 and 10,000 different products worldwide, operating in least 19 countries including Mexico, the United States, China, Spain, and others in Central and South America. It has at least 103 brands, which vary by country and market. They include Bimbo, Marinela, Milpa Real, Tia Rosa, Mrs. Baird's, Oroweat, Entenmann's, Thomas, Boboli, Barcel, Ricolino, La Corona, Pastelerías El Globo, and Sara Lee. It is one of the largest bakery companies in the world.

Bimbo adds new products and product lines through several strategies, all of which involve acquisition. While Bimbo has launched its own umbrella brands, like Tía Rosa (sweet breads and tortillas) and Marinela (snack cakes), much of its product line growth has come through the purchasing of other companies to enter the market for a certain product. For example, in 2004 Grupo Bimbo bought four confectionary companies in Mexico in order to enter the candy business.

To further consolidate its position in a specific product line and increase its market share, Bimbo also buys brand names in various markets, some of them iconic. For example, in 1986 Bimbo acquired the Wonder Bread brand in Mexico, gaining essentially a monopoly on the packaged bread market in that country. Bimbo greatly increased its presence and market share in the United States through acquisitions like Mrs. Baird's in 1998 and Sara Lee's bakery business in 2010.

Because the baking industry is often a local business, Bimbo enters new geographical markets through acquisition of smaller bakery concerns. In 2011 the brand recovered the Bimbo operation and brands in Spain and Portugal by acquiring the bakery business of Sara Lee in those countries, making Bimbo the industry leader in the Iberian Peninsula. In 2008 Bimbo bought the Nutrella Bakery in Brazil, entering the Brazilian market. Outside of Mexico, Bimbo marketed its various brands and products on a country level, sometimes even a city level, depending on the market. Emerging markets often had different strategies than established markets. About 40 percent of Bimbo's net sales came from Mexico and Latin America (in which, oddly, China was counted), 46 percent from the United States, and 14 percent from other countries.

BRAND EQUITY

- Nearly 62 percent of Bimbo's sales came from outside Mexico in 2011.
- Grupo Bimbo is the fourth-most-valuable brand in Mexico.
- In 2012 Bimbo had a brand value of US$2.634 billion.

Grupo Bimbo is a global market leader in bread baking and one of the biggest food companies in the world. About 62 percent of its sales came from outside Mexico in 2011. In the United States, Bimbo was a market leader for baked goods (bread, cakes, and pastries) in 2009, with a 16.2 percent market share. It dominated the Mexican market for bread, baked goods, and other products, and was that country's tenth largest company. In 2011 it was the fourth-most-valuable brand in Mexico, after Claro, Telcel, and Corona Extra, according to Brand Finance. In 2012 *Forbes* ranked Bimbo as number 1006 in its ranking of the Global 2000.

According to Brand Finance's *Global 500* for 2012, Grupo Bimbo had a brand value of US$2.634 billion, a brand rating of AA+, and an enterprise value of US$11.916 billion in 2012. It was ranked 444th. In 2010 its brand performance included a brand value of US$2.538 billion, a brand rating of AA, and an enterprise value of US$10.003 billion. It was ranked at 367. In 2009 Bimbo had a brand performance of US$1.346 billion, a brand rating of A+, and an enterprise value of US$4.399 billion. It was ranked 475th.

BRAND AWARENESS

- In Mexico, Grupo Bimbo has its highest brand awareness.
- In 2011 a survey of Mexican consumers ranked Bimbo second among companies with the best reputation.
- Bimbo pursued greater brand awareness through marketing and sponsorships in the United States.

Though Grupo Bimbo has more than 100 labels under which it markets its products, the overall Grupo Bimbo name is not thereby diluted but retains high brand awareness in Mexico. In a 2011 survey by the Reputation Institute and Inmark Mexico, Grupo Bimbo was ranked second in the list of companies with the best reputation in that country. Its score was 73.4 points on the RepTrak Pulso. Bimbo had a very positive reputation and was highly admired, trusted, and respected. Another survey by the Reputation Institute in 2009 ranked Bimbo at number 17 on the list of the global companies most respected by Mexican consumers. Bimbo was associated with soccer in Mexico and in other Central and South American countries because of its sports sponsorships.

Grupo Bimbo itself generally had less brand awareness in markets outside of Mexico, however. The exception was the United States, where there was strong brand awareness among Hispanic consumers in the growing Latino market. Marketing efforts like the "Say 'Beembo!'" campaign and MLS sponsorships helped build the brand in the United States and increase name recognition. Many of the umbrella brands in Grupo Bimbo's portfolio, like Sara Lee, are highly recognized in the United States and other countries.

BRAND OUTLOOK

- Grupo Bimbo had a strong economic outlook because of its strategic acquisitions and investment in innovative technologies.
- Bimbo released mission statement Vision 2015, which emphasized sustainability.
- In 2011 Bimbo was included in the sustainable IPC Index on the Mexican Stock Exchange.

Grupo Bimbo faced challenges like the higher cost of raw materials, rising labor costs in the United States, and continued economic instability in Europe. Nevertheless the brand has had climbing sales numbers since 2007. Bimbo's strong distribution network, its investment in innovative technologies, a company track record for successful strategic acquisitions, and increased consumer spending in the United States are factors that are expected to serve Bimbo well in the near future. In addition, Bimbo is positioned to capitalize on the growing health food market in China with selected bakery products.

Bimbo's mission statement for the early 21st century, Vision 2015, outlined major company goals, including becoming a leader in the food industry as well as the best global baking company. Vision 2015 also emphasized the importance of environmental initiatives. Bimbo has recognized the importance of sustainability as a means of helping to reduce costs. In 2008 it began using degradable polyethylene packaging for its products. The company worked to reduce its carbon footprint and built a wind farm in Mexico that will eventually supply enough energy for most of its plants in Mexico. In 2011 Bimbo was included in the sustainable IPC Index on the Mexican Stock Exchange and was labeled a Sustainable Enterprise.

FURTHER READING

Brand Finance. "Grupo Bimbo." *Brandirectory*. Accessed January 13, 2013. http://brandirectory.com/profile/grupo-bimbo.

Gammage, Jeff. "Union Soccer Team Wins Sponsorship from Bimbo Bakery." *Philadelphia Inquirer*, January 11, 2011.

"Global 2000 Leading Companies: Grupo Bimbo." *Forbes*. Accessed January 14, 2013. http://www.forbes.com/companies/grupo-bimbo/

"Grupo Bimbo S.A. de C.V." *International Directory of Company Histories*. Ed. Karen Hill. Vol. 128. Detroit, MI: St. James Press, 2012.

Schultz, E. J. "Bake Sale: Sara Lee Dumps Bread Unit." *AdvertisingAge*, November 9, 2010.

Sosland, Joshua. "Bimbo Leads by Example." *Baking & Snack International*, September 24, 2012.

———. "Servitje Says Global Reach Only a Part of Bimbo's Ambitions." *Baking & Snack International*, August 13, 2012.

York, Emily Bryson. "Sara Lee Bread Business Sale: Getting to Know Bimbo." *Chicago Tribune*, November 9, 2010.

GUCCI

AT A GLANCE

Brand Synopsis: Gucci products embody the "Made in Italy" qualities of the finest materials and craftsmanship.
Parent Company: Gucci Group N.V.
Rembrandt Tower
Amstelplein 1
Amsterdam 1096 HA
Netherlands
http://www.gucci.com
Sector: Consumer Discretionary
Industry Group: Consumer Durables and Apparel
Performance: Sales—US$4.2 billion (2011).
Principal Competitors: Chanel S.A.; LVMH Moët Hennessy Louis Vuitton S.A.; Compagnie Financiére Richemont S.A.

BRAND ORIGINS

- Guccio Gucci founded a fine leather goods firm in Florence in 1921
- After World War II, Gucci became an internationally renowned luxury brand.
- After family disputes, the Guccis lost control of the company in 1993.
- Pinault-Printemps-Redoute took control of Gucci in 1999.

Guccio Gucci founded his own luxury leather firm in his hometown of Florence, Italy, in 1921, and it quickly won favorable notice from the many international travelers in the city. Gucci's son Aldo set up a Gucci store in Rome in 1938, which after World War II did bustling business with Allied soldiers seeking gifts for women back home. This helped lead to the opening of a Gucci store in New York City in 1953. In the 1960s and 1970s, Gucci stores opened worldwide from London to Beverly Hills to Tokyo and Hong Kong, as the brand became a favorite of international celebrities and royalty. In 1972, Gucci started offering perfume and made a remarkably successful licensing deal for Gucci watches.

Even as the Gucci family became mired in infighting and legal problems during the 1980s, the brand remained prosperous, though it was losing some of its luster. However, in 1993, Maurizio Gucci, the last remaining Guccis to lead the parent company, sold his remaining stake to Bahraini investor Investcorp International. Under Investcorp's management, creative director Tom Ford revitalized the Gucci brand image through sexually charged promotions. In 1999, the company was acquired by French company Pinault-Printemps-Redoute (PPR) over heated opposition from domestic rival LVMH Moët Hennessy Louis Vuitton.

Gucci Group bought back some of its franchise operations and stores from outside operators and acquired several prominent fashion and luxury brands. The group continued opening new Gucci stores, especially in the burgeoning luxury markets of Asia. PPR bought out all of Gucci Group's outstanding shares in 2004 and took it private again. In February 2011 PPR dissolved Gucci Group and began administering Gucci and other brands separately.

BRAND ELEMENTS

- The Gucci brand is identified most widely by its distinctive interlocking "GG" logo.
- A horse bit motif and red–green–red stripes are also featured on many Gucci products.
- Gucci aggressively combats counterfeiters and competitors using the name "Gucci."
- Gucci has pursued lawsuits against Guess Inc. on charges of imitating Gucci's trademarks.

Since its founding, Gucci lines have featured a horse bit motif intended to connect the brand with the equestrian world and aristocracy. In the early 1960s, Gucci began printing a capital G logo on its canvas bags; soon a second interlocking capital G was added, and it became one of the most recognized luxury logos worldwide. A red–green–red striped pattern is also associated with Gucci, applied variously to luggage, denim pants, handbags, and cars. The firm developed its distinctive bamboo purse handle, which it attaches to materials ranging from canvas to crocodile skin, during the 1940s when fine leather was scarce in Italy.

Gucci fights to preserve the rights to its logo and its name. Most recently, in July 2012 an Italian court ruled that ToBeG Srl, a firm founded by relatives Guccio and Alessandro Gucci, was infringing on Gucci trademarks by using the word Gucci in its promotions. In May 2012 Gucci was awarded damages from mid-range fashion producer Guess Inc. for trademark dilution in a New York federal court. The company cooperates with government authorities and files frequent lawsuits against suspected counterfeiters and retailers that offer fake Gucci products.

BRAND IDENTITY

- Gucci's appeal rests on Italy's reputation for craftsmanship and style.
- Tom Ford developed a more up-to-date, sexually charged image for Gucci in the mid-1990s.
- Gucci designs its stores to reinforce its brand image.
- Gucci's "Forever Now" campaign celebrated the brand's 90th anniversary in 2011.

From its start, Gucci's appeal has rested on the image of Italy as the land of elegant design and fine craftsmanship, producing luxury items for which well-heeled customers are willing to pay a premium. Italy also became the land where silver screen royalty and actual royalty went on holiday and enjoyed showing off discreetly with Gucci clothing and accessories. In the mid-1990s, creative director Tom Ford aimed to update the brand's image with sexier fashion lines and advertising campaigns showing androgynous models in provocative poses. The appearances of celebrities wearing custom-made Gucci outfits at the Oscars and Grammys and high-society soirées also kept the brand name before the public.

Gucci imposed the same promotions and retail displays in all its international markets. The company restricted the brand's availability to selected department stores and its owner-operated boutiques, which by 1998 accounted for an estimated 70 percent of sales. After redesigning its product line, the company created a retail setting that would reinforce its projected image. The first new-model Gucci store opened in London in February 1998, and the company planned to renovate all the other outlets. The 14,000-square-foot store featured a dramatic limestone-lined entrance with stainless steel doors intended to evoke a bank vault, and the showrooms were equipped with elegant wooden moldings and custom-designed furniture.

After Tom Ford's departure from Gucci Group in 2004, Frida Giannini emerged as creative director of Gucci, shifting the brand to a more traditionally feminine image in women's wear and reconnecting with themes from Gucci's long history. In 2005 Gucci began developing a new retail concept, featuring a more spacious center aisle and white lacquer and steel fittings. Along with the new store format, Gucci revised its packaging scheme. The brand's familiar dark brown and black tones were replaced with gold and bronze, as the lettering changed from dark silver to gold, a color intended "to communicate a sensation of light and warmth" according to Giannini in a *Women's Wear Daily* article from July 28, 2006.

The 90th anniversary of its founding in 2011 prompted Gucci to reemphasize its heritage under the "Forever Now" campaign. Gucci launched the Collection 1921 and set up the Artisan Corner program in which the company's artisans demonstrated their skills in stores. The company opened the Museo Gucci in Florence, which displays Gucci items in a showroom-like format along with modern artworks. The Christie's auction house helped set up the "Gucci Collector" website that offers appraisals of Gucci items and assures purchasers of the genuineness of products for sale.

BRAND STRATEGY

- Gucci preserves its luxury positioning by restricting sales to its own branded outlets and high-end department stores.
- Gucci stores have expanded rapidly worldwide, especially in Asia.
- From the mid-1990s, Gucci has expanded its presence in jewelry, perfume, watches, and home furnishings.
- The La Pelle Guccissima line introduced in 2005 refreshed Gucci's reputation for fine leather goods.

Continuing international expansion is a key to Gucci's brand strategy. In the early 1970s Gucci had already opened stores in Tokyo and Hong Kong. In 1997 the first two stores opened in China, one each in Beijing and Shanghai, as well as a store in Moscow to cater to Russia's nouveau riche. Japanese tourists had flocked for many years to Gucci stores abroad, and Gucci opened dozens of new stores in Japan, which as of 2000 accounted for 21 percent of Gucci's total sales. Over 2007 and 2008 the company launched stores in such far-flung locales as Mumbai, New Delhi, Macau, Cape Town, Auckland, Ho Chi Minh City, Prague, and Budapest. Within China, Gucci stores spread to smaller regional cities. Gucci enjoyed success in this market by keeping prices relatively low as well as providing special offers such as the 8-8-2008 Limited Edition, which celebrated the Beijing Olympics. Late in 2009 Gucci unleashed Gucci Icon-Temporary, a roving sneaker store set up for two to three weeks at a time in New York, Miami Beach, London, Paris, Berlin, Hong Kong, and Tokyo.

In 1998 Gucci was one of the first luxury firms to offer branded jewelry, seeing tremendous growth opportunity in a $100 billion industry where branded products comprised minimal share. The brand also entered the luxury watch market, lured by strong demand for high-end timepieces despite economic recession. In 2003, Gucci rolled out an expanded home furnishings portfolio with furniture, wallpaper, home accessories, linens, towels, and blankets, at price points from $175 to $13,000. Meanwhile, Tom Ford oversaw the release of a stream of new perfume variants supported by steamy advertisements, starting with Gucci Envy in 1997 and followed by Gucci Rush for Women in 1999 and Rush for Men in 2000. Frida Giannini oversaw the creation of Gucci by Gucci, a women's fragrance introduced in 2007 which incorporated typically masculine scent elements and was promoted by a short film directed by David Lynch. Gucci Guilty, a scent for women launched in 2010, recovered an edgy appeal with provocative film noir-inspired video and print ads.

Leather goods still make up the largest share of Gucci sales. Giannini fostered the development of the La Pelle Guccissima line of fine handcrafted leather goods and silk and cashmere scarves, which was launched in July 2005. The possibilities of luxury branding were expanding as Gucci introduced leather cases for the Apple iPod and then for the iPad in June 2010. More extravagantly, the Aquariva by Gucci speedboat was offered in 2010 for $750,000, followed in 2011 by Fiat's 500 by Gucci, a sporty minicar marketed in the United States through Chrysler dealerships.

BRAND EQUITY

- In 2012 Gucci was ranked 38th among global brands according to Interbrand.
- Gucci is ranked second among luxury brands behind Louis Vuitton.
- In its core field of leather goods, Gucci ranked third internationally in 2003 according to *Market Share Reporter.*

According to Interbrand's *2012 Ranking of the Top 100 Brands,* Gucci ranked 38th with a brand value of $9.4 billion, up 8 percent from 2010. Gucci ranked second among luxury brands behind Louis Vuitton and first among all Italian brands. In 2011, Gucci reported total revenues of over 23.14 billion (US$4.2 billion) out of an overall world luxury market estimated at nearly US$200 billion. In particular sectors, in 2003 (the most recent information available in *Market Share Reporter*) Gucci ranked third worldwide among leather goods firms with 10.9 percent market share. Gucci ranked fifth in luxury jewelry with 2.9 percent share in 2006 and accounted for 1 percent world share of watches in 2009.

BRAND AWARENESS

- A Nielsen Group survey from November 2007 showed that Gucci was the most desirable luxury brand worldwide.
- According to a 2004 survey by *Women's Wear Daily,* the majority of American women are very familiar with Gucci.
- Numerous rappers have mentioned Gucci as a brand they aspire to, or sometimes disdain.

A Nielsen Group survey of consumers from 48 countries conducted in November 2007 revealed that Gucci was the most desirable brand. About 20 percent of respondents stated they would prefer to purchase Gucci products if price were no concern. The countries with peak demand for Gucci were India with 41 percent and the United Arab Emirates with 37 percent. A Bain & Co survey in 2010 of Chinese consumers found that Gucci was the third "most desired" luxury brand, mentioned by 22 percent of participants. In the United States, a survey of brand awareness among American women commissioned by *Women's Wear Daily* in 2004 rated Gucci third in accessories, "very familiar" to 53.8 percent of respondents, and fourth among fashion designers with 55.9 percent familiarity.

In the American hip-hop scene, by the early 2000s many famous rappers were fond of dropping the names of luxury brands in their songs. According to the Agenda.com advertising agency, in 2004 Gucci ranked fifth with 49 mentions in Billboard Top 20 singles, not far behind leading brands Cadillac and Hennessy (one of Gucci's direct competitors). However, musicians' embrace of luxury brands could turn sour, as demonstrated in 2011 when "Gucci, Gucci," a single by California-based rapper Kreayshawn, mocked famous labels as passé.

BRAND OUTLOOK

- Gucci is adapting to the social media world in which consumers have more power to shape brand perceptions.

- Gucci's website and Gucci Style app offer videos and interviews as well as shopping for online-only accessories.
- The booming China market has become central to Gucci's long-range strategy.

Gucci is adapting its brand positioning to the presence of widespread Internet access and use of social networks such as Facebook and Twitter, which are giving the public ever more power to shape brand perceptions, threatening to erode their luxury status. Gucci relaunched its website in September 2010, featuring videos and interviews presenting behind-the-scenes information about Gucci's production, as well as access to a collection of online-only accessories and Internet streaming of fashion shows. The year 2011 saw the launch of the Gucci Style app for the iPad and iPhone, which is available in eight languages and adds a travel guide and social media feeds.

Since the global economic crisis of 2008, luxury brands have been remarkably resilient, appealing to discerning consumers with deep pocketbooks. Sales are still growing in Gucci's original core markets in Europe and North America, and Gucci is eager to start cultivating the next generation of consumers with its Gucci Kids line. However, China and nearby Asian countries have become increasingly central to its long-range strategy. By 2012 China was ready to overtake the United States as the world's largest luxury market, with estimated growth falling to 13-18% from 35-40% in 2011. At the end of 2011 Gucci had 58 branded outlets in Greater China (including Macau and Hong Kong) with plans to open about 10 more in 2012.

FURTHER READING

Booker, Avery. "As China's Luxury Market Evolves, Who's Winning and Who's Losing?" *Jing Daily,* October 1, 2012.

Cardona, Mercedes M. "Trendsetting Brands Combat Knock-Offs; Word Of Mouth, Product Placement Are Key to Success." *Advertising Age,* August 21, 2000.

Colavita, Courtney. "Gucci Goes Gold with New Look for Packaging." Women's Wear Daily, July 28, 2006.

Conti, Samantha. "Baubles Galore: Luxe Firms Seek Piece of $100B Jewelry Sector." *Women's Wear Daily,* April 7, 2003.

———. "A Growing Conversation: Gucci Latest Luxe Brand Flocking to Social Media." *Women's Wear Daily,* October 15, 2009.

Cooperman, Jackie. "Gucci Guys Get Their Rush." *Women's Wear Daily,* June 30, 2000.

Ebenkamp, Becky. "Wrapping Up the Rap Sheet." *Brandweek,* January 17, 2005.

Edelson, Sharon. "Gucci Sneakers Set for Global Pop-up." *Women's Wear Daily,* August 5, 2009.

Epiro, Stephanie. "Gucci's New Blend: By Frida." *Women's Wear Daily,* July 13, 2007.

Fallon, James. "Gucci Makeover Set As New Store Format Is Ready For A Rollout." *Women's Wear Daily,* February 11, 1998.

Farrar, Lisa, and Hye-Seung Seo. "Gucci's Shanghai Statement." *Women's Wear Daily,* April 24, 2012.

"Gucci Group NV." *International Directory of Company Histories.* Vol. 115. Detroit, MI: St. James Press, 2010.

Ilari, Alessandra. "Gucci Icons." Women's Wear Daily, June 5, 2006.

———. "Gucci Project to Boost Leather." Women's Wear Daily, May 17, 2005.

Ilari, Alessandra, and Joelle Diderich. "Gucci Designs iPad Cases." *Women's Wear Daily,* June 7, 2010.

Kaiser, Amanda. "Gucci Expanding into Home." *Women's Wear Daily,* June 16, 2003.

Menkes, Suzy. "Gucci Feeds Its Florentine Roots." *New York Times,* September 27, 2011.

O'Loughlin, Sandra. "Modest Change: Retailing's Once-Risque Luxury Brands Have Fashioned A More Conservative Look In Their Advertising For Fall." *Adweek,* September 6, 2004.

Olsen, Kerry. "Gucci's Guilty Set to Launch." *Women's Wear Daily,* July 2, 2010.

Roberts, Andrew. "Nielsen Survey Finds Gucci Atop Luxe Heap." *Women's Wear Daily,* February 28, 2008.

Socha, Miles. "Pinault's Bold Move: Polet Exits Gucci as PPR Slims Down." *Women's Wear Daily,* February 18, 2011.

Zargani, Laura. "Gucci Hits New Markets for Growth." *Women's Wear Daily,* May 15, 2008.

———. "Gucci Wins Trade Suit." *Women's Wear Daily,* July 25, 2012.

———. "Setting the Retail Stage; Gucci's Stores Have Always Been About Elegance, Exclusivity And Service." *Women's Wear Daily,* June 5, 2006.

HARLEY-DAVIDSON

AT A GLANCE

Brand Synopsis: Harley-Davidsons are loud, powerful, high-quality, quintessentially American motorcycles that appeal to people's love of freedom, individualism, and adventure.
Parent Company: Harley-Davidson, Inc.
P.O. Box 653
Milwaukee, Wisconsin 53201-0653
United States
http://www.harley-davidson.com
Sector: Consumer Discretionary
Industry Group: Automobiles & Components
Performance: *Market share*—55.7 percent in the United States (2010). *Sales*—US$4.9 billion (2012).
Principal Competitors: Yamaha Motor Corporation, Ltd.; Honda Motor Company Ltd.; Suzuki Motor Corporation; Kawasaki Motors Corp.; Hero MotorCorp; KTM-Sportmotorcycle AG; BMW Motorrad; Piaggio & C. S.p.A; Polaris Industries

BRAND ORIGINS

- The Harley-Davidson brand was launched in 1903 by William S. Harley and two brothers named Arthur and Walter Davidson.
- The first Harley-Davidson motorcycle was simply a bicycle with a small engine attached to it.
- Only two U.S. motorcycle manufacturers survived the Great Depression, and Harley-Davidson was one of them.
- The brand declined after it was acquired by a conglomerate, then recovered after its own managers bought it.
- After a severe downturn in 2009, the brand rebounded via global expansion and broadening of its domestic customer base.

Although inventors had been experimenting with motorized two-wheeled vehicles since the 1700s, the Harley-Davidson was among the first models reliable enough to be used for transportation. The brand's original prototype, a bicycle with a three-horsepower engine, was designed and built in Milwaukee, Wisconsin, in 1903 by William S. Harley and brothers Arthur and Walter Davidson. Four years later the Harley-Davidson Motor Company was incorporated, and a third brother, William A. Davidson, joined the team. The venture produced 61 motorcycles that year and was soon competing with about 150 other companies. Many of those went out of business during the Great Depression of the 1930s, leaving only one competitor in America, the Indian brand made by Hendee Manufacturing.

Even though Harley-Davidson sales dropped from 24,000 motorcycles in 1929 to just 3,600 in 1933, the firm retained a customer base that included importers from Canada and Europe, the U.S. Postal Service, police departments, and the military. During World War I the U.S. military had transitioned from cavalry horses to 20,000 Harley-Davidson motorcycles, which amounted to almost half of the company's production. During World War II the firm sold almost all of its motorcycles for military use. About 100,000 were shipped overseas for the Allied forces.

After the Indian brand was discontinued in 1953, Harley-Davidson was for many years the only motorcycle manufacturer in the United States. In 1965, facing growing competition from Europe and Japan, the corporation went public, and the two founding families gave up their controlling interest in it. Four years later Harley-Davidson was acquired by a conglomerate named American Machine and Foundry (AMF), which invested heavily in new plants, equipment, and employees. Nevertheless, the quality of the brand declined, and its reputation was seriously damaged. Harley-Davidson's share of the U.S. market for super-heavyweight motorcycles tumbled from 80 percent in 1969 to 20 percent in 1979.

In 1981 the senior managers of Harley-Davidson purchased the business from AMF for US$81.5 million. To celebrate, they organized a motorcycle cavalcade that proceeded from the AMF-built assembly plant in Pennsylvania back to the company's original headquarters in Wisconsin. Following the example of their Japanese competitors, the new owners instituted innovative management techniques that helped the brand rebound.

Profits increased steadily until 2009, when widespread economic recession caused a sudden drop in demand for motorcycles, especially a brand as expensive as the Harley, which often cost as much as a new car. At the same time many of Harley-Davidson's customers had reached retirement age and no longer enjoyed their previous level of income. Banks hesitated to loan them money to buy motorcycles. Harley-Davidson's profits plummeted by 91 percent in one year. Its motorcycle sales dropped 30 percent worldwide and 35 percent in the United States. The company made another remarkable recovery, however, by expanding foreign operations and by broadening its appeal within the United States.

BRAND ELEMENTS

- Harley-Davidson motorcycles are long, low, heavyweight machines that make a characteristic deep rumbling sound.
- The brand's nickname is "Hog" because a 1920s motorcycle racing team used a pig as its mascot.
- The company added an eagle insignia to its motorcycles to stimulate sales during the Great Depression.

Harley-Davidson is a distinctive brand of long, low, noisy, heavyweight motorcycles that have inspired fanatical loyalty on the part of customers and almost unparalleled brand recognition, even among nonriders. Customers fondly refer to these motorcycles by the nickname "Hog" a tradition that originated in the 1920s when a motorcycle racing team began carrying its mascot, a pig, on a victory lap after each win.

A Harley-Davidson motorcycle has an unusually powerful engine that makes a deep rumbling sound like a husky voice muttering, "potato, potato." The distinctive and easily recognizable sound has become an essential element of the Harley-Davidson brand.

The brand's famous "bar and shield" logo, trademarked a hundred years ago, features a horizontal black rectangle with an orange pinstripe and white letters that read "Harley-Davidson." Behind it is a black shield with an orange pinstripe and the words "Motor Company" in orange letters.

An art-deco eagle became part of the brand's signature look during the Great Depression of the 1930s, when the company stimulated sales by painting the design on the gas tank of its motorcycles. In keeping with Harley's status as an iconic all-American brand complete with an American eagle, Harley riders often fly American flags on their motorcycles.

BRAND IDENTITY

- Harley-Davidson is a high-end brand with a "wow" factor, designed to give customers exactly what they want.
- The brand denotes quality and a free-spirited outlook.
- The typical Harley customer has been a middle-age white American male, but the brand is being marketed more broadly now.

Harley-Davidson is meant to be the brand with the "wow" factor, a high-quality motorcycle that is exactly what the buyer wants, a machine that fulfills a customer's dream. The company website says, "Every rider knows the feeling that comes from finding the one – the Harley-Davidson motorcycle that you simply can't live without."

From the beginning Harley was promoted as the brand that delivered power, reliability, durability, and speed. To some degree the company has embraced the notion that Harley motorcycles offer independence, enabling riders to rebel against authority and cultural conventions. However, the brand is also meant to appeal to a wider audience, especially in recent years as its core customers have reached middle age.

The typical Harley rider is a white American male about 50 years old, possibly bearded and tattooed, but also possibly a lawyer or doctor. Since there is not much room left for expansion within that demographic, the company has been reaching out more to women, younger riders, various ethnic groups, and foreign nations.

BRAND STRATEGY

- Harley-Davidson, Inc. has two divisions: a motorcycle company and a financial services business.

- Variations on the basic design of the Harley motorcycle have kept the brand flexible and relevant over the years.
- The company expects to prosper by focusing on its core brand instead of venturing into other product lines.

Harley-Davidson, Inc. operates in two business segments: the Harley-Davidson Motor Company and Harley-Davidson Financial Services. The financial services division often loans money to customers and motorcycle dealerships to help them purchase expensive Harley motorcycles. The corporation also runs a nonprofit charitable organization named the Harley-Davidson Foundation, Inc.

Harley-Davidson Motor Company manufactures heavyweight custom, cruiser, and touring motorcycles. It also sells Harley-Davidson motorcycle parts, accessories, related gear and clothing, and certain other merchandise such as motor oil.

Over the years the company has experimented with numerous variations on the basic Harley motorcycle. The Sportster model, launched in 1957, introduced an era of loud, powerful "superbikes" that endured through the 1960s. In the 1970s and 1980s a grandson of one of the founders, William G. Davidson, designed popular new models that helped save the business from failing. These included the custom-built Super Glide, the Low Rider, and the Wide Glide.

During the 1990s Harley-Davidson tried to diversify by manufacturing recreational vehicles, but this product line was unsuccessful because the company lacked expertise in that field. The corporation purchased a small American manufacturer of sport performance motorcycles, the Buell Motorcycle Company, in 1998 and operated it as a subsidiary until 2009, when the line was discontinued to allow "single-minded focus on the unique strengths of the Harley-Davidson brand." In 2010 the company divested itself of an Italian sport motorcycle business, MV Agusta, which it had owned for only 14 months. MV Agusta had been purchased to help Harley-Davidson increase its presence in Europe, but the company decided that promoting its own signature brand instead would lead to more sustainable growth in the future.

BRAND EQUITY

- During an economic recession, Harley slipped from number 206 to 449 on the "Global 500" list of top brands.
- The Harley-Davidson brand was valued at US$2.6 billion for 2011, down from a high of US$2.9 billion in 2009.
- Revenues for Harley-Davidson Motor Co. were US$11.9 billion in 2011.
- In 2011 the brand achieved its all-time high market share, 55.7 percent of the U.S. market for heavyweight motorcycles.

Harley-Davidson Motor Co. had revenues of US$11.9 billion in 2011, with sales of new Harley-Davidson motorcycles up 5.9 percent globally from the previous year. For heavyweight motorcycles with an engine displacement of at least 651 cubic centimeters, the Harley brand had 55.7 percent of the U.S. market in 2011. This was the brand's all-time high, up from 54.9 percent in 2010, having increased steadily from 45.0 percent in 2001. In Europe the brand had 13.7 percent of the market, up from 12.7 percent in 2010 and 7.1 percent in 2001.

Brand Finance calculated the brand value of Harley-Davidson at US$2.6 billion for 2011, up from US$2.6 billion for the previous year but down from US$2.9 billion in 2009. Brand Finance ranked Harley-Davidson at number 449 in its "Global 500" list of top brands in 2012, down from number 206 in 2008 when widespread economic recession diminished the market for motorcycles. The brand had been ranked number 150 in the "Global 250" list of top brands for 2007.

In 2011 the price of Harley-Davidson stock rose 12.1 percent, substantially outperforming the average stock listed on Standard & Poor's top 500.

BRAND AWARENESS

- Harley-Davidson is one of the most recognized brands in the world.
- Numerous Harley-Davidson customers have had the brand's logo tattooed on their chests.
- Many thousands of motorcyclists sometimes converge on Milwaukee to celebrate the birthday of Harley-Davidson.
- The Harley fan club has more than a million members.

Harley-Davidson is one of the world's most recognized brands, even among people who do not ride motorcycles. Harley has often been acknowledged as the only brand with customers who are so enthused that they commonly have the logo tattooed on their chests. For the company's 85th birthday, 40,000 motorcyclists from as far away as California and Florida converged on Milwaukee for a day of raucous fun that ended with thousands of people standing together, roaring and shaking clenched fists in the air as a demonstration of product loyalty. When the company celebrated its 90th anniversary with a "family reunion" in Milwaukee, about 100,000 motorcyclists paraded through the city. More than 3 million people have characterized Harley-Davidson as a "friend" at the Facebook social networking website; 40 percent of those are 18 to 34 years old.

In 1983 the company launched a fan club called the Harley Owners Group (HOG), which quickly grew to 100,000 members. Run by Harley employees, the club sponsored motorcycle events across America every summer. Rival manufacturer Honda tried to answer with a fan club of its own, but it soon dwindled away. Today the HOG has more than a million members who participate in rides and rallies together.

BRAND OUTLOOK

- By transforming the way it manufactures its products, Harley-Davidson is increasing flexibility, efficiency, and competitiveness.
- The company is experimenting with new ways of marketing its products in foreign countries.
- The brand is already popular in Europe, but India and Asia could eventually become its largest markets.
- Continuing economic recession could stifle growth in the near future.

Harley-Davidson has embarked on a massive transformation of the way it manufactures motorcycles, incorporating more flexibility and efficiency into its production process and aiming to reduce the time required to launch products by 30 percent. New models, innovative styling, and related accessories will be introduced in 2013. An Internet program will allow buyers to select options in more than 2,000 combinations, build a highly customized motorcycle on the computer screen, and order it online. These changes are meant to make the business more competitive and to broaden its customer base, particularly in foreign countries, since the brand already has a large percentage of the market in the United States.

Harley-Davidson is also initiating new ways of marketing its brand globally. For example, instead of exporting entire motorcycles to India, the second-largest market in the world, the company will try a new strategy of shipping component kits from the United States for assembly in India. In past years trade barriers have stymied Harley-Davidson's attempts to compete in India, but the company is now cultivating dealerships there.

India and Asia offer great possibilities for Harley-Davidson because the region has a rapidly increasing population and a long history of motorcycle use. Although customers there tend to purchase small, inexpensive brands, Harley hopes to appeal to a growing middle class of people who can afford leisure and high-end motorcycles. Because Harley enjoys an impressive reputation worldwide, some foreign customers are enthused about having the chance to buy one of their own. The brand is already popular and increasing its sales throughout Europe, especially in Sweden and Germany, and the firm has plans to enlarge its presence in Latin America and Africa.

In the United States the company is attempting to appeal more to women and young riders, but widespread economic troubles in the United States and Europe caused a precipitous drop in sales during the past few years and that could persist. Between August 2011 and August 2012, Harley sales decreased by 9 percent in Europe. Although sales during that period rose 4 percent in the United States, this growth was significantly slower than the previous year's 25 percent increase for the same quarter. Overall, the company forecasts a sales increase of 5 percent to 7 percent throughout 2012.

FURTHER READING

Hamner, Susanna. "Harley, You're Not Getting Any Younger." *New York Times*, March 22, 2009.

Hanlon, Mike. "The World's Largest Motorcycle Manufacturer Considers Ducati Purchase." *Gizmag*, March 6, 2012. Accessed September 18, 2012. http://www.gizmag.com/hero-motocorp-worlds-largest-motorcycle-manufacturer-ducati-purchase/21725/

"Harley-Davidson, Inc." *International Directory of Company Histories*. Ed. Derek Jacques and Paula Kepos. Vol. 106. Detroit, MI: St. James Press, 2010.

"Harley-Davidson, Inc." *Notable Corporate Chronologies*. Detroit, MI: Gale, 2009.

"Harley-Davidson Unveils New Single-Brand Strategy, Announcing Plans to Divest MV Agusta." *Investment Weekly News*, October 31, 2009.

Reid, Peter C. "How Harley Beat Back the Japanese." *CNN Money*, September 25, 1989. Accessed September 18, 2012. http://money.cnn.com/magazines/fortune/fortune_archive/1989/09/25/72503/index.htm

Taylor, Alex III. "Harley-Davidson's Aging Biker Problem." *CNN Money*, September 17, 2010. Accessed September 18, 2012. http://money.cnn.com/2010/09/17/autos/harley_davidson_fall.fortune/index.htm

U.S. Commercial Service. "Motorcycles; European Market Briefs 2011–2012." U.S. Department of Commerce. http://export.gov/build/groups/public/@eg_main/@byind/@autotrans/documents/webcontent/motocycles046223.pdf

Wicks, Frank. "Between the Horse and Car." *Mechanical Engineering-CIME*, July 2003. *Business Insights: Essentials*. Accessed September 19, 2012. http://bi.galegroup.com/essentials/article/GALE%7CA105477882/c09712dd4c442b0e3ab3e705998087c8

Yousuf, Hibah. "Harley-Davidson Shares Skid after Sales Miss." *CNN Money*, August 1, 2012. Accessed September 18, 2012. http://buzz.money.cnn.com/2012/08/01/harley-davidson-earnings/

HEINEKEN

AT A GLANCE

Brand Synopsis: Sold in 178 countries worldwide, Heineken, the first truly global and one of the most valuable international beer brands, is associated with high quality and a fashionable yet accessible brand identity.
Parent Company: Heineken N.V.
Tweede Weteringplantsoen 21
Amsterdam, 1017 ZD
The Netherlands
http://www.heineken.com/
Sector: Consumer Staples
Industry Group: Food, Beverage & Tobacco
Performance: *Market share*—11 percent of the global market and 20.5 percent of the international premium beer market (2011). *Sales*—EUR17.1 billion (US$22.5 billion) (2011).
Principal Competitors: Anheuser-Busch InBev; Asahi Breweries; Asia Pacific Breweries; Carlsberg A/S; Diageo plc; Grupo Modelo C.V. de S.A.; Kingway Brewery; Mendocino Brewing Company, Inc.; SAB Miller

BRAND ORIGINS

- Heineken lager was first brewed in Amsterdam in the late 19th century.
- In the mid-20th century Heineken's largest market outside the Netherlands was the United States.
- Heineken beer has been marketed as a premium, international lager since the 1950s.

The Dutch-based Heineken originated in the 1860s. Gerard Adriaan Heineken bought one of the largest breweries in Amsterdam, De Hooiberg, which translates to "the haystack" in English, in 1864. In striving to produce a lager that was better-tasting and of better quality than other beers available in the city, the talented brewer and businessman hoped to create a thriving beer culture in Amsterdam.

Sales of Heineken's signature lager grew quickly. Four years later, De Hooiberg could no longer keep up with demand, and Heineken founded a new brewery outside Amsterdam and another outside Rotterdam in 1874. In a move that would prove crucial to his brand's long term success, Heineken hired a pupil of scientist Louis Pasteur, Dr. H. Elion, to breed a type of yeast especially suitable for making beer. Elion's research produced the Heineken A-yeast, which has been a major determinant in the flavor of Heineken beer since 1888. The integration of the new yeast quickly led to more successes for the brand, including the brewery's winning the Grand Prix at the 1889 World's Fair in Paris and expansion outwards from the Netherlands into Dutch colonies around the world and, by 1900, parts of Asia.

Gerard Heineken retired in 1914, and his son, Dr. Henri Pierre Heineken, took over the company's brewing operations officially in 1917. One key decision for the company during the early years of the 20th century involved exporting to the United States. Although the first barrels of Heineken had reached the United States in 1880, it was not until the early 20th century that the beer was imported on a regular basis. New York City was the first major market for Heineken in the United States. Although Prohibition eliminated the U.S. market in the 1920s, the United States became Heineken's largest market outside the Netherlands after the repeal of Prohibition, and the beer became the top-selling import in the United States.

Henri Heineken's son, Alfred Henry Heineken, joined the family business during the World War II era. The younger Heineken implemented significant changes in the company's marketing strategy in the second half of the 20th century. Alfred Henry Heineken noted that many Americans bought beer in supermarkets for home consumption in addition to drinking beer in pubs, which was not the case in most European countries. In 1948 Heineken beer became available in Dutch grocery stores, extending the company's product reach. To further boost sales, Alfred Heineken also launched the company's first radio advertisements, which helped widen its distribution network.

By the 1970s, sales were generally strong worldwide although Heineken beer held only about 2.8 percent of the European market in 1971. By 1973 Heineken had become the number one imported beer in the United States once again. From the 1970s until the late 1980s, parent company Heineken N.V. expanded the number of markets where Heineken was sold and produced, adding such markets as Jamaica, Ireland, Italy, Japan, and Spain. By the 1980s, Heineken was also the leading imported beer in Japan, Canada, and Australia. In 1989 Heineken became the most widely sold international brand of beer, available in more than 170 countries, while Heineken N.V. became the second-largest brewer in the world.

In the 1980s, Heineken initiated a more focused international marketing and advertising strategy. With ads that featured slogans like "When you make a great beer, you don't have to make a great fuss," Heineken differentiated itself from cheaper beers by emphasizing Heineken as a status symbol and as a premium beer.

Heineken experienced challenges in the late 1990s, when sales began to decline in the United States. To address this downturn, Heineken shifted its advertising strategy to attract beer drinkers aged 21 to 35, producing such campaigns as "It's All about Beer," which focused on humor. "It's All about Beer" remained the brand's tagline throughout the late 1990s and early 2000s. The shift in advertising tone paid off as U.S. sales reached 35 million cases in 1995 and 54 million cases in 2000. The brand also experienced increased competition during this period, however, and in the late 1990s, Heineken was replaced as the best-selling imported beer in the United States by Corona Extra.

To retain and also expand its market in the new millennium, Heineken added new products such as Heineken Premium Light in 2005, began advertising on television again in 2007, and launched marketing partnerships with Google and Facebook in 2011. Visually engaging advertising campaigns, like 2011's "Open Your World," also attracted consumer attention. Despite a challenging postrecession market, Heineken N.V.'s revenues have continued to grow, reaching US$21.4 billion in 2010 and US$22.1 billion in 2011.

BRAND ELEMENTS

- Heineken's flavor is created through the use of Heineken A-yeast, developed in 1888.
- Alfred Heineken redesigned Heineken's brand elements in the mid-20th century.
- The Heineken green bottle has been shown to be the most recognizable beer bottle in the world.

For many beer drinkers, the Heineken brand is associated with an international, premium appeal. One aspect of this appeal is the taste and composition of the beer itself. Heineken is made with only four ingredients: malted barley, hops, water, and Heineken A-yeast. It is the yeast that is particularly important: it has been a major determinant of the flavor of the beer since Dr. Elion created the yeast in 1888. More than a century later, Heineken A-yeast is still used in Heineken lager as well as Heineken Premium Light.

Visually, Heineken is associated with a distinctive green color, known as Heineken green, which is used on the beer's label. Alfred Heineken, who was greatly interested in advertising, redesigned the brand elements in the mid-20th century. He introduced the brand's use of the red star, a symbol often associated with the Heineken brand and one of the most recognized beer symbols in the world.

Perhaps Alfred Heineken's greatest innovation was the introduction of the Heineken signature green bottle. Although the green bottles cost more, they added a distinctive look to the brand and made it more popular. Brand awareness studies have found that if the labels are removed from beer bottles, Heineken is the only brand that maintains product recognition among consumers based on the bottle alone.

Over the years, changes were made to Heineken's label and bottle. In 2010 the STR bottle made its debut. This aluminum bottle revealed a hidden pattern of stars when viewed under a black light. In late 2012 the classic green bottle underwent its first redesign since 1946. Dubbed the Star Bottle and expected to launch globally in 2013, the bottle remained green but was taller and thinner and featured an embossed thumb groove to improve grip.

BRAND IDENTITY

- Heineken assumed its identity as a global brand in the 1950s.
- Heineken is marketed as a high-quality, upscale beer.
- Many of Heineken's ads emphasize the beer's international identity.
- Heineken has been James Bond's beer of choice since 1998 through product placement in the James Bond films.

Although Heineken had been exported to markets outside the Netherlands since 1876, it was not until Alfred Heineken's tenure as head of the company in the 1950s that Heineken took on its identity as a global brand and international premium lager. During this time, exporting shifted from a distribution strategy to become the core of Heineken's brand identity. As the first truly international beer brand, Heineken sought and continues to seek new markets across the world, building on its reputation as a beer enjoyed globally.

Heineken is available in at least 178 countries. The Heineken name is associated with a fashionable, superior product accessible to the everyday beer drinker and produced according to high standards. Many of Heineken's advertisements emphasize the international, upscale lifestyle associated with the brand. In the 1980s, one of the brand's campaigns asserted, "When you make a great beer, you don't have to make a great fuss." In 2011 the brand launched a global campaign titled "Open Your World." The company's campaign-specific television ads consisted of short films emphasizing a fun, chic atmosphere. The campaign focused on the three categories of "Perfection," "Friendship," and "Something New" and was reinforced by the brand's Open Your World campaign webpage.

Heineken is closely identified with its distinctive green beer bottles, the red star featured on the product's labels and bottle caps, and the Heineken lettering on labels in Heineken green, red, and black. In 2007 Heineken Premium Light became available in 12-ounce slim cans that featured visual elements taken from the bottle but with new packaging to differentiate the product from Heineken lager. Launched in 2011, Heineken's new global company visual identity also played off of and reshaped the brand's basic elements.

Heineken has focused its marketing and branding strategies on sponsorships of select sports, films, music, and cultural events to emphasize the brand's core identity. Heineken was a sponsor of the 1928 Olympic Games, held in Amsterdam, and of the 2012 Summer Olympics, in London. It has also sponsored the U.S. Open tennis tournament, the Rugby World Cup, and UEFA Champions League soccer. Heineken has secured product placement in several James Bond films since 1998, including 2012's *Skyfall*. Heineken's music sponsorships include festivals such as Coachella and Ultra in the United States, Rock in Rio in Brazil, Oxegen in Ireland, and the Open'er Festival in Poland.

BRAND STRATEGY

- When Heineken Premium Light was introduced in 2005, it was the first major product addition in the company's history.
- Heineken strives to identify and pursue new markets each year, especially emerging markets in Africa, Asia, and Central and South America.
- Heineken debuted the global brand campaign "Open Your World" in 2011.

For much of its history, Heineken focused on one product, its premium lager. It was not until beer consumption was on the decline in the Europe and the United States in the early 21st century that Heineken introduced a new beer that would remain part of its long-term strategy. In 2005 Heineken Premium Light (also known as Heineken Light) made its debut in the United States. It was intended to tap into the growing light beer segment and was the first major product addition in the company's history. Other Heineken beers available only in certain markets or for limited times have included Heineken Dark, Heineken Extra Cold, Heineken Oud Bruin, and Heineken Tarwebok.

Heineken N.V.'s primary focus remains building the market for its flagship Heineken premium lager worldwide. The company strives to identify and pursue new markets each year, especially emerging markets in Africa, Asia, and Central and South America. Although Heineken has been available in many countries for decades, the brand sees the long-term potential for growth in markets such as Ethiopia, China, India, Brazil, and Mexico. Heineken's worldwide advertising efforts reflect this emphasis on the international nature of the brand. The company's 2011 global campaign was titled "Open Your World." Similarly, Heineken Premium Light's 2011 advertising campaign featured the slogan "Be a Man of the World."

BRAND EQUITY

- Heineken was the third-most valuable beer brand in the world in 2011.
- Heineken's sales increased in 2012 despite significant declines in its U.S. market share in previous years.
- Interbrand's Best Global Brands 2012 ranked Heineken 92nd among the top 100 brands, with a brand value of US$3.9 billion.

Heineken is a valuable international brand, and its efforts to market itself as a truly global beer have proved lucrative. According to the research company Millward Brown, which ranked the top ten most valuable beer brands in the world, Heineken was the third-most valuable brand in the world in 2011, after Bud Light and Budweiser. Heineken held a similar ranking in the BrandZ™ Top 100 Most Valuable Global Brands list of 2012. According to BrandZ™, Heineken was the third-most valuable beer brand in the world, with a brand value of US$6 billion. However, Heineken's brand value had slipped 8 percent from the previous year. Interbrand's Best Global Brands 2012 ranked Heineken 92nd among the top 100 brands, with a brand value of US$3.9 billion, an increase of 3 percent over 2011. Only Budweiser, in 31st place (US$11.9 billion), and Corona Extra, in 89th place (US$4 billion), were ranked higher.

Although Heineken, no longer the number one imported beer in the United States, faced a decline in U.S. market share between 2009 and 2011, the brand experienced growth in various markets in Europe, Africa, and the Americas in 2011. Focused marketing also led Heineken to increased sales worldwide in 2012.

BRAND AWARENESS

- Heineken was ranked second only to Budweiser in a global survey of consumers' awareness of beer brands in 2003.
- Heineken has cultivated top-of-mind brand awareness through its strategic digital campaigns.
- By 2012 Heineken had 5 million Facebook friends, the most of any beer brand.

Since Heineken began production in the late 19th century in the Netherlands, it has grown from a locally produced beer to one available in at least 178 countries across the globe. Its signature lager has remained essentially unchanged since 1888, and it has become one of the most recognized premium beer brands in the world. Heineken has worked to increase the number of markets in which it operates, remains highly valued by consumers, and stands essentially alone as a truly global beer brand in the minds of consumers around the world.

In 2003 a survey jointly undertaken by *Business Week* and Interbrand showed that Heineken is ranked second only to Budweiser where consumer brand awareness is concerned. Heineken remains the only beer brand that consumers easily recognize based on the bottle alone. Heineken leverages sponsorships of European soccer (UEFA Champions League), music festivals across the globe, and other events to increase its top-of-mind awareness. Strategic marketing partnerships with Google and Facebook also have helped the brand remain relevant globally and have underscored its status as a premium brand. Heineken has also promoted top-of-mind awareness through digital campaigns, including a strong web presence. By 2012 Heineken had 5 million friends on Facebook (the most of any beer brand), which has enabled the brand to connect with loyal customers in countries all over the world.

BRAND OUTLOOK

- Heineken faced weaker sales in certain markets due to factors like high unemployment between 2009 and 2011.
- The brand experienced growth of 5.4 percent overall between 2010 and 2011.
- Emerging markets accounted for more than half of Heineken N.V.'s revenues in the first half of 2011.

In 2011 annual report, Heineken N.V. laid out five key business priorities, including the importance of growing the Heineken brand. Although the report noted that Heineken was the leader in the international premium beer segment in 2011, the brand faced declining market share in the United States. Heineken remained the number two imported beer in the United States in 2011, however, as it had for over a decade. Weaker sales during this period—caused by weather, high unemployment, and declining consumer confidence—limited growth in Heineken's traditionally strong markets in Europe and the Americas.

Despite these challenges, coordinated marketing efforts resulted in an increase in sales volume in Western Europe, the Americas, Africa and the Middle East, and Asia Pacific between 2010 and 2011 and led to 5.4 percent growth overall for Heineken. By 2012 Heineken N.V. saw its sales turn around globally, especially in the United States and Mexico. Emerging markets accounted for more than half of the company's revenue in the first half of 2011, and it was in markets like China, Brazil, Nigeria, and Mexico where most future growth was expected to occur. Astute marketing choices, including online advertising and sponsorships of music festivals, soccer, and rugby, helped position Heineken for a strong future.

FURTHER READING

Haig, Matt. "Heineken: The Export Brand." *Brand Royalty*. London: Kogan Page, 2004.

"Heineken." *Best Global Brands 2012*. Interbrand. Accessed December 1, 2012. http://www.interbrand.com/en/best-global-brands/2012/Heineken.

"Heineken." *Encyclopedia of Consumer Brands*. Ed. Janice Jorgensen. Vol. 1. Detroit, MI: St. James Press, 1994.

"Heineken: Refreshing Parts Out of Reach." *Marketing Week*, November 20, 2008.

"Heineken Launches New 'Star Bottle' Design; Same World-Class Taste, Sleek New Look to Hit Select New York On-Premise Accounts." PR Newswire, September 17, 2012.

Heineken N.V. "Annual Report 2011." Accessed December 2, 2012. http://www.annualreport.heineken.com/pdf/heineken-nv-annual-report-2011-eng.pdf.

"Heineken to Fire up Its Engines of Growth in Emerging Markets." *Business Monitor International*, April 6, 2011. Accessed January 9, 2013. http://marketpublishers.com/lists/9830/news.html.

Highman, Beth Watson, David E. Salamie, and Christina Stansell Weaver. "Heineken N.V." *International Directory of Company Histories*. Ed Tina Grant. Vol. 90. Detroit, MI: St. James Press, 2008.

Lane, Mark. "Heineken USA Inc." *Encyclopedia of Major Marketing Campaigns*. Vol. 2. Detroit, MI: Gale, 2007.

Millward Brown. "Beers." *BrandZ Top 100 Most Valuable Global Brands*, 2012. Accessed January 9, 2013. http://www.millwardbrown.com/brandz/Top_100_Global_Brands/Categories/Beer.aspx.

Veen, Maaike. "Brewmaster Built Brand's Popularity; The Dutch Brewer Learned the Power of Mass Marketing and Advertising." *Globe and Mail* (Toronto), January 7, 2002: R7.

HEINZ

AT A GLANCE

Brand Synopsis: Heinz is the world's top ketchup brand, and a leader in sauces, beans, and other food categories.
Parent Company: H.J. Heinz Company
P.O. Box 57
Pittsburgh, Pennsylvania 15230-0057
United States
http://www.heinz.com
Sector: Consumer Staples
Industry Group: Food & Staples Retailing
Performance: *Market share*—60 percent in the United States, 70 percent in Canada, and 78 percent in the United Kingdom of the market for ketchup (2012). *Sales*—US$4.5 billion (2012).
Principal Competitors: Campbell Soup Company; ConAgra Foods Inc.; Nestlé S.A.; Associated British Foods plc; Kraft Foods Group Inc.

BRAND ORIGINS

- At the age of eight, H.J. Heinz Company founder Henry John Heinz began selling produce from his family's plot to nearby neighbors during the 1850s.
- In 1876 John Henry Heinz formed a partnership with his brother John and cousin Frederick named F&J Heinz, which became H.J. Heinz Company in 1888.
- H.J. Heinz Company's phrase "57 Varieties" was coined in 1892.
- The H.J. Heinz Company incorporated in 1900.
- H.J. Heinz Company founder Henry Heinz died at age 75 in 1919.

The origins of the H.J. Heinz Company can be traced to Sharpsburg, Pennsylvania, where eight-year-old Henry John Heinz began selling produce from his family's garden to nearby neighbors. By the time he was 16 Heinz had several employees and was making three deliveries a week to Pittsburgh grocers.

In 1869, after Heinz had graduated from a local business school, he and L.C. Noble formed a partnership called Heinz, Noble & Company to sell bottled horseradish. Their product line soon expanded to include sauerkraut, vinegar, and pickles. Following the panic of 1873 and subsequent economic chaos, the business failed in 1875, but Heinz quickly regrouped. With his brother John and cousin Frederick as partners and himself as manager, the following year Heinz formed the partnership of F&J Heinz to manufacture condiments, pickles, and other prepared food. Ketchup was added to the product line in 1876.

In 1888 the partnership was reorganized as H.J. Heinz Company after Heinz gained financial control of the firm. Soon Heinz was known throughout the country as the "pickle king." The phrase "57 Varieties" was coined in 1892. Tomato soup and beans in tomato sauce were quickly added to the product line. Even as "57 Varieties" became a household slogan, the company had more than 60 products. At the World's Columbian Exposition in

Chicago in 1893, Heinz had the largest exhibit of any U.S. food company.

By 1900, the year the company was incorporated, H.J. Heinz Company occupied a major niche in U.S. business. It was first in the production of ketchup, pickles, mustard, and vinegar and fourth in the packing of olives. Overall the company made more than 200 products. Still, Heinz liked the lilt of his original slogan and in 1900 put it up in lights in New York City's first large electric sign, at Fifth Avenue and 23rd Street. A total of 1,200 lights illuminated a 40-foot-long green pickle and its advertising message.

By 1905 the company had opened its first factory in England. Henry Heinz died at age 75 in 1919. At that time the company had a workforce of 6,500 employees and maintained 25 branch factories. Heinz was succeeded as president of the company by his son, Howard, who branched into two new areas: ready-to-eat soups and baby food. He remained president until his death in 1941. Howard's son, H.J. Heinz II (known as Jack), became president of the company at his father's death

From 1941, when Jack took over, to 1946, H.J. Heinz's sales nearly doubled. Jack Heinz's tenure was distinguished by expansion of the company, both internationally and at home. Subsidiaries were launched in the Netherlands, Venezuela, Japan, Italy, and Portugal. In 1960 and 1961, H.J. Heinz Company acquired the assets of Reymer & Bros., Inc., and Hachmeister, Inc. StarKist Foods was acquired in 1963 and Ore-Ida Foods, Inc., in 1965.

During the 25 years that H.J. Heinz II was chief executive, the food industry changed greatly. The era was marked by the rise of supermarket chains and the development of new distribution and marketing systems. In 1966 H. J. Heinz II stepped down as president and CEO, although he retained his position as chairperson until his death in February 1987.

BRAND ELEMENTS

- Coined in 1892, the Heinz tagline "57 Varieties" continues to appear on product packaging, even though the company offers more than 57 varieties of its brand.
- The Heinz brand is often represented by a classic white, shield-like logo that features the "Heinz" name at the top.
- The Heinz brand encompasses several products, including soups and beans, but is perhaps best known for its tomato ketchup.
- Heinz has been reluctant to modify the flavor of its ketchup.

The Heinz brand has been associated with the phrase "57 Varieties" since 1892. Although the number of products associated with the brand name quickly grew beyond 57, the tagline became a permanent part of Heinz's identity. During the early 21st century "57 Varieties" continued to appear on the labeling for Heinz Tomato Ketchup.

The Heinz brand is often represented by a classic white, shield-like logo that features the "Heinz" name at the top. The logo is outlined with gold and green borders. The product description, such as "tomato ketchup" or "yellow mustard," is sometimes featured in the center of the shield. However, marketing catchphrases sometimes replace the product description. Some Heinz labeling retains the shield-like outline and company name but uses entirely different color schemes.

Although the Heinz brand encompasses several products, including soups and beans, tomato ketchup is in many ways the masthead. H.J. Heinz Company's 2012 annual report, titled *Growing Ketchup Globally*, prominently features a bottle of Heinz Tomato Ketchup adorned with the flags of different nations. In the report, Chairman, President, and CEO William R. Johnson explained: "It is no accident that Ketchup & Sauces dominates our portfolio. It is our crown jewel, our founder's legacy and our fastest-growing core category."

Indeed, the glass Heinz Tomato Ketchup bottle with its white metal cap has achieved iconic status. By the early 21st century the majority of Heinz Tomato Ketchup was marketed to consumers in plastic, squeezable bottles, with glass bottles reserved for restaurants. In 2011 the company temporarily made available to the public the 14-ounce glass bottles, featuring a vintage Heinz label.

According to the October 26, 2011, issue of The New York Times, Heinz has been reluctant to modify the flavor of its ketchup. In 2000 Heinz introduced green and purple colorized versions of its ketchup formula, intended for children, which were removed from the market three years later. Nearly 10 years after the introduction of a hot and spicy variation, the company introduced Heinz Tomato Ketchup Blended with Balsamic Vinegar. The original Heinz Tomato Ketchup formula also has been modified to introduce versions for those with specific health needs. Examples include salt- and gluten-free versions.

BRAND IDENTITY

- Heinz's brand identity is virtually synonymous with its flagship tomato ketchup.
- Heinz has differentiated itself by offering tomato ketchup that is much thicker and richer than its competitors.
- Throughout the years, the popularity of Heinz ketchup has been reinforced by both consumer and celebrity endorsements.

Heinz's brand identity is virtually synonymous with its flagship tomato ketchup. Although condiments are often taken for granted, Heinz has differentiated itself by offering tomato ketchup that is much thicker and richer than its competitors. Beyond quality, the Heinz brand also has a strong reputation for innovation and value. These qualities have not gone unnoticed with consumers, who have developed a strong affinity for the brand. As *The Huffington Post* reported in its November 26, 2012, issue, Heinz is "easily the most well-known catch up in the U.S."

Throughout the years, the popularity of Heinz ketchup has been reinforced by both consumer and celebrity endorsements. For example, in 2003 Heinz's "talking labels campaign" gave consumers the opportunity to "Say Something Ketchuppy" by offering phrases for ketchup bottles that reflected their feelings about the brand. These reflections included phrases such as: "Makes Hot Dogs Chase Their Tails" and "Are Your French Fries Lonely?"

The following year, Heinz built on the momentum of the "Say Something Ketchuppy" campaign by engaging celebrities such as former Star Trek actor William Shatner to get their own takes on the brand. Accompanying Shatner's "Fixes Burgers at Warp Speed" were on-label phrases like "Burger-licious" from actress Lindsay Lohan.

Heinz's identity is a global one, and it was among the first American food brands to stake its claim in emerging markets during the late 1990s. By the early 21st-century Heinz had made significant inroads in Russia, for example, where Chairman, President and CEO William Johnson said tomato ketchup was "better than vodka," according to the August 21, 2008, edition of CNBC's *Mad Money*. Heinz ketchup, gravy, and other sauces were popular in emerging markets because they offered better flavor for cheaper cuts of meat purchased by emerging middle class consumers.

BRAND STRATEGY

- Heinz's success and longevity can be attributed to the brand's ability to adapt to changing consumer needs and tastes.
- Faced with a relatively mature domestic market, emerging countries are a key component of Heinz's brand strategy.
- During its 2012 fiscal year, a record 21 percent of the H.J. Heinz Company's sales were attributed to emerging markets, and the company generated approximately 66 percent of its sales beyond the United States.

As *The Huffington Post* reported in its November 26, 2012, issue, Heinz is "easily the most well-known catch up in the U.S." With a firmly established position in the United States, emerging markets represent the best opportunities for expanding the Heinz brand. Heinz gained an edge on competitors by being one of the first American food brands to stake its claim in emerging markets during the late 1990s.

By the early 21st-century Heinz had made significant inroads with its ketchup in several emerging markets, including China, Russia, and Brazil, where more consumers were "slathering the tomato-based sauce on their cuisines," according to the February 17, 2012, issue of *The Los Angeles Times*. Heinz ketchup, gravy, and other sauces were popular in emerging markets because they improved the flavor of cheaper cuts of meat purchased by the growing number of new middle class consumers. During its 2012 fiscal year, a record 21 percent of the H.J. Heinz Company's sales were attributed to emerging markets, and the company generated approximately 66 percent of its sales beyond the United States.

Great opportunity existed in China, where ketchup was just catching on and many consumers referred to it as "tomato sauce." The Russian market was a different story in that it had become the world's second-largest ketchup market. According to the August 21, 2008, edition of CNBC's *Mad Money*, Heinz Chairman, President, and CEO William Johnson said that in Russia tomato ketchup was "better than vodka." Heinz touted its ketchup brand with print advertising in cities like Moscow, where its ketchup label, complete with Russian text, was displayed not on glass bottles, but a brick-like pattern of chopped tomatoes.

Heinz's brand strategy also has involved staying connected with consumer's positive feelings about the brand. One excellent example of this is myHeinz.com. The website allowed customers to order customized bottles of Heinz ketchup or Dijon mustard with special messages or photos. From the classic 14 ounce glass bottle to containers like "The Little Guy" and "The Squeezable," consumers were able to celebrate special occasions like the birth of a child or a wedding with custom phrases.

Heinz's success and longevity can be attributed to the brand's ability to adapt to changing consumer needs, tastes, and busy lifestyles. In the United Kingdom Heinz introduced its Heinz Beanz Fridge Pack, a resealable container with a see-through window that offers convenient access to beans for breakfast or chili. Also in the United Kingdom, Heinz introduced a Spaghetti Hoops Fridge Pack, as well as Squeeze & Stir Soup packets.

BRAND EQUITY

- In 2012 the Heinz brand generated sales of nearly US$4.5 billion for the H.J. Heinz Company.
- Heinz placed 46th in Interbrand's ranking of the top 100 global brands in 2012.
- According to *Global 500*, Heinz was the ninth-most-valuable food brand in 2011.
- In 2011 the H.J. Heinz Co. was the sixth-most-valuable U.S. food production company, according to the *Financial Times'* FT 500.

Heinz's brand equity is reflected in its status as the world leader in the ketchup category. In addition, the brand also enjoys a second-leading global position in the sauces category. In more than 50 countries, Heinz-branded products enjoy market share of first or second place. In 2012 the brand produced sales of nearly US$4.5 billion for the H.J. Heinz Company. That year, Heinz ranked 46th on Interbrand's list of the best global brands.

Citing data from *Global 500, Market Share Reporter* indicated that Heinz was the ninth-most-valuable food brand in 2011. In addition, the H.J. Heinz Co. was the sixth-most-valuable U.S. food production company in 2011, according to the *Financial Times'* FT 500. In mid-2011 the publication *Investor's Business Daily* indicated that Heinz was one of the highest-rated stocks in its Food-Packaged industry grouping. Among 26 companies, Heinz ranked seventh. That year, Heinz also received Processor of the Year honors from *Food Processing*.

BRAND AWARENESS

- The strong awareness surrounding the Heinz brand is commensurate with a heritage spanning more than 140 years.
- The Heinz brand is well-known throughout the world, holding first- or second-place market share positions in more than 50 countries.
- The strong awareness surrounding the Heinz brand also has benefited from unexpected celebrity endorsements.
- In 2011 Heinz received a first-place ranking in the American Customer Satisfaction Index and was the leader among food manufacturers for the 12th straight year.

The strong awareness surrounding the Heinz brand is commensurate with a heritage spanning more than 140 years. As *The Huffington Post* reported in its November 26, 2012, issue, Heinz is "easily the most well-known catch up in the U.S." Beyond the United States, the brand is well-known throughout the world, holding first- or second-place market share positions in more than 50 countries. Heinz enjoys a global leadership position in the ketchup category, driven by top-of-mind awareness that drives the sale of approximately 650 million bottles annually.

The strong awareness surrounding the Heinz brand also has benefited from unexpected celebrity endorsements. For example, in late 2012 actor Jackson Rathbone, from the popular movie series, Twilight, surprised the public by having a Heinz ketchup tattoo on his right calf. Jackson revealed the tattoo in November, on *The Wendy Williams Show*, where he confessed a love for ketchup dating back to his childhood years.

Heinz has taken innovative steps to generate brand awareness. One example is the "Join the Growing Movement" campaign. After converting its 20-ounce ketchup bottles for restaurants to PlantBottles, a form of environmentally responsible packaging that was made of 30 percent sugarcane, the company adorned labels with QR codes linking customers with The Nature Conservancy. The campaign was an innovative way to reach customers while they waited for their restaurant order, generate brand excitement, and promote a greater cause at the same time.

In 2011 Heinz received a first-place ranking in the American Customer Satisfaction Index (ACSI). Among food manufacturers, Heinz was the leader for the 12th straight year. Its leading ranking stemmed from strong performance in categories such as consumer expectations, loyalty, quality, and value. In particular, Heinz has demonstrated the ability to adapt its offerings to continuously changing consumer needs and tastes. For example, Heinz offers organic and gluten-free variations of its popular ketchup.

BRAND OUTLOOK

- In 2012 Heinz Chairman, President, and CEO William R. Johnson indicated that the company had only scratched the surface of the global US$110 billion Ketchup & Sauces market.
- Faced with a relatively mature domestic market, Heinz looked to emerging countries for future growth.
- Heinz's commitment to new product development is evident via the formation of Innovation Centers in Europe and other global markets.

Heading into 2013, Heinz was in a strong position. On an annual basis, the brand generated approximately US$4.5 billion in sales for the H.J. Heinz Company. In addition, the Heinz name had gained the trust of consumers throughout the world.

Looking to the future, Heinz Chairman, President, and CEO William R. Johnson was optimistic about the brand's future prospects. In Heinz's *2012 Annual Report*, Johnson indicated that the company's Ketchup & Sauces category would continue to be a focal point. Calling it "our crown jewel, our founder's legacy and our fastest-growing core category," he explained that Heinz had only begun to tap into the global Ketchup & Sauces market, which was valued at US$110 billion. The category achieved 14 percent growth during the company's 2012 fiscal year alone, and was projected to account for 60 percent of total sales within three to five years.

Faced with a relatively mature domestic market, Heinz looked to other countries for future growth. Its strategy includes both organic and acquisition-related growth. For example, in addition to expanding Russian manufacturing capabilities, Heinz acquired an 80 percent ownership interest in Coniexpress S.A. Industrias Alimenticias, a Brazilian producer of ketchup, tomato paste, sauces, condiments, and vegetables.

Heinz's future success depends in part on its ability to continuously develop new offerings for consumers. Heinz's commitment to new product development was evident via the formation of a new Innovation Center in Europe. In addition, Heinz had plans to establish a similar facility in Asia.

Beyond Innovation Centers, Heinz was focused developing new product subcategories to drive sales in a challenging economy. In 2011 Heinz established its Explorer Group to help discover new product opportunities. The United Kingdom was an excellent example of the company's efforts in this area. By late 2012 Heinz had announced a two-year plan to double the number of new products and product variations, such as its Heinz Big Ready Meals.

FURTHER READING

"ACSI Taps Heinz No. 1 in Customer Satisfaction." *Professional Services Close-Up*, November 19, 2011.

"Best Global Brands 2012." Interbrand, 2012. Accessed February 28, 2013. http://www.interbrand.com/en/best-global-brands/2012/Best-Global-Brands-2012.aspx.

Fusaro, Dave. "Processor of the Year: H.J. Heinz Co." *Food Processing*, December 2011.

H.J. Heinz Company. "Celebrities Speak out on Heinz Ketchup Talking Labels; The Thick and Rich … and Famous Gets Four Stars." September 21, 2004. Accessed February 28, 2013. http://www.heinz.com/our-company/press-room/press-releases/press-release.aspx?ndmConfigId=1012072&newsId=20040921005128.

———. *2012 Annual Report. Growing Ketchup Globally*. Accessed February 28, 2013. http://www.heinz.com/AR_2012/Heinz_Annual_Report_2012.pdf.

"H.J. Heinz Company." *International Directory of Company Histories*. Ed. Jay P. Pederson. Vol. 99. Detroit, MI: St. James Press, 2009.

"Heinz CEO: Ketchup 'Better Than Vodka' in Russia." *Mad Money*, August 21, 2008.

"Heinz Jalapeno Ketchup Taste Test: Not Bad, but Can't Beat the Original." *Huffington Post*, November 26, 2012.

"Heinz: Ketchup Craze in Russia, China, Not So Much in the U.S." *Los Angeles Times*, February 17, 2012.

Joseph, Seb. "Heinz to Double Number of Product Innovations in UK." *Marketing Week*, September 13, 2012.

Mao, Vincent. "Heinz Targets Fast-Growing Economies." *Investor's Business Daily*, July 29, 2011.

Newman, Andrew Adam. "Ketchup Moves Upmarket, with a Balsamic Tinge." *New York Times*, October 26, 2011.

HERMÈS

AT A GLANCE

Brand Synopsis: One of the world's most elegant retailers, known for fine craftsmanship and luxury, Hermès specializes in leather handbags, luggage, and upscale apparel.
Parent Company: Hermès International
24, rue du Faubourg Saint-Honoré
75008 Paris
France
http://www.Hermès.com
Sector: Consumer Discretionary
Industry Group: Retailing
Performance: *Market share*—Hermès was the fourth-largest luxury goods firm worldwide in terms of sales (2009). *Sales*—US$3.6 billion (2011)
Principal Competitors: Louis Vuitton; Giorgio Armani; Gucci; Richemont; Burberry

BRAND ORIGINS

- Hermès was named for its founder, Thierry Hermès, in 1837.
- In the 1930s Hermès introduced some of its most iconic products, including silk scarves, ladies' purses, and the anchor chain bracelet.
- In the 1950s Hermès International began using the duc-carriage-and-horse as its logo.
- Hermès was run by members of the original family until 2006, when Patrick Thomas took over the company's leadership.

The Hermès Fashion House was founded in 1837 by Thierry Hermès, a German immigrant to France. The store initially served as a shop for leather harnesses. The brand's initial focus was to design and sell high-end harnesses to the European nobility. Hermès first mark of great success came in 1855, when he earned the first prize in class at the Exposition Universelle in Paris for his harness work. At the 1867 Exposition Universelle, Hermès won the First Class Medal for his harness work.

When Thierry Hermès's son, Charles-Émile, took over the shop in the 1880s, he moved the location from the Grands Boulevards location in Paris to 24, Faubourg Saint-Honoré, near the presidential Palais de l'Élysée. The move placed the store near the elite consumers of Paris. After the transition, Charles-Émile began selling fine saddles in addition to the already much-praised harnesses. Soon after, Charles-Émile was joined by his two sons, Adolphe and Émile-Maurice, and was able to attract a new clientele in Europe, as well as in North Africa, Asia, Russia, and the Americas.

In 1902, under the direction of Adolphe and Émile-Maurice, the name was changed to Hermès Frères, meaning "Hermès Brothers." The brothers entered the 20th century on a high note, further expanding the product line to include a unique bag called a "haut à courroies," designed to allow riders to carry their saddles. By the start of World War I, the brothers had a staff of more than 70 saddlers to keep up with their growing business. Concern was growing, however, due to the increasing presence of the automobile. Émile-Maurice discovered upon a trip to the United States that technology in general was rapidly advancing. With the greater ability to travel, there was also an increased need for luggage. During his U.S. trip, Émile-Maurice discovered the zipper, a new fastener at the time, and obtained exclusive rights to use the zipper for both clothing and leather goods in Europe. It was called the "fermeture Hermès" or "the Hermès fastener."

In 1919 Émile-Maurice began to run the company alone, without Adolphe. The name was changed back to Hermès. During the 1920s Émile-Maurice expanded the brand to create and sell a wider variety of products, such as handbags, luggage, and accessories, such as scarves and jewelry. Also at this time, Émile-Maurice employed three of his sons-in-law to help with the growing company. Hermès opened several more locations in France in the 1920s and opened its first location in the United States in 1924.

As the Great Depression loomed in the 1930s, Hermès responded by launching its most famous creations. In 1935 the company released its "sac à dépêches," a simple lady's purse designed for travel. In 1937 Hermès released its first line of silk scarves. The scarves were an instant success and immediately became the most popular fashion accessory for upscale consumers. The following year, Hermès revealed another innovative product: the "chaîne d'ancre" or "anchor chain" bracelet design.

Following the death of Émile-Maurice in 1951, his son-in-law Robert Dumas took over the company and changed the name to Dumas-Hermès. It was under his guidance that Hermès began using its now-iconic logo of a duc-carriage-and-horse as well as orange boxes for packaging. Dumas also began focusing his attention on the success of the silk scarves, pursuing more artistic fabrics and patterns. In the 1950s the Faubourg Saint-Honoré location, under the direction of Annie Beaumel, began altering its window displays, turning them into theatrical productions and drawing more tourists. It was also in the 1950s that Grace Kelly, the princess of Monaco, was photographed with a "sac à dépêches": the bag was thereafter known as the "Kelly bag."

Despite the fame of the company and its popularity among celebrities, Hermès suffered a dramatic decline in the 1970s. When Jean-Louis Dumas took over the company in 1978, however, he pushed for the company to concentrate on marketing to young consumers of all demographics. He also shifted the marketing focus to scarves, leather goods, and ready-to-wear items, adding new products and methods to coincide with the traditional. He brought in new designers and began featuring unusual materials, such as python and ostrich skin. Under Dumas's guidance in the 1980s, Hermès expanded its product line to include tableware.

In the 1990s Hermès was listed on the Paris Bourse, with the Hermès/Dumas family still holding 80 percent of the stock. In subsequent years, Dumas reduced the number of franchises of the brand and increased the number of company-owned stores in an effort to ensure the quality of product. Jean-Louis Dumas retired in 2006 and was replaced by Patrick Thomas, the first leader of the company who was not a member of the Hermès family.

BRAND ELEMENTS

- Hermès duc-carriage-and-horse logo was introduced in the 1950s as a tribute to the brand's origins.
- The company packages all of its products in a distinctive orange box with the Hermès logo stamped on top.
- Some Hermès bag designs are so well known to consumers that they are immediately identifiable as Hermès products and do not bear a tag.

Hermès International's name is derived from the company's founder, Thierry Hermès, who opened the first location as a harness shop in Paris. The name has undergone some slight changes throughout the years, going from Hermès to Hermès Frères, back to Hermès, then on to Hermès-Dumas, and back again to Hermès. Though the Hermès name has remained throughout the existence of the company, the brand is often better known for its specific product lines. The most famous creations of Hermès are the Kelly bag (made famous by Grace Kelly), the Birkin bag (named for actress Jane Birkin), and the Hermès silk scarf.

Hermès's iconic logo features a duc-carriage-and-horse, colored in orange. The logo was introduced under the direction of Robert Dumas in the 1950s. The concept behind the logo was a reference to Hermès's origin as a maker of harnesses and saddles in a horse-drawn world. The color orange on the logo corresponds to the packaging that is used for all Hermès products. The plain boxes have become collectibles by themselves, as they represent the elegance and luxury of Hermès. Additionally, because some Hermès products, such as the Birkin bag, are so rare, the orange box also symbolizes an exclusivity that a consumer does not encounter in dealing with more accessible brands.

It is also noteworthy that one of the most distinctive aspects of the Hermès logo is that it is not featured on the company's most successful and famous products. The Birkin and Kelly bags do not have a tag showing off the Hermès brand. Instead, the bag designs themselves have become so famous that the brand is recognizable strictly from the design.

BRAND IDENTITY

- Hermès identifies its brand as elite, luxurious, and exclusive.

- The exclusivity of the Hermès brand can be seen in its custom products and strict "no return" policy.
- Hermès's decision in the late 1970s to appeal to a younger demographic has had no negative effect on its status as a top luxury brand.

Since the 1800s Hermès has provided quality, hand-crafted products for the elite. Beginning with harnesses and saddles for the nobility, Hermès expanded its product line throughout the centuries. The Hermès brand has consistently maintained its association with high-quality products, many of which are still hand-crafted by artisans all over the globe.

The fine quality of Hermès' goods, as well as the brand's exclusivity, continues to identify the brand today. Due to the custom nature of its products, Hermès maintains a strict "no return" policy. Made-to-order leather items are given a number that links them to the craftsman who created them in the event that there are any flaws or need for repairs. This made-to-order philosophy further promotes the brand's exclusivity and makes it popular with the world's elite. Hermès leather handbags are a status symbol among celebrities.

An additional element of the brand's identity originated in the late 1970s, as a result of a downturn in sales, when Hermès revamped its brand image to focus on younger consumers. This focus continues today, as can be seen in the 2011 Collection "Contemporary Artisan." The line remains true to the original image of being elegant but accessible but does so in a trendy, chic manner. Though the shift toward a younger, more modern identity initially stirred controversy (critics thought it made the brand seem common), the strategy proved successful, and Hermès has since been able to appeal to a wider range of consumers, without sacrificing its identity as a top luxury brand.

BRAND STRATEGY

- Hermès's strategy has remained consistent from year to year: create new products, acquire new artisans, and expand into new global markets.
- In 2011, Hermès created two new product collections and made acquisitions in watchmaking, leather goods, furniture, upholstery fabrics, and wallpaper.
- In 2011 Hermès opened retail stores in three new countries and 13 new stores in international locations where other Hermès stores already exist.

Hermès brand strategy has remained fairly consistent over the last few years: to create simple yet elegant products, to make the innovations to produce these creations, and to sell its products on a global scale. According to the 2011 annual report, these strategies remain in place.

As of 2012 Hermès International had 14 product lines, including leather, perfumes, scarves, ties, menswear, women's fashion, watches, stationery, footwear, gloves, enamel, decorative arts, tableware, and jewelry. Each year, Hermès generates a new collection of goods for these categories. In 2011, Hermès created two collections that "remained faithful to the discreet style that has defined creation at Hermès since the very beginning." Additionally, Hermès made acquisitions in watchmaking and leather goods, as well as in furniture, upholstery fabrics, and wallpaper—all of which will enable the brand to offer a larger selection of unique and distinctive items.

In addition to product line extensions, Hermès has also continued to expand the number of its retail stores on an international level. In 2011 Hermès added stores in three new locations: Kuwait, Kazakhstan, and India, where, according to the annual report, the first street-side store was opened in the historic center of Mumbai. Moreover, the company added 13 new stores to international cities that already host a Hermès store. This type of expansion is what led Hermès to record-high sales in 2010 and 2011, and to the creation of 700 new jobs.

In 2012, one further strategy will be introduced: to focus on remodeling the existing Hermès stores so that a wider selection of artisan collections can be displayed. Employees will be trained to sell these goods in order to promote the brand in a unified manner throughout the world.

BRAND EQUITY

- One Hermès *carré* (scarf) is sold every 25 seconds, on average.
- In 2012 Hermès International's brand value was estimated at US$6.2 billion by brand consultancy Interbrand.
- Hermès International is the third-ranked luxury brand on Interbrand's list and the third-most successful luxury brand in the world.

Hermès International is the third-most successful company in the world in the luxury sector. Competitor Louis Vuitton is first and Armani comes in second. According to the *Daily Mail*, one Hermès silk scarf, or "carré," is sold every 25 seconds. That means, on average, there are 3,456 Hermès scarfs sold internationally every day.

According to Interbrand's 2012 ranking of the top 100 brands, Hermès International ranked 63rd with a brand value of US$6.2 billion, whereas Louis Vuitton was ranked 17th, with a brand value of US$23.57 billion. Hermès was ranked 3rd in the luxury sector, according to the same poll, placing below Gucci (ranked 38th overall) and above Cartier (ranked 68th overall). Brand Finance's ranked Hermès International 321st overall on its Global

500 list in 2012 and estimates its brand value at US$3.43 billion. Louis Vuitton was ranked 202nd in the same list.

BRAND AWARENESS

- The Birkin bag has no logo or tag to show that it's a Hermès, yet it is one of the products that contribute to the brand's high recall.
- Hermès's duc-carriage-and-horse logo and orange boxes are widely recognized as emblems of the brand.
- The 5-year waiting list for consumers wishing to own a Birkin bag points to both the exclusivity and wide fame of the Hermès brand.

Compared to that of other retailers, Hermès brand awareness is unusual in that some of its most exclusive—and most recognizable—products do not bear a logo or a label. Consumers who wish to purchase a Birkin bag must join an impressive 5-year waiting list and pay US$9,000 to US$150,000. The bag became attractive to the average consumer because of its being featured on television shows, such as *Sex and the City, Gossip Girl,* and *Beverly Hills, 90210.* The bag remains a symbol of high society and luxury.

The Hermès brand is also identifiable by the distinctive orange boxes used for packaging purchased goods. Designed in the 1950s, the box has remained a staple of all Hermès sales. It was also in the 1950s that Hermès released its duc-carriage-and-horse logo, which remains in use on all marketing materials for the company.

BRAND OUTLOOK

- Hermès enjoyed record growth in 2011 and 2012 despite the slow recovery from the economic recession of 2008. Hermès's quick global expansion has created a demand that has outpaced supply.
- Hermès will focus on expanding production to keep up with consumer demand, but it will not compromise the artisanal quality of its products.

Despite the global economy being weak for discretionary spending, Hermès enjoyed record growth in revenue in 2011, when sales rose from US$2.4 billion in 2010 to US$2.8 billion. For the past several years, the company has expanded quickly throughout the world and has profited by its network of retail stores. The company opened 16 new stores in 2011, which positioned the brand for a successful share of the luxury market as the economy continued to rebound.

However, by Hermès's own admittance, as reported in its annual report, its operations will be the focus of future expansion because demand for the brand's products has been outpacing supply. Hermès maintained that "this tension results from our sustained commitment to maintain high standards in all stages of our objects' creation, from selecting the finest materials through to respecting the expertise that guarantees the excellence of our creations, down to their tiniest details." The company has promised to expand production capabilities to keep up with additional sales growth.

FURTHER READING

Brand Finance. "Global 500 2012." *Brandirectory.* Accessed October 4, 2012. http://brandfinance.com/images/upload/bf_g500_2012_web_dp.pdf.

Harris, Heather and Paul Jarvis. "Hermès Shares Jump in Paris After LVMH Increases Holding to More than 20 Percent." *Bloomberg News,* December 22, 2010. Accessed October 2, 2012. http://www.bloomberg.com/news/2010-12-21/lvmh-raises-Hermès-stake-to-20-percent-defying-family-s-takeover-defense.html.

Hermès. "2011 Annual Report." Accessed October 1, 2012. http://finance-en.Hermès.com/content/download/596/4505/version/3/file/AG+2012_2011+Reference+document+-+Annual+report_GB.pdf.

"How the Hermès Scarf Has Become One of the World's Most Recogniseable Accessories." *Daily Mail Reporter,* August 15, 2012. Accessed October 3, 2012. http://www.dailymail.co.uk/femail/article-2189055/How-Hermès-scarf-worlds-recogniseable-accessories.html.

Interbrand. "2012 Ranking of the Top 100 Brands." Accessed October 3, 2012. http://www.interbrand.com/en/best-global-brands/2012/Best-Global-Brands-2012-Brand-View.aspx.

Mirchandani, Priya. "Magic in an Orange Box." *Verve Online,* July 7, 2010. Accessed October 1, 2012. http://www.verveonline.com/87/fashion/Hermès.shtml.

Titarenko, Olga. "Hermès Kelly: The Legendary Bag." *Haute Today,* September 7, 2011. Accessed October 3, 2012. https://hautetoday.wordpress.com/tag/sac-a-depeches/.

HITACHI

AT A GLANCE

Brand Synopsis: Hitachi, an overarching corporate brand for diversified conglomerate Hitachi, Ltd., promises to develop and apply new technologies in a mission to improve society.
Parent Company: Hitachi, Ltd.
6-6 Marrunouchi 1-Chrome
Tokyo
Japan
http://www.hitachi.com
Sector: Industrials; Consumer Discretionary; Information Technology; Utilities
Industry Group: Transportation; Consumer Durables & Apparel; Semiconductors & Semiconductor Equipment; Utilities
Performance: *Sales*—US$100 billion (2012).
Principal Competitors: Fujitsu Limited; Panasonic Corporation; Toshiba Corporation

BRAND ORIGINS

- Hitachi was founded in Japan in 1910 by Namihei Odaira.
- Hitachi was named after the town where Odaira made his first sale.
- Although it evolved into a diverse international conglomerate, Hitachi achieved its success with a scant marketing effort.
- A financial downturn led Hitachi to undertake a corporate branding effort in 1999.

Hitachi is the corporate brand for Hitachi, Ltd., a Japan-based multinational conglomerate offering a wide range of electronics products and home appliances, as well as automotive systems, railway systems, power and industrial systems, elevators and escalators, construction equipment and materials, information and telecommunication systems, and financial services. The company traces its lineage to Namihei Odaira, an engineer who was employed at a mining company in 1910 when he decided to strike out on his own to develop technologies for Japan, rather than see his country remain reliant on American and European manufacturers. He designed small electric motors that gave him a foothold in the market, and in 1920 he incorporated his company. Odaira named it for the town where he made his first sale: Hitachi.

Hitachi's growth mirrored that of Japan's economy. To meet the needs of an emerging industrial power, the company expanded into a variety of areas, mostly through the acquisition of companies involved with mechanical equipment, copper cable, metal-working, and railway locomotives and cars. During World War II, Hitachi supported Japan's military effort with the production of radar and sonar equipment. Although the company did not manufacture weapons, it was almost disbanded following Japan's defeat because of its role in the war. Hitachi managed to remain in business, and it was another war, albeit undeclared, in Korea that provided the means for revival: Hitachi became a defense contractor for the United States military.

Under the leadership of a new chief executive after the Korean War, Hitachi expanded into new markets, including computers, household appliances, and consumer electronics. While the company excelled in engineering and manufacturing, the same could not be said for its branding and marketing efforts. While the Hitachi brand gained currency in Japan, it was little-known outside of the country because Hitachi products were marketed under third-party labels. The company began to modernize its business practices in the mid-1980s, but in the 1990s it still remained very much a lumbering giant with a limited sense of branding. Technically, Hitachi was a match for rival Japanese firm Sony, but while the latter nurtured a reputation for excellence, Hitachi's brand identity was muddled at best. Despite its marketing shortcomings, Hitachi had evolved into a large and diverse multinational concern. It wasn't until the Asian economic crisis of 1997 led to a net loss of more than US$3 billion in fiscal 1998 that the company decided the time had come for a major restructuring. As part of that effort, Hitachi began a process in 1999 to craft the "Hitachi Brand Platform." For the first time in its history, this highly diversified company would be represented by a unifying, overarching Hitachi corporate brand.

BRAND ELEMENTS

- *Hitachi* means "rising sun" in Japanese.
- The Hitachi Mark superimposes the Chinese characters for "rising" and "sun" within a circle.
- The Hitachi Tree was introduced in a Japanese television commercial in 1973.
- The Hitachi logo includes the slogan, "Inspire the Next."

While Hitachi's founder Namihei Odaira chose the Hitachi name for personal reasons, it is an important brand element with great cultural resonance in Japan. *Hitachi* means "rising sun" in Japanese. The sun is an important symbol in Japanese culture, having appeared on flags for many hundreds of years. During World War II, the Japanese army and navy made use of a rising-sun flag (which is now considered offensive in many parts of the world devastated by Japanese forces). Hitachi had never used the rising sun as part of its imagery, just the phrase, which only has meaning for the Japanese market. From that perspective, Hitachi is associated with national pride.

Odaira did have the meaning of the word "Hitachi" in mind when he designed the Hitachi brand mark, another important brand element with great meaning in the Asian market. He superimposed the two Chinese characters for "sun" and "rise" and placed them within a circle. According to the company, this image "captured Odaira's vision of a man standing before the rising sun, planning a better future." His goal in creating the mark was to literally brand his products with it and to make it a symbol of quality. In this regard, Odaira's was a very modern approach to branding.

Another image important to the Hitachi brand is the Hitachi Tree. In 1973 the company aired a television commercial in Japan that featured a tree. It was used to symbolize the breadth of the company's products and services as well as the collective drive of Hitachi and its employees. The tree became a staple in Hitachi's visual iconography, and its meaning expanded over the years to portray Hitachi as an environmentally friendly company.

The Hitachi logo, which includes the corporate slogan and advertising tagline, is also a key brand element. Prior to the company's branding makeover at the turn of the millennium, the Hitachi logo was comprised of the Hitachi Mark and the Hitachi name, running left to right. In the updated version of the logo, the corporate mark was dropped in favor of a slogan that ran under the Hitachi name: "Inspire the Next." The logo also makes use of Hitachi Red. Another color, Hitachi Silver, is used in some communications to emphasize the innovative and technical attributes of the brand.

BRAND IDENTITY

- The Hitachi brand seeks to portray itself as dedicated to the use of new technologies to enrich the lives of its customers and to improve society.
- Hitachi's brand identity is richer in Japan than elsewhere.
- The tagline "Inspire the Next" suggests commitment to act as a catalyst for change.
- "Inspire the Next" invites the audience to fill in the missing ending.

Through its various elements, the Hitachi brand seeks to craft a generalized identity as a company with ample capabilities, a brand dedicated to developing and applying new technologies to enrich the lives of customers for the betterment of society. This corporate brand identity is overarching, meant to cover all aspects of the company's many and varied business interests. Moreover, Hitachi's identity is intended both to remain the same in Japan as it is in other countries around the world and to keep in step with societal changes over time.

It is in Japan where the power of the Hitachi brand is the greatest, due in no small measure to a wider range of branding tools in play. The Hitachi name, for example, possesses greater power in its native language. The Hitachi Mark and the Hitachi Tree also have a greater impact on the Japanese market than they do internationally. For a Japanese audience, the Hitachi name, the mark, and the tree readily suggest a progressive, expansive outlook, in keeping with Hitachi's identity.

Internationally, the tagline used in the Hitachi logo and advertising does most of the heavy lifting in establishing Hitachi's brand identity. Nevertheless, "Inspire the Next" is a curious phrase, especially for an English-speaking audience. In Japan, however, such combinations are commonplace. Many Japanese study English but few become fluent, and as a result foreign words and phrases gain acceptance simply because they are easy to say or they sound interesting. Accurate grammar is of secondary importance. Japanese consumer-electronics retailer Yamada Denki, for example, makes use of the slogan "For Your Just." The phrase is readily accepted by a Japanese audience, while it remains mystifying to outsiders.

Hitachi maintains that "Inspire the Next" espouses the commitment of the company to be a catalyst for positive societal changes. The company's marketers also argue that the use of "Next" was a conscious choice, part of an effort to make the slogan concise. Further, they say that the incomplete statement invited readers to supply their own answers, such as "idea," "product," "solution," or "generation." The slogan also includes something similar to an accent mark that emanates from the upper right arm of the "x" in "Next." This red mark is intended to symbolize the brand's commitment to take the lead in building a better future. The color red is meant to signify the burning passion of the brand for achieving this goal.

BRAND STRATEGY

- The core attributes of "trust" and "technical capability" became the focal points in crafting Hitachi's brand identity.
- The focus of the 2001 global branding campaign was on corporate middle-managers.
- Media buys for the 2001 global branding campaign focused on news cable networks and newspapers purveying both general and financial news.
- Consumer advertising in the early 2000s attempted to position Hitachi as a high-end brand.

When Hitachi began its corporate branding effort in 1999, it was a massive company, employing more than 300,000 in over 1,000 subsidiaries. The true scope of what Hitachi did was as much of a mystery to the public as what the Hitachi brand stood for. Hence a good deal of time was spent talking with customers as well as employees to learn what customers wanted from the brand and what employees wanted the brand to become. The brand developers focused on the attributes of trust and technical capability. These became the twin pillars of Hitachi's brand identity as a vehicle for societal change inspired by an unwavering commitment to innovation. The tagline "Inspire the Next" was intended, among other things, to express the brand's promise to the world. It was a statement that both described Hitachi's brand identity and served as a call to action for the company and the world.

Beyond establishing a brand promise to act as a positive change agent, the Hitachi team developed a brand strategy. The individual consumer viewed Hitachi as a maker of consumer electronics, such as television sets, but in truth, consumer electronics was perhaps the least important source of revenue for the company. There were about 10 other business units of greater importance to the balance sheet. This reality had a significant influence on Hitachi's branding campaign that broke in the fall of 2001. The focus of the campaign was less on individual consumers and more on business customers. In essence, Hitachi pursued a business-to-business branding strategy. The specific targets of the advertising were corporate middle-managers around the world, executives who made direct buying decisions in a wide range of industries. To reach such a divergent group, the company advertised its "Inspire the Next" message on cable television news and financial news programming. Advertising in print was done in the *Wall Street Journal* and other major financial and mass-circulation newspapers.

As the early 2000s unfolded, Hitachi emphasized certain aspects of its brand in pursuit of a brand strategy that made a greater appeal to consumers. A 2004 television campaign that used the theme "the beauty of science" emulated the spirit of the popular movie "The Matrix" to promote Hitachi's technology credentials. Two years later, Hitachi hired veteran television-commercial director Jean-Paul Goude, who had made his mark with luxury brands like Chanel No. 5 and Louis Vuitton. The spot he directed for Hitachi promoted a new plasma HDTV. It was supported by print, online, and in-store ads. The execution of the commercial created a high-end image for Hitachi. The goal was to better compete against the likes of Sony and the other brands that consistently outspent Hitachi on advertising. Hitachi's commitment to a luxury brand strategy was limited, however. The brand's focus remained on anonymous midlevel managers, many working in unglamorous industries far from the view of everyday consumers. With Hitachi's bottom line firmly in mind, it was a pragmatic and effective brand strategy.

BRAND EQUITY

- Hitachi enjoys greater brand equity in the East than in the West.
- According to Brand Finance, Hitachi possessed a brand value of US$16.391 billion at the end of 2011.

- Brand Finance ranked Hitachi 44th on its 2012 Global 500 list of the world's most valuable brands.
- Hitachi was number 84 on *Forbes*'s 2012 list of the World's Most Powerful Brands.
- Interbrand placed Hitachi 23rd on its 2012 list of Japan's Best Global Brands.

The common definition of brand equity is the difference in price between a branded product and a generic equivalent. In the case of Hitachi, the value of the brand is very dependent on the product category and the geographic market. In railroad rolling-stock and power systems, for example, the Hitachi brand is more highly regarded than it is in consumer electronics. The difference in brand equity between markets within a category varies as well. In the United States and other Western countries, Hitachi televisions fall far short of Sony in reputation. In Japan and the East, however, the Hitachi and Sony brands compete on a more level playing field.

In an effort to compare brands, brand consultancies have developed formulas that assign a monetary value to them. According to one of the more prominent of these agencies, Brand Finance, Hitachi had a brand value of US$16.391 billion at the end of 2011. It was a rating that garnered 44th place on Brand Finance's 2012 Global 500 list of the world's most valuable brands. According to *Fortune* magazine, Hitachi was the world's 38th-most-valuable brand in 2012, while *Forbes* placed Hitachi at number 84 on its 2012 ranking of the World's Most Powerful Brands. As for its place among Japanese brands, Hitachi was slotted number 23 on Interbrand's list of Japan's Best Global Brands in 2012.

BRAND AWARENESS

- Hitachi enjoys greater brand awareness in Japan and other Asian countries than in the West.
- Hitachi brand awareness varies between the industries served.
- Corporate middle managers are more familiar with the Hitachi brand than are general consumers.

As is the case with brand equity, the awareness of the Hitachi brand varies between industries and regions of the world. In some industries and countries, Hitachi has been well established for many decades, and as a result the brand achieves a high degree of familiarity. Hitachi has operated in Japan for more than a century and, accordingly, enjoys strong brand awareness with general consumers. In other Asian countries, Hitachi is also well known. In Europe and the United States, however, Hitachi is a minor player in consumer electronics. The brand is recognizable to many consumers, but its reputation falls short of the quality inherent in the products that carry the Hitachi name. Hitachi just does not come readily to consumers' minds, and so it is relegated to the level of a value-priced or bargain brand.

In fields far more important to the company's fiscal health, however, Hitachi enjoys strong brand awareness worldwide. It was not by accident that when Hitachi launched its global branding campaign, it focused on middle managers. In a host of industries, the executives who make decisions on equipment investments are well aware of Hitachi, and it also carries weight for them. The sales impact on this group means more to the Hitachi balance sheet than the sales of large quantities of low-margin television sets and other consumer electronics.

BRAND OUTLOOK

- The Hitachi brand improved its global standing from 82nd on Brand Finance's 2010 Global 500 to 44th place by 2012.
- About three-quarters of Hitachi's revenues in 2011 came from Japan and other Asian countries, and only 16 percent from North America and Europe.
- Hitachi has sought to create a "Social Innovation Business," focusing on units that foster advanced social infrastructure.
- Significant competition in all of Hitachi's business segments have made it imperative that the company devote more attention and resources to building the Hitachi brand.

Hitachi is one of the world's most valuable brands, and according to Brand Finance the brand has been increasing in value in recent years. After the company negotiated its way through some difficult economic conditions, the Hitachi brand improved its global standing from a number 82 ranking on Brand Finance's 2010 Global 500 to 44th place two years later. The company appeared to be positioned for further growth because of the breadth of its operations, both regionally and in terms of business diversity. More than half of its revenues in fiscal 2011 came from Japan, and another 22.3 percent came from other Asian countries. North America and Europe each accounted for only about 8 percent of revenues. Growing the brand in these markets would provide further financial security in the future.

Hitachi has taken steps to create what it calls a "Social Innovation Business," focusing on units that help to create advanced social infrastructure by providing information and communication technology. Beyond information and telecommunications, this sector includes railway systems, building systems, and smart power-grids. Another area of opportunity is consumer electronics. Should Hitachi succeed in developing some flagship products in this area, it could very well elevate its brand significantly with general consumers. There is significant competition in all of Hitachi's business segments, making it imperative that the company devote more attention and resources to building the Hitachi brand. In use for more than a decade, the "Inspire the Next" theme may have run its course. In order to remain true to its brand promise, Hitachi will likely have to embrace change and take a fresh approach to its brand strategy.

FURTHER READING

Brand Finance. "Global 500 2012." *Brandirectory*. Accessed February 14, 2013. http://brandirectory.com/league_tables/table/global-500-2012.

Brooks, Liz. "'Inspiring' the C-Level Audience." *Adweek Magazines' Technology Marketing*, February 2002.

Elliott, Stuart. "'Unleashing' a New Campaign." *New York Times*, August 21, 2006.

"Hitachi." *Marketing*, April 1, 2009.

"Hitachi Hikes Its Corporate Global Budget." *Marketing Week*, September 6, 2001.

"Hitachi, Ltd." *International Directory of Company Histories*. Ed. Jay P. Pederson. Vol. 108. Detroit, MI: St. James Press, 2010.

"World's Most Valuable Electronic and Electric Equipment Companies, 2011." *Financial Times*, June 24, 2011.

H&M

AT A GLANCE

Brand Synopsis: By virtue of its fashion aptitude and deftness at anticipating trends, H&M offers the latest fashion for all family members while maintaining quality at a low price.
Parent Company: H&M Hennes & Mauritz AB (H&M)
Master Samuelsgatan 49
Stockholm
Sweden
http://www.hm.com
Sector: Consumer Discretionary
Industry Group: Consumer Durables and Apparel
Performance: *Market share*—1 percent of the global apparel market (2008). *Sales*—SEK128.8 billion (US$19.8 billion) (2011).
Principal Competitors: Arcadia Group; The Gap, Inc.; Zara International, Inc.

BRAND ORIGINS

- H&M was founded in Sweden in 1947 by Erling Persson as the retail store Hennes, which sold women's clothing exclusively.
- Hennes began its expansion by opening stores in neighboring Scandinavian countries in the 1960s and in Great Britain in 1976.
- Persson bought the retail shop Mauritz Widforss in 1968 and changed the company name to Hennes & Mauritz to reflect broader offerings.

H&M was founded as Hennes in 1947 by Erling Persson. A former salesman and founder of another company, Pennspecialisten, in Västerås, Sweden, Persson had discovered a new clothing-store concept during a trip to the United States. Persson decided to import this concept of high turnover produced by low prices to Sweden. From the first Hennes store in Västerås, which featured exclusively women's clothing, Hennes expanded throughout Sweden, spreading across much of the country through the 1960s.

Hennes also began to export its low-price clothing concept, beginning in neighboring Norway in 1964, followed by Denmark in 1967. By the end of the 1960s Hennes looked to extend its range beyond women's clothing. The company also sought further expansion in Stockholm. These two goals were fulfilled with the purchase in 1968 of Mauritz Widforss, a hunting and gun shop on Stockholm's Sergelgatan. As part of the purchase, Hennes also received a large stock of men's clothing items, primarily sportswear.

The men's clothing was quickly added to the company's retail offering, and the company's name was changed to Hennes & Mauritz to reflect its expanded product range. At the same time, Hennes & Mauritz added a line of children's clothing to its stores, so that by 1970 the company offered clothing for much of the family. Two more segments, for teenagers and babies, were added in 1976 and 1978, respectively.

The Mauritz acquisition resulted in more than a name change and an expansion of the company's clothing range.

It also helped transform the company's product offering itself. The introduction of sportswear led the company to develop clothing that better reflected the spirit of the times, as a new generation of youth clamored for clothing that allowed them to express their individuality. H&M began to develop the casual, down-to-earth yet fashionable image that proved a success in its later expansion.

Seeking further growth, the company made a new acquisition in 1973, buying another Swedish company, Bekladnadskompaniet. In the next year, as H&M prepared for further international growth, the company went public with a listing on the Stockholm Stock Exchange. The Persson family, however, retained the largest share of the company stock, leaving control securely in the family's hands.

During the 1970s H&M began to look beyond its Scandinavian base. In 1976 the company entered the British market, with mixed results. While H&M's growth in British remained limited, the company posted better results on the European continent. At home, the company acquired the Rowells mail-order company in 1980, which led to the introduction of H&M Rowells, the company's mail-order subsidiary.

The next move for H&M was to Switzerland, which quickly became one of H&M's principal foreign markets. In 1980 H&M launched its first German store. The H&M concept somewhat revolutionized the German clothing retail market, which was considered rather stodgy. H&M's characteristic informality also caused a stir in Germany, where employees were more than encouraged to drop the formal "Sie" form in their conversations with other employees. Nevertheless, the H&M concept caught on well with the German consumer at a time when few other brands existed on the German retail scene.

A new generation took over leadership of H&M when Erling Persson turned over the position of managing director to his son Stefan. Under the younger Persson, H&M continued its international expansion while retaining tight control of the H&M image. H&M continued to increase its presence in its existing markets throughout the 1980s, steadily opening new stores.

In the late 1980s H&M attempted to diversify its brand line by opening the Galne Gunnar (Crazy Gunnar) chain of cut-price stores. Having expanded the chain to 18 stores in Sweden, the company decided to abandon the concept after ten years, redeveloping the existing Galne Gunnar stores as H&M stores. Sticking with the H&M name appeared to be the most profitable future for the company. Growth of the H&M chain, particularly in terms of foreign expansion, increased dramatically in the 1990s.

BRAND ELEMENTS

- H&M's memorable and bold logo features a bright red color.
- H&M stores are tightly controlled to create uniformity within the brand.
- Fast turnover of clothing encourages repeat shopping and excitement within the brand.

The name H&M refers to the company's owners, Hennes and Mauritz. The company logo features the letters H&M in bold, capital letters in a bright red color. The font is slightly slanted and gives a sense of movement. The red color makes the logo pop, whether on a storefront or in print.

H&M stores are closely guided from the company's Stockholm headquarters to achieve a uniform retail concept, and thus its merchandising plan can be considered an integral part of the brand. It has been said that a sweater featured in a window display in London was to be displayed in exactly the same way in all other H&M stores. Such control over its image has enabled H&M to build a consistent brand appeal throughout the wholly company-owned chain. New clothing products are introduced on a near-daily basis, breaking up the seasonal stock rotation traditionally found in the retail clothing industry. Clothing items rarely remain on H&M's shelves for more than a month. This rapid rotation encourages repeat shopping.

BRAND IDENTITY

- H&M began collaborating on collections with designers and celebrities in 2004.
- H&M's goal is to offer "fashion and quality at the best price."
- A 2012 collaboration with soccer star David Beckham produced a line of men's undergarments.

Stefan Persson had been quick to recognize the emergence of fashions and trends—born of MTV, Hollywood, Madison Avenue advertising, and the Internet—that transcended national borders to become what he termed "global fashion," or fads among youth and other age groups across the world. H&M, with its emphasis on uniformity across its stores, was well-positioned to appeal to this new generation of consumers.

H&M's strong brand image is associated with the value of quality pieces and stylish collections and enhanced by the collaborations with famous designers and celebrities. The instant name recognition and mass-market appeal of the collaborations have allowed H&M to deliver high-end fashion at the low cost that customers expect. In November 2004 the company partnered with designer Karl Lagerfeld. His collection helped boost 2004 fourth-quarter sales by more than 14 percent and profits by 23.9 percent. H&M joined forces with Stella McCartney in 2005 and with the Dutch design team of Viktor & Rolf in 2006. H&M also forged ties with Madonna when she and her crew opted to wear H&M clothing off-stage during her Confessions world tour. A new collection, "M by Madonna," made its debut in March 2007. In 2012 H&M collaborated with wildly popular soccer star David Beckham to launch a line of men's undergarments.

According to H&M's website, the company's goal is to offer "fashion and quality at the best price." In order to maintain high levels of excitement and surprise, H&M provides consumers a constant barrage of new products and new campaigns. It wants to be perceived as a cool and fun company that always has something new and interesting and fashionable to offer.

BRAND STRATEGY

- H&M continues to offer a wide range of products to appeal to the greatest number of consumers.
- Offering the very latest and innovative fashions is essential to the H&M brand.
- A core strategy for success at H&M relies on opening new stores in new markets and continuing expansion in existing markets.
- H&M has begun to diversify its brand by acquiring other apparel chains and expanding them under their own names.

As a result of its comprehensive vision, H&M is able to offer a huge assortment of clothing and accessories, so that every customer who walks into a store can find something that appeals to his or her individual taste. Focusing on the latest trends and quickly bringing them to the consumer remains H&M core strategy. Teams of designers travel the world to explore new art, music, and film. They talk to consumers in stores, members of the fashion press, and trend forecasters. The teams cover the fashion shows and fashion in the street to find inspiration for H&M collections.

H&M controls the fashions featured in its stores: almost all of its clothing sales come from the company's own range of brand designs. The company employs a staff of more than 50 designers who create the collections for H&M brands. The designers are able to view fashions on runways or on the street and move quickly to get H&M's version of those fashions into the stores.

H&M is also continuing its strategy of expansion by increasing the number of its stores by 10 percent to 15 percent per year while maintaining profitability at its current stores. In 2012 this translated to the planned opening of 275 new stores, with the United States, the United Kingdom, and China designated as the largest markets for expansion. Markets to receive their first H&M stores included Latvia, Bulgaria, Malaysia, and Mexico.

In 2007 the company launched a new chain store concept, COS, or Collection of Style. The new, more upscale chain offered modern fashion and made its debut in London. By 2008 H&M considered this foray into new concepts a success and decided to build on that expansion strategy. It purchased a stake in Fabric Scandinavien AB, parent company of the Swedish chains Monki, Weekday, and Cheap Monday and expanded the chains under their original names. A home textile collection was launched in 2009 under the name H&M Home.

BRAND EQUITY

- H&M consistently ranks as the top global apparel brand.
- In 2011 H&M's brand value was ranked 21st among top global brands.
- In 2012 H&M placed 105th among 500 global brands, well ahead of competitor Zara in 215th place.

According to Interbrand's *2011 Ranking of the Top 100 Brands*, H&M ranked 21st, the highest ranking among apparel companies on the list. Its brand value was estimated to be US$16 billion. Zara, the next-highest ranked apparel company, was ranked 44th, with a value of US$8 billion. Brand Finance's *Global 500 2012* ranked H&M 105th overall, with an estimated brand value of US$8.6 billion. Zara placed 215th on Brand Finance's list with a brand value of US$4.7 billion.

BRAND AWARENESS

- H&M has maintained a steady brand presence with contemporary fashions at low prices.
- Continuing global expansion has allowed H&M to broaden brand awareness.
- H&M enjoys exceptional brand awareness in Europe.

Since Erling Persson founded Hennes in 1947 with an emphasis on fast turnover of trendy merchandise coupled with attractive pricing, the core concepts and values at H&M have changed very little. H&M has built a brand following based on its ability to anticipate the latest fashion trends and to have items in stock that appeal to a wide range of tastes. Steady expansion into global markets has helped broaden brand awareness. In 2012 H&M ranked 19th on the Top-40 Strongest Retail Brands in Germany index. Germany is H&M's number-one market for revenue. In 2012 H&M placed sixth on the Top-100 Trends to Brand index, a ranking of companies that understand how to translate trends into their brands, and 44th among the Top-50 Europe's Brand Corporations, a listing of Europe's most valuable brand corporations.

H&M enjoys top-of-mind awareness in fashion retail in large part thanks to its heavy involvement with social media. In the early 21st century H&M launched its own YouTube channel, a space where the company could post videos about the latest styles, upcoming collections, collaborations, fashion advice, and beauty tips. By 2012

H&M had amassed 9.7 million friends on Facebook, all of whom receive updates on collections, store shipments, job opportunities, contests, events, and podcasts. H&M uses social media to show that the brand is about more than just clothes, and it has become a source of news and inspiration in the fashion world. This prowess with social media has garnered the brand a ranking of 93 out of more than 30,000 brands on the Social Business Index.

BRAND OUTLOOK

- The global recession has brought customers to H&M as they seek more value for their money.
- The ability to purchase online in more markets should broaden H&M's appeal even further as younger consumers take advantage of e-commerce.
- H&M is working to be more environmentally friendly by using more recycled materials and reducing carbon emissions.
- H&M is addressing questions regarding fair wages and working conditions at supplier factories.

H&M has weathered the economic downturns around the globe by remaining loyal to its core strategies and staying true to its image. In fact, the thrifty and conscious spending habits of many consumers during recent recessions have given rise to exactly the sort of customer base that H&M thrives upon. H&M and Inditex are expected to continue their neck-and-neck competition for market share. H&M should have the advantage, as it spends around 5 percent of its revenues on splashy advertising campaigns and events that reinforce the company's brand and image.

Although H&M has been thriving within social media spheres, it has been late to the game with its Internet retailing. While consumers in Scandinavian countries have been able to make purchases online since 1998, H&M has been gradually rolling out e-commerce in other markets, adding the Netherlands in 2006, the United Kingdom in 2010, and the United States in 2012. The opening of additional e-commerce sites should further boost H&M's brand awareness, given that purchases by many younger consumers are greatly influenced by the Internet.

Investors worldwide are also impressed with H&M's efforts to improve sustainability, from conserving natural resources to upgrading working conditions in supplier factories. In an effort to be more environmentally friendly, H&M has worked to reduce the use of chemicals in the production of cotton for their clothes, shrink their carbon footprint by relying less on air transportation, increase the use of recycled materials in mailings and plastic bags, and abandon the testing of its cosmetics on animals. H&M has also joined other retailers in addressing questions relating to fair wages and working environments at their suppliers in Bangladesh, China, Cambodia, and India and has joined with consumers in donating money to help provide clean drinking water, preventative health care, and education around the world.

FURTHER READING

Brand Finance. "Global 500 2012." *Brandirectory*. Accessed September 5, 2012. http://brandfinance.com/images/upload/bf_g500_2012_web_dp.pdf.

Cohen, M. L., and Christina M. Stansell. "H&M Hennes & Mauritz AB." *International Directory of Company Histories*. Ed. Tina Grant. Vol. 98. Detroit, MI: St. James Press, 2009.

Datamonitor. "H&M Hennes & Mauritz AB." Accessed September 5, 2012. http://www.datamonitor.com/store/Product/h_m_hennes_mauritz_ab?productid=F7E41ECA-902F-483F-B72C-A7FAEA92122E.

"Economic Slowdown for H&M an Opportunity to Expand." *Apparel Online*, July 17, 2012.

H&M. "About H&M." Accessed September 5, 2012. http://about.hm.com/content/hm/AboutSection/en/About.html.

———. *H&M Hennes & Mauritz AB Full-Year Report*. Accessed September 5, 2012. http://about.hm.com/content/dam/hm/about/documents/en/cision/1573157_en.pdf.

"H&M Hennes & Mauritz AB." *Global Markets Direct SWOT Reports, August 27, 2012*. Detroit, MI: Gale, 2012.

"Rankings per brand." RankingtheBrands.com. Accessed September 5, 2012. http://www.rankingthebrands.com/Brand-detail.aspx?brandID=36.

Santos, Alexander Abad. "This Week's Social Media Power Rankings: All Hail David Beckham." *Atlantic Wire*, August 31, 2012.

"Top Apparel Makers Worldwide, 2008." *Market Share Reporter*. Detroit, MI: Gale, 2012.

"2011 Ranking of the Top 100 Brands." Interbrand. Accessed September 5, 2012. http://interbrand.com/en/best-global-brands/best-global-brands-2008/best-global-brands-2011.aspx.

HOME DEPOT

AT A GLANCE

Brand Synopsis: The mission of Home Depot, the largest home improvement retailer in the United States, is to provide the products and know-how to enable people to take their dreams for their homes into their own hands.
Parent Company: The Home Depot, Inc.
2455 Paces Ferry Road NW
Atlanta, Georgia 30339-4024
United States
http://www.homedepot.com
Sector: Consumer Discretionary
Industry Group: Retail
Performance: *Market share*—World's number one home improvement retailer. *Sales*—US$67.9 billion (2011).
Principal Competitors: Lowe's Companies, Inc.; Menard, Inc.; True Value Company; Wal-Mart Stores, Inc.; Ace Hardware Corporation; Sears, Roebuck and Co.; Costco Wholesale Corporation

BRAND ORIGINS

- The Home Depot, Inc., was created in 1978 by Bernard Marcus and Arthur Blank in the Atlanta area.
- A large variety of merchandise, coupled with well-trained and knowledgeable employees, is key to Home Depot's customer satisfaction.
- Home Depot is the largest home-repair chain in the world and the second largest retailer in the United States.
- Home Depot's expansion into Canada and Mexico was successful, but its attempts to gain a foothold in South America and China were short lived.

The Home Depot was created in June 1978 as a result of a corporate management shake-up by the new ownership of the Handy Dan home center chain in Southern California. After being ousted in a managerial shuffle at Handy Dan, executives Bernard Marcus and Arthur Blank procured backing from a New York venture capital firm and formed The Home Depot, Inc., opening the company's first two stores in the Atlanta area in June 1979. The concept that helped secure financing for the project was that when the price of merchandise was marked down, sales increased and the cost of making those sales decreased.

Most discount retail operations suffered from poor service delivered by unskilled, low-paid employees. Marcus and Blank realized that recognizing customers' needs would be one of the most important elements in their company's growth. They were also aware that, at the time, do-it-yourselfers accounted for more than 60 percent of the building-supply industry's sales volume, but the majority of these customers did not have the technical expertise required to accomplish most home repair or improvement projects.

The management team made sure that all Home Depot stores were large enough to stock at least 25,000 different items. Their competitors' stores normally had room for only 10,000 items. The sales staff in each store were trained to help customers demystify their home improvement projects. Marcus and Blank believed that, with education provided by a knowledgeable sales staff, customers would gain the confidence to take on more projects at home and return to Home Depot outlets to purchase more goods and get additional advice.

This approach paid off. By 1984 the company was operating 19 stores and reported sales of US$256 million, a 118 percent increase over 1983. In 1986 Home Depot's sales reached the US$1 billion mark, and the company was operating 60 retail outlets by year's end. For the first time in the company's history, however, the cost of sales had also begun to increase. At the end of 1985, the company's stock price plummeted. It was clear that changes were needed if Home Depot was to continue to grow and prosper.

The company slowed its expansion, opening just 10 new stores in 1986, all of them in established markets, with the idea of completely capturing those markets instead of striking out into new regions of the country. Home Depot continued with conservative expansion and by 1989 had surpassed Lowe's Companies, Inc., in sales, becoming the largest home-repair chain in the United States. Home Depot was an emerging giant in the U.S. retail market.

The booming economic times of the late 1990s were good years for Home Depot. Americans bought new homes and remodeled existing ones at record rates, and the firm earned more than US$38 billion in revenues. The company's status as a retailing powerhouse was confirmed in 1999 when its stock became a component of the Dow Jones Industrial Average. Over the next several years, Home Depot's fortunes increased right along with the booming housing market, firmly entrenching the company as the number two retailer in the United States behind Wal-Mart Stores, Inc.

Home Depot entered the Canadian market in 1994 and the Mexican market in 2000, eventually becoming the largest home improvement retailer in each of those countries. In 1997, Home Depot entered the South American market in Chile and Argentina, but these expansions did not succeed. Within a few years, South American companies had bought out the Home Depot stores in both those countries. Similarly, Home Depot's ventures into China did not prove successful, and by late 2012, the *China Times* was reporting that Home Depot was closing all its stores in that country.

BRAND ELEMENTS

- Home Depot creates a unity across the brand with a vivid orange color emblazoned throughout the stores.
- Creative marketing campaigns shine the spotlight on Home Depot customers instead of the store.
- Marketing taglines demonstrate the role that Home Depot can play in assisting customers with various home improvement endeavors.

Vivid orange is the prominent color in the Home Depot logo and is splashed across all signs, shelving, bags, and product displays in stores. Employees "live the orange life" and fans of the store are said to "bleed orange." All employees wear bright orange aprons that make them visible at once to customers; children who participate in youth clinics are given their own orange aprons to keep. The bold, white lettering in which the brand name appears on the Home Depot logo is in all capital letters and appears to have been applied using a stencil, a style that calls to mind the construction tools and materials that fill the shelves, bins, and crates in a Home Depot store.

Home Depot marketing slogans over the years have proved to be memorable, with constant refrains heard on radio and television and seen on the Internet. "More saving. More doing" was introduced in 2009, replacing "You can do it. We can help." The campaigns emphasize what customers can do for themselves—with an assist from Home Depot—versus the traditional touting of products and stores of mainstream retail advertising.

BRAND IDENTITY

- The combination of knowledgeable employees and high-quality products has created a winning brand for Home Depot.
- Home Depot's corporate sponsorships expose the brand to diverse audiences.
- In partnership with Home Depot stores, the company encourages employees to contribute their time and talents to help improve their communities.

Since its founding in 1978, Home Depot has been guided by what it terms the customer "bill of rights," by which shoppers are entitled to good-quality merchandise at a fair price, knowledgeable salespeople, and superior customer service. Home Depot sought to revolutionize the home improvement industry by providing customers with the know-how to complete jobs themselves and the right tool at the right price.

Home Depot's strong brand image is associated with the value of the store's products, made possible by the company's exclusive relationships with selected suppliers to market products under a variety of well-recognized brand names. High-quality merchandise marketed by private label brands and carried only by the Home Depot, along with several house brands, has proven to draw shoppers into the stores.

Home Depot built its sales staff from dedicated do-it-yourselfers and professional tradespeople, eventually hiring more than 2,500 licensed plumbers and electricians not only to provide better service to customers but also to serve as expert trainers for other employees on the floor. The company scheduled in-store instructional workshops for its customers and brought in local contractors and tradespeople as teachers. Customers were urged to call the Home Depot store in their area if they had any problem or questions while they were making home repairs or improvements. Dedicated Home Depot salespeople became part of the living brand, contributing to improved customer satisfaction and spreading the Home Depot message.

In 1999 Home Depot began sponsoring the NASCAR Home Depot racing team, now considered an integral part of the brand. Home Depot then expanded its fan-favorite sports sponsorships to include ESPN's College GameDay program as well as numerous soccer teams across the United States and Mexico. Home Depot became the title sponsor of The Home Depot Center, a sports facility located in Carson, California, designated as an official U.S. Olympic training site and home to various tournaments and teams.

Created in 2002 the Home Depot Foundation, the philanthropic arm of the company, has contributed more than US$270 million in money, time, and products to causes that include aid to U.S. veterans, disaster relief, Habitat for Humanity, and other community programs. Thousands of Home Depot employees regularly donate their time and expertise to improvements within their own communities. The goal of Home Depot's philanthropy overlaps with the goal of the brand itself. According to the foundation's website, "The mission of The Home Depot Foundation is simple, to improve homes and improve lives. Through partnerships with local nonprofits and the volunteer efforts of Team Depot, we focus on repairing and refurbishing homes and facilities that serve disadvantaged families and individuals."

BRAND STRATEGY

- Several attempts to extend the Home Depot brand have resulted in loss of revenue and store closings.
- Home Depot's Eco Options program seeks to educate consumers about environmentally friendly options for home improvement projects.
- As part of its environmental initiatives, Home Depot announced plans in 2007 to plant more than three million trees.

Since the early 1990s, several efforts to extend the Home Depot brand have failed to prosper. The company opened EXPO Design Centers in 1991 to focus on the upscale interior design market; all stores were closed by 2009. HD Supply, a professional line serving contractors, was acquired in 2006 and sold in 2007 amid dwindling sales. Home Depot Landscape Supply, with only a few stores in the Atlanta and Dallas areas, was founded in 2002 and closed in late 2007. In 2006 Home Depot announced the acquisition of a Chinese home improvement retailer. The core demographics of the U.S. population of do-it-yourselfers did not translate to the China market, however, and all stores were closed by 2012.

Other lines have fared better. In September 2005 Home Depot Direct launched its high-end online home-furnishings store, 10 Crescent Lane, followed by the launch of Paces Trading Company, its high-end online lighting store. In mid-2006 Home Depot acquired Home Decorators Collection, which was placed as an additional brand in the Home Depot Direct Division.

Home Depot established an environmental marketing department to educate consumers about environmentally friendly product choices. Launched in 2007 Eco Options helps consumers choose among more than 4,500 products sold in Home Depot stores, from light bulbs to paint, that offer such benefits as sustainable forestry, energy efficiency, water conservation, clean air, and a healthy home. Home Depot also committed to improving the energy efficiency of its stores and to recycling, winning multiple awards for its good stewardship programs.

BRAND EQUITY

- Home Depot consistently outperforms Lowe's, its nearest rival in home improvement retail.
- Home Depot is ranked as the third most valuable U.S. retail brand, behind only Wal-Mart and Target.
- In 2012 *Fortune* placed Atlanta-based Home Depot on its list of the most admired companies in Georgia.

The Home Depot, Inc., the largest home improvement retailer in the world, operates more than 2,200 warehouse stores across the United States, Canada, Guam, and Mexico. In the United States, where Home Depot ranks as the second largest retailer behind only Wal-Mart Stores, Inc., there are roughly 1,950 Home Depot stores spread across all 50 states and employing approximately 321,000 people. In 2011 Home Depot registered sales of US$67.9 billion, outpacing its closest rival, Lowe's, which had sales of US$48.8 billion.

Home Depot placed higher than Lowe's in the *Financial Times*'s ranking of the world's most valuable general retailers in 2011; Home Depot ranked third, with a market value of US$60 billion, while Lowe's ranked ninth, with a market value of US$34.8 billion. According to Interbrand's *2012 Most Valuable U.S. Retail Brands*, Home Depot ranked third, behind Walmart and Target, with a brand value of US$22 billion. In 2012 Fortune listed Home Depot among the top ten most admired companies in Georgia, behind such companies as Delta Air Lines, Coca Cola, and UPS.

BRAND AWARENESS

- Home Depot has put the customer at the center of its business model.
- Continuing global expansion has allowed Home Depot to broaden brand awareness.
- Home Depot's business practices have earned it high rankings on lists of most-admired retailers.

In recent years, Home Depot has consistently scored as one of the most recognizable brands. In 2005, it was ranked fourth in terms of mindshare (customer awareness) of all the Fortune 1000 companies. In 2012, it ranked 23rd in Brandirectory's *Global 500* and 3rd in their *Best Retail Brands*. The 2012 Social Media Effectiveness Index ranked Home Depot as the number one retailer in terms of business-to-consumer interactions on social media like Facebook and Twitter.

Home Depot expanded into Canada in 1994 and Mexico in 2001 through acquisitions and has become a top retailer in both countries. In 2008 Home Depot was ranked seventh among the world's largest retail companies by the *Consumer Goods Registry*. In 2009 Home Depot ranked fifth among top Canadian retailers and second in *Fortune*'s 2010 list of the world's most admired specialty retailers.

BRAND OUTLOOK

- Home Depot was able to weather a global financial downturn and a collapse in the housing industry by focusing on customer service in existing stores.
- Forty-five percent of the 9.5 million customers per week who visit Home Depot online then continue shopping in a store, which translates to 225 customers per day in each location.
- Home Depot's social-media store associates are an integral part of the brand's embrace and expansion of digital platforms.

In 2007 a collapse in home sales and a rise in unemployment smothered the home-building industry, and consumers cut back on spending for home repairs. Home Depot saw its total sales decline for the first time in its history. In 2012, after several years of stagnant sales, consumer confidence revived, the housing market began to rebound, and Home Depot once again began to post gains, assuring investors of its dominance in the home improvement market.

Home Depot reinvigorated itself by shifting its focus from expansion and growth to the maximization of existing stores. Its divestiture of brand extensions that drained revenue helped to refocus attention on customer service. Additionally, the company implemented significant changes to store operations to make them simpler and more customer-friendly. The company also trimmed costs with initiatives such as reducing energy consumption within its stores.

Home Depot's strong brand recognition helps drive 9.5 million customers a week to the Home Depot website. Many of these customers then continue their shopping at a Home Depot store. The company also introduced mobile shopping applications for Windows, the Android, and the iPhone. Home Depot has also implemented a popular online how-to community staffed by social-media-savvy employees who answer questions with text postings or videos. These tools help Home Depot expand their brand and their sales, without draining capital in large expansions. With this strategy of improving efficiency, responding to consumer needs, and selling across multiple platforms in place, Home Depot hopes to maintain its number one position in the home improvement market.

FURTHER READING

Cheng, Andria. "Home Depot Catches up on Internet Sales." *MarketWatch*, August 14, 2011.

Home Depot. "Our Company." Accessed September 26, 2012. https://corporate.homedepot.com/OurCompany/Pages/default.aspx.

"The Home Depot, Inc." *International Directory of Company Histories*. Ed. Jay P. Pederson. Vol. 97. Detroit, MI: St. James Press, 2009.

Lazich, Robert S., and Virgil L. Burton III. "Leading Home Improvement Firms Worldwide, 2008." *Market Share Reporter*. Detroit, MI: Gale, 2011.

———. "Top Retailers in North America, 2007." *Market Share Reporter*. Detroit, MI: Gale, 2008.

"Top Global Retailers by Revenue, 2009." *Business Rankings Annual*. Ed. Deborah J. Draper. Detroit, MI: Gale, 2012.

"2012 Ranking of the Best Retail Brands." Interbrand. Accessed September 26, 2012. http://www.interbrand.com/en/BestRetailBrands/2012-Best-Retail-Brands.aspx#page-wrap.

"World's Most Valuable Retailer Brands, 2011." *Business Rankings Annual*. Ed. Deborah J. Draper. Detroit, MI: Gale, 2012.

Zmuda, Natalie. "Home Depot Puts a New Spin on the Idea of 'Sales Rep.'" *Advertising Age*, May 23, 2011.

HONDA

AT A GLANCE

Brand Synopsis: As a leading automobile, motorcycle, and power products brand, Honda connects with customers with "The Power of Dreams."
Parent Company: Honda Motor Company Ltd.
1-1, 2-chome, Minami-Aoyama, Minato-ku
Tokyo 107-8556
Japan
http://world.honda.com
Sector: Consumer Discretionary
Industry Group: Automobiles & Components
Performance: *Market share*—9.8 percent (2012).
Principal Competitors: Toyota Motor Corp.; Volkswagen AG; General Motors Co.; Ford Motor Co.; Chrysler Group L.L.C.

BRAND ORIGINS

- Honda Motor Company was founded by Soichiro Honda and Takeo Fujisawa.
- In 1959 Honda established a U.S. subsidiary named American Honda Motor Company, Inc.
- Building on its leadership position with motorcycles, in 1967 Honda diversified and began producing cars and trucks.

Honda traces its roots back to company founders Soichiro Honda and Takeo Fujisawa. Soichiro Honda's achievements as a mechanical engineer are said to have matched those of Henry Ford. Working in his Japanese machine shop in 1938, Honda concentrated his early efforts on casting a perfect piston ring. He soon succeeded in casting a ring that met his standards, and attempted to sell it to the Toyota Corporation.

Toyota rejected Honda's first batch of piston rings, but two years later the company finally placed a large order. Honda ultimately sold his piston ring operation to Toyota and went on to manufacture motorbikes. To form a company, Honda joined efforts with investor Takeo Fujisawa. In 1949 Fujisawa provided the capital, as well as financial and marketing strategies, to start the new company.

In 1950, after his first motorcycle had been introduced in Japan, Honda stunned the engineering world by doubling the horsepower of the conventional four-stroke engine. With this technological innovation, the company was poised for success. By the end of 1959 Honda had climbed into first place among Japanese motorcycle manufacturers, with sales of US$55 million. The company's total unit sales that year reached 285,000.

In 1959 Honda established a U.S. subsidiary named American Honda Motor Company, Inc., in a move that was in sharp contrast to other foreign manufacturers who relied on distributors. Honda's strategy was to create a market of customers who had never given a thought to owning a motorcycle. The company started its enterprise in America by producing the smallest, most lightweight motorcycles available. Honda's success in creating a demand for lightweight motorcycles was impressive. Its U.S. sales skyrocketed from US$500,000 in 1960 to US$77 million in 1965.

In 1967 Honda diversified and began producing cars and trucks. In addition, the company started to manufacture portable generators, power tillers, lawn mowers, pumps, and outboard motors. In 1967 and 1968 the company introduced two lightweight passenger cars that performed poorly in both the Japanese and U.S. markets. It was not until 1973 and the introduction of the Honda Civic that the company became a real presence on the international automobile market. The world was in the grip of the oil crisis, and the energy-efficient Japanese compacts suddenly found a worldwide market.

As sales of the Honda Civic surpassed the one million mark, the company introduced an upscale, higher priced model named the Accord in 1976. Sales of the Accord grew rapidly, not only in Japan, but especially in the United States. In 1982, as a result of the burgeoning U.S. market for Japanese cars, production of the Accord was started at Honda's Marysville, Ohio, manufacturing plant. Meanwhile, Honda's total motorcycle production had reached 3.5 million units per year, with one-third being produced or sold outside of Japan.

As the Accord became more and more popular with middle-class Americans looking for high-quality, reliable, and affordable cars, management was convinced that the company could succeed in entering the luxury car market. In 1986 Honda introduced the Acura, which immediately garnered large sales throughout Japan and the United States. By the end of the 1980s Honda had developed into one of the leading car manufacturers in the world.

By 1995 cumulative world production of all Honda automobiles had surpassed the 30 million unit mark. Late that year Honda introduced the CR-V sport-utility vehicle. At the end of the 20th century Honda was the number-two automaker (in terms of profitability), behind Toyota.

BRAND ELEMENTS

- The Honda brand is represented on automobiles by a stylized capital H.
- In type, the Honda brand name appears in all capital letters.
- Honda motorcycles utilize a Honda logo, dating back to the early 1970s, that features an image of wings atop the Honda name in all capital letters.
- In 2012 the Honda brand was associated with the tagline, "The Power of Dreams."

The Honda brand name is represented on automobiles by a stylized capital H. In type, the name appears in all capital letters. The Honda motorcycle logo, which dates back to the early 1970s, features an image of wings atop the Honda name displayed in all capital letters. The use of wings is said to have stemmed from Soichiro Honda's appreciation of Greek mythology. Different iterations of the winged motorcycle logo have been used over the years. These include versions with different color schemes, as well as a commemorative 40th anniversary edition that was unveiled in 1988.

In 2012 the Honda brand was associated with the concept of dreams. This was evident in the tagline, "The Power of Dreams." The previous year Honda unveiled "The Undying Dream," a short-film documentary, at the Sundance Film Festival. According to an article in the January 27, 2011, issue of *Manufacturing Close-Up*, the film brought a Honda corporate principle called "the challenging spirit," to life. Specifically, this encompassed "Honda's quest to pursue and achieve impossible dreams, which has led to the creation of products that enhance human mobility and advance environmental consciousness."

BRAND IDENTITY

- Individuality is at the heart of Honda's brand identity, and is reflected in the tagline, "The Power of Dreams."
- In 2011 Honda debuted a short-film documentary called "The Undying Dream" at the Sundance Film Festival, which reflected its appreciation of individuality.
- Honda's brand identity also embodies a company principle known as "The Three Joys," which include "The Joy of Buying," "The Joy of Selling," and "The Joy of Creating."

In 2012 the element of individuality was at the heart of Honda's brand identity. According to the company's 2012 annual report, a principle known as "Respect for the Individual" represented its "desire to respect the unique character and ability of each individual person." This principle also was embodied in Honda's tagline, "The Power of Dreams." In 2011 the company debuted a short-film documentary called "The Undying Dream" at the Sundance Film Festival. In the January 27, 2011, issue of *Manufacturing Close-Up*, American Honda Motor Corporate Advertising Manager Barbara Ponce explained that Honda encourages "an independent spirit, taking risks to bring forth bold ideas, and realizing the power of your own dreams in the process."

Joy is another key element of Honda's brand identity. This stems from three company principles: "The Joy of Buying," "The Joy of Selling," and "The Joy of Creating," which collectively are known as "The Three Joys." According to the company's 2012 annual report, these principles express its "belief and desire that each person working in or coming into contact with our company, directly or through our products, should share a sense of joy through that experience."

BRAND STRATEGY

- The creation of products that benefit society and enhance mobility is a key aspect of Honda's brand strategy.
- Honda's brand strategy is tailored to the different needs of its global customers through regionalized operations.
- Internationally, China has become an important market for the Honda brand because of its growing economy.

Honda's tagline in 2012 was "The Power of Dreams." More than just a catchy phrase, the tagline was truly reflective of Honda's global strategy. For example, that year the company's annual report explained: "Dreams inspire us to create innovative products that enhance mobility and benefit society. To meet the particular needs of customers in different regions around the world, we base our sales networks, research and development centers, and manufacturing facilities in each region."

New product development is critical to the continued evolution of the Honda brand. During Honda's 2012 fiscal year the company was impacted by several natural disasters that threatened its performance in this area. Specifically, the Great East Japan Earthquake caused substantial damage to Honda's Japanese automobile research and development facilities. The quick establishment of satellite research and development locations enabled Honda to minimize the impact of the earthquake on product development.

Examples of new products that were being developed during Honda's 2012 fiscal year included several motorcycles within the leisure segment, including the company's New Mid Concept series for European, Japanese, and North American customers, and improved offerings within the scooter category for commuters in Asian countries. Within the automobile category Honda was concentrating on enhancing its brand via the introduction of environmentally friendly technologies such "Earth Dreams," a next-generation engine and transmission series. In Japan Honda was concentrating on compact and minivehicles such as its N Box, which provided customers with both ample interior space and fuel efficiency. Honda's growth strategy for its power products business was focused on emerging countries like Africa and Asia.

Internationally, China had become an important market for the Honda brand because of its growing economy. The company continued to make inroads through its Guangqi Honda Automobile Co. joint venture. In 2011 the operation sold 362,000 vehicles. The following year, Guangqi Honda added hybrid versions of the Odyssey, Accord, and City, and announced plans to begin production of an all-electric version of the Fit for markets such as Shenzhen, Guangzhou, and Hangzhou.

BRAND EQUITY

- According to Interbrand, in 2012 the Honda brand was valued at US$17.3 billion, a decrease of 11 percent from 2011.
- Honda ranked 21st on Interbrand's list of the 100 Best Global Brands in 2012.
- Honda's research and development expenses totaled ¥519.8 billion during its 2012 fiscal year.
- By 2012 Honda had amassed an intellectual property portfolio that included 17,600 patents in its native Japan, as well as 25,300 international patents.

According to Interbrand, in 2012 the Honda brand was valued at US$17.3 billion, a decrease of 11 percent from 2011. That year Honda ranked 21st on Interbrand's listing of the 100 Best Global Brands, behind BMW, Mercedes-Benz, and Toyota. It also was in 2012 that Honda ranked 65th on Millward Brown Optimor's BrandZ Top 100 ranking, behind BMW, Mercedes-Benz, and Toyota.

Citing figures from IBIS World, *Market Share Reporter* indicated that Honda ranked fifth among the world's top auto and light duty vehicle makers in 2011. Honda's market share totaled 5 percent that year. By comparison, Ford Motor Company's market share totaled 6.9 percent, followed by General Motors Corp. (7 percent), Volkswagen AG (7.3 percent), and Toyota Motor Corp. (9.2 percent). That share increased to 9.8 percent the following year, according to an article in *Ward'sAuto*.

Honda's brand equity stems from decades of research and development. In this area the company operates independent subsidiaries throughout the world, in order to provide engineers and technicians with the freedom to innovate and meet the needs of specific markets. Honda's research and development expenses totaled ¥519.8 billion during its fiscal 2012 year. By that time the company had amassed an intellectual property portfolio that included 17,600 patents in its native Japan, as well as 25,300 international patents.

BRAND AWARENESS

- As part of its 2012 Brand Image Awards, Kelley Blue Book honored Honda with top honors in both the Most Trusted Brand and Best Value Brand categories.
- Honda received Brand of the Year honors within the Full Line Automotive category in Harris Interactive's 2012 Harris Poll EquiTrend Equity Study.
- In late 2012 Honda was preparing to strengthen consumer awareness with a US$250 million dealership advertising program.
- In addition to mass market advertising, the Honda brand has been promoted through campaigns targeted toward specific global markets, as well as different racial and ethnic groups.

The Honda brand name has long been associated with quality and reliability. This has resulted in a high degree of trust between consumers and the brand. Satisfied owners have championed the brand through positive word-of-mouth. Kelley Blue Book (KBB) uses consumer perception data gathered from its Brand Watch study as the basis of the annual Brand Image Awards, which recognize those automotive brands that garner the most positive attention among consumers. In 2012 KBB honored Honda with top honors in both the Most Trusted Brand and Best Value Brand categories.

The strong level of awareness surrounding the Honda name was evident when it received Brand of the Year honors within the Full Line Automotive category in Harris Interactive's 2012 Harris Poll EquiTrend Equity Study. Described as an "annual brand health assessment" in the July 14, 2012, issue of *Marketing Weekly News*, the study involved survey responses from thousands of consumers throughout the United States in key categories such as familiarity, purchase consideration, and quality.

In late 2012 Honda was preparing to strengthen consumer awareness with a US$250 million dealership advertising program. Focused on major metropolitan markets, the so-called Tier 2 program gave approximately 1,100 dealerships the financial resources to develop their own advertising, as long as they agreed to join a regional advertising association and adhere to certain requirements. Development of the program followed criticism from some dealers that competing brands had historically received stronger levels of advertising support.

In addition to mass market advertising, the Honda brand has been promoted through campaigns targeted toward specific global markets, as well as different racial and ethnic groups. For example, in 2012 a European campaign called "The Great Unknown" was created in conjunction with the introduction of the new Honda Civic. In the United States, multicultural marketing campaigns were developed for both Hispanic and African-American consumers in conjunction with the introduction of the 2013 Honda Accord.

BRAND OUTLOOK

- Honda has a long heritage of eclectic research interests, including its ASIMO humanoid robot, and has affirmed its continued commitment to humanoid robotics research.
- In 2012 Honda was concentrating on enhancing its brand via the introduction of environmentally friendly technologies, including its "Earth Dreams" next-generation automotive engine and transmission.
- By the second half of 2012 Honda was preparing to introduce new automobile models with improved performance and styling.
- Honda's growth strategy for its power products business was focused on emerging countries like Africa and Asia.

Robust research and development initiatives, and the new technologies and products that follow, are the lifeblood for any leading manufacturer, and Honda is no exception. In order to develop products that meet the needs of different global markets and provide engineers with the freedom to be innovative, the company maintains independent research subsidiaries throughout the world. By 2012 Honda had amassed an intellectual property portfolio that included 17,600 patents in its native Japan, as well as 25,300 international patents. That year, the company invested ¥519.8 billion in research and development initiatives.

Honda has a long heritage of eclectic research and development interests. For example, the company's engineers have studied the cockroach to gain new insights into anticollision technology. Honda also has developed a humanoid robot named ASIMO, which has the ability to climb stairs, shake hands, and perform many other functions. In 2012 Honda was developing new technologies to improve ASIMO's ability to walk, run, and perform tasks. In the company's 2012 annual report, Honda affirmed its continued commitment to humanoid robotics research, explaining that it planned to "take proactive steps to convert this research into products for mass production and practical or applied use."

The 2012 Civic was a major disappointment for Honda. For the first time, the car received lackluster reviews from *Consumer Reports* and other industry analysts. Criticisms ranged from an overall lack of character to a rough ride and cheap interior. The vehicle's release took place at a time when some observers felt the Honda brand was slipping. For example, in its December 6, 2010, issue, *Automotive News* had commented that "declining buyer consideration, an outdated inventory system and a sliding reputation among younger car shoppers suggest a brand that has lost some of its mojo."

By the second half of 2012 Honda was preparing to change this situation by introducing new models with improved performance and styling. In addition to a new CR-V, new offerings included redesigned versions of the Civic and Accord. Collectively, those three vehicles alone represented approximately 70 percent of Honda's sales in the United States. The company also was concentrating on enhancing its brand via the introduction of environmentally friendly technologies, including a next-generation engine and transmission series named "Earth Dreams." In Japan, Honda was focused on compact and minivehicles such as its N Box, which provided customers with both ample interior space and fuel efficiency.

Examples of other new products that held the potential to maintain or improve Honda's brand strength included several motorcycles within the leisure segment, such as the New Mid Concept series for European, Japanese, and North American customers. In order to meet the needs of a growing commuter base in Asian countries, Honda also improved its offerings within the scooter category. Honda's growth strategy for its power products business was focused on emerging countries like Africa and Asia.

FURTHER READING

"Honda Adds Second Shift as Civic Suffers Poor Review: Company Confident Sales Will Bounce Back." *Indianapolis Business Journal*, October 24, 2011.

"Honda Earns 2012 Kelley Blue Book Brand Image Awards for Best Value Brand and Most Trusted Brand." *Marketing Weekly News*, April 21, 2012.

Honda Motor Co., Ltd. *Annual Report 2012*. Accessed February 28, 2013. http://world.honda.com/investors/library/annual_report/2012/honda2012ar-all-e.pdf.

"Honda Motor Company Ltd." *International Directory of Company Histories*. Ed. Tina Grant. Vol. 96. Farmington Hills, MI: St. James Press, 2008.

"Honda Named 'Brand of the Year' in the 2012 Harris Poll EquiTrend Equity Study." *Marketing Weekly News*, July 14, 2012.

"Honda to Shower Its Dealers with up to $250 Million for Ads." *Advertising Age*, October 8, 2012.

"Honda Unveils 'The Undying Dream' Short-Film Documentary at Sundance." *Manufacturing Close-Up*, January 27, 2011.

Rechtin, Mark. "Honda Accord Campaign Targets Hispanics, Blacks." *Automotive News*, October 8, 2012.

———. "The Threat to Honda's Mojo; Year of Opportunity Goes in Reverse for Brand." *Automotive News*, December 6, 2010.

———. "3 Honda Upgrades Affect 70% of U.S. Volume." *Automotive News*, December 6, 2010, 18.

Schweinsberg, Christie. "Honda Back in Black with Growing Sales, Market Share." *Ward's Auto*, November 27, 2012.

"Toyota, Honda Betting on Performance, Styling." *Automotive News*, July 30, 2012.

HP

AT A GLANCE

Brand Synopsis: HP seeks to harness the power of technology to help customers achieve their goals.
Parent Company: Hewlett-Packard Company
3000 Hanover Street
Palo Alto, California 94304
United States
http://www.hp.com
Sector: Information Technology
Industry Group: Technology Hardware & Equipment
Performance: *Sales*—US$120.4 billion (2012).
Principal Competitors: International Business Machines Corporation; Dell Inc; Accenture plc

BRAND ORIGINS

- Hewlett-Packard was launched in a Palo Alto, California, garage.
- HP's focus for many years was on scientific instruments.
- With the introduction of the ThinkJet and LaserJet printers in 1984, HP became a dominant force in the printer market.
- For most of its history, HP was an industrial brand, spending little on advertising.
- HP became more consumer-oriented in the new century.

HP is the brand of Hewlett-Packard Company, which established the template for a multitude of Silicon Valley-startup technology companies. HP was launched in a garage by Stanford University graduates William Hewlett and David Packard. In 1938, encouraged by one of their professors to start their own business, they invested US$538 in seed money and used the garage behind Packard's rented Palo Alto, California, home to begin development on a resistance-capacity audio oscillator. It would be the first of many testing instruments the company produced over the years.

HP went public in 1957, expanded internationally, and broadened the scope of its product offerings. In the 1960s the company introduced the world's first desktop calculator, followed by the first handheld scientific calculator in 1972. These steps set the stage for HP to move into business computing with the introduction of a minicomputer. In 1980 HP gained a toehold in the consumer market with the introduction of its first personal computer. In 1984 it introduced the HP ThinkJet ink-jet printer and the HP LaserJet Printer, allowing the company to quickly become the dominant force in the printer market. In the early 1990s HP solidified its place by introducing a color LaserJet printer and the OfficeJet, which combined printer, fax machine, and copier.

HP also enjoyed success in selling PCs to corporate customers, and in the mid-1990s it attempted to grow its share of the home PC market with the introduction of the Pavilion line. Despite its growing consumer products business, HP remained very much an industrial brand, positioned as a provider of expensive scientific instruments rather than as a consumer-friendly company. As a result, it lagged well behind in ad spending compared to consumer-oriented companies.

Declining margins led HP to conduct a comprehensive review of its operations in late 1998. Early the following year, the company decided to spin off its noncomputing segments as a separate company, Agilent Technologies, as a way to bring focus and make HP more competitive in a world rapidly impacted by the Internet. A new chief executive, Carly Fiorina, was installed in July 1999 to oversee the restructuring, and before the year's end, HP introduced a new company logo and brand campaign. Fiorina also engineered the US$19 billion acquisition of Compaq Computer Corporation in 2002, further tilting HP in the direction of a consumer brand. It was the last major act of Fiorina, who was soon fired because of poor performance by HP's server and storage segment. Under the leadership of her successor, Mark Hurd, HP began the process of a brand redesign and the creation of a new identity in a world that had changed considerably since William Hewlett and David Packard began developing test instruments in a Palo Alto garage.

BRAND ELEMENTS

- The "HP" letters are at the core of the HP logo.
- The rectangular frame was eliminated from the most recent incarnation of the HP logo.
- HP slogans have shown little consistency over the years.

At the heart of the HP brand is the high quality of the products that bear the HP name. The company has a long history of technical achievements and has forged a well-earned reputation for its engineering prowess. While that heritage creates brand equity in certain sectors, it carries little weight with general consumers. Even people unaware of HP's lineage, however, recognize the brand's reputation for excellence.

The HP logo is another important brand element. For many years, the corporate logo was comprised of the letters "hp" placed within a circle that was in turn framed within a rounded rectangle. In the early 2000s, some HP divisions began to independently modify the logo, leading to inconsistencies and a decision by management to redesign the mark. The result was a simplified version of the previous logo. The letters were given precise horizontal alignment, and the rectangular frame was eliminated. Instead of dark "HP" letters within a circle, the "hp" was rendered in white within a blue circle, although in some applications in which the logo was set against a solid field, the coloring was reversed. The new logo was applied to all HP products and communications.

Less important to the HP brand is a tagline or slogan. In the late 1980s, the brand used "What If?" This was followed by such phrases as "Expanding Possibilities," "Everything is possible," "The computer is personal again," "Invent," and "Better Together." The most recent incarnation is "Make It Matter." With no consistency to the messaging, taglines have provided limited value to the HP brand.

BRAND IDENTITY

- Creating cutting-edge technology is at the heart of HP's identity.
- HP espouses an optimistic view of the future.
- HP wants to be seen as a caring, technological partner.

At the core of HP's identity has always been its association with cutting-edge technology. The company trades on its long history of innovation, a reputation that plays better to a professional segment of the market than to general consumers. As a result, HP has tried to connect technology to problem solving, as a means of improving the world as well as individual lives.

HP presents itself as an encouraging partner. The company is optimistic, viewing the future as a world of boundless opportunities. In addition to confidence, the HP brand is courageous and willing to march into the future. The brand also seeks to display tenacity and an unquenchable thirst for knowledge and discovery. Creativity is another trait HP espouses, promising customers that it has the ability to help solve their problems. In the end, the HP identity is that of a technologically proficient yet caring partner, devoted to helping others realize their potential. The greatest outward expressions of HP's identity are the products that bear the HP brand. Powerful and easy to use, they embody the belief in the power of technology and HP's willingness and ability to partner with individuals.

BRAND STRATEGY

- HP pursued a global branding campaign in the 1980s using the "What If?" tagline.
- The "Invent" branding message was used in the early 2000s.
- A review of HP's branding strategy was begun in 2008.
- HP moved from a house of brands to a branded house approach.

For most of its history, HP was an industrial brand, well known and highly respected by its core customers who understood and valued the company's technical proficiency. As it expanded into products, such as printers and computers, that could be marketed to businesses and consumers, HP took a decentralized approach to its branding efforts. The HP brand meant different things to different audiences, and the company devoted fewer marketing dollars than its competitors to making its message stick. The brand was well regarded by business customers, but transferring that image to consumer markets proved problematic.

In the late 1980s HP launched a global branding effort using the "What If?" tagline. A decade later, the company launched a consumer products brand initiative that employed the "Expanding Possibilities" theme. At the turn of the new century, HP pursued another global brand initiative, centered on the "Invent" concept. The campaign played on HP's heritage of invention and the vision of its founders, while making a call to action, suggesting customers could achieve their goals with HP's help. HP employees were also urged to rethink their views on production, innovation, and service delivery. "Invent" became the new HP mantra.

In 2002, after HP acquired PC manufacturer Compaq, the company rolled out another global branding campaign. It made use of the plus sign (+), which became a repeating motif as part of a brand theme of "you + HP = possibilities." A subsequent tagline exclaimed "Everything is possible." Another campaign, called "Change + HP," targeted enterprise customers. HP also tried to improve its image with consumers by aligning itself with the entertainment industry, touting in ads how its technology was used in the making of movies. In 2006 HP unveiled yet another new tagline to promote its PC business: "The computer is personal again."

Recognizing that the HP brand had lost much of its luster and that the company's approach to branding had become unfocused, HP began a lengthy process in 2008 to reconsider its branding philosophy. Rather than being a house of brands, the company concluded that it needed to be a branded house, one that developed a strong brand that could be used across product lines around the world. To support that vision, HP developed a set of general guidelines. To maintain brand consistency, the logo would be rarely used on non-HP offerings. New acquisitions would be quickly transitioned to HP naming and branding. Products would be given descriptive names, avoiding any names that could distract from or compete with the HP brand. Furthermore, no new logos would be developed internally.

A new HP logo was also crafted, and it would be applied consistently to reinforce HP's brand identity, which the company came to see as a commitment to human progress. This brand story reflected HP's belief that technology was the key to human progress. To its customers, HP wished to be seen as a force that could help spark the creation of new solutions to business as well as individual and societal problems. To its employees, HP wished to inspire, to urge them to embody the brand for its customers. The new branding campaign centered around the tagline "Make It Matter."

BRAND EQUITY

- Brand Finance Plc assigned a value of US$21.707 billion to the HP brand in 2012.
- HP ranked No. 21 on Brand Finance's Global 500 of the world's most valuable brands in 2012.
- Interbrand estimated HP's brand value at US$26.087 billion in 2012.
- HP ranked No. 26 on the BrandZ Top 100 in 2012.

Despite an inconsistent strategy, HP has long been one of the world's most valuable brands. A reputation for innovative and reliable products allows the company to charge higher prices than many of its competitors, providing a practical measure of HP's brand equity. Using a proprietary methodology to quantify the value of a brand, consultancy Brand Finance Plc assigned a value of US$21.707 billion to the HP brand in 2012, which placed HP at No. 21 on Brand Finance's Global 500 of the world's most valuable brands. It also marked a steady diminishment in HP's brand equity in recent years. A year earlier, HP had possessed a brand value of US$26.756 billion, good enough for the No. 13 position on the Global 500. And in 2008 HP had been the 8th most valuable brand, with an assigned value of US$32.427 billion.

Another brand consultancy, Interbrand, using its own method of determining brand value, estimated the worth of HP's brand at US$26.087 billion in 2012, down 8 percent from the previous year. As a result, HP was listed as Interbrand's 15th most valuable brand in the world. According to Interbrand, HP's decline was caused by internal instability that "resulted in the lack of a cohesive business strategy or brand strategy, which threatens both financial results and HP's reputation."

Global research agency Millward Brown offers its own list of the world's most valuable brands, called the "BrandZ Top 100." According to its valuation method, HP was worth US$22.898 billion and ranked No. 26 on the 2012 list of the most valuable brands. It was a 35 percent loss in brand value over the previous year. As a result, HP fell eight places on the list from the previous year. Among technology brands, HP was listed as the 8th most valuable, trailing upstarts such as Baidu, the Chinese search engine and internet services company, and well behind the category leader Apple, whose brand value topped US$180 billion.

BRAND AWARENESS

- HP's long history contributes to its brand awareness.
- HP is recognized as a world leader in several market segments.
- Worldwide operations reinforce HP's brand awareness.

HP enjoys strong brand recognition across many sectors in virtually every corner of the world. A major contributing factor is the company's longevity. HP laid the groundwork for Silicon Valley, establishing a strong reputation in many fields, from entertainment to research, with its breakthrough scientific instruments. As an industrial brand with little marketing investment, HP broke through to enjoy general recognition. With the introduction of revolutionary printing products in the mid-1980s, HP became a dominant force in both the business and consumer segments of the printing market, increasing the brand's recognition among consumers in addition to information technology professionals.

While most consumers are not aware of HP's scope, there is no doubt that the company's broad interests increase brand awareness. HP is the world's largest provider of PCs, industry-standard servers, and imaging and printing products. Moreover, the company maintains product development facilities, laboratories, and manufacturing sites throughout Europe and in Asia Pacific countries. Whether or not HP has promoted a consistent message over the years, the brand remains one of the most recognizable in the world.

BRAND OUTLOOK

- Having spun off its former core assets as Agilent Technologies, HP struggled in the early 2000s to find its footing in the information technology arena.
- HP released the Touchpad in July 2011, and it fell flat.
- HP's "Make It Matter" campaign offered some hope for success in its new, unified branding strategy.

HP has experienced a number of setbacks as it attempted to make the transition from an industrial brand to a true consumer brand. Having spun off its former core assets as Agilent Technologies, HP has struggled to find solid footing in the information technology arena, especially with consumers. In the early 2000s the company underwent regular changes at the top ranks of management, which only added to an inconsistent approach to business strategy as well as branding. In 2010 HP acquired Palm, Inc., to stake a claim in the smartphone and tablet PC markets. The release of the HP Touchpad in July 2011 fell flat, and the company quickly abandoned the market. HP also considered eliminating its PC division. Instead, CEO Leo Apotheker was replaced by a new chief executive, Meg Whitman, who talked about defending HP's PC business by challenging Apple on product design. According to *Forbes* market survey information, HP was ranked No. 10 in terms of Innovative Design, compared to Apple's top spot. It was not only a tall mountain to climb, there was every reason to believe that it might not be a mountain worth climbing, given that tablets and smartphones were in many ways rendering the PC obsolete.

In making a successful turnaround, HP faced both internal and external challenges. There was no shortage of nimble competitors. The new "Make It Matter" campaign offered some hope of a unified branding strategy, and the breadth of HP's products and services provided some measure of security. According to the assessment of Interbrand, "HP faces numerous challenges as it attempts to restore its reputation for innovation and foster momentum within the rapidly changing technology arena."

FURTHER READING

"Best Global Brands 2012." Interbrand. Accessed December 26, 2012. http://www.interbrand.com/en/best-global-brands/2012/Best-Global-Brands-2012.aspx

Brand Finance. "Global 500 2012." *Brandirectory*. Accessed December 28, 2012. http://brandirectory.com/league_tables/table/global-500-2012.

Bulik, Beth Snyder. "HP Big on Buzz and Bottom Line." *Advertising Age*, August 21, 2006.

———. "HP Sheds Stodgy Image, Goes Too Cool for School." *Advertising Age*, May 16, 2005.

Elkin, Tobi. "HP Unifies Branding with $200 Mil Push." *Advertising Age*, November 22, 1999.

"Hewlett-Packard Company." *International Directory of Company Histories*. Ed. Jay P. Pederson. Vol. 111. Detroit, MI: St. James Press, 2010.

"Hewlett-Packard Reinvents Itself." *Advertising Age*, January 31, 2000.

Hill, Jamie. "Can HP Add Colour to Its Boring, Grey Past?" *Marketing Week*, February 12, 2004.

Mazur, Laura. "High Tech Firms Are Backwards about Branding." *Marketing*, March 25, 1999.

Millward Brown. "Brandz Top 100 Most Valuable Global Brands 2012." Accessed January 17, 2013. http://www.millwardbrown.com/brandz/Top_100_Global_Brands.aspx

Passikoff, Robert. "Rebuilding the HP Brand." *Forbes*, September 18, 2012.

"Post-merger HP Invents New Image to Challenge Tech Foes IBM and Dell." *Brandweek*, November 18, 2002.

HSBC

AT A GLANCE

Brand Synopsis: HSBC, one of the world's largest banking and financial service providers, is committed to helping its clients achieve global success.
Parent Company: HSBC Holdings PLC
8 Canada Square
London E14 5HQ
United Kingdom
http://www.hsbcgroup.com
Sector: Financials
Industry Group: Banks
Performance: *Market share*—2.80%, worldwide (2008). *Operating income*—US$43.66 billion.
Principal Competitors: Barclays PLC; Citigroup, Inc.; The Royal Bank of Scotland Group PLC.

BRAND ORIGINS

- HSBC was originally founded as the Hongkong and Shanghai Banking Company, Ltd., in 1865.
- Hongkong Bank expanded into Japan, Thailand, the Philippines, Singapore, the United States, and other regions by 1900.
- Japan began its domination of China in the 1930s, and Hongkong Bank's operations were allowed to continue in certain occupied regions.
- In 1991 the bank created a new holding company, HSBC Holdings PLC, which made Hongkong Bank a subsidiary of the U.K.-incorporated HSBC Holdings.
- In 1998 HSBC announced that it would unify the HSBC group under the HSBC name, creating a globally unified brand.

HSBC was originally founded as the Hongkong and Shanghai Banking Company, Ltd. in 1865. At the time, Hong Kong's financial needs were supplied by European trading houses, a system that eventually deteriorated to make room for established banks in 1864. An office in London was opened a year after the Hongkong and Shanghai Banking Company was opened in order to prevent the success of a proposed "Bank of China." To avoid the necessity of a Royal Charter, or the need to comply with colonial banking regulations, the bank's founders designed their brand as a local concern. Hongkong Bank expanded into Japan, Thailand, the Philippines, Singapore, San Francisco, New York, Lyons, Hamburg, and the regions now known as Malaysia, Myanmar, Sri Lanka, and Vietnam by 1900. Hongkong Bank became the banker to the government of Hong Kong and acquired the Treasury Chest business for China and Japan, providing loans for wars waged between the countries, and for the enforcement of peace during internal conflicts as well as for infrastructural projects, including railroads and shipping lines.

World War I divided the bank, which eventually led to the resignation of German members of the board. Japan began its domination of China in the 1930s, and Hongkong Bank's operations were allowed to continue in occupied regions of Dairen, Mukden, and Harbin, though its services were restricted to foreign trade. Elsewhere in China the bank experienced increased competition from the Chinese financial community.

The Japanese occupation of China in the 1940s forced employees of Hongkong Bank to be repatriated or to flee the new regime. Employees in China managed to establish a new operation that opened in 1943. Following the end of the war, colonial authorities once again assumed control and began the process of assisting in the reconstruction of Hong Kong. The bank's branches, including those in Japan but excluding the Hamburg branch, were reopened, only to face the severe inflation and the increasing public disorder generated by civil war.

After all but the Shanghai branches in China were closed in 1955, the Hongkong Bank under Michael Turner began a new strategy of expansion using subsidiaries in order to reduce the bank's dependence on Hong Kong. As Britain had relinquished much of its empire following the war, the bank's expansion now depended on mergers, acquisitions, or nationalizations. Hongkong and Shanghai Bank began by buying the Mercantile Bank and the British Bank of the Middle East. These purchases made the Hongkong Bank the largest foreign bank in most countries from the Far East to southwest Asia. Hongkong Bank would continue to acquire and make strategic alliances with competing financiers throughout the 1980s and 1990s.

In 1991 the bank created a new holding company, HSBC Holdings PLC, which made Hongkong Bank a subsidiary of the U.K.-incorporated (albeit Hong Kong-based) HSBC Holdings. The following year, Hongkong Bank, which had acted as the quasi-central bank, was divested of many of its unofficial duties while HSBC Holdings continued to expand. In 1998 HSBC announced that it would unify the HSBC Group under the HSBC name, creating a globally unified brand.

BRAND ELEMENTS

- HSBC's logo consists of a red and white hexagon and the corporate logotype "HSBC."
- HSBC's logo is standardized worldwide so that every branch promotes the same awareness of the HSBC brand.
- HSBC has also achieved high visibility through its partnership with the Wimbledon Tennis Championships.

HSBC is immediately identifiable for its signature red and white hexagon and corporate logotype "HSBC." This logo frequently appears with HSBC's ad campaign "HSBC helps you unlock the world's potential." Its previous tagline "The world's local bank" was part of the bank's promotional effort to align its brand image with its core values: a brand open to new ideas, prepared to join with new global partners, and committed to a connection with customers and communities. Moreover, the brand's logo is standardized worldwide so that every branch is recognizable as a part of the HSBC brand. While this local emphasis still holds true, the brand also seeks to focus on its potential to gain new shares in emerging global markets.

HSBC enhances the visibility of its brand through many sponsorships, which include programs in education, health, and environmental conservation. In 2006 the brand announced a US$5 million association with SOS Children as part of the Future First campaign. HSBC also achieves visibility through its partnership with the Wimbledon Tennis Championships (by providing banking facilities on site) and the renaming of the Road to Wimbledon junior event as the HSBC Road to Wimbledon National 14 and Under Challenge.

BRAND IDENTITY

- In 2002 HSBC billed itself as "the world's local bank" and opened its new headquarters at London's Canary Wharf the following year.
- In 2012, HSBC launched a new brand strategy that linked its identity to a larger global scope.
- The future lies in international business, and so HSBC has realigned its ad campaigns to emphasize that aspect of its operations.

In 2002 HSBC billed itself as "the world's local bank" and opened its new headquarters at London's Canary Wharf the following year. Acquisitions in the early 2000s included the American financier Household International Inc. and the British Marks & Spencer's Financial Service Holdings. The group's consistent sensitivity to local cultural needs fueled the bank's reputation as a global bank prepared to adjust to fit the financial needs of local communities.

To signal its commitment to that adjustment, HSBC launched a slight rebranding effort in 2012. While the bank remained committed to its local communities, it sought to further identify the global aspect of its brand. The resulting advertising campaign is about the future—one that it is only attainable in a global climate. Each campaign begins with the phrase "In the future" and continues with focused statements from each of the bank's segments. Examples include: "In the future, even the smallest business will be multinational" and "In the future, there will be no markets left waiting to emerge." The banks shift away from the local aspect is an attempt to capitalize on the increasingly international activity of businesses.

BRAND STRATEGY

- Numerous acquisitions have led to HSBC's large global network.
- In 2002 HSBC launched a worldwide advertising campaign titled "the world's local bank" to unify its brand around the world.
- In 2012 HSBC launched a new campaign to communicate its changing business strategy, which included a focus on tapping new markets throughout the world.

HSBC expanded considerably throughout the 1980s and 1990s via the traditional methods of mergers and acquisitions. The bank acquired Concord International (a leasing and finance group), Anthony Gibbs (a British merchant bank), and the Bank of British Columbia between 1980 and 1986. The acquisition in 1992 of Midland Bank provided HSBC with a greater presence in Europe, doubled the new parent company's assets and work force, and attracted larger corporate customers to the brand.

In the 1990s HSBC's brand was divided among a disconnected group of banks around the world. HSBC built its brand image over the next five years largely through campaigns based on the acknowledgement that customers were individuals and communities were unique, and they required services specially tailored to their needs. The brand was faced with a "global-local" problem of deciding whether to strive for local relevance or global scale. The brand reconciled the two targets with the worldwide advertising campaign with the tagline "the world's local bank," which was designed by Peter Stringham (the then global head of marketing for HSBC) in 2002. The ad campaign carried the message that those who banked with HSBC would benefit from the services and advice of a company with international expertise and sensitivity to the community's unique needs.

Now that the world market has changed again, the brand has once again been shifting its strategy. According to Interbrand, "In an effort to consolidate in underperforming markets, HSBC is concentrating its presence in growth markets and businesses where wealth is being created." These markets are certainly found in emerging global economies. The company has suggested that for its bank, and its clients, to remain successful, the future must include global business. Its current ad campaign stresses this image as each ad focuses on one element of the future and one element of HSBC's global banking network.

BRAND EQUITY

- In their interim management report of 2012, HSBC reported profit before tax of US$757 million and total assets of US$878 billion.
- Interbrand ranked HSBC 33rd in its ranking of the top 100 brands, with a brand value of US$11.3 billion.
- HSBC ranked high on many brand valuations, placing 13th on Brand Finance's Global 500 and first in its Global Banking 500.

In their interim management report of 2012, HSBC reported profit before tax of US$757 million, 37 percent lower than the same term in 2011, and total assets of US$ 878 billion. HSBC's net operating income was US$6.81 billion, and total operating expenses were US$5.44 billion, up 20 percent from the previous year due to higher customer redress provisions in the United Kingdom. Foreign exchange revenue grew as a result of higher client revenues and a favorable trading environment for foreign exchange. The bank's net expense from financial instruments was US$9 million.

Based on its continued growth in foreign markets and its new cost-cutting strategies, HSBC, although down a few percentage points from 2011, still remained high atop the brand valuation rankings. In 2012 HSBC was ranked the 33rd best global brand by Interbrand, with a brand value of US$11.3 billion. Additionally, it was ranked 13th in Brand Finance's Global 500 list and first in the Brand Finance Global Banking 500 list. HBSC was rated the second-most valuable U.K. brand by Brand Finance and appeared in 19th place on Global Finance's list of the "World's 50 Safest Banks."

BRAND AWARENESS

- In 2012 HSBC sought the attention of the global commuter by buying advertising space in airports in 24 countries.
- In May 2011 HSBC launched its "In the future..." campaign to promote its various global business lines and its new brand strategy.
- Due to both its airport campaign and its aggressive brand strategy, HSBC has earned top-of-mind brand recall in the banking industry.

HSBC enjoys top-of-mind recall in the banking industry due, in part, to its inventive advertising and new brand image. Since 1998 HSBC has operated under the same brand name and hexagonal logo, but the visibility of the brand has benefited most from its iconic worldwide brand campaigns. In 2012, to support its new focus on global markets, HSBC decided to advertise in places that would catch the eye of globally minded consumers. HSBC sought the attention of the global commuter by buying advertising space in airports, beginning in the United Kingdom and New York, until the brand had ad visibility in 48 airports in 24 countries. The brand's ads are also featured on the Executive Club pages of British Airways' website.

BRAND OUTLOOK

- HSBC Holdings PLC is a leading international banking group, with 9,500 offices serving 120 million customers in approximately 80 countries.
- Efforts in rebranding and cost-cutting will help HSBC ensure its success in the future.
- By focusing on new markets like India and China, and diminishing operations in Europe, the brand hopes to strengthen its international interests.

HSBC Holdings PLC (also known as the HSBC Group) is a leading international banking group that operates in 9,500 offices serving 120 million customers in approximately 80 countries. The brand's global connections are what will support its ability to remain one of the world's most successful brands and one of the world's most successful banks. With a new brand strategy focused on this effort, HSBC has positioned itself for a bright tomorrow.

Additionally, new cost-cutting measures, including job cuts and a renewed focus on emerging global markets, will help the brand reach its objective of becoming the world's leading international bank. According to HSBC's 2011 annual review, restructuring costs of US$132 million were put towards this cost efficiency program, which includes continued investment in India and China and diminished operations in Europe, actions that were aimed at preparing the brand for a predicted regional shift in economic strength during the following year.

FURTHER READING

Agrayspace.com. "HSBC Brand-Basic Elements." Accessed October 9 2012. http://www.agrayspace.com/KCAI/styleguides/hsbc_brand_basic_elements.pdf

"Banking on Airports: Q&A with HSBC's Global Advertising Head." *Sparksheet*. Accessed October 9, 2012. http://sparksheet.com/banking-on-airports-qa-with-hsbcs-global-advertising-head/.

Blanden, Michael. "After the Dust of Battle." *Banker*, August 1992, 36.

Brand Finance. "Global 500 2012." *Brandirectory*. Accessed October 30, 2012. http://brandfinance.com/images/upload/bf_g500_2012_web_dp.pdf.

Collis, Maurice. *Wayfoong: The Hong Kong and Shanghai Banking Corporation*. London: Faber and Faber, 1965.

DuBlanc, Robin, David E. Salamie, and Frederick C. Ingram. "HSBC Holdings PLC." *International Directory of Company Histories*. Ed. Tina Grant. Vol. 80. Detroit: St. James Press, 2007. 155-163. *Gale Virtual Reference Library*. Accessed October 12, 2012. http://go.galegroup.com/ps/i.do?id=GALE%7CCX3483800045&v=2.1&u=itsbtrial&it=r&p=GVRL&sw=w.

Effective Brands. "Building the Global HSBC Brand." *The Global Brand CEO- Case Study: HSBC*. Accessed October 30, 2012. http://www.effectivebrands.com/EffectiveBrands/pdf/EB_HSBC-CaseStudy.pdf.

Engardio, Pete. "Global Banker." *Business Week*, May 24, 1993, 42–46.

Graham, George. "HSBC Reaps Fruits of Growth Strategy." *Financial Times*, February 24, 1998, 26.

HSBC. "HSBC: A Brief History: The Hongkong and Shanghai Banking Corporation Limited." http://www.hsbc.com/about-hsbc/-/media/HSBC-com/about-hsbc/history/pdfs/120607-hsbc-brief-history.ashx.

Interbrand. "Best Global Brands 2012." Accessed October 30, 2012. http://www.interbrand.com/en/best-global-brands/2012/Best-Global-Brands-2012.aspx

"World's 50 Safest Banks 2012." *Global Finance*, March 1, 2012. Accessed October 30, 2012. http://www.gfmag.com/tools/best-banks/11661-worlds-50-safest-banks-april-2012.html#axzz2AnB4AZEg

HTC

AT A GLANCE

Brand Synopsis: The Taiwanese brand HTC personifies high quality in smartphones, Internet tablets, and notebook computers.
Parent Company: HTC Corporation
23 Xinghua Rd., Taoyuan 330
Taiwan
http://www.htc.com
Sector: Electronics
Industry Group: Telecommunications
Performance: *Market share*—5.9 percent of the U.S. mobile market; 4.6 percent of the mobile market worldwide (2012).
Principal Competitors: Apple Inc.; Nokia Oyj; Samsung Electronics

BRAND ORIGINS

- HTC was founded as the High Tech Computer Company in Taiwan in 1997 by Peter Chou, Cher Wang, and H.T. Cho.
- The company released its first products under its own brand name in 2006.
- HTC reached great success in the United States in 2010 after releasing the HTC Evo 4G, the first 4G phone in the U.S.
- In 2011 HTC acquired S3 Graphics, Dashwire, and 51 percent of the shares of Beats Electronics, further expanding the company's mobile technology.

High Tech Computer Corporation, known as HTC, was founded in 1997 by Peter Chou, Cher Wang, and H.T. Cho as a manufacturer of notebook computers for American-based companies, including Hewlett-Packard and Microsoft. By 1998 the company had begun designing some of the world's first touch and wireless hand-held devices, creating one of the first touch-screen smartphones by 2000 for Palm, a subsidiary of HP. As a manufacturer, HTC was able to build relationships and close partnerships with important players in the mobile markets of Europe, Asia, and the United States. Prior to the company manufacturing products for its own brand, HTC created products such as the innovative Color Palm-size PC, the Compaq iPAQ, and the Microsoft Smart Music Phone.

In 2006 HTC began to manufacture products for its own brand instead of for other companies. Due to the success the company had as a manufacturer as well as the partnerships with major companies, after HTC launched its new brand *Business Week* magazine in 2007 ranked HTC as the second-best-performing technology company in Asia and the third-largest globally in 2006. After launching its own brand, HTC recorded a remarkably fast growth rate and its products proliferated around the world. Also in 2007 HTC acquired Dopod International, a Taiwan-based mobile device company, which placed HTC in competition within the Asian market with partner HP.

HTC brought its first HTC-branded product to the United States in 2010, the HTC Evo 4G, the first 4G-capable phone. The company had launched its first 4G phone, the Integrated GSM/WiMax 4G, in Russia in 2008. Also in 2010 HTC announced that it would now sell smartphones in China under the brand HTC instead of Dopod, as it had partnered with China Mobile, a state-owned telecommunication network. The following year, HTC was listed as the third-largest smartphone manufacturer in the world, behind Apple and Samsung. After the launch of HTC's 4G device in the United States, HTC's sales had increased by 111 percent from the previous year. Bloomberg reported in 2011 that HTC had become the largest smartphone vendor in the United States, with an increase of 10 percentage points in share up to 24 percent. In 2012, however, Apple and Samsung had regained control of the market, with HTC's share dropping back to under 5 percent.

In 2011 HTC acquired VIA Technology's stake in S3 Graphics, an American-based graphics company. Under HTC's direction S3 has moved from 3D computer graphics to exclusively designing graphics for mobile devices, although the company still produces graphics accelerators for PCs. Additionally in 2011, HTC acquired Dashwire, a virtual information cloud, for US$18.5 million. The same year, HTC went into partnership with Beats Electronics, acquiring 51 percent of the audio production company. The company released a smartphone in 2011, the HTC Rezound, which utilized Beats Audio.

BRAND ELEMENTS

- The company's brand name HTC was created at the founding of the company in 1997; the company's full name was High Tech Computer Corporation.
- The slogan used for brand marketing is "HTC Quietly Brilliant," subtly claiming to not need the extensive marketing that competitors are known for.
- The company logo is simple, using only the brand name HTC in simply styled typeface.

The company name HTC is the most immediately recognizable aspect of its brand. HTC has been operating under that name since the company was founded in 1997. The letters are an acronym for High Tech Computer Company, although the company has never used its full name in any product. Prior to manufacturing its own computers and mobile devices in 2006, the HTC name was unknown; the company was a manufacturer and creator for other computer companies, such as Microsoft and HP. Since 2006 the company has mostly operated under HTC, with the exception of utilizing the brand name Dopod after acquiring the company in 2007. The Dopod brand was eliminated in 2010 after HTC began selling the Dopod mobile devices under the HTC brand name. In the United States, HTC did not release a product under its name until it released the HTC Evo 4G in 2010.

HTC has had two major slogans: the first was "HTC Innovation," marketing the groundbreaking aspect of the company. The company has been cutting edge in many developmental aspects, releasing the first color touchscreen mobile device in 2000 and releasing the first 4G smartphone in the United States. In 2009 the company changed its slogan to "HTC Quietly Brilliant." The company trademarked the slogan the same year. The concept behind the newer slogan was to place the company away from competitors Apple and Samsung. Both Apple and Samsung rely on heavy marketing grabs, attracting consumers through clever television and internet marketing. HTC instead relies on the abilities and creativity of its products to further its brand, building the company off of its reputation for innovation.

The HTC logo used in marketing is simple, using only the letters of its name in a bright green digital typeface with the slogan "quietly brilliant" in black all-lowercase typeface. The HTC logo that appears on its products is the brand name written in the same simple typeface, matching the product's outer color.

BRAND IDENTITY

- HTC has been on the forefront of new mobile computer advances since the company was founded in 1997, striving "to integrate state-of-the-art technologies with effortless user experiences."
- Instead of relying heavily on marketing, HTC instead uses its reputation for innovative technology to further expose the brand.
- In 2011 HTC purchased Beats Electronics and S3 to take advantage of their innovative technology.

HTC's brand portrait is based on the company's history for releasing innovative products. Although the company did not release a product under its own name until 2006, the company had been manufacturing innovative products since the company was founded in 1997. Working as a product creator and manufacturer for Hewlett-Packard and Microsoft, HTC began its reputation for groundbreaking work. From releasing the first touchscreen color mobile device for Palm in 1999 to introducing Compaq's pocket PC in 2000, HTC placed itself as a manufacturer of innovation. The first product HTC released in the United States, the HTC Evo 4G, was the first 4G device used in the United States. Part of the company's innovative image is derived from the company's goal "to integrate state-of-the-art technologies with effortless user experiences," making products that not only feature new technology, but have made its accessibility easier for the consumer.

Additionally, HTC's slogan "Quietly Brilliant" explains a large portion of the company's identity. Instead of marketing heavily, HTC relies on the innovation of the product and reputation to further the brand. As the company had started as a manufacturer instead of an individual product brand, HTC has been behind the scenes for the majority of the company's history, building its reputation on the product alone, without any name recognition. As the company has released products under its own name, the company has remained original with product design, without utilizing heavy marketing. After purchasing Beats Electronics in 2011, HTC began utilizing the Beats Audio system, not only allowing for mobile users to have better music output, but allowing for better sound for every aspect of smartphones. HTC also states that its smartphone cameras rival leading point-and-shoot cameras. The company also purchased S3, a graphics company, in 2011 and since has utilized HD graphics on its smartphones.

BRAND STRATEGY

- After the company was founded, HTC acted solely as a computer and mobile manufacturer for other companies, such as Hewlett-Packard.
- HTC purchased Dopod in 2007, a Taiwanese-based mobile company, utilizing the already-established brand until it was phased out in 2010.
- The company gradually grew its own branding internationally, starting with the Asian market before venturing into the United States.

Initially, HTC products were not released under the company's brand name as the company was a creator and manufacturer for other computer and mobile companies, such as Hewlett-Packard. During HTC's period as a manufacturer, the company was able to build relationships with other companies, proving its innovation and reliability as a technology company. As the company successfully grew, HTC was able to utilize those relationships to further its own brand and continues to do so. As the company had built a relationship with Microsoft during its period as a manufacturer, HTC continues to work with Microsoft, releasing mobile devices that use the Microsoft software and, as of 2013, is in partnership with Google, utilizing the company's Android operating software.

HTC began releasing products under its brand name first in China in 2006, and from there gradually expanded its global product base. In 2007 HTC acquired the Taiwanese-based mobile company Dopod, which was the preferred mobile device choice for China Mobile, a state-owned telecommunications company. Dopod was founded in 2004 in Taipei, but quickly grew its reputation in the Asian mobile market. HTC continued the use of the Dopod name until 2010, when the company converted all of Dopod products to the HTC brand name.

In its effort to become a more global company, HTC released its first products under its own brand name to the Asian market. In 2008 HTC released its first 4G phone in Russia, introducing 4G to the country. Following in the same path, HTC released the first 4G phone in the United States in 2010. Although HTC did not initially launch as a multinational corporation, the company has since grown into a successful international brand.

BRAND EQUITY

- HTC is the fifth most successful mobile device manufacturer for products sold in the United States, holding 5.9 percent of the market as of November 2012.
- Interbrand ranked HTC as the 98th most valuable brand in 2011 with a value of US$33.492 billion.
- Brand Finance ranked HTC as the 252nd most valuable brand with a value of US$17.192 billion, where competitor Apple was ranked first with a value of US$70.605 billion.

The technology blog BGR states that HTC is the fifth most successful OEM (original equipment manager) for U.S. mobile subscribers, with Samsung, Apple, LG, and Motorola coming in ahead of HTC. Between August and November 2012, Samsung's share of the mobile market increased to 26.9 percent, up 1.2 percent. For the same period, HTC lost share of the market, falling 0.4 percent to having 5.9 percent of the market.

According to Interbrand's *2011 Ranking of the Top 100 Brands*, HTC ranked 98th with a brand value of US$3.6 billion, whereas Apple came in ranked at eighth, with a value of US$33.492 billion. Brand Finance's *Global 500 2012* ranked HTC 252nd overall and estimated its brand value at US$17.192 billion. Competitor Apple was ranked first in the same list, with a brand value of US$70.605 billion, and competitor Samsung ranked sixth with a value of US$38.197 billion.

BRAND AWARENESS

- The company started out as an OEM, not attaching its brand onto the products it was making.
- HTC's marketing is "Quietly Brilliant," meaning the company focuses less on brand marketing and more on research and product innovation.
- In 2013 HTC launched a television campaign for the Droid DNA emphasizing its availability through Verizon.

Unlike its competitors, HTC's top-of-mind recognition is limited. Due to the company's history of being an original equipment manufacturer for mobile devices and computers, the company did not advertise or expose the brand's name to end consumers. HTC has been using its own brand name since 2006, releasing mobile devices into the Asian market. The company did not launch its first product into the United States until 2010, but the product was the HTC Evo 4G, the first 4G device released in the United States. The Evo put the brand on the forefront of new mobile technology, adding competition to Apple's successful iPhone. Since then, HTC has mostly fallen back, becoming a less marketed brand. Even the company slogan was changed to "Quietly Brilliant," as the company does not rely on heavy marketing and advertising campaigns, as its major competitors do. In 2013 HTC launched a new television campaign for the Droid DNA, the advertising focusing more on its availability through the telecommunications company Verizon than the brand HTC. Due to a more subtle marketing plan, HTC's brand is not as well known to consumers as its competitors are.

BRAND OUTLOOK

- HTC's sales and market share in the United States decreased in 2012, dropping to 5.9 percent by November 2012.
- The company has acquired several other technology companies as part of an effort of releasing new products with better sound, graphics, and speed.
- In the Asian market, HTC remains strong, holding 13.3 percent market share in May 2012.

Although HTC was extremely successful when it first launched its brand into the U.S. market in 2010, releasing the HTC Evo 4G, the first 4G device in the United States, HTC has since dropped down in the market. At first the company was able to take on the already successful Apple and Samsung, but since the market share has been gradually lessening. Between August and November 2012, HTC's share of the U.S. mobile market decreased from 6.3 percent to 5.9 percent.

In 2011 HTC increased the capabilities of the company by acquiring the audio company Beats Audio, allowing HTC mobile devices to have improved sound. Also in 2011 HTC acquired the graphics company S3. The company had previously been known for its 3D graphics, but HTC has been using the research and development of S3 to increase the graphics capability on its mobile devices. The same year, HTC also acquired Dashwire, a virtual information cloud, further increasing the company's sources for new technology. In 2013 HTC launched the Droid DNA, a device that makes use of the Beats Audio technology as well as a high-speed operating system, with the expectation of regaining some of the lost market share in the United States.

Although the brand is not as successful as competitors in the United States, HTC's largest market remains in Asia, where the company has worked with China's state-run telecom company China Mobile since it acquired the Taiwanese-based Dopod. HTC has been doing increasingly well in the Asian market; the market share in Asia was 6.4 percent in April 2012 and increased to 13.3 percent by May 2012.

FURTHER READING

Brand Finance. "Global 500 2012." *Brandirectory*. Accessed December 12, 2012. http://brandfinance.com/images/upload/bf_g500_2012_web_dp.pdf.

Culpan, Tim, and Hugo Miller. "HTC Takes Lead in U.S. Smartphone Market as Apple, RIM Decline." *Bloomberg*, November 1, 2011.

Epstein, Zach. "Rim and HTC Are Q3S Biggest Smartphone Losers." *BGR*, November 8, 2012. Accessed January 3, 2013. http://bgr.com/2012/11/08/smartphone-market-share-q3-2012/.

Graziano, Dan. "Samsung and Apple Are Still the Only Winners in the Mobile Market." *BGR*, January 3, 2013. Accessed January 3, 2013. http://bgr.com/2013/01/03/samsung-apple-market-share-2012-280876/.

"HTC." Made in Taiwan. Accessed January 4, 2013. http://www.roc-taiwan-hn.com/htc.php.

"HTC Can Regain Market Share: Goldman Sachs." *Want China Times* (Taipei), July 18, 2012. Accessed January 9, 2013. http://www.wantchinatimes.com/news-subclass-cnt.aspx?id=20120718000063&cid=1102.

Myftiu, Matt. "Tech Time Review: Droid DNA by HTC Smartphone Offers Super-sharp Screen, Extra-fast Processor." *Heritage News* (Dearborn, MI), January 9, 2013.

Ricker, Thomas. "HTC Buyout of Dopod in Final Stages." *engadget*, September 19, 2006. Accessed January 4, 2013. http://www.engadget.com/2006/09/19/htc-buyout-of-dopod-in-final-stages-i-mate-o2-hp-wail/.

HYUNDAI

AT A GLANCE

Brand Synopsis: Originally positioned as a producer of budget automobiles, South Korea's Hyundai has expanded its product line and carved out an increasingly upscale niche to become the fastest-growing automotive brand in the world.
Parent Company: Hyundai Motor Company
231 Yangjae-dong, Seocho-gu
Seoul 137-938
South Korea
http://worldwide.hyundai.com
Sector: Consumer Discretionary
Industry Group: Automobiles & Components
Performance: *Market share*—5.1%, worldwide (2011). *Sales*—US$68.57 billion (2011).
Principal Competitors: Chrysler Group LLC; Ford Motor Company; General Motors Company; Honda Motor Company, Ltd.; Nissan Motor Company; Toyota Motor Corporation

BRAND ORIGINS

- Hyundai's parent, the Hyundai Group, was one of the largest South Korean *chaebol,* or corporate conglomerates, prior to its dismantling in 2003.
- Though dubbed "the first Korean car," Hyundai's Pony, introduced in 1975, involved collaboration with British, Italian, and Japanese personnel.
- With the low-budget subcompact Excel, Hyundai broke into the U.S. market in the mid-1980s.
- As a financial crisis swept Asia in the late 1990s, Hyundai purchased a controlling stake in its leading Korean competitor, Kia Motors.

The Hyundai brand had its origins in 1947, with the founding of the Hyundai Engineering and Construction Company. This company grew into the Hyundai Group, which became one of the largest of the South Korean *chaebol,* or corporate conglomerates. In 1967 the Hyundai *chaebol* established the Hyundai Motor Company, which in the following year produced its first model, the Cortina, in a joint venture with the Ford Motor Company. Seeking to manufacture automobiles under its own name, Hyundai began work on what would become the Pony in 1975. Ironically, the Pony—known as "the first Korean car"—was in part the result of a collaboration with British engineers, Italian stylists, and Japanese technicians.

The Pony proved a highly successful export model, particularly in Central America and later Canada, but it failed to crack the U.S. market because it did not meet federal emissions standards. Sales to the world's largest auto market began in 1985, with the establishment of Hyundai Motor America and the introduction of the Excel. A front-wheel drive version of the Pony, the Excel proved vastly superior to its leading competitor, the Yugoslav-produced Yugo, in the low-budget subcompact niche.

Yet, the very success of the Excel had a negative impact on Hyundai's brand image, which consumers came to associate with cheapness. In response, Hyundai began to reposition itself as a manufacturer of higher-end vehicles, such as the Sonata midsize sedan and the sporty Scoupe. Up to this point, Hyundai had not produced its own engines, but that changed with the introduction of the four-cylinder Alpha motor in 1991, and thenceforth the company began to steer its own course technologically.

In 1998, as a financial crisis swept Asia, Hyundai purchased a controlling stake in its leading Korean competitor, Kia Motors, thus forming the Hyundai Motor Group, of which the Hyundai Motor Company is the leading player. (Hyundai eventually reduced its interest in Kia to 34 percent.) The parent *chaebol* underwent a massive restructuring and was finally dismantled in 2003. In the early years of the 21st century, the value of the Hyundai brand began to steadily improve, making it the world's fastest-growing auto brand.

BRAND ELEMENTS

- The name *Hyundai* is derived from two Chinese characters that together translate as "modernity."
- The shape of the *H* in the Hyundai brand symbol is intended to resemble two people shaking hands, while the oval represents Hyundai's global market.
- Notable Hyundai advertising campaigns have included "Driving is believing," "Prepare to want one," "Always there for you," and "Drive your way."
- Hyundai's "Live brilliant" campaign, launched in 2012, is fully global, conveying the same message to all major markets.

The name *Hyundai* is derived from two Chinese characters that together translate as "modernity." The Hyundai logo includes both a stylized *H* and the brand name, rendered in baby-blue letters of equal size. All of the letters are capitals except the *n,* and all except the *Y* are composed using 90-degree angles; thus, the *U* and the *A* are nearly square, but with rounded corners.

The brand symbol features an *H* inside a horizontal oval, both of which are silver, with shading and highlights added to create the impression of a three-dimensional design. The four ends of the capital *H* are relatively thin at the tips, with the legs steadily widening as they get closer to the horizontal crossbar of the letter. The crossbar slants 45 degrees upward and to the right in a manner that suggests movement. The shape of the *H* is intended to resemble two people shaking hands, while the oval in which it is set symbolizes Hyundai's global market.

BRAND IDENTITY

- Hyundai has long cultivated the image of a forward-looking brand, as would be expected of a company whose name means "modernity."
- The Hyundai logo, which suggests two people shaking hands within the framework of a globe, reflects the company's core values.
- Hyundai's five core values are *Customer, Challenge, Collaboration, People,* and *Globality.*
- Early Hyundai advertising sometimes used self-deprecating humor—for instance, by comparing the humble Excel to the BMW 3 Series.

Hyundai has long cultivated an image of itself as a forward-looking brand, an idea that goes back at least two decades before the formation of the Hyundai Motor Company. When Hyundai's parent company was established in 1947, its founder chose a name that translated as "modernity," and this theme continues to define the Hyundai brand today. It is reflected in the carmaker's statement of its management philosophy: "Realize the dream of mankind by creating a new future through ingenious thinking and continuously challenging new frontiers."

Similarly, the design of Hyundai's logo—with an oval symbolizing the global market, and an *H* that resembles two people shaking hands—reflects elements of Hyundai's core values, as stated on the corporate website. Those values include *Customer* ("We promote a customer-driven corporate culture by providing the best quality and impeccable service with all values centered on our customers"), *Challenge, Collaboration, People,* and *Globality* ("We respect the diversity of cultures and customs, aspire to be the world's best at what we do, and strive to become a respected global corporate citizen.")

Despite these constants in its brand identity, Hyundai has evolved over time from being primarily a budget carmaker to becoming a brand with vehicles in a wide range of price points, and its advertising has developed apace. The low-priced Excel became an extraordinarily popular import in the United States and other global markets during the 1980s, and its advertising emphasized this fact—sometimes in a humorously self-deprecating fashion. A late 1980s TV spot, for example, compared the Excel to the BMW 3 Series, which of course was a high-precision machine with a price tag many times that of the humble Excel.

BRAND STRATEGY

- For the first two decades of its existence, Hyundai succeeded with a limited line of mostly low-budget vehicles.
- In 1985, the Excel sold nearly 169,000 units, setting a U.S. record for first-year sales of an import.
- In the 1990s, Hyundai took a number of steps, including investments in design, to counter consumers' perception of the brand as "cheap."
- Though it has dramatically broadened the range of vehicles it offers, Hyundai continues to emphasize value in its marketing campaigns.

For the first two decades of its existence, Hyundai succeeded with a limited line of mostly low-budget vehicles such as the Excel subcompact. In the year that followed its 1985 introduction to the U.S. market, the Excel sold nearly 169,000 units, setting a U.S. record for first-year sales of an import. Over time, however, consumers came to associate the Hyundai brand not only with low price but with low quality. Jokes abounded: the first-generation Accent subcompact acquired the nickname "Accident," for example, and one popular quip reconfigured the brand name as an acronym for "Hope you understand nothing's drivable and inexpensive."

To counter this image, Hyundai took a number of steps, including massive investment in design and quality improvements, as well as an expansion of its product line to include higher-end models such as the midsize Sonata. The latter made its first major impact on the global market with its second-generation Y2 series in 1988. Advertising for the Sonata during that year's Summer Olympic Games, which were held in the South Korean capital of Seoul, emphasized the achievements of the parent company as a means of building confidence in the automobile manufacturer. As John Holusha wrote in the *New York Times,* "The theme was that a company that can make huge industrial products has the technology to make consumer products as well."

In subsequent years, Hyundai has dramatically broadened the range of vehicles it offers, particularly in higher-end niches such as luxury sedans and sports cars, yet it has continued to emphasize value. The brand's 2003 "Always there for you" campaign, for example, made tongue-in-cheek comparisons between the second-generation Accent and other "great buys" in history, including Manhattan Island.

The "Drive your way" campaign, which debuted in 2005, was intended to impart a sense of both independence and refinement to the company's increasingly upmarket product line, but as times grew harder in the wake of the 2008 financial crisis, Hyundai advertising returned to the theme of affordability. With automobile sales plummeting, Hyundai launched a North American campaign built around the word "Smart," positioning itself as "The smart choice" by reminding potential customers that "Smart is in." Television spots concluded with a specific retail offer, known as the "Smart Advantage."

BRAND EQUITY

- Between 2008 and 2010, Hyundai enjoyed explosive growth, with net income climbing from US$863 million to more than US$7 billion.
- Hyundai rose from 69th place on Interbrand's list of the best global brands in 2009 to 61st place in 2011.
- The world's fastest-growing automotive brand for two years in a row, Hyundai had a brand value calculated at more than US$6 billion in 2011.
- Hyundai held a 5.1 percent market share worldwide in 2011, putting it in seventh place behind General Motors, Ford, Toyota, Chrysler, Honda, and Nissan.

Between 2008 and 2010, as the industrialized world struggled through the worst economic crisis since the Great Depression, Hyundai enjoyed explosive growth, with net income climbing from US$863 million in 2008 to nearly US$3.5 billion in 2009 and over US$7 billion in 2010. Accompanying this sales success has been a steady and decisive improvement in its brand equity as measured by Interbrand in its ranking of the best global brands. From 69th place in 2009, Hyundai rose 4 points in 2010 and another 4 points in the following year to place 61st on the 2011 list. This put it just above KFC and below Adidas, and 8th out of the 12 automotive-sector companies on the list. Interbrand calculated Hyundai's brand value to be about US$6 billion, a 19 percent improvement over the preceding year, which made Hyundai the fastest-growing automotive brand in the world for the second year in a row.

According to *Market Share Reporter,* Hyundai held a 5.1 percent market share among global automakers for 2011, putting it in seventh place behind General Motors, Ford, Toyota, Chrysler, Honda, and Nissan. Whereas some of the leading brands on that list saw their market share decline from 2010 to 2011, Hyundai's rose from 4.6 percent during the period. Hyundai held a 6 percent share among producers of low-cost vehicles and a 3.35 percent share among new-car loan providers worldwide in 2011. Hyundai came in seventh among automobile advertisers in 2009, with a more than 4 percent share of advertising dollars spent.

BRAND AWARENESS

- Hyundai vehicles are sold in some 6,000 dealerships to buyers in nearly 200 countries.
- In 2009, 60 percent of Americans were aware of the Hyundai brand and willing to buy a Hyundai product, compared to 40 percent in 2007.
- For many years, Hyundai suffered not so much from weak brand awareness as from consumers' perception of it as a cheap, low-quality brand.
- Hyundai edged out rivals Honda and Toyota to take the number-one spot in a 2011 Kelley Blue Book survey of brand loyalty.

With Hyundai vehicles sold in some 6,000 dealerships and showrooms to buyers in nearly 200 countries, awareness of the Hyundai brand is high and increasing. Hyundai earned recognition as "marketer of the year" for 2009 from *Advertising Age,* whose Jean Halliday praised it for a campaign that honestly addressed the financial challenges consumers faced amid a recessionary economy.

The brand's strategy of "Engaging with both the broken dreams [of consumers] and the intact ones through high-profile ad buys that garnered plenty of positive press," Halliday wrote, "was in sharp contrast to the tail-between-the-legs mode of Hyundai's rivals." A survey by CNW Marketing Research, noted in Halliday's article, found that 60 percent of Americans were aware of the Hyundai brand and willing to buy a Hyundai product, compared to 40 percent just two years earlier.

For Hyundai, the problem has not always been consumer awareness so much as image. The brand's reputation for cheap, no-frills cars made it easy fodder for late-night comedians such as Jay Leno and David Letterman. The jokes might have been funny to audiences, but Hyundai executives regarded the brand's image problems with deadly seriousness, and in the mid-1990s they launched a concerted effort to expand the Hyundai product line, improve the quality of its offerings, and enhance its marketing. By 2011, this undertaking had yielded impressive results, with Hyundai jumping four spots on Interbrand's global brand ranking and earning recognition as the fastest-growing automotive brand in the world for the second straight year.

Also in 2011, Hyundai edged out Honda and Toyota to take the number-one spot in a Kelley Blue Book survey of brand loyalty. A decade earlier, according to data from automotive marketing research firm Strategic Vision, only 8 percent of Hyundai buyers were repeat customers, but by 2011 that figure had tripled. Kelley Blue Book analyst Arthur Henry told the *Los Angeles Times,* "Hyundai's product renaissance is benefitting the company not just by attracting an all-new customer base, but by helping them to retain loyal Hyundai customers as well."

BRAND OUTLOOK

- Despite Hyundai's global focus, almost half its sales still came from South Korea in 2012.
- In 2011 Hyundai introduced a new brand direction, "modern premium," which it defined as being "about providing new values and experiences."
- The unusual three-door design of the Veloster, introduced in 2011, exemplified the company's new "modern premium" brand direction.
- Some analysts have questioned whether Hyundai's investment in research was sufficient to meet the demands of a more competitive future marketplace.

Like many successful brands, Hyundai has had a global vision almost from the beginning, and though a surprisingly large portion of its sales—almost half—still came from South Korean buyers in 2012, it marketed itself aggressively on a worldwide scale. Whereas all previous Hyundai advertising campaigns had a regional focus and execution, "Live brilliant," launched in April 2012, transmitted a single message to all major markets as a means of building a consistent global brand image.

The campaign furthered the company's brand direction, dubbed "modern premium." Introduced in 2011, modern premium "does not just mean luxury cars," according to the company website; rather, "it is about providing new values and experiences ... through ways that are unique to the brand and which go beyond what customers expect." Hyundai accompanied this new brand definition with the rollout of a vehicle designed to exemplify it: the Veloster. Its many technological features included proprietary Blue Link technology, which enable hands-free texting, but the Veloster's most unusual quality was its three-door design: whereas the passenger side would have two doors, the driver's side would feature only a single, wide door.

Even as it enjoyed a growing global presence and soaring reputation, the Hyundai brand faced creeping competition, and some analysts questioned whether the company's investment in research was adequate to meet the demands of the future. As Hyunjoo Jin and Ben Klayman noted in a Reuters report, maintaining its dominance would be "tough" for Hyundai "at a time when Chinese carmakers are the 'new Hyundai' of old—replicating its success in being competitive through cheap labour, an undervalued currency and government support for local carmakers." And whereas Volkswagen and BMW invested 5 percent of revenue in research and development, Hyundai spent less than 2 percent, leading an executive at a rival company to characterize its strategy as "maximum design, minimum investment."

Yet, the very fact that Hyundai was being compared to BMW served to illustrate the great distance that the brand had come from the days of the Excel. The success of its luxury Genesis and Equus models, a company executive told the *Korea Herald,* was "elevating the company's brand image in overseas markets" and in the process altering consumers' concept of Hyundai from that of "a 'cheap car' maker to a premium brand."

FURTHER READING

CASSIES. "The 2011 Cassies." Accessed September 14, 2012. http://cassies.ca/winners/2011/cassies.ca/winners/2011Winners/2011_winners_Hyundai.html.

Garfield, Bob. "We've Thought about It: Carless Ads Push Hyundai Upmarket." *Advertising Age,* September 10, 2007. Accessed September 14, 2012. http://adage.com/article/ad-review/thought-carless-ads-push-hyundai-upmarket/120323/.

Halliday, Jean. "Marketer of the Year: Hyundai." *Advertising Age,* November 9, 2009. Accessed September 14, 2012. http://adage.com/article/special-report-marketer-of-the-year-2009/hyundai-marketer-year-2009/140380/.

Hirsch, Jerry. "Hyundai Is Rated No. 1 in Brand Loyalty." *Los Angeles Times,* June 10, 2011. Accessed September 14,

2012. http://articles.latimes.com/2011/jul/19/business/la-fi-hyundai-20110719.

Holusha, John. "Hyundai's Bid to Move Up in Class." *New York Times,* November 2, 1988. Accessed September 14, 2012. http://www.nytimes.com/1988/11/02/business/hyundai-s-bid-to-move-up-in-class.html?scp=1&sq=hyundai%20holusha&st=Search.

"Hyundai Group." *International Directory of Company Histories.* Ed. Tina Grant. Vol. 56. Detroit: St. James Press, 2004. *Business Insights: Essentials.* Accessed September 14, 2012. http://bi.galegroup.com/essentials/article/GALE%7CI2501308152/696c2e17c21ba54934284f746db79811.

Hyundai Motor Company. "2010 Annual Report." Accessed September 14, 2012. http://worldwide.hyundai.com/wcm/idc/groups/sggeneralcontent/@hmc/documents/sitecontent/mdaw/mdi2/~edisp/hw026563.pdf.

"Hyundai Motor Launches New Global Brand Campaign 'Live Brilliant.'" *Cisionwire,* April 3, 2012. Accessed September 14, 2012. http://www.cisionwire.com/hyundai-motor-company/r/hyundai-motor-launches-new-global-brand-campaign--live-brilliant-,c9242730.

"Hyundai Motor Named 'The Fastest Growing Automotive Brand' for Second Straight Year." *Canada Free Press,* October 17, 2011. Accessed September 14, 2012. http://www.canadafreepress.com/index.php/article/41391.

Hyunjoo Jin and Ben Klayman. "More than Moving Metal; Hyundai Drives Brand Makeover." *Reuters,* April 10, 2012. Accessed September 14, 2012. http://www.reuters.com/article/2012/04/10/uk-hyundai-idUSLNE83900G20120410.

Interbrand. "2011 Ranking of the Top 100 Brands." Accessed September 14, 2012. http://www.interbrand.com/en/best-global-brands/best-global-brands-2008/best-global-brands-2011.aspx.

Kim Yon-se. "Hyundai Motor Strives to Become Premium Brand." *AsiaOne,* April 11, 2012. Accessed September 14, 2012. http://www.asiaone.com/print/Motoring/News/Story/A1Story20120411-338912.html.

Lee Ji-yoon. "Hyundai Motor Sheds 'Cheap Car' Image." *Korea Herald,* August 2, 2012. http://www.koreaherald.com/view.php?ud=20120802001069.

Maillie, David. "Hyundai Closing In on Honda as Their Brand Value Rises." *Streetdirectory.com,* n.d. Accessed September 14, 2012. http://www.streetdirectory.com/travel_guide/22496/car_focus/hyundai_closing_in_on_honda_as_their_brand_value_rises.html.

Peele, Robert. "Classic Ad: Hyundai Excel." *New York Times,* January 29, 2011. Accessed September 14, 2012. http://wheels.blogs.nytimes.com/2011/01/29/classic-ad-hyundai-excel/.

Snyder, Jesse. "Hyundai Moves from 'Value Brand to a Valuable Brand.'" *Automotive News,* April 13, 2012. Accessed September 14, 2012. http://edit.autonews.com/article/20120413/BLOG06/120419933&template=printart&nocache=1.

SyncForce. "Hyundai Brand Ranking." *Ranking the Brands,* 2012. Accessed September 14, 2012. http://www.rankingthebrands.com/Brand-detail.aspx?brandID=368.

IBM

AT A GLANCE

Brand Synopsis: The IBM brand, one of the most widely recognized brands in the world, has evolved over the years from a maker of mechanical business machines and computer hardware to a partner in business success through the development of innovative software and services.
Parent Company: International Business Machines Corp.
1 New Orchard Rd.
Armonk, New York 10504-1722
United States
http://www.ibm.com
Sector: Information Technology
Industry Group: Software & Services
Performance: *Market share*—45 percent in supercomputing worldwide (2011). *Sales*—US$44.9 billion in the Americas; US$107 billion worldwide (2011).
Principal Competitors: Accenture; Dell; Hewlett-Packard; Intel; Microsoft; Oracle; Unisys

BRAND ORIGINS

- IBM came into existence on June 16, 1911, when three corporations merged to form the Computing Tabulating Recording (CTR) Company.
- To more accurately reflect its broad product line and international scope, CTR became International Business Machines (IBM) Corporation in 1924.
- Among the innovations introduced by IBM were the magnetic hard disk drive (1956) and the floppy disk (1971).
- During the early 21st century the company emerged as a leading player in eBusiness—a term coined by IBM in 1996.

The company that would become IBM came into existence on June 16, 1911, with the merger of three corporations established in the late 19th and early 20th centuries: Washington, D.C.'s Tabulating Machine Company; the International Time Recording Company of Endicott, New York; and the Dayton, Ohio-based Computing Scale Company. Together, these formed the Computing Tabulating Recording (CTR) Company, which had a diverse product line that ranged from employee time-keeping systems and food-production machines to punched tabulating cards, a forerunner of computer software.

In order to more accurately reflect its broad product line and increasingly international scope, CTR became the International Business Machines (IBM) Corporation on February 14, 1924. IBM flourished amid the economic turmoil of the 1930s, and by the 1940s it dominated the robust electric typewriter market even as it laid the groundwork for technological breakthroughs that would collectively render typewriters obsolete.

In 1944 IBM introduced the world's first large-scale calculating computer, the Automatic Sequence Control Calculator (ASCC), or Mark I. It debuted the magnetic hard disk drive in 1956 and in 1957 introduced FORTRAN (Formula Translator), which soon became the most widely used computer programming language. Long before the advent of personal computers, in 1961 IBM launched the Selectric typewriter, which, with its memory function, pointed toward the future of word processing. The 1970s saw such innovations as the floppy disk (1971), the first major commercial laser printer (1976), and advances in information storage technology. In 1981 the company took its personal computer, or PC, to the mass market, helping ignite a revolution that led to *Time* magazine's naming the PC "Person of the Year" in 1982.

Despite these successes, a number of unfortunate marketing decisions in the 1980s brought about a string of billion-dollar losses in the early 1990s. To recover its market position, IBM began a shift away from hardware toward software, services, and technology, a move that restored the company's profitability later in the decade. During the early 21st century IBM emerged as a leading player in the world of eBusiness, a term it introduced in 1996 to describe the use of the Internet and other information and communication technologies to support business activities. IBM celebrated its centennial in June 2011 as one of the largest companies—and one of the most valuable brands—in the world.

BRAND ELEMENTS

- The IBM logo features the three-letter brand name spelled out in a series of alternating blue and white horizontal stripes.
- Designed by Paul Rand in 1972, IBM's "eight-bar logo" was intended to convey a sense of dynamic movement.
- The color of the IBM logo may be the source of the popular nickname "Big Blue," but there are a number of other theories regarding the origins of the name.
- During the 1940s and 1950s IBM used simplified logos consisting of the letters *IBM* before experimenting with an early version of the horizontal-stripe logo.
- For many years, IBM's most famous catchphrase was the one-word slogan "THINK."

Though the proper name of the company is International Business Machines Corporation, its brand name has long been simply the initials *IBM*. These make up the IBM logo, in which the letters are rendered in a series of horizontal stripes. The stripes are made up of alternating positive and negative space, with the negative space white and the positive space a robin's-egg shade.

The color of the IBM logo is so intricately tied with the brand's image that many people refer to it as "IBM blue." The shade may be the source of the company's well-known nickname, "Big Blue", but IBM historians cite a number of other theories regarding possible origins of the expression. These include the color of the large mainframe computers produced by IBM in the 1960s and early 1970s, the blue suits worn by IBM employees in compliance with a company dress code around the same time, and the "true-blue" loyalty of IBM customers.

Designed by Paul Rand in 1972 and still in use four decades later, the "eight-bar logo," as it is known, was intended to convey a sense of dynamic movement. As such it contrasts sharply with the ornate, highly stylized logos used by the Computing Tabulating Recording (CTR) Company and the firms that merged to form CTR in 1911. When CTR changed its name in 1924 to reflect its international scope and increasing focus on business technology, it reintroduced itself to the world with a bold, modern logo that resembled a globe. This first IBM trademark used the full company name, with *Business* and *Machines* in the northern and southern hemispheres respectively and *International* on a band around the equator of the globe.

In 1947 the company greatly simplified its logo, reducing it to the letters *IBM* in a sober-looking typeface known as Beton Bold. In 1956, when Thomas J. Watson, Jr., took over leadership from his father, who had served as chief executive for four decades, the company slightly altered its logo to convey a sense of continuity in change. Whereas the letters of the earlier logotype were formed with dark lines surrounding negative space, the new one, in a City Medium font, featured filled-in black letters. In the 1960s the company began experimenting with a "13-bar" logo before adopting Rand's design, with its reduced number of stripes.

Besides its logo and nickname, IBM was for many years associated with the one-word catchphrase "THINK," a slogan introduced by Watson in 1915. Among more recently coined taglines is "Solutions for a Small Planet," which accompanied the 1995 rollout of a large-scale advertising campaign that helped the company regain a leading position in the information technology market. Similarly, in 2008, the company launched its "Let's Build a Smarter Planet" campaign to tap into the perceived need for greener business practices.

BRAND IDENTITY

- CTR's chief executive, Thomas J. Watson, renamed his company after its Canadian subsidiary, International Business Machines, in 1924.
- Watson's slogan "THINK" became so widely known that it was parodied in *New Yorker* cartoons.
- As it shifted away from an emphasis on hardware, IBM sought to reshape its identity to stress creative thinking and innovation.

After the Computing Tabulating Recording (CTR) Company opened an office in Brazil and manufacturing facilities in Europe during the 1910s, chief executive Thomas J. Watson sought a new name to reflect the company's emerging global presence. He found what he was looking for in the title of a Canadian subsidiary, International Business Machines, and in 1924 CTR formally changed its name. The new name also reflected the company's decision to produce a broader array of equipment than just tabulators—equipment that would eventually come to include clocks, scales, typewriters, calculators, and both mainframe and personal computers. Thus was born what would become one of the world's most widely known brands, which thenceforth appeared on virtually all the company's products. (The designation "IBM 001" was retroactively assigned to a mechanical punch produced in 1910 by one of the firms that merged to form CTR.) As a result, for much of the 20th century, the brand's identity was that of a trusted maker of essential office machines.

IBM has used a number of advertising slogans with the public over the years, but perhaps its most well-known catchphrase is the one-word admonition "THINK." Introduced by Watson in 1915, it first appeared on signs in company facilities, but it eventually made such an impact on the public at large that it was parodied in *New Yorker* cartoons. Watson's slogan embodied an emphasis on creative thinking and innovation that is among the characteristics most widely associated with IBM.

As the company shifted away from the manufacture of hardware to more emphasis on software and services, it sought to reshape its identity so it would be known as one of the pioneers of information technology. In 2011, for the company's centennial, IBM put together an interactive page on its website that highlighted IBM's history as "the world's most forward-looking company." The page proclaims that IBM has always been a company defined, not by its products, but by its core values of dedication to the client's success; innovation that matters; and trust and responsibility in all relationships. The company's recent advertising slogans "Solutions for a Small Planet" and "Let's Build a Smarter Planet" stress the ideas of success, creativity, and innovation that are so central to IBM's identity.

BRAND STRATEGY

- Financier Charles Flint, who orchestrated the merger that created CTR in 1911, viewed its wide product line as a way of maintaining profitability.
- Over the years, IBM's product focus has shifted many times, but the broad-based approach introduced by Flint remains a key component of its business strategy.
- IBM made a major strategic shift in the mid-1990s, redirecting its focus from hardware to software, services, and technology solutions.
- The company announced in 2010 that it would invest some US$20 billion in acquisitions by 2015.
- With more than 50 overseas subsidiaries and a client base spread across some 170 countries, IBM derives more than half its revenues from international sales.

When financier Charles Flint orchestrated a three-company merger to form CTR in 1911, the result was a corporation with a wide product line that ranged from coffee grinders to time-keeping systems. Rather than narrow this broad base, Flint regarded it as means of maintaining CTR's profitability through both good and bad economic times. This has remained a key element of IBM's brand strategy even as its market focus has shifted with changing times.

IBM has abandoned whole product lines as these became obsolete or unprofitable, ceasing production of punch cards (often referred to colloquially as "IBM cards") in 1958, for example. It made an even more fundamental shift in the 1990s, as it sought to regain a position of strength in the information technology market that it had lost through several strategic errors, most notably by failing to capitalize on its early dominance in the personal computer market. Rather than attempt to retake ground it had already lost, the company began a move away from hardware toward software, services, and technology solutions. It divested itself of its printer and printer-supply operations, along with what remained of its typewriter business (which became the basis for Lexmark International), in 1991; acquired Lotus Development, thus becoming the world's largest software company, in 1995; and sold the PC division to Chinese manufacturer Lenovo in 2005.

Throughout its history, IBM has sought a dominant position at the forefront of business technology. Often it has advanced this goal through research and creativity, but the history of IBM is also replete with instances of shrewd business maneuvering. In 1933, for example, it purchased the Electromatic Typewriter Company primarily because the deal brought a great number of valuable patents under the IBM umbrella. Likewise, in 1964 the company changed the face of computer marketing with the IBM System/360, which introduced the now-familiar concept of a computer "family" line that included compatible machines of various sizes and applications. Another marketing milestone came in 1969, when IBM adopted the concept of "unbundling," or charging separately for various functions, thus helping to spawn a vast software and computer-services industry.

IBM has actively pursued a strategy of growth by purchasing more than 100 companies in the 21st century's first decade. The company announced in 2010 that it would invest some US$20 billion more in acquisitions by 2015. Particularly important to future IBM growth is an area in which the company has shown a strong interest throughout most of its history: global expansion. Not only does it own more than 50 subsidiaries in nations ranging from Austria to Zambia, but IBM sells to a client base spread across some 170 countries, and foreign sales make up more than half of its total revenues.

BRAND EQUITY

- IBM placed second, behind only Coca-Cola, on the Interbrand ranking of the top 100 global brands for 2011.
- In 2012 Interbrand estimated IBM's brand value at nearly US$70 billion.
- With more patents than any technology corporation in the United States, IBM has built its brand equity through technological achievement.
- IBM employees have earned five Nobel prizes, six Turing awards, five National Medals of Science, and nine National Medals of Technology.
- Among the countless inventions and processes introduced by IBM are the Universal Product Code (UPC), magnetic stripe cards, and the automated teller machine (ATM).

By almost any measure, IBM is among the world's strongest companies, and the IBM brand is among the most valuable. In terms of market capitalization, determined by multiplying share price by the total number of shares issued, IBM placed sixth on the *Financial Times* Global 500 ranking of publicly traded corporations for the second quarter of 2012. As for its brand value, it placed second—behind only Coca-Cola—on the Interbrand ranking of the top 100 global brands for 2011. Interbrand appraised IBM's brand value at nearly US$70 billion, an 8 percent increase over the previous year.

As of fall 2012, the company held a 16th-place position on the RankingTheBrands.com top 100 list, which is computed by compiling an aggregate of all reputable published brand rankings. Among the sources that contributed to this ranking were BrandZ, BrandFinance, and the European Brand Institute, which placed IBM second, fourth, and fifth on their respective lists of top global brands.

For a company in IBM's business sector, brand equity ultimately rests in a record of technological achievement, and here again the company's score sheet is an extraordinarily impressive one. Not only does IBM hold more patents than any technology corporation in the United States, but 2011 marked the 19th straight year in which it earned the largest number of U.S. patents among all companies for that period. As of 2012, IBM employees had earned five Nobel prizes, six Turing awards, five National Medals of Science, and nine National Medals of Technology.

Beyond its patents and awards, IBM has made an indelible impact on daily life that has served to bolster its brand equity beyond calculation. Among the countless inventions and processes introduced by IBM are the hard disk drive, floppy disks, the FORTRAN programming language, the Universal Product Code (UPC), magnetic stripe cards, and the automated teller machine (ATM). Additionally, IBM innovations made possible the personal computer, low-cost office printers, and mainframe computers. IBM's PC and ThinkPad laptop, though neither was the first of its kind, proved to be some of the world's most popular and widely known products of their type.

BRAND AWARENESS

- IBM's "Solutions for a Small Planet" advertising campaign, which it launched in 1995, was aimed at corporate leaders rather than technical specialists.
- The term "eBusiness," coined by IBM in 1996, has become a part of the English language.
- Its snappy, clever "eBusiness" marketing campaign helped IBM overcome a stodgy reputation—and greatly strengthened the bottom line in the late 1990s.
- The company's marketing success rests ultimately on its established reputation for producing innovative technology.

On the occasion of IBM's centennial in 2011, business commentator David Taylor referred to the brand name as "likely the most well-known [acronym] in the business world." Indeed, the name, logo, and lore of IBM are integral parts of modern life, making it one of the most widely recognized brands in the world. This visibility has been borne out in consistently high rankings for its brand value, including a second-place position on the 2011 list of "Top 100 Brands" published by Interbrand.

To an extent, IBM has fostered its high global visibility in the same way that any business does: through advertising. It has pursued large-scale campaigns such as "Solutions for a Small Planet," launched in 1995 as part of an effort to regain the brand's dominance in the business technology marketplace. Directed toward chief executive, information, and financial officers rather than technical specialists, the "Solutions" campaign built on IBM's high brand recognition to deliver a message that its product line could help users solve problems and reach their goals.

An even larger campaign appeared later in the decade to help position IBM at the forefront of electronic business or "eBusiness"—a term, created by the company in 1996, that has since become widely used. The eBusiness campaign included witty black-and-white television slots that had the look and feel of a chic independent film. These helped overcome IBM's traditional image, which Taylor summed up as "Solid. Corporate.... Maybe even a little boring?" Thanks in no small part to its eBusiness strategy, the IBM brand regained the strength it had lost in a number of marketing missteps in the late 1980s and early 1990s: stock prices, which had dipped below US$40 in 1993, reached nearly US$125 by the summer of 1999.

As important as these and other marketing campaigns have been to the public's high awareness of the IBM brand, however, the company's marketing success rests ultimately on its established reputation for producing innovative technology. Not only has IBM created a great number of tools used in the office and throughout daily life, but it has also greatly expanded the reach of products it did not invent. For instance, IBM did not create either the personal computer or the term "personal computer," but it radically transformed that market sector with its PC, introduced in 1981. Though IBM ceased production of the PC in 1987 and in 2005 sold its PC division to Chinese manufacturer Lenovo, *PC* remains a popular term for a type of product regardless of brand name, much like the names Kleenex or Band-Aid.

BRAND OUTLOOK

- Despite its many successes, the IBM brand is not invulnerable—a fact illustrated by the failure of the PCjr in 1983.
- IBM has recovered from market downturns in part because of its continued emphasis on innovation in areas such as nanotechnology and supercomputing.
- On the eve of IBM's centennial in 2011, its Watson supercomputer trounced *Jeopardy!* champs Ken Jennings and Brad Rutter in a series of competitions.
- As it entered the 21st century, IBM maintained a focus on emerging market sectors and global acquisitions.

Despite its many successes, the IBM brand is not invulnerable. The decade that began with the 1983 introduction of the PCjr, whose high price and incompatibility with the PC doomed it to failure, saw a number of other missteps. IBM lost its dominance in the personal computing market and, by refusing to shift its focus away from mainframe computers, failed to take advantage of the trend toward client-server computing. These mistakes helped bring about a string of billion-dollar losses in the early 1990s.

IBM recovered from these and other misfortunes, however, thanks in no small part to its continual emphasis on innovation. In the early 21st century the company regularly made headlines with ever more stunning technological breakthroughs. In 2000, for instance, IBM scientists developed a means of transporting information at an atomic level, using electrons rather than wiring, and in the following year company researchers began building computer circuits that would fit within a single molecule.

Even more attention-getting than these achievements in nanotechnology were advances in IBM supercomputers, which the company demonstrated to the public in ways certain to capture the imagination. In 1997 IBM's 32-node RS/6000 SP supercomputer, better known as "Deep Blue," became the first machine to defeat a reigning world chess champion—in this case, Gary Kasparov—in tournament-style competition. Three years later, IBM delivered ASCI White, which was a thousand times more powerful than Deep Blue and unquestionably the fastest supercomputer in the world, to the U.S. Department of Energy. In February 2011, on the eve of the company's centennial, the Watson supercomputer (named after IBM's first CEO, Thomas J. Watson) defeated *Jeopardy!* champions Ken Jennings and Brad Rutter in a series of competitions.

As it entered the 21st century, IBM maintained a focus on emerging market sectors such as cloud computing. The latter, which involves the use of computer resources delivered over a network, is a significant and growing area of IBM eBusiness. In addition to pursuing technological innovation, IBM has continued to grow through acquisitions.. With its business well established among the relatively mature markets of North America, western Europe, and the Pacific rim, IBM has pursued a strategy of expansion into the developing markets of Latin America, China and India, and the former Soviet bloc.

FURTHER READING

Harwood, John. *The Interface: IBM and the Transformation of Corporate Design, 1945–1976.* Minneapolis: University of Minnesota Press, 2011.

"IBM." *Brandirectory.* Brand Finance, September 5, 2011. Accessed September 7, 2012. http://brandirectory.com/profile/ibm.

"IBM." *Ranking the Brands.* RankingTheBrands.com. Accessed September 7, 2012. http://www.rankingthebrands.com/Brand-detail.aspx?brandID=6.

"IBM Logo History." *Best Logos—World's Best Logos and Brands.* Accessed September 7, 2012. http://www.worldsbestlogos.blogspot.com/search/label/IBM.

International Business Machines Corporation. "IBM at 100." Accessed September 7, 2012. http://www-03.ibm.com/ibm/history/ibm100/us/en/.

———. "2011 Annual Report." Accessed September 7, 2012. http://www.ibm.com/annualreport/2011/bin/assets/2011_ibm_annual.pdf.

"International Business Machines Corporation." *International Directory of Company Histories.* Ed. Jay P. Pederson. Vol. 130. Detroit, MI: St. James Press, 2012.

Maddox, Kate. "IBM Brand Must Continue to Reinvent Itself to Be Relevant." *BtoB,* June 13, 2011.

Neff, Jack. "2011 Marketer A-List: IBM." *Advertising Age,* November 7, 2011.

Taylor, David. "Lessons for Brand Success from Big Blue: IBM at 100 Years Old." *Central Penn Business Journal,* July 22, 2011.

"2011 Ranking of the Top 100 Brands." Interbrand. Accessed September 7, 2012. http://www.interbrand.com/en/best-global-brands/best-global-brands-2008/best-global-brands-2011.aspx.

ICBC

AT A GLANCE

Brand Synopsis: ICBC is the largest bank in China and one of the largest in the world; the ongoing expansion of its banking services for private customers and businesses in China and abroad has made ICBC a powerful global financial brand.
Parent Company: Industrial and Commercial Bank of China Limited
No. 55, FuXingMenNei Street, Xicheng District
Beijing
China
www.icbc-ltd.com
Sector: Financials
Industry Group: Banks
Performance: *Market share*—20 percent of retail banking in China (2010). *Net profit*—RMB208.4 billion (2011).
Principal Competitors: Bank of China; China Construction Bank; Agricultural Bank of China

BRAND ORIGINS

- Industrial and Commercial Bank of China Limited (ICBC) is one of China's "big four" banks. It is the largest of the four banks and one of the largest banks in the world.
- ICBC originated when the People's Bank shifted its assets to a new, government-owned bank dubbed the Industrial and Commercial Bank of China Limited in 1984.
- ICBC held several billion renminbi in savings accounts by 1985; in the 1990s it began handling international credit cards and opened its first overseas offices.
- ICBC began issuing its popular debit card, called the Peony Card, in 1997.
- In October 2006 ICBC participated in a public offering of stock, and American Express was among the international investors who bought a portion of the bank; the government of China continued to own a majority of ICBC.

Industrial and Commercial Bank of China Limited (ICBC) is one of the "big four" banks in China, along with China Construction Bank, the Bank of China, and the Agricultural Bank of China. ICBC is the largest of these four banks and one of the largest banks in the world; according to some calculations and categories, it is the biggest bank. In 2011 it had more than 408,000 employees and offices on several continents.

In the late 1970s and early 1980s China transitioned from a state-run economy under the communist system to a more market-based economy. During this time the government moved the agricultural segment from the People's Bank to form the Agricultural Bank of China. The People's Bank would eventually become the entity that determined China's economic policies, shifting its assets to a new, government-owned bank called the Industrial and Commercial Bank of China Limited in 1984.

ICBC continued to change and grow in the 1980s. It allowed a limited group of professionals to have checking accounts and extended a number of commercial loans. It held several billion Chinese renminbi in savings accounts by 1985, surpassing even the bank's expectations. To serve this large number of customers, ICBC opened several branches across the country and dispatched employees to private households to find more potential customers.

The number of employees and branches increased with ICBC's customer base: by 1990 it had 30,000 branches and 480,000 employees. During this time ICBC began handling international credit cards such as Visa, an illustration of its increasingly global business. It opened its first overseas office in Singapore in the 1990s, followed by offices in London, New York, Tokyo, Dubai, Seoul, and Sydney, Australia.

The bank did not neglect its home customers, though. It began issuing its popular Peony Card in 1997. Customers could use it as a debit card, for making deposits and transfers, and for use at restaurants. The card proved so popular that by the end of 2001 ICBC had issued 63 million Peony Cards that could be used at the bank's 10,000 automated teller machines. The Peony Card and ATM functions duplicated the operations of a number of ICBC's branches, so ICBC closed 20,000 of its 47,000 domestic branches in 2000.

ICBC conducted a public offering of stock in October 2006. Although the Chinese government remained as ICBC's majority owner, international investors bought percentages of the bank. These investors included American Express, which paid US$4 billion for 10 percent ownership. In the early 2000s ICBC bought a stake in the Standard Bank of South Africa, opened a branch in Dubai, and broadened its presence in Australia, Canada, the United States, and India.

BRAND ELEMENTS

- ICBC's logo is a ring surrounding two symmetrical objects that resemble the letter *H* turned on its side.
- ICBC's logo is often presented in red, reminiscent of the flag of the People's Republic of China.
- ICBC uses its logo on ICBC branches and offices (sometimes in large letters on the tops of buildings), on websites, and in television commercials.

ICBC's logo consists of a ring surrounding two symmetrical objects—resembling pictographic characters in written Chinese language—that form the outline of a shape similar to the letter *H* turned on its side. The logo often appears in red, reminiscent of the red flag of the People's Republic of China, and the company often uses red in signage, banners, and other visual images.

The logo appears on prominent signage and other places at ICBC's bank branches, at various ICBC offices (sometimes in large figures atop the buildings), and in other places, such as financial expos. ICBC commercials use this symbol multiple times, as do the company websites and other advertisements.

BRAND IDENTITY

- The ICBC logo appears on banking cards that ICBC issues to account holders, such as the Peony Card it began issuing in 1997, the Peony International debit card, and banking cards for other accounts and functions.
- ICBC's stated mission is "Excellence for You," and the bank says it is "committed to the philosophy of 'customer demand is the key, customer satisfaction is the criteria.'"
- On its web pages ICBC stresses that its values encompass "integrity, humanity, prudence, innovation, and excellence."

ICBC's red logo appears on the banking cards it issues to account holders, such as the Peony Card it began issuing in 1997. ICBC issues a Peony International debit card along with banking cards for other accounts as well as ICBC credit cards.

The bank defines its mission as "Excellence for You" and strives to provide this excellence through its client services, shareholder returns, benefits, and societal contributions. The bank reiterated this focus on helping people in a 2012 statement in which it explained that "ICBC is committed to the philosophy of 'customer demand is the key, customer satisfaction is the criteria.'"

"Integrity leads to prosperity" appears on ICBC web pages and represents the values the bank believes are in line with what customers want in a financial institution—an honest company that has integrity. ICBC adds that its values encompass "integrity, humanity, prudence, innovation, and excellence."

BRAND STRATEGY

- ICBC operates globally, and its advertising highlights its current business in different countries and its desire to conduct even more global business.
- Television promotional spots for ICBC Indonesia feature the logo and a drawing of a peacock on a red background, while Canadian television commercials are produced in Mandarin and Cantonese.
- ICBC's web presence features pages in many different languages, serving as an information resource for potential customers and as an online banking destination for customers.

ICBC operates globally, and the company's advertising reflects its global focus, highlighting ICBC's current business in various countries and its desire to expand its global operations. Television ads for ICBC Indonesia feature the ICBC logo and a drawing of a peacock on a red background. Commercials for ICBC Canada feature the logo on Canadian maps and are played in Mandarin and Cantonese versions.

The company projects its concern for providing excellent service domestically and internationally through its websites, which are presented in a number of different languages. These pages contain detailed information to help potential customers learn about ICBC and its services, and customers can open accounts and bank online.

BRAND EQUITY

- *Brandirectory* ranked ICBC as the seventh-most-valuable banking brand in the world in 2013 and as the second-most-valuable brand of any kind in China in 2011.
- "BrandZ Top 100 Most Valuable Global Brands" named ICBC the world's most valuable financial brand from 2009 through 2012.
- *Fortune* magazine included ICBC in its list of the top 500 global brands in all fields for 2010, 2011, and 2012.

Brandirectory's "Best Banking Brands 2013" ranked ICBC seventh in the world, with a brand value of US$19,820 million, and its "China 100 2011" had the bank ranked second among all brands in China, behind only China Mobile.

"BrandZ Top 100 Most Valuable Global Brands 2012" named ICBC the world's most valuable financial brand from 2009 through 2012. The 2012 edition of the "BrandZ Top 100 Most Valuable Global Brands" called ICBC the biggest "mover and shaker" among financial brands. It also ranked ICBC the second most valuable Chinese brand.

Fortune magazine included ICBC in its list of the top 500 global brands in all fields for 2010, 2011, and 2012.

BRAND AWARENESS

- A 2005 market-research survey found that 95.8 percent of Internet users in China were familiar with ICBC's online banking services and 76.7 percent had used those services.
- ICBC captured 20 percent of China's retail banking market in 2010 and held 35 percent of the savings deposits market among China's four biggest banks.
- A 2013 report in the *Sydney Morning Herald* written by Peter Cai called ICBC "the world's largest bank in terms of profitability, market capitalisation and customer deposits."

The Shanghai-based market research firm iResearch reported in 2005 that its survey found that 95.8 percent of Internet users in China had heard of ICBC's online banking services and that 76.7 percent of those Internet users had used ICBC's online banking services.

ICBC held a 20 percent share of the retail banking market in China in 2010 and held 35 percent of the savings deposits market among China's big four banks, with balances that made ICBC the largest bank in the country.

A 2013 report in the *Sydney Morning Herald* written by Peter Cai called ICBC "the world's largest bank in terms of profitability, market capitalisation and customer deposits."

BRAND OUTLOOK

- In 2012 ICBC announced plans to join with European insurance firm AXA-Minmetals to sell life insurance in China.
- ICBC bought a 70 percent interest in Bank of East Asia (Canada) in 2010 and changed the bank's name to ICBC (Canada) Limited; in 2012 it bought an 80 percent interest in the U.S. subsidiary of Bank of East Asia.
- ICBC acquired a license to operate in Mumbai in 2011 and opened a third Australian branch, in Melbourne, in 2012.

ICBC has demonstrated its intent to broaden its business and geographic interests. It acquired equity in the insurance firm AXA-Minmetals in 2010, and in 2012 the bank announced its intention to sell life insurance to the Chinese market. With this alliance with one of Europe's largest insurers ICBC aimed to bolster its presence there.

The company has intensified its efforts in the North American market as well. It bought a 70 percent interest in Bank of East Asia (Canada) in 2010 and changed the bank's name to ICBC (Canada) Limited. The bank targeted the large number of Chinese companies, students, and visitors in Canada and looked to provide services for both regions. Two years later ICBC bought an 80 percent interest in the U.S. subsidiary of the Bank of East Asia. According to a BBC report, the United States Federal Reserve had never before approved such a sale to a Chinese firm.

In 2011 ICBC acquired a license to operate in Mumbai, and the following year it expanded its operations in Australia by opening a third Australian branch in Melbourne.

FURTHER READING

"Brand Awareness of ICBC's E-banking Hits 95.8%." *SinoCast China Business Daily News*, June 27, 2005.

"BrandZ Top 100 Most Valuable Global Brands 2012." Millward Brown. Accessed January 9, 2013. http://www.millwardbrown.com/BrandZ/Top_100_Global_Brands.aspx.

Cai, Peter. "China's Biggest Bank, ICBC, Moves on Australian Expansion Plans." *Sydney Morning Herald*, November 13, 2012.

"China's Top Four Banks Set for Weakest Annual Profit Growth since IPOs." Reuters, November 1, 2012.

ICBC. "Corporate Culture." Accessed January 10, 2013. http://www.icbc-ltd.com/ICBCLtd/About%20Us/Corporate%20Culture/.

———. "ICBC Named World's Most Valuable Financial Brand for Four Years in Succession." June 13, 2012. Accessed January 9, 2013. http://www.icbc-ltd.com/ICBCLtd/About%20Us/News/icbc%20named%20worlds%20most%20valuable%20financial%20brand%20for%20four%20years%20in%20succession.htm.

———. "ICBC Sets up Branch in Canada." July 6, 2010. Accessed January 11, 2013. http://www.icbc-ltd.com/icbcltd/about%20us/news/icbc%20sets%20up%20branch%20in%20canada.htm.

"Industrial and Commercial Bank of China." RankingTheBrands.com. Accessed January 9, 2013. http://www.rankingthebrands.com/Brand-detail.aspx?brandID=1531.

"Industrial and Commercial Bank of China Ltd." *International Directory of Company Histories*. Ed. Derek Jacques and Paula Kepos. Vol. 109. Detroit, MI: St. James Press, 2010.

"Industrial and Commercial Bank of China (ICBC) Wins Two Awards—Best Retail Bank in China and Best Large-Scale Retail Bank in China for the Year 2010." *Asian Banker*, March 12, 2011.

IKEA

AT A GLANCE

Brand Synopsis: Swedish-based home furnishings retailer IKEA is known all over the world for its modern styles and affordable pricing.
Parent Company: INGKA Holding B.V. (a subsidiary of Stichting INGKA Foundation)
Bargelaan 20
2333 CT Leiden
Netherlands
31 71 565 7100
http://www.ikea.com
Sector: Consumer Discretionary
Industry Group: Consumer Durables & Apparel
Performance: Market share—6.3 percent (2011).
Sales—EUR 27.6 billion (US$36.7 billion) (2012).
Principal Competitors: Walmart, Target, Home Depot, Dania, Carrefour, Nitori

BRAND ORIGINS

- IKEA is an acronym for Ingvar Kamprad Elmtaryd Aggunaryd and was trademarked in 1943.
- IKEA began its global expansion in Norway in 1963 and has stores in 40 countries.
- IKEA was restructured in 1982, and franchises were developed under Inter IKEA Systems B.V.
- In 1986 Ingvar Kamprad retired from management of INGKA Group and became its senior advisor.
- IKEA made its appearance on the web in 1997 and introduced online shopping in 2000.

Ingvar Kamprad founded IKEA in Sweden in 1943 when he was 17 years old. The IKEA acronym is made up of Ingvar's initials and the first letters of the names of his family's farm (Elmataryd) and a nearby village (Aggunaryd). His original portfolio consisted of such household staples as matches, fish, seeds, and Christmas decorations. The company began selling furniture in 1948. From the beginning, Kamprad focused on selling everyday items at reduced prices.

When demand increased to the point where orders could not be delivered personally, Kamprad began to use a local milk van and the train station to distribute his products. His advertisements led to increased sales, and by the time he began working with local manufacturers to create furniture, he had an interested customer base.

During the 1950s, Kamprad's business continued to grow. He created the first IKEA catalog and opened the first showroom, which allowed customers see the quality of his low-priced furniture prior to purchase. In 1956 the concept of flat-packaging and self-assembly was born, making delivery easier and facilitating a novel approach to sales. In 1958 IKEA opened its first store in älmhult, Sweden, where for the first time customers could view furniture and buy on site.

In 1960 IKEA opened its first in-store restaurant. Today, IKEA restaurants and bistros still offer customers a taste of Swedish food at low prices. IKEA also began to develop some of its most popular furniture lines in the 1960s and 1970s. The Ögla and Poäng chairs, MTP and

Billy bookcases, and Klippan sofa have seen some alterations, but they are still sold today. In tandem with these developments, the company began to expand to other countries, opening stores in Norway, Denmark, Switzerland, Germany, Austria, the Netherlands, and Australia.

The company was restructured in 1982. Kamprad donated most of the IKEA organization to a Dutch company, and a franchise system was created under Inter IKEA Systems B.V. The Stichting INGKA Foundation was formed. The foundation owns the IKEA Group, while the parent company for the IKEA Group is INGKA Holding B.V. In turn, the IKEA Group is made up of many IKEA operations, including the Swedwood Industrial Group, whose primary task is "to ensure production capacity for IKEA." In 1986 Ingvar Kamprad retired from management of the INGKA Group and became its senior advisor.

In 1997 IKEA appeared on the web, and in 2000, the company began selling its products online. The shopping websites have helped reduce paper use and provided greater opportunity for interaction with customers.

BRAND ELEMENTS

- IKEA has kept its original name, established in 1943.
- The company has retained its original vision: "a better everyday life for the many people."
- The yellow and blue logo represents the store's Swedish background and efficient, straightforward business practices.
- In 2010 the logo's font was changed.

IKEA's trademark and concept are owned by Inter IKEA Systems, B.V. IKEA has kept its original name, created by Ingvar Kamprad in 1943. Since its founding, the company has continually enforced its vision: "a better everyday life for the many people" supported by a business idea of offering "a wide range of well-designed, functional home furnishing products at prices so low that as many people as possible will be able to afford them."

The company's logo has changed little since IKEA opened its first store. The yellow oval within the blue rectangle is easily recognizable; the colors represent the company's Swedish roots (blue and yellow are the Swedish national colors). The original font was a customized version of Futura, which aligned with the modernist movement and carried the look of efficiency and forwardness. These attributes tied in with Kamprad's vision. In 2010 the company changed the logo's font to Verdana, a move that was widely criticized because the new logo lacked the clean lines expected by consumers. IKEA's intention was to create a consistent font for its correspondence around the world, and despite the criticism, the company continues to use the new font.

BRAND IDENTITY

- IKEA's original focus was to make life better for many people with its inexpensive furniture.
- IKEA shifted its brand image from a seller of starter furniture to a seller of quality design.
- IKEA promotes its creative side with playful advertising campaigns.

In the past, IKEA's catalogs focused on starter furniture for young couples. As IKEA's customer base has broadened to include older consumers, the brand's focus has changed. To circumvent association of the brand with cheaply made products, marketing campaigns have shifted to showcase quality design (though still at affordable prices). In comparison to the ads of its competitor Target, which feature dorm furniture for the college-age generation, IKEA's marketing attempts to attract a wider audience with the tagline "The Life Improvement Store."

In addition to being associated with quality design, IKEA also promotes an image of creativity, playfulness, and fun. The website Toxel.com, for example, exhibits an array of global IKEA advertising stunts aimed to show how IKEA furniture can fit into any space. In Amsterdam an IKEA sofa was suspended in front of a billboard; an Australian newspaper ad mimics the sliding door of a closet; and the entire front of an apartment building in Frankfurt was redesigned using oversized mock-ups of IKEA drawers.

The IKEA brand embraces environmental and social responsibility. Its ambition is to "make products which have minimum impact on the environment and ... manufacture them in a socially responsible way." IKEA uses its website to communicate a great deal of information and promote transparency in its dealings with customers. It provides reports describing how the company is working toward sustainability and how customers can achieve a more sustainable lifestyle by using IKEA's products.

BRAND STRATEGY

- The layout of IKEA stores allows customers to view the entire stock and pull flat-packed products by themselves.
- All IKEA products are labeled as "Design and Quality, IKEA of Sweden."
- IKEA organizes its products under "systems" with Scandinavian names.

IKEA' brand strategy begins with the layout of its stores. The layout of IKEA stores is such that customers follow a path that takes them through the entire collection of products, which are displayed in various room arrangements. Customers are then able to pull the flat-packed items from a warehouse area they must pass through in order to exit. The cost of labor is thus lowered, and savings are passed on to the customer. In some of its international stores, this layout does not work; in Hong Kong, for example, space is limited and expensive. IKEA's solution to this problem was to build three smaller outlets and to place them throughout the city. In other countries, such as Germany, a one-story building is more affordable than a multistory one.

"The IKEA Way" is integral to its brand strategy. According to the IKEA website, "Anybody can make a good-quality product for a high price, or a poor-quality product for a low price. But to make good products at low prices, you need to develop methods that are both cost-effective and innovative." IKEA sells all its products under the IKEA brand (all products are labeled as "Design and Quality, IKEA of Sweden") but organizes many of its items under furniture "systems" with Scandinavian names, such as BILLY, GODMORGON, LACK, and GOSA.

BRAND EQUITY

- With few global competitors, IKEA ranked 52nd in the top 500 global brands in 2011.
- In the U.S. retail sector, IKEA was ranked the sixth most valuable brand in 2011 and 2012, while its competitor Target was ranked fifth.
- IKEA's brand value in 2012 was US$15.2 billion.

According to *Brandirectory,* IKEA's brand value in 2012 was US$15.2 billion, an increase from US$14.7 billion in 2011, and it was ranked 52nd among the top 500 global brands in 2011. In the U.S. retail sector, it was listed as the sixth most valuable brand in both 2011 and 2012, just behind Target, which was ranked fifth. *Interbrand*'s report on best global green brands in 2012 ranked IKEA 39th in the home furnishings sector, and in 2011 the company was ranked 31st in the global retail sector for home furnishings. *Interbrand* listed no other home furnishing retailers in the global green or retail sections of its reports.

BRAND AWARENESS

- In 2012, IKEA had stores in some 40 countries around the world.
- IKEA enjoys top-of-mind awareness and a nearly cult-like following.
- There are websites devoted to IKEA and its fans.

Customers associate Sweden, IKEA's home base, with social equity, ecological responsibility, and ethical practices. The company continues to have a reputation for offering quality furniture at low prices. Its inclusiveness of "the many people" is well known around the world, and it has used the same logo, with the exception of an adjustment to the font, since the early 1940s.

According to IKEA's website, IKEA has stores in some 40 countries. IKEA enjoys top-of-mind awareness and, according to *Interbrand*'s "Best Global Brands" 2010, IKEA's "awareness levels are incredibly high for a business of its size, which speaks to the high affinity for the brand." The IKEA brand is so popular, in fact, that it has achieved nearly cult-like status among many fans. There are websites devoted to IKEA and its fans, and according to *BloombergBusinessweek,* there is something known as "Ikea World, a state of mind that revolves around contemporary design, low prices, wacky promotions, and an enthusiasm that few institutions in or out of business can muster."

BRAND OUTLOOK

- IKEA's 2012 sales rose 9.5 percent to EUR 27.6 billion (US$36.7 billion).
- IKEA gained market share in every market in 2012.
- IKEA plans to double its store expansion rate after 2015.

IKEA continued its global expansion into the 2010s. In 2012 sales rose 9.5 percent to EUR 27.6 billion (US$36.7 billion). The company gained market share in every market, despite slumping economies across the globe. In fact, IKEA may have benefited from the recessions, as more consumers sought affordability. Since 2007 IKEA's sales have increased 38 percent, and the company has expanded into new territories, including the United Kingdom and Spain.

IKEA plans to continue moving boldly into the 21st century and forecasts increases in same-store sales of 5 percent annually. The company plans to double its new-store expansion rate after 2015. In order to protect itself from dependence on the unpredictable fossil fuel market, IKEA announced plans to spend nearly US$2 billion on renewable energy sources, such as wind farms and solar power. With an eye on the bottom line and a way with design, IKEA looked to be a solid performer for years to come.

FURTHER READING

Abend, Lisa. "The Font Wars: IKEA fans fume over Verdana." *Time Business*, August 28, 2009. Accessed August 28, 2012. http://www.time.com/time/business/article/0,8599,1919127,00.html.

Brand Finance. "IKEA." *Brandirectory.* Accessed August 30, 2012. http://brandirectory.com/profile/ikea.

FPO: IP Research & Communities. "Patents/Apps: IKEA." *Freepatentsonline.* Accessed August 27, 2012. http://www.freepatentsonline.com/result.html?p=11&query_txt=IKEA&sort=relevance&srch=top&patents=on.

IKEA. "About IKEA." Accessed August 26, 2012. http://www.ikea.com/ms/en_AA/about_ikea/index.html.

"Ikea." *BloombergBusinessweek*, November 13, 2005. Accessed March 4, 2013. http://www.businessweek.com/stories/2005-11-13/ikea.

"IKEA: Flat-pack Accounting." *Economist*, May 11, 2006. Accessed August 26, 2012. http://www.economist.com/node/6919139.

"IKEA's Global Marketing Strategy." *123HelpMe.com*. Accessed August 26, 2012. http://www.qweHelpMe.com/view.asp?id=165535.

Interbrand. "Best Global Green Brands in 2012." Accessed August 26, 2012. http://www.interbrand.com/en/best-global-brands/Best-Global-Green-Brands/2012-Report.aspx.

"Public's Disapproval of New Logo Shows IKEA's Brand Strength." *Beneath the World of Branding*. Accessed August 28, 2012. http://www.talentzoo.com/beneath-the-brand/blog_news.php?articleID=3029.

Shanley, Mia. "IKEA posts record profit, gains in almost all markets." *Reuters*, January 20, 2012. Accessed August 26, 2012. http://www.reuters.com/article/2012/01/20/ikea-earnings-idUSL6E8CG32Z20120120.

Toxel.com. "Clever and Creative IKEA Advertising." January 12, 2010. Accessed August 31, 2012. http://www.toxel.com/inspiration/2010/01/12/clever-and-creative-ikea-advertising/.

Vega, Tanzina. "A Focus on Families (and Furniture)." *New York Times*, September 13, 2010. Accessed August 29, 2012. http://www.nytimes.com/2010/09/13/business/media/13adco.html?_r=2.

ING

AT A GLANCE

Brand Synopsis: Based in the Netherlands and one of the largest banks in Europe, ING offers banking, insurance, investment, retirement, and other financial services to individuals and businesses in several countries; it is also a brand with a very strong visual identity and is visibly involved in endeavors such as fitness and sports.
Parent Company: ING Groep N.V. (ING Group)
Amsterdamse Poort
Bijlmerplein 888
1102 MG Amsterdam
The Netherlands
http://www.ing.com/Our-Company.htm
Sector: Financials
Industry Group: Banks; Insurance; Diversified Financials
Performance: *Sales*—EUR55.8 billion (2011).
Principal Competitors: Bidvest Group Ltd.; Royal Bank of Scotland Group PLC; Barclays Bank PLC; JPMorgan Chase and Co.; Bank of America Corporation; ABN AMRO Holding N.V.; UniCredit S.p.A.; Société Générale Group; Wells Fargo and Company; Sumitomo Mitsui Financial Group Inc.; Wachovia Corporation

BRAND ORIGINS

- NMB Postbank and Nationale-Nederlanden merged in 1991 to form Internationale Nederlanden Groep, a company later known as ING Groep N.V.
- Dutch insurers with the De Nederlanden name date to the 1800s.
- Nederlandsche Middenstandsbank was founded in 1927.
- ING offers banking, insurance, investment, and other services in the Netherlands, Belgium, and other European countries.
- Customers can conduct much of their ING banking business online or over the phone.

The ING Groep N.V., or the ING Group, is one of the largest banks and insurers in Europe. "The ING Groep N.V." is its whole name. This was formerly an abbreviation for Internationale Nederlanden Groep, a company formed in 1991 by the merger of the Dutch companies NMB Postbank and Nationale-Nederlanden.

Mergers and partnerships are a major part of ING's history. A number of Dutch insurance firms bearing a version of the De Nederlanden name date to the 1800s. These companies worked with other countries' insurance firms to create an international insurance network by 1900, and De Nederlanden later acquired firms in other countries. In 1962 De Nederlanden merged with fellow Dutch insurer Nationale Levensverzekeringen Bank to form Nationale-Nederlanden. This new company would acquire insurance companies in other countries, including the United States.

On the banking side of ING's history, NMB Postbank was itself the product of mergers and alliances. The Dutch bank Nederlandsche Middenstandsbank (NMB) was founded in 1927. Another Dutch bank, Postbank, was formed when Rijskpostspaarbank and Postcheque- en Girodienst (the Dutch form of the name) merged in 1986. Two years later, NMB and Postbank merged to form NMB Postbank.

ING offers banking, insurance, investment, and other services for clients in the Netherlands, Belgium, and other European countries. It has entered other countries as well. In India it partnered with Vysya Bank Ltd. to form ING Vysya Bank Ltd. and ING Vysya Life Insurance (with other partners), and it also operates ING Investment Management in that country. ING offers insurance, investment, and retirement services for clients in the United States, insurance products in Japan, and banking and insurance products for individuals and businesses in several countries in Europe, Asia, and South America.

Customers can conduct much of their banking business online or over the phone. Online banking is a major component of ING DIRECT, a division of ING, although it does have some physical branches. ING DIRECT operates worldwide, including in several European countries plus Australia. In 2012 other companies bought ING DIRECT's operations in the United States, Canada, and the United Kingdom.

BRAND ELEMENTS

- ING's orange lion relates to the history of its companies and to its home country, the Netherlands.
- Rijkspostspaarbank used the Dutch coat of arms with lions and other lion symbols before it became part of the ING Groep.
- Drawings of orange lions appear on ING's website, on its annual report, and in its commercials and print advertisements.
- ING DIRECT Italia uses a pumpkin as a symbol, a reminder of the ING brand's frequent use of orange.

ING's orange lion relates to the history of a number of its companies and to the corporation's home country, the Netherlands. Orange is the color of the Netherlands and its royalty, who are members of the House of Orange-Nassau. Lions appear on another Dutch symbol, the Netherlands coat of arms.

Government-owned bank Rijkspostspaarbank used the Dutch coat of arms, with its lions, and the company continued to use various lion symbols as it changed and merged and later became part of the ING Groep. ING's insurance companies have also used lions as symbols. One of these firms, De Nederlanden van 1845, incorporated the Dutch coat of arms, reminiscent of how Rijkspostspaarbank used the image.

The company uses this brand logo frequently. Drawings of orange lions appear on the company's website, in publications like its annual report, and in its commercials and print advertisements. ING Belgium offers a savings account, ING Lion Account, a savings account featuring cards with lions. People in orange lion suits even appear in ING commercials and print advertisements in the Netherlands, serving as ING brand mascots.

In addition to using orange lions as brand symbols, ING frequently uses the color orange and other orange items to represent itself. ING DIRECT uses an orange sphere as its logo. This sphere looks like an orange fruit, so the symbol is an orange-colored orange. ING DIRECT Italia bank branches use another orange symbol, the pumpkin. Pumpkin images appear in its commercials and websites, and in "Dentro la zucca" ("Inside the Pumpkin"), a short promotional piece about the bank. Branches of this bank also feature orange shapes that resemble pumpkins, as well as other orange designs. This bank offers a Conto Arancio, an Orange Account, and a Conto Corrente Arancio, an Orange Current Account. Although used in different ways and in different markets, the color orange provides a visual reminder of the ING brand.

BRAND IDENTITY

- ING describes ING House, the glass headquarters for ING's insurance operations, and the company itself as "innovative and transparent."
- Giant shoelaces atop ING House demonstrate the ING brand's commitment to fitness, acknowledgement of public opinion, and sense of humor.
- A 2006 print advertisement referred to ING Vysya, the Bangalore Lions field hockey team, and lions as "undisputed kings."

Depictions of lions appear at Amsterdam's ultramodern ING House, the custom-built headquarters for ING's insurance operations. The building itself symbolizes ING. The company has described both the large glass building and itself as "innovative and transparent." The company found that the structure's design, with its streamlined form and use of steel, glass, and open spaces, conveyed ING's self-image very effectively. Transparency and innovation are important for ING, which wants to convince customers and potential customers that it is a trustworthy and progressive business, a company worthy of customer investments of money and effort.

ING has used the building to say additional things about the brand. It sometimes adds long, thin tube-like material to the top of ING House. This tube-like material looks like enormous orange shoelaces, especially since ING House is shaped like a shoe. These laces echo the brand's involvement with the Orange Laces Nation fund-raising organization, the pro-fitness organization Run for Something Better, and several running races around the world.

The giant orange shoelaces help portray ING as a brand committed to fitness and to helping people improve their lives. The laces also indicate that ING has acknowledged comments that ING House looks like a shoe. Since ING reinforced these perceptions by adding giant shoelaces atop the building, it has portrayed itself as a brand that is aware of other people and their opinions; it also demonstrates that it is a brand with a sense of fun and a sense of humor about itself.

ING again employed lions in a highly symbolic advertisement. "The lions are the undisputed kings," declared a 2006 print advertisement for ING Vysya Life Insurance, a company formed when ING merged with India's Vysya. This phrase represented several things. At its most basic level, it congratulated the Bangalore Lions Indian field hockey team on winning the Premier Hockey League cup. The advertisement featured a photograph of a hockey player (with the orange uniform and lion logo from its sponsor, ING) and text about the Bangalore Lions' victory.

In this advertisement, ING called the Lions "undisputed kings," alluding to the lion's nickname as the "king of the jungle." ING also portrayed itself as a lion. It used lion drawings to represent ING Vysya and the ING-sponsored Bangalore Lions. ING Vysya then included itself among the "undisputed kings." This portrayal presented the ING brand, the athletes of the Bangalore Lions, and actual lions, as unquestionably strong and successful.

BRAND STRATEGY

- The ING website ingyournumber.com helps users determine how much money they need for retirement.
- Commercials for Spain's ING DIRECT España told viewers that "commission" was a useless word for people who hold an Orange Account.
- ING has sponsored marathons and other running events, such as the New York City Marathon.

As a company with banking, insurance, and other financial interests, ING deals with a lot numbers. The company refers to its experience and expertise with numbers on its website, ingyournumber.com. This site assists Internet users in completing a questionnaire that can help them determine how much money they need for retirement. Computer users can also search for and contact financial professionals and access information about ING's retirement planning services and other services. The company has also created commercials advertising their services and the ingyournumber.com site. Several of these commercials featured people carrying orange numbers that signified the amount of money they needed in order to retire. The commercials told viewers how they could use ING to find their own numbers.

Other ING commercials described its services. Commercials for Spain's ING DIRECT España told viewers that "commission" was a useless word for people who hold an Orange Account, or Cuenta Naranja, because in most cases there was no fee for stock market transactions. This commercial described the features of that savings account in a series of messages on orange backgrounds. These visuals, and the Orange Account name, again reiterated ING's use of the color orange while describing the company's services.

Other ING activities bring the company name to people. It has sponsored the New York City Marathon and other marathons, half marathons, and various running events throughout the United States. It is also involved in racing events for children and Run for Something Better, an organization promoting physical fitness for children. People can raise funds for Run for Something Better through the Orange Laces Nation organization, which actually gives participants orange shoelaces. With Orange Laces Nation, ING once again uses the color orange to refer to its company. Marathon participants with these orange shoelaces serve as moving advertisements for ING.

BRAND EQUITY

- In the Netherlands and Belgium, ING held significant chunks of the banking market.
- In 2010 ING was the "largest universal bank in Poland with a 6.5% market share."
- In 2012 ING Vysya Bank Ltd. had an estimated 4 percent to 5 percent share of the private banking industry in India.

The company held considerable market share in a number of banking categories in the Netherlands and Belgium, according to a 2012 report. ING was the leading bank for payments in the Netherlands, with a 30 percent market share. It also held 30 percent of the small and medium enterprises market, 22 percent of the mortgages, 20 percent of the mid-corporate banking market, 19 percent of savings, and 7 percent of the private banking market, all in the Netherlands. The same 2012 report stated that in Belgium, ING captured 25 percent of the mid-corporate banking market, 22 percent of the mortgages, 18 percent of the small and medium enterprises market, 16 percent of the private banking market, 15 percent of savings, and 13 percent of payments.

ING also has a market presence in other countries in Europe. A 2010 report by Pegasystems called ING the "largest universal bank in Poland with a 6.5% market share" and with "more than 2 million individual customers and over 150,000 small and large business customers."

This market presence even extends to other continents. India's ING Vysya Bank Ltd. was formed when Vysya Bank Ltd. and ING merged in 2002. In that year an ING Vysya Bank executive estimated that the bank had a 4 percent to 5 percent share of the private banking industry in India.

BRAND AWARENESS

- In 2005 marketing analysts noted that since ING began serving as the title sponsor for the New York City Marathon in 2003, it jumped from low

- awareness to awareness among around 80 percent of American consumers.
- ING sponsors the Netherlands national soccer team, who sport orange uniforms and use soccer balls with ING lion logos.
- In 2012 Australian commercials for ING DIRECT urged viewers to "Spend Your Life Well" and informed customers that ING DIRECT offered more than savings accounts.

The company's brand-building strategies have been effective. In 2005 marketing analysts noted that since ING began serving as the title sponsor for the New York City Marathon in 2003, it jumped from low awareness to awareness among around 80 percent of American consumers. The analysts cite ING's brand exposure to thousands of runners, millions of people watching the race in person, and millions more watching it worldwide on television broadcasts and highlights. It has produced extensive advertising relating to the marathon, sponsored its Run for Something Better racing initiative at the races, and used its name and logo in marathon guides.

ING has also sponsored other sporting endeavors to promote its brand. It sponsors the Netherlands national soccer team (known as a voetbal, or football, team), who sport orange uniforms and use soccer balls with ING lion logos. ING's orange lion mascots and other orange design elements appear in advertisements about ING and this soccer team. Although the team uses a lion symbol that is different from ING's lion symbol, its use evokes the ING lion.

ING DIRECT has made an effort to define itself and has taken steps to advertise itself, its companies, and its products in countries around the world. In 2012, for example, it launched an advertising campaign in Australia. Using the tagline "Spend Your Life Well," this campaign informed customers that ING DIRECT's services went beyond savings accounts to include investment services, home loans, pension products, and other services.

BRAND OUTLOOK

- In 2012 different companies bought ING DIRECT's operations in the United States, Canada, and the United Kingdom.
- Future ING strategies include strengthening its European banking operations, utilizing its international banking network, and continuing to repay the Dutch government for its 2008 state aid.
- ING has worked to separate its banking and insurance operations, as illustrated in the separate headquarters it provides each.

The years 2012 and 2013 were a time of transition for ING DIRECT. In February 2012 the American company Capital One bought ING DIRECT U.S.A., which offered banking, investment, and retirement services. In 2013 this company became known as Capital One 360. Also in 2012, Canada's Bank of Nova Scotia, also known as Scotiabank, bought ING DIRECT Canada, and the United Kingdom–based Barclays bought ING DIRECT UK.

Such sales of its companies are in keeping with one of ING's company strategies: to streamline its portfolio. Other ING strategies for the future include strengthening its European banking operations and utilizing its international banking network. In addition ING continued to repay the government of the Netherlands for the capital aid it gave the company during the worldwide financial crisis in 2008.

The company has also worked to separate its banking and insurance work. ING believed that such a separation would help satisfy "the widespread demand for greater simplicity, reliability and transparency." This division is symbolized by the physical separation of its offices. The headquarters for banking operations is housed at Amsterdamse Poort, while the head offices for insurance operations are situated at ING House. ING is obviously a company making constant physical and business transitions.

FURTHER READING

"Amazing ING Group Office at Amsterdam." Neeshu.com, September 17, 2010. Accessed January 29, 2013. http://neeshu.com/articles/amazing-ing-group-office-at-amsterdam.html.

Barman, Neelasri, and Vishwanath Nair. "ING Vysya Will Grow Faster than the Market and with Better Quality." *Daily News & Analysis*, April 12, 2012. Accessed December 28, 2012. http://www.dnaindia.com/money/report_ing-vysya-will-grow-faster-than-the-market-and-with-better-quality_1674684.

"ING Direct Launches New Brand Campaign." *Australian Banking and Finance*, August 13, 2012. Accessed December 28, 2012. http://www.australianbankingfinance.com/banking/ing-direct-launches-new-brand-campaign/.

ING Groep N.V. "The History of the ING Lion." March 5, 2012. Accessed December 26, 2012. http://www.ing.com/Our-Company/About-us/History-of-ING/History-of-ING-lion.htm.

———. "Mission & Strategy." December 18, 2012. Accessed December 28, 2012. http://www.ing.com/Our-Company/About-us/Mission-Strategy.htm.

———. *2011 Annual Report*. Accessed December 26, 2012. http://www.ing.com/Our-Company/Investor-relations/Annual-Reports.htm.

"ING Groep N.V." *International Directory of Company Histories*. Ed. Jay P. Pederson. Vol. 108. Detroit, MI: St. James Press, 2010.

Parry, Tim. "The Brand-Building Race: How ING Grew Awareness with NYC Marathon." *Chief Marketer*, October 17, 2005.

Pegasystems. *ING Poland: Focus on Emerging Financial Markets*. 2010. Accessed January 29, 2013. http://www.pega.com/sites/default/files/pega_cs_ING-Poland20101206.pdf.

van der Noordaa, Hans. *Reshaping ING in the Benelux*. *ING Investor Day*, January 13, 2012. Accessed January 29, 2013. http://www.slideshare.net/ING/ing-investor-day13january2012reshapinginginthebenelux.

INTEL

AT A GLANCE

Brand Synopsis: Intel leads the world in the production of semiconductor chips and dominates the microprocessor market. This success and promotions like its Intel Inside program have made Intel an internationally renowned brand.
Parent Company: Intel Corporation
2200 Mission College Blvd.
Santa Clara, California 95054-1549
United States
http://www.intel.com/content/www/us/en/homepage.html
Sector: Information Technology
Industry Group: Semiconductors & Semiconductor Equipment
Performance: *Sales*—US$54 billion (2011).
Principal Competitors: Advanced Micro Devices, Inc.; Samsung Electronics Co., Ltd.; Texas Instruments Incorporated; International Business Machines Corporation; STMicroelectronics N.V.

BRAND ORIGINS

- "Intel" is short for "integrated electronics."
- Robert Noyce and Gordon Moore, inventors of the integrated circuit, founded what became known as Intel in 1968.
- Early Intel creations included microchips featuring erasable, programmable, read-only memory.
- Intel produced microchips for a number of computer manufacturers and, in the 1990s, founded Intel Products Group.
- Intel products include the Pentium, Celeron, and Atom microprocessors.

Intel developed the first microprocessor in 1971 and would go on to dominate the global market for that product. The company's commitments to technological innovation and promotion would help it develop into one of the world's most successful and renowned companies.

Robert Noyce and Gordon Moore, inventors of the integrated circuit, founded N M Electronics in 1968 with venture capitalists Arthur Rock and Andrew Grove. They would serve as chief executive officers of the company soon known as "Intel," short for "integrated electronics." This new company developed a number of microprocessor chips for various uses and companies, including chips for use in International Business Machines (IBM) personal computers. IBM would own part of Intel until the 1980s. Other Intel creations included microchips featuring erasable, programmable, read-only memory, which allowed customers to use electricity and ultraviolet light to erase and program these chips.

The company expanded rapidly, from 12 employees in 1968 to 15,000 in 1980, and more than 82,000 worldwide by 2010. Throughout the 1980s, Intel developed additional microchips for various products. In the following decade, it topped US$1 billion in sales and expanded its business with the Intel Products Group, which sold network, communications, and personal conferencing products directly to PC users. Intel also introduced "Intel Inside" in the 1990s. This long-running brand campaign would go on to become a highly visible and recognizable brand element.

Intel's headquarters is in Santa Clara, California, and the company now has offices, laboratories, and factories all over the world. These sites help create its products, like Pentium, Celeron, Atom, Core i3, Core i5, and Core i7 microprocessors and also the Centrino chips used for wireless technology. This production illustrates Intel's continual commitment to producing innovative goods and services for various markets.

BRAND ELEMENTS

- The Intel logo is the company name in lowercase letters surrounded by a circle.
- Walter Werzowa composed a five-tone audio tone to signify Intel brand identity.
- Intel uses bunny suits—full-body suits with attached filtration systems and helmets used to keep products clean.
- The Intel Inside logo reminds people that Intel products are not readily visible or understood but are nonetheless important functioning parts for electronic products.

The Intel logo is the company name in lowercase letters surrounded by a circle. The company's Intel Inside brand campaign also utilizes this design. It features a circle surrounding the Intel Inside slogan. These logos often use the colors blue and white, a color scheme also used on its products, packaging, websites, office signs, merchandise, and other Intel material. Other Intel name logos include the word Intel in lowercase letters with the "e" lower than the other letters.

Intel also employs a particular sound to identify itself. It uses a five-tone musical phrase composed by Walter Werzowa. This phrase consists of a multi-instrument "sparkle" sound followed by a four-note percussive chime. The chime's four notes correspond to the four syllables of the words Intel Inside. As early as 1999 Intel employees noted the familiarity of this audio mark. This tone has appeared in products that use Intel, advertisements for Intel, and Internet sites, and can even be downloaded as a cell phone ringtone.

The company also uses bunny suits as a visual identifier. These suits are not rabbit suits but full-body suits, helmets, and attached filtration systems that look like hazardous materials (hazmat) suits or astronaut suits and helmets. Intel employees wear these bunny suits when working in clean rooms so they do not contaminate the tiny, delicate microchips being produced. Intel features this bunny suit in its advertisements and websites and has even sold dolls dressed in bunny suits with an "Intel Inside" logo on the front. Visitors can don these bunny suits when they visit the Intel Corporate Museum in Santa Clara, California. These ubiquitous suits symbolize Intel's technical work and promote the company itself.

A number of Intel products are hidden from everyday viewing and are highly technical in nature. The company then faces the challenge of reminding people that its products exist and are worthy of their patronage, even if they cannot be seen or immediately understood. This issue helped spur the creation of the Intel Inside program. Launched in 1991, this campaign reminds people that Intel products are not readily visible or understood but are nonetheless important, functioning parts for electronic products. The Intel Inside logo appears on various products as well as packaging, advertisements, merchandise, and other places.

BRAND IDENTITY

- By using the phrase "Sponsors of tomorrow," Intel refers to its role in developing and producing technological advances.
- The phrase "Visibly Smart" refers to Intel's intelligent, innovative practices and visible global reputation.
- An Intel processor powered the Infoscape, two walls of touch screens featuring more than 500 live Internet links.
- Intel's participation in electronics shows demonstrates the brand's position in the electronics field and its interest in innovation.

Intel has used the phrase "Sponsors of tomorrow." This phrase refers to the company's role in developing and producing technological advances. Its use of the word "tomorrow" implies a continued commitment to provide this innovation. Intel works internationally to produce innovation, and fittingly, "Sponsors of tomorrow" is part of the company's global promotional campaign. Yet another Intel campaign, "Visibly Smart," also refers to the company's intelligent, innovative practices and visible global reputation. It also slyly alludes to the fact that many of Intel's products are not usually visible.

Although Intel's products are usually hidden, the brand's work and achievements are not. The Infoscape was a highly visible example of its work. The Infoscape included two seven-foot-tall walls that functioned as touch screens with more than 500 live Internet links from 20,000 sources. People could touch any of the screens' live links to access Internet pages. Controlling these links was a laptop computer featuring an Intel Core i7 processor.

The wall-sized Infoscape and its huge number of links dramatically demonstrated the power of Intel's processors as well as Intel's expertise in creating this technology. Intel displayed the Infoscape at the 2010 International Consumer Electronic Show, an annual show that highlights new electronic products. Intel's participation in this show highlighted the brand's position as a prominent electronics brand and its continuing focus on innovation and the new, further evidenced by its Infoscape display.

BRAND STRATEGY

- In 2011 Intel spent US$8.4 billion in research.
- Intel websites use the words *breakthrough* and *innovation* repeatedly.
- The Intel Brand Advantage Program links Intel and other companies as cobrands in different ventures.

As one of the self-proclaimed "Sponsors of tomorrow," Intel invests heavily in research. The company spent US$6.6 billion in research and development in 2010 and US$8.4 billion in 2011. This spending illustrates its commitment to advancement and innovation. Intel websites also reflect these interests, using the word *innovation* multiple times as well as words such as *breakthrough*, *transformations*, and *advanced technology*.

The company has taken great efforts to explain its commitment to innovation. The Intel Corporate Museum educates visitors about the corporation, how it makes chips, and how Intel products affect everyday life. The museum offers a website called "How Intel Makes Chips: Transistors to Transformations" and also includes a physical and online store that sells products that promote the Intel brand. Intel thus has explained technology and its relevance while promoting its own role in developing and producing this technology, linking the Intel brand to technological advances.

Intel also links its brands with other brands through the Brand Advantage Program. In this program, companies use the Intel name and logo to help promote their own goods and services. Some of Intel's partners in this program include Germany's Wincor Nixdorf, the leading retail IT service-provider in Europe. Wincor Nixdorf's European retailers use Intel processors and this company features the Intel logo on its print materials, web pages, and in other instances. Intel also discusses its cobranding partners in its own marketing, so the Brand Advantage Program benefits both sides.

BRAND EQUITY

- In 2011 Intel held 80.1 percent of the global microprocessor market while competitor Advanced Micro Devices, Inc., held 19.7 percent for the same year.
- Intel led the global semiconductor market in 2012, capturing 15.7 percent of this market.
- In 2011 Intel earned 57 percent of its revenue in the Asia-Pacific region, 21 percent in the Americas, 13 percent in Europe, and 9 percent in Japan.
- Every year since 2008, Intel has ranked among the top-30 global companies in Brand Finance's "Global 500" list.

Intel's closest competitor in the field of microprocessors is Advanced Micro Devices (AMD), Inc. AMD made gains in the microprocessor market in 2011, but still trailed far behind Intel in market share. In 2011 Intel held 80.1 percent of the global microprocessor market, compared to AMD's 19.7 percent global percentage that same year.

Intel also led the global semiconductor market in 2011 and 2012. In 2012 it captured 15.7 percent of that market, ahead of nearest competitors Samsung Electronics and its 10.1 percent and Qualcomm and its 4.3 percent. The semiconductor market is more competitive and inclusive than the microprocessor market. The top 20 companies in semiconductors held a combined 65 percent of the global market, in sharp contrast with Intel and AMD's near-duopoly of the global microprocessor industry.

Intel is successful all over the world. In a breakdown of its 2011 revenues, Intel earned 57 percent of its revenue in the Asia-Pacific region, 21 percent in the Americas, 13 percent in Europe, and 9 percent in a single country, Japan.

Every year since 2008, Brand Finance has ranked the top international brands in its "Global 500" list. Intel has placed in the top 30 in every "Global 500" list. For example, it placed 20th on the 2012 list, with a brand value of US$21.9 billion.

BRAND AWARENESS

- Brand Finance called Intel a "market leader" in 2012 and noted that Intel continued to build its brand awareness.
- According to Brand Finance in 2012, Intel had "excellent brand consistency," partly through its longtime use of its audio mark in various places.
- In a 2011 *Marketing* magazine article, Belle Charlene Kwan noted that Intel dominated the microprocessing industry and that consumers assume that all computers will feature Intel products.

While discussing the 2012 "Global 500" rankings, Brand Finance called Intel a "market leader" and said the company continued to build brand awareness. It cited the large amounts of money Intel has spent on advertising. It also cited its "excellent brand consistency," including its use of its familiar audio mark in its advertising, products, and other places.

In a 2011 article published in *Marketing* magazine, Belle Charlene Kwan discussed this market position and consumers' assumptions about Intel. Kwan noted that there was no question that Intel dominated the microprocessing industry and that "there are consumers who, instead of thinking they can choose between Intel and another brand, take it for granted that Intel will be in all computers." These assumptions underscore Intel's market dominance and success in promoting its products.

BRAND OUTLOOK

- Intel has developed new products, including processors, drives, and software for Ultrabooks, slim, streamlined mobile computers that incorporate features from notebook and tablet computers.
- In 2010 Intel began providing processors for in-vehicle infotainment equipment in cars produced by Chinese automobile maker Hawtai Motor.
- Intel began using its Intel Inside tag on smartphones in the United Kingdom, Russia, India, and China in 2012, another instance of Intel promoting its technological accomplishments and its brand name.

Continuing its history of innovations, Intel has developed and marketed additional products. It developed processors, drives, and software for Ultrabooks, slim, streamlined mobile computers that incorporate features from notebook and tablet computers. Ultrabooks promote Intel by providing mobile examples of the company's technological expertise and innovative spirit.

Intel has also developed new products for new markets. In 2010 it began providing processors for in-vehicle infotainment (IVI) equipment in cars produced by Chinese automobile maker Hawtai Motor. Intel worked with Wuhan Bluestar Technology to create these IVI devices, which allow automobile drivers and passengers to receive entertainment content, make and receive phone calls and text, navigate, and perform other functions. Under the Brand Advantage Program, Intel and Hawtai Motor served as cobrands in this project. This venture marks Intel's participation in another new field, automotive electronics, and its involvement in the growing Chinese automotive market.

Intel Inside logos also appear in additional products and markets. In 2012 it began using the Intel Inside tag on smartphones in the United Kingdom, Russia, India, and China. The company hoped to establish a presence in a new product market and differentiate itself among less-well-known chip makers. Intel's creation of new products and entry into new markets demonstrates the company's continued growth and development, both technologically and as a brand.

FURTHER READING

Brand Finance. "Intel." *Brandirectory.* Accessed December 11, 2012. http://brandirectory.com/profile/intel.

Brew, Alan. "Intel Inside Smartphones: A Brand Disconnect?" *Branding Business with RiechesBaird,* September 27, 2012. Accessed December 11, 2012. http://www.brandingbusiness.com/2012/09/intel-inside-smartphones-a-brand-disconnect/.

Ford, Dale. "Qualcomm Rides Wireless Wave to Take Third Place in Global Semiconductor Market in 2012." IHS iSuppli, December 4, 2012. Accessed December 10, 2012. http://www.isuppli.com/Semiconductor-Value-Chain/News/Pages/Qualcomm-Rides-Wireless-Wave-to-Take-Third-Place-in-Global-Semiconductor-Market-in-2012.aspx.

Gianatasio, David. "Intel Intros 'Sponsors of Tomorrow.'" *Adweek,* May 6, 2009.

Intel. "Intel Inside® Program." Accessed December 10, 2012. http://www.intel.com/pressroom/intel_inside.htm.

———. *2011 Annual Report.* Accessed December 10, 2012. http://www.intc.com/intelAR2011/introduction/financial/.

"Intel Corporation." *International Directory of Company Histories.* Ed. Jay P. Pederson. Vol. 75. Detroit, MI: St. James Press, 2006.

Kaufman, Laura. "The Man Who Created Intel's Audio 'Signature.'" *Los Angeles Times,* October 20, 1999.

Kwan, Belle Charlene. "The Giant's Shoulder—Intel Brand Profile." *Marketing,* May 2011. Accessed December 12, 2012. http://www.marketingmag.com.au/blogs/the-giants-shoulder-intel-brand-profile-9188/.

Rau, Shane, and Michael Shirer. "Worldwide PC Microprocessor Revenues in 2011 Rise 13.2 percent Compared to 2010, According to IDC." International Data Corporation, March 15, 2012. Accessed December 10, 2012. http://www.idc.com/getdoc.jsp?containerId=prUS23376112.

ISUZU

AT A GLANCE

Brand Synopsis: Isuzu, the oldest automaker in Japan, is one of the world's leading manufacturers of diesel engines and trucks and other commercial vehicles.
Parent Company: Isuzu Motors Ltd.
26-1 Minami-Oi 6-chome
Shinagawa-ku
Tokyo 140
Japan
http://www.isuzu.co.jp/world/index.html
Sector: Consumer Discretionary.
Industry Group: Automobiles & Components.
Performance: *Market share*—26.4 percent of truck market, Japan (2004); 3 percent of heavy truck market, worldwide (2005). *Sales*—US$17.6 billion (2012).
Principal Competitors: Ford; General Motors; Hino; Honda; Mitsubishi; Nissan; Toyota

BRAND ORIGINS

- Under the name Tokyo Motors, the company began production of a truck under the nameplate Isuzu in 1938.
- During the 1950s Isuzu grew by becoming a supplier of industrial products to militaries around the world.
- In 1971 General Motors purchased a 34.2 percent share of Isuzu and began selling Isuzu's KB pickup truck in the United States in 1972.
- Rapid expansion hurt the brand and losses started to mount, including a loss of nearly US$500 million in 1991.
- By 2008 Isuzu's demise in the U.S. market was complete.

Isuzu Motors has its origin in a 1916 diversification plan undertaken by the Tokyo Ishikawajima Shipbuilding and Engineering Company. The company was established to build heavy ships but soon entered into a partnership with the Tokyo Gas and Electric Industrial Company to design cars and trucks. The partnership manufactured its first vehicle, the Type A truck, in 1918 and its first car, the A9, in 1922. Incorporated as Ishikawajima Automobile Manufacturing, Ltd in 1929, the company developed its first air-cooled diesel engine in 1934, helping to make it a leader in diesel technologies.

Under the name Tokyo Motors, the company began production of a truck under a new nameplate Isuzu (Japanese for "50 bells") in 1938. By this time, however, the military had gained control of the government and launched a war against China. As a result, Tokyo Motors came under government production plans and much of its output was earmarked for the military. Exposed to bombing raids during World War II, the company's production was disrupted until the war ended. Tokyo Motors was quick to recover from the war, however, and resumed production before the end of 1945. In 1946 the company introduced a new diesel truck called the TX80. According to Funding Universe.com, this product helped Tokyo Motors fund major investments in its facilities and expand the scope of its product research.

The company changed its name to Isuzu Motors, Ltd. in 1949. During the 1950s Isuzu was rebuilt as a company and as a brand first by supplying trucks, engines, and other industrial products to militaries around the world, with the US military one of its largest customers. The 1960s were a time of experimentation for the brand. In addition to launching several new successful truck models, the company attempted to equip an automobile with a diesel engine. While economical and reliable, the car was uncomely, noisy, and, ultimately, a commercial failure. Despite this failure, Isuzu introduced several new cars during the 1960s.

Although Isuzu was a recognized leader in the truck market, its rapid development of new models in the 1960s left it financially weakened. In 1971 General Motors purchased a 34.2 percent share of Isuzu, and Isuzu's KB pickup truck was sold through GM dealerships in the US beginning in 1972. General Motors saw the fuel efficiency of Isuzu models as a distinct competitive advantage in the American market. In 1976 GM started rebranding Isuzu vehicles under several of its other established nameplates, and in doing so displaced many of popular economical cars and trucks of the 1970s. However, due to a consumer revolt against little, underpowered vehicles, the Isuzu product line fell increasingly out of step with American tastes. Dismayed by the poor quality of many American models, consumers were drawn en masse to Toyota and Honda cars.

Isuzu's production for General Motors declined steadily from 1979 to 1981. Responding to what it felt was a loss of synergy with GM, Isuzu established its own dealer network in the United States, American Isuzu Motors. After an apparent power struggle which saw a GM attempt to partner with Honda and Suzuki instead, GM resolved to expand its relationship with Isuzu. The company established new contracts with GM, building a model called the Storm under an entirely new nameplate, Geo.

Isuzu's export sales surpassed three million units in 1986, but again, much of this growth occurred in Asian markets and was accounted for in truck sales. In fact, Isuzu became the world's largest truck manufacturer on a per-unit basis in 1987. The 1990s saw Isuzu expand into several developing markets, such as Thailand, Malaysia, and Egypt. Significant expansion led the brand to be spread too thin, and losses started to mount, including a loss of nearly US$500 million in 1991.

Isuzu's losses concerned General Motors, which owned 37.5 percent of the company at the time.

Therefore, Donald T. Sullivan was installed as executive vice-president of operations in 1992, the first non-Japanese speaking manager in a high position within a Japanese auto manufacturer. In addition to deciding on several innovative cost cutting measures, Sullivan determined that Isuzu was not profitably competitive in the automobile market and decided to focus on what Isuzu did best: trucks, recreational vehicles, and engines. These efforts appeared to have a positive effect on Isuzu's business, stemming losses while reversing a gradual decline in sales. By the end of Isuzu's 1993 fiscal year, the company reported a loss of only US$39 million. Although the 1994 fiscal year ended with even greater gains, Isuzu still carried a heavy debt burden, at US$7.4 billion.

While Sullivan helped Isuzu fit within General Motors' global strategy which led to a few hopeful ventures in the mid-1990s including a cooperative effort with Nissan, the brand's progress in the United States, however, was hurt in 1996 when *Consumer Reports* judged the Isuzu Trooper "not acceptable" due to what it suggested was a propensity to roll over. The National Highway Traffic Safety Administration found no proof of the magazine's claims. Still, the brand's name was damaged.

In order to rebound from the publicity damage in the U.S. and survive in this troubled economic climate throughout Asia, Isuzu began to seek ways in the late 1990s to strengthen its ties with General Motors. Since the company's diesel engine manufacturing operations offered it the greatest opportunity for long-term growth, Isuzu entered into a joint venture with GM in 1998, known as DMAX, to begin mass-producing diesel engines in the United States, with the aim of becoming the world's largest diesel engine manufacturer. To this end, GM invested US$456 million in Isuzu, increasing its stake in the Japanese automaker to 49 percent.

Still operating at a loss after the turn of the century, Isuzu began a series of radical streamlining efforts intended to reverse the company's poor financial performance. The efforts included relocating production facilities and cutting jobs; still, the losses were of grave concern to GM, which began to reconsider its relationship with the troubled Japanese firm. As part of a comprehensive recapitalization plan, Isuzu began the repurchase of its stock from shareholders, primarily GM, which reduced GM's 49 percent share to 12 percent. As part of this reorganization, GM gained full control of DMAX and Isuzu Motors of Poland, as well as ownership of all diesel engine designs from Isuzu.

Unfortunately, this fresh infusion of capital could do nothing to reverse the company's fortunes, and losses for the 2003 fiscal year were in excess of US$1 billion. Never recovering in the U.S. market, the company discontinued the Trooper model along with its two most popular models, the Axiom and the Rodeo, which comprised 71 percent of its total U.S. sales of slightly more than 27,000 units in 2004. This move left Isuzu with only two models in the U.S. market: the Ascender, a rebadged GMC

Envoy, and the i-series pickup truck, a rebadged Chevrolet Colorado. By 2005 Isuzu Motors America was primarily a distributor of medium duty commercial trucks and, due to its cuts and restructuring efforts, announced its first profit in years.

By 2006 Isuzu had repurchased all of its shares back from GM, and before the year was over the brand found a new investor, Toyota, which had a plan for Isuzu's reputable diesel engine technology. In 2008 Isuzu's demise on the U.S. market was complete, and the brand announced a complete withdrawal from the U.S. market by January 2009. In one of the greatest brand downfalls in American automotive history, the Isuzu brand went from selling a complete line of cars, trucks, and SUVs into being a specialized SUV maker, and finally selling only a pair of rebadged, General Motors trucks in less than a decade. Isuzu continues to sell commercial vehicles in the U.S. and has rebounded on the whole as the leading producer of trucks, engines, and buses of all shapes and sizes in the world.

BRAND ELEMENTS

- Isuzu means "50 bells" in Japanese. Originally derived from the Isuzu River, it has been the brand name since 1938.
- The logo is "Isuzu" in capital letters, usually red, with the "S" and "Z" rendered as mirror images of each other.
- A logo adopted in 1974 incorporated a graphic element: two pillars that were often placed inside a square or oval.
- An earlier logo featured a red circle with "Isuzu" in silver letters above a blue circle with Japanese symbols.

The brand derives its name from the Isuzu River, which flows past the Ise Shrine of Mie prefecture, the oldest shrine in Japan. Ishikawa Automotive Works introduced a car called the Isuzu in 1933, and five years later Isuzu was adopted as a brand name. By that time the firm was known as Tokyo Automobile Industries Co., Ltd. The company's name has been Isuzu Motors Limited since 1949. The word Isuzu is Japanese for "50 bells."

The brand's logo is "Isuzu" in capital letters, usually red, with the "S" and "Z" rendered as mirror images of each other. Previously the company used a two-pillar logo, a stylized representation of the first syllable in "Isuzu." This graphic symbol was sometimes done in black against a square background of tan, or in white against a red square with the word "Isuzu" in small letters beneath. Often the graphic symbol was positioned inside an oval, and sometimes the two in combination were placed above "Isuzu" in large black, brown, or red letters. This logo was introduced in 1974 to celebrate the brand's partnership with General Motors.

In its earlier days the brand had a round red logo with two wing-like projections and "Isuzu" written in silver letters that resembled Japanese script. Below the name was a blue circle with Japanese symbols and a curlicue border, both in silver.

BRAND IDENTITY

- Isuzu is positioned as a well-established brand known for innovation, reliability, and efficiency.
- The concepts of uncompromising excellence and respect for customers, society, and the environment are part of the Isuzu brand image.
- Isuzu wants to be known as the world's leading designer of diesel engines and vehicles that run on alternative energy.

Isuzu is positioned as a well-established, world-class brand, the first automaker in Japan, with a long history of delivering innovative, reliable, efficient vehicles, particularly diesel trucks for commercial uses. The firm emphasizes the concept of respect for its customers, for society, and for the environment. Isuzu, the company says, "is striving to gain the trust of each and every person around the world."

In addition, the corporate philosophy promises, "Isuzu will always mean the best." By aiming at excellence in business practices and in product design, the firm says it expects Isuzu to change global standards, to achieve "creation without compromise."

The company promotes Isuzu as the top brand in commercial vehicles and diesel engines, boldly accepting the challenge of global leadership while staying true to its traditions. For more than 50 years, Isuzu has been widely considered the leading designer of diesel engines. Looking to the future, Isuzu is presented as a modern, environmentally and socially responsible brand in the process of designing and launching efficient, low-emission vehicles, many of which will run on alternative fuels.

BRAND STRATEGY

- During the 1980s Isuzu's U.S. advertising starred David Leisure, a comedian who made outrageously false claims about the brand.
- Isuzu's current strategy emphasizes engineering, particularly the design of clean diesel engines.
- Isuzu is also striving to develop its line of low pollution alternative fuel vehicles.

In an effort to raise consciousness of the Isuzu name and boost sales of the company's trucks in the United States during the brand wars of the 1980s, Isuzu launched a revolutionary advertising campaign featuring the comedian David Leisure. The performer was portrayed as a spokesman named Joe Isuzu who made outrageously false claims about Isuzu products. A series of subtitles provided factual corrections as well as punch lines to Leisure's statements. The campaign easily could have failed had it not been for the comedian's wry delivery and obviously contrived smile. In one ad, Joe Isuzu concludes by saying, "May lightning strike me if I'm lying." At this point the actor is incinerated by a blinding light, leaving only a puff of smoke. Seconds later, the irrepressible spokesman falls out of the air and into the bed of an Isuzu truck. The ads were very effective in promoting Isuzu and launching Leisure's career, but they had only a limited impact on Isuzu's sales. In fact, the company experienced no significant gain in passenger car sales.

Isuzu's current strategy has returned to a focus on engineering. In emphasizing what it has done well for nearly a century, Isuzu is currently devoting its efforts to improving diesel technology, notably the design of clean diesel engines. Labeled by the brand as "its most critical management issue," diesel engine technology has presented manufacturers like Isuzu with difficulties to achieve progressively cleaner exhaust gas emissions. Isuzu is attempting to further improve the advantages of diesel engines, which include high performance and durability, while reducing their impact on the environment. In the process of its research and strategizing around engine technology, Isuzu is also working on low pollution alternative fuel vehicles, including Compressed Natural Gas (CNG) Vehicles, Dimethyl Ethel Engine (DME) Vehicles, Diesel Hybrid Vehicles, and advanced fuel cell vehicles, some of which are already on the roads across Asia.

BRAND EQUITY

- For decades Isuzu trucks have led their categories in markets including Japan, Hong Kong, Eqypt, Vietnam, and the United States.
- With a brand value of US$2.4 billion, Isuzu placed 485th on Brandirectory's list of "Top 500 Global Brands" in 2012.
- Isuzu's consolidated sales from April 2011 through March 2012 amounted to ¥1,400 billion (US$15.2 billion).

With Isuzu no longer manufacturing passenger cars and completely out of the U.S. consumer vehicle market, the brand largely exists as the leading commercial truck maker. While Isuzu still manufactures pickup trucks and SUVs, the brand does not compete as it once did with other vehicle manufacturers, given its increased attention to medium- and heavy-duty trucks and commercial buses.

The company reports that for several decades the Isuzu ELF was the leading light-duty truck in its category in Japan and Hong Kong. In 2009 it had 40 percent of the domestic market. Certain Isuzu trucks and pickups sold under the GM brand in Egypt have led the market there for more than 20 years. Isuzu N series light-duty trucks have about half of the market in Vietnam and are popular in many nearby countries. Isuzu N series vehicles are often used as delivery trucks in the United States, where they were number one in their category for 24 years and had 75 percent of the market in 2009.

Isuzu's placement on Brandirectory's "Top 500 Global Brands" may suggest that the brand is rebounding. After ranking 472nd on the list in 2008, Isuzu did not make the list at all for several years, then returned in 2012 in 485th position with a brand value of US$2.4 billion and a company value in excess of US$17 billion. In 15th place, rival Toyota had a brand value of US$24.5 billion, and Honda was 55th with US$15 billion.

In 2011 Isuzu sold more than 560,000 vehicles worldwide. Its consolidated sales from April 2011 through March 2012 amounted to ¥1,400 billion (US$15.2 billion), while nonconsolidated sales were ¥944 billion (US$10.3 billion).

BRAND AWARENESS

- Perhaps because of its focus on commercial vehicles, Isuzu seems to be engaging the general public less than other automakers.
- Auto racing and extensive dealer networks help keep Isuzu in the public eye.
- In a 2011 survey, U.S. consumers ranked Isuzu among the 10 worst automobile brands, far behind Toyota, Ford, and Honda.

Having changed its primary focus to manufacturing commercial vehicles, Isuzu does not appear to be engaging the general public as much as other automakers, or in the same way. The brand does enjoy publicity from its involvement in auto racing. The Isuzu D-MAX, for example, placed first among all diesel pickups in the Dakar 2009 Rally, the world's top rally competition. In addition, Isuzu is widely known in some countries because of extensive dealer networks and the service systems they provide.

Although Isuzu performs well in many countries, a 2011 survey by *Consumer Reports* found that U.S. consumers ranked Isuzu among the 10 worst automobile brands, with an overall brand perception score of 2. In first place, Toyota scored 147, Ford was second with 144, and Honda was third with 121. The ranking represented people's perception of the brand when scored across seven categories: safety, quality, value, performance, design/style, technology/innovation, and environmentally friendly/green.

Many studies of consumer perception, such as those conducted by J.D. Power and Associates, appear to no longer include Isuzu, even though the brand continues to manufacture pickup trucks and SUVs.

BRAND OUTLOOK

- Isuzu is expecting dramatic growth in emerging markets but little growth in developed countries such as the United States.
- Exports from China and Korea are expected to triple between 2007 and 2015, competing with Isuzu.
- Isuzu is developing fuel-efficient, eco-friendly cars, and futuristic vehicles that run on alternative energy.

In its mid-term business plan for April 2011 through March 2014, Isuzu predicted that in developed countries the market for automobiles would not grow substantially in the near future, due in large part to widespread economic recession. However, demand for vehicles was expected to continue increasing dramatically in emerging markets, which accounted for 41.3 percent of sales in 2007 and are expected to account for 61.4 percent of sales by 2015. Therefore, Isuzu intends to continue expansion into those countries, particularly in throughout Asia, while maintaining its current market share in developed countries.

The business plan also anticipates that exports by Chinese and Korean manufacturers will triple between 2007 and 2015, creating greater competition for Isuzu. In 2012 Isuzu entered India's fast-growing small commercial vehicle and multi-utility vehicle segment. In recent years the company has also strengthened its presence in Russia, Dubai, and Thailand.

Although Isuzu struggled to establish its own identity in the American auto market, the brand has continued to be successful in established Asian markets and developing markets around the globe. Isuzu Philippines Corporation, for example, exceeded its full-year sales for 2011 in less than eleven months in 2012, bucking the drop in industry sales. Isuzu's 11-month sales for 2012 were 22 percent higher than the 8,791 units sold in the same period in 2011.

As people buy more automobiles, demand for petroleum will increase, and so will demand for fuel efficiency and vehicles that operate on alternative fuels. In response, Isuzu has been developing new eco-friendly product lines and improving the performance of its diesel engines.

Now completely withdrawn from the U.S. consumer auto and truck market, Isuzu appears focused on what it has always done best: manufacturing diesel engines, trucks, and buses.

FURTHER READING

De Vera, Ben Arnold O. "Isuzu's 11-month sales exceed 2011 full-year performance." *Interacksyon Motoring,* December 19, 2012. Accessed December 22, 2012. http://www.interaksyon.com/motoring/isuzus-11-month-sales-exceed-2011-full-year-performance/.

"Ford Leads in the Factors That Matter Most to Car Shoppers." *Consumer Reports.* Accessed February 25, 2013. http://www.consumerreports.org/cro/cars/new-ars/news/2011/01/2011-car-brand-perception-survey/overview/index.htm.

Isuzu Motors. Tokyo: Isuzu Motors. Accessed December 18, 2012. http://www.isuzu.co.jp/world/corporate/about/global_02.html . 30 December 2012.

"Isuzu." *Brandirectory.* Accessed December 18, 2012. http://brandirectory.com/profile/isuzu.

"Isuzu Motors, Ltd. History." Funding Universe.com. Accessed December 21, 2012. http://www.fundinguniverse.com/company-histories/isuzu-motors-ltd-history/.

"Isuzu Motors Plans Rs 1000 Crore Plant in India." *The Economic Times (India),* July 18, 2012. Accessed December 22, 2012. http://www.ibef.org/artdisplay.aspx?cat_id=60&art_id=32062.

Isuzu North America Corporation. Accessed December 20, 2012. http://www.youtube.com/watch?v=J5IgatESU9A.

"Isuzu to Sever U.S. Sales Ties With GM." *Road & Track,* August 2, 2007. Accessed December 19, 2012. http://www.roadandtrack.com/rt-archive/isuzu-to-sever-us-sales-ties-with-gm.

Sarhan, Ayman. "Brand Repositioning Planning - DMAX (Saudi Arabia)." *Propaganda Advertising,* June 13, 2010. Accessed December 22, 2012. http://www.slideshare.net/101ayman/brand-repositioning-planning-isuzu-trucks-dmax-saudi-arabia.

ITAÚ

AT A GLANCE

Brand Synopsis: Itaú is a modern, reliable banking brand that promises steady growth through advanced technology, a full range of banking services, and a commitment to social and environmental responsibility.
Parent Company: Itaúsa (Investimentos Itaú S.A.)
Praça Alfredo Egydio de Souza Aranha 100
Torre Itaúsa, Parque Jabaquara
São Paulo, 04344-902
Brazil
http://www.itauunibanco.com.br/
Sector: Financials
Industry Group: Banks
Performance: *Market share*—25 percent of the Brazilian market (2011). *Sales*— US$422.52 billion in total assets (2011).
Principal Competitors: Banco do Brasil S.A.; Banco Bradesco S.A.; Caixa Economica Federal; Banco Santander (Brazil) S.A; HSBC Holdings Plc.; Banco Votorantim; BTG Pactuai; Banco Safra; Citibank; Banrisul; Deutsche Bank

BRAND ORIGINS

- The Itaú brand originated with Banco Central de Crédito, founded in São Paulo, Brazil, in 1945.
- In 1964 the company merged with a smaller firm, Banco Itaú, to form Banco Federal Itaú S.A.
- Itaú's brand grew rapidly because the company served urban areas during a time when many Brazilians were moving to cities.
- The Itaú brand was known primarily in Brazil until the 1990s, when the company began opening international offices.
- After merging with a primary competitor in 2008, Itaú became the largest nongovernmental bank in Latin America.

The Itaú brand traces its origins to Banco Central de Crédito (Central Bank of Credit), a financial institution founded in São Paulo, Brazil, in 1945. The firm started with only 10 million cruzeiros (US$513,000) in capital but doubled that within its first decade. Operating primarily in urban areas during a time when many Brazilians were moving into cities, the enterprise had grown to 30 branches by 1953, when its name was changed to Banco Federal de Crédito. In 1964 the business merged with a rural firm called Banco Itaú, forming Banco Federal Itaú S.A. Several large mergers followed, increasing the number of the company's branch locations to 561 nationwide by 1974 and making Itaú the second largest nongovernmental bank in Brazil.

During a period of economic turmoil in the 1980s, the bank more than tripled the number of its branches to accommodate customers who were transferring money every day in pursuit of the best interest rates. To halt rampant inflation, the government imposed strict regulations that forced many Brazilian banks to eliminate thousands of jobs, and Itaú's payroll dropped from 84,000 employees in 1988 to only 32,000 by 1996. Compensating for the loss of workers, the firm implemented technological improvements, including thousands of automated teller machines and an innovative telebanking network. This helped establish the brand's reputation for offering modern technology and excellent customer service.

In the mid-1990s Itaú operated more than 1,800 branches in 455 cities and claimed about 11 percent of the Brazilian retail banking market. During the decade the brand expanded internationally as subsidiaries were established in Argentina and other nearby countries and a few offices were opened in Europe and the United States. Affiliations with some of the world's largest and most influential banks helped Itaú diversify beyond retail banking and raise its brand awareness globally.

By 2005 Itaú had become the third-largest bank in Brazil, behind Banco Bradesco S.A. and Banco do Brasil. Three years later, Itaú merged with another of its primary Brazilian competitors, Unibanco, to form the largest privately operated bank in Latin America, employing about 100,000 people and calling itself "the global Latin American bank."

BRAND ELEMENTS

- The logo features "Itaú" in yellow letters on a navy blue square with rounded corners.
- The Itaú brand takes its name from the town of Itaú de Minas, the site of a bank absorbed by the conglomerate.
- After various mergers and name changes, the bank became Itaú Unibanco Holding S.A. in 2008.
- Itaú Unibanco is a subsidiary of Itaúsa, a huge parent company that controls numerous businesses.
- Itaú's parent company goes by a shortened name to emphasize the Itaú brand, which unites the entities that make up the conglomerate.

Itaú's logo features the name "Itaú" in yellow letters in the lower half of a navy blue square with rounded corners, often displayed against an orange background.

The brand was named after Itaú de Minas, a community in the state of Minas Gerais, the location of one of the first banks that became part of the corporation as it expanded. In 1964 Banco Itaú merged with Banco Federal de Crédito to form Banco Federal Itaú S.A. In 2008 the company merged with Unibanco (shortened from União de Bancos Brasileiros, which means "Union of Brazilian Banks") to create Itaú Unibanco Holding S.A., commonly known as Itaú Unibanco.

Itaú Unibanco is a financial institution operating as a subsidiary of a parent company that unites a large group of businesses under one umbrella. The parent company, Investimentos Itaú S.A., is commonly referred to as Itaúsa. This short form of the name was adopted to emphasize the Itaú brand, which remained the strong core of the conglomerate through several decades of mergers, acquisitions, and name changes.

Itaú Unibanco is a financial institution operating as a subsidiary of Itaúsa, a parent company first organized in 1966 to unite a group of businesses under the name Banco Federal Itaú de Investimentos S.A. The name was changed to Banco Itaú de Investimento S.A. in 1970, to Banco Itaú Português de Investimento S.A. in 1973, and then to Investimentos Itaú S.A. in 1974. At that time the organization was itself part of Instituições Financeiras Itaú, a holding company that controlled a group of more than 50 businesses. In 1991 the name was changed again to Investimentos Itaú S.A., commonly referred to as Itaúsa. This short form of the name was adopted to emphasize the Itaú brand, which had remained the strong core of the conglomerate through numerous mergers, acquisitions, and name changes.

BRAND IDENTITY

- Financial soundness, modern technology, and a full range of banking services are integral to the Itaú brand promise.
- Itaú emphasizes the word "sustainable" in its business structure and in its approach to the natural environment.
- Itaú describes itself as a "transformation agent" aiming to improve individuals, Brazilian society, and the world.
- The Itaú name is attached to various humanitarian endeavors that encourage a positive perception of the brand.

The Itaú brand is meant to convey a promise of steady growth, soundness, reliability, customer satisfaction, modern technology, and a full range of banking services for a wide variety of clients. The company also emphasizes the concept of sustainability in its business (ensuring that the brand will continue to perform well for clients, stockholders, and employees) and also environmental sustainability, to protect the planet. In 2011, for the seventh time, *Exame* magazine included Itaú Unibanco as one of the top 20 role model companies in its Guia Exame de Sustentabilidade (Sustainability Exame Guide). This was in recognition of the fact that when a business requested financing from Itaú, the bank first analyzed the social and environmental impacts of the proposed development.

Itaú is positioned as a forward-thinking brand that helps customers improve their financial status while also encouraging them to improve other aspects of their lives for the benefit of themselves and society in general. One of the brand's stated purposes is to be a "transformation agent," fostering literacy, cultural awareness, and concern for people and the natural environment. During the first half of 2012 Itaú Unibanco invested BRL84.3 million (US$31.1 million) in educational, cultural, and sports activities aimed at changing society. The conglomerate operates Fundação Itaú Social (Itaú Social Foundation), which launched a program called Itaú Criança (Itaú Child) in 2011 to encourage children to read. Funding was provided for 4,000 Bibliotecas Itaú Criança (Itaú Child Libraries) to distribute 400,000 books. The corporation also sponsors the Itaú-UNICEF Award to promote education in Brazil.

In 2011 Itaú Unibanco invested BRL53.3 million (US$19.7 million) in Itaú Cultural, an institute that promotes the visual arts, music, education, and culture. The organization has been in operation for 25 years and has partnerships with hundreds of television and radio stations. As manager of the historic Auditorium Ibirapuera in São Paulo, Itaú Cultural has exhibited the bank's various art collections and hosted numerous events that attracted more than 320,000 visitors during 2011.

BRAND STRATEGY

- The parent company Itaúsa remains focused primarily on banking but is also involved in such ventures as real estate.
- A large percentage of the conglomerate's businesses and products carry the Itaú brand name.
- Itaú Unibanco operates mostly in Latin America but has begun expanding its brand globally.

The Itaú brand name has been attached to various businesses, products, and services under the umbrella of the parent company Itaúsa. Although the conglomerate's interests have included insurance, building materials, chemicals, electronics, and real estate, its main focus has continued to be banking. The lead affiliate of the organization, Itaú Unibanco, provided assorted financial services under the Itaú name, in addition to other brand names.

The Itaúfone, Itaúfax, and Bankfone networks were launched for telebanking, and Itaú Bankline was created for online commerce. For consumer credit, the bank offered the Itaucard, and it also offered Hipercard, Redecard, and other cards via partnerships with other companies. This enabled Itaú Unibanco to lead the consumer credit segment in Brazil and to become a contender in Paraguay, Uruguay, Chile, Argentina, and Mexico.

By 2012 Itaú Unibanco had a presence in 18 foreign countries, mostly in Latin America but also in Europe, the United States, Dubai, and Asia. Among the first foreign subsidiaries were Banco Itaú Europa, Itaú Argentina (or Itaú Buen Ayre), and Itaú Bank (Cayman). Other subsidiaries have included Banco Francês e Brasileiro S.A., Itaú Corretora S.A., Itaúleasing S.A., Itaú Capitalização S.A., Itaú Bankers Trust S.A. (54 percent), and Itaúprevidência S.A.

BRAND EQUITY

- Itaú was rated as the most valuable brand in Brazil eight years in a row.
- The brand value of Itaú was an estimated BRL24.3 billion (US$9 billion) in 2011.
- Itaú Unibanco had a market value of BRL152.8 billion (US$56.4 billion) in 2011.
- In 2012 Itaú Unibanco was the largest private bank in Latin America and the 15th-largest bank in the world.

Interbrand, a brand valuation consultancy, calculated the brand value of Itaú at BRL24.3 billion (US$9 billion) in 2011, an increase of 18 percent since 2010. For the eighth year in a row, Interbrand rated Itaú as the most valuable brand in Brazil.

Banco Itaú had total assets of US$50.78 billion in 2003, which increased steadily to US$162.86 billion in 2007. After the merge with Unibanco in 2008, Itaú Unibanco claimed total assets of US$379.32 billion, which increased to US$422.52 billion in 2011.

Based on its market value of BRL152.8 billion (US$56.4 billion), Itaú Unibanco was the 8th largest bank in the world at the end of 2011, up from 10th place in 2010. By June 2012 the firm had dropped to 15th place, with a market value of BRL126.7 billion (US$46.7 billion).

In 2012 Itaú Unibanco was the largest privately operated bank in Latin America, with about 5,000 branch offices and other service centers. It led the industry in Brazil, with a market share of more than 25 percent. As the largest wealth manager in the country, Itaú had BRL110 billion (US$40.6 billion) in assets under management, an increase of 20 percent since 2010. *Banker* magazine ranked Itaú Unibanco number one in Latin America in 2012, with US$38.18 billion of Tier 1 capital. Banco do Brasil was second with US$32.33 billion, Bradesco was third with US$31.31 billion, and Caixa Economica was fourth with US$11.45 billion.

Parent corporation Itaúsa posted total sales of US$17.77 billion for the entire group of businesses in 2011, up from US$14 billion in 2010 and US$11.27 billion in 2009.

BRAND AWARENESS

- For three consecutive years, Itaú was the first brand customers recalled when asked to name a bank in Brazil.
- Itaú Unibanco won numerous awards in 2011, including bank of the year in Brazil and Latin America.
- The Itaú brand is promoted on Internet social networking sites, where it has many thousands of followers.

In 2011, for the third year in a row, a survey conducted by the Brazilian Advertisers Association and Consultoria Top-Brands found Itaú was "top of mind" in the banking category. This meant that when consumers were asked to recall the name of a bank, they most often thought of Itaú Unibanco.

Itaú Unibanco received many accolades in 2011, including Bank of the Year in Brazil and Latin America, an award administered by the *Banker* magazine. In its Top 1000 World Banks ranking, the *Banker* ranked Itaú Unibanco first in Brazil and 34th worldwide. *Carta Capital* magazine named Itaú Unibanco the most admired retail bank in Brazil and the sixth most-admired company of all types in Brazil. *Euromoney* magazine recognized Itaú's CEO, Roberto Setubal, as banker of the year. The British newspaper *Financial Times* and the International Finance Corporation (IFC), the financial institution of the World Bank, honored Itaú Unibanco as the World's Most Sustainable Bank in the FT/IFC Sustainable Finance Awards.

On Internet social networking sites, three million Facebook users indicated that they "liked" Itaú Unibanco; 80,000 were "following" Itaú in all of its profiles on Twitter; and 12,000 subscribed to Itaú's YouTube channels. The company promoted awareness of its brand on social networking sites by posting ad campaigns and tutorials on topics such as "The Responsible Use of Money," which received more than 20 million views in 2011.

BRAND OUTLOOK

- The Brazilian economy has remained stable despite the widespread recession that has devastated many other countries worldwide.
- Investors from economically distressed nations flooded Brazil with foreign money, threatening to destabilize the local currency.
- International banks have begun moving into Brazil and competing with the Itaú brand.
- The Itaú brand is expanding into Europe and other regions while maintaining slow, steady growth in Brazil.

While much of the world endured a deep economic recession that began in Europe in 2008, the economy of Brazil remained stable. Brazil's finance minister said in 2010 that the country was in an "international currency war" with the United States as the latter's economy floundered and, consequently, U.S. investors sought to harbor their money abroad. To slow the dramatic influx of foreign capital, which could have destabilized the Brazilian currency, the government imposed controls, including a higher tax on foreign ownership of financial assets. Nevertheless, the possibility remained that the global financial crisis could spread to Brazil.

By the end of 2011 Itaú Unibanco was anticipating that its brand would continue to prosper in Latin America, although it projected a growth rate of only 2 percent because the Brazilian economy had slowed. The Itaú brand also faced increasing competition from such foreign banks as Santander, Citibank, and Credit Suisse, which had begun to establish a presence in Brazil. Other foreign firms making preliminary moves to enter the region included Goldman Sachs, Bank of America Merrill Lynch, Royal Bank of Canada, and various Swiss enterprises.

As part of its own expansion abroad, in 2011 Itaú began establishing its brand in Colombia through the investment banking division Itaú BBA. Farther away, businesses such as Banco Itaú Suisse in Zurich, Switzerland, were opened to help Latin American clients with foreign investments. In 2012 it was announced that Banco Itaú BBA would join the International Forfaiting Association (IFA), where it would be represented by its subsidiary Banco Itaú BBA International, based in London.

FURTHER READING

"Banco Itaú S.A." *International Directory of Company Histories.* Ed. Tina Grant. Vol. 19. Detroit, MI: St. James Press, 1998.

"Banco Itaú Takes Top Market Spot in Brazil." *Global Banking News*, December 6, 2011.

Brand Finance. "Profile: Itaú." *Brandirectory*. Accessed October 15, 2012. http://brandirectory.com/profile/ita.

"Does Brazil Have a Credit Bubble?" *Banker*, April 1, 2011.

"Itaú Unibanco Flies through Turbulence after Banco do Brasil." *Euroweek*, June 17, 2011.

"Latin America's Top 100 Banks: Ranked by Assets in Millions of U.S. dollars, As of December 31, 2010." *Latin Trade*, September–October 2011.

"Ranking the Brands." RankingTheBrands.com. Accessed October 13, 2012. http://www.rankingthebrands.com/Brand-detail.aspx?brandID=1481.

"A Real Success Story." *Banker*, February 1, 2011.

"Top 1000 World Banks: Latin America—Colombia Rises in Latin Rankings." *Banker*, July 1, 2012.

JACK DANIEL'S

AT A GLANCE

Brand Synopsis: One of the top-selling whiskey brands in the world, Jack Daniel's remains strongly associated with its small-town roots in the American South.
Parent Company: Brown-Forman Corporation
850 Dixie Highway
Louisville, Kentucky 40210
United States
http://www.brown-forman.com
Sector: Consumer Staples
Industry Group: Food, Beverage & Tobacco
Performance: *Market share*—19 percent for Jack Daniel's Tennessee Honey in the flavored brown spirits category (2011). *Sales*—10.6 million cases worldwide (2011).
Principal Competitors: Bacardi Limited; Beam Inc.; Constellation Brands, Inc.; Corby Distilleries Limited; Diageo plc; Pernod Ricard S.A.

BRAND ORIGINS

- Jack Daniel's was founded in the mid-19th century by Jack Daniel, a native of Lynchburg, Tennessee.
- In 1866 Jack Daniel became the first whiskey maker to officially register his distillery with the federal government.
- In 1956 Jack Daniel's was sold to Brown-Forman Distillery Corporation, which in 2012 was still operating as the brand's parent company.
- By the early 21st century, Jack Daniel's had become the world's best-selling American whiskey brand, with 10.6 million cases sold in 2011.

Jack Daniel's, one of the world's most recognized whiskey brands, was founded in the mid-19th century by Jack Daniel in Lynchburg, Tennessee. As a child, Daniel had learned the secrets of sour-mash fermentation from Dan Call, a preacher and part-time whiskey distiller. Daniel eventually took over Call's business, soon discovering an underground cave spring that could act as a reliable, iron-free water source. The spring was situated close to hardwood sugar maples and rich agricultural lands, offering all the elements Daniel needed to make his whiskey.

The American Civil War broke out in 1861, and Daniel spread awareness of his whiskey brand by selling his Tennessee sour mash to Union and Confederate troops. After the war, Daniel acquired the cave spring and the 500 acres surrounding it, and in 1866 he became the first whiskey maker to officially register his distillery with the federal government, which had recently implemented a system for regulating and taxing the spirit industry. Soon after, all Jack Daniel's whiskey jugs were redesigned to include the phrase "The Oldest Registered Distillery in the United States."

Daniel was known for his small stature and big personality, and by the late 19th century he and his whiskey had become regional institutions. The distillery modernized and replaced its whiskey jugs with square bottles, an iconic symbol of the brand today. In 1906 Daniel deeded ownership of the distillery to his nephew Lem Motlow, although Daniel remained active in the business until his death in 1911.

Motlow and the Jack Daniel's brand faced serious challenges in the early 20th century, notably Tennessee's passing of a state-wide prohibition law in 1910, followed by the ratification of the 18th Amendment in 1919, which prohibited the manufacture and sale of alcohol throughout the United States. Even after Prohibition was repealed with the 21st Amendment in 1933, Tennessee remained dry until 1937, with some counties in the state continuing to prohibit liquor sales in the 21st century.

During Prohibition, Motlow focused on mule trading instead of alcohol production, an enterprise that helped him gain the capital necessary for plant renovation and expansion of the Jack Daniel's brand. After World War II, Motlow willed ownership of the business to his four sons, who ran the company until it was sold in the mid-1950s.

Motlow's sons increased sales of Jack Daniel's by word of mouth, regional advertisements, and some national advertising. Articles in the popular national magazines *Fortune* and *True* in the early 1950s also helped boost awareness of the brand. In 1955 the company announced a new "anti-Madison Avenue" marketing plan, which emphasized the brand's down-home Southern roots and long-standing relationship with the community of Lynchburg.

In 1956 Jack Daniel's became a wholly owned subsidiary of Kentucky-based Brown-Forman Distillery Corporation (later known simply as Brown-Forman Corporation). By the time of the sale, Jack Daniel's had already gained a national spotlight as the preferred whiskey of the "Rat Pack," a group of celebrity singers and actors that included Frank Sinatra and Sammy Davis, Jr. This association with Hollywood glamour gained Jack Daniel's even more popularity, but Brown-Forman did not have enough product to meet demand, and so, from the mid-1950s to the 1970s, the company sold Jack Daniel's on allocation.

By the time production caught up with demand, the Jack Daniel's brand was strong, with sales nearly tripling between 1973 and 1986. Following a few years of declining sales attributed to changing drinking habits among American consumers, Jack Daniel's renewed its solid sales track and began emphasizing marketing and sales overseas, eventually becoming one of the most popular liquor brands in the international marketplace.

In the late 1980s, to further expand its brand, Jack Daniel's began introducing new products, including the premium Gentleman Jack Rare Tennessee Whiskey and ready-to-drink beverages called Daniel's Country Cocktails. By 1991 Jack Daniel's had US$600 million in annual sales worldwide.

Jack Daniel's remained a market leader as it moved into the 21st century. By 2004 it had become the world's best-selling American whiskey brand, with worldwide sales reaching 10.6 million cases in 2011. The brand has continued successfully to introduce new products, including Jack Daniel's Tennessee Honey and the ready-to-drink beverages Jack Daniel's & Cola and Jack Daniel's & Ginger in 2011. In 2012 Jack Daniel's was Brown-Forman's top-selling and most prominent brand.

BRAND ELEMENTS

- In 1911 Jack Daniel's began using its distinctive black label with white lettering.
- The Jack Daniel's brand began using its iconic square bottle in 1895.
- In 2011 the Jack Daniel's black label was updated and simplified, while the square bottle was redesigned to be taller, slimmer, and more masculine.

Although Jack Daniel's had begun selling its whiskey in bottles by the early 20th century, it was not until 1911 that the brand began using its distinctive black label with white lettering. The black label was said to have been introduced to commemorate founder Jack Daniel's passing. The label for the brand's primary whiskey product, Jack Daniel's Tennessee Whiskey (also known as No. 7 Tennessee Whiskey or Old No. 7), originally included the Jack Daniel's name along with the words "Old No. 7 Brand," "Tennessee Sour Mash Whiskey," and the population of Lynchburg, Tennessee (at one time), 361. Other elements were added to the label over time, including the brand's claim of being the oldest registered distillery in the United States.

In 2011 the black label was updated and simplified in what the brand called a "refinement." Much of the extraneous text was removed, decluttering the label and making it more attractive to international consumers who are less likely to be interested in the brand's place in American history. The well-known black label has also been used on the packaging for other Jack Daniel's products, such as the aluminum bottles for Jack Daniel's & Cola and Jack Daniel's & Ginger, ready-to-drink products introduced in 2011.

Jack Daniel's whiskey is also known for its square bottle. Founder Jack Daniel made the switch from jugs to square bottles in 1895 to make his product stand out from other whiskey brands being sold at the time. The brand has used the square bottle since that time, except for a period during World War II when a glass shortage forced the company to use a round bottle. In 2011 the square bottle was redesigned to be taller and slimmer, with a more masculine silhouette and beveled corners.

BRAND IDENTITY

- Throughout its history Jack Daniel's has emphasized its connection to Lynchburg, Tennessee, where it began producing whiskey in the mid-19th century.

- Jack Daniel's has embraced alternative types of marketing and regularly seeks to associate itself with the music industry.
- By 2012 Jack Daniel's had more "fans" on its Facebook page than any other beverage alcohol brand.

From its earliest days, Jack Daniel's has emphasized its roots in the small town where it began producing whiskey in the mid-19th century. The brand's products, including Jack Daniel's Tennessee Whiskey, listed "Lynchburg, Tennessee" and its one-time population of 361 on their labels for decades. In 1955 the company launched a marketing campaign highlighting its heritage and long-standing relationship with the community of Lynchburg. The campaign's print ads included photographs showing how and where the whiskey was made, along with snapshots of real people from Lynchburg. The campaign lasted for decades, and by 2004 Jack Daniel's had run more than 1,000 ads in various media outlets featuring the small town where its whiskey is made.

Although Jack Daniel's did not regularly advertise on a national scale before the 1950s, the company has embraced many alternative types of marketing to effectively enhance its identity. Beginning in 1892, the company backed the Jack Daniel's Silver Cornet Band, a small band from Lynchburg that toured the United States, spreading the Jack Daniel's brand name in the process. The band was revived in 1978 and performed in cities across North America into the 1990s.

In the first decade of the 21st century, Jack Daniel's began focusing on music sponsorship and marketing opportunities in the United States and abroad to underscore its long-standing link with the music industry. In 2005 Jack Daniel's launched its Studio No. 7 music series, through which the company sponsored a number of concerts by unsigned musicians and bands from independent labels, later expanding the venture to include the Studio No. 7 Latino music series. Ideals like defiance and independence have also been cited in promoting the Jack Daniel's brand.

In recent years, Jack Daniel's has turned to the Internet and digital platforms for its marketing. By 2009 Jack Daniel's had joined popular microblogging service Twitter, and by 2012 the brand had 1.8 million "fans" on its Facebook page, more than any other beverage alcohol brand. In 2012 Jack Daniel's redesigned its website, which at that time was available in 185 countries.

BRAND STRATEGY

- In 1988 Jack Daniel's introduced Gentleman Jack Rare Tennessee Whiskey, its first new product in more than 100 years.
- Jack Daniel's entered the ready-to-drink market in 1992 by introducing Jack Daniel's Country Cocktails.
- Jack Daniel's Tennessee Honey, a blend of whiskey and honey liqueur, was introduced in 2011 and was immediately successful.
- By 2010 international markets accounted for almost half of Jack Daniel's sales.

Until the late 1980s, Jack Daniel's had only three products, all variations of its Tennessee Whiskey. In 1988 the distillery introduced its first new product in more than 100 years, Gentleman Jack Rare Tennessee Whiskey, an ultra-premium whiskey meant to appeal to female drinkers. To increase the new product's allure, Jack Daniel's severely limited production of the whiskey through the mid-1990s. Other new products followed, including Jack Daniel's Country Cocktails, a line of ready-to-serve beverages, in 1992, and Single Barrel Select, similar to a single-malt Scotch whiskey, in 1997. Jack Daniel's expanded its line of ready-to-drink beverages in 2011 with Jack Daniel's & Cola and Jack Daniel's & Ginger.

To further take advantage of strong growth in the spirits market, Jack Daniel's introduced Jack Daniel's Tennessee Honey, one of its most successful products, in the United States in 2011 and in select international markets in 2012 and 2013. The release of Tennessee Honey, a blend of whiskey and honey liqueur, was an attempt to broaden the audience for the Jack Daniel's brand, as its smoother, sweeter taste was designed to appeal to consumers who do not enjoy the taste of straight whiskey. Tennessee Honey immediately became a market leader in the flavored whiskey category in the United States and was the best-selling new spirits product in 2011, helping grow sales for the brand by 9 percent between 2010 and 2011.

Because of the strong growth of the international spirits market, Jack Daniel's has made a concerted effort to continue building its brand in its existing international markets and to introduce the brand to new markets. The 2011 simplification of the iconic Jack Daniel's black label, for example, was in part an effort to make the whiskey more attractive to international consumers who are uninterested in the brand's place in classic Americana. By 2010 nearly half of the company's sales were coming from outside the United States, and by 2012 Jack Daniel's was being sold on five continents. Although the brand and parent company Brown-Forman have struggled in Western Europe, where in recent years growth has been slower than in other markets, both companies have posted recent growth in Germany, the United Kingdom, and France. This growth has continued despite the brand raising its prices by 3 percent to 5 percent in 2012.

BRAND EQUITY

- By 2012 Jack Daniel's was one of the world's top-selling whiskey brands by volume, having sold 10.6 million cases worldwide in 2011.

- In 2012 Interbrand ranked Jack Daniel's 81st on its Best Global Brands list, giving it a brand value of US$4.4 billion.
- According to Brand Finance, in 2012 Jack Daniel's had a brand value of US$1.2 billion and ranked 10th on the Top 50 Brand Drinks list.

For decades, Jack Daniel's has been one of the world's top-selling whiskey brands by volume, and by 2004 it was the world's best-selling American whiskey brand. Worldwide sales of Jack Daniel's premium bourbon and Tennessee whiskey brands jumped 17 percent in 2010. The company sold 10.6 million cases worldwide in 2011, with nearly half of those sales occurring in international markets. In 2012 Jack Daniel's was the 19th best-selling liquor in the world.

Because of this success, Jack Daniel's enjoys a high brand value. In 2012 Interbrand ranked Jack Daniel's 81st on its Best Global Brands list, with a brand value of US$4.4 billion, an increase of 1 percent over 2011, the first year the company appeared on the list. In comparison, competitor Johnnie Walker was ranked 83rd on Interbrand's 2012 Best Global Brands list.

In 2012 Brand Finance gave Jack Daniel's a brand value of US$1.2 billion, a slight increase from 2011. Meanwhile, Jack Daniel's ranked 8th on Brand Finance's Top 50 Brand Drinks list in 2011 and 10th on the same list in 2012. Competitor Johnnie Walker, a Scotch whiskey maker, was first on the 2012 list, while Chivas Regal, also a maker of blended Scotch whiskey, was ranked fifth.

BRAND AWARENESS

- In the mid-1990s research sponsored by Brown-Forman showed Jack Daniel's to be a leader in top-of-mind awareness, unaided brand awareness, and total brand awareness.
- The Jack Daniel's brand is largely identified as distinctly American and is often associated with traits like authenticity, simplicity, and masculinity.
- In the 21st century, Jack Daniel's has used social media and mobile marketing to enhance its global brand awareness.

During the mid-1990s Jack Daniel's parent company Brown-Forman sponsored research showing that Jack Daniel's ranked first in the three all-important categories of top-of-mind awareness, unaided brand awareness, and total brand awareness. According to Brown-Forman, Jack Daniel's remains number one in brand awareness among liquor brands in the 21st century. The brand's classic Jack Daniel's No. 7 Tennessee Whiskey enjoys approximately 98 percent total brand awareness, and by the end of 2011, Jack Daniel's Tennessee Honey had 31 percent brand awareness, despite having been introduced in the United States that same year.

Jack Daniel's also holds a top position in global whiskey sales by volume, with sales continuing to increase as Jack Daniel's introduces its products in new markets. In the United States and other countries, the Jack Daniel's brand is most often perceived as being authentic, homespun, unpretentious, masculine, and uniquely American, qualities that have been reinforced by the brand's advertisements and marketing.

The company's brand recognition has also been enhanced by its global emphasis on social media, which includes an active presence on Facebook and Twitter. Jack Daniel's has also used mobile marketing, including a 2010 campaign that encouraged fans to scan mobile bar codes and sign a petition to make founder Jack Daniel's birthday a national holiday. Brand awareness has also been increased through the Jack Daniel's Studio No. 7 initiative, which presents exclusive-access shows for musicians across the United States. This sponsorship also serves to present Jack Daniel's as the drink of choice for musicians and music fans.

BRAND OUTLOOK

- Sales of Jack Daniel's were expected to continue to increase in the second decade of the 21st century.
- By 2012 Jack Daniel's had not emphasized developing markets like India and China, leaving it vulnerable to a loss in global market share.
- Jack Daniel's has implemented several environmental initiatives in recent years, including its support of the University of Tennessee Tree Improvement Program.

Sales of Jack Daniel's were expected to continue to increase in the second decade of the 21st century, due largely to the rapid growth of the spirits market globally and domestically. In recent years the brand has seen especially strong growth in Poland, Mexico, Russia, Turkey, and Australia.

Although Jack Daniel's has invested heavily in international markets in recent years, the brand has not yet put much focus on emerging markets like India and China, where growth in the spirits industry is expected to be strong for years to come. By focusing less on these markets and continuing to rely on overdeveloped markets, such as Western Europe and the United States, Jack Daniel's risks losing out on higher sales and revenues in the longer term.

In the United States and abroad, Jack Daniel's remains committed to the values of heritage, integrity, respect, excellence, and corporate citizenship. In 2010, in honor of the 150th anniversary of Jack Daniel's, parent company Brown-Forman announced a 10-year strategy called B-F (Building Forever) 150. The plan emphasized corporate responsibility, responsible drinking, and environmental sustainability. As a Brown-Forman brand,

Jack Daniel's will strive to be an environmental steward by encouraging conservation practices among its farmers, using less packaging, reducing overall waste, and expanding its reuse and recycling programs. Jack Daniel's has also partnered with the University of Tennessee Tree Improvement Program, which seeks to preserve and restore trees native to Tennessee, including the sugar maple.

FURTHER READING

"Best Global Brands 2012: Jack Daniel's." Interbrand. Accessed December 6, 2012. http://www.interbrand.com/en/best-global-brands/2012/JackDaniels.

Bird, Laura. "Preserving a Southern Tradition; Homespun Marketing, Like the Tennessee Squires International Mail Program, Have Made Jack Daniel's the Envy and Mystery of the Industry." *Adweek*, February 25, 2001.

Brown-Forman Corporation. "Enriching the Experience of Life: Corporate Responsibility Report 2011–12." Accessed December 6, 2012. http://www.brown-forman.com/_down/BF_CR_Report_2011-12.pdf.

Haig, Matt. "Jack Daniel's: The Personality Brand." *Brand Royalty*. London: Kogan Page, 2004.

"Jack Daniels." *Encyclopedia of Consumer Brands Volume 1: Consumable Products*. Ed. Janice Jorgensen. Detroit, MI: St. James Press, 1994.

Kim, Max. "It's Official: Jinro Soju Is the World's Best-Selling Liquor." *CNN Travel*, June 12, 2012. Accessed December 11, 2012. http://travel.cnn.com/seoul/drink/soju-most-sold-drink-world-930177.

Schreiner, Bruce. "Jack Daniel's Rolls out New Bottle for Black Label." Associated Press, May 16, 2011.

Shearman, Sarah. "Jack Daniel's to Boost Focus on Live Music Ties." *Marketing*, September 7, 2011.

Stengel, Jim. "Jack Daniel's Marketing Magic." *CNNMoney*, December 8, 2011.

Stout, Charles. "Four Principles of World Changing Brands: Creating Brands That Come to Life at Every Touchpoint." Interbrand. Accessed December 6, 2012. http://www.interbrand.com/Libraries/Articles/Interbrand_Four_Principles_Craig_Stout.sflb.ashx.

JOHN DEERE

AT A GLANCE

Brand Synopsis: Known for its leaping deer logo and green and yellow corporate colors, John Deere is a venerable American farming equipment brand that has been successfully extended to other products and markets around the world, embodying the values of integrity, quality, commitment, and innovation.
Parent Company: Deere & Company
One John Deere Place
Moline, Illinois 61265
United States
http://www.deere.com/
Sector: Industrials
Industry Group: Capital Goods
Performance: *Sales*—US$36.2 billion (2012).
Principal Competitors: Caterpillar Inc.; CNH Global N.W.; Kubota Corporation

BRAND ORIGINS

- Blacksmith John Deere became a manufacturer after inventing a new plow.
- Deere & Company was incorporated in 1868.
- The leaping deer trademark was introduced to help prevent copycat products.
- The Model D John Deere tractor was introduced in 1923.
- Deere began producing lawn care and gardening products during the 1960s.

The John Deere brand can be traced to a Vermont blacksmith of the same name who, because of difficult business conditions, moved to Grand Detour, Illinois, in 1836. It was there that he became aware of the problems that farmers encountered using cast-iron plows from the East that performed poorly in the soils found in the prairies. He invented a new type of plow, one that was polished and shaped to prevent the soil from clinging to the bottom. It was immediately embraced by midwestern farmers and laid the foundation for a manufacturing concern that he incorporated in 1868 as Deere & Company. Because manufacturing was conducted at a plant in Moline, Illinois, the plows were known as "Moline plows." To avoid the problem of copies, Deere registered his first trademark. It featured the name John Deere, "Moline, Ill.," and a picture of a deer leaping over a log—a visual pun on Deere's name. It was an image that would be modified over the years, but served as the enduring spirit of the brand.

Under the direction of Deere's son, Charles Deere, the company expanded into other lines of farm equipment. During the early 1900s the company increased its product list though a series of acquisitions. Soon, the animal-powered plows that had been Deere's core business for decades became outdated due to the rise of tractors. Deere sold third-party tractors until 1923, when it introduced its Model D tractor, ushering in the modern era for the company. As the century progressed, John Deere remained a prominent farm equipment brand in the United States. During the post–World War II economic boom Deere turned its sights overseas by establishing manufacturing operations in Canada, Western Europe, and Latin America.

During the late 1950s the John Deere brand was extended to construction and logging equipment. The company also recognized an opportunity in the vast suburbs that emerged during the postwar years. In 1963 the company began manufacturing lawn care and garden equipment. By the end of the decade the John Deere trademark could also be seen on chainsaws, hand tools, lanterns, and portable heaters. With the sale of farm equipment tailing off, Deere added to its construction equipment business during the 1970s. It also began selling snowmobiles, which were marketed with a tagline that would soon be applied to other Deere products: "Nothing runs likes a Deere."

The sale of farm equipment fell further during the early 1980s, when the agricultural sector fell into a deep slump. It was the sales of lawn tractors during this period that kept Deere afloat. At the turn of the 21st century Deere extended its brand on a number of fronts. Instead of focusing on the sale of farm equipment in North America, the company became more of a global company. Deere also paid more attention to the consumer sector. Through alliances with Home Depot and Lowe's, Deere opened up mass-market channels. During this period the company updated its iconic trademark, which was part of an effort to better manage the corporate brand on a global stage. Nevertheless, Deere remained committed to the core values that had been at the heart of the John Deere brand for well over 140 years.

BRAND ELEMENTS

- An African deer was used in the first John Deere trademark.
- The deer image underwent several changes since it was first introduced in 1876.
- The upgrade of the John Deere logo in 2000 depicted a deer jumping upward rather than landing.
- The "Nothing runs like a Deere" tagline was introduced during the early 1970s.
- John Deere green is closely associated with the brand.

The John Deere name is a key element of the John Deere brand. The patronym does not merely refer to the company's founder, it has since become associated with quality construction, performance, and durability. The leaping deer that was used in the company's first trademark and that became the dominant image of the corporate logo during the 19th and 20th centuries is a playful pun on the John Deere name while also reinforcing the brand's image of exceptional performance.

The deer image has changed over the years. The first incarnation in 1876 depicted an African deer leaping over a log. Later, a North American white-tailed deer rendered in more detail was used, along with the slogan "The Trade Mark of Quality Made Famous by Good Implements." The profile of the deer changed in 1936, when it became a solid silhouette. The deer's legs were now outstretched, creating a more powerful pose. The antlers were also adjusted in 1936, but a more significant change was made in 1940, when for the first time the antlers were turned forward. The 10-word slogan was dropped in 1937. Eventually, the phrase "Quality Farm Equipment" was employed, but it was eliminated in 1962, as Deer became known for products beyond agriculture. A more contemporary looking logo that featured a streamlined deer silhouette was introduced in 1968. It was used until 2000, when the deer image was refined further. The antlers were sharpened, the body made more muscular, and the front legs angled so that the deer was seen to be leaping upward rather than landing as in previous depictions.

The image of the John Deere brand is reinforced by the tagline the company has used since the early 1970s: "Nothing runs like a Deere." The phrase stakes a claim to high performance. Moreover, the tagline suggests that John Deere products are the best on the market, unmatched by the competition.

The John Deere brand is associated with the color green, so much so that the distinctive shade is known in many quarters as "John Deere Green." Distinctive colors were especially important in the farm equipment business, as each brand was strongly identified by a particular color. For example, International Harvester equipment was colored red and Ford equipment was blue.

As early as the 1800s Deere was painting its farm equipment in apple green, but because it did not finish well, the company switched to a bright green that was darkened as much as possible. Deere also uses yellow to provide highlights.

BRAND IDENTITY

- The John Deere brand reflects the corporate values of integrity, quality, commitment, and innovation.
- Consistent use of imagery implies integrity and commitment.
- The logo and tagline claim superior performance for John Deere products.
- John Deere earned a reputation for innovation that dates back to its founding.

John Deere has been reluctant over the years to alter one of the most iconic brands in the United States, maintaining that the company continues to espouse the core values that were handed down by its founder. They include integrity, quality, commitment, and innovation. The John Deere brand has been extended from the farming implement sector to construction products, logging products, and consumer goods. The brand has also expanded into new parts of the country beyond the midwestern United States, and made the transfer to countries across the globe. Across cultures, it is regarded as a premium brand.

The John Deere logo and "Nothing runs like a Deere" tagline reinforce the image the company wishes to convey. The leaping deer logo has remained relatively consistent since its introduction in 1876, lending a sense of stability to the brand, and with stability comes a feeling of integrity. The value of commitment is suggested as well. By remaining true to the outward elements of its brand—the logo, the slogan, and the corporate colors—Deere implies that it is also committed to its customers by providing them with the best products and service on the market.

The steady use of the green and yellow color scheme brings further consistency to the brand. The slogan "Nothing runs like a Deere" asserts that the performance of John Deere products is unmatched. The deer itself brings certain qualities to the brand as well. The deer is known for speed, agility, and grace. Even though these are not traits generally associated with farm equipment or other John Deere product lines, the brand benefits from this positive connection.

The idea of innovation has been at the heart of the brand since the beginning. The company was founded on an invention, a revolutionary new plow design. John Deere continued to refine his plow by tailoring it for different soil types. That inventive spirit was carried on after his death, as Deere & Company maintained its image as an innovative company. During the 1930s Deere introduced a combination unit that allowed a single farmer to bed, plant, and fertilize cotton 10 times faster than four men working with four mules. Later, the company brought advances to construction and logging equipment as well as to consumer products. As a result, John Deere enjoyed a well-earned reputation in the marketplace as a trustworthy premium brand, one that was justified in charging a higher price than most of its competition.

BRAND STRATEGY

- The original trademark was developed out of necessity.
- John Deere has taken a conservative approach to marketing throughout its history.
- A global branding strategy was adopted at the turn of 21st century.
- The latest logo features a deer jumping upward rather than landing.

Deere has generally taken a conservative approach to its brand strategy. For the most part, the John Deere brand evolved organically throughout the company's history. The trademark featuring a deer image was registered in 1876 primarily to ward off competitors selling so-called Moline plows. By placing the John Deere brand on the implements, the company protected its place in the market. The use of green also helped to distinguish Deere's products, but the shade was not selected with the kind of care taken by a focus-group culture of later generations. Changes to the John Deere imagery were seldom made, and marketing efforts were conservative as well. The company mostly relied on its distribution network to promote John Deere products.

Deere had been involved in construction and logging equipment for a number of years before it dropped the "Quality Farm Equipment" slogan from its logo in 1962, at a time when the brand was extended to lawn and garden care equipment. Early in the following decade the "Nothing runs like a Deer" slogan was first used to market a new John Deere snowmobile, which was part of a continued diversification effort that saw the John Deere name applied to a diverse group of new products. In the final years of the 20th century John Deere became involved in the mass market through an agreement with Home Depot to provide three midpriced lawn tractors. They were the first John Deere products to be sold outside of the dealership network, albeit they bore the Scotts brand. At the turn of the 21st century John Deere–branded products were being sold at Home Depot as well as at Lowe's.

Following World War II the John Deere brand was taken to a number of new countries. It was not until the 21st century, however, that Deere pursued an aggressive global strategy. As part of that effort, the company updated its leaping deer trade mark, altering the image while placing a greater emphasis on the John Deere name. Instead of landing, the deer was now leaping upward, suggesting that the company was itself leaping into the new millennium with the goal of seizing new opportunities.

BRAND EQUITY

- Revenues approached US$36.2 billion in 2012.
- With a brand value of US$3.6 billion, John Deere ranked number 296 on the Brand Finance list of the 500 most valuable global brands in 2012.
- Interbrand lists John Deere as number 85 on its "Best Global Brands 2012."
- *Forbes* ranks John Deere 89th on its 2012 list of the "World's Most Powerful Brands."

Brand equity is important to the fiscal health of Deere & Company, allowing it to command a higher price point than many of its competitors. Exactly how much a difference is difficult to determine, but brand equity plays an important role in the US$36.2 billion in revenues the company generated in 2012. The company's new global brand strategy also appeared to be paying dividends, given that net sales in 2000 were little more than US$11 billion.

The overall value of the John Deere brand has been calculated by outside parties. Brand Finance, a brand evaluation consultancy, assigned a brand value of US$3.6 billion to John Deere in 2012. It was performance that gave John Deere the 296th position on Brand Finance's list of the 500 most valuable global brands in 2012. It was a marked improvement over the previous year, when John Deere ranked 343th. Brand consultancy Interbrand uses its own methodology to determine brand value. It estimates that the John Deere brand is worth US$4.2 billion, giving John Deere the 85th position on its "Best Global Brands 2012" list. On the *Forbes*'s ranking of the "World's Most Powerful Brands," John Deere was listed at number 89 in 2012, with a brand value of US$5.7 billion.

BRAND AWARENESS

- John Deere enjoyed a 17 percent worldwide market share among the world's top lawn and garden equipment makers in 2010.
- The song "John Deere Green" revealed strong brand awareness.
- John Deere boasts 2 million Facebook and Twitter fans.

Doing business in more than 160 countries in North America, Latin America, Europe, and Asia, John Deere enjoys strong global brand awareness. Among the top lawn and garden equipment makers in the world in 2010, according to Freedonia Group, John Deere enjoyed a 17 percent market share, trailing only Husqvarna with 18 percent. In the United States, the John Deere name has been part of the culture for over 140 years. The John Deere logo is instantly recognized by most people, and the brand is widely associated with the color green. In 1993 the country music singer Joe Diffie recorded the song "John Deere Green," which became a hit. Prior to its release, Diffie approached Deere & Company about creating a promotion around the song that told of a farm boy who climbed a water tower to profess his love for his high school sweetheart by painting a heart in "John Deere Green." The company declined the offer as it did similar requests over the years.

Even though Deere & Company has been careful about managing the John Deere brand, it has not avoided newer forms of marketing, such as social media. In 2011 the company used Facebook in its "Can Do" project, which raised awareness of the role that farmers and ranchers play in providing food for a growing world population. Hundreds of thousands of cans were collected to build a full-sized replication of a John Deere combine. The effort helped establish a fan base of 2 million on Facebook and Twitter, another indication of strong brand awareness in the U.S. market.

BRAND OUTLOOK

- In the United States, suburbanites join farmers as John Deer enthusiasts.
- Deere & Company enjoyed a strong sales surge during the first decade of the 21st century.
- Brazil, China, India, and Russia offer future opportunities for John Deere products.

John Deere has been a well-known and successful brand for over 140 years. Even though its roots are deepest in the United States among the agriculture sector, the brand is well known to a broader segment of the population because of its strong brand image and expansion into new product categories. John Deere is also well known in most of the world, spurring a growth surge during the new century as revenues grew almost threefold between 2001 and 2011.

In the United States, John Deere will likely continue to grow its presence into mass channels through Home Depot and Lowe's and build brand loyalty with suburban property owners who buy mowers and garden equipment for their lawns. In foreign markets, John Deere appeared poised to enjoy increasing sales for its construction equipment, especially in markets such as Brazil, China, India, and Russia, where demand was beginning to climb. There was every reason to believe that the leaping deer logo and John Deere green would continue to resonate with consumers around the world for many years to come.

FURTHER READING

Beeler, Amanda. "Deere Goes beyond Famed Brand to Cultivate Ties with Customers." *Advertising Age*, May 22, 2000.

Bond, Patti. "Where Deeres and Homeowners Play." *Atlanta Journal-Constitution*, November 7, 1998.

Bluth, Andrew. "Old Colors Won't Fade in Tractor Deal." *New York Times*, May 23, 1999.

Brand Finance. "Global 500 2012." *Brandirectory*. Accessed January 9, 2013. http://brandirectory.com/league_tables/table/global-500-2012.

"Deere & Company." *International Directory of Company Histories*. Ed. Jay P. Pederson. Vol. 21. Detroit, MI: St. James Press, 1998.

Frazier, Mya. "John Deere Cultivates Its Image." *Advertising Age*, July 25, 2005.

Magee, David. *The John Deere Way*. Hoboken, NJ: John Wiley & Sons, Inc., 2005.

"Top Lawn & Garden Equipment Makers Worldwide, 2010." *Market Share Reporter*. Detroit, MI: Gale. 2012.

"2012 Ranking of the Top 100 Brands." Interbrand. Accessed January 9, 2013. http://www.interbrand.com/en/best-global-brands/2012/Best-Global-Brands-2012-Brand-View.aspx.

JOHNNIE WALKER

AT A GLANCE

Brand Synopsis: The best-selling blended scotch whisky brand in the world, Johnnie Walker is associated with qualities like masculine success and personal progress, especially through its iconic Striding Man logo.
Parent Company: Diageo plc
Lakeside Drive, Park Royal
London NW107HQ
United Kingdom
http://www.diageo.com/
Sector: Consumer Staples
Industry Group: Food, Beverage & Tobacco
Performance: *Market share*—Johnnie Walker is the number-one selling scotch whisky in the world and the best-selling spirit by value (2012). *Sales*—19 million volume units (2012).
Principal Competitors: Chivas Regal; Clan MacGregor; Cutty Sark; Dewar's; Inver House; Scoresby

BRAND ORIGINS

- Johnnie Walker has its roots in Scotland in a grocery store founded by John Walker in 1820.
- The brand's whiskies were introduced to the American market in the 1880s.
- By 1945 Johnnie Walker was the best-selling brand of scotch whisky in the world.

Johnnie Walker has its roots in a grocery store in Kilmarnock, Scotland, opened by John Walker in 1820, from which he sold spirits. For two decades Walker focused on local sales, primarily of single malt whiskies distilled by an independent maker. The business grew after a railway to the south opened in 1843 allowing access to the English market. After Walker's son Alexander joined the business in 1856, they moved into the wholesale whisky business. In 1857, after the death of John Walker, Alexander changed the production process when the Walkers adopted a new vatting process in which as many as 40 single malt whiskies were blended with neutral grain whiskies to produce a milder product with a more standardized taste.

During the 1880s Alexander Walker moved his family's whisky into markets in the United States by consigning its product via merchant vessels. To capture the English market, he opened an office in London. After Alexander Walker's death in 1889, his son, also named Alexander, became the head of John Walker and Sons. Assisted by James Stevenson, the pair transformed the brand.

In 1908 the Johnnie Walker brand name came into use along with the Striding Man logo and the slogan "Born 1820, still going strong." At the same time, the pair renamed its primary whiskies Johnnie Walker Red Label and Johnnie Walker Black Label. Between 1908 and the outbreak of World War I, the Johnnie Walker brand expanded very quickly. By 1914 Johnnie Walker had become the largest blender and bottler of scotch whisky in the world.

In the United States Prohibition was the era during which scotch whisky became dominant and associated with prestige. Johnnie Walker was exported to Canada, the British West Indies, and the Bahamas in this time period and regularly smuggled into the United States. By the 1920s Johnnie Walker was available in more than 120 countries. Walker and Stevenson floated John Walker & Sons Ltd. as a public company in 1923, then became a subsidiary of the dominant Distillers Company Limited (DCL) in 1925. In the 1930s Johnnie Walker was granted the Royal Warrant by King George VI.

Due to World War II in the early 1940s, the British government prohibited all distilling until 1949, while rationing of grain to distillers continued until 1953. Despite the impact on production, Johnnie Walker was the best-selling brand of scotch in the world by 1945. When John Walker & Sons was able to resume full-scale production, the United States was in the midst of a postwar economic boom in which scotch whisky, especially Johnnie Walker Black, was embraced as a sign of success.

From the early 1960s to the mid-1970s, Johnnie Walker was the number-one whisky in the world. Despite a lack of global marketing and the threat of new competitors, Johnnie Walker sales remained strong. The brand remained dominant until the mid-1970s, when American whisky became more popular than scotch whisky and a glut of scotch whisky led to lower prices and harmed its prestigious image.

Johnnie Walker's position and sales were somewhat revived after it was sold to Guinness PLC, the conglomerate that produced Guinness Stout, in 1986. Under new management, Johnnie Walker whiskies were marketed as status symbols. By the 1990s new advertising campaigns in the United States boosted Red Label into third place and Black Label into ninth among scotch whiskies. New whiskies were also introduced.

Though sales of blended scotch remained in a long-term decline from the 1980s and into the first years of the 2000s, Johnnie Walker sales generally remained strong. In the late 1990s Black Label became the number-one scotch whisky in its category. Johnnie Walker remained atop the world's scotch brands, though blended scotch whiskies lost 20 percent of its sales volume as young drinkers embraced clear liquors. To attract new, young liquor drinkers, the brand launched an effective global campaign, "Keep Walking," in 1999.

In the first decade of the 21st century, interest in scotch whisky was further revived by emerging markets like India and China. Though the worldwide economic downturn that began in late 2007 impacted consumer purchasing, scotch whiskies gained momentum. By 2012 there was a widespread resurgence in scotch whisky, and Johnnie Walker remained a market leader.

BRAND ELEMENTS

- Johnnie Walker whiskies are sold in distinctive square bottles designed by Alexander Walker.
- Johnnie Walker labels are angled at 24 degrees.
- In 1909 the brand began labeling its whiskies by color, beginning with Red Label and Black Label.

Nearly all Johnnie Walker whiskies are packaged in a distinctive square bottle closely identified with the brand. This bottle was designed by Alexander Walker and features a tall, slim body with a short neck. Introduced in 1870, it became standard across all of Johnnie Walker's blends in the 1920s. Its square shape was intended to protect the bottles when they were shipped.

Johnnie Walker's label is also distinctive. Johnnie Walker labels are applied at an angle of 24 degrees. Alexander Walker copyrighted the slanted label in 1877, and it became part of the brand's global identity. The original label registered by Walker was black and gold, similar to the one featured on Johnnie Walker Black Label.

The colors of Johnnie Walker's labels have become not only a key element of the brand but the name of the product as well. By the early 20th century, Johnnie Walker had three whiskies: Old Highland Whisky, Special Old Highland, and Extra Special Old Highland. Each one had its own colored label of white, red, and black, respectively. Customers began calling the whiskies by the color of the label, and the brand adapted the consumer practice. By 1909 the brand had made the switch and renamed its primary whiskies Johnnie Walker Red and Johnnie Walker Black. When new blends were introduced, new colors were added, including Gold, Blue, and Green.

When the Johnnie Walker brand name was introduced in 1908, it was accompanied by a poster painted by Tom Brown depicting a striding man who held a cane and wore a top hat, morning coat, and white trousers. This image of the Striding Man, along with the registered trademark slogan "Born 1820, still going strong," was found on Johnnie Walker bottles and in advertising through the early 21st century.

BRAND IDENTITY

- Scotch whisky is identified with masculine success, which is emphasized in Johnnie Walker's ads.
- Johnnie Walker introduced its "Keep Walking" campaign in 1999 to appeal to young drinkers.
- Johnnie Walker has sought to raise brand awareness by sponsoring elite sports like golf and Formula One racing.

For much of the 20th century, the drinking of scotch whisky was associated with masculine success. Originally this type of achievement meant being a successful businessman in the United States, for example. Johnnie Walker's advertising campaigns in the United States in the mid- to late 1960s reflected these values with slogans like "the luck of the Scotch" for Red Label and "Put your friends on 'Black' list" and "A small way of paying yourself back for all the years of struggle it took to get where you are" for Black Label.

As scotch whisky sales declined, Johnnie Walker continued to emphasize the link between scotch drinking and success. However, beginning in the late 1990s through the early 21st century, the definition of success was broadened to appeal to young drinkers to emphasize the spirit of progress. Concepts like maverick entrepreneurs, personal advancement, self-improvement, being a better man, and weathering obstacles became associated with the brand.

Johnnie Walker's advertising strategy reflected these changes in its first global branding campaign, "Keep Walking," which played on the concept of the Striding Man. Johnnie Walker later personalized the campaign for various markets. In 2003 in the United States, for example, a version of "Keep Walking" focused on life as a journey and Johnnie Walker as a product that could help drinkers navigate the uncertainties of that expedition.

Because of declining sales in Europe and a desire to appeal to a wider, international group of drinkers, especially in emerging markets in Africa, South America, and Asia, Johnnie Walker pursued new strategies. The brand partnered with HanHan, an influential Chinese blogger, and added its first Latino spokesperson, DJ Alex Sensation. In 2012 Johnnie Walker launched My Label Is Black, a social and support program in the United States that targeted the Hispanic community.

Johnnie Walker also linked its brand with sports associated with quality and elite status. Johnnie Walker had long been involved with Formula One (F1) racing, a sport popular in Europe among the wealthy but also growing in China. In 2005 Johnnie Walker partnered with F1 Team Vodafone McLaren Mercedes and in 2012 sponsored F1 driver Lewis Hamilton. The whisky was also identified with golf, a sport invented in Scotland, by sponsoring the Johnnie Walker Classic in Asia and the Johnnie Walker Championship in Scotland.

BRAND STRATEGY

- As scotch whisky sales declined, Johnnie Walker began introducing new whiskies like Blue Label, Green Label, and Gold Label in the early 1990s.
- The brand created excitement by introducing limited edition and one-off whiskies like King George V and Double Black.
- Johnnie Walker's campaign, "Where Flavor Is King," was intended to expand the brand's growth in emerging markets.

When Johnnie Walker officially became the brand name in 1908, the whiskies were identified by their label color. The first Johnny Walker scotch whiskies were Red Label and Black Label, and they still form the core of the Johnnie Walker brand and much of its sales. When scotch whisky sales began declining, Johnnie Walker began introducing new whiskies to broaden its brand line-up, appeal, and price points beginning in the early 1990s. In 1992 Blue Label, comprised of rarer whiskies blended in the style of John Walker, made its debut. Gold Label, which hit the market in 1995, was based on a special blend created for the brand's 100th anniversary in 1920. Green Label, introduced in 1997, featured malts without a grain base. In 2012 Platinum Label, another 18-year-old scotch whisky, was launched.

Johnnie Walker also created excitement among drinkers by introducing variations on Black, Blue, and Gold and creating one-off, limited edition, and regional scotch whiskies. Double Black, which debuted in the United States in 2011, was a popular limited edition whisky that amplified the style of Black. Gold Label Reserve, launched in 2012, was intended to appeal to non-whisky drinkers as the blend was more accessible and intended to be used for celebrations.

Johnnie Walker sought to sell all of its whiskies not only in established markets but also in emerging markets in the Asia-Pacific region, South America, and the Middle East. Though Johnnie Walker already controlled 30 percent of the Chinese market by 2012, it opened Johnnie Walker Houses in Shanghai and Beijing. These facilities featured a bar, museum shop, and exclusive membership and represented but one of the strategies intended to increase Johnnie Walker's presence in high-growth markets in the Asia-Pacific region.

Johnnie Walker also sought to appeal to the international market with a new global advertising campaign introduced in the fall of 2012. "Where Flavor Is King" emphasized and explained the many flavors found in the various blends of Johnnie Walker. The campaign targeted those who found Johnnie Walker whisky daunting, especially in emerging markets in Africa, Asia, and South America. The campaign had an accompanying Facebook app which explained the flavors and composition of the whiskies.

BRAND EQUITY

- In 2012 Johnnie Walker was considered one of the most valuable brands in the world.
- Interbrand ranked Johnnie Walker 83rd in its 2012 list of the best global brands.
- Johnnie Walker was ranked number one in the Just-Drinks/IWSR *Top Performing Spirits Brands* report.

By 2012 Johnnie Walker was the number-one premium scotch whisky and number-three premium spirit brand in the world. The scotch whisky enjoyed a high brand value. According to Brand Finance's 2012 list of the top 500 global brands, Johnnie Walker was the 484th most valuable brand in the world, though it had not been ranked in 2011. Its brand value was an estimated US$2.43 billion, while its enterprise value was US$11.74 billion. It also had a brand rating of AAA. On Interbrand's 2012 list of the best global brands, Johnnie Walker ranked 83rd, with a value of US$4.30 billion, an increase of 12 percent over the previous year.

In the Just-Drinks/IWSR second annual *Top Performing Spirits Brands* report, released in 2012, Johnnie Walker was ranked number one among 124 spirits brands. It received a number-one ranking in 2011 as well. In 2011 Johnnie Walker scored 4.19 out of a possible 5 in terms of brand strength and was seen as the brand with the most growth potential. In 2012 it scored 4.65 out of 5 and was named the most innovative scotch whisky brand by industry professionals. Johnnie Walker's wide geographic presence helped generate brand equity and provide new avenues for growth.

BRAND AWARENESS

- Johnnie Walker's Striding Man was one of the first global advertising icons.
- The Keep Walking campaign, launched in 1999, led to higher sales and greater brand awareness.
- In 2012 Johnnie Walker enjoyed 90 percent brand awareness among Thai drinkers.

For nearly a century, Johnnie Walker has been considered one of the most famous and most valuable brands in any category in the world. Its Striding Man became one of the first global advertising icons. The Keep Walking campaign, launched in 1999, capitalized on the brand's already high awareness ratings among consumers.

In 2003, when Johnnie Walker launched a new Striding Man campaign related to Keep Walking, it wanted to increase awareness of the Striding Man as a brand logo. Only 22 percent of consumers knew of the logo's connection to Johnnie Walker before the campaign, while 50 percent made the connection after the ads had been running for three months. Five years later, the Striding Man campaign won the Grand Prix at the 2008 IPA Effectiveness Awards, which honors campaigns that show commercial payback. Between 1999 and 2008, sales growth grew 48 percent as a result of the Keep Walking campaign and its variants.

Even in its smallest markets, Johnnie Walker has enjoyed high brand awareness. By 2012 more than 90 percent of Thai drinkers knew the brand, which has been sold in Thailand for more than a century. Despite its small size, Thailand is the third-largest market for Johnnie Walker in the world. As Interbrand remarked in its *Best Global Brands 2012,* "The brand's simple and elegant architecture translates into a clear differentiation from its competitors and strong understanding by consumers."

BRAND OUTLOOK

- Johnnie Walker saw worldwide volume growth of 17 percent between 2007 and 2012.
- North America remained Johnnie Walker's largest market, but the brand expects its strongest future growth to occur in the Asia-Pacific region.
- More than half of Johnnie Walker's sales in the Asia-Pacific region come from Thailand.

After decades of declining sales, the demand for scotch whisky finally began to rise, especially in the second decade of the 21st century. Available in 200 countries around the world, Johnnie Walker is the number-one scotch whisky in the world, with sales of more than US$5 billion in fiscal 2011 and volume growth of 17 percent between 2007 and 2012. It is positioned to take advantage of growing interest not only in established markets in the United States, Canada, and France but also in emerging markets like India, Brazil, Russia, China, South Africa, Kenya, Nigeria, Ghana, and various countries in the Middle East. Though North America remained Johnnie Walker's largest market, the brand has worked to increase sales worldwide.

A growing economy, boosted earnings, high purchasing power, and a desire for luxury products especially in the Asia-Pacific region are expected to lead to growth in sales for Johnnie Walker. By 2012 the brand controlled 30 percent of China's scotch whisky market by volume, a figure that is only expected to grow, in part because of the investments Johnnie Walker has made in the region. About 12 percent of Johnnie Walker's global sales came from the Asia-Pacific region in 2012, and that figure was expected to increase to 20 percent by 2015 as various brand investments come to fruition. More than half of Johnnie Walker's sales in the region come from Thailand, which remains a market with room for further growth.

FURTHER READING

Brand Finance. "Global 500 2012." *Brandirectory.* Accessed March 12, 2012. http://brandfinance.com/images/upload/bf_g500_2012_web_dp.pdf. Accessed December 18, 2012.

Carpenter, Julie. "Whisky Galore!: Scotch Has Become a Multi-Billion-Pound Boom Industry as Britain Rolls Out the Barrel for an Ever-Growing Global Market." *The Express,* June 8, 2012: 39.

Cooper, Ben. "Johnnie Walker Heads IWSR/just-drinks Rankings for Second Year." *Just-Drinks,* Oct. 8, 2012. Accessed October 8, 2012. http://www.just-drinks.com/news/johnnie-walker-heads-iwsrjust-drinks-rankings-for-second-year_id108299.aspx.

Interbrand. "Johnnie Walker." *Best Global Brands 2012.* Accessed December 18, 2012. http://www.interbrand.com/en/best-global-brands/2012/JohnnieWalker.

Jitpleecheep, Pitsinee. "It's Official: Thais Love Johnnie Walker." *Bangkok Post* (Thailand), October 18, 2012. http://www.bangkokpost.com/learning/learning-from-news/317667/johnnie-walker-thailand-3rd-in-world.

"Johnnie Walker." *Great Whiskeys: 500 of the Best from Around the World.* Ed. Charles Maclean. New York: DK Publishing, 2011, 206-07.

"Johnnie Walker Launches New Ad Campaign." *Beverage World,* September 10, 2012. Accessed December 18, 2012. http://www.beverageworld.com/articles/full/15285/johnnie-walker-launches-new-ad-campaign.

Lane, Mark, and Rebecca Stanfel. "Diageo plc." *Encyclopedia of Major Marketing Campaigns.* Vol. 2. Detroit: Gale, 2007. *Gale Virtual Reference Library.* http://go.galegroup.com/ps/i.do?id=GALE%7CCX3446600084&v=2.1&u=itsbtrial&it=r&p=GVRL&sw=w.

Walsh, Dominic. "Johnnie Walker Rests the Striding Man." *Times* (London), September 10, 2012, 43.

Wankoff, Jordan. "Johnnie Walker." *Encyclopedia of Consumer Brands: Consumable Products.* Ed. Janice Jorgensen. Detroit: St. James Press, 1994, 287-89.

JOHNSON & JOHNSON

AT A GLANCE

Brand Synopsis: Although it boasts a wide array of products, the "Johnson & Johnson" brand is best known for medical supplies that focus on family health.
Parent Company: Johnson & Johnson
One Johnson & Johnson Plaza
New Brunswick, New Jersey 08933
United States
http:// www.jnj.com
Sector: Health Care
Industry Group: Pharmaceuticals & Biotechnology
Performance: *Market share*—Personal products, 3.5 percent; health care equipment and supplies, 7.48 percent; pharmaceuticals, 29 percent (2011). *Sales*—US$65 billion (2011).
Principal Competitors: Pfizer; Novartis; Merck; Abbott Laboratories; GlaxoSmithKline; Roche Holding; AstraZeneca PLC; Cipla, Ltd.; Procter & Gamble

BRAND ORIGINS

- Incorporated in 1887 Johnson & Johnson adopted the slogan "The Most Trusted Name in Surgical Dressings."
- The company's decentralized structure includes three segments: consumer products, medical devices and diagnostics, and pharmaceuticals.
- Johnson & Johnson's consumer segment was originally based on improving the health of women and children.
- Johnson & Johnson's medical devices and diagnostics and pharmaceutical divisions focus on treating heart disease, diabetes, orthopedic problems, cancer, and infectious diseases.
- Controversy over brand ingredients and manufacturing procedures has been addressed quickly to preserve consumers' trust in the Johnson & Johnson brand.

In the late 1800s Robert Wood Johnson invented ways to lower postoperative infections with sterile surgical dressings. In 1887 he and his brothers James Wood Johnson and Edward Mead Johnson incorporated a medical products company called Johnson & Johnson. The company, based in New Brunswick, New Jersey, specialized in sterile surgical dressings. In 1888 the company published its first book, *Modern Methods of Antiseptic Wound Treatment*, a publication that became a standard teaching text around the world. As Johnson & Johnson's reputation spread, the company adopted the slogan "The Most Trusted Name in Surgical Dressings."

Robert Wood Johnson II became CEO in 1932. He established a global, decentralized family of companies and conceived the company credo of responsibility to customers, employees, the environment, and the community. This credo remains at the core of company operations today. Johnson & Johnson was listed on the New York Stock Exchange in 1944.

Johnson & Johnson expanded to Canada in 1919 and to the United Kingdom in 1924. By the mid-1980s Johnson & Johnson had increased the number of affiliations, with locations in Mexico, South Africa,

Australia, China, and Egypt. Per Johnson & Johnson's 2011 annual report, the company has grown to encompass 250 operating companies in 60 countries. Today's subsidiary brands fall within three segments: consumer personal products, medical devices and diagnostics, and pharmaceuticals.

The consumer segment began with the goal of improving the health of women and children. In 1894 the company launched maternity kits meant to make childbirth safer. The first sanitary pad was developed in 1896, and Ortho-Gynol, a prescription contraceptive gel, opened doors for family planning in 1931. Ortho Research Laboratories, Inc., was established in 1937 in Linden, New Jersey, specifically for the production of women's health products. The line of Johnson & Johnson baby care products expanded from Johnson's Baby Powder, which was launched in 1894, to Johnson's Baby Lotion, Johnson's Baby Oil, and, in 1954, Johnson's Baby Shampoo. One of Johnson & Johnson's most popular brands, Band-Aid, was created in 1921 and became so successful that people began to call all adhesive bandages "Band-Aids."

In 1994 the consumer segment grew again with the purchase of Neutrogena Corp. In 2006 Johnson & Johnson acquired Pfizer Consumer Healthcare and added the brands Listerine Antiseptic, Bengay, and Benadryl to the company umbrella.

In recent years, some Johnson & Johnson consumer products, especially those in baby care, have been scrutinized for formaldehyde-emitting ingredients, prompting the company to work toward removing all formaldehyde-causing ingredients from its products by 2015.

The company's medical devices and diagnostics segment became Ethicon, Incorporated, in 1949. During the late 1970s and 1980s, the company developed innovative mechanical wound closures and ways to manage diabetes. The purchase of Extracorporeal Medical Specialties enabled Johnson & Johnson to manufacture dialysis and intravenous treatment products. Johnson & Johnson also purchased lolab Corporation, which launched Acuvue brand contact lenses in 1987. When Johnson & Johnson acquired Cordis Corporation in the 1990s, it began to produce interventional vascular products and services. Coronary stents, such as the Palmaz-Schatz, led to major advances in cardiology.

Johnson & Johnson's presence in the pharmaceutical world began with the acquisition of McNeil Laboratories in 1959. The acquisition included Tylenol, a pain reliever that didn't contain aspirin. Tylenol was approved for over-the-counter use, and by 1976 it was the company's best-selling product.

The Tylenol brand was tainted in 1982 when seven people in the Chicago area died after ingesting cyanide-laced Tylenol capsules in an apparent case of product tampering. Johnson & Johnson recalled all Tylenol products and offered consumers an exchange of capsules for tablets, and then the company implemented tamper-resistant protection for its products. The cost in recalls, advertising, and repackaging exceeded $240 million.

Other important pharmaceutical products by Johnson & Johnson include RhoGAM, a treatment for hemolytic disease; Haldol, a standard treatment for schizophrenia; and Orthoclone OKT3, the first therapeutic monoclonal antibody to prevent rejection of organ transplants. In the early 2000s, the acquisition of Tibotec-Virco BVBA helped Johnson & Johnson research treatments for people with HIV/AIDS and other infectious diseases such as tuberculosis.

Johnson & Johnson faced controversy again in 2011 when its brand Doxil, a cancer-fighting drug, was suspended because of manufacturing inadequacies. The company applied to the U.S. Food and Drug Administration and the European Medicines Agency for approval of new manufacturing methods. The financial loss from Doxil was balanced by the success of the 2012 acquisition of Synthes, Incorporated, through which Johnson & Johnson was able to create a world-class orthopedic business.

BRAND ELEMENTS

- The name "Johnson & Johnson" has appeared in red, cursive letters with the red cross logo since 1894.
- Johnson & Johnson has used many slogans to differentiate its specialized brands and services.
- The goal of Johnson & Johnson is to improve the health and well-being of families everywhere.

The use of a red cross with the name "Johnson & Johnson" in the company's logo dates back as far as 1888, to the publication of *Modern Methods of Antiseptic Wound Treatment.* By 1894 the logo presented the name in red, cursive lettering. The name appeared as "Johnson" or "Johnson & Johnson," the form used exclusively in the company's current logo. The red cross continued to accompany the name, with the name sometimes appearing in white lettering inside the cross.

In 2007 "Johnson & Johnson" sued the American Red Cross over the use of the Red Cross logo. Ultimately, the two companies reached a settlement allowing both to continue using the Red Cross symbol to market themselves and their products.

In addition to its logo, Johnson & Johnson's brand is widely recognized by many of its famous slogans. The company adopted the slogan "The Most Trusted Name in Surgical Dressings" in 1892. Another early slogan was "The Family Company." More recognizable today is Johnson & Johnson's slogan for its gentle baby shampoo, "No More Tears," and the popular 1970s jingle "I am stuck on Band-Aid 'cause Band-Aid's stuck on me," written by pop star Barry Manilow. These slogans helped the Johnson & Johnson brand achieve its mission "to improve the health and well-being of families everywhere."

BRAND IDENTITY

- Johnson & Johnson's credo is to "put the needs and well-being of the people we serve first."
- Johnson & Johnson has demonstrated its commitment to its brand identity through philanthropic activities and a reduction of the negative environmental impacts of its operations.
- The company emphasizes transparency to consumers and is quick to address controversies regarding its subsidiary brands.

Robert Wood Johnson II's 1943 company credo states that Johnson & Johnson aims to "put the needs and well-being of the people we serve first." The company cares "for the world, one person at a time." Today, its credo remains the same. The company serves its customers first and foremost and does so in high-quality fashion.

Through the years, Johnson & Johnson has used charity work to build its brand and to promote an image of a charitable and caring brand. One of its first efforts involved a partnership with the American Red Cross to supply aid after the San Francisco earthquake in 1906. In 1987 the company became a founding partner in Safe Kids Worldwide, a global campaign to reduce accidental childhood injuries. Johnson & Johnson also supports the United Nations Millennium Development Goals, which include efforts to improve health care for mothers and children in developing countries.

Another way that Johnson & Johnson demonstrated its commitment to its brand identity was the 2011 launch of the Healthy Future 2015, a five-year plan with seven goals designed to improve the company's impact on the environment. According to Johnson & Johnson, the company is "striving for performance that does not merely comply with regulations but reduces our environmental impacts." As part of this campaign, Johnson & Johnson pledged to remove formaldehyde and other harmful materials from its consumer products.

Through these efforts, the brand intends to be transparent to its consumers. When consumer confidence in the brand waned because of controversies involving toxins in some products and questionable manufacturing practices of medical devices and pharmaceutical products, Johnson & Johnson responded, at great cost, to recover its integrity and demonstrate a concern for consumer safety. The efforts Johnson & Johnson makes today hope to circumvent any future problems.

BRAND STRATEGY

- Johnson & Johnson's decentralized structure has helped the company maintain close contact with consumers.
- Much of the company's success is due to strategic acquisitions, such as the purchases of Synthes and McNeil Laboratories, maker of Tylenol.
- Johnson & Johnson's acquisitions have gained exposure for the brand in new industries and new markets around the world.

Johnson & Johnson's decentralized organization has helped it grow into one of the world's most powerful brands. The company's 2010 annual report describes "a decentralized management approach that keeps our people close to customers; managing for the long term; and a focus on people and values."

A great deal of Johnson & Johnson's success stems from its strategic acquisitions. The acquisition of McNeil Laboratories yielded Tylenol, one of Johnson & Johnson's most recognizable brands. The 2006 purchase of Pfizer Consumer Healthcare generated large revenues from medical devices and pharmaceutical products. The acquisition of Kodak's Clinical Diagnostics business in 1994 added clinical chemistry and immuno-diagnostics to Johnson & Johnson's portfolio, making it the world's third-largest provider of diagnostic tests. SterilMed, acquired in 2011, reprocesses medical devices and sells decontaminated used devices such as catheters, improving Johnson & Johnson's environmental footprint. In 2012 Johnson & Johnson acquired Synthes, a leading global medical device company, and thereby gained greater exposure in China, Russia, and India.

BRAND EQUITY

- *Brandirectory* ranked Johnson & Johnson 128th in its "Global Top 500 2012."
- Interbrand ranked Johnson & Johnson 79th in "Best Global Brands" of 2012 and second in "Best Global Green Brands" for 2012.
- Johnson & Johnson received four Champion of Change awards at the 2012 CleanMed conference.

Johnson & Johnson ranked 128th in *Brandirectory's* "Global Top 500 2012," up from 132nd place in 2011. Its brand value for 2012 was listed at US$7.33 billion. Interbrand ranked Johnson & Johnson 79th in "Best Global Brands of 2012" and assigned a brand value of US$4.38 billion, up 4 percent from the previous year, noting that "Johnson & Johnson continues to expand its consumer health presence in emerging markets."

In Interbrand's "Fast Moving Consumer Goods" sector, Johnson & Johnson's brand value was listed at US$9.16 billion, a 9 percent increase from the previous year, and the company ranked second among the "Best Global Green Brands" for 2012." Interbrand called Johnson & Johnson "a global leader in sustainability initiatives for decades." The company received four Champion of Change awards at the 2012 CleanMed conference.

BRAND AWARENESS

- Popular slogans and jingles have helped give some Johnson & Johnson products top-of-mind awareness among consumers.
- Johnson & Johnson has paid fines and changed its formulas and manufacturing methods to rectify defects in certain brands.
- *Forbes* ranked Johnson & Johnson 50th on its "World's Most Powerful Brands" list.

From the beginning, Johnson & Johnson has been known for its innovative efforts to make surgery safer. Early cynicism about sterile techniques promoted by the company soon gave way to praise. The firm's first book, *Modern Methods of Antiseptic Wound Treatment,* became a standard teaching text around the world. Johnson & Johnson adopted the slogan "The Most Trusted Name in Surgical Dressings" and worked hard to promote a brand image that reflected that trustworthiness.

Not only were the company's early products for women and children trustworthy, they also often introduced new ways to improve health. Products such as Johnson's Baby Shampoo and Band-Aid bandages gained recognition through their clever slogans "No More Tears," and "I am stuck on Band-Aid 'cause Band-Aid's stuck on me." Band-Aid's top-of-mind status led consumers to begin referring to all adhesive bandages as "Band-Aids."

Johnson & Johnson products have also faced negative brand awareness. Tylenol had earned the status as the pain reliever doctors and pediatricians recommended most, but its popularity plummeted, first in 1982 after some capsules on store shelves were laced with cyanide in a tampering case, and later, when long-term side effects were discovered. Controversy also ensued regarding formaldehyde-forming ingredients in some consumer products, most notably the line of baby care products. The company has worked hard to remedy such problems in order to restore the brand's trustworthy reputation.

In April 2012, *Forbes* listed Johnson & Johnson as 50th on its list of the "World's Most Powerful Brands," again demonstrating Johnson & Johnson's remarkable brand awareness.

BRAND OUTLOOK

- Though overall sales for Johnson & Johnson decreased in 2012, sales in the pharmaceutical division increased on the strength of new drug introductions.
- Sales in the medical device and diagnostic segments increased in 2012, largely because of the acquisition of Synthes.
- In 2012 CEO Alan Gorsky said Johnson & Johnson needed to reevaluate its marketing of drugs and rebuild consumer confidence.

New York Stock Exchange figures in October 2012 showed Johnson & Johnson's price per share at US$68.22. Johnson & Johnson showed a greater decline in earnings for the year than its competitors, but some areas showed growth. Sales in the pharmaceutical division increased, due to new drugs that treat prostate cancer, schizophrenia, and hepatitis C. Partnerships with Astellas Pharma and GlaxoSmithKline, along with plans to open four innovation centers in California, China, London, and Boston, were intended to improve treatments for rheumatoid arthritis. These efforts speak to Johnson & Johnson's continued ability to care for their customers worldwide.

Some pharmaceutical sales decreased. Doxil's manufacturing process was found to be inadequate, and generic competition caused problems for the antibiotic Levaquin. Currency fluctuations during the second quarter also had a negative effect on the company's profitability. However, Johnson & Johnson's medical device and diagnostic segments did well, largely due to the acquisition of Synthes. According to *Seeking Alpha*, "Johnson & Johnson's pharmaceutical and medical device segments are the primary catalysts for long-term growth and increasing revenues."

Alan Gorsky became the CEO at Johnson & Johnson in April 2012, at a time when consumer confidence was down. He told the *New York Times*, "Johnson & Johnson needs to rethink the way it brings drugs to market, expand its reach into global markets and rebuild consumer confidence by returning recalled brands to pharmacy shelves." Additionally in 2012, the health care market underwent changes throughout the world as methods of pricing and reimbursing for health care were being revised. Gorsky said Johnson & Johnson considered the changes an opportunity. His statements pose Johnson & Johnson ready for change and growth in the long term.

FURTHER READING

"Best Global Brands 2012." Interbrand. Accessed October 10, 2012. http://www.interbrand.com/en/best-global-brands/2012/Best-Global-Brands-2012-Brand-View.aspx.

Black, Larry. "Johnson to Pay Dollars 1bn for Kodak's Diagnostics Arm: Healthcare Takeover Spree Continues." *Independent* (London), September 7, 1994.

Brand Finance. "Global 500 Top 2012." *Brandirectory*. Accessed October 10, 2012. http://brandirectory.com/league_tables/table/global-500-2012.

Brown, Abram. "Johnson & Johnson's $19.7 B Synthes Deal: A Surprise Earnings Boost." *Forbes*, June 3, 2012.

Gurowitz, Margaret. "Johnson & Johnson at BlogHer 2012—Come and See Us." *JNJ BTW*, August 2, 2012. Accessed October 16, 2012. http://www.jnjbtw.com/2012/08/johnson-johnson-at-blogher-2012-come-and-see-us-there/.

"Johnson & Johnson (US)." Adbrands.net, 2012. Accessed October 10, 2012. http://www.adbrands.net/us/johnsonandjohnson_us.htm.

"Johnson & Johnson." *New York Times*, August 16, 2012.

"Johnson and Johnson." *Notable Corporate Chronologies*. Farmington Hills, MI: Gale Group, 2009.

"Johnson & Johnson (JNJ)." Reuters, October 10, 2012. Accessed October 10, 2012. http://www.reuters.com/finance/stocks/companyProfile?rpc=66&symbol=JNJ.

ValueMax. "Uncertainty at Johnson & Johnson Created Risk." Seeking Alpha, October 10, 2012. Accessed October 10, 2012. http://seekingalpha.com/article/916711-uncertainty-at-johnson-johnson-creates-risk.

JOLLIBEE

AT A GLANCE

Brand Synopsis: As the company has expanded, Jollibee has held fast to its internal branding, which focuses on great taste and value, combined with a cheerful store experience.
Parent Company: Jollibee Foods Corporation
10/F Jollibee Plaza Building
Emerald Avenue
Ortigas Center
Pasig City, PH-1600
Philippines
www.jollibee.com.ph
Sector: Consumer Discretionary
Industry Group: Consumer Services; Restaurants
Performance: Market share—39% (Philippines, 2012). Sales—US$1.48 billion (2011).
Principal Competitors: Golden Arches Development Corp.; Pancake House Inc.; San Miguel Pure Foods Company Inc.; Sodexo Pass Inc.; Tropical Hut Food Market Inc.; Vitarich Corp.

BRAND ORIGINS

- The founder of Jollibee, Tony Tan Caktiong, graduated from the University of Santo Tomas in the Philippines with a degree in chemical engineering.
- Caktiong opened two Magnolia Ice Cream Parlors in 1975. In 1978 he changed the name of the restaurants to Jollibee and expanded the menu to include hamburgers.
- Jollibee was able to withstand the entry of McDonald's, Kentucky Fried Chicken, and Wendy's into the Philippine fast-food market through an intimate knowledge of Filipino food preferences.

Tony Tan Caktiong gained experience in the restaurant industry working as a waiter in his family's restaurant in Davao in the Philippines during the 1960s. Caktiong's father, a native of Fujian Province in China, had immigrated to the Philippines in order to escape poverty. After working as a chef at a Chinese temple in Manila, he was invited to start a restaurant business in Davao. The success of that business allowed Tony Tan Caktiong to attend the University of Santo Tomas, where he graduated with a degree in chemical engineering.

Caktiong's interest quickly returned to the restaurant business, however. Backed by the family's savings, Caktiong acquired the franchises to open two Magnolia Ice Cream Parlors, in Cubao and Quiapo, in 1975. Business was brisk and before long Caktiong had opened six restaurants. This led him to hire managers and train employees to take over the operation of the restaurants. By 1978 the company had added its own bakery operation as well.

After receiving a number of requests from customers for a more comprehensive food menu, Caktiong expanded his menu to include chicken and hamburgers. These items quickly became popular and soon began outselling ice cream at Caktiong's restaurants. McDonald's Corporation had begun preparations to enter the Philippines market during this time. Caktiong recognized the opportunity to develop his own U.S.-style fast-food format. In 1978 he changed the name and format of his restaurants to Jollibee, with a new menu featuring the Yumburger hamburger.

The company incorporated as Jollibee Foods in 1978, and operated seven restaurants in the metropolitan Manila region by the end of the year. Jollibee quickly expanded its menu, tailoring its foods to the Philippine palate. For example, in 1979 the company added a sweet spaghetti dish topped with hot dogs, a popular dish in the Philippines. Fries and a chicken dish, Chickenjoy, were added the following year.

Jollibee's knowledge of Filipino food preferences enabled the company to successfully compete with McDonald's, which entered the market in 1982, as well as other U.S. entrants, including Kentucky Fried Chicken and Wendy's. The company had opened its first franchised location by the early 1980s as well, on Ronquillo Street in Santa Cruz, Manila.

Jollibee launched its first international expansion effort in 1986, opening a restaurant in Taiwan. Jollibee also followed the large number of Filipinos working overseas, opening a location in Brunei and then Jakarta, Indonesia. New international locations quickly followed with sites in Dubai, Guam, Kuwait, Saudi Arabia, and the United Arab Emirates. The first Jollibee restaurant in Hong Kong opened in 1996, followed by an entry into the People's Republic of China with the opening of a store in Xiamen in 1997. The company then entered the United States through a joint venture, FSC Foods, opening its first Jollibee outlet in San Francisco in 1998.

BRAND ELEMENTS

- Jollibee's advertising focuses on the Filipino culture of large, closely knit families.
- Jollibee's primary mascot, a red and yellow bumblebee named Jollibee, is one of the most recognizable and iconic symbols in Filipino culture.
- The Jollibee slogan "Langhap-Sarap" means "delicious aroma" and implies that Jollibee food tastes as wonderful as it smells.

Jollibee's centers its advertising on children and family values, capitalizing on the Filipino culture of large, closely knit families. Jollibee advertisements feature children, parents, and grandparents enjoying Jollibee food together, creating a warm and friendly brand image. The wholesome scenes featured in Jollibee's branding and marketing campaigns aim to appeal to Filipino palates and hearts as well as to invoke a sense of national pride.

The company introduced its own mascot, a bumblebee, in 1980. The red and yellow Jollibee, which sports a chef's hat, shirt, and blazer, became hugely popular among Filipino children. A captivating cast of mascots was created to accompany the Jollibee bumblebee over the years, including Micro and Lady Moo, representing milkshakes; Mr. Champ, representing the Champ hamburger; Chickee, representing Chickenjoy chicken dinners; Mr. Yum, who loves science, symbolizing Yumburgers; Popo, a sports loving French fry mascot; Twirlie, the singing and dancing, performing Sundae mascot; and Hetty, with blonde spaghetti hair, representing spaghetti dishes.

In 2008, Jollibee the bumblebee and his friends began starring in their own television show. Jollibee, Mr. Yum, Twirlie, Hetty, and Popo appear each week in a half-hour format on Philippine television.

Created in 1982, Jollibee's slogan "Langhap-Sarap" has become an iconic part of Philippine culture. Translated from the Filipino language Tagalog, the phrase means "delicious aroma" or "deliciousness inhaled." The scent of food is as important as the taste in Filipino culture, and the tagline implies that from the smell alone, the food is already tasty and flavorful.

Jollibee outlets feature a cheerful, carnival atmosphere and are an important part of the Jollibee brand image. The playgrounds and bright colors of Jollibee restaurants aim to reflect the casual and lighthearted Filipino lifestyle, while fiestas, in-store activities, and promotions directed at children help to boost brand popularity among families as well as to reinforce Jollibee's fun-loving image.

BRAND IDENTITY

- Jollibee has aimed to promote a sense of Filipino pride with the creation of products and an atmosphere that typify national ideals.
- Jollibee marketing campaigns promote values such as family loyalty, respect for elders, and a sense of national pride.
- Many Filipinos living abroad visit international Jollibee establishments as a way to reconnect with their country's values and culture.

From the outset, Jollibee has endeavored to tap into Filipino culture, becoming an iconic brand along the way. As a counter to images of Westernized hamburger chains, Jollibee has tried to promote a sense of Filipino pride with the creation of products and an atmosphere that typify national ideals.

Jollibee marketing campaigns promote values such as family loyalty, respect for elders, and patriotism. The company understands that although many Filipinos identify as hardworking, it is their inherent happiness and hospitality that set the culture apart. Jollibee has endeavored to be seen as an extension of a Filipino family, with the happiness, security, and pride that a family creates.

Jollibee has developed a cult following among homesick Filipinos living abroad. For its international restaurants, Jollibee imports the ingredients to get the food and flavors exactly right. Restaurants outside the Philippines replicate everything you'd expect to find in a domestic Jollibee, down to the tables, chairs, and paintings on the walls. Jollibee also sells nostalgia alongside its hamburgers to further promote the brand's identity as a comforting reminder of home for Filipinos living abroad.

BRAND STRATEGY

- Jollibee restaurant menus feature items tailored specifically to Filipino tastes, such as spicy hamburgers and spaghetti with a sweet sauce topped with hot dogs.
- Jollibee owns the Philippine fast-food brands Greenwich Pizza, Chowking, Red Ribbon Bakeshop, and Mang Inasal.
- Jollibee owns the rights the United States-based Burger King franchise in the Philippines. Burger King products are considered premium pricing and target a more affluent clientele than Jollibee restaurants.

The Jollibee brand achieved dominant market position in the Philippines with their ability to tap into flavors that are specially suited to Filipino tastes. Jollibee's menu offers a variety of sweet and spicy hamburgers, seasoned chicken, traditional Filipino noodle dishes like Palabok Fiesta (thin rice noodles with a spiced sauce topped with pork rinds, shrimp, and a hard boiled egg), rice meals, and macaroni soup. Desserts feature peach mango pie and milkshakes made from purple yams. Jollibee serves meals with rice or noodles, and French fries are served with sweet ketchup made of bananas dyed red to look like tomatoes.

The company has taken the strategy of acquiring brands that already have a loyal following instead of opening exclusively Jollibee-brand restaurants. In 1994 Jollibee began its acquisitions of other brands, buying Greenwich Pizza, a small chain of pizza restaurants in the Philippines. Shortly after the acquisition, Jollibee introduced new pizza flavors and pastas along with new store formats. With over 200 restaurants, Greenwich Pizza is the largest pizza chain in the Philippines.

Jollibee acquired Chowking Food Corporation, the Philippine leader in Chinese fast-food restaurants, in 2000. Chowking's menu includes chow mein, dim sum, noodle soups, breakfast, chicken, and rice meals. The purchase helped transform the company into one of the region's leading restaurant groups. Chowking has restaurants in the Philippines, Indonesia, the United States, and the Middle East.

In 2005 Jollibee purchased Red Ribbon Bakeshop, a popular chain of fast-food style bakeries in the Philippines. Red Ribbon entered the United States market in 1984, opening stores in California, Nevada, New Jersey, New York, Arizona, and Virginia. Menu items include cakes, rolls, breads, pastries, and meat-filled pies and buns.

Jollibee acquired 70 percent of the Mang Inasal brand in 2010. In the Philippine Hiligaynon language, "Mang Inasal" means "Mr. Barbecue." Mang Inasal serves Filipino-style barbecue, with chicken, pork, and rice dishes on the menu in over 300 restaurants.

Jollibee took over the Philippine chain of United States-based Burger King restaurants in 2011. Although both Jollibee and Burger King have similar menus, Burger King items are priced approximately 30 percent higher than Jollibee items in the Philippines and are considered premium pricing. The addition of the Burger King brand to the Jollibee portfolio allows the company to compete for the growing affluence of many Filipinos.

Not all of the company's expansion efforts were successful. Jollibee attempted to enter the convenience store sector, operating under the Binggo format. This chain grew to just 20 locations, which did not provide sufficient volume to allow the company to compete against its larger rivals. Jollibee soon sold off its Binggo stores and returned its focus to its fast-growing restaurant businesses. The company also bought the Délifrance French bakery franchise in the Philippines in 1995. The company struggled to build this business, in part because the bread-based French food format failed to find a large customer base in the traditionally rice-oriented Filipino food culture. The company sold the Délifrance franchise in 2010.

BRAND EQUITY

- In 2012, Jollibee was world's fifth-fastest-growing restaurant company outside of the United States.
- Jollibee enjoys a 39-percent market share in the Philippines, outpacing main rival McDonald's.
- Jollibee has been ranked as the most admired retail company in Asia.

According to *Forbes Asia,* Jollibee dominates the fast-food hamburger market in the Philippines, with a 39-percent market share, outpacing main rival McDonald's with a 15-percent market share in 2012. In 2003 Jollibee had claimed a 65-percent market share of the hamburger market. *Euromonitor International* reports that in 2012 Jollibee was the world's fifth-fastest-growing restaurant company outside the United States in terms of sales.

Forbes Asia also recognized Jollibee in 2005 as one of the 200 best under a billion dollar companies in Asia out of 11,000 Asian public companies. London-based financial magazine *Euromoney* awarded Jollibee as "Best at Consumer Goods" in its 10th annual poll of *Asia's Best Managed Companies.*

In 2000 Jollibee was ranked as the most admired retail company in Asia, beating out rival McDonald's and Coca Cola. Jollibee was also ranked second on a listing of companies in the Philippines with the highest quality of products and services. In 1998 Jollibee was ranked first of leading companies in the Philippines, most emulated companies in the Philippines, and companies in the Philippines with the most innovative responses to customer needs.

BRAND AWARENESS

- Jollibee operates the largest fast-food network in the Philippines with 2,040 restaurants.
- Jollibee operates 541 restaurants outside of the Philippines.
- Jollibee brands are centered primarily in the Philippines and the Middle East, and Jollibee operates locations in 12 countries outside of the Philippines.

According to the company, Jollibee operates the largest fast-food network in the Philippines with 2,040 stores comprising the Jollibee, Chowking, Greenwich, Red Ribbon, Mang Inasal, and Burger King brands. Internationally the group operates 541 stores for a total of 2,581 stores worldwide. In the Philippines Jollibee is the undisputed champion of the fast-food market.

Jollibee brands are centered primarily in the Philippines and the Middle East. The company has outlets operating internationally in China, Hong Kong, Vietnam, Brunei, Indonesia, the United States, Malaysia, Saudi Arabia, United Arab Emirates, Qatar, Thailand, and Taiwan.

BRAND OUTLOOK

- Jollibee's greatest strengths come from its dominant market position in the Philippines and the incredible brand loyalty it has achieved both at home and abroad.
- The Jollibee, Greenwich Pizza, and Chowking restaurant brands remain strong and generate the highest growth and earnings for the company.
- Jollibee continues to expand in China through acquisitions of existing fast-food chains, including Yonghe King noodle shops, Hong Zhuang Yuan congee restaurants, and the San Pin Wang beef noodle chain.

Jollibee's greatest strengths come from its dominant market position in the Philippines and the incredible brand loyalty it has achieved both at home and abroad. There is a national pride in the company as it continues to grow internationally. Jollibee's twist on traditional menu offerings with unique products that emphasize local spices and taste preferences has given the company an edge over competitors.

Jollibee continues to dominate the fast food industry in the Philippines. The Jollibee, Greenwich Pizza, and Chowking restaurant brands remain strong and generate the highest growth and earnings for the company. The Mang Inasal and Burger King brand acquisitions provided the company with an even greater sales share.

Jollibee announced its intentions to continue international growth, hoping to achieve a 50-50 split between domestic and international sales by 2020. In 2011 the company maintained the steady pace of its expansion, opening nearly 300 restaurants, primarily in the Philippines and China. Jollibee plans to open its first store in Singapore in early 2013, but it may face stiff competition, where McDonald's is the leader with a 38-percent market share and KFC holds a 17-percent market share. The company has also announced plans to export the Mang Inasal format to the United States.

Jollibee continues to expand in China through acquisitions of existing fast-food chains. In 2004 it bought Yonghe King noodle shops and in 2008 acquired Hong Zhuang Yuan chain, a popular congee brand of restaurants. In 2012 Jollibee bought a 55-percent stake of Chinese beef noodle chain San Pin Wang. In each brand that it buys, Jollibee improves the taste and quality of the food, introduces new menu items, and redesigns the restaurants. Jollibee has seen double-digit returns on their investments in China and has announced their intentions to keep growing within China.

FURTHER READING

Almedral, Aurora. "Jollibee: A Taste of Home for Filipinos," *PRI's The World,* October 26, 2012. Accessed February 1, 2013. http://www.theworld.org/2012/10/jollibee-a-taste-of-home-for-filipinos.

Cohen, M. L. "Jollibee Foods Corporation." *International Directory of Company Histories.* Ed. Tina Grant. Vol. 134. Detroit: St. James Press, 2012. 170–173. *Gale Virtual Reference Library.* Web. Accessed February 1, 2013.

Conde, Carlos H. "Jollibee stings McDonald's in Philippines," *The New York Times,* May 31, 2005. Accessed February 1, 2013. http://www.nytimes.com/2005/05/30/business/worldbusiness/30iht-burger.html?pagewanted=all&_r=0.

Dumlao, Doris C. "Jollibee buys Burger King franchise in the Philippines," *Philippine Daily Inquirer,* October 1, 2011. Yahoo! News Philippines. Accessed February 1, 2013. http://ph.news.yahoo.com/jollibee-buys-burger-king-franchise-philippines-063005996.html.

Lichauco de Leno, Sunshine. "Billionaire Tony Tan Caktiong Takes Jollibee Foods Global," *Forbes Asia,* January 30, 2013. Accessed February 1, 2013. http://www.forbes.com/sites/forbesasia/2013/01/30/billionaire-tony-tan-caktiong-takes-jollibee-foods-global.

Solee, Tyrone. "Tony Tan Caktiong and Jollibee Success Story," MillionaireActs.com, January 30, 2009. Accessed February 1, 2013. http://www.millionaireacts.com/735/tony-tan-caktiong-and-jollibee-success-story.html.

Wells, Jennifer Schultz. "Hotelier Jennie Chua's New Challenge: Bringing Jollibee Fast Food to Singapore," *Forbes Asia,* December 10, 2012. Accessed February 1, 2013. http://www.forbes.com/sites/forbesasia/2012/11/28/hotelier-jennie-chuas-new-challenge-bringing-jollibee-fast-food-to-singapore.

JP MORGAN

AT A GLANCE

Brand Synopsis: JP Morgan is the investment banking brand of JPMorgan Chase & Co., projecting an image of a respected and trusted financial services firm that offers honest advice and innovative solutions.
Parent Company: JPMorgan Chase & Co.
270 Park Avenue
New York, New York 10017
United States
http://www.jpmorgan.com
Sector: Financials
Industry Group: Banks
Performance: *Brand value*—US$13.775 billion (2012).
Principal Competitors: Barclays plc; Citigroup Inc.; Bank of America Corporation

BRAND ORIGINS

- Banker John Pierpont Morgan was the man behind the JP Morgan brand name.
- Morgan was a controversial figure of his day.
- J.P. Morgan Jr. carried on the family's banking tradition until his death in 1943.
- The Chase Manhattan merger resulted in JPMorgan Chase & Co.
- The JP Morgan brand was revived in 2008.

JP Morgan, the investment banking brand of JPMorgan Chase & Co., is one of the United States' most venerable banking brands. The man behind the brand's name, John Pierpont Morgan, was a brand unto himself. Born the son of a successful banker, Morgan was just 17 when he entered his father's banking house in 1854. Only three years later, he founded J.P. Morgan and Company to serve as an agent for his father's bank. As he grew older, more respected, and more powerful, Morgan made his mark by organizing railroads. With the death of his father and his father's partners, he became an international banking figure as the head of houses in New York, Philadelphia, London, and Paris. In 1895 the J.P. Morgan & Co. name was adopted for the concern.

Morgan became more widely known to the citizens of his own country in the mid-1890s when he used his European connections to bolster U.S. gold reserves that had been depleted as a result of the Panic of 1893. It would not be the last time that Morgan performed such a civic duty while turning a handsome profit, nor would it be the last time the United States experienced a financial calamity that required his intervention.

Morgan refused to disclose his profits in the gold transaction to a congressional investigative committee. In many respects, Morgan answered to no one. He was a publicity-shy autocrat, due in part to a cankerous nose that marred his appearance. There was no doubt of his power, however. He helped to form the General Electric Company in the 1890s and at the turn of the century organized U.S. Steel Corporation, International Harvester Company, and Mercantile Marine Company.

Within the business community, Morgan was both respected and feared. In other quarters he was vilified as a robber baron. In a famous speech delivered in 1907 at a Gridiron Club dinner, President Theodore Roosevelt decried "the malefactors of great wealth" and urged business reform. According to reporters at the scene, Roosevelt glanced at Morgan when he uttered his famous phase. Later in 1907, when a botched corner on the copper market resulted in a bank run that threatened the country's financial stability, it was Morgan who organized a bailout. With Roosevelt's help, he resolved the crisis while managing to find a way to turn the situation to his advantage. It was the culmination of Morgan's career.

After Morgan's death, his son J.P. "Jack" Morgan Jr. became the head of the firm. He maintained the House of Morgan as well as the JP Morgan brand. As his father had done in 1907, Jack Morgan sought to avert a financial disaster in October 1929 when the stock market began to collapse. His efforts failed, however, and the crash of Wall Street led to the Great Depression of the 1930s, as well as to the Glass-Steagall Act that forced the separation of deposit and investment banking. As a result, J.P. Morgan & Co. became a private commercial bank, and a new investment banking concern was formed under the Morgan Stanley & Company name.

Jack Morgan died in 1943, and while there was no longer a living J.P. Morgan on the American banking scene, and J.P. Morgan & Co was little more than a midsized bank, the JP Morgan brand remained valuable. When in 1959 the bank merged with Guaranty Trust Company of New York, four times larger in size, the JP Morgan name was dropped in favor of Morgan Guaranty Trust Company. Before long, however, a holding company was formed under the J.P. Morgan & Co. name, and in 1988 the company elected to operate exclusively as J.P. Morgan & Co.

In the 1990s the restrictions imposed by Glass-Steagall were lifted, resulting in a return of commercial and investment banking combinations and a rash of large bank mergers. J.P. Morgan found a partner in Chase Manhattan Bank. A 2000 merger resulted in the creation of JPMorgan Chase & Co. There had been some talk of simply calling the firm "Morgan Chase." While the Morgan name was retained, the JP Morgan logo and brand were dropped. In 2008, during a modern financial crisis, the brand was revived once again, a century after the brand's namesake had dominated the American banking scene.

BRAND ELEMENTS

- The J.P. Morgan name is the most important element of the JP Morgan brand.
- The updated wordmark uses a thinner font.
- "Distinctively J.P. Morgan" has served as a tagline for the brand.
- Sporting and cultural event sponsorships support the JP Morgan brand.

The most important element of the JP Morgan brand is the name itself. The emotions aroused by John Pierpont Morgan dissipated long ago, and most people are unaware of the major deals he struck or his role in taming the Panic of 1907, but they know he was a banker. He is the only American banker most people can name. As a result, the Morgan name is highly valuable as a banking brand.

The JP Morgan name is so valuable that a wordmark is sufficient to serve as the brand's logo. After the Chase Manhattan merger, the company incorporated Chase's eight-sided logo that had been created in 1961 after Chase National Bank merged with the Bank of Manhattan Company. It was considered a radical design at the time but had become one of the world's most recognizable trademarks. The symbol was joined by the JPMorganChase wordmark. When the bank decided in 2008 to revive the JP Morgan brand for its institutional business, the old JP Morgan logo was updated and returned to use. The font was thinner and provided a more modern look, but it was reminiscent of the brand's classic appearance.

JP Morgan is not associated with a specific tagline, unlike its sister brand, which uses "Chase what matters." The corporate brand of JPMorgan Chase has also used "The Way Forward" as a slogan. In 2011 JP Morgan incorporated the word "distinctively" into its print ads. The result was "Distinctively J.P. Morgan," serving as a combination wordmark and tagline.

Another element of the JP Morgan brand is sponsorships. The bank aligns itself with specific sporting events and nonprofit arts and cultural organizations around the world that bring luster to the brand and are in keeping with its identity. JP Morgan sponsors the U.S. Open Tennis Championship, the Lord's Cricket Ground in London, squash's Tournament of Champions, and other niche sporting events. Cultural sponsorships include the San Francisco Museum of Modern Art, the Art Gallery of New South Wales in Australia, the New York City Ballet Traveling Tour, the Peking Opera, and the Today Art Museum in Beijing, China.

BRAND IDENTITY

- JP Morgan portrays itself as a respected and trusted financial services firm.
- Honest advice and innovative solutions are additional elements of JP Morgan's brand identity.
- The cultural resonance of the JP Morgan name supports the brand identity.
- Industry recognition reinforces JP Morgan's reputation for offering honest advice and innovative solutions.

JP Morgan's brand identity, the image the company projects to the world, is that of a respected and trusted financial services firm that offers honest advice and innovative solutions to its customers. The firm's superb execution is matched by its integrity; if faced with a choice, JP Morgan promises to do the right thing and not take the expedient path. Also part of JP Morgan's brand identity is an aspiration to be the best in the world in every business in which the firm operates.

The elements of the JP Morgan brand support its identity. With a deep cultural resonance, the JP Morgan name draws connections to a number of positive values, including longevity and stability. As a result, the brand is positioned as trustworthy. The name also suggests power and an ability to be effective. The "Distinctively J.P. Morgan" tagline supports the idea that the brand is venerable and reliable.

Neither the JP Morgan name nor the tagline suggest, in themselves, the established identity of being a provider of honest advice and innovative solutions. The firm's reputation in the marketplace does much of the heavy lifting in this area. JP Morgan is a global leader in all four of its major business lines: Investment Banking, Commercial Banking, Asset Management, and Treasury and Securities Services. The firm has also received a number of awards in recognition of its services to clients. In 2011 it was named among *Barron's* Most Respected Companies, Transition Manager of the Year by Global Pensions, Best Trade Bank in the World by *Trade & Forfaiting Review*, and *Euromoney's* Best Global Commodities House. The following year, JP Morgan was named *Risk's* Derivatives House of the Year, Asset Manager of the Year by *AsianInvestor*, the #1 Global Prime Broker by *Global Custodian*, and Euromoney's #1 Private Bank for the Ultra-High Net Worth globally and the High Net Worth in the United States. While such recognition did little to promote the JP Morgan brand identity with the general population, it did have an impact on the narrow slice of the global population to which the brand appealed.

BRAND STRATEGY

- The JP Morgan brand has proven too valuable to remain in permanent retirement.
- The merger with Chase Manhattan led to a hybrid brand, JPMorgan Chase.
- The JP Morgan name was reinstated in 2008 as the investment banking brand for JPMorgan Chase.

For more than a century the JP Morgan name has been synonymous with American banking. When the 1959 merger with Guaranty Trust Company of New York led to the retirement of the full name with the creation of the new Morgan Guaranty Trust, the brand was too powerful to lie dormant. It soon returned to its prominent place in the banking world. Again, at the turn of the millennium, a merger with Chase Manhattan resulted in the withdrawal of the JP Morgan brand. It was replaced by a hybrid brand, JPMorgan Chase, but the Chase brand elements took precedence, primarily the iconic Chase logo.

Changes in the marketplace, however, led to the return of the traditional JP Morgan brand. As a global financial crisis unfolded in 2008, JPMorgan Chase acquired the troubled Bear Stearns Companies, Inc., a global investment bank and securities trading and brokerage firm that had bet heavily and lost on the mortgage-backed assets that were at the core of a subprime mortgage crisis. An emergency loan from the Federal Reserve Bank of New York was unable to save Bear Stearns, and JPMorgan Chase stepped in to buy it.

Shortly after the acquisition, the Bear Stearns name was removed from the firm's New York City headquarters. Instead of being replaced by JPMorgan Chase, however, the new name was an old one: JP Morgan. Chase's eight-sided symbol was also eliminated. It was all part of a new branding strategy to segregate the consumer side of the business under the Chase name and the institutional businesses under the JP Morgan name.

Unlike many financial service firms, JPMorgan Chase was in a strong-enough position, not only to weather the financial storm but also to take advantage of it. Many bank clients during these uncertain times began turning to reputable, large, conservative firms. It was an environment in which the JP Morgan brand held great appeal, leading to its resurrection.

There was another reason for the reorganization of JPMorgan Chase. Given the severe problems experienced by the banking industry that many attributed to deregulation, there was some talk that Glass-Steagall might be reinstated in some form. Should retail banking and investment banking once again become separated, JPMorgan Chase would have already laid the groundwork by splitting its operations between two master brands. As time passed, such a possibility grew more remote. Nevertheless, JPMorgan Chase was better prepared than most to divide its business if necessary.

BRAND EQUITY

- Brand Finance estimated that at the end of 2012 JP Morgan had a brand value of US$13.775 billion.
- JP Morgan was ranked 15th on Brand Directory's 2013 Banking 500 list of the most valuable banking brands.
- Brand Finance listed JP Morgan as number 73 on the consultancy's 2012 Global 500 list of the world's most valuable brands.
- Interbrand assigned a US$11.471 billion valuation of JP Morgan.
- JP Morgan was listed as 32nd on Interbrand's Best Global Brands 2012.

The significant brand equity inherent in the JP Morgan name is vividly demonstrated by the fact that it was twice brought back from retirement. Few brands are ever successful in such an attempt. Not only has JP Morgan succeeded, but the brand was so powerful that its absence was not even perceived. It was as if it had never been gone. Thus, when clients were looking for safe havens during the financial crisis in 2008, many of them turned to a JP Morgan brand that had only just been brought out of mothballs.

Putting a monetary value on brand equity with any precision is a difficult task. In an attempt to do this to facilitate comparison of brand values, brand consultancies and business publications have developed their own methodologies. The Brand Finance brand consultancy estimated that at the end of 2012 JP Morgan had a brand value of US$13.775 billion. It was a performance that placed JP Morgan at 15th on Brand Directory's Banking 500 list of the most valuable banking brands in 2013. It ranked sixth among United States–based banking brands. JP Morgan was also listed at number 73 on the consultancy's 2012 Global 500 list of the world's most valuable brands.

Another brand consultancy, Interbrand, assigned a US$11.471 billion valuation to JP Morgan. As a result, JP Morgan was listed as 32nd on Interbrand's Best Global Brands 2012. The Millward Brown consultancy ranked JP Morgan number 83 on its BrandZ Top 100 in 2009 and number 93 in 2010, before it fell off the list because of an economic climate that adversely impacted JP Morgan's score.

BRAND AWARENESS

- The lasting fame of John Pierpont Morgan has redounded to benefit JP Morgan's brand awareness.
- JP Morgan's operations around the world help to build brand awareness.
- A recent study reveals high brand awareness of JP Morgan mutual funds, even though these are not a core product offering of the bank.

JP Morgan enjoys strong brand awareness with the general population, especially in the United States, as well as with the all-important pool of potential clients that includes corporations, institutions, and high-net-worth individuals. John Pierpont Morgan was a titan from another era, but his well-publicized exploits keep his name alive. The JP Morgan brand benefits from the memory of its namesake, whether the man is viewed with reverence or disdain.

The breadth of services and geographic reach are also important to JP Morgan's brand awareness. The brand is well entrenched in many categories. Its Treasury Services business, for example, has over 135,000 clients in more than 180 countries, including corporations, financial institutions, governments, and municipalities. JP Morgan's private banking unit maintains offices across the United States, as well as in Latin America, Africa, Asia, Europe, and the Middle East.

Brand awareness surveys are not generally available for public consumption. One study done in 2011 by Cogent Research that is accessible gives a sense of JP Morgan's brand awareness. The survey was conducted to determine the views of affluent and high-net-worth individuals regarding major banking brands and their asset management services. All told, 4,100 U.S. adults were surveyed online. JP Morgan Funds was one of only five mutual fund providers that were known by at least half of the respondents. It ranked fourth overall for brand awareness. In terms of unaided mentions, JP Morgan Funds ranked eighth. Mutual funds was not a sector closely associated with JP Morgan, but awareness of the overarching JP Morgan brand helped to improve the ranking of the banks' funds.

BRAND OUTLOOK

- In 2012 JPMorgan Chase reported a loss of US$2 billion that affected but did not break the powerful brand.
- As of 2013, the JP Morgan brand was well-positioned to deal with tighter financial regulations and other looming challenges.
- The reputation of the historical figure behind the JP Morgan name guarantees that the brand will continue to be associated with American banking in the future.

In 2012 JPMorgan Chase reported a US$2 billion loss that resulted from a poorly executed hedging strategy. The misstep generated a good deal of negative press that adversely impacted the JP Morgan brand. However, it was simply too powerful, and the bank's customer base too broad, for the brand to be derailed by the incident. Still, there was no lack of future challenges, including stiffer competition in the global financial services industry and economic imbalances around the world that could jeopardize the bank's position. The United States could also tighten regulations on the banking industry that would increase compliance costs and impact earnings. All things considered, the bank appeared well positioned for the future.

The JP Morgan brand has stood the test of time. The man behind the brand is part of the fabric of American history, and his legacy, both positive and negative, will live on. At the very least, the JP Morgan name will continue to be associated with American banking for many years to come. That simple name-recognition imparts value to the JP Morgan brand and will likely continue to do so well into the future.

FURTHER READING

Brand Finance. "J.P. Morgan." *Brandirectory*. Accessed February 19, 2013. http://brandirectory.com/profile/jp-morgan.

"J.P. Morgan." RankingTheBrands.com. Accessed February 19, 2013. http://www.rankingthebrands.com/Brand-detail.aspx?brandID=336.

"J.P. Morgan & Co. Incorporated." *International Directory of Company Histories*. Ed. Jay P. Pederson. Vol. 38. Detroit, MI: St. James Press, 2001.

"J.P. Morgan's Stately Old Logo Returns." *New York Times*, June 16, 2008.

"John Pierpont Morgan." *Dictionary of American Biography*. New York: Charles Scribner's Sons, 1936.

Planes, Alex. "What Makes JPMorgan Chase One of the Dow's Best Brands." Dailyfinance.com, October 21, 2012. Accessed February 26, 2013. http://www.fool.com/investing/general/2012/10/21/what-makes-jpmorgan-one-of-the-dows-best-brands.aspx

Roose, Kevin. "After JPMorgan Trading Debacle, a Chorus of Criticism." *New York Times*, May 11, 2012.

Silverstein, Barry. "Back to Basics: As Banks Look ahead, They Must Concentrate on Fundamentals." Brandchannel, July 13, 2010. Accessed February 19, 2013. http://www.brandchannel.com/features_effect.asp?pf_id=507